JAVA™

HOW TO PROGRAM
FOURTH EDITION

Deitel™ Books, Cyber Classrooms, Complete Training Courses and Web-Based Training published by Prentice Hall

***How to Program* Series**
Advanced Java™ 2 Platform How to Program
C How to Program, 3/E
C++ How to Program, 3/E
C# How to Program
e-Business and e-Commerce How to Program
Internet and World Wide Web How to Program, 2/E
Java™ How to Program, 4/E
Perl How to Program
Visual Basic® 6 How to Program
Visual Basic® .NET How to Program
Visual C++® .NET How to Program
Wireless Internet & Mobile Business How to Program
XML How to Program

***Multimedia Cyber Classroom* and *Web-Based Training* Series**
(for information regarding Deitel™ Web-based training visit **www.ptgtraining.com**)
Advanced Java™ 2 Platform Multimedia Cyber Classroom
C++ Multimedia Cyber Classroom, 3/E
C# Multimedia Cyber Classroom, 3/E
e-Business and e-Commerce Multimedia Cyber Classroom
Internet and World Wide Web Multimedia Cyber Classroom, 2/E
Java™ 2 Multimedia Cyber Classroom, 4/E
Perl Multimedia Cyber Classroom
Visual Basic® 6 Multimedia Cyber Classroom
Visual Basic® .NET Multimedia Cyber Classroom
Visual C++® .NET Multimedia Cyber Classroom
Wireless Internet & Mobile Business Programming Multimedia Cyber Classroom
XML Multimedia Cyber Classroom

***The Complete Training Course* Series**
The Complete Advanced Java™ 2 Platform Training Course
The Complete C++ Training Course, 3/E
The Complete C# Training Course, 3/E
The Complete e-Business and e-Commerce Programming Training Course
The Complete Internet and World Wide Web Programming Training Course
The Complete Java™ 2 Training Course, 3/E
The Complete Perl Training Course
The Complete Visual Basic® 6 Training Course
The Complete Visual Basic® .NET Training Course
The Complete Visual C++® .NET Training Course
The Complete Wireless Internet & Mobile Business Programming Training Course
The Complete XML Training Course

***.NET* Series**
C# How to Program
Visual Basic® .NET How to Program
Visual C++® .NET How to Program

***Visual Studio®* Series**
Getting Started with Microsoft® Visual C++™ 6 with an Introduction to MFC
Visual Basic® 6 How to Program
C# How to Program
Visual Basic® .NET How to Program
Visual C++® .NET How to Program

***For Managers* Series**
e-Business and e-Commerce for Managers

Coming Soon
e-books and e-whitepapers

To communicate with the authors, send email to:

deitel@deitel.com

For information on corporate on-site seminars and public seminars offered by Deitel & Associates, Inc. worldwide, visit:

www.deitel.com

For continuing updates on Prentice Hall and Deitel & Associates, Inc. publications visit the Prentice Hall Web site

www.prenhall.com/deitel

JAVA™

HOW TO PROGRAM
FOURTH EDITION

H. M. Deitel
Deitel & Associates, Inc.

P. J. Deitel
Deitel & Associates, Inc.

PRENTICE HALL, Upper Saddle River, New Jersey 07458

Library of Congress Cataloging-in-Publication Data

Deitel, Harvey M
Java : how to program / H.M. Deitel, P.J. Deitel.--4th ed.
p. cm.
Includes bibliographical references and index.
ISBN 0-13-034151-7
1. Java (computer program language) I. Deitel, Paul J. II. Title
QA76.73.J38 D45 2001
005.13'3--dc21 2001045143

Vice President and Editorial Director: ***Marcia Horton***
Acquisitions Editor: ***Petra J. Recter***
Assistant Editor: ***Sarah Burrows***
Project Manager: ***Crissy Statuto***
Editorial Assistant: ***Karen Schultz***
Vice President and Director of Production and Manufacturing, ESM: ***David W. Riccardi***
Executive Managing Editor: ***Vince O'Brien***
Managing Editor: ***David A. George***
Assistant Managing Editor: ***Camille Trentacoste***
Director of Creative Services: ***Paul Belfanti***
Creative Director: ***Carole Anson***
Chapter Opener and Cover Designer: ***Tamara Newnam***
Manufacturing Manager: ***Trudy Pisciotti***
Manufacturing Buyer: ***Lisa McDowell***
Marketing Manager: ***Jennie Burger***

The authors and publisher of this book have used their best efforts in preparing this book. These efforts include the development, research, and testing of the theories and programs to determine their effectiveness. The authors and publisher make no warranty of any kind, expressed or implied, with regard to these programs or to the documentation contained in this book. The authors and publisher shall not be liable in any event for incidental or consequential damages in connection with, or arising out of, the furnishing, performance, or use of these programs.

Many of the designations used by manufacturers and sellers to distinguish their products are claimed as trademarks and registered trademarks. Where those designations appear in this book, and Prentice Hall and the authors were aware of a trademark claim, the designations have been printed in initial caps or all caps. All product names mentioned remain trademarks or registered trademarks of their respective owners.

Printed in the United States of America

10 9 8 7 6 5 4 3 2 1

ISBN 0-13-0345151-7

Prentice-Hall International (UK) Limited, *London*
Prentice-Hall of Australia Pty. Limited, *Sydney*
Prentice-Hall Canada Inc., *Toronto*
Prentice-Hall Hispanoamericana, S.A., *Mexico*
Prentice-Hall of India Private Limited, *New Delhi*
Prentice-Hall of Japan, Inc., *Tokyo*
Pearson Education Asia Pte. Ltd., *Singapore*
Editora Prentice-Hall do Brasil, Ltda., *Rio de Janeiro*

To David Nelson and Gary Morin of Sun Microsystems:
We dedicate this book to you—our friends and our mentors—to whom we owe our decade-long relationship with Sun.

It was a privilege to be working with you and your colleagues at Sun when Java and the field of Java education were born.

Harvey and Paul Deitel

Trademarks

Contents

Preface xxxv

1 Introduction to Computers, the Internet and the Web 1

1.1 Introduction 2
1.2 What Is a Computer? 7
1.3 Computer Organization 7
1.4 Evolution of Operating Systems 8
1.5 Personal, Distributed and Client/Server Computing 9
1.6 Machine Languages, Assembly Languages and High-Level Languages 10
1.7 History of C++ 11
1.8 History of Java 12
1.9 Java Class Libraries 13
1.10 Other High-Level Languages 14
1.11 Structured Programming 14
1.12 The Internet and the World Wide Web 15
1.13 Basics of a Typical Java Environment 16
1.14 General Notes about Java and This Book 19
1.15 Thinking About Objects: Introduction to Object Technology and the Unified Modeling Language 22
1.16 Discovering Design Patterns: Introduction 26
1.17 Tour of the Book 28
1.18 (Optional) A Tour of the Case Study on Object-Oriented Design with the UML 41
1.19 (Optional) A Tour of the "Discovering Design Patterns" Sections 45

2 Introduction to Java Applications 55

2.1 Introduction 56
2.2 A First Program in Java: Printing a Line of Text 56
2.2.1 Compiling and Executing your First Java Application 61

2.3 Modifying Our First Java Program 62
2.3.1 Displaying a Single Line of Text with Multiple Statements 62
2.3.2 Displaying Multiple Lines of Text with a Single Statement 63
2.4 Displaying Text in a Dialog Box 65
2.5 Another Java Application: Adding Integers 69
2.6 Memory Concepts 75
2.7 Arithmetic 76
2.8 Decision Making: Equality and Relational Operators 79
2.9 (Optional Case Study) Thinking About Objects: Examining the Problem Statement 87

3 Introduction to Java Applets 105
3.1 Introduction 106
3.2 Sample Applets from the Java 2 Software Development Kit 107
3.2.1 The **TicTacToe** Applet 107
3.2.2 The **DrawTest** Applet 111
3.2.3 The **Java2D** Applet 112
3.3 A Simple Java Applet: Drawing a String 112
3.3.1 Compiling and Executing **WelcomeApplet** 118
3.4 Two More Simple Applets: Drawing Strings and Lines 120
3.5 Another Java Applet: Adding Floating-Point Numbers 123
3.6 Viewing Applets in a Web Browser 130
3.6.1 Viewing Applets in Netscape Navigator 6 131
3.6.2 Viewing Applets in Other Browsers Using the Java Plug-In 131
3.7 Java Applet Internet and World Wide Web Resources 134
3.8 (Optional Case Study) Thinking About Objects: Identifying the Classes in a Problem Statement135

4 Control Structures: Part 1 148
4.1 Introduction 149
4.2 Algorithms 149
4.3 Pseudocode 150
4.4 Control Structures 150
4.5 The **if** Selection Structure 153
4.6 The **if/else** Selection Structure 155
4.7 The **while** Repetition Structure 159
4.8 Formulating Algorithms: Case Study 1 (Counter-Controlled Repetition) 160
4.9 Formulating Algorithms with Top-Down, Stepwise Refinement: Case Study 2 (Sentinel-Controlled Repetition) 165
4.10 Formulating Algorithms with Top-Down, Stepwise Refinement: Case Study 3 (Nested Control Structures) 173
4.11 Assignment Operators 178
4.12 Increment and Decrement Operators 179
4.13 Primitive Data Types 182
4.14 (Optional Case Study) Thinking About Objects: Identifying Class Attributes 183

5 Control Structures: Part 2 197
5.1 Introduction 198
5.2 Essentials of Counter-Controlled Repetition 198
5.3 The **for** Repetition Structure 201
5.4 Examples Using the **for** Structure 205
5.5 The **switch** Multiple-Selection Structure 210
5.6 The **do/while** Repetition Structure 215
5.7 Statements **break** and **continue** 218
5.8 Labeled **break** and **continue** Statements 220
5.9 Logical Operators 222
5.10 Structured Programming Summary 229
5.11 (Optional Case Study) Thinking About Objects: Identifying Objects' States and Activities 234

6 Methods 246
6.1 Introduction 247
6.2 Program Modules in Java 247
6.3 **Math** Class Methods 249
6.4 Methods 249
6.5 Method Definitions 251
6.6 Argument Promotion 258
6.7 Java API Packages 259
6.8 Random-Number Generation 261
6.9 Example: A Game of Chance 265
6.10 Duration of Identifiers 274
6.11 Scope Rules 275
6.12 Recursion 278
6.13 Example Using Recursion: The Fibonacci Series 281
6.14 Recursion vs. Iteration 286
6.15 Method Overloading 288
6.16 Methods of Class **JApplet** 291
6.17 (Optional Case Study) Thinking About Objects: Identifying Class Operations 293

7 Arrays 313
7.1 Introduction 314
7.2 Arrays 315
7.3 Declaring and Allocating Arrays 317
7.4 Examples Using Arrays 317
7.4.1 Allocating an Array and Initializing Its Elements 318
7.4.2 Using an Initializer List to Initialize Elements of an Array 319
7.4.3 Calculating the Value to Store in Each Array Element 320
7.4.4 Summing the Elements of an Array 322
7.4.5 Using Histograms to Display Array Data Graphically 323
7.4.6 Using the Elements of an Array as Counters 324
7.4.7 Using Arrays to Analyze Survey Results 326

7.5 References and Reference Parameters 329
7.6 Passing Arrays to Methods 329
7.7 Sorting Arrays 332
7.8 Searching Arrays: Linear Search and Binary Search 335
7.8.1 Searching an Array with Linear Search 335
7.8.2 Searching a Sorted Array with Binary Search 338
7.9 Multiple-Subscripted Arrays 343
7.10 (Optional Case Study) Thinking About Objects: Collaboration Among Objects 350

8 Object-Based Programming 378
8.1 Introduction 379
8.2 Implementing a Time Abstract Data Type with a Class 380
8.3 Class Scope 388
8.4 Controlling Access to Members 388
8.5 Creating Packages 390
8.6 Initializing Class Objects: Constructors 394
8.7 Using Overloaded Constructors 395
8.8 Using *Set* and *Get* Methods 400
8.8.1 Executing an Applet that Uses Programmer-Defined Packages 409
8.9 Software Reusability 411
8.10 Final Instance Variables 412
8.11 Composition: Objects as Instance Variables of Other Classes 414
8.12 Package Access 417
8.13 Using the **this** Reference 419
8.14 Finalizers 426
8.15 Static Class Members 427
8.16 Data Abstraction and Encapsulation 432
8.16.1 Example: Queue Abstract Data Type 433
8.17 (Optional Case Study) Thinking About Objects: Starting to Program the Classes for the Elevator Simulation 434

9 Object-Oriented Programming 445
9.1 Introduction 446
9.2 Superclasses and Subclasses 449
9.3 **protected** Members 451
9.4 Relationship between Superclass Objects and Subclass Objects 452
9.5 Constructors and Finalizers in Subclasses 459
9.6 Implicit Subclass-Object-to-Superclass-Object Conversion 463
9.7 Software Engineering with Inheritance 464
9.8 Composition vs. Inheritance 465
9.9 Case Study: Point, Circle, Cylinder 465
9.10 Introduction to Polymorphism 472
9.11 Type Fields and **switch** Statements 473
9.12 Dynamic Method Binding 473
9.13 **final** Methods and Classes 474
9.14 Abstract Superclasses and Concrete Classes 474

9.15 Polymorphism Examples 475
9.16 Case Study: A Payroll System Using Polymorphism 477
9.17 New Classes and Dynamic Binding 485
9.18 Case Study: Inheriting Interface and Implementation 486
9.19 Case Study: Creating and Using Interfaces 494
9.20 Inner Class Definitions 501
9.21 Notes on Inner Class Definitions 512
9.22 Type-Wrapper Classes for Primitive Types 513
9.23 (Optional Case Study) Thinking About Objects: Incorporating Inheritance into the Elevator Simulation 513
9.24 (Optional) Discovering Design Patterns: Introducing Creational, Structural and Behavioral Design Patterns 520
9.24.1 Creational Design Patterns 521
9.24.2 Structural Design Patterns 523
9.24.3 Behavioral Design Patterns 524
9.24.4 Conclusion 526
9.24.5 Internet and World-Wide-Web Resources 526

10 Strings and Characters 536

10.1 Introduction 537
10.2 Fundamentals of Characters and Strings 538
10.3 **String** Constructors 538
10.4 **String** Methods **length**, **charAt** and **getChars** 540
10.5 Comparing **String**s 542
10.6 **String** Method **hashCode** 547
10.7 Locating Characters and Substrings in **String**s 549
10.8 Extracting Substrings from **String**s 551
10.9 Concatenating **String**s 552
10.10 Miscellaneous **String** Methods 553
10.11 Using **String** Method **valueOf** 555
10.12 **String** Method **intern** 557
10.13 **StringBuffer** Class 559
10.14 **StringBuffer** Constructors 560
10.15 **StringBuffer** Methods **length**, **capacity**, **setLength** and **ensureCapacity** 561
10.16 **StringBuffer** Methods **charAt**, **setCharAt**, **getChars** and **reverse** 563
10.17 **StringBuffer append** Methods 564
10.18 **StringBuffer** Insertion and Deletion Methods 566
10.19 **Character** Class Examples 568
10.20 Class **StringTokenizer** 576
10.21 Card Shuffling and Dealing Simulation 579
10.22 (Optional Case Study) Thinking About Objects: Event Handling 583

11 Graphics and Java2D 601

11.1 Introduction 602
11.2 Graphics Contexts and Graphics Objects 604

11.3 Color Control 605
11.4 Font Control 612
11.5 Drawing Lines, Rectangles and Ovals 618
11.6 Drawing Arcs 622
11.7 Drawing Polygons and Polylines 625
11.8 The Java2D API 628
11.9 Java2D Shapes 628
11.10 (Optional Case Study) Thinking About Objects: Designing Interfaces with the UML 635

12 Graphical User Interface Components: Part 1 646
12.1 Introduction 647
12.2 Swing Overview 649
12.3 **JLabel** 651
12.4 Event-Handling Model 654
12.5 **JTextField** and **JPasswordField** 656
12.5.1 How Event Handling Works 660
12.6 **JButton** 662
12.7 **JCheckBox** and **JRadioButton** 665
12.8 **JComboBox** 671
12.9 **JList** 673
12.10 Multiple-Selection Lists 676
12.11 Mouse Event Handling 678
12.12 Adapter Classes 683
12.13 Keyboard Event Handling 689
12.14 Layout Managers 692
12.14.1 **FlowLayout** 693
12.14.2 **BorderLayout** 696
12.14.3 **GridLayout** 699
12.15 Panels 701
12.16 (Optional Case Study) Thinking About Objects: Use Cases 703

13 Graphical User Interface Components: Part 2 720
13.1 Introduction 721
13.2 **JTextArea** 722
13.3 Creating a Customized Subclass of **JPanel** 725
13.4 Creating a Self-Contained Subclass of **JPanel** 730
13.5 **JSlider** 735
13.6 Windows 739
13.7 Designing Programs that Execute as Applets or Applications 741
13.8 Using Menus with Frames 747
13.9 Using **JPopupMenus** 755
13.10 Pluggable Look-and-Feel 758
13.11 Using **JDesktopPane** and **JInternalFrame** 762
13.12 Layout Managers 766
13.13 **BoxLayout** Layout Manager 767
13.14 **CardLayout** Layout Manager 770

13.15 **GridBagLayout** Layout Manager 774
13.16 **GridBagConstraints** Constants **RELATIVE** and **REMAINDER** 780
13.17 (Optional Case Study) Thinking About Objects: Model-View-Controller 783
13.18 (Optional) Discovering Design Patterns: Design Patterns Used in Packages **java.awt** and **javax.swing** 788
13.18.1 Creational Design Patterns 789
13.18.2 Structural Design Patterns 789
13.18.3 Behavioral Design Patterns 792
13.18.4 Conclusion 795

14 Exception Handling 804
14.1 Introduction 805
14.2 When Exception Handling Should Be Used 807
14.3 Other Error-Handling Techniques 807
14.4 Basics of Java Exception Handling 808
14.5 **try** Blocks 809
14.6 Throwing an Exception 809
14.7 Catching an Exception 810
14.8 Exception-Handling Example: Divide by Zero 812
14.9 Rethrowing an Exception 818
14.10 **throws** Clause 818
14.11 Constructors, Finalizers and Exception Handling 824
14.12 Exceptions and Inheritance 824
14.13 **finally** Block 825
14.14 Using **printStackTrace** and **getMessage** 830

15 Multithreading 837
15.1 Introduction 838
15.2 Class **Thread**: An Overview of the **Thread** Methods 840
15.3 Thread States: Life Cycle of a Thread 841
15.4 Thread Priorities and Thread Scheduling 842
15.5 Thread Synchronization 848
15.6 Producer/Consumer Relationship without Thread Synchronization 849
15.7 Producer/Consumer Relationship with Thread Synchronization 854
15.8 Producer/Consumer Relationship: The Circular Buffer 860
15.9 Daemon Threads 869
15.10 **Runnable** Interface 870
15.11 Thread Groups 876
15.12 (Optional Case Study) Thinking About Objects: Multithreading 877
15.13 (Optional) Discovering Design Patterns: Concurrent Design Patterns 886

16 Files and Streams 894
16.1 Introduction 895
16.2 Data Hierarchy 895
16.3 Files and Streams 897
16.4 Creating a Sequential-Access File 903
16.5 Reading Data from a Sequential-Access File 915

16.6 Updating Sequential-Access Files 927
16.7 Random-Access Files 928
16.8 Creating a Random-Access File 928
16.9 Writing Data Randomly to a Random-Access File 933
16.10 Reading Data Sequentially from a Random-Access File 939
16.11 Example: A Transaction-Processing Program 944
16.12 Class **File** 961

17 Networking 978

17.1 Introduction 979
17.2 Manipulating URIs 981
17.3 Reading a File on a Web Server 986
17.4 Establishing a Simple Server Using Stream Sockets 990
17.5 Establishing a Simple Client Using Stream Sockets 991
17.6 Client/Server Interaction with Stream Socket Connections 992
17.7 Connectionless Client/Server Interaction with Datagrams 1003
17.8 Client/Server Tic-Tac-Toe Using a Multithreaded Server 1011
17.9 Security and the Network 1026
17.10 DeitelMessenger Chat Server and Client 1026
17.10.1 **DeitelMessengerServer** and Supporting Classes 1027
17.10.2 **DeitelMessenger** Client and Supporting Classes 1036
17.11 (Optional) Discovering Design Patterns: Design Patterns Used in Packages **java.io** and **java.net** 1056
17.11.1 Creational Design Patterns 1056
17.11.2 Structural Design Patterns 1057
17.11.3 Architectural Patterns 1058
17.11.4 Conclusion 1060

18 Multimedia: Images, Animation, Audio and Video 1068

18.1 Introduction 1069
18.2 Loading, Displaying and Scaling Images 1070
18.3 Animating a Series of Images 1073
18.4 Customizing **LogoAnimator** via Applet Parameters 1077
18.5 Image Maps 1081
18.6 Loading and Playing Audio Clips 1084
18.7 Internet and World Wide Web Resources 1087

19 Data Structures 1094

19.1 Introduction 1095
19.2 Self-Referential Classes 1096
19.3 Dynamic Memory Allocation 1096
19.4 Linked Lists 1097
19.5 Stacks 1108
19.6 Queues 1113
19.7 Trees 1116

20 Java Utilities Package and Bit Manipulation 1147

20.1 Introduction 1148
20.2 **Vector** Class and **Enumeration** Interface 1148
20.3 **Stack** Class 1156
20.4 **Dictionary** Class 1160
20.5 **Hashtable** Class 1161
20.6 **Properties** Class 1168
20.7 **Random** Class 1174
20.8 Bit Manipulation and the Bitwise Operators 1175
20.9 **BitSet** Class 1190

21 Collections 1201

21.1 Introduction 1202
21.2 Collections Overview 1203
21.3 Class **Arrays** 1203
21.4 Interface **Collection** and Class **Collections** 1208
21.5 Lists 1208
21.6 Algorithms 1215
21.6.1 Algorithm **sort** 1215
21.6.2 Algorithm **shuffle** 1217
21.6.3 Algorithms **reverse**, **fill**, **copy**, **max** and **min** 1219
21.6.4 Algorithm **binarySearch** 1221
21.7 Sets 1223
21.8 Maps 1226
21.9 Synchronization Wrappers 1228
21.10 Unmodifiable Wrappers 1228
21.11 Abstract Implementations 1229
21.12 (Optional) Discovering Design Patterns: Design Patterns Used in Package **java.util** 1229
21.12.1 Creational Design Patterns 1229
21.12.2 Behavioral Design Patterns 1230
21.12.3 Conclusion 1230

22 Java Media Framework and Java Sound (on CD) 1236

22.1 Introduction 1237
22.2 Playing Media 1238
22.3 Formatting and Saving Captured Media 1249
22.4 RTP Streaming 1263
22.5 Java Sound 1277
22.6 Playing Sampled Audio 1278
22.7 Musical Instrument Digital Interface (MIDI) 1285
22.7.1 MIDI Playback 1286
22.7.2 MIDI Recording 1291
22.7.3 MIDI Synthesis 1295
22.7.4 Class **MidiDemo** 1299
22.8 Internet and World Wide Web Resources 1316

22.9 (Optional Case Study) Thinking About Objects: Animation and Sound in the View 1317

A Java Demos 1346
A.1 Introduction 1346
A.2 The Sites 1346

B Java Resources 1348
B.1 Resources 1348
B.2 Products 1349
B.3 FAQs 1350
B.4 Tutorials 1350
B.5 Magazines 1350
B.6 Java Applets 1350
B.7 Multimedia 1351
B.8 Newsgroups 1351

C Operator Precedence Chart 1353

D ASCII Character Set 1355

E Number Systems (on CD) 1356
E.1 Introduction 1357
E.2 Abbreviating Binary Numbers as Octal Numbers and Hexadecimal Numbers 1360
E.3 Converting Octal Numbers and Hexadecimal Numbers to Binary Numbers 1361
E.4 Converting from Binary, Octal, or Hexadecimal to Decimal 1361
E.5 Converting from Decimal to Binary, Octal, or Hexadecimal 1362
E.6 Negative Binary Numbers: Two's Complement Notation 1364

F Creating HTML Documentation with *javadoc* (on CD) 1369
F.1 Introduction 1370
F.2 Documentation Comments 1370
F.3 Documenting Java Source Code 1370
F.4 **javadoc** 1379
F.5 Files Produced by **javadoc** 1379

G Elevator Events and Listener Interfaces (on CD) 1384
G.1 Introduction 1384
G.2 Events 1384
G.3 Listeners 1388
G.4 Component Diagrams Revisited 1391

H Elevator Model (on CD) 1393
H.1 Introduction 1393
H.2 Class **ElevatorModel** 1393
H.3 Classes **Location** and **Floor** 1401
H.4 Class **Door** 1404
H.5 Class **Button** 1408

H.6 Class **ElevatorShaft** 1409
H.7 Classes **Light** and **Bell** 1416
H.8 Class **Elevator** 1420
H.9 Class **Person** 1429
H.10 Component Diagrams Revisited 1436
H.11 Conclusion 1436

I Elevator View (on CD) 1438

I.1 Introduction 1438
I.2 Class Objects 1455
I.3 Class Constants 1457
I.4 Class constructor 1458
I.5 Event Handling 1460
I.5.1 **ElevatorMoveEvent** types 1461
I.5.2 **PersonMoveEvent** types 1461
I.5.3 **DoorEvent** types 1462
I.5.4 **ButtonEvent** types 1462
I.5.5 **BellEvent** types 1463
I.5.6 **LightEvent** types 1463
I.6 Component Diagrams Revisited 1463
I.7 Conclusion 1463

J Career Opportunities (on CD) 1465

J.1 Introduction 1466
J.2 Resources for the Job Seeker 1467
J.3 Online Opportunities for Employers 1468
J.3.1 Posting Jobs Online 1470
J.3.2 Problems with Recruiting on the Web 1472
J.3.3 Diversity in the Workplace 1472
J.4 Recruiting Services 1473
J.4.1 Testing Potential Employees Online 1474
J.5 Career Sites 1475
J.5.1 Comprehensive Career Sites 1475
J.5.2 Technical Positions 1476
J.5.3 Wireless Positions 1477
J.5.4 Contracting Online 1477
J.5.5 Executive Positions 1478
J.5.6 Students and Young Professionals 1479
J.5.7 Other Online Career Services 1480
J.6 Internet and World Wide Web Resources 1481

K Unicode® (on CD) 1489

K.1 Introduction 1490
K.2 Unicode Transformation Formats 1491
K.3 Characters and Glyphs 1492
K.4 Advantages/Disadvantages of Unicode 1493
K.5 Unicode Consortium's Web Site 1493

K.6 Using Unicode 1494
K.7 Character Ranges 1497

Bibliography **1501**

Index **1506**

Illustrations

1 Introduction to Computers, the Internet and the Web
1.1 Typical Java environment. 17

2 Introduction to Java Applications
2.1 A first program in Java. 57
2.2 Executing **Welcome1** in a Microsoft Windows 2000 **Command Prompt**. 62
2.3 Printing a line of text with multiple statements. 63
2.4 Printing multiple lines of text with a single statement. 64
2.5 Some common escape sequences. 64
2.6 Displaying multiple lines in a dialog box. 66
2.7 A sample Netscape Navigator window with GUI components. 67
2.8 Message dialog box. 68
2.9 An addition program "in action." 69
2.10 Input dialog box. 72
2.11 Message dialog box customized with the four-argument version of method **showMessageDialog**. 74
2.12 **JOptionPane** constants for message dialogs. 75
2.13 Memory location showing the name and value of variable **number1**. 75
2.14 Memory locations after storing values for **number1** and **number2**. 76
2.15 Memory locations after calculating the **sum** of **number1** and **number2**. 76
2.16 Arithmetic operators. 77
2.17 Precedence of arithmetic operators. 78
2.18 Order in which a second-degree polynomial is evaluated. 80
2.19 Equality and relational operators. 80
2.20 Using equality and relational operators. 81
2.21 Precedence and associativity of the operators discussed so far. 86
2.22 Person moving towards elevator on the first floor. 89
2.23 Person riding the elevator to the second floor. 89

2.24 Person walking away from elevator. 90

3 Introduction to Java Applets

3.1 The examples from the **applets** directory. 108
3.2 Sample execution of the **TicTacToe** applet. 110
3.3 Selecting **Reload** from the **appletviewer**'s **Applet** menu. 110
3.4 Sample execution of applet **DrawTest**. 111
3.5 Sample execution of applet **Java2D**. 113
3.6 A first applet in Java and the applet's screen output. 113
3.7 **WelcomeApplet.html** loads class **WelcomeApplet** of Fig. 3.6 into the **appletviewer**. 119
3.8 Applet that displays multiple strings. 121
3.9 **WelcomeApplet2.html** loads class **WelcomeApplet2** of Fig. 3.8 into the **appletviewer**. 121
3.10 Drawing strings and lines. 122
3.11 The **WelcomeLines.html** file, which loads class **WelcomeLines** of Fig. 3.10 into the **appletviewer**. 122
3.12 An addition program "in action." 123
3.13 **AdditionApplet.html** loads class **AdditionApplet** of Fig. 3.12 into the **appletviewer**. 125
3.14 Applet of Fig. 3.10 executing in Netscape Navigator 6. 132
3.15 **Java Plug-in HTML Converter** window. 132
3.16 Selecting the directory containing HTML files to convert. 133
3.17 Selecting the template used to convert the HTML files. 134
3.18 Confirmation dialog after conversion completes. 134
3.19 Nouns (and noun phrases) in problem statement. 135
3.20 Representing a class in the UML. 138
3.21 Class diagram showing associations among classes. 139
3.22 Multiplicity types. 139
3.23 Class diagram for the elevator model. 140
3.24 Object diagram of an empty building in our elevator model. 141

4 Control Structures: Part 1

4.1 Flowcharting Java's sequence structure. 151
4.2 Java keywords. 152
4.3 Flowcharting the single-selection **if** structure. 154
4.4 Flowcharting the double-selection **if/else** structure. 155
4.5 Flowcharting the **while** repetition structure. 160
4.6 Pseudocode algorithm that uses counter-controlled repetition to solve the class-average problem. 161
4.7 Class-average program with counter-controlled repetition. 161
4.8 Pseudocode algorithm that uses sentinel-controlled repetition to solve the class-average problem. 168
4.9 Class-average program with sentinel-controlled repetition. 169
4.10 Pseudocode for examination-results problem. 175
4.11 Java program for examination-results problem. 176
4.12 Arithmetic assignment operators. 179

4.13 The increment and decrement operators. 179
4.14 The difference between preincrementing and postincrementing. 180
4.15 Precedence and associativity of the operators discussed so far. 182
4.16 The Java primitive data types. 183
4.17 Descriptive words and phrases from problem statement. 185
4.18 Classes with attributes. 187

5 Control Structures: Part 2

5.1 Counter-controlled repetition. 199
5.2 Counter-controlled repetition with the **for** structure. 201
5.3 Components of a typical **for** structure header. 202
5.4 Flowcharting a typical **for** repetition structure. 205
5.5 Summation with the **for** structure. 206
5.6 Calculating compound interest with the **for** structure. 207
5.7 An example using **switch**. 211
5.8 The **switch** multiple-selection structure. 214
5.9 Using the **do/while** repetition structure. 216
5.10 Flowcharting the **do/while** repetition structure. 217
5.11 Using the **break** statement in a **for** structure. 218
5.12 Using the **continue** statement in a **for** structure. 219
5.13 Using a labeled **break** statement in a nested **for** structure. 221
5.14 Using a labeled **continue** statement in a nested **for** structure. 223
5.15 Truth table for the **&&** (logical AND) operator. 224
5.16 Truth table for the **||** (logical OR) operator. 225
5.17 Truth table for the boolean logical exclusive OR (**^**) operator. 226
5.18 Truth table for operator **!** (logical negation, or logical NOT). 226
5.19 Demonstrating the logical operators. 227
5.20 Precedence and associativity of the operators discussed so far. 229
5.21 Java's single-entry/single-exit control structures. 230
5.22 Rules for forming structured programs. 231
5.23 The simplest flowchart. 231
5.24 Repeatedly applying Rule 2 of Fig. 5.22 to the simplest flowchart. 232
5.25 Applying Rule 3 of Fig. 5.22 to the simplest flowchart. 232
5.26 Stacked, nested and overlapped building blocks. 233
5.27 An unstructured flowchart. 233
5.28 Statechart diagram for **FloorButton** and **ElevatorButton** objects. 235
5.29 Activity diagram for a **Person** object. 236
5.30 Activity diagram for the **Elevator** object. 237

6 Methods

6.1 Hierarchical boss-method/worker-method relationship. 248
6.2 **Math** class methods. 250
6.3 Using programmer-defined method **square.** 252
6.4 Programmer-defined **maximum** method. 256
6.5 Allowed promotions for primitive data types. 258
6.6 Packages of the Java API. 259
6.7 Shifted and scaled random integers. 262

6.8 Rolling a six-sided die 6000 times. 263
6.9 Program to simulate the game of craps. 265
6.10 A scoping example. 276
6.11 Recursive evaluation of 5!. 279
6.12 Calculating factorials with a recursive method. 279
6.13 Recursively generating Fibonacci numbers. 282
6.14 Set of recursive calls to method **fibonacci** (**f** in this diagram). 285
6.15 Summary of recursion examples and exercises in this text. 287
6.16 Using overloaded methods. 289
6.17 Compiler error messages generated from overloaded methods with identical parameter lists and different return types. 290
6.18 **JApplet** methods that the applet container calls during an applet's execution. 292
6.19 Verb phrases for each class in simulator. 293
6.20 Classes with attributes and operations. 294
6.21 Values for the sides of triangles in Exercise 6.15. 306
6.22 The Towers of Hanoi for the case with four disks. 311

7 Arrays

7.1 A 12-element array. 315
7.2 Precedence and associativity of the operators discussed so far. 316
7.3 Initializing the elements of an array to zeros. 318
7.4 Initializing the elements of an array with a declaration. 319
7.5 Generating values to be placed into elements of an array. 321
7.6 Computing the sum of the elements of an array. 322
7.7 A program that prints histograms . 323
7.8 Die-rolling program using arrays instead of **switch**. 324
7.9 A simple student-poll analysis program. 326
7.10 Passing arrays and individual array elements to methods . 330
7.11 Sorting an array with bubble sort . 333
7.12 Linear search of an array. 336
7.13 Binary search of a sorted array 338
7.14 A double-subscripted array with three rows and four columns. 343
7.15 Initializing multidimensional arrays. 344
7.16 Example of using double-subscripted arrays. 347
7.17 Verb phrases for each class exhibiting behaviors in simulation. 350
7.18 Collaborations in the elevator system. 351
7.19 Collaboration diagram of a person pressing a floor button 352
7.20 Collaboration diagram for passengers exiting and entering the elevator. 353
7.21 The 36 possible outcomes of rolling two dice. 360
7.22 Determine what this program does. 360
7.23 Determine what this program does. 361
7.24 Turtle graphics commands. 363
7.25 The eight possible moves of the knight. 364
7.26 The 22 squares eliminated by placing a queen in the upper left corner. 367
7.27 Rules for adjusting the positions of the tortoise and the hare. 371

7.28 Simpletron Machine Language (SML) operation codes. 372
7.29 SML program that reads two integers and computes their sum. 373
7.30 SML program that reads two integers and determines which is larger. 373
7.31 Behavior of several SML instructions in the Simpletron. 375
7.32 A sample dump. 376

8 Object-Based Programming

8.1 Abstract data type **Time1** implementation as a class. 381
8.2 Using an object of class **Time1** in a program. 385
8.3 Erroneous attempt to access private members of class **Time1**. 389
8.4 Placing Class **Time1** in a package for reuse. 391
8.5 Using programmer-defined class **Time1** in a package. 393
8.6 Class **Time2** with overloaded constructors. 396
8.7 Using overloaded constructors to initialize objects of class **Time2**. 398
8.8 Class **Time3** with *set* and *get* methods. 401
8.9 Using class **Time3**'s *set* and *get* methods. 405
8.10 Contents of **TimeTest5.jar**. 410
8.11 Initializing a **final** variable. 412
8.12 Compiler error message as a result of not initializing increment. 413
8.13 **Date** class. 414
8.14 **Employee** class with member object references. 416
8.15 Demonstrating an object with a member object reference. 416
8.16 Package access to members of a class. 418
8.17 Using the **this** reference implicitly and explicitly. 419
8.18 Class **Time4** using **this** to enable chained method calls. 422
8.19 Concatenating method calls. 425
8.20 **Employee** class that uses a **static** class variable to maintain a count of the number of **Employee** objects in memory. 428
8.21 Using a **static** class variable to maintain a count of the number of objects of a class. 429
8.22 Complete class diagram with visibility notations. 435

9 Object-Oriented Programming

9.1 Some simple inheritance examples in which the subclass "is a" superclass. 449
9.2 An inheritance hierarchy for university **CommunityMember**s. 450
9.3 A portion of a **Shape** class hierarchy. 451
9.4 **Point** class definition. 453
9.5 **Circle** class definition. 454
9.6 Assigning subclass references to superclass references. 457
9.7 **Point** class definition to demonstrate when constructors and finalizers are called. 460
9.8 **Circle** class definition to demonstrate when constructors and finalizers are called. 461
9.9 Order in which constructors and finalizers are called. 462
9.10 **Point** class definition. 465
9.11 Testing class **Point**. 466
9.12 **Circle** class definition. 467

9.13 Testing class **Circle**. 468
9.14 Class **Cylinder** definition. 470
9.15 Testing class **Cylinder**. 471
9.16 **Employee abstract** superclass. 478
9.17 **Boss** extends **abstract** class **Employee**. 479
9.18 **CommissionWorker** extends **abstract** class **Employee**. 480
9.19 **PieceWorker** extends **abstract** class **Employee**. 481
9.20 **HourlyWorker** extends **abstract** class **Employee**. 482
9.21 Testing the **Employee** class hierarchy using an **abstract** superclass. 483
9.22 **Shape** abstract superclass for **Point**, **Circle**, **Cylinder** hierarchy. 487
9.23 **Point** subclass of abstract class **Shape**. 488
9.24 **Circle** subclass of **Point**—indirect subclass of **abstract** class **Shape**. 489
9.25 **Cylinder** subclass of **Circle**—indirect subclass of abstract class **Shape**. 490
9.26 **Shape**, **Point**, **Circle**, **Cylinder** hierarchy. 492
9.27 Point, circle, cylinder hierarchy with a **Shape** interface. 495
9.28 **Point** implementation of interface **Shape**. 495
9.29 **Circle** subclass of **Point**—indirect implementation of interface **Shape**. 497
9.30 **Cylinder** subclass of **Circle**—indirect implementation of interface **Shape**. 498
9.31 **Shape**, **Point**, **Circle**, **Cylinder** hierarchy. 499
9.32 **Time** class. 501
9.33 Demonstrating an inner class in a windowed application. 503
9.34 Demonstrating anonymous inner classes. 508
9.35 Attributes and operations of classes **FloorButton** and **ElevatorButton**. 514
9.36 Attributes and operations of classes **FloorDoor** and **ElevatorDoor**. 515
9.37 Generalization diagram of superclass **Location** and subclasses **Elevator** and **Floor**. 516
9.38 Class diagram of our simulator (incorporating inheritance). 517
9.39 Class diagram with attributes and operations (incorporating inheritance). 518
9.40 The 18 Gang-of-four design patterns discussed in *Java How to Program 4/e*. 520
9.41 Concurrent design patterns and architectural patterns discussed in *Java How to Program, 4/e*. 521
9.42 Class **Singleton** ensures that only one object of its class is created. 522
9.43 Class **SingletonExample** attempts to create **Singleton** object more than once. 523
9.44 Class **SingletonExample** output shows that the **Singleton** object may be created only once. 523
9.45 The **MyShape** hierarchy. 533
9.46 The **MyShape** hierarchy. 535

10 Strings and Characters

10.1 Demonstrating the **String** class constructors. 538
10.2 The **String** class character manipulation methods. 541

10.3 Demonstrating **String** comparisons. 543
10.4 **String** class **startsWith** and **endsWith** methods. 546
10.5 **String** class **hashCode** method. 548
10.6 The **String** class searching methods. 549
10.7 **String** class **substring** methods. 551
10.8 **String** method **concat**. 552
10.9 Miscellaneous **String** methods. 554
10.10 **String** class **valueOf** methods. 555
10.11 **String** class **intern** method. 557
10.12 **StringBuffer** class constructors. 560
10.13 **StringBuffer length** and **capacity** methods. 561
10.14 **StringBuffer** class character manipulation methods. 563
10.15 **StringBuffer** class **append** methods. 565
10.16 **StringBuffer** class **insert** and **delete** methods. 567
10.17 **static** character testing methods and case conversion methods of class **Character**. 569
10.18 **Character** class **static** conversion methods. 572
10.19 Non-**static** methods of class **Character**. 574
10.20 Tokenizing strings with a **StringTokenizer** object. 576
10.21 Card dealing program. 579
10.22 Class **ElevatorModelEvent** is the superclass for all other event classes in our model. 584
10.23 Class diagram that models the generalization between **ElevatorModelEvent** and its subclasses. 585
10.24 Triggering actions of the **ElevatorModelEvent** subclass events. 586
10.25 Modified collaboration diagram for passengers entering and exiting the **Elevator** on the first **Floor**. 587
10.26 Class **ElevatorMoveEvent**, a subclass of **ElevatorModelEvent**, is sent when the **Elevator** has arrived at or departed from, a **Floor**. 589
10.27 Interface **ElevatorMoveListener** provides the methods required to listen for **Elevator** departure and arrival events. 589
10.28 Class diagram of our simulator (including event handling). 590
10.29 Counts for the string **"Whether 'tis nobler in the mind to suffer"**. 597
10.30 The letters of the alphabet as expressed in international Morse code. 599

11 Graphics and Java2D

11.1 Some classes and interfaces used in this chapter from Java's original graphics capabilities and from the Java2D API. 603
11.2 Java coordinate system. Units are measured in pixels. 604
11.3 **Color** class **static** constants and RGB values 606
11.4 **Color** methods and color-related **Graphics** methods. 606
11.5 Demonstrating setting and getting a **Color.** 607
11.6 Demonstrating the **JColorChooser** dialog. 609
11.7 The **HSB** and **RGB** tabs of the **JColorChooser** dialog. 612
11.8 **Font** methods, constants and font-related **Graphics** methods. 613

11.9 Using **Graphics** method **setFont** to change **Font**s. 614
11.10 Font metrics. 616
11.11 **FontMetrics** and **Graphics** methods for obtaining font metrics. 616
11.12 Obtaining font metric information. 617
11.13 **Graphics** methods that draw lines, rectangles and ovals. 618
11.14 Demonstrating **Graphics** method **drawLine.** 620
11.15 The arc width and arc height for rounded rectangles. 622
11.16 An oval bounded by a rectangle. 622
11.17 Positive and negative arc angles. 623
11.18 **Graphics** methods for drawing arcs. 623
11.19 Demonstrating **drawArc** and **fillArc.** 623
11.20 **Graphics** methods for drawing polygons and class **Polygon** constructors. 625
11.21 Demonstrating **drawPolygon** and **fillPolygon**. 626
11.22 Demonstrating some Java2D shapes. 629
11.23 Demonstrating some Java2D shapes 633
11.24 Class diagram that models class **Person** realizing interface **DoorListener**. 636
11.25 Elided class diagram that models class **Person** realizing interface **DoorListener**. 636
11.26 Class **Person** is generated from Fig. 11.24. 636
11.27 Class diagram that models realizations in the elevator model. 637
11.28 Class diagram for listener interfaces. 638

12 Graphical User Interface Components: Part 1

12.1 A sample Netscape Navigator window with GUI components. 648
12.2 Some basic GUI components. 648
12.3 Common superclasses of many of the Swing components. 650
12.4 Demonstrating class **JLabel.** 651
12.5 Some event classes of package **java.awt.event**. 654
12.6 Event-listener interfaces of package **java.awt.event**. 655
12.7 Demonstrating **JTextField**s and **JPasswordField**s. 656
12.8 Event registration for **JTextField textField1**. 661
12.9 The button hierarchy. 662
12.10 Demonstrating command buttons and action events. 662
12.11 Program that creates two **JCheckBox** buttons. 665
12.12 Creating and manipulating radio button. 668
12.13 Program that uses a **JComboBox** to select an icon. 671
12.14 Selecting colors from a **JList**. 674
12.15 Using a multiple-selection **JList**. 676
12.16 **MouseListener** and **MouseMotionListener** interface methods. 679
12.17 Demonstrating mouse event handling. 680
12.18 Event adapter classes and the interfaces they implement. 683
12.19 Program that demonstrates adapter classes. 684
12.20 Distinguishing among left, center and right mouse-button clicks. 686

12.21 **InputEvent** methods that help distinguish among left-, center- and right-mouse-button clicks. 689
12.22 Demonstrating key event-handling. 689
12.23 Layout managers. 692
12.24 Program that demonstrates components in **FlowLayout**. 693
12.25 Demonstrating components in **BorderLayout**. 696
12.26 Program that demonstrates components in **GridLayout**. 699
12.27 A **JPanel** with five **JButton**s in a **GridLayout** attached to the **SOUTH** region of a **BorderLayout**. 701
12.28 Use-case diagram for elevator simulation from user's perspective. 704
12.29 Use-case diagram from the perspective of a **Person**. 705
12.30 Class **ElevatorController** processes user input. 706
12.31 Interface **ElevatorConstants** provides **Location** name constants. 708
12.32 Modified class diagram showing generalization of superclass **Location** and subclasses **Elevator** and **Floor**. 709

13 Graphical User Interface Components: Part 2

13.1 Copying selected text from one text area to another. 722
13.2 Defining a custom drawing area by subclassing **JPanel**. 727
13.3 Drawing on a customized subclass of class **JPanel**. 728
13.4 Customized subclass of **JPanel** that processes mouse events. 730
13.5 Capturing mouse events with a **JPanel**. 733
13.6 Horizontal **JSlider** component. 735
13.7 Custom subclass of **JPanel** for drawing circles of a specified diameter. 737
13.8 Using a **JSlider** to determine the diameter of a circle. 738
13.9 Creating a GUI-based application from an applet. 742
13.10 Using **JMenu**s and mnemonics. 748
13.11 Using a **PopupMenu** object. 755
13.12 Changing the look-and-feel of a Swing-based GUI. 759
13.13 Creating a multiple document interface. 763
13.14 Additional layout managers. 766
13.15 Demonstrating the **BoxLayout** layout manager. 767
13.16 Demonstrating the **CardLayout** layout manager. 771
13.17 Designing a GUI that will use **GridBagLayout**. 774
13.18 **GridBagConstraints** instance variables. 774
13.19 **GridBagLayout** with the weights set to zero. 776
13.20 Demonstrating the **GridBagLayout** layout manager. 776
13.21 Demonstrating the **GridBagConstraints** constants **RELATIVE** and **REMAINDER**. 780
13.22 Class diagram of the elevator simulation. 784
13.23 Component diagram for elevator simulation. 786
13.24 Class **ElevatorSimulation** is the application for the elevator simulation. 787
13.25 Inheritance hierarchy for class **JPanel**. 791
13.26 Basis for the Observer design pattern. 793

14 Exception Handling

14.1 Exception class **DivideByZeroException**. 813
14.2 A simple exception-handling example with divide by zero. 814
14.3 The **java.lang** package errors. 821
14.4 The **java.lang** package exceptions. 821
14.5 The java.util package exceptions. 822
14.6 The **java.io** package exceptions. 823
14.7 The **java.awt** package exceptions. 823
14.8 The java.net package exceptions. 824
14.9 Demonstration of the **try-catch-finally** exception-handling mechanism. 826
14.10 Demonstration of stack unwinding. 828
14.11 Using **getMessage** and **printStackTrace.** 831

15 Multithreading

15.1 State diagram showing the Life cycle of a thread. 842
15.2 Java thread priority scheduling. 844
15.3 Multiple threads printing at random intervals. 845
15.4 Class **ProduceInteger** represents the producer in a producer/consumer relationship. 850
15.5 Class **ConsumeInteger** represents the consumer in a producer/consumer relationship. 851
15.6 Class **HoldIntegerUnsynchronized** maintains the data shared between the producer and consumer threads. 852
15.7 Threads modifying a shared object without synchronization. 853
15.8 Class **ProduceInteger** represents the producer in a producer/consumer relationship. 854
15.9 Class **ConsumeInteger** represents the consumer in a producer/consumer relationship. 855
15.10 Class **HoldIntegerSynchronized** monitors access to a shared integer. 857
15.11 Threads modifying a shared object with synchronization. 859
15.12 **UpdateThread** used by **SwingUtilities** method **invokeLater** to ensure GUI updates properly. 861
15.13 Class **ProduceInteger** represents the producer in a producer/consumer relationship. 861
15.14 Class **ConsumeInteger** represents the consumer in a producer/consumer relationship. 862
15.15 Class **HoldIntegerSynchronized** monitors access to a shared array of integers. 863
15.16 Threads modifying a shared array of cells. 868
15.17 Demonstrating the **Runnable** interface, suspending threads and resuming threads. 871
15.18 Modified collaboration diagram with active classes for passengers entering and exiting the **Elevator**. 879
15.19 Sequence diagram for a single **Person** changing floors in system. 882
15.20 Final class diagram of the elevator simulation 884
15.21 Final class diagram with attributes and operations. 885

16 Files and Streams

16.1 The data hierarchy. 897
16.2 Java's view of a file of *n* bytes. 898
16.3 A portion of the class hierarchy of the **java.io** package. 899
16.4 **BankUI** contains a reusable GUI for several programs. 904
16.5 Class **AccountRecord** maintains information for one account. 906
16.6 Creating a sequential file. 908
16.7 Sample data for the program of Fig. 16.6. 915
16.8 Reading a sequential file. 915
16.9 Credit inquiry program. 921
16.10 Java's view of a random-access file. 929
16.11 **RandomAccessAccountRecord** class used in the random-access file programs. 929
16.12 Creating a random-access file sequentially. 931
16.13 Writing data randomly to a random-access file. 934
16.14 Reading a random-access file sequentially. 939
16.15 The initial **Transaction Processor** window. 945
16.16 Loading a record into the **Update Record** internal frame. 945
16.17 Inputting a transaction in the **Update Record** internal frame. 946
16.18 **New Record** internal frame. 946
16.19 **Delete Record** internal frame. 946
16.20 Transaction-processing program. 947
16.21 Some commonly used **File** methods. 962
16.22 Demonstrating class **File**. 963
16.23 Sample data for master file. 975
16.24 Sample data for transaction file. 975
16.25 Additional transaction records. 975
16.26 Data for Exercise 16.10. 976
16.27 Telephone keypad digits and letters. 976

17 Networking

17.1 HTML document to load **SiteSelector** applet. 981
17.2 Loading a document from a URL into a browser. 983
17.3 Reading a file by opening a connection through a **URL** 986
17.4 Server portion of a client/server stream-socket connection. 993
17.5 Demonstrating the client portion of a stream-socket connection between a client and a server. 998
17.6 Demonstrating the server side of connectionless client/server computing with datagrams. 1004
17.7 Demonstrating the client side of connectionless client/server computing with datagrams. 1008
17.8 Server side of client/server Tic-Tac-Toe program. 1012
17.9 Client side of client/server Tic-Tac-Toe program. 1019
17.10 Sample outputs from the client/server Tic-Tac-Toe program. 1025
17.11 **DeitelMessengerServer** application for managing a chat room. 1027

17.12 **SocketMessengerConstants** declares constants for use throughout the **DeitelMessengerServer** and **DeitelMessenger** applications. 1029
17.13 **MessageListener** interface that defines method **messageReceived** for receiving new chat messages. 1030
17.14 **ReceivingThread** for listening for new messages from **DeitelMessengerServer** clients in separate **Thread**s. 1031
17.15 **MulticastSendingThread** for delivering outgoing messages to a multicast group via **DatagramPacket**s. 1035
17.16 **MessageManager** interface that defines methods for communicating with a **DeitelMessengerServer**. 1037
17.17 **SocketMessageManager** implementation of interface **MessageManager** for communicating via **Socket**s and multicast **DatagramPacket**s. 1037
17.18 **SendingThread** for delivering outgoing messages to **DeitelMessengerServer**. 1041
17.19 **PacketReceivingThread** for listening for new multicast messages from **DeitelMessengerServer** in a separate **Thread**. 1042
17.20 **ClientGUI** subclass of **JFrame** for presenting a GUI for viewing and sending chat messages. 1046
17.21 **DeitelMessenger** application for participating in a **DeitelMessengerServer** chat session. 1054
17.22 Model-View-Controller Architecture. 1058
17.23 Three-tier application model. 1059

18 Multimedia: Images, Animation, Audio and Video

18.1 Loading and displaying an image in an applet. 1070
18.2 Animating a series of images. 1073
18.3 **LogoAnimator2** subclass of **LogoAnimator** (Fig. 18.2) adds a constructor for customizing the number of images, animation delay and base image name. 1078
18.4 Customizing an animation applet via the **param** HTML tag. 1079
18.5 Demonstrating an image map. 1081
18.6 Loading and playing an **AudioClip**. 1085

19 Data Structures

19.1 Two self-referential class objects linked together. 1097
19.2 A graphical representation of a linked list. 1099
19.3 Definitions of class **ListNode** and class **List**. 1099
19.4 Definition of class **EmptyListException**. 1102
19.5 Manipulating a linked list. 1103
19.6 The **insertAtFront** operation. 1105
19.7 A graphical representation of the **insertAtBack** operation. 1106
19.8 A graphical representation of the **removeFromFront** operation. 1107
19.9 A graphical representation of the **removeFromBack** operation. 1108
19.10 Class **StackInheritance** extends class **List**. 1109
19.11 A simple stack program. 1110
19.12 A simple stack class using composition. 1112

19.13 Class **QueueInheritance** extends class **List**. 1113
19.14 Processing a queue. 1114
19.15 A graphical representation of a binary tree. 1116
19.16 A binary search tree containing 12 values. 1117
19.17 Definitions of **TreeNode** and **Tree** for a binary search tree. 1117
19.18 Creating and traversing a binary tree. 1120
19.19 A binary search tree. 1122
19.20 A 15-node binary search tree. 1127
19.21 Sample output of recursive method **outputTree**. 1133
19.22 Simple commands. 1133
19.23 Simple program that determines the sum of two integers. 1134
19.24 Simple program that finds the larger of two integers. 1135
19.25 Calculate the squares of several integers. 1135
19.26 Writing, compiling and executing a Simple language program. 1137
19.27 SML instructions produced after the compiler's first pass. 1138
19.28 Symbol table for program of Fig. 19.27. 1139
19.29 Unoptimized code from the program of Fig. 19.25. 1143
19.30 Optimized code for the program of Fig. 19.27. 1144

20 Java Utilities Package and Bit Manipulation

20.1 Demonstrating class **Vector** of package **java.util**. 1149
20.2 Demonstrating class **Stack** of package **java.util**. 1156
20.3 Demonstrating class **Hashtable**. 1162
20.4 Demonstrating class **Properties**. 1168
20.5 The bitwise operators. 1176
20.6 Printing the bits in an integer. 1176
20.7 Results of combining two bits with the bitwise AND operator (**&**). 1179
20.8 Demonstrating the bitwise AND, bitwise inclusive OR, bitwise exclusive OR and bitwise complement operators. 1179
20.9 Results of combining two bits with the bitwise inclusive OR operator (**|**). 1184
20.10 Results of combining two bits with the bitwise exclusive OR operator (**^**). 1185
20.11 Demonstrating the bitwise shift operators. 1185
20.12 The bitwise assignment operators. 1190
20.13 Demonstrating the Sieve of Eratosthenes using a **BitSet**. 1191

21 Collections

21.1 Using methods of class **Arrays**. 1203
21.2 Using **static** method **asList**. 1206
21.3 Using an **ArrayList** to demonstrate interface **Collection**. 1209
21.4 Using **List**s and **ListIterator**s. 1211
21.5 Using method **toArray**. 1213
21.6 Using algorithm **sort**. 1215
21.7 Using a **Comparator** object in **sort**. 1216
21.8 Card shuffling and dealing example. 1217
21.9 Using algorithms **reverse**, **fill**, **copy**, **max** and **min**. 1220
21.10 Using algorithm **binarySearch**. 1222
21.11 Using a **HashSet** to remove duplicates. 1224

21.12 Using **SortedSet**s and **TreeSet**s. 1225
21.13 Using **HashMap**s and **Map**s. 1226
21.14 Synchronization wrapper methods. 1228
21.15 Unmodifiable wrapper methods. 1229

22 Java Media Framework and Java Sound (on CD)

22.1 Playing media with interface **Player**. 1239
22.2 Formatting and saving media from capture devices. 1250
22.3 Serving streaming media with RTP session managers. 1264
22.4 Application to test class **RTPServer** from Fig. 22.3. 1272
22.5 **ClipPlayer** plays an audio file. 1278
22.6 **ClipPlayerTest** enables the user to specify the name and location of the audio to play with **ClipPlayer**. 1283
22.7 **MidiData** loads MIDI files for playback. 1286
22.8 **MidiRecord** enables a program to record a MIDI sequence. 1292
22.9 **MidiSynthesizer** can generate notes and send them to another MIDI device. 1295
22.10 **MidiDemo** provides the GUI than enables users to interact with the application. 1300
22.11 Class diagram of elevator simulation view. 1318
22.12 Class **ImagePanel** represents and displays a stationary object from the model. 1319
22.13 Class **MovingPanel** represents and displays a moving object from the model. 1321
22.14 Class **AnimatedPanel** represents and displays an animated object from the model. 1323
22.15 Relationship between array **imageIcons** and **List frameSequences**. 1328
22.16 Class **SoundEffects** return **AudioClip** objects. 1328
22.17 Class **ElevatorMusic** plays music when a **Person** rides in the **Elevator**. 1329

C Operator Precedence Chart

C.1 Operator precedence chart. 1353

D ASCII Character Set

D.1 ASCII character set. 1355

E Number Systems (on CD)

E.1 Digits of the binary, octal, decimal and hexadecimal number systems. 1358
E.2 Comparing the binary, octal, decimal and hexadecimal number systems. 1358
E.3 Positional values in the decimal number system. 1358
E.4 Positional values in the binary number system. 1359
E.5 Positional values in the octal number system. 1359
E.6 Positional values in the hexadecimal number system. 1360
E.7 Decimal, binary, octal, and hexadecimal equivalents. 1360
E.8 Converting a binary number to decimal. 1362

E.9 Converting an octal number to decimal. 1362
E.10 Converting a hexadecimal number to decimal. 1362

F Creating HTML Documentation with javadoc (on CD)

F.1 Java API documentation. 1371
F.2 A Java source code file containing documentation comments. 1371
F.3 HTML documentation for class **Time3**. 1376
F.4 The **Parameters:** note generated by javadoc. 1377
F.5 HTML documentation for method **setTime**. 1377
F.6 HTML documentation for method **getHour**. 1378
F.7 Common **javadoc** tags. 1378
F.8 Using the **javadoc** tool. 1380
F.9 Class **Time3**'s **index.html**. 1381
F.10 **Tree** page. 1381
F.11 Time3's **index-all.html** page. 1382
F.12 Time3's **helpdoc.html** page. 1382

G Elevator Events and Listener Interfaces (on CD)

G.1 **ElevatorModelEvent** superclass for events in the elevator simulation model. 1384
G.2 **BellEvent ElevatorModelEvent** subclass indicating that the **Bell** has rung. 1385
G.3 **ButtonEvent ElevatorModelEvent** subclass indicating that a **Button** has changed state. 1386
G.4 **DoorEvent ElevatorModelEvent** subclass indicating that a **Door** has changed state. 1386
G.5 **ElevatorMoveEvent ElevatorModelEvent** subclass indicating on which **Floor** the **Elevator** has either arrived or departed. 1387
G.6 **LightEvent ElevatorModelEvent** subclass indicating on which **Floor** the **Light** has changed state. 1387
G.7 **PersonMoveEvent ElevatorModelEvent** subclass indicating that a **Person** has moved. 1387
G.8 Interface **BellListener** method when **Bell** has rung. 1388
G.9 Interface **ButtonListener** methods when **Button** has been either pressed or reset. 1389
G.10 Interface **DoorListener** methods when **Door** has either opened or closed. 1389
G.11 Interface **ElevatorMoveListener** methods when **Elevator** has either departed from or arrived on a **Floor**. 1389
G.12 Interface **LightListener** method for when **Light** has either turned on or off. 1390
G.13 Interface **PersonMoveListener** methods when **Person** has moved. 1390
G.14 Interface **ElevatorModelListener** allows the model to send all events to the view. 1391
G.15 Component diagram for package **event**. 1392

H Elevator Model (on CD)

H.1 Class **ElevatorModel** represents the model in our elevator simulation. 1393
H.2 Class diagram showing realizations in the elevator model (Part 1). 1400
H.3 Class diagram showing realizations in the elevator model (Part 2). 1401
H.4 Classes and implemented listener interfaces from Fig. H.2. 1401
H.5 **Location** abstract superclass that represents a location in the simulation. 1402
H.6 Class **Floor**—a subclass of **Location**—represents a **Floor** across which a **Person** walks to the **Elevator**. 1403
H.7 Class **Door**, which represents a **Door** in the model, informs listeners when a **Door** has opened or closed. 1404
H.8 Class **Button**, which represents a **Button** in the model, informs listeners when a **Button** has been pressed or reset. 1408
H.9 Class **ElevatorShaft**, which represents the **ElevatorShaft**, which sends events from the **Elevator** to the **ElevatorModel**. 1410
H.10 Class **Light** represents a **Light** on the **Floor** in the model. 1416
H.11 Class **Bell** represents the **Bell** in the model. 1419
H.12 Class **Elevator** represents the **Elevator** traveling between two **Floor**s, operating asynchronously with other objects. 1420
H.13 Class **Person** represents the **Person** that rides the **Elevator**. The **Person** operates asynchronously with other objects. 1429
H.14 Component diagram for package **model**. 1437

I Elevator View (on CD)

I.1 **ElevatorView** displays the elevator simulation model. 1438
I.2 Objects in the **ElevatorView** representing objects in the model. 1456
I.3 Objects in the **ElevatorView** not represented in the model. 1457
I.4 Object diagram for the **ElevatorView** after initialization. 1460
I.5 Component diagram for package view. 1464

J Career Opportunities (on CD)

J.1 The **Monster.com** home page. (Courtesy of **Monster.com**.) 1468
J.2 **FlipDog.com** job search. (Courtesy of **Flipdog.com**.) 1469
J.3 List of a job seeker's criteria. 1471
J.4 Advantage Hiring, Inc.'s Net-Interview™ service. (Courtesy of Advantage Hiring, Inc.) 1474
J.5 Cruel World online career services. (Courtesy of Cruel World.) 1476
J.6 **eLance.com** request for proposal (RFP) example. (Courtesy of eLance, Inc.) 1479

K Unicode® (on CD)

K.1 Correlation between the three encoding forms. 1492
K.2 Various glyphs of the character A. 1492
K.3 Java program that uses Unicode encoding. 1494
K.4 Some character ranges. 1497

Preface

Live in fragments no longer. Only connect.
Edward Morgan Forster

Welcome to *Java How to Program, Fourth Edition* and the exciting world of programming with the *Java™ 2 Platform, Standard Edition*. This book is by an old guy and a young guy. The old guy (HMD; Massachusetts Institute of Technology 1967) has been programming and/or teaching programming for 40 years. The young guy (PJD; MIT 1991) has been programming and/or teaching programming for 22 years, and is both a Sun Certified Java Programmer and a Sun Certified Java Developer. The old guy programs and teaches from experience; the young guy does so from an inexhaustible reserve of energy. The old guy wants clarity; the young guy wants performance. The old guy seeks elegance and beauty; the young guy wants results. We got together to produce a book we hope you will find informative, challenging and entertaining.

In November 1995, we attended an Internet/World Wide Web conference in Boston to hear about Java. A Sun Microsystems representative spoke on Java in a packed convention ballroom. During that presentation, we saw the future of programming unfold. The first edition of *Java How to Program* was born at that moment and was published as the world's first Java computer science textbook.

The world of Java is evolving so rapidly that *Java How to Program: Fourth Edition* is being published less than five years after the first edition. This creates tremendous challenges and opportunities for us as authors, for our publisher—Prentice Hall, for instructors, for students and for professional people.

Before Java appeared, we were convinced that C++ would replace C as the dominant application development language and systems programming language for the next decade. However, the combination of the World Wide Web and Java now increases the prominence of the Internet in information systems strategic planning and implementation. Organizations want to integrate the Internet "seamlessly" into their information systems. Java is more appropriate than C++ for this purpose.

New Features in *Java How to Program: Fourth Edition*

This edition contains many new features and enhancements including:

- ***Full-Color Presentation***. The book is now in full color. In the book's earlier two-color editions, the programs were displayed in black and the screen captures appeared in the second color. Full color enables readers to see sample outputs as they would appear on a color monitor. Also, we now syntax color all the Java code, as many of today's Java development environments do. Our syntax-coloring conventions are as follows:

```
comments appear in green
keywords appear in dark blue
constants and literal values appear in light blue
class, method and variable names appear in black
```

- ***"Code Washing."*** This is our own term for the process we used to convert all the programs in the book to a more open layout with enhanced commenting. We have grouped program code into small, well-documented pieces. This greatly improves code readability—an especially important goal for us given that this new edition contains more than 25,000 lines of code.
- ***Tune-Up.*** We performed a substantial tune-up of the book's contents based on our own notes from extensive teaching in our professional Java seminars. In addition, a distinguished team of reviewers read the third edition book and provided us with their comments and criticisms. There are literally thousands of fine-tuning improvements over the third edition.
- ***Thinking About Objects***. This optional 180-page case study introduces *object-oriented design* (*OOD*) with the *Unified Modeling Language* (the *UML*). Many chapters in this edition end with a "Thinking About Objects" section in which we present a carefully paced introduction to object orientation. Our goal in these sections is to help you develop an object-oriented way of thinking to be able to design and implement more substantial systems. These sections also introduce you to the Unified Modeling Language (UML). The UML is a graphical language that allows people who build systems (e.g., software architects, systems engineers and programmers) to represent their object-oriented designs using a common notation. The "Thinking About Objects" section in Chapter 1 introduces basic concepts and terminology. Chapters 2–13, 15 and 22 (22 is on the CD) and Appendices G, H and I (also on the CD) include optional "Thinking About Objects" sections that present a substantial object-oriented elevator case study that applies the techniques of *object-oriented design (OOD)*. Appendices G, H and I fully implement the case study design in Java code. This case study will help prepare you for the kinds of substantial projects you are likely to encounter in industry. If you are a student and your instructor does not plan to include this case study in your course, you may want to read the case study on your own. We believe it will be well worth your effort to walk through this large and challenging project. The material presented in the case-study sections reinforces the material covered in the corresponding chapters. You will experience a solid introduction to object-oriented design with the UML. Also, you will sharpen your code-reading skills by touring

a carefully written and well-documented 3,465-line Java program that completely solves the problem presented in the case study.

- ***Discovering Design Patterns***. These optional sections introduce popular object-oriented design patterns in use today. Most of the examples provided in this book contain fewer than 150 lines of code. Such small examples normally do not require an extensive design process. However, some programs, such as our optional elevator-simulation case study, are more complex—they can require thousands of lines of code. Larger systems, such as automated teller machines or air-traffic control systems, could contain millions, or even hundreds of millions, of lines of code. Effective design is crucial to the proper construction of such complex systems. Over the past decade, the software engineering industry has made significant progress in the field of *design patterns*—proven architectures for constructing flexible and maintainable object-oriented software.[1] Using design patterns can substantially reduce the complexity of the design process. We present several design patterns in Java, but these design patterns can be implemented in any object-oriented language, such as C++, C# or Visual Basic. We describe several design patterns used by Sun Microsystems in the Java API. We use design patterns in many programs in this book, which we will identify in our "Discovering Design Patterns" sections. These programs provide examples of using design patterns to construct reliable, robust object-oriented software.
- ***Chapter 22 (on the CD), Java Media Framework (JMF) and JavaSound***. This chapter introduces to Java's audio and video capabilities, enhancing our Chapter 18 multimedia coverage. With the Java Media Framework, a Java program can play audio and video media, and *capture* audio and video media from devices such as microphones and video cameras. The JMF enables Java developers to create *streaming media* applications, in which a Java program sends live or recorded audio or video feeds across the Internet to other computers, then applications on those other computers play the media as it arrives over the network. The JavaSound APIs enable programs to manipulate MIDI (Musical Instrument Digital Interface) sounds and captured media (i.e., media from a device such as a microphone). The chapter concludes with a substantial MIDI-processing application that enables users to record MIDI files or select MIDI files to play. Users can create their own MIDI music by interacting with the application's simulated synthesizer keyboard. The application can synchronize playing the notes in a MIDI file with pressing the keys on the simulated synthesizer keyboard—similar to a player piano. [*Note*: Chapters 18 and 22 both provide substantial sets of exercises. Each chapter also has a special section containing additional interesting and challenging multimedia projects. These are intended only as suggestions for major projects. Solutions are not provided for these additional exercises in either the *Instructor's Manual* or the *Java 2 Multimedia Cyber Classroom*.]
- ***Enhanced TCP/IP-Based Networking***. We include a new capstone example in Chapter 17 that introduces *multicasting* for sending information to groups of network clients. This Deitel Messenger case study emulates many of today's popular

1. Gamma, Erich, Richard Helm, Ralph Johnson, and John Vlissides. *Design Patterns; Elements of Reusable Object-Oriented Software*. (Massachusetts: Addison-Wesley, 1995).

instant-messaging applications that enable computer users to communicate with friends, relatives and co-workers over the Internet. This 1130-line, multithreaded, client/server Java program uses most of the techniques presented to this point in the book.

- ***Appendix J (on the CD), Career Opportunities***. This detailed appendix introduces career services on the Internet. We explore online career services from the employer and employee's perspective. We suggest sites on which you can submit applications, search for jobs and review applicants (if you are interested in hiring someone). We also review services that build recruiting pages directly into e-businesses. One of our reviewers told us that he had just gone through a job search largely using the Internet and this chapter would have really expanded his search dramatically.
- ***Appendix K (on the CD), Unicode***. This appendix overviews the *Unicode Standard.* As computer systems evolved worldwide, computer vendors developed numeric representations of character sets and special symbols for the local languages spoken in different countries. In some cases, different representations were developed for the same languages. Such disparate character sets made communication between computer systems difficult. Java supports the Unicode Standard (maintained by a non-profit organization called the *Unicode Consortium*), which defines a single character set with unique numeric values for characters and special symbols in most spoken languages. This appendix discusses the Unicode Standard, overviews the Unicode Consortium Web site (**`unicode.org`**) and shows a Java example that displays "Welcome" in eight different languages!
- ***Java 2 Plug-In Moved to Chapter 3, Introduction to Applets***. Students enjoy seeing immediate results as they execute their Java programs. This is difficult if those programs are Java applets that execute in Web browsers. Most of today's Web browsers (with the exception of Netscape Navigator 6) do not support Java 2 applets directly, so students must test their applet programs with the **`appletviewer`** utility. Sun Microsystems provides the Java 2 Plug-in to enable Java 2 applets to execute in a Web browser that does not support Java 2. The discussion of the Java Plug-in walks the student through the steps necessary to execute an applet in today's Web browsers.
- ***Chapter 22 and Appendices E-K on the CD.*** There are so many topics covered in this new edition that we could not fit them all in the book! On the CD that accompanies this book, you will find the following chapter and appendices: Chapter 22, Java Media Framework (JMF) and Java Sound; Appendix E, Number Systems; Appendix F, Creating HTML Documentation with **`javadoc`**; Appendix G, Elevator Events and Listener Interfaces; Appendix H, Elevator Model; Appendix I, Elevator View; Appendix J, Career Opportunities; and Appendix K, Unicode.
- ***Chapters Moved to* Advanced Java™ 2 Platform How to Program**. Four chapters from *Java How to Program, Third Edition* have been moved to our new book *Advanced Java 2 Platform How to Program* and greatly enhanced. These chapters are: Java Database Connectivity (JDBC), Servlets, Remote Method Invocation and JavaBeans. *Advanced Java 2 Platform How to Program* covers each of these topics in more depth. We present the Table of Contents of *Advanced Java 2 Platform How to Program* shortly.

Some Notes to Instructors

A World of Object Orientation

When we wrote the first edition of *Java How to Program*, universities were still emphasizing procedural programming in languages like Pascal and C. The leading-edge courses were using object-oriented C++, but these courses were generally mixing a substantial amount of procedural programming with object-oriented programming—something that C++ lets you do, but Java does not. By the third edition of *Java How to Program*, many universities were switching from C++ to Java in their introductory curricula, and instructors were emphasizing a pure object-oriented programming approach. In parallel with this activity, the software engineering community was standardizing its approach to modeling object-oriented systems with the UML, and the design-patterns movement was taking shape. *Java How to Program* has many audiences, so we designed the book to be customizable. In particular, we included more than 200 pages of optional material that introduces object-oriented design, the UML and design patterns, and presents a substantial case study in object-oriented design and programming. This material is carefully distributed throughout the book to enable instructors to emphasize "industrial-strength" object-oriented design in their courses.

Students Like Java

Students are highly motivated by the fact that they are learning a leading-edge language (Java) and a leading-edge programming paradigm (object-oriented programming) that will be immediately useful to them while in the university environment and when they head into a world in which the Internet and the World Wide Web have a massive prominence. Students quickly discover that they can do great things with Java, so they are willing to put in the extra effort. Java helps programmers unleash their creativity. We see this in the Java courses Deitel & Associates, Inc. teaches. Once our students enter lab, we can't hold them back. They eagerly experiment and explore portions of the Java class libraries that we haven't as yet covered in class. They produce applications that go well beyond anything we've ever tried in our introductory C and C++ courses. And they tell us about projects they "can't wait" to try after the course.

Focus of the Book

Our goal was clear—produce a Java textbook for introductory university-level courses in computer programming for students with little or no programming experience, yet offer the depth and the rigorous treatment of theory and practice demanded by traditional, upper-level courses and that satisfies professionals' needs. To meet these goals, we produced a comprehensive book, because our text patiently teaches the basics of computer programming and of the Java language (i.e., data types, control structures, methods, arrays, recursion and other "traditional" programming topics); presents key programming paradigms, including object-based programming, object-oriented programming, event-driven programming and concurrent programming; and provides an extensive treatment of the Java class libraries.

Evolution of Java How to Program

Java How to Program (first edition) was the world's first university computer science textbook on Java. We wrote it fresh on the heels of *C How to Program, Second Edition* and *C++ How to Program*. Hundreds of thousands of university students and professional people worldwide have learned C, C++ and Java from these texts. Upon publication in August, 2001 *Java How to Program, Fourth Edition* will be used in hundreds of universities and thousands of corporations and government organizations worldwide. Deitel & Associates, Inc. taught Java courses internationally to thousands of students as we were writing the various editions of *Java How to Program*. We carefully monitored the effectiveness of these courses and tuned the material accordingly.

Conceptualization of Java

We believe in Java. Its conceptualization (and public release in 1995) by Sun Microsystems, the creators of Java, was brilliant. Sun based the new language on two of the world's most widely used implementation languages, C and C++. This immediately gave Java a huge pool of highly skilled programmers who were implementing most of the world's new operating systems, communications systems, database systems, personal computer applications and systems software. Sun removed the messier, more complex and error-prone C/C++ features (such as pointers, operator overloading and multiple inheritance, among others). They kept the language concise by removing special-purpose features that were used by only small segments of the programming community. They made the language truly portable to be appropriate for implementing Internet-based and World-Wide-Web-based applications, and they built in the features people really need such as strings, graphics, graphical user interface components, exception handling, multithreading, multimedia (audio, images, animation and video), file processing, database processing, Internet and World Wide Web-based client/server networking and distributed computing, and prepackaged data structures. Then they made the language available *at no charge* to millions of potential programmers worldwide.

2.5 Million Java Developers

Java was promoted in 1995 as a means of adding "dynamic content" to World-Wide-Web pages. Instead of Web pages with only text and static graphics, people's Web pages could now "come alive" with audios, videos, animations, interactivity—and soon, three-dimensional imaging. But we saw much more in Java than this. Java's features are precisely what businesses and organizations need to meet today's information-processing requirements. So we immediately viewed Java as having the potential to become one of the world's key general-purpose programming languages. In fact, Java has revolutionized software development with multimedia-intensive, platform-independent, object-oriented code for conventional, Internet-, Intranet- and Extranet-based applications and applets. Java now has 2.5 million developers worldwide—a stunning accomplishment given that it has only been available publicly for six years. No other programming language has ever acquired such a large developer base so quickly.

Enabling Multimedia-Based Applications and Communications

The computer field has never seen anything like the Internet/World Wide Web/Java "explosion" occurring today. People want to communicate. People need to communicate. Sure they have been doing that since the dawn of civilization, but computer communications have been mostly limited to digits, alphabetic characters and special characters. Today, we are in the midst of a multimedia revolution. People want to transmit pictures and they want those pictures to be in color. They want to transmit voices, sounds, audio clips and full-motion color video (and they want nothing less than DVD quality). Eventually, people will insist on three-dimensional, moving-image transmission. Our current flat, two-dimensional televisions will eventually be replaced with three-dimensional versions that turn our living rooms into "theaters-in-the-round." Actors will perform their roles as if we were watching live theater. Our living rooms will be turned into miniature sports stadiums. Our business offices will enable video conferencing among colleagues half a world apart as if they were sitting around one conference table. The possibilities are intriguing and Java is playing a key role in turning many of them into reality.

Teaching Approach

Java How to Program, Fourth Edition contains a rich collection of examples, exercises, and projects drawn from many fields to provide the student with a chance to solve interesting real-world problems. The book concentrates on the principles of good software engineering and stresses program clarity. We avoid arcane terminology and syntax specifications in favor of teaching by example. Our code examples have been tested on popular Java platforms. We are educators who teach edge-of-the-practice topics in industry classrooms worldwide. The text emphasizes good pedagogy.

Learning Java via the Live-Code™ Approach

The book is loaded with live-code™ examples. This is the focus of the way we teach and write about programming, and the focus of each of our multimedia Cyber Classrooms and Web-based training courses as well. Each new concept is presented in the context of a complete, working Java program (application or applet) immediately followed by one or more screen captures showing the program's output. We call this style of teaching and writing our ***live-code™ approach***. *We use the language to teach the language.* Reading these programs (25,000+ lines of code) is much like entering and running them on a computer.

Java and Swing from Chapter Two!

Java How to Program, Fourth Edition "jumps right in" with object-oriented programming, applications and the Swing-style GUI components from Chapter 2! People tell us this is a "gutsy" move, but Java students really want to "cut to the chase." There is great stuff to be done in Java so let's get right to it! Java is not trivial by any means, but it's fun to program with and students can see immediate results. Students can get graphical, animated, multimedia-based, audio-intensive, multithreaded, database-intensive, network-based programs running quickly through Java's extensive class libraries of "reusable components." They can implement impressive projects. They are typically more creative and productive in a one- or two-semester course than in C and C++ introductory courses.

World Wide Web Access

All of the code for *Java How to Program* is on the CD that accompanies this book and is available on the Internet at the Deitel & Associates, Inc. Web site **`www.deitel.com`**. Please run each program as you read the text. Make changes to the code examples and see what happens. See how the Java compiler "complains" when you make various kinds of errors. Immediately see the effects of making changes to the code. It's a great way to learn programming by doing programming. [This is copyrighted material. Feel free to use it as you study Java, but you may not republish any portion of it without explicit permission from the authors and Prentice Hall.]

Objectives

Each chapter begins with a statement of objectives. This tells the student what to expect and gives the student an opportunity, after reading the chapter, to determine if he or she has met these objectives. It is a confidence builder and a source of positive reinforcement.

Quotations

The learning objectives are followed by quotations. Some are humorous, some are philosophical, and some offer interesting insights. Our students enjoy relating the quotations to the chapter material. The quotations are worth a "second look" after you read each chapter.

Outline

The chapter Outline helps the student approach the material in top-down fashion. This, too, helps students anticipate what is to come and set a comfortable and effective learning pace.

25,576 Lines of Code in 197 Example Programs (with Program Outputs)

We present Java features in the context of complete, working Java programs. The programs range from just a few lines of code to substantial examples with several hundred lines of code (and 3,465 lines of code for the optional object-oriented elevator simulator example). Students should use the program code from the CD that accompanies the book or download the code from our Web site (**`www.deitel.com`**) and run each program while studying that program in the text.

545 Illustrations/Figures

An abundance of charts, line drawings and program outputs is included. The discussion of control structures, for example, features carefully drawn flowcharts. [*Note*: We do not teach flowcharting as a program development tool, but we do use a brief, flowchart-oriented presentation to specify the precise operation of each of Java's control structures.]

605 Programming Tips

We have included programming tips to help students focus on important aspects of program development. We highlight hundreds of these tips in the form of *Good Programming Practices, Common Programming Errors, Testing and Debugging Tips, Performance Tips, Portability Tips, Software Engineering Observations* and *Look-and-Feel Observations.* These tips and practices represent the best we have gleaned from a combined six decades of programming and teaching experience. One of our students—a mathematics major—told us that she feels this approach is like the highlighting of axioms, theorems, and corollaries in mathematics books; it provides a basis on which to build good software.

97 Good Programming Practices

When we teach introductory courses, we state that the "buzzword" of each course is "clarity," and we highlight as Good Programming Practices *techniques for writing programs that are clearer, more understandable, more debuggable, and more maintainable.*

199 Common Programming Errors

Students learning a language tend to make certain errors frequently. Focusing on these Common Programming Errors *helps students avoid making the same errors and shortens lines outside instructors' offices during office hours!*

46 Testing and Debugging Tips

When we first designed this "tip type," we thought we would use it strictly to tell people how to test and debug Java programs. In fact, many of the tips describe aspects of Java that reduce the likelihood of "bugs" and thus simplify the testing and debugging process.

67 Performance Tips

In our experience, teaching students to write clear and understandable programs is by far the most important goal for a first programming course. But students want to write the programs that run the fastest, use the least memory, require the smallest number of keystrokes, or dazzle in other nifty ways. Students really care about performance. They want to know what they can do to "turbo charge" their programs. So we have included 67 Performance Tips *that highlight opportunities for improving program performance—making programs run faster or minimizing the amount of memory that they occupy.*

24 Portability Tips

One of Java's "claims to fame" is "universal" portability, so some programmers assume that if they implement an application in Java, the application will automatically be "perfectly" portable across all Java platforms. Unfortunately, this is not always the case. We include Portability Tips *to help students write portable code and to provide insights on how Java achieves its high degree of portability. We had many more portability tips in our books,* C How to Program *and* C++ How to Program. *We needed fewer* Portability Tips *in* Java How to Program *because Java is designed to be portable top-to-bottom (for the most part)—much less effort is required on the Java programmer's part to achieve portability than with C or C++.*

134 Software Engineering Observations

The object-oriented programming paradigm requires a complete rethinking about the way we build software systems. Java is an effective language for performing good software engineering. The Software Engineering Observations *highlight architectural and design issues that affect the construction of software systems, especially large-scale systems. Much of what the student learns here will be useful in upper-level courses and in industry as the student begins to work with large, complex real-world systems.*

38 Look-and-Feel Observations

We provide Look-and-Feel Observations *to highlight graphical user interface conventions. These observations help students design their own graphical user interfaces in conformance with industry norms.*

Summary (983 Summary bullets)

Each chapter ends with additional pedagogical devices. We present a thorough, bullet-list-style summary of the chapter. On average, there are 42 summary bullets per chapter. This helps the students review and reinforce key concepts.

Terminology (2171 Terms)

We include in a *Terminology* section an alphabetized list of the important terms defined in the chapter—again, further reinforcement. On average, there are 95 terms per chapter.

397 Self-Review Exercises and Answers (Count Includes Separate Parts)

Extensive self-review exercises and answers are included for self-study. This gives the student a chance to build confidence with the material and prepare for the regular exercises. Students should be encouraged to do all the self-review exercises and check their answers.

779 Exercises (Count Includes Separate Parts)

Each chapter concludes with a set of exercises including simple recall of important terminology and concepts; writing individual Java statements; writing small portions of Java methods and classes; writing complete Java methods, classes, applications and applets; and writing major term projects. The large number of exercises across a wide variety of areas enables instructors to tailor their courses to the unique needs of their audiences and to vary course assignments each semester. Instructors can use these exercises to form homework assignments, short quizzes and major examinations. The solutions for most of the exercises are included on the *Instructor's Manual* CD that is *available only to instructors* through their Prentice-Hall representatives. **[*NOTE*: Please do not write to us requesting the instructor's manual. Distribution of this publication is strictly limited to college professors teaching from the book. Instructors may obtain the solutions manual only from their regular Prentice Hall representatives. We regret that we cannot provide the solutions to professionals.]** Solutions to approximately half of the exercises are included on the *Java Multimedia Cyber Classroom, Fourth Edition* CD, which also is part of *The Complete Java 2 Training Course*. For ordering instructions, please see the last few pages of this book or visit **`www.deitel.com`**.

Approximately 5300 Index Entries (with approximately 9500 Page References)

We have included an extensive index at the back of the book. This helps the student find any term or concept by keyword. The index is useful to people reading the book for the first time and is especially useful to practicing programmers who use the book as a reference. The terms in the Terminology sections generally appear in the index (along with many more index items from each chapter). Students can use the index with the Terminology sections to be sure they have covered the key material of each chapter.

"Double Indexing" of Java Live-Code™ Examples and Exercises

Java How to Program has 197 live-code™ examples and 1176 exercises (including parts). Many of the exercises are challenging problems or projects requiring substantial effort. We have "double indexed" the live-code™ examples. For every Java source-code program in the book, we took the file name with the **`.java`** extension, such as **`LoadAudioAndPlay.java`** and indexed it both alphabetically (in this case under "L") and as a subindex item under "Examples." This makes it easier to find examples using particular features. The more substantial exercises, such as "Maze Generator and Walker," are indexed both alphabetically (in this case under "M") and as subindex items under "Exercises."

Bibliography

An extensive bibliography of books, articles and Sun Microsystems Java 2 documentation is included to encourage further reading.

Software Included with *Java How to Program, Fourth Edition*

There are a number of for-sale Java products available. However, you do not need them to get started with Java. We wrote *Java How to Program, Fourth Edition* using only the *Java 2 Software Development Kit (J2SDK)*. For your convenience, Sun's J2SDK version 1.3.1 is included on the CD that accompanies this book. The J2SDK also can be downloaded from the Sun Microsystems Java Web site **`java.sun.com`**. With Sun's cooperation, we also were able to include on the CD a powerful Java integrated development environment (IDE)—Sun Microsystems' *Forté for Java Community Edition*.

Forté for Java Community Edition is a professional IDE written in Java that includes a graphical user interface designer, code editor, compiler, visual debugger and more. J2SDK 1.3.1 must be installed before installing *Forté for Java Community Edition*. If you have any questions about using this software, please read the introductory *Forté* documentation on the CD. We will provide additional information on our Web site **`www.deitel.com`**.

The CD also contains the book's examples and an HTML Web page with links to the Deitel & Associates, Inc. Web site, the Prentice Hall Web site and the many Web sites listed in the appendices. If you have access to the Internet, this Web page can be loaded into your Web browser to give you quick access to all the resources. Finally, the CD contains Chapter 22 and Appendices E–K.

Ancillary Package for *Java How to Program, Fourth Edition*

Java How to Program, Fourth Edition has extensive ancillary materials for instructors teaching from the book. The Instructor's Manual CD contains solutions to the vast majority of the end-of-chapter exercises and a test bank of multiple choice questions (approximately 2 per book section). In addition, we provide PowerPoint® slides containing all the code and figures in the text. You are free to customize these slides to meet your own classroom needs. Prentice Hall provides a *Companion Web Site* (**`www.prenhall.com/deitel`**) that includes resources for instructors and students. For instructors, the Web site has a Syllabus Manager for course planning, links to the PowerPoint slides and reference materials from the appendices of the book (such as the operator precedence chart, character sets and Web resources). For students, the Web site provides chapter objectives, true/false exercises with instant feedback, chapter highlights and reference materials. [***NOTE*: Please do not write to us requesting the instructor's manual. Distribution of this publication is strictly limited to college professors teaching from the book. Instructors may obtain the solutions manual only from their regular Prentice Hall representatives. We regret that we cannot provide the solutions to professionals.**]

Java 2 Multimedia Cyber Classroom, Fourth Edition (CD and Web-Based Training Versions) and *The Complete Java 2 Training Course, Fourth Edition*

We have prepared an interactive, CD-based, software version of *Java How to Program, Fourth Edition* called the *Java 2 Multimedia Cyber Classroom, Fourth Edition*. It is loaded with features for learning and reference. The *Cyber Classroom* is wrapped with the textbook at a discount in *The Complete Java 2 Training Course, Fourth Edition*. If you already have the book and would like to purchase the *Java 2 Multimedia Cyber Classroom, Fourth Edition* separately, please visit **`www.informit.com/cyberclassrooms`**. The ISBN# for the *Java 2 Multimedia Cyber Classroom, Fourth Edition* is 0-13-064935-x. All Deitel *Cyber Classrooms* are generally available in CD and Web-based training formats.

The CD has an introduction with the authors overviewing the *Cyber Classroom*'s features. The 197 live-code™ example Java programs in the textbook truly "come alive" in the *Cyber Classroom*. If you are viewing a program and want to execute it, you simply click on the lightning bolt icon and the program will run. You will immediately see—and hear for the audio-based multimedia programs—the program's outputs. If you want to modify a program and see and hear the effects of your changes, simply click the floppy-disk icon that causes the source code to be "lifted off" the CD and "dropped into" one of your own directories so you can edit the text, recompile the program and try out your new version. Click the audio icon and Paul Deitel will talk about the program and "walk you through" the code.

The *Cyber Classroom* also provides navigational aids including extensive hyperlinking. The *Cyber Classroom* is browser based, so it remembers recent sections you have visited and allows you to move forward or backward among these sections. The thousands of index entries are hyperlinked to their text occurrences. You can key in a term using the "find" feature and the *Cyber Classroom* will locate its occurrences throughout the text. The Table of Contents entries are "hot"—so clicking a chapter name takes you to that chapter.

Students tell us that they particularly like the hundreds of solved problems from the textbook that are included with the *Cyber Classroom*. Studying and running these extra programs is a great way for students to enhance their learning experience.

Students and professional users of our Cyber Classrooms tell us they like the interactivity and that the Cyber Classroom is an effective reference because of the extensive hyperlinking and other navigational features. We received an email from a person who said that he lives "in the boonies" and cannot take a live course at a university, so the Cyber Classroom was the solution to his educational needs.

Professors tell us that their students enjoy using the *Cyber Classroom*, spend more time on the course and master more of the material than in textbook-only courses. We have published (and will be publishing) many other *Cyber Classroom* and *Complete Training Course* products. For a complete list of the available and forthcoming *Cyber Classrooms* and *Complete Training Courses*, see the *Deitel™ Series* page at the beginning of this book or the product listing and ordering information at the end of this book. You can also visit **`www.deitel.com`** or **`www.prenhall.com/deitel`** for more information.

Advanced Java™ 2 Platform How to Program

Our companion book—***Advanced Java 2 Platform How to Program***—focuses on the ***Java 2 Platform, Enterprise Edition (J2EE)***, presents advanced Java 2 Platform Standard Edition features and introduces the ***Java 2 Platform, Micro Edition (J2ME)***. This book is intended for developers and upper-level university students in advanced courses who already know Java and want a deeper treatment and understanding of the language. The book features our signature live-code™ approach of complete working programs and contains over 37,000 lines of code. The programs are more substantial than those presented in *Java How to Program, Fourth Edition*. The book expands the coverage of Java Database Connectivity (JDBC), remote method invocation (RMI), servlets and JavaBeans from *Java How to Program, Fourth Edition*. The book also covers emerging and more advanced Java technologies of concern to enterprise application developers. The Table of Contents for ***Advanced Java 2 Platform How to Program*** is: **Chapters**—Introduction; Advanced Swing Graphical User Interface Components; Model-View-Controller; Graphics Programming with Java 2D and Java 3D; Case Study: A Java2D Application; JavaBeans Component Model; Security; Java Database Connectivity (JDBC); Servlets; Java Server Pages (JSP); Case Study: Servlet and JSP Bookstore; Java 2 Micro Edition (J2ME) and Wireless Internet; Remote Method Invocation (RMI); Session Enterprise JavaBeans (EJBs) and Distributed Transactions; Entity EJBs; Java Message Service (JMS) and Message-Driven EJBs; Enterprise Java Case Study: Architectural Overview; Enterprise Java Case Study: Presentation and Controller Logic; Enterprise Java Case Study: Business Logic Part 1; Enterprise Java Case Study: Business Logic Part 2; Application Servers; Jini; JavaSpaces; Jiro; Java Management Extensions (JMX); Common Object Request Broker Architecture (CORBA): Part 1; Common Object Request Broker Architecture (CORBA): Part 2; Peer-to-Peer Networking; **Appendices**—Creating Markup with XML; XML Document Type Definitions; XML Document Object Model (DOM); XSL: Extensible Stylesheet Language Transformations; Downloading and Installing J2EE 1.2.1; Java Community Process (JCP); Java Native Interface (JNI); Career Opportunities; Unicode.

Acknowledgments

One of the great pleasures of writing a textbook is acknowledging the efforts of the many people whose names may not appear on the cover, but whose hard work, cooperation, friendship, and understanding were crucial to the production of the book.

Other people at Deitel & Associates, Inc. devoted long hours to this project. We would like to acknowledge the efforts of our full-time Deitel & Associates, Inc. colleagues Tem Nieto, Sean Santry, Jonathan Gadzik, Kate Steinbuhler, Rashmi Jayaprakash and Laura Treibick.

- Tem Nieto is a graduate of the Massachusetts Institute of Technology. Tem teaches XML, Java, Internet and Web, C, C++ and Visual Basic seminars and works with us on textbook writing, course development and multimedia authoring efforts. He is co-author with us of *Internet & World Wide Web How to Program (Second Edition), XML How to Program, Perl How to Program* and *Visual Basic 6 How to Program.* In *Java How to Program, Fourth Edition* Tem co-authored Chapters 11, 12, 13 and 21 and the Special Section entitled "Building Your Own Compiler" in Chapter 19.
- Sean Santry, a graduate of Boston College (Computer Science and Philosophy) and co-author of *Advanced Java 2 Platform How to Program*, edited Chapter 22 (Java Media Framework and Java Sound), helped update the programs in Chapter 15 (Multithreading), designed and implemented the Deitel Messenger networking application in Chapter 17 (Networking), helped design the optional case study on OOD/UML, reviewed the optional design patterns case study and reviewed the implementation of the elevator simulation for the OOD/UML case study.
- Jonathan Gadzik, a graduate of the Columbia University School of Engineering and Applied Science (BS in Computer Science) co-authored the optional OOD/UML case study and the optional "Discovering Design Patterns" sections. He also implemented the 3,465-line Java program that completely solves the object-oriented elevator simulation exercise presented in the OOD/UML case study.
- Kate Steinbuhler, a graduate of Boston College with majors in English and Communications, co-authored Appendix J, Career Opportunities, and managed the permissions process. Kate is moving on to law school at the University of Pittsburgh—good luck Kate! Thank you for your contributions to three Deitel publications.

- Rashmi Jayaprakash, a graduate of Boston University with a major in Computer Science, co-authored Appendix K, Unicode.
- Laura Treibick, a graduate of University of Colorado at Boulder with a major in Photography and Multimedia, created the delightful animated bug character for the implementation of the OOD/UML case study.

We would also like to thank the participants in our Deitel & Associates, Inc. College Internship Program.[2]

- Susan Warren, a Junior in Computer Science at Brown University, and Eugene Izumo, a Sophomore in Computer Science at Brown University, reviewed the entire *Fourth Edition*; reviewed and updated Chapter 22, Java Media Framework and Java Sound; and updated Appendix A (Java Demos) and Appendix B (Java Resources). Susan and Eugene also worked on many of the books's ancillary materials, including the solutions to the exercises, true/false questions for the companion Web site (**`www.prenhall.com/deitel`**), true/false questions for the Java 2 Multimedia Cyber Classroom and multiple choice questions for the Instructor's test bank.
- Vincent He, a Senior in Management and Computer Science at Boston College, co-authored Chapter 22, Java Media Framework and Java Sound—one of the most exciting and fun chapters in the book! We are sure you will enjoy the multimedia extravaganza Vincent created for you.
- Liz Rockett, a Senior in English at Princeton University edited and updated Chapter 22, Java Media Framework and Java Sound.
- Chris Henson, a graduate of Brandeis University (Computer Science and History), reviewed Chapter 22, Java Media Framework and Java Sound.
- Christina Carney, a Senior in Psychology and Business at Framingham State College, researched and updated the bibliography, helped prepare the Preface and performed the URL research for the OOD/UML case study and design patterns.
- Amy Gips, a Sophomore in Marketing and Finance at Boston College, updated and added URLs for applets, graphics, Java 2D and Multimedia in Appendices A and B. Amy also researched quotes for Chapter 22 and helped prepare the Preface.
- Varun Ganapathi, a Sophomore in Computer Science and Electrical Engineering at Cornell University, updated Appendix F, Creating HTML Documentation with **`javadoc`**.
- Reshma Khilnani, a Junior in Computer Science and Mathematics at the Massachusetts Institute of Technology, worked with Rashmi on the Unicode Appendix

We are fortunate to have been able to work on this project with the talented and dedicated team of publishing professionals at Prentice Hall. We especially appreciate the

---

2. The *Deitel & Associates, Inc. College Internship Program* offers a limited number of salaried positions to Boston-area college students majoring in Computer Science, Information Technology or Marketing. Students work at our corporate headquarters in Sudbury, Massachusetts full-time in the summers and part-time during the academic year. Full-time positions are available to college graduates. For more information about this competitive program, please contact Abbey Deitel at **`deitel@deitel.com`** and check our Web site, **`www.deitel.com`**.

extraordinary efforts of our computer science editor, Petra Recter and her boss—our mentor in publishing—Marcia Horton, Editor-in-Chief of Prentice-Hall's Engineering and Computer Science Division. Camille Trentacoste did a marvelous job as production manager.

The *Java 2 Multimedia Cyber Classroom, Fourth Edition* was developed in parallel with *Java How to Program, Fourth Edition*. We sincerely appreciate the "new media" insight, savvy and technical expertise of our e-media editor-in-chief, mentor and friend Mark Taub. He and our e-media editor, Karen Mclean, did a remarkable job bringing the *Java 2 Multimedia Cyber Classroom, Fourth Edition* to publication under a tight schedule. *Michael Ruel* did a marvelous job as Cyber Classroom project manager.

We owe special thanks to the creativity of Tamara Newnam Cavallo (**`smart_art@earthlink.net`**) who did the art work for our programming tips icons and the cover. She created the delightful bug creature who shares with you the book's programming tips.

We sincerely appreciate the efforts of our fourth edition reviewers:

Java How to Program, Fourth Edition Reviewers

Dibyendu Baksi (Sun Microsystems)
Tim Boudreau (Sun Microsystems)
Michael Bundschuh (Sun Microsystems)
Gary Ginstling (Sun Microsystems)
Tomas Pavek (Sun Microsystems)
Rama Roberts (Sun Microsystems)
Terry Hull (Sera Nova)
Ralph Johnson ("gang-of-four" co-author of the seminal book, *Design Patterns: Elements of Reusable Object-Oriented Software*, Addison Wesley, 1995)
Cameron Skinner (Embarcadero Technologies; OMG)
Michael Chonoles (Lockheed Martin Adv. Concepts; OMG)
Brian Cook (The Technical Resource Connection; OMG)
Akram Al-Rawi (Zayed University)
Charley Bay (Fronte Range Community College)
Clint Bickmore (Fronte Range Community College)
Ron Braithwaite (Nutriware)
Columbus Brown (IBM)
Larry Brown (co-author of *Core Web Programming*)
Dan Corkum (Trillium Software)
Jonathan Earl (Technical Training and Consulting)
Karl Frank (togethersoft.com)
Charles Fry (thesundancekid.org)
Kyle Gabhart (Objective Solutions)
Felipe Gaucho (Softexport)
Rob Gordon (SuffolkSoft, Inc.)
Michelle Guy (XOR)
Christopher Green (Colorado Springs Technical Consulting Group)
Kevlin Henney (Curbralan Limited)
Ethan Henry (Sitraka Software)
Faisal Kaleem (Florida International University)
Rob Kelly (SUNY)

Scott Kendall (Consultant, UML author)
Sachin Khana (Freelance Java Programmer)
Michael-Franz Mannion (Java Developer)
Julie McVicar (Oakland Community College)
Matt Mitton (Consultant)
Dan Moore (XOR)
Simon North (Synopsys)
Chetan Patel (Lexisnexis)
Brian Pontarelli (Consultant)
Kendall Scott (Consultant, UML author)
Craig Shofding (CAS Training Corp)
Spencer Roberts (Titus Corporation)
Toby Steel (CertaPay)
Stephen Tockey (Construx Software)
Kim Topley (Author of *Core Java Foundation Classes* and *Core Swing: Advanced Programming*, both published by Prentice Hall)
Gustavo Toretti (Java Programmer; Campinas University)
Michael Van Kleeck (Director of Technology, Learning.com)
Dave Wagstaff (Sungard)

Java How to Program, Third Edition Post-Publication Reviewers
Jonathan Earl (Technical Training Consultants)
Harry Foxwell (Sun Microsystems)
Terry Hull (Sera Nova)
Ron McCarty (Penn State University Behrend Campus)
Bina Ramamurthy (SUNY Buffalo)
Vadim Tkachenko (Sera Nova)

Under a tight time schedule, they scrutinized every aspect of the text and made countless suggestions for improving the accuracy and completeness of the presentation.

We would sincerely appreciate your comments, criticisms, corrections, and suggestions for improving the text. Please address all correspondence to:

`deitel@deitel.com`

We will respond immediately. Well, that's it for now. Welcome to the exciting world of Java programming. We hope you enjoy this look at leading-edge computer applications development. Good luck!

Dr. Harvey M. Deitel
Paul J. Deitel

About the Authors

Dr. Harvey M. Deitel, CEO of Deitel & Associates, Inc., has 40 years experience in the computing field including extensive industry and academic experience. He is one of the world's leading computer science instructors and seminar presenters. Dr. Deitel earned B.S. and M.S. degrees from the Massachusetts Institute of Technology and a Ph.D. from

Boston University. He has 20 years of college teaching experience including earning tenure and serving as the Chairman of the Computer Science Department at Boston College before founding Deitel & Associates, Inc. with his son Paul J. Deitel. He is author or co-author of several dozen books and multimedia packages and is currently writing many more. With translations published in Japanese, Russian, Spanish, Italian, Basic Chinese, Traditional Chinese, Korean, French, Polish and Portuguese, Dr. Deitel's texts have earned international recognition. Dr. Deitel has delivered professional seminars internationally to major corporations, government organizations and various branches of the military.

Paul J. Deitel, Chief Technical Officer of Deitel & Associates, Inc., is a graduate of the Massachusetts Institute of Technology's Sloan School of Management where he studied Information Technology. Through Deitel & Associates, Inc. he has delivered Internet and World Wide Web courses and programming language classes for industry clients including Sun Microsystems, EMC^2, IBM, BEA Systems, Visa International, Progress Software, Boeing, Fidelity, Hitachi, Cap Gemini, Compaq, Art Technology, White Sands Missile Range, NASA at the Kennedy Space Center, the National Severe Storm Laboratory, Rogue Wave Software, Lucent Technologies, Computervision, Cambridge Technology Partners, Adra Systems, Entergy, CableData Systems, Banyan, Stratus, Concord Communications and many other organizations. He has lectured on Java and C++ for the Boston Chapter of the Association for Computing Machinery, and has taught satellite-based courses through a cooperative venture of Deitel & Associates, Inc., Prentice Hall and the Technology Education Network. He and his father, Dr. Harvey M. Deitel, are the world's best-selling Computer Science textbook authors.

About Deitel & Associates, Inc.

Deitel & Associates, Inc. is an internationally recognized corporate training and content-creation organization specializing in Internet/World Wide Web software technology, e-business/e-commerce software technology and computer programming languages education. Deitel & Associates, Inc. is a member of the World Wide Web Consortium. The company provides courses on Internet and World Wide Web programming, object technology and major programming languages. The founders of Deitel & Associates, Inc. are Dr. Harvey M. Deitel and Paul J. Deitel. The company's clients include many of the world's largest computer companies, government agencies, branches of the military and business organizations. Through its publishing partnership with Prentice Hall, Deitel & Associates, Inc. publishes leading-edge programming textbooks, professional books, interactive CD-ROM-based multimedia *Cyber Classrooms*, satellite courses and Web-based training courses. Deitel & Associates, Inc. and the authors can be reached via e-mail at

`deitel@deitel.com`

To learn more about Deitel & Associates, Inc., its publications and its worldwide corporate on-site curriculum, see the last few pages of this book and visit:

`www.deitel.com`

Individuals wishing to purchase Deitel books, Cyber Classrooms, Complete Training Courses and Web-based training courses can do so through

`www.deitel.com`

Bulk orders by corporations and academic institutions should be placed directly with Prentice Hall. See the last few pages of this book for worldwide ordering details.

The World Wide Web Consortium (W3C)

W3C® MEMBER

Deitel & Associates, Inc. is a member of the *World Wide Web Consortium (W3C)*. The W3C was founded in 1994 "to develop common protocols for the evolution of the World Wide Web." As a W3C member, we hold a seat on the W3C Advisory Committee (our Advisory Committee representative is our Chief Technology Officer, Paul Deitel). Advisory Committee members help provide "strategic direction" to the W3C through meetings around the world. Member organizations also help develop standards recommendations for Web technologies (such as HTML, XML and many others) through participation in W3C activities and groups. Membership in the W3C is intended for companies and large organizations. For information on becoming a member of the W3C visit **`www.w3.org/Consortium/Prospectus/Joining`**.

1

Introduction to Computers, the Internet and the Web

Objectives

- To understand basic computer science concepts.
- To become familiar with different types of programming languages.
- To introduce the Java development environment.
- To understand Java's role in developing distributed client/server applications for the Internet and Web.
- To introduce object-oriented design with the UML and design patterns.
- To preview the remaining chapters of the book.

Our life is frittered away by detail ... Simplify, simplify.
Henry Thoreau

High thoughts must have high language.
Aristophanes

The chief merit of language is clearness.
Galen

My object all sublime
I shall achieve in time.
W. S. Gilbert

He had a wonderful talent for packing thought close, and rendering it portable.
Thomas Babington Macaulay

Egad, I think the interpreter is the hardest to be understood of the two!
Richard Brinsley Sheridan

Outline

1.1 Introduction
1.2 What Is a Computer?
1.3 Computer Organization
1.4 Evolution of Operating Systems
1.5 Personal, Distributed and Client/Server Computing
1.6 Machine Languages, Assembly Languages and High-Level Languages
1.7 History of C++
1.8 History of Java
1.9 Java Class Libraries
1.10 Other High-Level Languages
1.11 Structured Programming
1.12 The Internet and the World Wide Web
1.13 Basics of a Typical Java Environment
1.14 General Notes about Java and This Book
1.15 Thinking About Objects: Introduction to Object Technology and the Unified Modeling Language
1.16 Discovering Design Patterns: Introduction
1.17 Tour of the Book
1.18 (Optional) A Tour of the Case Study on Object-Oriented Design with the UML
1.19 (Optional) A Tour of the "Discovering Design Patterns" Sections

Summary • Terminology • Self-Review Exercises • Answers to Self-Review Exercises • Exercises

1.1 Introduction

Welcome to Java! We have worked hard to create what we hope will be an informative, entertaining and challenging learning experience for you. Java is a powerful computer programming language that is fun to use for novices and appropriate for experienced programmers building substantial information systems. *Java How to Program: Fourth Edition* is designed to be an effective learning tool for each of these audiences.

How can one book appeal to both groups? The answer is that the common core of the book emphasizes achieving program *clarity* through the proven techniques of *structured programming* and *object-oriented programming*. Nonprogrammers will learn programming the right way from the beginning. We have attempted to write in a clear and straightforward manner. The book is abundantly illustrated. Perhaps most importantly, the book presents hundreds of working Java programs and shows the outputs produced when those programs are run on a computer. We teach all Java features in the context of complete working Java programs. We call this the *live-code™ approach*. These examples are available from three locations—they are on the CD that accompanies this book, they may be downloaded from our Web site **www.deitel.com** and they are available on our interactive CD product, the *Java 2 Multimedia Cyber Classroom: Fourth Edition.* The Cyber Classroom's features and ordering information appear at the back of this book. The Cyber Classroom also contains answers to approximately half of the solved exercises in this book, including short answers, small programs and many full projects. If you purchased *The Complete Java 2 Training Course: Fourth Edition*, you already have the Cyber Classroom.

The early chapters introduce the fundamentals of computers, computer programming and the Java computer programming language. Novices who have taken our courses tell us that the material in those chapters presents a solid foundation for the deeper treatment of Java in the later chapters. Experienced programmers tend to read the early chapters quickly and find that the treatment of Java in the later chapters is rigorous and challenging.

Many experienced programmers have told us that they appreciate our structured programming treatment. Often, they have been programming in structured languages like C or Pascal, but they were never formally introduced to structured programming, so they are not writing the best possible code in these languages. As they review structured programming in the chapters "Control Structures: Part 1" and "Control Structures: Part 2," they are able to improve their C and Pascal programming styles as well. So whether you are a novice or an experienced programmer, there is much here to inform, entertain and challenge you.

Most people are familiar with the exciting tasks computers perform. Using this textbook, you will learn how to command computers to perform those tasks. It is *software* (i.e., the instructions you write to command computers to perform *actions* and make *decisions*) that controls computers (often referred to as *hardware*), and Java is one of today's most popular software-development languages. Java was developed by Sun Microsystems and an implementation of it is available free over the Internet from the Sun Web site

java.sun.com/j2se

This book is based on the *Java 2 Platform, Standard Edition*, which describes the Java language, libraries and tools. Other vendors can implement *Java development kits* based on the *Java 2 Platform.* Sun provides an implementation of the *Java 2 Platform, Standard Edition* called the *Java 2 Software Development Kit, Standard Edition (J2SDK)* that includes the minimum set of tools you need to write software in Java. At the time of this publication, the most recent version was J2SDK 1.3.1. You can download future updates to the J2SDK from the Sun Web site **java.sun.com/j2se**.

Computer use is increasing in almost every field of endeavor. In an era of steadily rising costs, computing costs have been decreasing dramatically due to rapid developments in both hardware and software technology. Computers that might have filled large rooms and cost millions of dollars two decades ago can now be inscribed on the surfaces of silicon chips smaller than a fingernail, costing perhaps a few dollars each. Ironically, silicon is one of the most abundant materials on earth—it is an ingredient in common sand. Silicon-chip technology has made computing so economical that hundreds of millions of general-purpose computers are in use worldwide helping people in business, industry, government, and in their personal lives. The number of computers worldwide easily could double in the next few years.

This book will challenge you for several reasons. For many years, students learned C or Pascal as their first programming language. They probably learned the programming methodology called *structured programming.* You will learn both structured programming and the exciting newer methodology, *object-oriented programming.* Why do we teach both? We believe that object orientation is the key programming methodology of the future. You will build and work with many *objects* in this course. However, you will discover that the internal structure of those objects is built with structured programming techniques. Also, the logic of manipulating objects is occasionally best expressed with structured programming.

Another reason we present both methodologies is the continuing migration from C-based systems (built primarily with structured programming techniques) to C++ and Java-based systems (built primarily with object-oriented programming techniques). There is a huge amount of so-called "legacy C code" in place, because C has been in use for over three decades. Once people learn C++ or Java, they find these languages to be more powerful than C. These people often choose to move their programming projects to C++ or Java. They begin converting their legacy systems and begin employing the object-oriented programming capabilities of C++ or Java to realize the full benefits of these languages. Often, the choice between C++ and Java is made based on the simplicity of Java compared to C++.

Java has become the language of choice for implementing Internet-based and Intranet-based applications and software for devices that communicate over a network. Do not be surprised when your new stereo and other devices in your home will be networked together by Java technology! Also, do not be surprised when your wireless devices, like cell phones, pagers and personal digital assistants (PDAs) communicate over the so-called Wireless Internet via the kind of Java-based networking protocols that you will learn in this book and its companion *Advanced Java 2 Platform How to Program.*

Java is a particularly attractive first programming language. At the JavaOne™ trade show in June 2001, it was announced that Java is now a required part of the programming languages curriculum in 56% of US colleges and universities. Also, 87% of US colleges and universities offer Java courses. Java is attractive to high schools as well. In 2003, the College Board will standardize on Java for Advanced Placement computer science courses.

Java has evolved rapidly into the large-scale applications arena. Java is no longer a language used simply to make World Wide Web pages "come alive." Java has become the preferred language for meeting many organizations' programming needs.

For many years, languages like C and C++ appealed to universities because of their portability. Introductory courses could be offered in these languages on any hardware/operating system combination, as long as a C/C++ compiler was available. However, the programming world has become more complex and more demanding. Today, users want applications with graphical user interfaces (GUIs). They want applications that use multimedia capabilities such as graphics, images, animation, audio and video. They want applications that can run on the Internet and the World Wide Web and communicate with other applications. They want applications that can take advantage of the flexibility and performance improvements of multithreading (which enables programmers to specify that several activities should occur in parallel). They want applications with richer file processing than is provided by C or C++. They want applications that are not limited to the desktop or even to some local computer network, but can integrate Internet components and remote databases as well. They want applications that can be written quickly and correctly in a manner that takes advantage of prebuilt software components. They want easy access to a growing universe of reusable software components. Programmers want all these benefits in a truly portable manner, so that applications will run without modification on a variety of *platforms* (i.e., different types of computers running different operating systems). Java offers all these benefits to the programming community.

Another reason Java is attractive for university courses is that it is fully object oriented. One reason that C++ use has grown so quickly is that it extends C programming into the arena of object orientation. For the huge community of C programmers, this has been a powerful advantage. C++ includes ANSI/ISO C and offers the ability to do object-oriented programming as well. (ANSI is the American National Standards Institute, and ISO is the International Standards Organization.) An enormous amount of C code has been written in industry over the last several decades. C++ is a superset of C, so many organizations find it to be an ideal next step. Programmers can take their C code, compile it (often with nominal changes) in a C++ compiler and continue writing C-like code while mastering the object paradigm. Then, the programmers can gradually migrate portions of the legacy C code into C++ as time permits. New systems can be entirely written in object-oriented C++. Such strategies have been appealing to many organizations. The downside is that, even after adopting this strategy, companies tend to continue producing C-like code for many years. This, of course, means that they do not realize the benefits of object-oriented programming quickly and could produce programs that are confusing and hard to maintain as a result of to their hybrid design. Many organizations would prefer to plunge 100% into object-oriented development, but the realities of mountains of legacy code and the temptation to take a C-programming approach often prevent this.

Java is a fully object-oriented language with strong support for proper software engineering techniques. It is difficult to write C-like, so-called procedural programs in Java. You must create and manipulate objects. Error processing is built into the language. Many of the complex details of C and C++ programming that prevent programmers from "looking at the big picture" are not included in Java. For universities, these features are powerfully appealing. Students will learn object-oriented programming from the start. They will simply think in an object-oriented manner.

Here, too, there is a trade-off. Organizations turning to Java for new applications development do not want to convert all their legacy code to Java. So Java allows for so-called *native code*. This means that existing C and C++ code can be integrated with Java code. Although this may seem a bit awkward (and it certainly can be), it presents a pragmatic solution to a problem most organizations face.

The fact that Java is free for download at the Sun Web site, **java.sun.com/j2se**, is appealing to universities facing tight budgets and lengthy budget planning cycles. Also, as bug fixes and new versions of Java are developed, these become available immediately over the Internet, so universities can keep their Java software current.

Can Java be taught in a first programming course—the intended audience for this book? We think so. Prior to writing this book, Deitel & Associates, Inc. instructors taught hundreds of Java courses to several thousand people at all levels of expertise, including many nonprogrammers. We found that nonprogrammers become productive faster with Java than with C or C++. They are anxious to experiment with Java's powerful features for graphics, graphical user interfaces, multimedia, animation, multithreading, networking and the like—and they are successful at building substantial Java programs even in their first courses.

For many years, the Pascal programming language was the preferred vehicle for use in introductory and intermediate programming courses. Many people said that C was too difficult a language for these courses. In 1992, we published the first edition of *C How to Program,* to encourage universities to try C instead of Pascal in these courses. We used the same pedagogic approach we had used in our university courses for a dozen years, but wrapped the concepts in C rather than Pascal. We found that students were able to handle C at about the same level as Pascal. However, there was one noticeable difference—students appreciated that they were learning a language (C) likely to be valuable to them in industry. Our industry clients appreciated the availability of C-literate graduates who could work immediately on substantial projects rather than first having to go through costly and time-consuming training programs.

The first edition of *C How to Program* included a 60-page introduction to C++ and object-oriented programming. We saw C++ coming on strong, but we felt it would be at least a few more years before the universities would be ready to teach C++ and object-oriented programming (OOP) in introductory courses.

During 1993, we saw a surge in interest in C++ and OOP among our industry clients, but we still did not sense that the universities were ready to switch to C++ and OOP en masse. So, in January 1994, we published the Second Edition of *C How to Program* with a 300-page section on C++ and OOP. In May 1994, we published the first edition of *C++ How to Program,* a 950-page book devoted to the premise that C++ and OOP were now ready for prime time in introductory university courses for many schools that wanted to be at the leading edge of programming-languages education.

In 1995, we were following the introduction of Java carefully. In November 1995, we attended an Internet conference in Boston. A representative from Sun Microsystems gave a presentation on Java that filled one of the large ballrooms at the Hynes Convention Center. As the presentation proceeded, it became clear to us that Java would play a significant part in the development of interactive, multimedia Web pages. We immediately saw a much greater potential for the language. We saw Java as the proper language for universities to teach first-year programming language students in this modern world of graphics, images, animation, audio, video, database, networking, multithreading and collaborative computing. At the time, we were busy writing the second edition of *C++ How to Program.* We discussed with our publisher, Prentice Hall, our vision of Java making a strong impact in the university curriculum. We all agreed to delay the second edition of *C++ How to Program* a bit so that we could get the first edition of *Java How to Program* (based on Java 1.0.2) to the market in time for fall 1996 courses.

As Java rapidly evolved to Java 1.1, we wrote *Java How to Program: Second Edition* in 1997, less than a year after the first edition reached bookstores. Hundreds of universities and corporate training programs worldwide used the second edition. To keep pace with the enhancements in Java, we published *Java How to Program: Third Edition* in 1999. The third edition was a major overhaul to upgrade the book to the *Java 2 Platform.*

Java continues to evolve rapidly, so we wrote this fourth edition of *Java How to Program*—our first book to reach a fourth edition—just five years after the first edition was published. This edition is based on the *Java 2 Platform, Standard Edition* (*J2SE*). Java has grown so rapidly over the last several years that it now has two other editions. The *Java 2 Platform, Enterprise Edition* (*J2EE*) is geared toward developing large-scale, distributed networking applications and Web-based applications. The *Java 2 Platform, Micro Edition* (*J2ME*) is geared toward development of applications for small devices (such as cell phones, pagers and personal digital assistants) and other memory-constrained applications. The number of topics to cover in Java has become far too large for one book. So, in parallel with *Java How to Program, Fourth Edition,* we are publishing *Advanced Java 2 Platform How to Program,* which emphasizes developing applications with J2EE and provides coverage of several high-end topics from the J2SE. In addition, this book also includes substantial materials on J2ME and wireless-application development.

So, there you have it! You are about to start on a challenging and rewarding path. As you proceed, please share your thoughts on Java and *Java How to Program: Fourth Edition* with us via e-mail at **`deitel@deitel.com`**. We will respond promptly.

Prentice Hall maintains **`www.prenhall.com/deitel`**—a Web site dedicated to our Prentice Hall publications, including textbooks, professional books, interactive multimedia CD-based *Cyber Classrooms*, *Complete Training Courses* (boxed products containing both a *Cyber Classroom* and the corresponding book), Web-based training, e-whitepapers, e-books and ancillary materials for all these products. For each of our books, the site contains companion Web sites that include frequently asked questions (FAQs), code downloads, errata, updates, additional text and examples, additional self-test questions and new developments in programming languages and object-oriented programming technologies. If you would like to learn more about the authors or Deitel & Associates, Inc. please visit **`www.deitel.com`**. Good luck!

1.2 What Is a Computer?

A *computer* is a device capable of performing computations and making logical decisions at speeds millions, even billions, of times faster than human beings can. For example, many of today's personal computers can perform hundreds of millions, even billions, of additions per second. A person operating a desk calculator might require decades to complete the same number of calculations a powerful personal computer can perform in one second. (*Points to ponder*: How would you know whether the person added the numbers correctly? How would you know whether the computer added the numbers correctly?) Today's fastest *supercomputers* can perform hundreds of billions of additions per second—about as many calculations as hundreds of thousands of people could perform in one year! And trillion-instruction-per-second computers are already functioning in research laboratories!

Computers process *data* under the control of sets of instructions called *computer programs*. These programs guide the computer through orderly sets of actions specified by people called *computer programmers*.

The various devices that comprise a computer system (such as the keyboard, screen, disks, memory and processing units) are referred to as *hardware*. The computer programs that run on a computer are referred to as *software*. Hardware costs have been declining dramatically in recent years, to the point that personal computers have become a commodity. Unfortunately, software-development costs have been rising steadily, as programmers develop ever more powerful and complex applications without being able to improve significantly the technology of software development. In this book, you will learn proven software-development methods that can reduce software-development costs—top-down stepwise refinement, functionalization and object-oriented programming. Object-oriented programming is widely believed to be the significant breakthrough that can greatly enhance programmer productivity.

1.3 Computer Organization

Regardless of differences in physical appearance, virtually every computer may be envisioned as being divided into six *logical units* or sections. These are as follows:

1. *Input unit.* This is the "receiving" section of the computer. It obtains information (data and computer programs) from *input devices* and places this information at the disposal of the other units so that the information may be processed. Most information is entered into computers today through typewriter-like keyboards, "mouse" devices and disks. In the future, most information will be entered by speaking to computers, by electronically scanning images and by video recording.
2. *Output unit.* This is the "shipping" section of the computer. It takes information processed by the computer and places it on various *output devices* to make the information available for use outside the computer. Information output from computers is displayed on screens, printed on paper, played through audio speakers, magnetically recorded on disks and tapes or used to control other devices.
3. *Memory unit.* This is the rapid-access, relatively low-capacity "warehouse" section of the computer. It retains information that has been entered through the input unit so that the information may be made immediately available for processing when it is needed. The memory unit also retains information that has already been processed until that information can be placed on output devices by the output unit. The memory unit often is called either *memory, primary memory* or *random-access memory (RAM).*
4. *Arithmetic and logic unit (ALU).* This is the "manufacturing" section of the computer. It is responsible for performing calculations such as addition, subtraction, multiplication and division. It contains the decision mechanisms that allow the computer, for example, to compare two items from the memory unit to determine whether they are equal.
5. *Central processing unit (CPU).* This is the "administrative" section of the computer. It is the computer's coordinator and is responsible for supervising the operation of the other sections. The CPU tells the input unit when information should be read into the memory unit, tells the ALU when information from the memory unit should be utilized in calculations and tells the output unit when to send information from the memory unit to certain output devices.
6. *Secondary storage unit.* This is the long-term, high-capacity "warehousing" section of the computer. Programs or data not being used by the other units are normally placed on secondary storage devices (such as disks) until they are needed, possibly hours, days, months or even years later. Information in secondary storage takes longer to access than information in primary memory. The cost per unit of secondary storage is much less than the cost per unit of primary memory.

1.4 Evolution of Operating Systems

Early computers were capable of performing only one *job* or *task* at a time. This form of computer operation is often called single-user *batch processing.* The computer runs a single program at a time while processing data in groups or *batches.* In these early systems, users generally submitted their jobs to the computer center on decks of punched cards. Users often had to wait hours or even days before printouts were returned to their desks.

Software systems called *operating systems* were developed to help make it more convenient to use computers. Early operating systems managed the smooth transition between jobs. This minimized the time it took for computer operators to switch between jobs and hence increased the amount of work, or *throughput,* computers could process.

As computers became more powerful, it became evident that single-user batch processing rarely utilized the computer's resources efficiently. Instead, it was thought that many jobs or tasks could be made to *share* the resources of the computer to achieve better utilization. This is called *multiprogramming.* Multiprogramming involves the "simultaneous" operation of many jobs on the computer—the computer shares its resources among the jobs competing for its attention. With early multiprogramming operating systems, users still submitted jobs on decks of punched cards and waited hours or days for results.

In the 1960s, several groups in industry and the universities pioneered *timesharing* operating systems. Timesharing is a special case of multiprogramming in which users access the computer through *terminals*, typically devices with keyboards and screens. In a typical timesharing computer system, there may be dozens or even hundreds of users sharing the computer at once. The computer does not actually run all the users' jobs simultaneously. Rather, it runs a small portion of one user's job and moves on to service the next user. The computer does this so quickly that it might provide service to each user several times per second. Thus the users' programs *appear* to be running simultaneously. An advantage of timesharing is that the user receives almost immediate responses to requests rather than having to wait long periods for results, as with previous modes of computing. Also, if a particular user is currently idle, the computer can continue to service other users rather than wait for one user.

1.5 Personal, Distributed and Client/Server Computing

In 1977, Apple Computer popularized the phenomenon of *personal computing.* Initially, it was a hobbyist's dream. Computers became economical enough for people to buy them for their own personal use. In 1981, IBM, the world's largest computer vendor, introduced the IBM Personal Computer. Almost overnight, personal computing became legitimate in business, industry and government organizations.

But these computers were "stand-alone" units—people did their work on their own machines and transported disks back and forth to share information. Although early personal computers were not powerful enough to timeshare several users, these machines could be linked together in computer networks, sometimes over telephone lines and sometimes in *local area networks (LANs)* within an organization. This led to the phenomenon of *distributed computing,* in which an organization's computing, instead of being performed strictly at some central computer installation, is distributed over networks to the sites at which the real work of the organization is performed. Personal computers were powerful enough both to handle the computing requirements of individual users and to handle the basic communications tasks of passing information back and forth electronically.

Today's most powerful personal computers are as powerful as the million-dollar machines of just a decade ago. The most powerful desktop machines—called *workstations*—provide individual users with enormous capabilities. Information is shared easily across computer networks where some computers called *file servers* offer a common store of programs and data that may be used by *client* computers distributed throughout the network (hence the term *client/server computing*). C and C++ have become and remain the languages of choice for writing operating systems. They also remain popular for writing computer networking, distributed client/server and Internet and Web applications, although

Java is now the dominant language in each of these areas. Many programmers have discovered that programming in Java helps them be more productive than programming in C or C++. Today's popular operating systems, such as UNIX, Linux, MacOS, Windows and Windows 2000, provide the kinds of capabilities discussed in this section.

1.6 Machine Languages, Assembly Languages and High-Level Languages

Programmers write instructions in various programming languages, some directly understandable by computers and others that require intermediate *translation* steps. Hundreds of computer languages are in use today. These may be divided into three general types:

1. Machine languages
2. Assembly languages
3. High-level languages

Any computer can directly understand only its own *machine language*. Machine language is the "natural language" of a particular computer. It is defined by the hardware design of that computer. Machine languages generally consist of strings of numbers (ultimately reduced to 1s and 0s) that instruct computers to perform their most elementary operations one at a time. Machine languages are *machine dependent* (i.e., a particular machine language can be used on only one type of computer). Machine languages are cumbersome for humans, as can be seen by the following section of a machine-language program that adds overtime pay to base pay and stores the result in gross pay.

```
+1300042774
+1400593419
+1200274027
```

As computers became more popular, it became apparent that machine-language programming was simply too slow and tedious for most programmers. Instead of using the strings of numbers that computers could directly understand, programmers began using English-like abbreviations to represent the elementary operations of computers. These English-like abbreviations formed the basis of *assembly languages. Translator programs* called *assemblers* were developed to convert assembly-language programs to machine language at computer speeds. The following section of an assembly-language program also adds overtime pay to base pay and stores the result in gross pay, but somewhat more clearly than its machine-language equivalent.

```
LOAD   BASEPAY
ADD    OVERPAY
STORE  GROSSPAY
```

Although such code is clearer to humans, it is incomprehensible to computers until translated to machine language.

Computer usage increased rapidly with the advent of assembly languages, but programming in these still required many instructions to accomplish even the simplest tasks. To speed the programming process, *high-level languages* were developed in which single statements could be written to accomplish substantial tasks. The translator programs that convert high-level language programs into machine language are called *compilers*. High-level languages allow programmers to write instructions that look almost like everyday English and contain commonly used mathematical notations. A payroll program written in a high-level language might contain a statement such as

```
grossPay = basePay + overTimePay
```

Obviously, high-level languages are much more desirable from the programmer's standpoint than either machine languages or assembly languages. C, C++ and Java are among the most powerful and most widely used high-level programming languages.

The process of compiling a high-level language program into machine language can take a considerable amount of computer time. *Interpreter* programs were developed to execute high-level language programs directly without the need for compiling those programs into machine language. Although compiled programs execute much faster than interpreted programs, interpreters are popular in program-development environments in which programs are recompiled frequently as new features are added and errors are corrected. Once a program is developed, a compiled version can be produced to run most efficiently. As we study Java, you will see that interpreters have played an especially important part in helping Java achieve its goal of portability across a great variety of platforms.

1.7 History of C++

C++ evolved from C, which evolved from two previous languages, BCPL and B. BCPL was developed in 1967 by Martin Richards as a language for writing operating-systems software and compilers. Ken Thompson modeled many features in his language B after their counterparts in BCPL and used B to create early versions of the UNIX operating system at Bell Laboratories in 1970 on a Digital Equipment Corporation PDP-7 computer. Both BCPL and B were "typeless" languages—every data item occupied one "word" in memory. For example, it was the programmer's responsibility to treat a data item as a whole number or a real number.

The C language was evolved from B by Dennis Ritchie at Bell Laboratories and was originally implemented on a DEC PDP-11 computer in 1972. C uses many important concepts of BCPL and B while adding data typing and other features. C initially became widely known as the development language of the UNIX operating system. Today, virtually all new major operating systems are written in C or C++. Over the past two decades, C has become available for most computers. C is hardware independent. With careful design, it is possible to write C programs that are *portable* to most computers.

By the late 1970s, C had evolved into what is now referred to as "traditional C," or "Kernighan and Ritchie C." The publication by Prentice Hall in 1978 of Kernighan and Ritchie's book, *The C Programming Language,* brought wide attention to the language. This publication became one of the most successful computer science books ever.

The widespread use of C with various types of computers (sometimes called *hardware platforms*) led to many variations. These were similar, but often incompatible. This was a serious problem for programmers who needed to write portable programs that would run on several platforms. It became clear that a standard version of C was needed. In 1983, the X3J11 technical committee was created under the American National Standards Committee on Computers and Information Processing (X3) to "provide an unambiguous and machine-independent definition of the language." In 1989, the standard was approved. ANSI cooperated with the International Standards Organization (ISO) to standardize C worldwide; the joint standard document was published in 1990 and is referred to as ANSI/ ISO 9899: 1990. The second edition of Kernighan and Ritchie,[1] published in 1988, reflects this version called ANSI C, a version of the language still used worldwide (Ke88).

C++, an extension of C, was developed by Bjarne Stroustrup in the early 1980s at Bell Laboratories. C++ provides a number of features that "spruce up" the C language, but more importantly, it provides capabilities for *object-oriented programming*. C++ was also standardized by the ANSI and ISO committees.

There is a revolution brewing in the software community. Building software quickly, correctly and economically remains an elusive goal, and this at a time when demands for new and more powerful software are soaring. *Objects* are essentially reusable software *components* that model items in the real world. Software developers are discovering that using a modular, object-oriented design and implementation approach can make software-development groups much more productive than is possible with previous popular programming techniques such as structured programming. Object-oriented programs are often easier to understand, correct and modify.

Many other object-oriented languages have been developed, including Smalltalk, developed at Xerox's Palo Alto Research Center (PARC). Smalltalk is a pure object-oriented language—literally everything is an object. C++ is a hybrid language—it is possible to program in either a C-like style, an object-oriented style or both.

1.8 History of Java

Perhaps the microprocessor revolution's most important contribution to date is that it made possible the development of personal computers, which now number in the hundreds of millions worldwide. Personal computers have had a profound impact on people and the way organizations conduct and manage their business.

Many people believe that the next major area in which microprocessors will have a profound impact is in intelligent consumer-electronic devices. Recognizing this, Sun Microsystems funded an internal corporate research project code-named Green in 1991. The project resulted in the development of a C- and C++-based language that its creator, James Gosling, called Oak after an oak tree outside his window at Sun. It was later discovered that there already was a computer language called Oak. When a group of Sun people visited a local coffee place, the name Java was suggested, and it stuck.

The Green project ran into some difficulties. The marketplace for intelligent consumer-electronic devices was not developing as quickly as Sun had anticipated. Worse yet, a major contract for which Sun competed was awarded to another company. So the project was in danger of being canceled. By sheer good fortune, the World Wide Web exploded in popularity in 1993, and Sun people saw the immediate potential of using Java to create Web pages with so-called *dynamic content*. This breathed new life into the project.

Sun formally announced Java at a major conference in May 1995. Ordinarily, an event like this would not have generated much attention. However, Java generated immediate interest in the business community because of the phenomenal interest in the World Wide Web. Java is now used to create Web pages with dynamic and interactive content, to develop large-scale enterprise applications, to enhance the functionality of World Wide

---

1. Kernighan, B. W., and D. M. Ritchie, *The C Programming Language* (Second Edition), Englewood Cliffs, NJ: Prentice Hall, 1988.

Web servers (the computers that provide the content we see in our Web browsers), to provide applications for consumer devices (such as cell phones, pagers and personal digital assistants) and for many other purposes.

1.9 Java Class Libraries

Java programs consist of pieces called *classes*. Classes consist of pieces called *methods* that perform tasks and return information when they complete their tasks. You can program each piece you may need to form a Java program. However, most Java programmers take advantage of rich collections of existing classes in *Java class libraries*. The class libraries are also known as the *Java APIs (Application Programming Interfaces)*. Thus, there are really two pieces to learning the Java "world." The first is learning the Java language itself so that you can program your own classes; the second is learning how to use the classes in the extensive Java class libraries. Throughout the book, we discuss many library classes. Class libraries are provided primarily by compiler vendors, but many class libraries are supplied by independent software vendors (ISVs). Also, many class libraries are available from the Internet and World Wide Web as *freeware* or *shareware*. You can download freeware products and use them for free—subject to any restrictions specified by the copyright owner. You also can download shareware products for free, so you can try the software. Shareware products often are free of charge for personal use. However, for shareware products that you use regularly or use for commercial purposes, you are expected to pay a fee designated by the copyright owner.

Many freeware and shareware products are also *open source*. The source code for open-source products is freely available on the Internet, which enables you to learn from the source code, validate that the code serves its stated purpose and even modify the code. Often, open-source products require that you publish any enhancements you make so the open-source community can continue to evolve those products. One example of a popular open-source product is the Linux operating system.

Software Engineering Observation 1.1

Use a building-block approach to creating programs. Avoid reinventing the wheel. Use existing pieces—this is called software reuse *and it is central to object-oriented programming.*

[*Note*: We will include many of these *Software Engineering Observations* throughout the text to explain concepts that affect and improve the overall architecture and quality of software systems, and particularly, of large software systems. We will also highlight *Good Programming Practices* (practices that can help you write programs that are clearer, more understandable, more maintainable and easier to test and debug), *Common Programming Errors* (problems to watch out for so you do not make these same errors in your programs), *Performance Tips* (techniques that will help you write programs that run faster and use less memory), *Portability Tips* (techniques that will help you write programs that can run, with little or no modifications, on a variety of computers; these tips also include general observations about how Java achieves its high degree of portability), *Testing and Debugging Tips* (techniques that will help you remove bugs from your programs and, more important, techniques that will help you write bug-free programs to begin with) and *Look and Feel Observations* (techniques that will help you design the "look" and "feel" of your graphical user interfaces for appearance and ease of use). Many of these techniques and practices are only guidelines; you will, no doubt, develop your own preferred programming style.]

Software Engineering Observation 1.2

When programming in Java, you will typically use the following building blocks: Classes from class libraries, classes and methods you create yourself and classes and methods other people create and make available to you.

The advantage of creating your own classes and methods is that you know exactly how they work and you can examine the Java code. The disadvantage is the time-consuming and complex effort that goes into designing and developing new classes and methods.

Performance Tip 1.1

Using Java API classes and methods instead of writing your own versions can improve program performance, because these classes and methods are carefully written to perform efficiently. This technique also improves the prototyping speed of program development (i.e., the time it takes to develop a new program and get its first version running).

Portability Tip 1.1

Using classes and methods from the Java API instead of writing your own versions improves program portability, because these classes and methods are included in every Java implementation (assuming the same version number).

Software Engineering Observation 1.3

Extensive class libraries of reusable software components are available over the Internet and the Web. Many of these libraries provide source code and are available at no charge.

1.10 Other High-Level Languages

Hundreds of high-level languages have been developed, but only a few have achieved broad acceptance. *Fortran* (FORmula TRANslator) was developed by IBM Corporation between 1954 and 1957 to be used for scientific and engineering applications that require complex mathematical computations. Fortran is still widely used.

COBOL (COmmon Business Oriented Language) was developed in 1959 by a group of computer manufacturers and government and industrial computer users. COBOL is used primarily for commercial applications that require precise and efficient manipulation of large amounts of data. Today, about half of all business software is still programmed in COBOL. Approximately one million people are actively writing COBOL programs.

Pascal was designed at about the same time as C. It was created by Professor Nicklaus Wirth and was intended for academic use. We discuss Pascal further in the next section.

Basic was developed in 1965 at Dartmouth College as a simple language to help novices become comfortable with programming. *Bill Gates* implemented Basic on several early personal computers. Today, *Microsoft*—the company Bill Gates created—is the world's leading software-development organization.

1.11 Structured Programming

During the 1960s, many large software-development efforts encountered severe difficulties. Software schedules were typically late, costs greatly exceeded budgets and the finished products were unreliable. People began to realize that software development was a far more complex activity than they had imagined. Research activity in the 1960s resulted in the evolution of *structured programming*—a disciplined approach to writing programs that are clearer than unstructured programs, easier to test and debug and easier to modify. Chapters 4 and 5 discuss the principles of structured programming.

One of the more tangible results of this research was the development of the Pascal programming language by Nicklaus Wirth in 1971. Pascal, named after the seventeenth-century mathematician and philosopher Blaise Pascal, was designed for teaching structured programming in academic environments and rapidly became the preferred programming language in most universities. Unfortunately, the language lacks many features needed to make it useful in commercial, industrial and government applications, so it has not been widely accepted in these environments.

The Ada programming language was developed under the sponsorship of the United States Department of Defense (DOD) during the 1970s and early 1980s. Hundreds of separate languages were being used to produce DOD's massive command-and-control software systems. DOD wanted a single language that would fill most of its needs. Pascal was chosen as a base, but the final Ada language is quite different from Pascal. The language was named after Lady Ada Lovelace, daughter of the poet Lord Byron. Lady Lovelace is credited with writing the world's first computer program in the early 1800s (for the Analytical Engine mechanical computing device designed by Charles Babbage). One important capability of Ada is called *multitasking*, which allows programmers to specify that many activities are to occur in parallel. The native capabilities of other widely used high-level languages we have discussed—including C and C++—generally allow the programmer to write programs that perform only one activity at a time. Java, through a technique we will explain called *multithreading*, also enables programmers to write programs with parallel activities. [*Note*: Most operating systems provide libraries specific to individual platforms (sometimes called *platform-dependent libraries*) that enable high-level languages like C and C++ to specify that many activities are to occur in parallel in a program.]

1.12 The Internet and the World Wide Web

The *Internet* was developed more than three decades ago with funding supplied by the Department of Defense. Originally designed to connect the main computer systems of about a dozen universities and research organizations, the Internet today is accessible by hundreds of millions of computers worldwide.

With the introduction of the *World Wide Web*—which allows computer users to locate and view multimedia-based documents on almost any subject—the Internet has exploded into one of the world's premier communication mechanisms.

The Internet and the World Wide Web will surely be listed among the most important and profound creations of humankind. In the past, most computer applications ran on computers that were not connected to one another. Today's applications can be written to communicate among the world's hundreds of millions of computers. The Internet mixes computing and communications technologies. It makes our work easier. It makes information instantly and conveniently accessible worldwide. It makes it possible for individuals and local small businesses to get worldwide exposure. It is changing the nature of the way business is done. People can search for the best prices on virtually any product or service. Special-interest communities can stay in touch with one another. Researchers can be made instantly aware of the latest breakthroughs worldwide.

Java How to Program: Fourth Edition presents programming techniques that allow Java applications to use the Internet and World Wide Web to interact with other applications. These capabilities, and the capabilities discussed in our companion book *Advanced Java 2 Platform How to Program*, allow Java programmers to develop the kind of enterprise-level distributed applications that are used in industry today. Java applications can be written to execute on any computer platform, yielding major savings in systems development time and cost for corporations. If you have been hearing a great deal about the Internet and World Wide Web lately, and if you are interested in developing applications to run over the Internet and the Web, learning Java may be the key to challenging and rewarding career opportunities for you.

1.13 Basics of a Typical Java Environment

Java systems generally consist of several parts: An environment, the language, the Java Applications Programming Interface (API) and various class libraries. The following discussion explains a typical Java program development environment, as shown in Fig. 1.1.

Java programs normally go through five phases to be executed (Fig. 1.1). These are: *edit, compile, load, verify* and *execute.* We discuss these concepts in the context of the *Java 2 Software Development Kit (J2SDK)* that is included on the CD that accompanies this book. *Carefully follow the installation instructions for the J2SDK provided on the CD to ensure that you set up your computer properly to compile and execute Java programs.* [*Note*: If you are not using UNIX/Linux, Windows 95/98/ME or Windows NT/2000, refer to the manuals for your system's Java environment or ask your instructor how to accomplish these tasks in your environment (which will probably be similar to the environment in Fig. 1.1).]

Phase 1 consists of editing a file. This is accomplished with an *editor program* (normally known as an *editor*). The programmer types a Java program, using the editor, and makes corrections, if necessary. When the programmer specifies that the file in the editor should be saved, the program is stored on a secondary storage device, such as a disk. Java program file names end with the **`.java`** *extension.* Two editors widely used on UNIX/Linux systems are **`vi`** and **`emacs`**. On Windows 95/98/ME and Windows NT/2000, simple edit programs like the DOS Edit command and the Windows Notepad will suffice. Java integrated development environments (IDEs), such as Forté for Java Community Edition, NetBeans, Borland's JBuilder, Symantec's Visual Cafe and IBM's VisualAge have built-in editors that are integrated into the programming environment. We assume the reader knows how to edit a file.

[Note that Forté for Java Community Edition is written in Java and is free for non-commercial use. It is included on the CD accompanying this book. Sun updates this software approximately twice a year. Newer versions can be downloaded from

`www.sun.com/forte/ffj`

Forté for Java Community Edition executes on most major platforms. This book is written for any generic Java 2 development environment. It is not dependent on Forté for Java Community Edition. Our example programs should operate properly with most Java integrated development environments.]

In Phase 2 (discussed again in Chapters 2 and 3), the programmer gives the command **`javac`** to *compile* the program. The Java compiler translates the Java program into *byte-*

codes—the language understood by the Java interpreter. To compile a program called **`Welcome.java`**, type

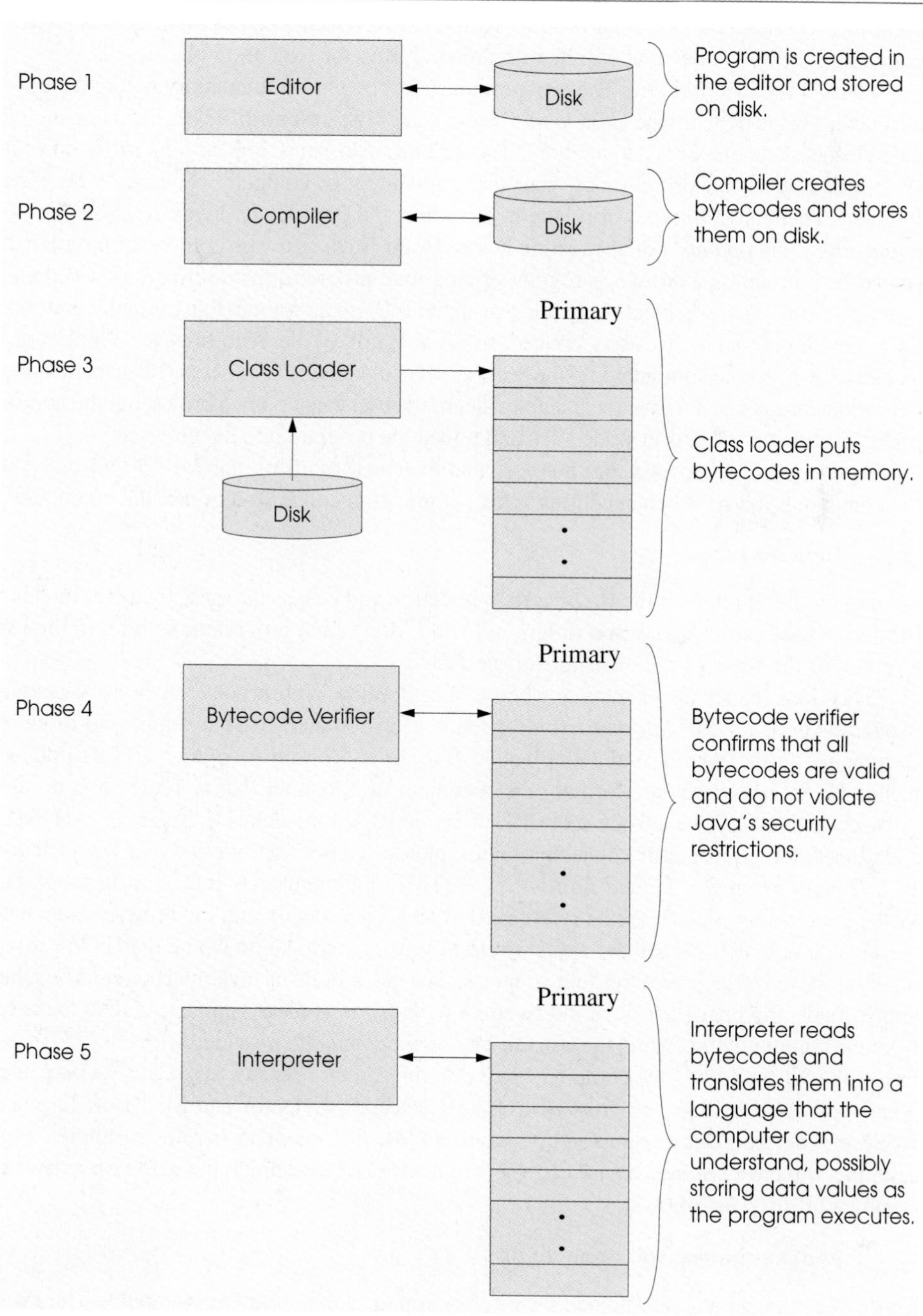

Fig. 1.1 Typical Java environment.

```
javac Welcome.java
```

at the command window of your system (i.e., the *MS-DOS prompt* in Windows, the *Command Prompt* in Windows NT/2000 or the *shell prompt* in UNIX/Linux). If the program compiles correctly, the compiler produces a file called **Welcome.class**. This is the file containing the bytecodes that will be interpreted during the execution phase.

Phase 3 is called *loading*. The program must first be placed in memory before it can be executed. This is done by the *class loader,* which takes the **.class** file (or files) containing the bytecodes and transfers it to memory. The **.class** file can be loaded from a disk on your system or over a network (such as your local university or company network or even the Internet). There are two types of programs for which the class loader loads **.class** files—*applications* and *applets*. An application is a program (such as a word-processor program, a spreadsheet program, a drawing program or an e-mail program) that normally is stored and executed from the user's local computer. An applet is a small program that normally is stored on a remote computer that users connect to via a World Wide Web browser. Applets are loaded from a remote computer into the browser, executed in the browser and discarded when execution completes. To execute an applet again, the user must point a browser at the appropriate location on the World Wide Web and reload the program into the browser.

Applications are loaded into memory and executed by using the *Java interpreter* via the command ***java***. When executing a Java application called **Welcome**, the command

```
java Welcome
```

invokes the interpreter for the **Welcome** application and causes the class loader to load information used in the **Welcome** program. [*Note*: Many Java programmers refer to the interpreter as the *Java Virtual Machine* or the *JVM*.]

The class loader also executes when a World Wide Web browser such as *Netscape Navigator* or *Microsoft Internet Explorer* loads a Java applet. Browsers are used to view documents on the World Wide Web called *Hypertext Markup Language* (*HTML*) documents. HTML describes the format of a document in a manner that is understood by the browser application (we introduce HTML in Section 3.4; for a detailed treatment of HTML and other Internet programming technologies, please see our text *Internet and World Wide Web How to Program, Second Edition*). An HTML document may refer to a Java applet. When the browser sees an applet referenced in an HTML document, the browser launches the Java class loader to load the applet (normally from the location where the HTML document is stored). Each browser that supports Java has a built-in Java interpreter. After the applet loads, the browser's Java interpreter executes the applet. Applets can also execute from the command line, using the ***appletviewer*** *command* provided with the J2SDK—the set of tools including the compiler (**javac**), interpreter (**java**), **appletviewer** and other tools used by Java programmers. Like Netscape Navigator and Microsoft Internet Explorer, the **appletviewer** requires an HTML document to invoke an applet. For example, if the **Welcome.html** file refers to the **Welcome** applet, the **appletviewer** command is used as follows:

```
appletviewer Welcome.html
```

This causes the class loader to load the information used in the **Welcome** applet. The **appletviewer** is a minimal browser—it knows only how to interpret references to applets and ignores all other HTML in a document.

Before the Java interpreter built into a browser or the **`appletviewer`** executes the bytecodes in an applet, the bytecodes are verified by the *bytecode verifier* in Phase 4. This ensures that the bytecodes for classes that are loaded from the Internet (referred to as *downloaded classes*) are valid and that they do not violate Java's security restrictions. Java enforces strong security, because Java programs arriving over the network should not be able to cause damage to your files and your system (as computer viruses might). Note that bytecode verification also occurs in applications that download classes from a network.

Finally, in Phase 5, the computer, under the control of its CPU, interprets the program one bytecode at a time, thus performing the actions specified by the program.

Programs might not work on the first try. Each of the preceding phases can fail because of various errors that we will discuss in this text. For example, an executing program might attempt to divide by zero (an illegal operation in Java just as it is in arithmetic). This would cause the Java program to print an error message. The programmer would return to the edit phase, make the necessary corrections and proceed through the remaining phases again to determine that the corrections work properly.

Common Programming Error 1.1

Errors like division-by-zero errors occur as a program runs, so these errors are called runtime errors *or* execution-time errors. Fatal runtime errors *cause programs to terminate immediately without having successfully performed their jobs.* Nonfatal runtime errors *allow programs to run to completion, often producing incorrect results.*

Most programs in Java input or output data. When we say that a program prints a result, we normally mean that the program displays results on the computer screen. Data may be output to other devices, such as disks and hardcopy printers.

1.14 General Notes about Java and This Book

Java is a powerful language. Experienced programmers sometimes take pride in being able to create some weird, contorted, convoluted usage of a language. This is a poor programming practice. It makes programs more difficult to read, more likely to behave strangely, more difficult to test and debug and more difficult to adapt to changing requirements. This book is also geared for novice programmers, so we stress *clarity.* The following is our first "good programming practice."

Good Programming Practice 1.1

Write your Java programs in a simple and straightforward manner. This is sometimes referred to as KIS ("keep it simple"). Do not "stretch" the language by trying bizarre usages.

You have heard that Java is a portable language and that programs written in Java can run on many different computers. For programming in general, *portability is an elusive goal.* For example, the ANSI C standard document[2] contains a lengthy list of portability issues, and complete books have been written that discuss portability.[3,4]

2. ANSI, *American National Standard for Information Systems–Programming Language C (ANSI Document ANSI/ISO 9899: 1990),* New York, NY: American National Standards Institute, 1990.
3. Jaeschke, R., *Portability and the C Language,* Indianapolis, IN: Hayden Books, 1989.
4. Rabinowitz, H., and C. Schaap, *Portable C,* Englewood Cliffs, NJ: Prentice Hall, 1990.

Portability Tip 1.2

Although it is easier to write portable programs in Java than in other programming languages, there are differences among compilers, interpreters and computers that can make portability difficult to achieve. Simply writing programs in Java does not guarantee portability. The programmer will occasionally need to deal with compiler and computer variations.

Testing and Debugging Tip 1.1

Always test your Java programs on all systems on which you intend to run those programs, to ensure that your Java programs will work correctly for their intended audience.

We have done a careful walkthrough of Sun's Java documentation and audited our presentation against it for completeness and accuracy. However, Java is a rich language, and there are some subtleties in the language and some topics we have not covered. If you need additional technical details on Java, we suggest that you read the most current Java documentation available over the Internet at **`java.sun.com`**. Our book contains an extensive bibliography of books and papers on the Java language in particular and on object-oriented programming in general. A Web-based version of the Java API documentation can be found at **`java.sun.com/j2se/1.3/docs/api/index.html`**. Also, you can download this documentation to your own computer from **`java.sun.com/j2se/1.3/docs.html`**.

Good Programming Practice 1.2

Read the documentation for the version of Java you are using. Refer to this documentation frequently to be sure you are aware of the rich collection of Java features and that you are using these features correctly.

Good Programming Practice 1.3

Your computer and compiler are good teachers. If, after carefully reading your Java documentation manual, you are not sure how a feature of Java works, experiment and see what happens. Study each error or warning message you get when you compile your programs, and correct the programs to eliminate these messages.

Good Programming Practice 1.4

The Java 2 Software Development Kit comes with the Java source code. Many programmers read the actual source code of the Java API classes to determine how those classes work and to learn additional programming techniques. If the Java API documentation is not clear on a particular topic, try studying the source code of the class.

In this book, we explain how Java works in its current implementations. Perhaps the most striking problem with the early versions of Java is that Java programs execute interpretively on the client's machine. Interpreters execute slowly compared to fully compiled machine code.

Performance Tip 1.2

Interpreters have an advantage over compilers for the Java world, namely that an interpreted program can begin execution immediately as soon as it is downloaded to the client's machine, whereas a source program to be compiled must first suffer a potentially long delay as the program is compiled before it can be executed.

Portability Tip 1.3

Although only Java interpreters were available to execute bytecodes at the client's site on early Java systems, compilers that translate Java bytecodes (or in some cases the Java source code) into the native machine code of the client's machine have been written for most popular platforms. These compiled programs perform comparably to compiled C or C++ code. However, there are not bytecode compilers for every Java platform, so Java programs will not perform at the same level on all platforms.

Applets present some more interesting issues. Remember, an applet could be coming from virtually any *Web server* in the world. So the applet will have to be able to run on any possible Java platform.

Portability Tip 1.4

Short, fast-executing Java applets can certainly still be interpreted. But what about more substantial, compute-intensive applets? Here, the user might be willing to suffer the compilation delay to get better execution performance. For some especially performance-intensive applets, the user might have no choice; interpreted code would run too slowly for the applet to perform properly, so the applet would have to be compiled.

Portability Tip 1.5

An intermediate step between interpreters and compilers is a just-in-time (JIT) compiler that, as the interpreter runs, produces compiled code for the programs and executes the programs in machine language rather than reinterpreting them. JIT compilers do not produce machine language that is as efficient as that from a full compiler.

Portability Tip 1.6

For the latest information on high-speed Java program translation, you might want to read about Sun's HotSpot™ compiler, so visit **`java.sun.com/products/hotspot`**. *The HotSpot compiler is a standard component of the Java 2 Software Development Kit.*

The Java compiler, **`javac`**, is not a traditional compiler in that it does not convert a Java program from source code into native machine code for a particular computer platform. Instead, the Java compiler translates source code into bytecodes. Bytecodes are the language of the Java Virtual Machine—a program that simulates the operation of a computer and executes its own machine language (i.e., Java bytecodes). The Java Virtual Machine is implemented in the J2SDK as the **`java`** interpreter, which translates the bytecodes into native machine language for the local computer platform.

Software Engineering Observation 1.4

For organizations wanting to do heavy-duty information systems development, Integrated Development Environments (IDEs) are available from many major software suppliers, including Sun Microsystems. The IDEs provide many tools for supporting the software-development process, such as editors for writing and editing programs, debuggers for locating logic errors in programs and many other features.

Software Engineering Observation 1.5

Sun Microsystems, Inc.'s powerful Java IDE—Forté for Java, Community Edition—is available on the CD that accompanies this book and can be downloaded from **`www.sun.com/forte/ffj`**.

1.15 Thinking About Objects: Introduction to Object Technology and the Unified Modeling Language

Now we begin our early introduction to object orientation. We will see that object orientation is a natural way of thinking about the world and a natural way of writing computer programs.

In the bodies of each of the first seven chapters, we concentrate on the "conventional" methodology of structured programming, because the objects we will build will be composed in part of structured-program pieces. However, we end each chapter with a "Thinking About Objects" section in which we present a carefully paced introduction to object orientation. Our goal in these "Thinking About Objects" sections is to help you develop an object-oriented way of thinking, so that you immediately can use the object-oriented programming techniques that we present starting in Chapter 8. The "Thinking About Objects" sections also introduce you to the *Unified Modeling Language (UML).* The UML is a graphical language that allows people who build systems (e.g., software architects, systems engineers, programmers and so on) to represent their object-oriented designs, using a common notation.

In this section, we introduce basic concepts (i.e., "object think") and terminology (i.e., "object speak"). Chapters 2–13, 15 and 22 and Appendices G–I include optional "Thinking About Objects" sections that present a substantial case study that applies the techniques of *object-oriented design (OOD).* The optional sections at the ends of Chapters 2 through 7 analyze a typical problem statement that requires a system to be built, determine the objects required to implement that system, determine the attributes the objects will have, determine the behaviors these objects will exhibit and specify how the objects will interact with one another to meet the system requirements. All this occurs *before* you learn to write object-oriented Java programs! The optional sections at the ends of Chapters 8–13 and 15 modify and enhance the design presented in Chapters 2–7. Chapter 22 presents how to display our multimedia-rich design on the screen. The optional "Thinking About Objects" sections in each chapter apply the concepts discussed in that chapter to the case study. In Appendices G, H and I, we present a complete Java implementation of the object-oriented system we design in the earlier chapters.

This case study will help prepare you for the kinds of substantial projects you are likely to encounter in industry. If you are a student and your instructor does not plan to include this case study in your course, you may want to cover it on your own time. We believe it will be well worth your time to walk through this large and challenging project, because the material presented in the case-study sections reinforces the material covered in the corresponding chapters. You will experience a solid introduction to object-oriented design with the UML. Also, you will sharpen your code-reading skills by touring a carefully written and well-documented 3,594-line Java program that completely solves the problem presented in the case study.

We begin our introduction to object orientation with some key terminology. Everywhere you look in the real world you see them—*objects*: People, animals, plants, cars, planes, buildings, computers and so on. Humans think in terms of objects. We possess the marvelous ability of *abstraction*, which enables us to view screen images such as people, planes, trees and mountains as objects, rather than as individual dots of color (called *pixels*—for "picture elements"). We can, if we wish, think in terms of beaches rather than grains of sand, forests rather than trees and houses rather than bricks.

We might be inclined to divide objects into two categories—animate objects and inanimate objects. Animate objects are "alive" in some sense; they move around and do things. Inanimate objects, on the other hand, seem not to do much at all. They do not move on their own. All these objects, however, do have some things in common. They all have *attributes* like size, shape, color, and weight, and they all exhibit *behaviors* (e.g., a ball rolls, bounces, inflates and deflates; a baby cries, sleeps, crawls, walks and blinks; a car accelerates, brakes and turns; a towel absorbs water).

Humans learn about objects by studying their attributes and observing their behaviors. Different objects can have similar attributes and can exhibit similar behaviors. Comparisons can be made, for example, between babies and adults and between humans and chimpanzees. Cars, trucks, little red wagons and roller skates have much in common.

Object-oriented design models real-world objects. It takes advantage of *class* relationships, where objects of a certain class—such as a class of vehicles—have the same characteristics. It takes advantage of *inheritance* relationships, and even *multiple-inheritance*[5] relationships, where newly created classes of objects are derived by absorbing characteristics of existing classes and adding unique characteristics of their own. An object of class "convertible" certainly has the characteristics of the more general class "automobile," plus a convertible's roof goes up and down.

Object-oriented design provides a more natural and intuitive way to view the design process—namely, by *modeling* real-world objects, their attributes, their behavior. OOD also models communication between objects. Just as people send *messages* to one another (e.g., a sergeant commanding a soldier to stand at attention), objects also communicate via messages.

OOD *encapsulates* data (attributes) and functions (behavior) into *objects;* the data and functions of an object are intimately tied together. Objects have the property of *information hiding*. This means that, although objects may know how to communicate with one another across well-defined *interfaces,* objects normally are not allowed to know how other objects are implemented—implementation details are hidden within the objects themselves. Surely, it is possible to drive a car effectively without knowing the details of how engines, transmissions and exhaust systems work internally. We will see why information hiding is so crucial to good software engineering.

Languages such as Java are *object-oriented*—programming in such a language is called *object-oriented programming* (*OOP*) and allows designers to implement the object-oriented design as a working system. Languages such as C, on the other hand, are *procedural programming languages,* so programming tends to be *action-oriented.* In C, the unit of programming is the *function.* In Java, the unit of programming is the *class* from which objects are eventually *instantiated* (a fancy term for "created"). Java classes contain *methods* (that implement class behaviors) and attributes (that implement class data).

C programmers concentrate on writing functions. Groups of actions that perform some common task are formed into functions, and functions are grouped to form programs. Data are certainly important in C, but the view is that data exist primarily in support of the actions that functions perform. The *verbs* in a system specification help the C programmer determine the set of functions needed to implement that system.

Java programmers concentrate on creating their own *user-defined types* called *classes* and *components.* Each class contains data and the set of functions that manipulate that data.

5. We will learn later that although Java—unlike C++—does not support multiple inheritance, it does offer most of the key benefits of this technology by supporting multiple interfaces per class.

The data components of a Java class are called *attributes*. The function components of a Java class are called *methods*. Just as an instance of a built-in type such as **`int`** is called a *variable*, an instance of a user-defined type (i.e., a class) is called an *object*. The programmer uses built-in types as the "building blocks" for constructing user-defined types. The focus in Java is on classes (out of which we make objects) rather than on functions. The *nouns* in a system specification help the Java programmer determine the set of classes from which objects will be created that will work together to implement the system.

Classes are to objects as blueprints are to houses. We can build many houses from one blueprint, and we can instantiate many objects from one class. Classes can also have relationships with other classes. For example, in an object-oriented design of a bank, the "bank-teller" class needs to relate to the "customer" class. These relationships are called *associations*.

We will see that, when software is packaged as classes, these classes can be *reused* in future software systems. Groups of related classes are often packaged as reusable *components*. Just as real-estate brokers tell their clients that the three most important factors affecting the price of real estate are "location, location and location," many people in the software community believe that the three most important factors affecting the future of software development are "reuse, reuse and reuse."

Indeed, with object technology, we can build much of the software we will need by combining "standardized, interchangeable parts" called classes. This book teaches you how to "craft valuable classes" for reuse. Each new class you create will have the potential to become a valuable software asset that you and other programmers can use to speed and enhance the quality of future software-development efforts—an exciting possibility.

Introduction to Object-Oriented Analysis and Design (OOAD)

You soon will be writing programs in Java. How will you create the code for your programs? If you are like many beginning programmers, you will simply turn on your computer and start typing. This approach may work for small projects, but what would you do if you were asked to create a software system to control the automated teller machines for a major bank? Such a project is too large and complex for you to sit down and simply start typing.

To create the best solutions, you should follow a detailed process for obtaining an *analysis* of your project's *requirements* and developing a *design* for satisfying those requirements. Ideally, you would go through this process and have its results reviewed and approved by your superiors before writing any code for your project. If this process involves analyzing and designing your system from an object-oriented point of view, we call it an *object-oriented analysis and design (OOAD) process*. Experienced programmers know that, no matter how simple a problem appears, time spent on analysis and design can save innumerable hours that might be lost from abandoning an ill-planned system-development approach part of the way through its implementation.

OOAD is the generic term for the ideas behind the process we employ to analyze a problem and develop an approach for solving it. Small problems like the ones discussed in these first few chapters do not require an exhaustive process. It may be sufficient to write *pseudocode* before we *begin* writing code. (Pseudocode is an informal means of expressing program code. It is not actually a programming language, but we can use it as a kind of "outline" to guide us as we write our code. We introduce pseudocode in Chapter 4.)

Pseudocode can suffice for small problems, but as problems and the groups of people solving these problems increase in size, the methods of OOAD become more involved. Ideally, a group should agree on a strictly defined process for solving the problem and on a uniform way of communicating the results of that process to one another. Although many different OOAD processes exist, a single graphical language for communicating the results of any OOAD process has become widely used. This language is known as the *Unified Modeling Language (UML)*. The UML was developed in the mid-1990s under the initial direction of three software methodologists: Grady Booch, James Rumbaugh and Ivar Jacobson.

History of the UML

In the 1980s, increasing numbers of organizations began using OOP to program their applications, and a need developed for an established process with which to approach OOAD. Many methodologists—including Booch, Rumbaugh and Jacobson—individually produced and promoted separate processes to satisfy this need. Each of these processes had its own notation, or "language" (in the form of graphical diagrams), to convey the results of analysis and design.

By the early 1990s, different companies, and even different divisions within the same company, were using different processes and notations. Additionally, these companies wanted to use software tools that would support their particular processes. With so many processes, software vendors found it difficult to provide such tools. Clearly, a standard notation and standard processes were needed.

In 1994, James Rumbaugh joined Grady Booch at Rational Software Corporation, and the two began working to unify their popular processes. They were soon joined by Ivar Jacobson. In 1996, the group released early versions of the UML to the software engineering community and requested feedback. Around the same time, an organization known as the *Object Management Group™ (OMG™)* invited submissions for a common modeling language. The OMG is a not-for-profit organization that promotes the use of object-oriented technology by issuing guidelines and specifications for object-oriented technologies. Several corporations—among them HP, IBM, Microsoft, Oracle and Rational Software—had already recognized the need for a common modeling language. These companies formed the *UML Partners* in response to the OMG's request for proposals. This consortium developed the UML version 1.1 and submitted it to the OMG. The OMG accepted the proposal and, in 1997, assumed responsibility for the continuing maintenance and revision of the UML. In 2001, the OMG released the UML version 1.4 (the current version at the time this book was published) and is working on version 2.0 (scheduled tentatively for release in 2002).

What is the UML?

The Unified Modeling Language is now the most widely used graphical representation scheme for modeling object-oriented systems. It has indeed unified the various popular notational schemes. Those who design systems use the language (in the form of graphical diagrams) to model their systems.

An attractive feature of the UML is its flexibility. The UML is extendable and is independent of the many OOAD processes. UML modelers are free to develop systems by using various processes, but all developers can now express those systems with one standard set of notations.

The UML is a complex, feature-rich graphical language. In our "Thinking About Objects" sections, we present a concise, simplified subset of these features. We then use this subset to guide the reader through a first design experience with the UML intended for the novice object-oriented designer/programmer. For a more complete discussion of the UML, refer to the Object Management Group's Web site (**www.omg.org**) and to the official UML 1.4 specifications document (**www.omg.org/uml**). In addition, many UML books have been published: *UML Distilled: Second Edition*, by Martin Fowler (with Kendall Scott) (ISBN #020165783X) provides a detailed introduction to the UML, with many examples. *The Unified Modeling Language User Guide* (ISBN #0201571684), written by Booch, Rumbaugh and Jacobson, is the definitive tutorial to the UML. The reader looking for an interactive learning product might consider Grady Booch's *The Complete UML Training Course* (ISBN #0130870145).

Object-oriented technology is ubiquitous in the software industry, and the UML is rapidly becoming so. Our goal in these "Thinking About Objects" sections is to encourage you to think in an object-oriented manner as early, and as often, as possible. In the "Thinking About Objects" section at the end of Chapter 2, you will begin to apply object technology to implement a solution to a substantial problem. We hope that you will find this optional project to be an enjoyable and challenging introduction to object-oriented design with the UML and to object-oriented programming.

1.16 Discovering Design Patterns: Introduction

This section begins our treatment of design patterns, entitled "Discovering Design Patterns." Most of the examples provided in this book contain fewer than 150 lines of code. These examples do not require an extensive design process, because they use only a few classes and illustrate introductory programming concepts. However, some programs, such as our optional elevator-simulation case study, are more complex—they can require thousands of lines of code or even more, contain many interactions among objects and involve many user interactions. Larger systems, such as automated teller machines or air-traffic control systems, could contain millions of lines of code. Effective design is crucial to the proper construction of such complex systems.

Over the past decade, the software engineering industry has made significant progress in the field of *design patterns*—proven architectures for constructing flexible and maintainable object-oriented software.[6] Using design patterns can substantially reduce the complexity of the design process. Designing an ATM system will be a somewhat less formidable task if developers use design patterns. In addition, well-designed object-oriented software allows designers to reuse and integrate preexisting components in future systems. Design patterns benefit system developers by

- helping to construct reliable software using proven architectures and accumulated industry expertise
- promoting design reuse in future systems
- helping to identify common mistakes and pitfalls that occur when building systems
- helping to design systems independently of the language in which they will ultimately be implemented

6. Gamma, Erich, Richard Helm, Ralph Johnson, and John Vlissides. *Design Patterns; Elements of Reusable Object-Oriented Software*. (Massachusetts: Addison-Wesley, 1995).

- establishing a common design vocabulary among developers
- shortening the design phase in a software-development process

The notion of using design patterns to construct software systems originated in the field of architecture. Architects use a set of established architectural design elements, such as arches and columns, when designing buildings. Designing with arches and columns is a proven strategy for constructing sound buildings—these elements may be viewed as architectural design patterns.

In software, design patterns are neither classes nor objects. Rather, designers use design patterns to construct sets of classes and objects. To use design patterns effectively, designers must familiarize themselves with the most popular and effective patterns used in the software-engineering industry. In this chapter, we discuss fundamental object-oriented design patterns and architectures, as well as their importance in constructing well-engineered software.

We present several design patterns in Java, but these design patterns can be implemented in any object-oriented language, such as C++ or Visual Basic. We describe several design patterns used by Sun Microsystems in the Java API. We use design patterns in many programs in this book, which we will identify throughout our discussion. These programs provide examples of using design patterns to construct reliable, robust object-oriented software.

History of Object-Oriented Design Patterns

During 1991–1994, Erich Gamma, Richard Helm, Ralph Johnson, and John Vlissides—collectively known as the "gang of four"—used their combined expertise to write the book *Design Patterns, Elements of Reusable Object-Oriented Software (Addison-Wesley: 1995).* This book described 23 design patterns, each providing a solution to a common software design problem in industry. The book groups design patterns into three categories—*creational design patterns, structural design patterns* and *behavioral design patterns.* Creational design patterns describe techniques to instantiate objects (or groups of objects). Structural design patterns allow designers to organize classes and objects into larger structures. Behavioral design patterns assign responsibilities to objects.

The gang-of-four book showed that design patterns evolved naturally through years of industry experience. In his article *Seven Habits of Successful Pattern Writers,*[7] John Vlissides states that "the single most important activity in pattern writing is reflection." This statement implies that, to create patterns, developers must reflect on, and document, their successes (and mistakes). Developers use design patterns to capture and employ this collective industry experience, which ultimately helps them avoid making the same mistakes twice.

New design patterns are being created all the time and being introduced rapidly to designers worldwide via the Internet. The topic of design patterns has generally been viewed as advanced, but authors such as ourselves are working this material into introductory and intermediate-level textbooks to help make this important knowledge available to a much wider audience.

Our treatment of design patterns begins with this required section in Chapter 1 and continues with five optional "Discovering Design Patterns" sections at the ends of Chapters 9, 13, 15, 17 and 21. Each of these sections is placed at the end of the chapter that introduces

---

7. Vlissides, John. *Pattern Hatching; Design Patterns Applied.* (Massachusetts: Addison-Wesley, 1998).

the necessary Java technologies. If you are a student and your instructor does not plan to include this material in your course, we encourage you to read this material on your own.

1.17 Tour of the Book

You are about to study one of today's most exciting and rapidly developing computer programming languages. Mastering Java will help you develop powerful business and personal computer-applications software. In this section, we take a tour of the many capabilities of Java you will study in *Java How to Program: Fourth Edition.*

Chapter 1—Introduction to Computers, the Internet and the Web—discusses what computers are, how they work and how they are programmed. The chapter gives a brief history of the development of programming languages from machine languages, to assembly languages, to high-level languages. The origin of the Java programming language is discussed. The chapter includes an introduction to a typical Java programming environment. The chapter also introduces object technology, the Unified Modeling Language and design patterns.

Chapter 2—Introduction to Java Applications—provides a lightweight introduction to programming *applications* in the Java programming language. The chapter introduces nonprogrammers to basic programming concepts and constructs. The programs in this chapter illustrate how to display (also called *outputting*) data on the screen to the user and how to obtain (also called *inputting*) data from the user at the keyboard. Some of the input and output is by performed using a *graphical user interface (GUI)* component called **`JOptionPane`** that provides predefined windows (called dialog boxes) for input and output. This allows a nonprogrammer to concentrate on fundamental programming concepts and constructs rather than on the more complex GUI event handling. Using **`JOptionPane`** here enables us to delay our introduction of GUI event handling to Chapter 6, "Methods." Chapter 2 also provides detailed treatments of *decision making* and *arithmetic operations*. After studying this chapter, the student will understand how to write simple, but complete, Java applications.

Chapter 3—Introduction to Java Applets—introduces another type of Java program, called an *applet*. Applets are Java programs designed to be transported over the Internet and executed in World Wide Web browsers (like Netscape Navigator and Microsoft Internet Explorer). The chapter introduces applets, using several of the demonstration applets supplied with the Java 2 Software Development Kit (J2SDK). We use **`appletviewer`** (a utility supplied with the J2SDK) or a Web browser to execute several sample applets. We then write Java applets that perform tasks similar to the programs of Chapter 2, and we explain the similarities and differences between applets and applications. After studying this chapter, the student will understand how to write simple, but complete, Java applets. The next several chapters use both applets and applications to demonstrate additional key programming concepts.

Chapter 4—Control Structures: Part 1—focuses on the program-development process. The chapter discusses how to take a *problem statement* (i.e., a *requirements document*) and from it develop a working Java program, including performing intermediate steps in pseudocode. The chapter introduces some fundamental data types and simple control structures used for decision making (**`if`** and **`if/else`**) and repetition (**`while`**). We examine counter-controlled repetition and sentinel-controlled repetition, and introduce Java's increment, decrement and assignment operators. The chapter uses simple flowcharts to show the flow of control through each of the control structures. The techniques discussed in Chapters 2 through 7 constitute a large part of what has been traditionally taught in the universities under the topic of structured programming. With Java, we do object-oriented programming. In doing so, we discover that the insides of the objects we build make abundant use of control structures. We have had a particularly positive experience assigning problems 4.11 through 4.14 in our introductory courses. Since these four problems have similar structure, doing all four is a nice way for students to "get the hang of" the program-development process. This chapter helps the student develop good programming habits in preparation for dealing with the more substantial programming tasks in the remainder of the text.

Chapter 5—Control Structures: Part 2—continues the discussions of Java control structures (**`for`**, the **`switch`** selection structure and the **`do/while`** repetition structure). The chapter explains the labeled **`break`** and **`continue`** statements with live-code examples. The chapter also contains a discussion of logical operators—**`&&`** (logical AND), **`&`** (boolean logical AND), **`||`** (logical OR), **`|`** (boolean logical inclusive OR), **`^`** (boolean logical exclusive OR) and **`!`** (NOT). There is a substantial exercise set including mathematical, graphical and business applications. Students will enjoy Exercise 5.25, which asks them to write a program with repetition and decision structures that prints the iterative song, "The Twelve Days of Christmas." The more mathematically inclined students will enjoy problems on binary, octal, decimal and hexadecimal number systems, calculating the mathematical constant π with an infinite series, Pythagorean triples and De Morgan's Laws. Our students particularly enjoy the challenges of triangle-printing and diamond-printing in Exercises 5.10, 5.18 and 5.20; these problems help students learn to deal with nested repetition structures—a complex topic to master in introductory courses.

Chapter 6—Methods—takes a deeper look inside objects. Objects contain data called instance variables and executable units called methods (these are often called *functions* in non-object-oriented procedural programming languages like C and *member functions* in C++). We explore methods in depth and include a discussion of methods that "call themselves," so-called recursive methods. We discuss class-library methods, programmer-defined methods and recursion. The techniques presented in Chapter 6 are essential to the production of properly structured programs, especially the kinds of larger programs and software that system programmers and application programmers are likely to develop in real-world applications. The "divide and conquer" strategy is presented as an effective means for solving complex problems by dividing them into simpler interacting components. Students enjoy the treatment of random numbers and simulation, and they appreciate the discussion of the dice game of craps that makes elegant use of control structures (this is one of our most successful lectures in our introductory courses). The chapter offers a solid introduction to recursion and includes a table summarizing the dozens of recursion examples and exercises distributed throughout the remainder of the book. Some texts leave recursion for a chapter late in the book; we feel this topic is best covered gradually throughout the text. The topic of method overloading (i.e., allowing multiple methods to have the same name as long as they have different "signatures") is motivated and explained clearly. We introduce *events* and *event handling*—elements required for programming graphical user interfaces. Events are notifications of state change such as button clicks, mouse clicks and pressing a keyboard key. Java allows programmers to specify the responses to events by coding methods called event handlers.

The extensive collection of exercises at the end of the chapter includes several classical recursion problems such as the Towers of Hanoi; we revisit this problem later in the text where we employ graphics, animation and sound to make the problem "come alive." There are many mathematical and graphical examples. Our students particularly enjoy the development of a "Computer-Assisted Instruction" system in Exercises 6.31 through 6.33; we ask students to develop a multimedia version of this system later in the book. Students will enjoy the challenges of the "mystery programs." The more mathematically inclined students will enjoy problems on perfect numbers, greatest common divisors, prime numbers and factorials.

Chapter 7—Arrays—explores the processing of data in lists and tables of values. Arrays in Java are processed as objects, further evidence of Java's commitment to almost 100% object orientation. We discuss the structuring of data into arrays, or groups, of related data items of the same type. The chapter presents numerous examples of both single-subscripted arrays and double-subscripted arrays. It is widely recognized that structuring data properly is just as important as using control structures effectively in the development of properly structured programs. Examples in the chapter investigate various common array manipulations, printing histograms, sorting data, passing arrays to methods and an introduction to the field of survey data analysis (with simple statistics). A feature of this chapter is the discussion of elementary sorting and searching techniques and the presentation of binary searching as a dramatic improvement over linear searching. The end-of-chapter exercises include a variety of interesting and challenging problems, such as improved sorting techniques, the design of an airline reservations system, an introduction to the concept of turtle graphics (made famous in the LOGO programming language) and the Knight's Tour and Eight Queens problems that introduce the notions of heuristic programming so widely employed in the field of artificial intelligence. The exercises conclude with a series of recursion problems including the selection sort, palindromes, linear search, binary search, the eight queens, printing an array, printing a string backwards and finding the minimum value in an array. The chapter exercises include a delightful simulation of the classic race between the tortoise and the hare, card shuffling and dealing algorithms, recursive quicksort and recursive maze traversals. A special section entitled "Building Your Own Computer" explains machine-language programming and proceeds with the design and implementation of a computer simulator that allows the reader to write and run machine language programs. This unique feature of the text will be especially useful to the reader who wants to understand how computers really work. Our students enjoy this project and often implement substantial enhancements; many enhancements are suggested in the exercises. In Chapter 19, another special section guides the reader through building a compiler; the machine language produced by the compiler is then executed on the machine language simulator produced in Chapter 7. Information is communicated from the compiler to the simulator in sequential files (presented in Chapter 16).

Chapter 8—Object-Based Programming—begins our deeper discussion of classes. The chapter represents a wonderful opportunity for teaching data abstraction the "right way"—through a language (Java) expressly devoted to implementing abstract data types (ADTs). The chapter focuses on the essence and terminology of classes and objects. What is an object? What is a class of objects? What does the inside of an object look like? How are objects created? How are they destroyed? How do objects communicate with one another? Why are classes such a natural mechanism for packaging software as reusable componentry? The chapter discusses implementing ADTs as Java-style classes, accessing class members, enforcing information hiding with **private** instance variables, separating interface from implementation, using access methods and utility methods and initializing objects with constructors (and using overloaded constructors). The chapter discusses declaring and using constant references, *composition*—the process of building classes that have as members references to objects, the **this** reference that enables an object to "know itself," dynamic memory allocation, **static** class members for containing and manipulating class-wide data and examples of popular abstract data types such as stacks and queues. The chapter introduces the **package** statement and discusses how to create reusable packages. The chapter also introduces creating *Java archive (JAR)* files and demonstrates how to use JAR files to deploy applets that consist of multiple classes. The chapter exercises challenge the student to develop classes for complex numbers, rational numbers, times, dates, rectangles, huge integers, a class for playing Tic-Tac-Toe, a savings-account class and a class for holding sets of integers.

Chapter 9—Object-Oriented Programming—discusses the relationships among classes of objects and programming with related classes. How can we exploit commonality between classes of objects to minimize the amount of work it takes to build large software systems? What is polymorphism? What does it mean to "program in the general" rather than "program in the specific?" How does programming in the general make it easy to modify systems and add new features with minimal effort? How can we program for a whole category of objects rather than programming individually for each type of object? The chapter deals with one of the most fundamental capabilities of object-oriented programming languages, inheritance, which is a form of software reusability in which new classes are developed quickly and easily by absorbing the capabilities of existing classes and adding appropriate new capabilities. The chapter discusses the notions of superclasses and subclasses, **protected** members, direct superclasses, indirect superclasses, use of constructors in superclasses and subclasses, and software engineering with inheritance. This chapter introduces *inner classes* that help hide implementation details. Inner classes are most frequently used to create GUI event handlers. Named inner classes can be declared inside other classes and are useful in defining common event handlers for several GUI components. Anonymous inner classes are declared inside methods and are used to create one object—typically an event handler for a specific GUI component. The chapter compares inheritance ("is a" relationships) with composition ("has a" relationships). A feature of the chapter is its several substantial case studies. In particular, a lengthy case study implements a point, circle and cylinder class hierarchy. The exercises ask the student to compare the creation of new classes by inheritance vs. composition; to extend the inheritance hierarchies discussed in the chapter; to write an inheritance hierarchy for quadrilaterals, trapezoids, parallelograms, rectangles and squares and to create a more general shape hierarchy with two-dimensional shapes and three-dimensional shapes. The chapter explains polymorphic behavior. When many classes are related through inheritance to a common superclass, each subclass object may be treated as a superclass object. This enables programs to be written in a general manner independent of the specific types of the subclass objects. New kinds of objects can be handled by the same program, thus making systems more extensible. Polymorphism enables programs to eliminate complex **switch** logic in favor of simpler "straight-line" logic. A video game screen manager, for example, can send a "draw" message to every object in a linked list of objects to be drawn. Each object knows how to draw itself. A new type of object can be added to the program without modifying that program as long as that new object also knows how to draw itself. This style of programming is typically used to implement today's popular graphical user interfaces. The chapter distinguishes between **abstract** classes (from which objects *cannot* be instantiated) and concrete classes (from which objects *can* be instantiated). The chapter also introduces interfaces—sets of methods that must be defined by any class that **implements** the interface. Interfaces are Java's replacement for the dangerous (albeit powerful) feature of C++ called multiple inheritance.

Abstract classes are useful for providing a basic set of methods and default implementation to classes throughout the hierarchy. Interfaces are useful in many situations similar to **abstract** classes; however, interfaces do not include any implementation—interfaces have no method bodies and no instance variables. A feature of the chapter is its three major polymorphism case studies—a payroll system, a shape hierarchy headed up by an **abstract** class and a shape hierarchy headed up by an interface. The chapter exercises ask the student to discuss a number of conceptual issues and approaches, work with **abstract** classes, develop a basic graphics package, modify the chapter's employee class—and pursue all these projects with polymorphic programming.

Chapter 10—Strings and Characters—deals with processing words, sentences, characters and groups of characters. The key difference between Java and C here is that Java strings are objects. This makes string manipulation more convenient and much safer than in C where string and array manipulations are based on dangerous pointers. We present classes **String**, **StringBuffer**, **Character** and **StringTokenizer**. For each, we provide extensive live-code examples demonstrating most of their methods "in action." In all cases, we show output windows so that the reader can see the precise effects of each of the string and character manipulations. Students will enjoy the card shuffling and dealing example (which they will enhance in the exercises to the later chapters on graphics and multimedia). A key feature of the chapter is an extensive collection of challenging string-manipulation exercises related to limericks, pig Latin, text analysis, word processing, printing dates in various formats, check protection, writing the word equivalent of a check amount, Morse Code and metric-to-English conversions. Students will enjoy the challenges of developing their own spell checker and crossword-puzzle generator.

Advanced Topics

Chapters 11, 12 and 13 were coauthored with our colleague, Mr. Tem Nieto of Deitel & Associates, Inc. Tem's infinite patience, attention to detail, illustration skills and creativity are apparent throughout these chapters. [Take a fast peek at Figure 12.19 to see what happens when we turn Tem loose!]

Chapter 11—Graphics and Java2D—is the first of several chapters that present the multimedia "sizzle" of Java. We consider Chapters 11 through 22 to be the book's advanced material. This is "fun stuff." Traditional C and C++ programming are pretty much confined to character-mode input/output. Some versions of C++ are supported by platform-dependent class libraries that can do graphics, but using these libraries makes your applications nonportable. Java's graphics capabilities are platform independent and hence, portable—and we mean portable in a worldwide sense. You can develop graphics-intensive Java applets and distribute them over the World Wide Web to colleagues everywhere, and they will run nicely on the local Java platforms. We discuss graphics contexts and graphics objects; drawing strings, characters and bytes; color and font control; screen manipulation and paint modes and drawing lines, rectangles, rounded rectangles, three-dimensional rectangles, ovals, arcs and polygons. We introduce the Java2D API, which provides powerful graphical manipulation tools. Figure 11.22 is an example of how easy it is to use the Java2D API to create complex graphics effects such as textures and gradients. The chapter has 23 figures that painstakingly illustrate each of these graphics capabilities with live-code™ examples, appealing screen outputs, detailed features tables and detailed line art. Some of the 27 exercises challenge students to develop graphical versions of their solutions to previous exercises on Turtle Graphics, the Knight's Tour, the Tortoise and the Hare simulation, Maze Traversal and the Bucket Sort. Our companion book, *Advanced Java 2 Platform How to Program*, presents the Java 3D API.

Chapter 12—Graphical User Interface Components: Part 1—introduces the creation of applets and applications with user-friendly graphical user interfaces (GUIs). This chapter focuses on Java's *Swing GUI components*. These *platform-independent* GUI components are written entirely in Java. This provides Swing GUI components with great flexibility—the GUI components can be customized to look like the computer platform on which the program executes, or they can use the standard Java look-and-feel that provides an identical user interface across all computer platforms. GUI development is a huge topic, so we divided it into two chapters. These chapters cover the material in sufficient depth to enable you to build "industrial-strength" GUI interfaces. We discuss the **`javax.swing`** package, which provides much more powerful GUI components than the **`java.awt`** components that originated in Java 1.0. Through its 16 programs and many tables and line drawings, the chapter illustrates GUI principles, the **`javax.swing`** hierarchy, labels, push buttons, lists, text fields, combo boxes, checkboxes, radio buttons, panels, handling mouse events, handling keyboard events and using three of Java's simpler GUI layout managers, namely, **`FlowLayout`**, **`BorderLayout`** and **`GridLayout`**. The chapter concentrates on the delegation event model for GUI processing. The 33 exercises challenge the student to create specific GUIs, exercise various GUI features, develop drawing programs that let the user draw with the mouse and control fonts.

Chapter 13—Graphical User Interface Components: Part 2—continues the detailed Swing discussion started in Chapter 12. Through its 13 programs, as well as tables and line drawings, the chapter illustrates GUI design principles, the **`javax.swing`** hierarchy, text areas, subclassing Swing components, sliders, windows, menus, pop-up menus, changing the look-and-feel, and using three of Java's advanced GUI layout managers, namely, **`BoxLayout`**, **`CardLayout`** and **`GridBagLayout`**. Two of the most important examples introduced in this chapter are a program that can run as either an applet or application and a program that demonstrates how to create a *multiple document interface* (*MDI*) graphical user interface. MDI is a complex graphical user interface in which one window—called the *parent*—acts as the controlling window for the application. This parent window contains one or more child windows—which are always graphically displayed within the parent window. Most word processors use MDI graphical user interfaces. The chapter concludes with a series of exercises that encourage the reader to develop substantial GUIs with the techniques and components presented in the chapter. One of the most challenging exercises in this chapter is a complete drawing application that asks the reader to create an object oriented-program that keeps track of the shapes the user has drawn. Other exercises use inheritance to subclass Swing components and reinforce layout manager concepts. The first six chapters of our companion book, *Advanced Java 2 Platform How to Program*, are designed for courses in advanced GUI programming.

Chapter 14—Exception Handling—is one of the most important chapters in the book from the standpoint of building so-called "mission-critical" or "business-critical" applications that require high degrees of robustness and fault tolerance. Things do go wrong, and at today's computer speeds—commonly hundreds of millions operations per second (with recent personal computers running at a billion or more instructions per second)—if they can go wrong they will, and rather quickly at that. Programmers are often a bit naive about using components. They ask, "How do I request that a component do something for me?" They also ask "What value(s) does that component return to me to indicate it has performed the job I asked it to do?" But programmers also need to be concerned with, "What happens when the component I call on to do a job experiences difficulty? How will that component signal that it had a problem?" In Java, when a component (e.g., a class object) encounters difficulty, it can "throw an exception." The environment of that component is programmed to "catch" that exception and deal with it. Java's exception-handling capabilities are geared to an object-oriented world in which programmers construct systems largely from reusable, prefabricated components built by other programmers. To use a Java component, you need to know not only how that component behaves when "things go well," but also what exceptions that component throws when "things go poorly." The chapter distinguishes between rather serious system **`Error`**s (normally beyond the control of most programs) and **`Exception`**s (which programs generally deal with to ensure robust operation). The chapter discusses the vocabulary of exception handling. The **`try`** block executes program code that either executes properly or **`throw`**s an exception if something goes wrong. Associated with each **`try`** block are one or more **`catch`** blocks that handle thrown exceptions in an attempt to restore order and keep systems "up and running" rather than letting them "crash." Even if order cannot be fully restored, the **`catch`** blocks can perform operations that enable a system to continue executing, albeit at reduced levels of performance—such activity is often referred to as "graceful degradation." Regardless of whether exceptions are thrown, a **`finally`** block accompanying a **`try`** block will always execute; the **`finally`** block normally performs cleanup operations like closing files and releasing resources acquired in the **`try`** block. The material in this chapter is crucial to many of the live-code examples in the remainder of the book. The chapter enumerates many of the **`Error`**s and **`Exception`**s of the Java packages. The chapter has some of the most appropriate quotes in the book, thanks to Barbara Deitel's painstaking research. The vast majority of the book's Testing and Debugging Tips emerged naturally from the material in Chapter 14.

Chapter 15—Multithreading—deals with programming applets and applications that can perform multiple activities in parallel. Although our bodies are quite good at this (breathing, eating, blood circulation, vision, hearing, etc. can all occur in parallel), our conscious minds have trouble with this. Computers used to be built with a single, rather expensive processor. Today, processors are becoming so inexpensive that it is possible to build computers with many processors that work in parallel—such computers are called *multiprocessors*. The trend is clearly towards computers that can perform many tasks in parallel. Most of today's programming languages, including C and C++, do not include built-in features for expressing parallel operations. These languages are often referred to as "sequential" programming languages or "single-thread-of-control" languages. Java includes capabilities to enable multithreaded applications (i.e., applications that can specify that multiple activities are to occur in parallel). This makes Java better prepared to deal with the more sophisticated multimedia, network-based multiprocessor-based applications programmers will develop. As we will see, multithreading is effective even on single-processor systems. For years, the "old guy" taught operating systems courses and wrote operating systems textbooks, but he never had a multithreaded language like Java available to demonstrate the concepts. In this chapter, we thoroughly enjoyed presenting multithreaded programs that demonstrate clearly the kinds of problems that can occur in parallel programming. There are all kinds of subtleties that develop in parallel programs that you simply never think about when writing sequential programs. A feature of the chapter is the extensive set of examples that show these problems and how to solve them. Another feature is the implementation of the "circular buffer," a popular means of coordinating control between asynchronous, concurrent "producer" and "consumer" processes that, if left to run without synchronization, would cause data to be lost or duplicated incorrectly, often with devastating results. We discuss the monitor construct developed by C. A. R. Hoare and implemented in Java; this is a standard topic in operating systems courses. The chapter discusses threads and thread methods. It walks through the various thread states and state transitions with a detailed line drawing showing the life-cycle of a thread. We discuss thread priorities and thread scheduling and use a line drawing to show Java's fixed-priority scheduling mechanism. We examine a producer/consumer relationship without synchronization, observe the problems that occur and solve the problem with thread synchronization. We implement a producer/consumer relationship with a circular buffer and proper synchronization with a monitor. We discuss daemon threads that "hang around" and perform tasks (e.g., "garbage collection") when processor time is available. We discuss interface **Runnable** which enables objects to run as threads without having to subclass class **Thread**. We close with a discussion of thread groups which, for example, enable separation to be enforced between system threads like the garbage collector and user threads. The chapter has a nice complement of exercises. The featured exercise is the classic readers and writers problem, a favorite in upper level operating systems courses; citations appear in the exercises for students who wish to research this topic. This is an important problem in database-oriented transaction-processing systems. It raises subtle issues of solving problems in concurrency control while ensuring that every separate activity that needs to receive service does so without the possibility of "indefinite postponement," that could cause some activities never to receive service—a condition also referred to as "starvation." Operating systems professors will enjoy the projects implemented by Java-literate students. We can expect substantial progress in the field of parallel programming as Java's multithreading capabilities enable large numbers of computing students to pursue parallel-programming class projects. As these students enter industry over the next several years, we expect a surge in parallel systems programming and parallel applications programming. We have been predicting this for decades—Java is making it a reality.

If this is your first Java book and you are an experienced computing professional, you may well be thinking, "Hey, this just keeps getting better and better. I can't wait to get started programming in this language. It will let me do all kinds of stuff I would like to do, but that was never easy for me to do with the other languages I have used." You've got it right. Java is an enabler. So, if you liked the multithreading discussion, hold onto your hat, because Java will let you program multimedia applications and make them available instantaneously over the World Wide Web.

Chapter 16—Files and Streams—deals with input/output that is accomplished through streams of data directed to and from files. This is one of the most important chapters for programmers who will be developing commercial applications. Modern business is centered around data. In this chapter, we translate data (objects) into a persistent format usable by other applications. Being able to store data in files or move it across networks (Chapter 17) makes it possible for programs to save data and to communicate with each other. This is the real strength of software today. The chapter begins with an introduction to the data hierarchy from bits, to bytes, to fields, to records, to files. Next, Java's simple view of files and streams is presented. We then present a walkthrough of the dozens of classes in Java's extensive input/output files and streams class hierarchy. We put many of these classes to work in live-code examples in this chapter and in Chapter 17. We show how programs pass data to secondary storage devices, like disks, and how programs retrieve data already stored on those devices. Sequential-access files are discussed using a series of three programs that show how to open and close files, how to store data sequentially in a file and how to read data sequentially from a file. Random-access files are discussed using a series of four programs that show how to create a file sequentially for random access, how to read and write data to a file with random access and how to read data sequentially from a randomly accessed file. The fourth random-access program combines many of the techniques of accessing files both sequentially and randomly into a complete transaction-processing program. We discuss buffering and how it helps programs that do significant amounts of input/output perform better. We discuss class **`File`** which programs use to obtain a variety of information about files and directories. We explain how objects can be output to, and input from, secondary storage devices. Students in our industry seminars have told us that, after studying the material on file processing, they were able to produce substantial file-processing programs that were immediately useful to their organizations. The exercises ask the student to implement a variety of programs that build and process sequential-access files and random-access files.

Chapter 17—Networking—deals with applets and applications that can communicate over computer networks. This chapter presents Java's lowest level networking capabilities. We write programs that "walk the Web." The chapter examples illustrate an applet interacting with the browser in which it executes, creating a mini Web browser, communicating between two Java programs using streams-based sockets and communicating between two Java programs using packets of data. A key feature of the chapter is the live-code implementation of a collaborative client/server Tic-Tac-Toe game in which two clients play Tic-Tac-Toe with one another arbitrated by a multithreaded server—great stuff! The multithreaded server architecture is exactly what is used today in popular UNIX and Windows NT network servers. The capstone example in the chapter is the Deitel Messenger case study, which simulates many of today's popular instant-messaging applications that enable computers users to communicate with friends, relatives and coworkers over the Internet. This 1130-line, multithreaded, client/server case study uses most of the programming techniques presented up to this point in the book. The messenger application also introduces multicasting, which enables a program to send packets of data to groups of clients. The chapter has a nice collection of exercises including several suggested modifications to the multithreaded server example. Our companion book, *Advanced Java 2 Platform*

How to Program, offers a much deeper treatment of networking and distributed computing, with topics including remote method invocation (RMI), servlets, JavaServer Pages (JSP), Java 2 Enterprise Edition, wireless Java (and the Java 2 Micro Edition) and Common Object Request Broker Architecture (CORBA).

Chapter 18—Multimedia: Images, Animation and Audio—is the first of two chapters that present Java's capabilities for making computer applications come alive. (Chapter 22 offers an extensive treatment of the Java Media Framework.) It is remarkable that students in first programming courses will be writing applications with all these capabilities. The possibilities are intriguing. Imagine having access (over the Internet and through CD-ROM technology) to vast libraries of graphics images, audios and videos and being able to weave your own together with those in the libraries to form creative applications. Already, most new computers sold come "multimedia equipped." Students can create extraordinary term papers and classroom presentations with components drawn from vast public-domain libraries of images, line drawings, voices, pictures, videos, animations and the like. A "paper" when many of us were in the earlier grades was a collection of characters, possibly handwritten, possibly typewritten. A "paper" today can be a multimedia "extravaganza" that makes the subject matter come alive. It can hold your interest, pique your curiosity and make you feel what the subjects of the paper felt when they were making history. Multimedia is making science labs much more exciting. Textbooks are coming alive. Instead of looking at a static picture of some phenomenon, you can watch that phenomenon occur in a colorful, animated, presentation with sounds, videos and various other effects, leveraging the learning process. People are able to learn more, learn it in more depth and experience more viewpoints.

The chapter discusses images and image manipulation, audios and animation. A feature of the chapter is the image maps that enable a program to sense the presence of the mouse pointer over a region of an image, without clicking the mouse. We present a live-code image-map application with the icons from the programming tips you have seen in this chapter and will see throughout the book. As the user moves the mouse pointer across the seven icon images, the type of tip is displayed, either "Good Programming Practice" for the thumbs-up icon, "Portability Tip" for the bug with the suitcase icon and so on. Once you have read the chapter, you will be eager to try out all these techniques, so we have included 35 problems to challenge and entertain you (more are provided in Chapter 22). Here are some of the exercises that you may want to turn into term projects:

15 Puzzle	*Game of Pool*	*One-Armed Bandit*
Analog Clock	*Horse Race*	*Random Inter-Image Transition*
Animation	*Image Flasher*	*Randomly Erasing an Image*
Artist	*Image Zooming*	*Reaction Time Tester*
Calendar/Tickler File	*Jigsaw Puzzle Generator*	*Rotating Images*
Calling Attention to an Image	*Kaleidoscope*	*Scrolling Image Marquee*
Coloring Black and White Images	*Limericks*	*Scrolling Text Marquee*
Crossword	*Maze Generator and Walker*	*Shuffleboard*
Fireworks Designer	*Multimedia Simpletron Simulator*	*Text Flasher*

You are going to have a great time attacking these problems! Some will take a few hours and some are great term projects. We see all kinds of opportunities for multimedia electives starting to appear in the university computing curriculum. We hope you will have contests with your classmates to develop the best solutions to several of these problems.

Chapter 19—Data Structures—is particularly valuable in second- and third-level university courses. The chapter discusses the techniques used to create and manipulate dynamic data structures, such as linked lists, stacks, queues (i.e., waiting lines) and trees. The chapter begins with discussions of self-referential classes and dynamic memory allocation. We proceed with a discussion of how to create and maintain various dynamic data structures. For each type of data structure, we present live-code programs and show sample outputs. Although it is valuable to know how these classes are implemented, Java programmers will quickly discover that many of the data structures they need are already available in class libraries, such as Java's own **`java.util`** that we discuss in Chapter 20 and Java **`Collections`** that we discuss in Chapter 21. The chapter helps the student master Java-style references (i.e., Java's replacement for the more dangerous pointers of C and C++). One problem when working with references is that students could have trouble visualizing the data structures and how their nodes are linked together. So we present illustrations that show the links and the sequence in which they are created. The binary tree example is a nice capstone for the study of references and dynamic data structures. This example creates a binary tree; enforces duplicate elimination and introduces recursive preorder, inorder and postorder tree traversals. Students have a genuine sense of accomplishment when they study and implement this example. They particularly appreciate seeing that the inorder traversal prints the node values in sorted order. The chapter includes a substantial collection of exercises. A highlight of the exercises is the special section "Building Your Own Compiler." This exercise is based on earlier exercises that walk the student through the development of an infix-to-postfix conversion program and a postfix-expression evaluation program. We then modify the postfix evaluation algorithm to generate machine-language code. The compiler places this code in a file (using techniques the student mastered in Chapter 16). Students then run the machine language produced by their compilers on the software simulators they built in the exercises of Chapter 7! The many exercises include a supermarket simulation using queueing, recursively searching a list, recursively printing a list backwards, binary tree node deletion, level-order traversal of a binary tree, printing trees, writing a portion of an optimizing compiler, writing an interpreter, inserting/deleting anywhere in a linked list, analyzing the performance of binary tree searching and sorting and implementing an indexed list class.

Chapter 20—Java Utilities Package and Bit Manipulation—walks through the classes of the **`java.util`** package and discusses each of Java's bitwise operators. This is a nice chapter for reinforcing the notion of reuse. When classes already exist, it is much faster to develop software by simply reusing these classes than by "reinventing the wheel." Classes are included in class libraries because the classes are generally useful, correct, performance tuned, portability certified and/or for a variety of other reasons. Someone has invested considerable work in preparing these classes so why should you write your own? The world's class libraries are growing at a phenomenal rate. Given this, your skill and value as a programmer will depend on your familiarity with what classes exist and how you can reuse them cleverly to develop high-quality software rapidly. University data structures courses will be changing drastically over the next several years because most important data structures are already implemented in widely available class libraries. This chapter discusses many classes. Two of the most useful are **`Vector`** (a dynamic array that can grow and shrink as necessary) and **`Stack`** (a dynamic data structure that allows insertions and deletions from only one end—called the top—thus ensuring last-in-first-out behavior). The beauty of studying these two classes is that they are related through inheritance, as is discussed in Chapter 9, so the **java.util** package itself implements some classes in terms of others, thus avoiding reinventing the wheel and taking advantage of reuse. We also discuss classes **Dictionary**, **Hashtable**, **Properties** (for creating and manipulating persistent **Hashtable**s), **Random** and **BitSet**. The discussion of **BitSet** includes live code for one of the classic applications of **BitSet**s, namely the *Sieve of Eratosthenes*, used for determining prime numbers. The chapter discusses in detail Java's powerful bit-manipulation capabilities, which enable programmers to exercise lower level hardware capabilities. This helps programs process bit strings, set individual bits on or off and store information more compactly. Such capabilities—inherited from C—are characteristic of low-level assembly languages and are valued by programmers writing system software such as operating systems and networking software.

Chapter 21—Collections—discusses many of the Java 2 classes (of the **java.util** package) that provide predefined implementations of many of the data structures discussed in Chapter 19. This chapter, too, reinforces the notion of reuse. These classes are modeled after a similar class library in C++—the Standard Template Library. Collections provide Java programmers with a standard set of data structures for storing and retrieving data and a standard set of algorithms (i.e., procedures) that allow programmers to manipulate the data (such as searching for particular data items and sorting data into ascending or descending order). The chapter examples demonstrate collections, such as linked lists, trees, maps and sets, and algorithms for searching, sorting, finding the maximum value, finding the minimum value and so on. Each example clearly shows how powerful and easy to use collections are. The exercises suggest modifications to the chapter examples and ask the reader to reimplement data structures presented in Chapter 19 using collections.

Chapter 22—Java Media Framework and Java Sound—is the second of our two chapters dedicated to Java's tremendous multimedia capabilities. This chapter focusses on the Java Media Framework (JMF) and the Java Sound API. The Java Media Framework provides both audio and video capabilities. With the JMF, a Java program can play audio and video media and capture audio and video media from devices such as microphones and video cameras. Many of today's multimedia applications involve sending audio or video feeds across the Internet. For example, you can visit the **cnn.com** Web site to watch or listen to live news conferences, and many people listen to Internet-based radio stations through their Web browsers. The JMF enables Java developers to create so-called *streaming media* applications, in which a Java program sends live or recorded audio or video feeds across the Internet to other computers, then applications on those other computers play the media as it arrives over the network. The JavaSound APIs enable programs to manipulate Musical Instrument Digital Interface (MIDI) sounds and captured media (i.e., media from a device such as a microphone). This chapter concludes with a substantial MIDI-processing application that enables users to select MIDI files to play and record new MIDI files. Users can create their own MIDI music by interacting with the application's simulated synthesizer keyboard. In addition, the application can synchronize playing the notes in a MIDI file with pressing the keys on the simulated synthesizer keyboard—similar to a player piano! As with Chapter 18, once you read this chapter, you will be eager to try all these techniques, so we have included 44 additional multimedia exercises to challenge and entertain you. Some of the interesting projects include the following:

Bouncing Ball Physics Demo
Craps
Digital Clock
Flight Simulator
Karaoke
Kinetics Physics Demo
Knight's Tour Walker
Morse Code
MP3 Player
Multimedia Authoring System
Pinball Machine
Roulette
Story Teller
Tic-Tac-Toe
Tortoise and the Hare
Towers of Hanoi
Video Conferencing
Video Games

Appendix A—Java Demos—presents a huge collection of some of the best Java demos available on the Web. Many of these sites make their source code available to you, so you can download the code and add your own features—a truly great way to learn Java! We encourage our students to do this, and we're amazed at the results! You should start your search by checking out the Sun Microsystems applet Web page, **`java.sun.com/applets`**. You can save time finding the best demos by checking out JARS (the Java Applet Rating Service) at **`www.jars.com`**. Here's a list of some of the demos mentioned in Appendix A (the URLs and descriptions of each are in Appendix A):

Animated SDSU Logo
Bumpy Lens 3D
Centipedo
Crazy Counter
Famous Curves Applet Index
Goldmine
Iceblox game
Java Game Park
Java4fun games
Missile Commando
PhotoAlbum II
Play A Piano
Sab's Game Arcade
SabBowl bowling game
Sevilla RDM 168
Stereoscopic 3D Hypercube
Teamball
Tube
Urbanoids
Warp 1.5

Appendix B—Java Resources—presents some of the best Java resources available on the Web. This is a great way for you to get into the "world of Java." The appendix lists various Java resources, such as consortia, journals and companies that make various key Java-related products. Here are some of the resources mentioned in Appendix B:

animated applets
applets/applications
arts and entertainment
audio sites
books
Borland JBuilder IDE
conferences
consultants
contests
CORBA homepage
current information
databases
demos (many with source code)
developer's kit
development tools
discussion groups
documentation
downloadable applets
FAQs (frequently asked ?s)
games
graphics
IBM Developers Java Zone
Intelligence.com
Java Applet Rating Service
Java Developer Connection
Java Developer's Journal
Java Media Framework
Java Report
Java tools
Java Toys
Java Users Group (JUGs)
Java Woman
`java.sun.com`
JavaWorld on-line magazine
learning Java
links to Java sites
lists of resources
lists of what is new and cool
live chat sessions on Java
multimedia collections
NASA multimedia gallery
NetBeans IDE
news
`news:comp.lang.java`
newsgroups
newsletters
Object Management Group
products
projects
publications
puzzles
reference materials
resources
seminars
sites
software
Sun Microsystems
SunWorld on-line magazine
Team Java
The Java Tutorial
trade shows
training (please call us!)
tutorials for learning java
URLs for Java applets
`www.javaworld.com`
Yahoo (Web search engine)

Appendix C—Operator Precedence Chart—lists each of the Java operators and indicates their relative precedence and associativity. We list each operator on a separate line and include the full name of the operator.

Appendix D—ASCII Character Set—lists the characters of the ASCII (American Standard Code for Information Interchange) character set and indicates the character code value for each. Java uses the Unicode character set with 16-bit characters for representing all of the characters in the world's "commercially significant" languages. Unicode includes ASCII as a subset. Currently, most English-speaking countries are using ASCII and just beginning to experiment with Unicode.

Appendix E—Number Systems—discusses the binary (base 2), decimal (base 10), octal (base 8) and hexadecimal (base 16) number systems. This material is valuable for introductory courses in computer science and computer engineering. The appendix is presented with the same pedagogic learning aids as the chapters of the book. A nice feature of the appendix is its 31 exercises, 19 of which are self-review exercises with answers.

Appendix F—Creating `javadoc` Documentation—introduces the `javadoc` documentation-generation tool. Sun Microsystems uses `javadoc` to document the Java APIs. The example in this appendix takes the reader through the `javadoc` documentation process. First, we introduce the comment style and tags that `javadoc` recognizes and uses to create documentation. Next, we discuss the commands and options used to run the utility. Finally, we examine the source files `javadoc` uses and the HTML files `javadoc` creates.

1.18 (Optional) A Tour of the Case Study on Object-Oriented Design with the UML

In this and the next section, we tour the two optional major features of the book—the optional case study of object-oriented design with the UML and our introduction to design patterns. The case study involving object-oriented design with the UML is an important addition to *Java How to Program, Fourth Edition.* This tour previews the contents of the "Thinking About Objects" sections and discusses how they relate to the case study. After completing this case study, you will have completed an object-oriented design and implementation for a significant Java application.

Section 1.15—Thinking About Objects: Introduction to Object Technology and the Unified Modeling Language

This section introduces the object-oriented design case study with the UML. We provide a general background of what objects are and how they interact with other objects. We also discuss briefly the state of the software-engineering industry and how the UML has influenced object-oriented analysis and design processes.

Section 2.9—(Optional Case Study) Thinking About Objects: Examining the Problem Statement

Our case study begins with a *problem statement* that specifies the requirements for a system that we will create. In this case study, we design and implement a simulation of an elevator system in a two-story building. The application user can "create" a person on either floor. This person then walks across the floor to the elevator, presses a button, waits for the elevator to arrive and rides it to the other floor. We provide the design of our elevator system after investigating the structure and behavior of object-oriented systems in general. We discuss how the UML will facilitate the design process in subsequent "Thinking About Object" sections by providing us with several types of diagrams to model our system. Finally, we provide a list of URL and book references on object-oriented design with the UML. You might find these references helpful as you proceed through our case-study presentation.

Section 3.8—(Optional Case Study) Thinking About Objects: Identifying the Classes in the Problem Statement

In this section, we design the elevator-simulation model, which represents the operations of the elevator system. We identify the classes, or "building blocks," of our model by extracting the nouns and noun phrases from the problem statement. We arrange these classes into a UML class diagram that describes the class structure of our model. The class diagram also describes relationships, known as *associations*, among classes (for example, a person has an association with the elevator, because the person rides the elevator). Lastly, we extract from the class diagram another type of diagram in the UML—the object diagram. The object diagram models the objects (instances of classes) at a specific time in our simulation.

Section 4.14—(Optional Case Study) Thinking About Objects: Identifying Class Attributes

A class contains both *attributes* (data) and *operations* (behaviors). This section focuses on the attributes of the classes discussed in Section 3.7. As we see in later sections, changes in an object's attributes often affect the behavior of that object. To determine the attributes for the classes in our case study, we extract the adjectives describing the nouns and noun phrases (which defined our classes) from the problem statement, then place the attributes in the class diagram we create in Section 3.7.

Section 5.11—(Optional Case Study) Thinking About Objects: Identifying Objects' States and Activities

An object, at any given time, occupies a specific condition called a *state*. A *state transition* occurs when that object receives a message to change state. The UML provides the *statechart diagram*, which identifies the set of possible states that an object may occupy and models that object's state transitions. An object also has an *activity*—the work performed by an object in its lifetime. The UML provides the *activity diagram*—a flowchart that models an object's *activity*. In this section, we use both types of diagrams to begin modeling specific behavioral aspects of our elevator simulation, such as how a person rides the elevator and how the elevator responds when a button is pressed on a given floor.

Section 6.16—(Optional Case Study) Thinking About Objects: Identifying Class Operations

In this section, we identify the operations, or services, of our classes. We extract from the problem statement the verbs and verb phrases that specify the operations for each class. We then modify the class diagram of Fig. 3.16 to include each operation with its associated class. At this point in the case study, we will have gathered all information possible from the problem statement. However, as future chapters introduce such topics as inheritance, event-handling and multithreading, we will modify our classes and diagrams.

Section 7.10—(Optional Case Study) Thinking About Objects: Collaboration Among Objects

At this point, we have created a "rough sketch" of the model for our elevator system. In this section, we see how it works. We investigate the behavior of the model by discussing *col-*

laborations—messages that objects send to each other to communicate. The class operations that we discovered in Section 6.16 turn out to be the collaborations among the objects in our system. We determine the collaborations in our system, then collect them into a *collaboration diagram*—the UML diagram for modeling collaborations. This diagram reveals which objects collaborate and when. We present a collaboration diagram of the people entering and exiting the elevator.

Section 8.17—(Optional Case Study) Thinking About Objects: Starting to Program the Classes for the Elevator Simulation

In this section, we take a break from designing the behavior of our system. We begin the implementation process to emphasize the material discussed in Chapter 8. Using the UML class diagram of Section 3.7 and the attributes and operations discussed in Sections 4.14 and 6.16, we show how to implement a class in Java from a design. We do not implement all classes—because we have not completed the design process. Working from our UML diagrams, we create code for the **`Elevator`** class.

Section 9.23—(Optional Case Study) Thinking About Objects: Incorporating Inheritance into the Elevator Simulation

Chapter 9 begins our discussion of object-oriented programming. We consider inheritance—classes sharing similar characteristics may inherit attributes and operations from a "base" class. In this section, we investigate how our elevator simulation can benefit from using inheritance. We document our discoveries in a class diagram that models inheritance relationships—the UML refers to these relationships as *generalizations*. We modify the class diagram of Section 3.7 by using inheritance to group classes with similar characteristics. We continue implementing the **`Elevator`** class of Section 8.17 by incorporating inheritance.

Section 10.22—(Optional Case Study) Thinking About Objects: Event Handling

In this section, we include interfaces necessary for the objects in our elevator simulation to send messages to other objects. In Java, objects often communicate by sending an *event*—a notification that some action has occurred. The object receiving the event then performs an action in response to the type of event received—this is known as *event handling*. In Section 7.10, we outlined the message passing, or the collaborations, in our model, using a collaboration diagram. We now modify this diagram to include event handling, and, as an example, we explain in detail how doors in our simulation open upon the elevator's arrival.

Section 11.10—(Optional Case Study) Thinking About Objects: Designing Interfaces with the UML

In this section, we design a class diagram that models the relationships between classes and interfaces in our simulation—the UML refers to these relationships as *realizations*. In addition, we list all operations that each interface provides to the classes. Lastly, we show how to create the Java classes that implement these interfaces. As in Section 8.17 and Section 9.23, we use class **`Elevator`** to demonstrate the implementation.

Section 12.16 - (Optional Case Study) Thinking About Objects: Use Cases

Chapter 12 discusses user interfaces that enable a user to interact with a program. In this section, we discuss the interaction between our elevator simulation and its user. Specifically, we investigate the scenarios that may occur between the application user and the simulation itself—this set of scenarios is called a *use case*. We model these interactions, using *use-case diagrams* of the UML. We then discuss the graphical user interface for our simulation, using our use-case diagrams.

Section 13.17—(Optional Case Study) Thinking About Objects: Model-View-Controller
We designed our system to consist of three components, each having a distinct responsibility. By this point in the case study, we have almost completed the first component, called the *model*, which contains data that represent the simulation. We design the *view*—the second component, dealing with how the model is displayed—in Section 22.8. We design the *controller*—the component that allows the user to control the model—in Section 12.16. A system such as ours that uses the model, view and controller components is said to adhere to *Model-View-Controller* (*MVC*) architecture. In this section, we explain the advantages of using this architecture to design software. We use the UML *component diagram* to model the three components, then implement this diagram as Java code.

Section 15.12—(Optional Case Study) Thinking About Objects: Multithreading
In the real world, objects operate and interact concurrently. Java is a *multithreaded* language, which enables the objects in our simulation to act seemingly independently from each other. In this section, we declare certain objects as "threads" to enable these objects to operate concurrently. We modify the collaboration diagram originally presented in Section 7.10 (and modified in Section 10.22) to incorporate multithreading. We present the UML *sequence diagram* for modeling interactions in a system. This diagram emphasizes the chronological ordering of messages. We use a sequence diagram to model how a person inside the simulation interacts with the elevator. This section concludes the design of the model portion of our simulation. We design how this model is displayed in Section 22.9, then implement this model as Java code in Appendix H.

Section 22.9—(Optional Case Study) Thinking About Objects: Animation and Sound in the View
This section designs the view, which specifies how the model portion of the simulation is displayed. Chapter 18 presents several techniques for integrating animation in programs, and Chapter 22 presents techniques for integrating sound. Section 22.9 uses some of these techniques to incorporate sound and animation into our elevator simulation. Specifically, this section deals with animating the movements of people and our elevator, generating sound effects and playing "elevator music" when a person rides the elevator. This section concludes the design of our elevator simulation. Appendices G, H and I implement this design as a 3,594-line, fully operational Java program.

Appendix G—Elevator Events and Listener Interfaces
[Note: This appendix is on the CD that accompanies this book.] As we discussed in Section 10.22, several objects in our simulation interact with each other by sending messages, called events, to other objects wishing to receive these events. The objects receiving the events are called *listener objects*—these must implement *listener interfaces*. In this section, we implement all event classes and listener interfaces used by the objects in our simulation.

Appendix H—Elevator Model
[Note: This appendix is on the CD that accompanies this book.] The majority of the case study involved designing the model (i.e., the data and logic) of the elevator simulation. In

this section, we implement that model in Java. Using all the UML diagrams we created, we present the Java classes necessary to implement the model. We apply the concepts of object-oriented design with the UML and object-oriented programming and Java that you learned in the chapters.

Appendix I—Elevator View
[Note: This appendix is on the CD that accompanies this book.] The final section implements how we display the model from Appendix H. We use the same approach to implement the view as we used to implement the model—we create all the classes required to run the view, using the UML diagrams and key concepts discussed in the chapters. By the end of this section, you will have completed an "industrial-strength" design and implementation of a large-scale system. You should feel confident tackling larger systems, such as the 8000-line Enterprise Java case study we present in our companion book *Advanced Java 2 Platform How to Program* and the kinds of applications that professional software engineers build. Hopefully, you will move on to even deeper study of object-oriented design with the UML.

1.19 (Optional) A Tour of the "Discovering Design Patterns" Sections

Our treatment of design patterns is spread over five optional sections of the book. We overview those sections here.

Section 9.24—(Optional) Discovering Design Patterns: Introducing Creational, Structural and Behavioral Design Patterns
This section provides tables that list the sections in which we discuss the various design patterns. We divide the discussion of each section into creational, structural and behavioral design patterns. Creational patterns provide ways to instantiate objects, structural patterns deal with organizing objects and behavioral patterns deal with interactions between objects. The remainder of the section introduces some of these design patterns, such as the Singleton, Proxy, Memento and State design patterns. Finally, we provide several URLs for further study on design patterns.

Section 13.18—(Optional) Discovering Design Patterns: Design Patterns Used in Packages `java.awt` and `javax.swing`
This section contains most of our design-patterns discussion. Using the material on Java Swing GUI components in Chapters 12 and 13, we investigate some examples of pattern use in packages **`java.awt`** and **`javax.swing`**. We discuss how these classes use the Factory Method, Adapter, Bridge, Composite, Chain-of-Responsibility, Command, Observer, Strategy and Template Method design patterns. We motivate each pattern and present examples of how to apply them.

Section 15.13—(Optional) Discovering Design Patterns: Concurrent Design Patterns
Developers have introduced several design patterns since those described by the gang of four. In this section, we discuss concurrency design patterns, including Single-Threaded Execution, Guarded Suspension, Balking, Read/Write Lock and Two-Phase Termination—these solve various design problems in multithreaded systems. We investigate how class **`java.lang.Thread`** uses concurrency patterns.

Section 17.11—(Optional) Discovering Design Patterns: Design Patterns Used in Packages **java.io** *and* **java.net**

Using the material on files, streams and networking in Chapters 16 and 17, we investigate some examples of pattern use in packages **java.io** and **java.net**. We discuss how these classes use the Abstract Factory, Decorator and Facade design patterns. We also consider architectural patterns, which specify a set of subsystems—aggregates of objects that each collectively comprise a major system responsibility—and how these subsystems interact with each other. We discuss the popular Model-View-Controller and Layers architectural patterns.

Section 21.12—(Optional) Discovering Design Patterns: Design Patterns Used in Package **java.util**

Using the material on data structures and collections in Chapters 19, 20 and 21, we investigate pattern use in package **java.util**. We discuss how these classes use the Prototype and Iterator design patterns. This section concludes the discussion on design patterns. After finishing the *Discovering Design Patterns* material, you should be able to recognize and use key design patterns and have a better understanding of the workings of the Java API. After completing this material, we recommend that you move on to the gang-of-four book.

Well, there you have it! We have worked hard to create this book and its optional Cyber Classroom version. The book is loaded with live-code examples, programming tips, self-review exercises and answers, challenging exercises and projects, and numerous study aids to help you master the material. Java is a powerful programming language that will help you write programs quickly and effectively. And Java is a language that scales nicely into the realm of enterprise-systems development to help organizations build their key information systems. As you read the book, if something is not clear, or if you find an error, please write to us at **deitel@deitel.com**. We will respond promptly, and we will post corrections and clarifications on our Web site,

www.deitel.com

We hope you enjoy learning with *Java How to Program: Fourth Edition* as much as we enjoyed writing it!

SUMMARY

- Software controls computers (often referred to as hardware).
- Java is one of today's most popular software-development languages.
- Java was developed by Sun Microsystems. Sun provides an implementation of the Java 2 Platform, Standard Edition called the Java 2 Software Development Kit (J2SDK), version 1.3.1 that includes the minimum set of tools you need to write software in Java.
- Java is a fully object-oriented language with strong support for proper software-engineering techniques.
- A computer is a device capable of performing computations and making logical decisions at speeds millions, even billions, of times faster than human beings can.
- Computers process data under the control of sets of instructions called computer programs. These computer programs guide the computer through orderly sets of actions specified by people called computer programmers.

- The various devices that comprise a computer system (such as the keyboard, screen, disks, memory and processing units) are referred to as hardware.
- The computer programs that run on a computer are referred to as software.
- The input unit is the "receiving" section of the computer. It obtains information (data and computer programs) from various input devices and places this information at the disposal of the other units so that the information may be processed.
- The output unit is the "shipping" section of the computer. It takes information processed by the computer and places it on output devices to make it available for use outside the computer.
- The memory unit is the rapid access, relatively low-capacity "warehouse" section of the computer. It retains information that has been entered through the input unit so that the information may be made immediately available for processing when it is needed and retains information that has already been processed until that information can be placed on output devices by the output unit.
- The arithmetic and logic unit (ALU) is the "manufacturing" section of the computer. It is responsible for performing calculations such as addition, subtraction, multiplication and division and for making decisions.
- The central processing unit (CPU) is the "administrative" section of the computer. It is the computer's coordinator and is responsible for supervising the operation of the other sections.
- The secondary storage unit is the long-term, high-capacity "warehousing" section of the computer. Programs or data not being used by the other units are normally placed on secondary storage devices (such as disks) until they are needed, possibly hours, days, months or even years later.
- Early computers were capable of performing only one job or task at a time. This form of computer operation often is called single-user batch processing.
- Software systems called operating systems were developed to help make it more convenient to use computers. Early operating systems managed the smooth transition between jobs and minimized the time it took for computer operators to switch between jobs.
- Multiprogramming involves the "simultaneous" operation of many jobs on the computer—the computer shares its resources among the jobs competing for its attention.
- Timesharing is a special case of multiprogramming in which dozens or even hundreds of users share a computer through terminals. The computer runs a small portion of one user's job, then moves on to service the next user. The computer does this so quickly that it might provide service to each user several times per second, so programs appear to run simultaneously.
- An advantage of timesharing is that the user receives almost immediate responses to requests rather than having to wait long periods for results, as with previous modes of computing.
- In 1977, Apple Computer popularized the phenomenon of personal computing.
- In 1981, IBM introduced the IBM Personal Computer. Almost overnight, personal computing became legitimate in business, industry and government organizations.
- Although early personal computers were not powerful enough to timeshare several users, these machines could be linked together in computer networks, sometimes over telephone lines and sometimes in local area networks (LANs) within an organization. This led to the phenomenon of distributed computing, in which an organization's computing is distributed over networks to the sites at which the real work of the organization is performed.
- Today, information is shared easily across computer networks where some computers called file servers offer a common store of programs and data that may be used by client computers distributed throughout the network—hence the term client/server computing.
- Java has become the language of choice for developing Internet-based applications (and for many other purposes).

- Computer languages may be divided into three general types: machine languages, assembly languages and high-level languages.
- Any computer can directly understand only its own machine language. Machine languages generally consist of strings of numbers (ultimately reduced to 1s and 0s) that instruct computers to perform their most elementary operations one at a time. Machine languages are machine dependent.
- English-like abbreviations formed the basis of assembly languages. Translator programs called assemblers convert assembly-language programs to machine language at computer speeds.
- Compilers translate high-level language programs into machine-language programs. High-level languages (like Java) contain English words and conventional mathematical notations.
- Interpreter programs directly execute high-level language programs without the need for compiling those programs into machine language.
- Although compiled programs execute much faster than interpreted programs, interpreters are popular in program-development environments in which programs are recompiled frequently as new features are added and errors are corrected.
- Objects are essentially reusable software components that model items in the real world. Modular, object-oriented design and implementation approaches make software-development groups more productive than is possible with previous popular programming techniques such as structured programming. Object-oriented programs are often easier to understand, correct and modify.
- Java originated at Sun Microsystems as a project for intelligent consumer-electronic devices.
- When the World Wide Web exploded in popularity in 1993, Sun people saw the immediate potential of using Java to create Web pages with so-called dynamic content.
- Java is now used to create Web pages with dynamic and interactive content, to develop large-scale enterprise applications, to enhance the functionality of Web servers, to provide applications for consumer devices and so on.
- Java programs consist of pieces called classes. Classes consist of pieces called methods that perform tasks and return information when they complete their tasks.
- Most Java programmers use rich collections of existing classes in Java class libraries.
- FORTRAN (FORmula TRANslator) was developed by IBM Corporation between 1954 and 1957 for scientific and engineering applications that require complex mathematical computations.
- COBOL (COmmon Business Oriented Language) was developed in 1959 by a group of computer manufacturers and government and industrial computer users. COBOL is used primarily for commercial applications that require precise and efficient manipulation of large amounts of data.
- Pascal was designed at about the same time as C. It was created by Professor Nicklaus Wirth and was intended for academic use.
- Basic was developed in 1965 at Dartmouth College as a simple language to help novices become comfortable with programming.
- Structured programming is a disciplined approach to writing programs that are clearer than unstructured programs, easier to test and debug and easier to modify.
- The Ada language was developed under the sponsorship of the United States Department of Defense (DOD) during the 1970s and early 1980s. One important capability of Ada is called multitasking; this allows programmers to specify that many activities are to occur in parallel.
- Most high-level languages—including C and C++—generally allow the programmer to write programs that perform only one activity at a time. Java, through a technique called multithreading, enables programmers to write programs with parallel activities.
- The Internet was developed more than three decades ago with funding supplied by the Department of Defense. Originally designed to connect the main computer systems of about a dozen universi-

ties and research organizations, the Internet today is accessible by hundreds of millions of computers worldwide.

- The Web allows computer users to locate and view multimedia-intensive documents over the Internet.
- Java systems generally consist of several parts: an environment, the language, the Java Applications Programming Interface (API) and various class libraries.
- Java programs normally go through five phases to be executed—edit, compile, load, verify and execute.
- Java program file names end with the **`.java`** extension.
- The Java compiler (**`javac`**) translates a Java program into bytecodes—the language understood by the Java interpreter. If a program compiles correctly, the compiler produces a file with the **`.class`** extension. This is the file containing the bytecodes that are interpreted during the execution phase.
- A Java program must first be placed in memory before it can execute. This is done by the class loader, which takes the **`.class`** file (or files) containing the bytecodes and transfers it to memory. The **`.class`** file can be loaded from a disk on your system or over a network.
- An application is a program that is normally stored and executed on the user's local computer.
- An applet is a small program that is normally stored on a remote computer that users connect to via a Web browser. Applets are loaded from a remote computer into the browser, executed in the browser and discarded when execution completes.
- Applications are loaded into memory, then executed by the **`java`** interpreter.
- Browsers are used to view HTML (Hypertext Markup Language) documents on the World Wide Web.
- When the browser sees an applet in an HTML document, the browser launches the Java class loader to load the applet. The browsers that support Java each have a built-in Java interpreter. Once the applet is loaded, the Java interpreter in the browser begins executing the applet.
- Applets can also be executed from the command line using the **`appletviewer`** command provided with the Java 2 Software Development Kit (J2SDK). The **`appletviewer`** is commonly referred to as the minimum browser—it knows only how to interpret applets.
- Before the bytecodes in an applet are executed by the Java interpreter built into a browser or the **`appletviewer`**, they are verified by the bytecode verifier to ensure that the bytecodes for downloaded classes are valid and that they do not violate Java's security restrictions.
- An intermediate step between interpreters and compilers is a just-in-time (JIT) compiler that, as the interpreter runs, produces compiled code for the programs and executes the programs in machine language rather than reinterpreting them. JIT compilers do not produce machine language that is as efficient as a full compiler.
- For organizations wanting to do heavy-duty information-systems development, Integrated Development Environments (IDEs) are available from the major software suppliers. The IDEs provide many tools for supporting the software-development process.
- Object orientation is a natural way of thinking about the world and of writing computer programs.
- The Unified Modeling Language (UML) is a graphical language that allows people who build systems to represent their object-oriented designs in a common notation.
- Humans think in terms of objects. We possess the marvelous ability of abstraction, which enables us to view screen images as people, planes, trees and mountains rather than as individual dots of color (called pixels—for "picture elements").

- Humans learn about objects by studying their attributes and observing their behaviors. Different objects can have similar attributes and can exhibit similar behaviors.
- Object-oriented design (OOD) models real-world objects. It takes advantage of class relationships, where objects of a certain class—such as a class of vehicles—have the same characteristics. It takes advantage of inheritance relationships, and even multiple-inheritance relationships, where newly created classes of objects are derived by absorbing characteristics of existing classes and adding unique characteristics of their own.
- OOD encapsulates data (attributes) and functions (behavior) into objects; the data and functions of an object are intimately tied together.
- Objects have the property of information hiding. This means that, although objects may know how to communicate with one another across well-defined interfaces, objects normally are not allowed to know how other objects are implemented.
- Languages such as Java are object-oriented—programming in such a language is called object-oriented programming (OOP) and allows designers to implement the object-oriented design as a working system.
- In Java, the unit of programming is the class from which objects are eventually instantiated (a fancy term for "created"). Java classes contain methods (which implement class behaviors) and attributes (which implement class data).
- Java programmers concentrate on creating their own user-defined types, called classes. Each class contains data and the set of functions that manipulate that data. The data components of a Java class are called attributes. The function components of a Java class are called methods.
- An instance of a user-defined type (i.e., a class) is called an object.
- Classes can also have relationships with other classes. These relationships are called associations.
- With object technology, we can build much of the software we will need by combining "standardized, interchangeable parts" called classes.
- The process of analyzing and designing a system from an object-oriented point of view is called object-oriented analysis and design (OOAD).
- The Unified Modeling Language (the UML) is now the most widely used graphical representation scheme for modeling object-oriented systems. Those who design systems use the language (in the form of graphical diagrams) to model their systems.
- Over the past decade, the software-engineering industry has made significant progress in the field of design patterns—proven architectures for constructing flexible and maintainable object-oriented software. Using design patterns can substantially reduce the complexity of the design process.
- Design patterns benefit system developers by helping to construct reliable software using proven architectures and accumulated industry expertise, promoting design reuse in future systems, identifying common mistakes and pitfalls that occur when building systems, helping to design systems independently of the language in which they will be implemented, establishing a common design vocabulary among developers and shortening the design phase in a software-development process.
- Designers use design patterns to construct sets of classes and objects.
- Creational design patterns describe techniques to instantiate objects (or groups of objects).
- Structural design patterns allow designers to organize classes and objects into larger structures.
- Behavioral design patterns assign responsibilities to objects.

TERMINOLOGY

abstraction
Ada
ALU (arithmetic and logic unit)
ANSI C

applet
appletviewer command
application
arithmetic and logic unit (ALU)
array
assembly language
attribute
Basic
behavior
behavioral design pattern
bytecode
bytecode verifier
C
C standard library
C++
central processing unit (CPU)
class
.class file
class libraries
class loader
client/server computing
COBOL
collections
compile phase
compiler
compile-time error
computer
computer program
computer programmer
condition
CPU (central processing unit)
creational design pattern
design pattern
disk
distributed computing
dynamic content
edit phase
editor
encapsulation
event-driven programming
execute phase
execution-time error
fatal runtime error
file server
Fortran
freeware
hardware
high-level language
HotSpot compiler
HTML (Hypertext Markup Language)
IDE (Integrated Development Environment)
information hiding
inheritance
input device
input unit
input/output (I/O)
instance variable
Internet
interpreter
Java
Java 2 Software Development Kit (J2SDK)
.java extension
java interpreter
Java Virtual Machine
javac compiler
JIT (just-in-time) compiler
KIS (keep it simple)
legacy systems
live-code™ approach
load phase
logic error
machine dependent
machine independent
machine language
memory unit
method
Microsoft
Microsoft Internet Explorer Web browser
modeling
multiprocessor
multitasking
multithreading
Netscape Navigator Web browser
nonfatal run-time error
object
object-oriented analysis and design (OOAD)
object-oriented design (OOD)
object-oriented programming (OOP)
open source
output device
output unit
Pascal
personal computing
platforms
portability
primary memory
problem statement
procedural programming
programming language
reference

requirements document
reusable componentry
runtime error
secondary storage unit
shareware
software
software reuse
structural design pattern
structured programming
Sun Microsystems
Swing GUI components
syntax error
throughput
throw an exception
timesharing
translator programs
Unified Modeling Language (UML)
verify phase
video
World Wide Web

SELF-REVIEW EXERCISES

1.1 Fill in the blanks in each of the following statements:

a) The company that popularized personal computing was ________.
b) The computer that made personal computing legitimate in business and industry was the ________.
c) Computers process data under the control of sets of instructions called ________.
d) The six key logical units of the computer are the ________, ________, ________, ________, ________ and ________.
e) The three classes of languages discussed in the chapter are ________, ________ and ________.
f) The programs that translate high-level language programs into machine language are called ________.

1.2 Fill in the blanks in each of the following sentences about the Java environment:

a) The ________ command from the Java 2 Software Development Kit executes a Java applet.
b) The ________ command from the Java 2 Software Development Kit executes a Java application
c) The ________ command from the Java 2 Software Development Kit compiles a Java program.
d) A(n) ________ file is required to invoke a Java applet.
e) A Java program file must end with the ________ file extension.
f) When a Java program is compiled, the file produced by the compiler ends with the ________ file extension.
g) The file produced by the Java compiler contains ________ that are interpreted to execute a Java applet or application.

1.3 Fill in the blanks in each of the following statements:

a) The ________ allows computer users to locate and view multimedia-based documents on almost any subject over the Internet.
b) Java ________ typically are stored on your computer and are designed to execute independent of a World Wide Web browsers.
c) Lists and tables of values are called ________.
d) The ________ GUI components are written completely in Java.
e) ________ allows an applet or application to perform multiple activities in parallel.
f) ________ provide Java programmers with a standard set of data structures for storing and retrieving data and a standard set of algorithms that allow programmers to manipulate the data.

1.4 Fill in the blanks in each of the following statements (based on Sections 1.15 and 1.16):
  a) Over the past decade, the software-engineering industry has made significant progress in the field of __________—proven architectures for constructing flexible and maintainable object-oriented software.
  b) Objects have the property of __________.
  c) Java programmers concentrate on creating their own user-defined types, called __________.
  d) Classes can also have relationships with other classes. These relationships are called __________.
  e) The process of analyzing and designing a system from an object-oriented point of view is called __________.

ANSWERS TO SELF-REVIEW EXERCISES

1.1 a) Apple. b) IBM Personal Computer. c) programs. d) input unit, output unit, memory unit, arithmetic and logic unit, central processing unit, secondary storage unit. e) machine languages, assembly languages, high-level languages. f) compilers.

1.2 a) **`appletviewer`**. b) **`java`**. c) **`javac`**. d) HTML. e) **`.java`**. f) **`.class`**. g) bytecodes.

1.3 a) World Wide Web. b) applications. c) arrays. d) Swing. e) Multithreading. f) Collections.

1.4 a) design patterns. b) information hiding. c) classes. d) associations. e) object-oriented analysis and design (OOAD).

EXERCISES

1.5 Categorize each of the following items as either hardware or software:
  a) CPU
  b) Java compiler
  c) ALU
  d) Java interpreter
  e) input unit
  f) editor

1.6 Why might you want to write a program in a machine-independent language instead of a machine-dependent language? Why might a machine-dependent language be more appropriate for writing certain types of programs?

1.7 Fill in the blanks in each of the following statements:
  a) Which logical unit of the computer receives information from outside the computer for use by the computer? __________.
  b) The process of instructing the computer to solve specific problems is called __________.
  c) What type of computer language uses English-like abbreviations for machine language instructions? __________.
  d) Which logical unit of the computer sends information that has already been processed by the computer to various devices so that the information may be used outside the computer? __________.
  e) Which logical unit of the computer retains information? __________.
  f) Which logical unit of the computer performs calculations? __________.
  g) Which logical unit of the computer makes logical decisions? __________.
  h) The level of computer language most convenient to the programmer for writing programs quickly and easily is __________.

i) The only language that a computer can directly understand is called that computer's __________.

j) Which logical unit of the computer coordinates the activities of all the other logical units? __________.

1.8 Distinguish between the terms fatal error and nonfatal error. Why might you prefer to experience a fatal error rather than a nonfatal error?

1.9 Fill in the blanks in each of the following statements:

a) Java __________ are designed to be transported over the Internet and executed in World Wide Web browsers.
b) __________ programming causes a program to perform a task in response to user interactions with graphical user interface (GUI) components.
c) Java's graphics capabilities are __________ and, hence portable.
d) The standard __________ can be used to provide identical user interfaces across all computer platforms.
e) Languages that cannot perform multiple activities in parallel are called __________ languages or __________ languages.
f) Aggregations of data such as linked lists, stacks, queues and trees are called __________.

1.10 Fill in the blanks in each of the following statements (based on Sections 1.15 and 1.16):

a) __________ design patterns describe techniques to instantiate objects (or groups of objects).
b) The __________ is now the most widely used graphical representation scheme for modeling object-oriented systems.
c) Java classes contain __________ (which implement class behaviors) and (which implement class data).
d) __________ design patterns allow designers to organize classes and objects into larger structures.
e) __________ design patterns assign responsibilities to objects.
f) In Java, the unit of programming is the __________, from which __________ are eventually instantiated.

Introduction to Java Applications

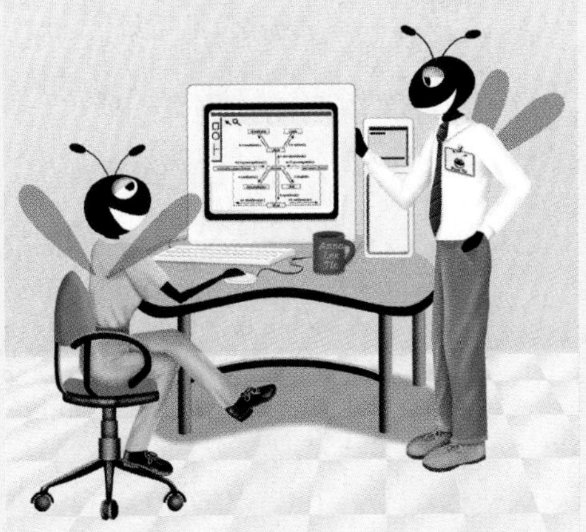

Objectives

- To be able to write simple Java applications.
- To be able to use input and output statements.
- To become familiar with primitive data types.
- To understand basic memory concepts.
- To be able to use arithmetic operators.
- To understand the precedence of arithmetic operators.
- To be able to write decision-making statements.
- To be able to use relational and equality operators.

Comment is free, but facts are sacred.
C. P. Scott

The creditor hath a better memory than the debtor.
James Howell

When faced with a decision, I always ask, "What would be the most fun?"
Peggy Walker

He has left his body to science—
and science is contesting the will.
David Frost

Classes struggle, some classes triumph, others are eliminated.
Mao Zedong

Equality, in a social sense, may be divided into that of condition and that of rights.
James Fenimore Cooper

Outline

2.1 Introduction
2.2 A First Program in Java: Printing a Line of Text
  2.2.1 Compiling and Executing your First Java Application
2.3 Modifying Our First Java Program
  2.3.1 Displaying a Single Line of Text with Multiple Statements
  2.3.2 Displaying Multiple Lines of Text with a Single Statement
2.4 Displaying Text in a Dialog Box
2.5 Another Java Application: Adding Integers
2.6 Memory Concepts
2.7 Arithmetic
2.8 Decision Making: Equality and Relational Operators
2.9 (Optional Case Study) Thinking About Objects: Examining the Problem Statement

Summary • Terminology • Self-Review Exercises • Answers to Self-Review Exercises • Exercises

2.1 Introduction

The Java language facilitates a disciplined approach to computer program design. We now introduce Java programming and present examples that illustrate several important features of Java. Each example is analyzed one line at a time. In this chapter and Chapter 3, we present two program types in Java—*applications* and *applets*. In Chapter 4 and Chapter 5, we present a detailed treatment of *program development* and *program control* in Java.

2.2 A First Program in Java: Printing a Line of Text

Java uses notations that may appear strange to nonprogrammers. We begin by considering a simple *application* that displays a line of text. An application is a program that executes using the **java** interpreter (discussed later in this section). The program and its output are shown in Fig. 2.1.

This program illustrates several important features of the Java language. We consider each line of the program in detail. Each program we present in this book has line numbers included for the reader's convenience; line numbers are not part of actual Java programs. Line 9 does the "real work" of the program, namely displaying the phrase **Welcome to Java Programming!** on the screen. But let us consider each line in order. Line 1,

```
// Fig. 2.1: Welcome1.java
```

begins with **//**, indicating that the remainder of the line is a *comment.* Programmers insert comments to *document* programs and improve program readability. Comments also help other people read and understand a program. Comments do not cause the computer to perform any action when the program is run. The Java compiler ignores comments. We begin every program with a comment indicating the figure number and file name (line 1).

```
// Fig. 2.1: Welcome1.java
// A first program in Java.

public class Welcome1 {

   // main method begins execution of Java application
   public static void main( String args[] )
   {
      System.out.println( "Welcome to Java Programming!" );

   }  // end method main

}  // end class Welcome1
```

```
Welcome to Java Programming!
```

Fig. 2.1 A first program in Java.

Good Programming Practice 2.1

Use comments to clarify difficult concepts used in a program.

A comment that begins with **//** is called a *single-line comment*, because the comment terminates at the end of the current line. A **//** comment can also begin in the middle of a line and continue until the end of that line.

Multiple-line comments can be written in two other forms. For example,

```
/* This is a multiple
   line comment. It can be
   split over many lines */
```

is a comment that can spread over several lines. This type of comment begins with delimiter **/*** and ends with delimiter ***/**; this type of comment may be called a *multiple-line comment*. All text between the delimiters of the comment is ignored by the compiler. A similar form of comment called a *documentation comment* is delimited by **/**** and ***/**.

Common Programming Error 2.1

Forgetting one of the delimiters of a multiple-line comment is a syntax error.

Java absorbed comments delimited with **/*** and ***/** from the C programming language and single-line comments delimited with **//** from the C++ programming language. Java programmers generally use C++-style single-line comments in preference to C-style comments. Throughout this book, we use C++-style single-line comments. The documentation comment syntax (**/**** and ***/**) is special to Java. It enables programmers to embed documentation for their programs directly in the programs. The ***javadoc*** utility program (provided by Sun Microsystems with the Java 2 Software Development Kit) reads those comments from the program and uses them to prepare your program's documentation. There are subtle issues to using **javadoc**-style comments properly. We do not use **javadoc**-style comments in the programs presented in this book. However, **javadoc**-style comments are explained thoroughly in Appendix F.

Line 2,

```
// A first program in Java.
```

is a single-line comment that describes the purpose of the program.

Good Programming Practice 2.2

Every program should begin with a comment describing the purpose of the program.

Line 3 is simply a blank line. Programmers use blank lines and space characters to make programs easier to read. Together, blank lines, space characters and tab characters are known as *white space*. (Space characters and tabs are known specifically as *white-space characters*.) Such characters are ignored by the compiler. We discuss conventions for using white-space characters in this chapter and the next several chapters, as these spacing conventions are needed in may Java programs.

Good Programming Practice 2.3

Use blank lines, space characters and tab characters to enhance program readability.

Line 4,

```
public class Welcome1 {
```

begins a *class definition* for class **Welcome1**. Every program in Java consists of at least one class definition that is defined by you—the programmer. These classes are known as *programmer-defined classes*, or *user-defined classes*. The ***class*** *keyword* introduces a class definition in Java and is immediately followed by the *class name* (**Welcome1** in this program). Keywords (or *reserved words*) are reserved for use by Java (we discuss the various keywords throughout the text) and are always spelled with all lowercase letters. The complete list of Java keywords is shown in Fig. 4.2.

By convention, all class names in Java begin with a capital letter and have a capital letter for every word in the class name (e.g., **SampleClassName**). The name of the class is called an *identifier*. An identifier is a series of characters consisting of letters, digits, underscores (_) and dollar signs (**$**) that does not begin with a digit and does not contain spaces. Some valid identifiers are **Welcome1**, **$value**, **_value**, **m_inputField1** and **button7**. The name **7button** is not a valid identifier, because it begins with a digit, and the name **input field** is not a valid identifier, because it contains a space. Java is *case sensitive*—i.e., uppercase and lowercase letters are different, so **a1** and **A1** are different identifiers.

Common Programming Error 2.2

Java is case sensitive. Not using the proper uppercase and lowercase letters for an identifier is normally a syntax error.

Good Programming Practice 2.4

By convention, you should always begin a class name with a capital letter.

Good Programming Practice 2.5

When reading a Java program, look for identifiers that start with capital letters. These identifiers normally represent Java classes.

Software Engineering Observation 2.1

*Avoid using identifiers that contain dollar signs (**$**), as the compiler often uses dollar signs to create identifier names.*

In Chapter 2 through Chapter 7, every class we define begins with the **`public`** *keyword*. For now, we will simply require this keyword. The **`public`** keyword is discussed in detail in Chapter 8. Also in that chapter, we discuss classes that do not begin with keyword **`public`**. [*Note*: Several times early in this text, we ask you to mimic certain Java features we introduce as you write your own Java programs. We specifically do this when it is not yet important for you to know all of the details of a feature in order for you to use that feature in Java. All programmers initially learn how to program by mimicking what other programmers have done before them. For each detail we ask you to mimic, we indicate where the full discussion will be presented later in the text.]

When you save your **`public`** class definition in a file, the file name must be the class name followed by the "**`.java`**" file-name extension. For our application, the file name is **`Welcome1.java`**. All Java class definitions are stored in files ending with the file-name extension "**`.java`**."

Common Programming Error 2.3

*It is an error for a **`public`** class if the file name is not identical to the class name (plus the **`.java`** extension) in terms of both spelling and capitalization. Therefore, it is also an error for a file to contain two or more **`public`** classes.*

Common Programming Error 2.4

*It is an error not to end a file name with the **`.java`** extension for a file containing an application's class definition. If the extension is missing, the Java compiler will not be able to compile the class definition.*

A *left brace* (at the end of line 4), **{**, begins the *body* of every class definition. A corresponding *right brace* (in line 13 in this program), **}**, must end each class definition. Notice that lines 6–11 are indented. This indentation is one of the spacing conventions mentioned earlier. We define each spacing convention as a *Good Programming Practice*.

Good Programming Practice 2.6

*Whenever you type an opening left brace, **{**, in your program, immediately type the closing right brace, **}**, then reposition the cursor between the braces to begin typing the body. This practice helps prevent errors due to missing braces.*

Good Programming Practice 2.7

*Indent the entire body of each class definition one "level" of indentation between the left brace, **{**, and the right brace, **}**, that define the body of the class. This format emphasizes the structure of the class definition and helps make the class definition easier to read.*

Good Programming Practice 2.8

Set a convention for the indent size you prefer, and then uniformly apply that convention. The Tab *key may be used to create indents, but tab stops may vary between editors. We recommend using three spaces to form a level of indent.*

Common Programming Error 2.5

If braces do not occur in matching pairs, the compiler indicates an error.

Line 5 is a blank line, inserted for program readability. Line 6,

```
// main method begins execution of Java application
```

is a single-line comment indicating the purpose of lines 6–11 of the program.

Line 7,

```
public static void main( String args[] )
```

is a part of every Java application. Java applications begin executing at **main**. The parentheses after **main** indicate that **main** is a program building block called a *method.* Java class definitions normally contain one or more methods. For a Java application class, exactly one of those methods must be called **main** and must be defined as shown on line 7; otherwise, the **java** interpreter will not execute the application. Methods are able to perform tasks and return information when they complete their tasks. The ***void*** keyword indicates that this method will perform a task (displaying a line of text, in this program), but will not return any information when it completes its task. Later, we will see that many methods return information when they complete their task. Methods are explained in detail in Chapter 6. For now, simply mimic **main**'s first line in your Java applications.

The left brace, **{**, on line 8 begins the *body of the method definition.* A corresponding right brace, **}**, must end the method definition's body (line 11 of the program). Notice that the line in the body of the method is indented between the braces.

Good Programming Practice 2.9

Indent the entire body of each method definition one "level" of indentation between the left brace, **{***, and the right brace,* **}***, that define the body of the method. This format makes the structure of the method stand out and helps make the method definition easier to read.*

Line 9,

```
System.out.println( "Welcome to Java Programming!" );
```

instructs the computer to perform an *action*, namely to print the *string* of characters contained between the double quotation marks. A string is sometimes called a *character string*, a *message* or a *string literal.* We refer to characters between double quotation marks generically as *strings*. White-space characters in strings are not ignored by the compiler.

System.out is known as the *standard output object.* **System.out** allows Java applications to display strings and other types of information in the *command window* from which the Java application executes. In Microsoft Windows 95/98/ME, the command window is the *MS-DOS prompt.* In Microsoft Windows NT/2000, the command window is the *Command Prompt* (***cmd.exe***). In UNIX, the command window is normally called a *command window*, a *command tool*, a *shell tool* or a *shell.* On computers running an operating system that does not have a command window (such as a Macintosh), the **java** interpreter normally displays a window containing the information the program displays.

Method ***System.out.println*** *displays* (or *prints*) *a line* of text in the command window. When **System.out.println** completes its task, it automatically positions the *output cursor* (the location where the next character will be displayed) to the beginning of the next line in the command window. (This move of the cursor is similar to you pressing the *Enter* key when typing in a text editor—the cursor appears at the beginning of the next line in your file.)

The entire line, including **System.out.println**, its *argument* in the parentheses (the string) and the *semicolon* (**;**), is a *statement*. Every statement must end with a semicolon (also known as the *statement terminator*). When the statement on line 9 of our program executes, it displays the message **Welcome to Java Programming!** in the command window.

Common Programming Error 2.6

Omitting the semicolon at the end of a statement is a syntax error. A syntax error *occurs when the compiler cannot recognize a statement. The compiler normally issues an error message to help the programmer identify and fix the incorrect statement. Syntax errors are violations of the language rules. Syntax errors are also called* compile errors, compile-time errors *or* compilation errors, *because the compiler detects them during the compilation phase. You will be unable to execute your program until you correct all of the syntax errors in it.*

Testing and Debugging Tip 2.1

When the compiler reports a syntax error, the error may not be on the line number indicated by the error message. First, check the line for which the error was reported. If that line does not contain syntax errors, check the preceding several lines in the program.

Some programmers find it difficult when reading and/or writing a program to match the left and right braces (**{** and **}**) that delimit the body of a class definition or a method definition. For this reason, some programmers prefer to include a single-line comment after a closing right brace (**}**) that ends a method definition and after a closing right brace that ends a class definition. For example, line 11,

```
} // end method main
```

specifies the closing right brace (**}**) of method **main**, and line 13,

```
} // end class Welcome1
```

specifies the closing right brace (**}**) of class **Welcome1**. Each comment indicates the method or class that the right brace terminates. We use such comments through Chapter 6 to help beginning programmers determine where each program component terminates. After Chapter 6, we use such comments when pairs of braces contain many statements, which makes the closing braces difficult to identify.

Good Programming Practice 2.10

*Some programmers prefer to follow the closing right brace (**}**) of a method body or class definition with a single-line comment indicating the method or class definition to which the brace belongs. This comment improves program readability.*

2.2.1 Compiling and Executing your First Java Application

We are now ready to compile and execute our program. To compile the program, we open a command window, change to the directory where the program is stored and type

```
javac Welcome1.java
```

If the program contains no syntax errors, the preceding command creates a new file called **Welcome1.class** containing the Java bytecodes that represent our application. These bytecodes will be interpreted by the **java** interpreter when we tell it to execute the program, as shown in the Microsoft Windows 2000 **Command Prompt** of Fig. 2.2.

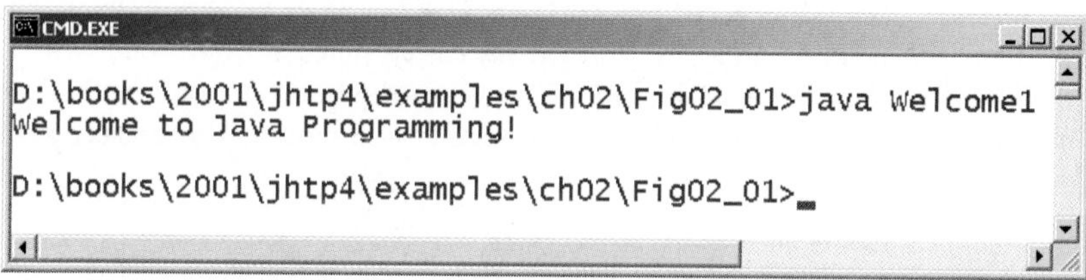

Fig. 2.2 Executing **Welcome1** in a Microsoft Windows 2000 **Command Prompt**.

In the command prompt of Figure 2.2, we typed

```
java Welcome1
```

to launch the **java** interpreter and indicate that it should load the "**.class**" file for class **Welcome1**. Note that the "**.class**" file-name extension is omitted from the preceding command; otherwise the interpreter will not execute the program. The interpreter automatically calls method **main**. Next, the statement on line 7 of **main** displays "**Welcome to Java Programming!**"

Testing and Debugging Tip 2.2

The Java compiler generates syntax error messages when the syntax of a program is incorrect. When you are learning how to program, sometimes it is helpful to "break" a working program so you can see the error messages produced by the compiler. Then, when you encounter that error message again, you will have an idea of the error's cause. Try removing a semicolon or curly brace from the program of Fig. 2.1, then recompile the program to see the error messages generated by the omission.

2.3 Modifying Our First Java Program

This section continues our introduction to Java programming with two examples that modify the example in Fig. 2.1 to print text on one line by using multiple statements and to print text on several lines by using a single statement.

2.3.1 Displaying a Single Line of Text with Multiple Statements

Welcome to Java Programming! can be displayed using several methods. Class **Welcome2**, shown in Fig. 2.3, uses two statements to produce the same output as that shown in Fig. 2.1.

Most of the program is identical to that of Fig. 2.1, so we discuss only the changes here. Line 2,

```
// Printing a line of text with multiple statements.
```

is a single-line comment stating the purpose of this program. Line 4 begins the definition of class **Welcome2**.

Lines 9–10 of method **main**,

```
System.out.print( "Welcome to " );
System.out.println( "Java Programming!" );
```

```
1  // Fig. 2.3: Welcome2.java
2  // Printing a line of text with multiple statements.
3
4  public class Welcome2 {
5
6     // main method begins execution of Java application
7     public static void main( String args[] )
8     {
9        System.out.print( "Welcome to " );
10       System.out.println( "Java Programming!" );
11
12    }  // end method main
13
14 }  // end class Welcome2
```

```
Welcome to Java Programming
```

Fig. 2.3 Printing a line of text with multiple statements.

display one line of text in the command window. The first statement uses **System.out**'s method **print** to display a string. The difference between **print** and **println** is that, after displaying its argument, **print** does not position the output cursor at the beginning of the next line in the command window; the next character the program displays in the command window will appear immediately after the last character that **print** displays. Thus, line 10 positions the first character in its argument, "**J**," immediately after the last character that line 9 displays (the space character at the end of the string on line 9). Each **print** or **println** statement resumes displaying characters from where the last **print** or **println** statement stopped displaying characters.

2.3.2 Displaying Multiple Lines of Text with a Single Statement

A single statement can display multiple lines by using *newline characters*. Newline characters are "special characters" that indicate to **System.out**'s **print** and **println** methods when they should position the output cursor to the beginning of the next line in the command window. Figure 2.4 outputs four lines of text, using newline characters to determine when to begin each new line.

Most of the program is identical to those of Fig. 2.1 and Fig. 2.3, so we discuss only the changes here. Line 2,

```
// Printing multiple lines of text with a single statement.
```

is a single-line comment stating the purpose of this program. Line 4 begins the definition of class **Welcome3**.

Line 9,

```
System.out.println( "Welcome\nto\nJava\nProgramming!" );
```

displays four separate lines of text in the command window. Normally, the characters in a string are displayed exactly as they appear in the double quotes. Notice, however, that the two characters **** and **n** are not printed on the screen. The *backslash* (****) is called an *escape character*. It indicates that a "special character" is to be output. When a backslash appears in a string of characters, Java combines the next character with the backslash to form an *escape sequence*. The escape sequence **\n** is the *newline character*. When a newline character appears in a string being output with **System.out**, the newline character causes the screen's output cursor to move to the beginning of the next line in the command window. Some other common escape sequences are listed in Fig. 2.5.

```
// Fig. 2.4: Welcome3.java
// Printing multiple lines of text with a single statement.

public class Welcome3 {

   // main method begins execution of Java application
   public static void main( String args[] )
   {
      System.out.println( "Welcome\nto\nJava\nProgramming!" );

   } // end method main

} // end class Welcome3
```

```
Welcome
to
Java
Programming!
```

Fig. 2.4 Printing multiple lines of text with a single statement.

Escape sequence	Description
`\n`	Newline. Position the screen cursor to the beginning of the next line.
`\t`	Horizontal tab. Move the screen cursor to the next tab stop.
`\r`	Carriage return. Position the screen cursor to the beginning of the current line; do not advance to the next line. Any characters output after the carriage return overwrite the characters previously output on that line.
`\\`	Backslash. Used to print a backslash character.
`\"`	Double quote. Used to print a double-quote character. For example, `System.out.println( "\"in quotes\"" );` displays `"in quotes"`

Fig. 2.5 Some common escape sequences.

2.4 Displaying Text in a Dialog Box

Although the first several programs presented in this chapter display output in the command window, many Java applications use windows or *dialog boxes* (also called *dialogs*) to display output. For example, World Wide Web browsers such as Netscape Navigator or Microsoft Internet Explorer display Web pages in their own windows. Email programs typically allow you to type and read messages in a window provided by the email program. Typically, dialog boxes are windows in which programs display important messages to the user of the program. Java's class ***JOptionPane*** provides prepackaged dialog boxes that enable programs to display messages to users. Figure 2.6 displays the same string as in Fig. 2.4 in a predefined dialog box known as a *message dialog*.

One of the great strengths of Java is its rich set of predefined classes that programmers can reuse rather than "reinventing the wheel." We use many of these classes throughout the book. Java's numerous predefined classes are grouped into categories of related classes called *packages*. The packages are referred to collectively as the *Java class library*, or the *Java applications programming interface* (*Java API*). The packages of the Java API are split into *core packages* and *extension packages*. The names of the packages begin with either "**java**" (core packages) or "**javax**" (extension packages). Many of the core and extension packages are included as part of the Java 2 Software Development Kit. We overview these included packages in Chapter 6. As Java continues to evolve, new packages are developed as extension packages. These extensions often can be downloaded from **java.sun.com** and used to enhance Java's capabilities. In this example, we use class **JOptionPane**, which Java defines for us in package ***javax.swing***.

Line 4,

```
// Java extension packages
```

is a single-line comment indicating the section of the program in which we specify **import** statements for classes in Java's extension packages. In every program that specifies **import** statements, we separate the import statements into the following groups: Java core packages (for package names starting with **java**), Java extension packages (for package names starting with **javax**) and Deitel packages (for our own packages defined later in the book).

Line 5,

```
import javax.swing.JOptionPane;  // import class JOptionPane
```

is an ***import*** statement. The compiler uses **import** statements to identify and load classes used in a Java program. When you use classes from the Java API, the compiler attempts to ensure that you use them correctly. The **import** statements help the compiler locate the classes you intend to use. For each new class we use from the Java API, we indicate the package in which you can find that class. This package information is important. It helps you locate descriptions of each package and class in the *Java API documentation*. A Web-based version of this documentation can be found at

java.sun.com/j2se/1.3/docs/api/index.html

Also, you can download this documentation to your own computer from

java.sun.com/j2se/1.3/docs.html

```
1  // Fig. 2.6: Welcome4.java
2  // Printing multiple lines in a dialog box
3
4  // Java extension packages
5  import javax.swing.JOptionPane;  // import class JOptionPane
6
7  public class Welcome4 {
8
9     // main method begins execution of Java application
10    public static void main( String args[] )
11    {
12       JOptionPane.showMessageDialog(
13          null, "Welcome\nto\nJava\nProgramming!" );
14
15       System.exit( 0 );  // terminate application
16
17    }  // end method main
18
19 }  // end class Welcome4
```

Message
Welcome
to
Java
Programming!
OK

Fig. 2.6 Displaying multiple lines in a dialog box.

We will provide an overview of the use of this documentation with the downloads and resources for *Java How to Program, Fourth Edition* on our Web site, **www.deitel.com**. Packages are discussed in detail in Chapter 8, Object-Based Programming.

Common Programming Error 2.7

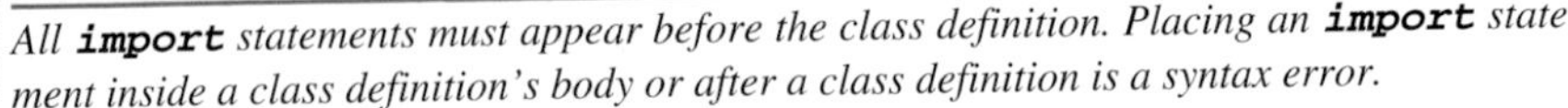

All ***import*** *statements must appear before the class definition. Placing an* ***import*** *statement inside a class definition's body or after a class definition is a syntax error.*

Line 5 tells the compiler to load the ***JOptionPane*** class from the ***javax.swing*** package. This package contains many classes that help Java programmers define *graphical user interfaces* (*GUIs*) for their application. *GUI components* facilitate data entry by the user of your program and formatting or presentation of data outputs to the user of your program. For example, Fig. 2.7 contains a Netscape Navigator window. In the window, there is a bar containing *menus* (**File**, **Edit**, **View**, etc.), called a *menu bar*. Below the menu bar is a set of *buttons* that each have a defined task in Netscape Navigator. Below the buttons there is a *text field* in which the user can type the name of the World Wide Web site to visit. The menus, buttons and text fields are part of Netscape Navigator's GUI. They enable you to interact with the Navigator program. Java contains classes that implement the GUI components described here and others that will be described in Chapter 12, Basic Graphical User Interface Components, and Chapter 13, Advanced Graphical User Interface Components.

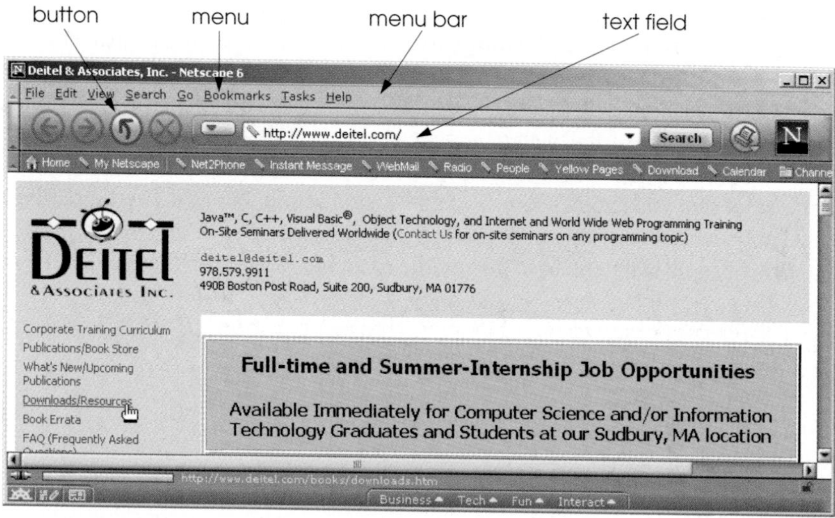

Fig. 2.7 A sample Netscape Navigator window with GUI components.

In method **main** of Fig. 2.6, lines 12–13,

```
JOptionPane.showMessageDialog(
   null, "Welcome\nto\nJava\nProgramming!" );
```

indicate a call to method ***showMessageDialog*** of class **JOptionPane**. The method requires two arguments. When a method requires multiple arguments, the arguments are separated with *commas* (**,**). Until we discuss **JOptionPane** in detail in Chapter 13, the first argument will always be the keyword ***null***. The second argument is the string to display. The first argument helps the Java application determine where to position the dialog box. When the first argument is **null**, the dialog box appears in the center of the computer screen. Most applications you use on your computer execute in their own window (e.g., email programs, Web browsers and word processors). When such an application displays a dialog box, it normally appears in the center of the application window, which is not necessarily the center of the screen. Later in this book, you will see more elaborate applications in which the first argument to method **showMessageDialog** will cause the dialog box to appear in the center of the application window, rather than the center of the screen.

Good Programming Practice 2.11

*Place a space after each comma (**,**) in an argument list, to make programs more readable.*

Method **JOptionPane.showMessageDialog** is a special method of class **JOptionPane** called a ***static*** *method*. Such methods are always called by using their class name followed by a dot operator (**.**) and the method name, as in

*ClassName***.***methodName***(** *arguments* **)**

Many of the predefined methods we introduce early in this book are **static** methods. We ask you to mimic this syntax for calling **static** methods until we discuss them in detail in Chapter 8, Object-Based Programming.

Executing the statement at lines 12–13 displays the dialog box in Fig. 2.8. The *title bar* of the dialog contains the string **Message** , to indicate that the dialog is presenting a message to the user. The dialog box automatically includes an **OK** button that allows the user to *dismiss (hide) the dialog* by pressing the button. This is accomplished by positioning the *mouse cursor* (also called the *mouse pointer*) over the **OK** button and clicking the left mouse button.

Remember that all statements in Java end with a semicolon (**;**). Therefore, lines 12–13 represent one statement. Java allows large statements to be split over many lines. However, you cannot split a statement in the middle of an identifier or in the middle of a string.

Common Programming Error 2.8

Splitting a statement in the middle of an identifier or a string is a syntax error.

Line 15,

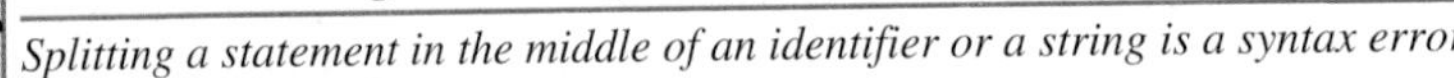

```
System.exit( 0 );   // terminate application
```

uses **static** method ***exit*** of class **System** to terminate the application. In any application that displays a graphical user interface, this line is required in order to terminate the application. Notice once again the syntax used to call the method—the class name (**System**), a dot (**.**) and the method name (**exit**). Remember that identifiers starting with capital letters normally represent class names. So, you can assume that **System** is a class. Class **System** is part of the package ***java.lang***. Notice that class **System** is not imported with an **import** statement at the beginning of the program. By default, package **java.lang** is imported in every Java program. Package **java.lang** is the only package in the Java API for which you are not required to provide an **import** statement.

The argument **0** to method **exit** indicates that the application has terminated successfully. (A nonzero value normally indicates that an error has occurred.) This value is passed to the command window that executed the program. The argument is useful if the program is executed from a *batch file* (on Windows 95/98/ME/NT/2000 systems) or a *shell script* (on UNIX/Linux systems). Batch files and shell scripts often execute several programs in sequence. When the first program ends, the next program begins execution automatically. It is possible to use the argument to method **exit** in a batch file or shell script to determine whether other programs should execute. For more information on batch files or shell scripts, see your operating system's documentation.

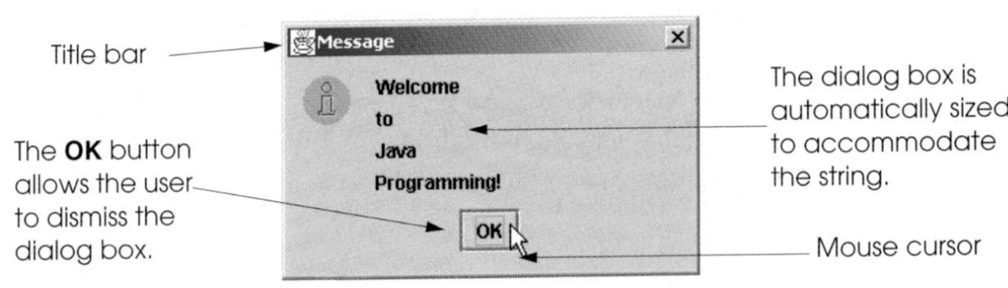

Fig. 2.8 Message dialog box.

Common Programming Error 2.9

Forgetting to call **System.exit** *in an application that displays a graphical user interface prevents the program from terminating properly. This omission normally results in the command window preventing you from typing any other commands. Chapter 14 discusses in more detail the reason that* **System.exit** *is required in GUI-based applications.*

2.5 Another Java Application: Adding Integers

Our next application inputs two *integers* (whole numbers, like –22, 7 and 1024) typed by a user at the keyboard, computes the sum of the values and displays the result. This program uses another predefined dialog box from class **JOptionPane** called an *input dialog* that allows the user to input a value for use in the program. The program also uses a message dialog to display the sum of the integers. Figure 2.9 shows the application and sample screen captures.

```
// Fig. 2.9: Addition.java
// An addition program.

// Java extension packages
import javax.swing.JOptionPane;   // import class JOptionPane

public class Addition {

   // main method begins execution of Java application
   public static void main( String args[] )
   {
      String firstNumber;      // first string entered by user
      String secondNumber;     // second string entered by user
      int number1;             // first number to add
      int number2;             // second number to add
      int sum;                 // sum of number1 and number2

      // read in first number from user as a String
      firstNumber =
         JOptionPane.showInputDialog( "Enter first integer" );

      // read in second number from user as a String
      secondNumber =
         JOptionPane.showInputDialog( "Enter second integer" );

      // convert numbers from type String to type int
      number1 = Integer.parseInt( firstNumber );
      number2 = Integer.parseInt( secondNumber );

      // add the numbers
      sum = number1 + number2;

      // display the results
      JOptionPane.showMessageDialog(
         null, "The sum is " + sum, "Results",
         JOptionPane.PLAIN_MESSAGE );
```

Fig. 2.9 An addition program "in action" (part 1 of 2).

```
37
38          System.exit( 0 );    // terminate application
39
40       }  // end method main
41
42    }  // end class Addition
```

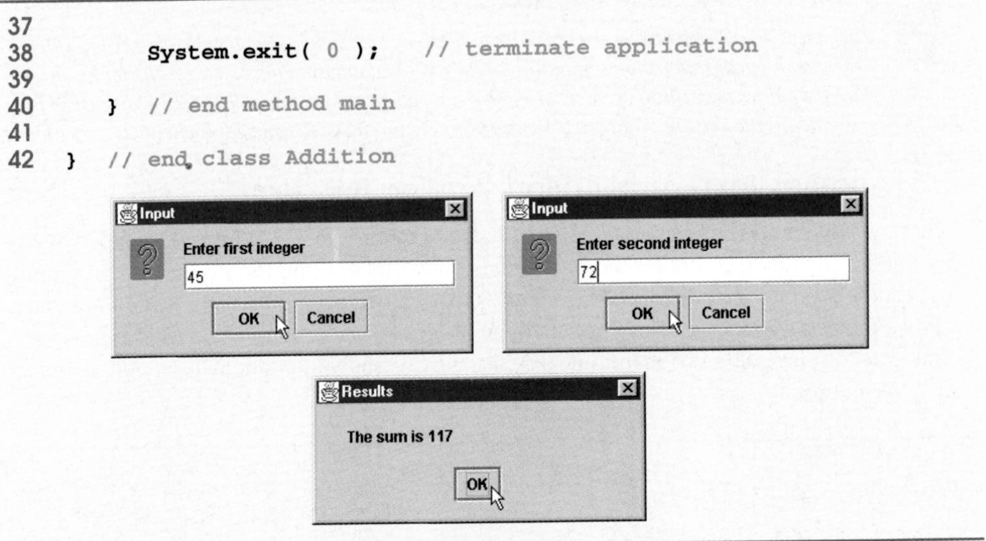

Fig. 2.9 An addition program "in action" (part 2 of 2).

Lines 1 and 2,

```
// Fig. 2.9: Addition.java
// An addition program.
```

are single-line comments stating the figure number, file name and purpose of the program.

Line 4,

```
// Java extension packages
```

is a single-line comment specifying that the next line imports a class from the Java extension packages.

Line 5,

```
import javax.swing.JOptionPane;   // import class JOptionPane
```

indicates that the compiler should load class **JOptionPane** for use in this application.

As stated earlier, every Java program consists of at least one class definition. Line 7,

```
public class Addition {
```

begins the definition of class **Addition**. The file name for this **public** class must be **Addition.java**.

Remember that all class definitions start with an opening left brace (at the end of line 7), **{**, and end with a closing right brace, **}** (in line 42).

As stated earlier, every application begins execution with method **main** (lines 10–40). The left brace (line 11) marks the beginning of **main**'s body and the corresponding right brace (line 36) marks the end of **main**'s body.

Lines 12–13,

```
String firstNumber;    // first string entered by user
String secondNumber;   // second string entered by user
```

are *declarations.* The words **firstNumber** and **secondNumber** are the names of *variables.* A variable is a location in the computer's memory where a value can be stored for use by a program. All variables must be declared with a name and a data type before they can be used in a program. This declaration specifies that the variables **firstNumber** and **secondNumber** are data of type ***String*** (located in package **java.lang**), which means that the variables will hold strings. A variable name can be any valid identifier. Like statements, declarations end with a semicolon (**;**). Notice the single-line comments at the end of each line. This use and placement of the comments is a common practice used by programmers to indicate the purpose of each variable in the program.

Good Programming Practice 2.12

Choosing meaningful variable names helps a program to be self-documenting *(i.e., it becomes easier to understand the program simply by reading it rather than by reading manuals or viewing an excessive number of comments).*

Good Programming Practice 2.13

By convention, variable-name identifiers begin with a lowercase letter. As with class names, every word in the name after the first word should begin with a capital letter. For example, identifier ***firstNumber*** *has a capital* ***N*** *in its second word,* ***Number****.*

Good Programming Practice 2.14

Some programmers prefer to declare each variable on a separate line. This format allows for easy insertion of a descriptive comment next to each declaration.

Software Engineering Observation 2.2

Java automatically imports classes from package ***java.lang****, such as class* ***String****. Therefore,* ***import*** *statements are not required for classes in package* ***java.lang****.*

Declarations can be split over several lines, with each variable in the declaration separated by a comma (i.e., a *comma-separated list* of variable names). Several variables of the same type may be declared in one declaration or in multiple declarations. Lines 12–13 can also be written as follows:

```
String firstNumber,    // first string entered by user
       secondNumber;   // second string entered by user
```

Lines 14–16,

```
int number1;           // first number to add
int number2;           // second number to add
int sum;               // sum of number1 and number2
```

declare that variables **number1**, **number2** and **sum** are data of type ***int***, which means that these variables will hold *integer* values (whole numbers such as 7, –11, 0 and 31,914). We will soon discuss the data types **float** and **double**, for specifying real numbers (numbers with decimal points, such as 3.4, 0.0 and –11.19), and variables of type **char**, for specifying character data. A **char** variable may hold only a single lowercase letter, a single uppercase letter, a single digit or a single special character (such as **x**, **$**, **7** and *****) and escape sequences (such as the newline character, **\n**). Java is capable of representing characters from many other spoken languages. Types such as **int**, **double** and **char** are often called *primitive data types,* or *built-in data types*. Primitive-type names are keywords;

thus, they must appear in all lowercase letters. Chapter 4 summarizes the eight primitive types (**boolean**, **char**, **byte**, **short**, **int**, **long**, **float** and **double**).

Line 18 is a single-line comment indicating that the next statement reads the first number from the user. Lines 19–20,

```
firstNumber =
   JOptionPane.showInputDialog( "Enter first integer" );
```

reads from the user a **String** representing the first of the two integers to add. Method **JOptionPane.showInputDialog** displays the input dialog in Fig. 2.10.

The argument to **showInputDialog** indicates what the user should type in the text field. This message is called a *prompt*, because it directs the user to take a specific action. The user types characters in the text field, and then clicks the **OK** button or presses the *Enter* key to return the string to the program. (If you type and nothing appears in the text field, position the mouse pointer in the text field and click the left mouse button to activate the text field.) Unfortunately, Java does not provide a simple form of input that is analogous to displaying output in the command window with **System.out**'s method **print** and **println**. For this reason, we normally receive input from a user through a GUI component (an input dialog box in this program).

Technically, the user can type anything in the text field of the input. Our program assumes that the user follows directions and enters a valid integer value. In this program, if the user either types a noninteger value or clicks the **Cancel** button in the input dialog, a runtime logic error will occur. Chapter 14, Exception Handling, discusses how to make your programs more robust by enabling them to handle such errors. This is also known as making your program *fault tolerant.*

The result of **JOptionPane** method **showInputDialog** (a **String** containing the characters typed by the user) is given to variable **firstNumber** by using the *assignment operator,* **=**. The statement (lines 19–20) is read as "**firstNumber** *gets* the value of **JOptionPane.showInputDialog("Enter first integer")**." The **=** operator is called a *binary operator*, because it has two *operands*: **firstNumber** and the result of the expression **JOptionPane.showInputDialog("Enter first integer")**. This whole statement is called an *assignment statement*, because it assigns a value to a variable. The expression to the right side of the assignment operator, **=**, is always evaluated first. In this case, the program calls method **showInputDialog**, and the value input by the user is assigned to **firstNumber**.

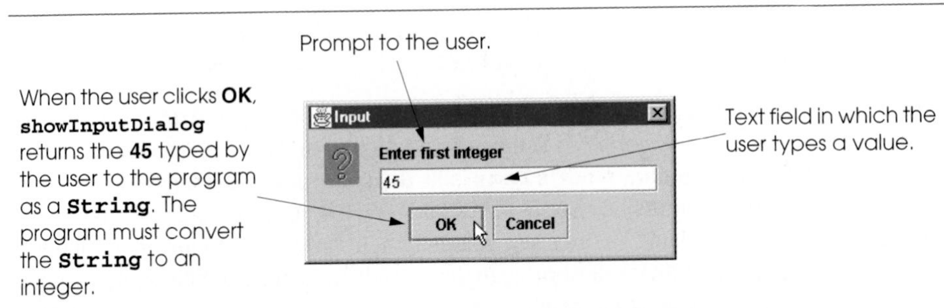
Prompt to the user.
When the user clicks OK, showInputDialog returns the 45 typed by the user to the program as a String. The program must convert the String to an integer.
Input
Enter first integer
45
OK
Cancel
Text field in which the user types a value.

Fig. 2.10 Input dialog box.

Line 22 is a single-line comment indicating that the next statement reads the second number from the user.

Lines 23–24,

```
secondNumber =
   JOptionPane.showInputDialog( "Enter second integer" );
```

display an input dialog in which the user types a **String** representing the second of the two integers to add.

Lines 27–28,

```
number1 = Integer.parseInt( firstNumber );
number2 = Integer.parseInt( secondNumber );
```

convert the two **String**s input by the user to **int** values that the program can use in a calculation. Method ***Integer.parseInt*** (a **static** method of class **Integer**) converts its **String** argument to an integer. Class **Integer** is defined in package **java.lang**. Line 27 assigns the **int** (integer) value that **Integer.parseInt** returns to variable **number1**. Line 28 assigns the **int** (integer) value that **Integer.parseInt** returns to variable **number2**.

Line 31,

```
sum = number1 + number2;
```

is an assignment statement that calculates the sum of the variables **number1** and **number2** and assigns the result to variable **sum** by using the assignment operator, **=**. The statement is read as, "**sum** *gets* the value of **number1 + number2**." Most calculations are performed in assignment statements. When the program encounters the addition operation, it uses the values stored in the variables **number1** and **number2** to perform the calculation. In the preceding statement, the addition operator is a binary operator: its two operands are **number1** and **number2**.

Good Programming Practice 2.15

Place spaces on either side of a binary operator. This format makes the operator stand out and makes the program more readable.

After the calculation has been performed, lines 34–36,

```
JOptionPane.showMessageDialog(
   null, "The sum is " + sum, "Results",
   JOptionPane.PLAIN_MESSAGE );
```

use method **JOptionPane.showMessageDialog** to display the result of the addition. This new version of **JOptionPane** method **showMessageDialog** requires four arguments. As in Fig. 2.6, the **null** first argument indicates that the message dialog will appear in the center of the screen. The second argument is the message to display. In this case, the second argument is the expression

```
"The sum is " + sum
```

which uses the operator **+** to "add" a **String** (the literal **"The sum is "**) and the value of variable **sum** (the **int** variable containing the result of the addition on line 31). Java has a version of the **+** operator for *string concatenation* that concatenates a **String** and a value of another data type (including another **String**); the result of this operation is a new (and normally longer) **String**. If we assume that **sum** contains the integer value **117**, the expression evaluates as follows:

1. Java determines that the two operands of the **+** operator (the string **"The sum is "** and the integer **sum**) are of different types and one of them is a **String**.
2. Java converts **sum** to a **String**.
3. Java appends the **String** representation of **sum** to the end of **"The sum is "**, resulting in the **String "The sum is 117"**.

Method **showMessageDialog** displays the resulting **String** in the dialog box. Note that the automatic conversion of integer **sum** occurs only because the addition operation concatenates the **String** literal **"The sum is "** and **sum**. Also, note that the space between **is** and **117** is part of the string **"The sum is "**. String concatenation is discussed in detail in Chapter 10, "Strings and Characters."

Common Programming Error 2.10

Confusing the **+** *operator used for string concatenation with the* **+** *operator used for addition can lead to strange results. For example, assuming that integer variable* **y** *has the value* **5**, *the expression* **"y + 2 = " + y + 2** *results in the string* **"y + 2 = 52"**, *not* **"y + 2 = 7"**, *because first the value of* **y** *is concatenated with the string* **"y + 2 = "**, *and then the value* **2** *is concatenated with the new larger string* **"y + 2 = 5"**. *The expression* **"y + 2 = " + (y + 2)** *produces the desired result.*

The third and fourth arguments of method **showMessageDialog** in Fig. 2.9 represent the string that should appear in the dialog box's *title bar* and the *dialog box type*, respectively. The fourth argument—**JOptionPane.PLAIN_MESSAGE**—is a value indicating the type of message dialog to display. This type of message dialog does not display an icon to the left of the message. Figure 2.11 illustrates the second and third arguments and shows that there is no icon in the window.

The message dialog types are shown in Fig. 2.12. All message dialog types except **PLAIN_MESSAGE** dialogs display an icon to the user indicating the type of message.

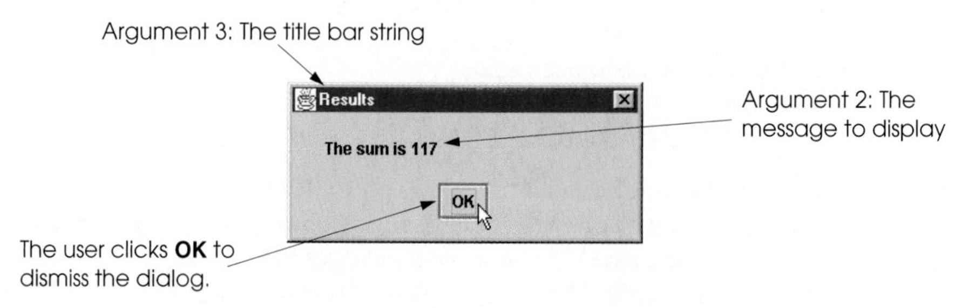

Fig. 2.11 Message dialog box customized with the four-argument version of method **showMessageDialog**.

Message dialog type	Icon	Description
JOptionPane.ERROR_MESSAGE		Displays a dialog that indicates an error to the user.
JOptionPane.INFORMATION_MESSAGE		Displays a dialog with an informational message to the user. The user can simply dismiss the dialog.
JOptionPane.WARNING_MESSAGE		Displays a dialog that warns the user of a potential problem.
JOptionPane.QUESTION_MESSAGE		Displays a dialog that poses a question to the user. This dialog normally requires a response, such as clicking on a **Yes** or a **No** button.
JOptionPane.PLAIN_MESSAGE	no icon	Displays a dialog that simply contains a message, with no icon.

Fig. 2.12 **JOptionPane** constants for message dialogs.

2.6 Memory Concepts

Variable names such as **number1**, **number2** and **sum** actually correspond to *locations* in the computer's memory. Every variable has a *name*, a *type*, a *size* and a *value*.

In the addition program of Fig. 2.9, when the statement

```
number1 = Integer.parseInt( firstNumber );
```

executes, the string previously typed by the user in the input dialog and stored in **firstNumber** is converted to an **int** and placed into a memory location to which the name **number1** has been assigned by the compiler. Suppose that the user enters the string **45** as the value for **firstNumber**. The program converts **firstNumber** to an **int**, and the computer places that integer value, **45**, into location **number1**, as shown in Fig. 2.13.

Whenever a value is placed in a memory location, the value replaces the previous value in that location. The previous value is destroyed (i.e., lost).

When the statement

```
number2 = Integer.parseInt( secondNumber );
```

executes, suppose that the user enters the string **72** as the value for **secondNumber**. The program converts **secondNumber** to an **int**, and the computer places that integer value, **72**, into location **number2**. The memory appears as shown in Fig. 2.14.

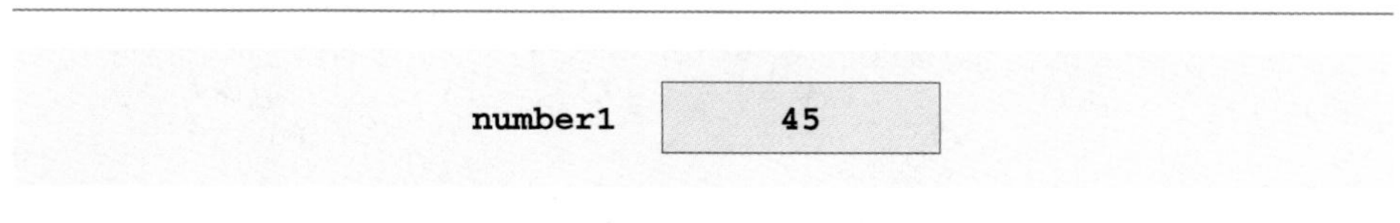

Fig. 2.13 Memory location showing the name and value of variable **number1**.

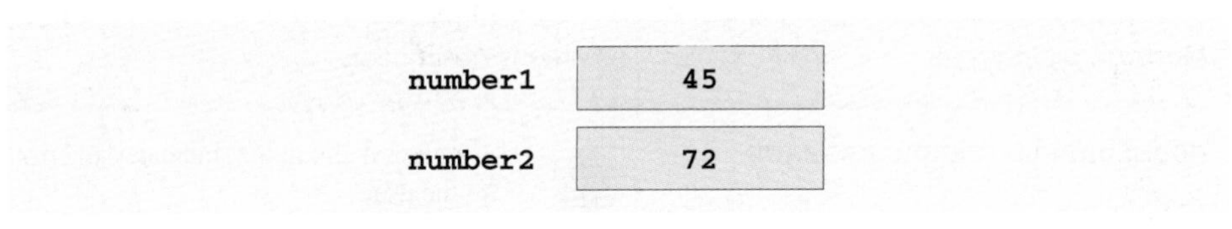

Fig. 2.14 Memory locations after storing values for **number1** and **number2**.

After the program of Fig. 2.9 obtains values for **number1** and **number2**, it adds the values and places the sum into variable **sum**. The statement

```
sum = number1 + number2;
```

performs the addition and also replaces **sum**'s previous value. After **sum** has been calculated, memory appears as shown in Fig. 2.15. Note that the values of **number1** and **number2** appear exactly as they did before they were used in the calculation of **sum**. These values were used, but not destroyed, as the computer performed the calculation. Thus, when a value is read from a memory location, the process is nondestructive.

2.7 Arithmetic

Most programs perform arithmetic calculations. The *arithmetic operators* are summarized in Fig. 2.16. Note the use of various special symbols not used in algebra. The *asterisk* (*****) indicates multiplication, and the *percent sign* (**%**) is the *modulus operator*, which is discussed shortly. The arithmetic operators in Fig. 2.16 are binary operators, because they each operate on two operands. For example, the expression **sum + value** contains the binary operator **+** and the two operands **sum** and **value**.

Integer division yields an integer quotient; for example, the expression **7 / 4** evaluates to **1**, and the expression **17 / 5** evaluates to **3**. Note that any fractional part in integer division is simply discarded (i.e., truncated)—no rounding occurs. Java provides the modulus operator, **%**, that yields the remainder after integer division. The expression **x % y** yields the remainder after **x** is divided by **y**. Thus, **7 % 4** yields **3**, and **17 % 5** yields **2**. This operator is most commonly used with integer operands, but also can be used with other arithmetic types. In later chapters, we consider many interesting applications of the modulus operator, such as determining if one number is a multiple of another. There is no arithmetic operator for exponentiation in Java. Chapter 5 shows how to perform exponentiation in Java. [*Note*: The modulus operator can be used with both integer and floating-point numbers.]

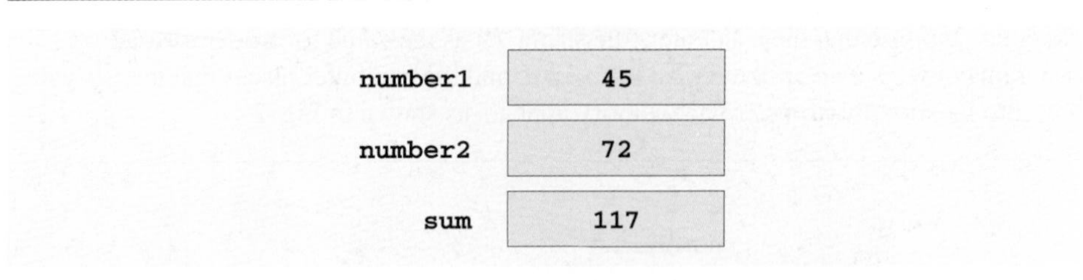

Fig. 2.15 Memory locations after calculating the **sum** of **number1** and **number2**.

Java operation	Arithmetic operator	Algebraic expression	Java expression
Addition	+	$f+7$	`f + 7`
Subtraction	-	$p-c$	`p - c`
Multiplication	*	bm	`b * m`
Division	/	x / y or $\frac{x}{y}$ or $x \div y$	`x / y`
Modulus	%	$r \bmod s$	`r % s`

Fig. 2.16 Arithmetic operators.

Arithmetic expressions in Java must be written in *straight-line form* to facilitate entering programs into the computer. Thus, expressions such as "**a** divided by **b**" must be written as **a / b**, so that all constants, variables and operators appear in a straight line. The following algebraic notation is generally not acceptable to compilers:

$$\frac{a}{b}$$

Parentheses are used in Java expressions in the same manner as in algebraic expressions. For example, to multiply **a** times the quantity **b + c**, we write

```
a * ( b + c )
```

Java applies the operators in arithmetic expressions in a precise sequence determined by the following *rules of operator precedence*, which are generally the same as those followed in algebra:

1. Operators in expressions contained within pairs of parentheses are evaluated first. Thus, *parentheses may be used to force the order of evaluation to occur in any sequence desired by the programmer.* Parentheses are at the highest level of precedence. In cases of *nested* or *embedded* parentheses, the operators in the innermost pair of parentheses are applied first.
2. Multiplication, division and modulus operations are applied next. If an expression contains several multiplication, division or modulus operations, the operators are applied from left to right. Multiplication, division and modulus operators have the same level of precedence.
3. Addition and subtraction operations are applied last. If an expression contains several addition and subtraction operations, the operators are applied from left to right. Addition and subtraction operators have the same level of precedence.

The rules of operator precedence enable Java to apply operators in the correct order. When we say that operators are applied from left to right, we are referring to the *associativity* of the operators. We will see that some operators associate from right to left. Figure 2.17 summarizes these rules of operator precedence. This table will be expanded as additional Java operators are introduced. A complete precedence chart is included in Appendix C.

Operator(s)	Operation(s)	Order of evaluation (precedence)
`( )`	Parentheses	Evaluated first. If the parentheses are nested, the expression in the innermost pair is evaluated first. If there are several pairs of parentheses on the same level (i.e., not nested), they are evaluated left to right.
`*`, `/` and `%`	Multiplication Division Modulus	Evaluated second. If there are several of this type of operator, they are evaluated from left to right.
`+` or `-`	Addition Subtraction	Evaluated last. If there are several of this type of operator, they are evaluated from left to right.

Fig. 2.17 Precedence of arithmetic operators.

Now, let us consider several expressions in light of the rules of operator precedence. Each example lists an algebraic expression and its Java equivalent.

The following is an example of an arithmetic mean (average) of five terms:

Algebra: $$m = \frac{a+b+c+d+e}{5}$$

Java:
```
m = ( a + b + c + d + e ) / 5;
```

The parentheses are required, because division has higher precedence than that of addition. The entire quantity **(a + b + c + d + e)** is to be divided by **5**. If the parentheses are erroneously omitted, we obtain **a + b + c + d + e / 5**, which evaluates as

$$a + b + c + d + \frac{e}{5}$$

The following is an example of the equation of a straight line:

Algebra: $y = mx + b$

Java:
```
y = m * x + b;
```

No parentheses are required. The multiplication operator is applied first, because multiplication has a higher precedence than that of addition. The assignment occurs last, because it has a lower precedence than that of multiplication and division.

The following example contains modulus (**%**), multiplication, division, addition and subtraction operations:

Algebra: $z = pr\%q + w/x - y$

Java:
```
z  =  p  *  r  %  q  +  w  /  x  -  y;
```

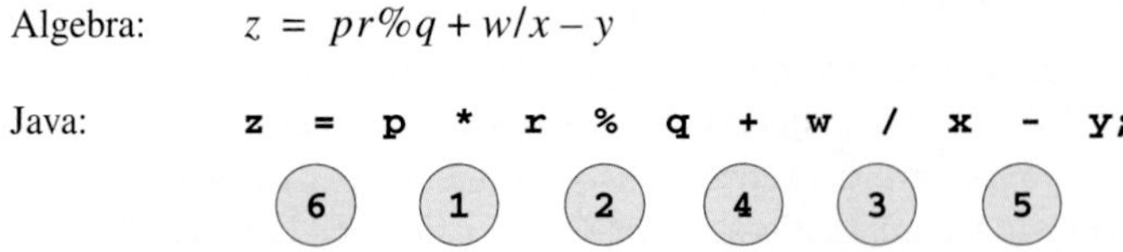

The circled numbers under the statement indicate the order in which Java applies the operators. The multiplication, modulus and division operations are evaluated first in left-to-right order (i.e., they associate from left to right), because they have higher precedence than that of addition and subtraction. The addition and subtraction operations are evaluated next. These operations are also applied from left to right.

Not all expressions with several pairs of parentheses contain nested parentheses. For example, the expression

```
a * ( b + c ) + c * ( d + e )
```

does not contain nested parentheses. Rather, these parentheses are on the same level.

To develop a better understanding of the rules of operator precedence, consider the evaluation of a second-degree polynomial ($y = ax^2 + bx + c$):

```
y  =  a  *  x  *  x  +  b  *  x  +  c;
   6     1     2     4     3     5
```

The circled numbers under the preceding statement indicate the order in which Java applies the operators. There is no arithmetic operator for exponentiation in Java; x^2 is represented as **`x * x`**.

Suppose that **`a`**, **`b`**, **`c`** and **`x`** are initialized as follows: **`a = 2`**, **`b = 3`**, **`c = 7`** and **`x = 5`**. Figure 2.18 illustrates the order in which the operators are applied in the preceding second-degree polynomial.

As in algebra, it is acceptable to place unnecessary parentheses in an expression to make the expression clearer. Such unnecessary parentheses are also called *redundant parentheses*. For example, the preceding assignment statement might be parenthesized as follows:

```
y = ( a * x * x ) + ( b * x ) + c;
```

Good Programming Practice 2.16

Using parentheses for complex arithmetic expressions, even when the parentheses are not necessary, can make the arithmetic expressions easier to read.

2.8 Decision Making: Equality and Relational Operators

This section introduces a simple version of Java's **`if`** *structure* that allows a program to make a decision based on the truth or falsity of some *condition*. If the condition is met (i.e., the condition is *true*), the statement in the body of the **`if`** structure is executed. If the condition is not met (i.e., the condition is *false*), the body statement does not execute. We will see an example shortly.

Conditions in **`if`** structures can be formed by using the *equality operators* and *relational operators* summarized in Fig. 2.19. The relational operators all have the same level of precedence and associate from left to right. The equality operators both have the same level of precedence, which is lower than the precedence of the relational operators. The equality operators also associate from left to right.

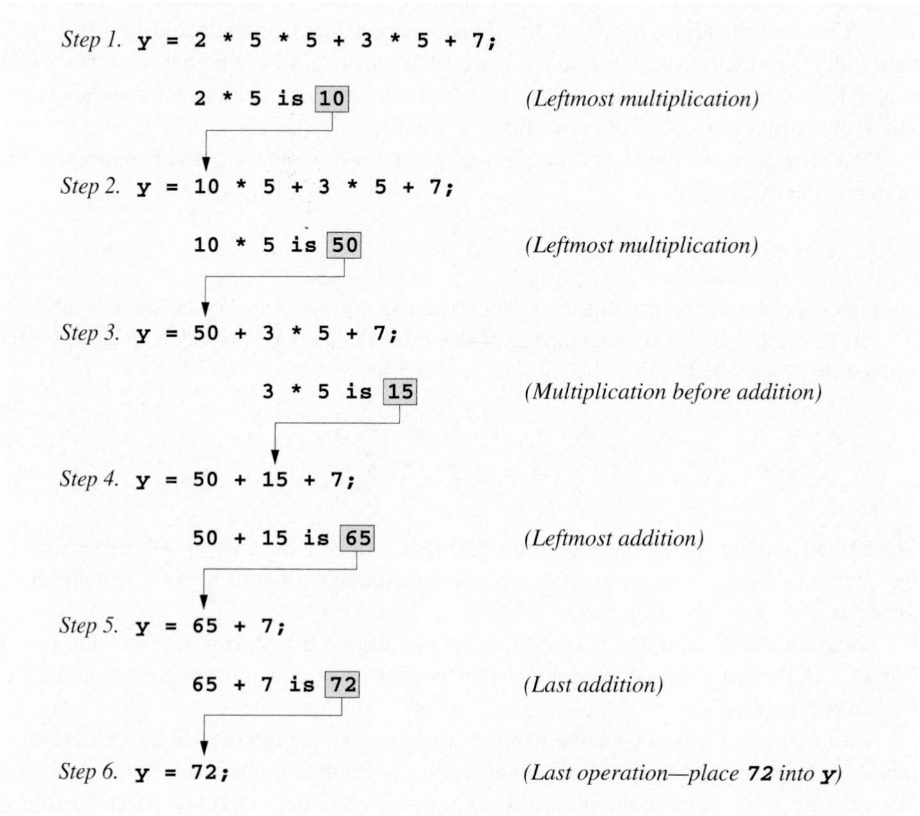
Step 1. y = 2 * 5 * 5 + 3 * 5 + 7;
2 * 5 is 10
(Leftmost multiplication)
Step 2. y = 10 * 5 + 3 * 5 + 7;
10 * 5 is 50
(Leftmost multiplication)
Step 3. y = 50 + 3 * 5 + 7;
3 * 5 is 15
(Multiplication before addition)
Step 4. y = 50 + 15 + 7;
50 + 15 is 65
(Leftmost addition)
Step 5. y = 65 + 7;
65 + 7 is 72
(Last addition)
Step 6. y = 72;
(Last operation—place 72 into y)

Fig. 2.18 Order in which a second-degree polynomial is evaluated.

Standard algebraic equality or relational operator	Java equality or relational operator	Example of Java condition	Meaning of Java condition
Equality operators			
=	`==`	`x == y`	**x** is equal to **y**
≠	`!=`	`x != y`	**x** is not equal to **y**
Relational operators			
>	`>`	`x > y`	**x** is greater than **y**
<	`<`	`x < y`	**x** is less than **y**
≥	`>=`	`x >= y`	**x** is greater than or equal to **y**
≤	`<=`	`x <= y`	**x** is less than or equal to **y**

Fig. 2.19 Equality and relational operators.

Common Programming Error 2.11

It is a syntax error if the operators **==**, **!=**, **>=** *and* **<=** *contain spaces between their symbols, as in* **= =**, **! =**, **> =** *and* **< =**, *respectively.*

Common Programming Error 2.12

Reversing the operators **!=**, **>=** *and* **<=**, *as in* **=!**, **=>** *and* **=<**, *is a syntax error.*

Common Programming Error 2.13

Confusing the equality operator, **==**, *with the assignment operator,* **=**, *can be a logic error or a syntax error. The equality operator should be read as "is equal to," and the assignment operator should be read as "gets" or "gets the value of." Some people prefer to read the equality operator as "double equals" or "equals equals."*

The next example uses six **if** structures to compare two numbers input into text fields by the user. If the condition in any of these **if** statements is true, the assignment statement associated with that **if** structure executes. The user inputs two values through input dialogs. Next, the program converts the input values to integers and stores them in variables **number1** and **number2**. Then, the program compares the numbers and displays the results of the comparisons in an information dialog. The program and sample outputs are shown in Fig. 2.20.

```
// Fig. 2.20: Comparison.java
// Compare integers using if structures, relational operators
// and equality operators.

// Java extension packages
import javax.swing.JOptionPane;

public class Comparison {

   // main method begins execution of Java application
   public static void main( String args[] )
   {
      String firstNumber;   // first string entered by user
      String secondNumber;  // second string entered by user
      String result;        // a string containing the output
      int number1;          // first number to compare
      int number2;          // second number to compare

      // read first number from user as a string
      firstNumber =
         JOptionPane.showInputDialog( "Enter first integer:" );

      // read second number from user as a string
      secondNumber =
         JOptionPane.showInputDialog( "Enter second integer:" );

```

Fig. 2.20 Using equality and relational operators (part 1 of 3).

```
      // convert numbers from type String to type int
      number1 = Integer.parseInt( firstNumber );
      number2 = Integer.parseInt( secondNumber );

      // initialize result to empty String
      result = "";

      if ( number1 == number2 )
         result = number1 + " == " + number2;

      if ( number1 != number2 )
         result = number1 + " != " + number2;

      if ( number1 < number2 )
         result = result + "\n" + number1 + " < " + number2;

      if ( number1 > number2 )
         result = result + "\n" + number1 + " > " + number2;

      if ( number1 <= number2 )
         result = result + "\n" + number1 + " <= " + number2;

      if ( number1 >= number2 )
         result = result + "\n" + number1 + " >= " + number2;

      // Display results
      JOptionPane.showMessageDialog(
         null, result, "Comparison Results",
         JOptionPane.INFORMATION_MESSAGE );

      System.exit( 0 );  // terminate application

   }  // end method main

}  // end class Comparison
```

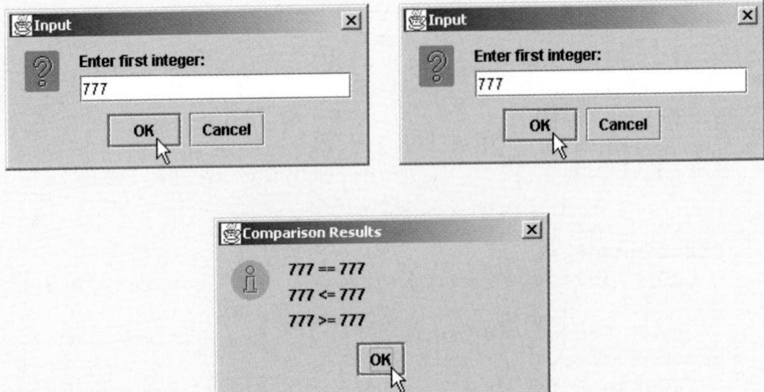

Fig. 2.20 Using equality and relational operators (part 2 of 3).

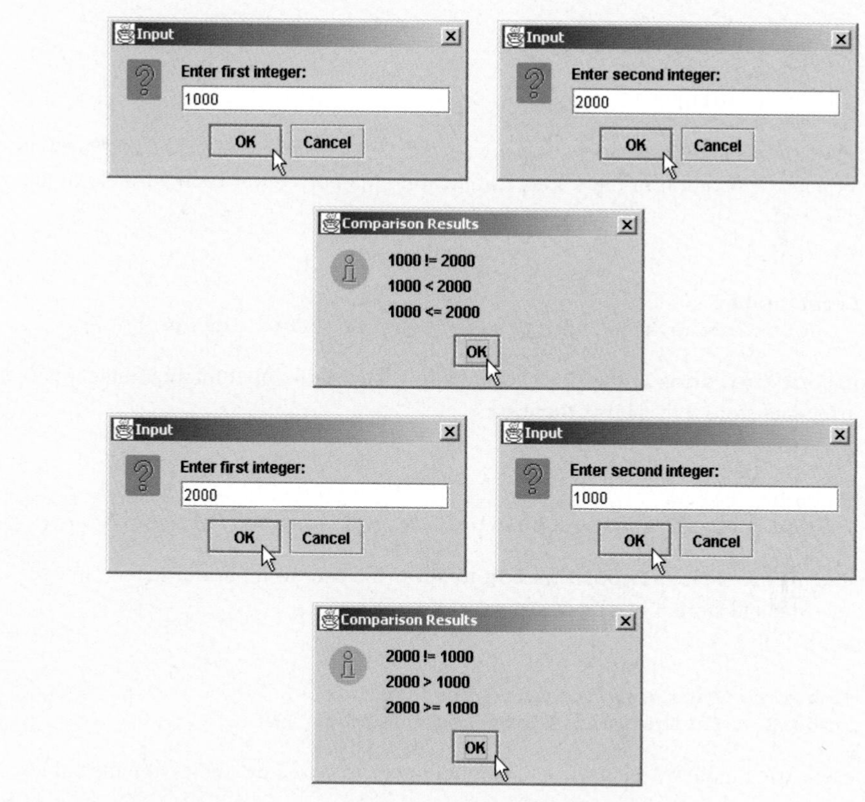

Fig. 2.20 Using equality and relational operators (part 3 of 3).

The definition of application class **Comparison** begins at line 8,

```
public class Comparison {
```

As discussed previously, method **main** (lines 11–59) begins the execution of every Java application.

Lines 13–17,

```
String firstNumber;   // first string entered by user
String secondNumber;  // second string entered by user
String result;        // a string containing the output
int number1;          // first number to compare
int number2;          // second number to compare
```

declare the variables used in method **main**. Note that there are three variables of type **String** and two variables of type **int**. Remember that variables of the same type may be declared in one declaration or in multiple declarations. If more than one name is declared in a declaration, the names are separated by commas (**,**), as in

```
String firstNumber, secondNumber, result;
```

or as in

```
String firstNumber,
       secondNumber,
       result;
```

This is set of names known as a *comma-separated list*. Once again, notice the comment at the end of each declaration in lines 13–17, indicating the purpose of each variable in the program.

Lines 20–21,

```
firstNumber =
   JOptionPane.showInputDialog( "Enter first integer:" );
```

use **JOptionPane.showInputDialog** to allow the user to input the first integer value as a string and store it in **firstNumber**.

Lines 24–25,

```
secondNumber =
   JOptionPane.showInputDialog( "Enter second integer:" );
```

use **JOptionPane.showInputDialog** to allow the user to input the second integer value as a string and store it in **secondNumber**.

Lines 28–29,

```
number1 = Integer.parseInt( firstNumber );
number2 = Integer.parseInt( secondNumber );
```

convert each string input by the user in the input dialogs to type **int** and assign the values to int variables **number1** and **number2**.

Line 32,

```
result = "";
```

assigns to **result** the *empty string*—a string containing no characters. Every variable declared in a method (such as **main**) must be *initialized* (given a value) before it can be used in an expression. Because we do not yet know what the final **result** string will be, we assign to **result** the empty string as a temporary initial value.

Common Programming Error 2.14

Not initializing a variable defined in a method before that variable is used in the method's body is a syntax error.

Lines 34–35,

```
if ( number1 == number2 )
   result = result + number1 + " == " + number2;
```

define an ***if*** *structure* that compares the values of the variables **number1** and **number2** to determine if they are equal. The **if** structure always begins with keyword **if**, followed by a condition in parentheses. The **if** structure expects one statement in its body. The indentation shown here is not required, but it improves the readability of the program by emphasizing that the statement in line 35 is part of the **if** structure that begins on line 34.

Good Programming Practice 2.17

Indent the statement i7n the body of an **if** *structure to make the body of the structure stand out and to enhance program readability.*

Good Programming Practice 2.18

Place only one statement per line in a program. This format enhances program readability

In the preceding **if** structure, if the values of variables **number1** and **number2** are equal, line 35 assigns to **result** the value of **result + number1 + " == " + number2**. As discussed in Fig. 2.9, the **+** operator in this expression performs string concatenation. For this discussion, we assume that each of the variables **number1** and **number2** has the value **123**. First, the expression converts **number1**'s value to a string and appends it to **result** (which currently contains the empty string) to produce the string **"123"**. Next, the expression appends **" == "** to **"123"** to produce the string **"123 == "**. Finally, the expression appends **number2** to **"123 == "** to produce the string **"123 == 123"**. The **String result** becomes longer as the program proceeds through the **if** structures and performs more concatenations. For example, given the value **123** for both **number1** and **number2** in this discussion, the **if** conditions at lines 46–47 (**<=**) and 49–50 (**>=**) are also true. So, the program displays the **result**

```
123 == 123
123 <= 123
123 >= 123
```

in a message dialog.

Common Programming Error 2.15

Replacing operator **==** *in the condition of an* **if** *structure, such as* **if (x == 1)**, *with operator* **=**, *as in* **if (x = 1)**, *is a syntax error.*

Common Programming Error 2.16

Forgetting the left and right parentheses for the condition in an **if** *structure is a syntax error. The parentheses are required.*

Notice that there is no semicolon (**;**) at the end of the first line of each **if** structure. Such a semicolon would result in a logic error at execution time. For example,

```
if ( number1 == number2 );   // logic error
   result = result + number1 + " == " + number2;
```

would actually be interpreted by Java as

```
if ( number1 == number2 )
   ;

result = result + number1 + " == " + number2;
```

where the semicolon on the line by itself—called the *empty statement*—is the statement to execute if the condition in the **if** structure is true. When the empty statement executes, no task is performed in the program. The program then continues with the assignment statement, which executes regardless of whether the condition is true or false.

Common Programming Error 2.17

Placing a semicolon immediately after the right parenthesis of the condition in an **`if`** *structure is normally a logic error. The semicolon will cause the body of the* **`if`** *structure to be empty, so the* **`if`** *structure itself will perform no action, regardless of whether its condition is true. Worse yet, the intended body statement of the* **`if`** *structure will now become a statement in sequence with the* **`if`** *structure and will always be executed.*

Notice the use of spacing in Fig. 2.20. Remember that white-space characters, such as tabs, newlines and spaces, are normally ignored by the compiler. So, statements may be split over several lines and may be spaced according to the programmer's preferences without affecting the meaning of a program. It is incorrect to split identifiers and string literals. Ideally, statements should be kept small, but it is not always possible to do so.

Good Programming Practice 2.19

A lengthy statement may be spread over several lines. If a single statement must be split across lines, choose breaking points that make sense, such as after a comma in a comma-separated list, or after an operator in a lengthy expression. If a statement is split across two or more lines, indent all subsequent lines until the end of the statement.

The chart in Fig. 2.21 shows the precedence of the operators introduced in this chapter. The operators are shown from top to bottom in decreasing order of precedence. Notice that all of these operators, with the exception of the assignment operator, **`=`**, associate from left to right. Addition is left associative, so an expression like **`x + y + z`** is evaluated as if it had been written as **`( x + y ) + z`**. The assignment operator, **`=`**, associates from right to left, so an expression like **`x = y = 0`** is evaluated as if it had been written as **`x = ( y = 0 )`**, which, as we will soon see, first assigns the value **`0`** to variable **`y`** and then assigns the result of that assignment, **`0`**, to **`x`**.

Good Programming Practice 2.20

Refer to the operator precedence chart (see the complete chart in Appendix C) when writing expressions containing many operators. Confirm that the operations in the expression are performed in the order you expect. If you are uncertain about the order of evaluation in a complex expression, use parentheses to force the order, exactly as you would do in algebraic expressions. Be sure to observe that some operators, such as assignment, **`=`**, *associate from right to left rather than from left to right.*

Operators	Associativity	Type
`()`	left to right	parentheses
`*  /  %`	left to right	multiplicative
`+  -`	left to right	additive
`<  <=  >  >=`	left to right	relational
`==  !=`	left to right	equality
`=`	right to left	assignment

Fig. 2.21 Precedence and associativity of the operators discussed so far.

We have introduced many important features of Java in this chapter, including displaying data on the screen, inputting data from the keyboard, performing calculations and making decisions. We should note that these applications are meant to introduce the reader to basic programming concepts. As you will see in later chapters, more substantial Java applications contain just a few lines of code in method **main** that creates the objects that perform the work of the application. In Chapter 3, we demonstrate many similar techniques as we introduce Java applet programming. In Chapter 4, we build on the techniques of Chapter 2 and Chapter 3 as we introduce *structured programming*. You will become more familiar with indentation techniques. We will study how to specify and vary the order in which statements are executed; this order is called *flow of control.*

2.9 (Optional Case Study) Thinking About Objects: Examining the Problem Statement

Now we begin our optional, object-oriented design and implementation case study. The "Thinking About Objects" sections at the ends of this and the next several chapters will ease you into object orientation by examining an elevator simulation case study. This case study will provide you with a substantial, carefully paced, complete design and implementation experience. In Chapters 3 through 13, Chapter 15 and Chapter 22, we will perform the various steps of an object-oriented design (OOD) process using the UML while relating to the object-oriented concepts discussed in the chapters. In Appendices G, H and I, we will implement the elevator simulator using the techniques of object-oriented programming (OOP) in Java. We present the complete case-study solution. This is not an exercise; rather, it is an end-to-end learning experience that concludes with a detailed walkthrough of the actual Java code. We have provided this case study so that you can become accustomed to the kinds of substantial problems encountered in industry. We hope you enjoy this learning experience.

Problem Statement

A company intends to build a two-floor office building and equip it with an elevator. The company wants you to develop an object-oriented *software-simulator application* in Java that models the operation of the elevator to determine whether it will meet the company's needs. The company wants the simulation to contain an elevator system. The application consists of three parts. The first and most substantial part is the simulator, which *models* the operation of the elevator system. The second part is the display of this model on screen so that the user may *view* it graphically. The final part is the *graphical user interface*, or *GUI*, that allows the user to *control* the simulation. Our design and implementation will follow the so-called *Model-View-Controller architecture* we will learn about in Section 13.17.

The elevator system consists of an elevator shaft and an elevator car. In our simulation, we model people who ride the elevator car (referred to as "the elevator") to travel between the floors in the elevator shaft, as shown in Fig. 2.22, Fig. 2.23 and Fig. 2.24.

The elevator contains a door (called the "elevator door") that opens upon the elevator's arrival at a floor and closes upon the elevator's departure from that floor. The elevator door is closed during the trips between floors to prevent the passenger from being injured by brushing against the wall of the elevator shaft. In addition, the elevator shaft connects to a door on each floor (referred to as the two "floor doors"), so people cannot fall down the shaft when the elevator is not at a floor. Note that we do not display the floor doors in the figures, because they would obscure the inside of the elevator (we use a mesh door to represent the elevator door because mesh allows us to see inside the elevator). The floor door opens concurrently with the elevator door, so it appears as if both doors open at the same time. A person sees only one door, depending on that person's location. When the person is inside the elevator, the person sees the elevator door and can exit the elevator when this door opens; when the person is outside the elevator, the person sees the floor door and can enter the elevator when that door opens[1].

The elevator starts on the first floor with all the doors closed. To conserve energy, the elevator moves only when necessary. For simplicity, the elevator and floors each have a capacity of only one person.[2]

The user of our application should, at any time, be able to create a unique person in the simulation and situate that person on either the first or second floor (Fig. 2.22[3]). When created, the person walks across the floor to the elevator. The person then presses a button on the floor next to the elevator shaft (referred to as a "floor button"). When pressed, that floor button illuminates, then requests the elevator. When summoned, the elevator travels to the person's floor. If the elevator is already on that person' floor, the elevator does not travel. Upon arrival, the elevator resets the button inside the elevator (called the "elevator button"), sounds the bell inside the elevator, then opens the elevator door (which opens the floor door on that floor). The elevator then signals the elevator shaft of the arrival. The elevator shaft, upon receiving this message, resets the floor button and illuminates the light on that floor.

Occasionally, a person requests the elevator when it is moving. If the request was generated at the floor from which the elevator just departed, the elevator must "remember" to revisit that floor after carrying the current passenger to the other floor.

When the floor door opens, the person enters the elevator after the elevator passenger (if there is one) exits. If a person neither enters nor requests the elevator, the elevator closes its door and remains on that floor until the next person presses a floor button to summon the elevator. When a person enters the elevator, that person presses the elevator button, which also illuminates when pressed. The elevator closes its door (which also closes the floor door on that floor) and moves to the opposite floor. The elevator takes five seconds to travel between floors. When the elevator arrives at the destination floor, the elevator door opens (along with the floor door on that floor) and the person exits the elevator.

The application user introduces a person onto the first or second floor by pressing the **First Floor** button or the **Second Floor** button, respectively. When the user presses the **First Floor** button, a person should be created (by the elevator simulation) and positioned on the first floor of the building. When the user presses the **Second Floor** button, a person should be created and positioned on the second floor. Over time, the user can create any number of people in the simulation, but the user cannot create a new person on an occupied floor. For example, Fig. 2.22 shows that the **First Floor** button is disabled to prevent the user from creating more than one person on the first floor. Figure 2.23 shows that this button is reenabled when the person rides the elevator.

---

1. Most people do not consider this when riding an elevator—they really think of one "elevator door," when in reality, there is a door in the elevator and a door on the floor, and these doors open and close in tandem.
2. After you have studied this case study, you may want to modify it to allow more than one person to ride the elevator at once and more than one person to wait on each floor at once.
3. To create portions of the graphics for the elevator simulation, we used images that Microsoft provides free for download at `msdn.microsoft.com/downloads/default.asp`. We created other graphics with Paint Shop Pro™ from Jasc® Software.

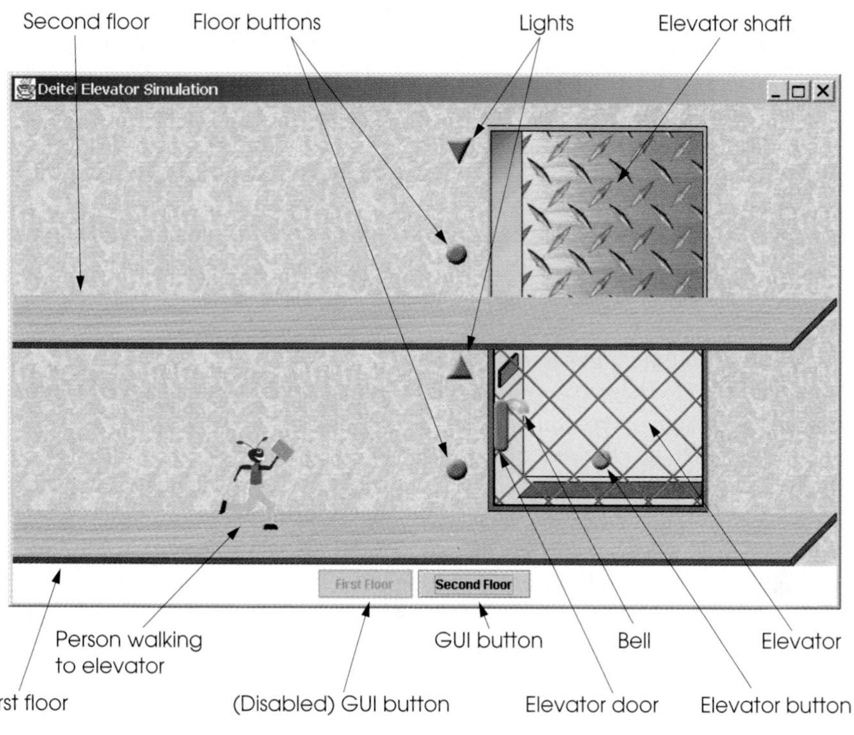

Fig. 2.22 Person moving towards elevator on the first floor.

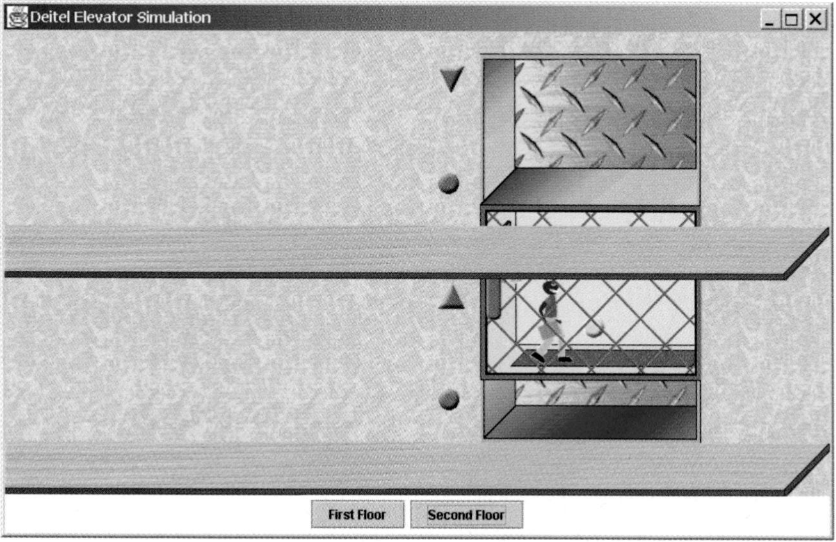

Fig. 2.23 Person riding the elevator to the second floor.

The company requests that we display the results of the simulation graphically, as shown in Fig. 2.22, Fig. 2.23 and Fig. 2.24. At various points in time, the screen should display a person walking to the elevator, pressing a button and entering, riding and exiting the elevator. The display also should also show the elevator moving, the doors opening, the lights turning on and off, the buttons illuminating when they are pressed and the buttons darkening when they are reset.

The company requests that audio be integrated into the simulation. For example, as a person walks, the application user should hear the footsteps. Each time a floor or elevator button is pressed or reset, the user should hear a click. The bell should ring upon the elevator's arrival, and doors should creak when they open or close. Lastly, "elevator music" should play as the elevator travels between floors.

Analyzing and Designing the Elevator System

We must analyze and design our system before we implement it as Java code. The output of the analysis phase is intended to specify clearly in a *requirements document* what the system is supposed to do. The requirements document for this case study is essentially the description of what the elevator simulator is supposed to do—presented informally in the last few pages. The output of the design phase should specify clearly *how* the system should be constructed to do what is needed. In the next several "Thinking About Objects" sections, we perform the steps of an object-oriented design (OOD) process on the elevator system. The UML is designed for use with any OOD process—many such processes exist. One popular method is the Rational Unified Process™ developed by Rational Software Corporation. For this case study, we present our own simplified design process. For many of our readers, this will be their first OOD/UML experience.

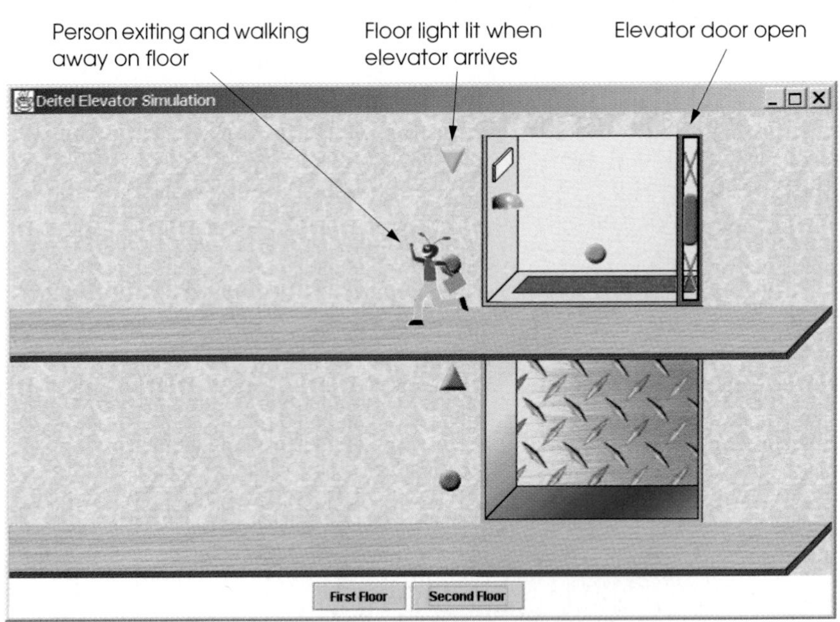

Fig. 2.24 Person walking away from elevator.

We now begin the design phase of our elevator system, which will span Chapters 2 through 13, Chapter 15 and Chapter 22, in which we gradually develop the design. Appendices G, H and I present the complete Java implementation.

A system is a set of components that interact to solve a problem. In our case study, the elevator-simulator application represents the system. A system may contain "subsystems," which are "systems within a system." Subsystems simplify the design process by managing subsets of system responsibilities. System designers may allocate system responsibilities among the subsystems, design the subsystems, then integrate the subsystems with the overall system. Our elevator-simulation system contains three subsystems, which are defined in the problem statement:

1. the simulator model (which represents the operation of the elevator system),
2. the display of this model on screen (so that the user may view it graphically), and
3. the graphical user interface (that allows the user to control the simulation).

We develop the simulator model gradually through Chapter 15 and present the implemented model in Appendix H. We discuss the GUI components allowing the user to control the model in Chapter 12 and introduce how the subsystems work together to form the system in Chapter 13. Finally, we introduce how to display the simulator model on the screen in Chapter 22 and conclude the display in Appendix I.

System *structure* describes the system's objects and their inter-relationships. System *behavior* describes how the system changes as its objects interact with each other. Every system has both structure and behavior—we must design both. However, there are several distinct *types* of system structures and behaviors. For example, the interaction among the objects in the system differs from the interaction between the user and the system, yet both are interactions that constitute the system behavior.

The UML specifies nine types of diagrams for modeling systems. Each diagram models a distinct characteristic of a system's structure or behavior—the first four diagrams relate to system structure; the remaining five diagrams relate to system behavior:

1. Class diagram
2. Object diagram
3. Component diagram
4. Deployment diagram
5. Activity diagram
6. Statechart diagram
7. Collaboration diagram
8. Sequence diagram
9. Use-Case diagram

Class diagrams, which we explain in "Thinking About Objects" Section 3.8, model the classes, or "building blocks," used to build a system. Each entity in the problem statement is a candidate to be a class in the system (i.e., **Person**, **Elevator**, **Floor**, etc.).

Object diagrams, which we also explain in Section 3.8, model a "snapshot" of the system by modeling a system's objects and their relationships at a specific point in time. Each object represents an instance of a class from the class diagram (e.g., the elevator object is an instance of class **Elevator**), and there may be several objects created from one class (e.g., both the first floor button object and the second floor button object are created from class **FloorButton**).

Component diagrams, presented in Section 13.17, model the *components*—resources (which include graphics and audio) and *packages* (which are groups of classes)—that make up the system.

Deployment diagrams model the runtime requirements of the system (such as the computer or computers on which the system will reside), memory requirements for the system, or other devices the system requires during execution. We do not present deployment diagrams in this case study, because we are not designing a "hardware-specific" system—our simulation requires only one computer containing the Java 2 runtime environment on which to run.

Statechart diagrams, which we introduce in Section 5.11, model *how* an object changes *state* (i.e., the condition of an object at a specific time). When an object changes state, that object may behave differently in the system.

Activity diagrams, which we also introduce in Section 5.11, model an object's *activity*—that object's workflow during program execution. An activity diagram is a flowchart that models the actions the object will perform and in what order.

Both *collaboration diagrams* and *sequence diagrams* model the interactions among the objects in a system. Collaboration diagrams emphasize what interactions occur, whereas sequence diagrams emphasize when interactions occur. We introduce these diagrams in Section 7.10 and Section 15.12, respectively.

Use-Case diagrams represent the interaction between the user and our system (i.e., all actions the user may perform on the system). We introduce use-case diagrams in Section 12.16, where we discuss user-interface issues.

In "Thinking About Objects" Section 3.17, we continue designing our elevator system by identifying the classes in the problem statement. We accomplish this by extracting all the nouns and noun clauses from the problem statement. Using these classes, we develop a class diagram that models the structure of our elevator simulation system.

Internet and World-Wide-Web Resources

Listed below are URLs and books on object-oriented design with the UML—you may find these references helpful as you study the remaining sections of our case-study presentation.

www.omg.com/technology/uml/index.htm

This is the UML resourse page from the Object Management Group, which provides specifications for various object-oriented technologies, such as the UML.

www.smartdraw.com/drawing/software/indexUML.asp

This site shows how to draw UML diagrams without the use of modeling tools.

www.rational.com/uml/index.jsp

This is the UML resource page for Rational Software Corporation—the company that created the UML.

microgold.com/Stage/UML_FAQ.html

This site provides the UML FAQ maintained by Rational Software.

www.softdocwiz.com/Dictionary.htm

This site hosts the Unified Modeling Language Dictionary, which lists and defines all terms used in the UML.

`www.embarcadero.com`
This site provides a free 30-day license to download a trial-version of Describe™— the new UML modeling tool from Embarcadero Technologies®.

`www.ics.uci.edu/pub/arch/uml/uml_books_and_tools.html`
This site lists books on the UML and software tools that use the UML, such as Rational Rose™ and Embarcadero Describe™.

`www.ootips.org/ood-principles.html`
This site provides answers to the question "what makes good OOD?"

`wdvl.internet.com/Authoring/Scripting/Tutorial/oo_design.html`
This site introduces OOD and provides OOD resources.

Bibliography

Booch, G., *Object-Oriented Analysis and Design with Applications.* Addison-Wesley. Massachusetts; 1994.

Folwer, M., and Scott, K., *UML Distilled Second Edition; A Brief Guide to the Standard Object Modeling Language.* Addison-Wesley. Massachusetts; 1999.

Larman, C., *Applying UML and Patterns; An Introduction to Object-Oriented Analysis and Design.* Prentice Hall. New Jersey; 1998.

Page-Jones, M., *Fundamentals of Object-Oriented Design in UML.* Addison-Wesley. Massachusetts; 1999.

Rumbaugh, J.; Jacobson, I.; and Booch, G., The *Unified Modeling Language Reference Manual.* Addison-Wesley. Massachusetts; 1999.

Rumbaugh, J.; Jacobson, I.; and Booch, G., *The Unified Modeling Language User Guide.* Addison-Wesley. Massachusetts; 1999.

Rumbaugh, J.; Jacobson, I.; and Booch, G., *The Complete UML Training Course.* Prentice Hall. New Jersey; 2000.

Rumbaugh, J.; Jacobson, I.; and Booch, G., *The Unified Software Development Process.* Addison-Wesley. Massachusetts; 1999.

Rosenburg, D., and Scott, K., *Applying Use Case Driven Object Modeling with UML: An Annotated e-Commerce Example.* Addison-Wesley. Massachusetts; 2001.

Schach, S., *Object-Oriented and Classical Software Engineering.* McGraw Hill. New York; 2001.

Schneider, G., and Winters, J., *Applying Use Cases.* Addison-Wesley. Massachusetts; 1998.

Scott, K., *UML Explained.* Addison-Wesley. Massachusetts; 2001.

Stevens, P., and Pooley, R.J., *Using UML: Software Engineering with Objects and Components Revised Edition.* Addison-Wesley; 2000.

SUMMARY

- An application is a program that executes using the **`java`** interpreter.
- A comment that begins with **`//`** is called a single-line comment. Programmers insert comments to document programs and improve program readability.
- A string of characters contained between double quotation marks is called a string, a character string, a message or a string literal.
- Blank lines, space characters, newline characters and tab characters are known as white-space characters. White-space characters outside strings are ignored by the compiler.

- Keyword **class** introduces a class definition and is immediately followed by the class name.
- Keywords (or reserved words) are reserved for use by Java. Keywords must appear in all lowercase letters.
- By convention, all class names in Java begin with a capital letter. If a class name contains more than one word, the first letter of each word should be capitalized.
- An identifier is a series of characters consisting of letters, digits, underscores (_) and dollar signs (**$**) that does not begin with a digit, does not contain any spaces and is not a keyword.
- Java is case sensitive—that is, uppercase and lowercase letters are different.
- A left brace, **{**, begins the body of every class definition. A corresponding right brace, **}**, ends each class definition.
- Java applications begin executing at method **main**.
- Methods are able to perform tasks and return information when they complete their tasks.
- The first line of method **main** must be defined as

```
public static void main( String args[] )
```

- A left brace, **{**, begins the body of a method definition. A corresponding right brace, **}**, ends the method definition's body.
- **System.out** is known as the standard output object. **System.out** allows Java applications to display strings and other types of information in the command window from which the Java application executes.
- The escape sequence **\n** indicates a newline character. Other escape sequences include **\t** (tab), **\r** (carriage return), **** (backslash) and **\"** (double quote).
- Method **println** of the **System.out** object displays (or prints) a line of information in the command window. When **println** completes its task, it automatically positions the output cursor to the beginning of the next line in the command window.
- Every statement must end with a semicolon (also known as the statement terminator).
- The difference between **System.out**'s **print** and **println** methods is that **print** does not position to the beginning of the next line in the command window when it finishes displaying its argument. The next character displayed in the command window appears immediately after the last character displayed with **print**.
- Java contains many predefined classes that are grouped into categories of related classes called packages. The packages are referred to collectively as the Java class library or the Java applications programming interface (Java API).
- Class **JOptionPane** is defined in package **javax.swing**. Class **JOptionPane** contains methods that display dialog boxes.
- The compiler uses **import** statements to locate classes required to compile a Java program.
- The **javax.swing** package contains many classes that help define a graphical user interface (GUI) for an application. GUI components facilitate data entry by the user of a program and data outputs by a program.
- Method **showMessageDialog** of class **JOptionPane** displays a dialog box containing a message to the user.
- A **static** method is called by following its class name by a dot (**.**) and the name of the method.
- Method **exit** of class **System** terminates an application. Class **System** is in package **java.lang**. All Java programs import package **java.lang** by default.

- A variable is a location in the computer's memory where a value can be stored for use by a program. The name of a variable is any valid identifier.
- All variables must be declared with a name and a data type before they can be used in a program.
- Declarations end with a semicolon (**;**) and can be split over several lines, with each variable in the declaration separated by a comma (forming a comma-separated list of variable names).
- Variables of type **int** hold integer values (whole numbers such as 7, –11, 0 and 31,914).
- Types such as **int**, **float**, **double** and **char** are primitive data types. Names of primitive data types are keywords of the Java programming language.
- A prompt directs the user to take a specific action.
- A variable is assigned a value by using an assignment statement, which uses the assignment operator, **=**. The **=** operator is called a binary operator, because it has two operands.
- Method **Integer.parseInt** (a **static** method of class **Integer**) converts its **String** argument to an **int** value.
- Java has a version of the **+** operator for string concatenation that enables a string and a value of another data type (including another string) to be concatenated.
- Every variable has a name, a type, a size and a value.
- When a value is placed in a memory location, the value replaces the value previously in that location. When a value is read out of a memory location, the variable's value remains unchanged.
- The arithmetic operators are binary operators, because they operate on two operands.
- Integer division yields an integer result.
- Arithmetic expressions in Java must be written in straight-line form to facilitate entering programs into the computer.
- Operators in arithmetic expressions are applied in a precise sequence determined by the rules of operator precedence.
- Parentheses may be used to force the order of evaluation of operators.
- When we say that operators are applied from left to right, we are referring to the associativity of the operators. Some operators associate from right to left.
- Java's **if** structure allows a program to make a decision based on the truth or falsity of a condition. If the condition is met (i.e., the condition is true), the statement in the body of the **if** structure executes. If the condition is not met (i.e., the condition is false), the body statement does not execute.
- Conditions in **if** structures can be formed by using the equality operators and relational operators.
- The empty string is a string containing no characters.
- Every variable declared in a method must be initialized before it can be used in an expression.

TERMINOLOGY

addition operator (**+**)
applet
application
argument to a method
arithmetic operators
assignment operator (**=**)
assignment statement
associativity of operators
backslash (****) escape character
binary operator
body of a class definition
body of a method definition
braces (**{** and **}**)
case sensitive
character string
class
class definition
.class file extension
class keyword
class name

command tool
command window
comma-separated list
comment (//)
compilation error
compile error
compiler
compile-time error
condition
decision
declaration
dialog
dialog box
division operator (/)
document a program
empty string ("")
equality operators
    == "is equal to"
    != "is not equal to"
escape sequence
exit method of System
false
graphical user interface (GUI)
identifier
if structure
import statement
input dialog
int primitive type
integer (int)
Integer class
integer division
interpreter
Java
Java 2 Software Development Kit (J2SDK)
Java applications programming interface (API)
Java class library
Java documentation comment
.java file extension
java interpreter
java.lang package
javax.swing package
JOptionPane class
JOptionPane.ERROR_MESSAGE
JOptionPane.INFORMATION_MESSAGE
JOptionPane.PLAIN_MESSAGE
JOptionPane.QUESTION_MESSAGE
JOptionPane.WARNING_MESSAGE
left brace, {, begins the body of a class
left brace, {, begins the body of a method
literal
main method
memory
memory location
message
message dialog
method
Microsoft Internet Explorer browser
modulus operator (%)
mouse cursor
mouse pointer
MS-DOS Prompt
multiple-line comment
multiplication operator (*)
nested parentheses
Netscape Navigator browser
newline character (\n)
object
operand
operator
package
parentheses ()
parseInt method of class Integer
precedence
primitive data type
programmer-defined class
prompt
public keyword
relational operators
    < "is less than"
    <= "is less than or equal to"
    > "is greater than
    >= "is greater than or equal to"
reserved words
right brace, }, ends the body of a class
right brace, }, ends the body of a method
right-to-left associativity
rules of operator precedence
semicolon (;) statement terminator
shell tool
showInputDialog method of JOptionPane
showMessageDialog method of
    JOptionPane
single-line comment
standard output object
statement
statement terminator (;)
static method
straight-line form
string
String class

string concatenation
string concatenation operator (**+**)
subtraction operator (**-**)
syntax error
System class
System.out object
System.out.print method
System.out.println method
title bar of a dialog
true
user-defined class
variable
variable name
variable value
void keyword
white-space characters

SELF-REVIEW EXERCISES

2.1 Fill in the blanks in each of the following statements:

a) The __________ begins the body of every method, and the __________ ends the body of every method.
b) Every statement ends with a __________.
c) The __________ structure is used to make decisions.
d) __________ begins a single-line comment.
e) __________, __________, __________ and __________ are called white-space characters.
f) Class __________ contains methods that display message dialogs and input dialogs.
g) __________ are reserved for use by Java.
h) Java applications begin execution at method __________.
i) Methods __________ and __________ display information in the command window.
j) A __________ method is always called using its class name followed by a dot (**.**) and its method name.

2.2 State whether each of the following is *true* or *false*. If *false*, explain why.

a) Comments cause the computer to print the text after the **//** on the screen when the program is executed.
b) All variables must be given a type when they are declared.
c) Java considers the variables **number** and **NuMbEr** to be identical.
d) The modulus operator (**%**) can be used only with integer operands.
e) The arithmetic operators *****, **/**, **%**, **+** and **-** all have the same level of precedence.
f) Method **Integer.parseInt** converts an integer to a **String**.

2.3 Write Java statements to accomplish each of the following tasks:

a) Declare variables **c**, **thisIsAVariable**, **q76354** and **number** to be of type **int**.
b) Display a dialog asking the user to enter an integer.
c) Convert a **String** to an integer, and store the converted value in integer variable **age**. Assume that the **String** is stored in **value**.
d) If the variable **number** is not equal to **7**, display **"The variable number is not equal to 7"** in a message dialog. [*Hint*: Use the version of the message dialog that requires two arguments.]
e) Print the message **"This is a Java program"** on one line in the command window.
f) Print the message **"This is a Java program"** on two lines in the command window; the first line should end with **Java**. Use only one statement.

2.4 Identify and correct the errors in each of the following statements:

a)
```
if ( c < 7 );
   JOptionPane.showMessageDialog( null,
      "c is less than 7" );
```
b)
```
if ( c => 7 )
   JOptionPane.showMessageDialog( null,
      "c is equal to or greater than 7" );
```

2.5 Write a statement (or comment) to accomplish each of the following tasks:

a) State that a program will calculate the product of three integers.
b) Declare the variables **x**, **y**, **z** and **result** to be of type **int**.
c) Declare the variables **xVal**, **yVal** and **zVal** to be of type **String**.
d) Prompt the user to enter the first value, read the value from the user and store it in the variable **xVal**.
e) Prompt the user to enter the second value, read the value from the user and store it in the variable **yVal**.
f) Prompt the user to enter the third value, read the value from the user and store it in the variable **zVal**.
g) Convert **xVal** to an **int**, and store the result in the variable **x**.
h) Convert **yVal** to an **int**, and store the result in the variable **y**.
i) Convert **zVal** to an **int**, and store the result in the variable **z**.
j) Compute the product of the three integers contained in variables **x**, **y** and **z**, and assign the result to the variable **result**.
k) Display a dialog containing the message **"The product is "** followed by the value of the variable **result**.
l) Return a value from the program indicating that the program terminated successfully.

2.6 Using the statements you wrote in Exercise 2.5, write a complete program that calculates and prints the product of three integers.

ANSWERS TO SELF-REVIEW EXERCISES

2.1 a) left brace (**{**), right brace (**}**). b) semicolon (**;**). c) **if**. d) **//**. e) Blank lines, space characters, newline characters and tab characters. f) **JOptionPane**. g) Keywords. h) **main**. i) **System.out.print** and **System.out.println**. j) **static**.

2.2 a) False. Comments do not cause any action to be performed when the program is executed. They are used to document programs and improve their readability.
b) True.
c) False. Java is case sensitive, so these variables are distinct.
d) False. The modulus operator can also be used with noninteger operands in Java.
e) False. The operators *****, **/** and **%** are on the same level of precedence, and the operators **+** and **-** are on a lower level of precedence.
f) False. **Integer.parseInt** method converts a **String** to an integer (**int**) value.

2.3 a) `int c, thisIsAVariable, q76354, number;`
b) `value = JOptionPane.showInputDialog( "Enter an integer" );`
c) `age = Integer.parseInt( value );`
d)
```
if ( number != 7 )
   JOptionPane.showMessageDialog( null,
      "The variable number is not equal to 7" );
```
e) `System.out.println( "This is a Java program" );`
f) `System.out.println( "This is a Java\nprogram" );`

2.4 The solutions to Self-Review Exercise 2.4 are as follows:

a) Error: Semicolon after the right parenthesis of the condition in the **if** statement.
Correction: Remove the semicolon after the right parenthesis. [*Note*: The result of this error is that the output statement will be executedregardless of whether the condition in the **if** statement is true. The semicolon after the right parenthesis is considered an empty statement—a statement that does nothing. We will learn more about the empty statement in the next chapter.]

b) Error: The relational operator `=>` is incorrect.
Correction: Change `=>` to `>=`.

2.5

a)
```
// Calculate the product of three integers
```
b)
```
int x, y, z, result;
```
c)
```
String xVal, yVal, zVal;
```
d)
```
xVal = JOptionPane.showInputDialog(
    "Enter first integer:" );
```
e)
```
yVal = JOptionPane.showInputDialog(
    "Enter second integer:" );
```
f)
```
zVal = JOptionPane.showInputDialog(
    "Enter third integer:" );
```
g)
```
x = Integer.parseInt( xVal );
```
h)
```
y = Integer.parseInt( yVal );
```
i)
```
z = Integer.parseInt( zVal );
```
j)
```
result = x * y * z;
```
k)
```
JOptionPane.showMessageDialog( null,
    "The product is " + result );
```
l)
```
System.exit( 0 );
```

2.6 The solution to Exercise 2.6 is as follows:

```
// Calculate the product of three integers

// Java extension packages
import javax.swing.JOptionPane;

public class Product {

   public static void main( String args[] )
   {
      int x, y, z, result;
      String xVal, yVal, zVal;

      xVal = JOptionPane.showInputDialog(
         "Enter first integer:" );
      yVal = JOptionPane.showInputDialog(
         "Enter second integer:" );
      zVal = JOptionPane.showInputDialog(
         "Enter third integer:" );

      x = Integer.parseInt( xVal );
      y = Integer.parseInt( yVal );
      z = Integer.parseInt( zVal );

      result = x * y * z;
      JOptionPane.showMessageDialog( null,
         "The product is " + result );

      System.exit( 0 );
   }
}
```

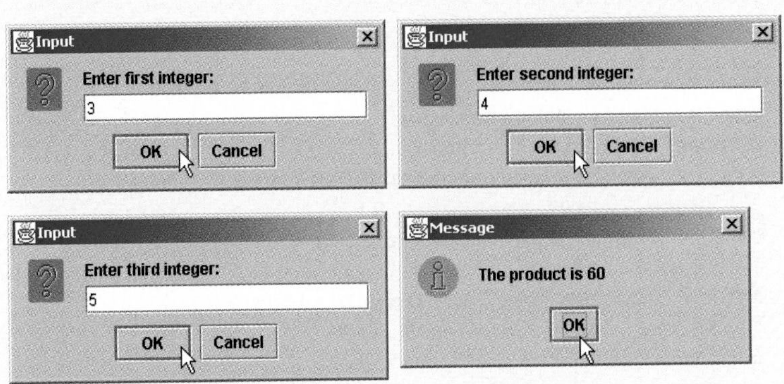

EXERCISES

2.7 Fill in the blanks in each of the following statements:

a) _________ are used to document a program and improve its readability.

b) An input dialog capable of receiving input from the user is displayed with method _________ of class _________.

c) A decision can be made in a Java program with an _________.

d) Calculations are normally performed by _________ statements.

e) A dialog capable of displaying a message to the user is displayed with method _________ of class _________.

2.8 Write Java statements that accomplish each of the following tasks:

a) Display the message **"Enter two numbers"**, using class **JOptionPane**.

b) Assign the product of variables **b** and **c** to variable **a**.

c) State that a program performs a sample payroll calculation (i.e., use text that helps to document a program).

2.9 State whether each of the following is *true* or *false*. If *false*, explain why.

a) Java operators are evaluated from left to right.

b) The following are all valid variable names: **_under_bar_**, **m928134**, **t5**, **j7**, **her_sales$**, **his_$account_total**, **a**, **b$**, **c**, **z**, **z2**.

c) A valid Java arithmetic expression with no parentheses is evaluated from left to right.

d) The following are all invalid variable names: **3g**, **87**, **67h2**, **h22**, **2h**.

2.10 Fill in the blanks in each of the following statements:

a) What arithmetic operations have the same precedence as multiplication? _________.

b) When parentheses are nested, which set of parentheses is evaluated first in an arithmetic expression? _________.

c) A location in the computer's memory that may contain different values at various times throughout the execution of a program is called a _________.

2.11 What displays in the message dialog when each of the given Java statements is performed? Assume that **x = 2** and **y = 3**.

a)
```
JOptionPane.showMessageDialog( null, "x = " + x );
```
b)
```
JOptionPane.showMessageDialog( null,
   "The value of x + x is " + ( x + x ) );
```
c)
```
JOptionPane.showMessageDialog( null, "x =" );
```
d)
```
JOptionPane.showMessageDialog( null,
   ( x + y ) + " = " + ( y + x ) );
```

2.12 Which of the following Java statements contain variables whose values are changed or replaced?

a) `p = i + j + k + 7;`

b) `JOptionPane.showMessageDialog( null,`
`"variables whose values are destroyed" );`

c) `JOptionPane.showMessageDialog( null, "a = 5" );`

d) `stringVal = JOptionPane.showInputDialog( "Enter string: );`

2.13 Given that $y = ax^3 + 7$, which of the following are correct Java statements for this equation?

a) `y = a * x * x * x + 7;`

b) `y = a * x * x * ( x + 7 );`

c) `y = ( a * x ) * x * ( x + 7 );`

d) `y = ( a * x ) * x * x + 7;`

e) `y = a * ( x * x * x ) + 7;`

f) `y = a * x * ( x * x + 7 );`

2.14 State the order of evaluation of the operators in each of the following Java statements, and show the value of **x** after each statement is performed:

a) `x = 7 + 3 * 6 / 2 - 1;`

b) `x = 2 % 2 + 2 * 2 - 2 / 2;`

c) `x = ( 3 * 9 * ( 3 + ( 9 * 3 / ( 3 ) ) ) );`

2.15 Write an application that displays the numbers 1 to 4 on the same line, with each pair of adjacent numbers separated by one space. Write the program using the following methods:

a) Using one **System.out** statement.

b) Using four **System.out** statements.

2.16 Write an application that asks the user to enter two numbers, obtains the numbers from the user and prints the sum, product, difference and quotient (division) of the numbers. Use the techniques shown in Fig. 2.9.

2.17 Write an application that asks the user to enter two integers, obtains the numbers from the user and displays the larger number followed by the words "**is larger**" in an information message dialog. If the numbers are equal, print the message "**These numbers are equal.**" Use the techniques shown in Fig. 2.20.

2.18 Write an application that inputs three integers from the user and displays the sum, average, product, smallest and largest of the numbers in an information message dialog. Use the GUI techniques shown in Fig. 2.20. [*Note*: The calculation of the average in this exercise should result in an integer representation of the average. So, if the sum of the values is 7, the average should be 2, not 2.3333….]

2.19 Write an application that inputs from the user the radius of a circle and prints the circle's diameter, circumference and area. Use the value 3.14159 for π. Use the GUI techniques shown in Fig. 2.9. [*Note*: You may also use the predefined constant **Math.PI** for the value of π. This constant is more precise than the value 3.14159. Class **Math** is defined in the **java.lang** package, so you do not need to **import** it.] Use the following formulas (*r* is the radius):

$$diameter = 2r$$
$$circumference = 2\pi r$$
$$area = \pi r^2$$

2.20 Write an application that displays in the command window a box, an oval, an arrow and a diamond using asterisks (*****), as follows:

```
*********     ***       *        *
*       *   *     *    ***      * *
*       *  *       *  *****    *   *
*       *  *       *    *     *     *
*       *  *       *    *    *       *
*       *  *       *    *     *     *
*       *  *       *    *      *   *
*       *   *     *     *       * *
*********     ***       *        *
```

2.21 Modify the program you created in Exercise 2.20 to display the shapes in a **JOptionPane.PLAIN_MESSAGE** dialog. Does the program display the shapes exactly as in Exercise 2.20?

2.22 What does the following code print?

```
System.out.println( "*\n**\n***\n****\n*****" );
```

2.23 What does the following code print?

```
System.out.println( "*" );
System.out.println( "***" );
System.out.println( "*****" );
System.out.println( "****" );
System.out.println( "**" );
```

2.24 What does the following code print?

```
System.out.print( "*" );
System.out.print( "***" );
System.out.print( "*****" );
System.out.print( "****" );
System.out.println( "**" );
```

2.25 What does the following code print?

```
System.out.print( "*" );
System.out.println( "***" );
System.out.println( "*****" );
System.out.print( "****" );
System.out.println( "**" );
```

2.26 Write an application that reads five integers and determines and prints the largest and the smallest integers in the group. Use only the programming techniques you learned in this chapter.

2.27 Write an application that reads an integer and determines and prints whether it is odd or even. [*Hint*: Use the modulus operator. An even number is a multiple of 2. Any multiple of 2 leaves a remainder of 0 when divided by 2.]

2.28 Write an application that reads in two integers and determines and prints if the first is a multiple of the second. [*Hint*: Use the modulus operator.]

2.29 Write an application that displays in the command window a checkerboard pattern as follows:

```
* * * * * * * *
 * * * * * * * *
* * * * * * * *
 * * * * * * * *
* * * * * * * *
 * * * * * * * *
* * * * * * * *
 * * * * * * * *
```

2.30 Modify the program you wrote in Exercise 2.29 to display the checkerboard pattern in a **JOptionPane.PLAIN_MESSAGE** dialog. Does the program display the shapes exactly as in Exercise 2.29?

2.31 Here's a peek ahead. In this chapter, you have learned about integers and the data type **int**. Java can also represent uppercase letters, lowercase letters and a considerable variety of special symbols. Every character has a corresponding integer representation. The set of characters a computer uses and the corresponding integer representations for those characters is called that computer's *character set*. You can indicate a character value in a program simply by enclosing that character in single quotes, as in **'A'**.

You can determine the integer equivalent of a character by preceding that character with **(int)**. This form is called a cast (we will say more about casts in Chapter 4) as in:

```
(int) 'A'
```

The following statement outputs a character and its integer equivalent:

```
System.out.println( "The character " + 'A' +
   " has the value " + ( int ) 'A' );
```

When the preceding statement executes, it displays the character **A** and the value **65** (from the so-called Unicode character set) as part of the string.

Write an application that displays the integer equivalents of some uppercase letters, lowercase letters, digits and special symbols. At a minimum, display the integer equivalents of the following: **A B C a b c 0 1 2 $ * + /** and the blank character.

2.32 Write an application that inputs one number consisting of five digits from the user, separates the number into its individual digits and prints the digits separated from one another by three spaces each. For example, if the user types in the number **42339**, the program should print

```
4   2   3   3   9
```

[*Hint*: It is possible to do this exercise with the techniques you learned in this chapter. You will need to use both division and modulus operations to "pick off" each digit.]

Assume that the user enters the correct number of digits. What happens when you execute the program and type a number with more than five digits? What happens when you execute the program and type a number with fewer than five digits?

2.33 Using only the programming techniques you learned in this chapter, write an application that calculates the squares and cubes of the numbers from 0 to 10 and prints the resulting values in table format as follows:

```
number  square  cube
0       0       0
1       1       1
2       4       8
3       9       27
4       16      64
5       25      125
6       36      216
7       49      343
8       64      512
9       81      729
10      100     1000
```

[*Note*: This program does not require any input from the user.]

2.34 Write a program that reads a first name and a last name from the user as two separate inputs and concatenates the first name and last name, separating them by a space. Display in a message dialog the concatenated name.

2.35 Write a program that inputs five numbers and determines and prints the number of negative numbers input, the number of positive numbers input and the number of zeros input.

Introduction to Java Applets

Objectives

- To observe some of Java's exciting capabilities through the Java 2 Software Development Kit's demonstration applets.
- To differentiate between applets and applications.
- To be able to write simple Java applets.
- To be able to write simple Hypertext Markup Language (HTML) files to load an applet into the **`appletviewer`** or a World Wide Web browser.
- To understand the difference between variables and references.
- To execute applets in World Wide Web browsers.

He would answer to "Hi!" or to any loud cry
Such as "Fry me!" or "Fritter my wig!"
To "What-you-may-call-um!" or "What-was-his-name!"
But especially "Thing-um-a-jig!"
Lewis Carroll

Painting is only a bridge linking the painter's mind with that of the viewer.
Eugène Delacroix

My method is to take the utmost trouble to find the right thing to say, and then to say it with the utmost levity.
George Bernard Shaw

Though this be madness, yet there is method in 't.
William Shakespeare

Outline

3.1 Introduction
3.2 Sample Applets from the Java 2 Software Development Kit
3.2.1 The TicTacToe Applet
3.2.2 The DrawTest Applet
3.2.3 The Java2D Applet
3.3 A Simple Java Applet: Drawing a String
3.3.1 Compiling and Executing **WelcomeApplet**
3.4 Two More Simple Applets: Drawing Strings and Lines
3.5 Another Java Applet: Adding Floating-Point Numbers
3.6 Viewing Applets in a Web Browser
3.6.1 Viewing Applets in Netscape Navigator 6
3.6.2 Viewing Applets in Other Browsers Using the Java Plug-In
3.7 Java Applet Internet and World Wide Web Resources
3.8 (Optional Case Study) Thinking About Objects: Identifying the Classes in a Problem Statement

Summary • Terminology • Self-Review Exercises • Answers to Self-Review Exercises • Exercises

3.1 Introduction

In Chapter 2, we introduced Java application programming and several important aspects of Java applications. This chapter introduces another type of Java program called a Java applet. Applets are Java programs that can be embedded in *Hypertext Markup Language (HTML) documents (i.e.,* Web pages). When a browser loads a Web page containing an applet, the applet downloads into the Web browser and begins execution.

The browser that executes an applet is generically known as the *applet container*. The Java 2 Software Development Kit (J2SDK) includes an applet container (called the **appletviewer**) for testing applets before you embed them in a Web page. Most Web browsers in use today do not support Java 2 directly. For this reason, we normally demonstrate our applets using the **appletviewer**. One browser that does support Java 2 is Netscape Navigator 6. To execute applets in other Web browsers such as Microsoft Internet Explorer or earlier versions of Netscape Navigator requires the *Java Plug-in*, which we discuss in Section 3.6.2 of this chapter.

Portability Tip 3.1

Most Web browsers in use today do not support applets written in Java 2. To execute applets in such browsers, you must use the Java Plug-in (see Section 3.6.2).

Testing and Debugging Tip 3.1

Test your applets in the **appletviewer** *applet container before executing them in a Web browser. This enables you to see error messages that may occur. Also, once an applet is executing in a browser, it is sometimes difficult to reload the applet after making changes to the applet's class definition.*

Testing and Debugging Tip 3.2

Test your applets in every Web browser in which the applets will execute to ensure that they operate correctly in each browser.

One of our goals in this chapter is to mimic several features presented in Chapter 2. This provides positive reinforcement of previous concepts. Another goal of this chapter is to begin using the object-oriented programming terminology introduced in Section 1.15.

As in Chapter 2, there are a few cases where we do not as yet provide all the details necessary to create complex applications and applets in Java. It is important to build your knowledge of fundamental programming concepts first. In Chapter 4 and Chapter 5, we present a detailed treatment of *program development* and *program control* in Java. As we proceed through the text, we present many substantial applications and applets.

3.2 Sample Applets from the Java 2 Software Development Kit

We begin by considering several sample applets provided with the Java 2 Software Development Kit (J2SDK) version 1.3. The applets we demonstrate give you a sense of Java's capabilities. Each of the sample programs provided with the J2SDK also comes with *source code* (the **.java** files containing the Java applet programs). This source code is helpful as you enhance your Java knowledge—you can read the source code provided to learn new and exciting features of Java. Remember, all programmers initially learn new features by mimicking their use in existing programs. The J2SDK comes with many such programs and there are a tremendous number of Java resources on the Internet and World Wide Web that include Java source code.

The demonstration programs provided with the J2SDK are located in your J2SDK install directory in a subdirectory called **demo**. For the Java 2 Software Development Kit version 1.3, the default location of the **demo** directory on Windows is

```
c:\jdk1.3\demo
```

On UNIX/Linux it is the directory in which you install the J2SDK followed by **jdk1.3/demo**—for example

```
/usr/local/jdk1.3/demo
```

For other platforms, there will be a similar directory (or folder) structure. For the purpose of this chapter, we assume on Windows that the J2SDK is installed in **c:\jdk1.3** and on UNIX that the J2SDK is installed in your home directory in **~/jdk1.3**. [*Note:* You may need to update these locations to reflect your chosen install directory and/or disk drive, or a newer version of the J2SDK.]

If you are using a Java Development tool that does not come with the Sun Java demos, you can download the J2SDK (with the demos) from the Sun Microsystems Java Web site

```
java.sun.com/j2se/1.3/
```

3.2.1 The TicTacToe Applet

The first applet we demonstrate from the J2SDK demos is the **TicTacToe** applet, which allows you to play Tic-Tac-Toe against the computer. To execute this applet, open a command window (*MS-DOS Prompt* on Windows 95/98/ME, *Command Prompt* on Windows NT/2000 or a *command tool/shell tool* on UNIX) and change directories to the J2SDK's **demo** directory. Both Windows and UNIX use command ***cd*** to ***c****hange* ***d****irectories*. For example, the command

```
cd c:\jdk1.3\demo
```

changes to the **demo** directory on Windows and the command

```
cd ~/jdk1.3/demo
```

changes to the **demo** directory on UNIX.

The **demo** directory contains four subdirectories—***applets***, ***jfc***, ***jpda*** and ***sound*** (you can see these directories by issuing in the command window the **dir** command on Windows or the **ls** command on UNIX). The **applets** directory contains many demonstration applets. The **jfc** (Java Foundation Classes) directory contains many examples of Java's newest graphics and GUI features (some of these examples are also applets). The **jdpa** directory contains examples of the *Java Platform Debugging Architecture* (beyond the scope of this book). The sound directory contains examples of the *Java Sound API* (covered in Chapter 18). For the demonstrations in this section, change directories to the **applets** directory by issuing the command

```
cd applets
```

on either Windows or UNIX.

Listing the contents of the **applets** directory (with the **dir** command on Windows or the **ls** command on UNIX) indicates that there are many examples. Figure 3.1 shows the subdirectories and provides a brief description of the examples in each subdirectory.

Example	Description
Animator	Performs one of four separate animations.
ArcTest	Demonstrates drawing arcs. You can interact with the applet to change attributes of the arc that is displayed.
BarChart	Draws a simple bar chart.
Blink	Displays blinking text in different colors.
CardTest	Demonstrates several GUI components and a variety of ways in which GUI components can be arranged on the screen (the arrangement of GUI components is also known as the *layout* of the GUI components).
Clock	Draws a clock with rotating "hands," the current date and the current time. The clock is updated once per second.
DitherTest	Demonstrates drawing with a graphics technique known as dithering that allows gradual transformation from one color to another.

Fig. 3.1 The examples from the **applets** directory (part 1 of 2).

Example	Description
DrawTest	Allows the user to drag the mouse to draw lines and points on the applet in different colors.
Fractal	Draws a fractal. Fractals typically require complex calculations to determine how they are displayed.
GraphicsTest	Draws a variety of shapes to illustrate graphics capabilities.
GraphLayout	Draws a graph consisting of many nodes (represented as rectangles) connected by lines. Drag a node to see the other nodes in the graph adjust on the screen and demonstrate complex graphical interactions.
ImageMap	Demonstrates an image with *hot spots*. Positioning the mouse pointer over certain areas of the image highlights the area and a message is displayed in the lower-left corner of the **appletviewer** window. Position over the mouth in the image to hear the applet say "hi."
JumpingBox	Moves a rectangle randomly around the screen. Try to catch it by clicking it with the mouse!
MoleculeViewer	Presents a three-dimensional view of several different chemical molecules. Drag the mouse to view the molecule from different angles.
NervousText	Draws text that jumps around the screen.
SimpleGraph	Draws a complex curve.
SortDemo	Compares three sorting techniques. Sorting (described in Chapter 7) arranges information in order—like alphabetizing words. When you execute the applet, three **appletviewer** windows appear. Click in each one to start the sort. Notice that the sorts all operate at different speeds.
SpreadSheet	Demonstrates a simple spreadsheet of rows and columns.
SymbolTest	Draws characters from the Java character set.
TicTacToe	Allows the user to play Tic-Tac-Toe against the computer.
WireFrame	Draws a three-dimensional shape as a wire frame. Drag the mouse to view the shape from different angles.

Fig. 3.1 The examples from the **applets** directory (part 2 of 2).

Change directories to subdirectory **TicTacToe**. In that directory you will find the HTML file **example1.html** that is used to execute the applet. In the command window, type the command

```
appletviewer example1.html
```

and press the *Enter* key. This executes the **appletviewer**. The **appletviewer** loads the HTML file specified as its *command-line argument* (**example1.html**), determines from the file which applet to load (we discuss the details of HTML files in Section 3.3) and begins executing the applet. Figure 3.2 shows several screen captures of playing Tic-Tac-Toe with this applet.

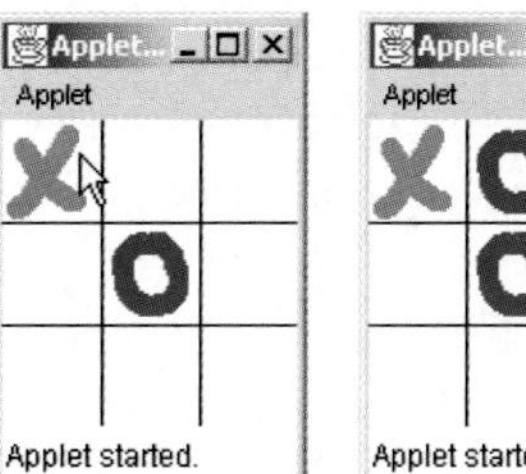

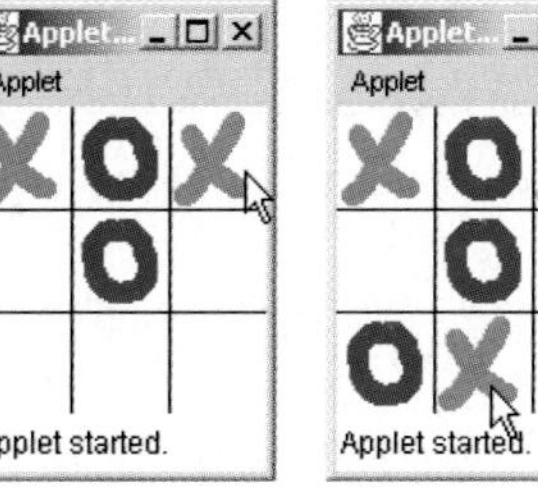

Fig. 3.2 Sample execution of the **`TicTacToe`** applet.

Testing and Debugging Tip 3.3

If the **`appletviewer`** *command does not work and/or the system indicates that the* **`appletviewer`** *command cannot be found, the* **`PATH`** *environment variable may not be defined properly on your computer. Review the installation directions for the Java 2 Software Development Kit to ensure that the* **`PATH`** *environment variable is defined correctly for your system (on some computers, you may need to restart your computer after modifying the* **`PATH`** *environment variable).*

You are player **X**. To interact with the applet, point the mouse at the square where you want to place an **X** and click the mouse button (normally, the left mouse button). The applet plays a sound (assuming your computer supports audio playback) and places an **X** in the square if the square is open. If the square is occupied, this is an invalid move and the applet plays a different sound indicating that you cannot make the specified move. After you make a valid move, the applet responds by making its own move (this happens quickly).

To play again, re-execute the applet by clicking the **`appletviewer`**'s ***Applet*** *menu* and selecting the ***Reload*** *menu item* (Fig. 3.3). To terminate the **`appletviewer`**, click the **`appletviewer`**'s **Applet** menu and select the ***Quit*** *menu item.*

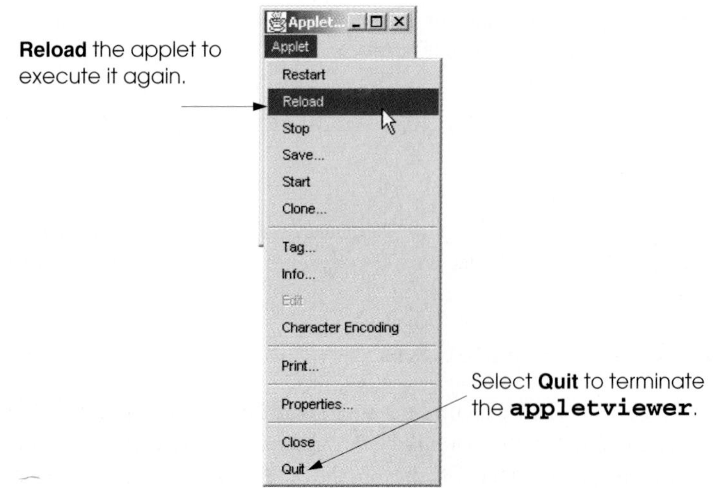

Fig. 3.3 Selecting **Reload** from the **`appletviewer`**'s **Applet** menu.

3.2.2 The DrawTest Applet

The next applet we demonstrate allows you to draw lines and points in different colors. To draw, you simply drag the mouse on the applet by pressing a mouse button and holding it while you drag the mouse. For this example, change directories to directory **applets**, then to subdirectory **DrawTest**. In that directory is the **example1.html** file that is used to execute the applet. In the command window, type the command

```
appletviewer example1.html
```

and press the *Enter* key. This executes the **appletviewer**. The **appletviewer** loads the HTML file specified as its command-line argument (**example1.html** again), determines from the file which applet to load and begins execution of the applet. Figure 3.4 shows a screen capture of this applet after drawing some lines and points.

The default shape to draw is a line and the default color is black, so you can draw black lines by dragging the mouse across the applet. To drag the mouse, press and hold the mouse button and move the mouse. Notice that the line follows the mouse pointer around the applet. The line is not permanent until you release the mouse button. You can then start a new line by repeating the process.

Select a color by clicking the circle inside one of the colored rectangles at the bottom of the applet. You can select from red, green, blue, pink, orange and black. The GUI components used to present these options are commonly known as *radio buttons*. If you think of a car radio, only one radio station can be selected at a time. Similarly, only one drawing color can be selected at a time.

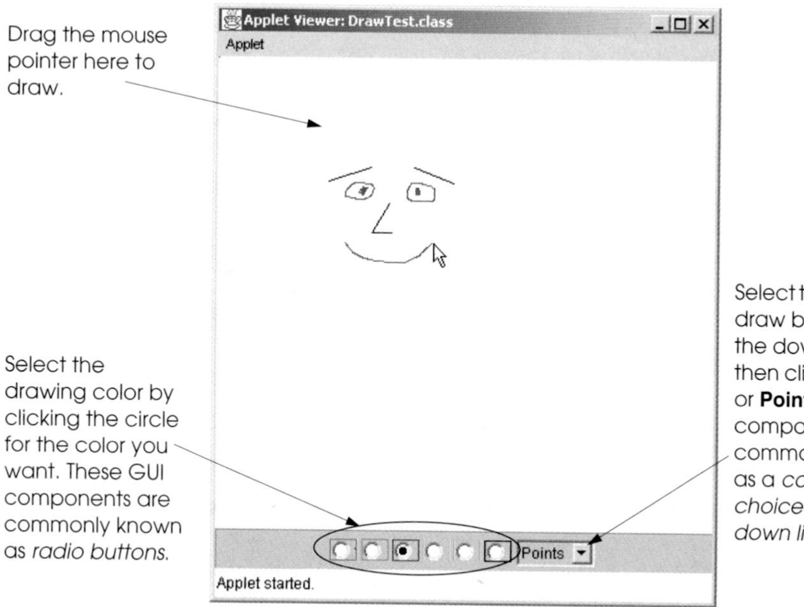
Applet Viewer: DrawTest.class
Applet
Drag the mouse pointer here to draw.
Select the drawing color by clicking the circle for the color you want. These GUI components are commonly known as *radio buttons*.
Select the shape to draw by clicking the down arrow, then clicking **Lines** or **Points**. This GUI component is commonly known as a *combo box*, *choice* or *drop-down list*.
Points
Applet started.

Fig. 3.4 Sample execution of applet **DrawTest**.

Try changing the shape to draw from **Lines** to **Points** by clicking the down arrow to the right of the word **Lines** at the bottom of the applet. A list drops down from the GUI component containing the two choices—**Lines** and **Points**. To select **Points**, click the word **Points** in the list. The GUI component closes the list and the current shape type is now **Points**. This GUI component is commonly known as a *choice*, *combo box* or *drop-down list*.

To start a new drawing, select **Reload** from the **appletviewer**'s **Applet** menu. To terminate the applet, select **Quit** from the **appletviewer**'s **Applet** menu.

3.2.3 The Java2D Applet

The last applet we demonstrate before defining applets of our own shows many of the complex new two-dimensional drawing capabilities built into Java 2—known as the *Java2D API*. For this example, change directories to the **jfc** directory in the J2SDK's **demo** directory, then change to the **Java2D** directory (you can move up the directory tree toward **demo** using the command "**cd ..**" in both Windows and UNIX/Linux). In that directory is an HTML file (**Java2Demo.html**) that is used to execute the applet. In the command window, type the command

```
appletviewer Java2Demo.html
```

and press the *Enter* key. This executes the **appletviewer**. The **appletviewer** loads the HTML file specified as its command-line argument (**Java2Demo.html**), determines from the file which applet to load and begins execution of the applet. This particular demo takes some time to load as it is quite large. Figure 3.5 shows a screen capture of one of this applet's many demonstrations of Java's two-dimensional graphics capabilities.

At the top of this demo you see tabs that look like file folders in a filing cabinet. This demo provides 12 different tabs with several different features on each tab. To change to a different part of the demo, simply click one of the tabs. Also, try changing the options in the upper-right corner of the applet. Some of these affect the speed with which the applet draws the graphics. For example, click the small box with a check in it (a GUI component known as a *checkbox*) to the left of the word **Anti-Aliasing** to turn off anti-aliasing (a graphics technique for producing smoother on-screen graphics in which the edges of the graphic are blurred). When this feature is turned off (i.e., its *checkbox* is unchecked), the animation speed increases for the animated shapes at the bottom of the demo shown in Fig. 3.5. This occurs because an animated shape displayed with anti-aliasing takes longer to draw than an animated shape without anti-aliasing.

3.3 A Simple Java Applet: Drawing a String

Now, let's get started with some applets of our own. Remember, we are just getting started—we have many more topics to learn before we can write applets similar to those demonstrated in Section 3.2. However, we will cover many of the same techniques in this book.

We begin by considering a simple applet that mimics the program of Fig. 2.1 by displaying the string **"Welcome to Java Programming!"**. The applet and its screen output are shown in Fig. 3.6. The HTML document to load the applet into the **appletviewer** is shown and discussed in Fig. 3.7.

Click a tab to select a two-dimensional graphics demo.

Try changing the options to see their effect on the demonstration.

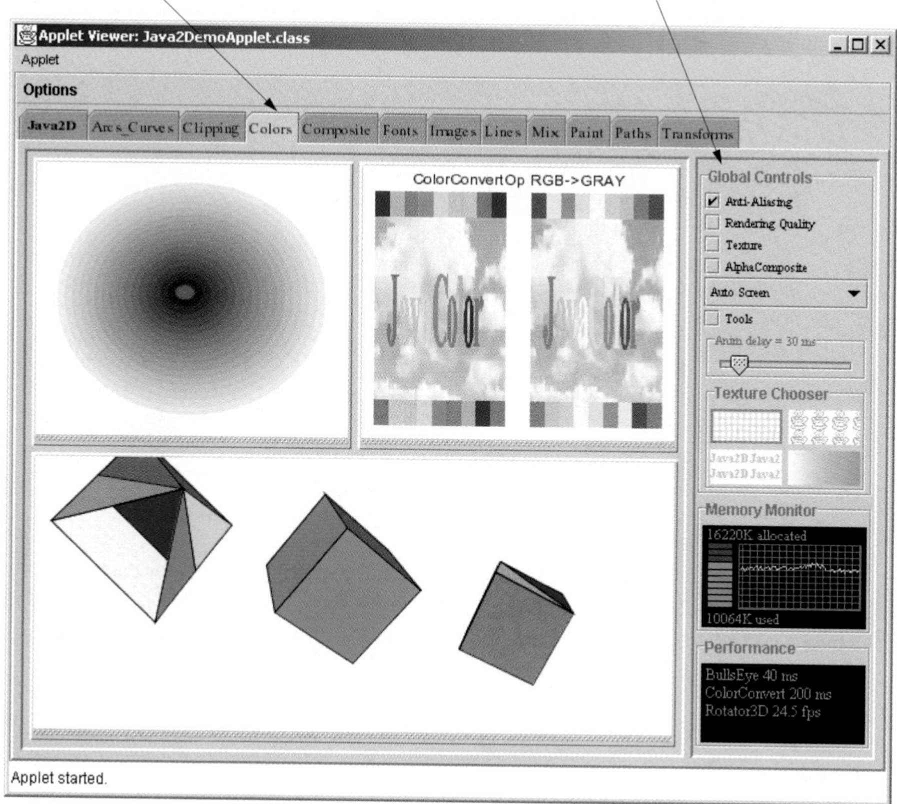

Fig. 3.5 Sample execution of applet **Java2D**.

```
// Fig. 3.6: WelcomeApplet.java
// A first applet in Java.

// Java core packages
import java.awt.Graphics;     // import class Graphics

// Java extension packages
import javax.swing.JApplet;  // import class JApplet

public class WelcomeApplet extends JApplet {

   // draw text on applet's background
   public void paint( Graphics g )
   {
      // call inherited version of method paint
      super.paint( g );
```

Fig. 3.6 A first applet in Java and the applet's screen output (part 1 of 2).

```
17
18        // draw a String at x-coordinate 25 and y-coordinate 25
19        g.drawString( "Welcome to Java Programming!", 25, 25 );
20
21     }  // end method paint
22
23  }  // end class WelcomeApplet
```

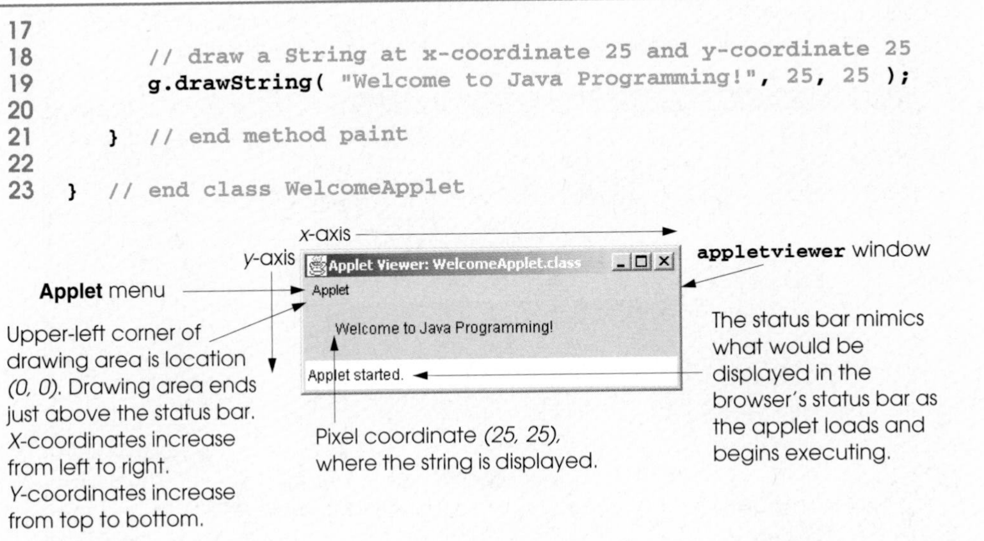

Fig. 3.6 A first applet in Java and the applet's screen output (part 2 of 2).

This program illustrates several important Java features. We consider each line of the program in detail. Line 19 does the "real work" of the program, namely drawing the string **`Welcome to Java Programming!`** on the screen. But let us consider each line of the program in order. Lines 1–2

```
// Fig. 3.6: WelcomeApplet.java
// A first applet in Java.
```

begin with **`//`**, indicating that the remainder of each line is a comment. The comment on line 1 indicates the figure number and file name for the applet source code. The comment on line 2 simply describes the purpose of the program.

As stated in Chapter 2, Java contains many predefined components called classes that are grouped into packages in the Java API. Line 5

```
import java.awt.Graphics;     // import class Graphics
```

is an **`import`** statement that tells the compiler load class ***`Graphics`*** from package ***`java.awt`*** for use in this Java applet. Class **`Graphics`** enables a Java applet to draw graphics such as lines, rectangles, ovals and strings of characters. Later in the book, you will see that class **`Graphics`** also enables applications to draw.

Line 8

```
import javax.swing.JApplet;  // import class JApplet
```

is an **`import`** statement that tells the compiler load class ***`JApplet`*** from package **`javax.swing`**. When you create an applet in Java, you normally import the **`JApplet`** class. [*Note:* There is an older class called ***`Applet`*** from package ***`java.applet`*** that is not used with Java's newest GUI components from the **`javax.swing`** package. In this book, we use only class **`JApplet`** with applets.]

As with applications, every Java applet you create contains at least one class definition. One key feature of class definitions that was not mentioned in Chapter 2 is that programmers rarely create class definitions "from scratch." In fact, when you create a class definition, you normally use pieces of an existing class definition. Java uses *inheritance* (introduced in Section 1.15 and discussed in detail in Chapter 9, "Object-Oriented Programming") to create new classes from existing class definitions. Line 10

```
public class WelcomeApplet extends JApplet {
```

begins a **class** definition for class **WelcomeApplet**. At the end of line 10, the left brace, **{**, begins the body of the class definition. The corresponding right brace, **}**, on line 23 ends the class definition. Keyword **class** introduces the class definition. **WelcomeApplet** is the class name. Keyword ***extends*** indicates that class **WelcomeApplet** inherits existing pieces from another class. The class from which **WelcomeApplet** inherits (**JApplet**) appears to the right of **extends**. In this inheritance relationship, **JApplet** is called the *superclass* or *base class* and **WelcomeApplet** is called the *subclass* or *derived class*. Using inheritance here results in a **WelcomeApplet** class definition that has the *attributes* (data) and *behaviors* (methods) of class **JApplet** as well as the new features we are adding in our **WelcomeApplet** class definition (specifically, the ability to draw **Welcome to Java Programming!** on the applet).

A key benefit of extending class **JApplet** is that someone else previously defined "what it means to be an applet." The **appletviewer** and World Wide Web browsers that support applets expect every Java applet to have certain capabilities (attributes and behaviors). Class **JApplet** already provides all those capabilities—programmers do not need to "reinvent the wheel" and define all these capabilities on their own. In fact, applet containers expect applets to have over 200 different methods. In our programs to this point, we defined one method in each program. If we had to define over 200 methods just to display **Welcome to Java Programming!**, we would never create an applet, because it would take too long to define one! Using **extends** to inherit from class **JApplet** enables applet programmers to create new applets quickly.

The inheritance mechanism is easy to use; the programmer does not need to know every detail of class **JApplet** or any other superclass from which a new class inherits. The programmer needs to know only that class **JApplet** defines the capabilities required to create the minimum applet. However, to make the best use of any class, programmers should study all the capabilities of the superclass.

Good Programming Practice 3.1

*Investigate the capabilities of any class in the Java API documentation (**java.sun.com/j2se/1.3/docs/api/index.html**) carefully before inheriting a subclass from it. This helps ensure that the programmer does not unintentionally "reinvent the wheel" by redefining a capability that the superclass already provides.*

Classes are used as "templates" or "blueprints" to *instantiate* (or *create*) *objects* for use in a program. An object (or *instance*) resides in the computer's memory and contains information used by the program. The term object normally implies that attributes (data) and behaviors (methods) are associated with the object. The object's methods use the attributes to provide useful services to the *client of the object* (i.e., the code in a program that calls the methods).

When an applet container (the **appletviewer** or browser in which the applet executes) loads our **WelcomeApplet** class, the applet container creates an object (instance) of class **WelcomeApplet** that implements the applet's attributes and behaviors. [*Note:* The terms instance and object are often used interchangeably.] Applet containers can create only objects of classes that are **public** and extend **JApplet**. Thus, applet containers require applet class definitions to begin with the keyword **public** (line 10). Otherwise, the applet container cannot load and execute the applet. The **public** keyword and related keywords (such as **private** and **protected**) are discussed in detail in Chapter 8, "Object-Based Programming." For now, we ask you simply to start all class definitions with the **public** keyword until the discussion of **public** in Chapter 8.

When you save a **public** class in a file, the file name must be the class name followed by the **.java** file name extension. For our applet, the file name must be **WelcomeApplet.java**. Please note that the class name part of the file name must use the same spelling as the class name, including identical use of uppercase and lowercase letters. For reinforcement, we repeat two Common Programming Errors from Chapter 2.

Common Programming Error 3.1

*It is an error for a **public** class if the file name is not identical to the class name (plus the **.java** extension) in both spelling and capitalization. Therefore, it is also an error for a file to contain two or more **public** classes.*

Common Programming Error 3.2

*It is an error not to end a file name with the **.java** extension for a file containing an application's class definition. The Java compiler will not be able to compile the class definition.*

Testing and Debugging Tip 3.4

*The compiler error message "Public class ClassName must be defined in a file called ClassName.java" indicates either that the file name does not exactly match the name of the **public** class in the file (including all uppercase and lowercase letters) or that you typed the class name incorrectly when compiling the class (the name must be spelled with the proper uppercase and lowercase letters).*

Line 13

```
public void paint( Graphics g )
```

begins the definition of the applet's ***paint** method*—one of three methods (behaviors) that the applet container calls for an applet when the container begins executing the applet. In order, these three methods are ***init*** (discussed later in this chapter), ***start*** (discussed in Chapter 6) and **paint**. Your applet class gets a "free" version of each of these methods from class **JApplet** when you specify **extends JApplet** in the first line of your applet's class definition. If you do not define these methods in your own applet, the applet container calls the versions inherited from **JApplet**. The inherited versions of methods **init** and **start** have empty bodies (i.e., their bodies do not contain statements, so they do not perform a task) and the inherited version of method **paint** does not draw anything on the applet. [*Note:* There are several other methods that an applet container calls during an applet's execution. We discuss these methods in Chapter 6, "Methods."]

To enable our applet to draw, class **WelcomeApplet** *overrides* (*replaces* or *redefines*) the default version of **paint** by placing statements in the body of **paint** that draw a message on the screen. When the applet container tells the applet to "draw itself" on the screen by calling method **paint**, our message **Welcome to Java Programming!** appears rather than a blank screen.

Lines 13–21 are the definition of **paint**. The task of method **paint** is to draw graphics (such as lines, ovals and strings of characters) on the screen. Keyword **void** indicates that this method does not return any results when it completes its task. The set of parentheses after **paint** defines the method's *parameter list*. The parameter list is where methods receive data required to perform their tasks. Normally, this data is passed by the programmer to the method through a *method call* (also known as *invoking a method* or *sending a message*). For example, in Chapter 2 we passed data to **JOptionPane**'s **showMessageDialog** method such as the message to display or the type of dialog box. However, when writing applets, the programmer does not call method **paint** explicitly. Rather, the applet container calls **paint** to tell the applet to draw and the applet container passes to the **paint** method the information **paint** requires to perform its task, namely a **Graphics** object (called **g**). It is the applet container's responsibility to create the **Graphics** object to which **g** refers. Method **paint** uses the **Graphics** object to draw graphics on the applet. The **public** keyword at the beginning of line 13 is required so the applet container can call your **paint** method. For now, all method definitions should begin with the **public** keyword. We introduce other alternatives in Chapter 8.

The left brace, **{**, on line 14 begins method **paint**'s body. The corresponding right brace, **}**, on line 21 ends **paint**'s body.

Line 16

```
super.paint( g );
```

calls the version of method **paint** inherited from superclass **JApplet**.[1]

Line 19

```
g.drawString( "Welcome to Java Programming!", 25, 25 );
```

instructs the computer to perform an action (or task), namely to draw the characters of the string **Welcome to Java Programming!** on the applet. This statement uses method **drawString** defined by class **Graphics** (this class defines all the drawing capabilities of a Java program, including strings of characters and shapes such as rectangles, ovals and lines). The statement calls method **drawString** using the **Graphics** object **g** (in **paint**'s parameter list) followed by a *dot operator* (**.**) followed by the method name **drawString**. The method name is followed by a set of parentheses containing the argument list **drawString** needs to perform its task.

The first argument to **drawString** is the **String** to draw on the applet. The last two arguments in the list—**25** and **25**—are the *x-y coordinates* (or *position*) at which the bottom-left corner of the string should be drawn on the applet. Drawing methods from class **Graphics** require coordinates to specify where to draw on the applet (later in the text we

1. For reasons that will become clear later in the text, this statement should be the first statement in every applet's **paint** method. Although the early examples of applets will work without this statement, omitting this statement causes subtle errors in more elaborate applets that combine drawing and GUI components. Including this statement now will get you in the habit of using it and will save time and effort as you build more substantial applets later.

demonstrate drawing in applications). The first coordinate is the *x-coordinate* (the number of pixels from the left side of the applet), and the second coordinate is the *y-coordinate* (representing the number of pixels from the top of the applet). Coordinates are measured from the upper-left corner of the applet in *pixels* (just below the **Applet** menu in the sample output window of Fig. 3.6). A pixel ("picture element") is the unit of display for your computer's screen. On a color screen, a pixel appears as one colored dot on the screen. Many personal computers have 800 pixels for the width of the screen and 600 pixels for the height of the screen, for a total of 800 times 600 or 480,000 displayable pixels. Many computers today have screens with higher screen resolutions, i.e., they have more pixels for the width and height of the screen. The size of an applet on the screen depends on the size and resolution of the screen. For screens with the same size, the applet will appear smaller on the screen with the higher resolution. Note that some older computers have screen resolutions lower than 800 by 600. The most common lower resolution is 640 by 480.

When line 19 executes, it draws the message **`Welcome to Java Programming!`** on the applet at the coordinates **`25`** and **`25`**. Note that the quotation marks enclosing the string are *not* displayed on the screen.

As an aside, why would you want free copies of methods **`init`**, **`start`** and **`paint`** if they do not perform a task? The predefined start-up sequence of method calls made by the **`appletviewer`** or browser for every applet is always **`init`**, **`start`** and **`paint`**—this provides an applet programmer a guarantee that these methods will be called as every applet begins execution. Every applet does not need all three of these methods. However, the **`appletviewer`** or browser expects each of these methods to be defined so it can provide a consistent start-up sequence for an applet. [Note: This is similar to applications always starting execution with **`main`**.] Inheriting the default versions of these methods guarantees the browser that it can treat each applet uniformly by calling **`init`**, **`start`** and **`paint`** as applet execution begins. Also, the programmer can concentrate on defining only the methods required for a particular applet.

3.3.1 Compiling and Executing `WelcomeApplet`

As with application classes, you must compile applet classes before they can execute. After defining class **`WelcomeApplet`** and saving it in **`WelcomeApplet.java`**, open a command window, change to the directory in which you saved the applet class definition and type the command

```
javac WelcomeApplet.java
```

to compile class **`WelcomeApplet`**. If there are no syntax errors, the resulting bytecodes are stored in the file **`WelcomeApplet.class`**.

Before you can execute the applet you must create an *HTML (Hypertext Markup Language)* file to load the applet into the applet container (**`appletviewer`** or a browser). Typically, an HTML file ends with the "**`.html`**" or "**`.htm`**" file name extension. Browsers display the contents of documents that contain text (also known as *text files*). To execute a Java applet, an HTML text file must indicate which applet the applet container should load and execute. Figure 3.7 shows a simple HTML file—**`WelcomeApplet.html`**—that loads into the applet defined in Fig. 3.6 into an applet container. [Note: For the early part of this book, we always demonstrate applets with the **`appletviewer`** applet container.]

```
1  <html>
2  <applet code = "WelcomeApplet.class" width = "300" height = "45">
3  </applet>
4  </html>
```

Fig. 3.7 **WelcomeApplet.html** loads class **WelcomeApplet** of Fig. 3.6 into the **appletviewer**.

Good Programming Practice 3.2

Always test a Java applet in the **appletviewer** *and ensure that it is executing correctly before loading the applet into a World Wide Web browser. Browsers often save a copy of an applet in memory until the current browsing session terminates (i.e., all browser windows are closed). Thus, if you change an applet, recompile the applet, then reload the applet in the browser, you may not see the changes because the browser may still be executing the original version of the applet. Close all your browser windows to remove the old version of the applet from memory. Open a new browser window and load the applet to see your changes.*

Software Engineering Observation 3.1

If your World Wide Web browser does not support Java 2, most of the applets in this book will not execute in your browser. This is because most of the applets in this book use features that are specific to Java 2 or are not provided by browsers that support Java 1.1. Section 3.6.2 discusses how to use the Java Plug-in to view applets in Web browsers that do not support Java 2.

Many HTML codes (or *tags*) come in pairs. For example, lines 1 and 4 of Fig. 3.7 indicate the beginning and the end, respectively, of the HTML tags in the file. All HTML tags begin with a *left angle bracket,* **<**, and end with a *right angle bracket,* **>**. Lines 2 and 3 are special HTML tags for Java applets. They tell the applet container to load a specific applet and define the size of the applet's display area (its *width* and *height* in pixels) in the **appletviewer** (or browser). Normally, the applet and its corresponding HTML file are stored in the same directory on disk. Typically, a browser loads an HTML file from a computer (other than your own) connected to the Internet. However, HTML files also can reside on your computer (as we demonstrated in Section 3.2). When an applet container encounters an HTML file that specifies an applet to execute, the applet container automatically loads the applet's **.class** file (or files) from the same directory on the computer in which the HTML file resides.

The ***<applet>*** *tag* has several *attributes*. The first attribute of the **<applet>** tag on line 2 (**code = "WelcomeApplet.class"**) indicates that the file **WelcomeApplet.class** contains the compiled applet class. Remember, when you compile your Java programs, every class is compiled into a separate file that has the same name as the class and ends with the **.class** extension. The second and third attributes of the **<applet>** tag indicate the ***width*** and the ***height*** of the applet in pixels. The upper-left corner of the applet's display area is always at *x*-coordinate 0 and *y*-coordinate 0. The width of this applet is 300 pixels and its height is 45 pixels. You may want (or need) to use larger **width** and **height** values to define a larger drawing area for your applets. The **</applet>** tag (line 3) terminates the **<applet>** tag that began on line 2. The **</html>** tag (line 4) specifies the end of the HTML tags that began on line 1 with **<html>**.

Software Engineering Observation 3.2

Generally, each applet should be less than 800 pixels wide and 600 pixels tall (most computer screens support these dimensions as the minimum width and height).

Common Programming Error 3.3

*Placing additional characters such as commas (**,**) between the attributes in the* **<applet>** *tag may cause the* **appletviewer** *or browser to produce an error message indicating a* **MissingResourceException** *when loading the applet.*

Common Programming Error 3.4

Forgetting the ending **</applet>** *tag prevents the applet from loading into the* **appletviewer** *or browser properly.*

Testing and Debugging Tip 3.5

If you receive a **MissingResourceException** *error message when loading an applet into the* **appletviewer** *or a browser, check the* **<applet>** *tag in the HTML file carefully for syntax errors. Compare your HTML file to the file in Fig. 3.7 to confirm proper syntax.*

The **appletviewer** understands only the **<applet>** and **</applet>** HTML tags, so it is sometimes referred to as the "minimal browser" (it ignores all other HTML tags). The **appletviewer** is an ideal place to test an applet and ensure that it executes properly. Once the applet's execution is verified, you can add the applet's HTML tags to an HTML file that will be viewed by people browsing the Internet.

To execute the **WelcomeApplet** in the **appletviewer** open a command window, change to the directory containing your applet and HTML file and type the command

```
appletviewer WelcomeApplet.html
```

Note that the **appletviewer** *requires* an HTML file to load an applet. This is different from the **java** interpreter for applications which requires only the class name of the application class. Also, the preceding command must be issued from the directory in which the HTML file and the applet's **.class** file are located.

Common Programming Error 3.5

Running the **appletviewer** *with a file name that does not end with* **.html** *or* **.htm** *is an error that prevents the* **appletviewer** *from loading your applet for execution.*

Portability Tip 3.2

Test your applets in every browser used by people who view your applet. This will help ensure that people who view your applet experience the functionality you expect. [Note: A goal of the Java Plug-In (discussed later in the book) is to provide consistent applet execution across many different browsers.]

3.4 Two More Simple Applets: Drawing Strings and Lines

Let us consider another applet. An applet can draw **Welcome to Java Programming!** several ways. For example, an applet can use two **drawString** statements in method **paint** to print multiple lines of text as in Fig. 3.8. The HTML file to load the applet into an applet container is shown in Fig. 3.9.

```
1  // Fig. 3.8: WelcomeApplet2.java
2  // Displaying multiple strings in an applet.
3
4  // Java core packages
5  import java.awt.Graphics;     // import class Graphics
6
7  // Java extension packages
8  import javax.swing.JApplet;   // import class JApplet
9
10 public class WelcomeApplet2 extends JApplet {
11
12    // draw text on applet's background
13    public void paint( Graphics g )
14    {
15       // call inherited version of method paint
16       super.paint( g );
17
18       // draw two Strings at different locations
19       g.drawString( "Welcome to", 25, 25 );
20       g.drawString( "Java Programming!", 25, 40 );
21
22    } // end method paint
23
24 } // end class WelcomeApplet2
```

Pixel coordinate *(25, 25)*, where **Welcome to** is displayed

Pixel coordinate *(25, 40)*, where **Java Programming!** is displayed

Applet Viewer: WelcomeApplet2.class
Applet
Welcome to
Java Programming!
Applet started.

Fig. 3.8 Applet that displays multiple strings.

```
<html>
<applet code = "WelcomeApplet2.class" width = "300" height = "60">
</applet>
</html>
```

Fig. 3.9 **WelcomeApplet2.html** loads class **WelcomeApplet2** of Fig. 3.8 into the **appletviewer**.

Note that each call to method **drawString** can draw at any pixel location on the applet. The reason the two output lines appear left aligned as shown in Fig. 3.8 is that both use the same *x* coordinate (**25**). Also, each **drawString** method call uses different *y* coordinates (**25** on line 19 and **40** on line 20), so the strings appear at different vertical locations on the applet. If we reverse lines 19 and 20 in the program, the output window will still appear as shown because the pixel coordinates specified in each **drawString** statement are independent of the coordinates specified in all other **drawString** statements (and all other drawing operations). When drawing graphics, lines of text are not separated by newline characters (as shown with methods **System.out**'s method **println** and **JOptionPane**'s method **showMessageDialog** in Chapter 2). In fact, if you try to output a string containing a newline character (**\n**), you will simply see a small black box at that position in the string.

To make drawing more interesting, the applet of Fig. 3.10 draws two lines and a string. The HTML file to load the applet into an applet container is shown in Fig. 3.11.

```java
// Fig. 3.10: WelcomeLines.java
// Displaying text and lines

// Java core packages
import java.awt.Graphics;     // import class Graphics

// Java extension packages
import javax.swing.JApplet;   // import class JApplet

public class WelcomeLines extends JApplet {

   // draw lines and a string on applet's background
   public void paint( Graphics g )
   {
      // call inherited version of method paint
      super.paint( g );

      // draw horizontal line from (15, 10) to (210, 10)
      g.drawLine( 15, 10, 210, 10 );

      // draw horizontal line from (15, 30) to (210, 30)
      g.drawLine( 15, 30, 210, 30 );

      // draw String between lines at location (25, 25)
      g.drawString( "Welcome to Java Programming!", 25, 25 );

   }  // end method paint

}  // end class WelcomeLines
```


Fig. 3.10 Drawing strings and lines.

```html
<html>
<applet code = "WelcomeLines.class" width = "300" height = "40">
</applet>
</html>
```

Fig. 3.11 The **WelcomeLines.html** file, which loads class **WelcomeLines** of Fig. 3.10 into the **appletviewer**.

Lines 19 and 22 of method **paint**

```
g.drawLine( 15, 10, 210, 10 );
g.drawLine( 15, 30, 210, 30 );
```

use *method* ***drawLine*** of class **Graphics** to indicate that the **Graphics** object that **g** refers to should draw lines. Method **drawLine** requires four arguments that represent the two end points of the line on the applet—the *x*-coordinate and *y*-coordinate of the first end point in the line and the *x*-coordinate and *y*-coordinate of the second end point in the line. All coordinate values are specified with respect to the upper-left corner *(0, 0)* coordinate of the applet. Method **drawLine** draws a straight line between the two end points.

3.5 Another Java Applet: Adding Floating-Point Numbers

Our next applet (Fig. 3.12) mimics the application of Fig. 2.9 for adding two integers. However, this applet requests that the user enter two *floating-point numbers* (i.e., numbers with a decimal point such as 7.33, 0.0975 and 1000.12345). To store floating-point numbers in memory we introduce primitive data type ***double***, which represents *double-precision floating-point* numbers. There is also primitive data type ***float*** for *storing single-precision floating-point* numbers. A **double** requires more memory to store a floating-point value, but stores it with approximately twice the precision of a **float** (15 significant digits for **double** vs. seven significant digits for **float**).

Once again, we use **JOptionPane.showInputDialog** to request input from the user. The applet computes the sum of the input values and displays the result by drawing a string inside a rectangle on the applet. The HTML file to load this applet into the **appletviewer** is shown in Fig. 3.13.

```
// Fig. 3.12: AdditionApplet.java
// Adding two floating-point numbers.

// Java core packages
import java.awt.Graphics;    // import class Graphics

// Java extension packages
import javax.swing.*;        // import package javax.swing

public class AdditionApplet extends JApplet {
   double sum;  // sum of values entered by user

   // initialize applet by obtaining values from user
   public void init()
   {
      String firstNumber;    // first string entered by user
      String secondNumber;   // second string entered by user
      double number1;        // first number to add
      double number2;        // second number to add

      // obtain first number from user
      firstNumber = JOptionPane.showInputDialog(
         "Enter first floating-point value" );
```

Fig. 3.12 An addition program "in action" (part 1 of 2).

```java

      // obtain second number from user
      secondNumber = JOptionPane.showInputDialog(
         "Enter second floating-point value" );

      // convert numbers from type String to type double
      number1 = Double.parseDouble( firstNumber );
      number2 = Double.parseDouble( secondNumber );

      // add numbers
      sum = number1 + number2;
   }

   // draw results in a rectangle on applet's background
   public void paint( Graphics g )
   {
      // call inherited version of method paint
      super.paint( g );

      // draw rectangle starting from (15, 10) that is 270
      // pixels wide and 20 pixels tall
      g.drawRect( 15, 10, 270, 20 );

      // draw results as a String at (25, 25)
      g.drawString( "The sum is " + sum, 25, 25 );

   } // end method paint

}  // end class AdditionApplet
```

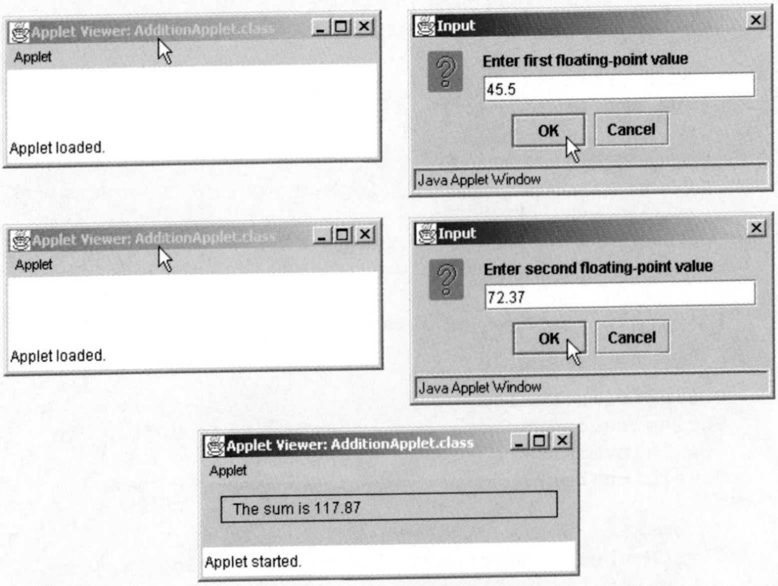

Fig. 3.12 An addition program "in action" (part 2 of 2).

```
<html>
<applet code = "AdditionApplet.class" width = "300" height = "65">
</applet>
</html>
```

Fig. 3.13 **AdditionApplet.html** loads class **AdditionApplet** of Fig. 3.12 into the **appletviewer**.

Lines 1–2

```
// Fig. 3.12: AdditionApplet.java
// Adding two floating-point numbers.
```

are single-line comments stating the figure number, file name and purpose of the program.

Line 5

```
import java.awt.Graphics;    // import class Graphics
```

imports class **Graphics** (package **java.awt**) for use in this applet. Actually, the **import** statement at line 5 is not required if we always use the complete name of class **Graphics**—***java.awt.Graphics***—which includes the full package name and class name. For example, the first line of method **paint** can be defined as

```
public void paint( java.awt.Graphics g )
```

Software Engineering Observation 3.3

The Java compiler does not require ***import*** *statements in a Java source code file if the complete class name—the full package name and class name (e.g.,* ***java.awt.Graphics****)—is specified every time a class name is used in the source code.*

Line 8

```
import javax.swing.*;        // import package javax.swing
```

specifies to the compiler that several classes from package **javax.swing** are used in this applet. The asterisk (*****) indicates that all classes in the **javax.swing** package (such as **JApplet** and **JOptionPane**) should be available to the compiler so the compiler can ensure that we use the classes correctly. This allows programmers to use the *shorthand name* (the class name by itself) of any class from the **javax.swing** package in the program. Remember that our last two programs imported only class **JApplet** from package **javax.swing**. In this program, we use classes **JApplet** and **JOptionPane** from that package. Importing an entire package into a program is also a shorthand notation so the programmer is not required to provide a separate **import** statement for every class used from that package. Remember that you can always use the complete name of every class, i.e., **javax.swing.JApplet** and **javax.swing.JOptionPane** rather than **import** statements.

Software Engineering Observation 3.4

The compiler does not load every class in a package when it encounters an ***import*** *statement that uses the* *** *** *(e.g.,* ***javax.swing.**** *) notation. The compiler loads from the package only those classes the program uses.*

Software Engineering Observation 3.5

Many packages have subpackages. For example, the **java.awt** *package has subpackage* **event** *for the package* **java.awt.event***. When the compiler encounters an* **import** *statement that uses the* * *(e.g.,* **java.awt.****) notation to indicate that a program uses multiple classes from a package, the compiler does not load classes from the subpackage* **event***. Thus, you cannot define an* **import** *of* **java.*** *to search for classes from all Java core packages.*

Software Engineering Observation 3.6

When using **import** *statements, separate* **import** *statements must be specified for each package used in a program.*

Common Programming Error 3.6

Assuming that an **import** *statement for an entire package (e.g.,* **java.awt.***) also* **imports** *classes from subpackages in that package (e.g.,* **java.awt.event.***) results in syntax errors for the classes from the subpackages. There must be separate import statements for every package from which classes are used.*

Remember that applets inherit from the **JApplet** class, so they have all the methods that an applet container requires to execute the applet. Line 10

```
public class AdditionApplet extends JApplet {
```

begins class **AdditionApplet**'s definition and indicates that it inherits from **JApplet**.

All class definitions start with an opening left brace (end of line 10), **{**, and end with a closing right brace, **}** (line 52).

Common Programming Error 3.7

If braces do not occur in matching pairs, the compiler indicates a syntax error.

Line 11

```
double sum;   // sum of values entered by user
```

is an *instance variable declaration*—every instance (object) of the class contains one copy of each instance variable. For example, if there are 10 instances of this applet executing, each instance has its own copy of **sum**. Thus, there would be 10 separate copies of **sum** (one per applet). Programmers declare instance variables in the body of the class definition, but outside the bodies of all the class's method definitions. The preceding declaration states that **sum** is a variable of primitive type **double**.

A benefit of instance variables is that all the methods of the class can use the instance variables. Until now, we declared all variables in an application's **main** method. Variables defined in the body of a method are known as *local variables* and can be used only in the body of the method in which they are defined. Another distinction between instance variables and local variables is that instance variables have default values and local variables do not. The default value of variable **sum** is 0.0, because **sum** is an instance variable.

Good Programming Practice 3.3

Explicitly initializing instance variables rather than relying on automatic initialization improves program readability.

The applet of Fig. 3.12 contains two methods—**init** (lines 14–35) and **paint** (lines 38–50). When an applet container loads an applet, the container creates an instance of the applet class and calls its **init** method. The applet container calls method **init** only once during an applet's execution. Method **init** normally *initializes* the applet's instance variables (if they need to be initialized to a value other than their default value) and performs tasks that should occur only once when the applet begins execution. As we will see in later chapters, the applet's **init** method typically creates the applet's graphical user interface.

Software Engineering Observation 3.7

The order in which methods are defined in a class definition has no effect on when those methods are called at execution time. However, following conventions for the order in which methods are defined improves program readability and maintainability.

The first line of the **init** method always appears as

```
public void init()
```

indicating that **init** is a **public** method that returns no information (**void**) when it completes and receives no arguments (empty parentheses after **init**) to perform its task.

The left brace (line 15) marks the beginning of **init**'s body, and the corresponding right brace (line 35) marks the end of **init**. Lines 16–17

```
String firstNumber;    // first string entered by user
String secondNumber;   // second string entered by user
```

declare local **String** variables **firstNumber** and **secondNumber** in which the program stores the **String**s input by the user.

Lines 18–19

```
double number1;        // first number to add
double number2;        // second number to add
```

declare local variables **number1** and **number2** of primitive data type **double**—these variables hold floating-point values. Unlike **sum**, **number1** and **number2** are not instance variables, so they are not initialized to 0.0 (the default value of **double** instance variables).

As an important aside, there are actually two types of variables in Java—*primitive data type variables* (normally called *variables*) and *reference variables* (normally called *references*). The identifiers **firstNumber** and **secondNumber** are actually references—names that are used to *refer to objects* in the program. Such references actually contain the location of an object in the computer's memory. In our preceding applets, method **paint** actually receives a reference called **g** that refers to a **Graphics** object. Statements in method **paint** use that reference to send messages to the **Graphics** object. These messages are calls to methods (like **drawString**, **drawLine** and **drawRect**) that enable the program to draw. For example, the statement

```
g.drawString( "Welcome to Java Programming!", 25, 25 );
```

sends the **drawString** message to the **Graphics** object to which **g** refers. As part of the message, which is simply a method call, we provide the data that **drawString** requires to do its task. The **Graphics** object uses this data to draw the **String** at the specified location.

The identifiers **number1**, **number2** and **sum** are the names of *variables.* A variable is similar to an object. The primary difference between a variable and an object is that an object is defined by a class definition that can contain both data (instance variables) and methods, whereas a variable is defined by a *primitive (or built-in) data type* (one of **char**, **byte**, **short**, **int**, **long**, **float**, **double** or **boolean**) that can contain only data. A variable can store exactly one value at a time, whereas one object may contain many individual pieces of data. The distinction between a variable and a reference is based on the data type of the identifier, which is stated in a declaration. If the data type is a class name, the identifier is a reference to an object and that reference can be used to send messages to (call methods on) that object. If the data type is one of the primitive data types, the identifier is a variable that can be used to store in memory or retrieve from memory a single value of the declared primitive type.

Software Engineering Observation 3.8

A hint to help you determine if an identifier is a variable or a reference is the variable's data type. By convention all class names in Java start with a capital letter. Therefore, if the data type starts with a capital letter, normally you can assume that the identifier is a reference to an object of the declared type (e.g., ***Graphics g*** *indicates that* ***g*** *is a reference to a* ***Graphics*** *object).*

Lines 22–23

```
// obtain first number from user
firstNumber = JOptionPane.showInputDialog(
   "Enter first floating-point value" );
```

read the first floating-point number from the user. **JOptionPane** method **showInputDialog** displays an input dialog that prompts the user to enter a value. The user types a value in the input dialog's text field, then clicks the **OK** button to return the string the user typed to the program. If you type and nothing appears in the text field, position the mouse pointer in the text field and click the mouse to make the text field active. Variable **firstNumber** is assigned the result of the call to **JOptionPane.showInputDialog** operation with an assignment statement. The statement is read as "**firstNumber** *gets* the value of **JOptionPane.showInputDialog("Enter first floating-point value")**."

In lines 22–23, notice the method call syntax. At this point, we have seen two different ways to call methods. This statement uses the **static** method call syntax introduced in Chapter 2. All **static** methods are called with the syntax

ClassName.*methodName*(*arguments*)

Also in this chapter, we have called methods of class **Graphics** with a similar syntax that started with a reference to a **Graphics** object. Generically, this syntax is

referenceName.*methodName*(*arguments*)

This syntax is used for most methods calls in Java. In fact, the applet container uses this syntax to call methods **init**, **start** and **paint** on your applets.

Lines 26–27

```
// obtain second number from user
secondNumber = JOptionPane.showInputDialog(
   "Enter second floating-point value" );
```

read the second floating-point value from the user by displaying an input dialog.

Lines 30–31

```
number1 = Double.parseDouble( firstNumber );
number2 = Double.parseDouble( secondNumber );
```

convert the two strings input by the user to **double** values for use in a calculation. Method ***Double.parseDouble*** (a **static** method of class **Double**) converts its **String** argument to a **double** floating-point value. Class **Double** is in package **java.lang**. The floating-point value returned by **parseDouble** in line 30 is assigned to variable **number1**. The floating-point value returned by **parseDouble** in line 31 is assigned to variable **number2**.

Software Engineering Observation 3.9

Each primitive data type (such as **int** *or* **double***) has a corresponding class (such as* **Integer** *or* **Double***) in package* **java.lang***. These classes (commonly known as* type-wrapper classes*) provide methods for processing primitive data type values (such as converting a* **String** *to a primitive data type value or converting a primitive data type value to a* **String***). Primitive data types do not have methods. Therefore, methods related to a primitive data type are located in the corresponding type-wrapper class (e.g., method* **parseDouble** *that converts a* **String** *to a* **double** *value is located in class* **Double***). See the online API documentation for the complete details of the methods in the type-wrapper classes.*

The assignment statement at line 34

```
sum = number1 + number2;
```

calculates the sum of the values stored in variables **number1** and **number2** and assigns the result to variable **sum** using the assignment operator **=**. The statement is read as "**sum** *gets* the value of **number1 + number2**." Notice that instance variable **sum** is used in method **init** even though **sum** was not defined in method **init**. We can use **sum** in **init** (and all other methods of the class), because **sum** is an instance variable.

At this point the applet's **init** method returns and the applet container calls the applet's **start** method. We did not define **start** in this applet, so the one inherited from class **JApplet** is called here. Normally, the **start** method is used with an advanced concept called multithreading. See Chapter 15 and Chapter 18 for typical uses of **start**.

Next, the applet container calls the applet's **paint** method. In this example, method **paint** draws a rectangle in which the result of the addition will appear. Line 45

```
g.drawRect( 15, 10, 270, 20 );
```

sends the **drawRect** message to the **Graphics** object to which **g** refers (calls the **Graphics** object's **drawRect** method). Method **drawRect** draws a rectangle based on its four arguments. The first two integer values represent the *upper-left x-coordinate* and *upper-left y-coordinate* where the **Graphics** object begins drawing the rectangle. The third and fourth arguments are non-negative integers that represent the *width* of the rectangle in pixels and the *height* of the rectangle in pixels, respectively. This particular statement draws a rectangle starting at coordinate *(15, 10)* that is 270 pixels wide and 20 pixels tall.

Common Programming Error 3.8

It is a logic error to supply a negative width or negative height as an argument to **Graphics** *method* **drawRect**. *The rectangle will not be displayed and no error will be indicated.*

Common Programming Error 3.9

It is a logic error to supply two points (i.e., pairs of x- and y-coordinates) as the arguments to **Graphics** *method* **drawRect**. *The third argument must be the width in pixels and the fourth argument must be the height in pixels of the rectangle to draw.*

Common Programming Error 3.10

It is normally a logic error to supply arguments to **Graphics** *method* **drawRect** *that cause the rectangle to draw outside the applet's viewable area (i.e., the width and height of the applet as specified in the HTML document that references the applet). Either increase the applet's width and height in the HTML document or pass arguments to method* **drawRect** *that cause the rectangle to draw inside the applet's viewable area.*

Line 48

```
g.drawString( "The sum is " + sum, 25, 25 );
```

sends the **drawString** message to the **Graphics** object to which **g** refers (calls the **Graphics** object's **drawString** method). The expression

```
"The sum is " + sum
```

from the preceding statement uses the string concatenation operator **+** to concatenate the string **"The sum is "** and **sum** (converted to a string) to create the string **drawString** displays. Notice again that the preceding statement uses the instance variable **sum** even though method **paint** does not define **sum** as a local variable.

The benefit of defining **sum** as an instance variable is that we were able to assign **sum** a value in **init** and use **sum**'s value in the **paint** method later in the program. All methods of a class are capable of using the instance variables in the class definition.

Software Engineering Observation 3.10

The only statements that should be placed in an applet's **init** *method are those that are directly related to the one-time initialization of an applet's instance variables. The applet's results should be displayed from other methods of the applet class. Results that involve drawing should be displayed from the applet's* **paint** *method.*

Software Engineering Observation 3.11

The only statements that should be placed in an applet's **paint** *method are those that are directly related to drawing (i.e., calls to methods of class* **Graphics***) and the logic of drawing. Generally, dialog boxes should not be displayed from an applet's* **paint** *method.*

3.6 Viewing Applets in a Web Browser

We demonstrated several applets in this chapter using the **appletviewer** applet container. As we mentioned, applets also can execute in Java-enabled Web browsers. Unfortunately, there are many different browser versions being used worldwide. Some support only Java 1.0 and many support Java 1.1. However, few support the Java 2 Platform. Also, even the browsers that support Java 1.1 do so inconsistently. In Section 3.6.1, we demonstrate an applet executing in Netscape Navigator 6, which supports Java 2. In Section 3.6.2, we demonstrate how to use the Java Plug-in to execute Java 2 applets in other Web browsers such as Microsoft Internet Explorer or earlier versions of Netscape Navigator.

Portability Tip 3.3

Not all Web browsers support Java. Those that do often support different versions and are not always consistent across all platforms.

3.6.1 Viewing Applets in Netscape Navigator 6

When you install Netscape Navigator 6, one of the browser components in the default installation is Java 2. Once installed, you can simply load an applet's HTML file into the browser to execute the applet. You can download and install Netscape 6 from

```
www.netscape.com
```

by clicking the **Download** button at the top of the Web page.

After installing the browser, open the program. On Windows, Netscape 6 typically places an icon on your desktop during the install process. In the **File** menu, click **Open File...** to select an HTML document from your local computer's hard disk. In the **Open File** dialog, navigate to the location of the HTML file of Fig. 3.11. Select the file name **`WelcomeLines.html`** by clicking it, then click the **Open** button to open the file in the browser. In a few moments, you should see the applet of Fig. 3.10 appear in the browser window as shown in Fig. 3.14.

3.6.2 Viewing Applets in Other Browsers Using the Java Plug-In

If you would like to use the features of the Java 2 platform in an applet and execute that applet in a browser that does not support Java 2, Sun provides the *Java Plug-in* to bypass a browser's Java support and use a complete version of the *Java 2 Runtime Environment (J2RE)* that is installed on the user's local computer. If the J2RE does not already exist on the client machine, it can be downloaded and installed dynamically.

Performance Tip 3.1

Because of the size of the Java Plug-in, it is difficult and inefficient to download the Plug-in for users with slower Internet connections. For this reason, the Plug-in is ideal for corporate intranets where users are connected to a high-speed network. Once the Plug-in is downloaded, it does not need to be downloaded again.

You must indicate in the HTML file containing an applet that the browser should use the Java Plug-in to execute the applet. To do so, requires that you convert the **`<applet>`** and **`</applet>`** tags into tags that load the Java Plug-in and execute the applet. Sun provides a conversion utility called the *Java Plug-in 1.3 HTML Converter*[2] that performs the conversion for you. Complete information on downloading and using the Java Plug-in and the HTML Converter are available at the Web site

```
java.sun.com/products/plugin/
```

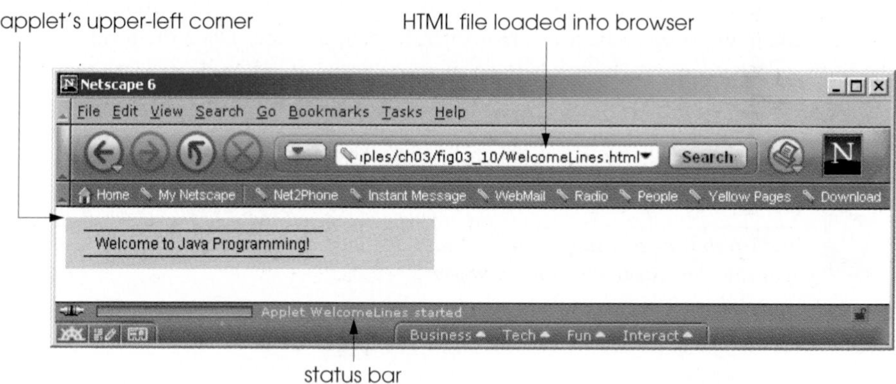

Fig. 3.14 Applet of Fig. 3.10 executing in Netscape Navigator 6.

Once you have downloaded and installed the Java Plug-in HTML converter, you can execute it via the batch file **`HTMLConverter.bat`** on Windows or the shell script **`HTMLConverter.sh`** on Linux/UNIX. These files are located in the **`converter`** directory's **`classes`** subdirectory. Figure 3.15 shows the **Java Plug in HTML Converter** window.

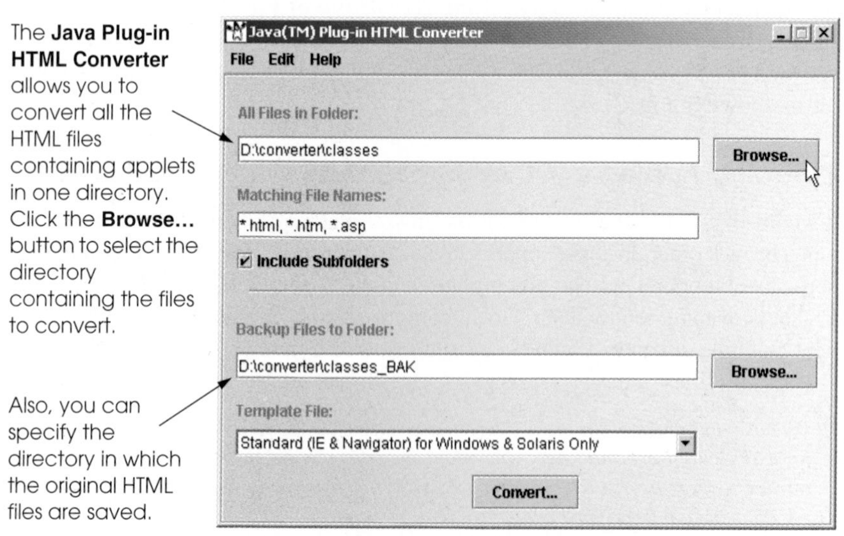

Fig. 3.15 **Java Plug-in HTML Converter** window.

2. As of Java 2 Software Development Kit version 1.3.1, a command-line version of the Java Plug-in HTML converter is one of the tools in the J2SDK. To use the command-line version, open a command window and change directories to the location that contains the HTML file to convert. In that directory type **`HTMLConverter`** *fileName*, where *fileName* is the HTML file to convert. Visit **`java.sun.com/products/plugin/1.3/docs/htmlconv.html`** for more details on the command-line HTML converter.

To perform the conversion, you must select the directory containing the HTML files to convert. You can either type the directory name in the text field below **All Files in Folder**, or you can select the directory by clicking the **Browse...** button to the right of that text field. We clicked the **Browse...** button to display the **Open** dialog in Fig. 3.16.

After selecting the directory containing files to convert, the **Java Plug in HTML Converter** window appears as in Fig. 3.17. The converter provides several conversion templates to support different combinations of browsers. The default template supports Netscape Navigator and Microsoft Internet Explorer. Figure 3.17 shows the expanded ***Template File*** drop-down list containing the pre-defined conversion templates. We selected the default template that enables Microsoft Internet Explorer and Netscape Navigator to use the plug-in to execute an applet.

After selecting the appropriate template file, click the ***Convert...*** button at the bottom of the **Java Plug in HTML Converter** window. Figure 3.18 shows the dialog box that appears containing the status and results of the conversion. At this point the applet's HTML file can be loaded into Netscape Navigator or Microsoft Internet Explorer to execute the applet. If the Java 2 Runtime Environment does not already exist on the user's computer, the converted HTML file contains information that enables the browser to prompt users to determine if they would like to download the plug-in.

In this chapter and Chapter 2, we have introduced many important features of Java, including applications, applets, displaying data on the screen, inputting data from the keyboard, performing calculations and making decisions. In Chapter 4, we build on these techniques as we introduce *structured programming*. Here, you will become more familiar with indentation techniques. We also study how to specify and vary the order in which a program executes statements—this order is called *flow of control.*

The **Open** dialog box allows you to select the directory containing the files to convert.

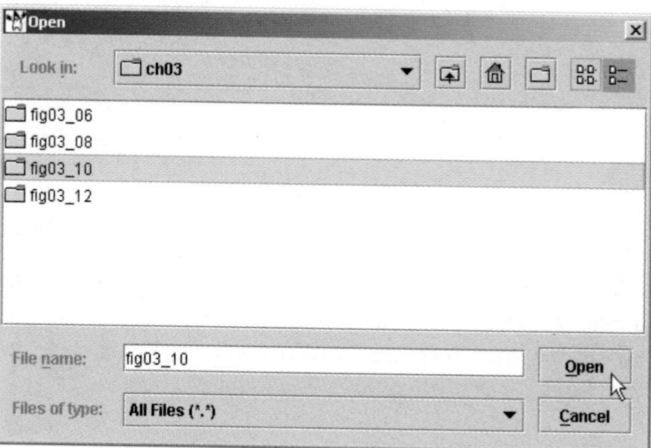

Fig. 3.16 Selecting the directory containing HTML files to convert.

The **Java Plug-in HTML Converter** window after selecting the directory containing files to convert.

The **Template File** drop-down list allows you to choose the browsers in which to use the plug-in to execute applets.

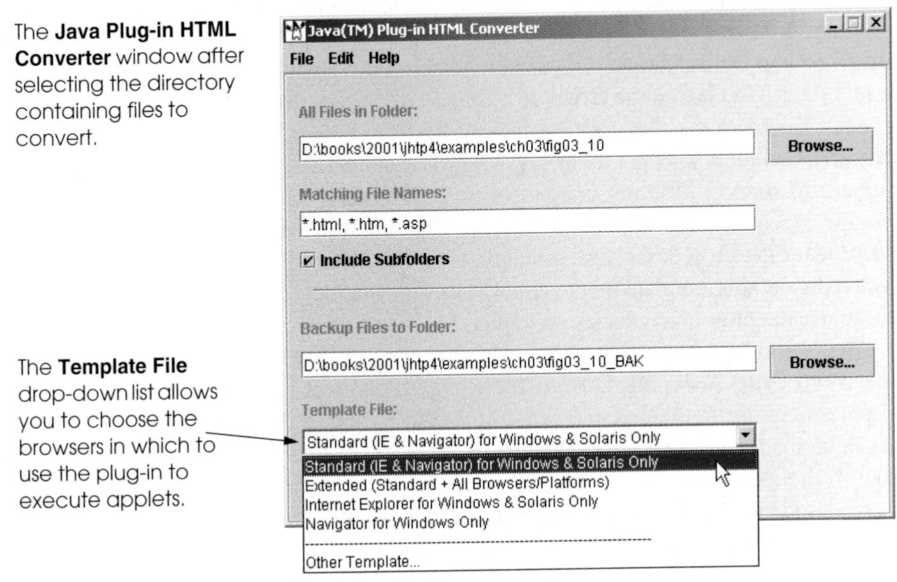

Fig. 3.17 Selecting the template used to convert the HTML files.

The confirmation dialog showing that the converter found and converted one applet in an HTML file in the specified directory.

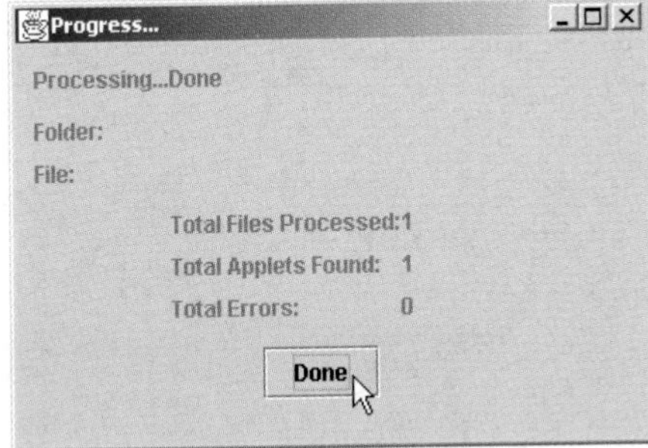

Fig. 3.18 Confirmation dialog after conversion completes.

3.7 Java Applet Internet and World Wide Web Resources

If you have access to the Internet and the World Wide Web, there are a large number of Java applet resources available to you. The best place to start is at the source—the Sun Microsystems, Inc. Java Web site **java.sun.com**. In the upper-left corner of the Web page is an ***Applets*** *hyperlink* that takes you to the Web page

java.sun.com/applets

This page contains a variety of Java applet resources, including free applets you can use on your own World Wide Web site, the demonstration applets from the J2SDK and a variety of other applets (many of which can be downloaded and used on your own computer).

There is also a section entitled "Applets at Work" where you can read about uses of applets in industry.

On the Sun Microsystems Java Web site, visit the *Java Developer Connection*

```
developer.java.sun.com/developer
```

This free site includes technical support, discussion forums, on-line training courses, technical articles, resources, announcements of new Java features, early access to new Java technologies, and links to other important Java Web sites. Even though the site is free, you must register to use it.

Another useful Web site is *JARS*—originally called the *Java Applet Rating Service*. The JARS site

```
www.jars.com
```

calls itself the "#1 Java Review Service." This site originally was a large Java repository for applets. Its benefit was that it rated every applet registered at the site as top 1%, top 5% and top 25%, so you could view the best applets on the Web. Early in the development of the Java language, having your applet rated here was a great way to demonstrate your Java programming abilities. JARS is now all-around resource for Java programmers.

The resources listed in this section provide hyperlinks to many other Java-related Web sites. If you have Internet access, spend some time browsing these sites, executing applets and reading the source code for the applets when it is available. This will help you rapidly expand your Java expertise. Appendix B contains many other Web-based Java resources.

3.8 (Optional Case Study) Thinking About Objects: Identifying the Classes in a Problem Statement

Now we begin the substantial task of designing the elevator simulator model, which represents the workings of the elevator system. We will design the user interaction and display of this model in Section 12.16 and Section 22.9, respectively.

Identifying the Classes in a System

The first step of our OOD process is to identify the classes in our model. We will eventually describe these classes in a formal way and implement them in Java. First, we review the problem statement and locate all the *nouns*; it is likely that these include most of the classes (or instances of classes) necessary to implement the elevator simulation. Figure 3.19 is a list of these nouns (and noun phrases) in the order of their appearance.

Nouns (and noun phrases) in the problem statement		
company	elevator system	graphical user interface (GUI)
office building	elevator shaft	elevator car
elevator	display	person
software-simulator application	model	floor (first floor; second floor)

Fig. 3.19 Nouns (and noun phrases) in problem statement (part 1 of 2).

Nouns (and noun phrases) in the problem statement		
passenger	bell inside the elevator	**First Floor** GUI button
floor door	light on that floor	**Second Floor** GUI button
user of our application	energy	audio
floor button	capacity	elevator music
elevator button		

Fig. 3.19 Nouns (and noun phrases) in problem statement (part 2 of 2).

We choose only the nouns that perform important duties in our model. For this reason we omit several nouns (the next paragraph explains why each is omitted):

- company
- office building
- display
- graphical user interface (GUI)
- user of our application
- energy
- capacity
- **First Floor** and **Second Floor** GUI buttons
- audio
- elevator music

We do not need to model "company," as a class, because the company is not part of the simulation; the company simply wants us to model the elevator. We do not model the office building, or the actual place the elevator is situated, because the building does not affect *how* our elevator simulation operates. The phrases "display," "audio" and "elevator music" pertain to the presentation of the model, but do not pertain to the model itself. We use these phrases when we construct the presentation in Section 22.9 and Appendix I. The phrases "graphical user interface," "user of our application" and "**First Floor** and **Second Floor** GUI buttons" pertain to how the user controls the model, but they do not represent the model. We use these phrases when we construct the user interface in Section 12.16. "Capacity" is a property of the elevator and of the floor—not a separate entity itself. Lastly, although we'll be saving energy with the policy of not moving the elevator until requested, we do not model "energy."

We determine the classes for our system by grouping the remaining nouns into categories. We discard "elevator system" for the time being—we focus on designing only the system's model and disregard how this model relates to the system as a whole. (We discuss the system as a whole in Section 13.17.) Using this logic, we discard "simulation," because the simulation *is* the system in our case study. Lastly, we combine "elevator" and "elevator car" into "elevator," because the problem statement uses the two words interchangeably. Each remaining noun from Fig. 3.19 refers to one or more of the following categories:

- model
- elevator shaft
- elevator
- person
- floor (first floor, second floor)
- elevator door
- floor door
- elevator button
- floor button
- bell
- light

These categories are likely to be classes we will need to implement our system. Notice that we create one category for the buttons on the floors and one category for the button on the elevator. The two types of buttons perform different duties in our simulation—the buttons on the floors summon the elevator, and the button in the elevator informs the elevator to move to the other floor.

We can now model the classes in our system based on the categories we created. By convention, we capitalize class names in the design process (as we will do when we write the actual Java program that implements our design). If the name of a class contains more than one word, we run the words together and capitalize each word (e.g., **`MultipleWordName`**). Using this convention, we create classes **`ElevatorModel`**,[3] **`ElevatorShaft`**, **`Elevator`**, **`Person`**, **`Floor`**, **`ElevatorDoor`**, **`FloorDoor`**, **`ElevatorButton`**, **`FloorButton`**, **`Bell`** and **`Light`**. We construct our system using all of these classes as building blocks. Before we begin building the system, however, we must gain a better understanding of how the classes relate to one another.

Class Diagrams

The UML enables us to model, via the *class diagram*, the classes in the elevator system and their interrelationships. Class diagrams model the structure of the system by providing the classes, or "building blocks," of the system. Figure 3.20 represents class **`Elevator`** using the UML. In a class diagram, each class is modeled as a rectangle. We then divide this rectangle into three parts. The top part contains the name of the class. The middle part contains the class' *attributes*. (We discuss attributes in "Thinking About Objects" Section 4.14 and Section 5.11.) The bottom part of the rectangle contains the class' *operations* (discussed in "Thinking About Objects," Section 6.17).

---

3. When we refer to the "elevator model," we imply all classes composing the model describing the operation of our elevator system—in other words, in our simulation, several classes comprise the model. We will see in Section 13.17 that our system requires a single class to represent the model—we create class **`ElevatorModel`** to act as the "representative" for the model, because, as we will see in Fig. 3.23, **`ElevatorModel`** is the class that aggregates all other classes comprising the model.

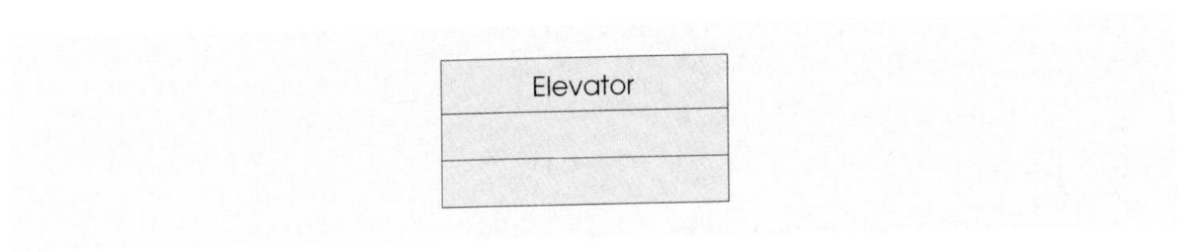

Fig. 3.20 Representing a class in the UML.

Classes relate to one another via *associations*. Figure 3.21 shows how our classes **ElevatorShaft**, **Elevator** and **FloorButton** relate to one another. Notice that the rectangles in this diagram are not subdivided into three sections. The UML allows the suppression of class attributes and operations in this manner to create more readable diagrams. Such a diagram is said to be an *elided diagram*, (i.e., some information, such as the contents for the second and bottom compartments), is not modeled. We place information in these compartments in Section 4.14 and Section 6.17, respectively.

In this class diagram, a solid line that connects classes represents an *association*. An association is a relationship between classes. The numbers near the lines express *multiplicity* values. Multiplicity values indicate how many objects of a class participate in the association. From the diagram, we see that two objects of class **FloorButton** participate in the association with one object of class **ElevatorShaft**, because the two **FloorButtons** are located on the **ElevatorShaft**. Therefore, class **FloorButton** has a *two-to-one* relationship with class **ElevatorShaft**; we can also say that class **ElevatorShaft** has a *one-to-two* relationship with class **FloorButton**. We also see that class **ElevatorShaft** has a *one-to-one* relationship with class **Elevator** and vice versa. Using the UML, we can model many types of multiplicity. Figure 3.22 shows the multiplicity types and how to represent them.

An association can be named. For example, the word **Requests** above the line connecting classes **FloorButton** and **Elevator** indicates the name of that association—the arrow shows the direction of the association. This part of the diagram reads "one object of class **FloorButton** requests one object of class **Elevator**." Note that associations are directional with the direction indicated by the arrowhead next to the association name—so it would be improper, for example, to read the preceding association as "one object of class **Elevator** requests one object of class **FloorButton**." In addition, the word **Resets** indicates that "one object of class **ElevatorShaft** resets two objects of class **FloorButton**." Lastly, the phrase **Signals arrival** indicates that "one object of class **Elevator** signals the **Elevator** object's arrival to one object of class **ElevatorShaft**."

The diamond attached to the association lines of class **ElevatorShaft** indicates that class **ElevatorShaft** has an *aggregation* relationship with classes **FloorButton** and **Elevator**. Aggregation implies a whole/part relationship. The class that has the aggregation symbol (the hollow diamond) on its end of an association line is the whole (in this case, **ElevatorShaft**), and the class on the other end of the association line is the part (in this case, classes **FloorButton** and **Elevator**). In this example, the elevator shaft "has an" elevator and two floor buttons. The "has a/has an" relationship defines aggregation (we will see in Section 9.23 that the "is a/is an" relationship defines inheritance).

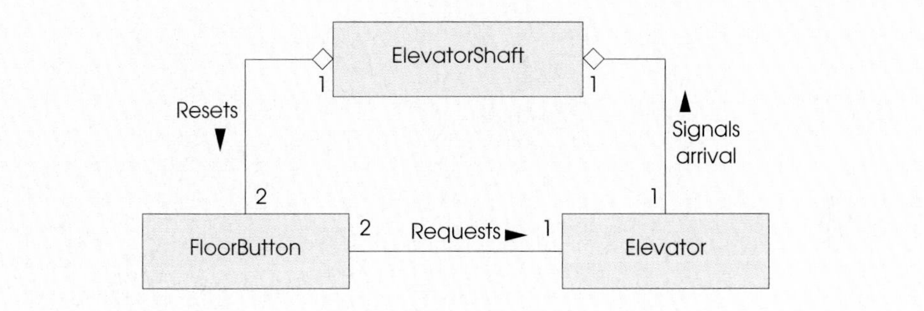

Fig. 3.21 Class diagram showing associations among classes.

Symbol	Meaning
0	None.
1	One.
m	An integer value.
0..1	Zero or one.
m, n	*m* or *n*
m..n	At least *m*, but not more than *n*.
*	Zero or more.
0..*	Zero or more
1..*	One or more

Fig. 3.22 Multiplicity types.

Figure 3.23 shows the complete class diagram for the elevator model. We model all classes that we created, as well as the associations between these classes. [*Note*: In Chapter 9, we expand our class diagram by using the object-oriented concept of *inheritance*.]

Class **ElevatorModel** is represented near the top of the diagram and aggregates one object of class **ElevatorShaft** and two objects of class **Floor**. The **ElevatorShaft** class is an aggregation of one object of class **Elevator** and two objects each of classes **Light**, **FloorDoor** and **FloorButton**. (Notice the two-to-one relationships between each of these classes and **ElevatorShaft**.) Class **Elevator** is an aggregation of classes **ElevatorDoor**, **ElevatorButton** and **Bell**. Class **Person** has associations with both **FloorButton** and **ElevatorButton** (and other classes, as we will soon see). The *association name* **Presses** and the *name-direction* arrowheads indicate that the object of class **Person** presses these buttons. The object of class **Person** also rides the object of class **Elevator** and walks across the object of class **Floor**. The name **Requests** indicates that an object of class **FloorButton** requests the object of class **Elevator**. The name **Signals to move** indicates that the object of class **ElevatorButton** signals the object of class **Elevator** to move to the other floor. The diagram indicates many other associations, as well.

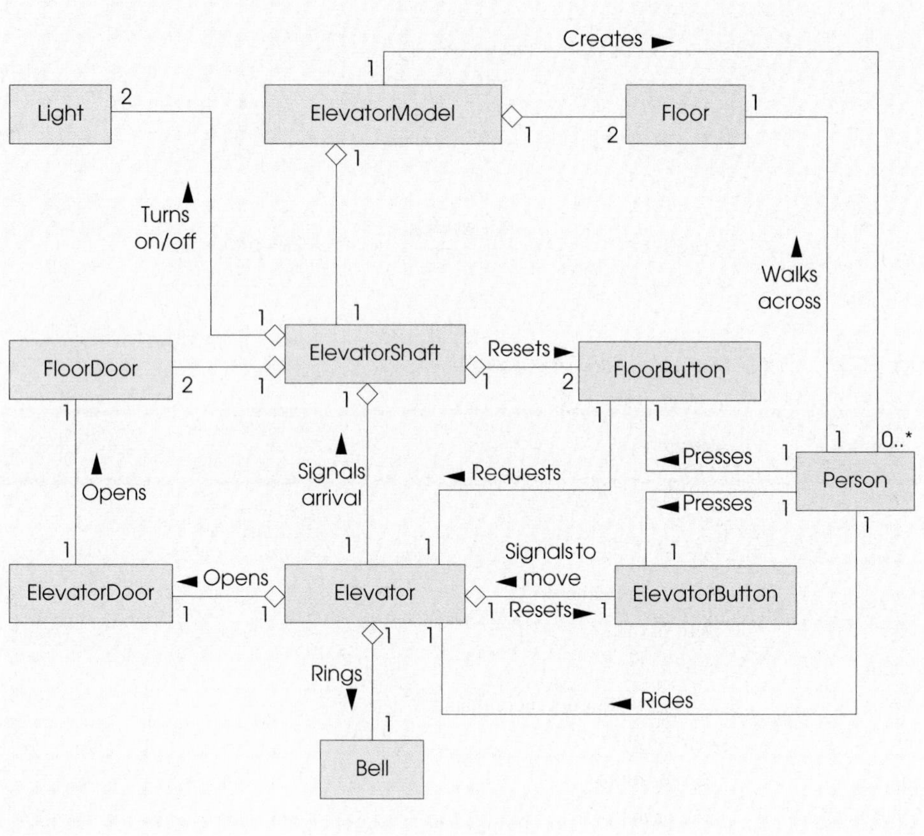

Fig. 3.23 Class diagram for the elevator model.

Object Diagrams

The UML also defines *object diagrams*, which are similar to class diagrams in that both diagrams model the structure of the system. However, object diagrams model objects (instances of classes) *at a specific time* in program execution. Object diagrams present a snapshot of the structure while the system is running, providing information about which objects are participating in the system at a definite point in time. Object diagrams represent relationships between objects as solid lines—these relationship are called *links*.

Figure 3.24 models a snapshot of the system when no people are in the building (i.e., no objects of class **`Person`** exist in the system at this point in time). Objects usually are written in the form **`objectName : ClassName`**—**`objectName`** refers to the name of the object, and **`ClassName`** refers to the class to which that object belongs. All names in an object diagram are underlined. The UML permits us to omit the object names for objects in the diagram where there exists only one object of that class (e.g., one object of class **`Bell`** at the bottom of the diagram). In large systems, object diagrams can contain many objects. This can result in cluttered, hard-to-read diagrams. If the name of a particular object is unknown, or if it is not necessary to include the name (i.e., we care only about the object type), we can disregard the object name and display only the colon and the class name.

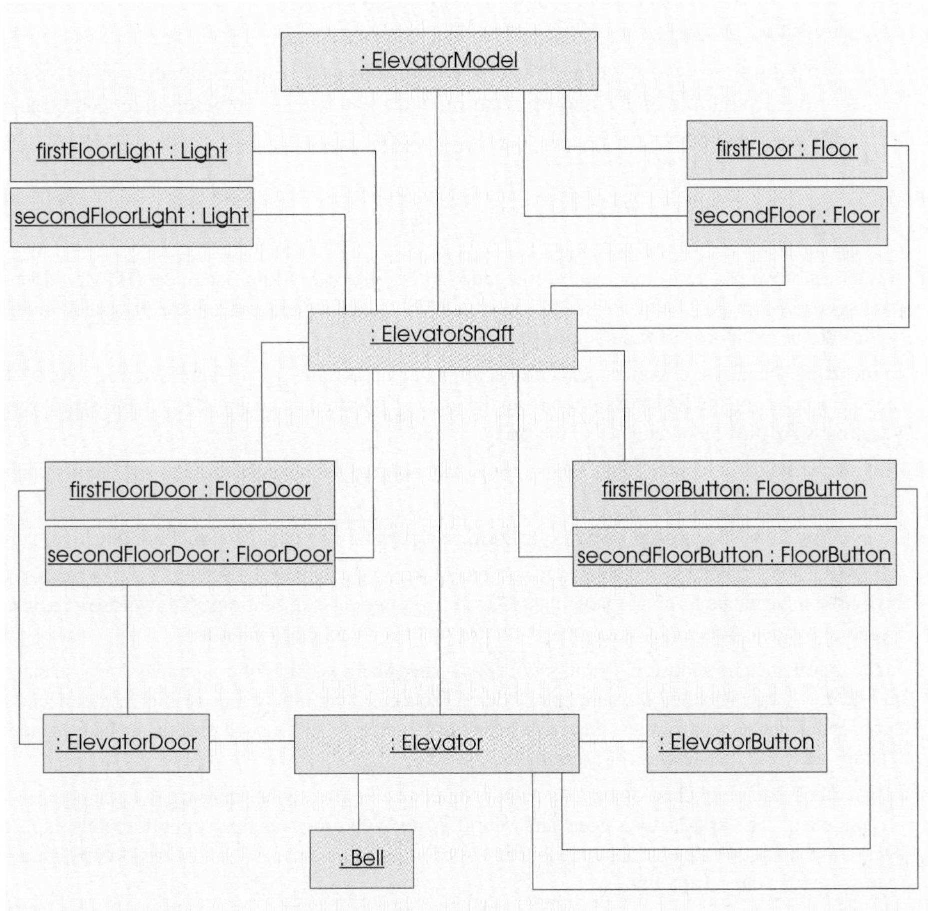

Fig. 3.24 Object diagram of an empty building in our elevator model.

Now we have identified the classes for our system (although we may discover others in later phases of the design process). In "Thinking About Objects," Section 4.14, we determine the attributes for each of these classes, and in "Thinking About Objects," Section 5.11, we use these attributes to examine how the system changes over time and to introduce its behavioral aspects. As we expand our knowledge, we will discover new information that will enable us to describe our classes more completely. Because the real world is inherently object oriented, it will be quite natural for you to pursue this project, even though you might have just begun your study of object orientation.

Questions

1. Why might it be more complicated to implement a three-story (or taller) building?
2. It is common for large buildings to have many elevators. We will see in Chapter 9 that once we have created one elevator object, it is easy to create as many as we like. What problems or opportunities do you foresee in having several elevators,

each of which may pick up and discharge passengers at every floor in a large building?

3. For simplicity, we have given our elevator and each floor a capacity of one passenger. What problems and opportunities do you foresee in being able to increase these capacities?

SUMMARY

- Applets are Java programs that can be embedded in Hypertext Markup Language (HTML) documents (i.e., Web pages). When a browser loads a Web page containing an applet, the applet downloads into the Web browser and begins execution.
- In the **appletviewer**, you can execute an applet again by clicking the appletviewer's **Applet** menu and selecting the **Reload** option from the menu. To terminate an applet, click the **appletviewer**'s **Applet** menu and select the **Quit** option.
- Class **Graphics** is located in package **java.awt**. Import the **Graphics** class so the program can draw graphics.
- Class **JApplet** is located in package **javax.swing**. When you create an applet in Java, you must import the **JApplet** class.
- Java uses inheritance to create new classes from existing class definitions. Keyword **extends** followed by a class name indicates the class from which a new class inherits.
- In the inheritance relationship, the class following **extends** is called the superclass or base class and the new class is called the subclass or derived class. Using inheritance results in a new class definition that has the attributes (data) and behaviors (methods) of the superclass as well as the new features added in the subclass definition.
- A benefit of extending class **JApplet** is that someone else already has defined "what it means to be an applet." The **appletviewer** and World Wide Web browsers that support applets expect every Java applet to have certain capabilities (attributes and behaviors), and class **JApplet** already provides those capabilities.
- Classes are used as "templates" or "blueprints" to instantiate (or create) objects in memory for use in a program. An object (or instance) is a region in the computer's memory in which information is stored for use by the program. The term object normally implies that attributes (data) and behaviors (methods) are associated with the object and that those behaviors perform operations on the attributes of the object.
- Method **paint** is one of three methods (behaviors) that an applet container calls when any applet begins execution. These three methods are **init**, **start** and **paint**, and they are guaranteed to be called in that order.
- The parameter list is where methods receive data required to complete their tasks. Normally, this data is passed by the programmer to the method through a method call (also known as invoking a method). In the case of method **paint**, the applet container calls the method and passes the **Graphics** argument.
- Method **drawString** of class **Graphics** draws a string at the specified location on the applet. The first argument to **drawString** is the **String** to draw. The last two arguments in the list are the coordinates (or position) at which the string should be drawn. Coordinates are measured from the upper-left (0, 0) coordinate of the applet in pixels.
- You must create an HTML (Hypertext Markup Language) file to load an applet into an applet container, so the applet container can execute the applet.

- Many HTML codes (referred to as tags) come in pairs. HTML tags begin with a left angle bracket **<** and end with a right angle bracket **>**.
- Normally, the applet and its corresponding HTML file are stored in the same directory on disk.
- The first component of the **<applet>** tag indicates the file containing the compiled applet class. The second and third components of the **<applet>** tag indicate the **width** and the **height** of the applet in pixels. Generally, each applet should be less than 800 pixels wide and 600 pixels tall.
- The **appletviewer** only understands the **<applet>** and **</applet>** HTML tags, so it is sometimes referred to as the "minimal browser." It ignores all other HTML tags.
- Method **drawLine** of class **Graphics** draws lines. The method requires four arguments representing the two end points of the line on the applet—the x-coordinate and y-coordinate of the first end point in the line and the x-coordinate and y-coordinate of the second end point in the line. All coordinate values are specified with respect to the upper-left corner (0, 0) coordinate of the applet.
- Primitive data type **double** stores double-precision floating-point numbers. Primitive data type **float** stores single-precision floating-point numbers. A **double** requires more memory to store a floating-point value, but stores it with approximately twice the precision of a **float** (15 significant digits for **double** vs. seven significant digits for **float**).
- The **import** statements are not required if you always use the complete name of a class, including the full package name and class name (e.g., **java.awt.Graphics**).
- The asterisk (*****) notation after a package name in an **import** indicates that all classes in the package should be available to the compiler so the compiler can ensure that the classes are used correctly. This allows programmers to use the shorthand name (the class name by itself) of any class from the package in the program.
- Every instance (object) of a class contains one copy of each of that class's instance variables. Instance variables are declared in the body of a class definition, but not in the body of any method of that class definition. An important benefit of instance variables is that their identifiers can be used in all methods of the class.
- Variables defined in the body of a method are known as local variables and can be used only in the body of the method in which they are defined.
- Instance variables are always assigned a default value, and local variables are not.
- Method **init** normally initializes the applet's instance variables (if they need to be initialized to a value other than their default value) and performs any tasks that should occur only once when the applet begins execution
- There are actually two types of variables in Java—primitive data type variables and references.
- References refer to objects in a program. References actually contain the location in the computer's memory of an object. A reference is used to send messages to (i.e., call methods on) the object in memory. As part of the message (method call), we provide the data (arguments) that the method requires to do its task.
- A variable is similar to an object. The primary difference between a variable and an object is that an object is defined by a class definition that can contain both data (instance variables) and methods, whereas a variable is defined by a primitive (or built-in) data type (one of **char**, **byte**, **short**, **int**, **long**, **float**, **double** or **boolean**) that can contain only data.
- A variable can store exactly one value at a time, whereas one object can contain many individual data members.
- If the data type used to declare a variable is a class name, the identifier is a reference to an object and that reference can be used to send messages to (call methods on) that object. If the data type used to declare a variable is one of the primitive data types, the identifier is a variable that can be used to store in memory or retrieve from memory a single value of the declared primitive type.

- Method **Double.parseDouble** (a **static** method of class **Double**) converts its **String** argument to a **double** floating-point value. Class **Double** is part of the package **java.lang**.
- Method **drawRect** draws a rectangle based on its four arguments. The first two integer values represent the upper-left x-coordinate and upper-left y-coordinate where the **Graphics** object begins drawing the rectangle. The third and fourth arguments are non-negative integers that represent the width of the rectangle in pixels and the height of the rectangle in pixels, respectively.
- To use the features of Java 2 in an applet, Sun provides the Java Plug-in to bypass a browser's Java support and use a complete version of the Java 2 Runtime Environment (J2RE) that is installed on the user's local computer.
- To specify that an applet should use the Java Plug-in rather than the browser's Java support, use the HTML Converter to convert the applet's **<applet>** and **</applet>** tags in the HTML file to indicate that the applet container should use the Plug-in to execute the applet. Sun provides the Java Plug-in 1.3 HTML Converter to perform the conversion for you.

TERMINOLOGY

applet
applet container
<applet> tag
Applet menu
appletviewer
boolean primitive type
browser
built-in data type
byte primitive type
char primitive type
command-line argument
coordinate
create an object
derived class
double primitive data type
Double.parseDouble method
double-precision floating-point number
drawLine method of class **Graphics**
drawRect method of class **Graphics**
drawString method of class **Graphics**
extends keyword
float primitive type
floating-point number
Graphics class
height of an applet
HTML Converter
HTML tag
Hypertext Markup Language (HTML)
import statement
information hiding
init method of class **JApplet**
instance variable
instantiate an object
int primitive type
interface
invoke a method
JApplet class
java.awt package
Java Plug-in
Java 2 Runtime Environment (J2RE)
javax.swing package
local variable
logic error
long primitive type
message
method call
Microsoft Internet Explorer
Netscape Communicator
object
paint method of class **JApplet**
parameter list
pixel (picture element)
primitive data type
Quit menu item
references
Reload menu item
short primitive type
single-precision floating-point number
source code
start method of class **JApplet**
subclass
superclass
text file
width of an applet
World Wide Web

SELF-REVIEW EXERCISES

3.1 Fill in the blanks in each of the following.

a) Class _________ provides methods for drawing.

b) Java applets begin execution with a series of three method calls: _________, _________ and _________.

c) Methods _________ and _________ display lines and rectangles.

d) Keyword _________ indicates that a new class is a subclass of an existing class.

e) Every Java applet should extend either class _________ or class _________.

f) Java's eight primitive data types are _________, _________, _________, _________, _________, _________, _________ and _________.

3.2 State whether each of the following is *true* or *false*. If *false*, explain why.

a) To draw a rectangle, method **drawRect** requires four arguments that specify two points on the applet.

b) Method **drawLine** requires four arguments that specify two points on the applet to draw a line.

c) Type **Double** is a primitive data type.

d) Data type **int** is used to declare a floating-point number.

e) Method **Double.parseDouble** converts a **String** to a primitive **double** value.

3.3 Write Java statements to accomplish each of the following:

a) Display a dialog asking the user to enter a floating-point number.

b) Convert a **String** to a floating-point number and store the converted value in **double** variable **age**. Assume that the **String** is stored in **stringValue**.

c) Draw the message **"This is a Java program"** on one line on an applet (assume you are defining this statement in the applet's **paint** method) at position *(10, 10)*.

d) Draw the message **"This is a Java program"** on two lines on an applet (assume these statements are defined in applet method **paint**) starting at position *(10, 10)* and where the first line ends with **Java**. Make the two lines start at the same *x* coordinate.

ANSWERS TO SELF-REVIEW EXERCISES

3.1 a) **Graphics**. b) **init**, **start**, **paint**. c) **drawLine**, **drawRect**. d) **extends**. e) **JApplet**, **Applet**. f) **byte**, **short**, **int**, **long**, **float**, **double**, **char** and **boolean**.

3.2 a) False. Method **drawRect** requires four arguments—two that specify the upper-left corner of the rectangle and two that specify the width and height of the rectangle. b) True. c) False. Type **Double** is a class in the **java.lang** package. Remember that names that start with a capital letter are normally class names. d) False. Data type **double** or data type **float** can be used to declare a floating-point number. Data type **int** is used to declare integers. e) True.

3.3 a)
```
stringValue = JOptionPane.showInputDialog(
   "Enter a floating-point number" );
```
b)
```
age = Double.parseDouble( stringValue );
```
c)
```
g.drawString( "This is a Java program", 10, 10 );
```
d)
```
g.drawString( "This is a Java", 10, 10 );
g.drawString( "program", 10, 25 );
```

EXERCISES

3.4 Fill in the blanks in each of the following:

a) Data type _________ declares a single-precision floating-point variable.

b) If class **Double** provides method **parseDouble** to convert a **String** to a **double** and class **Integer** provides method **parseInt** to convert a **String** to an **int**, then class **Float** probably provides method __________ to convert a **String** to a **float**.
c) Data type __________ declares a double-precision floating-point variable.
d) The __________ or a browser can be used to execute a Java applet.
e) To load an applet into a browser you must first define a(n) __________ file.
f) The __________ and __________ HTML tags specify that an applet should be loaded into an applet container and executed.

3.5 State whether each of the following is *true* or *false*. If *false*, explain why.
a) All browsers support Java 2.
b) When using an **import** of the form **javax.swing.***, all classes in the package are imported.
c) You do not need import statements if the full package name and class name are specified each time you refer to a class in a program.

3.6 Write an applet that asks the user to enter two floating-point numbers, obtains the two numbers from the user and draws the sum, product (multiplication), difference and quotient (division) of the two numbers. Use the techniques shown in Fig. 3.12.

3.7 Write an applet that asks the user to enter two floating-point numbers, obtains the numbers from the user and displays the larger number followed by the words "**is larger**" as a string on the applet. If the numbers are equal, print the message "**These numbers are equal**." Use the techniques shown in Fig. 3.12.

3.8 Write an applet that inputs three floating-point numbers from the user and displays the sum, average, product, smallest and largest of these numbers as strings on the applet. Use the techniques shown in Fig. 3.12.

3.9 Write an applet that inputs from the user the radius of a circle as a floating-point number and draws the circle's diameter, circumference and area. Use the value 3.14159 for π. Use the techniques shown in Fig. 3.12. [Note: You may also use the predefined constant **Math.PI** for the value of π. This constant is more precise than the value 3.14159. Class **Math** is defined in the **java.lang** package, so you do not need to **import** it.] Use the following formulas (r is the radius):

$$diameter = 2r$$
$$circumference = 2\pi r$$
$$area = \pi r^2$$

3.10 Write an applet that draws a box, an oval, an arrow and a diamond using asterisks (*****) as follows:

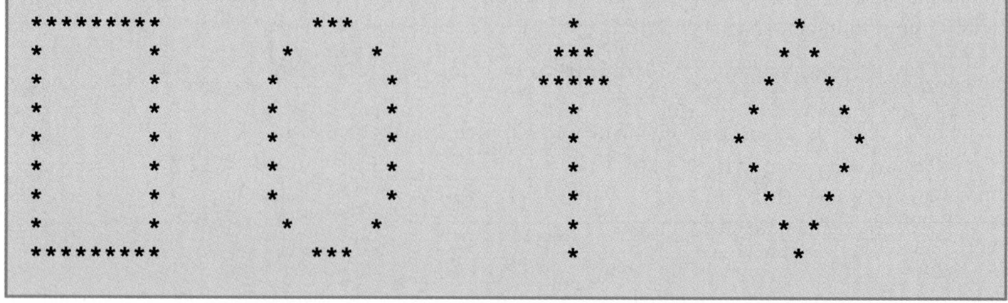

```
*********        ***          *            *
*       *      *     *       ***          * *
*       *     *       *     *****        *   *
*       *     *       *       *         *     *
*       *     *       *       *        *       *
*       *     *       *       *         *     *
*       *     *       *       *          *   *
*       *      *     *        *           * *
*********        ***          *            *
```

3.11 Write an applet that reads five integers and determines and prints the largest and smallest integers in the group. Use only the programming techniques you learned in this chapter and Chapter 2. Draw the results on the applet.

3.12 Write an applet that reads in two floating-point numbers and determines and prints if the first is a multiple of the second. (*Hint*: Use the modulus operator.) Use only the programming techniques you learned in this chapter and Chapter 2. Draw the results on the applet.

3.13 Write an applet that draws a checkerboard pattern as follows:

```
* * * * * * * *
 * * * * * * * *
* * * * * * * *
 * * * * * * * *
* * * * * * * *
 * * * * * * * *
* * * * * * * *
 * * * * * * * *
```

3.14 Write an applet that draws a variety of rectangles of different sizes and locations.

3.15 Write an applet that allows the user to input the four arguments required by method **drawRect**, then draws a rectangle using the four input values.

3.16 The **Graphics** class contains a **drawOval** method that takes the same four arguments as method **drawRect**. However, the arguments for method **drawOval** specify the "bounding box" for the oval. The sides of the bounding box are the boundaries of the oval. Write a Java applet that draws an oval and a rectangle with the same four arguments. You will see that the oval touches the rectangle at the center of each side.

3.17 Modify the solution to Exercise 3.16 to output a variety of ovals of different shapes and sizes.

3.18 Write an applet that allows the user to input the four arguments required by method **drawOval**, then draws an oval using the four input values.

3.19 What does the following code print?

```
g.drawString( "*", 25, 25 );
g.drawString( "***", 25, 55 );
g.drawString( "*****", 25, 85 );
g.drawString( "****", 25, 70 );
g.drawString( "**", 25, 40 );
```

3.20 Using only programming techniques from Chapter 2 and Chapter 3, write an applet that calculates the squares and cubes of the numbers from 0 to 10 and draws the resulting values in table format as follows:

```
number  square  cube
0       0       0
1       1       1
2       4       8
3       9       27
4       16      64
5       25      125
6       36      216
7       49      343
8       64      512
9       81      729
10      100     1000
```

[*Note*: This program does not require any input from the user.]

Control Structures: Part 1

Objectives

- To understand basic problem-solving techniques.
- To be able to develop algorithms through the process of top-down, stepwise refinement.
- To be able to use the **`if`** and **`if/else`** selection structures to choose among alternative actions.
- To be able to use the **`while`** repetition structure to execute statements in a program repeatedly.
- To understand counter-controlled repetition and sentinel-controlled repetition.
- To be able to use the increment, decrement and assignment operators.

Let's all move one place on.
Lewis Carroll

The wheel is come full circle.
William Shakespeare, *King Lear*

How many apples fell on Newton's head before he took the hint!
Robert Frost, comment

Outline

4.1 Introduction
4.2 Algorithms
4.3 Pseudocode
4.4 Control Structures
4.5 The `if` Selection Structure
4.6 The `if/else` Selection Structure
4.7 The `while` Repetition Structure
4.8 Formulating Algorithms: Case Study 1 (Counter-Controlled Repetition)
4.9 Formulating Algorithms with Top-Down, Stepwise Refinement: Case Study 2 (Sentinel-Controlled Repetition)
4.10 Formulating Algorithms with Top-Down, Stepwise Refinement: Case Study 3 (Nested Control Structures)
4.11 Assignment Operators
4.12 Increment and Decrement Operators
4.13 Primitive Data Types
4.14 (Optional Case Study) Thinking About Objects: Identifying Class Attributes

Summary • Terminology • Self-Review Exercises • Answers to Self-Review Exercises • Exercises

4.1 Introduction

Before writing a program to solve a problem, it is essential to have a thorough understanding of the problem and a carefully planned approach to solving the problem. When writing a program, it is equally essential to understand the types of building blocks that are available and to employ proven program construction principles. In this chapter and in Chapter 5, we discuss these issues in our presentation of the theory and principles of structured programming. The techniques you learn here are applicable to most high-level languages, including Java. When we study object-based programming in more depth in Chapter 8, we will see that control structures are helpful in building and manipulating objects.

4.2 Algorithms

Any computing problem can be solved by executing a series of actions in a specific order. A *procedure* for solving a problem in terms of

1. the *actions* to be executed and
2. the *order* in which the actions are to be executed

is called an *algorithm*. The following example demonstrates that correctly specifying the order in which the actions are to be executed is important.

Consider the "rise-and-shine algorithm" followed by one junior executive for getting out of bed and going to work: (1) Get out of bed, (2) take off pajamas, (3) take a shower, (4) get dressed, (5) eat breakfast, (6) carpool to work.

This routine gets the executive to work well prepared to make critical decisions. Suppose, however, that the same steps are performed in a slightly different order: (1) Get out of bed, (2) take off pajamas, (3) get dressed, (4) take a shower, (5) eat breakfast, (6) carpool to work.

In this case, our junior executive shows up for work soaking wet. Specifying the order in which statements are to be executed in a computer program is called *program control.* In this chapter and Chapter 5, we investigate the program control capabilities of Java.

4.3 Pseudocode

Pseudocode is an artificial and informal language that helps programmers develop algorithms. The pseudocode we present here is particularly useful for developing algorithms that will be converted to structured portions of Java programs. Pseudocode is similar to everyday English; it is convenient and user friendly, although it is not an actual computer programming language.

Pseudocode programs are not actually executed on computers. Rather, they help the programmer "think out" a program before attempting to write it in a programming language, such as Java. In this chapter, we give several examples of pseudocode programs.

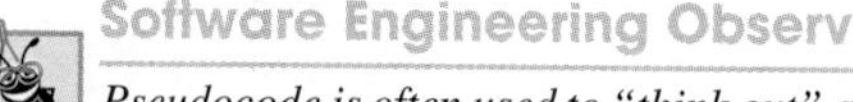

Software Engineering Observation 4.1

Pseudocode is often used to "think out" a program during the program design process. Then the pseudocode program is converted to Java.

The style of pseudocode we present consists purely of characters, so programmers may conveniently type pseudocode programs using an editor program. The computer can produce a freshly printed copy of a pseudocode program on demand. A carefully prepared pseudocode program may be converted easily to a corresponding Java program. This conversion is done in many cases simply by replacing pseudocode statements with their Java equivalents.

Pseudocode normally describes only executable statements—the actions that are performed when the program is converted from pseudocode to Java and is run. Declarations are not executable statements. For example, the declaration

```
int i;
```

tells the compiler the type of variable **i** and instructs the compiler to reserve space in memory for the variable. This declaration does not cause any action—such as input, output or a calculation—to occur when the program is executed. Some programmers choose to list variables and mention the purpose of each at the beginning of a pseudocode program.

4.4 Control Structures

Normally, statements in a program are executed one after the other in the order in which they are written. This process is called *sequential execution.* Various Java statements we will soon discuss enable the programmer to specify that the next statement to be executed may be other than the next one in sequence. This is called *transfer of control.*

During the 1960s, it became clear that the indiscriminate use of transfers of control was the root of much difficulty experienced by software development groups. The finger of blame was pointed at the **goto** *statement* (used in several programming languages, including C and Basic), which allows the programmer to specify a transfer of control to one of a very wide range of possible destinations in a program. The notion of so-called *structured programming* became almost synonymous with "**goto** elimination." Java does not have a **goto** statement; however, **goto** is a reserved word and should not be used in a Java program.

The research of Bohm and Jacopini[1] had demonstrated that programs could be written without any **goto** statements. The challenge of the era for programmers was to shift their styles to "**goto**-less programming." It was not until the 1970s that programmers started taking structured programming seriously. The results have been impressive, as software development groups have reported reduced development times, more frequent on-time delivery of systems and more frequent within-budget completion of software projects. The key to these successes is that structured programs are clearer, easier to debug and modify and more likely to be bug free in the first place.

Bohm and Jacopini's work demonstrated that all programs could be written in terms of only three *control structures*—namely, the *sequence structure*, the *selection structure* and the *repetition structure*. The sequence structure is built into Java. Unless directed otherwise, the computer executes Java statements one after the other in the order in which they are written. The *flowchart* segment in Fig. 4.1 illustrates a typical sequence structure in which two calculations are performed in order.

A flowchart is a graphical representation of an algorithm or a portion of an algorithm. Flowcharts are drawn using certain special-purpose symbols, such as rectangles, diamonds, ovals and small circles; these symbols are connected by arrows called *flowlines*, which indicate the order in which the actions of the algorithm execute.

Like pseudocode, flowcharts are often useful for developing and representing algorithms, although pseudocode is strongly preferred by many programmers. Flowcharts show clearly how control structures operate; that is all we use them for in this text. The reader should carefully compare the pseudocode and flowchart representations of each control structure.

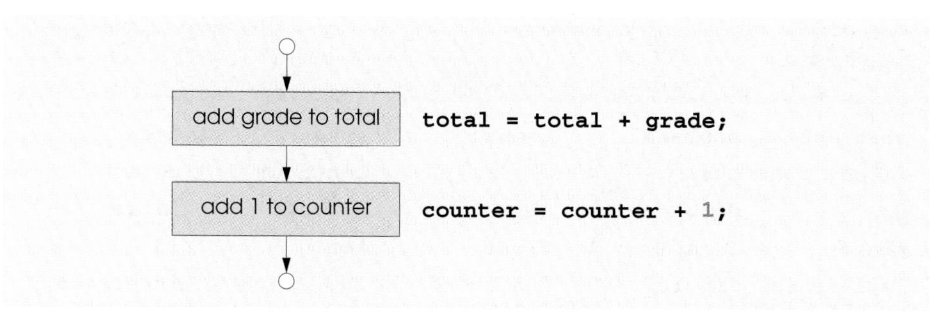

Fig. 4.1 Flowcharting Java's sequence structure.

1. Bohm, C., and G. Jacopini, "Flow Diagrams, Turing Machines, and Languages with Only Two Formation Rules," *Communications of the ACM*, Vol. 9, No. 5, May 1966, pp. 336–371.

Consider the flowchart segment for the sequence structure in Fig. 4.1. We use the *rectangle symbol*, also called the *action symbol*, to indicate any type of action, including a calculation or an input/output operation. The flowlines in the figure indicate the order in which the actions are to be performed; first, **grade** is to be added to **total**, and then **1** is to be added to **counter**. Java allows us to have as many actions as we want in a sequence structure. As we will soon see, anywhere a single action may be placed, we may instead place several actions in sequence.

When drawing a flowchart that represents a *complete* algorithm, an *oval symbol* containing the word "Begin" is the first symbol used in the flowchart; an oval symbol containing the word "End" indicates where the algorithm ends. When drawing only a portion of an algorithm, as in Fig. 4.1, the oval symbols are omitted in favor of *small circle symbols*, also called *connector symbols*.

Perhaps the most important flowcharting symbol is the *diamond symbol*, also called the *decision symbol*, which indicates that a decision is to be made. We will discuss the diamond symbol in the next section.

Java provides three types of selection structures; we discuss each in this chapter and in Chapter 5. The **if** selection structure either performs (selects) an action, if a condition is true, or skips the action, if the condition is false. The **if/else** selection structure performs an action if a condition is true and performs a different action if the condition is false. The **switch** selection structure (Chapter 5) performs one of many different actions, depending on the value of an expression.

The **if** structure is called a *single-selection structure*, because it selects or ignores a single action (or, as we will soon see, a single group of actions). The **if/else** structure is called a *double-selection structure*, because it selects between two different actions (or groups of actions). The **switch** structure is called a *multiple-selection structure*, because it selects among many different actions (or groups of actions).

Java provides three types of repetition structures—namely, **while**, **do/while** and **for**. (**do/while** and **for** are covered in Chapter 5.) Each of the words **if**, **else**, **switch**, **while**, **do** and **for** are Java *keywords*. These words are reserved by the language to implement various features, such as Java's control structures. Keywords cannot be used as identifiers, such as for variable names. A complete list of Java keywords is shown in Fig. 4.2.

Java Keywords				
abstract	**boolean**	**break**	**byte**	**case**
catch	**char**	**class**	**continue**	**default**
do	**double**	**else**	**extends**	**false**
final	**finally**	**float**	**for**	**if**
implements	**import**	**instanceof**	**int**	**interface**
long	**native**	**new**	**null**	**package**
private	**protected**	**public**	**return**	**short**

Fig. 4.2 Java keywords (part 1 of 2).

Java Keywords				
`static`	`super`	`switch`	`synchronized`	`this`
`throw`	`throws`	`transient`	`true`	`try`
`void`	`volatile`	`while`		
Keywords that are reserved, but not used, by Java				
`const`	`goto`			

Fig. 4.2 Java keywords (part 2 of 2).

Common Programming Error 4.1

Using a keyword as an identifier is a syntax error.

Well, that is all there is. Java has only seven control structures: the sequence structure, three types of selection structures and three types of repetition structures. Each program is formed by combining as many of each type of control structure as is appropriate for the algorithm the program implements. As with the sequence structure in Fig. 4.1, we will see that each control structure is flowcharted with two small circle symbols, one at the entry point to the control structure and one at the exit point.

Single-entry/single-exit control structures make it easy to build programs; the control structures are attached to one another by connecting the exit point of one control structure to the entry point of the next. This procedure is similar to the way in which a child stacks building blocks, so we call it *control-structure stacking*. We will learn that there is only one other way in which control structures may be connected: *control-structure nesting*. Thus, algorithms in Java programs are constructed from only seven different types of control structures, combined in only two ways.

4.5 The `if` Selection Structure

A selection structure is used to choose among alternative courses of action in a program. For example, suppose that the passing grade on an examination is 60 (out of 100). Then the pseudocode statement

If student's grade is greater than or equal to 60
    Print "Passed"

determines if the condition "student's grade is greater than or equal to 60" is true or false. If the condition is true, then "Passed" is printed, and the next pseudocode statement in order is "performed." (Remember that pseudocode is not a real programming language.) If the condition is false, the Print statement is ignored, and the next pseudocode statement in order is performed. Note that the second line of this selection structure is indented. Such indentation is optional, but it is highly recommended, because it emphasizes the inherent structure of structured programs. The Java compiler ignores white-space characters, like blanks, tabs and newlines, used for indentation and vertical spacing. Programmers insert these white-space characters to enhance program clarity.

Good Programming Practice 4.1

Consistently applying reasonable indentation conventions throughout your programs improves program readability. We suggest a fixed-size tab of about π inch or three spaces per indent.

The preceding pseudocode *if* statement may be written in Java as

```
if ( studentGrade >= 60 )
   System.out.println( "Passed" );
```

Notice that the Java code corresponds closely to the pseudocode. This attribute is a property of pseudocode that makes it a useful program development tool. The statement in the body of the **if** structure outputs the character string **"Passed"** in the command window.

The flowchart in Fig. 4.3 illustrates the single-selection **if** structure. This flowchart contains what is perhaps the most important flowcharting symbol—the *diamond symbol*, also called the *decision symbol*, which indicates that a decision is to be made. The decision symbol contains an expression, such as a condition, that can be either **true** or **false**. The decision symbol has two flowlines emerging from it. One indicates the direction to be taken when the expression in the symbol is true; the other indicates the direction to be taken when the expression is false. A decision can be made on any expression that evaluates to a value of Java's **boolean** type (i.e., any expression that evaluates to **true** or **false**).

Note that the **if** structure is a single-entry/single-exit structure. We will soon learn that the flowcharts for the remaining control structures also contain (besides small circle symbols and flowlines) only rectangle symbols, to indicate the actions to be performed, and diamond symbols, to indicate decisions to be made. This factor is indicative of the *action/decision model of programming* we have been emphasizing throughout this chapter.

We can envision seven bins, each containing only control structures of one of the seven types. These control structures are empty; nothing is written in the rectangles or in the diamonds. The programmer's task, then, is to assemble a program from as many of each type of control structure as the algorithm demands, combining the control structures in only two possible ways (stacking or nesting) and then filling in the actions and decisions in a manner appropriate for the algorithm. In this chapter we discuss the variety of ways in which actions and decisions may be written.

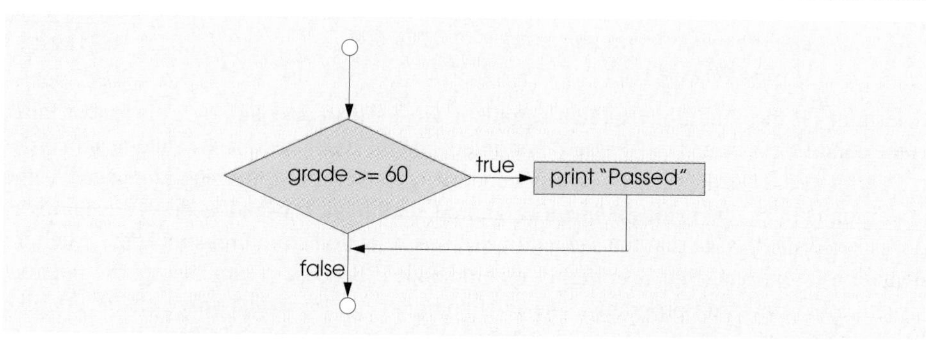

Fig. 4.3 Flowcharting the single-selection **if** structure.

4.6 The `if/else` Selection Structure

The **`if`** selection structure performs an indicated action only when the given condition evaluates to **`true`**; otherwise, the action is skipped. The **`if/else`** selection structure allows the programmer to specify that a different action is to be performed when the condition is true rather than when the condition is false. For example, the pseudocode statement

If student's grade is greater than or equal to 60
    Print "Passed"
else
    Print "Failed"

prints *Passed* if the student's grade is greater than or equal to 60 and prints *Failed* if the student's grade is less than 60. In either case, after printing occurs, the next pseudocode statement in sequence is "performed." Note that the body of the *else* is also indented.

Good Programming Practice 4.2

Indent both body statements of an **`if/else`** *structure.*

The indentation convention you choose should be carefully applied throughout your programs. It is difficult to read programs that do not use uniform spacing conventions.

The preceding pseudocode *If/else* structure may be written in Java as

```
if ( studentGrade >= 60 )
   System.out.println( "Passed" );
else
   System.out.println( "Failed" );
```

The flowchart in Fig. 4.4 nicely illustrates the flow of control in an **`if/else`** structure. Once again, note that, besides small circles and arrows, the only symbols in the flowchart are rectangles (for actions) and a diamond (for a decision). We continue to emphasize this action/decision model of computing. Imagine again a deep bin containing as many empty double-selection structures as might be needed to build a Java algorithm. The programmer's job is to assemble the selection structures (by stacking and nesting) with other control structures required by the algorithm and to fill in the empty rectangles and empty diamonds with actions and decisions appropriate to the algorithm being implemented.

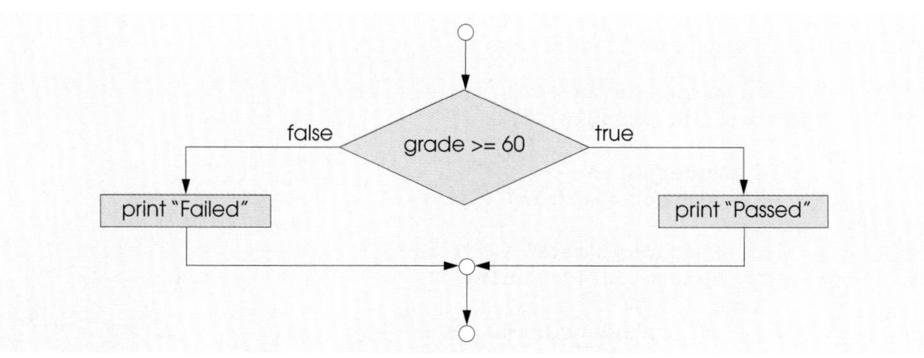

Fig. 4.4 Flowcharting the double-selection **`if/else`** structure.

The *conditional operator* (**?:**) is related to the **if/else** structure. **?:** is Java's only *ternary operator*—it takes three operands. The operands together with **?:** form a *conditional expression.* The first operand is a **boolean** expression, the second is the value for the conditional expression if the condition evaluates to **true** and the third is the value for the conditional expression if the condition evaluates to **false**. For example, the statement

```
System.out.println( studentGrade >= 60 ? "Passed" : "Failed" );
```

contains a conditional expression that evaluates to the string **"Passed"** if the condition **studentGrade >= 60** is true and to the string **"Failed"** if the condition is false. Thus, this statement with the conditional operator performs essentially the same function as the **if/else** statement given previously. The precedence of the conditional operator is low, so the entire conditional expression is normally placed in parentheses. We will see that conditional operators can be used in some situations where **if/else** statements cannot.

Good Programming Practice 4.3

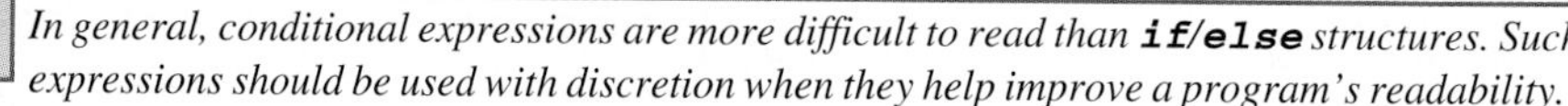

In general, conditional expressions are more difficult to read than **if/else** *structures. Such expressions should be used with discretion when they help improve a program's readability.*

Nested **if/else** *structures* test for multiple cases by placing **if/else** structures inside **if/else** structures. For example, the following pseudocode statement prints **A** for exam grades greater than or equal to 90, **B** for grades in the range 80 to 89, **C** for grades in the range 70 to 79, **D** for grades in the range 60 to 69 and **F** for all other grades:

```
If student's grade is greater than or equal to 90
    Print "A"
else
    If student's grade is greater than or equal to 80
        Print "B"
    else
        If student's grade is greater than or equal to 70
            Print "C"
        else
            If student's grade is greater than or equal to 60
                Print "D"
            else
                Print "F"
```

This pseudocode may be written in Java as

```
if ( studentGrade >= 90 )
   System.out.println( "A" );
else
   if ( studentGrade >= 80 )
      System.out.println( "B" );
   else
      if ( studentGrade >= 70 )
         System.out.println( "C" );
      else
         if ( studentGrade >= 60 )
            System.out.println( "D" );
         else
            System.out.println( "F" );
```

If **studentGrade** is greater than or equal to 90, the first four conditions will be true, but only the **System.out.println** statement after the first test will be executed. After that particular **System.out.println** is executed, the **else** part of the "outer" **if/else** statement is skipped.

Good Programming Practice 4.4

If there are several levels of indentation, each level should be indented by the same additional amount of space.

Most Java programmers prefer to write the preceding **if** structure as

```
if ( grade >= 90 )
   System.out.println( "A" );
else if ( grade >= 80 )
   System.out.println( "B" );
else if ( grade >= 70 )
   System.out.println( "C" );
else if ( grade >= 60 )
   System.out.println( "D" );
else
   System.out.println( "F" );
```

Both forms are equivalent. The latter form is popular because it avoids the deep indentation of the code to the right. Such deep indentation often leaves little room on a line, forcing lines to be split and decreasing program readability.

It is important to note that the Java compiler always associates an **else** with the previous **if** unless told to do otherwise by the placement of braces (**{}**). This attribute is referred to as the *dangling-else problem*. For example,

```
if ( x > 5 )
   if ( y > 5 )
      System.out.println( "x and y are > 5" );
else
   System.out.println( "x is <= 5" );
```

appears to indicate that if **x** is greater than **5**, the **if** structure in its body determines if **y** is also greater than **5**. If so, the string **"x and y are > 5"** is output. Otherwise, it *appears* that if **x** is not greater than **5**, the **else** part of the **if/else** structure outputs the string **"x is <= 5"**.

Beware! The preceding nested **if** structure does not execute as it would appear to. The compiler actually interprets the preceding structure as

```
if ( x > 5 )
   if ( y > 5 )
      System.out.println( "x and y are > 5" );
   else
      System.out.println( "x is <= 5" );
```

in which the body of the first **if** structure is an **if/else** structure. This structure tests if **x** is greater than **5**. If so, execution continues by testing if **y** is also greater than **5**. If the second condition is true, the proper string—**"x and y are > 5"**—is displayed. However, if the second condition is false, the string **"x is <= 5"** is displayed, even though we know that **x** is greater than **5**.

To force the preceding nested **if** structure to execute as it was originally intended, the structure must be written as follows:

```
if ( x > 5 ) {
   if ( y > 5 )
      System.out.println( "x and y are > 5" );
}
else
   System.out.println( "x is <= 5" );
```

The braces (**{}**) indicate to the compiler that the second **if** structure is in the body of the first **if** structure and that the **else** is matched with the first **if** structure. In Exercise 4.21 and Exercise 4.22, you will investigate the dangling-else problem further.

The **if** selection structure normally expects only one statement in its body. To include several statements in the body of an **if** structure, enclose the statements in braces (**{** and **}**). A set of statements contained within a pair of braces is called a *block*.

Software Engineering Observation 4.2

A block can be placed anywhere in a program that a single statement can be placed.

The following example includes a block in the **else** part of an **if/else** structure:

```
if ( grade >= 60 )
   System.out.println( "Passed" );
else {
   System.out.println( "Failed" );
   System.out.println( "You must take this course again." );
}
```

In this case, if **grade** is less than 60, the program executes both statements in the body of the **else** and prints

```
Failed.
You must take this course again.
```

Notice the braces surrounding the two statements in the **else** clause. These braces are important. Without the braces, the statement

```
System.out.println( "You must take this course again." );
```

would be outside the body of the **else** part of the **if** structure and would execute regardless of whether the grade is less than 60.

Common Programming Error 4.2

Forgetting one or both of the braces that delimit a block can lead to syntax or logic errors.

Syntax errors (such as when one brace in a block is left out of the program) are caught by the compiler. A *logic error* (such as when both braces in a block are left out of the program) has its effect at execution time. A *fatal logic error* causes a program to fail and terminate prematurely. A *nonfatal logic error* allows a program to continue executing, but the program produces incorrect results.

Software Engineering Observation 4.3

Just as a block can be placed anywhere a single statement can be placed, it is also possible to have no statement at all (i.e., the empty statement in such places). The empty statement is represented by placing a semicolon (`;`) where a statement would normally be.

Common Programming Error 4.3

Placing a semicolon after the condition in an `if` structure leads to a logic error in single-selection `if` structures and a syntax error in double-selection `if` structures (if the `if` part contains a nonempty body statement).

Good Programming Practice 4.5

Some programmers prefer to type the beginning and ending braces of blocks before typing the individual statements within the braces. This practice helps avoid omitting one or both of the braces.

In this section, we have introduced the notion of a block. A block may contain declarations (as does the body of **`main`**, for example). The declarations in a block commonly are placed first in the block before any action statements occur, but declarations may also be intermixed with action statements.

4.7 The `while` Repetition Structure

A *repetition structure* allows the programmer to specify that an action is to be repeated while some condition remains true. The pseudocode statement

While there are more items on my shopping list
    Purchase next item and cross it off my list

describes the repetition that occurs during a shopping trip. The condition "there are more items on my shopping list" may be true or false. If it is true, then the action "Purchase next item and cross it off my list" is performed. This action will be performed repeatedly while the condition remains true. The statement(s) contained in the *while* repetition structure constitute the body of the *while* structure. The body of the *while* structure may be a single statement or a block. Eventually, the condition will become false (when the last item on the shopping list has been purchased and crossed off the list). At this point, the repetition terminates, and the first pseudocode statement after the repetition structure is executed.

Common Programming Error 4.4

Not providing in the body of a `while` structure an action that eventually causes the condition in the `while` to become false is a logic error. Normally, such a repetition structure will never terminate—an error called an infinite loop.

Common Programming Error 4.5

Spelling the keyword `while` with an uppercase `W`, as in `While`, is a syntax error. (Remember that Java is a case-sensitive language.) All of Java's reserved keywords, such as `while`, `if` and `else`, contain only lowercase letters.

As an example of a **`while`** structure, consider a program segment designed to find the first power of 2 larger than 1000. Suppose that the **`int`** variable **`product`** has been initialized to **`2`**. When the following **`while`** structure finishes executing, **`product`** contains the result:

```
int product = 2;

while ( product <= 1000 )
   product = 2 * product;
```

The flowchart in Fig. 4.5 illustrates the flow of control of the preceding **while** repetition structure. Once again, note that, besides small circles and arrows, the flowchart contains only a rectangle symbol and a diamond symbol.

Imagine, again, a deep bin of empty **while** structures that may be stacked and nested with other control structures to form a structured implementation of an algorithm's flow of control. The empty rectangles and diamonds are then filled in with appropriate actions and decisions. The flowchart clearly shows the repetition. The flowline emerging from the rectangle wraps back to the decision, which is tested each time through the loop until the decision eventually becomes false. At this point, the **while** structure is exited, and control passes to the next statement in the program.

When the **while** structure is entered, **product** is 2. Variable **product** is repeatedly multiplied by 2, taking on the values 4, 8, 16, 32, 64, 128, 256, 512 and 1024 successively. When **product** becomes 1024, the condition **product <= 1000** in the **while** structure becomes **false**. This result terminates the repetition, with 1024 as **product**'s final value. Execution continues with the next statement after the **while**. [*Note*: If a **while** structure's condition is initially **false**, the body statement(s) will never be performed.]

4.8 Formulating Algorithms: Case Study 1 (Counter-Controlled Repetition)

To illustrate how algorithms are developed, we solve several variations of a class-averaging problem. Consider the following problem statement:

> *A class of ten students took a quiz. The grades (integers in the range 0 to 100) for this quiz are available to you. Determine the class average on the quiz.*

The class average is equal to the sum of the grades divided by the number of students. The algorithm for solving this problem on a computer must input each of the grades, perform the averaging calculation and print the result.

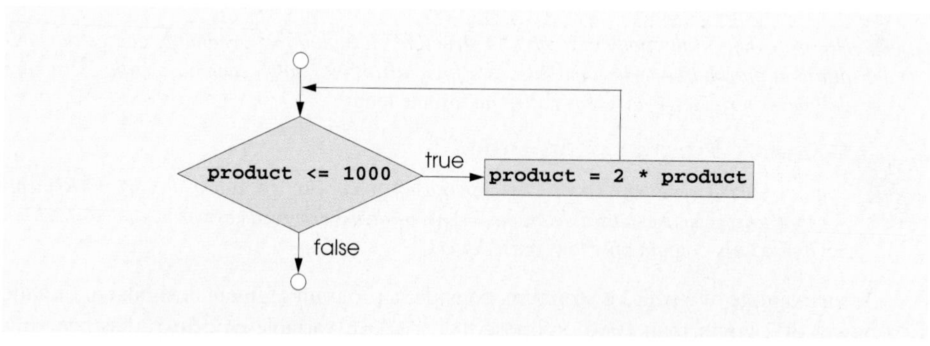

Fig. 4.5 Flowcharting the **while** repetition structure.

Let us use pseudocode to list the actions to be executed and specify the order in which these actions should be executed. We use *counter-controlled repetition* to input the grades one at a time. This technique uses a variable called a *counter* to control the number of times a set of statements will execute. In this example, repetition terminates when the counter exceeds 10. In this section, we present a pseudocode algorithm (Fig. 4.6) and the corresponding program (Fig. 4.7) to solve this probem using counter-controlled repetition. In the next section, we show how pseudocode algorithms are developed. Counter-controlled repetition is often called *definite repetition*, because the number of repetitions is known before the loop begins executing.

Note the references in the algorithm to a total and a counter. A *total* is a variable used to accumulate the sum of a series of values. A *counter* is a variable used to count—in this case, to count the number of grades entered. Variables used to store totals should normally be initialized to zero before being used in a program; otherwise, the sum would include the previous value stored in the total's memory location.

```
Set total to zero
Set grade counter to one

While grade counter is less than or equal to ten
    Input the next grade
    Add the grade into the total
    Add one to the grade counter

Set the class average to the total divided by ten
Print the class average
```

Fig. 4.6 Pseudocode algorithm that uses counter-controlled repetition to solve the class-average problem.

```java
// Fig. 4.7: Average1.java
// Class average program with counter-controlled repetition.

// Java extension packages
import javax.swing.JOptionPane;

public class Average1 {

   // main method begins execution of Java application
   public static void main( String args[] )
   {
      int total,          // sum of grades input by user
          gradeCounter,   // number of grades entered
          gradeValue,     // grade value
          average;        // average of all grades
      String grade;       // grade typed by user

```

Fig. 4.7 Class-average program with counter-controlled repetition (part 1 of 3).

```
      // Initialization Phase
      total = 0;              // clear total
      gradeCounter = 1;       // prepare to loop

      // Processing Phase
      while ( gradeCounter <= 10 ) {  // loop 10 times

         // prompt for input and read grade from user
         grade = JOptionPane.showInputDialog(
            "Enter integer grade: " );

         // convert grade from a String to an integer
         gradeValue = Integer.parseInt( grade );

         // add gradeValue to total
         total = total + gradeValue;

         // add 1 to gradeCounter
         gradeCounter = gradeCounter + 1;

      }  // end while structure

      // Termination Phase
      average = total / 10;  // perform integer division

      // display average of exam grades
      JOptionPane.showMessageDialog( null,
         "Class average is " + average, "Class Average",
         JOptionPane.INFORMATION_MESSAGE );

      System.exit( 0 );     // terminate the program

   }  // end method main

}  // end class Average1
```

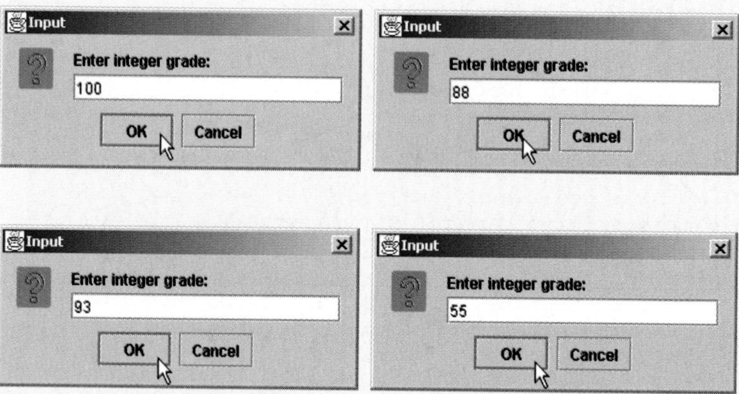

Fig. 4.7 Class-average program with counter-controlled repetition (part 2 of 3).

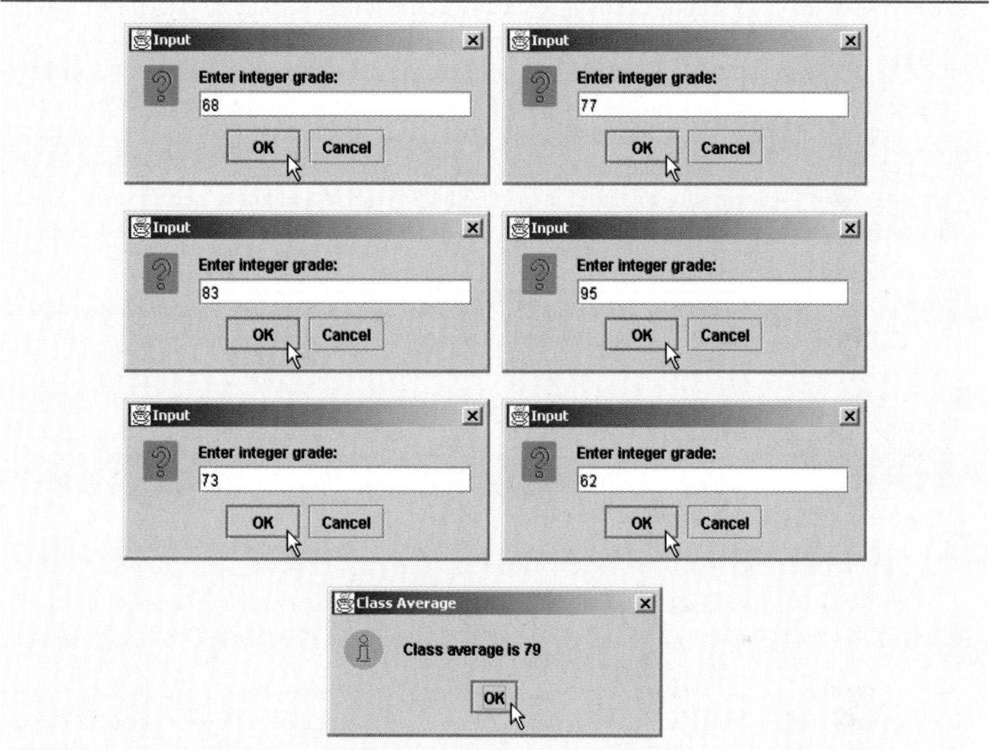

Fig. 4.7 Class-average program with counter-controlled repetition (part 3 of 3).

Good Programming Practice 4.6

Initialize counters and totals.

Line 5,

```
import javax.swing.JOptionPane;
```

imports class **JOptionPane** to enable the program to read data from the keyboard and output data to the screen using the input dialog and message dialog shown in Chapter 2.

Line 7 begins the definition of application class **Average1**. Remember that the definition of an application class must contain a **main** method (lines 10–49) in order for the application to be executed.

Lines 12–16,

```
int total,          // sum of grades
    gradeCounter,   // number of grades entered
    gradeValue,     // grade value
    average;        // average of all grades
String grade;       // grade typed by user
```

declare variables **total**, **gradeCounter**, **gradeValue** and **average** to be of type **int** and variable **grade** to be of type **String**. Variable **grade** stores the **String** the user types in the input dialog. Variable **gradeValue** stores the integer value of **grade** after the program converts it from a **String** to an **int**.

Notice that the preceding declarations appear in the body of method **main**. Remember that variables declared in a method definition's body are *local variables* and can be used only from the line of their declaration in the method to the closing right brace (**}**) of the method definition. A local variable's declaration must appear before the variable is used in that method. A local variable declared in one method of a class cannot be accessed directly by other methods of a class.

Good Programming Practice 4.7

Always place a blank line before a declaration that appears between executable statements. This format makes the declarations stand out in the program and contributes to program clarity.

Good Programming Practice 4.8

If you prefer to place declarations at the beginning of a method, separate the declarations from the executable statements in that method with one blank line, to highlight where the declarations end and the executable statements begin.

Common Programming Error 4.6

Attempting to use a local variable's value before initializing the variable (normally with an assignment statement) results in a compile error indicating that the variable may not have been initialized. The value of a local variable cannot be used until the variable is initialized. The program will not compile properly until the variable receives an initial value.

Lines 19–20,

```
total = 0;              // clear total
gradeCounter = 1;       // prepare to loop
```

are assignment statements that initialize **total** to **0** and **gradeCounter** to **1**. Note that these statements initialize variables **total** and **gradeCounter** before they are used in calculations.

Line 23,

```
while ( gradeCounter <= 10 ) {   // loop 10 times
```

indicates that the **while** structure should continue looping (also called *iterating*) as long as the value of **gradeCounter** is less than or equal to 10.

Lines 26–27,

```
grade = JOptionPane.showInputDialog(
   "Enter integer grade: " );
```

correspond to the pseudocode statement "*Input the next grade.*" The statement displays an input dialog with the prompt "**Enter integer grade:**" on the screen.

After the user enters the **grade**, the program converts it from a **String** to an **int** at line 30,

```
gradeValue = Integer.parseInt( grade );
```

Remember that class **Integer** is from package **java.lang** that the compiler imports in every Java program. The pseudocode for the class-average problem does not reflect the preceding statement. The pseudocode statement "*Input the next grade*" requires the programmer to implement the process of obtaining the value from the user and converting it to a type that can be used in calculating the average. As you learn to program, you will find that you require fewer pseudocode statements to help you implement a program.

Next, the program updates the **total** with the new **gradeValue** entered by the user. Line 33,

```
total = total + gradeValue;
```

adds **gradeValue** to the previous value of **total** and assigns the result to **total**.

Line 36,

```
gradeCounter = gradeCounter + 1;
```

adds **1** to **gradeCounter** to indicate that the program hasprocessed a grade and is ready to input the next grade from the user. Incrementing **gradeCounter** is necessary for the condition in the **while** structure to become **false** eventually and terminate the loop.

Line 41,

```
average = total / 10;  // perform integer division
```

assigns the results of the average calculation to variable **average**. Lines 44–46,

```
JOptionPane.showMessageDialog(
   null, "Class average is " + average, "Class Average",
   JOptionPane.INFORMATION_MESSAGE );
```

display an information message dialog containing the string **"Class average is "** followed by the value of variable **average**. The string "**Class Average**" (the third argument) is the title of the message dialog.

Line 48,

```
System.exit( 0 );        // terminate the program
```

terminates the application.

After compiling the class definition with **javac**, execute the application from the command window with the command

```
java Average1
```

This command executes the Java interpreter and tells it that the **main** method for this application is defined in class **Average1**.

Note that the averaging calculation in the program produced an integer result. Actually, the sum of the grade-point values in this example is 794, which, when divided by 10, should yield 79.4 (i.e., a number with a decimal point). We will see how to deal with such numbers (called *floating-point numbers*) in the next section.

4.9 Formulating Algorithms with Top-Down, Stepwise Refinement: Case Study 2 (Sentinel-Controlled Repetition)

Let us generalize the class-average problem. Consider the following problem:

> *Develop a class-averaging program that processes an arbitrary number of grades each time the program executes.*

In the first class-average example, the number of grades (10) was known in advance. In this example, no indication is given of how many grades the user will input. The program must process an arbitrary number of grades. How can the program determine when to stop the input of grades? How will it know when to calculate and print the class average?

One way to solve this problem is to use a special value called a *sentinel value* (also called a *signal value*, a *dummy value* or a *flag value*) to indicate the end of data entry. The user types grades in until all legitimate grades have been entered. The user then types the sentinel value to indicate that the last grade has been entered. Sentinel-controlled repetition is often called *indefinite repetition*, because the number of repetitions is not known before the loop begins executing.

Clearly, the sentinel value must be chosen so that it cannot be confused with an acceptable input value. Because grades on a quiz are normally nonnegative integers, –1 is an acceptable sentinel value for this problem. Thus, an execution of the class-average program might process a stream of inputs such as 95, 96, 75, 74, 89 and –1. In this case, the program would compute and print the class average for the grades 95, 96, 75, 74 and 89. (–1 is the sentinel value, so it should not enter into the averaging calculation.)

Common Programming Error 4.7

Choosing a sentinel value that is also a legitimate data value results in a logic error and may prevent a sentinel-controlled loop from terminating properly.

We approach the class-average program with a technique called *top-down, stepwise refinement*, a method that is essential to the development of well-structured algorithms. We begin with a pseudocode representation of the *top*:

Determine the class average for the quiz

The top is a single statement that conveys the overall function of the program. As such, the top is, in effect, a complete representation of a program. Unfortunately, the top rarely conveys a sufficient amount of detail from which to write the Java algorithm. So we now begin the refinement process. We divide the top into a series of smaller tasks and list these tasks in the order in which they need to be performed. This procedure results in the following *first refinement*:

Initialize variables
Input, sum up and count the quiz grades
Calculate and print the class average

This pseudocode uses only the sequence structure—the steps listed occur in order, one after the other.

Software Engineering Observation 4.4

Each refinement, as well as the top itself, is a complete specification of the algorithm; only the level of detail varies.

To proceed to the next level of refinement (i.e., the *second refinement*), we commit to specific variables. We need a running total of the grades, a count of how many grades have been processed, a variable to receive the value of each grade as it is input and a variable to store the calculated average. The pseudocode statement

Initialize variables

may be refined as follows:

Initialize total to zero
Initialize counter to zero

Notice that only the variables *total* and *counter* are initialized before they are used; the variables *average* and *grade* (for the calculated average and the user input, respectively) need not be initialized, because their values are replaced as they are calculated or input.

The pseudocode statement

Input, sum up and count the quiz grades

requires a repetition structure (i.e., a loop) that successively inputs each grade. We do not know how many grades the user will input, so the program will use sentinel-controlled repetition. The user at the keyboard inputs legitimate grades one at a time. After inputting the last legitimate grade, the user types the sentinel value. The program tests for the sentinel value after each grade is input and terminates the loop when the user inputs the sentinel value. The second refinement of the preceding pseudocode statement is then

Input the first grade (possibly the sentinel)

While the user has not as yet entered the sentinel
    Add this grade into the running total
    Add one to the grade counter
    Input the next grade (possibly the sentinel)

Notice that in pseudocode, we do not use braces around the pseudocode that forms the body of the *while* structure. We simply indent the pseudocode under the *while*, to show that it belongs to the *while*. Again, pseudocode is only an informal program development aid.

The pseudocode statement

Calculate and print the class average

may be refined as follows:

If the counter is not equal to zero
    Set the average to the total divided by the counter
    Print the average
else
    Print "No grades were entered"

Notice that we are testing for the possibility of division by zero—a *logic error* that, if undetected, would cause the program to produce invalid output. The complete second refinement of the pseudocode algorithm for the class-average problem is shown in Fig. 4.8.

Testing and Debugging Tip 4.1

When performing division by an expression whose value could be zero, explicitly test for this case and handle it appropriately in your program (such as by printing an error message) rather than allowing the division by zero to occur.

Good Programming Practice 4.9

Include completely blank lines in pseudocode programs to make the pseudocode more readable. The blank lines separate pseudocode control structures, as well as the phases of the programs.

```
Initialize total to zero
Initialize counter to zero

Input the first grade (possibly the sentinel)

While the user has not as yet entered the sentinel
     Add this grade into the running total
     Add one to the grade counter
     Input the next grade (possibly the sentinel)

If the counter is not equal to zero
     Set the average to the total divided by the counter
     Print the average
else
     Print "No grades were entered"
```

Fig. 4.8 Pseudocode algorithm that uses sentinel-controlled repetition to solve the class-average problem.

Software Engineering Observation 4.5

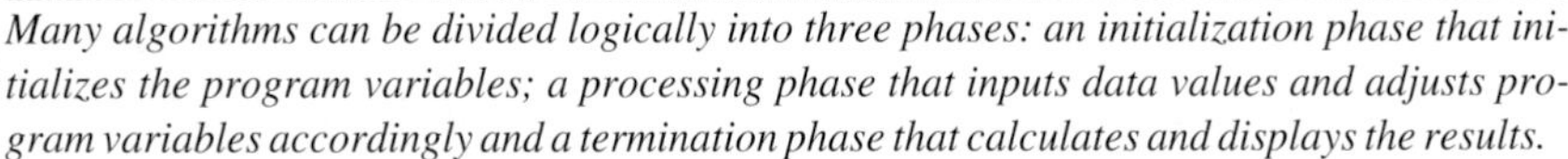

Many algorithms can be divided logically into three phases: an initialization phase that initializes the program variables; a processing phase that inputs data values and adjusts program variables accordingly and a termination phase that calculates and displays the results.

The pseudocode algorithm in Fig. 4.8 solves the more general class-averaging problem. This algorithm was developed after only two levels of refinement. Sometimes more levels are necessary.

Software Engineering Observation 4.6

The programmer terminates the top-down, stepwise refinement process when the pseudocode algorithm is specified in sufficient detail for the programmer to be able to convert the pseudocode to a Java applet or application. Normally, implementing the Java applet or application is then straightforward.

The Java application and a sample execution are shown in Fig. 4.9. Although each grade is an integer, the averaging calculation is likely to produce a number with a decimal point (i.e., a real number). The type **`int`** cannot represent real numbers (i.e., numbers with decimal points), so this program uses data type ***`double`*** to handle floating-point numbers. The program introduces a special operator called a *cast operator* to handle the type conversion we will need for the averaging calculation. These features are explained in detail in the discussion of the application.

In this example, we see that control structures may be stacked on top of one another (in sequence) just as a child stacks building blocks. The **`while`** structure (lines 33–47) is followed by an **`if/else`** structure (lines 52–63) in sequence. Much of the code in this program is identical to the code in Fig. 4.7, so we concentrate in this example on the new features and issues.

```
// Fig. 4.9: Average2.java
// Class average program with sentinel-controlled repetition.

// Java core packages
import java.text.DecimalFormat;

// Java extension packages
import javax.swing.JOptionPane;

public class Average2 {

   // main method begins execution of Java application
   public static void main( String args[] )
   {
      int gradeCounter,  // number of grades entered
          gradeValue,    // grade value
          total;         // sum of grades
      double average;    // average of all grades
      String input;      // grade typed by user

      // Initialization phase
      total = 0;         // clear total
      gradeCounter = 0;  // prepare to loop

      // Processing phase
      // prompt for input and read grade from user
      input = JOptionPane.showInputDialog(
         "Enter Integer Grade, -1 to Quit:" );

      // convert grade from a String to an integer
      gradeValue = Integer.parseInt( input );

      while ( gradeValue != -1 ) {

         // add gradeValue to total
         total = total + gradeValue;

         // add 1 to gradeCounter
         gradeCounter = gradeCounter + 1;

         // prompt for input and read grade from user
         input = JOptionPane.showInputDialog(
            "Enter Integer Grade, -1 to Quit:" );

         // convert grade from a String to an integer
         gradeValue = Integer.parseInt( input );
      }

      // Termination phase
      DecimalFormat twoDigits = new DecimalFormat( "0.00" );

      if ( gradeCounter != 0 ) {
         average = (double) total / gradeCounter;
```

Fig. 4.9 Class-average program with sentinel-controlled repetition (part 1 of 2).

```
54
55           // display average of exam grades
56           JOptionPane.showMessageDialog( null,
57              "Class average is " + twoDigits.format( average ),
58              "Class Average", JOptionPane.INFORMATION_MESSAGE );
59        }
60        else
61           JOptionPane.showMessageDialog( null,
62              "No grades were entered", "Class Average",
63              JOptionPane.INFORMATION_MESSAGE );
64
65        System.exit( 0 );    // terminate application
66
67     }  // end method main
68
69  }  // end class Average2
```

Fig. 4.9 Class-average program with sentinel-controlled repetition (part 2 of 2).

Line 18 declares **double** variable **average**. This change allows us to store the class average as a floating-point number. Line 23 initializes **gradeCounter** to **0**, because no grades have been entered yet. Remember that this program uses sentinel-controlled repetition. To keep an accurate record of the number of grades entered, variable **gradeCounter** is incremented only when the user inputs a valid grade value.

Notice the difference in program logic for sentinel-controlled repetition as compared with the counter-controlled repetition in Fig. 4.7. In counter-controlled repetition, each iteration (loop) of the **while** structure reads a value from the user, for the specified number of iterations. In sentinel-controlled repetition, the program reads and converts one value (lines 27–31) before reaching the **while** structure. This value determines whether the program's flow of control should enter the body of the **while** structure. If the condition of the **while** structure is **false**, the user entered the sentinel, so the body of the **while** structure does not execute (i.e., no grades were entered). If, on the other hand, the condition is **true**, the body begins execution, and the loop adds the value input by the user to the

total. After the value has been processed, lines 42–46 in the loop's body input the next value from the user before program control reaches the end of the **while** structure's body. As program control reaches the closing right brace (**}**) of the body at line 47, execution continues with the next test of the condition of the **while** structure (line 33). The condition uses the new value just input by the user to determine if the **while** structure's body should execute again. Notice that the next value always is input from the user immediately before the program tests the condition of the **while** structure. This structure allows the program to determine if the value just input by the user is the sentinel value *before* the program processes that value (i.e., adds it to the **total**). If the value input is the sentinel value, the **while** structure terminates, and the program does not add the value to the **total**.

Notice the block in the **while** loop in Fig. 4.9. Without the braces, the last four statements in the body of the loop would fall outside the loop, causing the computer to interpret the code incorrectly as follows:

```
while ( gradeValue != -1 )

   // add gradeValue to total
   total = total + gradeValue;

// add 1 to gradeCounter
gradeCounter = gradeCounter + 1;

// prompt for input and read grade from user
input = JOptionPane.showInputDialog(
   "Enter Integer Grade, -1 to Quit:" );

// convert grade from a String to an integer
gradeValue = Integer.parseInt( input );
```

This code would cause an infinite loop in the program if the user does not input the sentinel **-1** as the input value at lines 27–28 (before the **while** structure) in the program.

Common Programming Error 4.8

Omitting the curly braces that are needed to delineate a block can lead to logic errors such as infinite loops. To prevent this problem, some programmers enclose the body of every control structure in braces.

Good Programming Practice 4.10

In a sentinel-controlled loop, the prompts requesting data entry should explicitly remind the user of the value that represents the sentinel.

Line 50,

```
DecimalFormat twoDigits = new DecimalFormat( "0.00" );
```

declares **twoDigits** as a reference to an object of class ***DecimalFormat*** (package ***java.text***). **DecimalFormat** objects format numbers. In this example, we want to output the class average with two digits to the right of the decimal point (i.e., rounded to the nearest hundredth). The preceding line creates a **DecimalFormat** object that is initialized with the string **"0.00"**. Each **0** is a *format flag* that specifies a required digit position in the formatted floating-point number. This particular format indicates that every number formatted with **twoDigits** will have at least one digit to the left of the decimal point and exactly two digits to the right of the decimal point. If the number does not meet the formatting requirements, **0**s are inserted in the formatted number at the required positions. The ***new*** *operator* creates an object as the program executes by obtaining enough memory to store an object of the type specified to the right of **new**. The process of creating new objects is also known as *creating an instance*, or *instantiating an object.* Operator **new** is known as the *dynamic memory allocation operator*. The value in parentheses after the type in a **new** operation is used to *initialize* (i.e., give a value to) the new object. Reference **twoDigits** is assigned the result of the **new** operation by using the *assignment operator,* **=**. The statement is read as "**twoDigits** *gets* the value of **new DecimalFormat("0.00")**."

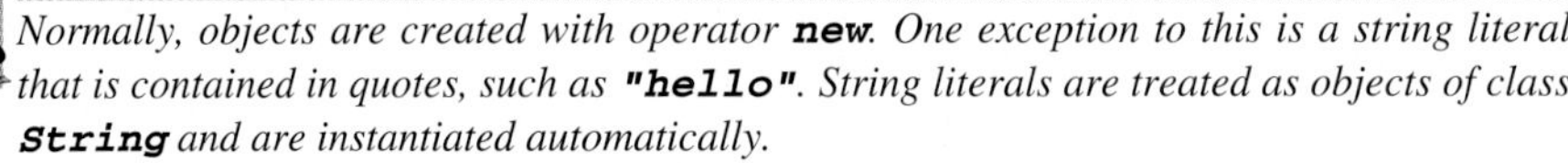

Software Engineering Observation 4.7

Normally, objects are created with operator ***new****. One exception to this is a string literal that is contained in quotes, such as* ***"hello"****. String literals are treated as objects of class* ***String*** *and are instantiated automatically.*

Averages do not always evaluate to integer values. Often, an average is a value that contains a fractional part, such as 3.333 or 2.7. These values are referred to as *floating-point numbers* and are represented by the data type **double**. The variable **average** is declared to be of type **double** to capture the fractional result of our calculation. However, the result of the calculation **total / gradeCounter** is an integer, because **total** and **gradeCounter** are both integer variables. Dividing two integers results in *integer division*—any fractional part of the calculation is lost (i.e., *truncated*). The fractional part of the calculation is lost before the result can be assigned to **average**, because the calculation is performed before the assignment occurs.

To perform a floating-point calculation with integer values, we must create temporary values that are floating-point numbers for the calculation. Java provides the *unary cast operator* to accomplish this task. Line 53,

```
average = (double) total / gradeCounter;
```

uses the cast operator ***(double)*** to create a temporary floating-point copy of its operand—**total**. Using a cast operator in this manner is called *explicit conversion*. The value stored in **total** is still an integer. The calculation now consists of a floating-point value (the temporary **double** version of **total**) divided by the integer **gradeCounter**. Java knows how to evaluate only arithmetic expressions in which the operands' data types are identical. To ensure that the operands are of the same type, Java performs an operation called *promotion* (or *implicit conversion*) on selected operands. For example, in an expression containing the data types **int** and **double**, the values of **int** operands are *promoted* to **double** values for use in the expression. In this example, Java promotes the value of **gradeCounter** to type **double**, and then the program performs the calculation and assigns the result of the floating-point division to **average**. Later in this chapter, we discuss all of the standard data types and their order of promotion.

Common Programming Error 4.9

The cast operator can be used to convert between primitive numeric types and to convert between related class types (as we discuss in Chapter 9). Casting a variable to the wrong type may cause compilation errors or runtime errors.

Cast operators are available for any data type. The cast operator is formed by placing parentheses around the name of a data type. The operator is a *unary operator* (i.e., an operator that takes only one operand). In Chapter 2, we studied the binary arithmetic operators. Java also supports unary versions of the plus (**+**) and minus (**-**) operators, so the programmer can write expressions like `-7` or `+5`. Cast operators associate from right to left and have the same precedence as other unary operators, such as unary `+` and unary `-`. This precedence is one level higher than that of the *multiplicative operators* `*`, `/` and `%` and one level lower than that of parentheses. (See the operator precedence chart in Appendix C.) We indicate the cast operator with the notation **(***type***)** in our precedence charts, to indicate that any type name can be used to form a cast operator.

Common Programming Error 4.10

Using floating-point numbers in a manner that assumes they are represented precisely can lead to incorrect results. Floating-point numbers are represented approximately by computers.

Common Programming Error 4.11

Assuming that integer division rounds (rather than truncates) can lead to incorrect results.

Good Programming Practice 4.11

Do not compare floating-point values for equality or inequality. Rather, test for whether the absolute value of the difference between two floating-point numbers is less than a specified small value.

Despite the fact that floating-point numbers are not always 100% precise, they have numerous applications. For example, when we speak of a "normal" body temperature of 98.6, we do not need to be precise to a large number of digits. When we view the temperature on a thermometer and read it as 98.6, it may actually be 98.5999473210643. The point here is that calling this number simply 98.6 is fine for most applications.

Another way in which floating-point numbers develop is through division. When we divide 10 by 3, the result is 3.3333333..., with the sequence of 3s repeating infinitely. The computer allocates only a fixed amount of space to hold such a value, so clearly the stored floating-point value can be only an approximation.

4.10 Formulating Algorithms with Top-Down, Stepwise Refinement: Case Study 3 (Nested Control Structures)

Let us work through another complete problem. We once again formulate the algorithm using pseudocode and top-down, stepwise refinement, and we develop a corresponding Java program. Consider the following problem statement:

> *A college offers a course that prepares students for the state licensing exam for real estate brokers. Last year, several of the students who completed this course took the licensing examination. Naturally, the college wants to know how well its students did on the exam. You have been asked to write a program to summarize the results. You have been given a list of these 10 students. Next to each name is written a 1 if the student passed the exam and a 2 if the student failed.*
>
> *Your program should analyze the results of the exam as follows:*
>
> 1. *Input each test result (i.e., a 1 or a 2). Display the message "Enter result" on the screen each time the program requests another test result.*
> 2. *Count the number of test results of each type.*
> 3. *Display a summary of the test results indicating the number of students who passed and the number of students who failed.*
> 4. *If more than 8 students passed the exam, print the message "Raise tuition."*

After reading the problem statement carefully, we make the following observations about the problem:

1. The program must process test results for 10 students. A counter-controlled loop will be used.
2. Each test result is a number—either a 1 or a 2. Each time the program reads a test result, the program must determine if the number is a 1 or a 2. We test for a 1 in our algorithm. If the number is not a 1, we assume that it is a 2. (An exercise at the end of the chapter considers the consequences of this assumption.)
3. Two counters are used to keep track of the exam results—one to count the number of students who passed the exam and one to count the number of students who failed the exam.
4. After the program has processed all the results, it must decide if more than eight students passed the exam.

Let us proceed with top-down, stepwise refinement. We begin with a pseudocode representation of the top:

Analyze exam results and decide if tuition should be raised

Once again, it is important to emphasize that the top is a complete representation of the program, but several refinements are likely before the pseudocode can evolve naturally into a Java program. Our first refinement is

Initialize variables
Input the ten exam grades and count passes and failures
Print a summary of the exam results and decide if tuition should be raised

Here, too, even though we have a complete representation of the entire program, further refinement is necessary. We now commit to specific variables. We need counters to record the passes and failures, a counter to control the looping process and a variable to store the user input. The pseudocode statement

Initialize variables

may be refined as follows:

Initialize passes to zero
Initialize failures to zero
Initialize student to one

Notice that only the counters for the number of passes, number of failures and number of students are initialized. The pseudocode statement

Input the ten quiz grades and count passes and failures

requires a loop that successively inputs the result of each exam. Here it is known in advance that there are precisely ten exam results, so counter-controlled looping is appropriate. Inside the loop (i.e., *nested* within the loop) a double-selection structure determines whether each exam result is a pass or a failure and increments the appropriate counter accordingly. The refinement of the preceding pseudocode statement is:

While student counter is less than or equal to ten
Input the next exam result

If the student passed
Add one to passes
else
Add one to failures

Add one to student counter

Notice the use of blank lines to set off the *if/else* control structure to improve program readability. The pseudocode statement

Print a summary of the exam results and decide if tuition should be raised

may be refined as follows:

Print the number of passes
Print the number of failures

If more than eight students passed
Print "Raise tuition"

The complete second refinement appears in Fig. 4.10. Notice that the pseudocode also uses blank lines to set off the *while* structure for program readability.

```
Initialize passes to zero
Initialize failures to zero
Initialize student to one

While student counter is less than or equal to ten
    Input the next exam result

    If the student passed
        Add one to passes
    else
        Add one to failures

    Add one to student counter

Print the number of passes
Print the number of failures

If more than eight students passed
    Print "Raise tuition"
```

Fig. 4.10 Pseudocode for examination-results problem.

This pseudocode is now sufficiently refined for conversion to Java. The Java program and two sample executions are shown in Fig. 4.11.

```
// Fig. 4.11: Analysis.java
// Analysis of examination results.

// Java extension packages
import javax.swing.JOptionPane;

public class Analysis {

   // main method begins execution of Java application
   public static void main( String args[] )
   {
      // initializing variables in declarations
      int passes = 0,                  // number of passes
          failures = 0,                // number of failures
          student = 1,                 // student counter
          result;                      // one exam result
      String input,                    // user-entered value
             output;                   // output string

      // process 10 students; counter-controlled loop
      while ( student <= 10 ) {

         // obtain result from user
         input = JOptionPane.showInputDialog(
            "Enter result (1=pass,2=fail)" );

         // convert result to int
         result = Integer.parseInt( input );

         // process result
         if ( result == 1 )
            passes = passes + 1;
         else
            failures = failures + 1;

         student = student + 1;
      }

      // termination phase
      output = "Passed: " + passes +
         "\nFailed: " + failures;

      if ( passes > 8 )
         output = output + "\nRaise Tuition";

      JOptionPane.showMessageDialog( null, output,
         "Analysis of Examination Results",
         JOptionPane.INFORMATION_MESSAGE );

      System.exit( 0 );  // terminate application
```

Fig. 4.11 Java program for examination-results problem (part 1 of 2).

```
51
52     }  // end method main
53
54  }  // end class Analysis
```

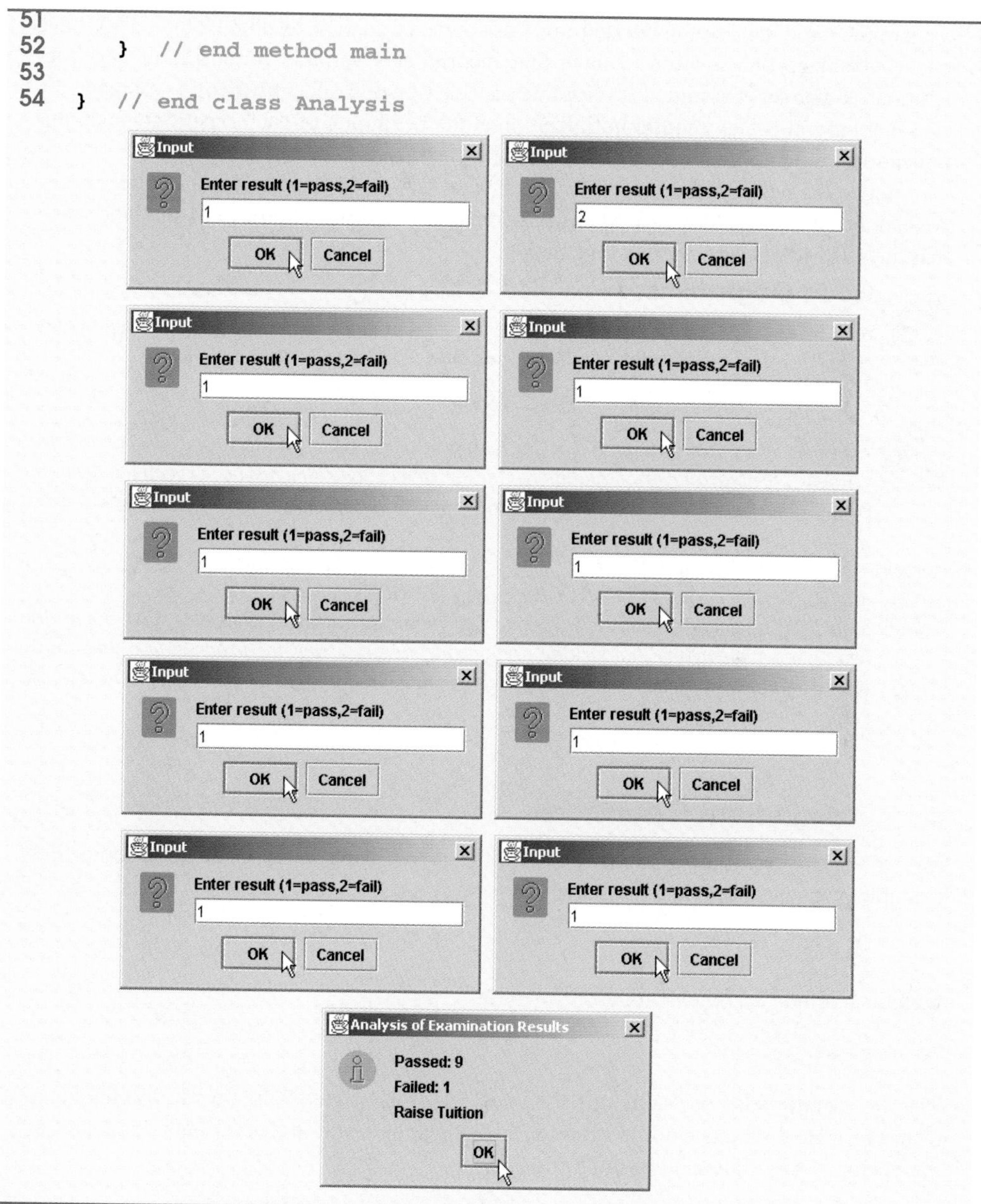

Fig. 4.11 Java program for examination-results problem (part 2 of 2).

Lines 13–18,

```
int passes = 0,          // number of passes
    failures = 0,        // number of failures
    student = 1,         // student counter
    result;              // one exam result
String input,            // user-entered value
       output;           // output string
```

declare the variables used in **main** to process the examination results. Note that we have taken advantage of a feature of Java that incorporates variable initialization into declarations (**passes** is assigned **0**, **failures** is assigned **0** and **student** is assigned **1**). Looping programs may require initialization at the beginning of each repetition; such initialization would normally occur in assignment statements.

Notice the nested **if/else** structure at lines 31–34 of the **while** structure's body. Also, notice the use of **String** reference **output** in lines 40, 41 and 44 to build the string that lines 46–48 display in a message dialog.

Good Programming Practice 4.12

Initializing local variables when they are declared in methods helps the programmer avoid compiler messages warning of uninitialized data.

Software Engineering Observation 4.8

Experience has shown that the most difficult part of solving a problem on a computer is developing the algorithm for the solution. Once a correct algorithm has been specified, the process of producing a working Java program from the algorithm is normally straightforward.

Software Engineering Observation 4.9

Many experienced programmers write programs without ever using program development tools like pseudocode. These programmers feel that their ultimate goal is to solve the problem on a computer and that writing pseudocode merely delays the production of final outputs. Although this method may work for simple and familiar problems, it can lead to serious errors in large, complex projects.

4.11 Assignment Operators

Java provides several assignment operators for abbreviating assignment expressions. For example, you can abbreviate the statement

```
c = c + 3;
```

with the *addition assignment operator*, **+=**, as

```
c += 3;
```

The **+=** operator adds the value of the expression on the right of the operator to the value of the variable on the left of the operator and stores the result in the variable on the left of the operator. Any statement of the form

variable **=** *variable operator expression***;**

where *operator* is one of the binary operators **+**, **-**, *****, **/** or **%** (or others we discuss later in the text), can be written in the form

*variable operator***=** *expression***;**

Thus, the assignment expression **c += 3** adds **3** to **c**. Figure 4.12 shows the arithmetic assignment operators, sample expressions using the operators and explanations of what the operators do.

Assignment operator	Sample expression	Explanation	Assigns
Assume: **int c = 3, d = 5, e = 4, f = 6, g = 12;**			
`+=`	`c += 7`	`c = c + 7`	`10` to `c`
`-=`	`d -= 4`	`d = d - 4`	`1` to `d`
`*=`	`e *= 5`	`e = e * 5`	`20` to `e`
`/=`	`f /= 3`	`f = f / 3`	`2` to `f`
`%=`	`g %= 9`	`g = g % 9`	`3` to `g`

Fig. 4.12 Arithmetic assignment operators.

Performance Tip 4.1

Programmers can write programs a bit faster and compilers can compile programs a bit faster when the abbreviated assignment operators are used. Some compilers generate code that runs faster when abbreviated assignment operators are used.

Performance Tip 4.2

Many of the performance tips we mention in this text result in nominal improvements, so the reader may be tempted to ignore them. Significant performance improvement is often realized when a supposedly nominal improvement is placed in a loop that may repeat a large number of times.

4.12 Increment and Decrement Operators

Java provides the unary *increment operator*, **++**, and the unary *decrement operator*, **--**, which are summarized in Fig. 4.13. A program can increment the value of a variable called **c** by 1 using the increment operator, **++**, rather than the expression **c = c + 1** or **c += 1**. If an increment or decrement operator is placed before a variable, it is referred to as the *preincrement* or *predecrement operator*, respectively. If an increment or decrement operator is placed after a variable, it is referred to as the *postincrement* or *postdecrement operator*, respectively.

Operator	Called	Sample expression	Explanation
`++`	preincrement	`++a`	Increment **a** by 1, then use the new value of **a** in the expression in which **a** resides.
`++`	postincrement	`a++`	Use the current value of **a** in the expression in which **a** resides, then increment **a** by 1.
`--`	predecrement	`--b`	Decrement **b** by 1, then use the new value of **b** in the expression in which **b** resides.
`--`	postdecrement	`b--`	Use the current value of **b** in the expression in which **b** resides, then decrement **b** by 1.

Fig. 4.13 The increment and decrement operators .

Preincrementing (predecrementing) a variable causes the variable to be incremented (decremented) by 1, and then the new value of the variable is used in the expression in which it appears. Postincrementing (postdecrementing) the variable causes the current value of the variable to be used in the expression in which it appears, and then the variable value is incremented (decremented) by 1.

The application in Fig. 4.14 demonstrates the difference between the preincrementing version and the postincrementing version of the **++** increment operator. Postincrementing the variable **c** causes it to be incremented after it is used in the **System.out.println** method call (line 13). Preincrementing the variable **c** causes it to be incremented before it is used in the **System.out.println** method call (line 20).

The program displays the value of **c** before and after the **++** operator is used. The decrement operator (**--**) works similarly.

Good Programming Practice 4.13

Unary operators should be placed next to their operands, with no intervening spaces.

```
1  // Fig. 4.14: Increment.java
2  // Preincrementing and postincrementing
3
4  public class Increment {
5
6     // main method begins execution of Java application
7     public static void main( String args[] )
8     {
9        int c;
10
11       c = 5;
12       System.out.println( c );   // print 5
13       System.out.println( c++ ); // print 5 then postincrement
14       System.out.println( c );   // print 6
15
16       System.out.println();      // skip a line
17
18       c = 5;
19       System.out.println( c );   // print 5
20       System.out.println( ++c ); // preincrement then print 6
21       System.out.println( c );   // print 6
22
23    }  // end method main
24
25 }  // end class Increment
```

```
5
5
6

5
6
6
```

Fig. 4.14 The difference between preincrementing and postincrementing.

Line 16,

```
System.out.println();       // skip a line
```

uses **System.out.println** to output a blank line. If **println** receives no arguments, it simply outputs a newline character.

The arithmetic assignment operators and the increment and decrement operators can be used to simplify program statements. For example, the three assignment statements in Fig. 4.11 (lines 32, 34 and 36),

```
passes = passes + 1;
failures = failures + 1;
student = student + 1;
```

can be written more concisely with assignment operators as

```
passes += 1;
failures += 1;
student += 1;
```

with preincrement operators as

```
++passes;
++failures;
++student;
```

or with postincrement operators as

```
passes++;
failures++;
student++;
```

It is important to note here that when incrementing or decrementing a variable in a statement by itself, the preincrement and postincrement forms have the same effect, and the predecrement and postdecrement forms have the same effect. It is only when a variable appears in the context of a larger expression that preincrementing and post-incrementing the variable have different effects (and similarly for predecrementing and postdecrementing).

Common Programming Error 4.12

Attempting to use the increment or decrement operator on an expression other than an lvalue *is a syntax error. An* lvalue *is a variable or expression that can appear on the left side of an assignment operation. For example, writing* **++(x + 1)** *is a syntax error, because* **(x + 1)** *is not an* lvalue.

The chart in Fig. 4.15 shows the precedence and associativity of the operators that have been introduced up to this point. The operators are shown from top to bottom in decreasing order of precedence. The second column describes the associativity of the operators at each level of precedence. Notice that the conditional operator (**?:**), the unary operators increment (**++**), decrement (**--**), plus (**+**), minus (**-**) and casts and the assignment operators **=**, **+=**, **-=**, ***=**, **/=** and **%=** associate from right to left. All other operators in the operator precedence chart in Fig. 4.15 associate from left to right. The third column names the groups of operators.

Operators	Associativity	Type
`()`	left to right	parentheses
`++ --`	right to left	unary postfix
`++ -- + - (type)`	right to left	unary
`* / %`	left to right	multiplicative
`+ -`	left to right	additive
`< <= > >=`	left to right	relational
`== !=`	left to right	equality
`?:`	right to left	conditional
`= += -= *= /= %=`	right to left	assignment

Fig. 4.15 Precedence and associativity of the operators discussed so far.

4.13 Primitive Data Types

The table in Fig. 4.16 lists the primitive data types in Java. The primitive types are the building blocks for more complicated types. Like its predecessor languages C and C++, Java requires all variables to have a type before they can be used in a program. For this reason, Java is referred to as a *strongly typed language*.

In C and C++ programs, programmers frequently had to write separate versions of programs to support different computer platforms, because the primitive data types were not guaranteed to be identical from computer to computer. For example, an **`int`** value on one machine might be represented by 16 bits (2 bytes) of memory, while an **`int`** value on another machine might be represented by 32 bits (4 bytes) of memory. In Java, **`int`** values are always 32 bits (4 bytes).

Portability Tip 4.1

Unlike in the programming languages C and C++, the primitive types in Java are portable across all computer platforms that support Java. This and many other portability features of Java enable programmers to write programs once, without knowing which computer platform will execute the program. This attribute is sometimes referred to as WORA *(Write Once Run Anywhere).*

Each data type in Fig. 4.16 is listed with its size in bits (there are eight bits to a byte) and its range of values. Because the designers of Java want it to be maximally portable, they chose to use internationally recognized standards for both character formats (Unicode) and floating-point numbers (IEEE 754).

When instance variables of the primitive data types are declared in a class, they are automatically assigned default values unless specified otherwise by the programmer. Instance variables of types **`char`**, **`byte`**, **`short`**, **`int`**, **`long`**, **`float`** and **`double`** are all given the value **`0`** by default. Variables of type **`boolean`** are given the value **`false`** by default.

Type	Size in bits	Values	Standard
`boolean`	8	`true` or `false`	
`char`	16	`'\u0000'` to `'\uFFFF'` (0 to 65535)	(ISO Unicode character set)
`byte`	8	–128 to +127 (-2^7 to $2^7 - 1$)	
`short`	16	–32,768 to +32,767 (-2^{15} to $2^{15} - 1$)	
`int`	32	–2,147,483,648 to +2,147,483,647 (-2^{31} to $2^{31} - 1$)	
`long`	64	–9,223,372,036,854,775,808 to +9,223,372,036,854,775,807 (-2^{63} to $2^{63} - 1$)	
`float`	32	*Negative range:* –3.4028234663852886E+38 to –1.40129846432481707e–45 *Positive range:* 1.40129846432481707e–45 to 3.4028234663852886E+38	(IEEE 754 floating point)
`double`	64	*Negative range:* –1.7976931348623157E+308 to –4.94065645841246544e–324 *Positive range:* 4.94065645841246544e–324 to 1.7976931348623157E+308	(IEEE 754 floating point)

Fig. 4.16 The Java primitive data types.

4.14 (Optional Case Study) Thinking About Objects: Identifying Class Attributes

In "Thinking About Objects," Section 3.8, we began the first phase of an object-oriented design (OOD) for our elevator simulator—identifying the classes needed to implement the simulator. We began by listing the nouns in the problem statement and then created a separate class for each category of noun and noun phrase that perform an important duty in the elevator simulation. We then represented the classes and their relationships in a UML class diagram (Fig. 3.23). Classes have *attributes* (data) and *operations* (behaviors). Class attributes are implemented in Java programs as variables; class behaviors are implemented as methods. In this section, we determine many of the class attributes needed to implement the elevator simulator. In Chapter 5, we examine how these attributes represent an object's *state*, or condition. In Chapter 6, we determine class behavior. In Chapter 7, we concentrate on the interactions, often called *collaborations*, between the objects in the elevator simulator.

Consider the attributes of some real-world objects: A person's attributes include height and weight, for example. A radio's attributes include its station setting, its volume setting and whether it is set to AM or FM. A car's attributes include its speedometer and odometer readings, the amount of gas in its tank, what gear it is in, etc. A personal computer's attributes include its manufacturer (e.g., Sun, Apple, IBM or Compaq), type of screen (e.g., monochrome or color), main memory size (in megabytes), hard disk size (in gigabytes), etc.

We can identify the attributes of the classes in our system by looking for descriptive words and phrases in the problem statement. For each descriptive word or phrase we find, we create an attribute and assign that attribute to a class. We also create attributes to represent any additional data that a class may need (as the need for this data becomes clear throughout the design process).

We begin examining the problem statement looking for attributes distinct to each class. Figure 4.17 lists the words or phrases from the problem statement that describe each class. The sentence "The user can create any number of people in the simulation" implies that the model will introduce several **Person** objects during execution. We require an integer value representing the number of people in the simulation at any given time, because we may wish to track, or identify, the people in our model. As mentioned in Section 2.9, the **ElevatorModel** object acts as the "representative" for the model (even though the model consists of several classes) for interactions with other parts of the system (in this case, the user is a part of the system), so we assign the **numberOfPeople** attribute to class **ElevatorModel**.

Class **Elevator** contains several attributes. The phrases "is moving" and "is summoned" describe possible states of **Elevator** (we introduce states in the next "Thinking About Objects" section), so we include **moving** and **summoned** as **boolean** attributes. **Elevator** also arrives at a "destination floor," so we include the attribute **destinationFloor**, representing the **Floor** at which the **Elevator** will arrive. Although the problem statement does not mention explicitly that the **Elevator** leaves from a current **Floor**, we may assume another attribute called **currentFloor** representing on which **Floor** the **Elevator** is resting. The problem statement specifies that "both the elevator and each floor have capacity for only one person," so we include the capacity attribute for class **Elevator** (and class **Floor**) and set the value to **1**. Lastly, the problem statement specifies that the elevator "takes five seconds to travel between floors," so we introduce the **travelTime** attribute and set the value to **5**.

Class **Person** contains several attributes. The user must be able to "create a unique person," which implies that each **Person** object should have a unique identifier. We assign integer attribute **ID** to the **Person** object. The **ID** attribute helps to identify that **Person** object. In addition, the problem statement specifies that the **Person** can be "waiting on that floor to enter the elevator." Therefore, "waiting" is a state that **Person** object may enter. Though not mentioned explicitly, if the **Person** is not waiting for the **Elevator**, the **Person** is moving to (or away from) the **Elevator**. We assign the **boolean** attribute **moving** to class **Person**. When this attribute is set to **false**, the **Person** is "waiting." Lastly, the phrase "on that floor" implies that the **Person** occupies a floor. We cannot assign a **Floor** reference to class **Person**, because we are interested only in attributes. However, we want to include the location of the **Person** object in the model, so we include the **currentFloor** attribute, which may have a value of either **1** or **2**.

Class **Floor** has a **capacity** attribute. The problem statement specified that the user could situate the person on either "the first or second floor"—therefore, a **Floor** object requires a value that distinguishes that **Floor** object as the first or second floor, so we include the **floorNumber** attribute.

According to the problem statement, the **ElevatorButton** and **FloorButton** are "pressed" by a **Person**. The buttons may be "reset" as well. The state of each button is either "pressed" or "reset." We include the **boolean** attribute **pressed** in both button classes. When **pressed** is **true**, the button object is pressed; when **pressed** is **false**, the button object is reset. Classes **ElevatorDoor** and **FloorDoor** exhibit similar characteristics. Both objects are either "open" or "closed," so we include the **boolean** attribute **open** in both door classes. Class **Light** also falls into this category—the light is either "illuminated" (turned on) or "turned off," so we include the **boolean** attribute **on** in class **Light**. Note that although the problem statement mentions that the bell rings, there is no mention of when the bell "is ringing," so we do not include a separate **ring** attribute for class **Bell**. As we progress through this case study, we will continue to add, modify and delete information about the classes in our system.

Class	Descriptive words and phrases
ElevatorModel	number of people in the simulation
ElevatorShaft	[no descriptive words or phrases]
Elevator	moving summoned current floor destination floor capacity of only one person five seconds to travel between floors
Person	unique waiting / moving current floor
Floor	first or second; capacity for only one person
FloorButton	pressed / reset
ElevatorButton	pressed / reset
FloorDoor	door closed / door open
ElevatorDoor	door closed / door open
Bell	[no descriptive words or phrases]
Light	illuminated / turned off

Fig. 4.17 Descriptive words and phrases from problem statement.

Figure 4.18 is a class diagram that lists some of the attributes for each class in our system—the descriptive words and phrases in Fig. 4.17 help us generate these attributes. Note that Fig. 4.18 does not show associations among objects—we showed these associations in Fig. 3.23. In the UML class diagram, a class's attributes are placed in the middle compartment of the class's rectangle. Consider the **open** attribute of class **ElevatorDoor**:

```
open : Boolean = false
```

This listing contains three pieces of information about the attribute. The *attribute name* is **open**. The *attribute type* is **Boolean**.[2] The type depends on the language used to write the software system. In Java, for example, the value can be a *primitive type*, such as **boolean** or **float**, as well as a user-defined type like a class—we begin our study of classes in Chapter 8, where we will see that each new class is a new data type.

We can also indicate an initial value for each attribute. The **open** attribute in class **ElevatorDoor** has an initial value of **false**. If a particular attribute has no initial value specified, only its name and type (separated by a colon) are shown. For example, the **ID** attribute of class **Person** is an integer—in Java, the **ID** attribute is of type **int**. Here we show no initial value, because the value of this attribute is a number that we do not yet know; this number will be determined by **ElevatorModel** at execution time. Integer attribute **currentFloor** for class **Person** is not determined until program execution as well—this attribute is determined when the simulation user decides on which **Floor** to place the **Person**. For now we do not concern ourselves with the types or initial values of the attributes. We include only the information we can glean easily from the problem statement.

Note that Fig. 4.18 does not include attributes for class **ElevatorShaft**. Actually, class **ElevatorShaft** contains seven attributes that we can determine from the class diagram of Fig. 3.23—references to the **Elevator** object, two **FloorButton** objects, two **FloorDoor** objects and two **Light** objects. Class **ElevatorModel** contains three user-defined attributes—two references to **Floor** objects and a reference to the **ElevatorShaft** object. Class **Elevator** also contains three user-defined attributes—reference to the **ElevatorButton** object, the **ElevatorDoor** object and the **Bell** object. To save space, we will not show these additional attributes in our class diagrams—we will, however, include them in the code in the appendices.

The class diagram of Fig. 4.18 provides a good basis for the structure of our model but the diagram is not fully complete. For example, the attribute **currentFloor** in class **Person** represents the floor on which a person is currently located. However, on what floor is the person when that person rides the elevator? These attributes do not yet sufficiently represent the structure of the model. As we present more of the UML and object-oriented design through Chapter 22, we will continue to strengthen the structure of our model.

---

2. Note that the attribute types in Fig. 4.18 are in UML notation. We will associate the attribute types **Boolean** and **Integer** in the UML diagram with the attribute types **boolean** and **int** in Java, respectively. We described in Chapter 3 that Java provides a "type-wrapper class" for each primitive data type. The Java type-wrapper classes have the same notation as the UML notation for attribute types; however, when we implement our design in Java starting in Chapter 8, we use primitive data types for simplification. Deciding whether to use primitive data types or type-wrapper classes is an implementation-specific issue that should not be mentioned in the UML.

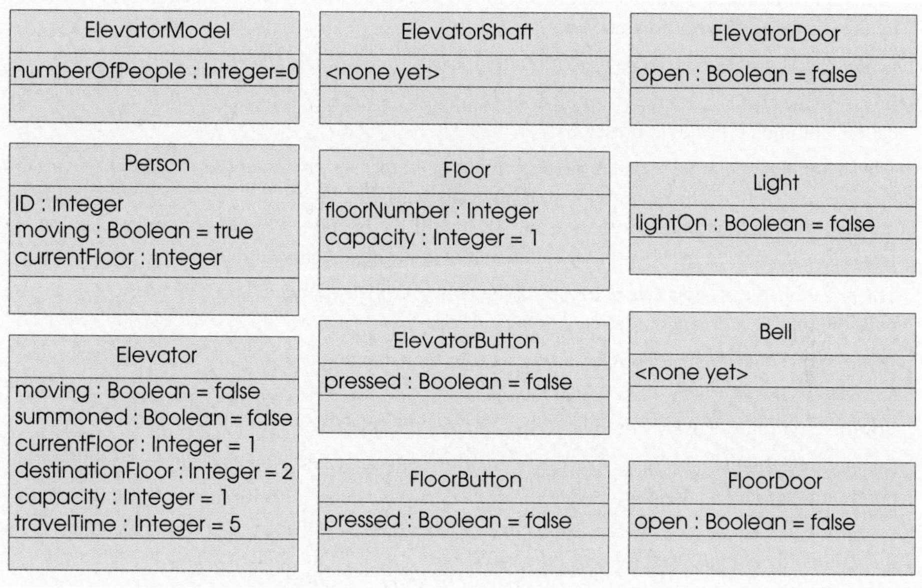

Fig. 4.18 Classes with attributes.

SUMMARY

- A procedure for solving a problem in terms of the actions to be executed and the order in which the actions should be executed is called an algorithm.
- Specifying the order in which statements execute in a computer program is called program control.
- Pseudocode helps the programmer "think out" a program before attempting to write it in a programming language, such as Java.
- Top-down, stepwise refinement is a process for refining pseudocode by maintaining a complete representation of the program during each refinement.
- Declarations are messages to the compiler telling it the names and attributes of variables and telling it to reserve space for variables.
- A selection structure chooses among alternative courses of action.
- The **`if`** selection structure executes an indicated action only when the condition is true.
- The **`if/else`** selection structure specifies separate actions to execute when the condition is true and when the condition is false.
- When more than one statement should execute where normally only a single statement appears, the statements must be enclosed in braces, forming a block. A block can be placed anywhere a single statement can be placed.
- An empty statement, indicating that no action is to be taken, is indicated by placing a semicolon (**`;`**) where a statement would normally be.
- A repetition structure specifies that an action is to be repeated while some condition remains true.
- The format for the **`while`** repetition structure is

```
while ( condition )
    statement
```

- A value that contains a fractional part is referred to as a floating-point number and is represented by the data type **`float`** or **`double`**.
- Unary cast operator **`(double)`** creates a temporary floating-point copy of its operand.
- Java provides the arithmetic assignment operators **`+=`**, **`-=`**, **`*=`**, **`/=`** and **`%=`**, which help abbreviate certain common types of expressions.
- The increment operator, **`++`**, and the decrement operator, **`--`**, increment or decrement a variable by 1, respectively. If the operator is prefixed to the variable, the variable is incremented or decremented by 1 first, and then used in its expression. If the operator is postfixed to the variable, the variable is used in its expression, and then incremented or decremented by 1.
- The primitive types (**`boolean`**, **`char`**, **`byte`**, **`short`**, **`int`**, **`long`**, **`float`** and **`double`**) are the building blocks for more complicated types in Java.
- Java requires all variables to have a type before they can be used in a program. For this reason, Java is referred to as a strongly typed language.
- Primitive types in Java are portable across all computer platforms that support Java.
- Java uses internationally recognized standards for both character formats (Unicode) and floating-point numbers (IEEE 754).
- Instance variables of types **`char`**, **`byte`**, **`short`**, **`int`**, **`long`**, **`float`** and **`double`** are all given the value **`0`** by default. Variables of type **`boolean`** are given the value **`false`** by default.

TERMINOLOGY

`--` operator
`?:` operator
`++` operator
action
action/decision model
algorithm
arithmetic assignment operators:
  `+=`, **`-=`**, **`*=`**, **`/=`** and **`%=`**
block
body of a loop
cast operator, **`(`** *type* **`)`**
conditional operator (**`?:`**)
control structure
counter-controlled repetition
decision
decrement operator (**`--`**)
definite repetition
`double`
double-selection structure
empty statement (**`;`**)
`if` selection structure
`if/else` selection structure
implicit conversion
increment operator (**`++`**)
indefinite repetition
infinite loop
initialization
integer division
ISO Unicode character set
logic error
loop counter
loop-continuation condition
nested control structures
postdecrement operator
postincrement operator
predecrement operator
preincrement operator
promotion
pseudocode
repetition
repetition structures
selection
sentinel value
sequential execution
single-entry/single-exit control structures
single-selection structure
stacked control structures
structured programming
syntax error
top-down, stepwise refinement
unary operator
`while` repetition structure
white-space characters

SELF-REVIEW EXERCISES

4.1 Fill in the blanks in each of the following statements:

a) All programs can be written in terms of three types of control structures: ________, ________ and ________.

b) The ________ selection structure is used to execute one action when a condition is true and another action when that condition is false.

c) Repeating a set of instructions a specific number of times is called ________ repetition.

d) When it is not known in advance how many times a set of statements will be repeated, a ________ value can be used to terminate the repetition.

4.2 Write four different Java statements that each add 1 to integer variable **x**.

4.3 Write Java statements to accomplish each of the following tasks:

a) Assign the sum of **x** and **y** to **z**, and increment the value of **x** by 1 after the calculation. Use only one statement.

b) Test if the value of the variable **count** is greater than 10. If it is, print **"Count is greater than 10"**.

c) Decrement the variable **x** by 1, and then subtract it from the variable **total**. Use only one statement.

d) Calculate the remainder after **q** is divided by **divisor**, and assign the result to **q**. Write this statement in two different ways.

4.4 Write a Java statement to accomplish each of the following tasks:

a) Declare variables **sum** and **x** to be of type **int**.

b) Assign **1** to variable **x**.

c) Assign **0** to variable **sum**.

d) Add variable **x** to variable **sum**, and assign the result to variable **sum**.

e) Print **"The sum is: "**, followed by the value of variable **sum**.

4.5 Combine the statements that you wrote in Exercise 4.4 into a Java application that calculates and prints the sum of the integers from 1 to 10. Use the **while** structure to loop through the calculation and increment statements. The loop should terminate when the value of **x** becomes 11.

4.6 Determine the value of each variable after the calculation is performed. Assume that when each statement begins executing, all variables have the integer value 5.

a) **product *= x++;**

b) **quotient /= ++x;**

4.7 Identify and correct the errors in each of the following sets of code:

a)
```
while ( c <= 5 ) {
   product *= c;
   ++c;
```

b)
```
if ( gender == 1 )
   System.out.println( "Woman" );
else;
   System.out.println( "Man" );
```

4.8 What is wrong with the following **while** repetition structure?

```
while ( z >= 0 )
   sum += z;
```

ANSWERS TO SELF-REVIEW EXERCISES

4.1 a) sequence, selection, repetition. b) **if/else**. c) counter-controlled, or definite. d) Sentinel, signal, flag or dummy.

4.2
```
x = x + 1;
x += 1;
++x;
x++;
```

4.3 a) `z = x++ + y;`
b)
```
if ( count > 10 )
   System.out.println( "Count is greater than 10" );
```
c) `total -= --x;`
d) `q %= divisor;`
`q = q % divisor;`

4.4 a) `int sum, x;`
b) `x = 1;`
c) `sum = 0;`
d) `sum += x;` or `sum = sum + x;`
e) `System.out.println( "The sum is: " + sum );`

4.5 The program is as follows:

```
// Calculate the sum of the integers from 1 to 10
public class Calculate {
   public static void main( String args[] )
   {
      int sum, x;

      x = 1;
      sum = 0;

      while ( x <= 10 ) {
         sum += x;
         ++x;
      }

      System.out.println( "The sum is: " + sum );
   }
}
```

4.6 a) `product = 25`, `x = 6`
b) `quotient = 0`, `x = 6`

4.7 a) Error: Missing the closing right brace of the **while** structure's body.
Correction: Add a closing right brace after the statement **++c;**.
b) Error: Semicolon after **else** results in a logic error. The second output statement will always be executed.
Correction: Remove the semicolon after **else**.

4.8 The value of the variable **z** is never changed in the **while** structure. Therefore, if the loop-continuation condition **(z >= 0)** is true, an infinite loop is created. To prevent an infinite loop from occurring, **z** must be decremented so that it eventually becomes less than 0.

EXERCISES

4.9 Identify and correct the errors in each of the following sets of code. [*Note*: There may be more than one error in each piece of code]:

a)
```
if ( age >= 65 );
    System.out.println( "Age greater than or equal to 65" );
else
    System.out.println( "Age is less than 65 )";
```

b)
```
int x = 1, total;
while ( x <= 10 ) {
    total += x;
    ++x;
}
```

c)
```
While ( x <= 100 )
    total += x;
    ++x;
```

d)
```
while ( y > 0 ) {
    System.out.println( y );
    ++y;
```

4.10 What does the following program print?

```
public class Mystery {

   public static void main( String args[] )
   {
      int y, x = 1, total = 0;

      while ( x <= 10 ) {
         y = x * x;
         System.out.println( y );
         total += y;
         ++x;
      }

      System.out.println( "Total is " + total );
   }
}
```

For Exercise 4.11 through Exercise 4.14, perform each of the following steps:

a) Read the problem statement.
b) Formulate the algorithm using pseudocode and top-down, stepwise refinement.
c) Write a Java program.
d) Test, debug and execute the Java program.
e) Process three complete sets of data.

4.11 Drivers are concerned with the mileage obtained by their automobiles. One driver has kept track of several tankfuls of gasoline by recording miles driven and gallons used for each tankful. Develop a Java application that will input the miles driven and gallons used (both as integers) for each tankful. The program should calculate and display the miles per gallon obtained for each tankful and print the combined miles per gallon obtained for all tankfuls up to this point. All averaging calculations should produce floating-point results. Use input dialogs to obtain the data from the user.

4.12 Develop a Java application that will determine if a department-store customer has exceeded the credit limit on a charge account. For each customer, the following facts are available:

a) account number,
b) balance at the beginning of the month,

c) total of all items charged by the customer this month,
d) total of all credits applied to the customer's account this month, and
e) allowed credit limit.

The program should input each of these facts from input dialogs as integers, calculate the new balance (= *beginning balance* + *charges* – *credits*), display the new balance and determine if the new balance exceeds the customer's credit limit. For those customers whose credit limit is exceeded, the program should display the message "Credit limit exceeded."

4.13 A large company pays its salespeople on a commission basis. The salespeople receive $200 per week, plus 9% of their gross sales for that week. For example, a salesperson who sells $5000 worth of merchandise in a week receives $200 plus 9% of $5000, or a total of $650. You have been supplied with a list of items sold by each salesperson. The values of these items are as follows:

Item	Value
1	239.99
2	129.75
3	99.95
4	350.89

Develop a Java application that inputs one salesperson's items sold for last week and calculates and displays that salesperson's earnings. There is no limit to the number of items that can be sold by a salesperson.

4.14 Develop a Java application that will determine the gross pay for each of three employees. The company pays "straight time" for the first 40 hours worked by each employee and pays "time and a half" for all hours worked in excess of 40 hours. You are given a list of the employees of the company, the number of hours each employee worked last week and the hourly rate of each employee. Your program should input this information for each employee and should determine and display the employee's gross pay. Use input dialogs to input the data.

4.15 The process of finding the largest value (i.e., the maximum of a group of values) is used frequently in computer applications. For example, a program that determines the winner of a sales contest would input the number of units sold by each salesperson. The salesperson who sells the most units wins the contest. Write a pseudocode program and then a Java application that inputs a series of 10 single-digit numbers as characters and determines and prints the largest of the numbers. *Hint*: Your program should use the following three variables:

a) **`counter`**: A counter to count to 10 (i.e., to keep track of how many numbers have been input and to determine when all 10 numbers have been processed);
b) **`number`**: The current digit input to the program;
c) **`largest`**: The largest number found so far.

4.16 Write a Java application that uses looping to print the following table of values:

```
N       10*N     100*N    1000*N

1       10       100      1000
2       20       200      2000
3       30       300      3000
4       40       400      4000
5       50       500      5000
```

4.17 Using an approach similar to that for Exercise 4.15, find the *two* largest values of the 10 digits entered. [*Note*: You may input each number only once.]

4.18 Modify the program in Fig. 4.11 to validate its inputs. For any input, if the value entered is other than 1 or 2, keep looping until the user enters a correct value.

4.19 What does the following program print?

```
public class Mystery2 {

   public static void main( String args[] )
   {
      int count = 1;

      while ( count <= 10 ) {
         System.out.println(
            count % 2 == 1 ? "****" : "++++++++" );
         ++count;
      }
   }
}
```

4.20 What does the following program print?

```
public class Mystery3 {

   public static void main( String args[] )
   {
      int row = 10, column;

      while ( row >= 1 ) {
         column = 1;

         while ( column <= 10 ) {
            System.out.print( row % 2 == 1 ? "<" : ">" );
            ++column;
         }

         --row;
         System.out.println();
      }
   }
}
```

4.21 *(Dangling-Else Problem)* Determine the output for each of the given sets of code when **x** is **9** and **y** is **11** and when **x** is **11** and **y** is **9**. Note that the compiler ignores the indentation in a Java program. Also, the Java compiler always associates an **else** with the previous **if** unless told to do otherwise by the placement of braces (**{}**). On first glance, the programmer may not be sure which **if** an **else** matches; this situation is referred to as the "dangling-else problem." We have eliminated the indentation from the following code to make the problem more challenging. [*Hint*: Apply indentation conventions you have learned.]

a)
```
if ( x < 10 )
if ( y > 10 )
System.out.println( "*****" );
else
System.out.println( "#####" );
System.out.println( "$$$$$" );
```

b)
```
if ( x < 10 ) {
if ( y > 10 )
System.out.println( "*****" );
}
else {
System.out.println( "#####" );
System.out.println( "$$$$$" );
}
```

4.22 *(Another Dangling-Else Problem)* Modify the given code to produce the output shown in each part of the problem. Use proper indentation techniques. You may not make any changes other than inserting braces and changing the indentation of the code. The compiler ignores indentation in a Java program. We have eliminated the indentation from the given code to make the problem more challenging. [*Note*: It is possible that no modification is necessary for some of the parts.]

```
if ( y == 8 )
if ( x == 5 )
System.out.println( "@@@@@" );
else
System.out.println( "#####" );
System.out.println( "$$$$$" );
System.out.println( "&&&&&" );
```

a) Assuming that **x = 5** and **y = 8**, the following output is produced:

```
@@@@@
$$$$$
&&&&&
```

b) Assuming that **x = 5** and **y = 8**, the following output is produced:

```
@@@@@
```

c) Assuming that **x = 5** and **y = 8**, the following output is produced:

```
@@@@@
&&&&&
```

d) Assuming that **x = 5** and **y = 7**, the following output is produced [*Note*: The last three output statements after the **else** are all part of a block]:]

```
#####
$$$$$
&&&&&
```

4.23 Write an applet that reads in the size of the side of a square and displays a hollow square of that size out of asterisks, by using the **drawString** method inside your applet's **paint** method.

Use an input dialog to read the size from the user. Your program should work for squares of all lengths of side between 1 and 20.

4.24 A palindrome is a number or a text phrase that reads the same backward as forward. For example, each of the following five-digit integers are palindromes: 12321, 55555, 45554 and 11611. Write an application that reads in a five-digit integer and determines whether or not it is a palindrome. If the number is not five digits long, display an error message dialog indicating the problem to the user. When the user dismisses the error dialog, allow the user to enter a new value.

4.25 Write an application that inputs an integer containing only 0s and 1s (i.e., a "binary" integer) and prints its decimal equivalent. [*Hint*: Use the modulus and division operators to pick off the "binary number's" digits one at a time, from right to left. Just as in the decimal number system, where the rightmost digit has a positional value of 1 and the next digit to the left has a positional value of 10, then 100, then 1000, etc., in the binary number system the rightmost digit has a positional value of 1, the next digit to the left has a positional value of 2, then 4, then 8, etc. Thus, the decimal number 234 can be interpreted as 4 * 1 + 3 * 10 + 2 * 100. The decimal equivalent of binary 1101 is 1 * 1 + 0 * 2 + 1 * 4 + 1 * 8, or 1 + 0 + 4 + 8 or, 13.]

4.26 Write an application that displays the following checkerboard pattern:

```
* * * * * * * *
 * * * * * * * *
* * * * * * * *
 * * * * * * * *
* * * * * * * *
 * * * * * * * *
* * * * * * * *
 * * * * * * * *
```

Your program may use only three output statements, one of the form

```
System.out.print( "* " );
```

one of the form

```
System.out.print( " " );
```

and one of the form

```
System.out.println();
```

Note that the preceding statement indicates that the program should output a single newline character to drop to the next line of the output. [*Hint*: Repetition structures are required in this exercise.]

4.27 Write an application that keeps displaying in the command window the multiples of the integer 2, namely 2, 4, 8, 16, 32, 64, etc. Your loop should not terminate (i.e., you should create an infinite loop). What happens when you run this program?

4.28 What is wrong with the following statement? Provide the correct statement to add one to the sum of **x** and **y**.

```
System.out.println( ++(x + y) );
```

4.29 Write an application that reads three nonzero values entered by the user in input dialogs and determines and prints if they could represent the sides of a triangle.

4.30 Write an application that reads three nonzero integers and determines and prints if they could represent the sides of a right triangle.

4.31 A company wants to transmit data over the telephone, but it is concerned that its phones may be tapped. All of its data are transmitted as four-digit integers. It has asked you to write a program that will encrypt its data so that the data may be transmitted more securely. Your application should read a four-digit integer entered by the user in an input dialog and encrypt it as follows: Replace each digit by *(the sum of that digit plus 7) modulus 10*. Then swap the first digit with the third, and swap the second digit with the fourth. Then print the encrypted integer. Write a separate application that inputs an encrypted four-digit integer and decrypts it to form the original number.

4.32 The factorial of a nonnegative integer n is written as $n!$ (pronounced "n factorial") and is defined as follows:

$$n! = n \cdot (n - 1) \cdot (n - 2) \cdot \ldots \cdot 1 \quad \text{(for values of } n \text{ greater than or equal to 1)}$$

and

$$n! = 1 \quad (\text{for } n = 0).$$

For example, $5! = 5 \cdot 4 \cdot 3 \cdot 2 \cdot 1$, which is 120.

a) Write an application that reads a nonnegative integer from an input dialog and computes and prints its factorial.

b) Write an application that estimates the value of the mathematical constant e by using the formula

$$e = 1 + \frac{1}{1!} + \frac{1}{2!} + \frac{1}{3!} + \ldots$$

c) Write an application that computes the value of e^x by using the formula:

$$e^x = 1 + \frac{x}{1!} + \frac{x^2}{2!} + \frac{x^3}{3!} + \ldots$$

Control Structures: Part 2

Objectives

- To be able to use the **`for`** and **`do/while`** repetition structures to execute statements in a program repeatedly.
- To understand multiple selection using the **`switch`** selection structure.
- To be able to use the **`break`** and **`continue`** program control statements.
- To be able to use the logical operators.

Who can control his fate?
William Shakespeare, *Othello*

The used key is always bright.
Benjamin Franklin

Man is a tool-making animal.
Benjamin Franklin

Intelligence … is the faculty of making artificial objects, especially tools to make tools.
Henri Bergson

Outline

5.1 Introduction
5.2 Essentials of Counter-Controlled Repetition
5.3 The **for** Repetition Structure
5.4 Examples Using the **for** Structure
5.5 The **switch** Multiple-Selection Structure
5.6 The **do/while** Repetition Structure
5.7 Statements **break** and **continue**
5.8 Labeled **break** and **continue** Statements
5.9 Logical Operators
5.10 Structured Programming Summary
5.11 (Optional Case Study) Thinking About Objects: Identifying Objects' States and Activities

Summary • Terminology • Self-Review Exercises • Answers to Self-Review Exercises • Exercises

5.1 Introduction

Chapter 4 began our introduction to the types of building blocks that are available for problem solving and used those building blocks to employ proven program construction principles. In this chapter, we continue our presentation of the theory and principles of structured programming by introducing Java's remaining control structures. As in Chapter 4, the Java techniques you learn here are applicable to most high-level languages. When we begin our formal treatment of object-based programming in Java in Chapter 8, we will see that the control structures we study in this chapter and Chapter 4 are helpful in building and manipulating objects.

5.2 Essentials of Counter-Controlled Repetition

Counter-controlled repetition requires the following:

1. the *name* of a control variable (or loop counter),
2. the *initial value* of the control variable,
3. the amount of *increment* (or *decrement*) by which the control variable is modified each time through the loop (also known as *each iteration of the loop*), and
4. the condition that tests for the *final value* of the control variable (i.e., whether looping should continue).

To see the four elements of counter-controlled repetition, consider the applet shown in Fig. 5.1, which draws 10 lines from the applet's **paint** method. Remember that an applet requires a separate HTML document to load the applet into the **appletviewer** or a browser. For the purpose of this applet, the **<applet>** tag specifies a width of **275** pixels and a height of **110** pixels.

```
1  // Fig. 5.1: WhileCounter.java
2  // Counter-controlled repetition
3
4  // Java core packages
5  import java.awt.Graphics;
6
7  // Java extension packages
8  import javax.swing.JApplet;
9
10 public class WhileCounter extends JApplet {
11
12    // draw lines on applet's background
13    public void paint( Graphics g )
14    {
15       // call inherited version of method paint
16       super.paint( g );
17
18       int counter = 1;                // initialization
19
20       while ( counter <= 10 ) {       // repetition condition
21          g.drawLine( 10, 10, 250, counter * 10 );
22          ++counter;                   // increment
23
24       } // end while structure
25
26    } // end method paint
27
28 } // end class WhileCounter
```

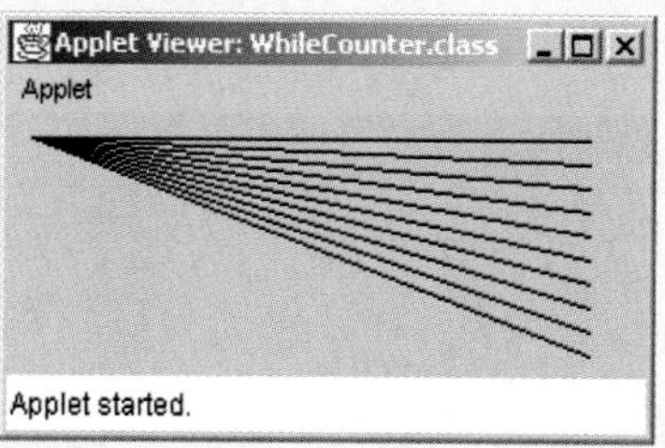

Fig. 5.1 Counter-controlled repetition.

The applet's **paint** method (that the applet container calls when it executes the applet) operates as follows: The declaration on line 18 *names* the control variable (**counter**), declares it to be an integer, reserves space for it in memory and sets it to an *initial value* of **1**. Declarations that include initialization are, in effect, executable statements. The declaration and initialization of **counter** could also have been accomplished with the declaration and statement

```
int counter;  // declare counter
counter = 1;  // initialize counter to 1
```

The declaration is not executable, but the assignment statement is. We use both methods of initializing variables throughout this book.

Line 21 in the **while** structure uses **Graphics** reference **g**, which refers to the applet's **Graphics** object, to send the **drawLine** message to the **Graphics** object, asking it to draw a line. Remember that "sending a message to an object" actually means calling a method to perform a task. One of the **Graphics** object's many services is to draw lines. In previous chapters, we also saw that the **Graphics** object's other services include drawing rectangles, strings and ovals. **Graphics** method **drawLine** requires four arguments, representing the line's first *x*-coordinate, first *y*-coordinate, second *x*-coordinate and second *y*-coordinate. In this example, the second *y*-coordinate changes value during each iteration of the loop with the calculation **counter * 10**. This change causes the second point (the end point of the line) in each call to **drawLine** to move 10 pixels down the applet's display area.

Line 22 in the **while** structure *increments* the control variable by 1 for each iteration of the loop. The loop-continuation condition in the **while** structure tests whether the value of the control variable is less than or equal to **10** (the *final value* for which the condition is **true**). Note that the program performs the body of this **while** structure even when the control variable is **10**. The loop terminates when the control variable exceeds **10** (i.e., **counter** becomes **11**).

The program in Fig. 5.1 can be made more concise by initializing **counter** to **0** and preincrementing **counter** in the **while** structure condition as follows:

```
while ( ++counter <= 10 )       // repetition condition
   g.drawLine( 10, 10, 250, counter * 10 );
```

This code saves a statement (and eliminates the need for braces around the loop's body), because the **while** condition performs the increment before testing the condition. (Remember that the precedence of **++** is higher than that of **<=**.) Coding in such a condensed fashion takes practice.

Good Programming Practice 5.1

Programs should control counting loops with integer values.

Common Programming Error 5.1

Because floating-point values may be approximate, controlling the counting of loops with floating-point variables may result in imprecise counter values and inaccurate tests for termination.

Good Programming Practice 5.2

Indent the statements in the body of each control structure.

Good Programming Practice 5.3

Put a blank line before and after each major control structure to make it stand out in the program.

Good Programming Practice 5.4

Too many levels of nesting can make a program difficult to understand. As a general rule, try to avoid using more than three levels of nesting.

Good Programming Practice 5.5

Vertical spacing above and below control structures, and indentation of the bodies of control structures within the control structures' headers, gives programs a two-dimensional appearance that enhances readability.

5.3 The `for` Repetition Structure

The **`for`** repetition structure handles all of the details of counter-controlled repetition. To illustrate the power of the **`for`** structure, let us rewrite the applet of Fig. 5.1. The result is shown in Fig. 5.2. Remember that this program requires a separate HTML document to load the applet into the **`appletviewer`**. For the purpose of this applet, the **`<applet>`** tag specifies a width of **`275`** pixels and a height of **`110`** pixels.

```java
// Fig. 5.2: ForCounter.java
// Counter-controlled repetition with the for structure

// Java core packages
import java.awt.Graphics;

// Java extension packages
import javax.swing.JApplet;

public class ForCounter extends JApplet {

   // draw lines on applet's background
   public void paint( Graphics g )
   {
      // call inherited version of method paint
      super.paint( g );

      // Initialization, repetition condition and incrementing
      // are all included in the for structure header.
      for ( int counter = 1; counter <= 10; counter++ )
         g.drawLine( 10, 10, 250, counter * 10 );

   }  // end method paint

}  // end class ForCounter
```

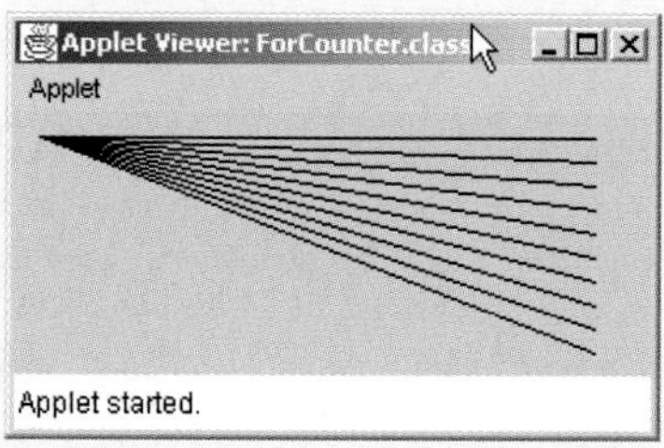

Fig. 5.2 Counter-controlled repetition with the **`for`** structure.

The applet's **paint** method operates as follows: When the **for** structure (lines 20–21) begins executing, the control variable **counter** is initialized to **1**. (The first two elements of counter-controlled repetition and the *name* of the control variable and its *initial value*.) Next, the program checks the loop-continuation condition, **counter <= 10**. The condition contains the *final value* (**10**) of the control variable. Because the initial value of **counter** is **1**, the condition is satisfied (**true**), so the body statement (line 21) draws a line. After executing the body of the loop, the program increments variable **counter** in the expression **counter++**. Then, the program performs the loop-continuation test again to determine whether the program should continue with the next iteration of the loop or whether it should terminate the loop. At this point, the control variable value is **2**, so the condition is true (i.e., the final value is not exceeded), and thus the program performs the body statement again (i.e., the next iteration of the loop). This process continues until the **counter**'s value becomes **11**, causing the loop-continuation test to fail and repetition to terminate. Then, the program performs the first statement after the **for** structure. (In this case, method **paint** terminates, because the program reaches the end of **paint**.)

Notice that Fig. 5.2 uses the loop-continuation condition **counter <= 10**. If the programmer incorrectly specified **counter < 10** as the condition, the loop would be executed only nine times. This mistake is a common logic error called an *off-by-one error.*

Common Programming Error 5.2

*Using an incorrect relational operator or using an incorrect final value of a loop counter in the condition of a **while**, **for** or **do/while** structure can cause an off-by-one error.*

Good Programming Practice 5.6

*Using the final value in the condition of a **while** or **for** structure and using the **<=** relational operator will help avoid off-by-one errors. For a loop that prints the values 1 to 10, the loop-continuation condition should be **counter <= 10** rather than **counter < 10** (which causes an off-by-one error) or **counter < 11** (which is correct). Many programmers prefer so-called zero-based counting, in which to count 10 times, **counter** would be initialized to zero and the loop-continuation test would be **counter < 10**.*

Figure 5.3 takes a closer look at the **for** structure of Fig. 5.2. The **for** structure's first line (including the keyword **for** and everything in parentheses after **for**) is sometimes called the ***for** structure header*. Notice that the **for** structure "does it all": It specifies each of the items needed for counter-controlled repetition with a control variable. If there is more than one statement in the body of the **for** structures, braces (**{** and **}**) are required to define the body of the loop.

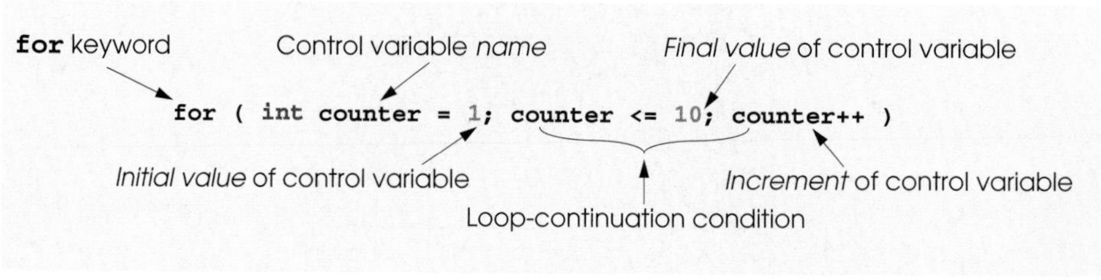

Fig. 5.3 Components of a typical **for** structure header.

The general format of the **for** structure is

```
for ( expression1; expression2; expression3 )
    statement
```

where *expression1* names the loop's control variable and provides its initial value, *expression2* is the loop-continuation condition (containing the control variable's final value) and *expression3* modifies the value of the control variable, so that the loop-continuation condition eventually becomes **false**. In most cases, the **for** structure can be represented with an equivalent **while** structure, with *expression1*, *expression2* and *expression3* placed as follows:

```
expression1;

while ( expression2 ) {
    statement
    expression3;
}
```

In Section 5.7, we show a case in which a **for** structure cannot be represented with an equivalent **while** structure.

If *expression1* (the initialization section) declares the control variable inside the parentheses of the header of the **for** structure (i.e., the control variable's type is specified before the name of the variable), the control variable can be used only in the **for** structure. This restricted use of the name of the control variable is known as the variable's *scope*. The scope of a variable defines where the program can use the variable. For example, we mentioned previously that a program can use a local variable only in the method that declares the variable. Scope is discussed in detail in Chapter 6, "Methods."

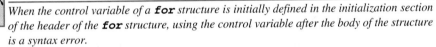

Common Programming Error 5.3

When the control variable of a **for** *structure is initially defined in the initialization section of the header of the* **for** *structure, using the control variable after the body of the structure is a syntax error.*

Sometimes, *expression1* and *expression3* in a **for** structure are comma-separated lists of expressions that enable the programmer to use multiple initialization expressions and/or multiple increment expressions. For example, there may be several control variables in a single **for** structure that must be initialized and incremented.

Good Programming Practice 5.7

Place only expressions involving the control variables in the initialization and increment sections of a **for** *structure. Manipulations of other variables should appear either before the loop (if they execute only once, like initialization statements) or in the body of the loop (if they execute once per iteration of the loop, like incrementing or decrementing statements).*

The three expressions in the **for** structure are optional. If *expression2* is omitted, Java assumes that the loop-continuation condition is **true**, thus creating an infinite loop. One might omit *expression1* if the program initializes the control variable before the loop. One might omit *expression3* if the program calculates the increment with statements in the loop's body or if the loop does not require an increment. The increment expression in the **for** structure acts as a stand-alone statement at the end of the body of the **for** structure, so the expressions

```
counter = counter + 1
counter += 1
++counter
counter++
```

are equivalent in the increment portion of the **for** structure. Many programmers prefer the form **counter++**, because a **for** structure increments its control variable after the body of the loop executes and placing **++** after the variable name increments the variable after the program uses its value. Therefore, the postincrementing form seems more natural. Preincrementing and postincrementing *have the same effect in the increment expression*, because the increment does not appear in a larger expression. The two semicolons in the **for** structure are required.

Common Programming Error 5.4

Using commas instead of the two required semicolons in a **for** *header is a syntax error.*

Common Programming Error 5.5

Placing a semicolon immediately to the right of the right parenthesis of a **for** *header makes the body of that* **for** *structure an empty statement. This is normally a logic error.*

The initialization, loop-continuation condition and increment portions of a **for** structure can contain arithmetic expressions. For example, assume that **x = 2** and **y = 10**. If **x** and **y** are not modified in the body of the loop, the statement

```
for ( int j = x; j <= 4 * x * y; j += y / x )
```

is equivalent to the statement

```
for ( int j = 2; j <= 80; j += 5 )
```

The increment of a **for** structure may also be negative, in which case it is really a decrement, and the loop actually counts downward.

If the loop-continuation condition is initially **false**, the program does not perform the body of the **for** structure. Instead, execution proceeds with the statement following the **for** structure.

Programs frequently display the control variable value or use it in calculations in loop body. However, this use is not required. It is common to use the control variable for controlling repetition while never mentioning it in the body of the **for** structure.

Testing and Debugging Tip 5.1

Although the value of the control variable can be changed in the body of a **for** *loop, avoid doing so, because this practice can lead to subtle errors.*

We flowchart the **for** structure much as we do the **while** structure. For example, the flowchart of the **for** statement

```
for ( int counter = 1; counter <= 10; counter++ )
   g.drawLine( 10, 10, 250, counter * 10 );
```

is shown in Fig. 5.4. This flowchart makes it clear that the initialization occurs only once and that the increment occurs each time *after* the program performs the body statement.

Note that, besides small circles and arrows, the flowchart contains only rectangle symbols and a diamond symbol. The programmer fills the rectangles and diamonds with actions and decisions appropriate to the algorithm.

5.4 Examples Using the `for` Structure

The examples given next show methods of varying the control variable in a **`for`** structure. In each case, we write the appropriate **`for`** structure header. Note the change in the relational operator for loops that decrement the control variable.

a) Vary the control variable from **`1`** to **`100`** in increments of **`1`**.

```
for ( int i = 1; i <= 100; i++ )
```

b) Vary the control variable from **`100`** to **`1`** in increments of **`-1`** (i.e., decrements of **`1`**).

```
for ( int i = 100; i >= 1; i-- )
```

c) Vary the control variable from **`7`** to **`77`** in steps of **`7`**.

```
for ( int i = 7; i <= 77; i += 7 )
```

d) Vary the control variable from **`20`** to **`2`** in steps of **`-2`**.

```
for ( int i = 20; i >= 2; i -= 2 )
```

e) Vary the control variable over the following sequence of values: **`2`**, **`5`**, **`8`**, **`11`**, **`14`**, **`17`**, **`20`**.

```
for ( int j = 2; j <= 20; j += 3 )
```

f) Vary the control variable over the following sequence of values: **`99`**, **`88`**, **`77`**, **`66`**, **`55`**, **`44`**, **`33`**, **`22`**, **`11`**, **`0`**.

```
for ( int j = 99; j >= 0; j -= 11 )
```

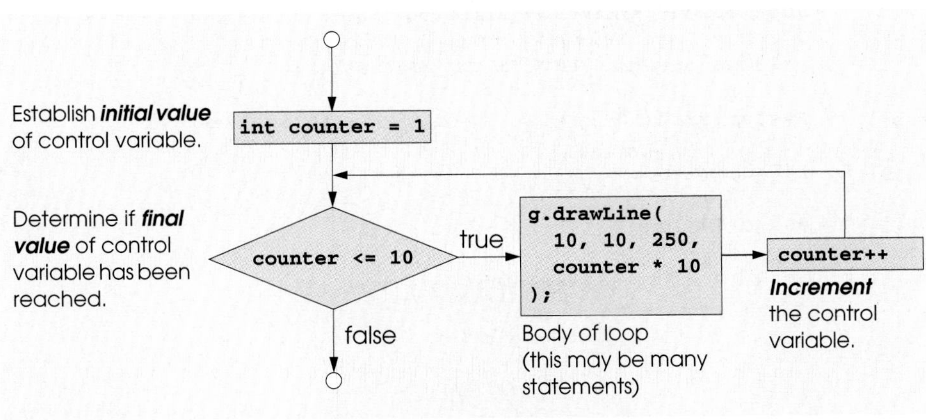

Fig. 5.4 Flowcharting a typical **`for`** repetition structure.

Common Programming Error 5.6

Not using the proper relational operator in the loop-continuation condition of a loop that counts downward (such as using **i <= 1** *in a loop counting down to 1) is usually a logic error and will yield incorrect results when the program runs.*

The next two sample programs demonstrate simple applications of the **for** repetition structure. The application in Fig. 5.5 uses the **for** structure to sum all the even integers from **2** to **100**. Remember that the **java** interpreter is used to execute an application from the command window.

Note that the body of the **for** structure in Fig. 5.5 could actually be merged into the rightmost portion of the **for** header by using a comma as follows:

```
for ( int number = 2;
      number <= 100;
      sum += number, number += 2 )
   ;  // empty statement
```

```
// Fig. 5.5: Sum.java
// Counter-controlled repetition with the for structure

// Java extension packages
import javax.swing.JOptionPane;

public class Sum {

   // main method begins execution of Java application
   public static void main( String args[] )
   {
      int sum = 0;

      // sum even integers from 2 through 100
      for ( int number = 2; number <= 100; number += 2 )
         sum += number;

      // display results
      JOptionPane.showMessageDialog( null, "The sum is " + sum,
         "Sum Even Integers from 2 to 100",
         JOptionPane.INFORMATION_MESSAGE );

      System.exit( 0 );   // terminate the application

   }  // end method main

}  // end class Sum
```

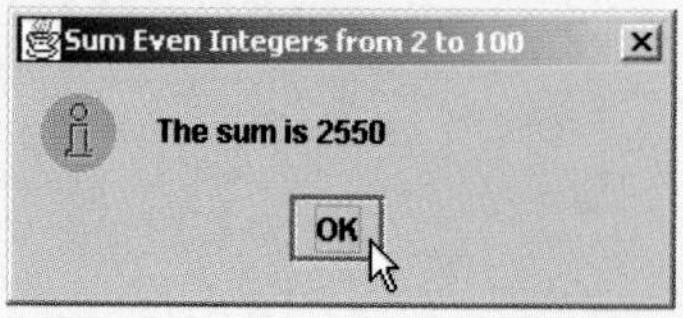

Sum Even Integers from 2 to 100

The sum is 2550

OK

Fig. 5.5 Summation with the **for** structure.

Similarly, the initialization **sum = 0** could be merged into the initialization section of the **for** structure.

Good Programming Practice 5.8

*Although statements preceding a **for** structure and statements in the body of a **for** structure can often be merged into the header of the **for** structure, avoid doing so, because it makes the program more difficult to read.*

Good Programming Practice 5.9

Limit the size of control structure headers to a single line. if possible.

The next example uses the **for** structure to compute compound interest. Consider the following problem:

> *A person invests $1000.00 in a savings account yielding 5% interest. Assuming that all interest is left on deposit, calculate and print the amount of money in the account at the end of each year for 10 years. Use the following formula to determine the amounts:*
>
> $a = p\,(1 + r)^{\,n}$
>
> *where*
>
> p is the original amount invested (i.e., the principal)
> r is the annual interest rate
> n is the number of years
> a is the amount on deposit at the end of the nth year.

This problem involves a loop that performs the indicated calculation for each of the 10 years the money remains on deposit. The solution is the application shown in Fig. 5.6.

```java
// Fig. 5.6: Interest.java
// Calculating compound interest

// Java core packages
import java.text.NumberFormat;
import java.util.Locale;

// Java extension packages
import javax.swing.JOptionPane;
import javax.swing.JTextArea;

public class Interest {

   // main method begins execution of Java application
   public static void main( String args[] )
   {
      double amount, principal = 1000.0, rate = 0.05;

      // create DecimalFormat to format floating-point numbers
      // with two digits to the right of the decimal point
      NumberFormat moneyFormat =
         NumberFormat.getCurrencyInstance( Locale.US );

```

Fig. 5.6 Calculating compound interest with the **for** structure (part 1 of 2).

```
24         // create JTextArea to display output
25         JTextArea outputTextArea = new JTextArea();
26
27         // set first line of text in outputTextArea
28         outputTextArea.setText( "Year\tAmount on deposit\n" );
29
30         // calculate amount on deposit for each of ten years
31         for ( int year = 1; year <= 10; year++ ) {
32
33            // calculate new amount for specified year
34            amount = principal * Math.pow( 1.0 + rate, year );
35
36            // append one line of text to outputTextArea
37            outputTextArea.append( year + "\t" +
38               moneyFormat.format( amount ) + "\n" );
39
40         }  // end for structure
41
42         // display results
43         JOptionPane.showMessageDialog( null, outputTextArea,
44            "Compound Interest", JOptionPane.INFORMATION_MESSAGE );
45
46         System.exit( 0 );  // terminate the application
47
48      }  // end method main
49
50   }  // end class Interest
```

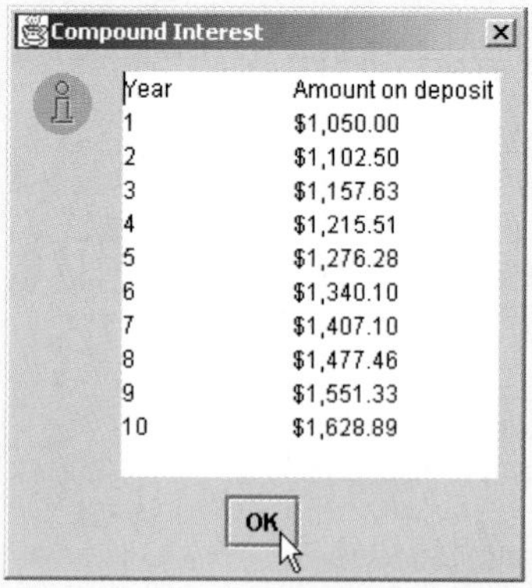

Compound Interest

Year	Amount on deposit
1	$1,050.00
2	$1,102.50
3	$1,157.63
4	$1,215.51
5	$1,276.28
6	$1,340.10
7	$1,407.10
8	$1,477.46
9	$1,551.33
10	$1,628.89

OK

Fig. 5.6 Calculating compound interest with the **for** structure (part 2 of 2).

Line 17 in method **main** declares three **double** variables and initializes two of them—**principal** to **1000.0** and **rate** to **.05**. Java treats floating-point constants, like **1000.0** and **.05** in Fig. 5.6, as type **double**. Similarly, Java treats whole number constants, like **7** and **-22**, as type **int**. Lines 21–22 declare ***NumberFormat*** reference **moneyFormat** and initialize it by calling **static** method ***getCurrencyInstance*** of class **NumberFormat**. This method returns a **NumberFormat** object that can format numeric values as currency (e.g., in the United States, currency values normally are preceded with a dollar sign, $). The argument to the method—**Locale.US**—indicates that the currency values should be displayed starting with a dollar sign ($), use a decimal point to separate dollars and cents and use a comma to delineate thousands (e.g., $1,234.56). Class **Locale** provides constants that can be used to customize this program to represent currency values for other countries, so that currency formats are displayed properly for each *locale* (i.e., each country's local-currency format). Class **NumberFormat** (imported at line 5) is located in package **java.text**, and class **Locale** (imported at line 6) is located in package ***java.util***.

Line 25 declares **JTextArea** reference **outputTextArea** and initializes it with a new object of class **JTextArea** (from package **javax.swing**). A **JTextArea** is a GUI component that can display many lines of text. The message dialog that displays the **JTextArea** determines the width and height of the **JTextArea**, based on the **String** it contains. We introduce this GUI component now because we will see many examples throughout the text in which the program outputs contain too many lines to display on the screen. This GUI component allows us to scroll through the lines of text so we can see all the program output. The methods for placing text in a **JTextArea** include ***setText*** and ***append***.

Line 28 uses **JTextArea** method **setText** to place a **String** in the **JTextArea** to which **outputTextArea** refers. Initially, a **JTextArea** contains an empty **String** (i.e., a **String** with no characters in it). The preceding statement replaces the empty **String** with one containing the column heads for our two columns of output—"**Year**" and "**Amount on Deposit**." The column heads are separated with a tab character (escape sequence **\t**). Also, the string contains the newline character (escape sequence **\n**), indicating that any additional text appended to the **JTextArea** should begin on the next line.

The **for** structure (lines 31–40) executes its body 10 times, varying control variable **year** from 1 to 10 in increments of 1. (Note that **year** represents n in the statement of the problem.) Java does not include an exponentiation operator. Instead, we use **static** method **pow** of class **Math** for this purpose. **Math.pow(x, y)** calculates the value of **x** raised to the **y**th power. Method **pow** takes two arguments of type **double** and returns a **double** value. Line 34 performs the calculation from the statement of the problem,

$$a = p\,(1 + r)^{\,n}$$

where a is **amount**, p is **principal**, r is **rate** and n is **year**.

Lines 37–38 **append** more text to the end of the **outputTextArea**. The text includes the current value of **year**, a tab character (to position to the second column), the result of the method call **moneyFormat.format(amount)**—which formats the **amount** as U. S. currency—and a newline character (to position the cursor in the **JTextArea** at the beginning of the next line).

Lines 43–44 display the results in a message dialog. Until now, the message displayed has always been a **String**. In this example, the second argument is **outputTextArea**—a GUI component. An interesting feature of class **JOptionPane** is that the message it displays with **showMessageDialog** can be a **String** or a GUI component, such as a **JTextArea**. In this example, the message dialog sizes itself to accommodate the **JTextArea**. We use this technique several times early in this chapter to display large text-based outputs. Later in this chapter, we demonstrate how to add a scrolling capability to the **JTextArea**, so the user can view a program's output that is too large to display in full on the screen.

Notice that the variables **amount**, **principal** and **rate** are of type **double**. We did this for simplicity, because we are dealing with fractional parts of dollars and thus need a type that allows decimal points in its values. Unfortunately, this setting can cause trouble. Here is a simple explanation of what can go wrong when using **float** or **double** to represent dollar amounts (assuming that dollar amounts are displayed with two digits to the right of the decimal point): Two **double** dollar amounts stored in the machine could be 14.234 (which would normally be rounded to 14.23 for display purposes) and 18.673 (which would normally be rounded to 18.67 for display purposes). When these amounts are added, they produce the internal sum 32.907, which would normally be rounded to 32.91 for display purposes. Thus, your printout could appear as

```
  14.23
+ 18.67
-------
  32.91
```

but a person adding the individual numbers as printed would expect the sum to be 32.90. You have been warned!

Good Programming Practice 5.10

Do not use variables of type **float** *or* **double** *to perform precise monetary calculations. The imprecision of floating-point numbers can cause errors that will result in incorrect monetary values. In the exercises, we explore the use of integers to perform monetary calculations. [*Note*: Some third-party vendors provide for-sale class libraries that perform precise monetary calculations.]*

Note that the body of the **for** structure contains the calculation **1.0 + rate**, which appears as an argument to the **Math.pow** method. In fact, this calculation produces the same result each time through the loop, so repeating the calculation every iteration of the loop is wasteful.

Performance Tip 5.1

Avoid placing expressions whose values do not change inside loops. But even if you do, many of today's sophisticated optimizing compilers will place such expressions outside loops in the generated compiled code.

Performance Tip 5.2

Many compilers contain optimization features that improve the code that you write, but it is still better to write good code from the start.

5.5 The `switch` Multiple-Selection Structure

We have discussed the **if** single-selection structure and the **if/else** double-selection structure. Occasionally, an algorithm contains a series of decisions in which the algorithm tests a variable or expression separately for each of the constant integral values (i.e., values of types **byte**, **short**, **int** and **char**) the variable or expression may assume and takes different actions based on those values. Java provides the **switch** multiple-selection structure to handle such decision making. The applet of Fig. 5.7 demonstrates drawing lines, rectangles or ovals, based on an integer the user inputs via an input dialog.

```java
// Fig. 5.7: SwitchTest.java
// Drawing lines, rectangles or ovals based on user input.

// Java core packages
import java.awt.Graphics;

// Java extension packages
import javax.swing.*;

public class SwitchTest extends JApplet {
   int choice;   // user's choice of which shape to draw

   // initialize applet by obtaining user's choice
   public void init()
   {
      String input;  // user's input

      // obtain user's choice
      input = JOptionPane.showInputDialog(
                 "Enter 1 to draw lines\n" +
                 "Enter 2 to draw rectangles\n" +
                 "Enter 3 to draw ovals\n" );

      // convert user's input to an int
      choice = Integer.parseInt( input );
   }

   // draw shapes on applet's background
   public void paint( Graphics g )
   {
      // call inherited version of method paint
      super.paint( g );

      // loop 10 times, counting from 0 through 9
      for ( int i = 0; i < 10; i++ ) {

         // determine shape to draw based on user's choice
         switch ( choice ) {

            case 1:
               g.drawLine( 10, 10, 250, 10 + i * 10 );
               break;  // done processing case

            case 2:
               g.drawRect( 10 + i * 10, 10 + i * 10,
                  50 + i * 10, 50 + i * 10 );
               break;  // done processing case

            case 3:
               g.drawOval( 10 + i * 10, 10 + i * 10,
                  50 + i * 10, 50 + i * 10 );
               break;  // done processing case

```

Fig. 5.7 An example using **switch** (part 1 of 3).

```
            default:
               g.drawString( "Invalid value entered",
                  10, 20 + i * 15 );

         }  // end switch structure

      }  // end for structure

   }  // end paint method

}  // end class SwitchTest
```

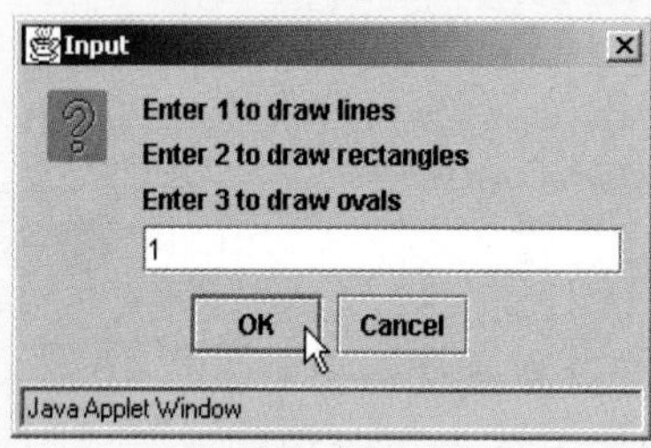

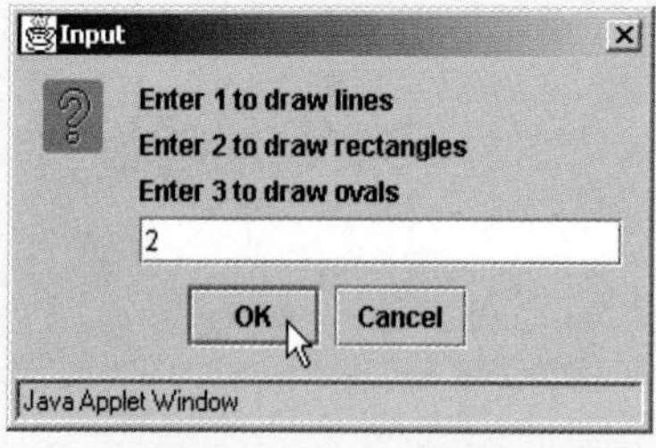

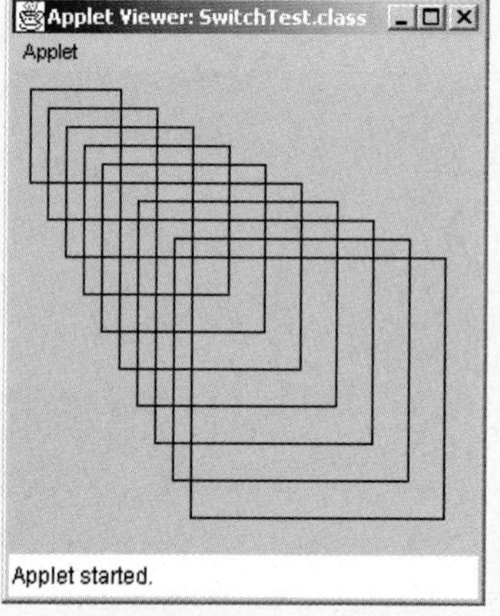

Fig. 5.7 An example using **`switch`** (part 2 of 3).

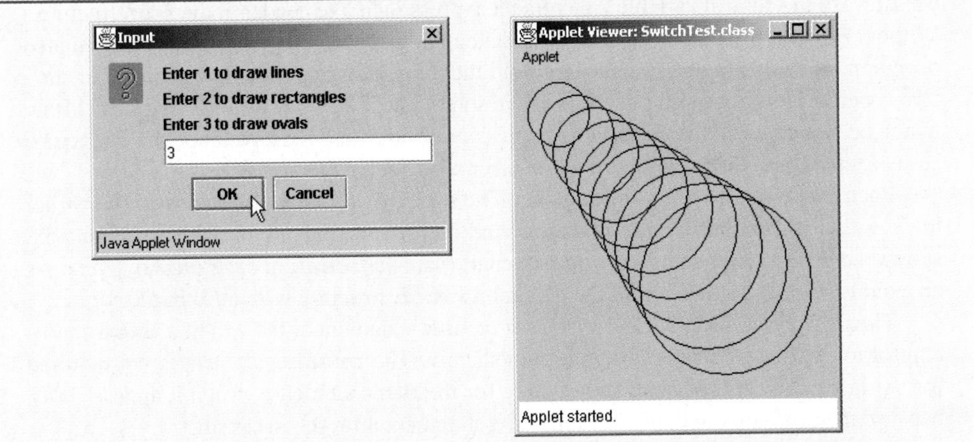

Fig. 5.7 An example using **switch** (part 3 of 3).

Line 11 in applet **SwitchTest** defines instance variable **choice** of type **int**. This variable stores the user's input that determines which type of shape to draw in **paint**.

Method **init** (lines 14–26) declares local variable **input** of type **String** in line 16. This variable stores the **String** the user types in the input dialog. Lines 19–22 display the input dialog with **static** method **JOptionPane.showInputDialog** and prompt the user to enter **1** to draw lines, **2** to draw rectangles or **3** to draw ovals. Line 25 converts input from a **String** to an **int** and assigns the result to **choice**.

Method **paint** (lines 29–62) contains a **for** structure (lines 35–60) that loops 10 times. In this example, the **for** structure's header, in line 35, uses zero-based counting. The values of **i** for the 10 iterations of the loop are 0, 1, 2, 3, 4, 5, 6, 7, 8 and 9, and the loop terminates when **i**'s value becomes 10. [*Note*: As you know, the applet container calls method **paint** after methods **init** and **start**. The applet container also calls method **paint** whenever the applet's screen area must be refreshed—e.g., after another window that covered the applet's area is moved to a different location on the screen.]

Nested in the **for** structure's body is a **switch** structure (lines 38–58) that draws shapes based on the integer value input by the user in method **init**. The **switch** structure consists of a series of ***case*** *labels* and an optional ***default*** *case*.

When the flow of control reaches the **switch** structure, the program evaluates the *controlling expression* (**choice**) in the parentheses following keyword **switch**. The program compares the value of the controlling expression (which must evaluate to an integral value of type **byte**, **char**, **short** or **int**) with each ***case*** *label*. Assume that the user entered the integer **2** as his or her choice. The program compares **2** with each **case** in the **switch**. If a match occurs (**case 2:**), the program executes the statements for that **case**. For the integer **2**, lines 44–47 draw a rectangle, using four arguments, representing the upper left *x*-coordinate, upper left *y*-coordinate, width and height of the rectangle, and the **switch** structure exits immediately with the **break** statement. Then, the program increments the counter variable in the **for** structure and reevaluates the loop-continuation condition to determine whether to perform another iteration of the loop.

The **break** statement causes program control to proceed with the first statement after the **switch** structure. (In this case, we reach the end of the **for** structure's body, so control flows to the control variable's increment expression in the header of the **for** structure.) Without **break**, the **case**s in a **switch** statement would run together. Each time a match occurs in the structure, the statements for all the remaining **case**s will execute. (This feature is perfect for programming the iterative song "The Twelve Days of Christmas.") If no match occurs between the controlling expression's value and a **case** label, the **default** case executes, and the program draws an error message on the applet.

Each **case** can have multiple actions. The **switch** structure differs from other structures in that it does not require braces around multiple actions in each **case**. Figure 5.8 shows the general **switch** structure flowchart (using a **break** in each **case**). [*Note*: As an exercise, make a flowchart of the general **switch** structure without **break**s.]

The flowchart makes it clear that each **break** statement at the end of a **case** causes control to exit the **switch** structure immediately. The **break** statement is not required for the last **case** in the **switch** structure (or the **default** case, when it appears last), because the program continues with the next statement after the **switch**.

Again, note that, besides small circles and arrows, the flowchart contains only rectangle and diamond symbols. It is the programmer's responsibility to fill the rectangles and diamonds with actions and decisions appropriate to the algorithm. Although nested control structures are common, it is rare to find nested **switch** structures in a program.

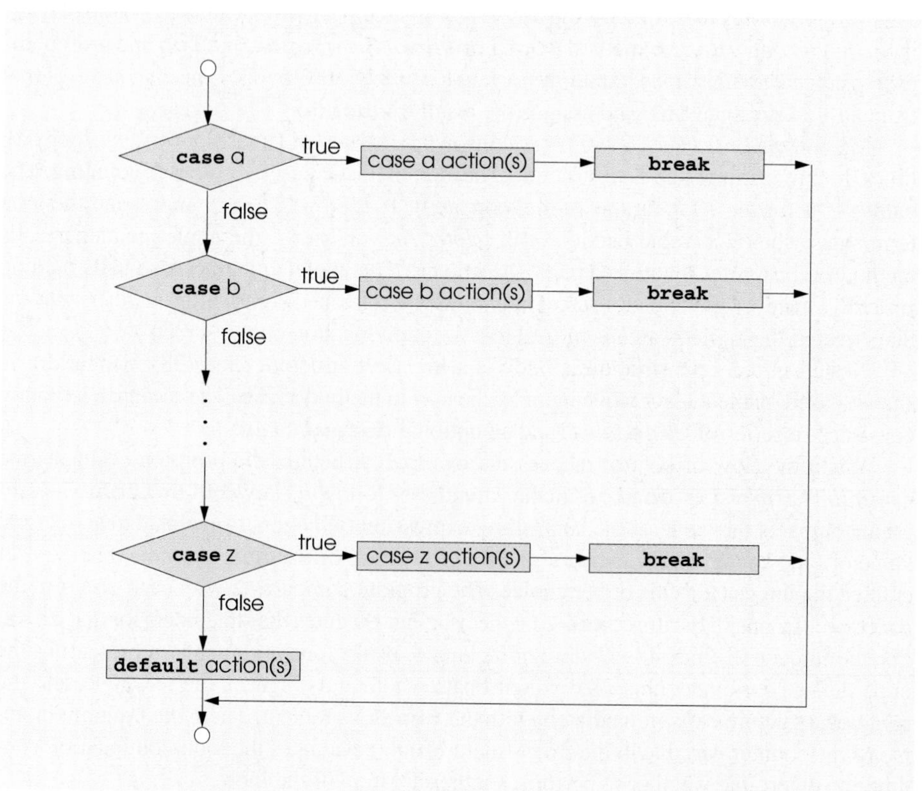

Fig. 5.8 The **switch** multiple-selection structure.

Common Programming Error 5.7

Forgetting a **break** *statement when one is needed in a* **switch** *structure is a logic error.*

Good Programming Practice 5.11

Provide a **default** *case in* **switch** *statements. Cases not explicitly tested in a* **switch** *statement without a* **default** *case are ignored. Including a* **default** *case focuses the programmer on the need to process exceptional conditions. There are situations in which no* **default** *processing is needed.*

Good Programming Practice 5.12

Although the **case***s and the* **default** *case in a* **switch** *structure can occur in any order, it is considered a good programming practice to place the* **default** *clause last.*

Good Programming Practice 5.13

In a **switch** *structure, when the* **default** *clause is listed last, the* **break** *for that* **case** *statement is not required. Some programmers include this* **break** *for clarity and symmetry with other cases.*

Note that listing **case** labels together (such as **case 1: case 2:** with no statements between the cases) performs the same set of actions for each case.

When using the **switch** structure, remember that the expression after each **case** can be only a *constant integral expression* (i.e., any combination of character constants and integer constants that evaluates to a constant integer value). A character constant is represented as the specific character in single quotes, such as **'A'**. An integer constant is simply an integer value. The expression after each **case** also can be a *constant variable*—i.e., a variable that contains a value which does not change for the entire program. Such a variable is declared with keyword ***final*** (discussed in Chapter 6). When we discuss object-oriented programming in Chapter 9, we present a more elegant way to implement **switch** logic. We use a technique called *polymorphism* to create programs that are often clearer, easier to maintain and easier to extend than programs using **switch** logic.

5.6 The do/while Repetition Structure

The **do/while** repetition structure is similar to the **while** structure. In the **while** structure, the program tests the loop-continuation condition at the beginning of the loop, before performing the body of the loop. The **do/while** structure tests the loop-continuation condition *after* performing the body of the loop; therefore, *the loop body always executes at least once*. When a **do/while** structure terminates, execution continues with the statement after the **while** clause. Note that it is not necessary to use braces in the **do/while** structure if there is only one statement in the body. However, most programmers include the braces, to avoid confusion between the **while** and **do/while** structures. For example,

```
while ( condition )
```

normally is the first line of a **while** structure. A **do/while** structure with no braces around a single-statement body appears as

```
do
   statement
while ( condition );
```

which can be confusing. Reader may misinterpret the last line—**while(** *condition* **);**— as a **while** structure containing an empty statement (the semicolon by itself). Thus, to avoid confusion, the **do/while** structure with one statement often is written as follows:

```
do {
    statement
} while ( condition );
```

Good Programming Practice 5.14

Some programmers always include braces in a **do/while** *structure, even if the braces are not necessary. This helps eliminate ambiguity between the* **while** *structure and the* **do/while** *structure containing only one statement.*

Common Programming Error 5.8

Infinite loops occur when the loop-continuation condition in a **while**, **for** *or* **do/while** *structure never becomes* **false**. *To prevent this situation, make sure that there is not a semicolon immediately after the header of a* **while** *or* **for** *structure. In a counter-controlled loop, ensure that the control variable is incremented (or decremented) in the body of the loop. In a sentinel-controlled loop, ensure that the sentinel value is eventually input.*

The applet in Fig. 5.9 uses a **do/while** structure to draw 10 nested circles, using **Graphics** method **drawOval**.

```
// Fig. 5.9: DoWhileTest.java
// Using the do/while repetition structure.

// Java core packages
import java.awt.Graphics;

// Java extension packages
import javax.swing.JApplet;

public class DoWhileTest extends JApplet {

   // draw lines on applet's background
   public void paint( Graphics g )
   {
      // call inherited version of method paint
      super.paint( g );

      int counter = 1;

      do {
         g.drawOval( 110 - counter * 10, 110 - counter * 10,
            counter * 20, counter * 20 );
         ++counter;
      } while ( counter <= 10 );  // end do/while structure

   }  // end method paint

}  // end class DoWhileTest
```

Fig. 5.9 Using the **do/while** repetition structure (part 1 of 2).

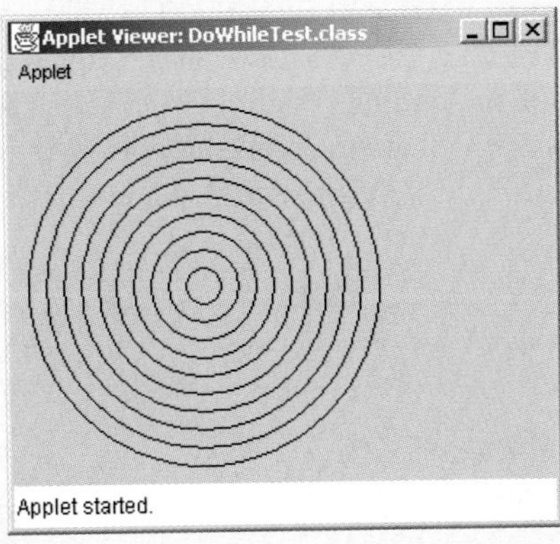

Fig. 5.9 Using the **do/while** repetition structure (part 2 of 2).

In method **paint** (lines 13–26), line 18 declares control variable **counter** and initializes it to **1**. Upon entering the **do/while** structure, lines 21–22 send the **drawOval** message to the **Graphics** object to which **g** refers. The four arguments that represent the upper left *x*-coordinate, upper left *y*-coordinate, width and height of the oval's *bounding box* (an imaginary rectangle in which the oval touches the center of all four sides of the rectangle) are calculated based on the value of **counter**. The program draws the innermost oval first. The bounding box's upper left corner for each subsequent oval moves closer to the upper left corner of the applet. At the same time, the width and height of the bounding box are increased, to ensure that each new oval contains all the previous ovals. Line 23 increments **counter**. Then, the program evaluates the loop-continuation test at the bottom of the loop. The **do/while** flowchart in Fig. 5.10 makes it clear that the program does not evaluate the loop-continuation condition until after the action executes once.

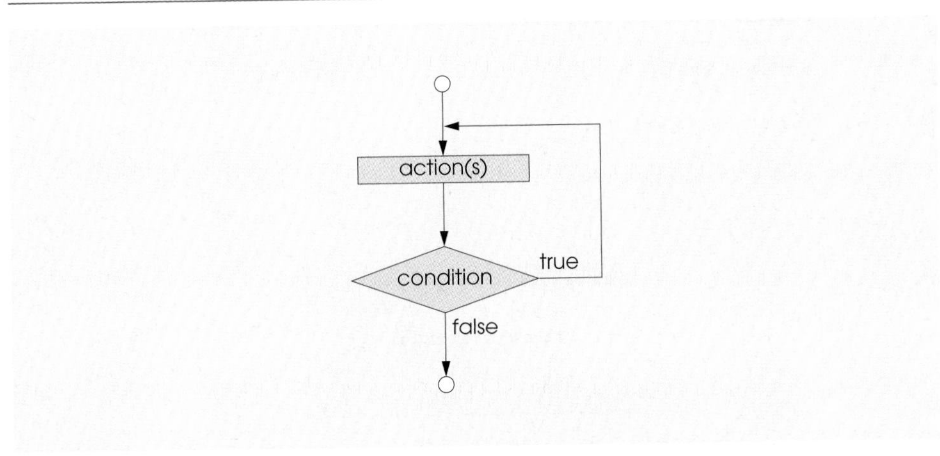

Fig. 5.10 Flowcharting the **do/while** repetition structure.

5.7 Statements **break** and **continue**

The ***break*** and ***continue*** statements alter the flow of control. The **break** statement, when executed in a **while**, **for**, **do/while** or **switch** structure, causes immediate exit from that structure. Execution continues with the first statement after the structure. Common uses of the **break** statement are to escape early from a loop or skip the remainder of a **switch** structure (as in Fig. 5.7). Figure 5.11 demonstrates the **break** statement in a **for** repetition structure.

```java
// Fig. 5.11: BreakTest.java
// Using the break statement in a for structure

// Java extension packages
import javax.swing.JOptionPane;

public class BreakTest {

   // main method begins execution of Java application
   public static void main( String args[] )
   {
      String output = "";
      int count;

      // loop 10 times
      for ( count = 1; count <= 10; count++ ) {

         // if count is 5, terminate loop
         if ( count == 5 )
            break;  // break loop only if count == 5

         output += count + " ";

      }  // end for structure

      output += "\nBroke out of loop at count = " + count;
      JOptionPane.showMessageDialog( null, output );

      System.exit( 0 );  // terminate application

   }  // end method main

}  // end class BreakTest
```

Fig. 5.11 Using the **break** statement in a **for** structure.

When the **if** structure at line 19 in the **for** structure detects that **count** is **5**, the **break** statement at line 20 executes. This statement terminates the **for** structure, and the program proceeds to line 26 (immediately after the **for**). Line 26 completes the string to display in a message dialog at line 27. The loop fully executes its body only four times.

The **continue** statement, when executed in a **while**, **for** or **do/while** structure, skips the remaining statements in the loop body and proceeds with the next iteration of the loop. In **while** and **do/while** structures, the program evaluates the loop-continuation test immediately after the **continue** statement executes. In **for** structures, the increment expression executes, then the program evaluates the loop-continuation test. Earlier, we stated that the **while** structure could be used in most cases to represent the **for** structure. The one exception occurs when the increment expression in the **while** structure follows the **continue** statement. In this case, the increment does not execute before the program evaluates the repetition-continuation condition, so the **while** structure does not execute in the same manner as does the **for** structure. Figure 5.12 uses the **continue** statement in a **for** structure to skip the string concatenation statement (line 22) when the **if** structure (line 18) determines that the value of **count** is **5**. When the **continue** statement executes, program control continues with the increment of the control variable in the **for** structure.

Good Programming Practice 5.15

Some programmers feel that **break** *and* **continue** *violate structured programming. Because the effects of these statements are achievable with structured programming techniques, these programmers do not use* **break** *and* **continue**.

```
1  // Fig. 5.12: ContinueTest.java
2  // Using the continue statement in a for structure
3
4  // Java extension packages
5  import javax.swing.JOptionPane;
6
7  public class ContinueTest {
8
9     // main method begins execution of Java application
10    public static void main( String args[] )
11    {
12       String output = "";
13
14       // loop 10 times
15       for ( int count = 1; count <= 10; count++ ) {
16
17          // if count is 5, continue with next iteration of loop
18          if ( count == 5 )
19             continue;  // skip remaining code in loop
20                        // only if count == 5
21
22          output += count + " ";
23
24       }  // end for structure
25
```

Fig. 5.12 Using the **continue** statement in a **for** structure (part 1 of 2).

```
        output += "\nUsed continue to skip printing 5";
        JOptionPane.showMessageDialog( null, output );

        System.exit( 0 );  // terminate application

    } // end method main

}  // end class ContinueTest
```

Message
1 2 3 4 6 7 8 9 10
Used continue to skip printing 5
OK

Fig. 5.12 Using the **continue** statement in a **for** structure (part 2 of 2).

Performance Tip 5.3

*The **break** and **continue** statements, when used properly, perform faster than the corresponding structured techniques.*

Software Engineering Observation 5.1

There is a tension between achieving quality software engineering and achieving the best performing software. Often, one of these goals is achieved at the expense of the other. For all but the most performance-intensive situations, apply the following rule of thumb: First, make your code simple and correct; then make it fast and small, but only if necessary.

5.8 Labeled break and continue Statements

The **break** statement can break out of only an immediately enclosing **while**, **for**, **do/while** or **switch** structure. To break out of a nested set of structures, you can use the *labeled* **break** *statement*. This statement, when executed in a **while**, **for**, **do/while** or **switch** structure, causes immediate exit from that structure and any number of enclosing repetition structures; program execution resumes with the first statement after the enclosing *labeled block* (i.e., a set of statements enclosed in curly braces and preceded by a label). The block can be either a repetition structure (the body would be the block) or a block in which the repetition structure is the first executable code. Labeled **break** statements are commonly used to terminate nested looping structures containing **while**, **for**, **do/while** or **switch** structures. Figure 5.13 demonstrates the labeled **break** statement in a nested **for** structure.

The block (lines 14–37) begins with a *label* (an identifier followed by a colon) at line 14; here, we use the label "**stop:**." The block is enclosed in braces at the end of line 14 and line 37 and includes the nested **for** structure (lines 17–32) and the string-concatenation statement at line 35. When the **if** structure at line 23 detects that **row** is equal to **5**, the **break** statement at line 24 executes. This statement terminates both the **for** structure at line 20 and its enclosing **for** structure at line 17. The program proceeds immediately to line 39—the first statement after the labeled block. The outer **for** structure fully executes its body only four times. Notice that the string-concatenation statement at line 35 never executes, because it is in the labeled block's body, and the outer **for** structure never completes.

```
1  // Fig. 5.13: BreakLabelTest.java
2  // Using the break statement with a label
3
4  // Java extension packages
5  import javax.swing.JOptionPane;
6
7  public class BreakLabelTest {
8
9     // main method begins execution of Java application
10    public static void main( String args[] )
11    {
12       String output = "";
13
14       stop: {   // labeled block
15
16          // count 10 rows
17          for ( int row = 1; row <= 10; row++ ) {
18
19             // count 5 columns
20             for ( int column = 1; column <= 5 ; column++ ) {
21
22                // if row is 5, jump to end of "stop" block
23                if ( row == 5 )
24                   break stop; // jump to end of stop block
25
26                output += "*  ";
27
28             }  // end inner for structure
29
30             output += "\n";
31
32          }  // end outer for structure
33
34          // the following line is skipped
35          output += "\nLoops terminated normally";
36
37       }  // end labeled block
38
39       JOptionPane.showMessageDialog(
40          null, output,"Testing break with a label",
41          JOptionPane.INFORMATION_MESSAGE );
42
43       System.exit( 0 );   // terminate application
44
45    }  // end method main
46
47 }  // end class BreakLabelTest
```

Fig. 5.13 Using a labeled **break** statement in a nested **for** structure (part 1 of 2).

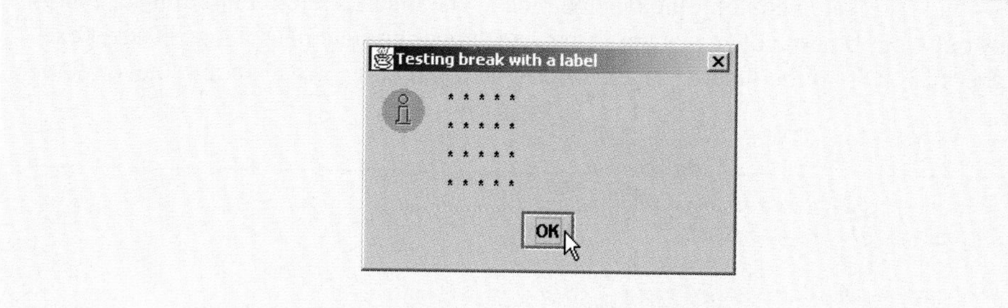

Fig. 5.13 Using a labeled **break** statement in a nested **for** structure (part 2 of 2).

The **continue** statement proceeds with the next iteration (repetition) of the immediately enclosing **while**, **for** or **do/while** structure. The *labeled **continue** statement*, when executed in a repetition structure (**while**, **for** or **do/while**), skips the remaining statements in that structure's body and any number of enclosing repetition structures and proceeds with the next iteration of the enclosing *labeled repetition structure* (i.e., a repetition structure preceded by a label). In labeled **while** and **do/while** structures, the program evaluates the loop-continuation test immediately after the **continue** statement executes. In a labeled **for** structure, the increment expression is executed, and then the loop-continuation test is evaluated. Figure 5.14 uses the labeled **continue** statement in a nested **for** structure to enable execution to continue with the next iteration of the outer **for** structure.

The labeled **for** structure (lines 14–32) starts at the **nextRow** label. When the **if** structure at line 24 in the inner **for** structure detects that **column** is greater than **row**, the **continue** statement at line 25 executes, and program control continues with the increment of the control variable of the outer **for** loop. Even though the inner **for** structure counts from 1 to 10, the number of ***** characters output on a row never exceeds the value of **row**.

Performance Tip 5.4

*The program in Fig. 5.14 can be made simpler and more efficient by replacing the condition in the **for** structure at line 21 with **column <= row** and removing the **if** structure at lines 24–25 from the program.*

5.9 Logical Operators

So far, we have studied only *simple conditions*, such as **count <= 10**, **total > 1000** and **number != sentinelValue**. These conditions were expressed in terms of the relational operators **>**, **<**, **>=** and **<=** and the equality operators **==** and **!=**. Each decision tested one condition. To test multiple conditions in the process of making a decision, we performed these tests in separate statements or in nested **if** or **if/else** structures.

Java provides *logical operators* to enable programmers to form more complex conditions by combining simple conditions. The logical operators are **&&** (*logical AND*), **&** (*boolean logical AND*), **||** (*logical OR*), **|** (*boolean logical inclusive OR*), **^** (*boolean logical exclusive OR*) and **!** (*logical NOT*, also called *logical negation*).

```
// Fig. 5.14: ContinueLabelTest.java
// Using the continue statement with a label

// Java extension packages
import javax.swing.JOptionPane;

public class ContinueLabelTest {

   // main method begins execution of Java application
   public static void main( String args[] )
   {
      String output = "";

      nextRow:   // target label of continue statement

         // count 5 rows
         for ( int row = 1; row <= 5; row++ ) {
            output += "\n";

            // count 10 columns per row
            for ( int column = 1; column <= 10; column++ ) {

               // if column greater than row, start next row
               if ( column > row )
                  continue nextRow; // next iteration of
                                    // labeled loop

               output += "*  ";

            }  // end inner for structure

         }  // end outer for structure

      JOptionPane.showMessageDialog(
         null, output,"Testing continue with a label",
         JOptionPane.INFORMATION_MESSAGE );

      System.exit( 0 );  // terminate application

   }  // end method main

}  // end class ContinueLabelTest
```

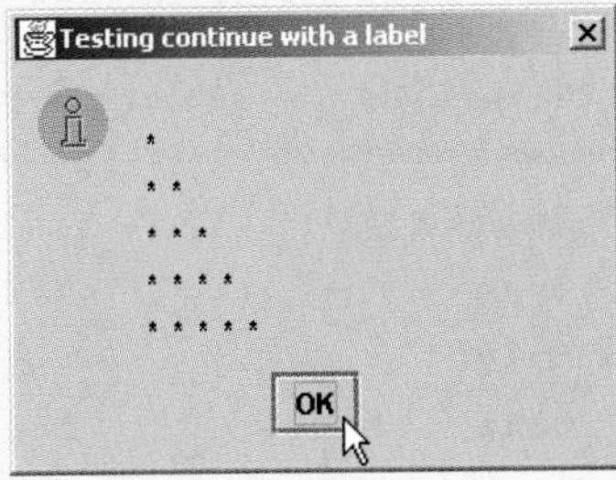

Fig. 5.14 Using a labeled **continue** statement in a nested **for** structure .

Suppose we wish to ensure at some point in a program that two conditions are *both* **true** before we choose a certain path of execution. In this case, we can use the logical **&&** operator, as follows:

```
if ( gender == 1 && age >= 65 )
   ++seniorFemales;
```

This **if** statement contains two simple conditions. The condition **gender == 1** might be evaluated, for example, to determine if a person is a female. The condition **age >= 65** is evaluated to determine if a person is a senior citizen. The two simple conditions are evaluated first, because the precedences of **==** and **>=** are both higher than the precedence of **&&**. The **if** statement then considers the combined condition

```
gender == 1 && age >= 65
```

This condition is **true** *if and only if* both of the simple conditions are **true**. If this combined condition is indeed **true**, the **if** structure's body statement increments variable **seniorFemales** by **1**. If either or both of the simple conditions are **false**, the program skips the increment and proceeds to the statement following the **if** structure. The preceding combined condition can be made more readable by adding redundant parentheses:

```
( gender == 1 ) && ( age >= 65 )
```

The table in Fig. 5.15 summarizes the **&&** operator. The table shows all four possible combinations of **false** and **true** values for *expression1* and *expression2*. Such tables are often called *truth tables*. Java evaluates to **false** or **true** all expressions that include relational operators, equality operators and/or logical operators.

Now let us consider the || (logical OR) operator. Suppose we wish to ensure that either *or* both of two conditions are **true** before we choose a certain path of execution. In this case, we use the || operator, as in the following program segment:

```
if ( semesterAverage >= 90 || finalExam >= 90 )
   System.out.println ( "Student grade is A" );
```

This statement also contains two simple conditions. The condition **semesterAverage >= 90** evaluates to determine if the student deserves an "A" in the course because of a solid performance throughout the semester. The condition **finalExam >= 90** evaluates to determine if the student deserves an "A" in the course because of an outstanding performance on the final exam. The **if** statement then considers the combined condition

expression1	expression2	expression1 && expression2
false	false	false
false	true	false
true	false	false
true	true	true

Fig. 5.15 Truth table for the && (logical AND) operator.

```
semesterAverage >= 90 || finalExam >= 90
```

and awards the student an "A" if either or both of the simple conditions are **true**. Note that the only time the message "**Student grade is A**" is *not* printed is when both of the simple conditions are **false**. Figure 5.16 is a truth table for the logical OR operator (**||**).

The **&&** operator has a higher precedence than the **||** operator. Both operators associate from left to right. An expression containing **&&** or **||** operators is evaluated only until truth or falsity is known. Thus, evaluation of the expression

```
gender == 1 && age >= 65
```

stops immediately if **gender** is not equal to **1** (i.e., the entire expression is **false**) and continues if **gender** is equal to **1** (i.e., the entire expression could still be **true** if the condition **age >= 65** is **true**). This performance feature for evaluation of logical AND and logical OR expressions is called *short-circuit evaluation.*

Common Programming Error 5.9

*In expressions using operator **&&**, it is possible that a condition—we will call this the dependent condition—may require another condition to be **true** for it to be meaningful to evaluate the dependent condition. In this case, the dependent condition should be placed after the other condition, or an error might occur.*

Performance Tip 5.5

*In expressions using operator **&&**, if the separate conditions are independent of one another, make the condition that is most likely to be **false** the leftmost condition. In expressions using operator **||**, make the condition that is most likely to be **true** the leftmost condition. This can reduce a program's execution time.*

The *boolean logical AND* (**&**) and *boolean logical inclusive OR* (**|**) operators work identically to the regular logical AND and logical OR operators, with one exception: The boolean logical operators always evaluate both of their operands (i.e., there is no short-circuit evaluation). Therefore, the expression

```
gender == 1 & age >= 65
```

evaluates **age >= 65** regardless of whether **gender** is equal to **1**. This method is useful if the right operand of the boolean logical AND or boolean logical inclusive OR operator has a required *side effect*—a modification of a variable's value. For example, the expression

expression1	expression2	expression1 || expression2
false	false	false
false	true	true
true	false	true
true	true	true

Fig. 5.16 Truth table for the || (logical OR) operator.

```
birthday == true | ++age >= 65
```

guarantees that the condition **++age >= 65** will be evaluated. Thus, the variable **age** is incremented in the preceding expression, regardless of whether the overall expression is **true** or **false**.

Good Programming Practice 5.16

For clarity, avoid expressions with side effects in conditions. The side effects may look clever, but they are often more trouble than they are worth.

A condition containing the *boolean logical exclusive OR* (**^**) operator is **true** *if and only if one of its operands results in a* **true** *value and one results in a* **false** *value.* If both operands are **true** or both are **false**, the result of the entire condition is **false**. Figure 5.17 is a truth table for the boolean logical exclusive OR operator (**^**). This operator is also guaranteed to evaluate both of its operands (i.e., there is no short-circuit evaluation).

Java provides the **!** (logical negation) operator to enable a programmer to "reverse" the meaning of a condition. Unlike the logical operators **&&**, **&**, **||**, **|** and **^**, which combine two conditions (i.e., they are binary operators), the logical negation operator has only a single condition as an operand (i.e., they are unary operator). The logical negation operator is placed before a condition to choose a path of execution if the original condition (without the logical negation operator) is **false**, such as in the following program segment:

```
if ( ! ( grade == sentinelValue ) )
   System.out.println( "The next grade is " + grade );
```

The parentheses around the condition **grade == sentinelValue** are needed, because the logical negation operator has a higher precedence than the equality operator. Figure 5.18 is a truth table for the logical negation operator.

In most cases, the programmer can avoid using logical negation by expressing the condition differently with an appropriate relational or equality operator. For example, the previous statement may also be written as follows:

expression1	expression2	expression1 ^ expression2
false	**false**	**false**
false	**true**	**true**
true	**false**	**true**
true	**true**	**false**

Fig. 5.17 Truth table for the boolean logical exclusive OR (**^**) operator .

expression	!expression
false	**true**
true	**false**

Fig. 5.18 Truth table for operator **!** (logical negation, or logical NOT).

```
if ( grade != sentinelValue )
   System.out.println( "The next grade is " + grade );
```

This flexibility can help a programmer express a condition in a more convenient manner.

The application in Fig. 5.19 demonstrates all of the logical operators and boolean logical operators by producing their truth tables. The program uses string concatenation to create the string that is displayed in a **JTextArea**.

```
// Fig. 5.19: LogicalOperators.java
// Demonstrating the logical operators

// Java extension packages
import javax.swing.*;

public class LogicalOperators {

   // main method begins execution of Java application
   public static void main( String args[] )
   {
      // create JTextArea to display results
      JTextArea outputArea = new JTextArea( 17, 20 );

      // attach JTextArea to a JScrollPane so user can
      // scroll through results
      JScrollPane scroller = new JScrollPane( outputArea );

      String output;

      // create truth table for && operator
      output = "Logical AND (&&)" +
         "\nfalse && false: " + ( false && false ) +
         "\nfalse && true: " + ( false && true ) +
         "\ntrue && false: " + ( true && false ) +
         "\ntrue && true: " + ( true && true );

      // create truth table for || operator
      output += "\n\nLogical OR (||)" +
         "\nfalse || false: " + ( false || false ) +
         "\nfalse || true: " + ( false || true ) +
         "\ntrue || false: " + ( true || false ) +
         "\ntrue || true: " + ( true || true );

      // create truth table for & operator
      output += "\n\nBoolean logical AND (&)" +
         "\nfalse & false: " + ( false & false ) +
         "\nfalse & true: " + ( false & true ) +
         "\ntrue & false: " + ( true & false ) +
         "\ntrue & true: " + ( true & true );

      // create truth table for | operator
      output += "\n\nBoolean logical inclusive OR (|)" +
         "\nfalse | false: " + ( false | false ) +
         "\nfalse | true: " + ( false | true ) +
```

Fig. 5.19 Demonstrating the logical operators (part 1 of 2).

```
46             "\ntrue | false: " + ( true | false ) +
47             "\ntrue | true: " + ( true | true );
48 
49          // create truth table for ^ operator
50          output += "\n\nBoolean logical exclusive OR (^)" +
51             "\nfalse ^ false: " + ( false ^ false ) +
52             "\nfalse ^ true: " + ( false ^ true ) +
53             "\ntrue ^ false: " + ( true ^ false ) +
54             "\ntrue ^ true: " + ( true ^ true );
55 
56          // create truth table for ! operator
57          output += "\n\nLogical NOT (!)" +
58             "\n!false: " + ( !false ) +
59             "\n!true: " + ( !true );
60 
61          outputArea.setText( output );  // place results in JTextArea
62 
63          JOptionPane.showMessageDialog( null, scroller,
64             "Truth Tables", JOptionPane.INFORMATION_MESSAGE );
65 
66          System.exit( 0 );  // terminate application
67 
68       }  // end method main
69 
70    }  // end class LogicalOperators
```

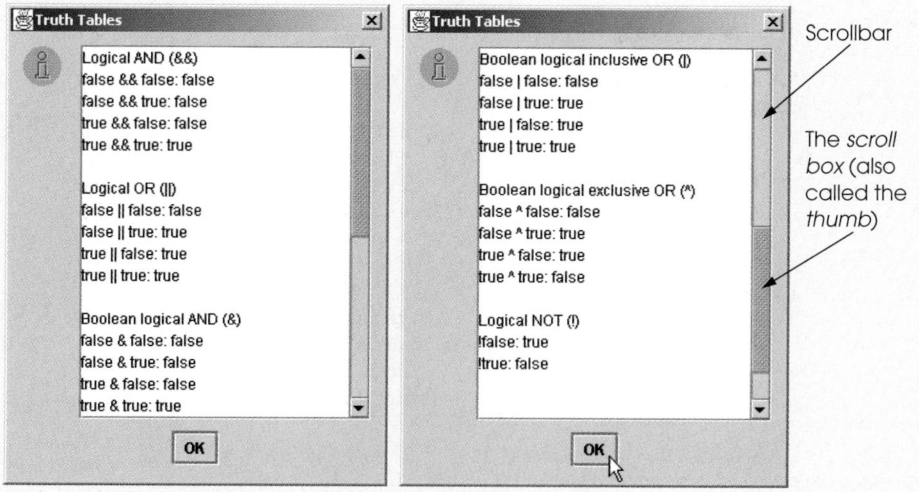

Truth Tables

Logical AND (&&)
false && false: false
false && true: false
true && false: false
true && true: true

Logical OR (||)
false || false: false
false || true: true
true || false: true
true || true: true

Boolean logical AND (&)
false & false: false
false & true: false
true & false: false
true & true: true

OK

Truth Tables

Boolean logical inclusive OR (|)
false | false: false
false | true: true
true | false: true
true | true: true

Boolean logical exclusive OR (^)
false ^ false: false
false ^ true: true
true ^ false: true
true ^ true: false

Logical NOT (!)
!false: true
!true: false

OK

Scrollbar

The *scroll box* (also called the *thumb*)

Fig. 5.19 Demonstrating the logical operators (part 2 of 2).

In the output of Fig. 5.19, the strings "true" and "false" indicate **true** and **false** for the operands in each condition. The result of the condition is shown as **true** or **false**. Note that when you concatenate a **boolean** value with a **String**, Java automatically adds the string "false" or "true," based on the **boolean** value.

Line 13 in method **main** creates a **JTextArea**. The numbers in the parentheses indicate that the **JTextArea** has 17 rows and 20 columns. Line 17 declares **JScrollPane** reference **scroller** and initializes it with a new **JScrollPane** object. Class

JScrollPane (from package **javax.swing**) provides a GUI component with scrolling functionality. A **JScrollPane** object is initialized with the GUI component for which it will provide scrolling functionality (**outputArea** in this example). This initialization attaches the GUI component to the **JScrollPane**. When you execute this application, notice the *scrollbar* on the right side of the **JTextArea**. You can click the *arrows* at the top or bottom of the scrollbar to scroll up or down, respectively, through the text in the **JTextArea** one line at a time. You can also drag the *scroll box* (also called the *thumb*) up or down to scroll through the text rapidly.

Lines 22–59 build the **output** string that is displayed in the **outputArea**. Line 61 uses method **setText** to replace the text in **outputArea** with the **output** string. Lines 63–64 display a message dialog. The second argument, **scroller**, indicates that the **scroller** (and the **outputArea** attached to it) should be displayed as the message in the message dialog.

The chart in Fig. 5.20 shows the precedence and associativity of the Java operators introduced up to this point. The operators are shown from top to bottom in decreasing order of precedence.

5.10 Structured Programming Summary

Just as architects design buildings by employing the collective wisdom of their profession, so should programmers design programs. Our field is younger than architecture is, and our collective wisdom is considerably sparser. We have learned that structured programming produces programs that are easier than unstructured programs to understand and hence are easier to test, debug, modify and even prove correct in a mathematical sense.

Operators	Associativity	Type
`()`	left to right	parentheses
`++ --`	right to left	unary postfix
`++ -- + - !` (*type*)	right to left	unary
`* / %`	left to right	multiplicative
`+ -`	left to right	additive
`< <= > >=`	left to right	relational
`== !=`	left to right	equality
`&`	left to right	boolean logical AND
`^`	left to right	boolean logical exclusive OR
`|`	left to right	boolean logical inclusive OR
`&&`	left to right	logical AND
`||`	left to right	logical OR
`?:`	right to left	conditional
`= += -= *= /= %=`	right to left	assignment

Fig. 5.20 Precedence and associativity of the operators discussed so far.

Figure 5.21 summarizes Java's control structures. Small circles are used in the figure to indicate the single entry and single exit points of each structure. Connecting individual flowchart symbols arbitrarily can lead to unstructured programs. Therefore, the programming profession has chosen to combine flowchart symbols to form a limited set of control structures, and to build structured programs by properly combining control structures in two simple ways.

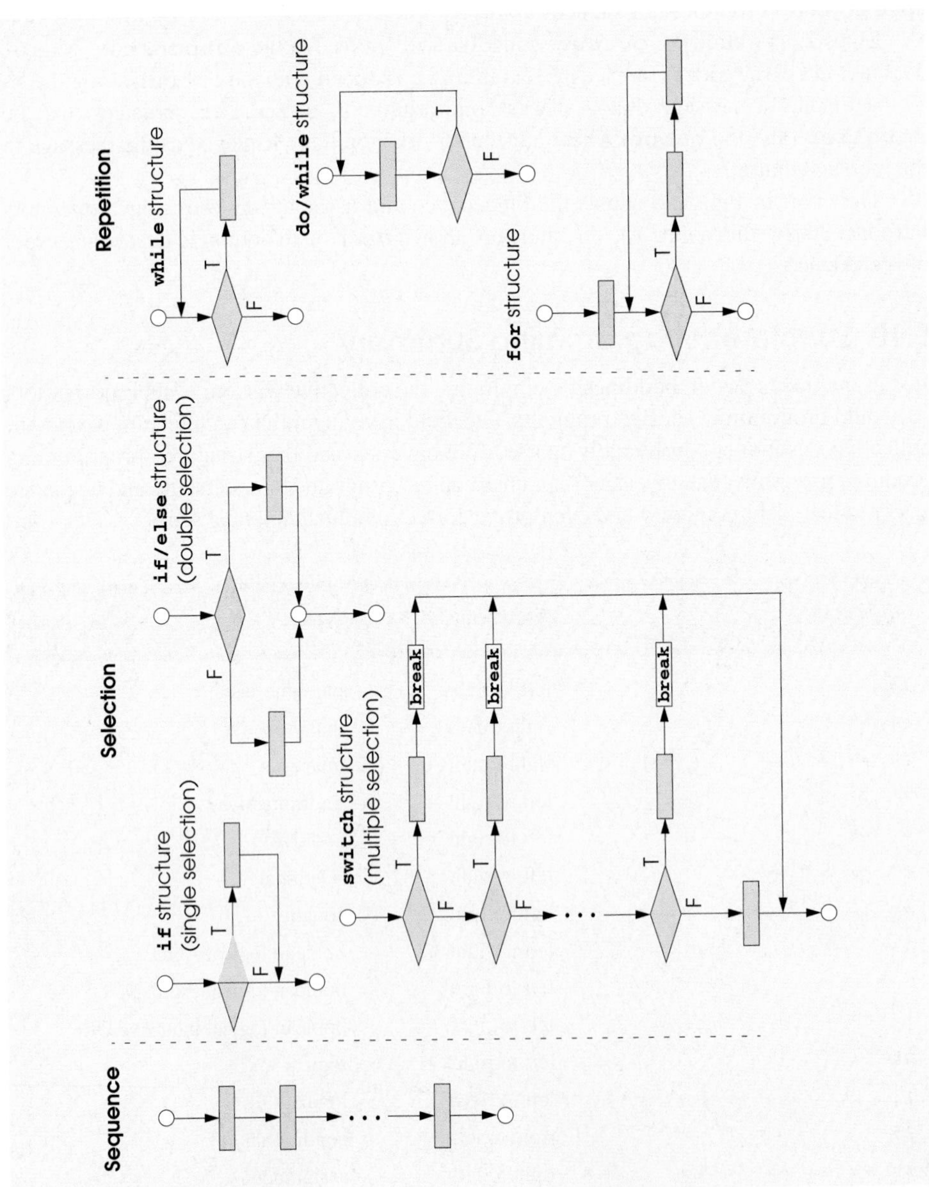

Fig. 5.21 Java's single-entry/single-exit control structures.

For simplicity, only single-entry/single-exit control structures are used; there is only one way to enter and only one way to exit each control structure. Connecting control structures in sequence to form structured programs is simple: The exit point of one control structure is connected to the entry point of the next control structure (i.e., the control structures are simply placed one after another in a program); we have called this method "control-structure stacking." The rules for forming structured programs also allow for control-structure nesting.

Figure 5.22 shows the rules for forming properly structured programs. The rules assume that the rectangle flowchart symbol may be used to indicate any action, including input/output.

Applying the rules of Fig. 5.22 always results in a structured flowchart with a neat, building-block-like appearance (Fig. 5.23). For example, repeatedly applying Rule 2 to the simplest flowchart results in a structured flowchart containing many rectangles in sequence (Fig. 5.24). Rule 2 generates a stack of control structures; so let us call Rule 2 the *stacking rule*. [*Note*: The symbols at the top and bottom of Fig. 5.23 represent the beginning and end of a program, respectively.]

Rule 3 is called the *nesting rule*. Repeatedly applying Rule 3 to the simplest flowchart results in a flowchart with neatly nested control structures. For example, in Fig. 5.25, the rectangle in the simplest flowchart is first replaced with a double-selection (**`if/else`**) structure. Then, Rule 3 is applied again to both of the rectangles in the double-selection structure, replacing each of the rectangles with double-selection structures. The dashed boxes around each of the double-selection structures represent the rectangle that was replaced with a double-selection structure.

Rules for Forming Structured Programs

1) Begin with the "simplest flowchart" (Fig. 5.23).
2) Any rectangle (action) can be replaced by two rectangles (actions) in sequence.
3) Any rectangle (action) can be replaced by any control structure (sequence, **`if`**, **`if/else`**, **`switch`**, **`while`**, **`do/while`** or **`for`**).
4) Rules 2 and 3 may be applied as often as you like and in any order.

Fig. 5.22 Rules for forming structured programs.

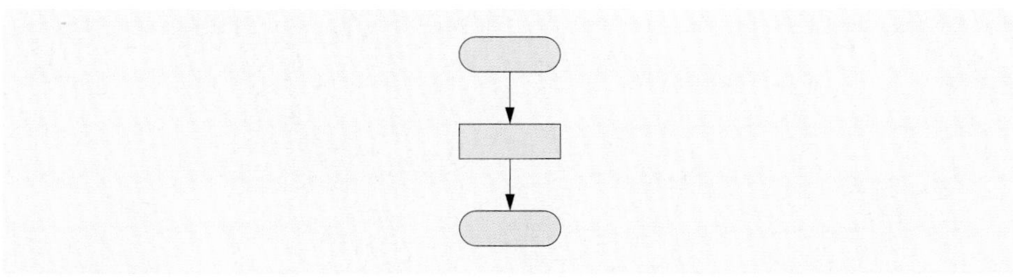

Fig. 5.23 The simplest flowchart.

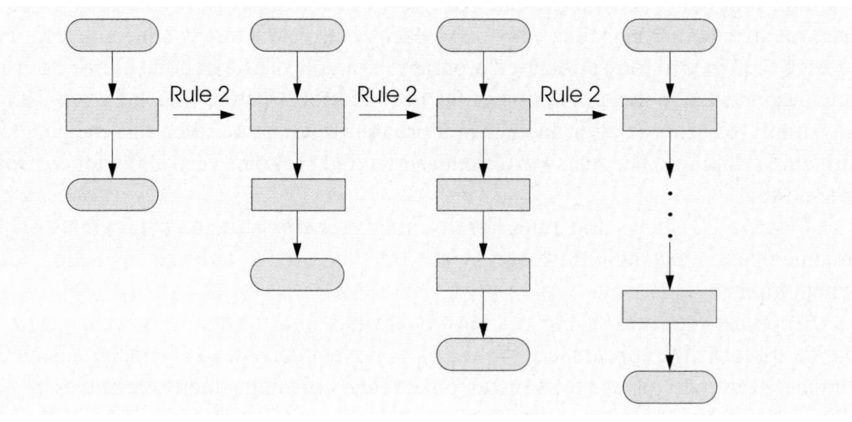

Fig. 5.24 Repeatedly applying Rule 2 of Fig. 5.22 to the simplest flowchart.

Rule 3

Rule 3

Rule 3

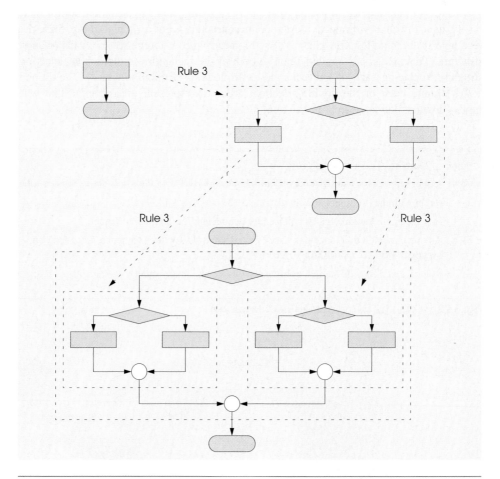

Fig. 5.25 Applying Rule 3 of Fig. 5.22 to the simplest flowchart.

Rule 4 generates larger, more involved and more deeply nested structures. The flowcharts that emerge from applying the rules in Fig. 5.22 constitute the set of all possible structured flowcharts and hence the set of all possible structured programs.

The beauty of the structured approach is that we use only seven simple single-entry/single-exit pieces and we assemble them in only two simple ways. Figure 5.26 shows the kinds of stacked building blocks that emerge from applying Rule 2 and the kinds of nested building blocks that emerge from applying Rule 3. The figure also shows the kind of overlapped building blocks that cannot appear in structured flowcharts (because of the elimination of the **goto** statement).

If the rules in Fig. 5.22 are followed, you cannot create an unstructured flowchart (such as that in Fig. 5.27). If you are uncertain if a particular flowchart is structured, apply the rules of Fig. 5.22 in reverse to try to reduce the flowchart to the simplest flowchart. If the flowchart is reducible to the simplest flowchart, the original flowchart is structured; otherwise, it is not.

Structured programming promotes simplicity. Bohm and Jacopini have shown that only three forms of control are needed—sequence, selection and repetition.

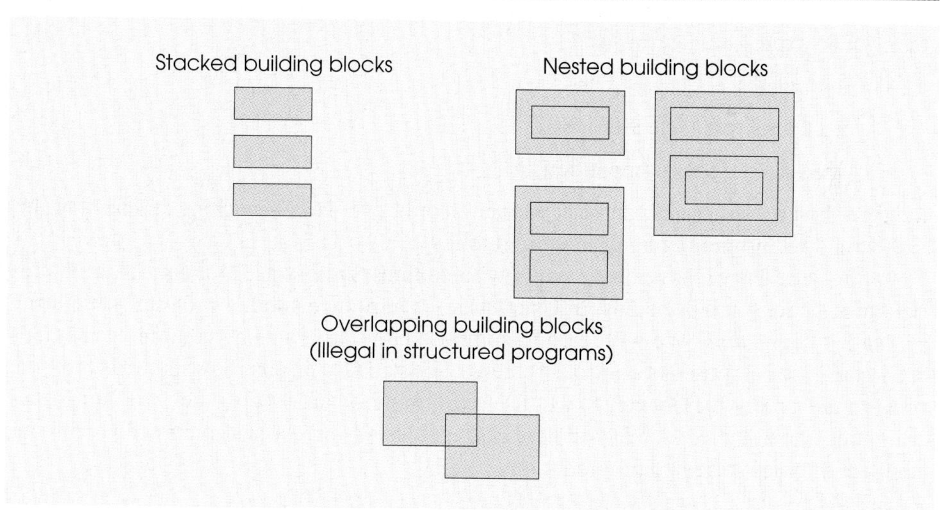

Fig. 5.26 Stacked, nested and overlapped building blocks.

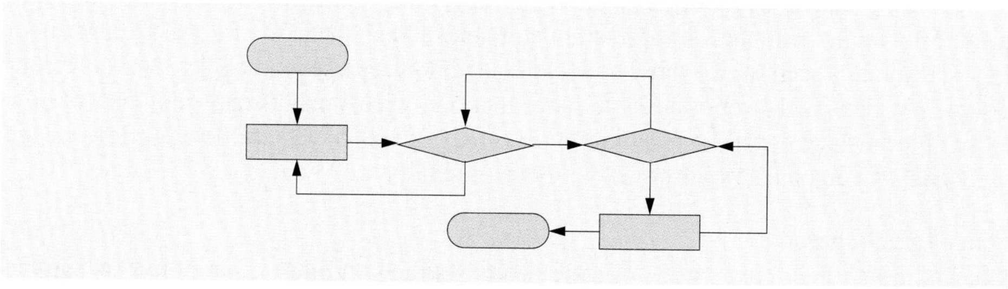

Fig. 5.27 An unstructured flowchart.

Sequence is trivial. Selection is implemented in one of three ways:

- an **if** structure (single selection),
- an **if/else** structure (double selection), or
- a **switch** structure (multiple selection).

In fact, it is straightforward to prove that the **if** structure is sufficient for any form of selection; everything that can be done with the **if/else** structure and the **switch** structure can be implemented by combining **if** structures (although perhaps not as elegantly).

Repetition is implemented in one of three ways:

- a **while** structure,
- a **do/while** structure, or
- a **for** structure.

It is straightforward to prove that the **while** structure is sufficient to provide any form of repetition. Everything that can be done with the **do/while** structure and the **for** structure can be done with the **while** structure (although perhaps not as elegantly).

Combining these results illustrates that any form of control ever needed in a Java program can be expressed in terms of

- a sequence,
- a **if** structure (selection), or
- a **while** structure (repetition).

And these control structures can be combined in only two ways—stacking and nesting. Indeed, structured programming promotes simplicity.

In this chapter, we have discussed how to compose programs from control structures containing actions and decisions. In Chapter 6, we introduce another program structuring unit, called the *method*. We will learn to compose large programs by combining methods that, in turn, are composed of control structures. We will also discuss how methods promote software reusability. In Chapter 8, we discuss in more detail Java's other program-structuring unit, called the *class*. We will then create objects from classes and proceed with our treatment of object-oriented programming.

5.11 (Optional Case Study) Thinking About Objects: Identifying Objects' States and Activities

In "Thinking About Objects," Section 4.14, we determined many of the class attributes needed to implement the elevator simulator and added them to the class diagram of Fig. 4.18. In this section, we show how these attributes represent an object's *state*, or condition. We identify the set of possible states that our objects may occupy and discuss how these objects change state in response to *messages*. We also discuss the workflow, or the *activities*, that an object performs in our elevator simulation.

Statechart Diagrams

Objects in a system have *states*. A state describes the condition of an object at a given time. *Statechart diagrams* (also called *state diagrams*) give us a way to express how, and under what conditions, the objects in a system change state. Unlike the class and object diagrams presented in earlier case-study sections, statechart diagrams model the behavior of the system.

Figure 5.28 is a simple statechart diagram that models the states of an object of either class **FloorButton** or class **ElevatorButton**. The UML represents each state in a statechart diagram as a *rounded rectangle* with the name of the state placed inside the rectangle. A *solid circle* with an attached arrowhead designates the initial state (in this case, the "Not pressed" state). Notice that this statechart diagram models the **boolean** attribute **pressed** in the class diagram of Fig. 4.18. The attribute is initialized to **false**, or the "Not pressed" state according to the statechart diagram.

The arrows indicate *transitions* between states. An object can transition from one state to another in response to a *message*. For example, the **FloorButton** and **ElevatorButton** objects change from the "Not pressed" state to the "Pressed" state in response to a **buttonPressed** message, and the **pressed** attribute changes to a value of **true**. The name of the message that causes a transition is written near the line that corresponds to that transition. (We explain messages in Section 7.10 and Section 10.22.)

Objects from other classes, such as **Light**, **Elevator** and **Person**, have similar statechart diagrams. Class **Light** has an "on" state or an "off" state—transitions between these states occur as a result of "turn on" and "turn off" events, respectively. Class **Elevator** and class **Person** each have a "moving" state and a "waiting" state—transitions between these states occur as a result of "start moving" and "stop moving" events, respectively.

Activity Diagrams

The *activity diagram* is similar to the statechart diagram in that they both model aspects of system behavior. Unlike a statechart diagram, an activity diagram models an object's workflow during program execution. An activity diagram is a flowchart that models the *actions* the object will perform and in what order. The activity diagram in Fig. 5.29 models the activities of a person. The diagram begins with the person moving toward the floor button. If the door is open, the person waits for the current elevator passenger (if one exists) to exit then enters the elevator.[1] If the door is closed, the person presses the floor button and waits for the elevator to open the door. When the door opens, the person waits for the elevator passenger to exit (if one exists) then enters the elevator. The person presses the elevator button, which causes the elevator to move to the other floor, unless the elevator already services that floor; the person then waits for the doors to re-open and exits the elevator after the doors open.

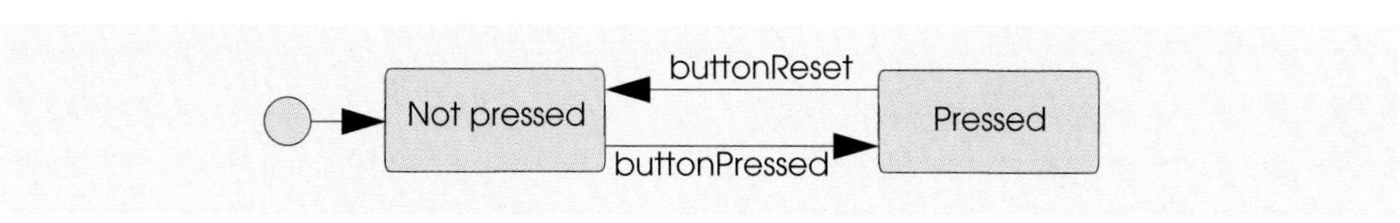

Fig. 5.28 Statechart diagram for **FloorButton** and **ElevatorButton** objects.

1. We use *multithreading* and **synchronized** *methods* in Section 15.12 to guarantee that the passenger riding the elevator will exit before the person waiting for the elevator will enter.

The UML represents activities as ovals in activity diagrams. The name of the activity is placed inside the oval. An arrow connects two activities, indicating the order in which the activities are performed. As with statechart diagrams, the *solid circle* indicates the starting activity. In this case, the person moving toward the floor button is the starting activity. The activity flow arrives at a *branch* (indicated by the *small diamond symbol*) after the person moves to the floor button. This point determines the next activity based on the associated *guard condition* (in square brackets above the transition), which states that the transition occurs if this condition is met. For example, in Fig. 5.29, if the floor door is closed, the person presses the floor button, waits for the door to open, waits for the passenger (if there is one) to exit the elevator, then enters the elevator. However, if the floor door is open, the person waits for the passenger (if there is one) to exit the elevator, then enters the elevator. Regardless of whether the floor door was open or closed at the last diamond symbol, the person now presses the elevator button (which causes the doors to close and the elevator to move to the other floor), the person waits for the elevator door to open—when this door opens, the person exits the elevator. Activity diagrams are similar to the flowcharts for control structures presented in Chapters 4 and 5—both diagram types employ diamond symbols to alter the flow of control between activities.

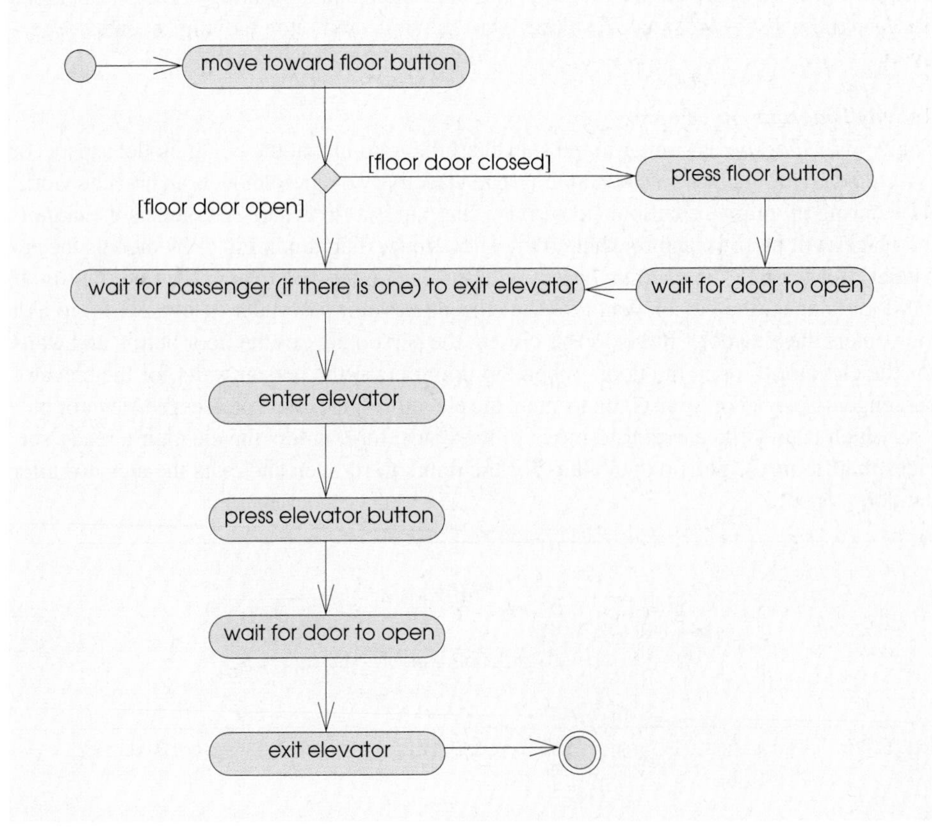

Fig. 5.29 Activity diagram for a `Person` object.

Figure 5.30 shows an activity diagram for the elevator. The diagram begins when a button is pressed. If the button is an elevator button, the elevator sets **summoned** to false (we explain this **boolean** variable in a moment), closes the elevator door, moves to the other floor, resets the elevator button, rings the bell and opens the elevator door. If the button is a floor button, the next branch determines the next transition, based on whether the elevator is moving. If the elevator is idle, the next branch determines which floor button generated the request. If the request originated from the current floor on which the elevator is located, the elevator resets its button, rings its bell and opens its door. If the request originated from the opposite floor, the elevator closes the door and moves to the opposite (destination) floor, where the elevator resets its button, rings its bell and opens its door. Now consider the activity if the elevator is moving. A separate branch determines which floor button generated the request. If the request originated from the destination floor, the elevator continues traveling to that floor. If the request originated from the floor from which the elevator departed, the elevator continues traveling to the destination floor, but must remember to return to the requesting floor. The **summoned** attribute, originally displayed in Fig. 4.18, is set to **true** so that the elevator knows to return to the other floor after the elevator opens its door.

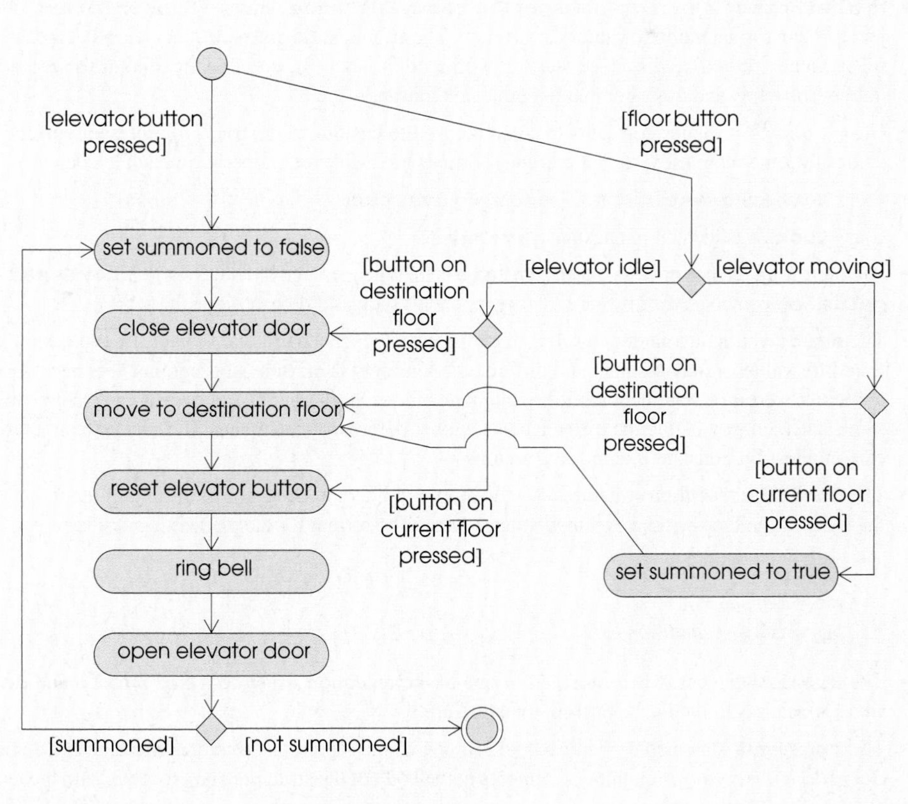

Fig. 5.30 Activity diagram for the **Elevator** object.

We have taken the first steps to modeling the behavior of the system and have shown how the attributes of an object determine that object's activity. In "Thinking About Objects," Section 6.17, we investigate the behaviors for all classes to give a more accurate interpretation of the system behavior by "filling in" the final compartment for the classes in our class diagram.

SUMMARY

- The **for** repetition structure handles all of the details of counter-controlled repetition. The general format of the **for** structure is

  for (*expression1*; *expression2*; *expression3*)
      statement

  where *expression1* initializes the loop's control variable, *expression2* is the loop-continuation condition and *expression3* modifies the control variable, so that the loop-continuation condition eventually becomes **false**.
- A **JTextArea** is a GUI component that is capable of displaying many lines of text.
- Method **setText** replaces the text in a **JTextArea**. Method **append** adds text to the end of the text in a **JTextArea**.
- **NumberFormat static** method **getCurrencyInstance** returns a **NumberFormat** object that can format numeric values as currency. The argument **Locale.US** indicates that the currency values should be displayed starting with a dollar sign ($), use a decimal point to separate dollars and cents and use a comma to delineate thousands.
- Class **Locale** provides constants that can be used to customize programs to represent currency values for other countries, so that currency formats are displayed properly for each locale.
- Class **NumberFormat** is located in package **java.text**.
- Class **Locale** is located in package ***java.util***.
- An interesting feature of class **JOptionPane** is that the message it displays with **showMessageDialog** can be a **String** or a GUI component, such as a **JTextArea**.
- The **switch** structure handles a series of decisions in which a particular variable or expression is tested for values it may assume, and different actions are taken. In most programs, it is necessary to include a **break** statement after the statements for each **case**. Several **case**s can execute the same statements by listing the **case** labels together before the statements. The **switch** structure can only test for constant integral expressions.
- The **do/while** repetition structure tests the loop-continuation condition at the end of the loop, so the body of the loop will be executed at least once. The format for the **do/while** structure is

  do {
      statement
  } while (*condition***);**

- The **break** statement, when executed in one of the repetition structures (**for**, **while** and **do/while**), causes immediate exit from the structure.
- The **continue** statement, when executed in one of the repetition structures (**for**, **while** and **do/while**), skips any remaining statements in the body of the structure and proceeds with the test for the next iteration of the loop.
- To break out of a nested set of structures, use the labeled **break** statement. This statement, when executed in a **while**, **for**, **do/while** or **switch** structure, causes immediate exit from that

structure and any number of enclosing repetition structures; program execution resumes with the first statement after the enclosing labeled block.

- The labeled **continue** statement, when executed in a repetition structure (**while**, **for** or **do/while**), skips the remaining statements in that structure's body and any number of enclosing repetition structures and proceeds with the next iteration of the enclosing labeled repetition structure.
- Logical operators may be used to form complex conditions by combining conditions. The logical operators are **&&**, **&**, **||**, **|**, **^** and **!**, meaning logical AND, boolean logical AND, logical OR, boolean logical inclusive OR, boolean logical exclusive OR and logical NOT (negation), respectively.
- Class **JScrollPane** provides a GUI component with scrolling functionality.

TERMINOLOGY

! operator
&& operator
|| operator
append method of class **JTextArea**
boolean logical AND (**&**)
boolean logical exclusive OR (**^**)
boolean logical inclusive OR (**|**)
break
case label
continue
counter-controlled repetition
default case in **switch**
definite repetition
do/while repetition structure
for repetition structure
infinite loop
java.text package
java.util package
JScrollPane class
JTextArea class
labeled **break** statement
labeled block
labeled **continue** statement
labeled repetition structure
Locale class
Locale.US
logical AND (**&&**)
logical negation (**!**)
logical operators
logical OR (**||**)
long
loop-continuation condition
multiple selection
nested control structures
NumberFormat class
off-by-one error
repetition structures
scroll box
scrollbar
short-circuit evaluation
single-entry/single-exit control structures
stacked control structures
switch selection structure
thumb of a scrollbar
while repetition structure

SELF-REVIEW EXERCISES

5.1 State whether each of the following is true or false. If false, explain why.

a) The **default** case is required in the **switch** selection structure.
b) The **break** statement is required in the default case of a **switch** selection structure.
c) The expression **(x > y && a < b)** is true if either **x > y** is true or **a < b** is true.
d) An expression containing the **||** operator is true if either or both of its operands is true.

5.2 Write a Java statement or a set of Java statements to accomplish each of the following tasks:

a) Sum the odd integers between 1 and 99, using a **for** structure. Assume that the integer variables **sum** and **count** have been declared.
b) Calculate the value of **2.5** raised to the power of **3**, using the **pow** method.
c) Print the integers from 1 to 20, using a **while** loop and the counter variable **x**. Assume that the variable **x** has been declared, but not initialized. Print only five integers per line. [*Hint*: Use the calculation **x % 5**. When the value of this expression is 0, print a newline character; otherwise, print a tab character. Assume that this code is an application; use

the **System.out.println()** method to output the newline character, and use the **System.out.print('\t')** method to output the tab character.]

d) Repeat Exercise 5.2 (c), using a **for** structure.

5.3 Find the error in each of the following code segments, and explain how to correct it:

a)
```
x = 1;

while ( x <= 10 );
   x++;
}
```
b)
```
for ( y = .1; y != 1.0; y += .1 )
   System.out.println( y );
```
c)
```
switch ( n ) {
   case 1:
      System.out.println( "The number is 1" );
   case 2:
      System.out.println( "The number is 2" );
      break;
   default:
      System.out.println( "The number is not 1 or 2" );
      break;
}
```
d) The following code should print the values 1 to 10.
```
n = 1;

while ( n < 10 )
   System.out.println( n++ );
```

ANSWERS TO SELF-REVIEW EXERCISES

5.1 a) False. The **default** case is optional. If no default action is needed, then there is no need for a **default** case. b) False. The **break** statement is used to exit the **switch** structure. The **break** statement is not required for the last case in a **switch** structure. c) False. Both of the relational expressions must be true for the entire expression to be true when using the **&&** operator. d) True.

5.2 The answers to Exercise 5.2 are as follows:

a)
```
sum = 0;
for ( count = 1; count <= 99; count += 2 )
   sum += count;
```
b)
```
Math.pow( 2.5, 3 )
```
c)
```
x = 1;

while ( x <= 20 ) {
   System.out.print( x );

   if ( x % 5 == 0 )
      System.out.println();
   else
      System.out.print( '\t' );

   ++x;
}
```

d)
```
for ( x = 1; x <= 20; x++ ) {
     System.out.print( x );

   if ( x % 5 == 0 )
      System.out.println();
   else
      System.out.print( '\t' );
}
```

or

```
for ( x = 1; x <= 20; x++ )

   if ( x % 5 == 0 )
      System.out.println( x );
   else
      System.out.print( x + "\t" );
```

5.3 The answers to Exercise 5.3 are as follows:

a) Error: The semicolon after the **while** header causes an infinite loop, and there is a missing left brace.
Correction: Replace the semicolon by a **{**, or remove both the **;** and the **}**.

b) Error: Using a floating-point number to control a **for** repetition structure may not work, because floating-point numbers are represented only approximately by most computers.
Correction: Use an integer, and perform the proper calculation in order to get the values you desire:
```
for ( y = 1; y != 10; y++ )
   System.out.println( ( float ) y / 10 );
```

c) Error: Missing **break** statement in the statements for the first **case**.
Correction: Add a **break** statement at the end of the statements for the first **case**. Note that this omission is not necessarily an error if the programmer wants the statement of **case 2:** to execute every time the **case 1:** statement executes.

d) Error: Improper relational operator used in the **while** repetition-continuation condition.
Correction: Use **<=** rather than **<**, or change **10** to **11**.

EXERCISES

5.4 Find the error(s) in each of the following segments of code:

a)
```
For ( x = 100, x >= 1, x++ )
   System.out.println( x );
```

b) The following code should print whether integer **value** is odd or even:
```
switch ( value % 2 ) {

   case 0:
      System.out.println( "Even integer" );

   case 1:
      System.out.println( "Odd integer" );
}
```

c) The following code should output the odd integers from 19 to 1:
```
for ( x = 19; x >= 1; x += 2 )
   System.out.println( x );
```

d) The following code should output the even integers from 2 to 100:

```
counter = 2;

do {
   System.out.println( counter );
   counter += 2;
} While ( counter < 100 );
```

5.5 What does the following program do?

```
public class Printing {

   public static void main( String args[] )
   {
      for ( int i = 1; i <= 10; i++ ) {

         for ( int j = 1; j <= 5; j++ )
            System.out.print( '@' );

         System.out.println();

      }

   }

}
```

5.6 Write an application that finds the smallest of several integers. Assume that the first value read specifies the number of values to input from the user.

5.7 Write an application that calculates the product of the odd integers from 1 to 15, and then displays the results in a message dialog.

5.8 The *factorial* method is used frequently in probability problems. The factorial of a positive integer *n* (written *n!* and pronounced "n factorial") is equal to the product of the positive integers from 1 to *n*. Write an application that evaluates the factorials of the integers from 1 to 5. Display the results in tabular format in a **JTextArea** that is displayed on a message dialog. What difficulty might prevent you from calculating the factorial of 20?

5.9 Modify the compound-interest program of Fig. 5.6 to repeat its steps for interest rates of 5, 6, 7, 8, 9 and 10%. Use a **for** loop to vary the interest rate. Add scrolling functionality to the **JTextArea**, so you can scroll through all the output.

5.10 Write an application that displays the following patterns separately one below the other. Use **for** loops to generate the patterns. All asterisks (*****) should be printed by a single statement of the form **System.out.print('*');**. (This statement causes the asterisks to print side by side.) A statement of the form **System.out.println();** can be used to position to the next line. A statement of the form **System.out.print(' ');** can be used to display a space for the last two patterns. There should be no other output statements in the program. [*Hint*: The last two patterns require that each line begin with an appropriate number of blank spaces.]

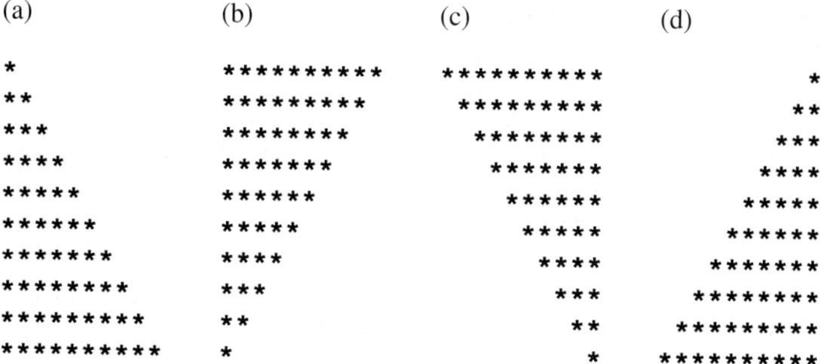

5.11 One interesting application of computers is drawing graphs and bar charts (sometimes called "histograms"). Write an applet that reads five numbers, each between 1 and 30. For each number read, your program should draw a line containing that number of adjacent asterisks. For example, if your program reads the number 7, it should display **`*******`**.

5.12 A mail-order house sells five different products whose retail prices are as follows: product 1, $2.98; product 2, $4.50; product 3, $9.98; product 4, $4.49; and product 5, $6.87. Write an application that reads a series of pairs of numbers as follows:

a) product number;
b) quantity sold for one day.

Your program should use a **`switch`** structure to help determine the retail price for each product. It should calculate and display the total retail value of all products sold last week. Use a **`TextField`** to obtain the product number from the user. Use a sentinel-controlled loop to determine when the program should stop looping and display the final results.

5.13 Modify the program in Fig. 5.6 to use only integers to calculate the compound interest. [*Hint*: Treat all monetary amounts as integral numbers of pennies. Then "break" the result into its dollar portion and cents portion by using the division and modulus operations, respectively. Insert a period between the dollars and the cents portions.]

5.14 Assume that **`i = 1`**, **`j = 2`**, **`k = 3`** and **`m = 2`**. What does each of the following statements print?

a) `System.out.println( i == 1 );`
b) `System.out.println( j == 3 );`
c) `System.out.println( i >= 1 && j < 4 );`
d) `System.out.println( m <= 99 & k < m );`
e) `System.out.println( j >= i || k == m );`
f) `System.out.println( k + m < j | 3 - j >= k );`
g) `System.out.println( !( k > m ) );`

5.15 Write an application that prints a table of the binary, octal, and hexadecimal equivalents of the decimal numbers in the range 1 through 256. If you are not familiar with these number systems, read Appendix E first. Place the results in a **`JTextArea`** with scrolling functionality. Display the **`JTextArea`** in a message dialog.

5.16 Calculate the value of π from the infinite series

$$\pi = 4 - \frac{4}{3} + \frac{4}{5} - \frac{4}{7} + \frac{4}{9} - \frac{4}{11} + \cdots$$

Print a table that shows the value of π approximated by one term of this series, by two terms, by three terms, etc. How many terms of this series do you have to use before you first get 3.14? 3.141? 3.1415? 3.14159?

5.17 (*Pythagorean Triples*) A right triangle can have sides whose lengths are all integers. The set of three integer values for the lengths of the sides of a right triangle is called a Pythagorean triple. The lengths of the three sides must satisfy the relationship that the sum of the squares of two of the sides is equal to the square of the hypotenuse. Write an application to find all Pythagorean triples for **`side1`**, **`side2`** and the **`hypotenuse`**, all no larger than 500. Use a triple-nested **`for`** loop that tries all possibilities. This method is an example of "brute force" computing. You will learn in more advanced computer science courses that there are large numbers of interesting problems for which there is no known algorithmic approach other than using sheer brute force.

5.18 Modify Exercise 5.10 to combine your code from the four separate triangles of asterisks into a single application that prints all four patterns side by side, making clever use of nested **`for`** loops.

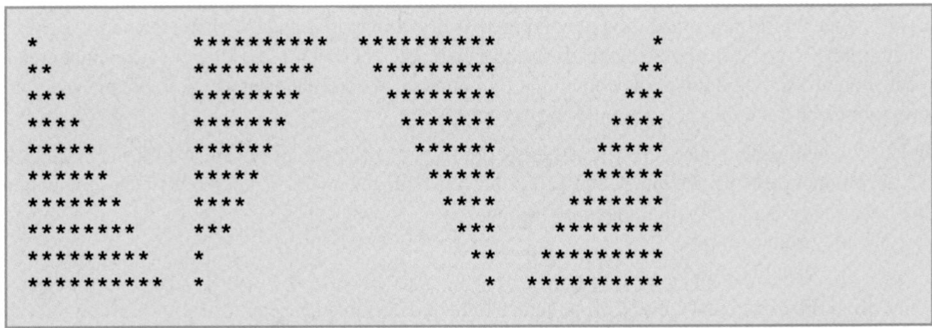

5.19 (*De Morgan's Laws*) In this chapter, we have discussed the logical operators **`&&`**, **`&`**, **`||`**, **`|`**, **`^`** and **`!`**. De Morgan's Laws can sometimes make it more convenient for us to express a logical expression. These laws state that the expression **`!(`***condition1* **`&&`** *condition2***`)`** is logically equivalent to the expression **`(!`***condition1* **`||`** **`!`***condition2***`)`**. Also, the expression **`!(`***condition1* **`||`** *condition2***`)`** is logically equivalent to the expression **`(!`***condition1* **`&&`** **`!`***condition2***`)`**. Use De Morgan's Laws to write equivalent expressions for each of the following, and then write a program to show that both the original expression and the new expression in each case are equivalent:

a) `!( x < 5 ) && !( y >= 7 )`
b) `!( a == b ) || !( g != 5 )`
c) `!( ( x <= 8 ) && ( y > 4 ) )`
d) `!( ( i > 4 ) || ( j <= 6 ) )`

5.20 Write an application that prints the following diamond shape. You may use output statements that print a single asterisk (**`*`**), a single space or a single newline character. Maximize your use of repetition (with nested **`for`** structures,) and minimize the number of output statements.

```
    *
   ***
  *****
 *******
*********
 *******
  *****
   ***
    *
```

5.21 Modify the program you wrote in Exercise 5.20 to read an odd number in the range 1 to 19 to specify the number of rows in the diamond. Your program should then display a diamond of the appropriate size.

5.22 A criticism of the **break** statement and the **continue** statement is that each is unstructured. Actually, **break** statements and **continue** statements can always be replaced by structured statements, although doing so can be awkward. Describe in general how you would remove any **break** statement from a loop in a program and replace that statement with some structured equivalent. [*Hint*: The **break** statement leaves a loop from within the body of the loop. The other way to leave is by failing the loop-continuation test. Consider using in the loop-continuation test a second test that indicates "early exit because of a 'break' condition."] Use the technique you developed here to remove the **break** statement from the program in Fig. 5.11.

5.23 What does the following program segment do?

```
for ( i = 1; i <= 5; i++ ) {

   for ( j = 1; j <= 3; j++ ) {

      for ( k = 1; k <= 4; k++ )
         System.out.print( '*' );

      System.out.println();
   }

   System.out.println();
}
```

5.24 Describe in general how you would remove any **continue** statement from a loop in a program and replace that statement with some structured equivalent. Use the technique you developed here to remove the **continue** statement from the program in Fig. 5.12.

5.25 (*"The Twelve Days of Christmas" Song*) Write an application that uses repetition and **switch** structures to print the song "The Twelve Days of Christmas." One **switch** structure should be used to print the day (i.e., "First," "Second," etc.). A separate **switch** structure should be used to print the remainder of each verse. Visit the Web site **www.12days.com/library/carols/12daysofxmas.htm** for the complete lyrics to the song.

6

Methods

Objectives

- To understand how to construct programs modularly from small pieces called *methods*.
- To introduce the common math methods available in the Java API.
- To be able to create new methods.
- To understand the mechanisms for passing information between methods.
- To introduce simulation techniques that use random-number generation.
- To understand how the visibility of identifiers is limited to specific regions of programs.
- To understand how to write and use methods that call themselves.

Form ever follows function.
Louis Henri Sullivan

E pluribus unum.
(One composed of many.)
Virgil

O! call back yesterday, bid time return.
William Shakespeare, *Richard II*

Call me Ishmael.
Herman Melville, *Moby Dick*

When you call me that, smile.
Owen Wister

Outline

6.1 Introduction
6.2 Program Modules in Java
6.3 `Math` Class Methods
6.4 Methods
6.5 Method Definitions
6.6 Argument Promotion
6.7 Java API Packages
6.8 Random-Number Generation
6.9 Example: A Game of Chance
6.10 Duration of Identifiers
6.11 Scope Rules
6.12 Recursion
6.13 Example Using Recursion: The Fibonacci Series
6.14 Recursion vs. Iteration
6.15 Method Overloading
6.16 Methods of Class `JApplet`
6.17 (Optional Case Study) Thinking About Objects: Identifying Class Operations

Summary • Terminology • Self-Review Exercises • Answers to Self-Review Exercises • Exercises

6.1 Introduction

Most computer programs that solve real-world problems are much larger than the programs presented in the first few chapters of this text. Experience has shown that the best way to develop and maintain a large program is to construct it from small, simple pieces, or *modules*. This technique is called *divide and conquer.* This chapter describes many key features of the Java language that facilitate the design, implementation, operation and maintenance of large programs.

6.2 Program Modules in Java

Modules in Java are called *methods* and *classes.* Java programs are written by combining new methods and classes the programmer writes with "prepackaged" methods and classes available in the *Java API* (also referred to as the *Java class library*) and in various other method and class libraries. In this chapter, we concentrate on methods; we begin to discuss classes in detail in Chapter 8.

The Java API provides a rich collection of classes and methods for performing common mathematical calculations, string manipulations, character manipulations, input/output operations, error checking and many other useful operations. This set of modules makes the programmer's job easier, because the modules provide many of the capabilities programmers need. The Java API methods are provided as part of the Java 2 Software Development Kit (J2SDK).

Good Programming Practice 6.1

Familiarize yourself with the rich collection of classes and methods in the Java API and with the rich collections of classes available in various class libraries.

Software Engineering Observation 6.1

Avoid reinventing the wheel. When possible, use Java API classes and methods instead of writing new classes and methods. This reduces program development time and avoids introducing programming errors.

Performance Tip 6.1

Do not try to rewrite existing Java API classes and methods to make them more efficient. You usually will not be able to increase the performance of these classes and methods.

The programmer can write methods to define specific tasks that a program may use many times during its execution. These are sometimes referred to as *programmer-defined methods.* The actual statements defining the methods are written only once and are hidden from other methods.

A method is *invoked* (i.e., made to perform its designated task) by a *method call.* The method call specifies the name of the method and provides information (as *arguments*) that the called method requires to perform its task. When the method call completes, the method either returns a result to the *calling method* (or *caller*) or simply returns control to the calling method. A common analogy for this program structure is the hierarchical form of management. A boss (the calling method, or caller) asks a worker (the *called method*) to perform a task and report back (i.e., *return*) the results after completing the task. The boss method does not know *how* the worker method performs its designated tasks. The worker may also call other worker methods, and the boss will be unaware of this occurrence. We will soon see how this "hiding" of implementation details promotes good software engineering. Figure 6.1 shows the **boss** method communicating with several worker methods in a hierarchical manner. Note that **worker1** acts as a "boss method" to **worker4** and **worker5**. Relationships among methods may also be different than the hierarchical structure shown in this figure.

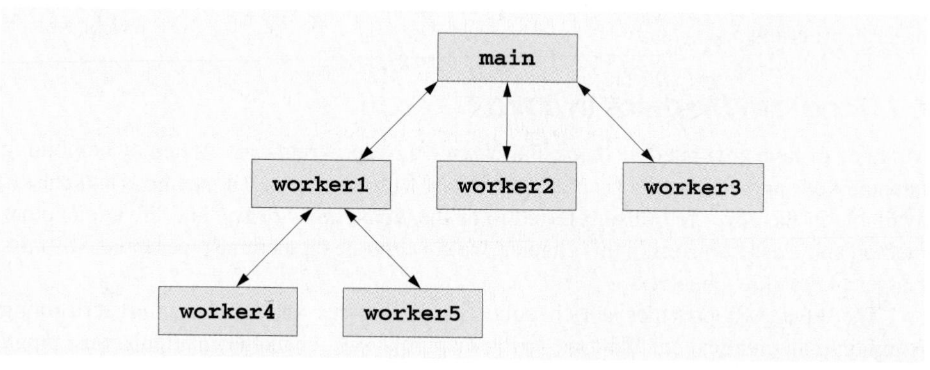

Fig. 6.1 Hierarchical boss-method/worker-method relationship.

6.3 Math Class Methods

Math class methods allow the programmer to perform certain common mathematical calculations. We use various **Math** class methods here to introduce the concept of methods. Throughout the book, we discuss many other methods from the classes of the Java API.

Methods are called by writing the name of the method, followed by a left parenthesis, followed by the *argument* (or a comma-separated list of arguments) of the method, followed by a right parenthesis. For example, a programmer desiring to calculate the square root of **900.0** might write

```
Math.sqrt( 900.0 )
```

When this statement executes, it calls **static Math** method **sqrt** to calculate the square root of the number contained in the parentheses (**900.0**). The number **900.0** is the *argument* of method **sqrt**. The preceding expression evaluates to **30.0**. Method **sqrt** method takes an argument of type **double** and returns a result of type **double**. Note that all **Math** class methods are **static**; therefore, they are invoked by preceding the name of the method with the class name **Math** and a dot (**.**) operator. To output the value of the preceding method call in the command window, a programmer might write

```
System.out.println( Math.sqrt( 900.0 ) );
```

In this statement, the value that **sqrt** returns becomes the argument to method **println**.

Software Engineering Observation 6.2

It is not necessary to import class **Math** *to use its methods.* **Math** *is part of the* **java.lang** *package, which is automatically imported by the compiler.*

Common Programming Error 6.1

Forgetting to invoke a **Math** *class method by preceding the name of the method with the class name* **Math** *and a dot operator (* **.** *) results in a syntax error.*

Method arguments may be constants, variables or expressions. If **c1 = 13.0**, **d = 3.0** and **f = 4.0**, then the statement

```
System.out.println( Math.sqrt( c1 + d * f ) );
```

calculates and prints the square root of **13.0 + 3.0 * 4.0 = 25.0**, namely **5.0**.

Some **Math** class methods are summarized in Fig. 6.2. In the figure, the variables **x** and **y** are of type **double**. The **Math** class also defines two commonly used mathematical constants: **Math.PI** and **Math.E**. The constant **Math.PI** (3.14159265358979323846) of class **Math** is the ratio of a circle's circumference to its diameter. The constant **Math.E** (2.7182818284590452354) is the base value for natural logarithms (calculated with static **Math** method **log**).

6.4 Methods

Methods allow the programmer to modularize a program. Variables declared in method definitions are *local variables*—only the method that defines them knows they exist. Most methods have a list of *parameters* that provide the means for communicating information between methods via method calls. A method's parameters are also local variables.

Method	Description	Example

`abs( x )`	absolute value of *x* (this method also has versions for **`float`**, **`int`** and **`long`** values)	`abs( 23.7 )` is `23.7`
		`abs( 0.0 )` is `0.0`
		`abs( -23.7 )` is `23.7`

`ceil( x )`	rounds *x* to the smallest integer not less than *x*	`ceil( 9.2 )` is `10.0` `ceil( -9.8 )` is `-9.0`
`cos( x )`	trigonometric cosine of *x* (*x* is in radians)	`cos( 0.0 )` is `1.0`
`exp( x )`	exponential method e^x	`exp( 1.0 )` is `2.71828` `exp( 2.0 )` is `7.38906`
`floor( x )`	rounds *x* to the largest integer not greater than *x*	`floor( 9.2 )` is `9.0` `floor( -9.8 )` is `-10.0`
`log( x )`	natural logarithm of *x* (base *e*)	`log( 2.718282 )` is `1.0` `log( 7.389056 )` is `2.0`
`max( x, y )`	larger value of *x* and *y* (this method also has versions for **`float`**, **`int`** and **`long`** values)	`max( 2.3, 12.7 )` is `12.7` `max( -2.3, -12.7 )` is `-2.3`
`min( x, y )`	smaller value of *x* and *y* (this method also has versions for **`float`**, **`int`** and **`long`** values)	`min( 2.3, 12.7 )` is `2.3` `min( -2.3, -12.7 )` is `-12.7`
`pow( x, y )`	*x* raised to power *y* (x^y)	`pow( 2.0, 7.0 )` is `128.0` `pow( 9.0, .5 )` is `3.0`
`sin( x )`	trigonometric sine of *x* (*x* is in radians)	`sin( 0.0 )` is `0.0`
`sqrt( x )`	square root of *x*	`sqrt( 900.0 )` is `30.0` `sqrt( 9.0 )` is `3.0`
`tan( x )`	trigonometric tangent of *x* (*x* is in radians)	`tan( 0.0 )` is `0.0`

Fig. 6.2 **`Math`** class methods.

There are several motivations for modularizing a program with methods. The divide-and-conquer approach makes program development more manageable. Another motivation is *software reusability*—using existing methods as building blocks to create new programs. With good method naming and definition, you can create programs from standardized methods rather than by building customized code. For example, we did not have to define how to convert **`String`**s to integers and floating-point numbers; Java already provides such methods for us in class **`Integer`** (**`parseInt`**) and class **`Double`** (**`parseDouble`**). A third motivation is to avoid repeating code in a program. Packaging code as a method allows a program to execute that code from several locations in a program simply by calling the method.

Software Engineering Observation 6.3

To promote software reusability, each method should be limited to performing a single, well-defined task, and the name of the method should express that task effectively.

Software Engineering Observation 6.4

If you cannot choose a concise name that expresses a method's task, it is possible that your method is attempting to perform too many diverse tasks. It is usually best to break such a method into several smaller method definitions.

6.5 Method Definitions

The programs presented up to this point each consisted of a class definition containing at least one method definition that called Java API methods to accomplish its tasks. We now consider how programmers write their own customized methods. Until we discuss more of the details of class definitions in Chapter 8, we use applets for all programs that contain two or more method definitions, for simplicity.

Consider an applet that uses a method **square** (invoked from the applet's **init** method) to calculate the squares of the integers from 1 to 10 (Fig. 6.3).

When the applet begins execution, the applet container calls the applet's **init** method. Line 16 declares **JTextArea** reference **outputArea** and initializes it with a new **JTextArea**. This **JTextArea** will display the program's results.

This program is the first in which we display a GUI component on an applet. The on-screen display area for a **JApplet** has a *content pane*, to which the GUI components must be attached so they can be displayed at execution time. The content pane is an object of class ***Container*** from the ***java.awt*** *package*. This class was **import**ed on line 5 for use in the applet. Line 19 declares **Container** reference **container** and assigns to it the result of a call to method ***getContentPane***—one of the many methods that our class **SquareInt** inherits from class **JApplet**. Method **getContentPane** returns a reference to the applet's content pane. The program uses that reference to attach GUI components, like a **JTextArea**, to the applet's user interface.

Line 22 places the **JTextArea** GUI component object to which **outputArea** refers on the applet. When the applet executes, any GUI components attached to it are displayed. **Container** method **add** attaches a GUI component to a container. For the moment, we can attach only one GUI component to the applet's content pane, and that GUI component will occupy the applet's entire drawing area on the screen (as defined by the **width** and **height** of the applet, in pixels, in the applet's HTML document). Later, we will discuss how to attach many GUI components to an applet by changing the applet's *layout*. The layout controls how the applet positions GUI components in its area on the screen.

Line 24 declares **int** variable **result** to store the result of each square calculation. Line 25 declares **String** reference **output** and initializes it with the empty string. This **String** will contain the results of squaring the values from 1 to 10. Lines 28–37 define a **for** repetition structure. Each iteration of this loop calculates the **square** of the current value of control variable **x**, stores the value in **result** and concatenates the **result** to the end of **output**.

The applet invokes (or calls) its **square** method on line 31 with the statement

```
result = square( counter );
```

The **()** after **square** represent the *method-call operator*, which has high precedence. At this point, the program makes a copy of the value of **counter** (the *argument* to the method call) and transfers program control to the first line of method **square** (defined at lines 44–

48). Method **square** receives the copy of the value of **counter** in the *parameter* **y**. Then, **square** calculates **y * y** (line 46). Method **square** uses a ***return*** statement to return (i.e., give back) the result of the calculation to the statement in **init** that invoked **square**. In method **init**, the return value is assigned to variable **result**. Lines 34–35 concatenate **"The square of "**, the value of **counter**, **" is "**, the value of **result** and a newline character to the end of **output**. This process repeats for each iteration of the **for** repetition structure. Line 39 uses method **setText** to set **outputArea**'s text to the **String output**.

```
1  // Fig. 6.3: SquareIntegers.java
2  // A programmer-defined square method
3
4  // Java core packages
5  import java.awt.Container;
6
7  // Java extension packages
8  import javax.swing.*;
9
10 public class SquareIntegers extends JApplet {
11
12    // set up GUI and calculate squares of integers from 1 to 10
13    public void init()
14    {
15       // JTextArea to display results
16       JTextArea outputArea = new JTextArea();
17
18       // get applet's content pane (GUI component display area)
19       Container container = getContentPane();
20
21       // attach outputArea to container
22       container.add( outputArea );
23
24       int result;  // store result of call to method square
25       String output = "";   // String containing results
26
27       // loop 10 times
28       for ( int counter = 1; counter <= 10; counter++ ) {
29
30          // calculate square of counter and store in result
31          result = square( counter );
32
33          // append result to String output
34          output += "The square of " + counter +
35                    " is " + result + "\n";
36
37       } // end for structure
38
39       outputArea.setText( output );   // place results in JTextArea
40
41    } // end method init
42
```

Fig. 6.3 Using programmer-defined method **square** (part 1 of 2).

```
43      // square method definition
44      public int square( int y )
45      {
46         return y * y;  // return square of y
47
48      }  // end method square
49
50   }  // end class SquareIntegers
```

```
Applet Viewer: SquareInteger...
Applet
The square of 1 is 1
The square of 2 is 4
The square of 3 is 9
The square of 4 is 16
The square of 5 is 25
The square of 6 is 36
The square of 7 is 49
The square of 8 is 64
The square of 9 is 81
The square of 10 is 100
Applet started.
```

Fig. 6.3 Using programmer-defined method **`square`** (part 2 of 2).

Note that we declared references **`output`**, **`outputArea`** and **`container`** and variable **`result`** as local variables in **`init`**, because they are used only in **`init`**. Variables should be declared as instance variables only if they are required for use in more than one method of the class or if the program should save their values between calls to the class's methods. Also, note that method **`init`** calls method **`square`** directly without preceding the method name with a class name and a dot operator or a reference name and a dot operator. Each method in a class is able to call the class's other methods directly. However, there is an exception to this rule. A class's **`static`** methods can call only other **`static`** methods of the class directly. Chapter 8 discusses **`static`** methods in detail.

The definition of method **`square`** (line 44) shows that **`square`** expects an integer parameter **`y`**; **`square`** uses this name to manipulate the value it receives. Keyword **`int`** preceding the name of the method indicates that **`square`** returns an integer result. The **`return`** statement in **`square`** passes the result of the calculation **`y * y`** back to the calling method. Note that the entire method definition appears between the braces of the class **`SquareInt`**. All methods must be defined inside a class definition.

Good Programming Practice 6.2

Place a blank line between method definitions to separate the methods and enhance program readability.

Common Programming Error 6.2

Defining a method outside the braces of a class definition is a syntax error.

The general format of a method definition is

```
return-value-type method-name( parameter-list )
{
    declarations and statements
}
```

The *method-name* is any valid identifier. The *return-value-type* is the data type of the result returned from the method to the caller. The *return-value-type* **void** indicates that a method does not return a value. Methods can return at most one value.

The *parameter-list* is a comma-separated list in which the method declares each parameter's type and name. There must be one argument in the method call for each parameter in the method definition. Each argument also must be compatible with the type of the corresponding parameter in the method definition. For example, a parameter of type **double** can receive values of 7.35, 22 or –0.03546, but not **"hello"** (because a **String** cannot be assigned to a **double** variable). If a method does not receive any values, the *parameter-list* is empty (i.e., the name of the method is followed by an empty set of parentheses). Each parameter in the parameter list of a method must be declared with a data type; otherwise, a syntax error occurs.

Following the first line of the method definition (also known as the *method header*), *declarations and statements* in braces form the *method body*. The method body is also referred to as a block. Variables can be declared in any block, and blocks can be nested. A method cannot be defined inside another method.

There are three ways to return control to the statement that invoked a method. If the method does not return a result, control returns when the program flow reaches the method-ending right brace or when the statement

```
return;
```

is executed. If the method returns a result, the statement

```
return expression;
```

evaluates the *expression*, then returns the resulting value to the caller. When a **return** statement executes, control returns immediately to the statement that invoked the method.

Note that the example in Fig. 6.3 actually contains two method definitions—**init** (lines 13–41) and **square** (line 44–48). Remember that the applet container calls method **init** to initialize the applet. In this example, method **init** repeatedly invokes the **square** method to perform a calculation, then places the results in the **JTextArea** that is attached to the applet's content pane. When the applet appears on the screen, the results are displayed in the **JTextArea**.

Notice the syntax used to invoke method **square**—we use just the name of the method, followed by the arguments to the method in parentheses. Methods in a class definition are allowed to invoke other methods in the same class definition by using this syntax. (There is an exception to this rule, discussed in Chapter 8.) Methods in the same class definition are both the methods defined in that class and the inherited methods (the methods from the class that the current class **extends**—**JApplet** in Fig. 6.3). We have now seen three ways to call a method: A method name by itself (as shown with **square(x)** in this example), a reference to an object followed by the dot (**.**) operator and the method name (such as **`g.drawLine( x1, y1, x2, y2 )`**), and a class name followed by a method name (such as **`Integer.parseInt( stringToConvert )`**). The last syntax is only for **`static`** methods of a class (discussed in detail in Chapter 8).

Common Programming Error 6.3

Omitting the return-value-type *in a method definition is a syntax error.*

Common Programming Error 6.4

Forgetting to return a value from a method that should return a value is a syntax error. If a return value type other than **`void`** *is specified, the method must contain a* **`return`** *statement.*

Common Programming Error 6.5

Returning a value from a method whose return type has been declared **`void`** *is a syntax error.*

Common Programming Error 6.6

Declaring method parameters of the same type as **`float x, y`** *instead of* **`float x, float y`** *is a syntax error, because types are required for each parameter in the parameter list.*

Common Programming Error 6.7

Placing a semicolon after the right parenthesis enclosing the parameter list of a method definition is a syntax error.

Common Programming Error 6.8

Redefining a method parameter in the method's body is a syntax error.

Common Programming Error 6.9

Passing to a method an argument that is not compatible with the corresponding parameter's type is a syntax error.

Common Programming Error 6.10

Defining a method inside another method is a syntax error.

Good Programming Practice 6.3

Avoid using the same names for instance variables and local variables. This helps readers of your program distinguish variables used in different parts of a class definition.

Good Programming Practice 6.4

Choosing meaningful method names and meaningful parameter names makes programs more readable and helps avoid excessive use of comments.

Software Engineering Observation 6.5

A method should usually be no longer than one page. Better yet, a method should usually be no longer than half a page. Regardless of how long a method is, it should perform one task well. Small methods promote software reusability.

Software Engineering Observation 6.6

Programs should be written as collections of small methods. This makes programs easier to write, debug, maintain and modify.

Software Engineering Observation 6.7

A method requiring a large number of parameters may be performing too many tasks. Consider dividing the method into smaller methods that perform the separate tasks. The method header should fit on one line if possible.

Software Engineering Observation 6.8

The method header and method calls must all agree in the number, type and order of parameters and arguments.

Testing and Debugging Tip 6.1

Small methods are easier to test, debug and understand than large ones.

The applet in our next example (Fig. 6.4) uses a programmer-defined method called **maximum** to determine and return the largest of three floating-point values.

```
// Fig. 6.4: Maximum.java
// Finding the maximum of three doubles

// Java core packages
import java.awt.Container;

// Java extension packages
import javax.swing.*;

public class Maximum extends JApplet {

   // initialize applet by obtaining user input and creating GUI
   public void init()
   {
      // obtain user input
      String s1 = JOptionPane.showInputDialog(
         "Enter first floating-point value" );
      String s2 = JOptionPane.showInputDialog(
         "Enter second floating-point value" );
      String s3 = JOptionPane.showInputDialog(
         "Enter third floating-point value" );

      // convert user input to double values
      double number1 = Double.parseDouble( s1 );
      double number2 = Double.parseDouble( s2 );
      double number3 = Double.parseDouble( s3 );

      // call method maximum to determine largest value
      double max = maximum( number1, number2, number3 );

      // create JTextArea to display results
      JTextArea outputArea = new JTextArea();

```

Fig. 6.4 Programmer-defined **maximum** method (part 1 of 2).

```
34        // display numbers and maximum value
35        outputArea.setText( "number1: " + number1 +
36           "\nnumber2: " + number2 + "\nnumber3: " + number3 +
37           "\nmaximum is: " + max );
38
39        // get the applet's GUI component display area
40        Container container = getContentPane();
41
42        // attach outputArea to Container c
43        container.add( outputArea );
44
45     }  // end method init
46
47     // maximum method uses Math class method max to help
48     // determine maximum value
49     public double maximum( double x, double y, double z )
50     {
51        return Math.max( x, Math.max( y, z ) );
52
53     }  // end method maximum
54
55  }  // end class Maximum
```

Fig. 6.4 Programmer-defined **maximum** method (part 2 of 2).

The three floating-point values are input by the user via input dialogs (lines 16–21 of **init**). Lines 24–26 use method **Double.parseDouble** to convert the **String**s input by the user to **double** values. Line 29 calls method **maximum** (defined on lines 49–53) to determine the largest **double** value of the three **double** values passed as arguments to the method. Method **maximum** returns the result to method **init**, using a **return** statement. The program assigns the result to variable **max**. Lines 35–37 use **String** concatenation to form a **String** containing the three **double** values input by the user and the **max** value and place the result in **JTextArea outputArea**.

Notice the implementation of the method **maximum** (lines 49–53). The first line indicates that the method returns a **double** floating-point value, that the method's name is **maximum** and that the method takes three **double** parameters (**x**, **y** and **z**) to accomplish its task. Also, the statement (line 51) in the body of the method returns the largest of the three floating-point values, using two calls to the **Math.max** method. First, the statement invokes method **Math.max** with the values of variables **y** and **z** to determine the larger of the two values. Next, the statement passes the value of variable **x** and the result of the first call to **Math.max** to method **Math.max**. Finally, the statement returns the result of the second call to **Math.max** to line 29 (the point at which method **init** invoked method **maximum**).

6.6 Argument Promotion

Another important feature of method definitions is the *coercion of arguments* (i.e., the forcing of arguments to the appropriate type to pass to a method). For example, a program can call **Math** method **sqrt** with an integer argument even though the method expects to receive a **double** argument. For example, the statement

```
System.out.println( Math.sqrt( 4 ) );
```

correctly evaluates **Math.sqrt(4)** and prints the value **2**. The method definition's parameter list causes Java to convert the integer value **4** to the **double** value **4.0** before passing the value to **sqrt**. In some cases, attempting these conversions leads to compiler errors if Java's *promotion rules* are not satisfied. The promotion rules specify how to convert types to other types without losing data. In our **sqrt** example above, an **int** is converted to a **double** without changing its value. However, converting a **double** to an **int** truncates the fractional part of the **double** value. Converting large integer types to small integer types (e.g., **long** to **int**) may also result in changed values.

The promotion rules apply to expressions containing values of two or more data types (also referred to as *mixed-type expressions*) and to primitive-data-type values passed as arguments to methods. The type of each value in a mixed-type expression is promoted to the "highest" type in the expression (actually, the expression uses a temporary copy of each value; the original values remain unchanged). The type of a method argument can be promoted to any "higher" type. Figure 6.5 lists the primitive data types and the types to which each is allowed to be promoted automatically.

Type	Allowed promotions
double	None
float	**double**
long	**float** or **double**
int	**long**, **float** or **double**
char	**int**, **long**, **float** or **double**
short	**int**, **long**, **float** or **double**
byte	**short**, **int**, **long**, **float** or **double**
boolean	None (**boolean** values are not considered to be numbers in Java)

Fig. 6.5 Allowed promotions for primitive data types.

Converting values to lower types can result in different values. Therefore, in cases where information may be lost due to conversion, the Java compiler requires the programmer to use a cast operator to force the conversion to occur. To invoke our **square** method, which uses an integer parameter with the **double** variable **y** (Fig. 6.3), we write the method call as **square((int) y)**. This method call explicitly casts (converts) the value of **y** to an integer for use in method **square**. Thus, if **y**'s value is **4.5**, method **square** returns **16**, not **20.25**.

Common Programming Error 6.11

Converting a primitive-data-type value to another primitive data type may change the value if the new data type is not an allowed promotion (e.g., **double** *to* **int***). Also, converting any integral value to a floating-point value and back to an integral value may introduce rounding errors into the result.*

6.7 Java API Packages

As we have seen, Java contains many predefined classes that are grouped into categories of related classes, called *packages*. Together, we refer to these packages as the *Java applications programming interface* (*Java API*), or the *Java class library*.

Throughout the text, **import** statements specify the classes required to compile a Java program. For example, a program uses the statement

```
import javax.swing.JApplet;
```

to tell the compiler to load the **JApplet** class from the **javax.swing** package. One of the great strengths of Java is the large number of classes in the packages of the Java API that programmers can reuse rather than "reinventing the wheel." We exercise a large number of these classes in this book. Figure 6.6 lists a subset of the many packages in the Java API and provides a brief description of each package. We use classes from these packages and others throughout this book. We provide this table to begin introducing you the variety of reusable components available in the Java API. When learning Java, you should spend time reading the descriptions of the packages and classes in the Java API documentation (**java.sun.com/j2se/1.3/docs/api**).

Package	Description
java.applet	*The Java Applet Package.* This package contains the **Applet** class and several interfaces that enable the creation of applets, interaction of applets with the browser and playing audio clips. In Java 2, class **javax.swing.JApplet** is used to define an applet that uses the *Swing GUI components*.
java.awt	*The Java Abstract Windowing Toolkit Package.* This package contains the classes and interfaces required to create and manipulate graphical user interfaces in Java 1.0 and 1.1. In Java 2, these classes can still be used, but the *Swing GUI components* of the **javax.swing** packages are often used instead.

Fig. 6.6 Packages of the Java API (part 1 of 2).

Package	Description
`java.awt.event`	*The Java Abstract Windowing Toolkit Event Package.* This package contains classes and interfaces that enable event handling for GUI components in both the **java.awt** and **javax.swing** packages.
`java.io`	*The Java Input/Output Package.* This package contains classes that enable programs to input and output data (see Chapter 16, Files and Streams).
`java.lang`	*The Java Language Package.* This package contains classes and interfaces required by many Java programs (many are discussed throughout this text) and is automatically imported by the compiler into all programs.
`java.net`	*The Java Networking Package.* This package contains classes that enable programs to communicate via networks (see Chapter 17, Networking).
`java.text`	*The Java Text Package.* This package contains classes and interfaces that enable a Java program to manipulate numbers, dates, characters and strings. It provides many of Java's internationalization capabilities i.e., features that enable a program to be customized to a specific locale (e.g., an applet may display strings in different languages, based on the user's country).
`java.util`	*The Java Utilities Package.* This package contains utility classes and interfaces, such as: date and time manipulations, random-number processing capabilities (**Random**), storing and processing large amounts of data, breaking strings into smaller pieces called *tokens* (**StringTokenizer**) and other capabilities (see Chapter 19, Data Structures, Chapter 20, Java Utilities Package and Bit Manipulation, and Chapter 21, The Collections API).
`javax.swing`	*The Java Swing GUI Components Package.* This package contains classes and interfaces for Java's Swing GUI components that provide support for portable GUIs.
`javax.swing.event`	*The Java Swing Event Package.* This package contains classes and interfaces that enable event handling for GUI components in the **javax.swing** package.

Fig. 6.6 Packages of the Java API (part 2 of 2).

The set of packages available in the Java 2 Software Development Kit (J2SDK) is quite large. In addition to the packages summarized in Fig. 6.6, the J2SDK includes packages for complex graphics, advanced graphical user interfaces, printing, advanced networking, security, database processing, multimedia, accessibility (for people with disabilities) and many other functions. For an overview of the packages in the J2SDK version 1.3, visit

java.sun.com/j2se/1.3/docs/api/overview-summary.html

Also, many other packages are available for download at **java.sun.com**.

6.8 Random-Number Generation

We now take a brief and, hopefully, entertaining diversion into a popular programming application, namely, simulation and game playing. In this section and the next section, we will develop a nicely structured game-playing program that includes multiple methods. The program uses most of the control structures we have studied to this point in the book and introduces several new concepts.

There is something in the air of a gambling casino that invigorates people—from the high rollers at the plush mahogany-and-felt craps tables to the quarter poppers at the one-armed bandits. It is the *element of chance*, the possibility that luck will convert a pocketful of money into a mountain of wealth. The element of chance can be introduced through the ***random*** method from the **Math** class. [Note: Java also provides a **Random** class in package java.util. Class **Random** is covered in Chapter 20.]

Consider the following statement:

```
double randomValue = Math.random();
```

The **random** method of class **Math** generates a random **double** value from 0.0 up to, but not including, 1.0. If method **random** truly produces values at random, then every value from 0.0 up to, but not including, 1.0 should have an equal *chance* (or *probability*) of being chosen each time method **random** is called. Note that the values returned by **random** are actually *pseudo-random numbers*—a sequence of values produced by a complex mathematical calculation. That calculation uses the current time of day to *seed* the random number generator, such that each execution of a program yields a different sequence of random values.

The range of values produced directly by method **random** often is different from the range of values required in a particular Java application. For example, a program that simulates coin tossing might require only 0 for "heads" and 1 for "tails." A program that simulates rolling a six-sided die would require random integers in the range from 1 to 6. A program that randomly predicts the next type of spaceship (out of four possibilities) that will fly across the horizon in a video game would require random integers in the range from 1 to 4.

To demonstrate method **random**, let us develop a program that simulates 20 rolls of a six-sided die and displays the value of each roll. We use the multiplication operator (*****) in conjunction with method **random** as follows to produce integers in the range from 0 to 5:

```
(int) ( Math.random() * 6 )
```

This manipulation is called *scaling* the range of values produced by **Math** method **random**. The number **6** in the preceding expression is called the *scaling factor*. The integer cast operator truncates the floating-point part (the part after the decimal point) of each value produced by the expression. Next, we *shift* the range of numbers produced by adding 1 to our previous result, as in

```
1 + (int) ( Math.random() * 6 )
```

Figure 6.7 confirms that the results of the preceding calculation are integers in the range from 1 to 6.

```java
// Fig. 6.7: RandomIntegers.java
// Shifted, scaled random integers.

// Java extension packages
import javax.swing.JOptionPane;

public class RandomIntegers {

   // main method begins execution of Java application
   public static void main( String args[] )
   {
      int value;
      String output = "";

      // loop 20 times
      for ( int counter = 1; counter <= 20; counter++ ) {

         // pick random integer between 1 and 6
         value = 1 + ( int ) ( Math.random() * 6 );

         output += value + "  ";  // append value to output

         // if counter divisible by 5,
         // append newline to String output
         if ( counter % 5 == 0 )
            output += "\n";

      }  // end for structure

      JOptionPane.showMessageDialog( null, output,
         "20 Random Numbers from 1 to 6",
         JOptionPane.INFORMATION_MESSAGE );

      System.exit( 0 );  // terminate application

   }  // end method main

}  // end class RandomIntegers
```

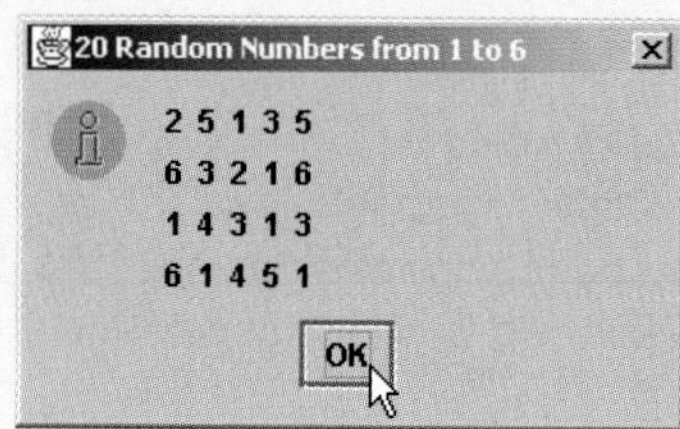

Fig. 6.7 Shifted and scaled random integers .

To show that these numbers occur with approximately equal likelihood, let us simulate 6000 rolls of a die with the program in Fig. 6.8. Each integer from 1 to 6 should appear approximately 1000 times.

```
// Fig. 6.8: RollDie.java
// Roll a six-sided die 6000 times.

// Java extension packages
import javax.swing.*;

public class RollDie {

   // main method begins execution of Java application
   public static void main( String args[] )
   {
      int frequency1 = 0, frequency2 = 0, frequency3 = 0,
          frequency4 = 0, frequency5 = 0, frequency6 = 0, face;

      // summarize results
      for ( int roll = 1; roll <= 6000; roll++ ) {
         face = 1 + ( int ) ( Math.random() * 6 );

         // determine roll value and increment appropriate counter
         switch ( face ) {

            case 1:
               ++frequency1;
               break;

            case 2:
               ++frequency2;
               break;

            case 3:
               ++frequency3;
               break;

            case 4:
               ++frequency4;
               break;

            case 5:
               ++frequency5;
               break;

            case 6:
               ++frequency6;
               break;

         }  // end switch structure

      }  // end for structure
```

Fig. 6.8 Rolling a six-sided die 6000 times (part 1 of 2).

```
49
50          JTextArea outputArea = new JTextArea();
51
52          outputArea.setText( "Face\tFrequency" +
53             "\n1\t" + frequency1 + "\n2\t" + frequency2 +
54             "\n3\t" + frequency3 + "\n4\t" + frequency4 +
55             "\n5\t" + frequency5 + "\n6\t" + frequency6 );
56
57          JOptionPane.showMessageDialog( null, outputArea,
58             "Rolling a Die 6000 Times",
59             JOptionPane.INFORMATION_MESSAGE );
60
61          System.exit( 0 );   // terminate application
62
63       }  // end method main
64
65    }  // end class RollDie
```

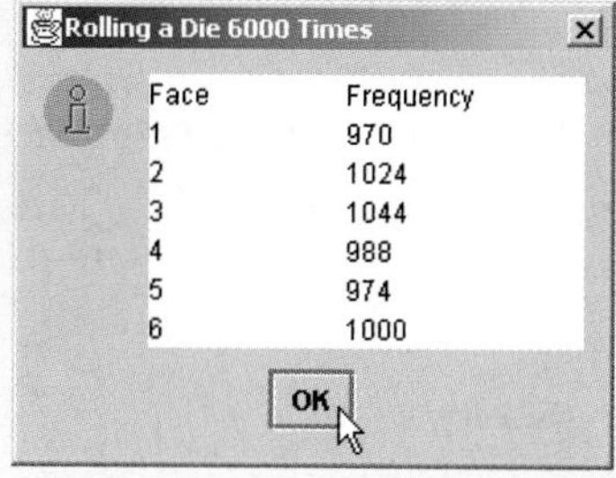

Fig. 6.8 Rolling a six-sided die 6000 times (part 2 of 2).

As the program output shows, scaling and shifting the values produced by method **random** enables the program to simulate realistically the rolling of a six-sided die. Note that the use of nested control structures in the program to determine the number of times each side of the six-sided die occurred. The **for** structure at lines 16–48 iterates 6000 times. During each iteration of the loop, line 17 produces a value from 1 to 6. The nested **switch** structure at lines 20–46 uses as its controlling expression the **face** value that was randomly chosen. Based on the value of **face**, the **switch** structure increments one of the six counter variables during each iteration of the loop. Note that the **switch** structure has no **default** case. When we study arrays in Chapter 7, we show how to replace the entire **switch** structure in this program with a single statement. Run the program several times, and observe the results. Notice that the program produces different results each time the program executes.

The values produced directly by **random** are always in the range

$$0.0 \le \texttt{Math.random()} < 1.0$$

Previously, we demonstrated how to write a single statement to simulate the rolling of a six-sided die with the statement

```
face = 1 + (int) ( Math.random() * 6 );
```

which always assigns an integer (at random) to variable **face** in the range $1 \le$ **face** ≤ 6. Note that the width of this range (i.e., the number of consecutive integers in the range) is 6, and the starting number in the range is 1. Referring to the preceding statement, we see that the width of the range is determined by the number used to scale **random** with the multiplication operator (i.e., 6), and the starting number of the range is equal to the number (i.e., 1) added to **(int) (Math.random() * 6)**. We can generalize this result as

```
n = a + (int) ( Math.random() * b );
```

where **a** is the *shifting value* (which is equal to the first number in the desired range of consecutive integers) and **b** is the *scaling factor* (which is equal to the width of the desired range of consecutive integers). In the exercises, we will see that it is possible to choose integers at random from sets of values other than ranges of consecutive integers.

6.9 Example: A Game of Chance

One of the most popular games of chance is a dice game known as "craps," which is played in casinos and back alleys throughout the world. The rules of the game are straightforward:

> *A player rolls two dice. Each die has six faces. These faces contain one, two, three, four, five and six spots, respectively. After the dice have come to rest, the sum of the spots on the two upward faces is calculated. If the sum is 7 or 11 on the first throw, the player wins. If the sum is 2, 3 or 12 on the first throw (called "craps"), the player loses (i.e., the "house" wins). If the sum is 4, 5, 6, 8, 9 or 10 on the first throw, that sum becomes the player's "point." To win, you must continue rolling the dice until you "make your point" (i.e., roll your point value). The player loses by rolling a 7 before making the point.*

The applet in Fig. 6.9 simulates the game of craps.

```
// Fig. 6.9: Craps.java
// Craps

// Java core packages
import java.awt.*;
import java.awt.event.*;

// Java extension packages
import javax.swing.*;

public class Craps extends JApplet implements ActionListener {

   // constant variables for game status
   final int WON = 0, LOST = 1, CONTINUE = 2;

   // other variables used
   boolean firstRoll = true;      // true if first roll of dice
   int sumOfDice = 0;             // sum of the dice
   int myPoint = 0;      // point if no win/loss on first roll
   int gameStatus = CONTINUE;     // game not over yet

```

Fig. 6.9 Program to simulate the game of craps (part 1 of 5).

```
   // graphical user interface components
   JLabel die1Label, die2Label, sumLabel, pointLabel;
   JTextField die1Field, die2Field, sumField, pointField;
   JButton rollButton;

   // set up GUI components
   public void init()
   {
      // obtain content pane and change its layout to
      // a FlowLayout
      Container container = getContentPane();
      container.setLayout( new FlowLayout() );

      // create label and text field for die 1
      die1Label = new JLabel( "Die 1" );
      container.add( die1Label );
      die1Field = new JTextField( 10 );
      die1Field.setEditable( false );
      container.add( die1Field );

      // create label and text field for die 2
      die2Label = new JLabel( "Die 2" );
      container.add( die2Label );
      die2Field = new JTextField( 10 );
      die2Field.setEditable( false );
      container.add( die2Field );

      // create label and text field for sum
      sumLabel = new JLabel( "Sum is" );
      container.add( sumLabel );
      sumField = new JTextField( 10 );
      sumField.setEditable( false );
      container.add( sumField );

      // create label and text field for point
      pointLabel = new JLabel( "Point is" );
      container.add( pointLabel );
      pointField = new JTextField( 10 );
      pointField.setEditable( false );
      container.add( pointField );

      // create button user clicks to roll dice
      rollButton = new JButton( "Roll Dice" );
      rollButton.addActionListener( this );
      container.add( rollButton );
   }

   // process one roll of dice
   public void actionPerformed( ActionEvent actionEvent )
   {
      // first roll of dice
      if ( firstRoll ) {
         sumOfDice = rollDice();      // roll dice
```

Fig. 6.9 Program to simulate the game of craps (part 2 of 5).

```

         switch ( sumOfDice ) {

            // win on first roll
            case 7: case 11:
               gameStatus = WON;
               pointField.setText( "" );   // clear point field
               break;

            // lose on first roll
            case 2: case 3: case 12:
               gameStatus = LOST;
               pointField.setText( "" );   // clear point field
               break;

            // remember point
            default:
               gameStatus = CONTINUE;
               myPoint = sumOfDice;
               pointField.setText( Integer.toString( myPoint ) );
               firstRoll = false;
               break;

         } // end switch structure

      } // end if structure body

      // subsequent roll of dice
      else {
         sumOfDice = rollDice();       // roll dice

         // determine game status
         if ( sumOfDice == myPoint )   // win by making point
            gameStatus = WON;
         else
            if ( sumOfDice == 7 )      // lose by rolling 7
               gameStatus = LOST;
      }

      // display message indicating game status
      displayMessage();

   } // end method actionPerformed

   // roll dice, calculate sum and display results
   public int rollDice()
   {
      int die1, die2, sum;

      // pick random die values
      die1 = 1 + ( int ) ( Math.random() * 6 );
      die2 = 1 + ( int ) ( Math.random() * 6 );

```

Fig. 6.9 Program to simulate the game of craps (part 3 of 5).

```
        sum = die1 + die2;   // sum die values

        // display results
        die1Field.setText( Integer.toString( die1 ) );
        die2Field.setText( Integer.toString( die2 ) );
        sumField.setText( Integer.toString( sum ) );

        return sum;  // return sum of dice

     } // end method rollDice

     // determine game status and display appropriate message
     // in status bar
     public void displayMessage()
     {
        // game should continue
        if ( gameStatus == CONTINUE )
           showStatus( "Roll again." );

        // game won or lost
        else {

           if ( gameStatus == WON )
              showStatus( "Player wins. " +
                 "Click Roll Dice to play again." );
           else
              showStatus( "Player loses. " +
                 "Click Roll Dice to play again." );

           // next roll is first roll of new game
           firstRoll = true;
        }

     } // end method displayMessage

  } // end class Craps
```

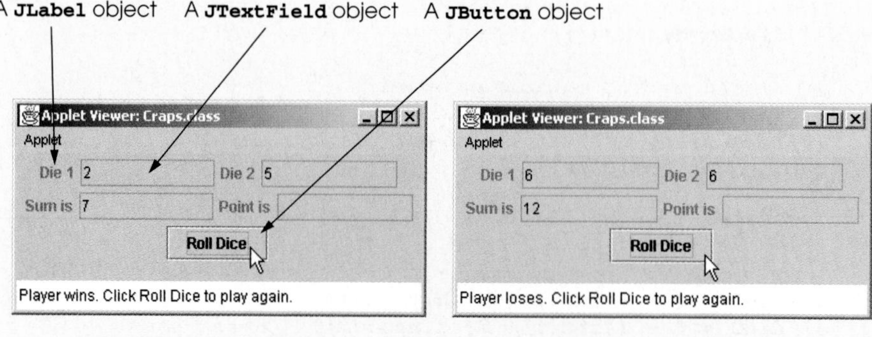

Fig. 6.9 Program to simulate the game of craps (part 4 of 5).

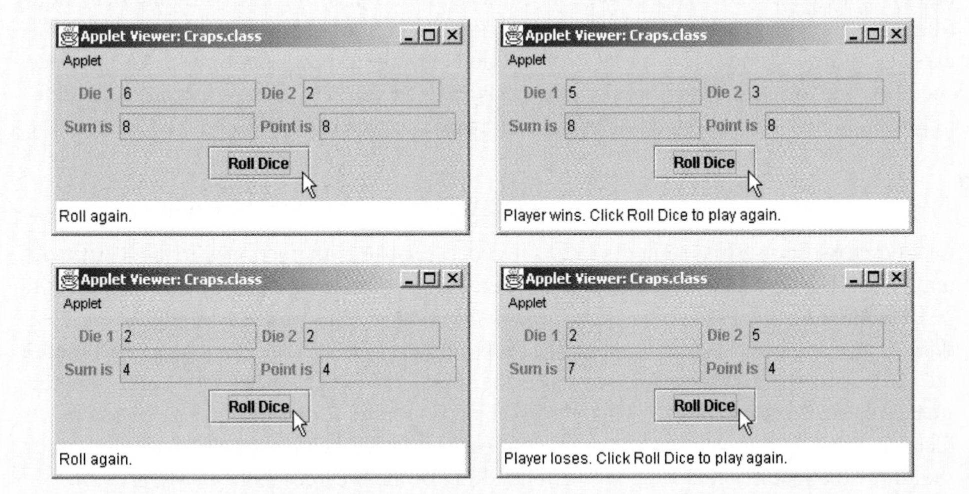

Fig. 6.9 Program to simulate the game of craps (part 5 of 5).

Notice that the player must roll two dice on the first and all subsequent rolls. When you execute the applet, click the **Roll Dice** button to play the game. The lower left corner of the **`appletviewer`** window displays the result of each roll. The screen captures show four separate executions of the applet (a win and a loss on the first roll, and a win and a loss after the first roll).

Until now, most user interactions in our programs have been through either an input dialog (in which the user could type an input value for the program) or a message dialog (in which a message was displayed to the user, and the user could click **OK** to dismiss the dialog). Although these dialogs are valid ways to receive input from a user and display output in a Java program, their capabilities are fairly limited—an input dialog can obtain only one value at a time from the user and a message dialog can display only one message. It is much more common to receive multiple inputs from the user at once (such as the user entering name and address information) or display many pieces of data at once (such as the values of the dice, the sum of the dice and the point, in this example). To begin our introduction to more elaborate user interfaces, this program illustrates two new graphical user interface concepts: Attaching several GUI components to an applet and GUI *event handling*. We discuss each of the new issues as they are encountered in the program.

The **`import`** statements in lines 5–9 enable the compiler to load the classes used in this applet. Line 5 specifies that the program uses classes from package **`java.awt`** (specifically, classes **`Container`** and ***`FlowLayout`***). Line 6 specifies that the program uses classes from package ***`java.awt.event`***. This package contains many data types that enable a program to process a user's interactions with a program's GUI. In this program, we use the ***`ActionListener`*** and ***`ActionEvent`*** data types from package **`java.awt.event`**. Line 9 specifies that the program uses classes from package **`javax.swing`** (specifically, **`JApplet`**, ***`JLabel`***, ***`JTextField`*** and ***`JButton`***).

As stated earlier, every Java program is based on at least one class definition that extends and enhances an existing class definition via inheritance. Remember that applets inherit from class **`JApplet`**. Line 11 indicates that class **`Craps`** inherits from **`JApplet`** and *implements* ***ActionListener***. A class can inherit existing attributes and behaviors (data and methods) from another class specified to the right of keyword **extends** in the class definition. In addition, a class can implement one or more *interfaces*. An interface specifies one or more behaviors (i.e., methods), which you must define in your class definition. Implementing interface **ActionListener** forces us to *define a method* with the first line

```
public void actionPerformed( ActionEvent actionEvent )
```

in our **Craps** class. This method's task is to process a user's interaction with the **JButton** (called **Roll Dice** on the user interface). When the user presses the button, this method will be called automatically in response to the user interaction. This process is called *event handling*. The *event* is the user interaction (i.e., pressing the button). The *event handler* is method **actionPerformed**. We discuss the details of this interaction and method **actionPerformed** shortly. Chapter 9, Object-Oriented Programming, discusses interfaces in detail. For now, as you develop your own applets that have graphical user interfaces, mimic the features that support event handling of the GUI components we present.

The game of craps is reasonably involved. The player may win or lose on the first roll, or may win or lose on any roll. Line 14 creates variables that define the three states of a game of craps: Game won (**WON**), game lost (**LOST**) or continue rolling the dice (**CONTINUE**). Keyword ***final*** at the beginning of the declaration indicates that these are *constant variables*. When a program declares a **final** variable, the program must initialize the variable before using the variable and cannot modify the variable thereafter. If the variable is an instance variable, this initialization normally occurs in the variable's declaration. The initialization also can occur in a special method of a class called a *constructor* (discussed in Chapter 8). Constant variables are often called *named constants* or *read-only variables*. We provide more details on keyword **final** in Chapter 7 and Chapter 8.

Common Programming Error 6.12

After declaring and initializing a ***final*** *variable, attempting to assign another value to that variable is a syntax error.*

Good Programming Practice 6.5

Use only uppercase letters (with underscores between words) in the names of ***final*** *variables. This format makes these constants stand out in a program.*

Good Programming Practice 6.6

Using meaningfully named ***final*** *variables rather than integer constants (such as 2) makes programs more readable.*

Lines 17–20 declare several instance variables that are used throughout the **Craps** applet. Variable **firstRoll** is a **boolean** variable that indicates whether the next roll of the dice is the first roll in the current game. Variable **sumOfDice** maintains the sum of the dice for the last roll. Variable **myPoint** stores the "point" if the player does not win or lose on the first roll. Variable **gameStatus** keeps track of the current state of the game (**WON**, **LOST** or **CONTINUE**).

Lines 23–25 declare references to the GUI components used in this applet's graphical user interface. References **die1Label**, **die2Label**, **sumLabel** and **pointLabel** all refer to ***JLabel*** *objects*. A **JLabel** contains a string of characters to be displayed on the screen. Normally, a **JLabel** indicates the purpose of another GUI component on the screen. In the screen captures of Fig. 6.9, the **JLabel** objects are the text to the left of each rectangle in the first two rows of the user interface. References **die1Field**, **die2Field**, **sumField** and **pointField** all refer to ***JTextField*** *objects*. **JTextField**s are used to get a single line of information from the user at the keyboard or to display information on the screen. The **JTextField** objects are the rectangles to the right of each **JLabel** in the first two rows of the user interface. *Reference* **rollButton** refers to a ***JButton*** *object*. When the user presses a **JButton**, the program normally responds by performing a task (rolling the dice, in this example). The **JButton** object is the rectangle containing the words **Roll Dice** at the bottom of the user interface shown in Fig. 6.9. We have seen **JButton**s in prior programs—every message dialog and every input dialog contained an **OK** button to dismiss the message dialog or send the user's input to the program. We also have seen **JTextField**s in prior programs—every input dialog contains a **JTextField** in which the user types an input value.

Method **init** (lines 28–67) creates the GUI component objects and attaches them to the user interface. Line 32 declares **Container** reference **container** and assigns to it the result method **getContentPane**. Remember, method **getContentPane** returns a reference to the applet's content pane that can be used to attach GUI components to the applet's user interface.

Line 33 uses **Container** method ***setLayout*** to specify the *layout manager* for the applet's user interface. Layout managers arrange GUI components on a **Container** for presentation purposes. The layout managers determine the position and size of every GUI component attached to the container, thereby processing most of the layout details and enabling the programmer to concentrate on the basic look and feel of the programs.

FlowLayout is the simplest layout manager. GUI components are placed from left to right in the order in which they are attached to the **Container** (the applet's content pane in this example) with method **add**. When the layout manager reaches the edge of the container, it begins a new row of components and continues laying out the components on that row. Line 33 creates a new object of class **FlowLayout** and passes it as the argument to method **setLayout**. Normally, the layout is set before any GUI components are added to a **Container**.

Common Programming Error 6.13

If a ***Container*** *is not large enough to display the GUI component attached to it, some or all of the GUI components simply will not display.*

[*Note*: Each **Container** can have only one layout manager at a time. Separate **Containers** in the same program can have different layout managers. Most Java programming environments provide GUI design tools that help a programmer graphically design a GUI; then the tools write Java code to create the GUI. Some of these GUI design tools also allow the programmer to use layout managers. Chapter 12 and Chapter 13 discuss several layout managers that allow more precise control over the layout of the GUI components.]

Lines 36–40, 43–47, 50–54 and 57–61 each create a **JLabel** and **JTextField** pair and attach them to the user interface. Since these sets of lines are all quite similar, we concentrate on lines 36–40. Line 36 creates a new **JLabel** object, initializes it with the string **"Die 1"** and assigns the object to reference **die1Label**. This procedure labels the corresponding **JTextField** (named **die1Field**) in the user interface, so the user can determine the purpose of the value displayed in **die1Field**. Line 37 attaches the **JLabel** to which **die1Label** refers to the applet's content pane. Line 38 creates a new **JTextField** object, initializes it to be **10** characters wide and assigns the object to reference **die1Field**. This **JTextField** displays the value of the first die after each roll of the dice. Line 39 uses **JTextField** method **setEditable** with the argument **false** to indicate that the user should not be able to type in the **JTextField**. This setting makes the **JTextField** *uneditable* and causes it to be displayed with a gray background by default. An editable **JTextField** has a white background (as seen in input dialogs). Line 32 attaches the **JTextField** to which **die1Field** refers to the applet's content pane.

Line 64 creates a new **JButton** object, initializes it with the string **"Roll Dice"** (this string will appear on the button) and assigns the object to reference **rollButton**.

Line 65 specifies that ***this*** applet should *listen* for events from the **rollButton**. The **this** keyword enables the applet to refer to itself. (We discuss **this** in detail in Chapter 8.) When the user interacts with a GUI component an *event* is sent to the applet. GUI events are messages (method calls) indicating that the user of the program has interacted with one of the program's GUI components. For example, when you press **rollButton** in this program, a message indicating the event that occurred is sent to the applet to notify the applet that you pressed the button. For a **JButton**, the message indicates to the applet that *an action was performed* by the user on the **JButton** and automatically calls method **actionPerformed** to process the user's interaction.

This style of programming is known as *event-driven programming*—the user interacts with a GUI component, the program is notified of the event and the program processes the event. The user's interaction with the GUI "drives" the program. The methods that are called when an event occurs are also known as *event-handling methods*. When a GUI event occurs in a program, Java creates an object containing information about the event that occurred and *calls* an appropriate event-handling method. Before any event can be processed, each GUI component must know which object in the program defines the event-handling method that will be called when an event occurs. In line 65, **JButton** method ***addActionListener*** is used to tell **rollButton** that the applet (**this**) can *listen* for *action events* and defines method **actionPerformed**. This procedure is called *registering the event handler* with the GUI component. (We also like to call it the *start-listening line*, because the applet is now listening for events from the button.) To respond to an action event, we must define a class that implements **ActionListener** (this requires that the class also define method **actionPerformed**), and we must register the event handler with the GUI component. Finally, the last line in **init** attaches the **JButton** to which **roll** refers to the applet's content pane, thus completing the user interface.

Method **actionPerformed** (lines 70–117) is one of several methods that process interactions between the user and GUI components. The first line of the method indicates that **actionPerformed** is a **public** method that returns nothing (**void**) when it completes its task. Method **actionPerformed** receives one argument—an **ActionEvent**—when it is called in response to an action performed on a GUI component by the user (in this case, pressing the **JButton**). The **ActionEvent** argument contains information about the action that occurred.

We define method **rollDice** (lines 120–137) to roll the dice and compute and display their sum. Method **rollDice** is defined once, but it is called from two places in the program (lines 74 and 104). Method **rollDice** takes no arguments, so it has an empty parameter list. Method **rollDice** returns the sum of the two dice, so a return type of **int** is indicated in the method's header.

The user clicks **Roll Dice** to roll the dice. This action invokes method **actionPerformed** (line 70) of the applet. Method **actionPerformed** checks the **boolean** variable **firstRoll** (line 73) to determine if it is **true** or **false**. If it is **true**, this roll is the first roll of the game. Line 74 calls **rollDice**, which picks two random values from 1 to 6, displays the value of the first die, second die and the sum of the dice in the first three **JTextField**s, respectively, and returns the sum of the dice. Note that the integer values are converted to **String**s (lines 131–133) with **static** method **Integer.toString**, because **JTextField**s can display only **String**s. After the first roll, the nested **switch** structure at line 76 in **actionPerformed** determines if the game has been won or lost, or if the game should continue with another roll. After the first roll, if the game is not over, **sumOfDice** is saved in **myPoint** and displayed in **pointField**.

Line 115 calls method **displayMessage** (defined at lines 141–161) to display the current status of the game. The **if/else** structure at line 144 uses applet method ***showStatus*** to display a **String** in the applet container's status bar. Line 145 displays

```
Roll again.
```

if **gameStatus** is equal to **CONTINUE**. Lines 150–151 display

```
Player wins. Click Roll Dice to play again.
```

if **gameStatus** is equal to **WON**. Lines 153–154 display

```
Player loses. Click Roll Dice to play again.
```

if **gameStatus** is equal to **LOST**. Method **showStatus** receives a **String** argument and displays it in the status bar of the applet container. If the game is over (i.e., it has been won or lost) line 158 sets **firstRoll** to **true** to indicate that the next roll of the dice is the first roll of the next game.

The program then waits for the user to click the **Roll Dice** button again. Each time the user presses **Roll Dice** button, method **actionPerformed** invokes method **rollDice** to produce a new **sumOfDice**. If the current roll is a continuation of an incomplete game, the code in lines 103–112 executes. In line 107, if **sumOfDice** matches **myPoint**, line 108 sets **gameStatus** to **WON**, and the game is complete. In line 110, if **sumOfDice** is equal to **7**, line 111 sets **gameStatus** to **LOST**, and the game is complete. When the game completes, **displayMessage** displays an appropriate message, and the user can click the **Roll Dice** button to begin a new game. Throughout the program, the four **JTextField**s are updated with the new values of the dice and the sum on each roll, and the **pointField** is updated each time a new game begins.

Note the interesting use of the various program control mechanisms we have discussed. The craps program uses four methods—**init**, **actionPerformed**, **rollDice** and **displayMessage**—and the **switch**, **if/else** and nested **if** structures. Note also the use of multiple **case** labels in the **switch** structure to execute the same statements (lines 79 and 85). Also, note that the event-handling mechanism acts as a form of program control. In this program, event-handling enables user-controlled repetition—each time the user clicks **Roll Dice**, the program rolls the dice again. In the exercises, we investigate various interesting characteristics of the game of craps.

6.10 Duration of Identifiers

Chapter 2 through Chapter 5 used identifiers for variable names and reference names. The attributes of variables and references include name, type, size and value. We also use identifiers as names for user-defined methods and classes. Actually, each identifier in a program has other attributes, including *duration* and *scope*.

An identifier's *duration* (also called its *lifetime*) is the period during which the identifier exists in memory. Some identifiers exist for brief periods of time and others exist for the entire execution of a program.

An identifier's *scope* defines where the identifier can be referenced in a program. Some identifiers can be referenced throughout a program, while others can be referenced only from limited portions of a program. This section discusses duration of identifiers. Section 6.11 discusses the scope of identifiers.

Identifiers that represent local variables in a method (i.e., parameters and variables declared in the body of the method) have *automatic duration*. Automatic-duration variables are created when program control reaches their declaration; they exist while the block in which they are declared is active; and they are destroyed when the block in which they are declared is exited. We will continue to refer to variables of automatic duration as *local variables*.

Performance Tip 6.2

Automatic duration is a means of conserving memory, because automatic-duration variables are created when program control reaches their declaration and are destroyed when the block in which they are declared is exited.

The instance variables of a class are initialized automatically by the compiler if the programmer does not provide explicit initial values. Variables of the primitive data types are initialized to zero, except **`boolean`** variables, which are initialized to **`false`**. References are initialized to **`null`**. Unlike instance variables of a class, automatic variables must be initialized by the programmer before they can be used.

Testing and Debugging Tip 6.2

If an automatic variable is not initialized before it is used in a method, the compiler issues an error message.

Java also has identifiers of *static duration*. Variables and references of static duration exist from the point at which the class that defines them is loaded into memory for execution until the program terminates. Their storage is allocated and initialized when their classes are loaded into memory. Even though static-duration variables and reference names exist when their classes are loaded into memory, these identifiers cannot necessarily be used throughout a program. Duration (an identifier's lifetime) and scope (where an identifier can be used) are separate issues, as shown in Section 6.11.

Software Engineering Observation 6.9

Automatic duration is an example of the principle of least privilege. *This principle states that each component of a system should have sufficient rights and privileges to accomplish its designated task, but no additional rights or privileges. This constraint helps prevent accidental and/or malicious errors from occurring in systems. Why have variables stored in memory and accessible when they are not needed?*

6.11 Scope Rules

The *scope* of an identifier for a variable, reference or method is the portion of the program that can reference the identifier. A local variable or reference declared in a block can be used only in that block or in blocks nested within that block. The scopes for an identifier are *class scope* and *block scope*. There is also a special scope for labels used with the **break** and **continue** statements (introduced in Chapter 5, "Control Structures: Part 2"). A label is visible only in the body of the repetition structure that immediately follows the label.

Methods and instance variables of a class have *class scope*. Class scope begins at the opening left brace, **{**, of the class definition and terminates at the closing right brace, **}**, of the class definition. Class scope enables methods of a class to invoke directly all methods defined in that same class or inherited into that class (such as the methods inherited into our applets from class **JApplet**) and to access directly all instance variables defined in the class. In Chapter 8, we will see that **static** methods are an exception to this rule. In a sense, all instance variables and methods of a class are *global* to the methods of the class in which they are defined (i.e., the methods can modify the instance variables directly and invoke other methods of the class). [*Note*: One of the reasons we use mainly applets in this chapter is to simplify our discussions. We have not as yet introduced a true windowed application in which the methods of our application class will have access to all the other methods of the class and the instance variables of the class.]

Identifiers declared inside a block have *block scope*. Block scope begins at the identifier's declaration and ends at the terminating right brace (**}**) of the block. Local variables of a method have block scope, as do method parameters, which are also local variables of the method. Any block may contain variable or reference declarations. When blocks are nested in a method's body and an identifier declared in an outer block has the same name as an identifier declared in an inner block, the compiler generates a syntax error stating that the variable is already defined. If a local variable in a method has the same name as an instance variable, the instance variable is "hidden" until the block terminates execution. In Chapter 8, we discuss how to access such "hidden" instance variables.

Common Programming Error 6.14

Accidentally using the same name for an identifier in an inner block of a method as is used for an identifier in an outer block of the same method results in a syntax error from the compiler.

Good Programming Practice 6.7

Avoid local-variable names that hide instance-variable names. This can be accomplished by avoiding the use of duplicate identifiers in a class.

The applet of Fig. 6.10 demonstrates scoping issues with instance variables and local variables.

This example uses the applet's **start** method (lines 27–40) for the first time. Remember, when an applet container loads an applet, the container first creates an instance of the applet class. It then calls the applet's **init**, **start** and **paint** methods. Method **start** always is defined with the line shown on line 27 as its first line.

```
// Fig. 6.10: Scoping.java
// A scoping example.

// Java core packages
import java.awt.Container;

// Java extension packages
import javax.swing.*;

public class Scoping extends JApplet {
   JTextArea outputArea;

   // instance variable accessible to all methods of this class
   int x = 1;

   // set up applet's GUI
   public void init()
   {
      outputArea = new JTextArea();
      Container container = getContentPane();
      container.add( outputArea );

   }  // end method init

   // method start called after init completes; start calls
   // methods useLocal and useInstance
   public void start()
   {
      int x = 5;   // variable local to method start

      outputArea.append( "local x in start is " + x );

      useLocal();      // useLocal has local x
      useInstance();   // useInstance uses instance variable x
      useLocal();      // useLocal reinitializes local x
      useInstance();   // instance variable x retains its value

      outputArea.append( "\n\nlocal x in start is " + x );

   }  // end method start

   // useLocal reinitializes local variable x during each call
   public void useLocal()
   {
      int x = 25;  // initialized each time useLocal is called

      outputArea.append( "\n\nlocal x in useLocal is " + x +
         " after entering useLocal" );
      ++x;
      outputArea.append( "\nlocal x in useLocal is " + x +
         " before exiting useLocal" );

   }  // end method useLocal
```

Fig. 6.10 A scoping example (part 1 of 2).

```
54
55      // useInstance modifies instance variable x during each call
56      public void useInstance()
57      {
58         outputArea.append( "\n\ninstance variable x is " + x +
59                            " on entering useInstance" );
60         x *= 10;
61         outputArea.append( "\ninstance variable x is " + x +
62                            " on exiting useInstance" );
63
64      }  // end method useInstance
65
66   }  // end class Scoping
```

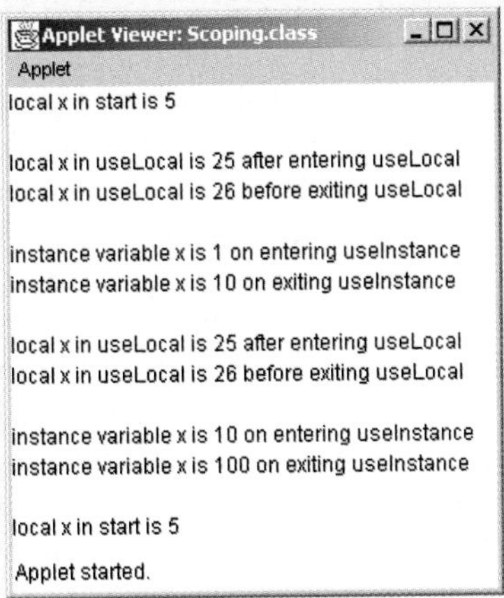

Fig. 6.10 A scoping example (part 2 of 2).

Line 14 declares and initializes instance variable **x** to **1**. This instance variable is hidden in any block (or method) that declares a variable named **x**. Method **start** declares a local variable **x** (line 29) and initializes it to **5**. This variable's value is displayed in the **JTextArea outputArea** to show that the instance variable **x** is hidden in **start**. The program defines two other methods—**useLocal** (lines 43–53) and **useInstance** (lines 56–64)—that each take no arguments and do not return results. Method **start** calls each of these methods twice. Method **useLocal** defines local (automatic) variable **x** (line 45). When **useLocal** is called (line 33), it creates local variable **x** and initializes **x** to **25**, displays the value of **x** in **outputArea**, increments **x** and displays the value of **x** again. When **uselLocal** is called again (line 35), it recreates local variable **x** and initializes **x** to **25**. Method **useInstance** does not declare any variables. Therefore, when it refers to variable **x**, the instance variable **x** is used. When **useInstance** is called (line 34), it displays the instance variable **x** in **outputArea**, multiplies the instance variable **x** by **10** and displays instance variable **x** again before returning. The next time method **useInstance** is called (line 36), the instance variable has its modified value, **10**. Finally, the program displays the local variable **x** in **start** again to show that none of the method calls modified the value of **x**, because the methods all referred to variables in other scopes.

6.12 Recursion

The programs we have discussed thus far are generally structured as methods that call one another in a disciplined, hierarchical manner. For some problems, however, it is useful to have methods call themselves. A *recursive method* is a method that calls itself either directly or indirectly through another method. Recursion is an important topic discussed at length in upper-level computer science courses. In this and the next section, simple examples of recursion are presented. This book contains an extensive treatment of recursion. Figure 6.15 (at the end of Section 6.14) summarizes the recursion examples and exercises in this book.

We consider recursion conceptually first. Then we examine several programs containing recursive methods. Recursive problem-solving approaches have a number of elements in common. A recursive method is called to solve a problem. The method actually knows how to solve only the simplest case(s) or so-called *base case(s)*. If the method is called with a base case, the method returns a result. If the method is called with a more complex problem, the method divides the problem into two conceptual pieces: a piece that the method knows how to do (base case) and a piece that the method does not know how to do. To make recursion feasible, the latter piece must resemble the original problem, but be a slightly simpler or slightly smaller version of the original problem. Because this new problem looks like the original problem, the method invokes (calls) a fresh copy of itself to go to work on the smaller problem; this procedure is referred to as a *recursive call* and is also called the *recursion step*. The recursion step also normally includes the keyword **return**, because its result will be combined with the portion of the problem the method knew how to solve to form a result that will be passed back to the original caller.

The recursion step executes while the original call to the method is still open (i.e., while it has not finished executing). The recursion step can result in many more recursive calls, as the method divides each new subproblem into two conceptual pieces. For the recursion eventually to terminate, each time the method calls itself with a slightly simpler version of the original problem, the sequence of smaller and smaller problems must converge on the base case. At that point, the method recognizes the base case, and returns a result to the previous copy of the method, and a sequence of returns ensues up the line until the original method call eventually returns the final result to the caller. This process sounds exotic when compared with the conventional problem solving we have performed to this point. As an example of these concepts at work, let us write a recursive program to perform a popular mathematical calculation.

The factorial of a nonnegative integer *n*, written *n!* (and pronounced "*n* factorial"), is the product

$$n \cdot (n - 1) \cdot (n - 2) \cdot \ldots \cdot 1$$

where 1! is equal to 1 and 0! is defined to be 1. For example, 5! is the product $5 \cdot 4 \cdot 3 \cdot 2 \cdot 1$, which is equal to 120.

The factorial of an integer, **number**, greater than or equal to 0, can be calculated *iteratively* (nonrecursively) using the **for** structure as follows:

```
factorial = 1;

for ( int counter = number; counter >= 1; counter-- )
   factorial *= counter;
```

A recursive definition of the factorial method is arrived at by observing the following relationship:

$$n! = n \cdot (n - 1)!$$

For example, 5! is clearly equal to 5 * 4!, as is shown by the following equations:

$$5! = 5 \cdot 4 \cdot 3 \cdot 2 \cdot 1$$
$$5! = 5 \cdot (4 \cdot 3 \cdot 2 \cdot 1)$$
$$5! = 5 \cdot (4!)$$

The evaluation of 5! would proceed as shown in Fig. 6.11. Figure 6.11 (a) shows how the succession of recursive calls proceeds until 1! is evaluated to be 1, which terminates the recursion. Figure 6.11 (b) shows the values returned from each recursive call to its caller until the final value is calculated and returned.

Figure 6.12 uses recursion to calculate and print the factorials of the integers from 0 to 10. (The choice of the data type **`long`** will be explained momentarily.) The recursive method **`factorial`** (lines 29–39) first tests to determine whether a terminating condition (line 32) is **`true`**. If **`number`** is less than or equal to **`1`** (the base case), **`factorial`** returns **`1`**, no further recursion is necessary and the method returns. If **`number`** is greater than **`1`**, line 37 expresses the problem as the product of **`number`** and a recursive call to **`factorial`** evaluating the factorial of **`number - 1`**. Note that **`factorial( number - 1 )`** is a slightly simpler problem than the original calculation **`factorial( number )`**.

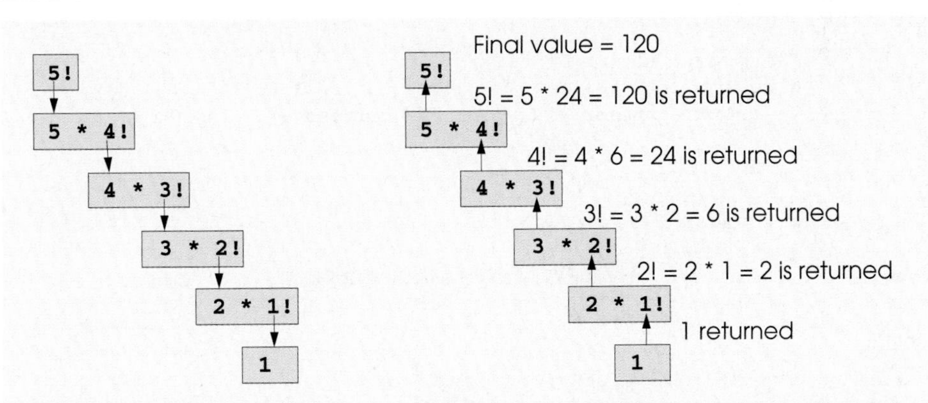

(a) Procession of recursive calls. (b) Values returned from each recursive call.

Fig. 6.11 Recursive evaluation of 5!.

```
1  // Fig. 6.12: FactorialTest.java
2  // Recursive factorial method
3
4  // Java core packages
5  import java.awt.*;
6
```

Fig. 6.12 Calculating factorials with a recursive method (part 1 of 2).

```
7  // Java extension packages
8  import javax.swing.*;
9
10 public class FactorialTest extends JApplet {
11    JTextArea outputArea;
12
13    // initialize applet by creating GUI and calculating factorials
14    public void init()
15    {
16       outputArea = new JTextArea();
17
18       Container container = getContentPane();
19       container.add( outputArea );
20
21       // calculate the factorials of 0 through 10
22       for ( long counter = 0; counter <= 10; counter++ )
23          outputArea.append( counter + "! = " +
24             factorial( counter ) + "\n" );
25
26    } // end method init
27
28    // Recursive definition of method factorial
29    public long factorial( long number )
30    {
31       // base case
32       if ( number <= 1 )
33          return 1;
34
35       // recursive step
36       else
37          return number * factorial( number - 1 );
38
39    } // end method factorial
40
41 } // end class FactorialTest
```

```
Applet Viewer: FactorialTest.class
Applet
0! = 1
1! = 1
2! = 2
3! = 6
4! = 24
5! = 120
6! = 720
7! = 5040
8! = 40320
9! = 362880
10! = 3628800

Applet started.
```

Fig. 6.12 Calculating factorials with a recursive method (part 2 of 2).

Method **factorial** (line 29) receives a parameter of type **long** and returns a result of type **long**. As can be seen in Fig. 6.12, factorial values become large quickly. We chose data type **long** so the program can calculate factorials greater than 20!. Unfortunately, the

factorial method produces large values so quickly that even **long** does not help us print many factorial values before the values exceed the size that can be stored in a **long** variable.

We explore in the exercises the fact that **float** and **double** may ultimately be needed by users desiring to calculate factorials of larger numbers. This situation points to a weakness in most programming languages, namely, that the languages are not easily extended to handle the unique requirements of various applications. As we will see in Chapter 9, Object-Oriented Programming, Java is an extensible language that allows us to create arbitrarily large integers if we wish. In fact, package **java.math** provides two classes—**BigInteger** and **BigDecimal**—explicitly for mathematical calculations of arbitrary precision that cannot be represented with Java's primitive data types.

Common Programming Error 6.15

Either omitting the base case or writing the recursion step incorrectly so that it does not converge on the base case will cause infinite recursion, eventually exhausting memory. This error is analogous to the problem of an infinite loop in an iterative (nonrecursive) solution.

6.13 Example Using Recursion: The Fibonacci Series

The Fibonacci series,

0, 1, 1, 2, 3, 5, 8, 13, 21, ...

begins with 0 and 1 and has the property that each subsequent Fibonacci number is the sum of the previous two Fibonacci numbers.

The series occurs in nature and, in particular, describes a form of spiral. The ratio of successive Fibonacci numbers converges on a constant value of 1.618.... This number, too, repeatedly occurs in nature and has been called the *golden ratio*, or the *golden mean*. Humans tend to find the golden mean aesthetically pleasing. Architects often design windows, rooms and buildings whose length and width are in the ratio of the golden mean. Postcards are often designed with a golden-mean length/width ratio.

The Fibonacci series may be defined recursively as follows:

$$\text{fibonacci}(0) = 0$$
$$\text{fibonacci}(1) = 1$$
$$\text{fibonacci}(n) = \text{fibonacci}(n-1) + \text{fibonacci}(n-2)$$

Note that there are two base cases for the Fibonacci calculation: fibonacci(0) is defined to be 0, and fibonacci(1) is defined to be 1. The applet of Fig. 6.13 calculates the ith Fibonacci number recursively, using method **fibonacci** (lines 68–78). The applet enables the user to input an integer in a **JTextField**. The value input indicates the ith Fibonacci number to calculate. When the user presses the *Enter* key, method **actionPerformed** executes in response to the user interface event and calls method **fibonacci** to calculate the specified Fibonacci number. Fibonacci numbers tend to become large quickly. Therefore, we use data type **long** as the parameter type and the return type of **fibonacci**. In Fig. 6.13, the screen captures show the results of calculating several Fibonacci numbers.

Once again, method **init** of this applet creates the GUI components and attaches them to the applet's content pane. The layout manager for the content pane is set to **FlowLayout** at line 22.

The event handling in this example is similar to the event handling of the **Craps** applet in Fig. 6.9. Line 34 specifies that **this** applet should listen for events from the **JTextField numberField**. Remember, the **this** keyword enables the applet to refer to itself. So, in line 34, the applet is telling **numberField** that the applet should be notified (with a call to the applet's **actionPerformed** method) when an action event occurs in the **numberField**. In this example, the user presses the *Enter* key while typing in the **numberField** to generate the action event. A message is then sent to the applet (i.e., a method—**actionPerformed**—is called on the applet) indicating that the user of the program has interacted with one of the program's GUI components (**numberField**). Remember that the statement to register the applet as the **numberField**'s listener will compile only if the applet class also implements **ActionListener** (line 12).

```
1   // Fig. 6.13: FibonacciTest.java
2   // Recursive fibonacci method
3
4   // Java core packages
5   import java.awt.*;
6   import java.awt.event.*;
7
8   // Java extension packages
9   import javax.swing.*;
10
11  public class FibonacciTest extends JApplet
12     implements ActionListener {
13
14     JLabel numberLabel, resultLabel;
15     JTextField numberField, resultField;
16
17     // set up applet's GUI
18     public void init()
19     {
20        // obtain content pane and set its layout to FlowLayout
21        Container container = getContentPane();
22        container.setLayout( new FlowLayout() );
23
24        // create numberLabel and attach it to content pane
25        numberLabel =
26           new JLabel( "Enter an integer and press Enter" );
27        container.add( numberLabel );
28
29        // create numberField and attach it to content pane
30        numberField = new JTextField( 10 );
31        container.add( numberField );
32
33        // register this applet as numberField's ActionListener
34        numberField.addActionListener( this );
35
36        // create resultLabel and attach it to content pane
37        resultLabel = new JLabel( "Fibonacci value is" );
38        container.add( resultLabel );
39
```

Fig. 6.13 Recursively generating Fibonacci numbers (part 1 of 3).

```
      // create numberField, make it uneditable
      // and attach it to content pane
      resultField = new JTextField( 15 );
      resultField.setEditable( false );
      container.add( resultField );

   }  // end method init

   // obtain user input and call method fibonacci
   public void actionPerformed( ActionEvent e )
   {
      long number, fibonacciValue;

      // obtain user's input and conver to long
      number = Long.parseLong( numberField.getText() );

      showStatus( "Calculating ..." );

      // calculate fibonacci value for number user input
      fibonacciValue = fibonacci( number );

      // indicate processing complete and display result
      showStatus( "Done." );
      resultField.setText( Long.toString( fibonacciValue ) );

   }  // end method actionPerformed

   // Recursive definition of method fibonacci
   public long fibonacci( long n )
   {
      // base case
      if ( n == 0 || n == 1 )
         return n;

      // recursive step
      else
         return fibonacci( n - 1 ) + fibonacci( n - 2 );

   }  // end method fibonacci

}  // end class FibonacciTest
```

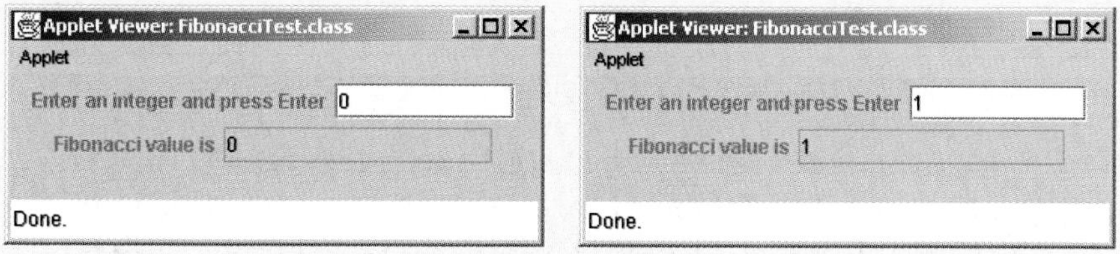

Applet Viewer: FibonacciTest.class
Applet
Enter an integer and press Enter 0
Fibonacci value is 0
Done.

Applet Viewer: FibonacciTest.class
Applet
Enter an integer and press Enter 1
Fibonacci value is 1
Done.

Fig. 6.13 Recursively generating Fibonacci numbers (part 2 of 3).

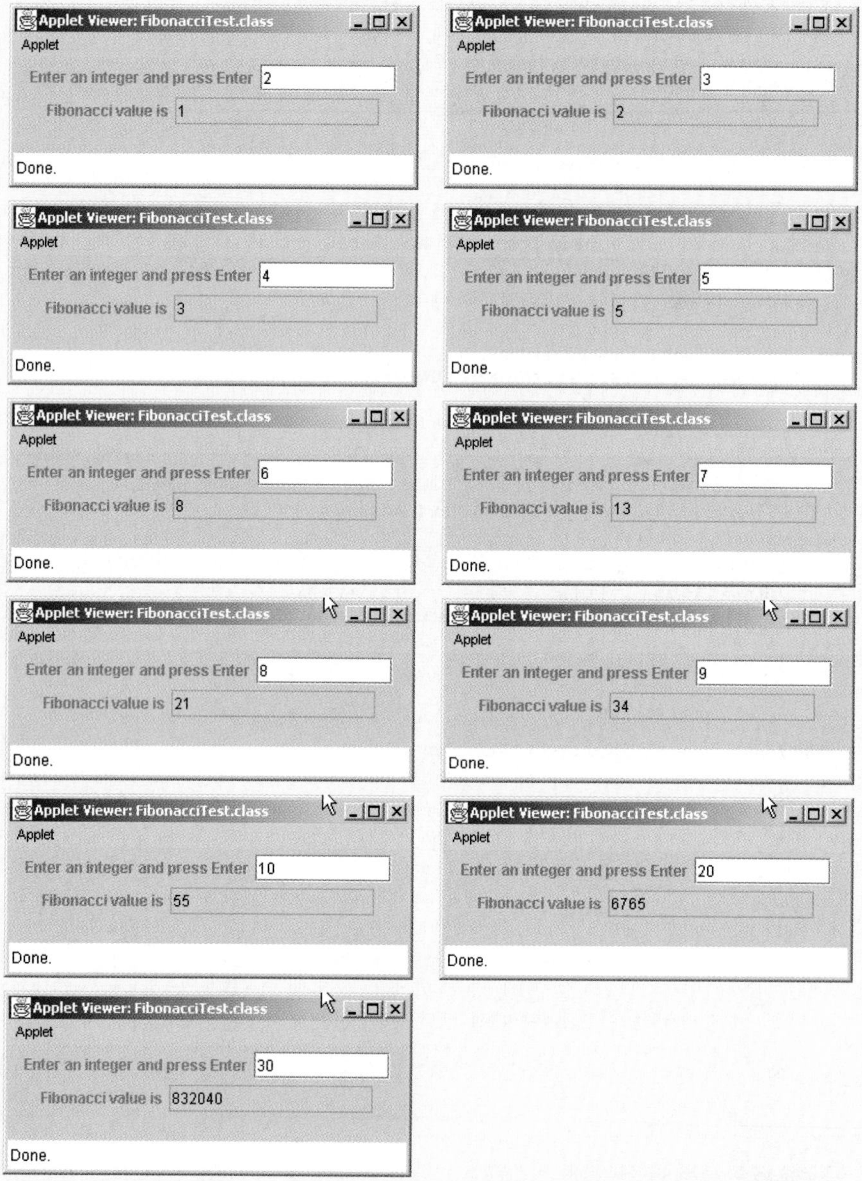

Fig. 6.13 Recursively generating Fibonacci numbers (part 3 of 3).

The call to **fibonacci** (line 59) from **actionPerformed** is not a recursive call, but all subsequent calls to **fibonacci** performed from the body of **fibonacci** are recursive. Each time **fibonacci** is invoked, it immediately tests for the base case—**n** equal to 0 or 1. If this condition is true, **fibonacci** returns **n** (fibonacci(0) is 0, and fibonacci(1) is 1). Interestingly, if **n** is greater than 1, the recursion step generates *two* recursive calls, each for a slightly simpler problem than the original call to **fibonacci**.

Figure 6.14 shows how method **fibonacci** evaluates **fibonacci(3)**. In the figure, **f** is an abbreviation for **fibonacci**.

Figure 6.14 raises some interesting issues about the order in which Java compilers evaluate the operands of operators. This issue is different than the order in which operators are applied to their operands, namely the order dictated by the rules of operator precedence. From Fig. 6.14, it appears that while **f(3)** is being evaluated, two recursive calls will be made, namely **f(2)** and **f(1)**. But in what order will these calls be made? Most programmers assume that the operands will be evaluated left to right. In Java, this assumption is true.

The C and C++ languages (on which many of Java's features are based) do not specify the order in which the operands of most operators (including **+**) are evaluated. Therefore, the programmer can make no assumption in those languages about the order in which the calls in this example execute. The calls could, in fact, execute **f(2)** first and **f(1)** second, or the calls could be executed in the reverse order: **f(1)**, then **f(2)**. In this program and in most other programs, it turns out that the final result would be the same for either case. But in some programs, the evaluation of an operand may have *side effects* that could affect the final result of the expression.

The Java language specifies that the order of evaluation of the operands is from left to right. Thus, the method calls are in fact **f(2)** first and **f(1)** second.

Good Programming Practice 6.8

Do not write expressions that depend on the order of evaluation of the operands of an operator. Use of such expressions often results in programs that are difficult to read, debug, modify and maintain.

A word of caution is in order about recursive programs like the one we use here to generate Fibonacci numbers. Each invocation of the **fibonacci** method that does not match one of the base cases (i.e., 0 or 1) results in two more recursive calls to the **fibonacci** method. This set of recursive calls rapidly gets out of hand. Calculating the Fibonacci value of 20 using the program in Fig. 6.13 requires 21,891 calls to the **fibonacci** method; calculating the Fibonacci value of 30 requires 2,692,537 calls to the **fibonacci** method.

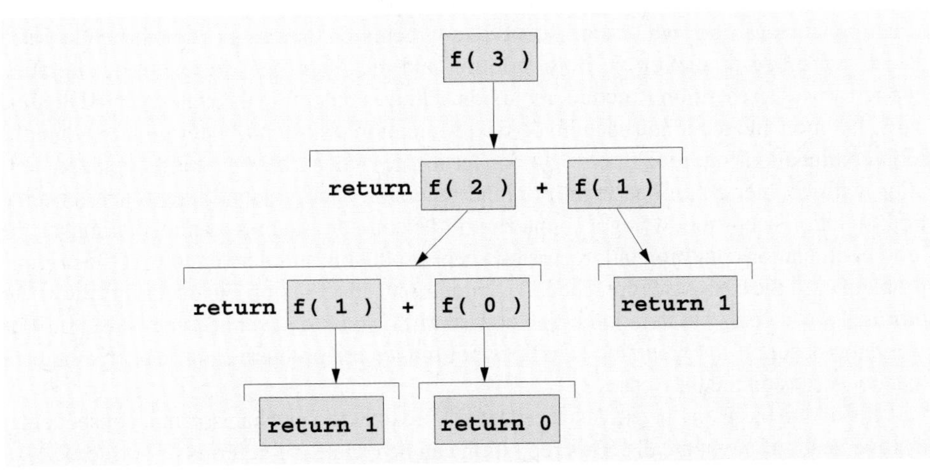

Fig. 6.14 Set of recursive calls to method **fibonacci** (**f** in this diagram).

As you try calculate larger Fibonacci values, you will notice that each consecutive Fibonacci number you ask the applet to calculate results in a substantial increase in calculation time and number of calls to the **fibonacci** method. For example, the Fibonacci value of 31 requires 4,356,617 calls, and the Fibonacci value of 32 requires 7,049,155 calls. As you can see, the number of calls to **fibonacci** is increasing quickly—1,664,080 additional calls between Fibonacci values of 30 and 31 and 2,692,538 additional calls between Fibonacci values of 31 and 32. This difference in number of calls made between Fibonacci values of 31 and 32 is more than 1.5 times the number of calls for Fibonacci values between 30 and 31. Problems of this nature humble even the world's most powerful computers! In the field of complexity theory, computer scientists study how hard algorithms work to complete their tasks. Complexity issues are discussed in detail in the upper-level computer science curriculum course generally called "Algorithms."

Performance Tip 6.3

Avoid Fibonacci-style recursive programs, which result in an exponential "explosion" of calls.

Testing and Debugging Tip 6.3

Try enhancing the Fibonacci program of Fig. 6.13 such that it calculates the approximate amount of time required to perform the calculation. For this purpose, call **static System** *method* **getCurrentTimeMillis***, which takes no arguments and returns the computer's current time in milliseconds. Call this method twice—once before the call to* **fibonacci** *and once after the call to* **fibonacci***. Save each of these values and calculate the difference in the times to determine how many milliseconds were required to perform the calculation. Display this result.*

6.14 Recursion vs. Iteration

In the previous sections, we studied two methods that can easily be implemented either recursively or iteratively. In this section,we compare the two approaches and discuss why the programmer might choose one approach over the other in a particular situation.

Both iteration and recursion are based on a control structure: Iteration uses a repetition structure (such as **for**, **while** or **do/while**); recursion uses a selection structure (such as **if**, **if/else** or **switch**). Both iteration and recursion involve repetition: Iteration explicitly uses a repetition structure; recursion achieves repetition through repeated method calls. Iteration and recursion each involve a termination test: Iteration terminates when the loop-continuation condition fails; recursion terminates when a base case is recognized. Iteration with counter-controlled repetition and recursion each gradually approach termination: Iteration keeps modifying a counter until the counter assumes a value that makes the loop-continuation condition fail; recursion keeps producing simpler versions of the original problem until the base case is reached. Both iteration and recursion can occur infinitely: An infinite loop occurs with iteration if the loop-continuation test never becomes false; infinite recursion occurs if the recursion step does not reduce the problem each time in a manner that converges on the base case.

Recursion has many negatives. It repeatedly invokes the mechanism and, consequently the overhead, of method calls. This repetition can be expensive in terms of both processor time and memory space. Each recursive call causes another copy of the method (actually, only the method's variables) to be created; this set of copies can consume considerable memory space. Iteration normally occurs within a method, so the overhead of repeated method calls and extra memory assignment is omitted. So why choose recursion?

Software Engineering Observation 6.10

Any problem that can be solved recursively can also be solved iteratively (nonrecursively). A recursive approach is normally preferred over an iterative approach when the recursive approach more naturally mirrors the problem and results in a program that is easier to understand and debug. Often, a recursive approach can be implemented with few lines of code and a corresponding iterative approach may take large amounts of code. Another reason to choose a recursive solution is that an iterative solution may not be apparent.

Performance Tip 6.4

Avoid using recursion in situations requiring performance. Recursive calls take time and consume additional memory.

Common Programming Error 6.16

Accidentally having a nonrecursive method call itself either directly or indirectly through another method can cause infinite recursion.

Most programming textbooks introduce recursion much later than we have done here. We feel that recursion is a sufficiently rich and complex topic that it is better to introduce it earlier and spread examples of it over the remainder of the text. Figure 6.15 summarizes the recursion examples and exercises in this text.

Chapter	Recursion examples and exercises
6	Factorial method
	Fibonacci method
	Greatest common divisor
	Sum of two integers
	Multiply two integers
	Raising an integer to an integer power
	Towers of Hanoi
	Visualizing recursion
7	Sum the elements of an array
	Print an array
	Print an array backward
	Check if a string is a palindrome
	Minimum value in an array
	Selection sort
	Eight Queens
	Linear search
	Binary search
	Quicksort
	Maze traversal
10	Printing a string input at the keyboard backward

Fig. 6.15 Summary of recursion examples and exercises in this text (part 1 of 2).

Chapter	Recursion examples and exercises
19	Linked-list insert Linked-list delete Search a linked list Print a linked list backward Binary-tree insert Preorder traversal of a binary tree Inorder traversal of a binary tree Postorder traversal of a binary tree

Fig. 6.15 Summary of recursion examples and exercises in this text (part 2 of 2).

Let us reconsider some observations we make repeatedly throughout this book. Good software engineering is important. High performance is often important. Unfortunately, these goals are often at odds with one another. Good software engineering is key to making more manageable the task of developing larger and more complex software systems. High performance in these systems is key to realizing the systems of the future, which will place ever greater computing demands on hardware. Where do methods fit in here?

Software Engineering Observation 6.11

Modularizing programs in a neat, hierarchical manner promotes good software engineering. But it has a price.

Performance Tip 6.5

A heavily modularized program—as compared with a monolithic (i.e., one-piece) program without methods—makes potentially large numbers of method calls, which consume execution time and space on a computer's processor(s). But monolithic programs are difficult to program, test, debug, maintain and evolve.

So modularize your programs judiciously, always keeping in mind the delicate balance between performance and good software engineering.

6.15 Method Overloading

Java enables several methods of the same name to be defined, as long as the methods have different sets of parameters (based on the number of parameters, the types of the parameters and the order of the parameters). This characteristic is called *method overloading*. When an overloaded method is called, the Java compiler selects the proper method by examining the number, types and order of the arguments in the call. Method overloading is commonly used to create several methods with the same name that perform similar tasks, but on different data types.

Good Programming Practice 6.9

Overloading methods that perform closely related tasks can make programs more readable and understandable.

Figure 6.16 uses overloaded method **`square`** to calculate the square of an **`int`** and the square of a **`double`**.

```
// Fig. 6.16: MethodOverload.java
// Using overloaded methods

// Java core packages
import java.awt.Container;

// Java extension packages
import javax.swing.*;

public class MethodOverload extends JApplet {

   // set up GUI and call versions of method square
   public void init()
   {
      JTextArea outputArea = new JTextArea();
      Container container = getContentPane();
      container.add( outputArea );

      outputArea.setText(
         "The square of integer 7 is " + square( 7 ) +
         "\nThe square of double 7.5 is " + square( 7.5 ) );
   }

   // square method with int argument
   public int square( int intValue )
   {
      System.out.println(
         "Called square with int argument: " + intValue );

      return intValue * intValue;

   }  // end method square with int argument

   // square method with double argument
   public double square( double doubleValue )
   {
      System.out.println(
         "Called square with double argument: " + doubleValue );

      return doubleValue * doubleValue;

   }  // end method square with double argument

}  // end class MethodOverload
```

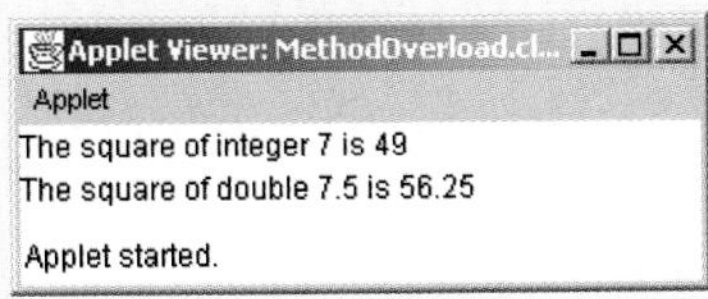

Fig. 6.16 Using overloaded methods (part 1 of 2).

```
Called square with int argument: 7
Called square with double argument: 7.5
```

Fig. 6.16 Using overloaded methods (part 2 of 2).

Overloaded methods are distinguished by their *signature*—a combination of the method's name and its parameter types. If the Java compiler looked only at method names during compilation, the code in Fig. 6.16 would be ambiguous—the compiler would not know how to distinguish between the two **square** methods. Logically, the compiler uses longer "mangled" or "decorated" names that include the original method name, the types of each parameter and the exact order of the parameters to determine if the methods in a class are unique in that class.

For example, in Fig. 6.16, the compiler might use the logical name "square of int" for the **square** method that specifies an **int** parameter and "square of double" for the **square** method that specifies a **double** parameter. If a method **foo**'s definition begins as

```
void foo( int a, float b )
```

then the compiler might use the logical name "foo of int and float." If the parameters are specified as

```
void foo( float a, int b )
```

then the compiler might use the logical name "foo of float and int." Note that the order of the parameters is important to the compiler. The preceding two **foo** methods are considered to be distinct by the compiler.

The logical names of methods used by the compiler did not mention the return types of the methods, because methods cannot be distinguished by return type. The program in Fig. 6.17 illustrates the compiler errors generated when two methods have the same signature and different return types. Overloaded methods can have different return types, but must have different parameter lists. Also, overloaded methods need not have the same number of parameters.

Common Programming Error 6.17

Creating overloaded methods with identical parameter lists and different return types is a syntax error.

```
// Fig. 6.17: MethodOverload.java
// Overloaded methods with identical signatures and
// different return types.

// Java extension packages
import javax.swing.JApplet;

```

Fig. 6.17 Compiler error messages generated from overloaded methods with identical parameter lists and different return types (part 1 of 2).

```
public class MethodOverload extends JApplet {

   // first definition of method square with double argument
   public int square( double x )
   {
      return x * x;
   }

   // second definition of method square with double argument
   // causes syntax error
   public double square( double y )
   {
      return y * y;
   }

}  // end class MethodOverload
```

```
MethodOverload.java:18: square(double) is already defined in
MethodOverload
   public double square( double y )
                 ^
MethodOverload.java:13: possible loss of precision
found    : double
required: int
      return x * x;
               ^
2 errors
```

Fig. 6.17 Compiler error messages generated from overloaded methods with identical parameter lists and different return types (part 2 of 2).

6.16 Methods of Class JApplet

We have written many applets to this point in the text, but we have not yet discussed the key methods of class **`JApplet`** that the applet container calls during the execution of an applet. Figure 6.18 lists the key methods of class **`JApplet`**, specifies when they get called and explains the purpose of each method.

These **`JApplet`** methods are defined by the Java API to do nothing unless you provide a definition in your applet's class definition. If you would like to use one of these methods in an applet you are defining, you *must* define the first line of each method as shown in Fig. 6.18. Otherwise, the applet container will not call your versions of the methods during the applet's execution. Defining the methods as discussed here is known as *overriding* the original method definition. The applet container will call the overridden version of a method for your applet before it attempts to call the default versions inherited from **`JApplet`**. Overriding is discussed in detail in Chapter 9.

Common Programming Error 6.18

Providing a definition for one of the **`JApplet`** *methods* **`init`**, **`start`**, **`paint`**, **`stop`** *or* **`destroy`** *that does not match the method headers shown in Figure 6.18 results in a method that will not be called automatically during execution of the applet.*

Method	When the method is called and its purpose
`public void init()`	This method is called once by the **`appletviewer`** or browser when an applet is loaded for execution. It performs initialization of an applet. Typical actions performed here are initialization of instance variables and GUI components of the applet, loading of sounds to play or images to display (see Chapter 18, Multimedia) and creation of threads (see Chapter 15, Multithreading).
`public void start()`	This method is called after the **`init`** method completes execution and every time the user of the browser returns to the HTML page on which the applet resides (after browsing another HTML page). This method performs any tasks that must be completed when the applet is loaded for the first time into the browser and that must be performed every time the HTML page on which the applet resides is revisited. Typical actions performed here include starting an animation see (Chapter 18, Multimedia) and starting other threads of execution (see Chapter 15, Multithreading).
`public void paint( Graphics g )`	This method is called after the **`init`** method completes execution and the **`start`** method has started executing to draw on the applet. It is also called automatically every time the applet needs to be repainted. For example, if the user covers the applet with another open window on the screen then uncovers the applet, the **`paint`** method is called. Typical actions performed here involve drawing with the **`Graphics`** object **`g`** that is automatically passed to the **`paint`** method for you.
`public void stop()`	This method is called when the applet should stop executing—normally, when the user of the browser leaves the HTML page on which the applet resides. This method performs any tasks that are required to suspend the applet's execution. Typical actions performed here are to stop execution of animations and threads.
`public void destroy()`	This method is called when the applet is being removed from memory—normally, when the user of the browser exits the browsing session. This method performs any tasks that are required to destroy resources allocated to the applet.

Fig. 6.18 **`JApplet`** methods that the applet container calls during an applet's execution .

Method ***`repaint`*** is also of interest to many applet programmers. The applet's **`paint`** method normally is called by the applet container. What if you would like to change the appearance of the applet in response to the user's interactions with the applet? In such situations, you may want to call **`paint`** directly. However, to call **`paint`**, we must pass it the **`Graphics`** parameter it expects. This requirement poses a problem for us. We do not have a **`Graphics`** object at our disposal to pass to **`paint`**. (We discuss this issue in Chapter 18, Multimedia.) For this reason, class **`JApplet`** provides method **`repaint`**. The statement

```
repaint();
```

obtains the **Graphics** object for you and invokes another method, called ***update***. Method **update** invokes method **paint** and passes to it the **Graphics** object. The **repaint** method is discussed in detail in Chapter 18, "Multimedia."

6.17 (Optional Case Study) Thinking About Objects: Identifying Class Operations

In the "Thinking About Objects" sections at the ends of Chapters 3, 4 and 5, we performed the first few steps in the object-oriented design for our elevator simulator. In Chapter 3, we identified the classes we need to implement. In Chapter 4, we created a class diagram that models the structure of our system. In Chapter 5, we examined objects' states and modeled objects' activities and state transitions.

In this section, we concentrate on determining the class *operations* (or *behaviors*) needed to implement the elevator simulator. In Chapter 7, we concentrate on the collaborations (interactions) between objects of our classes.

An operation of a class is a service that the class provides to "clients" (users) of that class. Consider the operations of some real-world classes. A radio's operations include setting its station and volume (typically invoked by a person adjusting the radio's controls). A car's operations include accelerating (invoked by the driver pressing the accelerator pedal), decelerating (invoked by the driver pressing the brake pedal and/or releasing the gas pedal), turning and shifting gears.

We can derive many of the operations of each class directly from the problem statement. To do so, we examine the verbs and verb phrases in the problem statement. We then relate each of these to particular classes in our system (Fig. 6.19). Many of the verb phrases in Fig. 6.19 help us determine the operations of our classes.

Class	Verb phrases
Elevator	moves to other floor, arrives at a floor, resets elevator button, rings elevator bell, signals its arrival, opens its door, closes its door
ElevatorShaft	turns off light, turns on light, resets floor button
Person	walks on floor, presses floor button, presses elevator button, rides elevator, enters elevator, exits elevator
Floor	[none in the problem statement]
FloorButton	requests elevator
ElevatorButton	closes elevator door, signals elevator to move to opposite floor
FloorDoor	signals person to enter elevator (by opening)
ElevatorDoor	signals person to exit elevator (by opening), opens floor door, closes floor door
Bell	[none in the problem statement]
Light	[none in the problem statement]
ElevatorModel	creates person

Fig. 6.19 Verb phrases for each class in simulator.

To create operations, we examine the verb phrases listed with each class. The phrase "moves to other floor" listed with class **Elevator** refers to the activity in which the elevator moves between floors. Should "moves" be an operation of class **Elevator**? The elevator decides to move in response to a button press. A button *signals* the elevator to move, but a button does not actually *move* the elevator—therefore, "moves to other floor" does not correspond to an operation. (We include the operations for informing the elevator to move to the other floor later in the discussion, when we discuss the verb phrases associated with the buttons.) The "arrives at a floor" phrase is also not an operation, because the elevator itself decides when to arrive on the floor after five seconds of travel.

The "resets elevator button" phrase associated with class **Elevator** implies that the elevator informs the elevator button to reset. Therefore, class **ElevatorButton** needs an operation to provide this service to the elevator. We place this operation (**resetButton**) in the bottom compartment of class **ElevatorButton** in our class diagram (Fig. 6.20).

We represent the names of the operations as method names (by following the names with a pair of parentheses) and include the return type after the colon:

```
resetButton() : void
```

The parentheses can contain a comma-separated list of the parameters that the operation takes—in this case, none. For the moment, most of our operations have no parameters and a **void** return type; this might change as our design and implementation processes proceed.

ElevatorModel
numberOfPeople : Integer=0
addPerson( ) : void

ElevatorShaft
<none yet>
<none yet>

ElevatorDoor
open : Boolean = false
openDoor( ) : void closeDoor( ) : void

Person
ID : Integer moving : Boolean = true
doorOpened( ) : void

Floor
floorNumber : Integer capacity : Integer = 1
<none yet>

Light
lightOn : Boolean = false
turnOnLight( ) : void turnOffLight( ) : void

Elevator
moving : Boolean = false summoned : Boolean = false currentFloor : Integer = 1 destinationFloor : Integer = 2 capacity : Integer = 1 travelTime : Integer = 5
ride( ) : void requestElevator( ) : void enterElevator( ) : void exitElevator( ) : void departElevator( ) : void

ElevatorButton
pressed : Boolean = false
resetButton( ) : void pressButton( ) : void

Bell
<none yet>
ringBell( ) : void

FloorButton
pressed : Boolean = false
resetButton( ) : void pressButton( ) : void

FloorDoor
open : Boolean = false
openDoor( ) : void closeDoor( ) : void

Fig. 6.20 Classes with attributes and operations.

From the "ring the elevator bell" phrase listed with class **Elevator**, we conclude that class **Bell** should have an operation that provides a service—namely, ringing. We list the **ringBell** operation under class **Bell**.

When arriving at a floor, the elevator "signals its arrival" to the doors. The elevator door responds by opening, as implied by the phrase "opens [the elevator's] door" associated with class **Elevator**. Therefore, class **ElevatorDoor** needs an operation that opens its door. We place the **openDoor** operation in the bottom compartment of this class. The phrase "closes [the elevator's] door" indicates that class **ElevatorDoor** needs an operation that closes its door, so we place the **closeDoor** operation in the same compartment.

Class **ElevatorShaft** lists "turns off light" and "turns on light" in its verb-phrases column, so we create the **turnOffLight** and **turnOnLight** operations and list them under class **Light**. The "resets floor button" phrase implies that the elevator instructs a floor button to reset. Therefore, class **FloorButton** needs a **resetButton** operation.

The phrase "walks on floor" listed by class **Person** is not an operation, because a person decides to walk across the floor in response to that person's creation. However, the phrases "presses floor button" and "presses elevator button" are operations pertaining to the button classes. We therefore place the **pressButton** operation under classes **FloorButton** and **ElevatorButton** in our class diagram (Fig. 6.20). The phrase "rides elevator" implies that **Elevator** needs a method that allows a person to ride the elevator, so we place operation **ride** in the bottom compartment of **Elevator**. The "enters elevator" and "exits elevator" phrases listed with class **Person** suggest that class **Elevator** needs operations that correspond to these actions.[1] We place operations **enterElevator** and **exitElevator** in the bottom compartment of class **Elevator**.

The "requests elevator" phrase listed under class **FloorButton** implies that class **Elevator** needs a **requestElevator** operation. The phrase "signals elevator to move to opposite floor" listed with class **ElevatorButton** implies that **ElevatorButton** informs **Elevator** to depart. Therefore, the **Elevator** needs to provide a "departure" service; we place a **departElevator** operation in the bottom compartment of **Elevator**.

The phrases listed with classes **FloorDoor** and **ElevatorDoor** mention that the doors—by opening—signal a **Person** object to enter or exit the elevator. Specifically, a door informs a person that the door has opened. (The person then enters or exits the elevator, accordingly.) We place the **doorOpened** operation in the bottom compartment for class **Person**. In addition, the **ElevatorDoor** opens and closes the **FloorDoor**, so we assign **openDoor** and **closeDoor** to the bottom compartment of class **FloorDoor**.

Lastly, the "creates person" action associated with class **ElevatorModel** refers to creating a **Person** object and adding it to the simulation. Although we can require **ElevatorModel** to send a "create person" and an "add person" message, an object of class **Person** cannot respond to these messages, because that object does not yet exist. We discuss new objects when we consider implementation in Chapter 8. We place the operation **addPerson** in the bottom compartment of **ElevatorModel** in the class diagram of Fig. 6.20 and anticipate that the application user will invoke this operation.

---

1. At this point, we can only guess what these operations do. For example, perhaps these operations model real-world elevators, some of which have sensors that detect when passengers enter and exit. For now, we simply list these operations. We will discover what, if any, actions these operations perform as we continue our design process.

For now, we do not concern ourselves with operation parameters or return types; we attempt to gain only a basic understanding of the operations of each class. As we continue our design process, the number of operations belonging to each class may vary—we might find that new operations are needed or that some current operations are unnecessary—and we might determine that some of our class operations need non-**void** return types.

SUMMARY

- The best way to develop and maintain a large program is to divide it into several smaller modules. Modules are written in Java as classes and methods.
- A method is invoked by a method call. The method call mentions the method by name and provides arguments in parentheses that the called method requires to perform its task. If the method is in another class, the call must be preceded by a reference name and a dot operator. If the method is **static**, it must be preceded by a class name and a dot operator.
- Each argument of a method may be a constant, a variable or an expression.
- A local variable is known only in a method definition. Methods are not allowed to know the implementation details of any other method (including its local variables).
- The on-screen display area for a **JApplet** has a content pane to which the GUI components must be attached so they can be displayed at execution time. The content pane is an object of class **Container** from the **java.awt** package.
- Method **getContentPane** of class **JApplet** returns a reference to the applet's content pane.
- The general format for a method definition is

  return-value-type method-name **(** *parameter-list* **)**
  {
  declarations and statements
  }

  The *return-value-type* states the type of the value returned to the calling method. If a method does not return a value, the *return-value-type* is **void**. The *method-name* is any valid identifier. The *parameter-list* is a comma-separated list containing the declarations of the variables that will be passed to the method. If a method does not receive any values, *parameter-list* is empty. The method body is the set of *declarations and statements* that constitute the method.
- The arguments passed to a method should match in number, type and order with the parameters in the method definition.
- When a program encounters a method, control transfers from the point of invocation to the called method, the method executes and control returns to the caller.
- A called method can return control to the caller in one of three ways. If the method does not return a value, control returns at the method-ending right brace or by executing the statement

  return;

  If the method does return a value, the statement

  return *expression***;**

  returns the value of *expression*.
- There are three ways to call a method—the method name by itself, a reference to an object followed by the dot (**.**) operator and the method name, and a class name followed by the dot (**.**) operator and a method name. The last syntax is for **static** methods of a class.

- An important feature of method definitions is the coercion of arguments. In many cases, argument values that do not correspond precisely to the parameter types in the method definition are converted to the proper type before the method is called. In some cases, these conversions can lead to compiler errors if Java's promotion rules are not followed.
- The promotion rules specify how types can be converted to other types without losing data. The promotion rules apply to mixed-type expressions. The type of each value in a mixed-type expression is promoted to the "highest" type in the expression.
- Method **Math.random** generates a double value from 0.0 up to, but not including, 1.0. Values produced by **Math.random** can be scaled and shifted to produce values in a range.
- The general equation for scaling and shifting a random number is

```
n = a + (int) ( Math.random() * b );
```

  where **a** is the shifting value (the first number in the desired range of consecutive integers) and **b** is the scaling factor (the width of the desired range of consecutive integers).
- A class can inherit existing attributes and behaviors (data and methods) from another class specified to the right of keyword **extends** in the class definition. In addition, a class can implement one or more *interfaces*. An interface specifies one or more behaviors (i.e., methods) that you must define in your class definition.
- The interface **ActionListener** specifies that a class must define a method with the first line

```
public void actionPerformed( ActionEvent actionEvent )
```

- The task of method **actionPerformed** is to process a user's interaction with a GUI component that generates an action event. This method is called in response to the user interaction (the event). This process is called *event handling*. The event handler is the **actionPerformed** method, which is called in response to the event. This style of programming is known as *event-driven programming*.
- Keyword **final** declares constant variables. Constant variables must be initialized before they are used in a program. Constant variables are often called *named constants* or *read-only variables*.
- A **JLabel** contains a string of characters to be displayed on the screen. Normally, a **JLabel** indicates the purpose of another GUI element on the screen.
- **JTextField**s get information from the user or displays information on the screen.
- When the user presses a **JButton**, the program normally responds by performing a task.
- **Container** method **setLayout** defines the layout manager for the applet's user interface. Layout managers are provided to arrange GUI components on a **Container** for presentation purposes.
- **FlowLayout** is the simplest layout manager. GUI components are placed on a **Container** from left to right in the order in which they are attached to the **Container** with method **add**. When the edge of the container is reached, components are continued on the next line.
- Before any event can be processed, each GUI component must know which object in the program defines the event-handling method that will be called when an event occurs. Method **addActionListener** is used to tell a **JButton** or **JTextField** that another object is listening for action events and defines method **actionPerformed**. This procedure is called *registering the event handler with the GUI component*. To respond to an action event, we must define a class that implements **ActionListener** and defines method **actionPerformed**. Also, we must register the event handler with the GUI component.
- Method **showStatus** displays a **String** in the applet container's status bar.

- Each variable identifier has the attributes duration (lifetime) and scope. An identifier's duration determines when that identifier exists in memory. An identifier's scope is where the identifier can be referenced in a program.
- Identifiers that represent local variables in a method have automatic duration. Automatic-duration variables are created when program control reaches their declaration; they exist while the block in which they are declared is active; and they are destroyed when the block in which they are declared is exited.
- Java also has identifiers of static duration. Variables and references of static duration exist from the point at which the class in which they are defined is loaded into memory for execution until the program terminates.
- The scopes for an identifier are class scope and block scope. An instance variable declared outside any method has class scope. Such an identifier is "known" in all methods of the class. Identifiers declared inside a block have block scope. Block scope ends at the terminating right brace (**}**) of the block.
- Local variables declared at the beginning of a method have block scope, as do method parameters, which are considered to be local variables of the method.
- Any block may contain variable declarations.
- A recursive method is a method that calls itself, either directly or indirectly.
- If a recursive method is called with a base case, the method returns a result. If the method is called with a more complex problem, the method divides the problem into two or more conceptual pieces: A piece that the method knows how to do and a slightly smaller version of the original problem. Because this new problem looks like the original problem, the method launches a recursive call to work on the smaller problem.
- For recursion to terminate, the sequence of smaller and smaller problems must converge to the base case. When the method recognizes the base case, the result is returned to the previous method call, and a sequence of returns ensues all the way up the line until the original call of the method returns the final result.
- Both iteration and recursion are based on a control structure: Iteration uses a repetition structure; recursion uses a selection structure.
- Both iteration and recursion involve repetition: Iteration explicitly uses a repetition structure; recursion achieves repetition through repeated method calls.
- Iteration and recursion each involve a termination test: Iteration terminates when the loop-continuation condition fails; recursion terminates when a base case is recognized.
- Iteration and recursion can occur infinitely: An infinite loop occurs with iteration if the loop-continuation test never becomes false; infinite recursion occurs if the recursion step does not reduce the problem in a manner that converges to the base case.
- Recursion repeatedly invokes the mechanism and, consequently the overhead, of method calls. This repetition can be expensive in terms of both processor time and memory space.
- The user presses the *Enter* key while typing in a **JTextField** to generate an action event. The event handling for this GUI component is set up like a **JButton**: Aclass must be defined that implements **ActionListener** and defines method **actionPerformed**. Also, the **JTextField**'s **addActionListener** method must be called to register the event.
- It is possible to define methods with the same name, but different parameter lists. This feature is called method overloading. When an overloaded method is called, the compiler selects the proper method by examining the arguments in the call.
- Overloaded methods can have different return values and must have different parameter lists. Two methods differing only by return type will result in a syntax error.

- The applet's **init** method is called once by the applet container when an applet is loaded for execution. It performs initialization of an applet. The applet's **start** method is called after the **init** method completes execution and every time the user of the browser returns to the HTML page on which the applet resides (after browsing another HTML page).
- The applet's **paint** method is called after the **init** method completes execution and the **start** method has started executing to draw on the applet. It is also called every time the applet needs to be repainted.
- The applet's **stop** method is called when the applet should suspend execution—normally, when the user of the browser leaves the HTML page on which the applet resides.
- The applet's **destroy** method is called when the applet is being removed from memory—normally, when the user of the browser exits the browsing session.
- Method **repaint** can be called in an applet to cause a fresh call to **paint**. Method **repaint** invokes another method called **update** and passes it the **Graphics** object. The **update** method invokes the **paint** method and passes it the **Graphics** object.

TERMINOLOGY

ActionEvent class
ActionListener interface
actionPerformed method
argument in a method call
automatic duration
automatic variable
base case in recursion
block
block scope
call a method
called method
caller
calling method
class
class scope
coercion of arguments
constant variable
copy of a value
destroy method of **JApplet**
divide and conquer
duration
element of chance
factorial method
final
FlowLayout class
init method of **JApplet**
invoke a method
iteration
Java API (Java class library)
JButton class of package **javax.swing**
JLabel class of package **javax.swing**
JTextField class of package **javax.swing**
local variable
Math class methods
Math.E
Math.PI
Math.random method
method
method call
method-call operator, **()**
method declaration
method definition
method overloading
mixed-type expression
modular program
named constant
overloading
paint method of **JApplet**
parameter in a method definition
programmer-defined method
promotion rules
random-number generation
read-only variable
recursion
recursion step
recursive call
recursive method
reference parameter
reference types
repaint method of **JApplet**
return
return-value type
scaling
scope
setLayout method of **JApplet**
shifting

showStatus method of **JApplet**
signature
simulation
software engineering
software reusability
start method of **JApplet**
static storage duration
stop method of **JApplet**
update method of **JApplet**
void

SELF-REVIEW EXERCISES

6.1 Fill in the blanks in each of the following statements:

a) Program modules in Java are called __________ and __________.
b) A method is invoked with a __________.
c) A variable known only within the method in which it is defined is called a __________.
d) The __________ statement in a called method can be used to pass the value of an expression back to the calling method.
e) The keyword __________ indicates that a method does not return a value.
f) The __________ of an identifier is the portion of the program in which the identifier can be used.
g) The three ways to return control from a called method to a caller are __________, __________ and __________.
h) The __________ method is invoked once when an applet begins execution.
i) The __________ method produces random numbers.
j) The __________ method is invoked each time the user of a browser revisits the HTML page on which an applet resides.
k) The __________ method is invoked to draw on an applet.
l) Variables declared in a block or in a method's parameter list are of __________ duration.
m) The __________ method invokes the applet's **update** method, which in turn invokes the applet's **paint** method.
n) The __________ method is invoked for an applet each time the user of a browser leaves an HTML page on which the applet resides.
o) A method that calls itself either directly or indirectly is a __________ method.
p) A recursive method typically has two components: one that provides a means for the recursion to terminate by testing for a __________ case and one that expresses the problem as a recursive call for a slightly simpler problem than does the original call.
q) In Java, it is possible to have various methods with the same name that each operate on different types and/or numbers of arguments. This feature is called method __________.
r) The __________ qualifier is used to declare read-only variables.

6.2 For the following program, state the scope (either class scope or block scope) of each of the following elements:

a) the variable **x**.
b) the variable **y**.
c) the method **cube**.
d) the method **paint**.
e) the variable **yPos**.

```
public class CubeTest extends JApplet {
   int x;

   public void paint( Graphics g )
   {
      int yPos = 25;
```

```
        for ( x = 1; x <= 10; x++ ) {
           g.drawString( cube( x ), 25, yPos );
           yPos += 15;
        }
    }

    public int cube( int y )
    {
        return y * y * y;
    }
}
```

6.3 Write an application that tests if the examples of the math-library method calls shown in Fig. 6.2 actually produce the indicated results.

6.4 Give the method header for each of the following methods:

a) Method **hypotenuse**, which takes two double-precision, floating-point arguments **side1** and **side2** and returns a double-precision, floating-point result.

b) Method **smallest**, which takes three integers **x**, **y** and **z** and returns an integer.

c) Method **instructions**, which does not take any arguments and does not return a value. [*Note*: Such methods are commonly used to display instructions to a user.]

d) Method **intToFloat**, which takes an integer argument **number** and returns a floating-point result.

6.5 Find the error in each of the following program segments. Explain how to correct the error.

a)
```
int g() {
   System.out.println( "Inside method g" );
   int h() {
      System.out.println( "Inside method h" );
   }
}
```

b)
```
int sum( int x, int y ) {
   int result;
   result = x + y;
}
```

c)
```
int sum( int n ) {
   if ( n == 0 )
      return 0;
   else
      n + sum( n - 1 );
}
```

d)
```
void f( float a ); {
   float a;
   System.out.println( a );
}
```

e)
```
void product() {
   int a = 6, b = 5, c = 4, result;
   result = a * b * c;
   System.out.println( "Result is " + result );
   return result;
}
```

6.6 Write a complete Java applet to prompt the user for the **`double`** radius of a sphere, and call method **`sphereVolume`** to calculate and display the volume of that sphere using the assignment

```
volume = ( 4.0 / 3.0 ) * Math.PI * Math.pow( radius, 3 )
```

The user should input the radius through a **`JTextField`**.

ANSWERS TO SELF-REVIEW EXERCISES

6.1 a) methods and classes. b) method call. c) local variable. d) **`return`**. e) **`void`**. f) scope. g) **`return;`** or **`return`** *expression***`;`** or encountering the closing right brace of a method. h) **`init`**. i) **`Math.random`**. j) **`start`**. k) **`paint`**. l) automatic. m) **`repaint`**. n) **`stop`**. o) recursive. p) base. q) overloading. r) **`final`**.

6.2 a) Class scope. b) Block scope. c) Class scope. d) Class scope. e) Block scope.

6.3 The following solution demonstrates the **`Math`** class methods in Fig. 6.2:

```
// Exercise 6.3: MathTest.java
// Testing the Math class methods

public class MathTest {
   public static void main( String args[] )
   {
      System.out.println( "Math.abs( 23.7 ) = " +
                          Math.abs( 23.7 ) );
      System.out.println( "Math.abs( 0.0 ) = " +
                          Math.abs( 0.0 ) );
      System.out.println( "Math.abs( -23.7 ) = " +
                          Math.abs( -23.7 ) );
      System.out.println( "Math.ceil( 9.2 ) = " +
                          Math.ceil( 9.2 ) );
      System.out.println( "Math.ceil( -9.8 ) = " +
                          Math.ceil( -9.8 ) );
      System.out.println( "Math.cos( 0.0 ) = " +
                          Math.cos( 0.0 ) );
      System.out.println( "Math.exp( 1.0 ) = " +
                          Math.exp( 1.0 ) );
      System.out.println( "Math.exp( 2.0 ) = " +
                          Math.exp( 2.0 ) );
      System.out.println( "Math.floor( 9.2 ) = " +
                          Math.floor( 9.2 ) );
      System.out.println( "Math.floor( -9.8 ) = " +
                          Math.floor( -9.8 ) );
      System.out.println( "Math.log( 2.718282 ) = " +
                          Math.log( 2.718282 ) );
      System.out.println( "Math.log( 7.389056 ) = " +
                          Math.log( 7.389056 ) );
      System.out.println( "Math.max( 2.3, 12.7 ) = v +
                          Math.max( 2.3, 12.7 ) );
      System.out.println( "Math.max( -2.3, -12.7 ) = " +
                          Math.max( -2.3, -12.7 ) );
      System.out.println( "Math.min( 2.3, 12.7 ) = " +
                          Math.min( 2.3, 12.7 ) );
      System.out.println( "Math.min( -2.3, -12.7 ) = " +
                          Math.min( -2.3, -12.7 ) );
```

```
        System.out.println( "Math.pow( 2, 7 ) = " +
                            Math.pow( 2, 7 ) );
        System.out.println( "Math.pow( 9, .5 ) = " +
                            Math.pow( 9, .5 ) );
        System.out.println( "Math.sin( 0.0 ) = " +
                            Math.sin( 0.0 ) );
        System.out.println( "Math.sqrt( 25.0 ) = " +
                            Math.sqrt( 25.0 ) );
        System.out.println( "Math.tan( 0.0 ) = " +
                            Math.tan( 0.0 ) );
    }
}
```

```
Math.abs( 23.7 ) = 23.7
Math.abs( 0.0 ) = 0
Math.abs( -23.7 ) = 23.7
Math.ceil( 9.2 ) = 10
Math.ceil( -9.8 ) = -9
Math.cos( 0.0 ) = 1
Math.exp( 1.0 ) = 2.71828
Math.exp( 2.0 ) = 7.38906
Math.floor( 9.2 ) = 9
Math.floor( -9.8 ) = -10
Math.log( 2.718282 ) = 1
Math.log( 7.389056 ) = 2
Math.max( 2.3, 12.7 ) = 12.7
Math.max( -2.3, -12.7 ) = -2.3
Math.min( 2.3, 12.7 ) = 2.3
Math.min( -2.3, -12.7 ) = -12.7
Math.pow( 2, 7 ) = 128
Math.pow( 9, .5 ) = 3
Math.sin( 0.0 ) = 0
Math.sqrt( 25.0 ) = 5
Math.tan( 0.0 ) = 0
```

6.4
a) `double hypotenuse( double side1, double side2 )`
b) `int smallest( int x, int y, int z )`
c) `void instructions()`
d) `float intToFloat( int number )`

6.5
a) Error: Method **`h`** is defined in method **`g`**.
Correction: Move the definition of **`h`** outside the definition of **`g`**.

b) Error: The method is supposed to return an integer, but does not.
Correction: Delete variable **`result`**, and place the statement

```
return x + y;
```

in the method, or add the following statement at the end of the method body:

```
return result;
```

c) Error: The result of **`n + sum( n - 1 )`** is not returned by this recursive method, resulting in a syntax error.
Correction: Rewrite the statement in the **`else`** clause as

```
return n + sum( n - 1 );
```

d) Error: Both the semicolon after the right parenthesis that encloses the parameter list and redefining the parameter **a** in the method definition are incorrect.
Correction: Delete the semicolon after the right parenthesis of the parameter list, and delete the declaration **float a;**.

e) Error: The method returns a value when it is not supposed to.
Correction: Change the return type to **int**.

6.6 The following solution calculates the volume of a sphere using the radius entered by the user:

```
// Exercise 6.6: SphereTest.java

// Java core packages
import java.awt.*;
import java.awt.event.*;

// Java extension packages
import javax.swing.*;

public class SphereTest extends JApplet
   implements ActionListener {

   JLabel promptLabel;
   JTextField inputField;

   public void init()
   {
      Container container = getContentPane();
      container.setLayout( new FlowLayout() );

      promptLabel = new JLabel( "Enter sphere radius: " );
      inputField = new JTextField( 10 );
      inputField.addActionListener( this );
      container.add( promptLabel );
      container.add( inputField );
   }

   public void actionPerformed( ActionEvent actionEvent )
   {
      double radius =
         Double.parseDouble( actionEvent.getActionCommand() );

      showStatus( "Volume is " + sphereVolume( radius ) );
   }

   public double sphereVolume( double radius )
   {
      double volume =
         ( 4.0 / 3.0 ) * Math.PI * Math.pow( radius, 3 );

      return volume;
   }
}
```

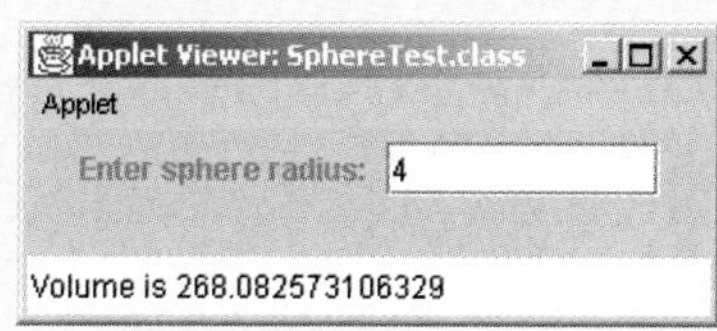

EXERCISES

6.7 What is the value of **x** after each of the following statements is performed?

a) **x = Math.abs(7.5);**
b) **x = Math.floor(7.5);**
c) **x = Math.abs(0.0);**
d) **x = Math.ceil(0.0);**
e) **x = Math.abs(-6.4);**
f) **x = Math.ceil(-6.4);**
g) **x = Math.ceil(-Math.abs(-8 + Math.floor(-5.5)));**

6.8 A parking garage charges a $2.00 minimum fee to park for up to three hours. The garage charges an additional $0.50 per hour for each hour *or part thereof* in excess of three hours. The maximum charge for any given 24-hour period is $10.00. Assume that no car parks for longer than 24 hours at a time. Write an applet that calculates and displays the parking charges for each customer who parked a car in this garage yesterday. You should enter in a **JTextField** the hours parked for each customer. The program should display the charge for the current customer and should calculate and display the running total of yesterday's receipts. The program should use the method **calculateCharges** to determine the charge for each customer.

6.9 An application of method **Math.floor** is rounding a value to the nearest integer. The statement

```
y = Math.floor( x + .5 );
```

will round the number **x** to the nearest integer and assign the result to **y**. Write an applet that reads **double** values and uses the preceding statement to round each of the numbers to the nearest integer. For each number processed, display both the original number and the rounded number.

6.10 **Math.floor** may be used to round a number to a specific decimal place. The statement

```
y = Math.floor( x * 10 + .5 ) / 10;
```

rounds **x** to the tenths position (i.e., the first position to the right of the decimal point). The statement

```
y = Math.floor( x * 100 + .5 ) / 100;
```

rounds **x** to the hundredths position (i.e., the second position to the right of the decimal point). Write an applet that defines four methods to round a number **x** in various ways:

a) **roundToInteger(number)**
b) **roundToTenths(number)**
c) **roundToHundredths(number)**
d) **roundToThousandths(number)**

For each value read, your program should display the original value, the number rounded to the nearest integer, the number rounded to the nearest tenth, the number rounded to the nearest hundredth and the number rounded to the nearest thousandth.

6.11 Answer each of the following questions:

a) What does it mean to choose numbers "at random?"
b) Why is the **Math.random** method useful for simulating games of chance?
c) Why is it often necessary to scale and/or shift the values produced by **Math.random**?
d) Why is computerized simulation of real-world situations a useful technique?

6.12 Write statements that assign random integers to the variable n in the following ranges:

a) $1 \leq n \leq 2$
b) $1 \leq n \leq 100$
c) $0 \leq n \leq 9$
d) $1000 \leq n \leq 1112$
e) $-1 \leq n \leq 1$
f) $-3 \leq n \leq 11$

6.13 For each of the following sets of integers, write a single statement that will print a number at random from the set:

a) 2, 4, 6, 8, 10.
b) 3, 5, 7, 9, 11.
c) 6, 10, 14, 18, 22.

6.14 Write a method **integerPower(base, exponent)** that returns the value of

$$base^{exponent}$$

For example, **integerPower(3, 4)** calculates 3^4 (or **3 * 3 * 3 * 3**). Assume that **exponent** is a positive, nonzero integer and that **base** is an integer. Method **integerPower** should use **for** or **while** to control the calculation. Do not use any math library methods. Incorporate this method into an applet that reads integer values from **JTextField**s for **base** and **exponent** from the user and performs the calculation with the **integerPower** method. [*Note*: Register for event handling on only the second **JTextField**. The user should interact with the program by typing numbers in both **JTextField**s and pressing *Enter* only in the second **JTextField**.]

6.15 Define a method **hypotenuse** that calculates the length of the hypotenuse of a right triangle when the other two sides are given (sample data appear in Fig. 6.21). The method should take two arguments of type **double** and return the hypotenuse as a **double**. Incorporate this method into an applet that reads values for **side1** and **side2** from **JTextField**s and performs the calculation with the **hypotenuse** method. Determine the length of the hypotenuse for each of the following triangles. [*Note*: Register for event handling on only the second **JTextField**. The user should interact with the program by typing numbers in both **JTextField**s and pressing *Enter* only in the second **JTextField**.]

Triangle	Side 1	Side 2
1	3.0	4.0
2	5.0	12.0
3	8.0	15.0

Fig. 6.21 Values for the sides of triangles in Exercise 6.15.

6.16 Write a method `multiple` that determines for a pair of integers whether the second integer is a multiple of the first. The method should take two integer arguments and return `true` if the second is a multiple of the first and `false` otherwise. Incorporate this method into an applet that inputs a series of pairs of integers (one pair at a time using `JTextField`s). [Note: Register for event handling on only the second `JTextField`. The user should interact with the program by typing numbers in both `JTextField`s and pressing *Enter* only in the second `JTextField`.]

6.17 Write a method `isEven` that uses the modulus operator to determine if an integer is even. The method should take an integer argument and return `true` if the integer is even and `false` otherwise. Incorporate this method into an applet that inputs a series integers (one at a time using a `JTextField`).

6.18 Write a method `squareOfAsterisks` that displays a solid square of asterisks whose side is specified in integer parameter `side`. For example, if `side` is `4`, the method displays

```
****
****
****
****
```

Incorporate this method into an applet that reads an integer value for `side` from the user at the keyboard and performs the drawing with the `squareOfAsterisks` method. Note that this method should be called from the applet's `paint` method and should be passed the `Graphics` object from `paint`.

6.19 Modify the method created in Exercise 6.18 to form the square out of whatever character is contained in character parameter `fillCharacter`. Thus, if `side` is `5` and `fillCharacter` is "`#`", the method should print

```
#####
#####
#####
#####
#####
```

6.20 Use techniques similar to those developed in Exercise 6.18 and Exercise 6.19 to produce a program that graphs a wide range of shapes.

6.21 Modify the program of Exercise 6.18 to draw a solid square with the `fillRect` method of the `Graphics` class. Method `fillRect` receives four arguments: *x*-coordinate, *y*-coordinate, width and height. Allow the user to input the coordinates at which the square should appear.

6.22 Write program segments that accomplish each of the following tasks:

a) Calculate the integer part of the quotient when integer `a` is divided by integer `b`.

b) Calculate the integer remainder when integer `a` is divided by integer `b`.

c) Use the program pieces developed in parts a) and b) to write a method `displayDigits` that receives an integer between `1` and `99999` and prints it as a series of digits, each pair of which is separated by two spaces. For example, the integer `4562` should be printed as

```
4  5  6  2
```

d) Incorporate the method developed in part c) into an applet that inputs an integer from an input dialog and invokes `displayDigits` by passing the method the integer entered. Display the results in a message dialog.

6.23 Implement the following integer methods:

a) Method **celsius** returns the Celsius equivalent of a Fahrenheit temperature, using the calculation

```
C = 5.0 / 9.0 * ( F - 32 );
```

b) Method **fahrenheit** returns the Fahrenheit equivalent of a Celsius temperature, using the calculation

```
F = 9.0 / 5.0 * C + 32;
```

c) Use these methods to write an applet that enables the user to enter either a Fahrenheit temperature and display the Celsius equivalent or enter a Celsius temperature and display the Fahrenheit equivalent.

[*Note*: This applet will require two **JTextField** objects that have registered action events. When **actionPerformed** is invoked, the **ActionEvent** parameter has method **getSource()** to determine the GUI component with which the user interacted. Your **actionPerformed** method should contain an **if/else** structure of the form

```
if ( actionEvent.getSource() == input1 ) {
   // process input1 interaction here
}
else {   // e.getSource() == input2
   // process input2 interaction here
}
```

where **input1** and **input2** are **JTextField** references.]

6.24 Write a method **minimum3** that returns the smallest of three floating-point numbers. Use the **Math.min** method to implement **minimum3**. Incorporate the method into an applet that reads three values from the user and determines the smallest value. Display the result in the status bar.

6.25 An integer number is said to be a *perfect number* if its factors, including 1 (but not the number itself), sum to the number. For example, 6 is a perfect number, because 6 = 1 + 2 + 3. Write a method **perfect** that determines if parameter **number** is a perfect number. Use this method in an applet that determines and displays all the perfect numbers between 1 and 1000. Print the factors of each perfect number to confirm that the number is indeed perfect. Challenge the computing power of your computer by testing numbers much larger than 1000. Display the results in a **JTextArea** that has scrolling functionality.

6.26 An integer is said to be *prime* if it is divisible only by 1 and itself. For example, 2, 3, 5 and 7 are prime, but 4, 6, 8 and 9 are not.

a) Write a method that determines if a number is prime.

b) Use this method in an applet that determines and prints all the prime numbers between 1 and 10,000. How many of these 10,000 numbers do you really have to test before being sure that you have found all the primes? Display the results in a **JTextArea** that has scrolling functionality.

c) Initially, you might think that $n/2$ is the upper limit for which you must test to see if a number is prime, but you need only go as high as the square root of n. Why? Rewrite the program, and run it both ways. Estimate the performance improvement.

6.27 Write a method that takes an integer value and returns the number with its digits reversed. For example, given the number 7631, the method should return 1367. Incorporate the method into an applet that reads a value from the user. Display the result of the method in the status bar.

6.28 The *greatest common divisor* (*GCD*) of two integers is the largest integer that evenly divides each of the two numbers. Write a method **gcd** that returns the greatest common divisor of two integers. Incorporate the method into an applet that reads two values from the user. Display the result of the method in the status bar.

6.29 Write a method **qualityPoints** that inputs a student's average and returns **4** if a student's average is 90–100, **3** if the average is 80–89, **2** if the average is 70–79, **1** if the average is 60–69 and **0** if the average is lower than 60. Incorporate the method into an applet that reads a value from the user. Display the result of the method in the status bar.

6.30 Write an applet that simulates coin tossing. Let the program toss a coin each time the user presses the **"Toss"** button. Count the number of times each side of the coin appears. Display the results. The program should call a separate method **flip** that takes no arguments and returns **false** for tails and **true** for heads. [*Note*: If the program realistically simulates coin tossing, each side of the coin should appear approximately half the time.]

6.31 Computers are playing an increasing role in education. Write a program that will help an elementary school student learn multiplication. Use **Math.random** to produce two positive one-digit integers. The program should then display a question in the status bar, such as

```
How much is 6 times 7?
```

The student then types the answer into a **JTextField**. Next, the program checks the student's answer. If it is correct, draw the string **"Very good!"** on the applet and ask another multiplication question. If the answer is wrong, draw the string **"No. Please try again."** on the applet and let the student try the same question again repeatedly until the student finally gets it right. A separate method should be used to generate each new question. This method should be called once when the applet begins execution and each time the user answers the question correctly. All drawing on the applet should be performed by the **paint** method.

6.32 The use of computers in education is referred to as *computer-assisted instruction* (*CAI*). One problem that develops in CAI environments is student fatigue. This problem can be eliminated by varying the computer's dialogue to hold the student's attention. Modify the program of Exercise 6.31 so the various comments are printed for each correct answer and each incorrect answer as follows:

Responses to a correct answer

```
Very good!
Excellent!
Nice work!
Keep up the good work!
```

Responses to an incorrect answer

```
No. Please try again.
Wrong. Try once more.
Don't give up!
No. Keep trying.
```

Use random-number generation to choose a number from 1 to 4 that will be used to select an appropriate response to each answer. Use a **switch** structure in the **paint** method to issue the responses.

6.33 More sophisticated computer-aided instruction systems monitor the student's performance over a period of time. The decision to begin a new topic is often based on the student's success with previous topics. Modify the program of Exercise 6.32 to count the number of correct and incorrect responses typed by the student. After the student types 10 answers, your program should calculate the percentage of correct responses. If the percentage is lower than 75%, print **Please ask your instructor for extra help** and reset the program so another student can try the program.

6.34 Write an applet that plays the "guess the number" game as follows: Your program chooses the number to be guessed by selecting a random integer in the range 1 to 1000. The applet displays the prompt **Guess a number between 1 and 1000** next to a **JTextField**. The player types a first guess into the **JTextField** and presses the *Enter* key. If the player's guess is incorrect, your program should display **Too high. Try again.** or **Too low. Try again.** in the status bar to help the player "zero in" on the correct answer and should clear the **JTextField** so the user can enter the next guess. When the user enters the correct answer, display **Congratulations. You guessed the number!** in the status bar and clear the **JTextField** so the user can play again. [*Note*: The guessing technique employed in this problem is similar to a *binary search.*]

6.35 Modify the program of Exercise 6.34 to count the number of guesses the player makes. If the number is 10 or fewer, print **Either you know the secret or you got lucky!** If the player guesses the number in 10 tries, print **Aha! You know the secret!** If the player makes more than 10 guesses, print **You should be able to do better!** Why should it take no more than 10 guesses? Well, with each "good guess" the player should be able to eliminate half of the numbers. Now show why any number from 1 to 1000 can be guessed in 10 or fewer tries.

6.36 Write a recursive method **power(base, exponent)** that when invoked returns

$$base^{\,exponent}$$

For example, **power(3, 4) = 3 * 3 * 3 * 3**. Assume that **exponent** is an integer greater than or equal to 1. (*Hint*: The recursion step should use the relationship

$$base^{\,exponent} = base \cdot base^{\,exponent\,-\,1}$$

and the terminating condition occurs when **exponent** is equal to **1**, because

$$base^1 = base$$

Incorporate this method into an applet that enables the user to enter the **base** and **exponent**.)

6.37 *(Towers of Hanoi)* Every budding computer scientist must grapple with certain classic problems, and the *Towers of Hanoi* (see Fig. 6.22) is one of the most famous. Legend has it that in a temple in the Far East, priests are attempting to move a stack of disks from one peg to another. The initial stack has 64 disks threaded onto one peg and arranged from bottom to top by decreasing size. The priests are attempting to move the stack from this peg to a second peg under the constraints that exactly one disk is moved at a time and at no time may a larger disk be placed above a smaller disk. A third peg is available for temporarily holding disks. Supposedly, the world will end when the priests complete their task, so there is little incentive for us to facilitate their efforts.

Let us assume that the priests are attempting to move the disks from peg 1 to peg 3. We wish to develop an algorithm that will print the precise sequence of peg-to-peg disk transfers.

If we were to approach this problem with conventional methods, we would rapidly find ourselves hopelessly knotted up in managing the disks. Instead, if we attack the problem with recursion in mind, it immediately becomes tractable. Moving n disks can be viewed in terms of moving only $n - 1$ disks (and hence the recursion) as follows:

a) Move $n - 1$ disks from peg 1 to peg 2, using peg 3 as a temporary holding area.
b) Move the last disk (the largest) from peg 1 to peg 3.
c) Move the $n - 1$ disks from peg 2 to peg 3, using peg 1 as a temporary holding area.

The process ends when the last task involves moving $n = 1$ disk (i.e., the base case). This task is accomplished by simply moving the disk, without the need for a temporary holding area.

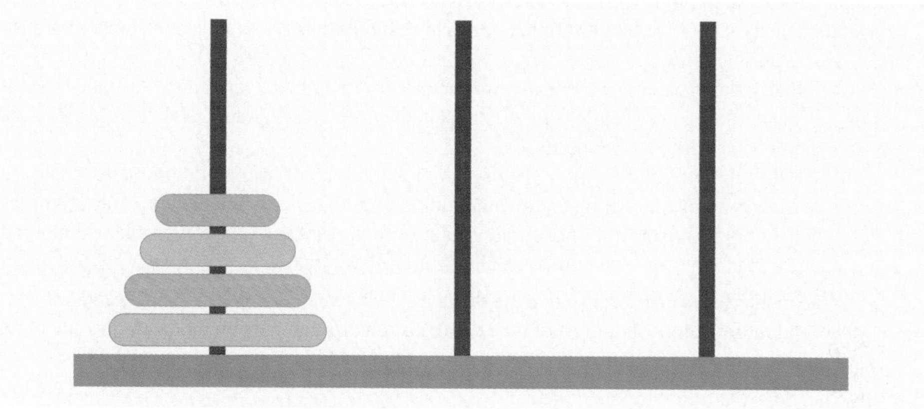

Fig. 6.22 The Towers of Hanoi for the case with four disks.

Write an applet to solve the Towers of Hanoi problem. Allow the user to enter the number of disks in a **JTextField**. Use a recursive **tower** method with four parameters:

a) the number of disks to be moved,
b) the peg on which these disks are initially threaded,
c) the peg to which this stack of disks is to be moved, and
d) the peg to be used as a temporary holding area.

Your program should display in a **JTextArea** with scrolling functionality the precise instructions it will take to move the disks from the starting peg to the destination peg. For example, to move a stack of three disks from peg 1 to peg 3, your program should print the following series of moves:

1 → **3** (This notation means move one disk from peg 1 to peg 3.)
1 → **2**
3 → **2**
1 → **3**
2 → **1**
2 → **3**
1 → **3**

6.38 Any program that can be implemented recursively can be implemented iteratively, although sometimes with more difficulty and less clarity. Try writing an iterative version of the Towers of Hanoi. If you succeed, compare your iterative version with the recursive version you developed in Exercise 6.37. Investigate issues of performance, clarity and your ability to demonstrate the correctness of the programs.

6.39 (*Visualizing Recursion*) It is interesting to watch recursion "in action." Modify the factorial method of Fig. 6.12 to print its local variable and recursive-call parameter. For each recursive call, display the outputs on a separate line, and add a level of indentation. Do your utmost to make the outputs clear, interesting and meaningful. Your goal here is to design and implement an output format that helps a person understand recursion better. You may want to add such display capabilities to the many other recursion examples and exercises throughout the text.

6.40 The greatest common divisor of integers **x** and **y** is the largest integer that evenly divides into both **x** and **y**. Write a recursive method **gcd** that returns the greatest common divisor of **x** and **y**. The **gcd** of **x** and **y** is defined recursively as follows: If **y** is equal to **0**, then **gcd(x, y)** is **x**; otherwise, **gcd(x, y)** is **gcd(y, x % y)**, where **%** is the modulus operator. Use this method to replace the one you wrote in the applet of Exercise 6.28.

6.41 Exercise 6.31 through Exercise 6.33 developed a computer-assisted instruction program to teach an elementary school student multiplication. This exercise suggests enhancements to that program.

a) Modify the program to allow the user to enter a grade-level capability. A grade level of 1 means to use only single-digit numbers in the problems, a grade level of 2 means to use numbers as large as two digits, etc.
b) Modify the program to allow the user to pick the type of arithmetic problems he or she wishes to study. An option of **1** means addition problems only, **2** means subtraction problems only, **3** means multiplication problems only, **4** means division problems only and **5** means to intermix randomly problems of all these types.

6.42 Write method **distance**, to calculate the distance between two points ($x1$, $y1$) and ($x2$, $y2$). All numbers and return values should be of type **double**. Incorporate this method into an applet that enables the user to enter the coordinates of the points.

6.43 What does the following method do?

```
// Parameter b must be a positive
// integer to prevent infinite recursion
public int mystery( int a, int b )
{
   if ( b == 1 )
      return a;
   else
      return a + mystery( a, b - 1 );
}
```

6.44 After you determine what the program in Exercise 6.43 does, modify the method to operate properly after removing the restriction of the second argument being nonnegative. Also, incorporate the method into an applet that enables the user to enter two integers, and test the method.

6.45 Write an application that tests as many of the math-library methods in Fig. 6.2 as you can. Exercise each of the methods by having your program print out tables of return values for a diversity of argument values.

6.46 Find the error in the following recursive method, and explain how to correct it:

```
public int sum( int n )
{
   if ( n == 0 )
      return 0;
   else
      return n + sum( n );
}
```

6.47 Modify the craps program of Fig. 6.9 to allow wagering. Initialize variable **bankBalance** to 1000 dollars. Prompt the player to enter a **wager**. Check that **wager** is less than or equal to **bankBalance**, and if not, have the user reenter **wager** until a valid **wager** is entered. After a correct **wager** is entered, run one game of craps. If the player wins, increase **bankBalance** by **wager**, and print the new **bankBalance**. If the player loses, decrease **bankBalance** by **wager**, print the new **bankBalance**, check if **bankBalance** has become zero, and if so, print the message **"Sorry. You busted!"** As the game progresses, print various messages to create some "chatter," such as **"Oh, you're going for broke, huh?"** or **"Aw c'mon, take a chance!"** or **"You're up big. Now's the time to cash in your chips!"**. Implement the "chatter" as a separate method that randomly chooses the string to display.

6.48 Write an applet that uses a method **circleArea** to prompt the user for the radius of a circle and to calculate and print the area of that circle.

7

Arrays

Objectives

- To introduce the array data structure.
- To understand the use of arrays to store, sort and search lists and tables of values.
- To understand how to declare an array, initialize an array and refer to individual elements of an array.
- To be able to pass arrays to methods.
- To understand basic sorting techniques.
- To be able to declare and manipulate multiple-subscript arrays.

With sobs and tears he sorted out
Those of the largest size ...
Lewis Carroll

Attempt the end, and never stand to doubt;
Nothing's so hard, but search will find it out.
Robert Herrick

Now go, write it before them in a table,
and note it in a book.
Isaiah 30:8

'Tis in my memory lock'd,
And you yourself shall keep the key of it.
William Shakespeare

Outline

7.1 Introduction
7.2 Arrays
7.3 Declaring and Allocating Arrays
7.4 Examples Using Arrays
  7.4.1 Allocating an Array and Initializing Its Elements
  7.4.2 Using an Initializer List to Initialize Elements of an Array
  7.4.3 Calculating the Value to Store in Each Array Element
  7.4.4 Summing the Elements of an Array
  7.4.5 Using Histograms to Display Array Data Graphically
  7.4.6 Using the Elements of an Array as Counters
  7.4.7 Using Arrays to Analyze Survey Results
7.5 References and Reference Parameters
7.6 Passing Arrays to Methods
7.7 Sorting Arrays
7.8 Searching Arrays: Linear Search and Binary Search
  7.8.1 Searching an Array with Linear Search
  7.8.2 Searching a Sorted Array with Binary Search
7.9 Multiple-Subscripted Arrays
7.10 (Optional Case Study) Thinking About Objects: Collaboration Among Objects

Summary • Terminology • Self-Review Exercises • Answers to Self-Review Exercises • Exercises • Recursion Exercises • Special Section: Building Your own Computer

7.1 Introduction

This chapter serves as an introduction to the important topic of data structures. *Arrays* are data structures consisting of related data items of the same type. Arrays are "static" entities, in that they remain the same size once they are created, although an array reference may be reassigned to a new array of a different size. Chapter 19, "Data Structures," introduces dynamic data structures, such as lists, queues, stacks and trees, that can grow and shrink as programs execute. Chapter 20, "Java Utilities Package and Bit Manipulation," discusses class **`Vector`**, which is an array-like class whose objects can grow and shrink in response to a Java program's changing storage requirements. Chapter 21, "The Collections API," introduces Java's predefined data structures that enable the programmer to use existing data structures for lists, queues, stacks and trees rather than "reinventing the wheel." The Collections API also provides class **`Arrays`**, which defines a set of utility methods for array manipulation.

7.2 Arrays

An array is a group of contiguous memory locations that all have the same name and the same type. To refer to a particular location or element in the array, we specify the name of the array and the *position number* (or *index* or *subscript*) of the particular element in the array.

Figure 7.1 shows an integer array called **c**. This array contains 12 *elements.* A program refers to any one of these elements by giving the name of the array followed by the position number of the particular element in square brackets (**[]**). The first element in every array has *position number zero* (sometimes called the *zeroth element).* Thus, the first element of array **c** is **c[0]**, the second element of array **c** is **c[1]**, the seventh element of array **c** is **c[6]**, and, in general, the *i*th element of array **c** is **c[i - 1]**. Array names follow the same conventions as other variable names.

Formally, the position number in square brackets is called a subscript (or an index). A subscript must be an integer or an integer expression. If a program uses an expression as a subscript, the program evaluates the expression to determine the subscript. For example, if we assume that variable **a** is **5** and that variable **b** is **6**, then the statement

```
c[ a + b ] += 2;
```

adds 2 to array element **c[11]**. Note that a subscripted array name is an *lvalue*—it can be used on the left side of an assignment to place a new value into an array element.

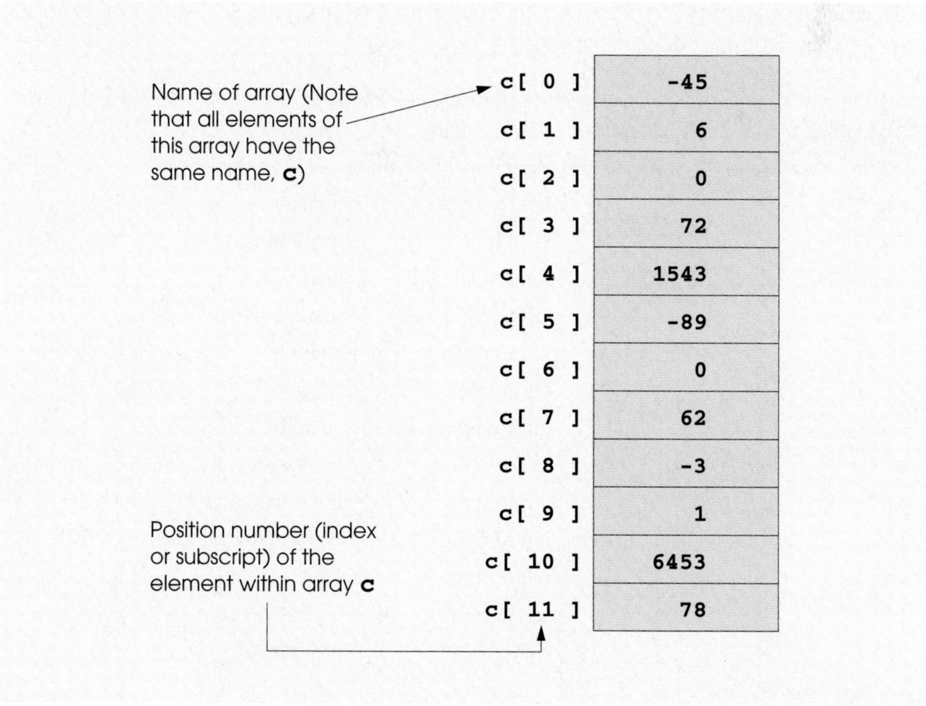

Name of array (Note that all elements of this array have the same name, **c**)

c[0]	-45
c[1]	6
c[2]	0
c[3]	72
c[4]	1543
c[5]	-89
c[6]	0
c[7]	62
c[8]	-3
c[9]	1
c[10]	6453
c[11]	78

Position number (index or subscript) of the element within array **c**

Fig. 7.1 A 12-element array.

Let us examine array **c** in Figure 7.1 more closely. The *name* of the array is **c**. Every array in Java *knows* its own length and maintains this information in a variable called ***length***. The expression **c.length** accesses array **c**'s **length** variable to determine the length of the array. The array's 12 elements are referred to as **c[0]**, **c[1]**, **c[2]**, ..., **c[11]**. The *value* of **c[0]** is **-45**, the value of **c[1]** is **6**, the value of **c[2]** is **0**, the value of **c[7]** is **62** and the value of **c[11]** is **78**. To calculate the sum of the values contained in the first three elements of array **c** and store the result in variable **sum**, we would write

```
sum = c[ 0 ] + c[ 1 ] + c[ 2 ];
```

To divide the value of the seventh element of array **c** by **2** and assign the result to the variable **x**, we would write

```
x = c[ 6 ] / 2;
```

Common Programming Error 7.1

It is important to note the difference between the "seventh element of the array" and "array element seven." Because array subscripts begin at 0, the "seventh element of the array" has a subscript of 6, while "array element seven" has a subscript of 7 and is actually the eighth element of the array. This confusion is a source of "off-by-one" errors.

The brackets used to enclose the subscript of an array are one of Java's many operators. Brackets are in the highest level of precedence in Java. The chart in Fig. 7.2 shows the precedence and associativity of the operators introduced so far. They are shown top to bottom in decreasing order of precedence with their associativity and type. See Appendix C for the complete operator precedence chart.

Operators	Associativity	Type
`() [] .`	left to right	highest
`++ --`	right to left	unary postfix
`++ -- + - !` (*type*)	right to left	unary
`* / %`	left to right	multiplicative
`+ -`	left to right	additive
`< <= > >=`	left to right	relational
`== !=`	left to right	equality
`&`	left to right	boolean logical AND
`^`	left to right	boolean logical exclusive OR
`|`	left to right	boolean logical inclusive OR
`&&`	left to right	logical AND
`||`	left to right	logical OR
`?:`	right to left	conditional
`= += -= *= /= %=`	right to left	assignment

Fig. 7.2 Precedence and associativity of the operators discussed so far.

7.3 Declaring and Allocating Arrays

Arrays are objects that occupy space in memory. All objects in Java (including arrays) must be allocated dynamically with operator **new**. For an array, the programmer specifies the type of the array elements and the number of elements as part of the **new** operation. To allocate 12 elements for integer array **c** in Fig. 7.1, use the declaration

```
int c[] = new int[ 12 ];
```

The preceding declaration also can be performed in two steps as follows:

```
int c[];                 // declares the array
c = new int[ 12 ];       // allocates the array
```

When allocating an array, each element of the array receives a default value–zero for the numeric primitive-data-type elements, **false** for **boolean** elements or **null** for references (any nonprimitive type).

Common Programming Error 7.2

Unlike array declarations in several other programming languages (such as C and C++), Java array declarations must not specify the number of array elements in the square brackets after the array name; otherwise, a syntax error occurs. For example, the declaration ***int c[12];*** *causes a syntax error.*

A program can allocate memory for several arrays with a single declaration. The following declaration reserves 100 elements for **String** array **b** and 27 elements for **String** array **x**:

```
String b[] = new String[ 100 ], x[] = new String[ 27 ];
```

When declaring an array, the type of the array and the square brackets can be combined at the beginning of the declaration to indicate that all identifiers in the declaration represent arrays, as in

```
double[] array1, array2;
```

which declares both **array1** and **array2** as arrays of **double** values. As shown previously, the declaration and initialization of the array can be combined in the declaration. The following declaration reserves 10 elements for **array1** and 20 elements for **array2**:

```
double[] array1 = new double[ 10 ],
         array2 = new double[ 20 ];
```

A program can declare arrays of any data type. It is important to remember that every element of a primitive data type array contains one value of the declared data type. For example, every element of an **int** array contains an **int** value. However, in an array of a nonprimitive type, every element of the array is a reference to an object of the array's declared data type. For example, every element of a **String** array is a reference to a **String**. In arrays that store references, the references have the value **null** by default.

7.4 Examples Using Arrays

This section presents several examples using arrays that demonstrate declaring arrays, allocating arrays, initializing arrays and manipulating array elements in various ways. For simplicity, the examples in this section use arrays that contain elements of type **int**. Please remember that a program can declare an array of any data type.

7.4.1 Allocating an Array and Initializing Its Elements

The application of Figure 7.3 uses operator **new** to allocate dynamically an array of 10 **int** elements, which are initially zero (the default value in an array of type **int**). The program displays the array elements in tabular format in a **JTextArea**.

Line 12 declares **array**—a reference capable of referring to an array of **int** elements. Line 14 allocates the 10 elements of the array with **new** and initializes the reference. The program builds its output in the **String** called **output** that will be displayed in a **JTextArea** on a message dialog. Line 16 appends to **output** the headings for the columns displayed by the program. The columns represent the subscript for each array element and the value of each array element, respectively.

Lines 19–20 use a **for** structure to append the subscript number (represented by **counter**) and value of each array element to **output**. Note the use of zero-based counting (remember, subscripts start at 0), so that the loop can access every array element. Also, note the expression **array.length** in the **for** structure condition to determine the length of the array. In this example, the length of the array is 10, so the loop continues executing as long as the value of control variable **counter** is less than 10. For a 10-element array, the subscript values are 0 through 9, so using the less than operator **<** guarantees that the loop does not attempt to access an element beyond the end of the array.

```
1  // Fig. 7.3: InitArray.java
2  // Creating an array.
3
4  // Java extension packages
5  import javax.swing.*;
6
7  public class InitArray {
8
9     // main method begins execution of Java application
10    public static void main( String args[] )
11    {
12       int array[];                // declare reference to an array
13
14       array = new int[ 10 ];  // dynamically allocate array
15
16       String output = "Subscript\tValue\n";
17
18       // append each array element's value to String output
19       for ( int counter = 0; counter < array.length; counter++ )
20          output += counter + "\t" + array[ counter ] + "\n";
21
22       JTextArea outputArea = new JTextArea();
23       outputArea.setText( output );
24
```

Fig. 7.3 Initializing the elements of an array to zeros (part 1 of 2).

```
        JOptionPane.showMessageDialog( null, outputArea,
           "Initializing an Array of int Values",
           JOptionPane.INFORMATION_MESSAGE );

        System.exit( 0 );
    }
 }
```

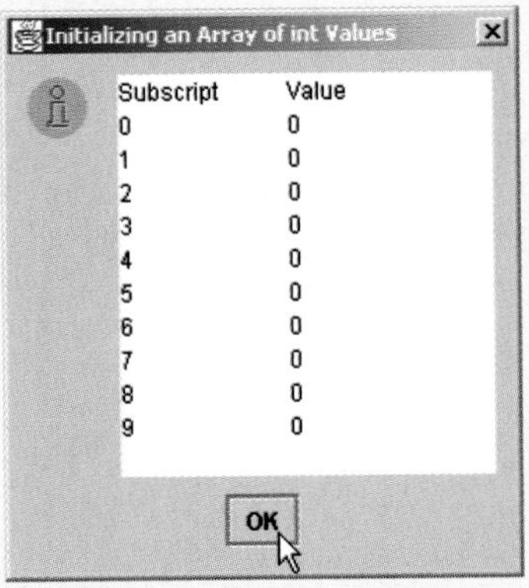

Initializing an Array of int Values

Subscript	Value
0	0
1	0
2	0
3	0
4	0
5	0
6	0
7	0
8	0
9	0

OK

Fig. 7.3 Initializing the elements of an array to zeros (part 2 of 2).

7.4.2 Using an Initializer List to Initialize Elements of an Array

A program can allocate and initialize the elements of an array in the array declaration by following the declaration with an equal sign and a comma-separated *initializer list* enclosed in braces (**{** and **}**). In this case, the array size is determined by the number of elements in the initializer list. For example, the declaration

```
int n[] = { 10, 20, 30, 40, 50 };
```

creates a five-element array with subscripts of **0**, **1**, **2**, **3** and **4**. Note that the preceding declaration does not require the **new** operator to create the array object. When the compiler encounters an array declaration that includes an initializer list, the compiler counts the number of initializers in the list and sets up a new operation to allocate the appropriate number of array elements.

The application of Fig. 7.4 initializes an integer array with 10 values (line 14) and displays the array in tabular format in a **JTextArea** on a message dialog. The code for displaying the array elements is identical to that of Fig. 7.3.

```
1  // Fig. 7.4: InitArray.java
2  // Initializing an array with a declaration.
3
4  // Java extension packages
5  import javax.swing.*;
6
```

Fig. 7.4 Initializing the elements of an array with a declaration (part 1 of 2).

```java
public class InitArray {

   // main method begins execution of Java application
   public static void main( String args[] )
   {
      // initializer list specifies number of elements and
      // value for each element
      int array[] = { 32, 27, 64, 18, 95, 14, 90, 70, 60, 37 };

      String output = "Subscript\tValue\n";

      // append each array element's value to String output
      for ( int counter = 0; counter < array.length; counter++ )
         output += counter + "\t" + array[ counter ] + "\n";

      JTextArea outputArea = new JTextArea();
      outputArea.setText( output );

      JOptionPane.showMessageDialog( null, outputArea,
         "Initializing an Array with a Declaration",
         JOptionPane.INFORMATION_MESSAGE );

      System.exit( 0 );
   }
}
```

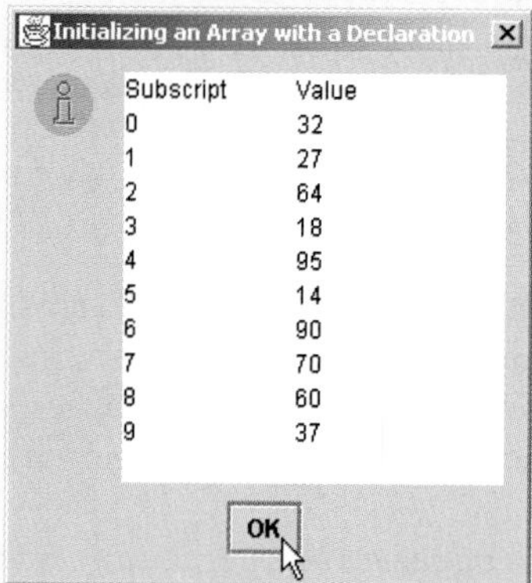

Fig. 7.4 Initializing the elements of an array with a declaration (part 2 of 2).

7.4.3 Calculating the Value to Store in Each Array Element

Some programs calculate the value stored in each array element. The application of Fig. 7.5 initializes the elements of a 10-element array to the even integers from 2 to 20 (**2**, **4**, **6**, …, **20**) and displays the array in tabular format. The **for** structure at lines 18–19 generates an array element's value by multiplying the current value of **counter** (the control variable of the loop) by **2** and adding **2**.

```
// Fig. 7.5: InitArray.java
// Initialize array with the even integers from 2 to 20.

// Java extension packages
import javax.swing.*;

public class InitArray {

   // main method begins execution of Java application
   public static void main( String args[] )
   {
      final int ARRAY_SIZE = 10;
      int array[];                        // reference to int array

      array = new int[ ARRAY_SIZE ];  // allocate array

      // calculate value for each array element
      for ( int counter = 0; counter < array.length; counter++ )
         array[ counter ] = 2 + 2 * counter;

      String output = "Subscript\tValue\n";

      for ( int counter = 0; counter < array.length; counter++ )
         output += counter + "\t" + array[ counter ] + "\n";

      JTextArea outputArea = new JTextArea();
      outputArea.setText( output );

      JOptionPane.showMessageDialog( null, outputArea,
         "Initializing to Even Numbers from 2 to 20",
         JOptionPane.INFORMATION_MESSAGE );

      System.exit( 0 );
   }
}
```

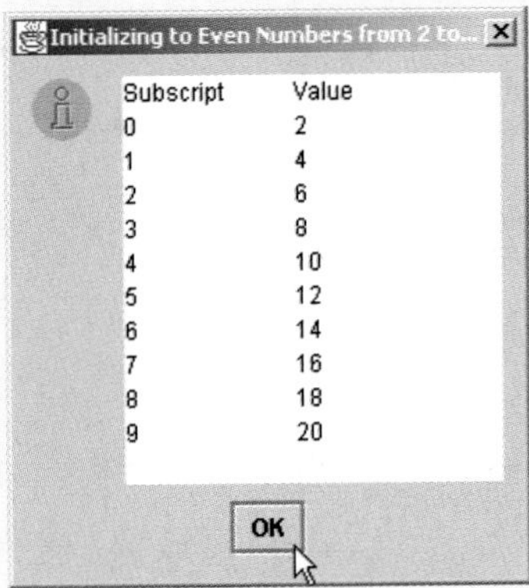

Fig. 7.5 Generating values to be placed into elements of an array.

Line 12 uses the **final** qualifier to declare constant variable **ARRAY_SIZE**, whose value is **10**. Remember that constant variables must be initialized before they are used and cannot be modified thereafter. If an attempt is made to modify a **final** variable after it is declared as shown on line 12, the compiler issues a message like

cannot assign a value to final variable *variableName*

If an attempt is made to use a **final** variable before it is initialized, the compiler issues the error message

Variable *variableName* **may not have been initialized**

Constant variables also are called *named constants* or *read-only variables.* Such variables often can make programs more readable. Note that the term "constant variable" is an oxymoron—a contradiction in terms—like "jumbo shrimp" or "freezer burn."

Common Programming Error 7.3

Assigning a value to a constant variable after the variable has been initialized is a syntax error.

7.4.4 Summing the Elements of an Array

Often, the elements of an array represent a series of values to use in a calculation. For example, if the elements of an array represent the grades for an exam in a class, the professor may wish to total the elements of an array, then calculate the class average for the exam.

The application of Fig. 7.6 sums the values contained in the 10-element integer array. The program declares, allocates and initializes the array at line 12. The **for** structure at lines 16–17 performs the calculations. [*Note*: It is important to remember that the values being supplied as initializers for **array** normally would be read into the program. For example, in an applet the user could enter the values through a **JTextField**, or in an application the values could be read from a file on disk (discussed in Chapter 16). Reading the data into a program makes the program more flexible, because it can be used with different sets of data.]

```
1  // Fig. 7.6: SumArray.java
2  // Total the values of the elements of an array.
3
4  // Java extension packages
5  import javax.swing.*;
6
7  public class SumArray {
8
9     // main method begins execution of Java application
10    public static void main( String args[] )
11    {
12       int array[] = { 1, 2, 3, 4, 5, 6, 7, 8, 9, 10 };
13       int total = 0;
14
```

Fig. 7.6 Computing the sum of the elements of an array (part 1 of 2).

```
      // add each element's value to total
      for ( int counter = 0; counter < array.length; counter++ )
         total += array[ counter ];

      JOptionPane.showMessageDialog( null,
         "Total of array elements: " + total,
         "Sum the Elements of an Array",
         JOptionPane.INFORMATION_MESSAGE );

      System.exit( 0 );
   }
}
```

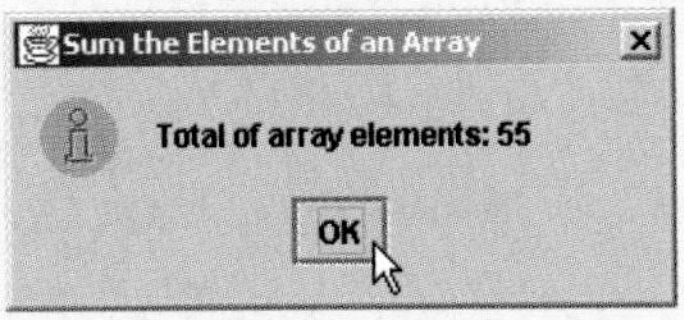

Sum the Elements of an Array

Total of array elements: 55

OK

Fig. 7.6 Computing the sum of the elements of an array (part 2 of 2).

7.4.5 Using Histograms to Display Array Data Graphically

Many programs present data to users in a graphical manner. For example, numeric values are often displayed as bars in a bar chart. In such a chart, longer bars represent larger numeric values. One simple way to display numeric data graphically is with a *histogram* that shows each numeric value as a bar of asterisks (*).

Our next application (Fig. 7.7) reads numbers from an array and graphs the information in the form of a bar chart (or histogram). The program displays each number followed by a bar consisting of that many asterisks. The nested **for** loop (lines 17–24) appends the bars to the **String** that will be displayed in **JTextArea outputArea** on a message dialog. Note the loop continuation condition of the inner **for** structure at line 22 (**stars <= array[counter]**). Each time the program reaches the inner **for** structure, the loop counts from **1** to **array[counter]**, thus using a value in **array** to determine the final value of the control variable **stars** and the number of asterisks to display.

```
1  // Fig. 7.7: Histogram.java
2  // Histogram printing program.
3
4  // Java extension packages
5  import javax.swing.*;
6
7  public class Histogram {
8
9     // main method begins execution of Java application
10    public static void main( String args[] )
11    {
12       int array[] = { 19, 3, 15, 7, 11, 9, 13, 5, 17, 1 };
13
14       String output = "Element\tValue\tHistogram";
```

Fig. 7.7 A program that prints histograms (part 1 of 2).

```

      // for each array element, output a bar in histogram
      for ( int counter = 0; counter < array.length; counter++ ) {
         output +=
            "\n" + counter + "\t" + array[ counter ] + "\t";

         // print bar of asterisks
         for ( int stars = 0; stars < array[ counter ]; stars++ )
            output += "*";
      }

      JTextArea outputArea = new JTextArea();
      outputArea.setText( output );

      JOptionPane.showMessageDialog( null, outputArea,
         "Histogram Printing Program",
         JOptionPane.INFORMATION_MESSAGE );

      System.exit( 0 );
   }
}
```

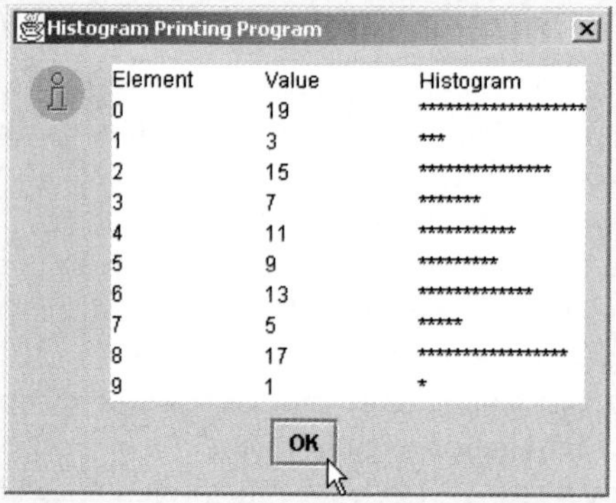

Histogram Printing Program

Element	Value	Histogram
0	19	*******************
1	3	***
2	15	***************
3	7	*******
4	11	***********
5	9	*********
6	13	*************
7	5	*****
8	17	*****************
9	1	*

OK

Fig. 7.7 A program that prints histograms (part 2 of 2).

7.4.6 Using the Elements of an Array as Counters

Sometimes programs use a series of counter variables to summarize data, such as the results of a survey. In Chapter 6, we used a series of counters in our die-rolling program to track the number of occurrences of each side on a six-sided die as the program rolled the die 6000 times. We also indicated that there is a more elegant method of writing the program of Fig. 6.8. An array version of this application is shown in Fig. 7.8.

```
// Fig. 7.8: RollDie.java
// Roll a six-sided die 6000 times

// Java extension packages
import javax.swing.*;

```

Fig. 7.8 Die-rolling program using arrays instead of **switch** (part 1 of 2).

```
7  public class RollDie {
8
9     // main method begins execution of Java application
10    public static void main( String args[] )
11    {
12       int face, frequency[] = new int[ 7 ];
13
14       // roll die 6000 times
15       for ( int roll = 1; roll <= 6000; roll++ ) {
16          face = 1 + ( int ) ( Math.random() * 6 );
17
18          // use face value as subscript for frequency array
19          ++frequency[ face ];
20       }
21
22       String output = "Face\tFrequency";
23
24       // append frequencies to String output
25       for ( face = 1; face < frequency.length; face++ )
26          output += "\n" + face + "\t" + frequency[ face ];
27
28       JTextArea outputArea = new JTextArea();
29       outputArea.setText( output );
30
31       JOptionPane.showMessageDialog( null, outputArea,
32          "Rolling a Die 6000 Times",
33          JOptionPane.INFORMATION_MESSAGE );
34
35       System.exit( 0 );
36    }
37 }
```

Rolling a Die 6000 Times

Face	Frequency
1	1007
2	1033
3	1016
4	979
5	999
6	966

OK

Fig. 7.8 Die-rolling program using arrays instead of **`switch`** (part 2 of 2).

The program uses the seven-element array **`frequency`** to count the occurrences of each side of the die. This program replaces lines 20–46 of Fig. 6.8 with line 19 of this program. Line 19 uses the random **`face`** value as the subscript for array **`frequency`** to determine which element the program should increment during each iteration of the loop. Since the random number calculation on line 19 produces numbers from 1 to 6 (the values for a six-sided die), the **`frequency`** array must be large enough to store six counters. However, in this program, we chose to use a seven-element array. We ignore the first array element, **`frequency[ 0 ]`**, because it is more logical to have the face value 1 increment

frequency[1] than **frequency[0]**. This allows us to use each face value directly as a subscript for the **frequency** array.

Good Programming Practice 7.1

Strive for program clarity. It is sometimes worthwhile to trade off the most efficient use of memory or processor time in favor of writing clearer programs.

Performance Tip 7.1

Sometimes performance considerations far outweigh clarity considerations.

Also, lines 25–26 of this program replace lines 52–55 from Fig. 6.8. We can loop through array **frequency**, so we do not have to enumerate each line of text to display in the **JTextArea** as we did in Fig. 6.8.

7.4.7 Using Arrays to Analyze Survey Results

Our next example uses arrays to summarize the results of data collected in a survey. Consider the problem statement:

> *Forty students were asked to rate the quality of the food in the student cafeteria on a scale of 1 to 10 (1 means awful and 10 means excellent). Place the 40 responses in an integer array and summarize the results of the poll.*

This is a typical array processing application (see Fig. 7.9). We wish to summarize the number of responses of each type (i.e., 1 through 10). The array **responses** is a 40-element integer array of the students' responses to the survey. We use an 11-element array **frequency** to count the number of occurrences of each response. As in Fig. 7.8, we ignore the first element (**frequency[0]**) because it is more logical to have the response 1 increment **frequency[1]** than **frequency[0]**. This allows us to use each response directly as a subscript on the **frequency** array. Each element of the array is used as a counter for one of the survey responses.

```
// Fig. 7.9: StudentPoll.java
// Student poll program

// Java extension packages
import javax.swing.*;

public class StudentPoll {

   // main method begins execution of Java application
   public static void main( String args[] )
   {
      int responses[] = { 1, 2, 6, 4, 8, 5, 9, 7, 8, 10,
                          1, 6, 3, 8, 6, 10, 3, 8, 2, 7,
                          6, 5, 7, 6, 8, 6, 7, 5, 6, 6,
                          5, 6, 7, 5, 6, 4, 8, 6, 8, 10 };
      int frequency[] = new int[ 11 ];

```

Fig. 7.9 A simple student-poll analysis program (part 1 of 2).

```
18        // for each answer, select value of an element of
19        // responses array and use that value as subscript in
20        // frequency array to determine element to increment
21        for ( int answer = 0; answer < responses.length; answer++ )
22           ++frequency[ responses[ answer ] ];
23
24        String output = "Rating\tFrequency\n";
25
26        // append frequencies to String output
27        for ( int rating = 1; rating < frequency.length; rating++ )
28           output += rating + "\t" + frequency[ rating ] + "\n";
29
30        JTextArea outputArea = new JTextArea();
31        outputArea.setText( output );
32
33        JOptionPane.showMessageDialog( null, outputArea,
34           "Student Poll Program",
35           JOptionPane.INFORMATION_MESSAGE );
36
37        System.exit( 0 );
38     }
39  }
```

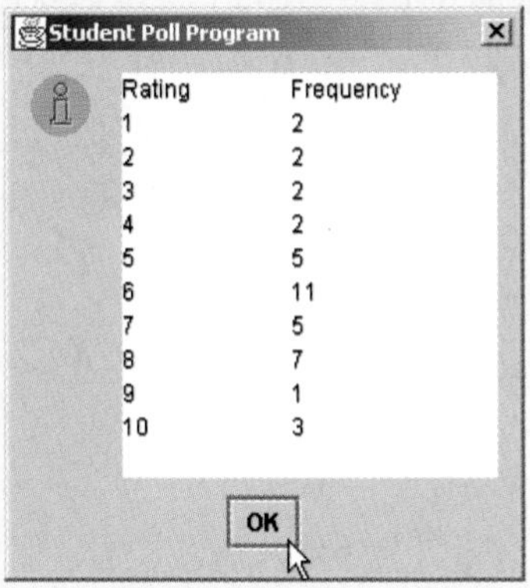

Student Poll Program

Rating	Frequency
1	2
2	2
3	2
4	2
5	5
6	11
7	5
8	7
9	1
10	3

OK

Fig. 7.9 A simple student-poll analysis program (part 2 of 2).

The **for** loop (lines 21–22) takes the responses one at a time from array **responses** and increments one of the 10 counters in the **frequency** array (**frequency[1]** to **frequency[10]**). The key statement in the loop is line 22, which increments the appropriate **frequency** counter, depending on the value of **responses[answer]**.

Let's consider several iterations of the **for** loop. When counter **answer** is **0**, **responses[answer]** is the value of the first element of array **responses** (i.e., **1**), so the program interprets **++frequency[responses[answer]];** as

```
++frequency[ 1 ];
```

which increments the value in array element one. To evaluate the expression, start with the value in the innermost set of square brackets (**answer**). Once you know the value of **answer**, plug that value into the expression and evaluate the next outer set of square brackets (**responses[answer]**). Then, use that value as the subscript for the **frequency** array to determine which counter to increment.

When **answer** is **1**, **responses[answer]** is the value of **responses**' second element (**2**), so the program interprets **++frequency[responses[answer]];** as

```
++frequency[ 2 ];
```

which increments array element two (the third element of the array).

When **answer** is **2**, **responses[answer]** is the value of **responses**' third element (**6**), so the program interprets **++frequency[responses[answer]];** as

```
++frequency[ 6 ];
```

which increments array element six (the seventh element of the array), and so on. Regardless of the number of responses processed in the survey, the program requires only an 11-element array (ignoring element zero) to summarize the results, because all the response values are between 1 and 10 and the subscript values for an 11-element array are 0 through 10. Also, note that the summarized results are correct, because the elements of array **frequency** were initialized to zero when the array was allocated with **new**.

If the data contained invalid values, such as 13, the program would attempt to add **1** to **frequency[13]**. This is outside the bounds of the array. In the C and C++ programming languages, such a reference would be allowed by the compiler and at execution time. The program would "walk" past the end of the array to where it thought element number 13 was located and add 1 to whatever happened to be at that location in memory. This could potentially modify another variable in the program or even result in premature program termination. Java provides mechanisms to prevent accessing elements outside the bounds of the array.

Common Programming Error 7.4

Referring to an element outside the array bounds is a logic error.

Testing and Debugging Tip 7.1

When a Java program executes, the Java interpreter checks array element subscripts to be sure they are valid (i.e., all subscripts must be greater than or equal to 0 and less than the length of the array). If there is an invalid subscript, Java generates an exception.

Testing and Debugging Tip 7.2

Exceptions indicate that an error occurred in a program. A programmer can write code to recover from an exception and continue program execution instead of abnormally terminating the program. When an invalid array reference occurs, Java generates an **ArrayIndexOutOfBoundsException***. Chapter 14 covers exception handling in detail.*

Testing and Debugging Tip 7.3

When looping through an array, the array subscript should never go below 0 and should always be less than the total number of elements in the array (one less than the size of the array). The loop terminating condition should prevent accessing elements outside this range.

Testing and Debugging Tip 7.4

Programs should validate all input values to prevent erroneous information from affecting a program's calculations.

7.5 References and Reference Parameters

Two ways to pass arguments to methods (or functions) in many programming languages (like C and C++) are *pass-by-value* and *pass-by-reference* (also called *call-by-value* and *call-by-reference*). When an argument is passed by value, a *copy* of the argument's value is made and passed to the called method.

Testing and Debugging Tip 7.5

With pass-by-value, changes to the called method's copy do not affect the original variable's value in the calling method. This prevents the accidental side effects that so greatly hinder the development of correct and reliable software systems.

When an argument is passed by reference, the caller gives the called method the ability to access the caller's data directly and to modify that data if the called method so chooses. Pass-by-reference improves performance, because it eliminates the overhead of copying large amounts of data.

Software Engineering Observation 7.1

Unlike other languages, Java does not allow the programmer to choose whether to pass each argument by value or by reference. Primitive data type variables are always passed by value. Objects are not passed to methods; rather, references to objects are passed to methods. The references themselves are passed by value—a copy of a reference is passed to a method. When a method receives a reference to an object, the method can manipulate the object directly.

Software Engineering Observation 7.2

When returning information from a method via a **`return`** *statement, primitive-data-type variables are always returned by value (i.e., a copy is returned) and objects are always returned by reference (i.e., a reference to the object is returned).*

To pass a reference to an object into a method, simply specify the reference name in the method call. Mentioning the reference by its parameter name in the body of the called method actually refers to the original object in memory, and the original object can be accessed directly by the called method.

Arrays are treated as objects by Java; therefore, arrays are passed to methods by reference—a called method can access the elements of the caller's original arrays. The name of an array is actually a reference to an object that contains the array elements and the **`length`** instance variable, which indicates the number of elements in the array. In the next section, we demonstrate pass-by-value and pass-by-reference using arrays.

Performance Tip 7.2

Passing arrays by reference makes sense for performance reasons. If arrays were passed by value, a copy of each element would be passed. For large, frequently passed arrays, this would waste time and would consume considerable storage for the copies of the arrays.

7.6 Passing Arrays to Methods

To pass an array argument to a method, specify the name of the array without any brackets. For example, if array **`hourlyTemperatures`** is declared as

```
int hourlyTemperatures[] = new int[ 24 ];
```

the method call

```
modifyArray( hourlyTemperatures );
```

passes array **hourlyTemperatures** to method **modifyArray**. In Java, every array object "knows" its own size (via the **length** instance variable). Thus, when we pass an array object into a method, we are not required to pass the size of the array as an additional argument.

Although entire arrays and objects referred to by individual elements of a nonprimitive-type array are passed by reference, individual array elements of primitive data types are passed by value exactly as simple variables are. Such simple single pieces of data are called *scalars* or *scalar quantities.* To pass an array element to a method, use the subscripted name of the array element as an argument in the method call.

For a method to receive an array through a method call, the method's parameter list must specify an array parameter (or several if more than one array is to be received). For example, the method header for method **modifyArray** might be written as

```
void modifyArray( int b[] )
```

indicating that **modifyArray** expects to receive an integer array in parameter **b**. Since arrays are passed by reference, when the called method uses the array name **b**, it refers to the actual array in the caller (array **hourlyTemperatures** in the preceding call).

The applet of Fig. 7.10 demonstrates the difference between passing an entire array and passing an array element. Once again, we use an applet here, because we have not yet defined an application that contains methods other than **main**. We are still taking advantage of some of the features provided for free in an applet (such as the automatic creation of an applet object and the automatic calls to **init**, **start** and **paint** by the applet container). In Chapter 9, Object-Oriented Programming, we introduce applications that execute in their own windows. At that point, we will begin to see application classes containing several methods.

Lines 15–17 in method **init** define the **JTextArea** called **outputArea** and attach it to the applet's content pane. The **for** structure at lines 26–27 appends the five elements of **array** (an array of **int** values) to the **String** called **output**. Line 29 invokes method **modifyArray** and passes it **array** as an argument. Method **modifyArray** (lines 50–54) multiplies each element by 2. To illustrate that **array**'s elements were modified, the **for** structure at lines 34–35 appends the five elements of **array** to **output** again. As the screen capture shows, method **modifyArray** did change the value of each element.

```
1  // Fig. 7.10: PassArray.java
2  // Passing arrays and individual array elements to methods
3
4  // Java core packages
5  import java.awt.Container;
6
7  // Java extension packages
8  import javax.swing.*;
9
```

Fig. 7.10 Passing arrays and individual array elements to methods (part 1 of 3).

```
public class PassArray extends JApplet {

   // initialize applet
   public void init()
   {
      JTextArea outputArea = new JTextArea();
      Container container = getContentPane();
      container.add( outputArea );

      int array[] = { 1, 2, 3, 4, 5 };

      String output =
         "Effects of passing entire array by reference:\n" +
         "The values of the original array are:\n";

      // append original array elements to String output
      for ( int counter = 0; counter < array.length; counter++ )
         output += "   " + array[ counter ];

      modifyArray( array );  // array passed by reference

      output += "\n\nThe values of the modified array are:\n";

      // append modified array elements to String output
      for ( int counter = 0; counter < array.length; counter++ )
         output += "   " + array[ counter ];

      output += "\n\nEffects of passing array " +
                "element by value:\n" +
                "a[3] before modifyElement: " + array[ 3 ];

      // attempt to modify array[ 3 ]
      modifyElement( array[ 3 ] );

      output += "\na[3] after modifyElement: " + array[ 3 ];
      outputArea.setText( output );

   } // end method init

   // multiply each element of an array by 2
   public void modifyArray( int array2[] )
   {
      for ( int counter = 0; counter < array2.length; counter++ )
         array2[ counter ] *= 2;
   }

   // multiply argument by 2
   public void modifyElement( int element )
   {
      element *= 2;
   }

} // end class PassArray
```

Fig. 7.10 Passing arrays and individual array elements to methods (part 2 of 3).

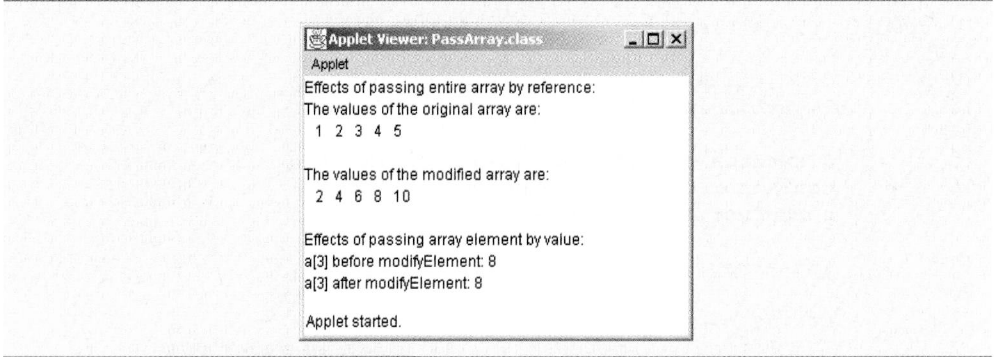

Fig. 7.10 Passing arrays and individual array elements to methods (part 3 of 3).

Next, the program demonstrates that individual elements of primitive-type arrays are passed to methods by value. To show the value of **array[3]** before calling method **modifyElement**, lines 37–39 append the value of **array[3]** (and other information) to **output**. Line 42 invokes method **modifyElement** and passes **array[3]** as an argument. Remember that **array[3]** is actually one **int** value in **array**. Also, remember that values of primitive types are passed to methods by value. Therefore, the program passes a copy of **array[3]**. Method **modifyElement** multiplies its argument by 2 and stores the result in its parameter **element**. Method parameters are local variables, so when **modifyElement** terminates, the local variable **element** is destroyed. Thus, when the program returns control to **init**, line 44 appends the unmodified value of **array[3] output**. Line 45 displays the results in the **JTextArea**.

7.7 Sorting Arrays

Sorting data (i.e., placing the data into some particular order such as ascending or descending) is one of the most important computing applications. A bank sorts all checks by account number so that it can prepare individual bank statements at the end of each month. Telephone companies sort their lists of accounts by last name and, within that, by first name, to make it easy to find phone numbers. Virtually every organization must sort some data and in many cases massive amounts of data. Sorting data is an intriguing problem that has attracted some of the most intense research efforts in the field of computer science. In this chapter, we discuss one of the simplest sorting schemes. In the exercises in this chapter, Chapter 19 and Chapter 21, we investigate more complex schemes that yield superior performance.

Performance Tip 7.3

Sometimes, the simplest algorithms perform poorly. Their virtue is that they are easy to program, test and debug. Sometimes, more complex algorithms are required to realize maximum performance.

Figure 7.11 sorts the values of **array** (a the 10-element array of **int** values) into ascending order. The technique we use is called the *bubble sort* or the *sinking sort*, because the smaller values gradually "bubble" their way to the top of the array (i.e., toward the first element) like air bubbles rising in water, while the larger values sink to the bottom (end) of the array. The technique uses nested loops to make several passes through the array. Each pass compares successive pairs of elements. If a pair is in increasing order (or the values are equal), the bubble sort leaves the values as they are. If a pair is in decreasing order, the bubble sort swaps their values in the array. The applet contains methods **init**, **bubbleSort** and **swap**. Method **init** (lines 13–36) initializes the applet. Method **bubbleSort** (lines 39–58) is called from **init** to sort the elements of **array**. Method **bubbleSort** calls method **swap** (lines 61–68) as necessary to exchange two elements of the array.

Lines 24–25 append the original values of **array** to the **String** called **output**. Line 27 invokes method **bubbleSort** and passes **array** as the array to sort.

Method **bubbleSort** receives the array as parameter **array2**. The nested **for** structure at lines 42–56 performs the sort. The outer loop controls the number of passes of the array. The inner loop controls the comparisons and swapping (if necessary) of the elements during each pass.

```
1  // Fig. 7.11: BubbleSort.java
2  // Sort an array's values into ascending order.
3
4  // Java core packages
5  import java.awt.*;
6
7  // Java extension packages
8  import javax.swing.*;
9
10 public class BubbleSort extends JApplet {
11
12    // initialize applet
13    public void init()
14    {
15       JTextArea outputArea = new JTextArea();
16       Container container = getContentPane();
17       container.add( outputArea );
18
19       int array[] = { 2, 6, 4, 8, 10, 12, 89, 68, 45, 37 };
20
21       String output = "Data items in original order\n";
22
23       // append original array values to String output
24       for ( int counter = 0; counter < array.length; counter++ )
25          output += "   " + array[ counter ];
26
27       bubbleSort( array );  // sort array
28
29       output += "\n\nData items in ascending order\n";
30
31       // append sorted\ array values to String output
32       for ( int counter = 0; counter < array.length; counter++ )
33          output += "   " + array[ counter ];
34
35       outputArea.setText( output );
36    }
37
```

Fig. 7.11 Sorting an array with bubble sort (part 1 of 2).

```java
    // sort elements of array with bubble sort
    public void bubbleSort( int array2[] )
    {
       // loop to control number of passes
       for ( int pass = 1; pass < array2.length; pass++ ) {

          // loop to control number of comparisons
          for ( int element = 0;
                element < array2.length - 1;
                element++ ) {

             // compare side-by-side elements and swap them if
             // first element is greater than second element
             if ( array2[ element ] > array2[ element + 1 ] )
                swap( array2, element, element + 1 );

          }  // end loop to control comparisons

       }  // end loop to control passes

    }  // end method bubbleSort

    // swap two elements of an array
    public void swap( int array3[], int first, int second )
    {
       int hold;  // temporary holding area for swap

       hold = array3[ first ];
       array3[ first ] = array3[ second ];
       array3[ second ] = hold;
    }

 }  // end class BubbleSort
```

Applet Viewer: BubbleSort.class
Applet
Data items in original order
2 6 4 8 10 12 89 68 45 37

Data items in ascending order
2 4 6 8 10 12 37 45 68 89
Applet started.

Fig. 7.11 Sorting an array with bubble sort (part 2 of 2).

Method **bubbleSort** first compares **array2[0]** to **array2[1]**, then **array2[1]** to **array2[2]**, then **array2[2]** to **array2[3]** so on until it completes the pass by comparing **array2[8]** to **array2[9]**. Although there are 10 elements, the comparison loop performs only nine comparisons. The comparisons performed in a bubble sort could cause a large value to move down the array (sink) many positions on a single pass. However, a small value may move up (bubble) only one position per pass. On the first pass, the largest value is guaranteed to sink to the bottom element of the array,

array2[9]. On the second pass, the second largest value is guaranteed to sink to **array2[8]**. On the ninth pass, the ninth largest value sinks to **array2[1]**. This leaves the smallest value in **array2[0]**, so only nine passes are required to sort a 10-element array.

If a comparison reveals that the two elements are in descending order, **bubbleSort** calls method **swap** to exchange the two elements, so they will be in ascending order in the array. Method **swap** receives a reference to the array (which it calls **array3**) and two integers representing the subscripts of the two elements of the array to exchange. The exchange is performed by the three assignments

```
hold = array3[ first ];
array3[ first ] = array3[ second ];
array3[ second ] = hold;
```

where the extra variable **hold** temporarily stores one of the two values being swapped. The swap cannot be performed with only the two assignments

```
array3[ first ] = array3[ second ];
array3[ second ] = array3[ first ];
```

If **array3[first]** is **7** and **array3[second]** is **5**, after the first assignment both array elements contain **5** and the value **7** is lost, hence the need for the extra variable **hold**.

The chief virtue of the bubble sort is that it is easy to program. However, the bubble sort runs slowly. This becomes apparent when sorting large arrays. In Exercise 7.11, we ask you to develop more efficient versions of the bubble sort. Other exercises investigate some sorting algorithms that are far more efficient than the bubble sort. More advanced courses (often titled "Data Structures," "Algorithms" or "Computational Complexity") investigate sorting and searching in greater depth.

7.8 Searching Arrays: Linear Search and Binary Search

Often, a programmer will be working with large amounts of data stored in arrays. It may be necessary to determine whether an array contains a value that matches a certain *key value*. The process of locating a particular element value in an array is called *searching*. In this section, we discuss two searching techniques—the simple *linear search* technique and the more efficient *binary search* technique. Exercise 7.31 and Exercise 7.32 at the end of this chapter ask you to implement recursive versions of the linear search and the binary search.

7.8.1 Searching an Array with Linear Search

In the applet of Fig. 7.12, method **linearSearch** (defined at lines 52–62) uses a **for** structure (lines 55–59) containing an **if** structure to compare each element of an array with a *search key*. If the search key is found, the method returns the subscript value for the element to indicate the exact position of the search key in the array. If the search key is not found, the method returns **-1** to indicate that the search key was not found. We return **-1** because it is not a valid subscript number. If the array being searched is not in any particular order, it is just as likely that the search key will be found in the first element as the last. On average, therefore, the program will have to compare the search key with half the elements of the array.

Figure 7.12 contains a 100-element array filled with the even integers from 0 to 198. The user types the search key in a **JTextField** and presses *Enter* to start the search. [*Note*: We pass the array to **linearSearch** even though the array is an instance variable of the class. We do this because an array normally is passed to a method of another class for sorting. For example, class **Arrays** (see Chapter 21) contains a variety of **static** methods for sorting arrays, searching arrays, comparing the contents of arrays and filling arrays of all the primitive types, **Object**s and **String**s.]

```
// Fig. 7.12: LinearSearch.java
// Linear search of an array

// Java core packages
import java.awt.*;
import java.awt.event.*;

// Java extension packages
import javax.swing.*;

public class LinearSearch extends JApplet
   implements ActionListener {

   JLabel enterLabel, resultLabel;
   JTextField enterField, resultField;
   int array[];

   // set up applet's GUI
   public void init()
   {
      // get content pane and set its layout to FlowLayout
      Container container = getContentPane();
      container.setLayout( new FlowLayout() );

      // set up JLabel and JTextField for user input
      enterLabel = new JLabel( "Enter integer search key" );
      container.add( enterLabel );

      enterField = new JTextField( 10 );
      container.add( enterField );

      // register this applet as enterField's action listener
      enterField.addActionListener( this );

      // set up JLabel and JTextField for displaying results
      resultLabel = new JLabel( "Result" );
      container.add( resultLabel );

      resultField = new JTextField( 20 );
      resultField.setEditable( false );
      container.add( resultField );

      // create array and populate with even integers 0 to 198
      array = new int[ 100 ];
```

Fig. 7.12 Linear search of an array (part 1 of 2).

```
      for ( int counter = 0; counter < array.length; counter++ )
         array[ counter ] = 2 * counter;

   }  // end method init

   // Search array for specified key value
   public int linearSearch( int array2[], int key )
   {
      // loop through array elements
      for ( int counter = 0; counter < array2.length; counter++ )

         // if array element equals key value, return location
         if ( array2[ counter ] == key )
            return counter;

      return -1;  // key not found
   }

   // obtain user input and call method linearSearch
   public void actionPerformed( ActionEvent actionEvent )
   {
      // input also can be obtained with enterField.getText()
      String searchKey = actionEvent.getActionCommand();

      // Array a is passed to linearSearch even though it
      // is an instance variable. Normally an array will
      // be passed to a method for searching.
      int element =
         linearSearch( array, Integer.parseInt( searchKey ) );

      // display search result
      if ( element != -1 )
         resultField.setText( "Found value in element " +
            element );
      else
         resultField.setText( "Value not found" );
   }

}  // end class LinearSearch
```


Fig. 7.12 Linear search of an array (part 2 of 2).

The linear search method works well for small arrays or for unsorted arrays. However, for large arrays, linear searching is inefficient. If the array is sorted, the high-speed *binary search* technique presented in the next section can be used.

7.8.2 Searching a Sorted Array with Binary Search

The binary search algorithm eliminates half of the elements in the array being searched after each comparison. The algorithm locates the middle array element and compares it to the search key. If they are equal, the search key has been found and binary search returns the subscript of that element. Otherwise, binary search reduces the problem to searching half of the array. If the search key is less than the middle array element, the first half of the array will be searched; otherwise, the second half of the array will be searched. If the search key is not the middle element in the specified subarray (piece of the original array), the algorithm repeats on one quarter of the original array. The search continues until the search key is equal to the middle element of a subarray or until the subarray consists of one element that is not equal to the search key (i.e., the search key is not found).

In a worst-case scenario, searching a sorted array of 1024 elements will take only 10 comparisons using a binary search. Repeatedly dividing 1024 by 2 (because after each comparison we are able to eliminate half of the array) yields the values 512, 256, 128, 64, 32, 16, 8, 4, 2 and 1. The number 1024 (2^{10}) is divided by 2 only ten times to get the value 1. Dividing by 2 is equivalent to one comparison in the binary search algorithm. An array of 1,048,576 (2^{20}) elements takes a maximum of 20 comparisons to find the key. An array of one billion elements takes a maximum of 30 comparisons to find the key. This is a tremendous increase in performance over the linear search that required comparing the search key to an average of half the elements in the array. For a one-billion-element array, this is a difference between an average of 500 million comparisons and a maximum of 30 comparisons! The maximum number of comparisons needed for the binary search of any sorted array is the exponent of the first power of 2 greater than the number of elements in the array.

Figure 7.13 presents the iterative version of method **binarySearch** (lines 85–116). The method receives two arguments—an integer array called **array2** (the array to search) and an integer **key** (the search key). The program passes the array to **binarySearch** even though the array is an instance variable of the class. Once again, we do this because an array normally is passed to a method of another class for sorting. If **key** matches the **middle** element of a subarray, **binarySearch** returns **middle** (the subscript of the current element) to indicate that the value was found and the search is complete. If **key** does not match the **middle** element of a subarray, **binarySearch** adjusts the **low** subscript or **high** subscript (both declared in the method), to continue the search using a smaller subarray. If **key** is less than the middle element, the **high** subscript is set to **middle - 1** and the search continues on the elements from **low** to **middle - 1**. If **key** is greater than the middle element, the **low** subscript is set to **middle + 1** and the search continues on the elements from **middle + 1** to **high**. Method **binarySearch** performs these comparisons in the nested **if/else** structure at lines 102–111.

```
1  // Fig. 7.13: BinarySearch.java
2  // Binary search of an array
3
4  // Java core packages
5  import java.awt.*;
6  import java.awt.event.*;
7  import java.text.*;
```

Fig. 7.13 Binary search of a sorted array (part 1 of 5)

```
// Java extension packages
import javax.swing.*;

public class BinarySearch extends JApplet
   implements ActionListener {

   JLabel enterLabel, resultLabel;
   JTextField enterField, resultField;
   JTextArea output;

   int array[];
   String display = "";

   // set up applet's GUI
   public void init()
   {
      // get content pane and set its layout to FlowLayout
      Container container = getContentPane();
      container.setLayout( new FlowLayout() );

      // set up JLabel and JTextField for user input
      enterLabel = new JLabel( "Enter integer search key" );
      container.add( enterLabel );

      enterField = new JTextField( 10 );
      container.add( enterField );

      // register this applet as enterField's action listener
      enterField.addActionListener( this );

      // set up JLabel and JTextField for displaying results
      resultLabel = new JLabel( "Result" );
      container.add( resultLabel );

      resultField = new JTextField( 20 );
      resultField.setEditable( false );
      container.add( resultField );

      // set up JTextArea for displaying comparison data
      output = new JTextArea( 6, 60 );
      output.setFont( new Font( "Monospaced", Font.PLAIN, 12 ) );
      container.add( output );

      // create array and fill with even integers 0 to 28
      array = new int[ 15 ];

      for ( int counter = 0; counter < array.length; counter++ )
         array[ counter ] = 2 * counter;

   } // end method init

```

Fig. 7.13 Binary search of a sorted array (part 2 of 5)

```
   // obtain user input and call method binarySearch
   public void actionPerformed( ActionEvent actionEvent )
   {
      // input also can be obtained with enterField.getText()
      String searchKey = actionEvent.getActionCommand();

      // initialize display string for new search
      display = "Portions of array searched\n";

      // perform binary search
      int element =
         binarySearch( array, Integer.parseInt( searchKey ) );

      output.setText( display );

      // display search result
      if ( element != -1 )
         resultField.setText(
            "Found value in element " + element );
      else
         resultField.setText( "Value not found" );

   } // end method actionPerformed

   // method to perform binary search of an array
   public int binarySearch( int array2[], int key )
   {
      int low = 0;                    // low element subscript
      int high = array.length - 1;    // high element subscript
      int middle;                     // middle element subscript

      // loop until low subscript is greater than high subscript
      while ( low <= high ) {

         // determine middle element subscript
         middle = ( low + high ) / 2;

         // display subset of array elements used in this
         // iteration of binary search loop
         buildOutput( array2, low, middle, high );

         // if key matches middle element, return middle location
         if ( key == array[ middle ] )
            return middle;

         // if key less than middle element, set new high element
         else if ( key < array[ middle ] )
            high = middle - 1;

         // key greater than middle element, set new low element
         else
            low = middle + 1;
      }
```

Fig. 7.13 Binary search of a sorted array (part 3 of 5)

```

      return -1;    // key not found

   }  // end method binarySearch

   // build row of output showing subset of array elements
   // currently being processed
   void buildOutput( int array3[],
      int low, int middle, int high )
   {
      // create 2-digit integer number format
      DecimalFormat twoDigits = new DecimalFormat( "00" );

      // loop through array elements
      for ( int counter = 0; counter < array3.length;
         counter++ ) {

         // if counter outside current array subset, append
         // padding spaces to String display
         if ( counter < low || counter > high )
            display += "    ";

         // if middle element, append element to String display
         // followed by asterisk (*) to indicate middle element
         else if ( counter == middle )
            display +=
               twoDigits.format( array3[ counter ] ) + "* ";

         // append element to String display
         else
            display +=
               twoDigits.format( array3[ counter ] ) + "  ";

      }  // end for structure

      display += "\n";

   }  // end method buildOutput

}  // end class BinarySearch
```

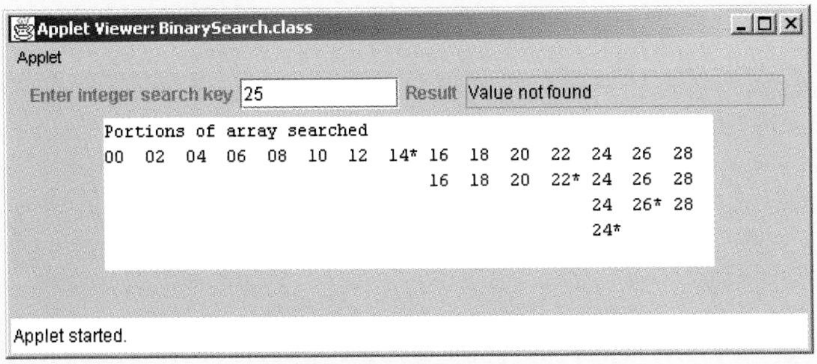

```
Applet Viewer: BinarySearch.class
Applet
Enter integer search key 25    Result Value not found
Portions of array searched
00  02  04  06  08  10  12  14* 16  18  20  22  24  26  28
                                16  18  20  22* 24  26  28
                                                24  26* 28
                                                24*
Applet started.
```

Fig. 7.13 Binary search of a sorted array (part 4 of 5)

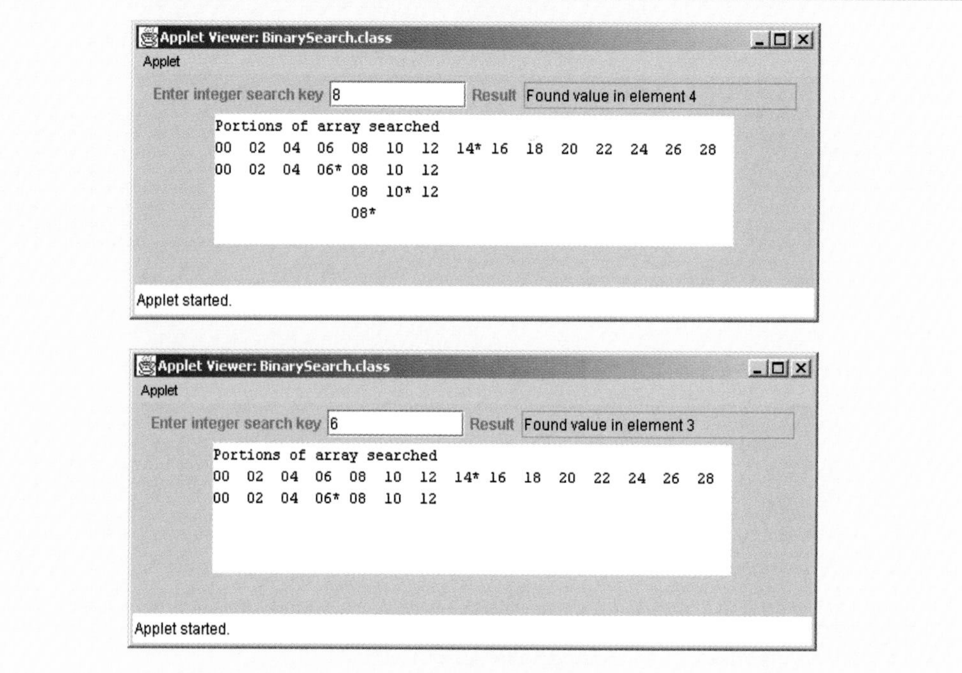

Fig. 7.13 Binary search of a sorted array (part 5 of 5)

The program uses a 15-element array. The first power of 2 greater than the number of array elements is 16 (2^4); therefore, **`binarySearch`** requires at most four comparisons to find the **`key`**. To illustrate this, line 99 of method **`binarySearch`** calls method **`buildOutput`** (defined at lines 120–150) to output each subarray during the binary search process. Method **`buildOutput`** marks the middle element in each subarray with an asterisk (**`*`**) to indicate the element to which the **`key`** is compared. Each search in this example results in a maximum of four lines of output—one per comparison.

`JTextArea output` uses *Monospaced* font (a *fixed-width font*—i.e., all characters are the same width) to help align the displayed text in each line of output. Line 49 uses method **`setFont`** to change the font displayed in **`output`**. Method **`setFont`** can change the font of text displayed on most GUI components. The method requires a ***`Font`*** (package **`java.awt`**) object as its argument. A **`Font`** object is initialized with three arguments—the **`String`** name of the font (**`"Monospaced"`**), an **`int`** representing the style of the font (***`Font.PLAIN`*** is a constant integer defined in class **`Font`** that indicates plain font) and an **`int`** representing the point size of the font (**`12`**). Java provides generic names for several fonts available on every Java platform. *Monospaced* font is also called *Courier*. Other common fonts include *Serif* (also called *TimesRoman*) and *SansSerif* (also called *Helvetica*). Java 2 actually provides access to all fonts on your system through methods of class ***`GraphicsEnvironment`***. The style can also be ***`Font.BOLD`***, ***`Font.ITALIC`*** or **`Font.BOLD + Font.ITALIC`**. The point size represents the size of the font—there are 72 points to an inch. The actual size of the text as it appears on the screen may vary based on the size of the screen and the screen resolution. We discuss font manipulation again in Chapter 11.

7.9 Multiple-Subscripted Arrays

Multiple-subscripted arrays with two subscripts are often used to represent *tables* of values consisting of information arranged in *rows* and *columns*. To identify a particular table element, we must specify the two subscripts—by convention, the first identifies the element's row and the second identifies the element's column. Arrays that require two subscripts to identify a particular element are called *double-subscripted arrays* or *two-dimensional arrays*. Note that multiple-subscripted arrays can have more than two subscripts. Java does not support multiple-subscripted arrays directly, but does allow the programmer to specify single-subscripted arrays whose elements are also single-subscripted arrays, thus achieving the same effect. Figure 7.14 illustrates a double-subscripted array, **a**, containing three rows and four columns (i.e., a 3-by-4 array). In general, an array with *m* rows and *n* columns is called an *m-by-n array*.

Every element in array **a** is identified in Fig. 7.14 by an element name of the form **a[row][column]**; **a** is the name of the array and **row** and **column** are the subscripts that uniquely identify the row and column of each element in **a**. Notice that the names of the elements in the first row all have a first subscript of **0**; the names of the elements in the fourth column all have a second subscript of **3**.

Multiple-subscripted arrays can be initialized with initializer lists in declarations like a single-subscripted array. A double-subscripted array **b[2][2]** could be declared and initialized with

```
int b[][] = { { 1, 2 }, { 3, 4 } };
```

The values are grouped by row in braces. So, **1** and **2** initialize **b[0][0]** and **b[0][1]**, and **3** and **4** initialize **b[1][0]** and **b[1][1]**. The compiler determines the number of rows by counting the number of initializer sublists (represented by sets of braces) in the initializer list. The compiler determines the number of columns in each row by counting the number of initializer values in the initializer sublist for that row.

Multiple-subscripted arrays are maintained as arrays of arrays. The declaration

```
int b[][] = { { 1, 2 }, { 3, 4, 5 } };
```

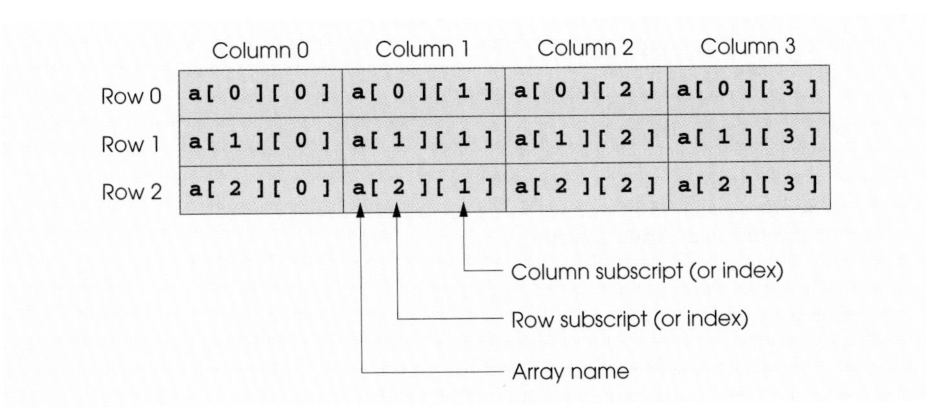

Fig. 7.14 A double-subscripted array with three rows and four columns.

creates integer array **b** with row **0** containing two elements (**1** and **2**) and row **1** containing three elements (**3**, **4** and **5**).

A multiple-subscripted array with the same number of columns in every row can be allocated dynamically. For example, a 3-by-4 array is allocated as follows:

```
int b[][];
b = new int[ 3 ][ 4 ];
```

In this case, we the literal values **3** and **4** to specify the number of rows and number of columns, respectively. Note that programs also can use variables to specify array dimensions. As with single-subscripted arrays, the elements of a double-subscripted array are initialized when **new** creates the array object.

A multiple-subscripted array in which each row has a different number of columns can be allocated dynamically as follows:

```
int b[][];
b = new int[ 2 ][ ];     // allocate rows
b[ 0 ] = new int[ 5 ]; // allocate columns for row 0
b[ 1 ] = new int[ 3 ]; // allocate columns for row 1
```

The preceding code creates a two-dimensional array with two rows. Row **0** has five columns and row **1** has three columns.

The applet of Fig. 7.15 demonstrates initializing double-subscripted arrays in declarations and using nested **for** loops to traverse the arrays (i.e., manipulate every element of the array).

```
// Fig. 7.15: InitArray.java
// Initializing multidimensional arrays

// Java core packages
import java.awt.Container;

// Java extension packages
import javax.swing.*;

public class InitArray extends JApplet {
   JTextArea outputArea;

   // set up GUI and initialize applet
   public void init()
   {
      outputArea = new JTextArea();
      Container container = getContentPane();
      container.add( outputArea );

      int array1[][] = { { 1, 2, 3 }, { 4, 5, 6 } };
      int array2[][] = { { 1, 2 }, { 3 }, { 4, 5, 6 } };

      outputArea.setText( "Values in array1 by row are\n" );
      buildOutput( array1 );
```

Fig. 7.15 Initializing multidimensional arrays (part 1 of 2).

```
25
26          outputArea.append( "\nValues in array2 by row are\n" );
27          buildOutput( array2 );
28       }
29
30       // append rows and columns of an array to outputArea
31       public void buildOutput( int array[][] )
32       {
33          // loop through array's rows
34          for ( int row = 0; row < array.length; row++ ) {
35
36             // loop through columns of current row
37             for ( int column = 0;
38                   column < array[ row ].length;
39                   column++ )
40                outputArea.append( array[ row ][ column ] + "  " );
41
42             outputArea.append( "\n" );
43          }
44       }
45    }
```

```
Applet Viewer: InitArray.class
Applet
Values in array1 by row are
1 2 3
4 5 6

Values in array2 by row are
1 2
3
4 5 6
Applet started.
```

Fig. 7.15 Initializing multidimensional arrays (part 2 of 2).

The program declares two arrays in method **init**. The declaration of **array1** (line 20) provides six initializers in two sublists. The first sublist initializes the first row of the array to the values 1, 2 and 3. The second sublist initializes the second row of the array to the values 4, 5 and 6. The declaration of **array2** (line 21) provides six initializers in three sublists. The sublist for the first row explicitly initializes the first row to have two elements with values 1 and 2, respectively. The sublist for the second row initializes the second row to have one element with value 3. The sublist for the third row initializes the third row to the values 4, 5 and 6.

Line 24 of method **init** calls method **buildOutput** (defined at lines 31–44) to append each array's elements to **outputArea** (a **JTextArea**). Method **buildOutput** specifies the array parameter as **int array[][]** to indicate that the method receives a double-subscripted array as an argument. Note the use of a nested **for** structure (lines 34–43) to output the rows of a double-subscripted array. In the outer **for** structure, the expression **array.length** determines the number of rows in the array. In the inner **for** structure, the expression **array[row].length** determines the number of columns in the current row of the array. This condition enables the loop to determine the exact number of columns in each row.

Many common array manipulations use **for** repetition structures. For example, the following **for** structure sets all the elements in the third row of array **a** in Fig. 7.14 to zero:

```
for ( int column = 0; column < a[ 2 ].length; column++)
   a[ 2 ][ column ] = 0;
```

We specified the *third* row; therefore, we know that the first subscript is always **2** (**0** is the first row and **1** is the second row). The **for** loop varies only the second subscript (i.e., the column subscript). The preceding **for** structure is equivalent to the assignment statements

```
a[ 2 ][ 0 ] = 0;
a[ 2 ][ 1 ] = 0;
a[ 2 ][ 2 ] = 0;
a[ 2 ][ 3 ] = 0;
```

The following nested **for** structure totals the values of all the elements in array **a**.

```
int total = 0;

for ( int row = 0; row < a.length; row++ )

   for ( int column = 0; column < a[ row ].length; column++ )

      total += a[ row ][ column ];
```

The **for** structure totals the elements of the array one row at a time. The outer **for** structure begins by setting the **row** subscript to **0** so that the elements of the first row may be totaled by the inner **for** structure. The outer **for** structure then increments **row** to **1** so that the second row can be totaled. Then, the outer **for** structure increments **row** to **2** so that the third row can be totaled. The result can be displayed when the nested **for** structure terminates.

The applet of Fig. 7.16 performs several other common array manipulations on 3-by-4 array **grades**. Each row of the array represents a student, and each column represents a grade on one of the four exams the students took during the semester. Four methods perform the array manipulations. Method **minimum** (lines 52–69) determines the lowest grade of any student for the semester. Method **maximum** (lines 72–89) determines the highest grade of any student for the semester. Method **average** (lines 93–103) determines a particular student's semester average. Method **buildString** (lines 106–121) appends the double-subscripted array to **String output** in a tabular format.

Methods **minimum**, **maximum** and **buildString** each use array **grades** and the variables **students** (number of rows in the array) and **exams** (number of columns in the array). Each method loops through array **grades** by using nested **for** structures—for example, the nested **for** structure from the definition of method **minimum** (lines 58–66). The outer **for** structure sets **row** (the row subscript) to **0** so that the elements of the first row can be compared to variable **lowGrade** in the body of the inner **for** structure. The inner **for** structure loops through the four grades of a particular row and compares each grade to **lowGrade**. If a grade is less than **lowGrade**, **lowGrade** is set to that grade. The outer **for** structure then increments the row subscript by **1**. The elements of the second row are compared to variable **lowGrade**. The outer **for** structure then increments the row subscript to **2**. The elements of the third row are compared to variable **lowGrade**. When execution of the nested structure is complete, **lowGrade** contains the smallest grade in the double-subscripted array. Method **maximum** works similarly to method **minimum**.

```
// Fig. 7.16: DoubleArray.java
// Double-subscripted array example

// Java core packages
import java.awt.*;

// Java extension packages
import javax.swing.*;

public class DoubleArray extends JApplet {
   int grades[][] = { { 77, 68, 86, 73 },
                      { 96, 87, 89, 81 },
                      { 70, 90, 86, 81 } };

   int students, exams;
   String output;
   JTextArea outputArea;

   // initialize instance variables
   public void init()
   {
      students = grades.length;      // number of students
      exams = grades[ 0 ].length;    // number of exams

      // create JTextArea and attach to applet
      outputArea = new JTextArea();
      Container container = getContentPane();
      container.add( outputArea );

      // build output string
      output = "The array is:\n";
      buildString();

      // call methods minimum and maximum
      output += "\n\nLowest grade: " + minimum() +
                "\nHighest grade: " + maximum() + "\n";

      // call method average to calculate each student's average
      for ( int counter = 0; counter < students; counter++ )
         output += "\nAverage for student " + counter + " is " +
            average( grades[ counter ] );

      // change outputArea's display font
      outputArea.setFont(
         new Font( "Courier", Font.PLAIN, 12 ) );

      // place output string in outputArea
      outputArea.setText( output );
   }
```

Fig. 7.16 Example of using double-subscripted arrays (part 1 of 3).

```java

   // find minimum grade
   public int minimum()
   {
      // assume first element of grages array is smallest
      int lowGrade = grades[ 0 ][ 0 ];

      // loop through rows of grades array
      for ( int row = 0; row < students; row++ )

         // loop through columns of current row
         for ( int column = 0; column < exams; column++ )

            // Test if current grade is less than lowGrade.
            // If so, assign current grade to lowGrade.
            if ( grades[ row ][ column ] < lowGrade )
               lowGrade = grades[ row ][ column ];

      return lowGrade;  // return lowest grade
   }

   // find maximum grade
   public int maximum()
   {
      // assume first element of grages array is largest
      int highGrade = grades[ 0 ][ 0 ];

      // loop through rows of grades array
      for ( int row = 0; row < students; row++ )

         // loop through columns of current row
         for ( int column = 0; column < exams; column++ )

            // Test if current grade is greater than highGrade.
            // If so, assign current grade to highGrade.
            if ( grades[ row ][ column ] > highGrade )
               highGrade = grades[ row ][ column ];

      return highGrade;  // return highest grade
   }

   // determine average grade for particular
   // student (or set of grades)
   public double average( int setOfGrades[] )
   {
      int total = 0;  // initialize total

      // sum grades for one student
      for ( int count = 0; count < setOfGrades.length; count++ )
         total += setOfGrades[ count ];

```

Fig. 7.16 Example of using double-subscripted arrays (part 2 of 3).

```
101         // return average of grades
102         return ( double ) total / setOfGrades.length;
103      }
104
105      // build output string
106      public void buildString()
107      {
108         output += "              ";  // used to align column heads
109
110         // create column heads
111         for ( int counter = 0; counter < exams; counter++ )
112            output += "[" + counter + "]  ";
113
114         // create rows/columns of text representing array grades
115         for ( int row = 0; row < students; row++ ) {
116            output += "\ngrades[" + row + "]     ";
117
118            for ( int column = 0; column < exams; column++ )
119               output += grades[ row ][ column ] + "    ";
120         }
121      }
122   }
```

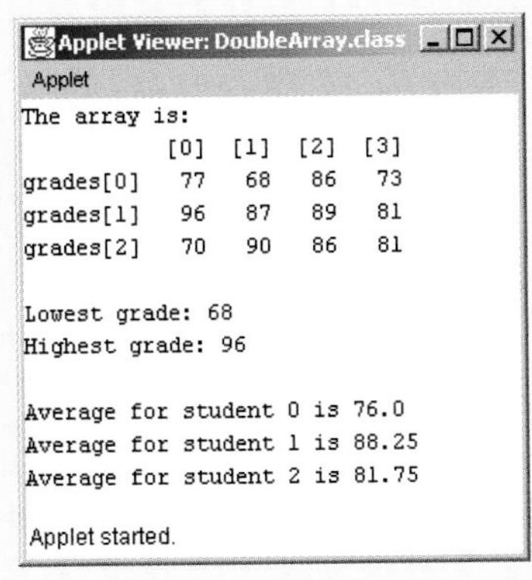

Fig. 7.16 Example of using double-subscripted arrays (part 3 of 3).

Method **average** takes one argument—a single-subscripted array of test results for a particular student. When line 41 calls **average**, the argument is **grades[counter]**, which specifies that a particular row of the double-subscripted array **grades** should be passed to **average**. For example, the argument **grades[1]** represents the four values (a single-subscripted array of grades) stored in the second row of the double-subscripted array **grades**. Remember that, in Java, a double-subscripted array is an array with elements that are single-subscripted arrays. Method **average** calculates the sum of the array elements, divides the total by the number of test results and returns the floating-point result as a **double** value.

7.10 (Optional Case Study) Thinking About Objects: Collaboration Among Objects

In this section, we concentrate on the collaborations (interactions) among objects. When two objects communicate with each other to accomplish a task, they are said to *collaborate*—objects do this by invoking one another's operations. We say that objects send *messages* to other objects. We explain how messages are sent and received in Java in Section 10.22. A *collaboration* consists of an object of one class sending a particular message to an object of another class.

The message sent by the first object invokes an operation of the second object. In "Thinking About Objects" Section 6.17, we determined many of the operations of the classes in our system. In this section, we concentrate on the messages that invoke these operations. Figure 7.17 is the table of classes and verb phrases from Section 6.17. We have removed all the verb phrases in classes **Elevator** and **Person** that do not correspond to operations. The remaining phrases are our first estimate of the collaborations in our system. As we proceed through this and the remaining "Thinking About Objects" sections, we will discover additional collaborations.

We examine the list of verb phrases to determine the collaborations in our system. For example, class **Elevator** lists the phrase "resets elevator button." To accomplish this task, an object of class **Elevator** sends the **resetButton** message to an object of class **ElevatorButton** (invoking the **resetButton** operation of **ElevatorButton**). Figure 7.18 lists all the collaborations that can be gleaned from our table of verb phrases. According to Fig. 7.17, the **Elevator**[1] rings the **Bell** and opens (and closes) the **ElevatorDoor**, so we include a **ringBell**, **openDoor** and **closeDoor** message in Fig. 7.18. However, we must consider how the **FloorDoors** open and close. According to the class diagram of Fig. 3.23, **ElevatorShaft** is the only class that associates with **FloorDoor**. The **Elevator** signals its arrival (we assume to the **ElevatorShaft**) by sending an **elevatorArrived** message. The **ElevatorShaft** responds to this message by resetting the appropriate **FloorButton** and turning on the appropriate **Light**—the **ElevatorShaft** sends **resetButton** and **turnOnLight** messages. At this point in the design, we may assume that the **Elevator** also signals its departure—that is, the **ElevatorShaft** sends an **elevatorDeparted** message to the **ElevatorShaft**, which then turns off the appropriate **Light** by sending it a **turnOffLight** message.

Class	Verb phrases
Elevator	Resets elevator button, rings elevator bell, signals its arrival, signals its departure, opens its door, closes its door.
ElevatorShaft	Turns off light, turns on light, resets floor button.

Fig. 7.17 Verb phrases for each class exhibiting behaviors in simulation (part 1 of 2).

1. We refer to an object by using that object's class name preceded by an article ("a," "an" or "the")—for example, the **Elevator** refers to the object of class **Elevator**. Our syntax avoids redundancy—i.e., we avoid repeating the phrase "an object of class...."

Class	Verb phrases
Person	Presses floor button, presses elevator button, rides elevator, enters elevator, exits elevator.
FloorButton	Summons (requests) elevator.
ElevatorButton	Signals elevator to move to opposite floor.
FloorDoor	Signals person to enter elevator (by opening).
ElevatorDoor	Signals person to exit elevator (by opening), opens floor door, closes floor door.
ElevatorModel	Creates person.

Fig. 7.17 Verb phrases for each class exhibiting behaviors in simulation (part 2 of 2).

An object of class...	Sends the message...	To an object of class...
Elevator	**resetButton**	**ElevatorButton**
	ringBell	**Bell**
	elevatorArrived	**ElevatorShaft**
	elevatorDeparted	**ElevatorShaft**
	openDoor	**ElevatorDoor**
	closeDoor	**ElevatorDoor**
ElevatorShaft	**resetButton**	**FloorButton**
	turnOnLight	**Light**
	turnOffLight	**Light**
Person	**pressButton**	**FloorButton, ElevatorButton**
	enterElevator	**Elevator**
	exitElevator	**Elevator**
FloorButton	**requestElevator**	**Elevator**
ElevatorButton	**moveElevator**	**Elevator**
FloorDoor	**doorOpened**	**Person**
	doorClosed	**Person**
ElevatorDoor	**doorOpened**	**Person**
	doorClosed	**Person**
	openDoor	**FloorDoor**
	closeDoor	**FloorDoor**

Fig. 7.18 Collaborations in the elevator system.

A **Person** may press either a **FloorButton** or the **ElevatorButton**. A **Person** object may enter and exit the **Elevator**. Therefore, a **Person** may send **pressButton**, **enterElevator** and **exitElevator** messages. A **FloorButton** requests, or summons, the **Elevator**, so a **FloorButton** may send a **requestElevator** message. The **ElevatorButton** signals the **Elevator** to begin moving to the other floor, so the **ElevatorButton** may send a **moveElevator** message.

Both a **FloorDoor** and the **ElevatorDoor** inform a **Person** that they have opened or closed, so both objects send **doorOpened** and **doorClosed** messages.[2] Finally, the **ElevatorModel** creates a **Person**, but the **ElevatorModel** cannot send a **personCreated** message, because that **Person** does not yet exist. We discover, in Section 8.6, how to use a special method that creates, or *instantiates*, new objects. This method is referred to as an *constructor*—the **ElevatorModel** will create a **Person** by calling that **Person**'s constructor (which is similar to sending the **personCreated** message).

Lastly, the **ElevatorDoor** must send **openDoor** and **closeDoor** messages to a **FloorDoor** to guarantee that these doors open and close together.

Collaboration Diagrams

Now let us consider the objects that must interact so that people in our simulation can enter and exit the elevator when it arrives on a floor. The UML provides the *collaboration diagram* to model such interactions. Collaboration diagrams are a type of *interaction diagram*; they model the behavioral aspects of the system by providing information about how objects interact. Collaboration diagrams emphasize which objects participate in the interactions. The other type of interaction diagram is the *sequence diagram*, which we present in Chapter 15. Figure 7.19 shows a collaboration diagram that models a person who is pressing a floor button. An object in a collaboration diagram is represented as a rectangle that encloses the object's name. We write object names in the collaboration diagram by using the convention we introduced in the object diagram of Fig. 3.24—objects are written in the form **objectName : ClassName**. In this example, we disregard the object name, because we care only about the object type. Collaborating objects are connected with solid lines, and messages are passed between objects along these lines in the direction shown by arrows. The name of the message, which appears next to the arrow, is the name of a method belonging to the receiving object—think of the name as a "service" that the receiving object (a "server") provides for its sending objects (its "clients").

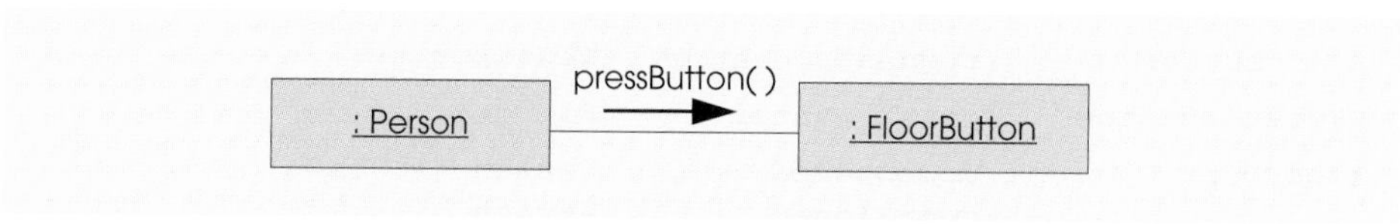

Fig. 7.19 Collaboration diagram of a person pressing a floor button

The arrow in Fig. 7.19 represents a message in the UML and a method—or *synchronous call*—in Java. This arrow indicates that the flow of control is from the sending object to the receiving object—the sending object may not send another message until the receiving object processes the message and returns control to the sending object. For example, in Fig. 7.19, a **Person** calls method **pressButton** of a **FloorButton** and

2. Note that most of the messages perform some specific action on the receiving object; for example, the **Elevator** resets the **ElevatorButton**. However, other messages inform receiving objects of *events* that have already happened; for example, the **FloorDoor** informs the **Person** that the **FloorDoor** has opened. In Section 10.22, we elaborate on the topic of events—for now, however, we proceed as if the two types of messages are indistinguishable.

may not send another message to an object until **pressButton** has finished and returns control to that **Person**. If our program contains a **FloorButton** object called **first-FloorButton**, and we assume that the **Person** manages the flow of control, the Java code implementation in class **Person** that represents this collaboration diagram is

```
firstFloorButton.pressButton();
```

Figure 7.20 shows a collaboration diagram that models the interactions among objects in the system while objects of class **Person** enter and exit the elevator. The collaboration begins when the **Elevator** arrives on a **Floor**. The number to the left of the message name indicates the order in which the message is passed. The *sequence of messages* in a collaboration diagram progresses in numerical order from least to greatest. In this diagram, the numbering starts with message **1** and ends with message **4.2**. The sequence of passing messages follows a nested structure—for example, message **1.1** is the *first message* nested in message **1**, and message **3.2** is the *second message* nested in message **3**. Message **3.2.1** would be the *first message* nested in message **3.2**. A message may be passed only when all nested messages from the previous message have been passed. For example, in Fig. 7.20, the **Elevator** passes message **4** after message **3**, message **3.1**, message **3.1.1**, message **3.1.1.1**, message **3.2** and message **3.2.1** are passed.

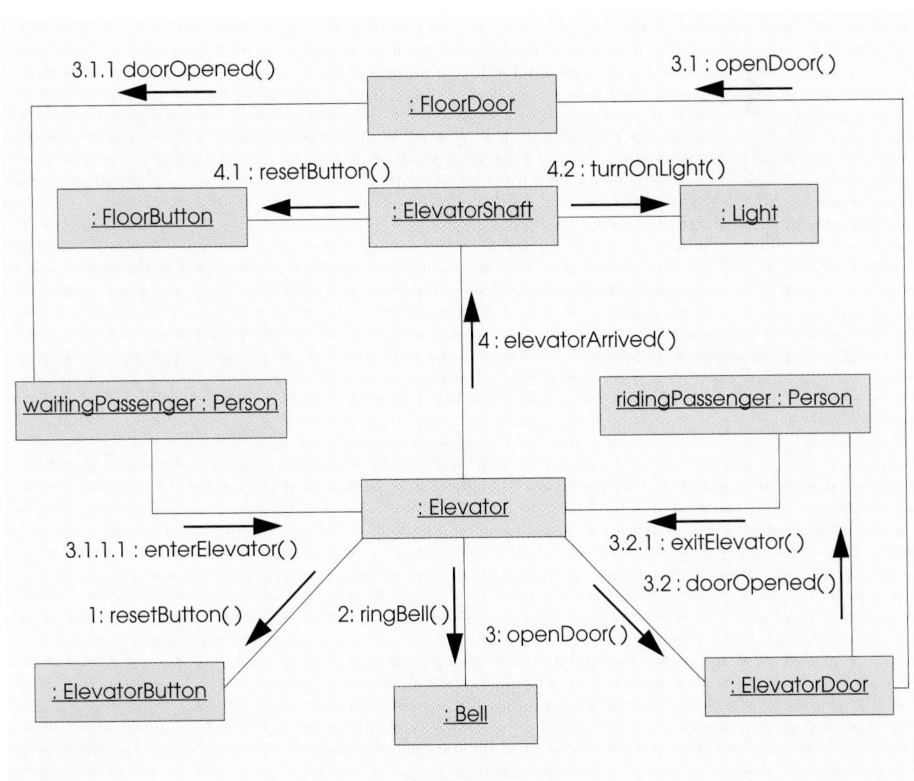

Fig. 7.20 Collaboration diagram for passengers exiting and entering the elevator.

The **Elevator** sends the **resetButton** message (message **1**) to the **ElevatorButton** to reset the **ElevatorButton**. The **Elevator** sends the **ringBell** message (message **2**) to the **Bell**, then opens the **ElevatorDoor** by passing the **openDoor** message (message **3**). The **ElevatorDoor** then opens the **FloorDoor** by sending an **openDoor** message (message **3.1** at the top of the diagram) to that **FloorDoor**. The **FloorDoor** informs the **waitingPassenger** that the **FloorDoor** has opened (message **3.1.1**), and the **waitingPassenger** enters the **Elevator** (message **3.1.1.1**). The **ElevatorDoor** then informs the **ridingPassenger** that the **ElevatorDoor** has opened (message **3.2**), so that the **ridingPassenger** may exit the **Elevator** (message **3.2.1**). Lastly, the **Elevator** informs the **ElevatorShaft** of the arrival (message **4**), so that the **ElevatorShaft** can reset the **FloorButton** (message **4.1**) and turn on the **Light** (message **4.2**).

Unfortunately, this design creates a problem. According to the diagram, the **waitingPassenger** enters the **Elevator** (message **3.1.1.1**) before the **ridingPassenger** (message **3.2.1**) exits. In "Thinking About Objects" Section 15.12, we apply multithreading, synchronization and active classes to our collaboration diagram, to force the **waitingPassenger** to wait for the **ridingPassenger** to exit the **Elevator**. Before we correct this problem, we modify this diagram to indicate more accurately the message passing in Section 10.22 when we discuss *event handling*.

SUMMARY

- Java stores lists of values in arrays. An array is a contiguous group of related memory locations. These locations are related by the fact that they all have the same name and the same type. To refer to a particular location or element within the array, we specify the name of the array and the subscript (or index or position number) of the element.
- Each array a **length** member that is set to the number of elements in the array at the time the program creates the array object.
- A subscript may be an integer or an integer expression. If a program uses an expression as a subscript, the program evaluates the expression to determine the particular element of the array.
- Java arrays always begin with element 0; thus, it is important to note the difference when referring to the "seventh element of the array" as opposed to "array element seven." The seventh element has a subscript of **6**, while array element seven has a subscript of **7** (actually the eighth element of the array).
- Arrays occupy space in memory and are considered to be objects. Operator **new** must be used to reserve space for an array. For example, the following creates an array of 100 **int** values:

```
int b[] = new int[ 100 ];
```

- When declaring an array, the type of the array and the square brackets can be combined at the beginning of the declaration to indicate that all identifiers in the declaration represent arrays, as in

```
double[] array1, array2;
```

- The elements of an array can be initialized with initializer lists in a declaration and by input.
- Java prevents referencing elements beyond the bounds of an array. If this occurs during program execution, an **ArrayIndexOutOfBoundsException** occurs.
- Constant variables must be initialized with a constant expression before they are used and cannot be modified thereafter.

- To pass an array to a method, pass the name of the array. To pass a single element of an array to a method, simply pass the name of the array followed by the subscript of the particular element.
- Arrays are passed to methods as references—therefore, the called methods can modify the element values in the caller's original arrays. Single elements of primitive-data-type arrays are passed to methods by value.
- To receive an array argument, the method must specify an array parameter in the parameter list.
- An array can be sorted by using the bubble-sort technique. Several passes of the array are made. On each pass, successive pairs of elements are compared. If a pair is in order (or the values are identical), it is left as is. If a pair is out of order, the values are swapped. For small arrays, the bubble sort is acceptable, but for larger arrays it is inefficient compared to more sophisticated sorting algorithms.
- The linear search compares each element of the array with the search key. If the array is not in any particular order, it is just as likely that the value will be found in the first element as the last. On average, therefore, the program will have to compare the search key with half the elements of the array. Linear search works well for small arrays and is acceptable even for large unsorted arrays.
- For sorted arrays, the binary search eliminates from consideration one half of the elements in the array after each comparison. The algorithm locates the middle element of the array and compares it with the search key. If they are equal, the search key is found and the array subscript of that element is returned. Otherwise, the problem is reduced to searching one half of the array that is still under consideration. In a worst-case scenario, searching a sorted array of 1024 elements will take only 10 comparisons using a binary search.
- Most GUI components have method **`setFont`** to change the font of the text on the GUI component. The method requires a **`Font`** (package **`java.awt`**) object as its argument.
- A **`Font`** object is initialized with three arguments—a **`String`** representing the name of the font, an **`int`** representing the style of the font and an **`int`** representing the point size of the font. The style can be **`Font.PLAIN`**, **`Font.BOLD`**, **`Font.ITALIC`** or **`Font.BOLD + Font.ITALIC`**. The point size represents the size of the font—there are 72 points to an inch. The actual screen size may vary based on the size of the screen and the screen resolution.
- Arrays may be used to represent tables of values consisting of information arranged in rows and columns. To identify a particular element of a table, two subscripts are specified: The first identifies the row in which the element is contained, and the second identifies the column in which the element is contained. Tables or arrays that require two subscripts to identify a particular element are called double-subscripted arrays.
- A double-subscripted array can be initialized with an initializer list of the form

  arrayType arrayName`[][] = { {` *row1 sublist* `}, {` *row2 sublist* `}, ... };`

- To dynamically create an array with a fixed number of rows and columns, use

  arrayType arrayName`[][] = new` *arrayType*`[` *numRows* `][` *numColumns* `];`

- To pass one row of a double-subscripted array to a method that receives a single-subscripted array, simply pass the name of the array followed by only the row subscript.

TERMINOLOGY

`a[ i ]`
`a[ i ][ j ]`
array
array initializer list
binary search of an array
bounds checking
bubble sort
column subscript
constant variable
declare an array
double-subscripted array
element of an array

final
Font class from **java.awt**
Font.BOLD
Font.ITALIC
Font.PLAIN
index
initialize an array
initializer
linear search of an array
lvalue
m-by-n array
multiple-subscripted array
name of an array
named constant
off-by-one error
pass of a bubble sort
pass-by-reference
pass-by-value
passing arrays to methods
position number
row subscript
search key
searching an array
setFont method
single-subscripted array
sinking sort
sorting
sorting an array
square brackets, **[]**
subscript
table of values
tabular format
temporary area for exchange of values
value of an element
zeroth element

SELF-REVIEW EXERCISES

7.1 Fill in the blank(s) in each of the following statements:

a) Lists and tables of values can be stored in __________.
b) The elements of an array are related by the fact that they have the same __________ and __________.
c) The number used to refer to a particular element of an array is called its __________.
d) The process of placing the elements of an array in order is called __________ the array.
e) Determining if an array contains a certain key value is called __________ the array.
f) An array that uses two subscripts is referred to as a __________ array.

7.2 State whether each of the following is *true* or *false*. If *false*, explain why.

a) An array can store many different types of values.
b) An array subscript should normally be of data type **float**.
c) An individual array element that is passed to a method and modified in that method will contain the modified value when the called method completes execution.

7.3 Answer the following questions regarding an array called **fractions**:

a) Define a constant variable **ARRAY_SIZE** initialized to 10.
b) Declare an array with **ARRAY_SIZE** elements of type **float** and initialize the elements to **0**.
c) Name the fourth element of the array.
d) Refer to array element 4.
e) Assign the value **1.667** to array element 9.
f) Assign the value **3.333** to the seventh element of the array.
g) Sum all the elements of the array using a **for** repetition structure. Define the integer variable **x** as a control variable for the loop.

7.4 Answer the following questions regarding an array called **table**:

a) Declare and create the array as an integer array and with 3 rows and 3 columns. Assume the constant variable **ARRAY_SIZE** has been defined to be 3.
b) How many elements does the array contain?
c) Use a **for** repetition structure to initialize each element of the array to the sum of its subscripts. Assume the integer variables **x** and **y** are declared as control variables.

7.5 Find the error in each of the following program segments and correct the error:

a)
```
final int ARRAY_SIZE = 5;
ARRAY_SIZE = 10;
```
b) Assume `int b[] = new int[ 10 ];`
```
for ( int i = 0; i <= b.length; i++ )
   b[ i ] = 1;
```
c) Assume `int a[][] = { { 1, 2 }, { 3, 4 } };`
```
   a[ 1, 1 ] = 5;
```

ANSWERS TO SELF-REVIEW EXERCISES

7.1 a) arrays. b) name, type. c) subscript (or index or position number). d) sorting. e) searching. f) double-subscripted (or two-dimensional).

7.2
a) False. An array can store only values of the same type.
b) False. An array subscript must be an integer or an integer expression.
c) False for individual primitive-data-type elements of an array because they are passed by value. If a reference to an array is passed, then modifications to the array elements are reflected in the original. Also, an individual element of a nonprimitive type is passed by reference, and changes to the object will be reflected in the original array element.

7.3
a) `final int ARRAY_SIZE = 10;`
b) `float fractions[] = new float[ ARRAY_SIZE ];`
c) `fractions[ 3 ]`
d) `fractions[ 4 ]`
e) `fractions[ 9 ] = 1.667;`
f) `fractions[ 6 ] = 3.333;`
g)
```
float total = 0;
for ( int x = 0; x < fractions.length; x++ )
   total += fractions[ x ];
```

7.4
a) `int table[][] = new int[ ARRAY_SIZE ][ ARRAY_SIZE ];`
b) Nine.
c)
```
for ( int x = 0; x < table.length; x++ )
   for ( int y = 0; y < table[ x ].length; y++ )
      table[ x ][ y ] = x + y;
```

7.5 The solutions to Exercise 7.5 are as follows:
a) Error: Assigning a value to a constant variable after it has been initialized.
Correction: Assign the correct value to the constant variable in a **final int ARRAY_SIZE** declaration or create another variable.
b) Error: Referencing an array element outside the bounds of the array (**b[10]**).
Correction: Change the **<=** operator to **<**.
c) Error: Array subscripting performed incorrectly.
Correction: Change the statement to **a[1][1] = 5;**.

EXERCISES

7.6 Fill in the blanks in each of the following:
a) Java stores lists of values in __________.
b) The elements of an array are related by the fact that they __________.
c) When referring to an array element, the position number contained within brackets is called a __________.

d) The names of the four elements of array **p** are __________, __________, __________ and __________.
e) Naming an array, stating its type and specifying the number of dimensions in the array is called __________ the array.
f) The process of placing the elements of an array into either ascending or descending order is called __________.
g) In a double-subscripted array, the first subscript identifies the __________ of an element and the second subscript identifies the __________ of an element.
h) An m-by-n array contains __________ rows, __________ columns and __________ elements.
i) The name of the element in row 3 and column 5 of array **d** is __________.

7.7 State whether each of the following is *true* or *false*. If *false*, explain why.
a) To refer to a particular location or element within an array, we specify the name of the array and the value of the particular element.
b) An array declaration reserves space for the array.
c) To indicate that 100 locations should be reserved for integer array **p**, the programmer writes the declaration

```
p[ 100 ];
```

d) A Java program that initializes the elements of a 15-element array to zero must contain at least one **for** statement.
e) A Java program that totals the elements of a double-subscripted array must contain nested **for** statements.

7.8 Write Java statements to accomplish each of the following:
a) Display the value of the seventh element of character array **f**.
b) Initialize each of the five elements of single-subscripted integer array **g** to **8**.
c) Total the elements of floating-point array **c** of 100 elements.
d) Copy 11-element array **a** into the first portion of array **b**, containing 34 elements.
e) Determine and print the smallest and largest values contained in 99-element floating-point array **w**.

7.9 Consider a 2-by-3 integer array **t**.
a) Write a statement that declares and creates **t**.
b) How many rows does **t** have?
c) How many columns does **t** have?
d) How many elements does **t** have?
e) Write the names of all the elements in the second row of **t**.
f) Write the names of all the elements in the third column of **t**.
g) Write a single statement that sets the element of **t** in row 1 and column 2 to zero.
h) Write a series of statements that initializes each element of **t** to zero. Do not use a repetition structure.
i) Write a nested **for** structure that initializes each element of **t** to zero.
j) Write a nested **for** structure that inputs the values for the elements of **t** from the keyboard.
k) Write a series of statements that determines and prints the smallest value in array **t**.
l) Write a statement that displays the elements of the first row of **t**.
m) Write a statement that totals the elements of the fourth column of **t**.
n) Write a series of statements that prints the array **t** in neat, tabular format. List the column subscripts as headings across the top and list the row subscripts at the left of each row.

7.10 Use a single-subscripted array to solve the following problem: A company pays its salespeople on a commission basis. The salespeople receive $200 per week plus 9% of their gross sales for that week. For example, a salesperson who grosses $5000 in sales in a week receives $200 plus 9% of $5000 or a total of $650. Write an applet (using an array of counters) that determines how many of the salespeople earned salaries in each of the following ranges (assume that each salesperson's salary is truncated to an integer amount):

a) $200-$299
b) $300-$399
c) $400-$499
d) $500-$599
e) $600-$699
f) $700-$799
g) $800-$899
h) $900-$999
i) $1000 and over

The applet should use the GUI techniques introduced in Chapter 6. Display the results in a **JTextArea**. Use **JTextArea** method **setText** to update the results after each value input by the user.

7.11 The bubble sort presented in Fig. 7.11 is inefficient for large arrays. Make the following simple modifications to improve the performance of the bubble sort:

a) After the first pass, the largest number is guaranteed to be in the highest-numbered element of the array; after the second pass, the two highest numbers are "in place"; and so on. Instead of making nine comparisons on every pass, modify the bubble sort to make eight comparisons on the second pass, seven on the third pass and so on.
b) The data in the array may already be in the proper order or near-proper order, so why make nine passes if fewer will suffice? Modify the sort to check at the end of each pass if any swaps have been made. If none have been made, the data must already be in the proper order, so the program should terminate. If swaps have been made, at least one more pass is needed.

7.12 Write statements that perform the following single-subscripted array operations:

a) Set the 10 elements of integer array **counts** to zeros.
b) Add 1 to each of the 15 elements of integer array **bonus**.
c) Print the five values of integer array **bestScores** in column format.

7.13 Use a single-subscripted array to solve the following problem: Write an applet that inputs 20 numbers, each of which is between 10 and 100, inclusive. As each number is read, display it only if it is not a duplicate of a number already read. Provide for the "worst case" in which all 20 numbers are different. Use the smallest possible array to solve this problem. The applet should use the GUI techniques introduced in Chapter 6. Display the results in a **JTextArea**. Use **JTextArea** method **setText** to update the results after each value input by the user.

7.14 Label the elements of 3-by-5 double-subscripted array **sales** to indicate the order in which they are set to zero by the following program segment:

```
for ( int row = 0; row < sales.length; row++ )

   for ( int col = 0; col < sales[ row ].length; col++ )

      sales[ row ][ col ] = 0;
```

7.15 Write an applet to simulate the rolling of two dice. The program should use **Math.random** to roll the first die and should use **Math.random** again to roll the second die. The sum of the two values should then be calculated. [*Note*: Each die can show an integer value from 1 to 6, so the sum of the values will vary from 2 to 12, with 7 being the most frequent sum and 2 and 12 being the least frequent sums. Figure 7.21 shows the 36 possible combinations of the two dice. Your program should

	1	2	3	4	5	6
1	2	3	4	5	6	7
2	3	4	5	6	7	8
3	4	5	6	7	8	9
4	5	6	7	8	9	10
5	6	7	8	9	10	11
6	7	8	9	10	11	12

Fig. 7.21 The 36 possible outcomes of rolling two dice.

roll the dice 36,000 times. Use a single-subscripted array to tally the numbers of times each possible sum appears. Display the results in a **JTextArea** in tabular format. Also, determine whether the totals are reasonable (i.e., there are six ways to roll a 7, so approximately one sixth of all the rolls should be 7). The applet should use the GUI techniques introduced in Chapter 6. Provide a **JButton** to allow the user of the applet to roll the dice another 36,000 times. The applet should reset the elements of the single-subscripted array to 0 before rolling the dice again.

7.16 What does the program of Fig. 7.22 do?

```
// Exercise 7.16: WhatDoesThisDo.java

// Java core packages
import java.awt.*;

// Java extension packages
import javax.swing.*;

public class WhatDoesThisDo extends JApplet {
   int result;

   public void init()
   {
      int array[] = { 1, 2, 3, 4, 5, 6, 7, 8, 9, 10 };

      result = whatIsThis( array, array.length );

      Container container = getContentPane();
      JTextArea output = new JTextArea();
      output.setText( "Result is: " + result );
      container.add( output );
   }

   public int whatIsThis( int array2[], int size )
   {
      if ( size == 1 )
         return array2[ 0 ];
```

Fig. 7.22 Determine what this program does.

```
         else
            return array2[ size - 1 ] +
               whatIsThis( array2, size - 1 );
      }
   }
```

Fig. 7.22 Determine what this program does.

7.17 Write a program that runs 1000 games of craps (Fig. 6.9) and answers the following questions:

a) How many games are won on the first roll, second roll, …, twentieth roll and after the twentieth roll?
b) How many games are lost on the first roll, second roll, …, twentieth roll and after the twentieth roll?
c) What are the chances of winning at craps? [*Note*: You should discover that craps is one of the fairest casino games. What do you suppose this means?]
d) What is the average length of a game of craps?
e) Do the chances of winning improve with the length of the game?

7.18 (*Airline Reservations System*) A small airline has just purchased a computer for its new automated reservations system. You have been asked to program the new system. You are to write an applet to assign seats on each flight of the airline's only plane (capacity: 10 seats).

Your program should display the following alternatives:

```
Please type 1 for "smoking"
Please type 2 for "nonsmoking"
```

If the person types 1, your program should assign a seat in the smoking section (seats 1-5). If the person types 2, your program should assign a seat in the nonsmoking section (seats 6-10). Your program should then print a boarding pass indicating the person's seat number and whether it is in the smoking or nonsmoking section of the plane.

Use a single-subscripted array of primitive type **boolean** to represent the seating chart of the plane. Initialize all the elements of the array to **false** to indicate that all seats are empty. As each seat is assigned, set the corresponding elements of the array to **true** to indicate that the seat is no longer available.

Your program should, of course, never assign a seat that has already been assigned. When the smoking section is full, your program should ask the person if it is acceptable to be placed in the nonsmoking section (and vice versa). If yes, make the appropriate seat assignment. If no, print the message **"Next flight leaves in 3 hours."**

7.19 What does the program of Fig. 7.23 do?

```
// Exercise 7.19: WhatDoesThisDo2.java

// Java core packages
import java.awt.*;

// Java extension packages
import javax.swing.*;

```

Fig. 7.23 Determine what this program does.

```
public class WhatDoesThisDo2 extends JApplet {

   public void init()
   {
      int array[] = { 1, 2, 3, 4, 5, 6, 7, 8, 9, 10 };
      JTextArea outputArea = new JTextArea();

      someFunction( array, 0, outputArea );

      Container container = getContentPane();
      container.add( outputArea );
   }

   public void someFunction( int array2[], int x, JTextArea out )
   {
      if ( x < array2.length ) {
         someFunction( array2, x + 1, out );
         out.append( array2[ x ] + "  " );
      }
   }
}
```

Fig. 7.23 Determine what this program does.

7.20 Use a double-subscripted array to solve the following problem. A company has four salespeople (1 to 4) who sell five different products (1 to 5). Once a day, each salesperson passes in a slip for each different type of product sold. Each slip contains the following:

a) The salesperson number
b) The product number
c) The total dollar value of that product sold that day

Thus, each salesperson passes in between 0 and 5 sales slips per day. Assume that the information from all of the slips for last month is available. Write an applet that will read all this information for last month's sales and summarize the total sales by salesperson by product. All totals should be stored in the double-subscripted array **sales**. After processing all the information for last month, display the results in tabular format with each of the columns representing a particular salesperson and each of the rows representing a particular product. Cross total each row to get the total sales of each product for last month; cross total each column to get the total sales by salesperson for last month. Your tabular printout should include these cross totals to the right of the totaled rows and to the bottom of the totaled columns. Display the results in a **JTextArea**.

7.21 (*Turtle Graphics*) The Logo language, which is popular among young computer users, made the concept of *turtle graphics* famous. Imagine a mechanical turtle that walks around the room under the control of a Java program. The turtle holds a pen in one of two positions, up or down. While the pen is down, the turtle traces out shapes as it moves; while the pen is up, the turtle moves about freely without writing anything. In this problem you will simulate the operation of the turtle and create a computerized sketchpad as well.

Use a 20-by-20 array **floor** that is initialized to zeros. Read commands from an array that contains them. Keep track of the current position of the turtle at all times and whether the pen is currently up or down. Assume that the turtle always starts at position 0,0 of the floor with its pen up. The set of turtle commands your program must process are shown in Fig. 7.24.

Command	Meaning
1	Pen up
2	Pen down
3	Turn right
4	Turn left
5,10	Move forward 10 spaces (or a number other than 10)
6	Print the 20-by-20 array
9	End of data (sentinel)

Fig. 7.24 Turtle graphics commands.

Suppose that the turtle is somewhere near the center of the floor. The following "program" would draw and print a 12-by-12 square, leaving the pen in the up position:

```
2
5,12
3
5,12
3
5,12
3
5,12
1
6
9
```

As the turtle moves with the pen down, set the appropriate elements of array **floor** to **1**s. When the **6** command (print) is given, wherever there is a **1** in the array, display an asterisk or some other character you choose. Wherever there is a zero, display a blank. Write a Java applet to implement the turtle graphics capabilities discussed here. The applet should display the turtle graphics in a **JTextArea**, using Monospaced font. Write several turtle graphics programs to draw interesting shapes. Add other commands to increase the power of your turtle graphics language.

7.22 (*Knight's Tour*) One of the more interesting puzzlers for chess buffs is the Knight's Tour problem, originally proposed by the mathematician Euler. The question is this: Can the chess piece called the knight move around an empty chessboard and touch each of the 64 squares once and only once? We study this intriguing problem in depth here.

The knight makes L-shaped moves (over two in one direction and then over one in a perpendicular direction). Thus, from a square in the middle of an empty chessboard, the knight can make eight different moves (numbered 0 through 7) as shown in Fig. 7.25.

a) Draw an 8-by-8 chessboard on a sheet of paper and attempt a Knight's Tour by hand. Put a **1** in the first square you move to, a **2** in the second square, a **3** in the third, etc. Before starting the tour, estimate how far you think you will get, remembering that a full tour consists of 64 moves. How far did you get? Was this close to your estimate?

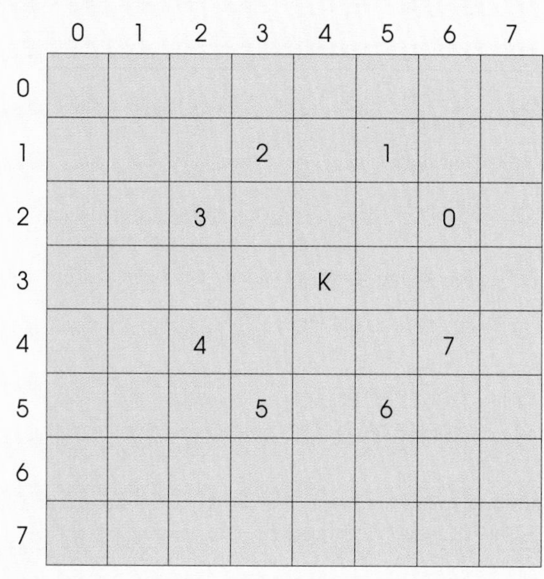

Fig. 7.25 The eight possible moves of the knight.

b) Now let us develop an applet that will move the knight around a chessboard. The board is represented by an 8-by-8 double-subscripted array **board**. Each of the squares is initialized to zero. We describe each of the eight possible moves in terms of both their horizontal and vertical components. For example, a move of type 0 as shown in Fig. 7.25 consists of moving two squares horizontally to the right and one square vertically upward. Move 2 consists of moving one square horizontally to the left and two squares vertically upward. Horizontal moves to the left and vertical moves upward are indicated with negative numbers. The eight moves may be described by two single-subscripted arrays, **horizontal** and **vertical**, as follows:

```
horizontal[ 0 ] = 2
horizontal[ 1 ] = 1
horizontal[ 2 ] = -1
horizontal[ 3 ] = -2
horizontal[ 4 ] = -2
horizontal[ 5 ] = -1
horizontal[ 6 ] = 1
horizontal[ 7 ] = 2

vertical[ 0 ] = -1
vertical[ 1 ] = -2
vertical[ 2 ] = -2
vertical[ 3 ] = -1
vertical[ 4 ] = 1
vertical[ 5 ] = 2
vertical[ 6 ] = 2
vertical[ 7 ] = 1
```

Let the variables **currentRow** and **currentColumn** indicate the row and column of the knight's current position. To make a move of type **moveNumber**, where **moveNumber** is between 0 and 7, your program uses the statements

```
currentRow += vertical[ moveNumber ];
currentColumn += horizontal[ moveNumber ];
```

Keep a counter that varies from **1** to **64**. Record the latest count in each square the knight moves to. Test each potential move to see if the knight already visited that square. Test every potential move to ensure that the knight does not land off the chessboard. Write a program to move the knight around the chessboard. Run the program. How many moves did the knight make?

c) After attempting to write and run a Knight's Tour program, you have probably developed some valuable insights. We will use these to develop a *heuristic* (or strategy) for moving the knight. Heuristics do not guarantee success, but a carefully developed heuristic greatly improves the chance of success. You may have observed that the outer squares are more troublesome than the squares nearer the center of the board. In fact, the most troublesome or inaccessible squares are the four corners.

Intuition may suggest that you should attempt to move the knight to the most troublesome squares first and leave open those that are easiest to get to so when the board gets congested near the end of the tour there will be a greater chance of success.

We could develop an "accessibility heuristic" by classifying each of the squares according to how accessible they are, then always moving the knight (using the knight's L-shaped moves) to the most inaccessible square. We label a double-subscripted array **accessibility** with numbers indicating from how many squares each particular square is accessible. On a blank chessboard, each center square is rated as **8**, each corner square is rated as **2** and the other squares have accessibility numbers of **3**, **4** or **6** as follows:

```
2 3 4 4 4 4 3 2
3 4 6 6 6 6 4 3
4 6 8 8 8 8 6 4
4 6 8 8 8 8 6 4
4 6 8 8 8 8 6 4
4 6 8 8 8 8 6 4
3 4 6 6 6 6 4 3
2 3 4 4 4 4 3 2
```

Write a version of the Knight's Tour using the accessibility heuristic. The knight should always move to the square with the lowest accessibility number. In case of a tie, the knight may move to any of the tied squares. Therefore, the tour may begin in any of the four corners. [*Note*: As the knight moves around the chessboard, your program should reduce the accessibility numbers as more squares become occupied. In this way, at any given time during the tour, each available square's accessibility number will remain equal to precisely the number of squares from which that square may be reached.] Run this version of your program. Did you get a full tour? Modify the program to run 64 tours, one starting from each square of the chessboard. How many full tours did you get?

d) Write a version of the Knight's Tour program that, when encountering a tie between two or more squares, decides what square to choose by looking ahead to those squares reachable from the "tied" squares. Your program should move to the square for which the next move would arrive at a square with the lowest accessibility number.

7.23 (*Knight's Tour: Brute Force Approaches*) In Exercise 7.22, we developed a solution to the Knight's Tour problem. The approach used, called the "accessibility heuristic," generates many solutions and executes efficiently.

As computers continue increasing in power, we will be able to solve more problems with sheer computer power and relatively unsophisticated algorithms. Let us call this approach "brute force" problem solving.

a) Use random number generation to enable the knight to walk around the chessboard (in its legitimate L-shaped moves, of course) at random. Your program should run one tour and print the final chessboard. How far did the knight get?
b) Most likely, the preceding program produced a relatively short tour. Now modify your program to attempt 1000 tours. Use a single-subscripted array to keep track of the number of tours of each length. When your program finishes attempting the 1000 tours, it should print this information in neat tabular format. What was the best result?
c) Most likely, the preceding program gave you some "respectable" tours, but no full tours. Now "pull all the stops out" and simply let your program run until it produces a full tour. (*Caution*: This version of the program could run for hours on a powerful computer.) Once again, keep a table of the number of tours of each length and print this table when the first full tour is found. How many tours did your program attempt before producing a full tour? How much time did it take?
d) Compare the brute force version of the Knight's Tour with the accessibility-heuristic version. Which required a more careful study of the problem? Which algorithm was more difficult to develop? Which required more computer power? Could we be certain (in advance) of obtaining a full tour with the accessibility-heuristic approach? Could we be certain (in advance) of obtaining a full tour with the brute force approach? Argue the pros and cons of brute force problem solving in general.

7.24 (*Eight Queens*) Another puzzler for chess buffs is the Eight Queens problem. Simply stated: Is it possible to place eight queens on an empty chessboard so that no queen is "attacking" any other, i.e., no two queens are in the same row, in the same column or along the same diagonal? Use the thinking developed in Exercise 7.22 to formulate a heuristic for solving the Eight Queens problem. Run your program. (*Hint*: It is possible to assign a value to each square of the chessboard indicating how many squares of an empty chessboard are "eliminated" if a queen is placed in that square. Each of the corners would be assigned the value 22, as in Figure 7.26.) Once these "elimination numbers" are placed in all 64 squares, an appropriate heuristic might be: Place the next queen in the square with the smallest elimination number. Why is this strategy intuitively appealing?

7.25 (*Eight Queens: Brute Force Approaches*) In this exercise, you will develop several brute force approaches to solving the Eight Queens problem introduced in Exercise 7.24.

a) Solve the Eight Queens exercise, using the random brute force technique developed in Exercise 7.23.
b) Use an exhaustive technique (i.e., try all possible combinations of eight queens on the chessboard).
c) Why do you suppose the exhaustive brute force approach may not be appropriate for solving the Knight's Tour problem?
d) Compare and contrast the random brute force and exhaustive brute force approaches.

7.26 (*Knight's Tour: Closed Tour Test*) In the Knight's Tour, a full tour occurs when the knight makes 64 moves touching each square of the chessboard once and only once. A closed tour occurs when the 64th move is one move away from the square in which the knight started the tour. Modify the program you wrote in Exercise 7.22 to test for a closed tour if a full tour has occurred.

7.27 (*The Sieve of Eratosthenes*) A prime integer is any integer that is evenly divisible only by itself and 1. The Sieve of Eratosthenes is a method of finding prime numbers. It operates as follows:

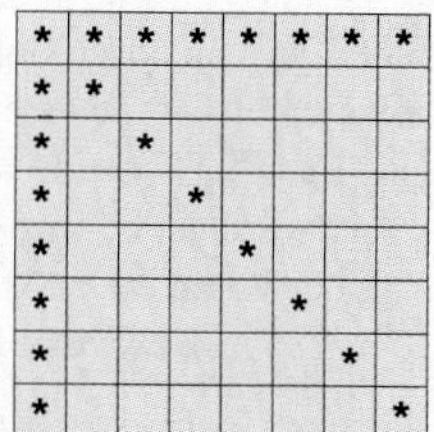

Fig. 7.26 The 22 squares eliminated by placing a queen in the upper left corner.

a) Create a primitive type **`boolean`** array with all elements initialized to **`true`**. Array elements with prime subscripts will remain **`true`**. All other array elements will eventually be set to **`false`**.

b) Starting with array subscript 2 (subscript 1 must be prime), determine whether a given element is **`true`**. If so, loop through the remainder of the array and set to **`false`** every element whose subscript is a multiple of the subscript for the element with value **`true`**. Then, continue the process with the next element with value **`true`**. For array subscript 2, all elements beyond element 2 in the array that have subscripts which are multiples of 2 will be set to **`false`** (subscripts 4, 6, 8, 10, etc.); for array subscript 3, all elements beyond element 3 in the array that have subscripts which are multiples of 3 will be set to **`false`** (subscripts 6, 9, 12, 15, etc.); and so on.

When this process is complete, the array elements that are still **`true`** indicate that the subscript is a prime number. These subscripts can be displayed. Write a program that uses an array of 1000 elements to determine and print the prime numbers between 1 and 999. Ignore element 0 of the array.

7.28 (*Bucket Sort*) A bucket sort begins with a single-subscripted array of positive integers to be sorted and a double-subscripted array of integers with rows subscripted from 0 to 9 and columns subscripted from 0 to n - 1, where n is the number of values in the array to be sorted. Each row of the double-subscripted array is referred to as a bucket. Write an applet containing a method called **`bucketSort`** that takes an integer array as an argument and performs as follows:

a) Place each value of the single-subscripted array into a row of the bucket array based on the value's ones digit. For example, 97 is placed in row 7, 3 is placed in row 3 and 100 is placed in row 0. This is called a "distribution pass."

b) Loop through the bucket array row by row and copy the values back to the original array. This is called a "gathering pass." The new order of the preceding values in the single-subscripted array is 100, 3 and 97.

c) Repeat this process for each subsequent digit position (tens, hundreds, thousands, etc.).

On the second pass, 100 is placed in row 0, 3 is placed in row 0 (because 3 has no tens digit) and 97 is placed in row 9. After the gathering pass, the order of the values in the single-subscripted array is 100, 3 and 97. On the third pass, 100 is placed in row 1, 3 is placed in row 0 and 97 is placed in row 0 (after the 3). After the last gathering pass, the original array is now in sorted order.

Note that the double-subscripted array of buckets is ten times the size of the integer array being sorted. This sorting technique provides better performance than a bubble sort, but requires much more memory. The bubble sort requires space for only one additional element of data. This is an example of the space-time trade-off: The bucket sort uses more memory than the bubble sort, but performs better. This version of the bucket sort requires copying all the data back to the original array on each pass. Another possibility is to create a second double-subscripted bucket array and repeatedly swap the data between the two bucket arrays.

RECURSION EXERCISES

7.29 (*Selection Sort*) A selection sort searches an array looking for the smallest element in the array, then swaps that element with the first element of the array. The process is repeated for the subarray beginning with the second element. Each pass of the array places one element in its proper location. For an array of *n* elements, *n* - 1 passes must be made, and for each subarray, *n* - 1 comparisons must be made to find the smallest value. When the subarray being processed contains one element, the array is sorted. Write recursive method **selectionSort** to perform this algorithm.

7.30 (*Palindromes*) A palindrome is a string that is spelled the same way forward and backward. Some examples of palindromes are "radar," "able was i ere i saw elba" and (if blanks are ignored) "a man a plan a canal panama." Write a recursive method **testPalindrome** that returns **boolean** value **true** if the string stored in the array is a palindrome and **false** otherwise. The method should ignore spaces and punctuation in the string. [Hint: Use **String** method **toCharArray**, which takes no arguments, to get a **char** array containing the characters in the **String**. Then, pass the array to method testPalindrome.]

7.31 (*Linear Search*) Modify Figure 7.12 to use recursive method **linearSearch** to perform a linear search of the array. The method should receive an integer array, the array size and the search key as arguments. If the search key is found, return the array subscript; otherwise, return –1.

7.32 (*Binary Search*) Modify the program of Figure 7.13 to use a recursive method **binarySearch** to perform the binary search of the array. The method should receive an integer array and the starting subscript and ending subscript as arguments. If the search key is found, return the array subscript; otherwise, return –1.

7.33 (*Eight Queens*) Modify the Eight Queens program you created in Exercise 7.24 to solve the problem recursively.

7.34 (*Print an array*) Write a recursive method **printArray** that takes an array of **int** values and the size of the array as arguments and returns nothing. The method should stop processing and return when it receives an array of size 0.

7.35 (*Print a string backward*) Write a recursive method **stringReverse** that takes a character array containing a string as an argument, prints the string backward and returns nothing.

7.36 (*Find the minimum value in an array*) Write a recursive method **recursiveMinimum** that takes an integer array and the array size as arguments and returns the smallest element of the array. The method should stop processing and return when it receives an array of one element.

7.37 (*Quicksort*) In the examples and exercises of this chapter, we discussed the sorting techniques bubble sort, bucket sort and selection sort. We now present the recursive sorting technique called Quicksort. The basic algorithm for a single-subscripted array of values is as follows:

a) *Partitioning Step*: Take the first element of the unsorted array and determine its final location in the sorted array (i.e., all values to the left of the element in the array are less than the element, and all values to the right of the element in the array are greater than the element). We now have one element in its proper location and two unsorted subarrays.
b) *Recursive Step*: Perform step 1 on each unsorted subarray.

Each time step 1 is performed on a subarray, another element is placed in its final location of the sorted array and two unsorted subarrays are created. When a subarray consists of one element, it must be sorted therefore, that element is in its final location.

The basic algorithm seems simple enough, but how do we determine the final position of the first element of each subarray? As an example, consider the following set of values (the element in bold is the partitioning element—it will be placed in its final location in the sorted array):

37 2 6 4 89 8 10 12 68 45

a) Starting from the rightmost element of the array, compare each element to **37** until an element less than **37** is found, then swap **37** and that element. The first element less than **37** is 12, so **37** and 12 are swapped. The new array is

12 2 6 4 89 8 10 **37** 68 45

Element 12 is in italic to indicate that it was just swapped with **37**.

b) Starting from the left of the array, but beginning with the element after 12, compare each element to **37** until an element greater than **37** is found, then swap **37** and that element. The first element greater than **37** is 89, so **37** and 89 are swapped. The new array is

12 2 6 4 **37** 8 10 *89* 68 45

c) Starting from the right, but beginning with the element before 89, compare each element to **37** until an element less than **37** is found, then swap **37** and that element. The first element less than **37** is 10, so **37** and 10 are swapped. The new array is

12 2 6 4 *10* 8 **37** 89 68 45

d) Starting from the left, but beginning with the element after 10, compare each element to **37** until an element greater than **37** is found, then swap **37** and that element. There are no more elements greater than **37**, so when we compare **37** to itself we know that **37** has been placed in its final location of the sorted array.

Once the partition has been applied on the previous array, there are two unsorted subarrays. The subarray with values less than 37 contains 12, 2, 6, 4, 10 and 8. The subarray with values greater than 37 contains 89, 68 and 45. The sort continues with both subarrays being partitioned in the same manner as the original array.

Based on the preceding discussion, write recursive method **`quickSort`** to sort a single-subscripted integer array. The method should receive as arguments an integer array, a starting subscript and an ending subscript. Method **`partition`** should be called by **`quickSort`** to perform the partitioning step.

7.38 (*Maze Traversal*) The following grid of **#**s and dots (**.**) is a double-subscripted array representation of a maze.

```
# # # # # # # # # # # #
# . . . # . . . . . . #
. . # . # . # # # # . #
# # # . # . . . . # . #
# . . . . # # # . # . .
# # # # . # . # . # . #
# . . # . # . # . # . #
# # . # . # . # . # . #
# . . . . . . . . # . #
# # # # # # . # # # . #
# . . . . . . # . . . #
# # # # # # # # # # # #
```

In the preceding double-subscripted array, the **#**s represent the walls of the maze, and the dots represent squares in the possible paths through the maze. Moves can be made only to a location in the array that contains a dot.

There is a simple algorithm for walking through a maze that guarantees finding the exit (assuming there is an exit). If there is not an exit, you will arrive at the starting location again. Place your right hand on the wall to your right and begin walking forward. Never remove your hand from the wall. If the maze turns to the right, you follow the wall to the right. As long as you do not remove your hand from the wall, eventually you will arrive at the exit of the maze. There may be a shorter path than the one you have taken, but you are guaranteed to get out of the maze if you follow the algorithm.

Write recursive method **mazeTraverse** to walk through the maze. The method should receive as arguments a 12-by-12 character array representing the maze and the starting location of the maze. As **mazeTraverse** attempts to locate the exit from the maze, it should place the character **X** in each square in the path. The method should display the maze after each move so the user can watch as the maze is solved.

7.39 (*Generating Mazes Randomly*) Write a method **mazeGenerator** that takes as an argument a double-subscripted 12-by-12 character array and randomly produces a maze. The method should also provide the starting and ending locations of the maze. Try your method **mazeTraverse** from Exercise 7.38, using several randomly generated mazes.

7.40 (*Mazes of Any Size*) Generalize methods **mazeTraverse** and **mazeGenerator** of Exercise 7.38 and Exercise 7.39 to process mazes of any width and height.

7.41 (*Simulation: The Tortoise and the Hare*) In this problem, you will recreate one of the truly great moments in history, namely the classic race of the tortoise and the hare. You will use random number generation to develop a simulation of this memorable event.

Our contenders begin the race at "square 1" of 70 squares. Each square represents a possible position along the race course. The finish line is at square 70. The first contender to reach or pass square 70 is rewarded with a pail of fresh carrots and lettuce. The course weaves its way up the side of a slippery mountain, so occasionally the contenders lose ground.

There is a clock that ticks once per second. With each tick of the clock, your applet should adjust the position of the animals according to the rules in Fig. 7.27

Use variables to keep track of the positions of the animals (i.e., position numbers are 1–70). Start each animal at position 1 (i.e., the "starting gate"). If an animal slips left before square 1, move the animal back to square 1.

Generate the percentages in the preceding table by producing a random integer, i, in the range $1 \le i \le 10$. For the tortoise, perform a "fast plod" when $1 \le i \le 5$, a "slip" when $6 \le i \le 7$ or a "slow plod" when $8 \le i \le 10$. Use a similar technique to move the hare.

Begin the race by printing

```
BANG !!!!!
AND THEY'RE OFF !!!!!
```

Then, for each tick of the clock (i.e., each repetition of a loop), print a 70-position line showing the letter **T** in the position of the tortoise and the letter **H** in the position of the hare. Occasionally, the contenders will land on the same square. In this case, the tortoise bites the hare, and your program should print **OUCH!!!** beginning at that position. All print positions other than the **T**, the **H** or the **OUCH!!!** (in case of a tie) should be blank.

After each line is printed, test for whether either animal has reached or passed square 70. If so, print the winner and terminate the simulation. If the tortoise wins, print **TORTOISE WINS!!! YAY!!!** If the hare wins, print **Hare wins. Yuch.** If both animals win on the same tick of the clock, you may want to favor the turtle (the "underdog") or you may want to print **It's a tie**. If neither animal wins, perform the loop again to simulate the next tick of the clock. When you are ready to run your program, assemble a group of fans to watch the race. You'll be amazed at how involved your audience gets!

Later in the book, we introduce a number of Java capabilities, such as graphics, images, animation, sound and multithreading. As you study those features, you might enjoy enhancing your tortoise and hare contest simulation.

Animal	Move type	Percentage of the time	Actual move
Tortoise	Fast plod	50%	3 squares to the right
	Slip	20%	6 squares to the left
	Slow plod	30%	1 square to the right
Hare	Sleep	20%	No move at all
	Big hop	20%	9 squares to the right
	Big slip	10%	12 squares to the left
	Small hop	30%	1 square to the right
	Small slip	20%	2 squares to the left

Fig. 7.27 Rules for adjusting the positions of the tortoise and the hare.

SPECIAL SECTION: BUILDING YOUR OWN COMPUTER

In the next several problems, we take a temporary diversion away from the world of high-level language programming. We "peel open" a computer and look at its internal structure. We introduce machine-language programming and write several machine-language programs. To make this an especially valuable experience, we then build a computer (through the technique of software-based *simulation)* on which you can execute your machine-language programs!

7.42 (*Machine-Language Programming*) Let us create a computer we will call the Simpletron. As its name implies, it is a simple machine, but as we will soon see, a powerful one as well. The Simpletron runs programs written in the only language it directly understands, that is, Simpletron Machine Language or SML for short.

The Simpletron contains an *accumulator*—a "special register" in which information is put before the Simpletron uses that information in calculations or examines it in various ways. All information in the Simpletron is handled in terms of *words*. A word is a signed four-digit decimal number such as `+3364`, `-1293`, `+0007`, `-0001`, etc. The Simpletron is equipped with a 100-word memory and these words are referenced by their location numbers `00`, `01`, `...`, `99`.

Before running an SML program, we must *load* or place the program into memory. The first instruction (or statement) of every SML program is always placed in location `00`. The simulator will start executing at this location.

Each instruction written in SML occupies one word of the Simpletron's memory (and hence instructions are signed four-digit decimal numbers). We shall assume that the sign of an SML instruction is always plus, but the sign of a data word may be either plus or minus. Each location in the Simpletron's memory may contain either an instruction, a data value used by a program or an unused (and hence undefined) area of memory. The first two digits of each SML instruction are the *operation code* specifying the operation to be performed. SML operation codes are summarized in Fig. 7.28.

The last two digits of an SML instruction are the *operand*—the address of the memory location containing the word to which the operation applies. Let's consider several simple SML programs.

Operation code	Meaning
Input/output operations:	
`final int READ = 10;`	Read a word from the keyboard into a specific location in memory.
`final int WRITE = 11;`	Write a word from a specific location in memory to the screen.
Load/store operations:	
`final int LOAD = 20;`	Load a word from a specific location in memory into the accumulator.
`final int STORE = 21;`	Store a word from the accumulator into a specific location in memory.
Arithmetic operations:	
`final int ADD = 30;`	Add a word from a specific location in memory to the word in the accumulator (leave result in the accumulator).
`final int SUBTRACT = 31;`	Subtract a word from a specific location in memory from the word in the accumulator (leave result in the accumulator).
`final int DIVIDE = 32;`	Divide a word from a specific location in memory into the word in the accumulator (leave result in the accumulator).
`final int MULTIPLY = 33;`	Multiply a word from a specific location in memory by the word in the accumulator (leave result in the accumulator).
Transfer of control operations:	
`final int BRANCH = 40;`	Branch to a specific location in memory.
`final int BRANCHNEG = 41;`	Branch to a specific location in memory if the accumulator is negative.
`final int BRANCHZERO = 42;`	Branch to a specific location in memory if the accumulator is 0.
`final int HALT = 43;`	Halt—the program has completed its task.

Fig. 7.28 Simpletron Machine Language (SML) operation codes .

The first SML program (Fig. 7.29) reads two numbers from the keyboard and computes and prints their sum. The instruction **+1007** reads the first number from the keyboard and places it into location **07** (which has been initialized to 0). Then, instruction **+1008** reads the next number into location **08**. The *load* instruction, **+2007**, puts the first number into the accumulator, and the *add* instruction, **+3008**, adds the second number to the number in the accumulator. *All SML arithmetic instructions leave their results in the accumulator.* The *store* instruction, **+2109**, places the result back into memory location **09** from which the *write* instruction, **+1109**, takes the number and prints it (as a signed four-digit decimal number). The *halt* instruction, **+4300**, terminates execution.

Location	Number	Instruction
00	`+1007`	(Read A)
01	`+1008`	(Read B)
02	`+2007`	(Load A)
03	`+3008`	(Add B)
04	`+2109`	(Store C)
05	`+1109`	(Write C)
06	`+4300`	(Halt)
07	`+0000`	(Variable A)
08	`+0000`	(Variable B)
09	`+0000`	(Result C)

Fig. 7.29 SML program that reads two integers and computes their sum.

The second SML program (Fig. 7.30) reads two numbers from the keyboard and determines and prints the larger value. Note the use of the instruction **`+4107`** as a conditional transfer of control, much the same as Java's **`if`** statement.

Now write SML programs to accomplish each of the following tasks:

a) Use a sentinel-controlled loop to read 10 positive numbers. Compute and print their sum.
b) Use a counter-controlled loop to read seven numbers, some positive and some negative, and compute and print their average.
c) Read a series of numbers and determine and print the largest number. The first number read indicates how many numbers should be processed.

Location	Number	Instruction
00	`+1009`	(Read A)
01	`+1010`	(Read B)
02	`+2009`	(Load A)
03	`+3110`	(Subtract B)
04	`+4107`	(Branch negative to 07)
05	`+1109`	(Write A)
06	`+4300`	(Halt)
07	`+1110`	(Write B)
08	`+4300`	(Halt)
09	`+0000`	(Variable A)
10	`+0000`	(Variable B)

Fig. 7.30 SML program that reads two integers and determines which is larger.

7.43 (*A Computer Simulator*) It may at first seem outrageous, but in this problem you are going to build your own computer. No, you will not be soldering components together. Rather, you will use the powerful technique of *software-based simulation* to create an object-oriented *software model* of the Simpletron. You will not be disappointed. Your Simpletron simulator will turn the computer you are using into a Simpletron, and you will actually be able to run, test and debug the SML programs you wrote in Exercise 7.42. Your Simpletron will be an event-driven applet—you will click a button to execute each SML instruction and you will be able to see the instruction "in action."

When you run your Simpletron simulator, it should begin by displaying:

```
*** Welcome to Simpletron! ***
*** Please enter your program one instruction  ***
*** (or data word) at a time into the input    ***
*** text field. I will display the location    ***
*** number and a question mark (?). You then   ***
*** type the word for that location. Press the ***
*** Done button to stop entering your program. ***
```

The program should display an **input JTextField** in which the user will type each instruction one at a time and a **Done** button for the user to click when the complete SML program has been entered. Simulate the memory of the Simpletron with a single-subscripted array **memory** that has 100 elements. Now assume that the simulator is running and let us examine the dialog as we enter the program of Fig. 7.30 (Exercise 7.42):

```
00 ? +1009
01 ? +1010
02 ? +2009
03 ? +3110
04 ? +4107
05 ? +1109
06 ? +4300
07 ? +1110
08 ? +4300
09 ? +0000
10 ? +0000
```

Your program should use a **JTextField** to display the memory location followed by a question mark. Each of the values to the right of a question mark is typed by the user into the **input JTextField**. When the **Done** button is clicked, the program should display:

```
*** Program loading completed ***
*** Program execution begins  ***
```

The SML program has now been placed (or loaded) in array **memory**. The Simpletron should provide an "**Execute next instruction**" button the user can click to execute each instruction in your SML program. Execution begins with the instruction in location **00** and, like Java, continues sequentially, unless directed to some other part of the program by a transfer of control.

Use the variable **accumulator** to represent the accumulator register. Use the variable **instructionCounter** to keep track of the location in memory that contains the instruction being performed. Use the variable **operationCode** to indicate the operation currently being performed (i.e., the left two digits of the instruction word). Use the variable **operand** to indicate the memory location on which the current instruction operates. Thus, **operand** is the rightmost two digits of the instruction currently being performed. Do not execute instructions directly from memory. Rather, transfer the next instruction to be performed from memory to a variable called **instructionRegister**. Then "pick off" the left two digits and place them in **operation-**

Code and "pick off" the right two digits and place them in **operand**. Each of the preceding registers should have a corresponding **JTextField** in which its current value can be displayed at all times. When Simpletron begins execution, the special registers are all initialized to 0.

Now, let us "walk through" execution of the first SML instruction, **+1009** in memory location **00**. This is called an *instruction execution cycle.*

The **instructionCounter** tells us the location of the next instruction to be performed. We *fetch* the contents of that location from **memory** by using the Java statement

```
instructionRegister = memory[ instructionCounter ];
```

The operation code and the operand are extracted from the instruction register by the statements

```
operationCode = instructionRegister / 100;
operand = instructionRegister % 100;
```

Now the Simpletron must determine that the operation code is actually a *read* (versus a *write*, a *load*, etc.). A **switch** differentiates among the twelve operations of SML.

In the **switch** structure, the behavior of various SML instructions is simulated as shown in Fig. 7.31. We discuss branch instructions shortly and leave the others to the reader.

When the SML program completes execution, the name and contents of each register as well as the complete contents of memory should be displayed. Such a printout is often called a *computer dump* (and, no, a computer dump is not a place where old computers go). To help you program your dump method, a sample dump format is shown in Fig. 7.32. Note that a dump after executing a Simpletron program would show the actual values of instructions and data values at the moment execution terminated. The sample dump assumes the output will be sent to the display screen with a series of **System.out.print** and **System.out.println** method calls. However, we encourage you to experiment with a version that can be displayed on the applet using a **JTextArea** or an array of **JTextField** objects.

Let us proceed with the execution of our program's first instruction, namely the **+1009** in location **00**. As we have indicated, the **switch** statement simulates this by prompting the user to enter a value into the input dialog, reading the value, converting the value to an integer and storing it in memory location **memory[operand]**. Since your Simpletron is event driven, it waits for the user to type a value into the **input JTextField** and press the *Enter key.* The value is then read into location **09**.

At this point, simulation of the first instruction is completed. All that remains is to prepare the Simpletron to execute the next instruction. Since the instruction just performed was not a transfer of control, we need merely increment the instruction counter register as follows:

```
++instructionCounter;
```

Instruction	Description
read:	Display an input dialog with the prompt "**Enter an integer**." Convert the input value to an integer and store it in location **memory[operand]**.
load:	**accumulator = memory[operand];**
add:	**accumulator += memory[operand];**

Fig. 7.31 Behavior of several SML instructions in the Simpletron.

```
REGISTERS:
accumulator            +0000
instructionCounter        00
instructionRegister    +0000
operationCode             00
operand                   00

MEMORY:
       0     1     2     3     4     5     6     7     8     9
 0 +0000 +0000 +0000 +0000 +0000 +0000 +0000 +0000 +0000 +0000
10 +0000 +0000 +0000 +0000 +0000 +0000 +0000 +0000 +0000 +0000
20 +0000 +0000 +0000 +0000 +0000 +0000 +0000 +0000 +0000 +0000
30 +0000 +0000 +0000 +0000 +0000 +0000 +0000 +0000 +0000 +0000
40 +0000 +0000 +0000 +0000 +0000 +0000 +0000 +0000 +0000 +0000
50 +0000 +0000 +0000 +0000 +0000 +0000 +0000 +0000 +0000 +0000
60 +0000 +0000 +0000 +0000 +0000 +0000 +0000 +0000 +0000 +0000
70 +0000 +0000 +0000 +0000 +0000 +0000 +0000 +0000 +0000 +0000
80 +0000 +0000 +0000 +0000 +0000 +0000 +0000 +0000 +0000 +0000
90 +0000 +0000 +0000 +0000 +0000 +0000 +0000 +0000 +0000 +0000
```

Fig. 7.32 A sample dump.

This completes the simulated execution of the first instruction. When the user clicks the **Execute next instruction** button, the entire process (i.e., the instruction execution cycle) begins again with the fetch of the next instruction to be executed.

Now let us consider how the branching instructions—the transfers of control—are simulated. All we need to do is adjust the value in the instruction counter appropriately. Therefore, the unconditional branch instruction (**40**) is simulated within the **switch** as

```
instructionCounter = operand;
```

The conditional "branch if accumulator is zero" instruction is simulated as

```
if ( accumulator == 0 )
   instructionCounter = operand;
```

At this point, you should implement your Simpletron simulator and run each of the SML programs you wrote in Exercise 7.42. You may embellish SML with additional features and provide for these in your simulator.

Your simulator should check for various types of errors. During the program loading phase, for example, each number the user types into the Simpletron's **memory** must be in the range **-9999** to **+9999**. Your simulator should test that each number entered is in this range, and, if not, keep prompting the user to reenter the number until the user enters a correct number.

During the execution phase, your simulator should check for various serious errors, such as attempts to divide by zero, attempts to execute invalid operation codes, accumulator overflows (i.e., arithmetic operations resulting in values larger than **+9999** or smaller than **-9999**) and the like. Such serious errors are called *fatal errors*. When a fatal error is detected, your simulator should print an error message such as:

```
*** Attempt to divide by zero ***
*** Simpletron execution abnormally terminated ***
```

and should print a full computer dump in the format we discussed previously. This will help the user locate the error in the program.

7.44 (*Modifications to the Simpletron Simulator*) In Exercise 7.43, you wrote a software simulation of a computer that executes programs written in Simpletron Machine Language (SML). In this exercise, we propose several modifications and enhancements to the Simpletron Simulator. In Exercise 19.26 and Exercise 19.27, we propose building a compiler that converts programs written in a high-level programming language (a variation of Basic) to Simpletron Machine Language. Some of the following modifications and enhancements may be required to execute the programs produced by the compiler:

a) Extend the Simpletron Simulator's memory to contain 1000 memory locations to enable the Simpletron to handle larger programs.
b) Allow the simulator to perform modulus calculations. This requires an additional Simpletron Machine Language instruction.
c) Allow the simulator to perform exponentiation calculations. This requires an additional Simpletron Machine Language instruction.
d) Modify the simulator to use hexadecimal values rather than integer values to represent Simpletron Machine Language instructions.
e) Modify the simulator to allow output of a newline. This requires an additional Simpletron Machine Language instruction.
f) Modify the simulator to process floating-point values in addition to integer values.
g) Modify the simulator to handle string input. [*Hint*: Each Simpletron word can be divided into two groups, each holding a two-digit integer. Each two-digit integer represents the ASCII decimal equivalent of a character. Add a machine-language instruction that will input a string and store the string beginning at a specific Simpletron memory location. The first half of the word at that location will be a count of the number of characters in the string (i.e., the length of the string). Each succeeding half-word contains one ASCII character expressed as two decimal digits. The machine-language instruction converts each character into its ASCII equivalent and assigns it to a "half-word."]
h) Modify the simulator to handle output of strings stored in the format of part g). [*Hint*: Add a machine-language instruction that will print a string beginning at a certain Simpletron memory location. The first half of the word at that location is a count of the number of characters in the string (i.e., the length of the string). Each succeeding half-word contains one ASCII character expressed as two decimal digits. The machine-language instruction checks the length and prints the string by translating each two-digit number into its equivalent character.]

7.45 The Fibonacci series

0, 1, 1, 2, 3, 5, 8, 13, 21, …

begins with the terms 0 and 1 and has the property that each succeeding term is the sum of the two preceding terms.

a) Write a *nonrecursive* method **`fibonacci( n )`** that calculates the *n*th Fibonacci number. Incorporate this method into an applet that enables the user to enter the value of **`n`**.
b) Determine the largest Fibonacci number that can be printed on your system.
c) Modify the program of part a) to use **`double`** instead of **`int`** to calculate and return Fibonacci numbers and use this modified program to repeat part b).

Object-Based Programming

Objectives

- To understand encapsulation and data hiding.
- To understand the notions of data abstraction and abstract data types (ADTs).
- To create Java ADTs, namely, classes.
- To be able to create, use and destroy objects.
- To be able to control access to object instance variables and methods.
- To appreciate the value of object orientation.
- To understand the use of the **`this`** reference.
- To understand class variables and class methods.

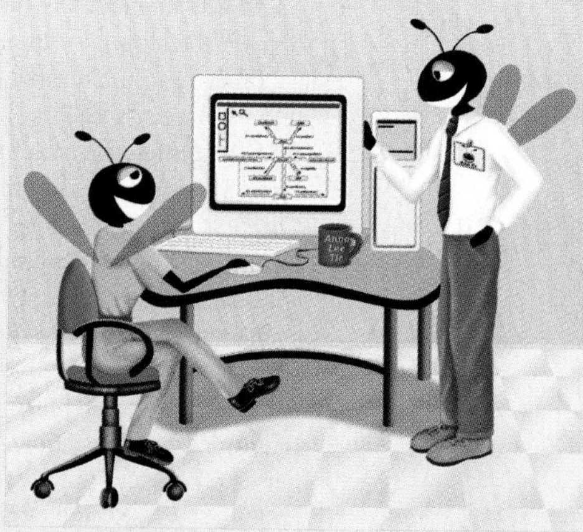

My object all sublime
I shall achieve in time.
W. S. Gilbert

Is it a world to hide virtues in?
William Shakespeare, Twelfth Night

Your public servants serve you right.
Adlai Stevenson

But what, to serve our private ends,
Forbids the cheating of our friends?
Charles Churchill

This above all: to thine own self be true.
William Shakespeare, Hamlet

Have no friends not equal to yourself.
Confucius

Outline

8.1 Introduction
8.2 Implementing a Time Abstract Data Type with a Class
8.3 Class Scope
8.4 Controlling Access to Members
8.5 Creating Packages
8.6 Initializing Class Objects: Constructors
8.7 Using Overloaded Constructors
8.8 Using Set and Get Methods
8.8.1 Executing an Applet that Uses Programmer-Defined Packages
8.9 Software Reusability
8.10 Final Instance Variables
8.11 Composition: Objects as Instance Variables of Other Classes
8.12 Package Access
8.13 Using the `this` Reference
8.14 Finalizers
8.15 Static Class Members
8.16 Data Abstraction and Encapsulation
8.16.1 Example: Queue Abstract Data Type
8.17 (Optional Case Study) Thinking About Objects: Starting to Program the Classes for the Elevator Simulation

Summary • Terminology • Self-Review Exercises • Answers to Self-Review Exercises • Exercises

8.1 Introduction

Now we investigate object orientation in Java in greater depth. Why did we defer this until now? First, the objects we will build will be composed in part of structured program pieces, so we needed to establish a basis in structured programming with control structures. Second, we wanted to study methods in depth. Third, we wanted to familiarize the reader with arrays that are Java objects.

Through our discussions of object-oriented Java programs in Chapter 2 through Chapter 7, we introduced many basic concepts (i.e., "object think") and terminology (i.e., "object speak") of object-oriented programming in Java. We also discussed our program-development methodology: We analyzed many typical problems that required a program—either a Java applet or a Java application—to be built, determined what classes from the Java API were needed to implement the program, determined what instance variables were needed, determined what methods were needed and specified how an object of our class collaborated with objects of Java API classes to accomplish the overall goals of the program.

Let us briefly review some key concepts and terminology of object orientation. OOP *encapsulates* data (*attributes*) and methods (*behaviors*) into *objects;* the data and methods of an object are intimately tied together. Objects have the property of *information hiding.* This means that although objects might know how to communicate with one another across well-defined *interfaces,* objects normally are not allowed to know how other objects are implemented—implementation details are hidden within the objects themselves. Surely it is possible to drive a car effectively without knowing the details of how engines, transmissions and exhaust systems work internally. We will see why information hiding is so crucial to good software engineering.

In C and other *procedural programming languages,* programming tends to be *action-oriented.* In Java, programming is *object-oriented.* In C, the unit of programming is the *function* (called *methods* in Java). In Java, the unit of programming is the *class* from which objects are eventually *instantiated* (i.e., created). Functions do not disappear in Java; rather, they are encapsulated as methods with the data they process within the "walls" of classes.

C programmers concentrate on writing functions. Groups of actions that perform some task are formed into functions, and functions are grouped to form programs. Data is certainly important in C, but the view is that data exists primarily in support of the actions that functions perform. The *verbs* in a system-requirements document help the C programmer determine the set of functions that will work together to implement the system.

Java programmers concentrate on creating their own *user-defined types* called *classes.* Classes are also referred to as *programmer-defined types.* Each class contains data as well as the set of methods that manipulate the data. The data components of a class are called *instance variables* (these are called *data members* in C++). Just as an instance of a built-in type such as **int** is called a *variable,* an instance of a user-defined type (i.e., a class) is called an *object.* The focus of attention in Java is on objects rather than methods. The *nouns* in a system-requirements document help the Java programmer determine an initial set of classes with which to begin the design process. These classes are then used to instantiate objects that will work together to implement the system.

This chapter explains how to create and use objects, a subject called *object-based programming (OBP).* Chapter 9 introduces *inheritance* and *polymorphism*—two key technologies that enable true *object-oriented programming (OOP).* Although inheritance is not discussed in detail until Chapter 9, inheritance is part of every Java class definition.

Performance Tip 8.1

When passing an object to a method in Java, only a reference to the object is passed, not a copy of a possibly large object (as would be the case in a pass by value).

Software Engineering Observation 8.1

It is important to write programs that are understandable and easy to maintain. Change is the rule rather than the exception. Programmers should anticipate their code's being modified. As we will see, classes facilitate program modifiability.

8.2 Implementing a Time Abstract Data Type with a Class

The next example consists of two classes—**Time1** (Fig. 8.1) and **TimeTest** (Fig. 8.2). Class **Time1** is defined in file **Time1.java**. Class **TimeTest** is defined in a separate file called **TimeTest.java**. It is important to note that these classes *must* be defined in separate files, because they are both **public** classes. [*Note:* The output of this program appears in Fig. 8.2.]

```
// Fig. 8.1: Time1.java
// Time1 class definition maintains the time in 24-hour format.

// Java core packages
import java.text.DecimalFormat;

public class Time1 extends Object {
   private int hour;     // 0 - 23
   private int minute;   // 0 - 59
   private int second;   // 0 - 59

   // Time1 constructor initializes each instance variable
   // to zero. Ensures that each Time1 object starts in a
   // consistent state.
   public Time1()
   {
      setTime( 0, 0, 0 );
   }

   // Set a new time value using universal time. Perform
   // validity checks on the data. Set invalid values to zero.
   public void setTime( int h, int m, int s )
   {
      hour = ( ( h >= 0 && h < 24 ) ? h : 0 );
      minute = ( ( m >= 0 && m < 60 ) ? m : 0 );
      second = ( ( s >= 0 && s < 60 ) ? s : 0 );
   }

   // convert to String in universal-time format
   public String toUniversalString()
   {
      DecimalFormat twoDigits = new DecimalFormat( "00" );

      return twoDigits.format( hour ) + ":" +
         twoDigits.format( minute ) + ":" +
         twoDigits.format( second );
   }

   // convert to String in standard-time format
   public String toString()
   {
      DecimalFormat twoDigits = new DecimalFormat( "00" );

      return ( (hour == 12 || hour == 0) ? 12 : hour % 12 ) +
         ":" + twoDigits.format( minute ) +
         ":" + twoDigits.format( second ) +
         ( hour < 12 ? " AM" : " PM" );
   }

}  // end class Time1
```

Fig. 8.1 Abstract data type **Time1** implementation as a class.

Software Engineering Observation 8.2

Class definitions that begin with keyword **public** *must be stored in a file that has exactly the same name as the class and ends with the* **.java** *file name extension.*

Common Programming Error 8.1

Defining more than one **public** *class in the same file is a syntax error.*

Figure 8.1 contains a simple definition for class **Time1**. Our **Time1** class definition begins with line 6, which indicates that class **Time1 extends** class ***Object*** (from package **java.lang**). Remember that you never create a class definition "from scratch." In fact, when you create a class definition, you always use pieces of an existing class definition. Java uses *inheritance* to create new classes from existing class definitions. Keyword **extends** followed by class name **Object** indicates the class (in this case **Time1**) from which our new class inherits existing pieces. In this inheritance relationship, **Object** is called the *superclass* or *base class* and **Time1** is called the *subclass* or *derived class*. Using inheritance results in a new class definition that has the *attributes* (data) and *behaviors* (methods) of class **Object** as well as new features we add in our **Time1** class definition. Every class in Java is a subclass of **Object** (directly or indirectly). Therefore, every class inherits the 11 methods defined by class **Object**. One key **Object** method is ***toString***, discussed later in this section. Other methods of class **Object** are discussed as they are needed throughout the text. For a complete list of class Object's methods, see the online API documentation at

java.sun.com/j2se/1.3/docs/api/index.html

Software Engineering Observation 8.3

Every class defined in Java must extend another class. If a class does not explicitly use the keyword ***extends*** *in its definition, the class implicitly* ***extends Object****.*

The *body* of the class definition is delineated with left and right braces (**{** and **}**) on lines 7 and 50. Class **Time1** contains three integer instance variables—**hour**, **minute** and **second**—that represent the time in *universal-time* format (*24-hour clock* format).

Keywords ***public*** and ***private*** are *member access modifiers.* Instance variables or methods declared with member access modifier **public** are accessible wherever the program has a reference to a **Time1** object. Instance variables or methods declared with member access modifier **private** are accessible *only* to methods of the class in which they are defined. Every instance variable or method definition should be preceded by a member access modifier.

The three integer instance variables **hour**, **minute** and **second** are each declared (lines 8–10) with member access modifier **private**, indicating that these instance variables are accessible only to methods of the class. When a program creates (instantiates) an object of the class, such instance variables are encapsulated in the object and can be accessed only through methods of that object's class (normally through the class's **public** methods). Typically, instance variables are declared **private**, and methods are declared **public**. It is possible to have **private** methods and **public** data, as we will see later. The **private** methods are known as *utility methods* or *helper methods* because they can be called only by other methods of that class and are used to support the operation of those methods. Using **public** data is uncommon and is a dangerous programming practice.

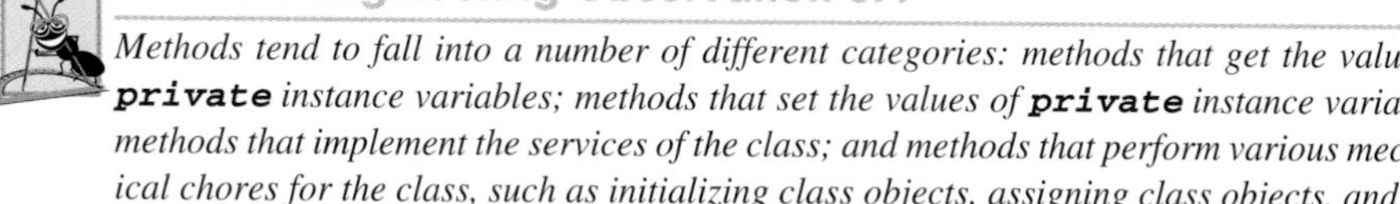

Software Engineering Observation 8.4

*Methods tend to fall into a number of different categories: methods that get the values of **private** instance variables; methods that set the values of **private** instance variables; methods that implement the services of the class; and methods that perform various mechanical chores for the class, such as initializing class objects, assigning class objects, and converting between classes and built-in types or between classes and other classes.*

Access methods can read or display data. Another common use for access methods is to test whether a condition is true or false—such methods are often called *predicate methods.* An example of a predicate method would be an **isEmpty** method for any container class—a class capable of holding many objects—such as a linked list, a stack or a queue (these data structures are discussed in depth in Chapter 19, Chapter 20 and Chapter 21). A program might test **isEmpty** before attempting to read another item from the container object. A program might test **isFull** before attempting to insert another item into the container object.

Class **Time1** contains the following **public** methods—**Time1** (lines 15–18), **setTime** (lines 22–27), **toUniversalString** (lines 30–37) and **toString** (line 40–48). These are the ***public*** *methods,* ***public*** *services* or ***public*** *interface* of the class. These methods are used by *clients* (i.e., portions of a program that are users of a class) of the class to manipulate the data stored in objects of the class.

The clients of a class use references to interact with an object of the class. For example, method **paint** in an applet is a client of class **Graphics**. Method **paint** uses a reference to a **Graphics** object (such as **g**) that it receives as an argument to draw on the applet by calling methods that are **public** services of class **Graphics** (such as **drawString**, **drawLine**, **drawOval** and **drawRect**).

Notice the method with the same name as the class (lines 15–18); it is the *constructor* method of that class. A constructor is a special method that initializes the instance variables of a class object. Java calls a class's constructor method when a program instantiates an object of that class. In this example, the constructor simply calls the class's **setTime** method (discussed shortly) with hour, minute and second values specified as 0.

It is common to have several constructors for a class; this is accomplished through *method overloading* (as we will see Fig. 8.6). Constructors can take arguments but cannot specify a return data type. Implicitly, the constructor returns a reference to the instantiated object. An important difference between constructors and other methods is that constructors *are not allowed to specify a return data type* (not even **void**). Normally, constructors are **public** methods of a class. Non**public** methods are discussed later.

Common Programming Error 8.2

*Attempting to declare a return type for a constructor and/or attempting to **return** a value from a constructor is a logic error. Java allows other methods of the class to have the same name as the class and to specify return types. Such methods are not constructors and will not be called when an object of the class is instantiated.*

Method **setTime** (lines 22–27) is a **public** method that receives three integer arguments and uses them to set the time. Each argument is tested in a conditional expression that determines whether the value is in range. For example, the **hour** value must be greater than or equal to 0 and less than 24 because we represent the time in universal time format (0–23 for the hour, 0–59 for the minute and 0–59 for the second). Any value outside this range is an invalid value and is set to zero—ensuring that a **Time1** object always contains valid data. This is also known as *keeping the object in a consistent state* or *maintaining the object's integrity*. In cases where invalid data is supplied to **setTime**, the program may want to indicate that an invalid time setting was attempted. We explore this possibility in the exercises.

Good Programming Practice 8.1

Always define a class so its instance variables are maintained in a consistent state.

Method **toUniversalString** (lines 30–37) takes no arguments and returns a **String**. This method produces a universal-time-format string consisting of six digits—two for the hour, two for the minute and two for the second. For example, 13:30:07 represents 1:30:07 PM. Line 32 creates an instance of class **DecimalFormat** (from package **java.text** imported at line 3) to help format the universal time. Object **twoDigits** is initialized with the *format control string* **"00"**, which indicates that the number format should consist of two digits—each **0** is a placeholder for a digit. If the number being formatted is a single digit, it is automatically preceded by a leading **0** (i.e., **8** is formatted as **08**). The **return** statement at lines 34–36 uses method **format** (which returns a formatted **String** containing the number) from object **twoDigits** to format the **hour**, **minute** and **second** values into two-digit strings. Those strings are concatenated with the **+** operator (separated by colons) and returned from method **toUniversalString**.

Method **toString** (line 40–48) takes no arguments and returns a **String**. This method produces a standard-time-format string consisting of the **hour**, **minute** and **second** values separated by colons and an AM or PM indicator, as in **1:27:06 PM**. This method uses the same **DecimalFormat** techniques as method **toUniversalString** to guarantee that the **minute** and **second** values each appear with two digits. Method **toString** is special, in that we inherited from class **Object** a **toString** method with exactly the same first line as our **toString** on line 40. The original **toString** method of class **Object** is a generic version that is used mainly as a placeholder that can be redefined by a subclass (similar to methods **init**, **start** and **paint** from class **JApplet**). Our version replaces the version we inherited to provide a **toString** method that is more appropriate for our class. This is known as *overriding* the original method definition (discussed in detail in Chapter 9).

Once the class has been defined, it can be used as a type in declarations such as

```
Time1 sunset,          // reference to object of type Time1
      timeArray[];     // reference to array of Time1 objects
```

The class name is a new type specifier. There may be many objects of a class, just as there may be many variables of a primitive data type such as **int**. The programmer can create new class types as needed; this is one of the reasons that Java is known as an *extensible language*.

The **TimeTest1** application of Fig. 8.2 uses class **Time1**. Method **main** of class **TimeTest1** declares and initializes an instance of class **Time1** called **time** in line 12. When the object is instantiated, operator **new** allocates the memory in which the **Time1** object will be stored; then **new** calls the **Time1** constructor to initialize the instance variables of the new **Time1** object. The constructor invokes method **setTime** to explicitly initialize each private instance variable to **0**. Operator **new** then returns a reference to the new object, and that reference is assigned to **time**. Similarly, line 32 in class **Time1** (Fig. 8.1) uses **new** to allocate the memory for a **DecimalFormat** object, then calls the **DecimalFormat** constructor with the argument **"00"** to indicate the number format control string.

Software Engineering Observation 8.5

Every time **new** *creates an object of a class, that class's constructor is called to initialize the instance variables of the new object.*

Note that class **Time1** was not **import**ed into the **TimeTest1.java** file. Actually, every class in Java is part of a *package* (like the classes from the Java API). If the programmer does not specify the package for a class, the class is automatically placed in the *default package*, which includes the compiled classes in the current directory. If a class is in the same package as the class that uses it, an **import** statement is not required. We import classes from the Java API because their **.class** files are not in the same package with each program we write. Section 8.5 illustrates how to define your own packages of classes for reuse.

```java
// Fig. 8.2: TimeTest1.java
// Class TimeTest1 to exercise class Time1

// Java extension packages
import javax.swing.JOptionPane;

public class TimeTest1 {

   // create Time1 object and manipulate it
   public static void main( String args[] )
   {
      Time1 time = new Time1();  // calls Time1 constructor

      // append String version of time to String output
      String output = "The initial universal time is: " +
         time.toUniversalString() +
         "\nThe initial standard time is: " +  time.toString() +
         "\nImplicit toString() call: " + time;

      // change time and append String version of time to output
      time.setTime( 13, 27, 6 );
      output += "\n\nUniversal time after setTime is: " +
         time.toUniversalString() +
         "\nStandard time after setTime is: " + time.toString();

      // use invalid values to change time and append String
      // version of time to output
      time.setTime( 99, 99, 99 );
      output += "\n\nAfter attempting invalid settings: " +
         "\nUniversal time: " + time.toUniversalString() +
         "\nStandard time: " + time.toString();

```

Fig. 8.2 Using an object of class **Time1** in a program (part 1 of 2).

```
33          JOptionPane.showMessageDialog( null, output,
34             "Testing Class Time1",
35             JOptionPane.INFORMATION_MESSAGE );
36
37          System.exit( 0 );
38       }
39
40    }  // end class TimeTest1
```

Testing Class Time1

The initial universal time is: 00:00:00
The initial standard time is: 12:00:00 AM
Implicit toString() call: 12:00:00 AM

Universal time after setTime is: 13:27:06
Standard time after setTime is: 1:27:06 PM

After attempting invalid settings:
Universal time: 00:00:00
Standard time: 12:00:00 AM

OK

Fig. 8.2 Using an object of class **Time1** in a program (part 2 of 2).

The statement at lines 15–18 defines a **String** reference **output**, which stores the string containing the results that will be displayed in a message box. Initially, the program assigns to **output** the time in universal-time format (by sending message **toUniversalString** to the object to which **time** refers) and standard-time format (by sending message **toString** to the object to which **time** refers) to confirm that the data were initialized properly. Note that line 18 uses a special string concatenation feature of Java. Concatenating a **String** with any object results in an implicit call to the object's **toString** method to convert the object to a **String**; then the **String**s are concatenated. Lines 17–18 illustrate that you can call **toString** both explicitly and implicitly in a **String** concatenation operation.

Line 21 sends the **setTime** message to the object to which **time** refers to change the time. Then lines 22–24 append the time to **output** again in both formats to confirm that the time was set correctly.

To illustrate that method **setTime** validates the values passed to it, line 28 calls method **setTime** and attempts to set the instance variables to invalid values. Then lines 29–31 append the time to **output** again in both formats to confirm that **setTime** validated the data. Lines 33–35 display a message box with the results of our program. Notice in the last two lines of the output window that the time is set to midnight—the default value of a **Time1** object.

Now that we have seen our first non-applet, non-application class, let us consider several issues of class design.

Again, note that the instance variables **hour**, **minute** and **second** are each declared **private**. Instance variables declared **private** are not accessible outside the class in which they are defined. The philosophy here is that the actual data representation used within the class is of no concern to the class's clients. For example, it would be perfectly reasonable for the class to represent the time internally as the number of seconds since midnight. Clients could use the same **public** methods and get the same results without being aware of this. In this sense, implementation of a class is said to be *hidden* from its clients. Exercise 8.18 asks you to make precisely this modification to the **Time1** class of Figure 8.1 and show that there is no change visible to the clients of the class.

Software Engineering Observation 8.6

Information hiding promotes program modifiability and simplifies the client's perception of a class. The client should not require knowledge of a class's implementation (known as implementation knowledge) to be able to reuse a class.

Software Engineering Observation 8.7

Clients of a class can (and should) use the class without knowing the internal details of how the class is implemented. If the class implementation is changed (to improve performance, for example), the class clients' source code need not change, provided that the class's interface remains constant. This makes it much easier to modify systems.

In this program, the **Time1** constructor simply initializes the instance variables to 0 (i.e., the universal time equivalent of 12 AM). This ensures that the object is created in a *consistent state* (i.e., all instance variable values are valid). Invalid values cannot be stored in the instance variables of a **Time1** object, because the constructor is automatically called when the **Time1** object is created and subsequent attempts by a client to modify the instance variables are scrutinized by the method **setTime**.

Instance variables can be initialized where they are declared in the class body, by the class's constructor, or they can be assigned values by "set" methods. (Remember, instance variables that are not initialized explicitly receive default values (primitive numeric variables are set to 0, **boolean**s are set to **false** and references are set to **null**).

Good Programming Practice 8.2

Initialize instance variables of a class in that class's constructor.

Every class may include a *finalizer* method called **finalize** that does "termination housekeeping" on each class object before the memory for the object is garbage collected by the system. We will discuss garbage collection and finalizers in detail in Section 8.14 and Section 8.15.

It is interesting that the **toUniversalString** and **toString** methods take no arguments. This is because these methods implicitly know that they are to manipulate the instance variables of the particular **Time1** object for which they are invoked. This makes method calls more concise than conventional function calls in procedural programming. It also reduces the likelihood of passing the wrong arguments, the wrong types of arguments and/or the wrong number of arguments, as often happens in C function calls.

Software Engineering Observation 8.8

Using an object-oriented programming approach can often simplify method calls by reducing the number of parameters to be passed. This benefit of object-oriented programming derives from the fact that encapsulation of instance variables and methods within an object gives the methods the right to access the instance variables.

Classes simplify programming because the client (or user of the class object) need only be concerned with the **public** operations encapsulated in the object. Such operations are usually designed to be client oriented rather than implementation oriented. Clients need not be concerned with a class's implementation. Interfaces do change, but less frequently than implementations. When an implementation changes, implementation-dependent code must change accordingly. By hiding the implementation, we eliminate the possibility of other program parts becoming dependent on the details of the class implementation.

Often, classes do not have to be created "from scratch." Rather, they can be *derived* from other classes that provide operations the new classes can use, or classes can include objects of other classes as members. Such *software reuse* can greatly enhance programmer productivity. Deriving new classes from existing classes is called *inheritance*—a distinguishing feature between object-based programming and object-oriented programming—and is discussed in detail in Chapter 9. Including class objects as members of other classes is called *composition* or *aggregation* and is discussed later in this chapter.

8.3 Class Scope

A class's instance variables and methods belong to that *class's scope*. Within a class's scope, class members are accessible to all of that class's methods and can be referenced simply by name. Outside a class's scope, class members cannot be referenced directly by name. Those class members (such as **public** members) that are visible can be accessed only through a "handle" (i.e., primitive data type members can be referred to by *objectReferenceName*.*primitiveVariableName* and object members can be referenced by *objectReferenceName*.*objectMemberName*). For example, a program can determine the number of elements in an array object by accessing the array's **public** member **length** as in *arrayName*.**length**.

Variables defined in a method are known only to that method (i.e., they are local variables to that method). Such variables are said to have block scope. If a method defines a variable with the same name as a variable with class scope (i.e., an instance variable), the class-scope variable is hidden by the method-scope variable in the method scope. A hidden instance variable can be accessed in the method by preceding its name with the keyword **this** and the dot operator, as in **this.***variableName*. Keyword **this** is discussed Section 8.13.

8.4 Controlling Access to Members

The member access modifiers **public** and **private** control access to a class's instance variables and methods. (In Chapter 9, we will introduce the additional access modifier **protected**.) As we stated previously, the primary purpose of **public** methods is to present to the class's clients a view of the *services* the class provides (i.e., the public interface of the class). Clients of the class need not be concerned with how the class accomplishes its tasks. For this reason, the **private** instance variables and **private** methods of a class (i.e., the class's implementation details) are not accessible to the clients of a class. Restricting access to class members via keyword **private** is called *encapsulation*.

Common Programming Error 8.3

An attempt by a method that is not a member of a particular class to access a **private** *member of that class is a syntax error.*

Figure 8.3 demonstrates that **private** class members are not accessible by name outside the class. Line 10 attempts to access directly the **private** instance variable **hour** of the **Time1** object to which **time** refers. When this program is compiled, the compiler generates an error stating that the **private** member **hour** is not accessible. [Note: This program assumes that the **Time1** class from Figure 8.1 is used.]

Good Programming Practice 8.3

Our preference is to list the **private** *instance variables of a class first, so that, as you read the code, you see the names and types of the instance variables before they are used in the methods of the class.*

Software Engineering Observation 8.9

Keep all the instance variables of a class **private***. When necessary, provide* **public** *methods to set the values of* **private** *instance variables and to get the values of* **private** *instance variables. This architecture helps hide the implementation of a class from its clients, which reduces bugs and improves program modifiability.*

Access to **private** data should be controlled carefully by the class's methods. For example, to allow clients to read the value of **private** data, the class can provide a *"get" method* (also called an *accessor method*). To enable clients to modify **private** data, the class can provide a *"set" method* (also called a *mutator method*). Such modification would seem to violate the notion of **private** data, but a *set* method can provide data validation capabilities (such as range checking) to ensure that the value is set properly. A *set* method can also translate between the form of the data used in the interface and the form used in the implementation. A *get* method need not expose the data in "raw" format; rather, the *get* method can edit the data and limit the view of the data the client will see.

Software Engineering Observation 8.10

Class designers use **private** *data and* **public** *methods to enforce the notion of information hiding and the principle of least privilege. If the client of a class needs access to data in the class, provide that access through* **public** *methods of the class. By doing so, the programmer of the class controls how the class's data is manipulated (e.g., data validity checking can prevent invalid data from being stored in an object). This is the principle of data encapsulation.*

```
// Fig. 8.3: TimeTest2.java
// Demonstrate errors resulting from attempts
// to access private members of class Time1.
public class TimeTest2 {

   public static void main( String args[] )
   {
      Time1 time = new Time1();

      time.hour = 7;
   }
}
```

```
TimeTest2.java:10: hour has private access in Time1
      time.hour = 7;
          ^
1 error
```

Fig. 8.3 Erroneous attempt to access private members of class **Time1**.

Software Engineering Observation 8.11

The class designer need not provide set *and/or* get *methods for each* **`private`** *data member; these capabilities should be provided only when it makes sense and after careful thought by the class designer.*

Testing and Debugging Tip 8.1

Making the instance variables of a class **`private`** *and the methods of the class* **`public`** *facilitates debugging because problems with data manipulations are localized to the class's methods.*

8.5 Creating Packages

As we have seen in almost every example in the text, classes and *interfaces* (discussed in Chapter 9) from preexisting libraries, such as the Java API, can be imported into a Java program. Each class and interface in the Java API belongs to a specific package that contains a group of related classes and interfaces. As applications become more complex, packages help programmers manage the complexity of application components. Packages also facilitate software reuse by enabling programs to import classes from other packages (as we have done in almost every example to this point). Another benefit of packages is that they provide a convention for *unique class names*. With hundreds of thousands of Java programmers around the world, there is a good chance that the names you choose for classes will conflict with the names that other programmers choose for their classes. This section introduces how to create your own packages and discusses the standard distribution mechanism for packages.

The application of Fig. 8.4 and Fig. 8.5 illustrates how to create your own package and use a class from that package in a program. The steps for creating a reusable class are:

1. Define a **`public`** class. If the class is not **`public`**, it can be used only by other classes in the same package.
2. Choose a package name, and add a ***`package`*** statement to the source code file for the reusable class definition. [Note: There can be only one **`package`** statement in a Java source code file.]
3. Compile the class so it is placed in the appropriate package directory structure.
4. Import the reusable class into a program, and use the class.

Common Programming Error 8.4

A syntax error occurs if any code appears in a Java file before the **`package`** *statement (if there is one) in the file.*

We chose to demonstrate *Step 1* by modifying the **`public`** class **`Time1`** defined in Fig. 8.1. The new version is shown in Fig. 8.4. No modifications have been made to the implementation of the class, so we will not discuss the implementation details of the class again here.

To satisfy *Step 2*, we added a **`package`** statement at the beginning of the file. Line 3 uses a **`package`** *statement* to define a **`package`** named **`com.deitel.jhtp4.ch08`**. Placing a **`package`** statement at the beginning of a Java source file indicates that the class defined in the file is part of the specified package. The only types of statements in Java that can appear outside the braces of a class definition are **`package`** statements and **`import`** statements.

```
// Fig. 8.4: Time1.java
// Time1 class definition in a package
package com.deitel.jhtp4.ch08;

// Java core packages
import java.text.DecimalFormat;

public class Time1 extends Object {
   private int hour;     // 0 - 23
   private int minute;   // 0 - 59
   private int second;   // 0 - 59

   // Time1 constructor initializes each instance variable
   // to zero. Ensures that each Time1 object starts in a
   // consistent state.
   public Time1()
   {
      setTime( 0, 0, 0 );
   }

   // Set a new time value using universal time. Perform
   // validity checks on the data. Set invalid values to zero.
   public void setTime( int h, int m, int s )
   {
      hour = ( ( h >= 0 && h < 24 ) ? h : 0 );
      minute = ( ( m >= 0 && m < 60 ) ? m : 0 );
      second = ( ( s >= 0 && s < 60 ) ? s : 0 );
   }

   // convert to String in universal-time format
   public String toUniversalString()
   {
      DecimalFormat twoDigits = new DecimalFormat( "00" );

      return twoDigits.format( hour ) + ":" +
         twoDigits.format( minute ) + ":" +
         twoDigits.format( second );
   }

   // convert to String in standard-time format
   public String toString()
   {
      DecimalFormat twoDigits = new DecimalFormat( "00" );

      return ( (hour == 12 || hour == 0) ? 12 : hour % 12 ) +
         ":" + twoDigits.format( minute ) +
         ":" + twoDigits.format( second ) +
         ( hour < 12 ? " AM" : " PM" );
   }

}  // end class Time1
```

Fig. 8.4 Placing Class **Time1** in a package for reuse.

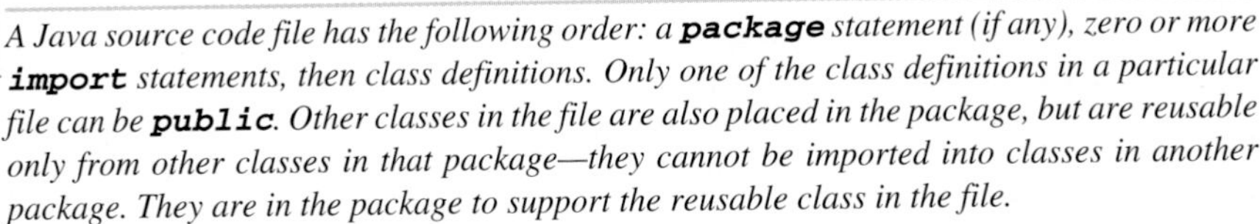

Software Engineering Observation 8.12

A Java source code file has the following order: a **package** *statement (if any), zero or more* **import** *statements, then class definitions. Only one of the class definitions in a particular file can be* **public**. *Other classes in the file are also placed in the package, but are reusable only from other classes in that package—they cannot be imported into classes in another package. They are in the package to support the reusable class in the file.*

In an effort to provide unique names for every package, Sun Microsystems specifies a convention for package naming that all Java programmers should follow. Every package name should start with your Internet domain name in reverse order. For example, our Internet domain name is **deitel.com**, so we began our package name with **com.deitel**. If your domain name is *yourcollege*.**edu**, the package name you would use is **edu.***yourcollege*. After the domain name is reversed, you can choose any other names you want for your package. If you are part of a company with many divisions or a university with many schools, you may want to use the name of your division or school as the next name in the package. We chose to use **jhtp4** as the next name in our package name to indicate that this class is from *Java How to Program: Fourth Edition*. The last name in our package name specifies that this package is for Chapter 8 (**ch08**). [Note: We use our own packages several times throughout the book. You can determine the chapter in which one of our reusable classes is defined by looking at the last part of the package name in the **import** statement. This appears before the name of the class being imported or before the * if a particular class is not specified.]

Step 3 is to compile the class so it is stored in the appropriate package. When a Java file containing a **package** statement is compiled, the resulting **.class** file is placed in the directory structure specified by the **package** statement. The preceding **package** statement indicates that class **Time1** should be placed in the directory **ch08**. The other names—**com**, **deitel** and **jhtp4**—are also directories. The directory names in the **package** statement specify the exact location of the classes in the package. If these directories do not exist before the class is compiled, the compiler creates them.

When compiling a class in a package, there is an extra option (**-d**) that must be passed to the **javac** compiler. This option specifies where to create (or locate) the directories in the **package** statement. For example, we used the compilation command

```
javac -d . Time1.java
```

to specify that the first directory specified in our package name should be placed in the current directory. The **.** after **-d** in the preceding command represents the current directory on the Windows, UNIX and Linux operating systems (and several others as well). After executing the compilation command, the current directory contains a directory called **com**, **com** contains a directory called **deitel**, **deitel** contains a directory called **jhtp4** and **jhtp4** contains a directory called **ch08**. In the **ch08** directory, you can find the file **Time1.class**.

The **package** directory names become part of the class name when the class is compiled. The class name in this example is actually **com.deitel.jhtp4.ch08.Time1** after the class is compiled. You can use this *fully qualified* name in your programs or you can **import** the class and use its short name (**Time1**) in the program. If another package also contains a **Time1** class, the fully qualified class names can be used to distinguish between the classes in the program and prevent a naming conflict (also called a name collision).

Once the class is compiled and stored in its package, the class can be imported into programs (*Step 4*). The **TimeTest3** application of Fig. 8.5, line 8 specifies that class **Time1** should be **import**ed for use in class **TimeTest3**.

At compile time for class **TimeTest3**, **javac** must locate **.class** file for **Time1**, so **javac** can ensure that class **TimeTest3** uses class **Time1** correctly. The compiler follows a specific search order to locate the classes it needs. It begins by searching the standard Java classes that are bundled with the J2SDK. Then it searches for *extension classes*. Java 2 provides an *extensions mechanism* that enables new packages to be added to Java for development and execution purposes. [*Note*: The extensions mechanism is beyond the scope of this book. For more information, visit **java.sun.com/j2se/1.3/docs/guide/extensions**.] If the class is not found in the standard Java classes or in the extension classes, the complier searches the *class path*. By default, the class path consists only of the current directory. However, the class path can be modified by:

```
1  // Fig. 8.5: TimeTest3.java
2  // Class TimeTest3 to use imported class Time1
3
4  // Java extension packages
5  import javax.swing.JOptionPane;
6
7  // Deitel packages
8  import com.deitel.jhtp4.ch08.Time1;  // import Time1 class
9
10 public class TimeTest3 {
11
12    // create an object of class Time1 and manipulate it
13    public static void main( String args[] )
14    {
15       Time1 time = new Time1();    // create Time1 object
16
17       time.setTime( 13, 27, 06 );  // set new time
18       String output =
19          "Universal time is: " + time.toUniversalString() +
20          "\nStandard time is: " + time.toString();
21
22       JOptionPane.showMessageDialog( null, output,
23          "Packaging Class Time1 for Reuse",
24          JOptionPane.INFORMATION_MESSAGE );
25
26       System.exit( 0 );
27    }
28
29 }  // end class TimeTest3
```

Packaging Class Time1 for Reuse

Universal time is: 13:27:06

Standard time is: 1:27:06 PM

OK

Fig. 8.5 Using programmer-defined class **Time1** in a package.

1. providing the ***-classpath*** option to the **javac** compiler, or
2. setting the ***CLASSPATH*** environment variable (a special variable that you define and the operating system maintains so that applications can search for classes in the specified locations).

In each case, the class path consists of a list of directories and/or *archive files* separated by semicolons (**;**). Archive files are individual files that contain directories of other files, typically in compressed format. For example, the standard classes of Java are contained in the archive file **rt.jar** that is installed with the J2SDK. Archive files normally end with the **.jar** or **.zip** file name extensions. The directories and archive files specified in the class path contain the classes you wish to make available to the Java compiler. For more information on the class path, visit **java.sun.com/j2se/1.3/docs/tooldocs/win32/classpath.html** for Windows or **java.sun.com/j2se/1.3/docs/tooldocs/solaris/classpath.html** for Solaris/Linux. [*Note*: We discuss archive files in more detail in Section 8.8.]

Common Programming Error 8.5

*Specifying an explicit class path eliminates the current directory from the class path. This prevents classes in the current directory from loading properly. If classes must be loaded from the current directory, include the current directory (**.**) in the explicit class path.*

Software Engineering Observation 8.13

*In general, it is a better practice to use the **-classpath** option of the compiler, rather than the **CLASSPATH** environment variable, to specify the class path for a program. This enables each application to have its own class path.*

Testing and Debugging Tip 8.2

*Specifying the class path with the **CLASSPATH** environment variable can cause subtle and difficult-to-locate errors in programs that use different versions of the same packages.*

For the example of Fig. 8.4 and Fig. 8.5, we did not specify an explicit class path. Thus, to locate the classes in the **com.deitel.jhtp4.ch08** package from this example, the compiler looks in the current directory for the first name in the package—**com**. Next, the compiler navigates the directory structure. Directory **com** contains the subdirectory **deitel**. Directory **deitel** contains the subdirectory **jhtp4**. Finally, directory **jhtp4** contains subdirectory **ch08**. In the **ch08** directory is the file **Time1.class**, which is loaded by the compiler to ensure that the class is used properly in our program.

Locating the classes to execute the program is similar to locating the classes to compile the program. Like the compiler, the **java** interpreter searches the standard classes and extension classes first, then searches the class path (the current directory by default). The class path for the interpreter can be specified explicitly by using either of the techniques discussed for the compiler. As with the compiler, it is better to specify an individual program's class path via command-line options to the interpreter. You can specify the class path to the **java** interpreter via the **-classpath** or **-cp** command line options followed by a list of directories and/or archive files separated by semicolons (**;**).

8.6 Initializing Class Objects: Constructors

When an object is created, its members can be initialized by a *constructor* method. A constructor is a method with the same name as the class (including case sensitivity). The programmer of a class can define the class's constructor, which is invoked each time the program instantiates an object of that class. Instance variables can be initialized implicitly to their default values (**0** for primitive numeric types, **false** for **boolean**s and **null** for references), they can be initialized in a constructor of the class or their values can be set later after the object is created. Constructors cannot specify return types or return values. A class can contain overloaded constructors to provide a variety of means for initializing objects of that class.

When a program instantiates an object of a class, the program can supply *initializers* in parentheses to the right of the class name. These initializers are passed as arguments to the class's constructor. This technique is demonstrated in the example of Section 8.7. We have also seen this technique several times previously as we created new objects of classes like **DecimalFormat**, **JLabel**, **JTextField**, **JTextArea** and **JButton**. For each of these classes, we have seen statements of the form

ref = new *ClassName*(*arguments*);

where **ref** is a reference of the appropriate data type, **new** indicates that a new object is being created, *ClassName* indicates the type of the new object and *arguments* specifies the values used by the class's constructor to initialize the object.

If no constructors are defined for a class, the compiler creates a *default constructor* that takes no arguments (also called a *no-argument constructor*). The default constructor for a class calls the default constructor for its superclass (the class it extends), then proceeds to initialize the instance variables in the manner we discussed previously. If the class that this class extends does not have a default constructor, the compiler issues an error message. It is also possible for the programmer to provide a no-argument constructor, as we showed in class **Time1** and will see in the next example. If any constructors are defined for a class by the programmer, Java will not create a default constructor for the class.

Good Programming Practice 8.4

When appropriate (almost always), provide a constructor to ensure that every object is properly initialized with meaningful values.

Common Programming Error 8.6

If constructors are provided for a class, but none of the **public** *constructors are no-argument constructors, and an attempt is made to call a no-argument constructor to initialize an object of the class, a syntax error occurs. A constructor can be called with no arguments only if there are no constructors for the class (the default constructor is called) or if there is a no-argument constructor.*

8.7 Using Overloaded Constructors

Methods of a class can be *overloaded* (i.e., several methods in a class may have exactly the same name as defined in Chapter 6, Methods). To overload a method of a class, simply provide a separate method definition with the same name for each version of the method. Remember that overloaded methods *must* have different parameter lists.

Common Programming Error 8.7

Attempting to overload a method of a class with another method that has the exact same signature (name and parameters) is a syntax error.

The **Time1** constructor in Fig. 8.1 initialized **hour**, **minute** and **second** to **0** (i.e., 12 midnight in universal time) with a call to the class's **setTime** method. Figure 8.6

overloads the constructor method to provide a convenient variety of ways to initialize objects of the new class **Time2**. The constructors guarantee that every object begins its existence in a consistent state. In this program, each constructor calls method **setTime** with the values passed to the constructor, to ensure that the value supplied for **hour** is in the range 0 to 23 and that the values for **minute** and **second** are each in the range 0 to 59. If a value is out of range, it is set to zero by **setTime** (once again ensuring that each instance variable remains in a consistent state). The appropriate constructor is invoked by matching the number, types and order of the arguments specified in the constructor call with the number, types and order of the parameters specified in each constructor definition. The matching constructor is called automatically. Figure 8.7 uses class **Time2** to demonstrate its constructors.

```
// Fig. 8.6: Time2.java
// Time2 class definition with overloaded constructors.
package com.deitel.jhtp4.ch08;

// Java core packages
import java.text.DecimalFormat;

public class Time2 extends Object {
   private int hour;     // 0 - 23
   private int minute;   // 0 - 59
   private int second;   // 0 - 59

   // Time2 constructor initializes each instance variable
   // to zero. Ensures that Time object starts in a
   // consistent state.
   public Time2()
   {
      setTime( 0, 0, 0 );
   }

   // Time2 constructor: hour supplied, minute and second
   // defaulted to 0
   public Time2( int h )
   {
      setTime( h, 0, 0 );
   }

   // Time2 constructor: hour and minute supplied, second
   // defaulted to 0
   public Time2( int h, int m )
   {
      setTime( h, m, 0 );
   }

   // Time2 constructor: hour, minute and second supplied
   public Time2( int h, int m, int s )
   {
      setTime( h, m, s );
   }
```

Fig. 8.6 Class **Time2** with overloaded constructors (part 1 of 2).

```
40
41      // Time2 constructor: another Time2 object supplied
42      public Time2( Time2 time )
43      {
44         setTime( time.hour, time.minute, time.second );
45      }
46
47      // Set a new time value using universal time. Perform
48      // validity checks on data. Set invalid values to zero.
49      public void setTime( int h, int m, int s )
50      {
51         hour = ( ( h >= 0 && h < 24 ) ? h : 0 );
52         minute = ( ( m >= 0 && m < 60 ) ? m : 0 );
53         second = ( ( s >= 0 && s < 60 ) ? s : 0 );
54      }
55
56      // convert to String in universal-time format
57      public String toUniversalString()
58      {
59         DecimalFormat twoDigits = new DecimalFormat( "00" );
60
61         return twoDigits.format( hour ) + ":" +
62            twoDigits.format( minute ) + ":" +
63            twoDigits.format( second );
64      }
65
66      // convert to String in standard-time format
67      public String toString()
68      {
69         DecimalFormat twoDigits = new DecimalFormat( "00" );
70
71         return ( (hour == 12 || hour == 0) ? 12 : hour % 12 ) +
72            ":" + twoDigits.format( minute ) +
73            ":" + twoDigits.format( second ) +
74            ( hour < 12 ? " AM" : " PM" );
75      }
76
77   }  // end class Time2
```

Fig. 8.6 Class **Time2** with overloaded constructors (part 2 of 2).

Most of the code in class **Time2** is identical to that in class **Time1**, so we concentrate on only the new features here (i.e., the constructors). Lines 16–19 define the no-argument (default) constructor. Lines 23–26 define a **Time2** constructor that receives a single **int** argument representing the **hour**. Lines 30–33 defines a **Time2** constructor that receives two **int** arguments representing the **hour** and **minute**. Lines 36–39 define a **Time2** constructor that receives three **int** arguments representing the **hour**, **minute** and **second**. Lines 42–45 define a **Time2** constructor that receives a **Time2** reference to another **Time2** object. In this case, the values from the **Time2** argument are used to initialize the **hour**, **minute** and **second**. Notice that none of the constructors specifies a return data type (remember, this is not allowed for constructors). Also, notice that all the constructors receive different numbers of arguments and/or different types of arguments. Even though only two of the constructors receive values for the **hour**, **minute** and **second**, all the constructors call **setTime** with values for **hour**, **minute** and **second** and substitute zeros for the missing values to satisfy **setTime**'s requirement of three arguments.

Notice in particular the constructor at lines 42–45, which uses the **hour**, **minute** and **second** values of its argument **time** to initialize the new **Time2** object. Even though we know that **hour**, **minute** and **second** are declared as **private** variables of class **Time2**, we are able to access these values directly by using the expressions **time.hour**, **time.minute** and **time.second**. This is due to a special relationship between objects of the same class. When one object of a class has a reference to another object of the same class, the first object can access *all* the second object's data and methods.

Class **TimeTest4** (Fig. 8.7) creates six **Time2** objects (lines 17–22) to demonstrate how to invoke the different constructors of the class. Line 17 shows that the no-argument constructor is invoked by placing an empty set of parentheses after the class name when allocating a **Time2** object with **new**. Lines 18–22 of the program demonstrate passing arguments to the **Time2** constructors. Remember that the appropriate constructor is invoked by matching the number, types and order of the arguments specified in the constructor call with the number, types and order of the parameters specified in each method definition. So, line 18 invokes the constructor at line 23 of Fig. 8.6. Line 19 invokes the constructor at line 30 of Fig. 8.6. Lines 20–21 invoke the constructor at line 36 of Fig. 8.6. Line 22 invokes the constructor at line 42 of Fig. 8.6.

Note that each **Time2** constructor in Fig. 8.6 could be written to include a copy of the appropriate statements from method **setTime**. This could be slightly more efficient, because the extra call to **setTime** is eliminated. However, consider changing the representation of the time from three **int** values (requiring 12 bytes of memory) to a single **int** value representing the total number of seconds that have elapsed in the day (requiring 4 bytes of memory). Coding the **Time2** constructors and method **setTime** identically makes such a change in this class definition more difficult. If the implementation of method **setTime** changes, the implementation of the **Time2** constructors would need to change accordingly. Having the **Time2** constructors call **setTime** directly requires any changes to the implementation of **setTime** to be made only once. This reduces the likelihood of a programming error when altering the implementation.

Software Engineering Observation 8.14

If a method of a class already provides all or part of the functionality required by a constructor (or other method) of the class, call that method from the constructor (or other method). This simplifies the maintenance of the code and reduces the likelihood of an error if the implementation of the code is modified. It is also an effective example of reuse.

```
1  // Fig. 8.7: TimeTest4.java
2  // Using overloaded constructors
3
4  // Java extension packages
5  import javax.swing.*;
6
```

Fig. 8.7 Using overloaded constructors to initialize objects of class **Time2** (part 1 of 3).

```java
// Deitel packages
import com.deitel.jhtp4.ch08.Time2;

public class TimeTest4 {

   // test constructors of class Time2
   public static void main( String args[] )
   {
      Time2 t1, t2, t3, t4, t5, t6;

      t1 = new Time2();                   // 00:00:00
      t2 = new Time2( 2 );                // 02:00:00
      t3 = new Time2( 21, 34 );           // 21:34:00
      t4 = new Time2( 12, 25, 42 );       // 12:25:42
      t5 = new Time2( 27, 74, 99 );       // 00:00:00
      t6 = new Time2( t4 );               // 12:25:42

      String output = "Constructed with: " +
         "\nt1: all arguments defaulted" +
         "\n       " + t1.toUniversalString() +
         "\n       " + t1.toString();

      output += "\nt2: hour specified; minute and " +
         "second defaulted" +
         "\n       " + t2.toUniversalString() +
         "\n       " + t2.toString();

      output += "\nt3: hour and minute specified; " +
         "second defaulted" +
         "\n       " + t3.toUniversalString() +
         "\n       " + t3.toString();

      output += "\nt4: hour, minute, and second specified" +
         "\n       " + t4.toUniversalString() +
         "\n       " + t4.toString();

      output += "\nt5: all invalid values specified" +
         "\n       " + t5.toUniversalString() +
         "\n       " + t5.toString();

      output += "\nt6: Time2 object t4 specified" +
         "\n       " + t6.toUniversalString() +
         "\n       " + t6.toString();

      JOptionPane.showMessageDialog( null, output,
         "Demonstrating Overloaded Constructors",
         JOptionPane.INFORMATION_MESSAGE );

      System.exit( 0 );
   }

}  // end class TimeTest4
```

Fig. 8.7 Using overloaded constructors to initialize objects of class **Time2** (part 2 of 3).

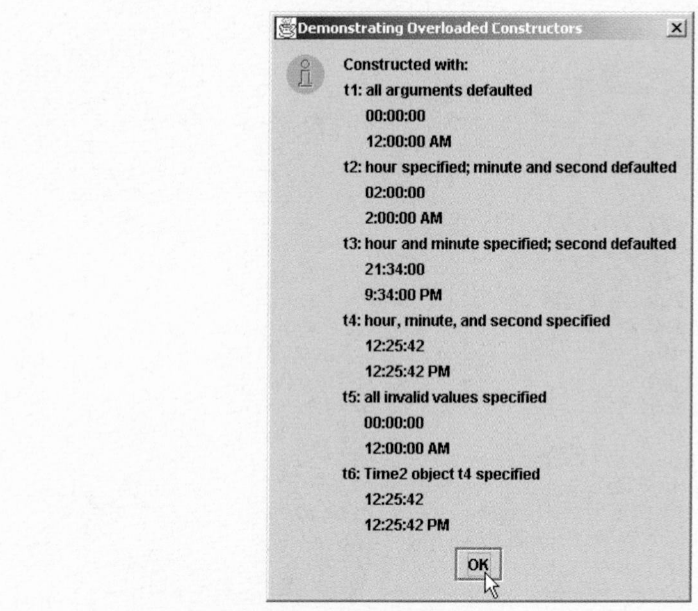

Fig. 8.7 Using overloaded constructors to initialize objects of class **`Time2`** (part 3 of 3).

8.8 Using *Set* and *Get* Methods

Private instance variables can be manipulated only by methods of the class. A typical manipulation might be the adjustment of a customer's bank balance (e.g., a **`private`** instance variable of a class **`BankAccount`**) by a method **`computeInterest`**.

Classes often provide **`public`** methods to allow clients of the class to *set* (i.e., assign values to) or *get* (i.e., obtain the values of) **`private`** instance variables. These methods need not be called *set* and *get*, but they often are.

As a naming example, a method that sets instance variable **`interestRate`** would typically be named **`setInterestRate`** and a method that gets the **`interestRate`** would typically be called **`getInterestRate`**. *Get* methods are also commonly called *accessor methods* or *query methods. Set* methods are also commonly called *mutator methods* (because they typically change a value).

It would seem that providing *set* and *get* capabilities is essentially the same as making the instance variables **`public`**. This is another subtlety of Java that makes the language so desirable for software engineering. If an instance variable is **`public`**, the instance variable can be read or written at will by any method in the program. If an instance variable is **`private`**, a **`public`** *get* method certainly seems to allow other methods to read the data at will but the *get* method controls the formatting and display of the data. A **`public`** *set* method can—and most likely will—carefully scrutinize attempts to modify the instance variable's value. This ensures that the new value is appropriate for that data item. For example, an attempt to *set* the day of the month for a date to 37 would be rejected, an attempt to *set* a person's weight to a negative value would be rejected, and so on. So, although *set* and *get* methods could provide access to **private** data, the access is restricted by the programmer's implementation of the methods.

The benefits of data integrity are not automatic simply because instance variables are made **private**—the programmer must provide validity checking. Java provides the framework in which programmers can design better programs in a convenient manner.

Software Engineering Observation 8.15

Methods that set the values of **private** *data should verify that the intended new values are proper; if they are not, the* set *methods should place the* **private** *instance variables into an appropriate consistent state.*

A class's *set* methods can return values indicating that attempts were made to assign invalid data to objects of the class. This enables clients of the class to test the return values of *set* methods to determine whether the objects they are manipulating are valid and to take appropriate action if the objects are not valid. In Chapter 14, Exception Handling, we illustrate a more robust way in which clients of a class can be notified if an object is not valid.

Good Programming Practice 8.5

Every method that modifies the private instance variables of an object should ensure that the data remains in a consistent state.

The applet of Fig. 8.8 (class **Time3**) and Fig. 8.9 (class **TimeTest5**) enhances our **Time** class (now called **Time3**) to include *get* and *set* methods for the **hour**, **minute** and **second private** instance variables. The *set* methods strictly control the setting of the instance variables to valid values. Attempts to set any instance variable to an incorrect value cause the instance variable to be set to zero (thus leaving the instance variable in a consistent state). Each *get* method simply returns the appropriate instance variable's value. This applet introduces enhanced GUI event handling techniques as we move toward defining our first full-fledged windowed application. After discussing the code, we introduce how to set up an applet to use classes in programmer-defined packages.

```
// Fig. 8.8: Time3.java
// Time3 class definition with set and get methods
package com.deitel.jhtp4.ch08;

// Java core packages
import java.text.DecimalFormat;

public class Time3 extends Object {
   private int hour;     // 0 - 23
   private int minute;   // 0 - 59
   private int second;   // 0 - 59

   // Time3 constructor initializes each instance variable
   // to zero. Ensures that Time object starts in a
   // consistent state.
   public Time3()
   {
      setTime( 0, 0, 0 );
   }
```

Fig. 8.8 Class **Time3** with *set* and *get* methods (part 1 of 3).

```
   // Time3 constructor: hour supplied, minute and second
   // defaulted to 0
   public Time3( int h )
   {
      setTime( h, 0, 0 );
   }

   // Time3 constructor: hour and minute supplied, second
   // defaulted to 0
   public Time3( int h, int m )
   {
      setTime( h, m, 0 );
   }

   // Time3 constructor: hour, minute and second supplied
   public Time3( int h, int m, int s )
   {
      setTime( h, m, s );
   }

   // Time3 constructor: another Time3 object supplied
   public Time3( Time3 time )
   {
      setTime( time.getHour(), time.getMinute(),
         time.getSecond() );
   }

   // Set Methods
   // Set a new time value using universal time. Perform
   // validity checks on data. Set invalid values to zero.
   public void setTime( int h, int m, int s )
   {
      setHour( h );     // set the hour
      setMinute( m );   // set the minute
      setSecond( s );   // set the second
   }

   // validate and set hour
   public void setHour( int h )
   {
      hour = ( ( h >= 0 && h < 24 ) ? h : 0 );
   }

   // validate and set minute
   public void setMinute( int m )
   {
      minute = ( ( m >= 0 && m < 60 ) ? m : 0 );
   }

```

Fig. 8.8 Class **Time3** with *set* and *get* methods (part 2 of 3).

```
70      // validate and set second
71      public void setSecond( int s )
72      {
73         second = ( ( s >= 0 && s < 60 ) ? s : 0 );
74      }
75
76      // Get Methods
77      // get hour value
78      public int getHour()
79      {
80         return hour;
81      }
82
83      // get minute value
84      public int getMinute()
85      {
86         return minute;
87      }
88
89      // get second value
90      public int getSecond()
91      {
92         return second;
93      }
94
95      // convert to String in universal-time format
96      public String toUniversalString()
97      {
98         DecimalFormat twoDigits = new DecimalFormat( "00" );
99
100        return twoDigits.format( getHour() ) + ":" +
101           twoDigits.format( getMinute() ) + ":" +
102           twoDigits.format( getSecond() );
103     }
104
105     // convert to String in standard-time format
106     public String toString()
107     {
108        DecimalFormat twoDigits = new DecimalFormat( "00" );
109
110        return ( ( getHour() == 12 || getHour() == 0 ) ?
111           12 : getHour() % 12 ) + ":" +
112           twoDigits.format( getMinute() ) + ":" +
113           twoDigits.format( getSecond() ) +
114           ( getHour() < 12 ? " AM" : " PM" );
115     }
116
117  }  // end class Time3
```

Fig. 8.8 Class **Time3** with *set* and *get* methods (part 3 of 3).

The new *set* methods of the class are defined in Fig. 8.8 at lines 59–62, 65–68 and 71–74, respectively. Notice that each method performs the same conditional statement that was previously in method **setTime** for setting the **hour**, **minute** or **second**. The addition of these methods caused us to redefine the body of method **setTime** to follow *Software Engineering Observation 8.14*—if a method of a class already provides all or part of the functionality required by another method of the class, call that method from the other method. Notice that **setTime** (lines 51–56) now calls methods **setHour**, **setMinute** and **setSecond**—each of which performs part of **setTime**'s task.

The new *get* methods of the class are defined at lines 78–81, 84–87 and 90–93, respectively. Notice that each method simply returns the **hour**, **minute** or **second** value (a copy of each value is returned, because these are all primitive data type variables). The addition of these methods caused us to redefine the bodies of methods **toUniversalString** (lines 96–103) and **toString** (lines 106–115) to follow *Software Engineering Observation 8.14*. In both cases, every use of instance variables **hour**, **minute** and **second** is replaced with a call to **getHour**, **getMinute** and **getSecond**.

Due to the changes in class **Time3** just described, we have minimized the changes that will have to occur in the class definition if the data representation is changed from **hour**, **minute** and **second** to another representation (such as total elapsed seconds in the day). Only the new *set* and *get* method bodies will have to change. This allows the programmer to change the implementation of the class without affecting the clients of the class (as long as all the **public** methods of the class are still called the same way).

The **TimeTest5** applet (Fig. 8.9) provides a graphical user interface that enables the user to exercise the methods of class **Time3**. The user can set the hour, minute or second value by typing a value in the appropriate **JTextField** and pressing the *Enter* key. The user can also click the "**Add 1 to second**" button to increment the time by one second. The **JTextField** and **JButton** events in this applet are all processed in method **actionPerformed** (lines 66–94). Notice that lines 34, 41, 48 and 59 all call **addActionListener** to indicate that the applet should start listening to **JTextField**s **hourField**, **minuteField**, **secondField** and **JButton tickButton**, respectively. Also, notice that all four calls use **this** as the argument, indicating that the object of our applet class **TimeTest5** has its **actionPerformed** method invoked for each user interaction with these four GUI components. This poses an interesting question—how do we determine the GUI component with which the user interacted?

In **actionPerformed**, notice the use of **actionEvent.getSource()** to determine which GUI component generated the event. For example, line 69 determines whether **tickButton** was clicked by the user. If so, the body of the **if** structure executes. Otherwise, the program tests the condition in the **if** structure at line 73, and so on. Every event has a *source*—the GUI component with which the user interacted to signal the program to do a task. The **ActionEvent** parameter contains a reference to the source of the event. The condition in line 69 simply asks, "Is the *source* of the event the **tickButton**?" This condition compares the references on either side of the **==** operator to determine whether they refer to the same object. In this case, if they both refer to the **JButton**, then the program knows that the user pressed the button. Remember that the source of the event calls **actionPerformed** in response to the user interaction.

After each operation, the resulting time is displayed as a string in the status bar of the applet. The output windows in Fig. 8.9 illustrate the applet before and after the following operations: setting the hour to 23, setting the minute to 59, setting the second to 58 and incrementing the second twice with the "**Add 1 to second**" button.

```
// Fig. 8.9: TimeTest5.java
// Demonstrating the Time3 class set and get methods.

// Java core packages
import java.awt.*;
import java.awt.event.*;

// Java extension packages
import javax.swing.*;

// Deitel packages
import com.deitel.jhtp4.ch08.Time3;

public class TimeTest5 extends JApplet
   implements ActionListener {

   private Time3 time;
   private JLabel hourLabel, minuteLabel, secondLabel;
   private JTextField hourField, minuteField,
      secondField, displayField;
   private JButton tickButton;

   // Create Time3 object and set up GUI
   public void init()
   {
      time = new Time3();

      Container container = getContentPane();
      container.setLayout( new FlowLayout() );

      // set up hourLabel and hourField
      hourLabel = new JLabel( "Set Hour" );
      hourField = new JTextField( 10 );
      hourField.addActionListener( this );
      container.add( hourLabel );
      container.add( hourField );

      // set up minuteLabel and minuteField
      minuteLabel = new JLabel( "Set minute" );
      minuteField = new JTextField( 10 );
      minuteField.addActionListener( this );
      container.add( minuteLabel );
      container.add( minuteField );

      // set up secondLabel and secondField
      secondLabel = new JLabel( "Set Second" );
      secondField = new JTextField( 10 );
      secondField.addActionListener( this );
      container.add( secondLabel );
      container.add( secondField );

      // set up displayField
      displayField = new JTextField( 30 );
```

Fig. 8.9 Using class **Time3**'s *set* and *get* methods (part 1 of 4).

```
      displayField.setEditable( false );
      container.add( displayField );

      // set up tickButton
      tickButton = new JButton( "Add 1 to Second" );
      tickButton.addActionListener( this );
      container.add( tickButton );

      updateDisplay();  // update text in displayField
   }

   // handle button and text field events
   public void actionPerformed( ActionEvent actionEvent )
   {
      // process tickButton event
      if ( actionEvent.getSource() == tickButton )
         tick();

      // process hourField event
      else if ( actionEvent.getSource() == hourField ) {
         time.setHour(
            Integer.parseInt( actionEvent.getActionCommand() ) );
         hourField.setText( "" );
      }

      // process minuteField event
      else if ( actionEvent.getSource() == minuteField ) {
         time.setMinute(
            Integer.parseInt( actionEvent.getActionCommand() ) );
         minuteField.setText( "" );
      }

      // process secondField event
      else if ( actionEvent.getSource() == secondField ) {
         time.setSecond(
            Integer.parseInt( actionEvent.getActionCommand() ) );
         secondField.setText( "" );
      }

      updateDisplay();  // update displayField and status bar
   }

   // update displayField and applet container's status bar
   public void updateDisplay()
   {
      displayField.setText( "Hour: " + time.getHour() +
         "; Minute: " + time.getMinute() +
         "; Second: " + time.getSecond() );

      showStatus( "Standard time is: " + time.toString() +
         "; Universal time is: " + time.toUniversalString() );
   }

```

Fig. 8.9 Using class **Time3**'s *set* and *get* methods (part 2 of 4).

```
   // add one to second and update hour/minute if necessary
   public void tick()
   {
      time.setSecond( ( time.getSecond() + 1 ) % 60 );

      if ( time.getSecond() == 0 ) {
         time.setMinute( ( time.getMinute() + 1 ) % 60 );

         if ( time.getMinute() == 0 )
            time.setHour( ( time.getHour() + 1 ) % 24 );
      }
   }

}  // end class TimeTest5
```

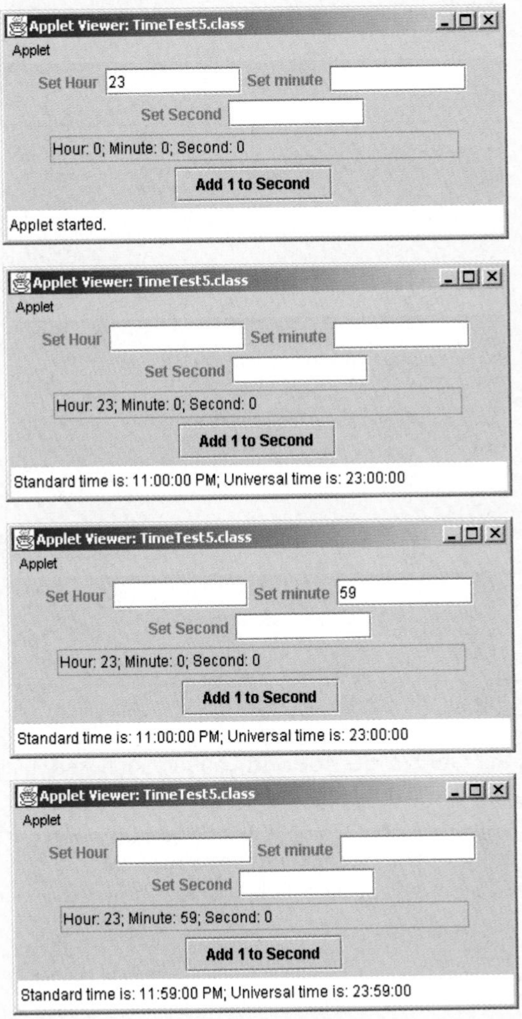

Applet Viewer: TimeTest5.class
Applet
Set Hour 23 Set minute
Set Second
Hour: 0; Minute: 0; Second: 0
Add 1 to Second
Applet started.

Applet Viewer: TimeTest5.class
Applet
Set Hour Set minute
Set Second
Hour: 23; Minute: 0; Second: 0
Add 1 to Second
Standard time is: 11:00:00 PM; Universal time is: 23:00:00

Applet Viewer: TimeTest5.class
Applet
Set Hour Set minute 59
Set Second
Hour: 23; Minute: 0; Second: 0
Add 1 to Second
Standard time is: 11:00:00 PM; Universal time is: 23:00:00

Applet Viewer: TimeTest5.class
Applet
Set Hour Set minute
Set Second
Hour: 23; Minute: 59; Second: 0
Add 1 to Second
Standard time is: 11:59:00 PM; Universal time is: 23:59:00

Fig. 8.9 Using class **`Time3`**'s *set* and *get* methods (part 3 of 4).

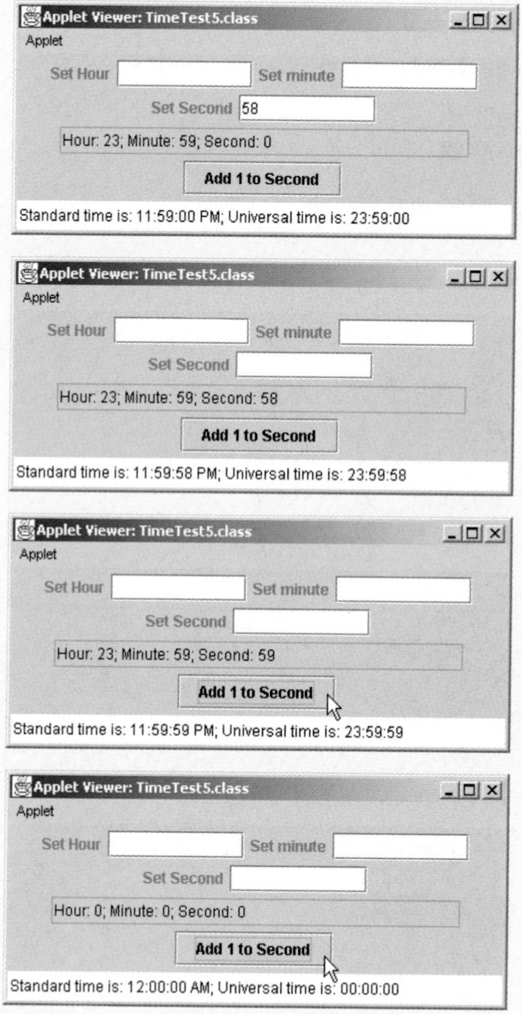

Fig. 8.9 Using class **`Time3`**'s *set* and *get* methods (part 4 of 4).

Note that when the "**`Add 1 to second`**" button is clicked, method **`actionPerformed`** calls the applet's **`tick`** method (defined at lines 108–118). Method **`tick`** uses all the new *set* and *get* methods to increment the second properly. Although this works, it incurs the performance burden of issuing multiple method calls. In Section 8.12, we discuss the notion of package access as a means of eliminating this performance burden.

Common Programming Error 8.8

A constructor can call other methods of the class, such as set *or* get *methods. However, the instance variables might not yet be in a consistent state, because the constructor is in the process of initializing the object. Using instance variables before they have been initialized properly is a logic error.*

Set methods are certainly important from a software engineering standpoint, because they can perform validity checking. *Set* and *get* methods have another important software engineering advantage, discussed in the following *Software Engineering Observation.*

Software Engineering Observation 8.16

Accessing **`private`** *data through* set *and* get *methods not only protects the instance variables from receiving invalid values, but also insulates clients of the class from the representation of the instance variables. Thus, if the representation of the data changes (typically, to reduce the amount of storage required, improve performance or enhance the class in other ways), only the method implementations need to change—the clients need not change as long as the interface provided by the methods remains the same.*

8.8.1 Executing an Applet that Uses Programmer-Defined Packages

After compiling the classes in Fig. 8.8 and Fig. 8.9, you can execute the applet from a command window with the command

```
appletviewer TimeTest5.html
```

As we discussed when we introduced packages earlier in this chapter, the interpreter can locate packaged classes in the current directory. The **`appletviewer`** is a Java application that executes a Java applet. Like the interpreter, the **`appletviewer`** can load standard Java classes and extension classes installed on the local computer. However, the **`appletviewer`** does not use the class path to locate classes in programmer-defined packages. For an applet, such classes should be bundled with the applet class in an archive file called a *Java Archive (JAR)* file. Remember that applets normally are downloaded from the Internet into a Web browser (see Chapter 3 for more information). Bundling the classes and packages that compose an applet enables the applet and its supporting classes to be downloaded as a unit, then executed in the browser (or via the Java Plug-in for browsers that do not support Java 2).

To bundle the classes in Fig. 8.8 and Fig. 8.9, open a command window and change directories to the location in which **`TimeTest5.class`** is stored. In that same directory should be the **`com`** directory that begins the package directory structure for class **`Time3`**. In that directory, issue the following command

```
jar cf TimeTest5.jar TimeTest5.class com\*.*
```

to create the JAR file. [*Note:* This command uses **`\`** as the directory separator from the MS-DOS prompt. UNIX would use **`/`** as the directory separator.] In the preceding command, **`jar`** is the *Java archive utility* used to create JAR files. Next are the options for the **`jar`** utility—**`cf`**. The letter **`c`** indicates that we are creating a JAR file. The letter **`f`** indicates that the next argument in the command line (**`TimeTest5.jar`**) is the name of the JAR file to create. Following the options and JAR file name are the actual files that will be included in the JAR file. We specified **`TimeTest5.class`** and **`com\*.*`**, indicating that **`TimeTest5.class`** and all the files in the **`com`** directory should be included in the JAR file. The **`com`** directory begins the package that contains the **`.class`** file for the **`Time3`**. [*Note:* You can include selected files by specifying the path and file name for each individual file.] It is important that the directory structure in the JAR file match the directory structure for the packaged classes. Therefore, we executed the **jar** command from the directory in which **com** is located.

To confirm that the files were archived directly, you can issue the command

```
jar tvf TimeTest5.jar
```

which produces the listing in Fig. 8.10. In the preceding command, the options for the **jar** utility are ***tvf***. The letter **t** indicates that the table of contents for the JAR should be listed. The letter ***v*** indicates that the output should be verbose (the verbose output includes the file size in bytes and the date and time each file was created, in addition to the directory structure and file name). The letter ***f*** specifies that the next argument on the command line is the JAR file to use.

The only remaining issue is to specify the archive as part of the applet's HTML file. In prior examples, **<applet>** tags had the form

```
<applet code = "ClassName.class" width = "width" height = "height">
</applet>
```

To specify that the applet classes are located in a JAR file, use an **<applet>** tag of the form:

```
<applet code = "ClassName.class" archive = "archiveList"
   width = "width" height = "height">
</applet>
```

The ***archive*** *attribute* can specify a comma-separated list of archive files for use in an applet. Each file in the **archive** list will be downloaded by the browser when it encounters the **<applet>** tags in the HTML document. For the TimeTest5 applet, the applet tag would be

```
<applet code = "TimeTest5.class" archive = "TimeTest5.jar"
   width = "400" height = "115">
</applet>
```

Try loading this applet into your Web browser. Remember that you *must* either have a browser that supports Java 2 (such as Netscape Navigator 6) or convert the HTML file for use with the Java Plug-in (as discussed in Chapter 3).

```
   0 Fri May 25 14:13:14 EDT 2001 META-INF/
  71 Fri May 25 14:13:14 EDT 2001 META-INF/MANIFEST.MF
2959 Fri May 25 13:42:32 EDT 2001 TimeTest5.class
   0 Fri May 18 17:35:18 EDT 2001 com/deitel/
   0 Fri May 18 17:35:18 EDT 2001 com/deitel/jhtp4/
   0 Fri May 18 17:35:18 EDT 2001 com/deitel/jhtp4/ch08/
1765 Fri May 18 17:35:18 EDT 2001 com/deitel/jhtp4/ch08/Time3.class
```

Fig. 8.10 Contents of **TimeTest5.jar**.

8.9 Software Reusability

Java programmers concentrate on crafting new classes and reusing existing classes. Many *class libraries* exist, and others are being developed worldwide. Software is then constructed from existing, well-defined, carefully tested, well-documented, portable, widely available components. This kind of software reusability speeds the development of powerful, high-quality software. *Rapid applications development (RAD)* is of great interest today.

Java programmers now have thousands of classes in the Java API from which to choose to help them implement Java programs. Indeed, Java is not just a programming language. It is a framework in which Java developers can work to achieve true reusability and rapid applications development. Java programmers can focus on the task at hand when developing their programs and leave the lower-level details to the classes of the Java API. For example, to write a program that draws graphics, a Java programmer does not require knowledge of graphics on every computer platform where the program will execute. Instead, a Java programmer concentrates on learning Java's graphics capabilities (which are quite substantial and growing) and writes a Java program that draws the graphics, using Java's API classes such as **`Graphics`**. When the program executes on a given computer, it is the job of the interpreter to translate Java commands into commands that the local computer can understand.

The Java API classes enable Java programmers to bring new applications to market faster by using preexisting, tested components. Not only does this reduce development time, it also improves programmers' ability to debug and maintain applications. To take advantage of Java's many capabilities, it is essential that programmers take the time to familiarize themselves with the variety of packages and classes in the Java API. There are many Web-based resources at java.sun.com to help you with this task. The primary resource for learning about the Java API is the *Java API documentation*, which can be found at

`java.sun.com/j2se/1.3/docs/api/index.html`

In addition, **`java.sun.com`** provides many other resources, including tutorials, articles and sites specific to individual Java topics. Java developers should also register (for free) at the Java Developer Connection

`developer.java.sun.com`

This site provides additional resources that Java developers will find useful, including more tutorials and articles, and links to other Java resources. See Appendix B for a more complete list of Java-related Internet and World Wide Web resources.

Good Programming Practice 8.6

Avoid reinventing the wheel. Study the capabilities of the Java API. If the API already contains a class that meets the requirements of your program, use that class rather than creating your own.

In general, to realize the full potential of software reusability, we need to improve cataloging schemes, licensing schemes, protection mechanisms that ensure master copies of classes are not corrupted, description schemes that system designers use to determine if existing objects meet their needs, browsing mechanisms that determine what classes are available and how closely they meet software developer requirements, and the like. Many interesting research and development problems have been solved and many more need to be solved; these problems will be solved because the potential value of software reuse is enormous.

8.10 Final Instance Variables

We have emphasized repeatedly the *principle of least privilege* as one of the most fundamental principles of good software engineering. Let us see one way in which this principle applies to instance variables.

Some instance variables need to be modifiable and some do not. The programmer can use the keyword **final** to specify that a variable is not modifiable and that any attempt to modify the variable is an error. For example,

```
private final int INCREMENT = 5;
```

declares a constant instance variable **INCREMENT** of type **int** and initializes it to 5.

Software Engineering Observation 8.17

Declaring an instance variable as **final** *helps enforce the principle of least privilege. If an instance variable should not be modified, declare it to be* **final** *to expressly forbid modification.*

Testing and Debugging Tip 8.3

Accidental attempts to modify a **final** *instance variable are caught at compile time rather than causing execution-time errors. It is always preferable to get bugs out at compile time, if possible, rather than allowing them to slip through to execution time (where studies have found that the cost of repair is often as much as ten times more expensive).*

Common Programming Error 8.9

Attempting to modify a **final** *instance variable after it is initialized is a syntax error.*

The applet of Fig. 8.11 creates a **final** instance variable **INCREMENT** of type **int** and initializes it to 5 in its declaration (line 15). A **final** variable cannot be modified by assignment after it is initialized. Such a variable can be initialized in its declaration or in every constructor of the class.

Common Programming Error 8.10

Not initializing a **final** *instance variable in its declaration or in every constructor of the class is a syntax error.*

```
1  // Fig. 8.11: Increment.java
2  // Initializing a final variable
3
4  // Java core packages
5  import java.awt.*;
6  import java.awt.event.*;
7
```

Fig. 8.11 Initializing a **final** variable (part 1 of 2).

```
// Java extension packages
import javax.swing.*;

public class Increment extends JApplet
   implements ActionListener {

   private int count = 0, total = 0;
   private final int INCREMENT = 5;   // constant variable

   private JButton button;

   // set up GUI
   public void init()
   {
      Container container = getContentPane();

      button = new JButton( "Click to increment" );
      button.addActionListener( this );
      container.add( button );
   }

   // add INCREMENT to total when user clicks button
   public void actionPerformed( ActionEvent actionEvent )
   {
      total += INCREMENT;
      count++;
      showStatus( "After increment " + count +
         ": total = " + total );
   }

} // end class Increment
```

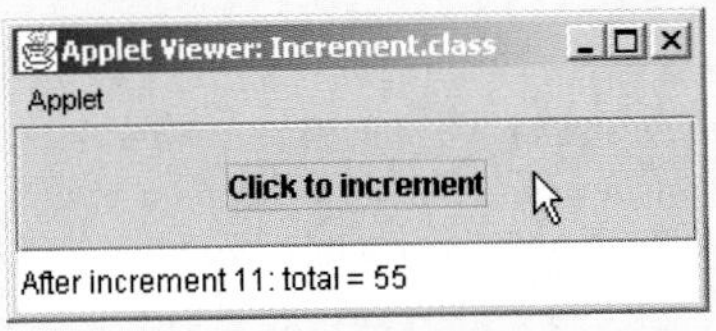

Applet Viewer: Increment.class
Applet
Click to increment
After increment 11: total = 55

Fig. 8.11 Initializing a **`final`** variable (part 2 of 2).

Figure 8.12 illustrates compiler errors produced for the program of Fig. 8.11 if instance variable **`INCREMENT`** is declared **`final`**, but is not initialized in the declaration.

```
Increment.java:11: variable INCREMENT might not have been
   initialized
public class Increment extends JApplet
       ^
1 error
```

Fig. 8.12 Compiler error message as a result of not initializing increment.

8.11 Composition: Objects as Instance Variables of Other Classes

An **AlarmClock** class object needs to know when it is supposed to sound its alarm, so why not include a reference to a **Time** object as a member of the **AlarmClock** object? Such a capability is called *composition.* A class can have references to objects of other classes as members.

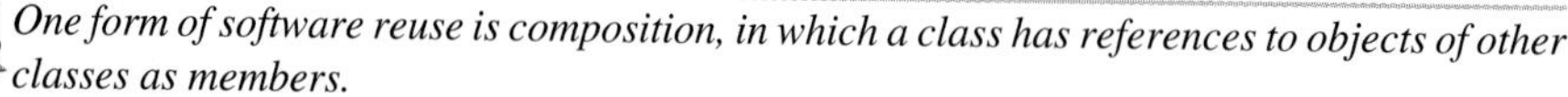

Software Engineering Observation 8.18

One form of software reuse is composition, in which a class has references to objects of other classes as members.

The next program contains three classes—**Date** (Fig. 8.13), **Employee** (Fig. 8.14) and **EmployeeTest** (Fig. 8.15). Class **Employee** contains instance variables **firstName**, **lastName**, **birthDate** and **hireDate**. Members **birthDate** and **hireDate** are references to **Date**s that contain instance variables **month**, **day** and **year**. This demonstrates that a class can contain references to objects of other classes. Class **EmployeeTest** instantiates an **Employee** and initializes and displays its instance variables. The **Employee** constructor (Fig. 8.14, lines 12–20) takes eight arguments—**first**, **last**, **birthMonth**, **birthDay**, **birthYear**, **hireMonth**, **hireDay** and **hireYear**. Arguments **birthMonth**, **birthDay** and **birthYear** are passed to the **Date** constructor (Fig. 8.13, lines 13–28) to initialize the **birthDate** object and **hireMonth**, **hireDay** and **hireYear** are passed to the **Date** constructor to initialize the **hireDate** object.

A member object does not need to be initialized immediately with constructor arguments. If an empty argument list is provided when a member object is created, the object's default constructor (or no-argument constructor if one is available) will be called automatically. Values, if any, established by the default constructor (or no-argument constructor) can then be replaced by *set* methods.

Performance Tip 8.2

Initialize member objects explicitly at construction time by passing appropriate arguments to the constructors of the member objects. This eliminates the overhead of initializing member objects twice—once when the member object's default constructor is called and again when set *methods are used to provide initial values for the member object.*

Note that both class **Date** (Fig. 8.13) and class **Employee** (Fig. 8.14) are defined as part of the package **com.deitel.jhtp4.ch08** as specified on line 3 of each file. Because they are in the same package (i.e., the same directory), class **Employee** does not need to import class **Date** to use it. When the compiler searches for the file **Date.class**, the compiler knows to search the directory where **Employee.class** is located. Classes in a package never need to import other classes from the same package.

```
1  // Fig. 8.13: Date.java
2  // Declaration of the Date class.
3  package com.deitel.jhtp4.ch08;
4
5  public class Date extends Object {
6     private int month;  // 1-12
```

Fig. 8.13 **Date** class (part 1 of 2).

```
   private int day;     // 1-31 based on month
   private int year;    // any year

   // Constructor: Confirm proper value for month;
   // call method checkDay to confirm proper
   // value for day.
   public Date( int theMonth, int theDay, int theYear )
   {
      if ( theMonth > 0 && theMonth <= 12 )  // validate month
         month = theMonth;
      else {
         month = 1;
         System.out.println( "Month " + theMonth +
            " invalid. Set to month 1." );
      }

      year = theYear;                     // could validate year
      day = checkDay( theDay );           // validate day

      System.out.println(
         "Date object constructor for date " + toString() );
   }

   // Utility method to confirm proper day value
   // based on month and year.
   private int checkDay( int testDay )
   {
      int daysPerMonth[] =
         { 0, 31, 28, 31, 30, 31, 30, 31, 31, 30, 31, 30, 31 };

      // check if day in range for month
      if ( testDay > 0 && testDay <= daysPerMonth[ month ] )
         return testDay;

      // check for leap year
      if ( month == 2 && testDay == 29 &&
           ( year % 400 == 0 ||
              ( year % 4 == 0 && year % 100 != 0 ) ) )
         return testDay;

      System.out.println( "Day " + testDay +
         " invalid. Set to day 1." );

      return 1;  // leave object in consistent state
   }

   // Create a String of the form month/day/year
   public String toString()
   {
      return month + "/" + day + "/" + year;
   }

}  // end class Date
```

Fig. 8.13 **Date** class (part 2 of 2).

```java
// Fig. 8.14: Employee.java
// Definition of class Employee.
package com.deitel.jhtp4.ch08;

public class Employee extends Object {
   private String firstName;
   private String lastName;
   private Date birthDate;
   private Date hireDate;

   // constructor to initialize name, birth date and hire date
   public Employee( String first, String last,
     int birthMonth, int birthDay, int birthYear,
     int hireMonth, int hireDay, int hireYear )
   {
      firstName = first;
      lastName = last;
      birthDate = new Date( birthMonth, birthDay, birthYear );
      hireDate = new Date( hireMonth, hireDay, hireYear );
   }

   // convert Employee to String format
   public String toString()
   {
      return lastName + ", " + firstName +
         "  Hired: " + hireDate.toString() +
         "  Birthday: " + birthDate.toString();
   }

}  // end class Employee
```

Fig. 8.14 **Employee** class with member object references.

```java
// Fig. 8.15: EmployeeTest.java
// Demonstrating an object with a member object.

// Java extension packages
import javax.swing.JOptionPane;

// Deitel packages
import com.deitel.jhtp4.ch08.Employee;

public class EmployeeTest {

   // test class Employee
   public static void main( String args[] )
   {
      Employee employee = new Employee( "Bob", "Jones",
         7, 24, 49, 3, 12, 88 );

```

Fig. 8.15 Demonstrating an object with a member object reference (part 1 of 2).

```
        JOptionPane.showMessageDialog( null,
           employee.toString(), "Testing Class Employee",
           JOptionPane.INFORMATION_MESSAGE );

        System.exit( 0 );
     }

  }  // end class EmployeeTest
```

```
Testing Class Employee
Jones, Bob Hired: 3/12/88 Birthday: 7/24/49
OK
```

```
Date object constructor for date 7/24/1949
Date object constructor for date 3/12/1988
```

Fig. 8.15 Demonstrating an object with a member object reference (part 2 of 2).

8.12 Package Access

When no member access modifier is provided for a method or variable when it is defined in a class, the method or variable is considered to have *package access*. If your program consists of one class definition, this has no specific effects on the program. However, if your program uses multiple classes from the same package (i.e., a group of related classes), these classes can access each other's package-access methods and data directly through a reference to an object.

Performance Tip 8.3

Package access enables objects of different classes to interact without the need for set *and* get *methods that provide access to data, thus eliminating some of the method call overhead.*

Let us consider a mechanical example of package access. The application of Fig. 8.16 contains two classes—the **PackageDataTest** application class (lines 8–34) and the **PackageData** class (lines 37–54). In the **PackageData** class definition, lines 38–39 declare the instance variables **number** and **string** with no member access modifiers; therefore, these are package access instance variables. The **PackageDataTest** application's **main** method creates an instance of the **PackageData** class (line 13) to demonstrate the ability to modify the **PackageData** instance variables directly (as shown on lines 20–21). The results of the modification can be seen in the output window.

When you compile this program, the compiler produces two separate files—a **.class** file for class **PackageData** and a **.class** file for class **PackageDataTest**. Every Java class has its own **.class** file. These two **.class** files are placed in the same directory by the compiler automatically and are considered to be part of the same package (they are certainly related by the fact that they are in the same file). Because they are part of the same package, class **PackageDataTest** is allowed to modify the package access data of objects of class **PackageData**.

```java
// Fig. 8.16: PackageDataTest.java
// Classes in the same package (i.e., the same directory) can
// use package access data of other classes in the same package.

// Java extension packages
import javax.swing.JOptionPane;

public class PackageDataTest {

   // Java extension packages
   public static void main( String args[] )
   {
      PackageData packageData = new PackageData();

      // append String representation of packageData to output
      String output =
         "After instantiation:\n" + packageData.toString();

      // change package access data in packageData object
      packageData.number = 77;
      packageData.string = "Good bye";

      // append String representation of packageData to output
      output += "\nAfter changing values:\n" +
         packageData.toString();

      JOptionPane.showMessageDialog( null, output,
         "Demonstrating Package Access",
         JOptionPane.INFORMATION_MESSAGE );

      System.exit( 0 );
   }

}  // end class PackageDataTest

// class with package access instance variables
class PackageData {
   int number;      // package access instance variable
   String string;   // package access instance variable

   // constructor
   public PackageData()
   {
      number = 0;
      string = "Hello";
   }

   // convert PackageData object to String representation
   public String toString()
   {
      return "number: " + number + "    string: " + string;
   }

```

Fig. 8.16 Package access to members of a class (part 1 of 2).

```
} // end class PackageData
```

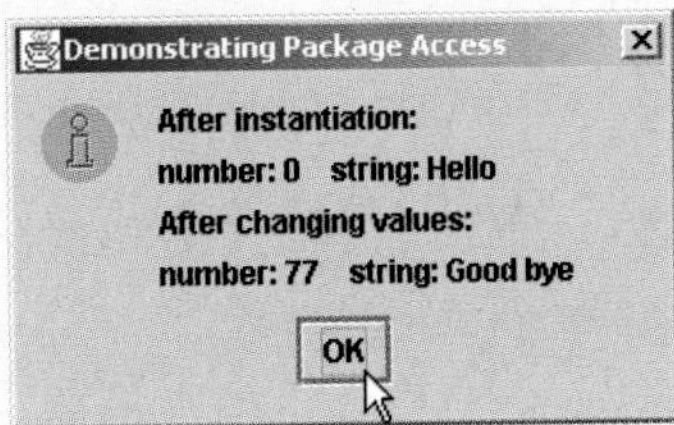

Fig. 8.16 Package access to members of a class (part 2 of 2).

Software Engineering Observation 8.19

Some people in the OOP community feel that package access corrupts information hiding and weakens the value of the object-oriented design approach, because the programmer must assume responsibility for error checking and data validation in any code that manipulates the package access data members.

8.13 Using the `this` Reference

When a method of a class references another member of that class for a specific object of that class, how does Java ensure that the proper object is referenced? The answer is that each object has access to a reference to itself—called the ***this*** *reference.*

The **this** reference is used implicitly to refer to both the instance variables and methods of an object. We begin with a simple example of using the **this** reference explicitly; a subsequent example shows some substantial and subtle examples of using **this**.

Performance Tip 8.4

Java conserves storage by maintaining only one copy of each method per class; this method is invoked by every object of that class. Each object, on the other hand, has its own copy of the class's instance variables.

The application of Fig. 8.17 demonstrates implicit and explicit use of the **this** reference to enable the **main** method of class **ThisTest** to display the **private** data of a **SimpleTime** object.

```
// Fig. 8.17: ThisTest.java
// Using the this reference to refer to
// instance variables and methods.

// Java core packages
import java.text.DecimalFormat;

// Java extension packages
import javax.swing.*;

```

Fig. 8.17 Using the **this** reference implicitly and explicitly (part 1 of 3).

```
public class ThisTest {

   // test class SimpleTime
   public static void main( String args[] )
   {
      SimpleTime time = new SimpleTime( 12, 30, 19 );

      JOptionPane.showMessageDialog( null, time.buildString(),
         "Demonstrating the \"this\" Reference",
         JOptionPane.INFORMATION_MESSAGE );

      System.exit( 0 );
   }

}  // end class ThisTest

// class SimpleTime demonstrates the "this" reference
class SimpleTime {
   private int hour, minute, second;

   // constructor uses parameter names identical to instance
   // variable names, so "this" reference required to distinguish
   // between instance variables and parameters
   public SimpleTime( int hour, int minute, int second )
   {
      this.hour = hour;        // set "this" object's hour
      this.minute = minute;    // set "this" object's minute
      this.second = second;    // set "this" object's second
   }

   // call toString explicitly via "this" reference, explicitly
   // via implicit "this" reference, implicitly via "this"
   public String buildString()
   {
      return "this.toString(): " + this.toString() +
         "\ntoString(): " + toString() +
         "\nthis (with implicit toString() call): " + this;
   }

   // convert SimpleTime to String format
   public String toString()
   {
      DecimalFormat twoDigits = new DecimalFormat( "00" );

      // "this" not required, because toString does not have
      // local variables with same names as instance variables
      return twoDigits.format( this.hour ) + ":" +
         twoDigits.format( this.minute ) + ":" +
         twoDigits.format( this.second );
   }

}  // end class SimpleTime
```

Fig. 8.17 Using the **this** reference implicitly and explicitly (part 2 of 3).

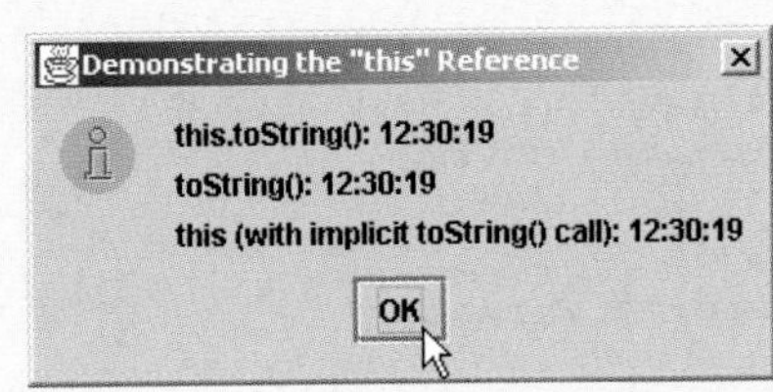

Fig. 8.17 Using the **this** reference implicitly and explicitly (part 3 of 3).

Class **SimpleTime** (lines 8–60) defines three **private** instance variables—**hour**, **minute** and **second**. The constructor (lines 34–39) receives three **int** arguments to initialize a **SimpleTime** object. Notice that the parameter names for the constructor are the same as the instance variable names. Remember that a local variable of a method with the same name as an instance variable of a class hides the instance variable in the scope of the method. For this reason, we use the **this** reference to refer explicitly to the instance variables on lines 36–38.

Common Programming Error 8.11

In a method in which a method parameter has the same name as one of the class members, use **this** *explicitly if you want to access the class member; otherwise, you will incorrectly reference the method parameter.*

Good Programming Practice 8.7

Avoid using method parameter names that conflict with class member names.

Method **buildString** (lines 43–48) returns a **String** created with a statement that uses the **this** reference three ways. Line 45 explicitly invokes the class's **toString** method via **this.toString()**. Line 46 implicitly uses the **this** reference to perform the same task. Line 47 appends **this** to the string that will be returned. Remember that the **this** reference is a reference to an object—the current **SimpleTime** object being manipulated. As before, any reference added to a **String** results in a call to the **toString** method for the referenced object. Method **buildString** is invoked at line 18 to display the results of the three calls to **toString**. Note that the same time is displayed on all three lines of the output because all three calls to **toString** are for the same object.

Another use of the **this** reference is in enabling *concatenated method calls* (also called *cascaded method calls* or *method call chaining*). Figure 8.18 illustrates returning a reference to a **Time4** object to enable method calls of class **Time4** to be concatenated. Methods **setTime** (lines 50–57), **setHour** (lines 60–65), **setMinute** (line 68–74) and **setSecond** (lines 77–83) each have a return type of **Time4** and each has as its last statement

```
return this;
```

to indicate that a reference to the **Time4** object being manipulated should be returned to the caller of the method.

```
// Fig. 8.18: Time4.java
// Time4 class definition
package com.deitel.jhtp4.ch08;

// Java core packages
import java.text.DecimalFormat;

public class Time4 extends Object {
   private int hour;     // 0 - 23
   private int minute;   // 0 - 59
   private int second;   // 0 - 59

   // Time4 constructor initializes each instance variable
   // to zero. Ensures that Time object starts in a
   // consistent state.
   public Time4()
   {
      this.setTime( 0, 0, 0 );
   }

   // Time4 constructor: hour supplied, minute and second
   // defaulted to 0
   public Time4( int hour )
   {
      this.setTime( hour, 0, 0 );
   }

   // Time4 constructor: hour and minute supplied, second
   // defaulted to 0
   public Time4( int hour, int minute )
   {
      this.setTime( hour, minute, 0 );
   }

   // Time4 constructor: hour, minute and second supplied
   public Time4( int hour, int minute, int second )
   {
      this.setTime( hour, minute, second );
   }

   // Time4 constructor: another Time4 object supplied.
   public Time4( Time4 time )
   {
      this.setTime( time.getHour(), time.getMinute(),
         time.getSecond() );
   }

   // Set Methods
   // set a new Time value using universal time
   public Time4 setTime( int hour, int minute, int second )
   {
      this.setHour( hour );        // set hour
```

Fig. 8.18 Class **Time4** using **this** to enable chained method calls (part 1 of 3).

```
      this.setMinute( minute );  // set minute
      this.setSecond( second );  // set second

      return this;     // enables chaining
   }

   // validate and set hour
   public Time4 setHour( int hour )
   {
      this.hour = ( hour >= 0 && hour < 24 ? hour : 0 );

      return this;     // enables chaining
   }

   // validate and set minute
   public Time4 setMinute( int minute )
   {
      this.minute =
         ( minute >= 0 && minute < 60 ) ? minute : 0;

      return this;     // enables chaining
   }

   // validate and set second
   public Time4 setSecond( int second )
   {
      this.second =
         ( second >= 0 && second < 60 ) ? second : 0;

      return this;     // enables chaining
   }

   // Get Methods
   // get value of hour
   public int getHour() { return this.hour; }

   // get value of minute
   public int getMinute() { return this.minute; }

   // get value of second
   public int getSecond() { return this.second; }

   // convert to String in universal-time format
   public String toUniversalString()
   {
      DecimalFormat twoDigits = new DecimalFormat( "00" );

      return twoDigits.format( this.getHour() ) + ":" +
         twoDigits.format( this.getMinute() ) + ":" +
         twoDigits.format( this.getSecond() );
   }

```

Fig. 8.18 Class **Time4** using **this** to enable chained method calls (part 2 of 3).

```
    // convert to String in standard-time format
    public String toString()
    {
        DecimalFormat twoDigits = new DecimalFormat( "00" );

        return ( this.getHour() == 12 || this.getHour() == 0 ?
            12 : this.getHour() % 12 ) + ":" +
            twoDigits.format( this.getMinute() ) + ":" +
            twoDigits.format( this.getSecond() ) +
            ( this.getHour() < 12 ? " AM" : " PM" );
    }

} // end class Time4
```

Fig. 8.18 Class **Time4** using **this** to enable chained method calls (part 3 of 3).

The example again demonstrates the explicit use of the **this** reference inside the body of a class. In class **Time4**, every use of an instance variable of the class and every call to another method in class **Time4** uses the **this** reference explicitly. Most programmers prefer not to use the **this** reference unless it is required or helps clarify a piece of code.

Good Programming Practice 8.8

Explicitly using **this** *can increase program clarity in some contexts in which* **this** *is optional.*

In application class **TimeTest6** (Fig. 8.19), line 18 and line 26 both demonstrate method call chaining. Why does the technique of returning the **this** reference work? Let us discuss line 18. The dot operator (**.**) associates from left to right, so the expression

```
time.setHour( 18 ).setMinute( 30 ).setSecond( 22 );
```

first evaluates **time.setHour(18)**, then returns a reference to object **time** as the result of this method call. Any time you have a reference in a program (even as the result of a method call), the reference can be followed by a dot operator and a call to one of the methods of the reference type. Thus, the remaining expression is interpreted as

```
time.setMinute( 30 ).setSecond( 22 );
```

The **time.setMinute(30)** call executes and returns a reference to **time**. The remaining expression is interpreted as

```
time.setSecond( 22 );
```

When the statement is complete, the time is **18** for the **hour**, **30** for the **minute** and **22** from the **second**.

Note that the calls on line 26

```
time.setTime( 20, 20, 20 ).toString();
```

also use the concatenation feature. These method calls must appear in this order in this expression because **toString** as defined in the class does not return a reference to a **Time4** object. Placing the call to **toString** before the call to **setTime** causes a syntax error. Note that **toString** returns a reference to a **String** object. Therefore, a method of class **String** could be concatenated to the end of line 26.

```java
// Fig. 8.19: TimeTest6.java
// Chaining method calls together with the this reference

// Java extension packages
import javax.swing.*;

// Deitel packages
import com.deitel.jhtp4.ch08.Time4;

public class TimeTest6 {

   // test method call chaining with object of class Time4
   public static void main( String args[] )
   {
      Time4 time = new Time4();

      // chain calls to setHour, setMinute and setSecond
      time.setHour( 18 ).setMinute( 30 ).setSecond( 22 );

      // use method call chaining to set new time and get
      // String representation of new time
      String output =
         "Universal time: " + time.toUniversalString() +
         "\nStandard time: " + time.toString() +
         "\n\nNew standard time: " +
         time.setTime( 20, 20, 20 ).toString();

      JOptionPane.showMessageDialog( null, output,
         "Chaining Method Calls",
         JOptionPane.INFORMATION_MESSAGE );

      System.exit( 0 );
   }

}  // end class TimeTest6
```

Chaining Method Calls

Universal time: 18:30:22
Standard time: 6:30:22 PM

New standard time: 8:20:20 PM

OK

Fig. 8.19 Concatenating method calls.

Note that the purpose of the example in Fig. 8.18 and Fig. 8.19 is to demonstrate the mechanics of concatenated method calls. Many Java methods return references to objects that can be used in the manner shown here. It is important to understand concatenated method calls as they appear frequently in Java programs.

Good Programming Practice 8.9

For program clarity, avoid using concatenated method calls.

8.14 Finalizers

We have seen that constructor methods are capable of initializing data in an object of a class when the class is created. Often, constructors acquire various system resources such as memory (when the **new** operator is used). We need a disciplined way to give resources back to the system when they are no longer needed to avoid resource leaks. The most common resource acquired by constructors is memory. Java performs automatic *garbage collection* of memory to help return memory back to the system. When an object is no longer used in the program (i.e., there are no references to the object), the object is *marked for garbage collection.* The memory for such an object can be reclaimed when the *garbage collector* executes. Therefore, memory leaks that are common in other languages like C and C++ (because memory is not automatically reclaimed in those languages) are less likely to happen in Java. However, other resource leaks can occur.

Performance Tip 8.5

Extensive use of local variables that refer to objects can degrade performance. When a local variable is the only reference to an object, the object is marked for garbage collection as the local variable goes out of scope. If this happens frequently in short time periods, large numbers of objects could be marked for garbage collection, thus placing a performance burden on the garbage collector.

Every class in Java can have a *finalizer method* that returns resources to the system. The finalizer method for an object is guaranteed to be called to perform *termination housekeeping* on the object just before the garbage collector reclaims the memory for the object. A class's finalizer method always has the name **finalize**, receives no parameters and returns no value (i.e., its return type is **void**). A class should have only one **finalize** method that takes no arguments. Method **finalize** is defined originally in class **Object** as a placeholder that does nothing. This guarantees that every class has a **finalize** method for the garbage collector to call.

Good Programming Practice 8.10

The last statement in a **finalize** *method should always be* **super.finalize();** *to ensure that the superclass's* **finalize** *method is called.*

Software Engineering Observation 8.20

The garbage collector is not guaranteed to execute; therefore, an object's **finalize** *method is not guaranteed to get called. You should not architect classes that rely on the garbage collector calling an object's* **finalize** *method to deallocate resources.*

Finalizers have not been provided for the classes presented so far. Actually, finalizers are rarely used in industrial Java applications. We will see a sample **finalize** method and discuss the garbage collector further in Figure 8.20.

Testing and Debugging Tip 8.4

Several professional Java developers who reviewed this book indicated that method **finalize** *is not useful in industrial Java applications, because it is not guaranteed to get called. For this reason, you should search your Java programs for any use of method* **finalize** *to ensure that the program does not rely on calls to method* **finalize** *for proper deallocation of resources. In fact, you might consider removing method* **finalize** *entirely* *and using other techniques to ensure proper resource deallocation. We present one such technique in Chapter 14, Exception Handling.*

8.15 Static Class Members

Each object of a class has its own copy of all the instance variables of the class. In certain cases, only one copy of a particular variable should be shared by all objects of a class. A ***static** class variable* is used for these and other reasons. A **static** class variable represents *class-wide information*—all objects of the class share the same piece of data. The declaration of a **static** member begins with the keyword **static**.

Let us motivate the need for **static** class-wide data with a video game example. Suppose we have a video game with **Martian**s and other space creatures. Each **Martian** tends to be brave and willing to attack other space creatures when the **Martian** is aware that there are at least five **Martian**s present. If there are fewer than five **Martian**s present, each **Martian** becomes cowardly. So each **Martian** needs to know the **martianCount**. We could endow class **Martian** with **martianCount** as instance data. If we do this, then every **Martian** will have a separate copy of the instance data and every time we create a new **Martian** we will have to update the instance variable **martianCount** in every **Martian**. This wastes space with the redundant copies and wastes time in updating the separate copies. Instead, we declare **martianCount** to be **static**. This makes **martianCount** class-wide data. Every **Martian** can see the **martianCount** as if it were instance data of the **Martian**, but only one copy of the static **martianCount** is maintained by Java. This saves space. We save time by having the **Martian** constructor increment the static **martianCount**. Because there is only one copy, we do not have to increment separate copies of **martianCount** for each **Martian** object.

Performance Tip 8.6

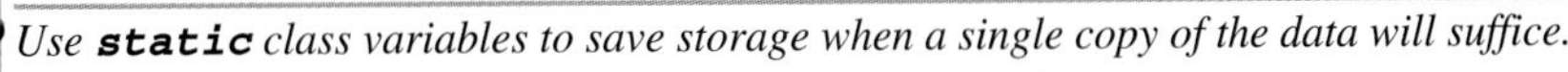

*Use **static** class variables to save storage when a single copy of the data will suffice.*

Although **static** class variables may seem like global variables, **static** class variables have class scope. A class's **public static** class members can be accessed through a reference to any object of that class, or they can be accessed through the class name by using the dot operator (e.g., **Math.random()**). A class's **private static** class members can be accessed only through methods of the class. Actually, **static** class members exist even when no objects of that class exist—they are available as soon as the class is loaded into memory at execution time. To access a **public static** class member when no objects of the class exist, simply prefix the class name and the dot operator to the class member. To access a **private static** class member when no objects of the class exist, a **public static** method must be provided and the method must be called by prefixing its name with the class name and dot operator.

Our next program defines two classes—**Employee** (Fig. 8.20) and **EmployeeTest** (Fig. 8.21). Class **Employee** defines a **private static** class variable and a **public static** method. The class variable **count** (Fig. 8.20, line 6) is initialized to zero by default. Class variable **count** maintains a count of the number of objects of class **Employee** that have been instantiated and currently reside in memory. This includes objects that have already been marked for garbage collection but have not yet been reclaimed.

```
1 // Fig. 8.20: Employee.java
2 // Employee class definition.
3 public class Employee extends Object {
4    private String firstName;
5    private String lastName;
6    private static int count;  // number of objects in memory
7
8    // initialize employee, add 1 to static count and
9    // output String indicating that constructor was called
10   public Employee( String first, String last )
11   {
12      firstName = first;
13      lastName = last;
14
15      ++count;  // increment static count of employees
16      System.out.println( "Employee object constructor: " +
17         firstName + " " + lastName );
18   }
19
20   // subtract 1 from static count when garbage collector
21   // calls finalize to clean up object and output String
22   // indicating that finalize was called
23   protected void finalize()
24   {
25      --count;  // decrement static count of employees
26      System.out.println( "Employee object finalizer: " +
27         firstName + " " + lastName + "; count = " + count );
28   }
29
30   // get first name
31   public String getFirstName()
32   {
33      return firstName;
34   }
35
36   // get last name
37   public String getLastName()
38   {
39      return lastName;
40   }
41
42   // static method to get static count value
43   public static int getCount()
44   {
45      return count;
46   }
47
48 }  // end class Employee
```

Fig. 8.20 **Employee** class that uses a **static** class variable to maintain a count of the number of **Employee** objects in memory.

When objects of class **Employee** exist, member **count** can be used in any method of an **Employee** object—in this example, **count** is incremented (line 15) by the constructor and decremented (line 25) by the finalizer. When no objects of class **Employee** exist, member **count** can still be referenced, but only through a call to **public static** method **getCount** (lines 43–46), as in:

```
Employee.getCount()
```

which determines the number of **Employee** objects currently in memory. Note that when there are no objects instantiated in the program, the **Employee.getCount()** method call is issued. However, when there are objects instantiated, method **getCount** can also be called through a reference to one of the objects, as in

```
e1.getCount()
```

Good Programming Practice 8.11

Always invoke **static** *methods by using the class name and the dot operator (.). This emphasizes to other programmers reading your code that the method being called is a* **static** *method.*

Notice that the **Employee** class has a **finalize** method (lines 23–28). This method is included to show when it is called by the garbage collector in a program. Method **finalize** normally is declared ***protected*** so it is not part of the **public** services of a class. We will discuss the **protected** access modifier in detail in Chapter 9.

Method **main** of the **EmployeeTest** application class (Fig. 8.21) instantiates two **Employee** objects (lines 16–17). When each **Employee** object's constructor is invoked, lines 12–13 of Fig. 8.20 store references to that **Employee**'s first name and last name **String** objects. Note that these two statements *do not* make copies of the original **String**s arguments. Actually, **String** objects in Java are *immutable*—they cannot be modified after they are created (class **String** does not provide any *set* methods). Because a reference cannot be used to modify a **String**, it is safe to have many references to one **String** object in a Java program. This is not normally the case for most other classes in Java. If Java String objects are immutable, why are we able to use the + and += operators to concatenate Strings? As we discuss in Chapter 10, Strings and Characters, the **String** concatenation operations actually result in the creation of new **String** objects containing the concatenated values. The original **String** objects actually are not modified.

When **main** is done with the two **Employee** objects, the references **e1** and **e2** are set to **null** at lines 37–38. At this point references **e1** and **e2** no longer refer to the objects that were instantiated on lines 16–17. This *marks the objects for garbage collection* because there are no more references to the objects in the program.

```
1  // Fig. 8.21: EmployeeTest.java
2  // Test Employee class with static class variable,
3  // static class method, and dynamic memory.
4  import javax.swing.*;
5
```

Fig. 8.21 Using a **static** class variable to maintain a count of the number of objects of a class (part 1 of 3).

```
public class EmployeeTest {

   // test class Employee
   public static void main( String args[] )
   {
      // prove that count is 0 before creating Employees
      String output = "Employees before instantiation: " +
         Employee.getCount();

      // create two Employees; count should be 2
      Employee e1 = new Employee( "Susan", "Baker" );
      Employee e2 = new Employee( "Bob", "Jones" );

      // Prove that count is 2 after creating two Employees.
      // Note: static methods should be called only via the
      // class name for the class in which they are defined.
      output += "\n\nEmployees after instantiation: " +
         "\nvia e1.getCount(): " + e1.getCount() +
         "\nvia e2.getCount(): " + e2.getCount() +
         "\nvia Employee.getCount(): " + Employee.getCount();

      // get names of Employees
      output += "\n\nEmployee 1: " + e1.getFirstName() +
         " " + e1.getLastName() + "\nEmployee 2: " +
         e2.getFirstName() + " " + e2.getLastName();

      // If there is only one reference to each employee (as
      // on this example), the following statements mark
      // those objects for garbage collection. Otherwise,
      // these statement simply decrement the reference count
      // for each object.
      e1 = null;
      e2 = null;

      System.gc(); // suggest call to garbage collector

      // Show Employee count after calling garbage collector.
      // Count displayed may be 0, 1 or 2 depending on
      // whether garbage collector executed immediately and
      // number of Employee objects it collects.
      output += "\n\nEmployees after System.gc(): " +
         Employee.getCount();

      JOptionPane.showMessageDialog( null, output,
         "Static Members and Garbage Collection",
         JOptionPane.INFORMATION_MESSAGE );

      System.exit( 0 );
   }

}  // end class EmployeeTest
```

Fig. 8.21 Using a `static` class variable to maintain a count of the number of objects of a class (part 2 of 3).

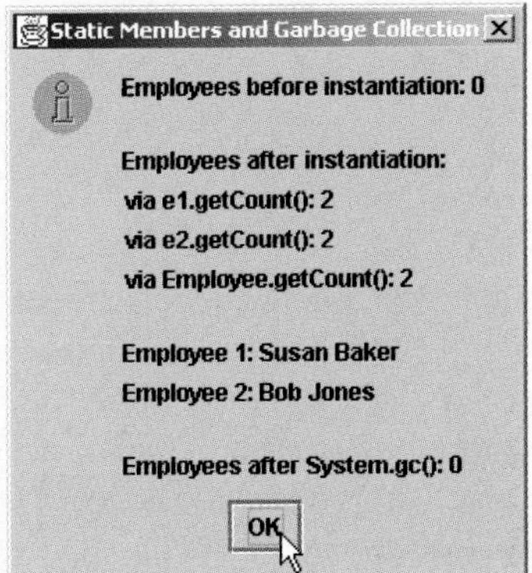


```
Employee object constructor: Susan Baker
Employee object constructor: Bob Jones
Employee object finalizer: Susan Baker; count = 1
Employee object finalizer: Bob Jones; count = 0
```

Fig. 8.21 Using a **static** class variable to maintain a count of the number of objects of a class (part 3 of 3).

Eventually, the garbage collector reclaims the memory for these objects (or the memory is reclaimed by the operating system when the program terminates). Because it is not guaranteed when the garbage collector will execute, we make an explicit call to the garbage collector with line 40, which uses **public static** method **gc** from class **System** (**java.lang** package) to indicate that the garbage collector immediately should make a best effort attempt to collect objects that have been marked for garbage collection. However, this is just a best effort—it is possible that no objects or a subset of the garbage objects will be collected. In our example, the garbage collector did execute before lines 49–51 displayed the results of the program. The last line of the output indicates that the number of **Employee** objects in memory is 0 after the call to **System.gc()**. Also, the last two lines of the command window output show that the **Employee** object for **Susan Baker** was finalized before the **Employee** object for **Bob Jones**. Remember, the garbage collector is not guaranteed to execute when **System.gc()** is invoked nor is it guaranteed to collect objects in a specific order, so it is possible that the output of this program on your system may differ.

[*Note*: A method declared **static** cannot access non**static** class members. Unlike non**static** methods, a **static** method has no **this** reference because, **static** class variables and **static** class methods exist independent of any objects of a class and before any objects of the class have been instantiated.]

Common Programming Error 8.12

Referring to the **this** *reference in a* **static** *method is a syntax error.*

Common Programming Error 8.13

It is a syntax error for a **static** *method to call an instance method or to access an instance variable.*

Software Engineering Observation 8.21

Any **`static`** *class variables and* **`static`** *class methods exist and can be used even if no objects of that class have been instantiated.*

8.16 Data Abstraction and Encapsulation

Classes normally hide their implementation details from the clients of the classes. This is called *encapsulation* or *information hiding*. As an example of encapsulation, let us consider a data structure called a *stack*.

Think of a stack in terms of a pile of dishes. When a dish is placed on the pile, it is always placed at the top (referred to as *pushing* the dish onto the stack), and when a dish is removed from the pile, it is always removed from the top (referred to as *popping* the dish off the stack). Stacks are known as *last-in, first-out (LIFO) data structures*—the last item pushed (inserted) on the stack is the first item popped (removed) from the stack.

The programmer can create a stack class and hide from its clients implementation of the stack. Stacks can easily be implemented with arrays and other methods (such as linked lists; see Chapter 19, "Data Structures," and Chapter 20, "Java Utilities Packages and Bit Manipulation"). A client of a stack class need not know how the stack is implemented. The client simply requires that when data items are placed in the stack, they will be recalled in last-in, first-out order. This concept is referred to as *data abstraction,* and Java classes define abstract data types (ADTs). Although users might happen to know the details of how a class is implemented, users may not write code that depends on these details. This means that a particular class (such as one that implements a stack and its operations of *push* and *pop*) can be replaced with another version without affecting the rest of the system, as long as the public services of that class does not change (i.e., every method still has the same name, return type and parameter list in the new class definition).

The job of a high-level language is to create a view convenient for programmers to use. There is no single accepted standard view—that is one reason why there are so many programming languages. Object-oriented programming in Java presents yet another view.

Most programming languages emphasize actions. In these languages, data exists in support of the actions programs need to take. Data is "less interesting" than actions, anyway. Data is "crude." There are only a few built-in data types, and it is difficult for programmers to create their own new data types.

This view changes with Java and the object-oriented style of programming. Java elevates the importance of data. The primary activity in Java is creating new data types (i.e., classes) and expressing the interactions among objects of those data types.

To move in this direction, the programming-languages community needed to formalize some notions about data. The formalization we consider is the notion of *abstract data types (ADTs).* ADTs receive as much attention today as structured programming did over the last two decades. ADTs do not replace structured programming. Rather, they provide an additional formalization to further improve the program development process.

What is an abstract data type? Consider the built-in type **`int`**. What comes to mind is the notion of an integer in mathematics, but **`int`** on a computer is not precisely what an integer is in mathematics. In particular, computer **`int`**s are normally quite limited in size. For example, **`int`** on a 32-bit machine is limited approximately to the range –2 billion to +2 billion. If the result of a calculation falls outside this range, an error occurs and the machine responds in some machine-dependent manner, including the possibility of "quietly" producing an incorrect result. Mathematical integers do not have this problem. So the notion of a computer **int** is really only an approximation to the notion of a real-world integer. The same is true with **float**.

The point is that even the built-in data types provided with programming languages like Java are really only approximations or models of real-world concepts and behaviors. We have taken **int** for granted until this point, but now you have a new perspective to consider. Types like **int**, **float**, **char** and others are all examples of abstract data types. They are essentially ways of representing real-world notions to some satisfactory level of precision within a computer system.

An abstract data type actually captures two notions, namely a *data representation* and the *operations* that are allowed on that data. For example, the notion of **int** defines addition, subtraction, multiplication, division and modulus operations in Java, but division by zero is undefined. Another example is the notion of negative integers whose operations and data representation are clear, but the operation of taking the square root of a negative integer is undefined. In Java, the programmer uses classes to implement abstract data types.

Java has a small set of primitive types. ADTs extend the base programming language.

Software Engineering Observation 8.22

The programmer is able to create new types through the use of the class mechanism. These new types can be designed to be used as conveniently as the built-in types. Thus, Java is an extensible language. Although the language is easy to extend with these new types, the base language itself is not changeable.

New Java classes can be proprietary to an individual, to small groups, to companies, and so on. Many classes are placed in standard *class libraries* intended for wide distribution. This does not necessarily promote standards, although de facto standards are emerging. The full value of Java will be realized only when substantial, standardized class libraries become more widely available than they are today. In the United States, such standardization often happens through *ANSI*, the *American National Standards Institute*. Worldwide standardization often happens through *ISO, the International Standards Organization*. Regardless of how these libraries ultimately appear, the reader who learns Java and object-oriented programming will be ready to take advantage of the new kinds of rapid, component-oriented software development made possible with class libraries.

8.16.1 Example: Queue Abstract Data Type

Each of us stands in line from time to time. A waiting line is also called a *queue*. We wait in line at the supermarket checkout counter, we wait in line to get gasoline, we wait in line to board a bus, we wait in line to pay a toll on the highway, and students know all too well about waiting in line during registration to get the courses they want. Computer systems use many waiting lines internally, so we write programs that simulate what queues are and do.

A queue is a good example of an abstract data type. A queue offers well-understood behavior to its clients. Clients put things in a queue one at a time—using an *enqueue* operation, and the clients get those things back one at a time on demand—using a *dequeue* operation. Conceptually, a queue can become infinitely long. A real queue, of course, is finite. Items are returned from a queue in *first-in, first-out (FIFO)* order—the first item inserted in the queue is the first item removed from the queue.

The queue hides an internal data representation that keeps track of the items currently waiting in line, and it offers a set of operations to its clients, namely *enqueue* and *dequeue*. The clients are not concerned about implementation of the queue. Clients merely want the queue to operate "as advertised." When a client enqueues a new item, the queue should accept that item and place it internally in some kind of first-in, first-out data structure. When the client wants the next item from the front of the queue, the queue should remove the item from its internal representation and should deliver the item to the outside world in FIFO order (i.e., the item that has been in the queue the longest should be the next one returned by the next *dequeue* operation).

The queue ADT guarantees the integrity of its internal data structure. Clients must not manipulate this data structure directly. Only the queue ADT has access to its internal data (i.e., the queue ADT encapsulates its data). Clients must cause only allowable operations to be performed on the data representation; operations not provided in the ADT's public interface are rejected by the ADT in some appropriate manner. This could mean issuing an error message, terminating execution, or simply ignoring the operation request.

8.17 (Optional Case Study) Thinking About Objects: Starting to Program the Classes for the Elevator Simulation

In the "Thinking About Objects" sections in Chapters 1 through 7, we introduced the fundamentals of object orientation and developed an object-oriented design for our elevator simulation. In Chapter 8, we introduced the details of programming with Java classes. We now begin implementing our object-oriented design in Java. At the end of this section, we show how to generate code in Java, working from class diagrams. This process is referred to as *forward engineering.*[1]

Visibility

Before we begin implementing our design in Java, we apply *member-access modifiers* (see Section 8.2) to the members of our classes. In Chapter 8, we introduced the access specifiers **`public`** and **`private`**—these determine the *visibilities* of an object's attributes and methods to other objects. Before we create class files, we consider which attributes and methods of our classes should be **`public`** and which should be **`private`**.

Each element of a class should have **`private`** *visibility unless it can be proven that the element needs* **`public`** *visibility.*

In Chapter 8, we discussed how attributes generally should be **`private`**, but what about the operations of a class—its methods? These operations are invoked by clients of that class; therefore, the methods normally should be **`public`**. In the UML, **`public`** visibility is indicated by placing a plus sign (+) before a particular element (i.e., a method or an attribute); a minus sign (-) indicates **`private`** visibility. Figure 8.22 shows our updated class diagram with visibility notations included.

---

1. G. Booch, *The Unified Modeling Language User Guide*. Massachusetts: Addison Wesley Longman, Inc., 1999: 16. [Once code exists, the process of going backward from the code to reproduce design documents is called *reverse engineering*.]

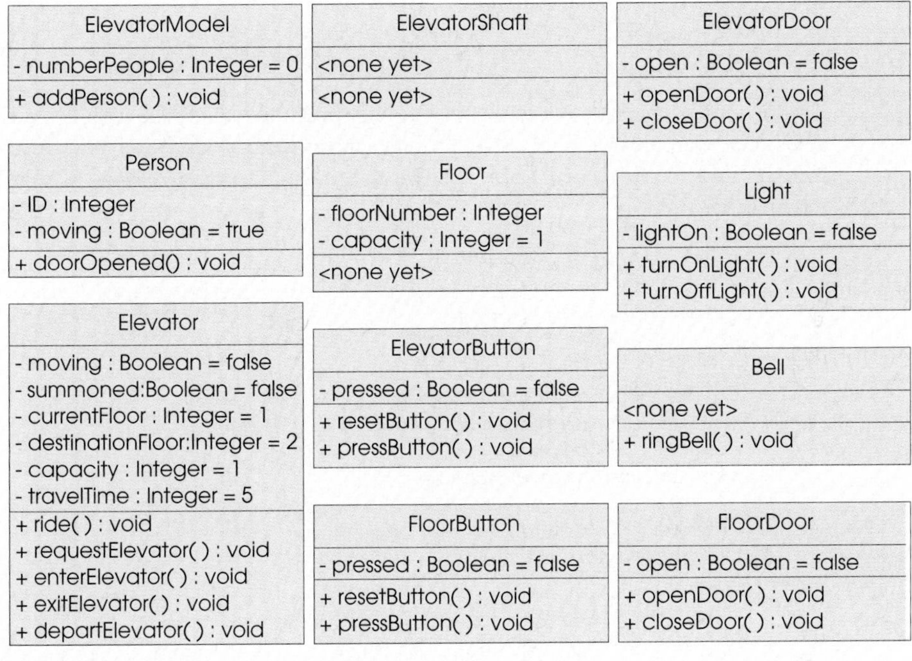

Fig. 8.22 Complete class diagram with visibility notations.

Implementation: Forward Engineering

Forward engineering is the process of transforming a design, such as that in a class diagram, into code of a specific programming language, such as Java. Now that we have discussed programming Java classes, we forward engineer the class diagram of Fig. 8.22 into the Java code for our elevator simulator. The generated code will represent only the "skeleton," or the structure, of the model.[2] In Chapters 9 and 10, we modify the code to incorporate inheritance and interfaces, respectively. In Appendix G, Appendix H and Appendix I, we present the complete, working Java code for our model.

As an example, we forward engineer class **`Elevator`** from Fig. 8.22. We use this figure to determine the attributes and operations of that class. We use the class diagram of Fig. 3.23 to determine associations (and aggregations) among classes. We adhere to the following four guidelines:

1. Use the name located in the first compartment to declare the class as a **`public`** class with an empty constructor. For example, class **`Elevator`** yields

2. So far, we have presented only about half of the case-study material—we have not yet discussed inheritance, event handling, multithreading and animation. The standard development process recommends finishing the design process before starting the coding process. Technically, we will not have finished designing our system until we have discussed these additional topics, so our current code implementation might seem premature. We present only a partial implementation illustrating the topics covered in Chapter 8.

```
public class Elevator {

   public Elevator() {}
}
```

2. Use the attributes located in the second compartment to declare the member variables. For example, the **private** attributes **moving**, **summoned**, **currentFloor**, **destinationFloor**, **capacity** and **travelTime** of class **Elevator** yield

```
public class Elevator {

   // class attributes
   private boolean moving;
   private boolean summoned;
   private int currentFloor = 1;
   private int destinationFloor = 2;
   private int capacity = 1;
   private int travelTime = 5;

   // class constructor
   public Elevator() {}
}
```

3. Use the associations described in the class diagram to generate the references to other objects. For example, according to Fig. 3.23, **Elevator** contains one object each of classes **ElevatorDoor**, **ElevatorButton** and **Bell**. This yields

```
public class Elevator {

   // class attributes
   private boolean moving;
   private boolean summoned;
   private int currentFloor = 1;
   private int destinationFloor = 2;
   private int capacity = 1;
   private int travelTime = 5;

   // class objects
   private ElevatorDoor elevatorDoor;
   private ElevatorButton elevatorButton;
   private Bell bell;

   // class constructor
   public Elevator() {}
}
```

4. Use the operations located in the third compartment of Fig. 8.22 to declare the methods. For example, the **public** operations **ride**, **requestElevator**, **enterElevator**, **exitElevator** and **departElevator** in **Elevator** yield

```java
public class Elevator {

   // class attributes
   private boolean moving;
   private boolean summoned;
   private int currentFloor = 1;
   private int destinationFloor = 2;
   private int capacity = 1;
   private int travelTime = 5;

   // class objects
   private ElevatorDoor elevatorDoor;
   private ElevatorButton elevatorButton;
   private Bell bell;

   // class constructor
   public Elevator() {}

   // class methods
   public void ride() {}
   public void requestElevator() {}
   public void enterElevator() {}
   public void exitElevator() {}
   public void departElevator() {}
}
```

This concludes the basics of forward engineering. We return to this example at the ends of "Thinking About Objects" Section 9.23 and Section 10.22 to incorporate inheritance, interfaces and event handling.

SUMMARY

- OOP encapsulates data (attributes) and methods (behaviors) into objects; the data and methods of an object are intimately tied together.
- Objects have the property of information hiding. Objects might know how to communicate with one another across well-defined interfaces, but they normally are not allowed to know how other objects are implemented.
- Java programmers concentrate on creating their own user-defined types called classes.
- The non-**static** data components of a class are called instance variables. The **static** data components of a class are called class variables.
- Java uses inheritance to create new classes from existing class definitions.
- Every class in Java is a subclass of **Object**. Thus, every new class definition has the attributes (data) and behaviors (methods) of class **Object**.
- Keywords **public** and **private** are member access modifiers.
- Instance variables and methods declared with member access modifier **public** are accessible wherever the program has a reference to an object of the class in which they are defined.
- Instance variables and methods declared with member access modifier **private** are accessible only to methods of the class in which they are defined.
- Instance variables are normally declared **private** and methods are normally declared **public**.
- The **public** methods (or **public** services) of a class are used by clients of the class to manipulate the data stored in objects of the class.

- A constructor is a method with the exact same name as the class that initializes the instance variables of an object of the class when the object is instantiated. Constructor methods can be overloaded for a class. Constructors can take arguments but cannot specify a return value type.
- Constructors and other methods that change instance variable values should always maintain objects in a consistent state.
- Method **toString** takes no arguments and returns a **String**. The original **toString** method of class **Object** is a placeholder that is normally redefined by a subclass.
- When an object is instantiated, operator **new** allocates the memory for the object, then **new** calls the constructor for the class to initialize the instance variables of the object.
- If the **.class** files for the classes used in a program are in the same directory as the class that uses them, **import** statements are not required.
- Concatenating a **String** and any object results in an implicit call to the object's **toString** method to convert the object to a **String**, then the **String**s are concatenated.
- Within a class's scope, class members are accessible to all of that class's methods and can be referenced simply by name. Outside a class's scope, class members can only be accessed off a "handle" (i.e., a reference to an object of the class).
- If a method defines a variable with the same name as a variable with class scope, the class-scope variable is hidden by the method-scope variable in the method. A hidden instance variable can be accessed in the method by preceding its name with the keyword **this** and the dot operator.
- Each class and interface in the Java API belongs to a specific package that contains a group of related classes and interfaces.
- Packages are actually directory structures used to organize classes and interfaces. Packages provide a mechanism for software reuse and a convention for unique class names.
- Creating a reusable class requires: defining a **public** class, adding a **package** statement to the class definition file, compiling the class into the appropriate package directory structure and importing the class into a program.
- When compiling a class in a package, the option **-d** must be passed to the compiler to specify where to create (or locate) all the directories in the **package** statement.
- The **package** directory names become part of the class name when the class is compiled. Use this fully qualified name in programs or **import** the class and use its short name (the name of the class by itself) in the program.
- If no constructors are defined for a class, the compiler creates a default constructor.
- When one object of a class has a reference to another object of the same class, the first object can access all the second object's data and methods.
- Classes often provide **public** methods to allow clients of the class to *set* (i.e., assign values to) or *get* (i.e., obtain the values of) **private** instance variables. *Get* methods are also commonly called accessor methods or query methods. *Set* methods are also commonly called mutator methods (because they typically change a value).
- Every event has a source—the GUI component with which the user interacted to signal the program to do a task.
- Use the keyword **final** to specify that a variable is not modifiable and that any attempt to modify the variable is an error. A **final** variable cannot be modified by assignment after it is initialized. Such a variable must be initialized in its declaration or in every constructor of the class.
- With composition, a class has references to objects of other classes as members.
- When no member access modifier is provided for a method or variable when it is defined in a class, the method or variable is considered to have package access.

- If a program uses multiple classes from the same package, these classes can access each other's package-access methods and data directly through a reference to an object.
- Each object has access to a reference to itself called the **this** reference that can be used inside the methods of the class to refer to the object's data and other methods explicitly.
- Any time you have a reference in a program (even as the result of a method call), the reference can be followed by a dot operator and a call to one of the methods for the reference type.
- Java performs automatic garbage collection of memory. When an object is no longer used in the program (i.e., there are no references to the object), the object is marked for garbage collection.
- Every class in Java can have a finalizer method that returns resources to the system. A class's finalizer method always has the name **finalize**, receives no parameters and returns no value. Method **finalize** is originally defined in class **Object** as a placeholder that does nothing. This guarantees that every class has a **finalize** method for the garbage collector to call.
- A **static** class variable represents class-wide information—all objects of the class share the same piece of data. A class's **public static** members can be accessed through a reference to any object of that class, or they can be accessed through the class name using the dot operator.
- **public static** method **gc** from class **System** suggests that the garbage collector immediately make a best effort attempt to collect garbage objects.The garbage collector is not guaranteed to collect objects in a specific order.
- A method declared **static** cannot access non**static** class members. Unlike non**static** methods, a **static** method has no **this** reference, because **static** class variables and **static** class methods exist independent of any objects of a class.
- **static** class members exist even when no objects of that class exist—they are available as soon as the class is loaded into memory at execution time.

TERMINOLOGY

abstract data type (ADT)
access method
aggregation
attribute
behavior
cascaded method calls
class
class definition
class library
class method (**static**)
class scope
class variable
client of a class
composition
concatenated method calls
consistent state for an instance variable
constructor
container class
-d compiler option
data type
default constructor
dot operator (**.**)
encapsulation
extends
extensibility
finalizer
get method
helper method
implementation of a class
information hiding
initialize a class object
instance method
instance of a class
instance variable
instantiate an object of a class
interface to a class
member access control
member access modifiers
member access operator (**.**)
message
method
method calls
mutator method
new operator
no-argument constructor
object

object-based programming (OBP)
object-oriented programming (OOP)
package access
package statement
predicate method
principle of least privilege
private
programmer-defined type
public
public interface of a class
query method
rapid applications development (RAD)
reusable code
services of a class
set method
software reusability
static class variable
static method
this reference
user-defined type
utility method

SELF-REVIEW EXERCISES

8.1 Fill in the blanks in each of the following statements:

a) Class members are accessed via the _________ operator in conjunction with a reference to an object of the class.
b) Members of a class specified as _________ are accessible only to methods of the class.
c) A _________ is a special method used to initialize the instance variables of a class.
d) A _________ method is used to assign values to **private** instance variables of a class.
e) Methods of a class are normally made _________ and instance variables of a class are normally made _________.
f) A _________ method is used to retrieve values of **private** data of a class.
g) The keyword _________ introduces a class definition.
h) Members of a class specified as _________ are accessible anywhere an object of the class is in scope.
i) The _________ operator dynamically allocates memory for an object of a specified type and returns a _________ to that type.
j) A _________ instance variable represents class-wide information.
k) The keyword _________ specifies that an object or variable is not modifiable after it is initialized.
l) A method declared **static** cannot access _________ class members.

ANSWERS TO SELF-REVIEW EXERCISES

8.1 a) dot (**.**). b) **private**. c) constructor. d) set. e) **public**, **private**. f) get. g) **class**. h) **public**. i) **new**, reference. j) **static**. k) **final**. l) non**static**.

EXERCISES

8.2 Create a class called **Complex** for performing arithmetic with complex numbers. Write a driver program to test your class.

Complex numbers have the form

```
realPart + imaginaryPart * i
```

where *i* is

$$\sqrt{-1}$$

Use floating-point variables to represent the **private** data of the class. Provide a constructor method that enables an object of this class to be initialized when it is declared. Provide a no-argument constructor with default values in case no initializers are provided. Provide **public** methods for each of the following:

a) Addition of two **Complex** numbers: The real parts are added together and the imaginary parts are added together.
b) Subtraction of two **Complex** numbers: The real part of the right operand is subtracted from the real part of the left operand and the imaginary part of the right operand is subtracted from the imaginary part of the left operand.
c) Printing **Complex** numbers in the form **(a, b)**, where **a** is the real part and **b** is the imaginary part.

8.3 Create a class called **Rational** for performing arithmetic with fractions. Write a driver program to test your class.

Use integer variables to represent the **private** instance variables of the class—the **numerator** and the **denominator**. Provide a constructor method that enables an object of this class to be initialized when it is declared. The constructor should store the fraction in reduced form (i.e., the fraction

```
2/4
```

would be stored in the object as 1 in the **numerator** and 2 in the **denominator**). Provide a no-argument constructor with default values in case no initializers are provided. Provide **public** methods for each of the following:

a) Addition of two **Rational** numbers. The result of the addition should be stored in reduced form.
b) Subtraction of two **Rational** numbers. The result of the subtraction should be stored in reduced form.
c) Multiplication of two **Rational** numbers. The result of the multiplication should be stored in reduced form.
d) Division of two **Rational** numbers. The result of the division should be stored in reduced form.
e) Printing **Rational** numbers in the form **a/b**, where **a** is the **numerator** and **b** is the **denominator**.
f) Printing **Rational** numbers in floating-point format. (Consider providing formatting capabilities that enable the user of the class to specify the number of digits of precision to the right of the decimal point.)

8.4 Modify the **Time3** class of Fig. 8.8 to include the **tick** method that increments the time stored in a **Time3** object by one second. Also provide method **incrementMinute** to increment the minute and method **incrementHour** to increment the hour. The **Time3** object should always remain in a consistent state. Write a driver program that tests the **tick** method, the **incrementMinute** method and the **incrementHour** method to ensure that they work correctly. Be sure to test the following cases:

a) incrementing into the next minute.
b) incrementing into the next hour.
c) incrementing into the next day (i.e., 11:59:59 PM to 12:00:00 AM).

8.5 Modify the **Date** class of Fig. 8.13 to perform error-checking on the initializer values for instance variables **month**, **day** and **year** (currently it validates only the month and day). Also, provide a method **nextDay** to increment the day by one. The **Date** object should always remain in a consistent state. Write a driver program that tests the **nextDay** method in a loop that prints the date during each iteration of the loop to illustrate that the **nextDay** method works correctly. Be sure to test the following cases:

a) incrementing into the next month.
b) incrementing into the next year.

8.6 Combine the modified **Time3** class of Exercise 8.5 and the modified **Date** class of Exercise 8.5 into one class called **DateAndTime**. Modify the **tick** method to call the **nextDay** method if the time is incremented into the next day. Modify methods **toString** and **toUniversal-String()** to output the date in addition to the time. Write a driver program to test the new class **DateAndTime**. Specifically test incrementing the time to the next day.

8.7 Modify the set methods in class **Time3** of Fig. 8.8 to return appropriate error values if an attempt is made to set one of the instance variables **hour**, **minute** or **second** of an object of class **Time** to an invalid value. (*Hint*: Use **boolean** return types on each method.)

8.8 Create a class **Rectangle**. The class has attributes **length** and **width**, each of which defaults to 1. It has methods that calculate the **perimeter** and the **area** of the rectangle. It has *set* and *get* methods for both **length** and **width**. The *set* methods should verify that **length** and **width** are each floating-point numbers larger than 0.0 and less than 20.0. Write a program to test class **Rectangle**.

8.9 Create a more sophisticated **Rectangle** class than the one you created in Exercise 8.8. This class stores only the Cartesian coordinates of the four corners of the rectangle. The constructor calls a *set* method that accepts four sets of coordinates and verifies that each of these is in the first quadrant with no single *x*- or *y*-coordinate larger than 20.0. The *set* method also verifies that the supplied coordinates do, in fact, specify a rectangle. Provide methods to calculate the **length**, **width**, **perimeter** and **area**. The length is the larger of the two dimensions. Include a predicate method **isSquare** which determines whether the rectangle is a square. Write a program to test class **Rectangle**.

8.10 Modify the **Rectangle** class of Exercise 8.9 to include a **draw** method that displays the rectangle inside a 25-by-25 box enclosing the portion of the first quadrant in which the rectangle resides. Use the methods of the **Graphics** class to help output the **Rectangle**. If you feel ambitious, you might include methods to scale the size of the rectangle, rotate it and move it around within the designated portion of the first quadrant.

8.11 Create a class **HugeInteger** which uses a 40-element array of digits to store integers as large as 40 digits each. Provide methods **inputHugeInteger**, **outputHugeInteger**, **addHugeIntegers** and **substractHugeIntegers**. For comparing **HugeInteger** objects, provide methods **isEqualTo**, **isNotEqualTo**, **isGreaterThan**, **isLessThan**, **IsGreaterThanOrEqualTo** and **isLessThanOrEqualTo**—each of these is a "predicate" method that simply returns **true** if the relationship holds between the two **HugeInteger**s and returns **false** if the relationship does not hold. Provide a predicate method **isZero**. If you feel ambitious, also provide the method **multiplyHugeIntegers**, the method **divideHugeIntegers** and the method **modulusHugeIntegers**.

8.12 Create a class **TicTacToe** that will enable you to write a complete program to play the game of Tic-Tac-Toe. The class contains as private data a 3-by-3 double array of integers. The constructor should initialize the empty board to all zeros. Allow two human players. Wherever the first player moves, place a 1 in the specified square; place a 2 wherever the second player moves. Each move must be to an empty square. After each move determine whether the game has been won and whether the game is a draw. If you feel ambitious, modify your program so that the computer makes the moves for one of the players automatically. Also, allow the player to specify whether he or she wants to go first or second. If you feel exceptionally ambitious, develop a program that will play three-dimensional Tic-Tac-Toe on a 4-by-4-by-4 board [Note: This is a challenging project that could take many weeks of effort!].

8.13 Explain the notion of package access in Java. Explain the negative aspects of package access as described in the text.

8.14 What happens when a return type, even **void**, is specified for a constructor?

8.15 Create a **Date** class with the following capabilities:

a) Output the date in multiple formats such as

```
MM/DD/YYYY
June 14, 1992
DDD YYYY
```

b) Use overloaded constructors to create **Date** objects initialized with dates of the formats in part a).

[Hint: You can compare **String**s using method equals. Suppose you have two **String** references **s1** and **s2**, if those **String**s are equal, **s1.equals(s2)** returns **true**; otherwise, it returns **false**.]

8.16 Create class **SavingsAccount**. Use a **static** class variable to store the **annualInterestRate** for all account holders. Each object of the class contains a **private** instance variable **savingsBalance** indicating the amount the saver currently has on deposit. Provide method **calculateMonthlyInterest** to calculate the monthly interest by multiplying the **savingsBalance** by **annualInterestRate** divided by 12; this interest should be added to **savingsBalance**. Provide a **static** method **modifyInterestRate** that sets the **annualInterestRate** to a new value. Write a driver program to test class **SavingsAccount**. Instantiate two **savingsAccount** objects, **saver1** and **saver2**, with balances of $2000.00 and $3000.00, respectively. Set **annualInterestRate** to 4%, then calculate the monthly interest and print the new balances for each of the savers. Then set the **annualInterestRate** to 5% and calculate the next month's interest and print the new balances for each of the savers.

8.17 Create class **IntegerSet**. Each object of the class can hold integers in the range 0 through 100. A set is represented internally as an array of **boolean**s. Array element **a[i]** is **true** if integer *i* is in the set. Array element **a[j]** is **false** if integer *j* is not in the set. The no-argument constructor initializes a set to the so-called "empty set" (i.e., a set whose array representation contains all **false** values).

Provide the following methods: Method **unionOfIntegerSets** creates a third set which is the set-theoretic union of two existing sets (i.e., an element of the third set's array is set to **true** if that element is **true** in either or both of the existing sets; otherwise, the element of the third set is set to **false**). Method **intersectionOfIntegerSets** creates a third set which is the set-theoretic intersection of two existing sets i.e., an element of the third set's array is set to **false** if that element is **false** in either or both of the existing sets; otherwise, the element of the third set is set to **true**). Method **insertElement** inserts a new integer *k* into a set (by setting **a[k]** to **true**). Method **deleteElement** deletes integer *m* (by setting **a[m]** to **false**). Method **setPrint** prints a set as a list of numbers separated by spaces. Print only those elements that are present in the set. Print **---** for an empty set. Method **isEqualTo** determines if two sets are equal. Write a program to test your **IntegerSet** class. Instantiate several **IntegerSet** objects. Test that all your methods work properly.

8.18 It would be perfectly reasonable for the **Time1** class of Figure 8.1 to represent the time internally as the number of seconds since midnight rather than the three integer values **hour**, **minute** and **second**. Clients could use the same **public** methods and get the same results. Modify the **Time1** class of Figure 8.1 to implement the **Time1** as the number of seconds since midnight and show that there is no change visible to the clients of the class.

8.19 *(Drawing Program)* Create a drawing applet that randomly draws lines, rectangles and ovals. For this purpose, create a set of "smart" shape classes where objects of these classes know how to draw themselves if provided with a **Graphics** object that tells them where to draw (i.e., the applet's **Graphics** object allows a shape to draw on the applet's background). The class names should be **MyLine**, **MyRect** and **MyOval**.

The data for class **MyLine** should include *x1*, *y1*, *x2* and *y2* coordinates. Method **drawLine** method of class **Graphics** will connect the two points supplied with a line. The data for classes **MyRect** and **MyOval** should include an upper-left *x*-coordinate value, an upper-left *y*-coordinate value, a *width* (must be nonnegative) and a *height* (must be nonnegative). All data in each class must be **private**.

In addition to the data, each class should define at least the following **public** methods:

a) A constructor with no arguments that sets the coordinates to 0.
b) A constructor with arguments that sets the coordinates to the supplied values.
c) Set methods for each individual piece of data that allow the programmer to independently set any piece of data in a shape (e.g., if you have an instance variable **x1**, you should have a method **setX1**).
d) Get methods for each individual piece of data that allow the programmer to independently retrieve any piece of data in a shape (e.g., if you have an instance variable **x1**, you should have a method **getX1**).
e) A **draw** method with the first line

```
public void draw( Graphics g )
```

will be called from the applet's **paint** method to draw a shape onto the screen.

The preceding methods are required. If you would like to provide more methods for flexibility, please do so.

Begin by defining class **MyLine** and an applet to test your classes. The applet should have a **MyLine** instance variable **line** that can refer to one **MyLine** object (created in the applet's **init** method with random coordinates). The applet's **paint** method should draw the shape with a statement like

```
line.draw( g );
```

where **line** is the **MyLine** reference and **g** is the **Graphics** object that the shape will use to draw itself on the applet.

Next, change the single **MyLine** reference into an array of **MyLine** references and hard code several **MyLine** objects into the program for drawing. The applet's **paint** method should walk through the array of **MyLine** objects and draw every one.

After the preceding part is working, you should define the **MyOval** and **MyRect** classes and add objects of these classes into the **MyRect** and **MyOval** arrays. The applet's **paint** method should walk through each array and draw every shape. Create five shapes of each type.

Once the applet is running, select **Reload** from the **appletviewer**'s **Applet** menu to reload the applet. This will cause the applet to choose new random numbers for the shapes and draw the shapes again.

In Chapter 9, we will modify this exercise to take advantage of the similarities between the classes and to avoid reinventing the wheel.

Object-Oriented Programming

Objectives

- To understand inheritance and software reusability.
- To understand superclasses and subclasses.
- To appreciate how polymorphism makes systems extensible and maintainable.
- To understand the distinction between abstract classes and concrete classes.
- To learn how to create abstract classes and interfaces.

Say not you know another entirely, till you have divided an inheritance with him.
Johann Kasper Lavater

This method is to define as the number of a class the class of all classes similar to the given class.
Bertrand Russell

Good as it is to inherit a library, it is better to collect one.
Augustine Birrell

General propositions do not decide concrete cases.
Oliver Wendell Holmes

A philosopher of imposing stature doesn't think in a vacuum. Even his most abstract ideas are, to some extent, conditioned by what is or is not known in the time when he lives.
Alfred North Whitehead

Outline

9.1 Introduction
9.2 Superclasses and Subclasses
9.3 `protected` Members
9.4 Relationship between Superclass Objects and Subclass Objects
9.5 Constructors and Finalizers in Subclasses
9.6 Implicit Subclass-Object-to-Superclass-Object Conversion
9.7 Software Engineering with Inheritance
9.8 Composition vs. Inheritance
9.9 Case Study: Point, Circle, Cylinder
9.10 Introduction to Polymorphism
9.11 Type Fields and `switch` Statements
9.12 Dynamic Method Binding
9.13 `final` Methods and Classes
9.14 Abstract Superclasses and Concrete Classes
9.15 Polymorphism Examples
9.16 Case Study: A Payroll System Using Polymorphism
9.17 New Classes and Dynamic Binding
9.18 Case Study: Inheriting Interface and Implementation
9.19 Case Study: Creating and Using Interfaces
9.20 Inner Class Definitions
9.21 Notes on Inner Class Definitions
9.22 Type-Wrapper Classes for Primitive Types
9.23 (Optional Case Study) Thinking About Objects: Incorporating Inheritance into the Elevator Simulation
9.24 (Optional) Discovering Design Patterns: Introducing Creational, Structural and Behavioral Design Patterns

Summary • Terminology • Self-Review Exercises • Answers to Self-Review Exercises • Exercises

9.1 Introduction

In this chapter, we discuss object-oriented programming (OOP) and its key component technologies—*inheritance* and *polymorphism.* Inheritance is a form of software reusability in which new classes are created from existing classes by absorbing their attributes and behaviors and adding new capabilities the new classes require. Inheritance takes advantage of *class* relationships where objects of a certain class—such as a class of vehicles—have the same characteristics. Newly created classes of objects are derived by absorbing characteristics of existing classes and adding unique characteristics of their own. An object of class "convertible" certainly has the characteristics of the more general class "automobile," but a convertible's roof goes up and down.

Software reusability saves time in program development. It encourages reuse of proven and debugged high-quality software, thus reducing problems after a system becomes operational. These are exciting possibilities. Polymorphism enables us to write programs in a general fashion to handle a wide variety of existing and yet-to-be-specified related classes. Polymorphism makes it easy to add new capabilities to a system. Inheritance and polymorphism are effective techniques for dealing with software complexity.

When creating a new class, instead of writing completely new instance variables and instance methods, the programmer can designate that the new class is to *inherit* the instance variables and instance methods of a previously defined *superclass.* The new class is referred to as a *subclass.* Each subclass itself becomes a candidate to be a superclass for some future subclass.

The *direct superclass* of a class is the superclass from which the class explicitly inherits (via the keyword **extends**). An indirect superclass is inherited from two or more levels up the class hierarchy. For example, class **JApplet** (package **javax.swing**) extends class **Applet** (package **java.applet**). Thus, each applet class we have defined is a direct subclass of **JApplet** and an indirect subclass of **Applet**.

With *single inheritance,* a class is derived from one superclass. Java does not support *multiple inheritance* (as C++ does) but it does support the notion of *interfaces.* Interfaces help Java achieve many of the advantages of multiple inheritance without the associated problems. We will discuss the details of interfaces in this chapter. We consider both general principles and a detailed specific example of creating and using interfaces.

A subclass normally adds instance variables and instance methods of its own, so a subclass is generally larger than its superclass. A subclass is more specific than its superclass and represents a smaller, more specialized group of objects. With single inheritance, the subclass starts out essentially the same as the superclass. The real strength of inheritance comes from the ability to define in the subclass additions to, or replacements for, the features inherited from the superclass.

Every subclass object is also an object of that class's superclass. For example, every applet we have defined is considered to be an object of class **JApplet**. Also, because **JApplet** extends **Applet**, every applet we have defined is considered to be an **Applet**. This information is critical when developing applets, because an applet container can execute a program only if it is an **Applet**. Although a subclass object always can be treated as one of its superclass types, superclass objects are not considered to be objects of their subclass types. We will take advantage of this "subclass-object-is-a-superclass-object" relationship to perform some powerful manipulations. For example, a drawing application can maintain a list of shapes to display. If all the shape types extend the same superclass directly or indirectly, the drawing program can store all the shapes in an array (or other data structure) of superclass objects. As we will see in this chapter, this ability to process a set of objects as a single type is a key thrust of object-oriented programming.

We add a new form of member access control in this chapter, namely **protected** access. Subclass methods and methods of other classes in the same package as the superclass can access **protected** superclass members.

Experience in building software systems indicates that significant portions of the code deal with closely related special cases. It becomes difficult in such systems to see the "big picture" because the designer and the programmer become preoccupied with the special cases. Object-oriented programming provides several ways of "seeing the forest through the trees."

The programmer and designer concentrate on the big picture—the commonality among objects in the system—rather than the special cases. This process is called *abstraction.*

If a procedural program has many closely related special cases, then it is common to see **`switch`** structures or nested **`if/else`** structures that distinguish among the special cases and provide the processing logic to deal with each case individually. We will show how to use inheritance and polymorphism to replace such **`switch`** logic with much simpler logic.

We distinguish between the *"is a" relationship* and the *"has a" relationship.* "Is a" is inheritance. In an "is a" relationship, an object of a subclass type may also be treated as an object of its superclass type. "Has a" is composition (as we discussed in Chapter 8). In a "has a" relationship, a class object has one or more objects of other classes as members. For example, a car *has a* steering wheel.

A subclass's methods might need to access certain of its superclass's instance variables and methods. A crucial aspect of software engineering in Java is that a subclass cannot access the **`private`** members of its superclass. If a subclass could access the superclass's **`private`** members, this would violate information hiding in the superclass.

Software Engineering Observation 9.1

A subclass cannot directly access **`private`** *members of its superclass.*

Testing and Debugging Tip 9.1

Hiding **`private`** *members is a tremendous help in testing, debugging and correctly modifying systems. If a subclass could access its superclass's* **`private`** *members, it would be possible for classes derived from that subclass to access that data as well, and so on. This would propagate access to what is supposed to be* **`private`** *data, and the benefits of information hiding would be lost throughout the class hierarchy.*

However, a subclass can access the ***`public`*** and ***`protected`*** members of its superclass. A subclass also can use the package access members of its superclass if the subclass and superclass are in the same package. Superclass members that should not be accessible to a subclass via inheritance are declared ***`private`*** in the superclass. A subclass can effect state changes in superclass ***`private`*** members only through ***`public`***, ***`protected`*** and package access methods provided in the superclass and inherited into the subclass. [*Note*: We use **`protected`** instance variables in this chapter to demonstrate how they work. Several of the exercises in this chapter require that you use only private instance variables, to maintain encapsulation.]

Software Engineering Observation 9.2

To preserve encapsulation, all instance variables should be declared **`private`** *and should be accessible only via* set *and* get *methods of the class.*

A problem with inheritance is that a subclass can inherit methods that it does not need or should not have. It is the class designer's responsibility to ensure that the capabilities provided by a class are appropriate for future subclasses. Even when the superclass methods are appropriate for the subclasses, it is common for a sublcass to require the method to perform a task in a manner that is specific to the subclass. In such cases, the superclass method can be *overridden* (redefined) in the subclass with an appropriate implementation.

Perhaps most exciting is the notion that new classes can inherit from abundant *class libraries*, such as those provided with the Java API. Organizations develop their own class libraries and can take advantage of other libraries available worldwide. Someday, most software might be constructed from *standardized reusable components*, just as hardware is often constructed today. This will help meet the challenges of developing the ever more powerful software we will need in the future.

9.2 Superclasses and Subclasses

Often an object of one class "is an" object of another class as well. A rectangle certainly *is a* quadrilateral (as are squares, parallelograms and trapezoids). Thus, class **Rectangle** can be said to *inherit* from class **Quadrilateral**. In this context, class **Quadrilateral** is a superclass, and class **Rectangle** is a subclass. A rectangle *is a* specific type of quadrilateral, but it is incorrect to claim that a quadrilateral *is a* rectangle (the quadrilateral could be a parallelogram). Figure 9.1 shows several simple inheritance examples of superclasses and potential subclasses.

Inheritance normally produces subclasses with *more* features than their superclasses, so the terms superclass and subclass can be confusing. There is another way, however, to view these terms that makes perfectly good sense. Because every subclass object "is an" object of its superclass, and because one superclass can have many subclasses, the set of objects represented by a superclass is normally larger than the set of objects represented by any of that superclass's subclasses. For example, the superclass **Vehicle** represents in a generic manner all vehicles, such as cars, trucks, boats, bicycles and so on. However, subclass **Car** represents only a small subset of all the **Vehicle**s in the world.

Inheritance relationships form tree-like hierarchical structures. A superclass exists in a hierarchical relationship with its subclasses. A class can certainly exist by itself, but it is when a class is used with the mechanism of inheritance that the class becomes either a superclass that supplies attributes and behaviors to other classes or a subclass that inherits those attributes and behaviors. Frequently, one class is both a subclass and a superclass.

Superclass	Subclasses
Student	**GraduateStudent** **UndergraduateStudent**
Shape	**Circle** **Triangle** **Rectangle**
Loan	**CarLoan** **HomeImprovementLoan** **MortgageLoan**
Employee	**FacultyMember** **StaffMember**
Account	**CheckingAccount** **SavingsAccount**

Fig. 9.1 Some simple inheritance examples in which the subclass "is a" superclass.

Let us develop a simple inheritance hierarchy. A typical university community has thousands of people who are community members. These people consist of employees, students and alumni. Employees are either faculty members or staff members. Faculty members are either administrators (such as deans and department chairpersons) or teaching faculty. This yields the inheritance hierarchy shown in Fig. 9.2. Note that the inheritance hierarchy could contain many other classes. For example, students can be graduate students or undergraduate students. Undergraduate students can be freshman, sophomores, juniors, and seniors. And so on. The arrows in the hierarchy represent the "is a" relationship. For example, based on this class hierarchy that we can state, "an **Employee** *is a* **CommunityMember**," or "a **Teacher** *is a* **Faculty** member." **CommunityMember** is the *direct superclass* of **Employee**, **Student** and **Alumni**. **CommunityMember** is an *indirect superclass* of all the other classes in the hierarchy diagram. Note that class **Employee** is both a subclass of **CommunityMember** and a superclass of **Faculty** and **Staff**.

Also, starting from the bottom of the diagram, you can follow the arrows and apply the *is a* relationship all the way up to the topmost superclass in the hierarchy. For example, an **Administrator** *is a* **Faculty** member, *is an* **Employee** and *is a* **CommunityMember**. And, in Java, an **Administrator** also *is an* **Object** because all classes in Java have **Object** as one of their direct or indirect superclasses. Thus, all classes in Java are related in a hierarchical relationship in which they share the 11 methods defined by class **Object**, which include the **toString** and **finalize** methods discussed previously. Other methods of class **Object** are discussed as they are needed in the text.

Another substantial inheritance hierarchy is the **Shape** hierarchy of Figure 9.3. There are abundant examples of hierarchies in the real world, but students are not accustomed to categorizing the real world in this manner, so it takes some adjustment in their thinking. Actually, biology students have had some practice with hierarchies. Everything we study in biology is grouped into a hierarchy headed by living things and these can be plants or animals and so on.

To specify that class **TwoDimensionalShape** is derived from (or inherits from) class **Shape**, class **TwoDimensionalShape** could be defined in Java as follows:

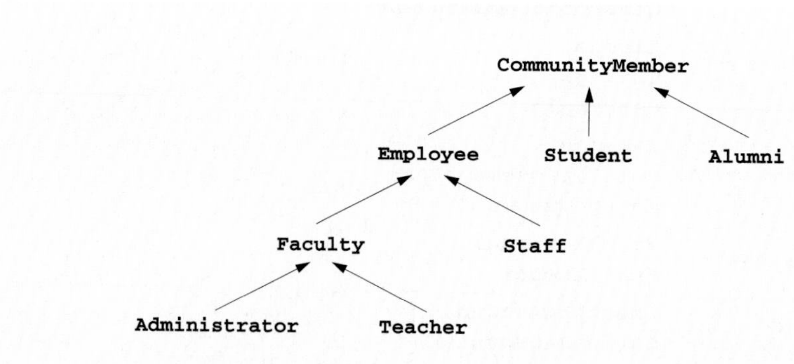

Fig. 9.2 An inheritance hierarchy for university **CommunityMembers**.

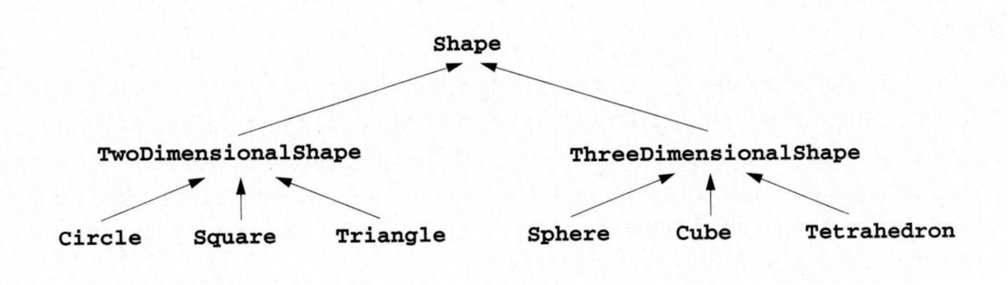

Fig. 9.3 A portion of a **Shape** class hierarchy.

```
public class TwoDimensionalShape extends Shape {
   ...
}
```

With inheritance, **private** members of a superclass are not directly accessible from that class's subclasses. Package access members of the superclass are accessible in a subclass only if both the superclass and its subclass are in the same package. All other superclass members become members of the subclass, using their original member access (i.e., **public** members of the superclass become **public** members of the subclass, and **protected** members of the superclass become **protected** members of the subclass).

Software Engineering Observation 9.3

Constructors are never inherited—they are specific to the class in which they are defined.

It is possible to treat superclass objects and subclass objects similarly; that commonality is expressed in the attributes and behaviors of the superclass. Objects of all classes derived from a common superclass can all be treated as objects of that superclass.

We will consider many examples in which we can take advantage of this inheritance relationship with an ease of programming not available in non-object-oriented languages such as C.

9.3 protected Members

A superclass's **public** members are accessible anywhere the program has a reference to that superclass type or one of its subclass types. A superclass's **private** members are accessible only in methods of that superclass.

A superclass's **protected** access members serve as an intermediate level of protection between **public** and **private** access. A superclass's **protected** members may be accessed only by methods of the superclass, by methods of subclasses and by methods of other classes in the same package (**protected** members have package access).

Subclass methods can normally refer to **public** and **protected** members of the superclass simply by using the member names. When a subclass method overrides a superclass method, the superclass method may be accessed from the subclass by preceding the superclass method name with keyword **super** followed by the dot operator (**.**). This technique is illustrated several times throughout the chapter.

9.4 Relationship between Superclass Objects and Subclass Objects

An object of a subclass can be treated as an object of its superclass. This makes possible some interesting manipulations. For example, despite the fact that objects of a variety of classes derived from a particular superclass might be quite different from one another, we can create an array of references to them—as long as we treat them as superclass objects. But the reverse is not true: A superclass object cannot always be treated a subclass object. For example, a **Shape** is not always a **Circle**.

However, an explicit cast can be used to convert a superclass reference to a subclass reference. This can be done only when the superclass reference is referencing a subclass object; otherwise, Java will indicate a ***ClassCastException***—an indication that the cast operation is not allowed. Exceptions are discussed in detail in Chapter 14.

Common Programming Error 9.1

Assigning an object of a superclass to a subclass reference (without a cast) is a syntax error.

Software Engineering Observation 9.4

If an object has been assigned to a reference of one of its superclasses, it is acceptable to cast that object back to its own type. In fact, this must be done in order to send that object any of its messages that do not appear in that superclass.

Our first example consists of two classes. Figure 9.4 shows a **Point** class definition. Figure 9.5 shows a **Circle** class definition. We will see that class **Circle** inherits from class **Point**. Figure 9.6 shows application class **InheritanceTest**, which demonstrates assigning subclass references to superclass references and casting superclass references to subclass references.

Every applet defined previously has used some of the techniques presented here. We now formalize the inheritance concept. In Chapter 3, we stated that every class definition in Java must extend another class. However, notice in Fig. 9.4 that class **Point** (line 4) does not use the **extends** keyword explicitly. If a new class definition does not extend an existing class definition explicitly, Java implicitly uses class **Object** (package **java.lang**) as the superclass for the new class definition. Class **Object** provides a set of methods that can be used with any object of any class.

Software Engineering Observation 9.5

Every class in Java implicitly extends **Object**, *unless it is specified otherwise in the first line of the class definition, in which case the class indirectly extends* **Object**. *Thus, class* **Object** *is the superclass of the entire Java class hierarchy.*

Let us first examine the **Point** class definition (Fig. 9.4). The **public** services of class **Point** include methods **setPoint**, **getX**, **getY**, **toString** and two **Point** constructors. The instance variables **x** and **y** of **Point** are specified as **protected**. This prevents clients of **Point** objects from accessing the data directly (unless they are classes in the same package), but enables classes derived from **Point** to access the inherited instance variables directly. If the data were specified as **private**, the non**private** methods of **Point** would have to be used to access the data, even by subclasses. Note that class **Point**'s **toString** method overrides the original **toString** method inherited from class **Object**.

```
1  // Fig. 9.4: Point.java
2  // Definition of class Point
3
4  public class Point {
5     protected int x, y; // coordinates of Point
6
7     // No-argument constructor
8     public Point()
9     {
10       // implicit call to superclass constructor occurs here
11       setPoint( 0, 0 );
12    }
13
14    // constructor
15    public Point( int xCoordinate, int yCoordinate )
16    {
17       // implicit call to superclass constructor occurs here
18       setPoint( xCoordinate, yCoordinate );
19    }
20
21    // set x and y coordinates of Point
22    public void setPoint( int xCoordinate, int yCoordinate )
23    {
24       x = xCoordinate;
25       y = yCoordinate;
26    }
27
28    // get x coordinate
29    public int getX()
30    {
31       return x;
32    }
33
34    // get y coordinate
35    public int getY()
36    {
37       return y;
38    }
39
40    // convert into a String representation
41    public String toString()
42    {
43       return "[" + x + ", " + y + "]";
44    }
45
46 }  // end class Point
```

Fig. 9.4 **Point** class definition.

Class **Point**'s constructors (lines 8–12 and 15–19) must call class **Object**'s constructor. In fact, every subclass constructor is required to call its direct superclass's constructor as its first task, either implicitly or explicitly (the syntax for this call is discussed with class **Circle** momentarily). If there is no explicit call to the superclass constructor,

Java automatically attempts to call the superclass's default constructor. Note that lines 10 and 17 are comments indicating where the call to the superclass **Object**'s default constructor occurs.

Software Engineering Observation 9.6

Every subclass constructor must call one of the direct superclass constructors explicitly or implicitly. Implicit calls can be made only to the no-argument constructor of the superclass. If the superclass does not provide a no-argument constructor, all direct subclasses of that class must call one of superclass's constructors explicitly.

Class **Circle** (Fig. 9.5) inherits from class **Point** as specified with the **extends** keyword on line 4. Keyword **extends** in the class definition indicates inheritance. All the (non**private**) members of class **Point** (except the constructors) are inherited into class **Circle**. Thus, the **public** interface to **Circle** includes the **Point** class's **public** methods as well as the two overloaded **Circle** constructors and **Circle** methods **setRadius**, **getRadius**, **area** and **toString**. Notice that method **area** (lines 38–41) uses predefined constant ***Math.PI*** from class **Math** (package **java.lang**) to calculate the area of a circle.

```
1  // Fig. 9.5: Circle.java
2  // Definition of class Circle
3
4  public class Circle extends Point {  // inherits from Point
5     protected double radius;
6
7     // no-argument constructor
8     public Circle()
9     {
10       // implicit call to superclass constructor occurs here
11       setRadius( 0 );
12    }
13
14    // constructor
15    public Circle( double circleRadius, int xCoordinate,
16       int yCoordinate )
17    {
18       // call superclass constructor to set coordinates
19       super( xCoordinate, yCoordinate );
20
21       // set radius
22       setRadius( circleRadius );
23    }
24
25    // set radius of Circle
26    public void setRadius( double circleRadius )
27    {
28       radius = ( circleRadius >= 0.0 ? circleRadius : 0.0 );
29    }
30
```

Fig. 9.5 **Circle** class definition (part 1 of 2).

invoke method **toString** to append the **String** representation of the **Circle**. Lines 39–40 append the **area** of the **Circle** to **output**.

Next, the **if/else** structure at lines 43–48 attempts a dangerous cast in line 44. We cast **point1**, which refers to a Point object, to a **Circle**. If the program attempts to execute this statement, Java would determine that **point1** really refers to a **Point**, recognize the cast to **Circle** as being dangerous and indicate an improper cast with **ClassCastException** message. However, we prevent this statement from executing with the **if** condition

```
if ( point1 instanceof Circle ) {
```

that uses operator ***instanceof*** to determine whether the object to which **point1** refers *is a* **Circle**. This condition evaluates to **true** only if the object to which **point1** refers *is a* **Circle**; otherwise, the condition evaluates to **false**. Reference **point1** does not refer to a **Circle**, so the condition fails, and a **String** indicating that **point1** does not refer to a **Circle** is appended to **output**.

If we remove the **if** test from the program and execute the program, the following message is generated at execution time:

```
Exception in thread "main" java.lang.ClassCastException: Point
        at InheritanceTest.main(InheritanceTest.java:43)
```

Such error messages normally include the file name (**InheritanceTest.java**) and line number at which the error occurred (**43**) so you can go to that specific line in the program for debugging.

9.5 Constructors and Finalizers in Subclasses

When an object of a subclass is instantiated, the superclass's constructor should be called to do any necessary initialization of the superclass instance variables of the subclass object. An explicit call to the superclass constructor (via the **super** reference) can be provided as the first statement in the subclass constructor. Otherwise, the subclass constructor will call the superclass default constructor (or no-argument constructor) implicitly.

Superclass constructors are not inherited by subclasses. Subclass constructors, however, can call superclass constructors via the **super** reference.

Software Engineering Observation 9.10

When an object of a subclass is created, first the subclass constructor calls the superclass constructor (explicitly via **super** *or implicitly), the superclass constructor executes, then the remainder of the subclass constructor's body executes.*

If the classes in your class hierarchy define **finalize** methods, the subclass **finalize** method as its last action should invoke the superclass **finalize** method to ensure that all parts of an object are finalized properly if the garbage collector reclaims the memory for the object.

The application of Fig. 9.7–Fig. 9.9 shows the order in which superclass and subclass constructors and finalizers are called. For the purpose of this example, class **Point** and class **Circle** are simplified.

Class **Point** (Fig. 9.7) contains two constructors, a finalizer, a **toString** method and **protected** instance variables **x** and **y**. The constructor and finalizer each print that they are executing, then display the **Point** for which they are invoked. Note the use of

this in the **System.out.println** calls to cause an implicit call to method **toString**. Notice the first line of the **finalize** method (line 23). Method **finalize** should always be defined as **protected** so subclasses have access to the method but classes that simply use **Point** objects do not.

Class **Circle** (Fig. 9.8) derives from **Point** and contains two constructors, a finalizer, a **toString** method and protected instance variable **radius**. The constructor and finalizer each print that they are executing, then display the **Circle** for which they are invoked. Note that the **Circle** method **toString** invokes **Point**'s **toString** via **super** (line 19).

Software Engineering Observation 9.11

When a superclass method is overridden in a subclass, it is common to have the subclass version call the superclass version and do some additional work. In this scenario, the superclass method performs the tasks common to all subclasses of that class, and the subclass method performs additional tasks specific to a given subclass.

```
1  // Fig. 9.7: Point.java
2  // Definition of class Point
3  public class Point extends Object {
4     protected int x, y; // coordinates of the Point
5
6     // no-argument constructor
7     public Point()
8     {
9        x = 0;
10       y = 0;
11       System.out.println( "Point constructor: " + this );
12    }
13
14    // constructor
15    public Point( int xCoordinate, int yCoordinate )
16    {
17       x = xCoordinate;
18       y = yCoordinate;
19       System.out.println( "Point constructor: " + this );
20    }
21
22    // finalizer
23    protected void finalize()
24    {
25       System.out.println( "Point finalizer: " + this );
26    }
27
28    // convert Point into a String representation
29    public String toString()
30    {
31       return "[" + x + ", " + y + "]";
32    }
33
34 } // end class Point
```

Fig. 9.7 **Point** class definition to demonstrate when constructors and finalizers are called.

```java
// Fig. 9.8: Circle.java
// Definition of class Circle
public class Circle extends Point {   // inherits from Point
   protected double radius;

   // no-argument constructor
   public Circle()
   {
      // implicit call to superclass constructor here
      radius = 0;
      System.out.println( "Circle constructor: " + this );
   }

   // Constructor
   public Circle( double circleRadius, int xCoordinate,
      int yCoordinate )
   {
      // call superclass constructor
      super( xCoordinate, yCoordinate );

      radius = circleRadius;
      System.out.println( "Circle constructor: " + this );
   }

   // finalizer
   protected void finalize()
   {
      System.out.println( "Circle finalizer: " + this );
      super.finalize();  // call superclass finalize method
   }

   // convert the Circle to a String
   public String toString()
   {
      return "Center = " + super.toString() +
             "; Radius = " + radius;
   }

}  // end class Circle
```

Fig. 9.8 **`Circle`** class definition to demonstrate when constructors and finalizers are called.

Common Programming Error 9.5

*When an overridden method calls the superclass version of the same method, not using keyword **`super`** to reference the superclass's method causes infinite recursion, because the subclass method actually calls itself.*

Common Programming Error 9.6

*Cascading **`super`** reference to refer to a member (method or variable) several levels up the hierarchy (as in **`super.super.x`**) is a syntax error.*

Application class **Test** (Fig. 9.9) uses this **Point/Circle** inheritance hierarchy. The application begins in method **main** by instantiating **Circle** object **circle1** (line 11). This invokes the **Circle** constructor at line 15 of Fig. 9.8, which immediately invokes the **Point** constructor at line 15 of Fig. 9.7. The **Point** constructor outputs the values received from the **Circle** constructor by implicitly calling method **toString** and returns program control to the **Circle** constructor. Then the **Circle** constructor outputs the complete **Circle** by calling method **toString**. Notice that the first two lines of the output from this program both show values for **x**, **y** and **radius**. Polymorphism is once again causing the **Circle**'s **toString** method to execute because it is a **Circle** object that is being created. When **toString** is invoked from the **Point** constructor, **0.0** is displayed for the **radius** because the **radius** has not yet been initialized in the **Circle** constructor.

Circle object **circle2** is instantiated next. Again, the **Point** and **Circle** constructors both execute. Notice, in the command-line output window, that the body of the **Point** constructor is performed before the body of the **Circle** constructor, showing that objects are constructed "inside out."

```
1  // Fig. 9.9: Test.java
2  // Demonstrate when superclass and subclass
3  // constructors and finalizers are called.
4  public class Test {
5
6     // test when constructors and finalizers are called
7     public static void main( String args[] )
8     {
9        Circle circle1, circle2;
10
11       circle1 = new Circle( 4.5, 72, 29 );
12       circle2 = new Circle( 10, 5, 5 );
13
14       circle1 = null;  // mark for garbage collection
15       circle2 = null;  // mark for garbage collection
16
17       System.gc();     // call the garbage collector
18    }
19
20 }  // end class Test
```

```
Point constructor: Center = [72, 29]; Radius = 0.0
Circle constructor: Center = [72, 29]; Radius = 4.5
Point constructor: Center = [5, 5]; Radius = 0.0
Circle constructor: Center = [5, 5]; Radius = 10.0
Circle finalizer: Center = [72, 29]; Radius = 4.5
Point finalizer: Center = [72, 29]; Radius = 4.5
Circle finalizer: Center = [5, 5]; Radius = 10.0
Point finalizer: Center = [5, 5]; Radius = 10.0
```

Fig. 9.9 Order in which constructors and finalizers are called.

Lines 14–15 set **circle1** to **null**, then set **circle2** to **null**. Each of these objects is no longer needed in the program, so Java marks the memory occupied by **circle1** and **circle2** for *garbage collection.* Java guarantees that, before the garbage collector runs to reclaim the space for each of these objects, the **finalize** methods for each object will be called. The garbage collector is a low-priority thread that runs automatically whenever processor time is available. We choose here to ask the garbage collector to run with a call to class **System**'s **static** method **gc** in line 17. Java does not guarantee the order in which objects will be garbage collected; therefore, it cannot guarantee which object's finalizer will execute first. Notice, in the command-line output window, that **finalize** methods are called for both the **Circle** and **Point** when each **Circle** object is garbage collected.

9.6 Implicit Subclass-Object-to-Superclass-Object Conversion

Despite the fact that a subclass object also "is a" superclass object, the subclass type and the superclass type are different. Subclass objects can be treated as superclass objects. This makes sense because the subclass has members corresponding to each of the superclass members—remember that the subclass normally has more members than the superclass has. Assignment in the other direction is not allowed because assigning a superclass object to a subclass reference would leave the additional subclass members undefined.

A reference to a subclass object could be implicitly converted into a reference to a superclass object because a subclass object *is a* superclass object through inheritance.

There are four possible ways to mix and match superclass references and subclass references with superclass objects and subclass objects:

1. Referring to a superclass object with a superclass reference is straightforward.
2. Referring to a subclass object with a subclass reference is straightforward.
3. Referring to a subclass object with a superclass reference is safe, because the subclass object *is an* object of its superclass as well. Such code can refer only to superclass members. If this code refers to subclass-only members through the superclass reference, the compiler will report a syntax error.
4. Referring to a superclass object with a subclass reference is a syntax error.

As convenient as it might be to treat subclass objects as superclass objects, and to do this by manipulating all these objects with superclass references, there appears to be a problem. In a payroll system, for example, we would like to be able to walk through an array of employees and calculate the weekly pay for each person. But intuition suggests that using superclass references would enable the program to call only the superclass payroll calculation routine (if indeed there is such a routine in the superclass). We need a way to invoke the proper payroll calculation routine for each object, whether it is a superclass object or a subclass object, and to do this simply by using the superclass reference. Actually, this is precisely how Java behaves and is discussed in this chapter when we consider polymorphism and dynamic binding.

9.7 Software Engineering with Inheritance

We can use inheritance to customize existing software. When we use inheritance to create a new class from an existing class, the new class inherits the attributes and behaviors of an existing class; then we can add attributes and behaviors or override superclass behaviors to customize the class to meet our needs.

It can be difficult for students to appreciate the problems faced by designers and implementers on large-scale software projects in industry. People experienced on such projects will invariably state that a key to improving the software development process is encouraging software reuse. Object-oriented programming in general, and Java in particular, certainly does this.

It is the availability of substantial and useful class libraries that delivers the maximum benefits of software reuse through inheritance. As interest in Java grows, interest in Java class libraries will increase. Just as shrink-wrapped software produced by independent software vendors became an explosive growth industry with the arrival of the personal computer, so, too, will the creation and sale of Java class libraries. Application designers will build their applications with these libraries, and library designers will be rewarded by having their libraries wrapped with the applications. What we see coming is a massive worldwide commitment to the development of Java class libraries for a huge variety of applications arenas.

Software Engineering Observation 9.12

Creating a subclass does not affect its superclass's source code or the superclass's Java bytecodes; the integrity of a superclass is preserved by inheritance.

A superclass specifies commonality. All classes derived from a superclass inherit the capabilities of that superclass. In the object-oriented design process, the designer looks for commonality among a set of classes and factors it out to form desirable superclasses. Subclasses are then customized beyond the capabilities inherited from the superclass.

Software Engineering Observation 9.13

Just as the designer of non-object-oriented systems should avoid unnecessary proliferation of functions, the designer of object-oriented systems should avoid unnecessary proliferation of classes. Proliferating classes creates management problems and can hinder software reusability, simply because it is more difficult for a potential user of a class to locate that class in a huge collection. The trade-off is to create fewer classes, each providing substantial additional functionality, but such classes might be too rich for certain users.

Performance Tip 9.1

When creating a new class, inherit from the class "closest" to what you need—i.e., the one that provides the minimum set of capabilities required for a new class to perform its tasks. Subclasses could inherit data and functionality that they will not use, in which case memory and processing resources may be wasted.

Note that reading a set of subclass declarations can be confusing because inherited members are not shown, but inherited members are nevertheless present in the subclasses. A similar problem can exist in the documentation of subclasses.

Software Engineering Observation 9.14

In an object-oriented system, classes are often closely related. "Factor out" common attributes and behaviors and place these in a superclass. Then use inheritance to form subclasses without having to repeat common attributes and behaviors.

Software Engineering Observation 9.15

Modifications to a superclass do not require subclasses to change as long as the public interface to the superclass remains unchanged.

9.8 Composition vs. Inheritance

We have discussed *is a* relationships that are implemented by inheritance. We have also discussed *has a* relationships (and seen examples in preceding chapters) in which a class has objects of other classes as members—such relationships create new classes by *composition* of existing classes. For example, given the classes **Employee**, **BirthDate** and **TelephoneNumber**, it is improper to say that an **Employee** *is a* **BirthDate** or that an **Employee** *is a* **TelephoneNumber**. But it is certainly appropriate to say that an **Employee** *has a* **BirthDate** and that an **Employee** *has a* **TelephoneNumber**.

9.9 Case Study: Point, Circle, Cylinder

Now let us consider a substantial inheritance example. We consider a point, circle, cylinder hierarchy. First we develop and use class **Point** (Fig. 9.10 and Fig. 9.11). Then we present an example in which we derive class **Circle** from class **Point** (Fig. 9.12 and Fig. 9.13). Finally, we present an example in which we derive class **Cylinder** from class **Circle** (Fig. 9.14 and Fig. 9.15).

Figure 9.10 is the class **Point** definition. Class **Point** is defined as part of package **com.deitel.jhtp4.ch09** (line 3). Note that **Point**'s instance variables are **protected**. Thus, when class **Circle** is derived from class **Point**, the methods of class **Circle** will be able to reference coordinates **x** and **y** directly rather than using access methods. This could result in better performance.

```
1  // Fig. 9.10: Point.java
2  // Definition of class Point
3  package com.deitel.jhtp4.ch09;
4
5  public class Point {
6     protected int x, y; // coordinates of Point
7
8     // No-argument constructor
9     public Point()
10    {
11       // implicit call to superclass constructor occurs here
12       setPoint( 0, 0 );
13    }
14
15    // constructor
16    public Point( int xCoordinate, int yCoordinate )
17    {
18       // implicit call to superclass constructor occurs here
19       setPoint( xCoordinate, yCoordinate );
20    }
21
```

Fig. 9.10 **Point** class definition (part 1 of 2).

```
   // set x and y coordinates of Point
   public void setPoint( int xCoordinate, int yCoordinate )
   {
      x = xCoordinate;
      y = yCoordinate;
   }

   // get x coordinate
   public int getX()
   {
      return x;
   }

   // get y coordinate
   public int getY()
   {
      return y;
   }

   // convert into a String representation
   public String toString()
   {
      return "[" + x + ", " + y + "]";
   }

}  // end class Point
```

Fig. 9.10 **Point** class definition (part 2 of 2).

Figure 9.11 shows a **Test** application for testing class **Point**. The **main** method must use **getX** and **getY** to read the values of **protected** instance variables **x** and **y**. Remember that **protected** instance variables are accessible only to methods of their class, their subclasses and other classes in the same package. Also, note the implicit call to **toString** when **point** is added to a **String** at line 25.

```
1  // Fig. 9.11: Test.java
2  // Applet to test class Point
3
4  // Java extension packages
5  import javax.swing.JOptionPane;
6
7  // Deitel packages
8  import com.deitel.jhtp4.ch09.Point;
9
10 public class Test {
11
12    // test class Point
13    public static void main( String args[] )
14    {
15       Point point = new Point( 72, 115 );
16
```

Fig. 9.11 Testing class **Point** (part 1 of 2).

```
      // get coordinates
      String output = "X coordinate is " + point.getX() +
               "\nY coordinate is " + point.getY();

      // set coordinates
      point.setPoint( 10, 10 );

      // use implicit call to point.toString()
      output += "\n\nThe new location of point is " + point;

      JOptionPane.showMessageDialog( null, output,
         "Demonstrating Class Point",
         JOptionPane.INFORMATION_MESSAGE );

      System.exit( 0 );
   }

}  // end class Test
```

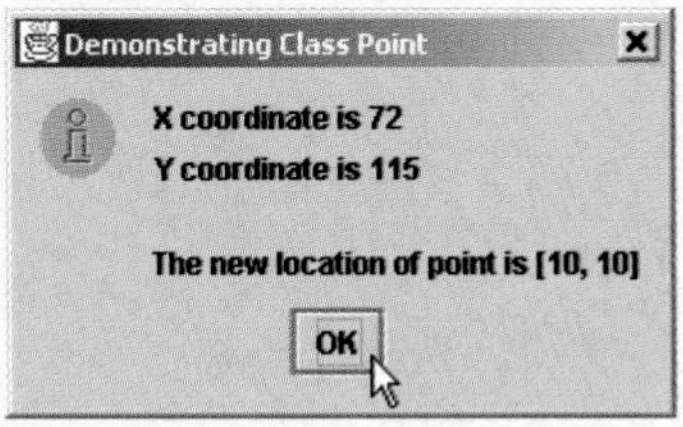

Demonstrating Class Point

X coordinate is 72
Y coordinate is 115

The new location of point is [10, 10]

OK

Fig. 9.11 Testing class **Point** (part 2 of 2).

Our next example imports the **Point** class definition from Fig. 9.10, so we do not show the class definition again here. Figure 9.12 shows the **Circle** class definition with the **Circle** method definitions. Note that class **Circle extends** class **Point**. This means that the **public** interface to **Circle** includes the **Point** methods as well as the **Circle** methods **setRadius**, **getRadius**, **area**, **toString** and the **Circle** constructors.

```
// Fig. 9.12: Circle.java
// Definition of class Circle
package com.deitel.jhtp4.ch09;

public class Circle extends Point {  // inherits from Point
   protected double radius;

   // no-argument constructor
   public Circle()
   {
      // implicit call to superclass constructor occurs here
      setRadius( 0 );
   }

```

Fig. 9.12 **Circle** class definition (part 1 of 2).

```
    // constructor
    public Circle( double circleRadius, int xCoordinate,
       int yCoordinate )
    {
       // call superclass constructor to set coordinates
       super( xCoordinate, yCoordinate );

       // set radius
       setRadius( circleRadius );
    }

    // set radius of Circle
    public void setRadius( double circleRadius )
    {
       radius = ( circleRadius >= 0.0 ? circleRadius : 0.0 );
    }

    // get radius of Circle
    public double getRadius()
    {
       return radius;
    }

    // calculate area of Circle
    public double area()
    {
       return Math.PI * radius * radius;
    }

    // convert the Circle to a String
    public String toString()
    {
       return "Center = " + "[" + x + ", " + y + "]" +
             "; Radius = " + radius;
    }

 }  // end class Circle
```

Fig. 9.12 **Circle** class definition (part 2 of 2).

Application **Test** (Fig. 9.13) instantiates an object of class **Circle** (line 19), then uses *get* methods to obtain the information about the **Circle** object. Method **main** indirectly references the **protected** data of class **Circle** through method calls. Method **main** then uses *set* methods **setRadius** and **setPoint** to reset the radius and coordinates of the center of the circle. Finally, **main** displays the **Circle** object **circle** and calculates and displays its area.

```
1  // Fig. 9.13: Test.java
2  // Applet to test class Circle
3
```

Fig. 9.13 Testing class **Circle** (part 1 of 2).

```
// Java core packages
import java.text.DecimalFormat;

// Java extension packages
import javax.swing.JOptionPane;

// Deitel packages
import com.deitel.jhtp4.ch09.Circle;

public class Test {

   // test class Circle
   public static void main( String args[] )
   {
      // create a Circle
      Circle circle = new Circle( 2.5, 37, 43 );
      DecimalFormat precision2 = new DecimalFormat( "0.00" );

      // get coordinates and radius
      String output = "X coordinate is " + circle.getX() +
               "\nY coordinate is " + circle.getY() +
               "\nRadius is " + circle.getRadius();

      // set coordinates and radius
      circle.setRadius( 4.25 );
      circle.setPoint( 2, 2 );

      // get String representation of Circle and calculate area
      output +=
         "\n\nThe new location and radius of c are\n" + circle +
         "\nArea is " + precision2.format( circle.area() );

      JOptionPane.showMessageDialog( null, output,
         "Demonstrating Class Circle",
         JOptionPane.INFORMATION_MESSAGE );

      System.exit( 0 );
   }

}  // end class Test
```

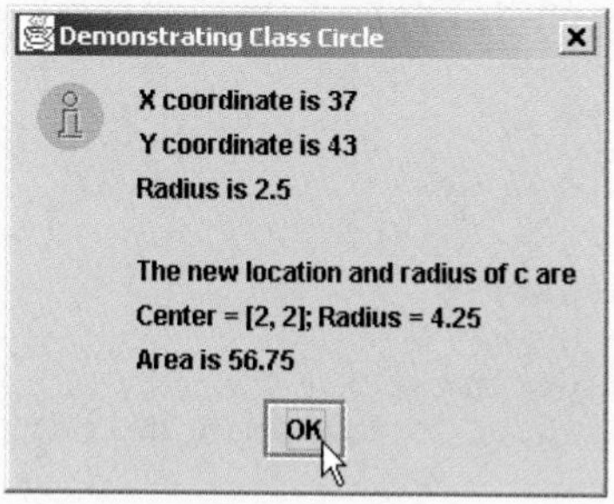

Demonstrating Class Circle
X coordinate is 37
Y coordinate is 43
Radius is 2.5

The new location and radius of c are
Center = [2, 2]; Radius = 4.25
Area is 56.75
OK

Fig. 9.13 Testing class **Circle** (part 2 of 2).

Our last example is shown in Fig. 9.14 and Fig. 9.15. Figure 9.14 shows the **Cylinder** class definition with the **Cylinder** method definitions. Note that class **Cylinder extends** class **Circle**. This means that the **public** interface to **Cylinder** includes the **Circle** methods and **Point** methods as well as the **Cylinder** constructor and **Cylinder** methods **setHeight**, **getHeight**, **area** (which overrides the **Circle area** method), **volume** and **toString**.

```
// Fig. 9.14: Cylinder.java
// Definition of class Cylinder
package com.deitel.jhtp4.ch09;

public class Cylinder extends Circle {
   protected double height;  // height of Cylinder

   // no-argument constructor
   public Cylinder()
   {
      // implicit call to superclass constructor here
      setHeight( 0 );
   }

   // constructor
   public Cylinder( double cylinderHeight, double cylinderRadius,
      int xCoordinate, int yCoordinate )
   {
      // call superclass constructor to set coordinates/radius
      super( cylinderRadius, xCoordinate, yCoordinate );

      // set cylinder height
      setHeight( cylinderHeight );
   }

   // set height of Cylinder
   public void setHeight( double cylinderHeight )
   {
      height = ( cylinderHeight >= 0 ? cylinderHeight : 0 );
   }

   // get height of Cylinder
   public double getHeight()
   {
      return height;
   }

   // calculate area of Cylinder (i.e., surface area)
   public double area()
   {
      return 2 * super.area() +
             2 * Math.PI * radius * height;
   }

```

Fig. 9.14 Class **Cylinder** definition (part 1 of 2).

```
    // calculate volume of Cylinder
    public double volume()
    {
       return super.area() * height;
    }

    // convert the Cylinder to a String
    public String toString()
    {
       return super.toString() + "; Height = " + height;
    }

 }  // end class Cylinder
```

Fig. 9.14 Class **Cylinder** definition (part 2 of 2).

Method **main** of the **Test** application (Fig. 9.15) instantiates an object of class **Cylinder** (line 19), then uses *get* methods (lines 23–26) to obtain information about the **Cylinder** object. Again, the **Test** applications's **main** method cannot reference directly the **protected** data of class **Cylinder**. Method **main** uses *set* methods **setHeight**, **setRadius** and **setPoint** (lines 29–31) to reset the **height**, **radius** and coordinates of the **Cylinder**. Then **main** uses **toString**, **area** and **volume** to print the attributes and some facts about the **Cylinder**. Figure 9.15 is a **Test** application to test class **Cylinder**'s capabilities.

```
1  // Fig. 9.15: Test.java
2  // Application to test class Cylinder
3
4  // Java core packages
5  import java.text.DecimalFormat;
6
7  // Java extension packages
8  import javax.swing.JOptionPane;
9
10 // Deitel packages
11 import com.deitel.jhtp4.ch09.Cylinder;
12
13 public class Test {
14
15    // test class Cylinder
16    public static void main( String args[] )
17    {
18       // create Cylinder
19       Cylinder cylinder = new Cylinder( 5.7, 2.5, 12, 23 );
20       DecimalFormat precision2 = new DecimalFormat( "0.00" );
21
22       // get coordinates, radius and height
23       String output = "X coordinate is " + cylinder.getX() +
24          "\nY coordinate is " + cylinder.getY() +
25          "\nRadius is " + cylinder.getRadius() +
26          "\nHeight is " + cylinder.getHeight();
```

Fig. 9.15 Testing class **Cylinder** (part 1 of 2).

```java

      // set coordinates, radius and height
      cylinder.setHeight( 10 );
      cylinder.setRadius( 4.25 );
      cylinder.setPoint( 2, 2 );

      // get String representation of Cylinder and calculate
      // area and volume
      output += "\n\nThe new location, radius " +
         "and height of cylinder are\n" + cylinder +
         "\nArea is " + precision2.format( cylinder.area() ) +
         "\nVolume is " + precision2.format( cylinder.volume() );

      JOptionPane.showMessageDialog( null, output,
         "Demonstrating Class Cylinder",
         JOptionPane.INFORMATION_MESSAGE );

      System.exit( 0 );
   }

}  // end class Test
```

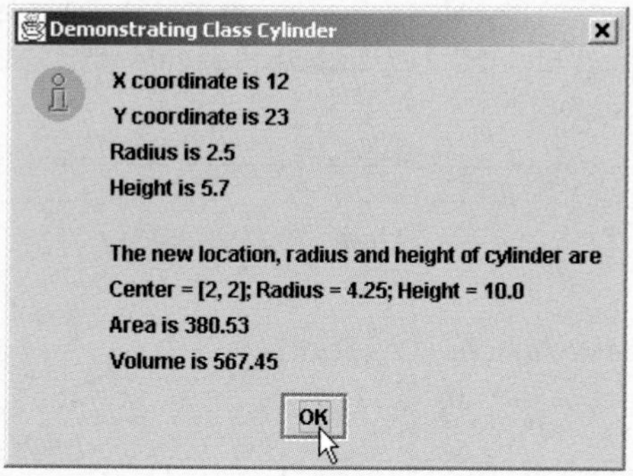

Demonstrating Class Cylinder

X coordinate is 12
Y coordinate is 23
Radius is 2.5
Height is 5.7

The new location, radius and height of cylinder are
Center = [2, 2]; Radius = 4.25; Height = 10.0
Area is 380.53
Volume is 567.45

OK

Fig. 9.15 Testing class **Cylinder** (part 2 of 2).

The series of examples in this section nicely demonstrates inheritance and defining and referencing **protected** instance variables. The reader should now be confident with the basics of inheritance. In the next several sections, we show how to program with inheritance hierarchies in a general manner, using polymorphism. Data abstraction, inheritance and polymorphism are the crux of object-oriented programming.

9.10 Introduction to Polymorphism

With *polymorphism,* it is possible to design and implement systems that are more easily *extensible.* Programs can be written to process generically—as superclass objects—objects of all existing classes in a hierarchy. Classes that do not exist during program development can be added with little or no modifications to the generic part of the program—as long as those classes are part of the hierarchy that is being processed generically. The only parts of a program that need modification are those parts that require direct knowledge of the particular class that is added to the hierarchy. We will study two substantial class hierarchies and will show how objects throughout those hierarchies are manipulated polymorphically.

9.11 Type Fields and `switch` Statements

One means of dealing with objects of many different types is to use a **`switch`** statement to take an appropriate action on each object, based on that object's type. For example, in a hierarchy of shapes in which each shape has a **`shapeType`** instance variable, a **`switch`** structure could determine which **`print`** method to call based on the object's **`shapeType`**.

There are many problems with using **`switch`** logic. The programmer might forget to make such a type test when one is warranted. The programmer might forget to test all possible cases in a **`switch`**. If a **`switch`**-based system is modified by adding new types, the programmer might forget to insert the new cases in existing **`switch`** statements. Every addition or deletion of a class demands that every **`switch`** statement in the system be modified; tracking these down can be time consuming and error prone.

As we will see, polymorphic programming can eliminate the need for **`switch`** logic. The programmer can use Java's polymorphism mechanism to perform the equivalent logic automatically, thus avoiding the kinds of errors typically associated with **`switch`** logic.

Testing and Debugging Tip 9.2

An interesting consequence of using polymorphism is that programs take on a simplified appearance. They contain less branching logic in favor of simpler sequential code. This simplification facilitates testing, debugging, and program maintenance.

9.12 Dynamic Method Binding

Suppose a set of shape classes such as **`Circle`**, **`Triangle`**, **`Rectangle`**, **`Square`**, are all derived from superclass **`Shape`**. In object-oriented programming, each of these classes might be endowed with the ability to draw itself. Each class has its own **`draw`** method, and the **`draw`** method implementation for each shape is quite different. When drawing a shape, whatever that shape may be, it would be nice to be able to treat all these shapes generically as objects of the superclass **`Shape`**. Then, to draw any shape, we could simply call method **`draw`** of superclass **`Shape`** and let the program determine dynamically (i.e., at execution time) which subclass **`draw`** method to use from the actual object's type.

To enable this kind of behavior, we declare **`draw`** in the superclass, and then we override **`draw`** in each of the subclasses to draw the appropriate shape.

Software Engineering Observation 9.16

When a subclass chooses not to redefine a method, the subclass simply inherits its immediate superclass's method definition.

If we use a superclass reference to refer to a subclass object and invoke the **`draw`** method, the program will choose the correct subclass's **`draw`** method dynamically (i.e., at execution time). This is called *dynamic method binding*. Dynamic method binding is an important mechanism for implementing polymorphic processing of objects and will be illustrated in the case studies later in this chapter

9.13 `final` Methods and Classes

We saw in Chapter 7 that variables can be declared **`final`** to indicate that they cannot be modified after they are declared and that they must be initialized when they are declared. It is also possible to define methods and classes with the **`final`** modifier.

A method that is declared **`final`** cannot be overridden in a subclass. Methods that are declared **`static`** and methods that are declared **`private`** are implicitly **`final`**. Because a **`final`** method's definition can never change, the compiler can optimize the program by removing calls to **`final`** methods and replacing them with the expanded code of their definitions at each method call location—a technique known as *inlining the code.*

A class that is declared **`final`** cannot be a superclass (i.e., a class cannot inherit from a **`final`** class). All methods in a **`final`** class are implicitly **`final`**.

Performance Tip 9.2

*The compiler can decide to inline a **`final`** method call and will do so for small, simple **`final`** methods. Inlining does not violate encapsulation or information hiding (but does improve performance because it eliminates the overhead of making a method call).*

Software Engineering Observation 9.17

*A class declared **`final`** cannot be extended, and every method in it is implicitly **`final`**.*

Software Engineering Observation 9.18

*In the Java API, the vast majority of the thousands of classes are not declared **`final`**. This enables inheritance and polymorphic processing—the fundamental capabilities of object-oriented programming. However, in some cases it is important to declare classes **`final`**—typically for security[1] or performance reasons.*

9.14 Abstract Superclasses and Concrete Classes

When we think of a class as a type, we assume that objects of that type will be instantiated. However, there are cases in which it is useful to define classes for which the programmer never intends to instantiate any objects. Such classes are called *abstract classes.* Because these are used as superclasses in inheritance situations, we will normally refer to them as *abstract superclasses.* No objects of abstract superclasses can be instantiated.

The sole purpose of an abstract class is to provide an appropriate superclass from which other classes may inherit interface and/or implementation (we will see examples of each shortly). Classes from which objects can be instantiated are called *concrete classes.*

---

1. Class **`String`** is an example of a **`final`** class. This class cannot be extended, so programs that use **`String`**s can rely on the functionality of **`String`** objects as specified in the Java API. Making the class **`final`** also prevents programmers from creating subclasses that might bypass security restrictions. For example, when a Java program attempts to open a file on your computer, the program supplies a **`String`** representing the name of the file. In many cases, opening a file is subject to security restrictions. If it were possible to create a subclass of **`String`**, that subclass might be implemented in a manner that enables it to specify one **`String`** to pass a security or permissions test, then specify a different name when the program actually opens the file. For more information on final classes and methods visit: **`java.sun.com/docs/books/tutorial/java/javaOO/final.html`** [*Note*: **`String`**s are covered in detail in Chapter 10 and file processing is covered in detail in Chapter 16.]

We could have an abstract superclass **TwoDimensionalObject** and derive concrete classes, such as **Square**, **Circle**, **Triangle**. We could also have an abstract superclass **ThreeDimensionalObject** and derive such concrete classes as **Cube**, **Sphere** and **Cylinder**. Abstract superclasses are too generic to define real objects; we need to be more specific before we can think of instantiating objects. For example, if someone tells you to "draw the shape," what shape would you draw? Concrete classes provide the specifics that make it reasonable to instantiate objects.

A class is made abstract by declaring it with keyword **abstract**. A hierarchy does not need to contain any **abstract** classes, but, as we will see, many good object-oriented systems have class hierarchies headed by **abstract** superclasses. In some cases, **abstract** classes constitute the top few levels of the hierarchy. A good example of this is the shape hierarchy in Fig. 9.3. The hierarchy begins with **abstract** superclass **Shape**. On the next level down we have two more **abstract** superclasses, namely **TwoDimensionalShape** and **ThreeDimensionalShape**. The next level down would start defining concrete classes for such two-dimensional shapes as **Circle** and **Square** and for such three-dimensional shapes as **Sphere** and **Cube**.

9.15 Polymorphism Examples

Here is an example of polymorphism. If class **Rectangle** is derived from class **Quadrilateral**, then a **Rectangle** object *is a* more specific version of a **Quadrilateral** object. An operation (such as calculating the perimeter or the area) that can be performed on an object of class **Quadrilateral** can also be performed on an object of class **Rectangle**. Such operations can also be performed on other "kinds of" **Quadrilaterals**, such as **Squares**, **Parallelograms** and **Trapezoids**. When a request is made through a superclass reference to use a method, Java chooses the correct overridden method polymorphically in the appropriate subclass associated with the object.

Here is another example of polymorphism. Suppose we have a video game that manipulates objects of many varieties, including objects of class **Martian**, **Venutian**, **Plutonian**, **SpaceShip**, **LaserBeam** and the like. Each of these classes extends a common superclass, **GamePiece**, that contains a method called **drawYourself**. This method is defined by each subclass. A Java screen manager program would simply maintain some kind of collection (such as a **GamePiece** array) of references to objects of these various classes. To refresh the screen periodically, the screen manager would simply send each object the same message, namely **drawYourself**. Each object would respond in its own unique way. A **Martian** object would draw itself with the appropriate number of antennae. A **SpaceShip** object would draw itself bright and silvery. A **LaserBeam** object would draw itself as a bright red beam across the screen. Thus, the same message sent to a variety of objects would have "many forms" of results—hence the term *polymorphism*.

Such a polymorphic screen manager makes it especially easy to add new types of objects to a system with minimal impact. Suppose we want to add **Mercurians** to our video game. We certainly have to build a new class **Mercurian** that extends **GamePiece** and provides its own definition of the **drawYourself** method. Then, when objects of class **Mercurian** appear in the collection, the screen manager need not be modified. It simply sends the message **drawYourself** to every object in the collection regardless of the object's type, so the new **Mercurian** objects just "fit right in." Thus, with polymorphism, new types of objects not even envisioned when a system is created can be added without modifications to the system (other than the new class itself, of course).

Through the use of polymorphism, one method call can cause different actions to occur, depending on the type of the object receiving the call. This gives the programmer tremendous expressive capability. We will see examples of the power of polymorphism in the next several sections.

Software Engineering Observation 9.19

With polymorphism, the programmer can deal in generalities and let the execution-time environment concern itself with the specifics. The programmer can command a wide variety of objects to behave in manners appropriate to those objects without even knowing the types of those objects.

Software Engineering Observation 9.20

Polymorphism promotes extensibility: Software written to invoke polymorphic behavior is written independent of the types of the objects to which messages (i.e., method calls) are sent. Thus, new types of objects that can respond to existing messages can be added into such a system without modifying the base system.

Software Engineering Observation 9.21

If a method is declared **final***, it cannot be overridden in subclasses, so method calls may not be sent polymorphically to objects of those subclasses. The method call may still be sent to subclasses, but they will all respond identically rather than polymorphically.*

Software Engineering Observation 9.22

An **abstract** *class defines a common interface for the various members of a class hierarchy. The* **abstract** *class contains methods that will be defined in the subclasses. All classes in the hierarchy can use this same interface through polymorphism.*

Although we cannot instantiate objects of **abstract** superclasses, we *can* declare references to **abstract** superclasses. Such references can be used to enable polymorphic manipulations of subclass objects when such objects are instantiated from concrete classes.

Let us consider more applications of polymorphism. A screen manager needs to display a variety of objects, including new types of objects that will be added to the system even after the screen manager is written. The system may need to display various shapes (the superclass is **Shape**), such as **Circle**, **Triangle** and **Rectangle**. Each shape class is derived from superclass **Shape**. The screen manager uses superclass **Shape** references to manage the objects to be displayed. To draw any object (regardless of the level at which that object appears in the inheritance hierarchy), the screen manager uses a superclass reference to the object and simply sends a **draw** message to the object. Method **draw** has been declared **abstract** in superclass **Shape** and has been overridden in each of the subclasses. Each **Shape** object knows how to draw itself. The screen manager does not have to worry about what type each object is or whether the screen manager has seen objects of that type before—the screen manager simply tells each object to **draw** itself.

Polymorphism is particularly effective for implementing layered software systems. In operating systems, for example, each type of physical device could operate quite differently from the others. Even so, commands to *read* or *write* data from and to devices can have a certain uniformity. The *write* message sent to a device-driver object needs to be interpreted specifically in the context of that device driver and how that device driver manipulates devices of a specific type. However, the *write* call itself is really no different from the *write* to any other device in the system—simply place some number of bytes from memory onto that device. An object-oriented operating system might use an **abstract** superclass to provide an interface appropriate for all device drivers. Then, through inheritance from that **abstract** superclass, subclasses are formed that all operate similarly. The capabilities (i.e., the **public** interface) offered by the device drivers are provided as **abstract** methods in the **abstract** superclass. The implementations of these **abstract** methods are provided in the subclasses that correspond to the specific types of device drivers.

It is common in object-oriented programming to define an *iterator class* that can walk through all the objects in a collection (such as an array). If you want to print a list of objects in a linked list, for example, an iterator object can be instantiated that will return the next element of the linked list each time the iterator is called. Iterators are commonly used in polymorphic programming to walk through an array or a linked list of objects from various levels of a hierarchy. The references in such a list would all be superclass references (see Chapter 19, Data Structures, for more on linked lists). A list of objects of superclass class **TwoDimensionalShape** could contain objects from the classes **Square**, **Circle**, **Triangle** and so on. Sending a **draw** message to each object in the list would, using polymorphism, draw the correct picture on the screen.

9.16 Case Study: A Payroll System Using Polymorphism

Let us use **abstract** classes, **abstract** methods and polymorphism to perform payroll calculations based on the type of employee (Fig. 9.16). We use an **abstract** superclass **Employee**. The subclasses of **Employee** are **Boss** (Fig. 9.17)—paid a fixed weekly salary regardless of the number of hours worked, **CommissionWorker** (Fig. 9.18)—paid a flat base salary plus a percentage of sales, **PieceWorker** (Fig. 9.19)—paid by the number of items produced and **HourlyWorker** (Fig. 9.20)—paid by the hour and receives overtime pay. Each subclass of **Employee** has been declared **final**, because we do not intend to inherit from them again.

An **earnings** method call certainly applies generically to all employees. But the way each person's earnings are calculated depends on the class of the employee, and these classes are all derived from the superclass **Employee**. So **earnings** is declared **abstract** in superclass **Employee** and appropriate implementations of **earnings** are provided for each of the subclasses. Then, to calculate any employee's earnings, the program simply uses a superclass reference to that employee's object and invokes the **earnings** method. In a real payroll system, the various **Employee** objects might be referenced by individual elements in an array of **Employee** references. The program would simply walk through the array one element at a time, using the **Employee** references to invoke the **earnings** method of each object.

Software Engineering Observation 9.23

If a subclass is derived from a superclass with an **abstract** *method, and if no definition is supplied in the subclass for that* **abstract** *method (i.e., if that method is not overridden in the subclass), that method remains* **abstract** *in the subclass. Consequently, the subclass is also an* **abstract** *class and must be explicitly declared as an* **abstract** *class.*

Software Engineering Observation 9.24

The ability to declare an **`abstract`** *method gives the class designer considerable power over how subclasses will be implemented in a class hierarchy. Any new class that wants to inherit from this class is forced to override the* **`abstract`** *method (either directly or by inheriting from a class that has overridden the method). Otherwise, that new class will contain an* **`abstract`** *method and thus be an* **`abstract`** *class, unable to instantiate objects.*

Software Engineering Observation 9.25

An **`abstract`** *can still have instance data and non***`abstract`** *methods subject to the normal rules of inheritance by subclasses. An* **`abstract`** *class can also have constructors.*

Common Programming Error 9.7

Attempting to instantiate an object of an **`abstract`** *class (i.e., a class that contains one or more* **`abstract`** *methods) is a syntax error.*

Common Programming Error 9.8

It is a syntax error if a class with one or more **`abstract`** *methods is not explicitly declared* **`abstract`**.

Let us consider the **`Employee`** class (Fig. 9.16). The **`public`** methods include a constructor that takes the first name and last name as arguments; a **`getFirstName`** method that returns the first name; a **`getLastName`** method that returns the last name; a **`toString`** method that returns the first name and last name separated by a space; and an **`abstract`** method—**`earnings`**. Why is this method **`abstract`**? The answer is that it does not make sense to provide an implementation of this method in the **`Employee`** class. We cannot calculate the earnings for a generic employee—we must first know *what kind of* employee it is. By making this method **`abstract`** we are indicating that we will provide an implementation in each concrete subclass, but not in the superclass itself.

```java
// Fig. 9.16: Employee.java
// Abstract base class Employee.

public abstract class Employee {
   private String firstName;
   private String lastName;

   // constructor
   public Employee( String first, String last )
   {
      firstName = first;
      lastName = last;
   }

   // get first name
   public String getFirstName()
   {
      return firstName;
   }

```

Fig. 9.16 **`Employee abstract`** superclass (part 1 of 2).

```
   // get last name
   public String getLastName()
   {
      return lastName;
   }

   public String toString()
   {
      return firstName + ' ' + lastName;
   }

   // Abstract method that must be implemented for each
   // derived class of Employee from which objects
   // are instantiated.
   public abstract double earnings();

}  // end class Employee
```

Fig. 9.16 **Employee abstract** superclass (part 2 of 2).

Class **Boss** (Fig. 9.17) is derived from **Employee**. The **public** methods include a constructor that takes a first name, a last name and a weekly salary as arguments and passes the first name and last name to the **Employee** constructor to initialize the **firstName** and **lastName** members of the superclass part of the subclass object. Other **public** methods include a **setWeeklySalary** method to assign a new value to **private** instance variable **weeklySalary**; an **earnings** method defining how to calculate a **Boss**'s earnings; and a **toString** method that forms a **String** containing the type of the employee (i.e., **"Boss: "**) followed by the boss's name.

```
// Fig. 9.17: Boss.java
// Boss class derived from Employee.

public final class Boss extends Employee {
   private double weeklySalary;

   // constructor for class Boss
   public Boss( String first, String last, double salary )
   {
      super( first, last );  // call superclass constructor
      setWeeklySalary( salary );
   }

   // set Boss's salary
   public void setWeeklySalary( double salary )
   {
      weeklySalary = ( salary > 0 ? salary : 0 );
   }

```

Fig. 9.17 **Boss** extends **abstract** class **Employee**.

```
   // get Boss's pay
   public double earnings()
   {
      return weeklySalary;
   }

   // get String representation of Boss's name
   public String toString()
   {
      return "Boss: " + super.toString();
   }

}  // end class Boss
```

Fig. 9.17 **Boss** extends **abstract** class **Employee**.

Class **CommissionWorker** (Fig. 9.18) is derived from **Employee**. The **public** methods include a constructor that takes a first name, a last name, a salary, a commission and a quantity of items sold as arguments and passes the first name and last name to the **Employee** constructor; *set* methods to assign new values to instance variables **salary**, **commission** and **quantity**; an **earnings** method to calculate a **CommissionWorker**'s earnings; and a **toString** method that forms a **String** containing the employee type (i.e., **"Commission worker: "**) followed by the worker's name.

```
// Fig. 9.18: CommissionWorker.java
// CommissionWorker class derived from Employee

public final class CommissionWorker extends Employee {
   private double salary;      // base salary per week
   private double commission;  // amount per item sold
   private int quantity;       // total items sold for week

   // constructor for class CommissionWorker
   public CommissionWorker( String first, String last,
      double salary, double commission, int quantity )
   {
      super( first, last );  // call superclass constructor
      setSalary( salary );
      setCommission( commission );
      setQuantity( quantity );
   }

   // set CommissionWorker's weekly base salary
   public void setSalary( double weeklySalary )
   {
      salary = ( weeklySalary > 0 ? weeklySalary : 0 );
   }

```

Fig. 9.18 **CommissionWorker** extends **abstract** class **Employee** (part 1 of 2).

```
    // set CommissionWorker's commission
    public void setCommission( double itemCommission )
    {
       commission = ( itemCommission > 0 ? itemCommission : 0 );
    }

    // set CommissionWorker's quantity sold
    public void setQuantity( int totalSold )
    {
       quantity = ( totalSold > 0 ? totalSold : 0 );
    }

    // determine CommissionWorker's earnings
    public double earnings()
    {
       return salary + commission * quantity;
    }

    // get String representation of CommissionWorker's name
    public String toString()
    {
       return "Commission worker: " + super.toString();
    }

 } // end class CommissionWorker
```

Fig. 9.18 **CommissionWorker** extends **abstract** class **Employee** (part 2 of 2).

Class **PieceWorker** (Fig. 9.19) is derived from **Employee**. The **public** methods include a constructor that takes a first name, a last name, a wage per piece and a quantity of items produced as arguments and passes the first name and last name to the **Employee** constructor; *set* methods to assign new values to instance variables **wagePerPiece** and **quantity**; an **earnings** method defining how to calculate a **PieceWorker**'s earnings; and a **toString** method that forms a **String** containing the type of the employee (i.e., **"Piece worker: "**) followed by the pieceworker's name.

```
// Fig. 9.19: PieceWorker.java
// PieceWorker class derived from Employee

public final class PieceWorker extends Employee {
   private double wagePerPiece; // wage per piece output
   private int quantity;        // output for week

   // constructor for class PieceWorker
   public PieceWorker( String first, String last,
      double wage, int numberOfItems )
   {
      super( first, last );  // call superclass constructor
      setWage( wage );
      setQuantity( numberOfItems);
  }
```

Fig. 9.19 **PieceWorker** extends **abstract** class **Employee** (part 1 of 2).

```

   // set PieceWorker's wage
   public void setWage( double wage )
   {
      wagePerPiece = ( wage > 0 ? wage : 0 );
   }

   // set number of items output
   public void setQuantity( int numberOfItems )
   {
      quantity = ( numberOfItems > 0 ? numberOfItems : 0 );
   }

   // determine PieceWorker's earnings
   public double earnings()
   {
      return quantity * wagePerPiece;
   }

   public String toString()
   {
      return "Piece worker: " + super.toString();
   }

}  // end class PieceWorker
```

Fig. 9.19 **PieceWorker** extends **abstract** class **Employee** (part 2 of 2).

Class **HourlyWorker** (Fig. 9.20) is derived from **Employee**. The **public** methods include a constructor that takes a first name, a last name, a wage and the number of hours worked as arguments and passes the first name and last name to the **Employee** constructor; *set* methods to assign new values to instance variables **wage** and **hours**; an **earnings** method defining how to calculate an **HourlyWorker**'s earnings; and a **toString** method that forms a **String** containing the type of the employee (i.e., **"Hourly worker: "**) followed by the hourly worker's name.

```
// Fig. 9.20: HourlyWorker.java
// Definition of class HourlyWorker

public final class HourlyWorker extends Employee {
   private double wage;   // wage per hour
   private double hours;  // hours worked for week

   // constructor for class HourlyWorker
   public HourlyWorker( String first, String last,
      double wagePerHour, double hoursWorked )
   {
      super( first, last );   // call superclass constructor
      setWage( wagePerHour );
      setHours( hoursWorked );
   }
```

Fig. 9.20 **HourlyWorker** extends **abstract** class **Employee** (part 1 of 2).

```java

   // Set the wage
   public void setWage( double wagePerHour )
   {
      wage = ( wagePerHour > 0 ? wagePerHour : 0 );
   }

   // Set the hours worked
   public void setHours( double hoursWorked )
   {
      hours = ( hoursWorked >= 0 && hoursWorked < 168 ?
         hoursWorked : 0 );
   }

   // Get the HourlyWorker's pay
   public double earnings() { return wage * hours; }

   public String toString()
   {
      return "Hourly worker: " + super.toString();
   }

}  // end class HourlyWorker
```

Fig. 9.20 **HourlyWorker** extends **abstract** class **Employee** (part 2 of 2).

Method **main** of the **Test** application (Fig. 9.21) begins by declaring **Employee** reference, **ref**. Each of the types of **Employee**s is handled similarly in **main**, so we will discuss only the case in which **main** deals with a **Boss** object.

```java
// Fig. 9.21: Test.java
// Driver for Employee hierarchy

// Java core packages
import java.text.DecimalFormat;

// Java extension packages
import javax.swing.JOptionPane;

public class Test {

   // test Employee hierarchy
   public static void main( String args[] )
   {
      Employee employee;  // superclass reference
      String output = "";

      Boss boss = new Boss( "John", "Smith", 800.0 );

```

Fig. 9.21 Testing the **Employee** class hierarchy using an **abstract** superclass.

```
      CommissionWorker commisionWorker =
         new CommissionWorker(
            "Sue", "Jones", 400.0, 3.0, 150 );

      PieceWorker pieceWorker =
         new PieceWorker( "Bob", "Lewis", 2.5, 200 );

      HourlyWorker hourlyWorker =
         new HourlyWorker( "Karen", "Price", 13.75, 40 );

      DecimalFormat precision2 = new DecimalFormat( "0.00" );

      // Employee reference to a Boss
      employee = boss;

      output += employee.toString() + " earned $" +
         precision2.format( employee.earnings() ) + "\n" +
         boss.toString() + " earned $" +
         precision2.format( boss.earnings() ) + "\n";

      // Employee reference to a CommissionWorker
      employee = commissionWorker;

      output += employee.toString() + " earned $" +
         precision2.format( employee.earnings() ) + "\n" +
         commissionWorker.toString() + " earned $" +
         precision2.format(
            commissionWorker.earnings() ) + "\n";

      // Employee reference to a PieceWorker
      employee = pieceWorker;

      output += employee.toString() + " earned $" +
         precision2.format( employee.earnings() ) + "\n" +
         pieceWorker.toString() + " earned $" +
         precision2.format( pieceWorker.earnings() ) + "\n";

      // Employee reference to an HourlyWorker
      employee = hourlyWorker;

      output += employee.toString() + " earned $" +
         precision2.format( employee.earnings() ) + "\n" +
         hourlyWorker.toString() + " earned $" +
         precision2.format( hourlyWorker.earnings() ) + "\n";

      JOptionPane.showMessageDialog( null, output,
         "Demonstrating Polymorphism",
         JOptionPane.INFORMATION_MESSAGE );

      System.exit( 0 );
   }

}  // end class Test
```

Fig. 9.21 Testing the **Employee** class hierarchy using an **abstract** superclass.

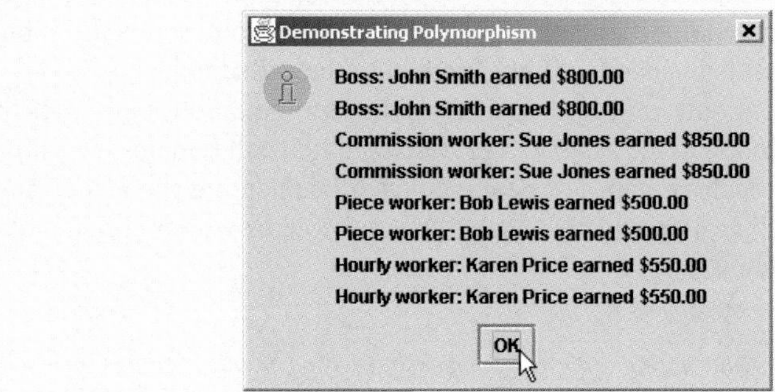

Fig. 9.21 Testing the **Employee** class hierarchy using an **abstract** superclass.

Line 18 instantiates subclass object class **Boss** and provides various constructor arguments, including a first name, a last name and a fixed weekly salary. The new object is assigned to **Boss** reference **boss**.

Line 33 assigns to superclass **Employee** reference **employee** a reference to the subclass **Boss** object to which **boss** refers. This is precisely what we must do to effect polymorphic behavior.

The method call in line 35 invokes the **toString** method of the object referenced by **employee**. The system determines that the referenced object is a **Boss** and invokes subclass **Boss**'s **toString** method—again, polymorphic behavior. This method call is an example of dynamic method binding—the decision as to what method to invoke is deferred until execution time.

The method call in line 36 invokes the **earnings** method of the object to which **employee** refers. The system determines that the object is a **Boss** and invokes the subclass **Boss**'s **earnings** method rather than the superclass's **earnings** method. This is also an example of dynamic method binding.

The method call in line 37 explicitly invokes the **Boss** version of method **toString** by following reference **boss** with the dot operator. We included line 37 for comparison purposes to ensure that the dynamically bound method invoked with **employee.toString()** was indeed the proper method.

The method call in line 38 explicitly invokes the **Boss** version of method **earnings** by using the dot operator with the specific **Boss** reference **boss**. This call is also included for comparison purposes to ensure that the dynamically bound method invoked with **employee.earnings()** was indeed the proper method.

To prove that the superclass reference **employee** can be used to invoke **toString** and **earnings** for the other types of employees, lines 41, 50 and 58 each assign a different type of employee object (**CommissionWorker**, **PieceWorker** and **HourlyWorker**, respectively) to the superclass reference **employee**; then the two methods are called after each assignment to show that Java is always capable of determining the type of the referenced object before invoking a method.

9.17 New Classes and Dynamic Binding

Polymorphism certainly works nicely when all possible classes are known in advance. But it also works when new kinds of classes are added to systems.

New classes are accommodated by dynamic method binding (also called *late binding*). An object's type need not be known at compile time for a polymorphic call to be compiled. At execution time, the call is matched with the method of the called object.

A screen manager program can now handle (without recompilation) new types of display objects as they are added to the system. The **draw** method call remains the same. The new objects themselves each contain a **draw** method implementing the actual drawing capabilities. This makes it easy to add new capabilities to systems with minimal impact. It also promotes software reuse.

Performance Tip 9.3

The kinds of polymorphic manipulations made possible with dynamic binding can also be accomplished by using hand-coded **switch** *logic based on type fields in objects. The polymorphic code generated by the Java compiler runs with performance comparable to that of efficiently coded* **switch** *logic.*

Software Engineering Observation 9.26

Java provides mechanisms for loading classes into a program dynamically to enhance the functionality of an executing program. In particular, **static** *method* **forName** *of class* **Class** *(package* **java.lang***) can be used to load a class definition, then create new objects of that class for use in a program. This concept is beyond the scope of this book. For more information, see the online API documentation for* **Class***.*

9.18 Case Study: Inheriting Interface and Implementation

Our next example (Fig. 9.22–Fig. 9.26) reexamines the **Point**, **Circle**, **Cylinder** hierarchy, except that we now head the hierarchy with **abstract** superclass **Shape** (Fig. 9.22). This hierarchy mechanically demonstrates the power of polymorphism. In the exercises, we explore a more realistic hierarchy of shapes.

Shape contains **abstract** method **getName**, so **Shape** must be declared an **abstract** superclass. **Shape** contains two other methods, **area** and **volume**, each of which has an implementation that returns zero by default. **Point** inherits these implementations from **Shape**. This makes sense because both the area and volume of a point are zero. **Circle** inherits the **volume** method from **Point**, but **Circle** provides its own implementation for the **area** method. **Cylinder** provides its own implementations for both the **area** (interpreted as the surface area of the cylinder) and **volume** methods.

In this example, class **Shape** is used to define a set of methods that all **Shape**s in our hierarchy have in common. Defining these methods in class **Shape** enables us to generically call these methods through a **Shape** reference. Remember, the only methods that can be called through any reference are those **public** methods defined in the reference's declared class type and any **public** methods inherited into that class. Thus, we can call **Object** and **Shape** methods through a **Shape** reference.

Note that although **Shape** is an **abstract** superclass, it still contains implementations of methods **area** and **volume**, and these implementations are inheritable. The **Shape** class provides an inheritable interface (set of services) in the form of three methods that all classes of the hierarchy will contain. The **Shape** class also provides some implementations that subclasses in the first few levels of the hierarchy will use.

This case study emphasizes that a subclass can inherit interface and/or implementation from a superclass.

Software Engineering Observation 9.27

Hierarchies designed for implementation inheritance tend to have their functionality high in the hierarchy—each new subclass inherits one or more methods that were defined in a superclass and uses the superclass definitions.

Software Engineering Observation 9.28

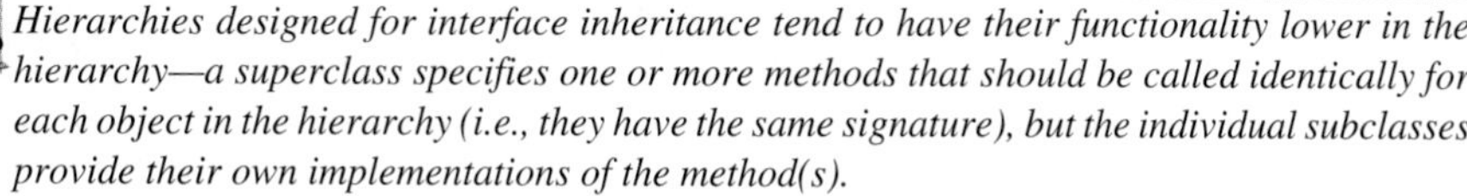

Hierarchies designed for interface inheritance tend to have their functionality lower in the hierarchy—a superclass specifies one or more methods that should be called identically for each object in the hierarchy (i.e., they have the same signature), but the individual subclasses provide their own implementations of the method(s).

Superclass **Shape** (Fig. 9.22) extends **Object**, consists of three **public** methods and does not contain any data (although it could). Method **getName** is **abstract**, so it is overridden in each of the subclasses. Methods **area** and **volume** are defined to return **0.0**. These methods are overridden in subclasses when it is appropriate for those classes to have a different **area** calculation (classes **Circle** and **Cylinder**) and/or a different **volume** calculation (class **Cylinder**).

Class **Point** (Fig. 9.23) is derived from **Shape**. A **Point** has an area of 0.0 and a volume of 0.0, so the superclass methods **area** and **volume** are not overridden here—they are inherited as defined in **Shape**. Other methods include **setPoint** to assign new **x** and **y** coordinates to a **Point** and **getX** and **getY** to return the **x** and **y** coordinates of a **Point**. Method **getName** is an implementation of the **abstract** method in the superclass. If this method were not defined, class **Point** would be an abstract class.

```
// Fig. 9.22: Shape.java
// Definition of abstract base class Shape

public abstract class Shape extends Object {

   // return shape's area
   public double area()
   {
      return 0.0;
   }

   // return shape's volume
   public double volume()
   {
      return 0.0;
   }

   // abstract method must be defined by concrete subclasses
   // to return appropriate shape name
   public abstract String getName();

}  // end class Shape
```

Fig. 9.22 **Shape** abstract superclass for **Point**, **Circle**, **Cylinder** hierarchy.

```
// Fig. 9.23: Point.java
// Definition of class Point

public class Point extends Shape {
   protected int x, y; // coordinates of the Point

   // no-argument constructor
   public Point()
   {
      setPoint( 0, 0 );
   }

   // constructor
   public Point( int xCoordinate, int yCoordinate )
   {
      setPoint( xCoordinate, yCoordinate );
   }

   // set x and y coordinates of Point
   public void setPoint( int xCoordinate, int yCoordinate )
   {
      x = xCoordinate;
      y = yCoordinate;
   }

   // get x coordinate
   public int getX()
   {
      return x;
   }

   // get y coordinate
   public int getY()
   {
      return y;
   }

   // convert point into String representation
   public String toString()
   {
      return "[" + x + ", " + y + "]";
   }

   // return shape name
   public String getName()
   {
      return "Point";
   }

}  // end class Point
```

Fig. 9.23 **Point** subclass of abstract class **Shape**.

Class **Circle** (Fig. 9.24) is derived from **Point**. A **Circle** has a volume of 0.0, so superclass method **volume** is not overridden—it is inherited from class **Point**, which inherited it from **Shape**. A **Circle** has an area different from that of a **Point**, so the **area** method is overridden. Method **getName** is an implementation of the **abstract** method in the superclass. If this method is not overridden here, the **Point** version of **getName** would be inherited. Other methods include **setRadius** to assign a new **radius** to a **Circle** and **getRadius** to return the **radius** of a **Circle**.

```
// Fig. 9.24: Circle.java
// Definition of class Circle

public class Circle extends Point {  // inherits from Point
   protected double radius;

   // no-argument constructor
   public Circle()
   {
      // implicit call to superclass constructor here
      setRadius( 0 );
   }

   // constructor
   public Circle( double circleRadius, int xCoordinate,
      int yCoordinate )
   {
      // call superclass constructor
      super( xCoordinate, yCoordinate );

      setRadius( circleRadius );
   }

   // set radius of Circle
   public void setRadius( double circleRadius )
   {
      radius = ( circleRadius >= 0 ? circleRadius : 0 );
   }

   // get radius of Circle
   public double getRadius()
   {
      return radius;
   }

   // calculate area of Circle
   public double area()
   {
      return Math.PI * radius * radius;
   }

```

Fig. 9.24 **Circle** subclass of **Point**—indirect subclass of **abstract** class **Shape** (part 1 of 2).

```
   // convert Circle to a String represention
   public String toString()
   {
      return "Center = " + super.toString() +
         "; Radius = " + radius;
   }

   // return shape name
   public String getName()
   {
      return "Circle";
   }

}  // end class Circle
```

Fig. 9.24 **Circle** subclass of **Point**—indirect subclass of **abstract** class **Shape** (part 2 of 2).

Software Engineering Observation 9.29

A subclass always inherits the most recently defined version of each **public** *and* **protected** *method from its direct and indirect superclasses.*

Class **Cylinder** (Fig. 9.25) is derived from **Circle**. A **Cylinder** has area and volume different from those of class **Circle**, so the **area** and **volume** methods are both overridden. Method **getName** is an implementation of the **abstract** method in the superclass. If this method had not been overridden here, the **Circle** version of **getName** would be inherited. Other methods include **setHeight** to assign a new **height** to a **Cylinder** and **getHeight** to return the **height** of a **Cylinder**.

```
// Fig. 9.25: Cylinder.java
// Definition of class Cylinder.

public class Cylinder extends Circle {
   protected double height;  // height of Cylinder

   // no-argument constructor
   public Cylinder()
   {
      // implicit call to superclass constructor here
      setHeight( 0 );
   }

   // constructor
   public Cylinder( double cylinderHeight,
      double cylinderRadius, int xCoordinate,
      int yCoordinate )
   {
      // call superclass constructor
      super( cylinderRadius, xCoordinate, yCoordinate );
```

Fig. 9.25 **Cylinder** subclass of **Circle**—indirect subclass of abstract class **Shape** (part 1 of 2).

```java

      setHeight( cylinderHeight );
   }

   // set height of Cylinder
   public void setHeight( double cylinderHeight )
   {
      height = ( cylinderHeight >= 0 ? cylinderHeight : 0 );
   }

   // get height of Cylinder
   public double getHeight()
   {
      return height;
   }

   // calculate area of Cylinder (i.e., surface area)
   public double area()
   {
      return 2 * super.area() + 2 * Math.PI * radius * height;
   }

   // calculate volume of Cylinder
   public double volume()
   {
      return super.area() * height;
   }

   // convert Cylinder to a String representation
   public String toString()
   {
      return super.toString() + "; Height = " + height;
   }

   // return shape name
   public String getName()
   {
      return "Cylinder";
   }

}  // end class Cylinder
```

Fig. 9.25 **Cylinder** subclass of **Circle**—indirect subclass of abstract class **Shape** (part 2 of 2).

Method **main** of class **Test** (Fig. 9.26) instantiates **Point** object **point**, **Circle** object **circle** and **Cylinder** object **cylinder** (lines 16–18). Next, array **arrayOf-Shapes** is instantiated (line 21). This array of superclass **Shape** references will refer to each subclass object instantiated. At line 24, the reference **point** is assigned to array element **arrayOfShapes[0]**. At line 27, the reference **circle** is assigned to array element **arrayOfShapes[1]**. At line 30, the reference **cylinder** is assigned to array element **arrayOfShapes[2]**. Now, each superclass **Shape** reference in the array refers to a subclass object of type **Point**, **Circle** or **Cylinder**.

```
// Fig. 9.26: Test.java
// Class to test Shape, Point, Circle, Cylinder hierarchy

// Java core packages
import java.text.DecimalFormat;

// Java extension packages
import javax.swing.JOptionPane;

public class Test {

   // test Shape hierarchy
   public static void main( String args[] )
   {
      // create shapes
      Point point = new Point( 7, 11 );
      Circle circle = new Circle( 3.5, 22, 8 );
      Cylinder cylinder = new Cylinder( 10, 3.3, 10, 10 );

      // create Shape array
      Shape arrayOfShapes[] = new Shape[ 3 ];

      // aim arrayOfShapes[ 0 ] at subclass Point object
      arrayOfShapes[ 0 ] = point;

      // aim arrayOfShapes[ 1 ] at subclass Circle object
      arrayOfShapes[ 1 ] = circle;

      // aim arrayOfShapes[ 2 ] at subclass Cylinder object
      arrayOfShapes[ 2 ] = cylinder;

      // get name and String representation of each shape
      String output =
         point.getName() + ": " + point.toString() + "\n" +
         circle.getName() + ": " + circle.toString() + "\n" +
         cylinder.getName() + ": " + cylinder.toString();

      DecimalFormat precision2 = new DecimalFormat( "0.00" );

      // loop through arrayOfShapes and get name,
      // area and volume of each shape in arrayOfShapes
      for ( int i = 0; i < arrayOfShapes.length; i++ ) {
         output += "\n\n" + arrayOfShapes[ i ].getName() +
            ": " + arrayOfShapes[ i ].toString() +
            "\nArea = " +
            precision2.format( arrayOfShapes[ i ].area() ) +
            "\nVolume = " +
            precision2.format( arrayOfShapes[ i ].volume() );
      }

      JOptionPane.showMessageDialog( null, output,
         "Demonstrating Polymorphism",
         JOptionPane.INFORMATION_MESSAGE );
```

Fig. 9.26 **Shape**, **Point**, **Circle**, **Cylinder** hierarchy (part 1 of 2).

```
54
55          System.exit( 0 );
56      }
57
58  }  // end class Test
```

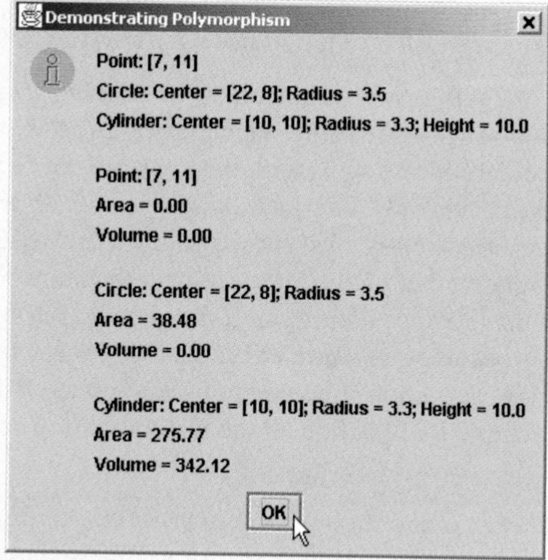

Fig. 9.26 **Shape**, **Point**, **Circle**, **Cylinder** hierarchy (part 2 of 2).

Lines 33 through 36 invoke methods **getName** and **toString** to illustrate that the objects are initialized correctly (as in the first three lines of the screen capture).

Next, the **for** structure at lines 42–49 walks through **arrayOfShapes**, and the following calls are made during each iteration of the loop:

```
arrayOfShapes[ i ].getName()
arrayOfShapes[ i ].toString()
arrayOfShapes[ i ].area()
arrayOfShapes[ i ].volume()
```

Each of these method calls is invoked on the object to which **arrayOfShapes[i]** currently refers. When the compiler looks at each of these calls, it is simply trying to determine whether a **Shape** reference (**arrayOfShapes[i]**) can be used to call these methods. For methods **getName**, **area** and **volume** the answer is yes, because each of these methods is defined in class **Shape**. For method **toString**, the compiler first looks at class **Shape** to determine that **toString** is not defined there, then the compiler proceeds to **Shape**'s superclass (**Object**) to determine whether **Shape** inherited a **toString** method that takes no arguments (as it did, because all **Object**s have a **toString** method).

The screen capture illustrates that all four methods are invoked properly based on the type of the referenced object. First, the string **"Point: "** and the coordinates of the object **point** (**arrayOfShapes[0]**) are output; the area and volume are both **0**. Next, the string **"Circle: "**, the coordinates of object **circle**, and the radius of object **circle** (**arrayOfShapes[1]**) are output; the area of **circle** is calculated and the volume is

0. Finally, the string **"Cylinder: "**, the coordinates of object **cylinder**, the radius of object **cylinder** and the height of object **cylinder** (**arrayOfShapes[2]**) are output; the area of **cylinder** is calculated and the volume of **cylinder** is calculated. All the method calls to **getName**, **toString**, **area** and **volume** are resolved at run-time with dynamic binding.

9.19 Case Study: Creating and Using Interfaces

Our next example (Fig. 9.27–Fig. 9.31) reexamines the **Point**, **Circle**, **Cylinder** hierarchy one last time, replacing **abstract** superclass **Shape** with the interface **Shape** (Fig. 9.27). An interface definition begins with the keyword ***interface*** and contains a set of **public abstract** methods. Interfaces may also contain **public static final** data. To use an interface, a class must specify that it **implements** the interface and the class must define every method in the interface with the number of arguments and the return type specified in the interface definition. If the class leaves any method of the interface undefined, the class becomes an **abstract** class and must be declared **abstract** in the first line of its class definition. Implementing a interface is like signing a contract with the compiler that states, "I will define all the methods specified by the interface."

Common Programming Error 9.9

*Leaving a method of an **interface** undefined in a class that **implements** the interface results in a compile error indicating that the class must be declared **abstract**.*

Software Engineering Observation 9.30

*Declaring a **final** reference indicates that the reference always refers to the same object. However, this does not affect the object to which the reference refers—the object's data still can be modified.*

We started using the concept of an interface when we introduced GUI event handling in Chapter 6, "Methods." Recall that our applet class included **implements ActionListener** (an interface in package **java.awt.event**). The reason we were required to define **actionPerformed** in the applets with event handling is that **ActionListener** is an interface that specifies that **actionPerformed** must be defined. Interfaces are an important part of GUI event handling, as we will discuss in the next section.

An interface is typically used in place of an **abstract** class when there is no default implementation to inherit—i.e., no instance variables and no default method implementations. Like **public abstract** classes, **interface**s are typically **public** data types, so they are normally defined in files by themselves with the same name as the interface and the **.java** extension.

The definition of interface **Shape** begins in Fig. 9.27 at line 4. Interface **Shape** has **abstract** methods **area**, **volume** and **getName**. By coincidence, all three methods take no arguments. However, this is not a requirement of methods in an interface.

In Fig. 9.28, line 4 indicates that class **Point** extends class **Object** and implements interface **Shape**. Class **Point** provides definitions of all three methods in the interface. Method **area** is defined at lines 45–48. Method **volume** is defined at lines 51–54. Method **getName** is defined at lines 57–60. These three methods satisfy the implementation requirement for the three methods defined in the interface. We have fulfilled our contract with the compiler.

```
// Fig. 9.27: Shape.java
// Definition of interface Shape

public interface Shape {

   // calculate area
   public abstract double area();

   // calculate volume
   public abstract double volume();

   // return shape name
   public abstract String getName();
}
```

Fig. 9.27 Point, circle, cylinder hierarchy with a **Shape** interface.

```
// Fig. 9.28: Point.java
// Definition of class Point

public class Point extends Object implements Shape {
   protected int x, y; // coordinates of the Point

   // no-argument constructor
   public Point()
   {
      setPoint( 0, 0 );
   }

   // constructor
   public Point( int xCoordinate, int yCoordinate )
   {
      setPoint( xCoordinate, yCoordinate );
   }

   // Set x and y coordinates of Point
   public void setPoint( int xCoordinate, int yCoordinate )
   {
      x = xCoordinate;
      y = yCoordinate;
   }

   // get x coordinate
   public int getX()
   {
      return x;
   }

```

Fig. 9.28 **Point** implementation of interface **Shape** (part 1 of 2).

```
    // get y coordinate
    public int getY()
    {
       return y;
    }

    // convert point into String representation
    public String toString()
    {
       return "[" + x + ", " + y + "]";
    }

    // calculate area
    public double area()
    {
       return 0.0;
    }

    // calculate volume
    public double volume()
    {
       return 0.0;
    }

    // return shape name
    public String getName()
    {
       return "Point";
    }

 }  // end class Point
```

Fig. 9.28 **Point** implementation of interface **Shape** (part 2 of 2).

When a class implements an interface, the same *is a* relationship provided by inheritance applies. For example, class **Point** implements **Shape**. Therefore, a **Point** object *is a* **Shape**. In fact, objects of any class that extends **Point** are also **Shape** objects. Using this relationship, we have maintained the original definitions of class **Circle**, class **Cylinder** and application class **Test** from Section 9.18 (repoeated in Fig. 9.29–Fig. 9.31) to illustrate that an interface can be used instead of an **abstract** class to process **Shape**s polymorphically. Notice that the output for the program (Fig. 9.31) is identical to Fig. 9.22. Also, notice that **Object** method **toString** is called through a **Shape** interface reference (line 44).

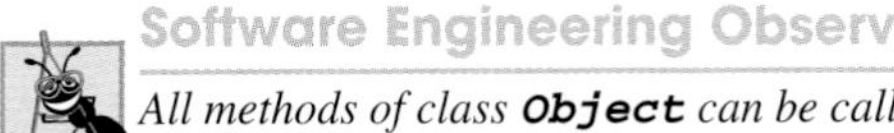

Software Engineering Observation 9.31

All methods of class **Object** *can be called by using a reference of an interface data type—a reference refers to an object, and all objects have the methods defined by class* **Object**.

One benefit of using interfaces is that a class can implement as many interfaces as it needs in addition to extending a class. To implement more than one interface, simply provide a comma-separated list of interface names after keyword **implements** in the class definition. This is particularly useful in the GUI event-handling mechanism. A class that implements more than one event-listener interface (such as **ActionListener** in earlier examples) can process different types of GUI events, as we will see in Chapter 12 and Chapter 13.

```
// Fig. 9.29: Circle.java
// Definition of class Circle

public class Circle extends Point {  // inherits from Point
   protected double radius;

   // no-argument constructor
   public Circle()
   {
      // implicit call to superclass constructor here
      setRadius( 0 );
   }

   // constructor
   public Circle( double circleRadius, int xCoordinate,
      int yCoordinate )
   {
      // call superclass constructor
      super( xCoordinate, yCoordinate );

      setRadius( circleRadius );
   }

   // set radius of Circle
   public void setRadius( double circleRadius )
   {
      radius = ( circleRadius >= 0 ? circleRadius : 0 );
   }

   // get radius of Circle
   public double getRadius()
   {
      return radius;
   }

   // calculate area of Circle
   public double area()
   {
      return Math.PI * radius * radius;
   }

   // convert Circle to a String represention
   public String toString()
   {
      return "Center = " + super.toString() +
         "; Radius = " + radius;
   }
```

Fig. 9.29 **Circle** subclass of **Point**—indirect implementation of interface **Shape** (part 1 of 2).

```java

    // return shape name
    public String getName()
    {
       return "Circle";
    }

 }  // end class Circle
```

Fig. 9.29 **Circle** subclass of **Point**—indirect implementation of interface **Shape** (part 2 of 2).

```java
// Fig. 9.30: Cylinder.java
// Definition of class Cylinder.

public class Cylinder extends Circle {
   protected double height;  // height of Cylinder

   // no-argument constructor
   public Cylinder()
   {
      // implicit call to superclass constructor here
      setHeight( 0 );
   }

   // constructor
   public Cylinder( double cylinderHeight,
      double cylinderRadius, int xCoordinate,
      int yCoordinate )
   {
      // call superclass constructor
      super( cylinderRadius, xCoordinate, yCoordinate );

      setHeight( cylinderHeight );
   }

   // set height of Cylinder
   public void setHeight( double cylinderHeight )
   {
      height = ( cylinderHeight >= 0 ? cylinderHeight : 0 );
   }

   // get height of Cylinder
   public double getHeight()
   {
      return height;
   }

   // calculate area of Cylinder (i.e., surface area)
   public double area()
   {
```

Fig. 9.30 **Cylinder** subclass of **Circle**—indirect implementation of interface **Shape** (part 1 of 2).

```
         return 2 * super.area() + 2 * Math.PI * radius * height;
      }

      // calculate volume of Cylinder
      public double volume()
      {
         return super.area() * height;
      }

      // convert Cylinder to a String representation
      public String toString()
      {
         return super.toString() + "; Height = " + height;
      }

      // return shape name
      public String getName()
      {
         return "Cylinder";
      }

   }  // end class Cylinder
```

Fig. 9.30 **Cylinder** subclass of **Circle**—indirect implementation of interface **Shape** (part 2 of 2).

```
// Fig. 9.31: Test.java
// Test Point, Circle, Cylinder hierarchy with interface Shape.

// Java core packages
import java.text.DecimalFormat;

// Java extension packages
import javax.swing.JOptionPane;

public class Test {

   // test Shape hierarchy
   public static void main( String args[] )
   {
      // create shapes
      Point point = new Point( 7, 11 );
      Circle circle = new Circle( 3.5, 22, 8 );
      Cylinder cylinder = new Cylinder( 10, 3.3, 10, 10 );

      // create Shape array
      Shape arrayOfShapes[] = new Shape[ 3 ];

      // aim arrayOfShapes[ 0 ] at subclass Point object
      arrayOfShapes[ 0 ] = point;

```

Fig. 9.31 **Shape**, **Point**, **Circle**, **Cylinder** hierarchy (part 1 of 2).

```
      // aim arrayOfShapes[ 1 ] at subclass Circle object
      arrayOfShapes[ 1 ] = circle;

      // aim arrayOfShapes[ 2 ] at subclass Cylinder object
      arrayOfShapes[ 2 ] = cylinder;

      // get name and String representation of each shape
      String output =
         point.getName() + ": " + point.toString() + "\n" +
         circle.getName() + ": " + circle.toString() + "\n" +
         cylinder.getName() + ": " + cylinder.toString();

      DecimalFormat precision2 = new DecimalFormat( "0.00" );

      // loop through arrayOfShapes and get name,
      // area and volume of each shape in arrayOfShapes
      for ( int i = 0; i < arrayOfShapes.length; i++ ) {
         output += "\n\n" + arrayOfShapes[ i ].getName() +
            ": " + arrayOfShapes[ i ].toString() +
            "\nArea = " +
            precision2.format( arrayOfShapes[ i ].area() ) +
            "\nVolume = " +
            precision2.format( arrayOfShapes[ i ].volume() );
      }

      JOptionPane.showMessageDialog( null, output,
         "Demonstrating Polymorphism",
         JOptionPane.INFORMATION_MESSAGE );

      System.exit( 0 );
   }

}  // end class Test
```

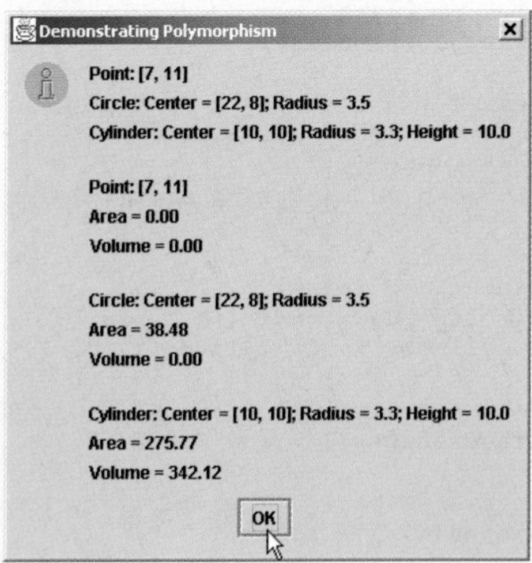

Fig. 9.31 **Shape**, **Point**, **Circle**, **Cylinder** hierarchy (part 2 of 2).

Another use of interfaces is to define a set of constants that can be used in many class definitions. Consider interface **Constants**

```
public interface Constants {
   public static final int ONE = 1;
   public static final int TWO = 2;
   public static final int THREE = 3;
}
```

Classes that implement interface **Constants** can use **ONE**, **TWO** and **THREE** anywhere in the class definition. A class can even use these constants by importing the interface, then referring to each constant as **Constants.ONE**, **Constants.TWO** and **Constants.THREE**. There are no methods declared in this interface, so a class that implements the interface is not required to provide any method implementations.

9.20 Inner Class Definitions

All the class definitions discussed so far were defined at file scope. For example, if a file contained two classes, one class was not nested in the body of the other class. Java provides a facility called *inner classes*, in which classes can be defined inside other classes. Such classes can be complete class definitions or *anonymous inner class* definitions (classes without a name). Inner classes are used mainly in event handling. However, they have other benefits. For example, the implementation of the queue abstract data type discussed in Section 8.16.1 might use an inner class to represent the objects that store each item currently in the queue. Only the queue data structure requires knowledge of how the objects are stored internally, so the implementation can be hidden by defining an inner class as part of class **Queue**.

Inner classes frequently are used with GUI event handling, we take this opportunity not only to show you inner class definitions, but also to demonstrate an application that executes in its own window. After you complete this example, you will be able to use in your applications the GUI techniques shown only in applets so far.

To demonstrate an inner class definition, Fig. 9.33 uses a simplified version of the **Time3** class (renamed **Time** in Fig. 9.32) from Figure 8.8. Class **Time** provides a default constructor, the same *set/get* methods as Figure 8.8 and a **toString** method. Also, this program defines class **TimeTestWindow** as an application. The application executes in its own window. [*Note*: We do not discuss class Time here, because all its features were discussed in Chapter 8.]

```
// Fig. 9.32: Time.java
// Time class definition.

// Java core packages
import java.text.DecimalFormat;

// This class maintains the time in 24-hour format
public class Time extends Object {
   private int hour;      // 0 - 23
   private int minute;    // 0 - 59
   private int second;    // 0 - 59
```

Fig. 9.32 **Time** class (part 1 of 3).

```

   // Time constructor initializes each instance variable
   // to zero. Ensures that Time object starts in a
   // consistent state.
   public Time()
   {
      setTime( 0, 0, 0 );
   }

   // Set a new time value using universal time. Perform
   // validity checks on the data. Set invalid values to zero.
   public void setTime( int hour, int minute, int second )
   {
      setHour( hour );
      setMinute( minute );
      setSecond( second );
   }

   // validate and set hour
   public void setHour( int h )
   {
      hour = ( ( h >= 0 && h < 24 ) ? h : 0 );
   }

   // validate and set minute
   public void setMinute( int m )
   {
      minute = ( ( m >= 0 && m < 60 ) ? m : 0 );
   }

   // validate and set second
   public void setSecond( int s )
   {
      second = ( ( s >= 0 && s < 60 ) ? s : 0 );
   }

   // get hour
   public int getHour()
   {
      return hour;
   }

   // get minute
   public int getMinute()
   {
      return minute;
   }

   // get second
   public int getSecond()
   {
      return second;
   }
```

Fig. 9.32 **Time** class (part 2 of 3).

```

   // convert to String in standard-time format
   public String toString()
   {
      DecimalFormat twoDigits = new DecimalFormat( "00" );

      return ( ( getHour() == 12 || getHour() == 0 ) ?
         12 : getHour() % 12 ) + ":" +
         twoDigits.format( getMinute() ) + ":" +
         twoDigits.format( getSecond() ) +
         ( getHour() < 12 ? " AM" : " PM" );
   }

}  // end class Time
```

Fig. 9.32 **Time** class (part 3 of 3).

```
// Fig. 9.33: TimeTestWindow.java
// Demonstrating the Time class set and get methods

// Java core packages
import java.awt.*;
import java.awt.event.*;

// Java extension packages
import javax.swing.*;

public class TimeTestWindow extends JFrame {
   private Time time;
   private JLabel hourLabel, minuteLabel, secondLabel;
   private JTextField hourField, minuteField,
      secondField, displayField;
   private JButton exitButton;

   // set up GUI
   public TimeTestWindow()
   {
      super( "Inner Class Demonstration" );

      time = new Time();

      // create an instance of inner class ActionEventHandler
      ActionEventHandler handler = new ActionEventHandler();

      // set up GUI
      Container container = getContentPane();
      container.setLayout( new FlowLayout() );

      hourLabel = new JLabel( "Set Hour" );
      hourField = new JTextField( 10 );
      hourField.addActionListener( handler );
```

Fig. 9.33 Demonstrating an inner class in a windowed application (part 1 of 4).

```
      container.add( hourLabel );
      container.add( hourField );

      minuteLabel = new JLabel( "Set minute" );
      minuteField = new JTextField( 10 );
      minuteField.addActionListener( handler );
      container.add( minuteLabel );
      container.add( minuteField );

      secondLabel = new JLabel( "Set Second" );
      secondField = new JTextField( 10 );
      secondField.addActionListener( handler );
      container.add( secondLabel );
      container.add( secondField );

      displayField = new JTextField( 30 );
      displayField.setEditable( false );
      container.add( displayField );

      exitButton = new JButton( "Exit" );
      exitButton.addActionListener( handler );
      container.add( exitButton );

   }  // end constructor

   // display time in displayField
   public void displayTime()
   {
      displayField.setText( "The time is: " + time );
   }

   // create TimeTestWindow and display it
   public static void main( String args[] )
   {
      TimeTestWindow window = new TimeTestWindow();

      window.setSize( 400, 140 );
      window.setVisible( true );
   }

   // inner class definition for handling JTextField and
   // JButton events
   private class ActionEventHandler
      implements ActionListener {

      // method to handle action events
      public void actionPerformed( ActionEvent event )
      {
         // user pressed exitButton
         if ( event.getSource() == exitButton )
            System.exit( 0 );   // terminate the application

```

Fig. 9.33 Demonstrating an inner class in a windowed application (part 2 of 4).

```
         // user pressed Enter key in hourField
         else if ( event.getSource() == hourField ) {
            time.setHour(
               Integer.parseInt( event.getActionCommand() ) );
            hourField.setText( "" );
         }

         // user pressed Enter key in minuteField
         else if ( event.getSource() == minuteField ) {
            time.setMinute(
               Integer.parseInt( event.getActionCommand() ) );
            minuteField.setText( "" );
         }

         // user pressed Enter key in secondField
         else if ( event.getSource() == secondField ) {
            time.setSecond(
               Integer.parseInt( event.getActionCommand() ) );
            secondField.setText( "" );
         }

         displayTime();
      }

   }  // end inner class ActionEventHandler

}  // end class TimeTestWindow
```

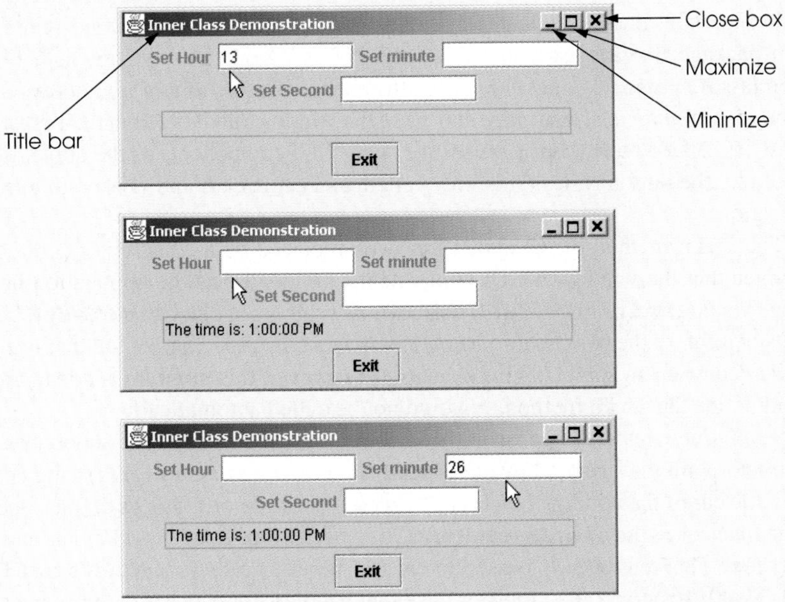

Fig. 9.33 Demonstrating an inner class in a windowed application (part 3 of 4).

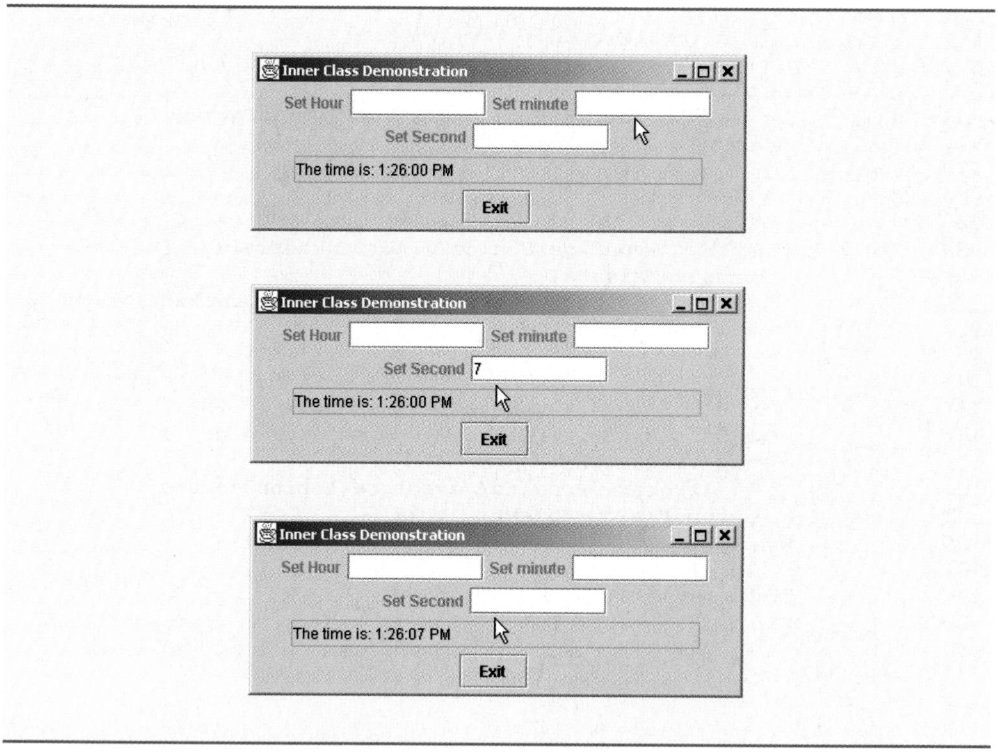

Fig. 9.33 Demonstrating an inner class in a windowed application (part 4 of 4).

In Fig. 9.33, line 11 indicates that class **TimeTestWindow** extends class ***JFrame*** (from package **javax.swing**) rather than class **JApplet** (as shown in Figure 8.8). Superclass **JFrame** provides the basic attributes and behaviors of a window—a *title bar* and buttons to *minimize*, *maximize* and *close* the window (all labeled in the first screen capture). Class **TimeTestWindow** uses the same GUI components as the applet of Fig. 8.8, except that the button (line 16) is now called **exitButton** and is used to terminate the application.

The **init** method of the applet has been replaced by a constructor (lines 19–54) to guarantee that the window's GUI components are created as the application begins executing. Method **main** (lines 67–73) defines a **new** object of class **TimeTestWindow** that results in a call to the constructor. Remember, **init** is a special method that is guaranteed to be called when an applet begins execution. However, this program is not an applet, so if we did define the **init** method, it would not be called automatically.

Several new features appear in the constructor. Line 21 calls the superclass **JFrame** constructor with the string **"Inner Class Demonstration"**. This string is displayed in the title bar of the window by class **JFrame**'s constructor. Line 26 defines one instance of our inner class **ActionEventHandler** (defined at lines 77–111) and assigns it to **handler**. This reference is passed to each of the four calls to **addActionListener** (lines 34, 40, 46 and 55) that register the event handlers for each GUI component that generates events in this example (**hourField**, **minuteField**, **secondField** and **exitButton**). Each call to **addActionListener** requires an object of type

ActionListener to be passed as an argument. Actually, **handler** *is an* **ActionListener**. Line 77 (the first line of the inner class definition) indicates that inner class **ActionEventHandler** implements **ActionListener**. Thus, every object of type **ActionEventHandler** *is an* **ActionListener**. The requirement that **addActionListener** be passed an object of type **ActionListener** is satisfied! The *is a* relationship is used extensively in the GUI event-handling mechanism, as you will see over the next several chapters. The inner class is defined as **private** because it will be used only in this class definition. Inner classes can be **private**, **protected** or **public**.

An inner class object has a special relationship with the outer class object that creates it. The inner class object is allowed to access directly all the instance variables and methods of the outer class object. The **actionPerformed** method (line 77–105) of class **ActionEventHandler** does just that. Throughout the method, the instance variables **time**, **exitButton**, **hourField**, **minuteField** and **secondField** are used, as is method **displayTime**. Notice that none of these needs a "handle" to the outer class object. This is a free relationship created by the compiler between the outer class and its inner classes.

Software Engineering Observation 9.32

An inner class object is allowed to access directly all the variables and methods of the outer class object that defined it.

This application must be terminated by pressing the **Exit** button. Remember, an application that displays a window must be terminated with a call to **System.exit(0)**. Also note that a window in Java is 0 pixels wide, 0 pixels tall and not displayed by default. Lines 71–72 use methods **resize** and **setVisible** to size the window and display it on the screen. These methods are defined in class **java.awt.Component** originally and inherited into class **JFrame**.

An inner class can also be defined inside a method of a class. Such an inner class has access to its outer class's members. However, it has limited access to the local variables for the method in which it is defined.

Software Engineering Observation 9.33

An inner class defined in a method is allowed to access directly all the instance variables and methods of the outer class object that defined it and any **final** *local variables in the method.*

The application of Fig. 9.34 modifies class **TimeTestWindow** of Fig. 9.33 to use *anonymous inner classes* defined in methods. An anonymous inner class has no name, so one object of the anonymous inner class must be created at the point where the class is defined in the program. We demonstrate anonymous inner classes two ways in this example. First, we use separate anonymous inner classes that implement an interface (**ActionListener**) to create event handlers for each of the three **JTextField**s **hourField**, **minuteField** and **secondField**. We also demonstrate how to terminate an application when the user clicks the Close box on the window. The event handler is defined as an anonymous inner class that extends a class (**WindowAdapter**). The **Time** class used is identical to Fig. 9.32, so it is not included here. Also, the **Exit** button has been removed from this example.

```
// Fig. 9.34: TimeTestWindow.java
// Demonstrating the Time class set and get methods

// Java core packages
import java.awt.*;
import java.awt.event.*;

// Java extension packages
import javax.swing.*;

public class TimeTestWindow extends JFrame {
   private Time time;
   private JLabel hourLabel, minuteLabel, secondLabel;
   private JTextField hourField, minuteField,
      secondField, displayField;

   // set up GUI
   public TimeTestWindow()
   {
      super( "Inner Class Demonstration" );

      // create Time object
      time = new Time();

      // create GUI
      Container container = getContentPane();
      container.setLayout( new FlowLayout() );

      hourLabel = new JLabel( "Set Hour" );
      hourField = new JTextField( 10 );

      // register hourField event handler
      hourField.addActionListener(

         // anonymous inner class
         new ActionListener() {

            public void actionPerformed( ActionEvent event )
            {
               time.setHour(
                  Integer.parseInt( event.getActionCommand() ) );
               hourField.setText( "" );
               displayTime();
            }

         } // end anonymous inner class

      ); // end call to addActionListener

      container.add( hourLabel );
      container.add( hourField );

```

Fig. 9.34 Demonstrating anonymous inner classes (part 1 of 4).

```
      minuteLabel = new JLabel( "Set minute" );
      minuteField = new JTextField( 10 );

      // register minuteField event handler
      minuteField.addActionListener(

         // anonymous inner class
         new ActionListener() {

            public void actionPerformed( ActionEvent event )
            {
               time.setMinute(
                  Integer.parseInt( event.getActionCommand() ) );
               minuteField.setText( "" );
               displayTime();
            }

         } // end anonymous inner class

      ); // end call to addActionListener

      container.add( minuteLabel );
      container.add( minuteField );

      secondLabel = new JLabel( "Set Second" );
      secondField = new JTextField( 10 );

      secondField.addActionListener(

         // anonymous inner class
         new ActionListener() {

            public void actionPerformed( ActionEvent event )
            {
               time.setSecond(
                  Integer.parseInt( event.getActionCommand() ) );
               secondField.setText( "" );
               displayTime();
            }

         } // end anonymous inner class

      ); // end call to addActionListener

      container.add( secondLabel );
      container.add( secondField );

      displayField = new JTextField( 30 );
      displayField.setEditable( false );
      container.add( displayField );
   }

```

Fig. 9.34 Demonstrating anonymous inner classes (part 2 of 4).

```
    // display time in displayField
    public void displayTime()
    {
       displayField.setText( "The time is: " + time );
    }

    // create TimeTestWindow, register for its window events
    // and display it to begin application's execution
    public static void main( String args[] )
    {
       TimeTestWindow window = new TimeTestWindow();

       // register listener for windowClosing event
       window.addWindowListener(

          // anonymous inner class for windowClosing event
          new WindowAdapter() {

             // terminate application when user closes window
             public void windowClosing( WindowEvent event )
             {
                System.exit( 0 );
             }

          }  // end anonymous inner class

       ); // end call to addWindowListener

       window.setSize( 400, 120 );
       window.setVisible( true );
    }

 }  // end class TimeTestWindow
```

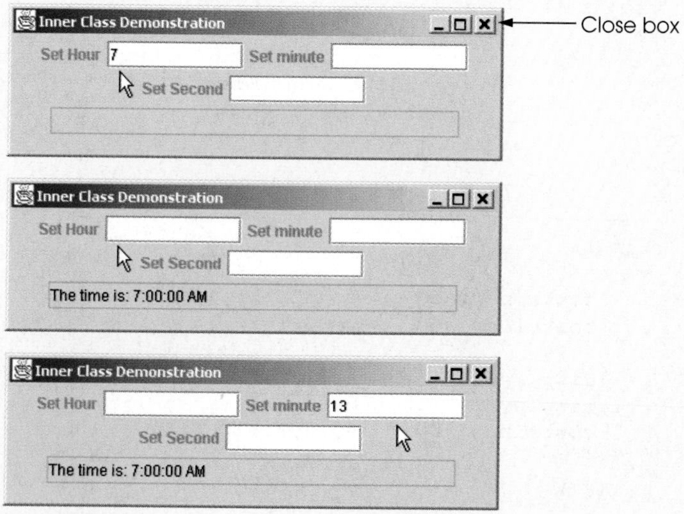

Fig. 9.34 Demonstrating anonymous inner classes (part 3 of 4).

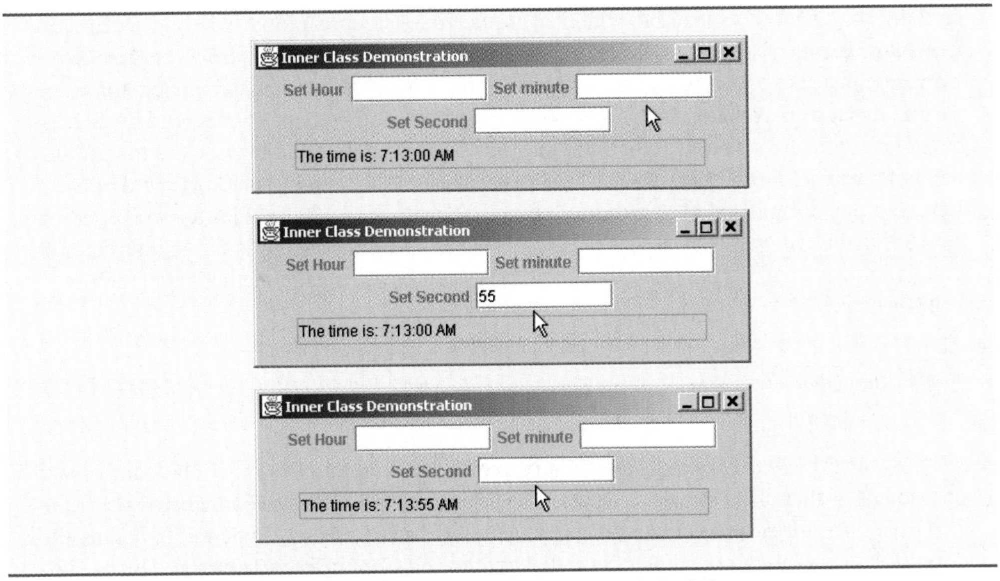

Fig. 9.34 Demonstrating anonymous inner classes (part 4 of 4).

Each of the three **JTextField**s that generate events in this program has a similar anonymous inner class to handle its events, so we discuss only the anonymous inner class for **hourField** here. Lines 33–48 are a call to **hourField**'s **addActionListener** method. The argument to this method must be an object that *is an* **ActionListener** (i.e., any object of a class that implements **ActionListener**). Lines 36–46 use special Java syntax to define an anonymous inner class and create one object of that class that is passed as the argument to **addActionListener**. Line 36 uses operator **new** to create an object. The syntax **ActionListener()** begins the definition of an anonymous inner class that implements interface **ActionListener**. This is similar to beginning a class definition with

```
public class MyHandler implements ActionListener {
```

The parentheses after **ActionListener** indicate a call to the default constructor of the anonymous inner class.

The opening left brace (**{**) at the end of line 36 and the closing right brace (**}**) at line 46 define the body of the class. Lines 38–44 define the **actionPerformed** method that is required in any class that implements **ActionListener**. Method **actionPerformed** is called when the user presses *Enter* while typing in **hourField**.

When an anonymous inner class implements an interface, the class must define every method in the interface.

Method **main** creates one instance of class **TimeTestWindow** (line 115), sizes the window (line 133) and displays the window (line 134).

Windows generate a variety of events that are discussed in Chapter 13. For this example we discuss the one event generated when the user clicks the window's close box—a *window closing event.* Lines 118–131 enable the user to terminate the application by clicking the window's close box (labeled in the first screen capture). Method ***addWindowListener*** registers a window event listener. The argument to **addWindowListener** must be a reference to an object that *is a* ***WindowListener*** (package **java.awt.event**) (i.e., any object of a class that implements **WindowListener**). However, there are seven different methods that must be defined in every class that implements **WindowListener** and we only need one in this example—***windowClosing***. For event handling interfaces with more than one method, Java provides a corresponding class (called an *adapter class*) that already implements all the methods in the interface for you. All you need to do is extend the adapter class and override the methods you require in your program.

Common Programming Error 9.10

Extending an adapter class and misspelling the name of the method you are overriding is a logic error.

Lines 121–129 use special Java syntax to define an anonymous inner class and create one object of that class that is passed as the argument to **addWindowListener**. Line 118 uses operator **new** to create an object. The syntax **WindowAdapter()** begins the definition of an anonymous inner class that extends class **WindowAdapter**. This is similar to beginning a class definition with

```
public class MyHandler extends WindowAdapter {
```

The parentheses after **WindowAdapter** indicate a call to the default constructor of the anonymous inner class. Class **WindowAdapter** implements interface **WindowListener**, so every **WindowAdapter** object *is a* **WindowListener**—the exact type required for the argument to **addWindowListener**.

The opening left brace (**{**) at the end of line 121 and the closing right brace (**}**) at line 129 define the body of the class. Lines 124–127 override the **windowClosing** method of **WindowAdapter** that is called when the user clicks the window's close box. In this example, **windowClosing** terminates the application.

In the last two examples, we have seen that inner classes can be used to create event handlers and that separate anonymous inner classes can be defined to handle events individually for each GUI component. In Chapter 12 and Chapter 13, we revisit this concept as we discuss the event handling mechanism in detail.

9.21 Notes on Inner Class Definitions

This section presents several notes of interest to programmers regarding the definition and use of inner classes.

1. Compiling a class that contains inner classes results in a separate **.class** file for every class. Inner classes with names have the file name *OuterClassName*$*InnerClassName*.class. Anonymous inner classes have the file name *OuterClassName*$*#*.class, where # starts at 1 and is incremented for each anonymous inner class encountered during compilation.
2. Inner classes with class names can be defined as **public**, **protected**, package access or **private** and are subject to the same usage restrictions as other members of a class.

3. To access the outer class's **this** reference, use *OuterClassName*.**this**.
4. The outer class is responsible for creating objects of its inner classes. To create an object of another class's inner class, first create an object of the outer class and assign it to a reference (we will call it **ref**). Then use a statement of the following form to create an inner class object:

   OuterClassName.*InnerClassName* **innerRef = ref.new** *InnerClassName*();

5. An inner class can be declared **static**. A **static** inner class does not require an object of its outer class to be defined (whereas a non**static** inner class does). A **static** inner class does not have access to the outer class's non**static** members.

9.22 Type-Wrapper Classes for Primitive Types

Each of the primitive types has a *type-wrapper class*. These classes are called **Character**, **Byte**, **Short**, **Integer**, **Long**, **Float**, **Double** and **Boolean**. Each type-wrapper class enables you to manipulate primitive types as objects of class **Object**. Therefore, values of the primitive data types can be processed polymorphically if they are maintained as objects of the type-wrapper classes. Many of the classes we will develop or reuse manipulate and share **Object**s. These classes cannot polymorphically manipulate variables of primitive types, but they can polymorphically manipulate objects of the type-wrapper classes, because every class ultimately is derived from class **Object**.

Each of the numeric classes—**Byte**, **Short**, **Integer**, **Long**, **Float** and **Double**—inherits from class **Number**. Each of the type wrappers is declared **final**, so their methods are implicitly **final** and may not be overridden. Note that many of the methods that process the primitive data types are defined as **static** methods of the type-wrapper classes. If you need to manipulate a primitive value in your program, first refer to the documentation for the type-wrapper classes—the method you need might already be defined. We will use the type-wrapper classes polymorphically in our study of data structures in Chapters 22 and 23.

9.23 (Optional Case Study) Thinking About Objects: Incorporating Inheritance into the Elevator Simulation

We now examine our elevator simulator design to see whether it might benefit from inheritance. In previous chapters, we have been treating **ElevatorButton** and **FloorButton** as separate classes. These classes, however, have much in common—both have attribute **pressed** and behaviors **pressButton** and **resetButton**. To apply inheritance, we first look for commonality between these classes. We extract this commonality, place it into superclass **Button**, then derive subclasses **ElevatorButton** and **FloorButton** from **Button**.

Let us now examine the similarities between classes **ElevatorButton** and **FloorButton**. Figure 9.35 shows the attributes and operations of each class. Both classes have their attribute (**pressed**) and operations (**pressButton** and **resetButton**) in common.

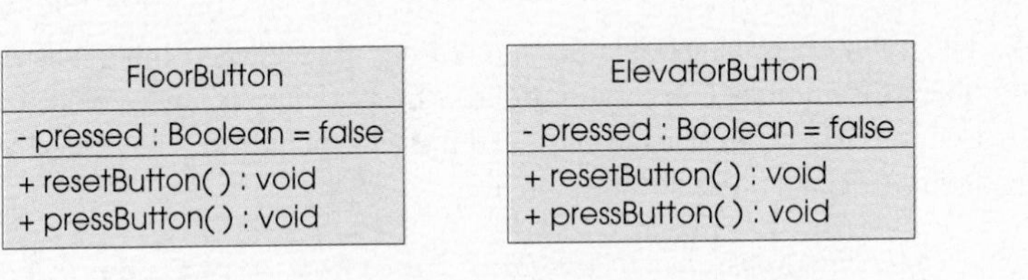

Fig. 9.35 Attributes and operations of classes **FloorButton** and **ElevatorButton**.

We must now examine whether these objects exhibit distinct behavior. If the **ElevatorButton** and **FloorButton** objects have the same behavior, then we cannot justify using two separate classes to instantiate these objects. However, if these objects have distinct behaviors, we can place the common attributes and operations in a superclass **Button**; then **ElevatorButton** and **FloorButton** inherit both the attributes and operations of **Button**.

We have been treating the **FloorButton** as if it behaves differently from the **ElevatorButton**—the **FloorButton** requests the **Elevator** to move to the **Floor** of the request, and the **ElevatorButton** signals the **Elevator** to move to the opposite **Floor**. Under closer scrutiny, we notice that both the **FloorButton** and the **ElevatorButton** signal the **Elevator** to move to a **Floor**, and the **Elevator** decides whether to move. The **Elevator** will sometimes move in response to a signal from the **FloorButton**, and the **Elevator** will always move in response to a signal from the **ElevatorButton**—however, neither the **FloorButton** nor the **ElevatorButton** decides for the **Elevator** that the **Elevator** must move to the other **Floor**. We conclude that both **FloorButton** and **ElevatorButton** have the same behavior—both signal the **Elevator** to move—so we *combine* (not inherit) classes into one **Button** class and discard class **FloorButton** and **ElevatorButton** from our case study.

We turn our attention to classes **ElevatorDoor** and **FloorDoor**. Figure 9.36 shows the attributes and operations of classes **ElevatorDoor** and **FloorDoor**—these two classes are structurally similar to each other as well, because both classes possess the attribute **open** and the two operations **openDoor** and **closeDoor**. In addition, both the **ElevatorDoor** and **FloorDoor** have the same behavior—they inform a **Person** that a door in the simulation has opened. The **Person** then decides either to enter or exit the **Elevator**, depending on which door opened. In other words, neither the **ElevatorDoor** nor the **FloorDoor** decides for the **Person** that the **Person** must enter or exit the **Elevator**. We combine both **ElevatorDoor** and **FloorDoor** into one **Door** class and eliminate classes **ElevatorDoor** and **FloorDoor** from our case study.[2]

2. As we continue to discuss inheritance throughout this section, we refer to the class diagram of Fig. 3.23 to determine similarities among objects. However, this diagram contains classes **FloorButton** and **ElevatorButton**, which we have eliminated recently from the case study. Therefore, during our discussion of inheritance, when we mention the **FloorButton**, we refer to that **Floor**'s **Button** object, and when we mention the **ElevatorButton**, we refer to the **Elevator**'s **Button** object.

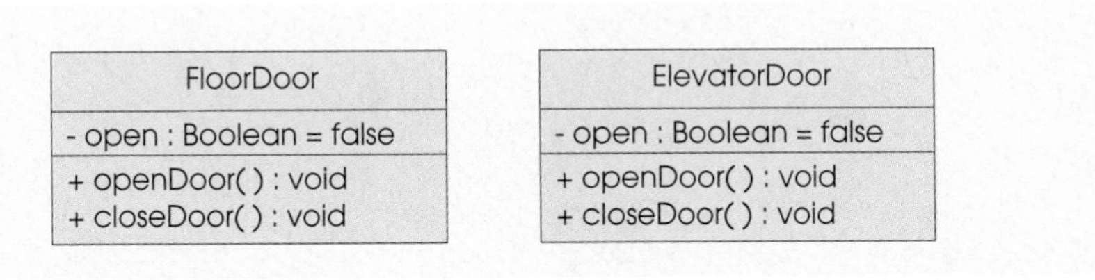

Fig. 9.36 Attributes and operations of classes **FloorDoor** and **ElevatorDoor**.

In Section 4.14, we encountered the problem of representing the location of the **Person**—on what **Floor** is the **Person** located when riding in the **Elevator**? Using inheritance, we may now model a solution. Both the **Elevator** and the two **Floor**s are locations at which the **Person** exists in the simulator. In other words, the **Elevator** and the **Floor**s are *types of* locations. Therefore, classes **Elevator** and **Floor** should inherit from an abstract superclass called **Location**. We declare class **Location** as abstract, because, for the purposes of our simulation, a location is too generic a term to define a real object. The UML requires that we place abstract class names (and abstract methods) in italics. Superclass **Location** contains the **protected** attribute **locationName**, which contains a **String** value of **"firstFloor"**, **"secondFloor"** or **"elevator"**. Therefore, only classes **Elevator** and **Floor** have access to **locationName**. In addition, we include the **public** method **getLocationName** to return the name of the location.

We search for more similarities between classes **Floor** and **Elevator**. First of all, according to the class diagram of Fig. 3.23, **Elevator** contains a reference to both a **Button** and a **Door**—the **ElevatorButton** (the **Elevator**'s **Button**) and the **ElevatorDoor** (the **Elevator**'s **Door**). Class **Floor**, through its association with class **ElevatorShaft** (class **ElevatorShaft** "connects" class **Floor**), also contains a reference to a **Button** and a **Door**—the **FloorButton** (that **Floor**'s **Button**) and the **FloorDoor** (that **Floor**'s **Door**). Therefore, in our simulation, the **Location** class, which is the superclass of classes **Elevator** and **Floor**, will contain **public** methods **getButton** and **getDoor**, which return a **Button** or **Door** reference, respectively. Class **Floor** overrides these methods to return the **Button** and **Door** references of that **Floor**, and class **Elevator** overrides these methods to return the **Button** and **Door** references of the **Elevator**. In other words, class **Floor** and **Elevator** exhibit distinct behavior from each other but share attribute **locationName** and methods **getButton** and **getDoor**—therefore, we may use inheritance for these classes.

The UML offers a relationship called a *generalization* to model inheritance. Figure 9.35 is the generalization diagram of superclass **Location** and subclasses **Elevator** and **Floor**. The empty-head arrows specify that classes **Elevator** and **Floor** inherit from class **Location**. Note that attribute **locationName** has an *access modifier* that we have not yet seen—the pound sign (**#**), indicating that **locationName** is a **protected** member, so **Location** subclasses may access this attribute. Note that classes **Floor** and **Elevator** contain additional attributes and methods that further distinguish these classes.

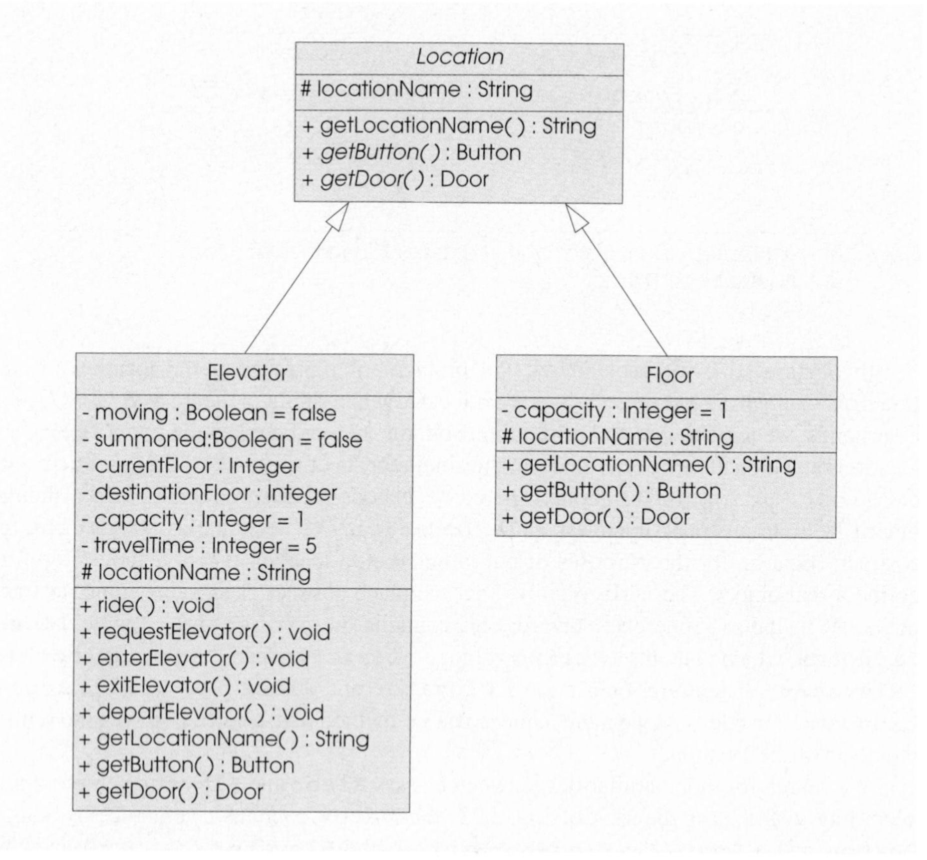

Fig. 9.37 Generalization diagram of superclass **Location** and subclasses **Elevator** and **Floor**.

Classes **Floor** and **Elevator** override methods **getButton** and **getDoor** from their superclass **Location**. In Fig. 9.37, these methods are italicized in class **Location**, indicating that they are *abstract methods*. However, the methods in the subclasses are not italicized—these methods became *concrete methods* by overriding the abstract methods. Class **Person** now contains a **Location** object representing whether the **Person** is on the first or second **Floor** or inside the **Elevator**. We remove the association between **Person** and **Elevator** and the association between **Person** and **Floor** from the class diagram, because the **Location** object acts as both the **Elevator** and **Floor** reference for the **Person**. A **Person** sets its **Location** object to reference the **Elevator** when that **Person** enters the **Elevator**. A **Person** sets its **Location** object to reference a **Floor** when the **Person** is on that **Floor**. Lastly, we assign class **Elevator** two **Location** objects to represent the **Elevator**'s reference to the current **Floor** and destination **Floor** (we originally used integers to describe these references). Figure 9.38 provides an updated class diagram of our model by incorporating inheritance and eliminating classes **FloorButton**, **ElevatorButton**, **FloorDoor** and **ElevatorDoor**.

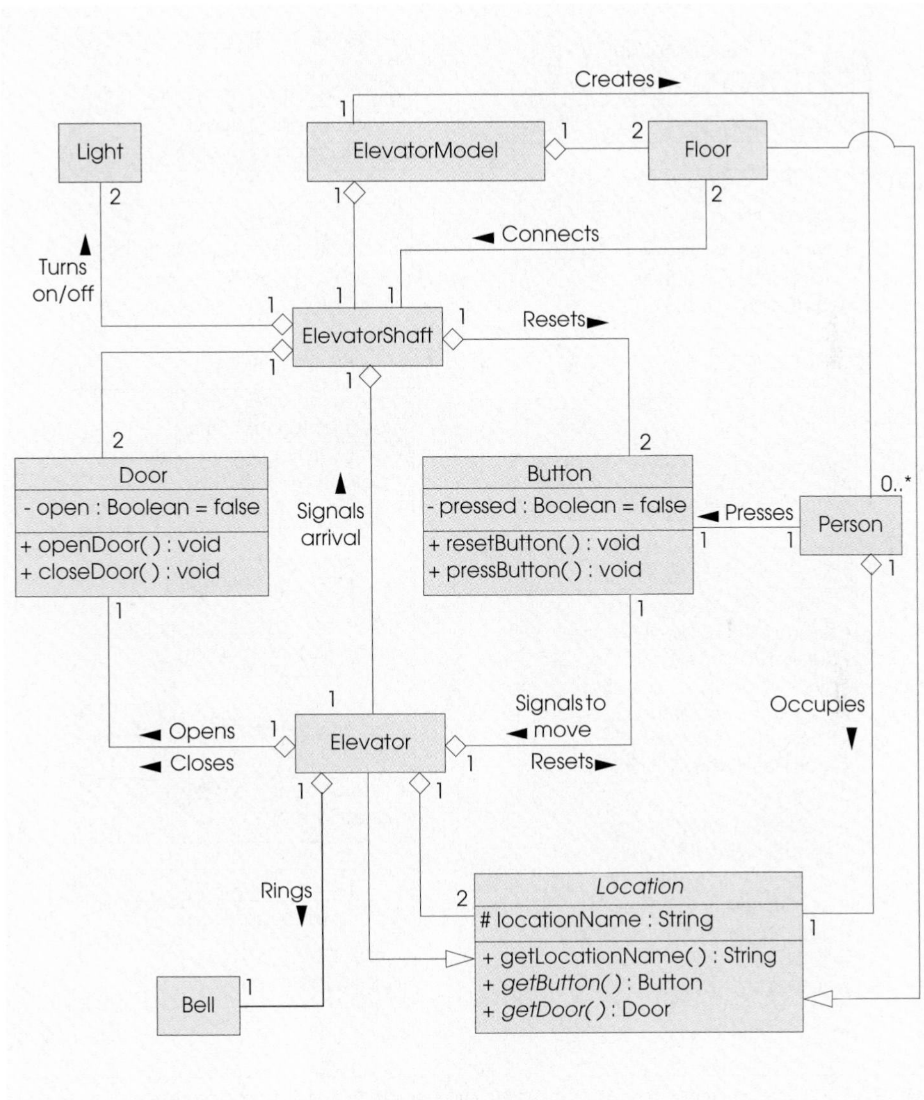

Fig. 9.38 Class diagram of our simulator (incorporating inheritance).

We have allowed a **`Person`**, occupying a **`Location`**, to interact with several of the objects in the simulator. For example, a **`Person`** can press a **`Button`** or be informed when a **`Door`** opens from that **`Person`**'s specific **`Location`**. In addition, because a **`Person`** may occupy only one **`Location`** at a time, that **`Person`** may interact with only the objects known to that **`Location`**—a **`Person`** will never perform an illegal action, such as pressing the first **`Floor`**'s **`Button`** while riding the **`Elevator`**.

We presented the class attributes and operations with access modifiers in Fig. 8.22. Now, we present a modified diagram incorporating inheritance in Fig. 9.39.

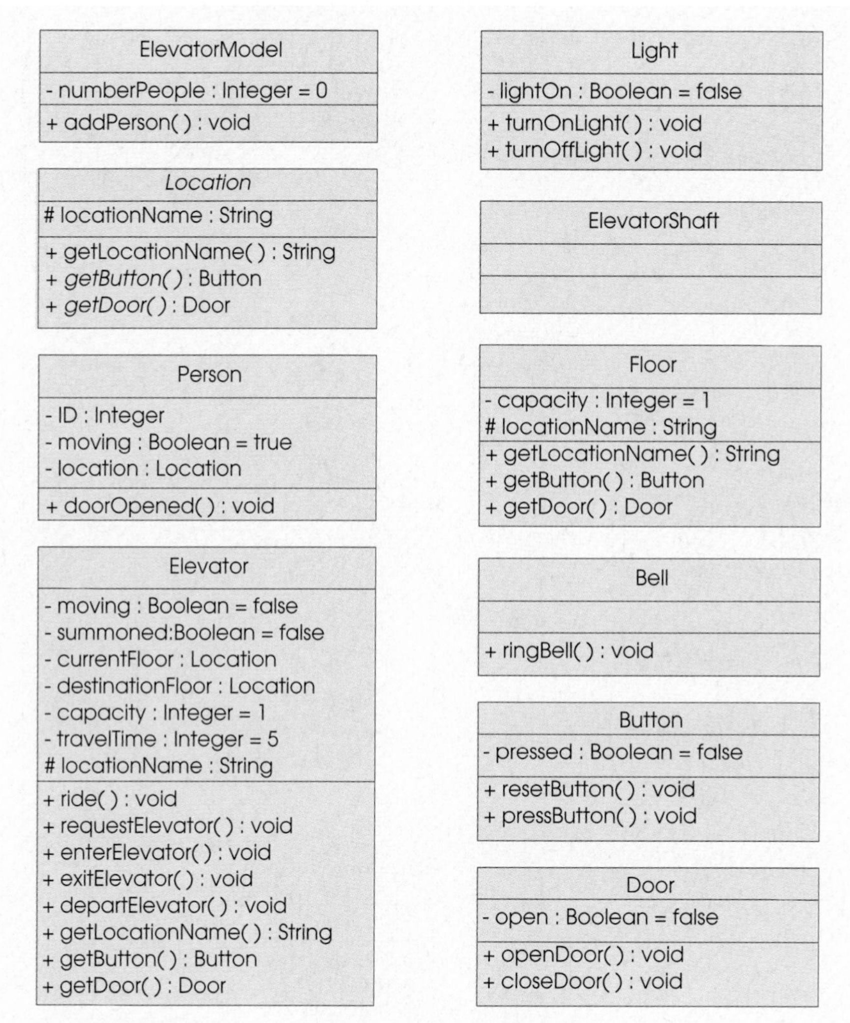

Fig. 9.39 Class diagram with attributes and operations (incorporating inheritance).

Class **`Elevator`** now contains two **`Location`** objects, called **`currentFloor`** and **`destinationFloor`**, replacing the integer values we used previously to describe the **`Floor`**s. Lastly, **`Person`** contains a **`Location`** object named **`location`**, which indicates whether **`Person`** is on a **`Floor`** or in the **`Elevator`**.

Implementation: Forward Engineering (Incorporating Inheritance)

"Thinking About Objects" Section 8.17 used the UML to express the Java class structure for our simulation. We continue our implementation while incorporating inheritance, using class **`Elevator`** as an example. For each class in the class diagram of Fig. 9.38,

1. If a class **A** is a subclass of class **B**, then **A** extends **B** in the class declaration and calls the constructor of **B**. For example, class **Elevator** is a subclass of abstract superclass **Location**, so the class declaration should read

```
public class Elevator extends Location {

   public Elevator
   {
      super();
   }
...
```

2. If class **B** is an abstract class and class **A** is a subclass of class **B**, then class **A** must override the abstract methods of class **B** (if class **A** is to be a concrete class). For example, class **Location** contains abstract methods **getLocationName**, **getButton** and **getDoor**, so class **Elevator** must override these methods (note that **getButton** returns the **Elevator**'s **Button** object, and **getDoor** returns the **Elevator**'s **Door** object—**Elevator** contains associations with both objects, according to the class diagram of Fig. 9.38).

```
public class Elevator extends Location {

   // class attributes
   private boolean moving;
   private boolean summoned;
   private Location currentFloor;
   private Location destinationFloor;
   private int capacity = 1;
   private int travelTime = 5;

   // class objects
   private Button elevatorButton;
   private Door elevatorDoor;
   private Bell bell;

   // class constructor
   public Elevator()
   {
      super();
   }

   // class methods
   public void ride() {}
   public void requestElevator() {}
   public void enterElevator() {}
   public void exitElevator() {}
   public void departElevator() {}

   // method overriding getLocationName
   public String getLocationName()
   {
      return "elevator";
   }
```

```
         // method overriding getButton
         public Button getButton() {}
         {
            return elevatorButton;
         }

         // method overriding getDoor
         public Door getDoor() {}
         {
            return elevatorDoor;
         }
      }
```

Using forward engineering provides a sound beginning for code implementation in any language. "Thinking About Objects" Section 11.10 returns to interactions and focuses on how objects generate and handle the messages passed in collaborations. In addition, we forward engineer more class diagrams to implement these interactions. Eventually, we present the Java code for our simulator in Appendix G, Appendix H and Appendix I.

9.24 (Optional) Discovering Design Patterns: Introducing Creational, Structural and Behavioral Design Patterns

Now that we have introduced object-oriented programming, we begin our deeper presentation of design patterns. In Section 1.17, we mentioned that the "gang of four" described 23 design patterns using three categories—creational, structural and behavioral. In this and the remaining "Discovering Design Patterns" sections, we discuss the design patterns of each type and their importance, and we mention how each pattern relates to the Java material in the book. For example, several Java Swing components that we introduce in Chapters 12 and 13 use the Composite design pattern, so we introduce the Composite design pattern in Section 13.18. Figure 9.40 identifies the 18 gang-of-four design patterns discussed in this book.

Figure 9.40 lists 18 of the most widely used patterns in the software-engineering industry. There are many popular patterns that have been documented since the gang-of-four book—these include the *concurrent design patterns*, which are especially helpful in the design of multithreaded systems. Section 15.13 discusses some of these patterns used in industry. Architectural patterns, as we discuss in Section 17.11, specify how subsystems interact with each other. Figure 9.41 specifies the concurrency patterns and architectural patterns that we discuss in this book.

Section	Creational design patterns	Structural design patterns	Behavioral design patterns
9.24	Singleton	Proxy	Memento State

Fig. 9.40 The 18 Gang-of-four design patterns discussed in *Java How to Program 4/e* (part 1 of 2).

Section	Creational design patterns	Structural design patterns	Behavioral design patterns
13.18	Factory Method	Adapter Bridge Composite	Chain-of-Responsibility Command Observer Strategy Template Method
17.11	Abstract Factory	Decorator Facade	
21.12	Prototype		Iterator

Fig. 9.40 The 18 Gang-of-four design patterns discussed in *Java How to Program 4/e* (part 2 of 2).

Section	Concurrent design patterns	Architectural patterns
15.13	Single-Threaded Execution Guarded Suspension Balking Read/Write Lock Two-Phase Termination	
17.11		Model-View-Controller Layers

Fig. 9.41 Concurrent design patterns and architectural patterns discussed in *Java How to Program, 4/e*.

9.24.1 Creational Design Patterns

Creational design patterns address issues related to the creation of objects, such as preventing a system from creating more than one object of a class (the Singleton creational design pattern) or deferring until execution time the decision as to what types of objects are going to be created (the purpose of the other creational design patterns discussed here). For example, suppose we are designing a 3-D drawing program, in which the user can create several 3-D geometric objects, such as cylinders, spheres, cubes, tetrahedrons, etc. At compile time, the program does not know what shapes the user will choose to draw. Based on user input, this program should be able to determine the class from which to instantiate an object. If the user creates a cylinder in the GUI, our program should "know" to instantiate an object of class **`Cylinder`**. When the user decides what geometric object to draw, the program should determine the specific subclass from which to instantiate that object.

The gang-of-four book describes five creational patterns (four of which we discuss in this book):

- Abstract Factory (Section 17.11)
- Builder (not discussed)

- Factory Method (Section 13.18)
- Prototype (Section 21.12)
- Singleton (Section 9.24)

Singleton

Occasionally, a system should contain exactly one object of a class—that is, once the program instantiates that object, the program should not be allowed to create additional objects of that class. For example, some systems connect to a database using only one object that manages database connections, which ensures that other objects cannot initialize unnecessary connections that would slow the system. The *Singleton design pattern* guarantees that a system instantiates a maximum of one object of a class.

Figure 9.42 demonstrates Java code using the Singleton design pattern. Line 5 declares class **Singleton** as **final**, so methods in this class cannot be overridden to handle multiple instantiations. Lines 11–14 declare a **private** constructor—only class **Singleton** can instantiate a **Singleton** object using this constructor. The **static** method **getSingletonInstance** (lines 17–24) allows the one-time instantiation of a **static** **Singleton** object (declared on line 8) by calling the **private** constructor. If the **Singleton** object has been created, line 23 merely returns a reference to the previously instantiated **Singleton** object.

Lines 10–11 of class **SingletonExample** (Fig. 9.43) declare two references to **Singleton** objects—**firstSingleton** and **secondSingleton**. Lines 14–15 call method **getSingletonInstance** and assign **Singleton** references to **firstSingleton** and **secondSingleton**, respectively. Line 18 tests if these objects reference the same **Singleton** object. Figure 9.44 shows that **firstSingleton** and **secondSingleton** share the same reference to the **Singleton** object, because each time method **getSingletonInstance** is called, it returns a reference to the same **Singleton** object.

```
1  // Singleton.java
2  // Demonstrates Singleton design pattern
3  package com.deitel.jhtp4.designpatterns;
4
5  public final class Singleton {
6
7     // Singleton object returned by method getSingletonInstance
8     private static Singleton singleton;
9
10    // constructor prevents instantiation from other objects
11    private Singleton()
12    {
13       System.err.println( "Singleton object created." );
14    }
15
16    // create Singleton and ensure only one Singleton instance
17    public static Singleton getSingletonInstance()
18    {
```

Fig. 9.42 Class **Singleton** ensures that only one object of its class is created (part 1 of 2).

```
      // instantiate Singleton if null
      if ( singleton == null )
         singleton = new Singleton();

      return singleton;
   }
}
```

Fig. 9.42 Class **Singleton** ensures that only one object of its class is created (part 2 of 2).

```
// SingletonExample.java
// Attempt to create two Singleton objects
package com.deitel.jhtp4.designpatterns;

public class SingletonExample {

   // run SingletonExample
   public static void main( String args[] )
   {
      Singleton firstSingleton;
      Singleton secondSingleton;

      // create Singleton objects
      firstSingleton = Singleton.getSingletonInstance();
      secondSingleton = Singleton.getSingletonInstance();

      // the "two" Singletons should refer to same Singleton
      if ( firstSingleton == secondSingleton )
         System.out.println( "firstSingleton and " +
            "secondSingleton refer to the same Singleton " +
            "object" );
   }
}
```

Fig. 9.43 Class **SingletonExample** attempts to create **Singleton** object more than once.

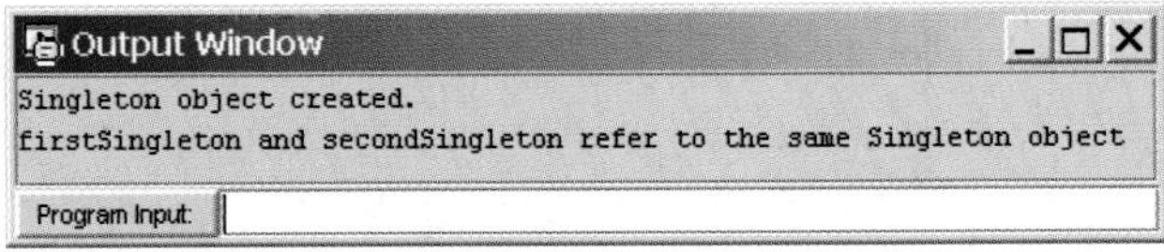

Fig. 9.44 Class **SingletonExample** output shows that the **Singleton** object may be created only once.

9.24.2 Structural Design Patterns

Structural design patterns describe common ways to organize classes and objects in a system. The gang-of-four book describes seven structural design patterns (six of which we discuss in this book):

- Adapter (Section 13.18)
- Bridge (Section 13.18)
- Composite (Section 13.18)
- Decorator (Section 17.11)
- Facade (Section 17.11)
- Flyweight (not discussed)
- Proxy (Section 9.24)

Proxy

An applet should always display something while images load. Whether that "something" is a smaller image or a string of text informing the user that the images are loading, the *Proxy design pattern* can be applied to achieve this effect. This pattern allows one object to act as a replacement for another. Consider loading several large images (several megabytes) in a Java applet. Ideally, we would like to see these images instantaneously—however, loading large images into memory can take time to complete (especially on a slow processor). The Proxy design pattern allows the system to use one object—called a *proxy object*—in place of another. In our example, the proxy object could be a gauge that informs the user of what percentage of a large image has been loaded. When this image finishes loading, the proxy object is no longer needed—the applet can then display an image instead of the proxy.

9.24.3 Behavioral Design Patterns

There are many different examples of *behavioral design patterns*, which provide proven strategies to model how objects collaborate with one another in a system and offer special behaviors appropriate for a wide variety of applications. Let us consider the Observer behavioral design pattern—a classic example of a design pattern illustrating collaborations between objects. For example, GUI components collaborate with their listeners to respond to user interactions. GUI components use this pattern to process user interface events. A listener observes state changes in a particular GUI component by registering to handle that GUI component's events. When the user interacts with that GUI component, the component notifies its listeners (also known as its observers) that the GUI component's state has changed (e.g., a button has been pressed).

Another pattern we consider is the Memento behavioral design pattern—an example of offering special behavior for a wide variety of applications. The Memento pattern enables a system to save an object's state, so that state can be restored at a later time. For example, many applications provide an "undo" capability that allows users to revert to previous versions of their work.

The gang-of-four book describes 11 behavioral design patterns (eight of which we discuss in this book):

- Chain-of-Responsibility (Section 13.18)
- Command (Section 13.18)
- Interpreter (not discussed)
- Iterator (Section 21.12)

- Mediator (not discussed)
- Memento (Section 9.24)
- Observer (Section 13.18)
- State (Section 9.24)
- Strategy (Section 13.18)
- Template Method (Section 13.18)
- Visitor (not discussed)

Memento

Consider a painting program. This type of program allows a user to create graphics. Occasionally the user may position a graphic improperly in the drawing area. Painting programs offer an "undo" feature that allows the user to unwind such an error. Specifically, the program restores the drawing area's state to that before the user placed the graphic. More sophisticated painting programs offer a *history*, which stores several states in a list, so the user can restore the program to any state in the history.The *Memento design pattern* allows an object to save its state, so that—if necessary—the object can be restored to its former state.

The Memento design pattern requires three types of objects. The *originator object* occupies some *state*—the set of attribute values at a specific time in program execution. In our painting-program example, the drawing area acts as the originator, because it contains attribute information describing its state—when the program first executes, the area contains no elements. The *memento object* stores a copy of all attributes associated with the originator's state—i.e., the memento saves the drawing area's state. The memento is stored as the first item in the history list, which acts as the *caretaker object*—the object that contains references to all memento objects associated with the originator.

Now, suppose the user draws a circle in the drawing area. The area contains different information describing its state—a circle object centered at specified *x-y* coordinates. The drawing area then uses another memento to store this information. This memento is stored as the second item in the history list. The history list displays all mementos on screen, so the user can select which state to restore. Suppose the user wishes to remove the circle—if the user selects the first memento from the list, the drawing area uses the first memento to restore itself to a blank area.

State

In certain designs, we must convey an object's state information or represent the various states that an object can occupy. Our optional elevator simulation case study in the "Thinking About Objects" sections uses the *State design pattern*. Our simulation includes an elevator that moves between floors in a two-story building. A person walks across a floor and rides the elevator to the other floor. Originally, we used an integer value to represent on which floor the person is walking. However, we encountered a problem when we tried to answer the question "on what floor is the person when riding the elevator?" Actually, the person is located on neither floor—rather the person is located inside the elevator. We also realized that the elevator and the floors are locations that the person can occupy in our simulation. We created an abstract superclass called **`Location`** to represent a "location." Subclasses **`Elevator`** and **`Floor`** inherit from superclass **`Location`**. Class **`Person`** contains a reference to a **`Location`** object, which represents the current location—elevator, first floor or second floor—of that person. Because a superclass reference can hold a subclass reference, the person's **Location** attribute references the appropriate **Floor** object when that person is on a floor and references the **Elevator** object when that person is inside the elevator.

The elevator and floors contain buttons. (The elevator's button signals the elevator to move to the other floor, and the floors' buttons summon the elevator to the floor of the request.) Because all locations in our simulation contain buttons, class **Location** provides abstract method **getButton**. Class **Elevator** implements method **getButton** to return a reference to the **Button** object inside the elevator, and class **Floor** implements method **getButton** to return a reference to the **Button** object on the floor. Using its **Location** reference, the person is able to press the correct button—i.e., the person will not press a floor's button when inside the elevator and will not press the elevator's button when on a floor.

The State design pattern uses an abstract superclass—called the *State class*—which contains methods that describe behaviors for states that an object (called the *context object*) can occupy. In our elevator simulation, the State class is superclass **Location**, and the context object is the object of class **Person**. Note that class **Location** does not describe all states of class **Person** (e.g., whether that person is walking or waiting for the elevator)—class **Location** describes only the location the **Person** and contains method **getButton** so the **Person** can access the **Button** object at various locations.

A *State subclass*, which extends the State class, represents an individual state that the context can occupy. The State subclasses in our simulation are classes **Elevator** and **Floor**. Each State subclass contains methods that implement the State class' abstract methods. For example, both classes **Elevator** and **Floor** implement method **getButton**.

The context contains exactly one reference to an object of the State class—this reference is called the *state object*. In the simulation, the state object is the object of class **Location**. When the context changes state, the state object references the State subclass object associated with that new state. For example, when the person walks from the floor into the elevator, the **Person** object's **Location** is changed from referencing one of the **Floor** objects to referencing the **Elevator** object. When the person walks onto the floor from the elevator, the **Person** object's **Location** references the appropriate **Floor** object.

9.24.4 Conclusion

In "Discovering Design Patterns" Section 9.24, we listed the three types of design patterns introduced in the gang-of-four book, we identified 18 of these design patterns that we discuss in this book and we discussed specific design patterns, including Singleton, Proxy, Memento and State. In "Discovering Design Patterns" Section 13.18, we introduce some design patterns associated with AWT and Swing GUI components. After reading this section, you should understand better how Java GUI components take advantage of design patterns.

9.24.5 Internet and World-Wide-Web Resources

The following URLs provide further information on the nature, importance and applications of design patterns.

Design Patterns

www.hillside.net/patterns
This page displays links to information on design patterns and languages.

www.hillside.net/patterns/books/
This site lists books on design patterns.

www.netobjectives.com/design.htm
This site introduces the importance of design patterns.

umbc7.umbc.edu/~tarr/dp/dp.html
This site links to design patterns Web sites, tutorials and papers.

www.links2go.com/topic/Design_Patterns
This site links to sites and information on design patterns.

www.c2.com/ppr/
This site discusses recent advances in design patterns and ideas for future projects.

Design Patterns in Java

www.research.umbc.edu/~tarr/cs491/fall00/cs491.html
This site is for a Java design patterns course at the University of Maryland and contains numerous examples of how to apply design patterns in Java.

www.enteract.com/~bradapp/javapats.html
This site discusses Java design patterns and presents design patterns in distributed computing.

www.meurrens.org/ip-Links/java/designPatterns/
This site displays numerous links to resources and information on Java design patterns.

Design Patterns in C++ & Visual Basic

journal.iftech.com/articles/9904_shankel_patterns/
This site provides insight to design patterns (the Iterator design pattern, in particular) in C++.

mspress.microsoft.com/prod/books/sampchap/2322.htm
This site overviews the book, *Microsoft Visual Basic Design Patterns* (Microsoft Press: 2000).

Architectural Patterns

compsci.about.com/science/compsci/library/weekly/aa030600a.htm
This site provides an overview the Model-View-Controller architecture.

www.javaworld.com/javaworld/jw-04-1998/jw-04-howto.html
This site contains an article discussing how Swing components use Model-View-Controller architecture.

www.ootips.org/mvc-pattern.html
This site provides information and tips on using MVC.

www.ftech.co.uk/~honeyg/articles/pda.htm
This site contains an article on the importance of architectural patterns in software.

www.tml.hut.fi/Opinnot/Tik-109.450/1998/niska/sld001.htm
This site provides information on architectural patterns, design pattern, and idioms (patterns targeting a specific language).

SUMMARY

- One of the keys to the power of object-oriented programming is achieving software reusability through inheritance.
- Through inheritance, a new class inherits the instance variables and methods of a previously defined superclass. In this case, the new class is referred to as a subclass.
- With single inheritance, a class is derived from one superclass. With multiple inheritance, a subclass inherits from multiple superclasses. Java does not support multiple inheritance, but Java does provide the notion of interfaces, which offer many of the benefits of multiple inheritance.
- A subclass normally adds instance variables and methods of its own, so a subclass generally is larger than its superclass. A subclass represents a smaller set of more specific objects than its superclass.
- A subclass cannot access the **private** members of its superclass. A subclass can, however, access the **public**, **protected** and package access members of its superclass. The subclass must be in the superclass's package to use superclass members with package access.
- A subclass constructor always calls the constructor for its superclass first (either explicitly or implicitly) to create and initialize the subclass members inherited from the superclass.
- Inheritance enables software reusability, which saves time in development and encourages the use of previously proven and debugged high-quality software.
- An object of a subclass can be treated as an object of its corresponding superclass, but the reverse is not true.
- A superclass exists in a hierarchical relationship with its subclasses.
- When a class is used with the mechanism of inheritance, it becomes either a superclass that supplies attributes and behaviors to other classes or a subclass that inherits those attributes and behaviors.
- An inheritance hierarchy can be arbitrarily deep within the physical limitations of a particular system, but most inheritance hierarchies have only a few levels.
- Hierarchies are useful for understanding and managing complexity. With software becoming increasingly complex, Java provides mechanisms for supporting hierarchical structures through inheritance and polymorphism.
- Modifier **protected** serves as an intermediate level of protection between **public** access and **private** access. Superclass **protected** members may be accessed by methods of the superclass, by methods of subclasses and by methods of classes in the same package.
- A superclass may be either a direct superclass or an indirect superclass. A direct superclass is the class that a subclass explicitly **extends**. An indirect superclass is inherited from several levels up the class hierarchy tree.
- When a superclass member is inappropriate for a subclass, the programmer must override that member in the subclass.
- In a "has a" relationship, a class object has a reference to an object of another class as a member. In an "is a" relationship, an object of a subclass type may also be treated as an object of the superclass type. "Is a" is inheritance. "Has a" is composition.
- A reference to a subclass object may be converted implicitly to a reference for a superclass object.
- It is possible to convert a superclass reference to a subclass reference by using an explicit cast. If the target object is not a subclass object, a **ClassCastException** is thrown.
- A superclass specifies commonality. All classes derived from a superclass inherit the capabilities of that superclass. In the object-oriented design process, the designer looks for commonality among classes and factors it out to form superclasses. Then, subclasses are customized beyond the capabilities inherited from the superclass.

- Reading a set of subclass declarations can be confusing, because inherited superclass members are not listed in the subclass declarations, but these members are indeed present in the subclasses.
- With polymorphism, it becomes possible to design and implement systems that are more extensible. Programs can be written to process objects of types that may not exist when the program is under development.
- Polymorphic programming can eliminate the need for **`switch`** logic, thus avoiding the kinds of errors associated with **`switch`** logic.
- An abstract method is declared by preceding the method's definition with the keyword **`abstract`** in the superclass.
- There are many situations in which it is useful to define classes for which the programmer never intends to instantiate any objects. Such classes are called **`abstract`** classes. Because these are used only as superclasses, typically they are called **`abstract`** superclasses. A program cannot instantiate objects of an **`abstract`** class.
- Classes from which a program can instantiate objects are called concrete classes.
- A class is made abstract by declaring it with the keyword **`abstract`**.
- If a subclass is derived from a superclass with an **`abstract`** method without supplying a definition for that **`abstract`** method in the subclass, that method remains **`abstract`** in the subclass. Consequently, the subclass is also an **`abstract`** class.
- When a request is made through a superclass reference to use a method, Java chooses the correct overridden method in the subclass associated with the object.
- Through the use of polymorphism, one method call can cause different actions to occur, depending on the type of the object receiving the call.
- Although we cannot instantiate objects of **`abstract`** superclasses, we can declare references to **`abstract`** superclasses. Such references can then be used to enable polymorphic manipulations of subclass objects when such objects are instantiated from concrete classes.
- New classes are regularly added to systems. New classes are accommodated by dynamic method binding (also called late binding). The type of an object need not be known at compile time for a method call to be compiled. At execution time, the appropriate method of the receiving object is selected.
- With dynamic method binding, at execution time the call to a method is routed to the method version appropriate for the class of the object receiving the call.
- When a superclass provides a method, subclasses can override the method, but they do not have to override it. Thus a subclass can use a superclass's version of a method.
- An interface definition begins with the keyword **`interface`** and contains a set of **`public abstract`** methods. Interfaces may also contain **`public static final`** data.
- To use an interface, a class must specify that it **`implements`** the interface and that class must define every method in the interface with the number of arguments and the return type specified in the interface definition.
- An interface is typically used in place of an abstract class when there is no default implementation to inherit.
- When a class implements an interface, the same "is a" relationship provided by inheritance applies.
- To implement more than one interface, simply provide a comma-separated list of interface names after keyword **`implements`** in the class definition.
- Inner classes are defined inside the scope of other classes.

- An inner class can also be defined inside a method of a class. Such an inner class has access to its outer class's members and to the **final** local variables for the method in which it is defined.
- Inner class definitions are used mainly in event handling.
- Class **JFrame** provides the basic attributes and behaviors of a window—a title bar and buttons to minimize, maximize and close the window.
- An inner class object has access to all the variables and methods of the outer class object.
- Because an anonymous inner class has no name, one object of the anonymous inner class must be created at the point where the class is defined in the program.
- An anonymous inner class can implement an interface or extend a class.
- The event generated when the user clicks the window's close box is a window closing event.
- Method **addWindowListener** registers a window event listener. The argument to **addWindowListener** must be a reference to an object that is a **WindowListener** (package **java.awt.event**).
- For event handling interfaces with more than one method, Java provides a corresponding class (called an adapter class) that already implements all the methods in the interface for you. Class **WindowAdapter** implements interface **WindowListener**, so every **WindowAdapter** object *is a* **WindowListener**.
- Compiling a class that contains inner classes results in a separate **.class** file for every class.
- Inner classes with class names can be defined as **public**, **protected**, package access or **private** and are subject to the same usage restrictions as other members of a class.
- To access the outer class's **this** reference, use *OuterClassName*.**this**.
- The outer class is responsible for creating objects of its non**static** inner classes.
- An inner class can be declared **static**.

TERMINOLOGY

abstract class
abstract method
abstract superclass
abstraction
anonymous inner class
base class
Boolean class
Character class
class hierarchy
client of a class
composition
direct superclass
Double class
dynamic method binding
extends
extensibility
final class
final instance variable
final method
garbage collection
"has a" relationship
hierarchical relationship
implementation inheritance
implicit reference conversion
indirect superclass
infinite recursion error
inheritance
inheritance hierarchy
inner class
Integer class
interface
interface inheritance
"is a" relationship
JFrame class
late binding
Long class
member access control
member object
method overriding
multiple inheritance
Number class
Object class

object-oriented programming (OOP)
override a method
override an **abstract** method
overriding vs. overloading
polymorphism
protected member of a class
reference to an **abstract** class
setSize method
setVisible method
single inheritance
software reusability
standardized software components
subclass
subclass constructor
subclass reference
super
superclass
superclass constructor
superclass reference
switch logic
this
type-wrapper class
"uses a" relationship
WindowAdapter class
windowClosing method
WindowEvent class
WindowListener interface

SELF-REVIEW EXERCISES

9.1 Fill in the blanks in each of the following statements:

a) If the class **Alpha** inherits from the class **Beta**, class **Alpha** is called the _________ class and class **Beta** is called the _________ class.
b) Inheritance enables _________, which saves time in development and encourages using previously proven and high-quality software components.
c) An object of a _________ class can be treated as an object of its corresponding _________ class.
d) The four member access specifiers are _________, _________, _________ and _________.
e) A "has a" relationship between classes represents _________ and an "is a" relationship between classes represents _________.
f) Using polymorphism helps eliminate _________ logic.
g) If a class contains one or more **abstract** methods, it is an _________class.
h) A method call resolved at run-time is referred to as _________ binding.
i) A subclass may call any non**private** superclass method by prepending _________ to the method call.

9.2 State whether each of the following statements is *true* or *false*. If *false*, explain why.

a) A superclass typically represents a larger number of objects than its subclass represents (true/false).
b) A subclass typically encapsulates less functionality than does its superclass. (true/false).

ANSWERS TO SELF-REVIEW EXERCISES

9.1 a) sub, super. b) software reusability. c) sub, super. d) **public**, **protected**, **private** and package access. e) composition, inheritance. f) **switch**. g) **abstract**. h) dynamic. i) **super**.

9.2 a) True.
b) False. A subclass includes all the functionality of its superclass.

EXERCISES

9.3 Consider the class **Bicycle**. Given your knowledge of some common components of bicycles, show a class hierarchy in which the class **Bicycle** inherits from other classes, which, in turn, inherit from yet other classes. Discuss the instantiation of various objects of class **Bicycle**. Discuss inheritance from class **Bicycle** for other closely related subclasses.

9.4 Define each of the following terms: single inheritance, multiple inheritance, interface, superclass and subclass.

9.5 Discuss why casting a superclass reference to a subclass reference is potentially dangerous.

9.6 Distinguish between single inheritance and multiple inheritance. What feature of Java helps realize the benefits of multiple inheritance?

9.7 (*True/False*) A subclass is generally smaller than its superclass.

9.8 (*True/False*) A subclass object is also an object of that subclass's superclass.

9.9 Some programmers prefer not to use **`protected`** access because it breaks information hiding in the superclass. Discuss the relative merits of using **`protected`** access vs. **`private`** access in superclasses.

9.10 Many programs written with inheritance could be solved with composition instead, and vice versa. Discuss the relative merits of these approaches in the context of the **`Point`**, **`Circle`**, **`Cylinder`** class hierarchy in this chapter. Rewrite the program of Fig. 9.22–Fig. 9.26 (and the supporting classes) to use composition rather than inheritance. After you do this, reassess the relative merits of the two approaches both for the **`Point`**, **`Circle`**, **`Cylinder`** problem and for object-oriented programs in general.

9.11 Rewrite the **`Point`**, **`Circle`**, **`Cylinder`** program of Fig. 9.22–Fig. 9.26 as a **`Point`**, **`Square`**, **`Cube`** program. Do this two ways—once with inheritance and once with composition.

9.12 In the chapter, we stated, "When a superclass method is inappropriate for a subclass, that method can be overridden in the subclass with an appropriate implementation." If this is done, does the subclass-is-a-superclass-object relationship still hold? Explain your answer.

9.13 Study the inheritance hierarchy of Fig. 9.2. For each class, indicate some common attributes and behaviors consistent with the hierarchy. Add some other classes (e.g., **`UndergraduateStudent`**, **`GraduateStudent`**, **`Freshman`**, **`Sophomore`**, **`Junior`**, **`Senior`**), to enrich the hierarchy.

9.14 Write an inheritance hierarchy for classes **`Quadrilateral`**, **`Trapezoid`**, **`Parallelogram`**, **`Rectangle`** and **`Square`**. Use **`Quadrilateral`** as the superclass of the hierarchy. Make the hierarchy as deep (i.e., as many levels) as possible. The **`private`** data of **`Quadrilateral`** should include the *(x, y)* coordinate pairs for the four endpoints of the **`Quadrilateral`**. Write a driver program that instantiates and displays objects of each of these classes. [In Chapter 11, "Graphics and Java2D," you will learn how to use Java's drawing capabilities.]

9.15 Write down all the shapes you can think of—both two-dimensional and three-dimensional—and form those shapes into a shape hierarchy. Your hierarchy should have superclass **`Shape`**, from which class **`TwoDimensionalShape`** and class **`ThreeDimensionalShape`** are derived. Once you have developed the hierarchy, define each of the classes in the hierarchy. We will use this hierarchy in the exercises to process all shapes as objects of superclass **`Shape`**.

9.16 How is it that polymorphism enables you to program "in the general" rather than "in the specific"? Discuss the key advantages of programming "in the general."

9.17 Discuss the problems of programming with **`switch`** logic. Explain why polymorphism is an effective alternative to using **`switch`** logic.

9.18 Distinguish between inheriting interface and inheriting implementation. How do inheritance hierarchies designed for inheriting interface differ from those designed for inheriting implementation?

9.19 Distinguish between non**`abstract`** methods and **`abstract`** methods.

9.20 (*True/False*) All methods in an **`abstract`** superclass must be declared **`abstract`**.

9.21 Suggest one or more levels of **`abstract`** superclasses for the **`Shape`** hierarchy discussed in the beginning of this chapter (the first level is **`Shape`** and the second level consists of the classes **`TwoDimensionalShape`** and **`ThreeDimensionalShape`**).

9.22 How does polymorphism promote extensibility?

9.23 You have been asked to develop a flight simulator that will have elaborate graphical outputs. Explain why polymorphic programming would be especially effective for a problem of this nature.

9.24 Develop a basic graphics package. Use the **Shape** class inheritance hierarchy from Figure 9.3. Limit yourself to two-dimensional shapes such as squares, rectangles, triangles and circles. Interact with the user. Let the user specify the position, size, shape and fill colors to be used in drawing each shape. The user can specify many items of the same shape. As you create each shape, place a **Shape** reference to each new **Shape** object into an array. Each class has its own **draw** method. Write a polymorphic screen manager that walks through the array sending **draw** messages to each object in the array to form a screen image. Redraw the screen image each time the user specifies an additional shape. Investigate the methods of class **Graphics** to help draw each shape.

9.25 Modify the payroll system of Fig. 9.16–Fig. 9.21 to add **private** instance variables **birthDate** (use class **Date** from Figure 8.13) and **departmentCode** (an **int**) to class **Employee**. Assume this payroll is processed once per month. Then, as your program calculates the payroll for each **Employee** (polymorphically), add a $100.00 bonus to the person's payroll amount if this is the month in which the **Employee**'s birthday occurs.

9.26 In Exercise 9.15, you developed a **Shape** class hierarchy and defined the classes in the hierarchy. Modify the hierarchy so that class **Shape** is an **abstract** superclass containing the interface to the hierarchy. Derive **TwoDimensionalShape** and **ThreeDimensionalShape** from class **Shape**—these classes should also be **abstract**. Use an **abstract print** method to output the type and dimensions of each class. Also include **area** and **volume** methods so these calculations can be performed for objects of each concrete class in the hierarchy. Write a driver program that tests the **Shape** class hierarchy.

9.27 Rewrite your solution to Exercise 9.26 to use a **Shape** interface instead of an abstract **Shape** class.

9.28 *(Drawing Application)* Modify the drawing program of Exercise 8.19 to create a drawing application that draws random lines, rectangles and ovals. [*Note:* Like an applet, a **JFrame** has a **paint** method that you can override to draw on the background of the **JFrame**.]

For this exercise, modify the **MyLine**, **MyOval** and **MyRect** classes of Exercise 8.19 to create the class hierarchy in Fig. 9.45. The classes of the **MyShape** hierarchy should be "smart" shape classes where objects of these classes know how to draw themselves (if provided with a **Graphics** object that tells them where to draw). The only **switch** or **if/else** logic in this program should be to determine the type of shape object to create (use random numbers to pick the shape type and the coordinates of each shape). Once an object from this hierarchy is created, it will be manipulated for the rest of its lifetime as a superclass **MyShape** reference.

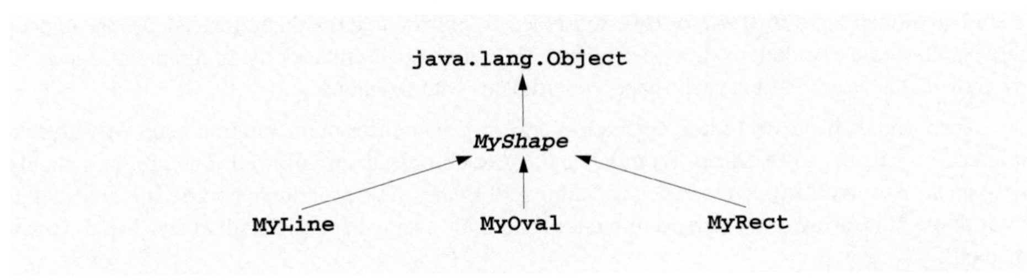

Fig. 9.45 The **MyShape** hierarchy.

Class **MyShape** in Fig. 9.45 *must* be **abstract**. The only data representing the coordinates of the shapes in the hierarchy should be defined in class **MyShape**. Lines, rectangles and ovals can all be drawn if you know two points in space. Lines require *x1*, *y1*, *x2* and *y2* coordinates. The **drawLine** method of the **Graphics** class will connect the two points supplied with a line. If you have the same four coordinate values (*x1*, *y1*, *x2* and *y2*) for ovals and rectangles, you can calculate the four arguments needed to draw them. Each requires an upper-left *x*-coordinate value (minimum of the two *x*-coordinate values), an upper-left *y*-coordinate value (minimum of the two *y* coordinate values), a *width* (difference between the two *x*-coordinate values; must be nonnegative) and a *height* (difference between the two *y*-coordinate values; must be nonnegative). [*Note*: In Chapter 12, each *x,y* pair will be captured by using mouse events from mouse interactions between the user and the program's background. These coordinates will be stored in an appropriate shape object as selected by the user. As you begin the exercise, you will use random coordinate values as arguments to the constructor.]

In addition to the data for the hierarchy, class **MyShape** should define at least the following methods:

a) A constructor with no arguments that sets the coordinates to 0.
b) A constructor with arguments that sets the coordinates to the supplied values.
c) Set methods for each individual piece of data that allow the programmer to independently set any piece of data for a shape in the hierarchy (e.g., if you have an instance variable **x1**, you should have a method **setX1**).
d) Get methods for each individual piece of data that allow the programmer to independently retrieve any piece of data for a shape in the hierarchy (e.g., if you have an instance variable **x1**, you should have a method **getX1**).
e) The **abstract** method

```
public abstract void draw( Graphics g );
```

This method will be called from the program's **paint** method to draw a shape onto the screen.

The preceding methods are required. If you would like to provide more methods for flexibility, please do so. However, be sure that any method you define in this class is a method that would be used by *all* shapes in the hierarchy.

All data *must* be **private** to class **MyShape** in this exercise (this forces you to use proper encapsulation of the data and provide proper *set/get* methods to manipulate the data). You are not allowed to define new data that can be derived from existing information. As explained previously, the upper-left *x*, upper-left *y*, *width* and *height* needed to draw an oval or rectangle can be calculated if you already know two points in space. All subclasses of **MyShape** should provide two constructors that mimic those provided by class **MyShape**.

Objects of the **MyOval** and **MyRect** classes should not calculate their upper-left *x*-coordinate, upper-left *y*-coordinate, *width* and *height* until they are about to draw. Never modify the *x1*, *y1*, *x2* and *y2* coordinates of a **MyOval** or **MyRect** object to prepare to draw them. Instead, use the temporary results of the calculations described above. This will help us enhance the program in Chapter 12 by allowing the user to select each shape's coordinates with the mouse.

There should be no **MyLine**, **MyOval** or **MyRect** references in the program—only **MyShape** references that refer to **MyLine**, **MyOval** and **MyRect** objects are allowed. The program should keep an array of **MyShape** references containing all shapes. The program's **paint** method should walk through the array of **MyShape** references and draw every shape (i.e., call every shape's **draw** method).

Begin by defining class **MyShape**, class **MyLine** and an application to test your classes. The application should have a **MyShape** instance variable that can refer to one **MyLine** object (created in the application's constructor). The **paint** method (for your subclass of **JFrame**) should draw the shape with a statement like

```
currentShape.draw( g );
```

where **currentShape** is the **MyShape** reference and **g** is the **Graphics** object that the shape will use to draw itself on the background of the window.

9.29 Next, change the single **MyShape** reference into an array of **MyShape** references and hard code several **MyLine** objects into the program for drawing. The application's **paint** method should walk through the array of shapes and draw every shape.

After the preceding part is working, you should define the **MyOval** and **MyRect** classes and add objects of these classes into the existing array. For now, all the shape objects should be created in the constructor for your subclass of **JFrame**. In Chapter 12, we will create the objects when the user chooses a shape and begins drawing it with the mouse.

In Exercise 9.28, you defined a **MyShape** hierarchy in which classes **MyLine**, **MyOval** and **MyRect** subclass **MyShape** directly. If the hierarchy was properly designed, you should be able to see the tremendous similarities between the **MyOval** and **MyRect** classes. Redesign and reimplement the code for the **MyOval** and **MyRect** classes to "factor out" the common features into the **abstract** class **MyBoundedShape** to produce the hierarchy in Fig. 9.46.

Class **MyBoundedShape** should define two constructors that mimic the constructors of class **MyShape** and methods that calculate the upper-left *x*-coordinate, upper-left *y*-coordinate, *width* and *height*. No new data pertaining to the dimensions of the shapes should be defined in this class. Remember, the values needed to draw an oval or rectangle can be calculated from two *(x,y)* coordinates. If designed properly, the new **MyOval** and **MyRect** classes should each have two constructors and a **draw** method.

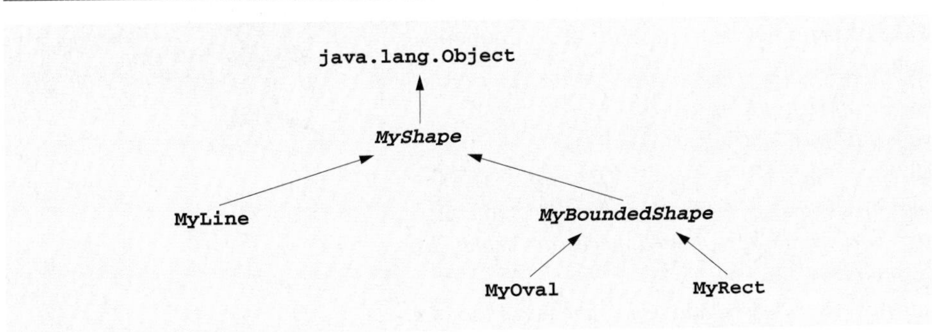

Fig. 9.46 The **MyShape** hierarchy.

10

Strings and Characters

Objectives

- To be able to create and manipulate nonmodifiable character string objects of class **`String`**.
- To be able to create and manipulate modifiable character string objects of class **`StringBuffer`**.
- To be able to create and manipulate objects of class **`Character`**.
- To be able to use a **`StringTokenizer`** object to break a **`String`** object into individual components called tokens.

The chief defect of Henry King
Was chewing little bits of string.
Hilaire Belloc

Vigorous writing is concise. A sentence should contain no unnecessary words, a paragraph no unnecessary sentences.
William Strunk, Jr.

I have made this letter longer than usual, because I lack the time to make it short.
Blaise Pascal

The difference between the almost-right word & the right word is really a large matter—it's the difference between the lightning bug and the lightning.
Mark Twain

Mum's the word.
Miguel de Cervantes, *Don Quixote de la Mancha*

Outline

10.1 Introduction
10.2 Fundamentals of Characters and Strings
10.3 `String` Constructors
10.4 `String` Methods `length`, `charAt` and `getChars`
10.5 Comparing `String`s
10.6 `String` Method `hashCode`
10.7 Locating Characters and Substrings in `String`s
10.8 Extracting Substrings from `String`s
10.9 Concatenating `String`s
10.10 Miscellaneous `String` Methods
10.11 Using `String` Method `valueOf`
10.12 `String` Method `intern`
10.13 `StringBuffer` Class
10.14 `StringBuffer` Constructors
10.15 `StringBuffer` Methods `length`, `capacity`, `setLength` and `ensureCapacity`
10.16 `StringBuffer` Methods `charAt`, `setCharAt`, `getChars` and `reverse`
10.17 `StringBuffer` `append` Methods
10.18 `StringBuffer` Insertion and Deletion Methods
10.19 `Character` Class Examples
10.20 Class `StringTokenizer`
10.21 Card Shuffling and Dealing Simulation
10.22 (Optional Case Study) Thinking About Objects: Event Handling

Summary • Terminology • Self-Review Exercises • Answers to Self-Review Exercises • Exercises • Special Section: Advanced String Manipulation Exercises • Special Section: Challenging String Manipulation Projects

10.1 Introduction

In this chapter, we introduce Java's string and character-processing capabilities. The techniques discussed here are appropriate for validating program input, displaying information to users and other text-based manipulations. The techniques also are appropriate for developing text editors, word processors, page-layout software, computerized typesetting systems and other kinds of text-processing software. We have already presented several string-processing capabilities in the text. This chapter discusses in detail the capabilities of class ***`String`***, class ***`StringBuffer`*** and class ***`Character`*** from the **`java.lang`** package and class ***`StringTokenizer`*** from the **`java.util`** package. These classes provide the foundation for string and character manipulation in Java.

10.2 Fundamentals of Characters and Strings

Characters are the fundamental building blocks of Java source programs. Every program is composed of a sequence of characters that—when grouped together meaningfully—is interpreted by the computer as a series of instructions used to accomplish a task. A program might contain *character constants.* A character constant is an integer value represented as a character in single quotes. As we stated previously, the value of a character constant is the integer value of the character in the *Unicode character set.* For example, **'z'** represents the integer value of **z**, and **'\n'** represents the integer value of newline. See Appendix D for the integer equivalents of these characters.

A string is a series of characters treated as a single unit. A string may include letters, digits and various *special characters,* such as **+**, **-**, *****, **/**, **$** and others. A string is an object of class **String**. *String literals* or *string constants* (often called *anonymous* ***String*** *objects*) are written as a sequence of characters in double quotation marks as follows:

```
"John Q. Doe"                       (a name)
"9999 Main Street"                  (a street address)
"Waltham, Massachusetts"            (a city and state)
"(201) 555-1212"                    (a telephone number)
```

A **String** may be assigned in a declaration to a **String** reference. The declaration

```
String color = "blue";
```

initializes **String** reference **color** to refer to the anonymous **String** object **"blue"**.

Performance Tip 10.1

Java treats all anonymous ***Strings*** *with the same contents as one anonymous* ***String*** *object that has many references. This conserves memory.*

10.3 `String` Constructors

Class **String** provides nine constructors for initializing **String** objects in a variety of ways. Seven of the constructors are demonstrated in Fig. 10.1. All the constructors are used in the **StringConstructors** application's **main** method.

Line 25 instantiates a new **String** object and assigns it to reference **s1**, using class **String**'s default constructor. The new **String** object contains no characters (the *empty string*) and has a length of 0.

Line 26 instantiates a new **String** object and assigns it to reference **s2**, using class **String**'s copy constructor. The new **String** object contains a copy of the characters in the **String** object **s** that is passed as an argument to the constructor.

```
1  // Fig. 10.1: StringConstructors.java
2  // This program demonstrates the String class constructors.
3
4  // Java extension packages
5  import javax.swing.*;
6
```

Fig. 10.1 Demonstrating the **String** class constructors (part 1 of 2).

```
public class StringConstructors {

   // test String constructors
   public static void main( String args[] )
   {
      char charArray[] = { 'b', 'i', 'r', 't', 'h', ' ',
                           'd', 'a', 'y' };
      byte byteArray[] = { ( byte ) 'n', ( byte ) 'e',
         ( byte ) 'w', ( byte ) ' ', ( byte ) 'y',
         ( byte ) 'e', ( byte ) 'a', ( byte ) 'r' };

      StringBuffer buffer;
      String s, s1, s2, s3, s4, s5, s6, s7, output;

      s = new String( "hello" );
      buffer = new StringBuffer( "Welcome to Java Programming!" );

      // use String constructors
      s1 = new String();
      s2 = new String( s );
      s3 = new String( charArray );
      s4 = new String( charArray, 6, 3 );
      s5 = new String( byteArray, 4, 4 );
      s6 = new String( byteArray );
      s7 = new String( buffer );

      // append Strings to output
      output = "s1 = " + s1 + "\ns2 = " + s2 + "\ns3 = " + s3 +
         "\ns4 = " + s4 + "\ns5 = " + s5 + "\ns6 = " + s6 +
         "\ns7 = " + s7;

      JOptionPane.showMessageDialog( null, output,
         "Demonstrating String Class Constructors",
         JOptionPane.INFORMATION_MESSAGE );

      System.exit( 0 );
   }

}  // end class StringConstructors
```

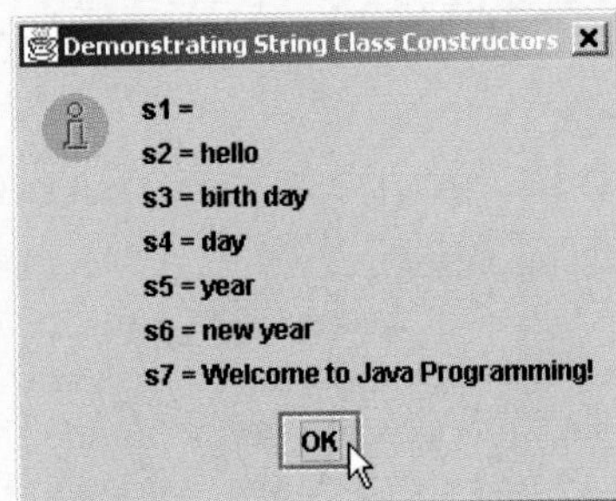

Fig. 10.1 Demonstrating the `String` class constructors (part 2 of 2).

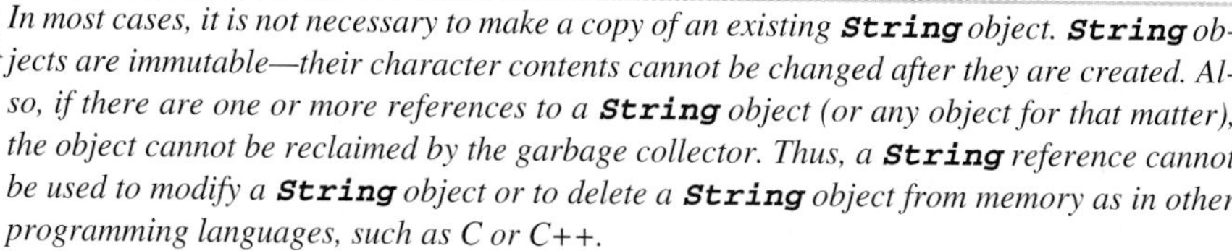

Software Engineering Observation 10.1

In most cases, it is not necessary to make a copy of an existing **String** *object.* **String** *objects are immutable—their character contents cannot be changed after they are created. Also, if there are one or more references to a* **String** *object (or any object for that matter), the object cannot be reclaimed by the garbage collector. Thus, a* **String** *reference cannot be used to modify a* **String** *object or to delete a* **String** *object from memory as in other programming languages, such as C or C++.*

Line 27 instantiates a new **String** object and assigns it to reference **s3** using class **String**'s constructor that takes a character array as an argument. The new **String** object contains a copy of the characters in the array.

Line 28 instantiates a new **String** object and assigns it to reference **s4** using class **String**'s constructor that takes a **char** array and two integers as arguments. The second argument specifies the starting position (the ***offset***) from which characters in the array are copied. The third argument specifies the number of characters (the ***count***) to be copied from the array. The new **String** object contains a copy of the specified characters in the array. If the **offset** or the **count** specified as arguments result in accessing an element outside the bounds of the character array, a **StringIndexOutOfBoundsException** is thrown. We discuss exceptions in detail in Chapter 14.

Line 29 instantiates a new **String** object and assigns it to reference **s5** using class **String**'s constructor that receives a **byte** array and two integers as arguments. The second and third arguments specify the **offset** and **count**, respectively. The new **String** object contains a copy of the specified **byte**s in the array. If the **offset** or the **count** specified as arguments result in accessing an element outside the bounds of the character array, a **StringIndexOutOfBoundsException** is thrown.

Line 30 instantiates a new **String** object and assigns it to reference **s6** using class **String**'s constructor that takes a **byte** array as an argument. The new **String** object contains a copy of the bytes in the array.

Line 31 instantiates a new **String** object and assigns it to reference **s7** using class **String**'s constructor that receives a **StringBuffer** as an argument. A **StringBuffer** is a dynamically resizable and modifiable string. The new **String** object contains a copy of the characters in the **StringBuffer**. Line 22 creates a new object of class **StringBuffer** using the constructor that receives a **String** argument (in this case **"Welcome to Java Programming"**) and assign the new object to reference **buffer**. We discuss **StringBuffer**s in detail later in this chapter. The screen capture for the program displays the contents of each **String**.

10.4 String Methods length, charAt and getChars

The application of Fig. 10.2 presents **String** methods ***length***, ***charAt*** and ***getChars***, which determine the length of a **String**, get the character at a specific location in a **String** and get the entire set of characters in a **String**, respectively.

Line 28 uses **String** method **length** to determine the number of characters in **String s1**. Like arrays, **String**s always know their own size. However, unlike arrays, **String**s do not have a **length** instance variable that specifies the number of elements in a **String**.

```
// Fig. 10.2: StringMiscellaneous.java
// This program demonstrates the length, charAt and getChars
// methods of the String class.
//
// Note: Method getChars requires a starting point
// and ending point in the String. The starting point is the
// actual subscript from which copying starts. The ending point
// is one past the subscript at which the copying ends.

// Java extension packages
import javax.swing.*;

public class StringMiscellaneous {

   // test miscellaneous String methods
   public static void main( String args[] )
   {
      String s1, output;
      char charArray[];

      s1 = new String( "hello there" );
      charArray = new char[ 5 ];

      // output the string
      output = "s1: " + s1;

      // test length method
      output += "\nLength of s1: " + s1.length();

      // loop through characters in s1 and display reversed
      output += "\nThe string reversed is: ";

      for ( int count = s1.length() - 1; count >= 0; count-- )
         output += s1.charAt( count ) + " ";

      // copy characters from string into char array
      s1.getChars( 0, 5, charArray, 0 );
      output += "\nThe character array is: ";

      for ( int count = 0; count < charArray.length; count++ )
         output += charArray[ count ];

      JOptionPane.showMessageDialog( null, output,
         "Demonstrating String Class Constructors",
         JOptionPane.INFORMATION_MESSAGE );

      System.exit( 0 );
   }

}  // end class StringMiscellaneous
```

Fig. 10.2 The `String` class character manipulation methods (part 1 of 2).

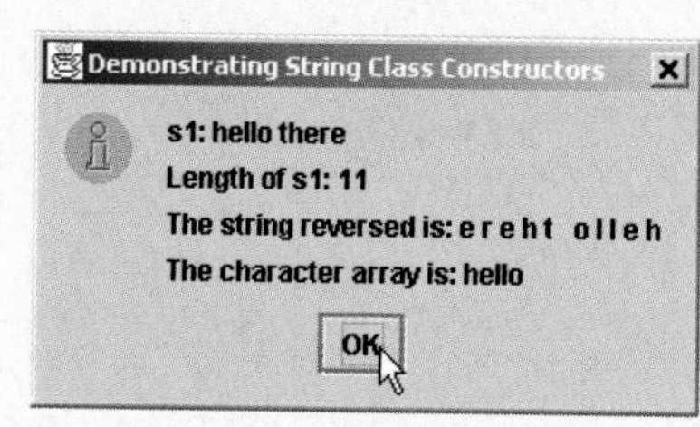

Fig. 10.2 The **String** class character manipulation methods (part 2 of 2).

Common Programming Error 10.1

Attempting to determine the length of a **String** *via an instance variable called* **length** *(e.g.,* **s1.length***) is a syntax error. The* **String** *method* **length** *must be used. (e.g.,* **s1.length()***).*

The **for** structure at lines 33–34 appends to **output** the characters of the **String** **s1** in reverse order. The **String** method **charAt** returns the character at a specific position in the **String**. Method **charAt** receives an integer argument that is used as the *position number* (or *index*) and returns the character at that position. Like arrays, the first element of a **String** is considered to be at position 0.

Common Programming Error 10.2

Attempting to access a character that is outside the bounds of a **String** *(i.e., an index less than 0 or an index greater than or equal to the* **String***'s length) results in a* **String-IndexOutOfBoundsException***.*

Line 37 uses **String** method **getChars** to copy the characters of a **String** into a character array. The first argument is the starting index from which characters are copied in the **String**. The second argument is the index that is one past the last character to be copied from the **String**. The third argument is the character array into which the characters are copied. The last argument is the starting index where the copied characters are placed in the character array. Next, the **char** array contents are appended one character at a time to **String output** with the **for** structure at lines 40–41 for display purposes.

10.5 Comparing Strings

Java provides a variety of methods for comparing **String** objects; these are demonstrated in the next two examples. To understand just what it means for one string to be "greater than" or "less than" another string, consider the process of alphabetizing a series of last names. The reader would, no doubt, place "Jones" before "Smith" because the first letter of "Jones" comes before the first letter of "Smith" in the alphabet. But the alphabet is more than just a list of 26 letters—it is an ordered list of characters. Each letter occurs in a specific position within the list. "Z" is more than just a letter of the alphabet; "Z" is specifically the twenty-sixth letter of the alphabet.

How does the computer know that one letter comes before another? All characters are represented inside the computer as numeric codes (see Appendix D). When the computer compares two strings, it actually compares the numeric codes of the characters in the strings.

Figure 10.3 demonstrates the **`String`** methods ***`equals`***, ***`equalsIgnoreCase`***, ***`compareTo`*** and ***`regionMatches`*** and demonstrates using the equality operator **`==`** to compare **`String`** objects.

```
// Fig. 10.3: StringCompare.java
// This program demonstrates the methods equals,
// equalsIgnoreCase, compareTo, and regionMatches
// of the String class.

// Java extension packages
import javax.swing.JOptionPane;

public class StringCompare {

   // test String class comparison methods
   public static void main( String args[] )
   {
      String s1, s2, s3, s4, output;

      s1 = new String( "hello" );
      s2 = new String( "good bye" );
      s3 = new String( "Happy Birthday" );
      s4 = new String( "happy birthday" );

      output = "s1 = " + s1 + "\ns2 = " + s2 +
         "\ns3 = " + s3 + "\ns4 = " + s4 + "\n\n";

      // test for equality
      if ( s1.equals( "hello" ) )
         output += "s1 equals \"hello\"\n";
      else
         output += "s1 does not equal \"hello\"\n";

      // test for equality with ==
      if ( s1 == "hello" )
         output += "s1 equals \"hello\"\n";
      else
         output += "s1 does not equal \"hello\"\n";

      // test for equality (ignore case)
      if ( s3.equalsIgnoreCase( s4 ) )
         output += "s3 equals s4\n";
      else
         output += "s3 does not equal s4\n";

      // test compareTo
      output +=
         "\ns1.compareTo( s2 ) is " + s1.compareTo( s2 ) +
         "\ns2.compareTo( s1 ) is " + s2.compareTo( s1 ) +
         "\ns1.compareTo( s1 ) is " + s1.compareTo( s1 ) +
         "\ns3.compareTo( s4 ) is " + s3.compareTo( s4 ) +
         "\ns4.compareTo( s3 ) is " + s4.compareTo( s3 ) +
         "\n\n";
```

Fig. 10.3 Demonstrating **`String`** comparisons (part 1 of 2).

```
50
51         // test regionMatches (case sensitive)
52         if ( s3.regionMatches( 0, s4, 0, 5 ) )
53            output += "First 5 characters of s3 and s4 match\n";
54         else
55            output +=
56               "First 5 characters of s3 and s4 do not match\n";
57
58         // test regionMatches (ignore case)
59         if ( s3.regionMatches( true, 0, s4, 0, 5 ) )
60            output += "First 5 characters of s3 and s4 match";
61         else
62            output +=
63               "First 5 characters of s3 and s4 do not match";
64
65         JOptionPane.showMessageDialog( null, output,
66            "Demonstrating String Class Constructors",
67            JOptionPane.INFORMATION_MESSAGE );
68
69         System.exit( 0 );
70      }
71
72   }  // end class StringCompare
```

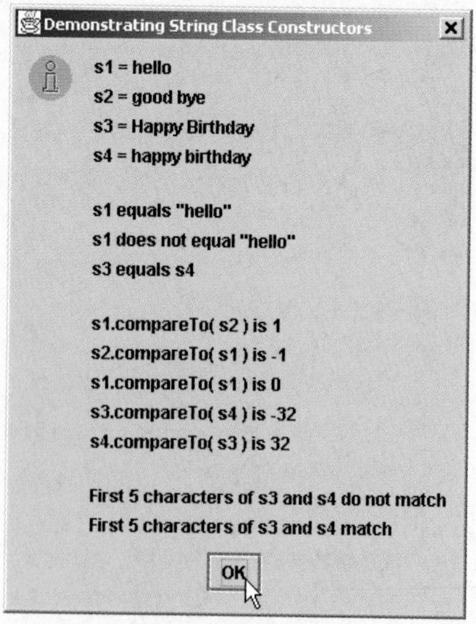

Demonstrating String Class Constructors

s1 = hello
s2 = good bye
s3 = Happy Birthday
s4 = happy birthday

s1 equals "hello"
s1 does not equal "hello"
s3 equals s4

s1.compareTo(s2) is 1
s2.compareTo(s1) is -1
s1.compareTo(s1) is 0
s3.compareTo(s4) is -32
s4.compareTo(s3) is 32

First 5 characters of s3 and s4 do not match
First 5 characters of s3 and s4 match

OK

Fig. 10.3 Demonstrating **`String`** comparisons (part 2 of 2).

The condition in the **`if`** structure at line 25 uses method **`equals`** to compare **`String s1`** and anonymous **`String "hello"`** for equality. Method **`equals`** (inherited into **`String`** from its superclass **`Object`**) tests any two objects for equality—the contents of the two objects are identical. The method returns **`true`** if the objects are equal and **`false`** otherwise. The preceding condition is **`true`** because **`String s1`** was initialized with a copy of the anonymous **`String "hello"`**. Method **`equals`** uses a *lexicographical comparison*—the integer Unicode values that represent each character in each **`String`** are compared. Thus, if the **String "hello"** is compared with the **String "HELLO"**, the result is **false**, because the integer representation of a lowercase letter is different from that of the corresponding uppercase letter.

The condition in the **if** structure at line 31 uses the equality operator **==** to compare **String s1** for equality with the anonymous **String "hello"**. *Operator == has different functionality when it is used to compare references and when it is used to compare values of primitive data types.* When primitive data type values are compared with **==**, the result is **true** if both values are identical. When references are compared with **==**, the result is **true** if both references *refer to the same object in memory.* To compare the actual contents (or state information) of objects for equality, methods (such as **equals**) must be invoked. The preceding condition evaluates to **false** in this program because the reference **s1** was initialized with the statement

```
s1 = new String( "hello" );
```

which creates a new **String** object with a copy of anonymous **String "hello"** and assigns the new object to reference **s1**. If **s1** had been initialized with the statement

```
s1 = "hello";
```

which directly assigns the anonymous **String "hello"** to the reference **s1**, the condition would be **true**. Remember that Java treats all anonymous **String** objects with the same contents as one anonymous **String** object that has many references. Thus, lines 16, 25 and 31 all refer to the same anonymous **String** object **"hello"** in memory.

Common Programming Error 10.3

Comparing references with **==** *can lead to logic errors, because* **==** *compares the references to determine whether they refer to the same object, not whether two objects have the same contents. When two identical (but separate) objects are compared with* **==**, *the result will be* **false**. *When comparing objects to determine whether they have the same contents, use method* **equals**.

If you are sorting **String**s, you may compare them for equality with method **equalsIgnoreCase**, which ignores the case of the letters in each **String** when performing the comparison. Thus, the **String "hello"** and the **String "HELLO"** compare as equal. The **if** structure at line 37 uses **String** method **equalsIgnoreCase** to compare **String s3**—**Happy Birthday**—for equality with **String s4**—**happy birthday**. The result of this comparison is **true**, because the comparison ignores case sensitivity.

Lines 44–48 use **String** method **compareTo** to compare **String** objects. For example, line 44 compares **String s1** to **String s2**. Method **compareTo** returns 0 if the **Strings** are equal, a negative number if the **String** that invokes **compareTo** is less than the **String** that is passed as an argument and a positive number if the **String** that invokes **compareTo** is greater than the **String** that is passed as an argument. Method **compareTo** uses a *lexicographical comparison*—it compares the numeric values of corresponding characters in each **String**.

The condition in the **if** structure at line 52 uses **String** method **regionMatches** to compare portions of two **String** objects for equality. The first argument is the starting index in the **String** that invokes the method. The second argument is a comparison

String. The third argument is the starting index in the comparison **String**. The last argument is the number of characters to compare between the two **String**s. The method returns **true** only if the specified number of characters are lexicographically equal.

Finally, the condition in the **if** structure at line 59 uses a second version of **String** method **regionMatches** to compare portions of two **String** objects for equality. If the first argument is **true**, the method ignores the case of the characters being compared. The remaining arguments are identical to those described for the for-argument **regionMatches** method.

The second example of this section (Fig. 10.4) demonstrates the ***startsWith*** and ***endsWith*** methods of class **String**. Application **StringStartEnd**'s **main** method defines an array of **String**s called **strings** containing **"started"**, **"starting"**, **"ended"** and **"ending"**. The remainder of method **main** consists of three **for** structures that test the elements of the array to determine whether they start with or end with a particular set of characters.

```
// Fig. 10.4: StringStartEnd.java
// This program demonstrates the methods startsWith and
// endsWith of the String class.

// Java extension packages
import javax.swing.*;

public class StringStartEnd {

   // test String comparison methods for beginning and end
   // of a String
   public static void main( String args[] )
   {
      String strings[] =
         { "started", "starting", "ended", "ending" };
      String output = "";

      // test method startsWith
      for ( int count = 0; count < strings.length; count++ )

         if ( strings[ count ].startsWith( "st" ) )
            output += "\"" + strings[ count ] +
               "\" starts with \"st\"\n";

      output += "\n";

      // test method startsWith starting from position
      // 2 of the string
      for ( int count = 0; count < strings.length; count++ )

         if ( strings[ count ].startsWith( "art", 2 ) )
            output += "\"" + strings[ count ] +
               "\" starts with \"art\" at position 2\n";

      output += "\n";
```

Fig. 10.4 **String** class **startsWith** and **endsWith** methods (part 1 of 2).

```
36
37         // test method endsWith
38         for ( int count = 0; count < strings.length; count++ )
39
40            if ( strings[ count ].endsWith( "ed" ) )
41               output += "\"" + strings[ count ] +
42                  "\" ends with \"ed\"\n";
43
44         JOptionPane.showMessageDialog( null, output,
45            "Demonstrating String Class Comparisons",
46            JOptionPane.INFORMATION_MESSAGE );
47
48         System.exit( 0 );
49      }
50
51   }  // end class StringStartEnd
```

Demonstrating String Class Comparisons

"started" starts with "st"
"starting" starts with "st"

"started" starts with "art" at position 2
"starting" starts with "art" at position 2

"started" ends with "ed"
"ended" ends with "ed"

OK

Fig. 10.4 **`String`** class **`startsWith`** and **`endsWith`** methods (part 2 of 2).

The first **`for`** structure (lines 19–23) uses the version of method **`startsWith`** that takes a **`String`** argument. The condition in the **`if`** structure (line 21) determines whether the **`String`** at location **`count`** of the array starts with the characters **`"st"`**. If so, the method returns **`true`** and the program appends **`strings[ count ]`** to **`output`** for display purposes.

The second **`for`** structure (lines 29–33) uses the version of method **`startsWith`** that takes a **`String`** and an integer as arguments. The integer argument specifies the index at which the comparison should begin in the **`String`**. The condition in the **`if`** structure (line 31) determines whether the **`String`** at location **`count`** of the array starts with the characters **`"art"`** beginning with the character at index **2** in each **`String`**. If so, the method returns **`true`** and the program appends **`strings[ count ]`** to **`output`** for display purposes.

The third **`for`** structure (line 38–42) uses method **`endsWith`**, which takes a **`String`** argument. The condition in the **`if`** structure (40) determines whether the **`String`** at location **`count`** of the array ends with the characters **`"ed"`**. If so, the method returns **`true`** and the program appends **`strings[ count ]`** to **`output`** for display purposes.

10.6 `String` Method `hashCode`

Often, it is necessary to store **`String`**s and other data types in a manner that allows the information to be found quickly. One of the best ways to store information for fast lookup is a *hash table*. A hash table stores information using a special calculation on the object to be stored that produces a *hash code*. The hash code is used to choose the location in the table at which to store the object. When the information needs to be retrieved, the same calculation is performed, the hash code is determined and a lookup of that location in the table results in the value that was stored there previously. Every object has the ability to be stored in a hash table. Class **Object** defines method ***hashCode*** to perform the hash code calculation. This method is inherited by all subclasses of **Object**. Method **hashCode** is overridden by **String** to provide a good hash code distribution based on the contents of the **String**. We will say more about hashing in Chapter 20.

The example in Fig. 10.5 demonstrates the **hashCode** method for two **String**s containing **"hello"** and **"Hello"**. Note that the hash code value for each **String** is different. That is because the **String**s themselves are lexicographically different.

```
// Fig. 10.5: StringHashCode.java1
// This program demonstrates the method
// hashCode of the String class.

// Java extension packages
import javax.swing.*;

public class StringHashCode {

   // test String hashCode method
   public static void main( String args[] )
   {
      String s1 = "hello", s2 = "Hello";

      String output =
         "The hash code for \"" + s1 + "\" is " +
         s1.hashCode() +
         "\nThe hash code for \"" + s2 + "\" is " +
         s2.hashCode();

      JOptionPane.showMessageDialog( null, output,
         "Demonstrating String Method hashCode",
         JOptionPane.INFORMATION_MESSAGE );

      System.exit( 0 );
   }

}  // end class StringHashCode
```

Demonstrating String Method hashCode

The hash code for "hello" is 99162322
The hash code for "Hello" is 69609650

OK

Fig. 10.5 **String** class **hashCode** method.

10.7 Locating Characters and Substrings in `Strings`

Often it is useful to search for a character or set of characters in a **String**. For example, if you are creating your own word processor, you might want to provide a capability for searching through the document. The application of Fig. 10.6 demonstrates the many versions of **String** methods ***indexOf*** and ***lastIndexOf*** that search for a specified character or substring in a **String**. All the searches in this example are performed on the **String letters** (initialized with **"abcdefghijklmabcdefghijklm"**) in method **main** of class **StringIndexMethods**.

```
// Fig. 10.6: StringIndexMethods.java
// This program demonstrates the String
// class index methods.

// Java extension packages
import javax.swing.*;

public class StringIndexMethods {

   // String searching methods
   public static void main( String args[] )
   {
      String letters = "abcdefghijklmabcdefghijklm";

      // test indexOf to locate a character in a string
      String output = "'c' is located at index " +
         letters.indexOf( 'c' );

      output += "\n'a' is located at index " +
         letters.indexOf( 'a', 1 );

      output += "\n'$' is located at index " +
         letters.indexOf( '$' );

      // test lastIndexOf to find a character in a string
      output += "\n\nLast 'c' is located at index " +
         letters.lastIndexOf( 'c' );

      output += "\nLast 'a' is located at index " +
         letters.lastIndexOf( 'a', 25 );

      output += "\nLast '$' is located at index " +
         letters.lastIndexOf( '$' );

      // test indexOf to locate a substring in a string
      output += "\n\n\"def\" is located at index " +
         letters.indexOf( "def" );

      output += "\n\"def\" is located at index " +
         letters.indexOf( "def", 7 );

```

Fig. 10.6 The **String** class searching methods (part 1 of 2).

```
42          output += "\n\"hello\" is located at index " +
43             letters.indexOf( "hello" );
44
45          // test lastIndexOf to find a substring in a string
46          output += "\n\nLast \"def\" is located at index " +
47             letters.lastIndexOf( "def" );
48
49          output += "\nLast \"def\" is located at index " +
50             letters.lastIndexOf( "def", 25 );
51
52          output += "\nLast \"hello\" is located at index " +
53             letters.lastIndexOf( "hello" );
54
55          JOptionPane.showMessageDialog( null, output,
56             "Demonstrating String Class \"index\" Methods",
57             JOptionPane.INFORMATION_MESSAGE );
58
59          System.exit( 0 );
60       }
61
62    }  // end class StringIndexMethods
```

Demonstrating String Class "index" ...

'c' is located at index 2
'a' is located at index 13
'$' is located at index -1

Last 'c' is located at index 15
Last 'a' is located at index 13
Last '$' is located at index -1

"def" is located at index 3
"def" is located at index 16
"hello" is located at index -1

Last "def" is located at index 16
Last "def" is located at index 16
Last "hello" is located at index -1

OK

Fig. 10.6 The **String** class searching methods (part 2 of 2).

The statements at lines 16–23 use method **indexOf** to locate the first occurrence of a character in a **String**. If **indexOf** finds the character, **indexOf** returns the index of that character in the **String**; otherwise, **indexOf** returns –1. There are two versions of **indexOf** that search for characters in a **String**. The expression on line 17 uses method **indexOf** that takes one integer argument, which is the integer representation of a character. Remember that a character constant in single quotes is of type **char** and specifies the integer representation of the character in the Unicode character set. The expression at line 20 uses the second version of method **indexOf**, which takes two integer arguments—the integer representation of a character and the starting index at which the search of the **String** should begin.

The statements at lines 26–33 use method **lastIndexOf** to locate the last occurrence of a character in a **String**. Method **lastIndexOf** performs the search from the end of the **String** toward the beginning of the **String**. If method **lastIndexOf** finds the character, **lastIndexOf** returns the index of that character in the **String**; otherwise, **lastIndexOf** returns –1. There are two versions of **lastIndexOf** that search for characters in a **String**. The expression at line 27 uses the version of method **lastIndexOf** that takes one integer argument that is the integer representation of a character. The expression at line 30 uses the version of method **lastIndexOf** that takes two integer arguments—the integer representation of a character and the highest index from which to begin searching backward for the character.

Lines 36–53 of the program demonstrate versions of methods **indexOf** and **lastIndexOf** that each take a **String** as the first argument. These versions of the methods perform identically to those described above except that they search for sequences of characters (or substrings) that are specified by their **String** arguments.

10.8 Extracting Substrings from Strings

Class **String** provides two ***substring*** methods to enable a new **String** object to be created by copying part of an existing **String** object. Each method returns a new **String** object. Both methods are demonstrated in Fig. 10.7.

```
// Fig. 10.7: SubString.java
// This program demonstrates the
// String class substring methods.

// Java extension packages
import javax.swing.*;

public class SubString {

   // test String substring methods
   public static void main( String args[] )
   {
      String letters = "abcdefghijklmabcdefghijklm";

      // test substring methods
      String output = "Substring from index 20 to end is " +
         "\"" + letters.substring( 20 ) + "\"\n";

      output += "Substring from index 0 up to 6 is " +
         "\"" + letters.substring( 0, 6 ) + "\"";

      JOptionPane.showMessageDialog( null, output,
         "Demonstrating String Class Substring Methods",
         JOptionPane.INFORMATION_MESSAGE );

      System.exit( 0 );
   }

}  // end class SubString
```

Fig. 10.7 **String** class **substring** methods (part 1 of 2).

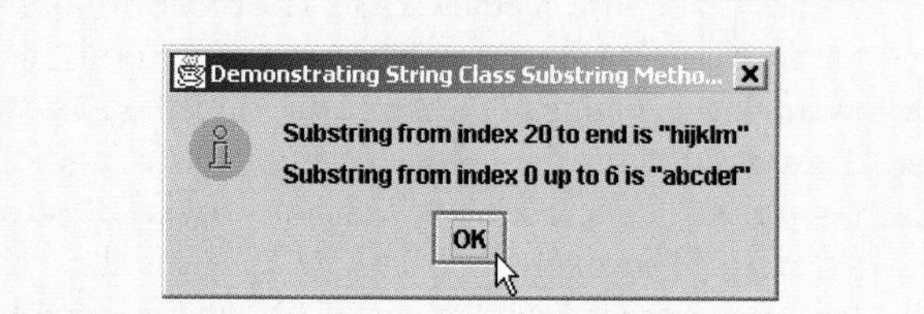

Fig. 10.7 **`String`** class **`substring`** methods (part 2 of 2).

The expression **`letters.substring( 20 )`** from line 17 uses the **`substring`** method that takes one integer argument. The argument specifies the starting index from which characters are copied in the original **`String`**. The substring returned contains a copy of the characters from the starting index to the end of the **`String`**. If the index specified as an argument is outside the bounds of the **`String`**, the program generates a **`StringIndexOutOfBoundsException`**.

The expression **`letters.substring( 0, 6 )`** from line 17 uses the **`substring`** method that takes two integer arguments. The first argument specifies the starting index from which characters are copied in the original **`String`**. The second argument specifies the index one beyond the last character to be copied (i.e., copy up to, but not including, that index in the **`String`**). The substring returned contains copies of the specified characters from the original **`String`**. If the arguments are outside the bounds of the **`String`**, the program generates a **`StringIndexOutOfBoundsException`**.

10.9 Concatenating `Strings`

The **`String`** method **`concat`** (Fig. 10.8) concatenates two **`String`** objects and returns a new **`String`** object containing the characters from both original **`String`**s. If the argument **`String`** has no characters in it, the original **`String`** is returned. The expression **`s1.concat( s2 )`** at line 20 appends the characters from the **`String s2`** to the end of the **`String s1`**. The original **`String`**s to which **`s1`** and **`s2`** refer are not modified.

Performance Tip 10.2

*In programs that frequently perform **`String`** concatenation, or other **`String`** modifications, it is more efficient to implement those modifications with class **`StringBuffer`** (covered in Section 10.13–Section 10.18).*

```
1  // Fig. 10.8: StringConcatenation.java
2  // This program demonstrates the String class concat method.
3  // Note that the concat method returns a new String object. It
4  // does not modify the object that invoked the concat method.
5
6  // Java extension packages
7  import javax.swing.*;
8
9  public class StringConcatenation {
10
```

Fig. 10.8 **`String`** method **`concat`** (part 1 of 2).

```
   // test String method concat
   public static void main( String args[] )
   {
      String s1 = new String( "Happy " ),
             s2 = new String( "Birthday" );

      String output = "s1 = " + s1 + "\ns2 = " + s2;

      output += "\n\nResult of s1.concat( s2 ) = " +
         s1.concat( s2 );

      output += "\ns1 after concatenation = " + s1;

      JOptionPane.showMessageDialog( null, output,
         "Demonstrating String Method concat",
         JOptionPane.INFORMATION_MESSAGE );

      System.exit( 0 );
   }

}  // end class StringConcatenation
```

Demonstrating String Method concat

s1 = Happy
s2 = Birthday

Result of s1.concat(s2) = Happy Birthday
s1 after concatenation = Happy

OK

Fig. 10.8 `String` method `concat` (part 2 of 2).

10.10 Miscellaneous `String` Methods

Class **`String`** provides several methods that return modified copies of **`String`**s or that return a character array. These methods are demonstrated in the application of Fig. 10.9.

Line 22 uses **`String`** method **`replace`** to return a new **`String`** object in which the method replaces every occurrence in **`String s1`** of character **`'l'`** (el) with character **`'L'`**. Method **`replace`** leaves the original **`String`** unchanged. If there are no occurrences of the first argument in the **`String`**, Method **`replace`** returns the original **`String`**.

Line 26 uses **`String`** method **`toUpperCase`** to generate a new **`String`** object with uppercase letters where corresponding lowercase letters reside in **`s1`**. The method returns a new **`String`** object containing the converted **`String`** and leaves the original **`String`** unchanged. If there are no characters to convert to uppercase letters, method **`toUpperCase`** returns the original **`String`**.

Line 27 uses **`String`** method **`toLowerCase`** to return a new **`String`** object with lowercase letters where corresponding uppercase letters reside in **`s1`**. The original **`String`** remains unchanged. If there are no characters to convert to lowercase letters, method **`toLowerCase`** returns the original **`String`**.

```java
// Fig. 10.9: StringMiscellaneous2.java
// This program demonstrates the String methods replace,
// toLowerCase, toUpperCase, trim, toString and toCharArray

// Java extension packages
import javax.swing.*;

public class StringMiscellaneous2 {

   // test miscellaneous String methods
   public static void main( String args[] )
   {
      String s1 = new String( "hello" ),
         s2 = new String( "GOOD BYE" ),
         s3 = new String( "   spaces   " );

      String output = "s1 = " + s1 + "\ns2 = " + s2 +
         "\ns3 = " + s3;

      // test method replace
      output += "\n\nReplace 'l' with 'L' in s1: " +
         s1.replace( 'l', 'L' );

      // test toLowerCase and toUpperCase
      output +=
         "\n\ns1.toUpperCase() = " + s1.toUpperCase() +
         "\ns2.toLowerCase() = " + s2.toLowerCase();

      // test trim method
      output += "\n\ns3 after trim = \"" + s3.trim() + "\"";

      // test toString method
      output += "\n\ns1 = " + s1.toString();

      // test toCharArray method
      char charArray[] = s1.toCharArray();

      output += "\n\ns1 as a character array = ";

      for ( int count = 0; count < charArray.length; ++count )
         output += charArray[ count ];

      JOptionPane.showMessageDialog( null, output,
         "Demonstrating Miscellaneous String Methods",
         JOptionPane.INFORMATION_MESSAGE );

      System.exit( 0 );
   }

}  // end class StringMiscellaneous2
```

Fig. 10.9 Miscellaneous `String` methods (part 1 of 2).

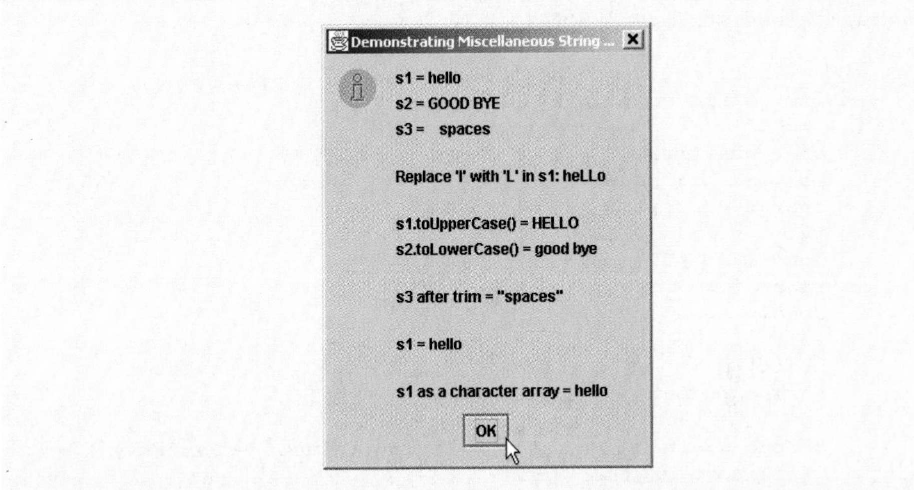

Fig. 10.9 Miscellaneous **`String`** methods (part 2 of 2).

Line 30 uses **`String`** method **`trim`** to generate a new **`String`** object that removes all white-space characters that appear at the beginning or end of the **`String`** to which the **`trim`** message is sent. The method returns a new **`String`** object containing the **`String`** without leading or trailing white-space characters. The original **`String`** remains unchanged.

Line 33 uses **`String`** method **`toString`** to return the **`String s1`**. Why is the **`toString`** method provided for class **`String`**? All objects can be converted to **`String`**s in Java by using method **`toString`**, which originates in class **`Object`**. If a class that inherits from **`Object`** (such as **`String`**) does not override method **`toString`**, the default version from class **`Object`** is used. The default version in **`Object`** creates a **`String`** consisting of the object's class name and the hash code for the object. The **`toString`** method normally is used to express the contents of an object as text. Method **`toString`** is provided in class **`String`** to ensure that the proper **`String`** value is returned.

Line 36 creates a new character array containing a copy of the characters in **`String s1`** and assigns it to **`charArray`**.

10.11 Using `String` Method `valueOf`

Class **`String`** provides a set of **`static`** class methods that take arguments of various types, convert those arguments to **`String`**s and return them as **`String`** objects. Class **`StringValueOf`** (Fig. 10.10) demonstrates the **`String`** class ***`valueOf`*** methods.

```
// Fig. 10.10: StringValueOf.java
// This program demonstrates the String class valueOf methods.

// Java extension packages
import javax.swing.*;

```

Fig. 10.10 **`String`** class **`valueOf`** methods (part 1 of 2).

```
 7  public class StringValueOf {
 8
 9     // test String valueOf methods
10     public static void main( String args[] )
11     {
12        char charArray[] = { 'a', 'b', 'c', 'd', 'e', 'f' };
13        boolean b = true;
14        char c = 'Z';
15        int i = 7;
16        long l = 10000000;
17        float f = 2.5f;
18        double d = 33.333;
19
20        Object o = "hello";  // assign to an Object reference
21        String output;
22
23        output = "char array = " + String.valueOf( charArray ) +
24           "\npart of char array = " +
25           String.valueOf( charArray, 3, 3 ) +
26           "\nboolean = " + String.valueOf( b ) +
27           "\nchar = " + String.valueOf( c ) +
28           "\nint = " + String.valueOf( i ) +
29           "\nlong = " + String.valueOf( l ) +
30           "\nfloat = " + String.valueOf( f ) +
31           "\ndouble = " + String.valueOf( d ) +
32           "\nObject = " + String.valueOf( o );
33
34        JOptionPane.showMessageDialog( null, output,
35           "Demonstrating String Class valueOf Methods",
36           JOptionPane.INFORMATION_MESSAGE );
37
38        System.exit( 0 );
39     }
40
41  }  // end class StringValueOf
```

Demonstrating String Class valueOf ...

char array = abcdef
part of char array = def
boolean = true
char = Z
int = 7
long = 10000000
float = 2.5
double = 33.333
Object = hello

OK

Fig. 10.10 **`String`** class **`valueOf`** methods (part 2 of 2).

The expression **`String.valueOf( charArray )`** from line 23 copies the contents of the character array **`charArray`** into a new **`String`** object and returns the new **`String`**. The expression **`String.valueOf( charArray, 3, 3 )`** from line 25 copies a portion of the contents of the character array **charArray** into a new **String** object and returns the new **String**. The second argument specifies the starting index from which the characters are copied. The third argument specifies the number of characters to copy.

There are seven other versions of method **valueOf**, which take arguments of type **boolean**, **char**, **int**, **long**, **float**, **double** and **Object**, respectively. These are demonstrated in lines 26–32 of the program. Note that the version of **valueOf** that takes an **Object** as an argument can do so because all **Object**s can be converted to **String**s with method **toString**.

10.12 String Method intern

Comparing large **String** objects is a relatively slow operation. **String** method ***intern*** can improve **String** comparison performance. When **String** method **intern** is invoked on a **String** object, it returns a reference to a **String** object that is guaranteed to have the same contents as the original **String**. Class **String** maintains the resulting **String** during program execution. Subsequently, if the program invokes method **intern** on other **String** objects with contents identical to the original **String**, method **intern** returns a reference to the copy of the **String** maintained in memory by class **String**. If a program uses **intern** on extremely large **String**s, the program can compare those **String**s faster by using the **==** operator, which simply compares two references—a fast operation. Using standard **String** methods such as **equals** and **equalsIgnoreCase** can be slower, because they compare corresponding characters in each **String**. For large **String**s, this is a time-consuming, iterative operation. The program of Fig. 10.11 demonstrates the **intern** method.

The program declares five **String** references—**s1**, **s2**, **s3**, **s4** and **output**. **String**s **s1** and **s2** are initialized with new **String** objects that each contain a copy of **"hello"**. The first **if** structure (lines 20–23) uses operator **==** to determine that **String**s **s1** and **s2** are the same object. References **s1** and **s2** refer to different objects, because they were initialized with new **String** objects.

The second **if** structure (lines 26–29) uses method **equals** to determine that the contents of **String**s **s1** and **s2** are equal. They were each initialized with copies of **"hello"**, so they have the same contents.

```
1   // Fig. 10.11: StringIntern.java
2   // This program demonstrates the intern method
3   // of the String class.
4
5   // Java extension packages
6   import javax.swing.*;
7
8   public class StringIntern {
9
10     // test String method intern
11     public static void main( String args[] )
12     {
13        String s1, s2, s3, s4, output;
```

Fig. 10.11 **String** class **intern** method (part 1 of 3).

```
      s1 = new String( "hello" );
      s2 = new String( "hello" );

      // test strings to determine if they are same
      // String object in memory
      if ( s1 == s2 )
         output = "s1 and s2 are the same object in memory";
      else
         output = "s1 and s2 are not the same object in memory";

      // test strings for equality of contents
      if ( s1.equals( s2 ) )
         output += "\ns1 and s2 are equal";
      else
         output += "\ns1 and s2 are not equal";

      // use String intern method to get a unique copy of
      // "hello" referred to by both s3 and s4
      s3 = s1.intern();
      s4 = s2.intern();

      // test strings to determine if they are same
      // String object in memory
      if ( s3 == s4 )
         output += "\ns3 and s4 are the same object in memory";
      else
         output +=
            "\ns3 and s4 are not the same object in memory";

      // determine if s1 and s3 refer to same object
      if ( s1 == s3 )
         output +=
            "\ns1 and s3 are the same object in memory";
      else
         output +=
            "\ns1 and s3 are not the same object in memory";

      // determine if s2 and s4 refer to same object
      if ( s2 == s4 )
         output += "\ns2 and s4 are the same object in memory";
      else
         output +=
            "\ns2 and s4 are not the same object in memory";

      // determine if s1 and s4 refer to same object
      if ( s1 == s4 )
         output += "\ns1 and s4 are the same object in memory";
      else
         output +=
            "\ns1 and s4 are not the same object in memory";

```

Fig. 10.11 `String` class `intern` method (part 2 of 3).

```
66        JOptionPane.showMessageDialog( null, output,
67           "Demonstrating String Method intern",
68           JOptionPane.INFORMATION_MESSAGE );
69
70        System.exit( 0 );
71     }
72
73  }  // end class StringIntern
```

Demonstrating String Method intern

s1 and s2 are not the same object in memory
s1 and s2 are equal
s3 and s4 are the same object in memory
s1 and s3 are not the same object in memory
s2 and s4 are not the same object in memory
s1 and s4 are not the same object in memory

OK

Fig. 10.11 **`String`** class **`intern`** method (part 3 of 3).

Line 33 uses method **`intern`** to get a reference to a **`String`** with the same contents as object **`s1`** and assigns the reference to **`s3`**. The **`String`** to which s3 refers is maintained in memory by class **`String`**. Line 34 also uses method **`intern`** to get a reference to a **`String`** object. However, because **`String s1`** and **`String s2`** have the same contents, the reference returned by this call to **`intern`** is a reference to the same **`String`** object returned by **`s1.intern()`**. The third **`if`** structure (lines 38–42) uses operator **`==`** to determine that **`String`**s **`s3`** and **`s4`** refer to the same object.

The fourth **`if`** structure (lines 45–50) uses operator **`==`** to determine that **`String`**s **`s1`** and **`s3`** are *not* the same object. Technically, they could refer to the same object, but they are not guaranteed to refer to the same object unless the objects they refer to were returned by calls to **`intern`** on **`String`**s with the same contents. In this case, **`s1`** refers to the **`String`** it was assigned in method **`main`** and **`s3`** refers to the **`String`** with the same contents maintained by class **`String`**.

The fifth **`if`** structure (lines 53–57) uses operator **`==`** to determine that **`String`**s **`s2`** and **`s4`** are *not* the same object, because the second **`intern`** call results in a reference to the same object returned by **`s1.intern()`**, not **`s2`**. Similarly, the sixth **`if`** structure (lines 60–64) uses operator **`==`** to determine that **`String`**s **`s1`** and **`s4`** are not the same object, because the second **`intern`** call results in a reference to the same object returned by **`s1.intern()`**, not **`s1`**.

10.13 `StringBuffer` Class

The **`String`** class provides many capabilities for processing **`String`**s. However, once a **`String`** object is created, its contents can never change. The next several sections discuss the features of class **`StringBuffer`** for creating and manipulating dynamic string information—i.e., modifiable **`String`**s. Every **`StringBuffer`** is capable of storing a number of characters specified by its capacity. If the capacity of a **`StringBuffer`** is exceeded, the capacity is automatically expanded to accommodate the additional characters. As we will see, class **StringBuffer** is also used to implement operators **+** and **+=** for **String** concatenation.

Performance Tip 10.3

***String** objects are constant strings and **StringBuffer** objects are modifiable strings. Java distinguishes constant strings from modifiable strings for optimization purposes; in particular, Java can perform certain optimizations involving **String** objects (such as sharing one **String** object among multiple references) because it knows these objects will not change.*

Performance Tip 10.4

*When given the choice between using a **String** object to represent a string versus a **StringBuffer** object to represent that string, always use a **String** object if indeed the object will not change; this improves performance.*

Common Programming Error 10.4

*Invoking **StringBuffer** methods that are not methods of class **String** on **String** objects is a syntax error.*

10.14 StringBuffer Constructors

Class **StringBuffer** provides three constructors (demonstrated in Fig. 10.12). Line 14 uses the default **StringBuffer** constructor to create a **StringBuffer** with no characters in it and an initial capacity of 16 characters. Line 15 uses **StringBuffer** constructor that takes an integer argument to create a **StringBuffer** with no characters in it and the initial capacity specified in the integer argument (i.e., **10**). Line 16 uses the **StringBuffer** constructor that takes a **String** argument to create a **StringBuffer** containing the characters of the **String** argument. The initial capacity is the number of characters in the **String** argument plus 16.

The statement on lines 18–21 uses **StringBuffer** method **toString** to convert the **StringBuffers** into **String** objects that can be displayed with **drawString**. Note the use of operator **+** to concatenate **Strings** for output. In Section 10.17, we discuss how Java uses **StringBuffers** to implement the **+** and **+=** operators for **String** concatenation.

```
1  // Fig. 10.12: StringBufferConstructors.java
2  // This program demonstrates the StringBuffer constructors.
3
4  // Java extension packages
5  import javax.swing.*;
6
7  public class StringBufferConstructors {
8
9     // test StringBuffer constructors
10    public static void main( String args[] )
11    {
12       StringBuffer buffer1, buffer2, buffer3;
13
```

Fig. 10.12 StringBuffer class constructors (part 1 of 2).

```
        buffer1 = new StringBuffer();
        buffer2 = new StringBuffer( 10 );
        buffer3 = new StringBuffer( "hello" );

        String output =
           "buffer1 = \"" + buffer1.toString() + "\"" +
           "\nbuffer2 = \"" + buffer2.toString() + "\"" +
           "\nbuffer3 = \"" + buffer3.toString() + "\"";

        JOptionPane.showMessageDialog( null, output,
           "Demonstrating StringBuffer Class Constructors",
           JOptionPane.INFORMATION_MESSAGE );

        System.exit( 0 );
    }

}  // end class StringBufferConstructors
```

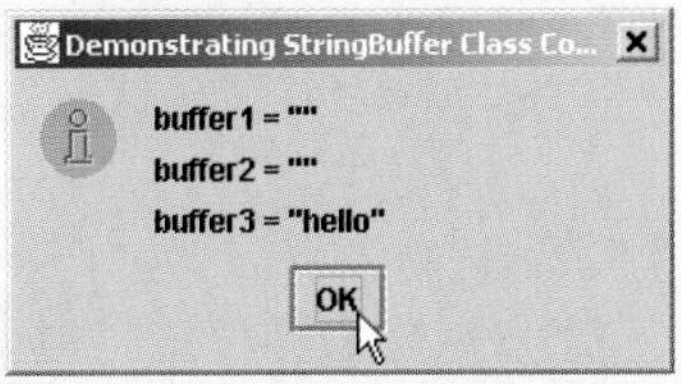

Demonstrating StringBuffer Class Co...

buffer1 = ""
buffer2 = ""
buffer3 = "hello"

OK

Fig. 10.12 **`StringBuffer`** class constructors (part 2 of 2).

10.15 `StringBuffer` Methods `length`, `capacity`, `setLength` and `ensureCapacity`

Class **`StringBuffer`** provides the **`length`** and **`capacity`** methods to return the number of characters currently in a **`StringBuffer`** and the number of characters that can be stored in a **`StringBuffer`** without allocating more memory, respectively. Method **`ensureCapacity`** is provided to allow the programmer to guarantee that a **`StringBuffer`** has a minimum capacity. Method **`setLength`** is provided to enable the programmer to increase or decrease the length of a **`StringBuffer`**. The program of Fig. 10.13 demonstrates these methods.

```
// Fig. 10.13: StringBufferCapLen.java
// This program demonstrates the length and
// capacity methods of the StringBuffer class.

// Java extension packages
import javax.swing.*;

public class StringBufferCapLen {

   // test StringBuffer methods for capacity and length
   public static void main( String args[] )
   {
```

Fig. 10.13 **`StringBuffer length`** and **`capacity`** methods (part 1 of 2).

```
13          StringBuffer buffer =
14             new StringBuffer( "Hello, how are you?" );
15
16          String output = "buffer = " + buffer.toString() +
17             "\nlength = " + buffer.length() +
18             "\ncapacity = " + buffer.capacity();
19
20          buffer.ensureCapacity( 75 );
21          output += "\n\nNew capacity = " + buffer.capacity();
22
23          buffer.setLength( 10 );
24          output += "\n\nNew length = " + buffer.length() +
25             "\nbuf = " + buffer.toString();
26
27          JOptionPane.showMessageDialog( null, output,
28             "StringBuffer length and capacity Methods",
29             JOptionPane.INFORMATION_MESSAGE );
30
31          System.exit( 0 );
32       }
33
34    }  // end class StringBufferCapLen
```

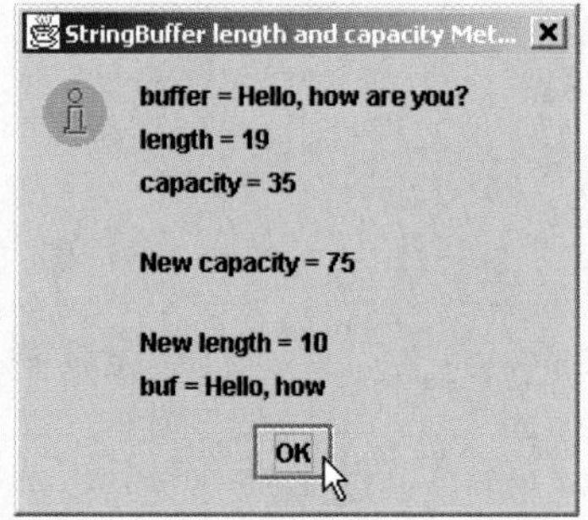

Fig. 10.13 **`StringBuffer`** **`length`** and **`capacity`** methods (part 2 of 2).

The program contains one **`StringBuffer`** called **`buffer`**. Lines 13–14 of the program use the **`StringBuffer`** constructor that takes a **`String`** argument to instantiate and initialize the **`StringBuffer`** with **`"Hello, how are you?"`**. Lines 16–18 append to **`output`** the contents, the length and the capacity of the **`StringBuffer`**. Notice in the output window that the capacity of the **`StringBuffer`** is initially 35. Remember that the **`StringBuffer`** constructor that takes a **`String`** argument creates a **`StringBuffer`** object with an initial capacity that is the length of the **`String`** passed as an argument plus 16.

Line 20 expands the capacity of the **`StringBuffer`** to a minimum of 75 characters. Actually, if the original capacity is less than the argument, the method ensures a capacity that is the greater of the number specified as an argument or twice the original capacity plus 2. If the **`StringBuffer`**'s current capacity is more than the specified capacity, the **`StringBuffer`**'s capacity remains unchanged.

Line 23 uses method **`setLength`** to set the length of the **`StringBuffer`** to 10. If the specified length is less than the current number of characters in the **`StringBuffer`**, the characters are truncated to the specified length (i.e., the characters in the **StringBuffer** after the specified length are discarded). If the specified length is greater than the number of characters currently in the **StringBuffer**, null characters (characters with the numeric representation 0) are appended to the **StringBuffer** until the total number of characters in the **StringBuffer** is equal to the specified length.

10.16 StringBuffer Methods charAt, setCharAt, getChars and reverse

Class **StringBuffer** provides the **charAt**, **setCharAt**, **getChars** and **reverse** methods to manipulate the characters in a **StringBuffer**. Method **charAt** takes an integer argument and returns the character in the **StringBuffer** at that index. Method **setCharAt** takes an integer and a character argument and sets the character at the specified position to the character argument. The index specified in the **charAt** and **setCharAt** methods must be greater than or equal to 0 and less than the **StringBuffer** length; otherwise, a **StringIndexOutOfBoundsException** is generated.

Common Programming Error 10.5

Attempting to access a character that is outside the bounds of a ***StringBuffer*** *(i.e., an index less than 0 or an index greater than or equal to the* ***StringBuffer****'s length) results in a* ***StringIndexOutOfBoundsException****.*

Method **getChars** returns a character array containing a copy of the characters in the **StringBuffer**. This method takes four arguments—the starting index from which characters should be copied in the **StringBuffer**, the index one past the last character to be copied from the **StringBuffer**, the character array into which the characters are to be copied and the starting location in the character array where the first character should be placed. Method **reverse** reverses the contents of the **StringBuffer**. Each of these methods is demonstrated in Fig. 10.14.

```
// Fig. 10.14: StringBufferChars.java
// The charAt, setCharAt, getChars, and reverse methods
// of class StringBuffer.

// Java extension packages
import javax.swing.*;

public class StringBufferChars {

   // test StringBuffer character methods
   public static void main( String args[] )
   {
      StringBuffer buffer = new StringBuffer( "hello there" );

      String output = "buffer = " + buffer.toString() +
         "\nCharacter at 0: " + buffer.charAt( 0 ) +
         "\nCharacter at 4: " + buffer.charAt( 4 );

```

Fig. 10.14 **StringBuffer** class character manipulation methods.

```
      char charArray[] = new char[ buffer.length() ];
      buffer.getChars( 0, buffer.length(), charArray, 0 );
      output += "\n\nThe characters are: ";

      for ( int count = 0; count < charArray.length; ++count )
         output += charArray[ count ];

      buffer.setCharAt( 0, 'H' );
      buffer.setCharAt( 6, 'T' );
      output += "\n\nbuf = " + buffer.toString();

      buffer.reverse();
      output += "\n\nbuf = " + buffer.toString();

      JOptionPane.showMessageDialog( null, output,
         "Demonstrating StringBuffer Character Methods",
         JOptionPane.INFORMATION_MESSAGE );

      System.exit( 0 );
   }

}  // end class StringBufferChars
```

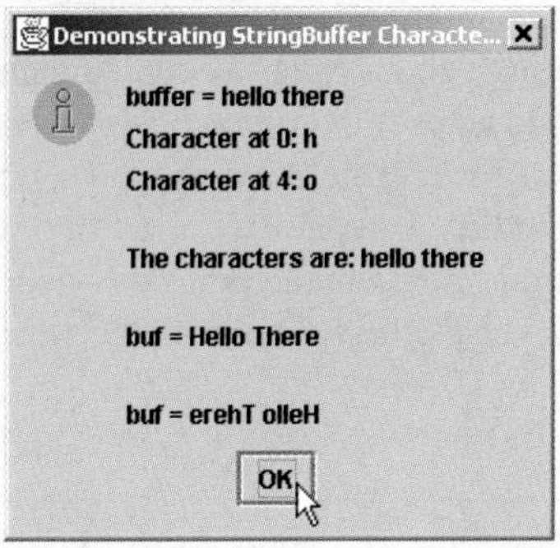

Fig. 10.14 **`StringBuffer`** class character manipulation methods.

10.17 `StringBuffer` append Methods

Class **`StringBuffer`** provides 10 overloaded **`append`** methods to allow various data-type values to be added to the end of a **`StringBuffer`**. Versions are provided for each of the primitive data types and for character arrays, **`String`**s and **`Object`**s. (Remember that method **`toString`** produces a **`String`** representation of any **`Object`**.) Each of the methods takes its argument, converts it to a **`String`** and appends it to the **`StringBuffer`**. The **`append`** methods are demonstrated in Fig. 10.15. [Note: Line 20 specifies the literal value **`2.5f`** as the initial value of a **`float`** variable. Normally, Java treats a floating-point literal value as type **`double`**. Appending the letter **`f`** to the literal **`2.5`** indicates to the compiler that **`2.5`** should be treated as type **`float`**. Without this indication the compiler generates a syntax error, because a **`double`** value cannot be assigned directly to a **`float`** variable in Java.]

```java
// Fig. 10.15: StringBufferAppend.java
// This program demonstrates the append
// methods of the StringBuffer class.

// Java extension packages
import javax.swing.*;

public class StringBufferAppend {

   // test StringBuffer append methods
   public static void main( String args[] )
   {
      Object o = "hello";
      String s = "good bye";
      char charArray[] = { 'a', 'b', 'c', 'd', 'e', 'f' };
      boolean b = true;
      char c = 'Z';
      int i = 7;
      long l = 10000000;
      float f = 2.5f;
      double d = 33.333;
      StringBuffer buffer = new StringBuffer();

      buffer.append( o );
      buffer.append( "  " );

      buffer.append( s );
      buffer.append( "  " );
      buffer.append( charArray );
      buffer.append( "  " );
      buffer.append( charArray, 0, 3 );
      buffer.append( "  " );
      buffer.append( b );
      buffer.append( "  " );
      buffer.append( c );
      buffer.append( "  " );
      buffer.append( i );
      buffer.append( "  " );
      buffer.append( l );
      buffer.append( "  " );
      buffer.append( f );
      buffer.append( "  " );
      buffer.append( d );

      JOptionPane.showMessageDialog( null,
         "buffer = " + buffer.toString(),
         "Demonstrating StringBuffer append Methods",
         JOptionPane.INFORMATION_MESSAGE );

      System.exit( 0 );
   }

}  // end StringBufferAppend
```

Fig. 10.15 `StringBuffer` class **`append`** methods (part 1 of 2).

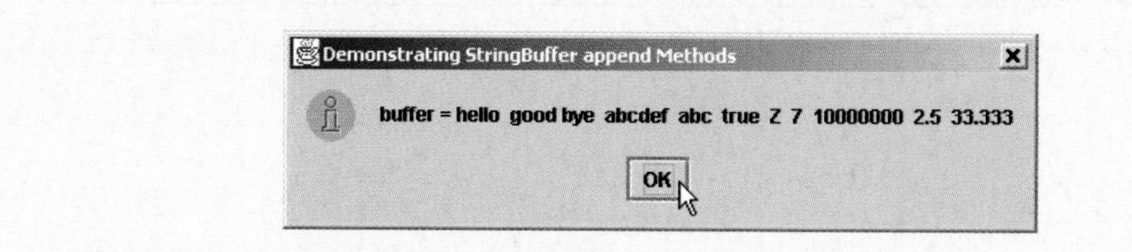

Fig. 10.15 **`StringBuffer`** class **`append`** methods (part 2 of 2).

Actually, **`StringBuffer`**s and the **`append`** methods are used by the compiler to implement the **+** and **+=** operators for concatenating **`String`**s. For example, assuming the following declarations:

```
String string1 = "hello";
String string2 = "BC"
int value = 22;
```

the statement

```
String s = string1 + string2 + value;
```

concatenates **`"hello"`**, **`"BC"`** and **`22`**. The concatenation is performed as follows:

```
new StringBuffer().append( "hello" ).append( "BC" ).append(
   22 ).toString();
```

First, Java creates a **`StringBuffer`**, then appends to the **`StringBuffer`** the **`String`** **`"hello"`**, the **`String`** **`"BC"`** and the integer **`22`**. Next, **`StringBuffer`**'s **`toString`** converts the **`StringBuffer`** to a **`String`** representation and the result is assigned to **`String s`**. The statement

```
s += "!";
```

is performed as follows:

```
s = new StringBuffer().append( s ).append( "!" ).toString()
```

First, Java creates a **`StringBuffer`**, then appends to the **`StringBuffer`** the current contents of **`s`** followed by **`"!"`**. Next, **`StringBuffer`**'s **`toString`** converts the **`StringBuffer`** to a **`String`** representation and the result is assigned to **`s.`**

10.18 `StringBuffer` Insertion and Deletion Methods

Class **`StringBuffer`** provides nine overloaded **`insert`** methods to allow various data-type values to be inserted at any position in a **`StringBuffer`**. Versions are provided for each of the primitive data types and for character arrays, **`String`**s and **`Object`**s. (Remember that method **`toString`** produces a **`String`** representation of any **`Object`**.) Each of the methods takes its second argument, converts it to a **`String`** and inserts it preceding the index specified by the first argument. The index specified by the first argument must be greater than or equal to **`0`** and less than the length of the **`StringBuffer`**; otherwise, a **`StringIndexOutOfBoundsException`** is generated. Class **`StringBuffer`** also provides methods ***`delete`*** and ***`deleteCharAt`*** for deleting characters at any position in a **StringBuffer**. Method **delete** takes two arguments—the starting subscript and the subscript one past the end of the characters to delete. All characters beginning at the starting subscript up to, but not including the ending subscript are deleted. Method **deleteCharAt** takes one argument—the subscript of the character to delete. Invalid subscripts cause both methods to throw a **StringIndexOutOfBoundsException**. The **insert** and delete methods are demonstrated in Fig. 10.16.

```
// Fig. 10.16: StringBufferInsert.java
// This program demonstrates the insert and delete
// methods of class StringBuffer.

// Java extension packages
import javax.swing.*;

public class StringBufferInsert {

   // test StringBuffer insert methods
   public static void main( String args[] )
   {
      Object o = "hello";
      String s = "good bye";
      char charArray[] = { 'a', 'b', 'c', 'd', 'e', 'f' };
      boolean b = true;
      char c = 'K';
      int i = 7;
      long l = 10000000;
      float f = 2.5f;
      double d = 33.333;
      StringBuffer buffer = new StringBuffer();

      buffer.insert( 0, o );
      buffer.insert( 0, "  " );
      buffer.insert( 0, s );
      buffer.insert( 0, "  " );
      buffer.insert( 0, charArray );
      buffer.insert( 0, "  " );
      buffer.insert( 0, b );
      buffer.insert( 0, "  " );
      buffer.insert( 0, c );
      buffer.insert( 0, "  " );
      buffer.insert( 0, i );
      buffer.insert( 0, "  " );
      buffer.insert( 0, l );
      buffer.insert( 0, "  " );
      buffer.insert( 0, f );
      buffer.insert( 0, "  " );
      buffer.insert( 0, d );

      String output =
         "buffer after inserts:\n" + buffer.toString();

```

Fig. 10.16 **StringBuffer** class **insert** and **delete** methods (part 1 of 2).

```
         buffer.deleteCharAt( 10 );  // delete 5 in 2.5
         buffer.delete( 2, 6 );      // delete .333 in 33.333

         output +=
            "\n\nbuffer after deletes:\n" + buffer.toString();

         JOptionPane.showMessageDialog( null, output,
            "Demonstrating StringBufferer Inserts and Deletes",
            JOptionPane.INFORMATION_MESSAGE );

         System.exit( 0 );
      }

   }  // end class StringBufferInsert
```

Demonstrating StringBufferer Inserts and Deletes

buffer after inserts:
33.333 2.5 10000000 7 K true abcdef good bye hello

buffer after deletes:
33 2. 10000000 7 K true abcdef good bye hello

OK

Fig. 10.16 **`StringBuffer`** class **`insert`** and **`delete`** methods (part 2 of 2).

10.19 `Character` Class Examples

Java provides a number of classes that enable primitive variables to be treated as objects. The classes are **`Boolean`**, **`Character`**, **`Double`**, **`Float`**, **`Byte`**, **`Short`**, **`Integer`** and **`Long`**. These classes (except **`Boolean`** and **`Character`**) are derived from **`Number`**. These eight classes are known as *type wrappers*, and they are part of the **`java.lang`** package. Objects of these classes can be used anywhere in a program that an **`Object`** or a **`Number`** is expected. In this section, we present class **`Character`**—the type-wrapper class for characters.

Most **`Character`** class methods are **`static`**, take at least a character argument and perform either a test or a manipulation of the character. This class also contains a constructor that receives a **`char`** argument to initialize a **`Character`** object and several non-**`static`** methods. Most of the methods of class **`Character`** are presented in the next three examples. For more information on class **`Character`** (and all the wrapper classes), see the **`java.lang`** package in the Java API documentation.

Figure 10.17 demonstrates some **`static`** methods that test characters to determine whether they are a specific character type and the **`static`** methods that perform case conversions on characters. Each method is used in method **`buildOutput`** of class **`StaticCharMethods`**. You can enter any character and apply the preceding methods to the character. Note the use of inner classes for the event handling as demonstrated in Chapter 9.

Line 63 uses **`Character`** method **`isDefined`** to determine if character **`c`** is defined in the Unicode character set. If so, the method returns **`true`**; otherwise, it returns **`false`**.

```
1  // Fig. 10.17: StaticCharMethods.java
2  // Demonstrates the static character testing methods
3  // and case conversion methods of class Character
4  // from the java.lang package.
5
6  // Java core packages
7  import java.awt.*;
8  import java.awt.event.*;
9
10 // Java extension packages
11 import javax.swing.*;
12
13 public class StaticCharMethods extends JFrame {
14    private char c;
15    private JLabel promptLabel;
16    private JTextField inputField;
17    private JTextArea outputArea;
18
19    // set up GUI
20    public StaticCharMethods()
21    {
22       super( "Static Character Methods" );
23
24       Container container = getContentPane();
25       container.setLayout( new FlowLayout() );
26
27       promptLabel =
28          new JLabel( "Enter a character and press Enter" );
29       container.add( promptLabel );
30
31       inputField = new JTextField( 5 );
32
33       inputField.addActionListener(
34
35          // anonymous inner class
36          new ActionListener() {
37
38             // handle text field event
39             public void actionPerformed( ActionEvent event )
40             {
41                String s = event.getActionCommand();
42                c = s.charAt( 0 );
43                buildOutput();
44             }
45
46          }  // end anonymous inner class
47
48       ); // end call to addActionListener
```

Fig. 10.17 **`static`** character testing methods and case conversion methods of class **`Character`** (part 1 of 3).

```
      container.add( inputField );

      outputArea = new JTextArea( 10, 20 );
      container.add( outputArea );

      setSize( 300, 250 );  // set the window size
      show();               // show the window
   }

   // display character info in outputArea
   public void buildOutput()
   {
      outputArea.setText(
         "is defined: " + Character.isDefined( c ) +
         "\nis digit: " + Character.isDigit( c ) +
         "\nis Java letter: " +
         Character.isJavaIdentifierStart( c ) +
         "\nis Java letter or digit: " +
         Character.isJavaIdentifierPart( c ) +
         "\nis letter: " + Character.isLetter( c ) +
         "\nis letter or digit: " +
         Character.isLetterOrDigit( c ) +
         "\nis lower case: " + Character.isLowerCase( c ) +
         "\nis upper case: " + Character.isUpperCase( c ) +
         "\nto upper case: " + Character.toUpperCase( c ) +
         "\nto lower case: " + Character.toLowerCase( c ) );
   }

   // execute application
   public static void main( String args[] )
   {
      StaticCharMethods application = new StaticCharMethods();

      application.addWindowListener(

         // anonymous inner class
         new WindowAdapter() {

            // handle event when user closes window
            public void windowClosing( WindowEvent windowEvent )
            {
               System.exit( 0 );
            }

         }  // end anonymous inner class

      ); // end call to addWindowListener

   }  // end method main

}  // end class StaticCharMethods
```

Fig. 10.17 `static` character testing methods and case conversion methods of class `Character` (part 2 of 3).

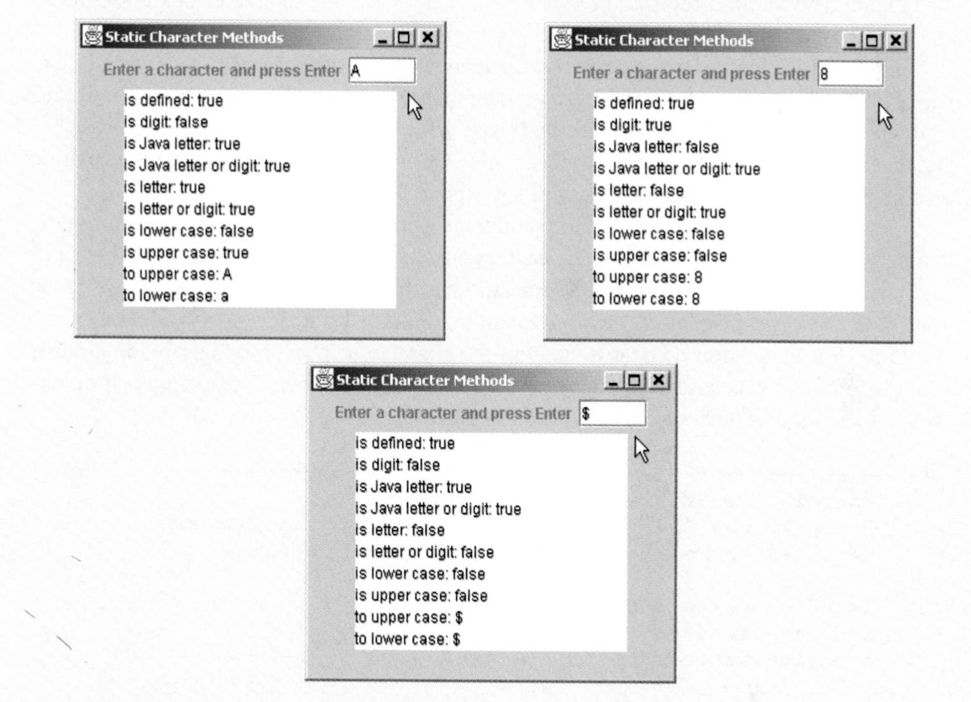

Fig. 10.17 **`static`** character testing methods and case conversion methods of class **`Character`** (part 3 of 3).

Line 64 uses **`Character`** method **`isDigit`** to determine whether character **`c`** is a defined Unicode digit. If so, the method returns **`true`**; otherwise, it returns **`false`**.

Line 66 uses **`Character`** method **`isJavaIdentifierStart`** to determine whether **`c`** is a character that can be used as the first character of an identifier in Java—i.e., a letter, an underscore (_) or a dollar sign (**`$`**). If so, the method returns **`true`**; otherwise, it returns **`false`**. Line 68 uses method **`Character`** method **`isJavaIdentifier-Part`** to determine whether character **`c`** is a character that can be used in an identifier in Java—i.e., a digit, a letter, an underscore (_) or a dollar sign (**`$`**). If so, the method returns **`true`**; otherwise, it returns **`false`**.

Line 69 uses method **`Character`** method **`isLetter`** to determine whether character **`c`** is a letter. If so, the method returns **`true`**; otherwise, it returns **`false`**. Line 71 uses method **`Character`** method **`isLetterOrDigit`** to determine whether character **`c`** is a letter or a digit. If so, the method returns **`true`**; otherwise, it returns **`false`**.

Line 72 uses method **`Character`** method **`isLowerCase`** to determine whether character **`c`** is a lowercase letter. If so, the method returns **`true`**; otherwise, it returns **`false`**. Line 73 uses method **`Character`** method **`isUpperCase`** to determine whether character **`c`** is an uppercase letter. If so, the method returns **`true`**; otherwise, it returns **`false`**.

Line 74 uses method **`Character`** method **`toUpperCase`** to convert the character **`c`** to its uppercase equivalent. The method returns the converted character if the character has an uppercase equivalent; otherwise, the method returns its original argument. Line 75 uses method **`Character`** method **`toLowerCase`** to convert the character **`c`** to its lowercase equivalent. The method returns the converted character if the character has a lowercase equivalent; otherwise, the method returns its original argument.

Figure 10.18 demonstrates **static Character** methods **digit** and **forDigit**, which perform conversions between characters and digits in different number systems. Common number systems include decimal (base 10), octal (base 8), hexadecimal (base 16) and binary (base 2). The base of a number is also known as its *radix*. For more information on conversions between number systems, see Appendix E.

Line 52 uses method **forDigit** to convert the integer **digit** into a character in the number system specified by the integer **radix** (also known as the base of the number). For example, the integer **13** in base 16 (the **radix**) has the character value **'d'**. Note that the lowercase and uppercase letters are equivalent in number systems.

Line 77 uses method **digit** to convert the character **c** into an integer in the number system specified by the integer **radix** (i.e., the base of the number). For example, the character **'A'** in base 16 (the **radix**) has the integer value 10.

```
1  // Fig. 10.18: StaticCharMethods2.java
2  // Demonstrates the static character conversion methods
3  // of class Character from the java.lang package.
4
5  // Java core packages
6  import java.awt.*;
7  import java.awt.event.*;
8
9  // Java extension packages
10 import javax.swing.*;
11
12 public class StaticCharMethods2 extends JFrame {
13    private char c;
14    private int digit, radix;
15    private JLabel prompt1, prompt2;
16    private JTextField input, radixField;
17    private JButton toChar, toInt;
18
19    public StaticCharMethods2()
20    {
21       super( "Character Conversion Methods" );
22
23       // set up GUI and event handling
24       Container container = getContentPane();
25       container.setLayout( new FlowLayout() );
26
27       prompt1 = new JLabel( "Enter a digit or character " );
28       input = new JTextField( 5 );
29       container.add( prompt1 );
30       container.add( input );
31
32       prompt2 = new JLabel( "Enter a radix " );
33       radixField = new JTextField( 5 );
34       container.add( prompt2 );
35       container.add( radixField );
```

Fig. 10.18 Character class **static** conversion methods (part 1 of 3).

```

      toChar = new JButton( "Convert digit to character" );

      toChar.addActionListener(

         // anonymous inner class
         new ActionListener() {

            // handle toChar JButton event
            public void actionPerformed( ActionEvent actionEvent )
            {
               digit = Integer.parseInt( input.getText() );
               radix =
                  Integer.parseInt( radixField.getText() );
               JOptionPane.showMessageDialog( null,
                  "Convert digit to character: " +
                  Character.forDigit( digit, radix ) );
            }

         }  // end anonymous inner class

      ); // end call to addActionListener

      container.add( toChar );

      toInt = new JButton( "Convert character to digit" );

      toInt.addActionListener(

         // anonymous inner class
         new ActionListener() {

            // handle toInt JButton event
            public void actionPerformed( ActionEvent actionEvent )
            {
               String s = input.getText();
               c = s.charAt( 0 );
               radix =
                  Integer.parseInt( radixField.getText() );
               JOptionPane.showMessageDialog( null,
                  "Convert character to digit: " +
                  Character.digit( c, radix ) );
            }

         }  // end anonymous inner class

      ); // end call to addActionListener

      container.add( toInt );

      setSize( 275, 150 );  // set the window size
      show();               // show the window
   }
```

Fig. 10.18 `Character` class `static` conversion methods (part 2 of 3).

```java

   // execute application
   public static void main( String args[] )
   {
      StaticCharMethods2 application = new StaticCharMethods2();

      application.addWindowListener(

         // anonymous inner class
         new WindowAdapter() {

            // handle event when user closes window
            public void windowClosing( WindowEvent windowEvent )
            {
               System.exit( 0 );
            }

         }  // end anonymous inner class

      ); // end call to addWindowListener

   }  // end method main

}  // end class StaticCharMethods2
```

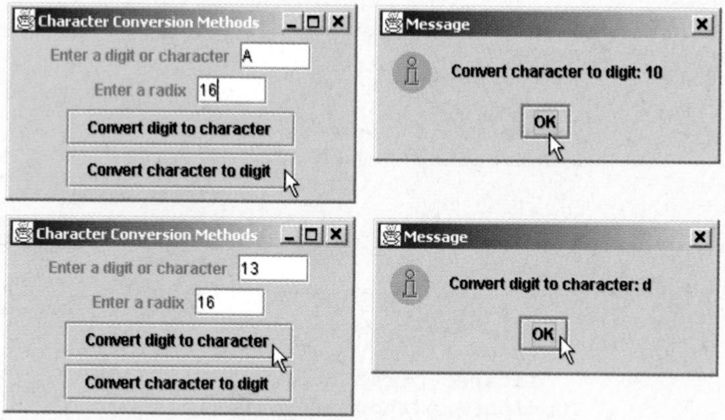

Character Conversion Methods
Enter a digit or character A
Enter a radix 16
Convert digit to character
Convert character to digit

Message
Convert character to digit: 10
OK

Character Conversion Methods
Enter a digit or character 13
Enter a radix 16
Convert digit to character
Convert character to digit

Message
Convert digit to character: d
OK

Fig. 10.18 `Character` class `static` conversion methods (part 3 of 3).

The program in Fig. 10.19 demonstrates the non**`static`** methods of class **`Character`**—the constructor, **`charValue`**, **`toString`**, **`hashCode`** and **`equals`**.

```java
// Fig. 10.19: OtherCharMethods.java
// Demonstrate the non-static methods of class
// Character from the java.lang package.

// Java extension packages
import javax.swing.*;
```

Fig. 10.19 Non-`static` methods of class `Character` (part 1 of 2).

```
7
8  public class OtherCharMethods {
9
10    // test non-static Character methods
11    public static void main( String args[] )
12    {
13       Character c1, c2;
14
15       c1 = new Character( 'A' );
16       c2 = new Character( 'a' );
17
18       String output = "c1 = " + c1.charValue() +
19          "\nc2 = " + c2.toString() +
20          "\n\nhash code for c1 = " + c1.hashCode() +
21          "\nhash code for c2 = " + c2.hashCode();
22
23       if ( c1.equals( c2 ) )
24          output += "\n\nc1 and c2 are equal";
25       else
26          output += "\n\nc1 and c2 are not equal";
27
28       JOptionPane.showMessageDialog( null, output,
29          "Demonstrating Non-Static Character Methods",
30          JOptionPane.INFORMATION_MESSAGE );
31
32       System.exit( 0 );
33    }
34
35 }  // end class OtherCharMethods
```

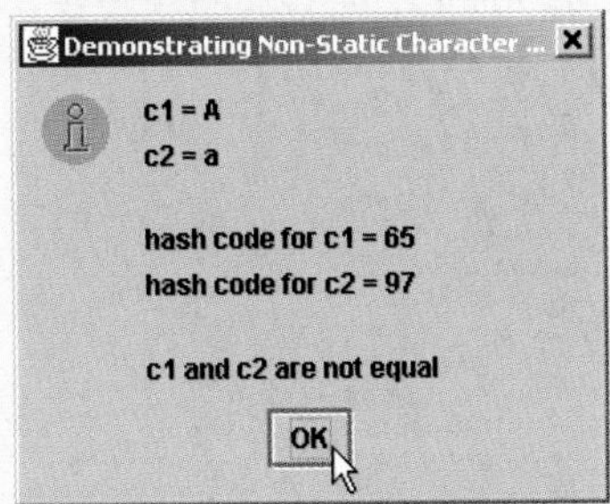

Fig. 10.19 Non-**static** methods of class **Character** (part 2 of 2).

Lines 15–16 instantiate two **Character** objects and pass character literals to the constructor to initialize those objects.

Line 18 uses **Character** method **charValue** to return the **char** value stored in **Character** object **c1**. Line 19 returns a **String** representation of **Character** object **c2** using method **toString**.

Lines 20–21perform **hashCode** calculations on the **Character** objects **c1** and **c2**, respectively. Remember that hash code values are used to store objects in hash tables for fast lookup capabilities (see Chapter 20).

The condition in the **if** structure on line 23 uses method **equals** to determine whether the object **c1** has the same contents as the object **c2** (i.e., the characters inside each object are equal).

10.20 Class StringTokenizer

When you read a sentence, your mind breaks the sentence into individual words and punctuation, or *tokens,* each of which conveys meaning to you. Compilers also perform tokenization. They break up statements into individual pieces like keywords, identifiers, operators and other elements of a programming language. In this section, we study Java's **StringTokenizer** class (from package **java.util**), which breaks a string into its component tokens. Tokens are separated from one another by delimiters, typically white-space characters such as blank, tab, newline and carriage return. Other characters can also be used as delimiters to separate tokens. The program in Fig. 10.20 demonstrates class **StringTokenizer**. The window for class **TokenTest** displays a **JTextField** where the user types a sentence to tokenize. Output in this program is displayed in a **JTextArea**.

When the user presses the *Enter* key in the **JTextField**, method **actionPerformed** (lines 37–49) is invoked. Lines 39–40 assign **String** reference **stringToTokenize** the value in the text in the **JTextField** returned by calling **event.getActionCommand()**. Next, lines 41–42 create an instance of class **StringTokenizer**. This **StringTokenizer** constructor takes a **String** argument and creates a **StringTokenizer** for **stringToTokenize** that will use the default delimiter string **" \n\t\r"** consisting of a space, a newline, a tab and a carriage return for tokenization. There are two other constructors for class **StringTokenizer**. In the version that takes two **String** arguments, the second **String** is the delimiter **String**. In the version that takes three arguments, the second **String** is the delimiter **String** and the third argument (a **boolean**) determines whether the delimiters are also returned as tokens (only if the argument is **true**). This is useful if you need to know what the delimiters are.

```
1  // Fig. 10.20: TokenTest.java
2  // Testing the StringTokenizer class of the java.util package
3
4  // Java core packages
5  import java.util.*;
6  import java.awt.*;
7  import java.awt.event.*;
8
9  // Java extension packages
10 import javax.swing.*;
11
12 public class TokenTest extends JFrame {
13    private JLabel promptLabel;
14    private JTextField inputField;
15    private JTextArea outputArea;
16
```

Fig. 10.20 Tokenizing strings with a **StringTokenizer** object (part 1 of 3).

```
   // set up GUI and event handling
   public TokenTest()
   {
      super( "Testing Class StringTokenizer" );

      Container container = getContentPane();
      container.setLayout( new FlowLayout() );

      promptLabel =
         new JLabel( "Enter a sentence and press Enter" );
      container.add( promptLabel );

      inputField = new JTextField( 20 );

      inputField.addActionListener(

         // anonymous inner class
         new ActionListener() {

            // handle text field event
            public void actionPerformed( ActionEvent event )
            {
               String stringToTokenize =
                  event.getActionCommand();
               StringTokenizer tokens =
                  new StringTokenizer( stringToTokenize );

               outputArea.setText( "Number of elements: " +
                  tokens.countTokens() + "\nThe tokens are:\n" );

               while ( tokens.hasMoreTokens() )
                  outputArea.append( tokens.nextToken() + "\n" );
            }

         }  // end anonymous inner class

      ); // end call to addActionListener

      container.add( inputField );

      outputArea = new JTextArea( 10, 20 );
      outputArea.setEditable( false );
      container.add( new JScrollPane( outputArea ) );

      setSize( 275, 260 );  // set the window size
      show();               // show the window
   }

   // execute application
   public static void main( String args[] )
   {
      TokenTest application = new TokenTest();

```

Fig. 10.20 Tokenizing strings with a **StringTokenizer** object (part 2 of 3).

```
70          application.addWindowListener(
71
72             // anonymous inner class
73             new WindowAdapter() {
74
75                // handle event when user closes window
76                public void windowClosing( WindowEvent windowEvent )
77                {
78                   System.exit( 0 );
79                }
80
81             }  // end anonymous inner class
82
83          ); // end call to addWindowListener
84
85       }  // end method main
86
87    }  // end class TokenTest
```

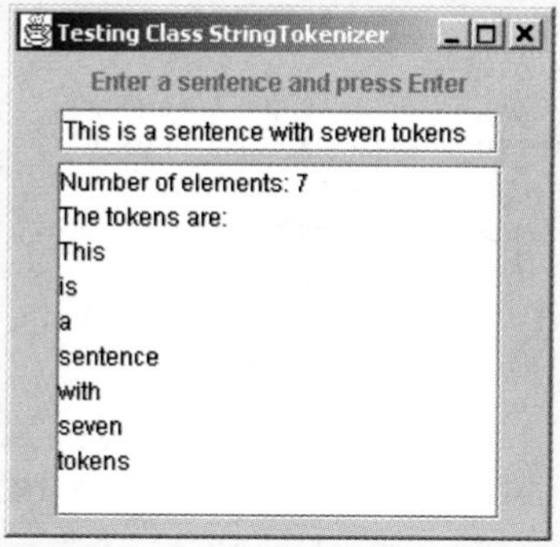

Testing Class StringTokenizer

Enter a sentence and press Enter

This is a sentence with seven tokens

Number of elements: 7
The tokens are:
This
is
a
sentence
with
seven
tokens

Fig. 10.20 Tokenizing strings with a **`StringTokenizer`** object (part 3 of 3).

The statement at lines 44–45 uses the **`StringTokenizer`** method **`countTokens`** to determine the number of tokens in the **`String`** to be tokenized.

The condition in the **`while`** structure at lines 47–48 **`StringTokenizer`** method **`hasMoreTokens`** to determine whether there are more tokens in the **`String`** being tokenized. If so, the **`append`** method is invoked for the **`JTextArea outputArea`** to append the next token to the **`String`** in the **`JTextArea`**. The next token is obtained with a call to **`StringTokenizer`** method **`nextToken`** that returns a **`String`**. The token is output followed by a newline character, so subsequent tokens appear on separate lines.

If you would like to change the delimiter **`String`** while tokenizing a **`String`**, you may do so by specifying a new delimiter string in a **`nextToken`** call as follows:

```
tokens.nextToken( newDelimiterString );
```

This feature is not demonstrated in the program.

10.21 Card Shuffling and Dealing Simulation

In this section, we use random number generation to develop a card shuffling and dealing simulation program. This program can then be used to implement programs that play specific card games.

We develop application **DeckOfCards** (Fig. 10.21), which creates a deck of 52 playing cards using **Card** objects, then enables the user to deal each card by clicking on a "**Deal card**" button. Each card dealt is displayed in a **JTextField**. The user can also shuffle the deck at any time by clicking on a "**Shuffle cards**" button.

```
// Fig. 10.21: DeckOfCards.java
// Card shuffling and dealing program

// Java core packages
import java.awt.*;
import java.awt.event.*;

// Java extension packages
import javax.swing.*;

public class DeckOfCards extends JFrame {
   private Card deck[];
   private int currentCard;
   private JButton dealButton, shuffleButton;
   private JTextField displayField;
   private JLabel statusLabel;

   // set up deck of cards and GUI
   public DeckOfCards()
   {
      super( "Card Dealing Program" );

      String faces[] = { "Ace", "Deuce", "Three", "Four",
         "Five", "Six", "Seven", "Eight", "Nine", "Ten",
         "Jack", "Queen", "King" };
      String suits[] =
         { "Hearts", "Diamonds", "Clubs", "Spades" };

      deck = new Card[ 52 ];
      currentCard = -1;

      // populate deck with Card objects
      for ( int count = 0; count < deck.length; count++ )
         deck[ count ] = new Card( faces[ count % 13 ],
            suits[ count / 13 ] );

      // set up GUI and event handling
      Container container = getContentPane();
      container.setLayout( new FlowLayout() );

      dealButton = new JButton( "Deal card" );
```

Fig. 10.21 Card dealing program (part 1 of 4).

```
      dealButton.addActionListener(

         // anonymous inner class
         new ActionListener() {

            // deal one card
            public void actionPerformed( ActionEvent actionEvent )
            {
               Card dealt = dealCard();

               if ( dealt != null ) {
                  displayField.setText( dealt.toString() );
                  statusLabel.setText( "Card #: " + currentCard );
               }
               else {
                  displayField.setText(
                     "NO MORE CARDS TO DEAL" );
                  statusLabel.setText(
                     "Shuffle cards to continue" );
               }
            }

         }  // end anonymous inner class

      ); // end call to addActionListener

      container.add( dealButton );

      shuffleButton = new JButton( "Shuffle cards" );
      shuffleButton.addActionListener(

         // anonymous inner class
         new ActionListener() {

            // shuffle deck
            public void actionPerformed( ActionEvent actionEvent )
            {
               displayField.setText( "SHUFFLING ..." );
               shuffle();
               displayField.setText( "DECK IS SHUFFLED" );
            }

         }  // end anonymous inner class

      ); // end call to addActionListener

      container.add( shuffleButton );

      displayField = new JTextField( 20 );
      displayField.setEditable( false );
      container.add( displayField );

      statusLabel = new JLabel();
```

Fig. 10.21 Card dealing program (part 2 of 4).

```
      container.add( statusLabel );

      setSize( 275, 120 );  // set window size
      show();               // show window
   }

   // shuffle deck of cards with one-pass algorithm
   public void shuffle()
   {
      currentCard = -1;

      // for each card, pick another random card and swap them
      for ( int first = 0; first < deck.length; first++ ) {
         int second =  ( int ) ( Math.random() * 52 );
         Card temp = deck[ first ];
         deck[ first ] = deck[ second ];
         deck[ second ] = temp;
      }

      dealButton.setEnabled( true );
   }

   // deal one card
   public Card dealCard()
   {
      if ( ++currentCard < deck.length )
         return deck[ currentCard ];
      else {
         dealButton.setEnabled( false );
         return null;
      }
   }

   // execute application
   public static void main( String args[] )
   {
      DeckOfCards app = new DeckOfCards();

      app.addWindowListener(

         // anonymous inner class
         new WindowAdapter() {

            // terminate application when user closes window
            public void windowClosing( WindowEvent windowEvent )
            {
               System.exit( 0 );
            }

         }  // end anonymous inner class

      ); // end call to addWindowListener

```

Fig. 10.21 Card dealing program (part 3 of 4).

```
148    }  // end method main
149
150 }  // end class DeckOfCards
151
152 // class to represent a card
153 class Card {
154    private String face;
155    private String suit;
156
157    // constructor to initialize a card
158    public Card( String cardFace, String cardSuit )
159    {
160       face = cardFace;
161       suit = cardSuit;
162    }
163
164    // return String represenation of Card
165    public String toString()
166    {
167       return face + " of " + suit;
168    }
169
170 }  // end class Card
```

Fig. 10.21 Card dealing program (part 4 of 4).

Class **Card** (lines 153–170) contains two **String** instance variables—**face** and **suit**—that are used to store references to the face name and suit name for a specific **Card**. The constructor for the class receives two **String**s that it uses to initialize **face** and **suit**. Method **toString** is provided to create a **String** consisting of the **face** of the card, the string **" of "** and the **suit** of the card.

Class **DeckOfCards** (lines 11–150) consists of an array **deck** of 52 **Card**s, an integer **currentCard** representing the most recently dealt card in the deck array (–1 if no cards have been dealt yet) and the GUI components used to manipulate the deck of cards. The constructor method of the application instantiates the **deck** array (line 29) and uses the **for** structure at lines 33–35 to fill the **deck** array with **Card**s. Note that each **Card** is instantiated and initialized with two **String**s—one from the **faces** array (**String**s **"Ace"** through **"King"**) and one from the **suits** array (**"Hearts"**, **"Diamonds"**, **"Clubs"** and **"Spades"**). The calculation **count % 13** always results in a value from 0 to 12 (the thirteen subscripts of the **faces** array), and the calculation **count / 13** always results in a value from 0 to 3 (the four subscripts in the **suits** array). When the **deck** array is initialized, it contains the cards with faces ace through king in order for each suit.

When the user clicks the **Deal card** button, method **actionPerformed** at lines 48–62 invokes method **dealCard** (defined at lines 118–126) to get the next card in the array. If the **deck** is not empty, a **Card** object reference is returned; otherwise, **null** is returned. If the reference is not **null**, lines 53–54 display the **Card** in the **JTextField displayField** and display the card number in the **JLabel statusLabel**. If the reference returned by **dealCard** was **null**, the **String** "**NO MORE CARDS TO DEAL**" is displayed in the **JTextField** and the **String** "**Shuffle cards to continue**" is displayed in the **JLabel**.

When the user clicks the **Shuffle cards** button, its **actionPerformed** method at lines 77–82 invokes method **shuffle** (defined on lines 102–115) to shuffle the cards. The method loops through all 52 cards (array subscripts 0 to 51). For each card, a number between 0 and 51 is picked randomly. Next, the current **Card** object and the randomly selected **Card** object are swapped in the array. A total of only 52 swaps are made in a single pass of the entire array, and the array of **Card** objects is shuffled! When the shuffling is complete, the **String** "**DECK IS SHUFFLED**" is displayed in the **JTextField**.

Notice the use of method **setEnabled** at lines 114 and 123 to activate and deactivate the **dealButton**. Method **setEnabled** can be used on many GUI components. When it is called with a **false** argument, the GUI component for which it is called is disabled so the user cannot interact with it. To reactivate the button, method **setEnabled** is called with a **true** argument.

10.22 (Optional Case Study) Thinking About Objects: Event Handling

Objects do not ordinarily perform their operations spontaneously. Rather, a specific operation is normally invoked when a sending object (a *client object*) sends a *message* to a receiving object (a *server object*) requesting that the receiving object perform that specific operation. In earlier sections, we mentioned that objects interact by sending and receiving messages. We began to model the behavior of our elevator system by using statechart and activity diagrams in Section 5.11 and collaboration diagrams in Section 7.10. In this section, we discuss how the objects of the elevator system interact.

Events

In Fig. 7.19, we presented an example of a person pressing a button by sending a **pressButton** message to the button—specifically, the **Person** object called method **pressButton** of the **Button** object. This message describes an action that is currently happening; in other words, the **Person** presses a **Button**. In general, the message name structure is a verb preceding a noun—e.g., the name of the **pressButton** message consists of the verb "press" followed by the noun "button."

An *event* is a message that notifies an object of an action that has already happened. For example, in this section, we modify our simulation so the **Elevator** sends an **elevatorArrived** event to the **Elevator**'s **Door** when the **Elevator** arrives at a **Floor**. In Section 7.10, the **Elevator** opens this **Door** directly by sending an **openDoor** message. Listening for an **elevatorArrived** event allows the **Door** to determine the actions to take when the **Elevator** has arrived, such as notifying the **Person** that the **Door** has opened. This reinforces the OOD principle of encapsulation and models the real world more closely. In reality, the door—not the elevator—"notifies" a person of a door's opening.

Notice that the event-naming structure is the inverse of the first type of message's naming structure. By convention, the event name consists of the noun preceding the verb. For instance, the **elevatorArrived** event name consists of the noun "elevator" preceding the verb "arrived."

In our simulation, we create a superclass called **ElevatorModelEvent** (Fig. 10.22) that represents an event in our model. **ElevatorModelEvent** contains a **Location** reference (line 11) that represents the location where the event was generated and an **Object** reference (line 14) to the source of the event. In our simulation, objects use instances of **ElevatorModelEvent** to send events to other objects. When an object receives an event, that object may use method **getLocation** (lines 31–34) and method **getSource** (lines 43–46) to determine the event's location and origin.

```
1  // ElevatorModelEvent.java
2  // Basic event packet holding Location object
3  package com.deitel.jhtp4.elevator.event;
4
5  // Deitel packages
6  import com.deitel.jhtp4.elevator.model.*;
7
8  public class ElevatorModelEvent {
9
10    // Location that generated ElevatorModelEvent
11    private Location location;
12
13    // source of generated ElevatorModelEvent
14    private Object source;
15
16    // ElevatorModelEvent constructor sets Location
17    public ElevatorModelEvent( Object source,
18       Location location )
19    {
20       setSource( source );
21       setLocation( location );
22    }
23
24    // set ElevatorModelEvent Location
25    public void setLocation( Location eventLocation )
26    {
27       location = eventLocation;
28    }
29
30    // get ElevatorModelEvent Location
31    public Location getLocation()
32    {
33       return location;
34    }
```

Fig. 10.22 Class **ElevatorModelEvent** is the superclass for all other event classes in our model (part 1 of 2).

```

   // set ElevatorModelEvent source
   private void setSource( Object eventSource )
   {
      source = eventSource;
   }

   // get ElevatorModelEvent source
   public Object getSource()
   {
      return source;
   }
}
```

Fig. 10.22 Class **ElevatorModelEvent** is the superclass for all other event classes in our model (part 2 of 2).

For example, a **Door** may send an **ElevatorModelEvent** to a **Person** when opening or closing, and the **Elevator** may send an **ElevatorModelEvent** informing a person of a departure or arrival. Having different objects send the same event type to describe different actions could be confusing. To eliminate ambiguity as we discuss what events are sent by objects, we create several **ElevatorModelEvent** subclasses in Fig. 10.23, so we will have an easier time associating each event with its sender. According to Fig. 10.23, classes **BellEvent**, **PersonMoveEvent**, **LightEvent**, **ButtonEvent**, **ElevatorMoveEvent** and **DoorEvent** are subclasses of class **ElevatorModelEvent**. Using these event subclasses, a **Door** sends a different event (a **DoorEvent**) than does a **Button** (which sends a **ButtonEvent**). Figure 10.24 displays the triggering actions of the subclass events. Note that all actions in Fig. 10.24 appear in the form "noun" + "verb".

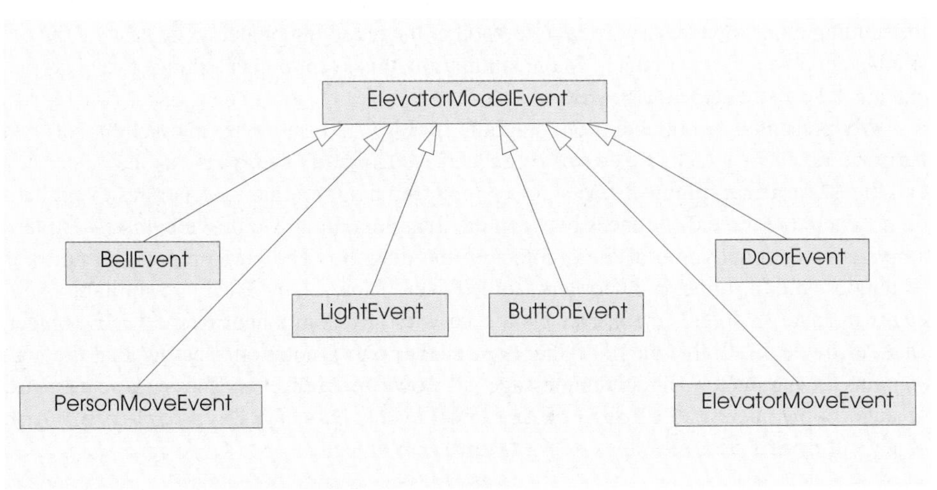

Fig. 10.23 Class diagram that models the generalization between **ElevatorModelEvent** and its subclasses.

Event	Sent when (triggering action)	Sent by object of class
BellEvent	the **Bell** has rung	**Bell**
ButtonEvent	a **Button** has been pressed a **Button** has been reset	**Button** **Button**
DoorEvent	a **Door** has opened a **Door** has closed	**Door** **Door**
LightEvent	a **Light** has turned on a **Light** has turned off	**Light**
PersonMoveEvent	a **Person** has been created a **Person** has arrived at the **Elevator** a **Person** has entered the **Elevator** a **Person** has exited the **Elevator** a **Person** has pressed a **Button** a **Person** has exited the simulation	**Person**
ElevatorMoveEvent	the **Elevator** has arrived at a **Floor** the **Elevator** has departed from a **Floor**	**Elevator**

Fig. 10.24 Triggering actions of the **ElevatorModelEvent** subclass events.

Event Handling

The concept of event handling in Java is similar to the concept of a *collaboration* described in Section 7.10. Event handling consists of an object of one class sending a particular message (which Java calls an *event*) to objects of other classes *listening for that type of message.*[1] The difference is that the objects receiving the message must *register* to receive the message; therefore, event handling describes *how* an object sends an event to other objects "listening" for that type of event—these objects are called *event listeners*. To send an event, the sending object invokes a particular method of the receiving object while passing the desired event object as a parameter. In our simulation, this event object belongs to a class that extends **ElevatorModelEvent**.

We presented a collaboration diagram in Fig. 7.20 showing interactions of two **Person** objects—**waitingPassenger** and **ridingPassenger**—as they enter and exit the **Elevator**. Figure 10.25 shows a modified diagram that incorporates event handling. There are three differences between the diagrams. First, we provide *notes*—explanatory remarks about some of the graphics in the diagram. The UML represents notes as rectangles with the upper right corners "folded over." Notes in the UML are similar to *comments* in Java. A dotted line associates a note with any component of the UML (object, class, arrow, etc.). In this diagram, the **<<parameter>>** notation specifies that the note contains the parameters of a given message: all **doorOpened** events pass a **DoorEvent** object as a parameter; all **elevatorArrived** events pass an **ElevatorMoveEvent** object; all **openDoor** messages pass a **Location** object.

1. Technically, one object sends a notification of an event—or some triggering action—to another object. However, Java parlance refers to sending this notification as "sending an event."

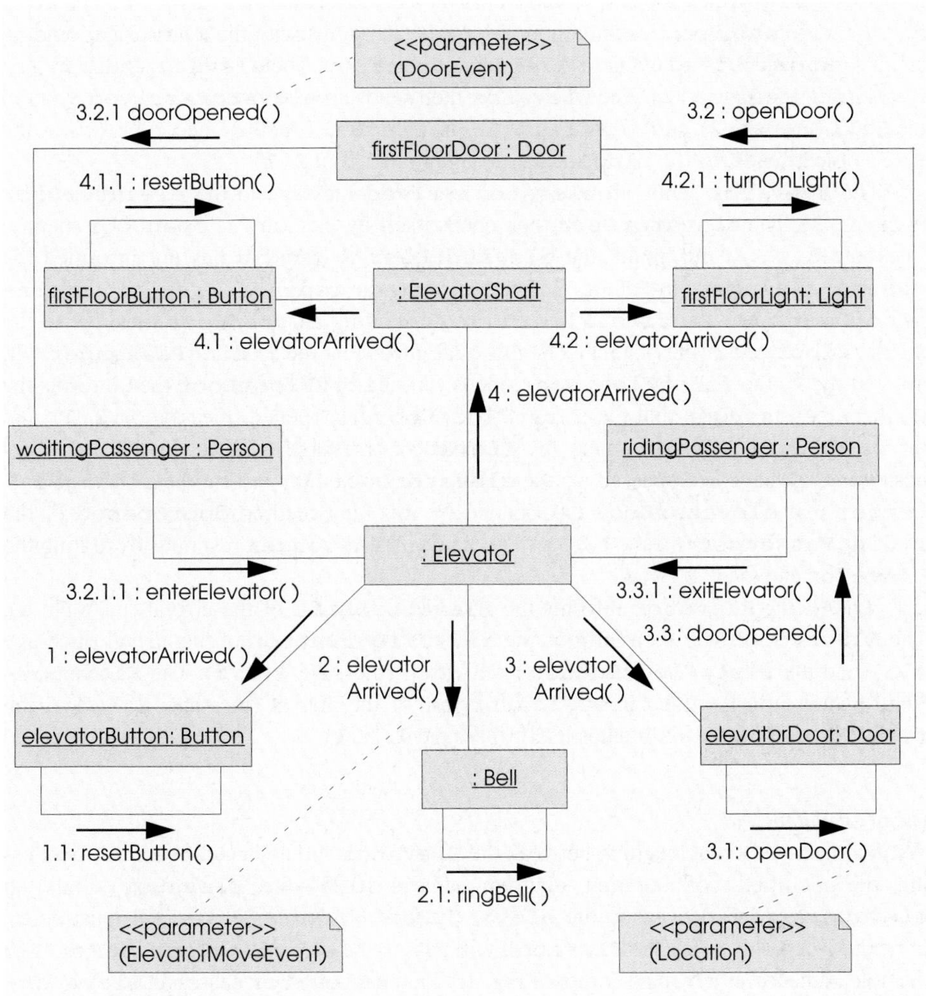

Fig. 10.25 Modified collaboration diagram for passengers entering and exiting the **`Elevator`** on the first **`Floor`**.

The second difference between the diagrams is that the interactions of Fig. 10.25 occur on the first **`Floor`**. This allows us to name all **`Button`** and **`Door`** objects (**`firstFloorDoor`** and **`firstFloorButton`**) to eliminate ambiguity, because the **`Button`** and **`Door`** classes each have three objects in our simulation. The interactions that occur on the second **`Floor`** are identical to the ones that occur on the first **`Floor`**.

The most substantial difference between Fig. 10.25 and Fig. 7.20 is that the **`Elevator`** *informs* objects (via an event) of an action *that has already happened*—the **`Elevator`** *has arrived.* The objects that receive the event then perform some action in response to the type of message they receive.

According to messages **`1`**, **`2`**, **`3`** and **`4`**, the **`Elevator`** performs only one action—it sends **`elevatorArrived`** events to objects interested in receiving those events. Specifically, the **Elevator** object sends an **ElevatorMoveEvent** using the receiving object's **elevatorArrived** method. Figure 10.25 begins with the **Elevator** sending an **elevatorArrived** event to the **elevatorButton**. The **elevatorButton** then *resets itself* (message **1.1**). The **Elevator** then sends an **elevatorArrived** event to the **Bell** (message **2**), and the **Bell** invokes its **ringBell** method, accordingly (i.e., the **Bell** object sends *itself* a **ringBell** message in message **2.1**).

The **Elevator** sends an **elevatorArrived** message to the **elevatorDoor** (message **3**). The **elevatorDoor** then opens itself by invoking its **openDoor** method (message **3.1**). At this point, the **elevatorDoor** is open but has not informed the **ridingPassenger** of opening. Before informing the **ridingPassenger**, the **elevatorDoor** opens the **firstFloorDoor** by sending an **openDoor** message to the **firstFloorDoor** (message **3.2**)—this guarantees that the **ridingPassenger** will not exit before the **firstFloorDoor** opens. The **firstFloorDoor** then informs the **waitingPassenger** that the **firstFloorDoor** has opened (message **3.2.1**), and the **waitingPassenger** enters the **Elevator** (message **3.2.1.1**). All messages nested in **3.2** have been passed, so the **elevatorDoor** may inform the **ridingPassenger** that **elevatorDoor** has opened by invoking method **doorOpened** of the **ridingPassenger** (message **3.3**). The **ridingPassenger** responds by exiting the **Elevator** (message **3.3.1**).[2]

Lastly, the **Elevator** informs the **ElevatorShaft** of the arrival (message **4**). The **ElevatorShaft** then informs the **firstFloorButton** of the arrival (message **4.1**), and the **firstFloorButton** resets itself (message **4.1.1**). The **ElevatorShaft** then informs the **firstFloorLight** of the arrival (message **4.2**), and the **firstFloorLight** illuminates itself (message **4.2.1**).

Event Listeners

We demonstrated event handling between the **Elevator** and object **elevatorDoor** using the modified collaboration diagram of Fig. 10.25—the **Elevator** sends an **elevatorArrived** event to the **elevatorDoor** (message **3**). We first must determine the event object that the **Elevator** will pass to the **elevatorDoor**. According to the note in the lower left-hand corner of Fig. 10.25, the **Elevator** passes an **ElevatorMoveEvent** (Fig. 10.26) object when the **Elevator** invokes an **elevatorArrived** method. The generalization diagram of Fig. 10.23 indicates that **ElevatorMoveEvent** is a subclass of **ElevatorModelEvent**, so **ElevatorMoveEvent** inherits the **Object** and **Location** references from **ElevatorModelEvent**.[3]

---

2. The problem of the **waitingPassenger** entering the **Elevator** (message **3.2.1.1**) before the **ridingPassenger** has exited (message **3.3.1**) remains in our collaboration diagram. We show in "Thinking About Objects" Section 15.12 how to solve this problem by using multithreading, synchronization and active classes.
3. In our simulation, all event classes have this structure—that is, the structure of class **ElevatorMoveEvent** is identical to the structure of class **DoorEvent**, **ButtonEvent**, etc. When you have finished reading the material in this section, we recommend that you view the implementation of the events in Appendix G to attain a better comprehension of the structure of our system events—Fig. G.1–G.7 present the code for the events, and Fig. G.8–G.14 present the code for the event listeners.

```
// ElevatorMoveEvent.java
// Indicates on which Floor the Elevator arrived or departed
package com.deitel.jhtp4.elevator.event;

// Deitel package
import com.deitel.jhtp4.elevator.model.*;

public class ElevatorMoveEvent extends ElevatorModelEvent {

   // ElevatorMoveEvent constructor
   public ElevatorMoveEvent( Object source, Location location )
   {
      super( source, location );
   }
}
```

Fig. 10.26 Class **ElevatorMoveEvent**, a subclass of **ElevatorModelEvent**, is sent when the **Elevator** has arrived at or departed from, a **Floor**.

The **elevatorDoor** must implement an interface that "listens" for an **ElevatorMoveEvent**—this makes the **elevatorDoor** an event listener. Interface **ElevatorMoveListener** (Fig. 10.27) provides methods **elevatorDeparted** (line 8) and **elevatorArrived** (line 11) that enable the **Elevator** to notify the **ElevatorMoveListener** when the **Elevator** has arrived or departed. An interface that provides the methods for an event listener, such as **ElevatorMoveListener**, is called an *event listener interface*.

Methods **elevatorArrived** and **elevatorDeparted** each receive an **ElevatorMoveEvent** (Fig. 10.26) object as an argument. Therefore, when the **Elevator** "sends an **elevatorArrived** event" to another object, the **Elevator** passes an **ElevatorMoveEvent** object as an argument to the receiving object's **elevatorArrived** method. We implement class **Door**—the class of which the **elevatorDoor** is an instance—in Appendix H, after we continue refining our design and learning more Java capabilities.

```
1  // ElevatorMoveListener.java
2  // Methods invoked when Elevator has either departed or arrived
3  package com.deitel.jhtp4.elevator.event;
4
5  public interface ElevatorMoveListener {
6
7     // invoked when Elevator has departed
8     public void elevatorDeparted( ElevatorMoveEvent moveEvent );
9
10    // invoked when Elevator has arrived
11    public void elevatorArrived( ElevatorMoveEvent moveEvent );
12 }
```

Fig. 10.27 Interface **ElevatorMoveListener** provides the methods required to listen for **Elevator** departure and arrival events.

Class Diagram Revisited

Figure 10.28 modifies the associations in the class diagram of Fig. 9.19 to include event handling. Note that like the collaboration diagram of Fig. 10.25, Fig. 10.28 indicates that an object informs, or *signals*, another object that some event has occurred. If an object receiving the event invokes a **`private`** method, the class diagram represents this method invocation as a *self association*—that is, the class contains an association with itself. The **`Button`**, **`Door`**, **`Light`** and **`Bell`** classes contain self associations; note that the association does not include an arrowhead indicating the direction of the association, because the class's association is with itself. Lastly, the diagram includes an association between class **`Door`** and class **`Person`** (the **`Door`** informs a **`Person`** that the **`Door`** has opened), because we established the relationship between all **`Door`** objects and a **`Person`** object.

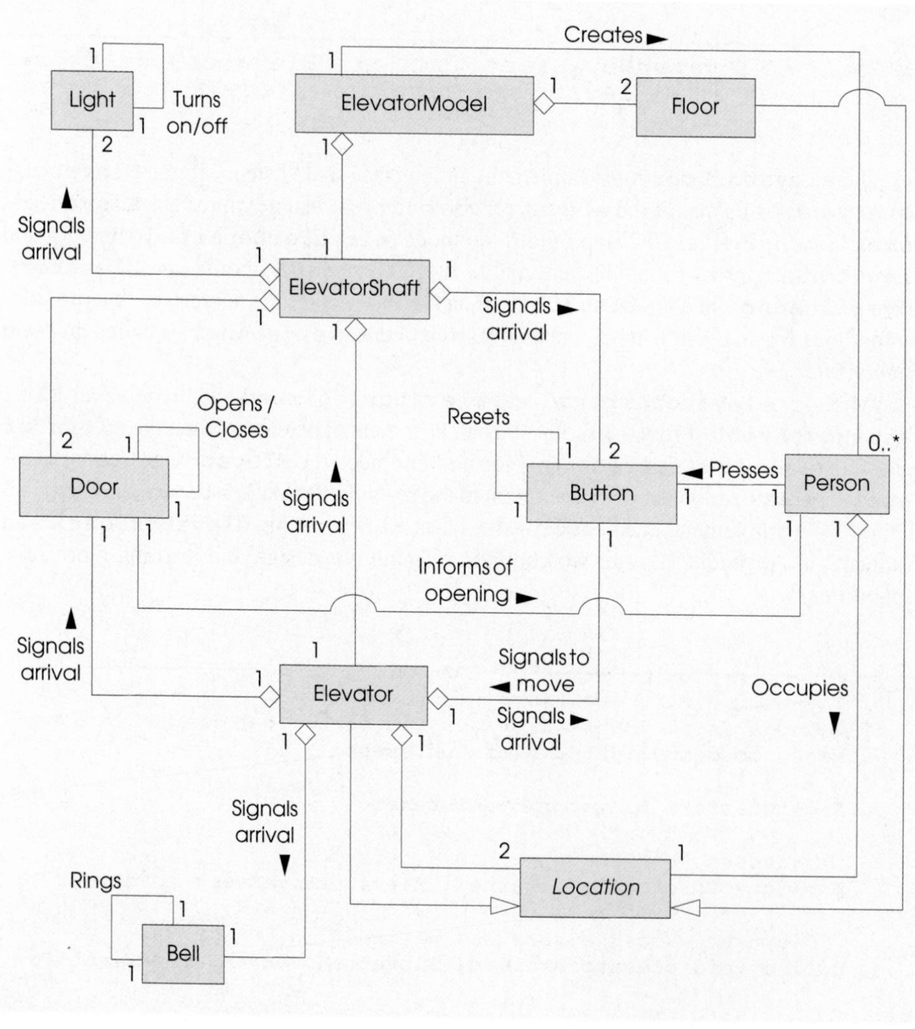

Fig. 10.28 Class diagram of our simulator (including event handling).

SUMMARY

- A character constant's value is its integer value in the Unicode character set. Strings can include letters, digits and special characters such as **+**, **-**, *****, **/** and **$**. A string in Java is an object of class **String**. String literals or string constants are often referred to as *anonymous* ***String*** *objects* and are written in double quotes in a program.
- Class **String** provides nine constructors.
- **String** method **length** returns the number of characters in a **String**.
- **String** method **charAt** returns the character at a specific position.
- Method **equals** is used to test any two objects for equality (i.e., the contents of the two objects are identical). The method returns **true** if the objects are equal, **false** otherwise. Method **equals** uses a *lexicographical comparison* for **String**s.
- When primitive-data type values are compared with **==**, the result is **true** if both values are identical. When references are compared with **==**, the result is **true** if both references refer to *the same object in memory.*
- Java treats all anonymous **String**s with the same contents as one anonymous **String** object.
- **String** method **equalsIgnoreCase** performs a case-insensitive **String** comparison.
- **String** method **compareTo** returns 0 if the **Strings** it is comparing are equal, a negative number if the **String** that invokes **compareTo** is less than the **String** that is passed as an argument and a positive number if the **String** that invokes **compareTo** is greater than the **String** that is passed as an argument. Method **compareTo** uses a lexicographical comparison.
- **String** method **regionMatches** compares portions of two **String**s for equality.
- **String** method **startsWith** determines whether a **String** starts with the characters specified as an argument. **String** method **endsWith** determines whether a **String** ends with the characters specified as an argument.
- Method **hashCode** performs a hash code calculation that enables a **String** object to be stored in a hash table. This method is inherited from **Object** and overridden by **String**.
- **String** method **indexOf** locates the first occurrence of a character or a substring in a **String**. Method **lastIndexOf** locates the last occurrence of a character or a substring in a **String**.
- **String** method **substring** copies and returns part of an existing **String** object.
- **String** method **concat** concatenates two **String** objects and returns a new **String** object containing the characters from both original **Strings**.
- **String** method **replace** returns a new **String** object that replaces every occurrence in a **String** of its first character argument with its second character argument.
- **String** method **toUpperCase** returns a new **String** with uppercase letters in the positions where the original **String** had lowercase letters. Method **toLowerCase** returns a new **String** with lowercase letters in the positions where the original **String** had uppercase letters.
- **String** method **trim** returns a new **String** object in which all white-space characters (such as spaces, newlines and tabs) have been removed from the beginning or end of a **String**.
- **String** method **toCharArray** returns a new character array containing a copy of the characters in a **String**.
- **String** class method **valueOf** returns its argument converted to a string.
- The first time **String** method **intern** is invoked on a **String** it returns a reference to that **String** object. Subsequent invocations of **intern** on different **String** objects that have the same contents as the original **String** result in multiple references to the original **String** object.

- Class **StringBuffer** provides three constructors that enable **StringBuffer**s to be initialized with no characters and an initial capacity of 16 characters; with no characters and an initial capacity specified in the integer argument or with a copy of the characters of the **String** argument and an initial capacity that is the number of characters in the **String** argument plus 16.
- **StringBuffer** method **length** returns the number of characters currently stored in a **StringBuffer**. Method **capacity** returns the number of characters that can be stored in a **StringBuffer** without allocating more memory.
- Method **ensureCapacity** ensures that a **StringBuffer** has a minimum capacity. Method **setLength** increases or decreases the length of a **StringBuffer**.
- **StringBuffer** method **charAt** returns the character at the specified index. Method **setCharAt** sets the character at the specified position. Method **getChars** returns a character array containing a copy of the characters in the **StringBuffer**.
- Class **StringBuffer** provides overloaded **append** methods to add primitive data-type, character array, **String** and **Object** values to the end of a **StringBuffer**.
- **StringBuffer**s and the **append** methods are used by the Java compiler to implement the **+** and **+=** operators for concatenating **String**s.
- Class **StringBuffer** provides overloaded **insert** methods to insert primitive data-type, character array, **String** and **Object** values at any position in a **StringBuffer**.
- Class **Character** provides a constructor that takes a character argument.
- **Character** method **isDefined** determines whether a character is defined in the Unicode character set. If so, the method returns **true**; otherwise, it returns **false**.
- **Character** method **isDigit** determines whether a character is a defined Unicode digit. If so, the method returns **true**; otherwise, it returns **false**.
- **Character** method **isJavaIdentifierStart** determines whether a character is a character that can be used as the first character of an identifier in Java [i.e., a letter, an underscore (_) or a dollar sign (**$**)]. If so, the method returns **true**; otherwise, it returns **false**.
- **Character** method **isJavaIdentifierPart** determines whether a character is a character that can be used in an identifier in Java [i.e., a digit, a letter, an underscore (_) or a dollar sign (**$**)]. If so, the method returns **true**; otherwise, it returns **false**. Method **isLetter** determines whether a character is a letter. If so, the method returns **true**; otherwise, it returns **false**. Method **isLetterOrDigit** determines whether a character is a letter or a digit. If so, the method returns **true**; otherwise, it returns **false**.
- **Character** method **isLowerCase** determines whether a character is a lowercase letter. If so, the method returns **true**; otherwise, **false**. **Character** method **isUpperCase** determines if a character is an uppercase letter. If so, the method returns **true**; otherwise, **false**.
- **Character** method **toUpperCase** converts a character to its uppercase equivalent. Method **toLowerCase** converts a character to its lowercase equivalent.
- **Character** method **digit** converts its character argument into an integer in the number system specified by its integer argument **radix**. Method **forDigit** converts its integer argument **digit** into a character in the number system specified by its integer argument **radix**.
- **Character** method **charValue** returns the **char** stored in a **Character** object. Method **toString** returns a **String** representation of a **Character**.
- **Character** method **hashCode** performs a hash code calculation on a **Character**.
- **StringTokenizer**'s default constructor creates a **StringTokenizer** for its **String** argument that will use the default delimiter string **" \n\t\r"**, consisting of a space, a newline, a tab and a carriage return for tokenization.

- **StringTokenizer** method **countTokens** returns the number of tokens in a **String** to be tokenized.
- **StringTokenizer** method **hasMoreTokens** determines if there are more tokens in the **String** being tokenized.
- **StringTokenizer** method **nextToken** returns a **String** with the next token.

TERMINOLOGY

append method of class **StringBuffer**
appending strings to other strings
array of strings
capacity method of class **StringBuffer**
Character class
character code
character constant
character set
charAt method of class **String**
charAt method of class **StringBuffer**
charValue method of class **Character**
compareTo method of class **String**
comparing strings
concat method of class **String**
concatenation
copying strings
countTokens method (**StringTokenizer**)
delimiter
digit method of class **Character**
endsWith method of class **String**
equals method of class **String**
equalsIgnoreCase method of **String**
forDigit method of class **Character**
getChars method of class **String**
getChars method of class **StringBuffer**
hash table
hashCode method of class **Character**
hashCode method of class **String**
hasMoreTokens method
hexadecimal digits
indexOf method of class **String**
insert method of class **StringBuffer**
intern method of class **String**
isDefined method of class **Character**
isDigit method of class **Character**
isJavaIdentifierPart method
isJavaIdentifierStart method
isLetter method of class **Character**
isLetterOrDigit method of **Character**
isLowerCase method of class **Character**
isUpperCase method of class **Character**
lastIndexOf method of class **String**
length method of class **String**
length method of class **StringBuffer**
length of a string
literal
nextToken method of **StringTokenizer**
numeric code representation of a character
printing character
regionMatches method of class **String**
replace method of class **String**
search string
setCharAt method of class **StringBuffer**
startsWith method of class **String**
string
String class
string concatenation
string constant
string literal
string processing
StringBuffer class
StringIndexOutOfBoundsException
StringTokenizer class
substring method of **String** class
toCharArray method of class **String**
token
tokenizing strings
toLowerCase method of class **Character**
toLowerCase method of class **String**
toString method of class **Character**
toString method of class **String**
toString method of class **StringBuffer**
toUpperCase method of class **Character**
toUpperCase method of class **String**
trim method of class **String**
Unicode
valueOf method of class **String**
white-space characters
word processing

SELF-REVIEW EXERCISES

10.1 State whether each of the following is *true* or *false*. If *false*, explain why.
a) When **String** objects are compared with **==**, the result is **true** if the **String**s contain the same values.
b) A **String** can be modified after it is created.

10.2 For each of the following, write a single statement that performs the indicated task.
a) Compare the string in **s1** to the string in **s2** for equality of contents.
b) Append the string **s2** to the string **s1**, using **+=**.
c) Determine the length of the string in **s1**.

ANSWERS TO SELF-REVIEW EXERCISES

10.1 a) False. **String** objects that are compared with operator **==** are actually compared to determine if they are the same object in memory.
b) False. **String** objects are constant and cannot be modified after they are created. **StringBuffer** objects can be modified after they are created.

10.2 a) **s1.equals(s2)**
b) **s1 += s2;**
c) **s1.length()**

EXERCISES

Exercises 10.3 through 10.6 are reasonably challenging. Once you have done these problems, you ought to be able to implement most popular card games easily.

10.3 Modify the program in Fig. 10.21 so that the card-dealing method deals a five-card poker hand. Then write the following additional methods:
a) Determine if the hand contains a pair.
b) Determine if the hand contains two pairs.
c) Determine if the hand contains three of a kind (e.g., three jacks).
d) Determine if the hand contains four of a kind (e.g., four aces).
e) Determine if the hand contains a flush (i.e., all five cards of the same suit).
f) Determine if the hand contains a straight (i.e., five cards of consecutive face values).
g) Determine if the hand contains a full house (i.e., two cards of one face value and three cards of another face value).

10.4 Use the methods developed in Exercise 10.3 to write a program that deals two five-card poker hands, evaluates each hand and determines which is the better hand.

10.5 Modify the program developed in Exercise 10.4 so that it can simulate the dealer. The dealer's five-card hand is dealt "face down" so the player cannot see it. The program should then evaluate the dealer's hand and, based on the quality of the hand, the dealer should draw one, two or three more cards to replace the corresponding number of unneeded cards in the original hand. The program should then reevaluate the dealer's hand. (*Caution*: This is a difficult problem!)

10.6 Modify the program developed in Exercise 10.5 so that it can handle the dealer's hand automatically, but the player is allowed to decide which cards of the player's hand to replace. The program should then evaluate both hands and determine who wins. Now, use this new program to play 20 games against the computer. Who wins more games, you or the computer? Have one of your friends play 20 games against the computer. Who wins more games? Based on the results of these games, make appropriate modifications to refine your poker-playing program. (This, too, is a difficult problem.) Play 20 more games. Does your modified program play a better game?

10.7 Write an application that uses `String` method `compareTo` to compare two strings input by the user. Output whether the first string is less than, equal to or greater than the second.

10.8 Write an application that uses `String` method `regionMatches` to compare two strings input by the user. The program should input the number of characters to be compared and the starting index of the comparison. The program should state whether the first string is less than, equal to or greater than the second string. Ignore the case of the characters when performing the comparison.

10.9 Write an application that uses random number generation to create sentences. Use four arrays of strings called `article`, `noun`, `verb` and `preposition`. Create a sentence by selecting a word at random from each array in the following order: `article`, `noun`, `verb`, `preposition`, `article` and `noun`. As each word is picked, concatenate it to the previous words in the sentence. The words should be separated by spaces. When the final sentence is output, it should start with a capital letter and end with a period. The program should generate 20 sentences and output them to a text area.

The arrays should be filled as follows: The article array should contain the articles `"the"`, `"a"`, `"one"`, `"some"` and `"any"`; the noun array should contain the nouns `"boy"`, `"girl"`, `"dog"`, `"town"` and `"car"`; the verb array should contain the verbs `"drove"`, `"jumped"`, `"ran"`, `"walked"` and `"skipped"`; the preposition array should contain the prepositions `"to"`, `"from"`, `"over"`, `"under"` and `"on"`.

After the preceding program is written, modify the program to produce a short story consisting of several of these sentences. (How about the possibility of a random term paper writer!)

10.10 *(Limericks)* A limerick is a humorous five-line verse in which the first and second lines rhyme with the fifth, and the third line rhymes with the fourth. Using techniques similar to those developed in Exercise 10.9, write a Java program that produces random limericks. Polishing this program to produce good limericks is a challenging problem, but the result will be worth the effort!

10.11 *(Pig Latin)* Write an application that encodes English language phrases into pig Latin. Pig Latin is a form of coded language often used for amusement. Many variations exist in the methods used to form pig Latin phrases. For simplicity, use the following algorithm:

To form a pig Latin phrase from an English language phrase, tokenize the phrase into words with an object of class StringTokenizer. To translate each English word into a pig Latin word, place the first letter of the English word at the end of the word and add the letters "ay." Thus, the word "jump" becomes "umpjay," the word "the" becomes "hetay," and the word "computer" becomes "omputercay." Blanks between words remain as blanks. Assume the following: The English phrase consists of words separated by blanks, there are no punctuation marks and all words have two or more letters. Method `printLatinWord` should display each word. Each token returned from `nextToken` is passed to method `printLatinWord` to print the pig Latin word. Enable the user to input the sentence. Keep a running display of all the converted sentences in a text area.

10.12 Write an application that inputs a telephone number as a string in the form `(555) 555-5555`. The program should use an object of class `StringTokenizer` to extract the area code as a token, the first three digits of the phone number as a token and the last four digits of the phone number as a token. The seven digits of the phone number should be concatenated into one string. The program should convert the area code string to `int` (remember `parseInt`!) and convert the phone number string to `long`. Both the area code and the phone number should be printed. Remember that you will have to change delimiter characters during the tokenization process.

10.13 Write an application that inputs a line of text, tokenizes the line with an object of class `StringTokenizer` and outputs the tokens in reverse order.

10.14 Use the string comparison methods discussed and the techniques for sorting arrays developed in Chapter 7 to write a program that alphabetizes a list of strings. Allow the user to enter the strings in a text field. Display the results in a text area.

10.15 Write an application that inputs text and outputs the text in uppercase and lowercase letters.

10.16 Write an application that inputs several lines of text and a search character and uses method **`String`** method **`indexOf`** to determine the number of occurrences of the character in the text.

10.17 Write an application based on the program in Exercise 10.16 that inputs several lines of text and uses **`String`** method **`indexOf`** to determine the total number of occurrences of each letter of the alphabet in the text. Uppercase and lowercase letters should be counted together. Store the totals for each letter in an array and print the values in tabular format after the totals have been determined.

10.18 Write an application that reads a series of strings and outputs only those strings beginning with the letter "**`b`**." The results should be output to a text area.

10.19 Write an application that reads a series of strings and prints only those strings ending with the letters "**`ED`**." The results should be output to a text area.

10.20 Write an application that inputs an integer code for a character and displays the corresponding character. Modify this program so that it generates all possible three-digit codes in the range form 000 to 255 and attempts to print the corresponding characters. Display the results in a text area.

10.21 Write your own versions of the **`String`** methods for searching strings.

10.22 Write a program that reads a five-letter word from the user and produces all possible three-letter words that can be derived from the letters of the five-letter word. For example, the three-letter words produced from the word "bathe" include the commonly used words "ate," "bat," "bet," "tab," "hat," "the" and "tea."

SPECIAL SECTION: ADVANCED STRING MANIPULATION EXERCISES

The preceding exercises are keyed to the text and designed to test the reader's understanding of fundamental string-manipulation concepts. This section includes a collection of intermediate and advanced string-manipulation exercises. The reader should find these problems challenging, yet entertaining. The problems vary considerably in difficulty. Some require an hour or two of program writing and implementation. Others are useful for lab assignments that might require two or three weeks of study and implementation. Some are challenging term projects.

10.23 *(Text Analysis)* The availability of computers with string-manipulation capabilities has resulted in some rather interesting approaches to analyzing the writings of great authors. Much attention has been focused on whether William Shakespeare ever lived. Some scholars believe there is substantial evidence indicating that Christopher Marlowe or other authors actually penned the masterpieces attributed to Shakespeare. Researchers have used computers to find similarities in the writings of these two authors. This exercise examines three methods for analyzing texts with a computer.

a) Write an application that reads several lines of text from the keyboard and prints a table indicating the number of occurrences of each letter of the alphabet in the text. For example, the phrase

```
To be, or not to be: that is the question:
```

contains one "a," two "b's," no "c's," etc.

b) Write an application that reads several lines of text and prints a table indicating the number of one-letter words, two-letter words, three-letter words, etc. appearing in the text. For example, Fig. 10.29 shows the counts for the phrase

```
Whether 'tis nobler in the mind to suffer
```

Word length	Occurrences
1	0
2	2
3	1
4	2 (including **'tis**)
5	0
6	2
7	1

Fig. 10.29 Counts for the string **"Whether 'tis nobler in the mind to suffer"**.

c) Write an application that reads several lines of text and prints a table indicating the number of occurrences of each different word in the text. The first version of your program should include the words in the table in the same order in which they appear in the text. For example, the lines

```
To be, or not to be: that is the question:
Whether 'tis nobler in the mind to suffer
```

contain the words "to" three times, the word "be" two times, the word "or" once, etc. A more interesting (and useful) printout should then be attempted in which the words are sorted alphabetically.

10.24 *(Printing Dates in Various Formats)* Dates are printed in several common formats. Two of the more common formats are

```
04/25/1955 and April 25, 1955
```

Write an application that reads a date in the first format and prints that date in the second format.

10.25 *(Check Protection)* Computers are frequently employed in check-writing systems such as payroll and accounts payable applications. Many strange stories circulate regarding weekly paychecks being printed (by mistake) for amounts in excess of $1 million. Incorrect amounts are printed by computerized check-writing systems because of human error and/or machine failure. Systems designers build controls into their systems to prevent such erroneous checks from being issued.

Another serious problem is the intentional alteration of a check amount by someone who intends to cash a check fraudulently. To prevent a dollar amount from being altered, most computerized check-writing systems employ a technique called *check protection.*

Checks designed for imprinting by computer contain a fixed number of spaces in which the computer may print an amount. Suppose a paycheck contains eight blank spaces in which the computer is supposed to print the amount of a weekly paycheck. If the amount is large, then all eight of those spaces will be filled, for example:

1,230.60 *(check amount)*

12345678 *(position numbers)*

On the other hand, if the amount is less than $1000, then several of the spaces would ordinarily be left blank. For example,

```
   99.87
--------
12345678
```

contains three blank spaces. If a check is printed with blank spaces, it is easier for someone to alter the amount of the check. To prevent a check from being altered, many check-writing systems insert *leading asterisks* to protect the amount as follows:

```
***99.87
--------
12345678
```

Write an application that inputs a dollar amount to be printed on a check, then prints the amount in check-protected format with leading asterisks if necessary. Assume that nine spaces are available for printing the amount.

10.26 *(Writing the Word Equivalent of a Check Amount)* Continuing the discussion of the previous exercise, we reiterate the importance of designing check-writing systems to prevent alteration of check amounts. One common security method requires that the check amount be written both in numbers and "spelled out" in words as well. Even if someone is able to alter the numerical amount of the check, it is extremely difficult to change the amount in words.

a) Many computerized check-writing systems do not print the amount of the check in words. Perhaps the main reason for this omission is the fact that most high-level languages used in commercial applications do not contain adequate string-manipulation features. Another reason is that the logic for writing word equivalents of check amounts is somewhat involved.
b) Write an application that inputs a numeric check amount and writes the word equivalent of the amount. For example, the amount 112.43 should be written as

```
ONE HUNDRED TWELVE and 43/100
```

10.27 *(Morse Code)* Perhaps the most famous of all coding schemes is the Morse code, developed by Samuel Morse in 1832 for use with the telegraph system. The Morse code assigns a series of dots and dashes to each letter of the alphabet, each digit, and a few special characters (such as period, comma, colon and semicolon). In sound-oriented systems, the dot represents a short sound and the dash represents a long sound. Other representations of dots and dashes are used with light-oriented systems and signal-flag systems.

Separation between words is indicated by a space, or, quite simply, the absence of a dot or dash. In a sound-oriented system, a space is indicated by a short period of time during which no sound is transmitted. The international version of the Morse code appears in Fig. 10.30.

Write an application that reads an English language phrase and encodes the phrase into Morse code. Also write a program that reads a phrase in Morse code and converts the phrase into the English language equivalent. Use one blank between each Morse-coded letter and three blanks between each Morse-coded word.

10.28 *(A Metric Conversion Program)* Write an application that will assist the user with metric conversions. Your program should allow the user to specify the names of the units as strings (i.e., centimeters, liters, grams, etc. for the metric system and inches, quarts, pounds, etc. for the English system) and should respond to simple questions such as

```
"How many inches are in 2 meters?"
"How many liters are in 10 quarts?"
```

Character	Code	Character	Code
A	.-	T	-
B	-...	U	..-
C	-.-.	V	...-
D	-..	W	.--
E	.	X	-..-
F	..-.	Y	-.--
G	--.	Z	--..
H	....		
I	..	Digits	
J	.---	1	.----
K	-.-	2	..---
L	.-..	3	...--
M	--	4	....-
N	-.	5	.....
O	---	6	-....
P		7	--...
Q	--.-	8	---..
R	.-.	9	----.
S	...	0	-----

Fig. 10.30 The letters of the alphabet as expressed in international Morse code .

Your program should recognize invalid conversions. For example, the question

```
"How many feet in 5 kilograms?"
```

is not a meaningful question because **`"feet"`** is a unit of length while **`"kilograms"`** is a unit of mass.

SPECIAL SECTION: CHALLENGING STRING MANIPULATION PROJECTS

10.29 *(Project: A Spelling Checker)* Many popular word processing software packages have built-in spell checkers.

In this project, you are asked to develop your own spell-checker utility. We make suggestions to help get you started. You should then consider adding more capabilities. Use a computerized dictionary (if you have access to one) as a source of words.

Why do we type so many words with incorrect spellings? In some cases, it is because we simply do not know the correct spelling, so we make a "best guess." In some cases, it is because we transpose two letters (e.g., "defualt" instead of "default"). Sometimes we double-type a letter accidentally (e.g., "hanndy" instead of "handy"). Sometimes we type a nearby key instead of the one we intended (e.g., "biryhday" instead of "birthday"), and so on.

Design and implement a spell-checker application in Java. Your program should maintain an array **`wordList`** of strings. Enable the user to enter these strings. [*Note*: In Chapter 17, we introduce file processing. Once you have this capability, you can obtain the words for the spell checker from a computerized dictionary stored in a file.]

Your program should ask a user to enter a word. The program should then look up that word in the **`wordList`** array. If the word is present in the array, your program should print "**`Word is spelled correctly`**."

If the word is not present in the array, your program should print "**`word is not spelled correctly`**." Then your program should try to locate other words in **`wordList`** that might be the word the user intended to type. For example, you can try all possible single transpositions of adjacent letters to discover that the word "default" is a direct match to a word in **`wordList`**. Of course, this implies that your program will check all other single transpositions, such as "edfault," "dfeault," "deafult," "defalut," and "defautl." When you find a new word that matches one in **`wordList`**, print that word in a message, such as "**`Did you mean "default?"`**."

Implement other tests, such as replacing each double letter with a single letter and any other tests you can develop to improve the value of your spell-checker.

10.30 *(Project: A Crossword Puzzle Generator)* Most people have worked a crossword puzzle, but few have ever attempted to generate one. Generating a crossword puzzle is suggested here as a string-manipulation project requiring substantial sophistication and effort.

There are many issues the programmer must resolve to get even the simplest crossword puzzle-generator program working. For example, how does one represent the grid of a crossword puzzle inside the computer? Should one use a series of strings, or should double-subscripted arrays be used?

The programmer needs a source of words (i.e., a computerized dictionary) that can be directly referenced by the program. In what form should these words be stored to facilitate the complex manipulations required by the program?

The really ambitious reader will want to generate the "clues" portion of the puzzle, in which the brief hints for each "across" word and each "down" word are printed for the puzzle worker. Merely printing a version of the blank puzzle itself is not a simple problem.

11

Graphics and Java2D

Objectives

- To understand graphics contexts and graphics objects.
- To understand and be able to manipulate colors.
- To understand and be able to manipulate fonts.
- To use **`Graphics`** methods to draw lines, rectangles, rectangles with rounded corners, three-dimensional rectangles, ovals, arcs and polygons.
- To use methods of class **`Graphics2D`** from the Java2D API to draw lines, rectangles, rectangles with rounded corners, ellipses, arcs and general paths.
- To be able to specify **`Paint`** and **`Stroke`** characteristics of shapes displayed with **`Graphics2D`**.

One picture is worth ten thousand words.
Chinese proverb

Treat nature in terms of the cylinder, the sphere, the cone, all in perspective.
Paul Cezanne

Nothing ever becomes real till it is experienced—even a proverb is no proverb to you till your life has illustrated it.
John Keats

A picture shows me at a glance what it takes dozens of pages of a book to expound.
Ivan Sergeyevich Turgenev

Outline

11.1 Introduction
11.2 Graphics Contexts and Graphics Objects
11.3 Color Control
11.4 Font Control
11.5 Drawing Lines, Rectangles and Ovals
11.6 Drawing Arcs
11.7 Drawing Polygons and Polylines
11.8 The Java2D API
11.9 Java2D Shapes
11.10 (Optional Case Study) Thinking About Objects: Designing Interfaces with the UML

Summary • Terminology • Self-Review Exercises • Answers to Self-Review Exercises • Exercises

11.1 Introduction

In this chapter, we overview several of Java's capabilities for drawing two-dimensional shapes, controlling colors and controlling fonts. One of Java's initial appeals was its support for graphics that enabled Java programmers to visually enhance their applets and applications. Java now contains many more sophisticated drawing capabilities as part of the *Java2D API*. This chapter begins with an introduction to many of the original drawing capabilities of Java. Next, we present several of the new and more powerful Java2D capabilities, such as controlling the style of lines used to draw shapes and controlling how shapes are filled with color and patterns.

Figure 11.1 shows a portion of the Java class hierarchy that includes several of the basic graphics classes and Java2D API classes and interfaces covered in this chapter. Class **`Color`** contains methods and constants for manipulating colors. Class **`Font`** contains methods and constants for manipulating fonts. Class **`FontMetrics`** contains methods for obtaining font information. Class **`Polygon`** contains methods for creating polygons. Class **`Graphics`** contains methods for drawing strings, lines, rectangles and other shapes. The bottom half of the figure lists several classes and interfaces from the Java2D API. Class **`BasicStroke`** helps specify the drawing characteristics of lines. Classes **`GradientPaint`** and **`TexturePaint`** help specify the characteristics for filling shapes with colors or patterns. Classes **`GeneralPath`**, **`Arc2D`**, **`Ellipse2D`**, **`Line2D`**, **`Rectangle2D`** and **`RoundRectangle2D`** define a variety of Java2D shapes.

To begin drawing in Java, we must first understand Java's *coordinate system* (Figure 11.2), which is a scheme for identifying every possible point on the screen. By default, the upper-left corner of a GUI component (such as an applet or a window) has the coordinates (0, 0). A coordinate pair is composed of an *x-coordinate* (the *horizontal coordinate*) and a *y-coordinate* (the *vertical coordinate*). The *x*-coordinate is the horizontal distance moving right from the upper-left corner. The *y*-coordinate is the vertical distance moving down from the upper-left corner. The *x-axis* describes every horizontal coordinate, and the *y-axis* describes every vertical coordinate.

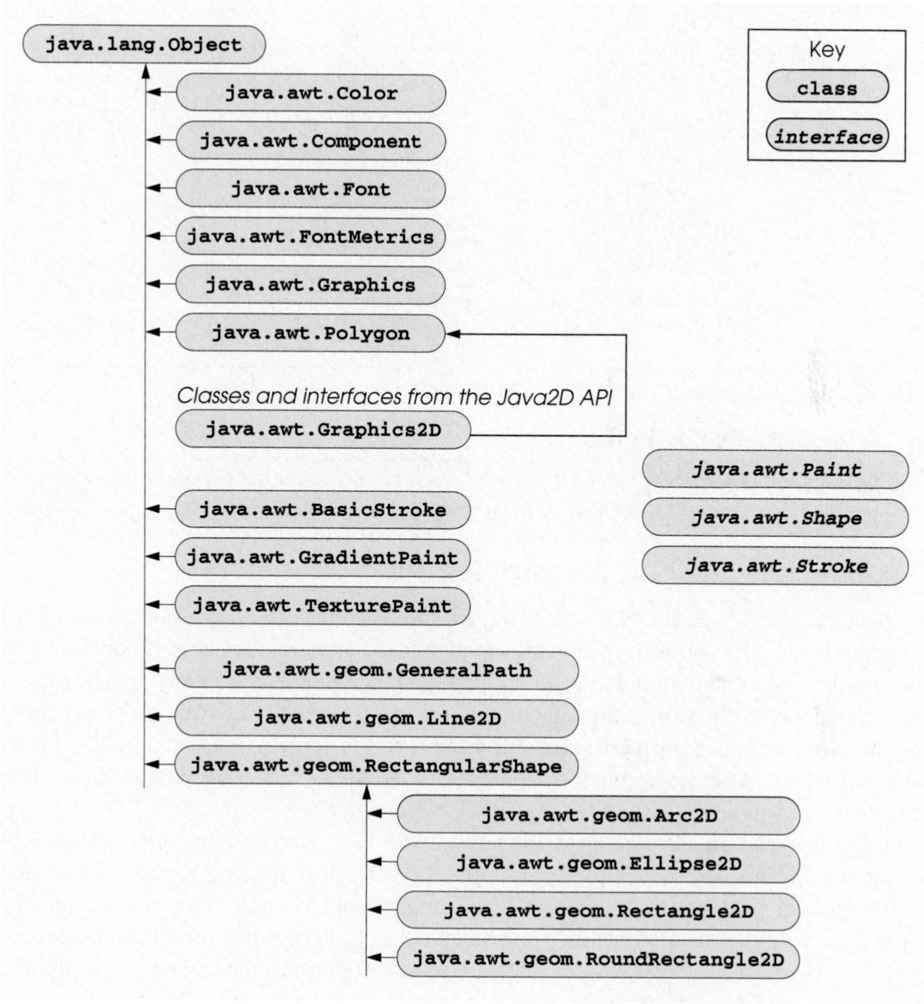

Fig. 11.1 Some classes and interfaces used in this chapter from Java's original graphics capabilities and from the Java2D API.

Software Engineering Observation 11.1

The upper-left coordinate (0, 0) of a window is actually behind the title bar of the window. For this reason, drawing coordinates should be adjusted to draw inside the borders of the window. Class **`Container`** *(a superclass of all windows in Java) has method* **`getInsets`**, *which returns an* **`Insets`** *object (package* **`java.awt`**) *for this purpose. An* **`Insets`** *object has four* **`public`** *members—***`top`**, **`bottom`**, **`left`** *and* **`right`**—*that represent the number of pixels from each edge of the window to the drawing area for the window.*

Text and shapes are displayed on the screen by specifying coordinates. Coordinate units are measured in *pixels*. A pixel is a display monitor's smallest unit of resolution.

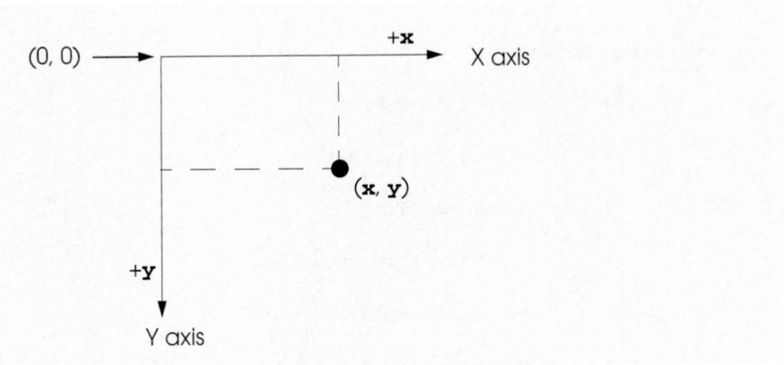

Fig. 11.2 Java coordinate system. Units are measured in pixels.

Portability Tip 11.1

Different display monitors have different resolutions (i.e., the density of pixels varies). This can cause graphics to appear to be different sizes on different monitors.

11.2 Graphics Contexts and Graphics Objects

A Java *graphics context* enables drawing on the screen. A Graphics object manages a graphics context by controlling how information is drawn. Graphics objects contain methods for drawing, font manipulation, color manipulation and the like. Every applet we have seen in the text that performs drawing on the screen has used the **`Graphics`** object **`g`** (the argument to the applet's **`paint`** method) to manage the applet's graphics context. In this chapter, we demonstrate drawing in applications. However, every technique shown here can be used in applets.

The **`Graphics`** class is an **`abstract`** class (i.e., **`Graphics`** objects cannot be instantiated). This contributes to Java's portability. Because drawing is performed differently on each platform that supports Java, there cannot be one class that implements drawing capabilities on all systems. For example, the graphics capabilities that enable a PC running Microsoft Windows to draw a rectangle are different from the graphics capabilities that enable a UNIX workstation to draw a rectangle—and those are both different from the graphics capabilities that enable a Macintosh to draw a rectangle. When Java is implemented on each platform, a derived class of **`Graphics`** is created that actually implements all the drawing capabilities. This implementation is hidden from us by the **`Graphics`** class, which supplies the interface that enables us to write programs that use graphics in a platform-independent manner.

Class **`Component`** is the superclass for many of the classes in the **`java.awt`** package (we discuss class **`Component`** in Chapter 12). **`Component`** method **`paint`** takes a **`Graphics`** object as an argument. This object is passed to the **`paint`** method by the system when a **`paint`** operation is required for a **`Component`**. The header for the **`paint`** method is

```
public void paint( Graphics g )
```

The **`Graphics`** object **`g`** receives a reference to an object of the system's derived **`Graphics`** class. The preceding method header should look familiar to you—it is the same one we have been using in our applet classes. Actually, the **Component** class is an indirect base class of class **JApplet**—the superclass of every applet in this book. Many capabilities of class **JApplet** are inherited from class **Component**. The paint method defined in class **Component** does nothing by default—it must be overridden by the programmer.

The paint method is seldom called directly by the programmer because drawing graphics is an *event-driven process*. When an applet executes, the paint method is automatically called (after calls to the **JApplet**'s **init** and **start** methods). For paint to be called again, an *event* must occur (such as covering and uncovering the applet). Similarly, when any **Component** is displayed, that **Component**'s **paint** method is called.

If the programmer needs to call **paint**, a call is made to the **Component** class **repaint** method. Method **repaint** requests a call to the **Component** class **update** method as soon as possible to clear the **Component**'s background of any previous drawing, then **update** calls **paint** directly. The repaint method is frequently called by the programmer to force a paint operation. Method **repaint** should not be overridden, because it performs some system-dependent tasks. The **update** method is seldom called directly and sometimes overridden. Overriding the **update** method is useful for "smoothing" animations (i.e., reducing "flicker") as we will discuss in Chapter 18, Multimedia. The headers for **repaint** and **update** are

```
public void repaint()
public void update( Graphics g )
```

Method **update** takes a **Graphics** object as an argument, which is supplied automatically by the system when **update** is called.

In this chapter, we focus on the **paint** method. In the next chapter, we concentrate more on the event-driven nature of graphics and discuss the **repaint** and **update** methods in more detail. We also discuss in that chapter class **JComponent**—a superclass of many GUI components in package **javax.swing**. Subclasses of **JComponent** typically paint from their **paintComponent** methods.

11.3 Color Control

Colors enhance the appearance of a program and help convey meaning. For example, a traffic light has three different color lights—red indicates stop, yellow indicates caution and green indicates go.

Class ***Color*** defines methods and constants for manipulating colors in a Java program. The predefined color constants are summarized in Fig. 11.3, and several color methods and constructors are summarized in Fig. 11.4. Note that two of the methods in Fig. 11.4 are **Graphics** methods that are specific to colors.

Every color is created from a red, a green and a blue component. Together these components are called *RGB values*. All three RGB components can be integers in the range from 0 to 255, or all three RGB parts can be floating-point values in the range 0.0 to 1.0. The first RGB part defines the amount of red, the second defines the amount of green and the third defines the amount of blue. The larger the RGB value, the greater the amount of that particular color. Java enables the programmer to choose from $256 \times 256 \times 256$ (or approximately 16.7 million) colors. However, not all computers are capable of displaying all these colors. If this is the case, the computer will display the closest color it can.

Color Constant	Color	RGB value
`public final static Color orange`	orange	255, 200, 0
`public final static Color pink`	pink	255, 175, 175
`public final static Color cyan`	cyan	0, 255, 255
`public final static Color magenta`	magenta	255, 0, 255
`public final static Color yellow`	yellow	255, 255, 0
`public final static Color black`	black	0, 0, 0
`public final static Color white`	white	255, 255, 255
`public final static Color gray`	gray	128, 128, 128
`public final static Color lightGray`	light gray	192, 192, 192
`public final static Color darkGray`	dark gray	64, 64, 64
`public final static Color red`	red	255, 0, 0
`public final static Color green`	green	0, 255, 0
`public final static Color blue`	blue	0, 0, 255

Fig. 11.3 `Color` class **`static`** constants and RGB values

Method	Description
`public Color( int r, int g, int b )`	Creates a color based on red, green and blue contents expressed as integers from 0 to 255.
`public Color( float r, float g, float b )`	Creates a color based on red, green and blue contents expressed as floating-point values from 0.0 to 1.0.
`public int getRed()    // Color class`	Returns a value between 0 and 255 representing the red content.
`public int getGreen()    // Color class`	Returns a value between 0 and 255 representing the green content.
`public int getBlue()    // Color class`	Returns a value between 0 and 255 representing the blue content.
`public Color getColor()    // Graphics class`	Returns a **`Color`** object representing the current color for the graphics context.
`public void setColor( Color c ) // Graphics class`	Sets the current color for drawing with the graphics context.

Fig. 11.4 **`Color`** methods and color-related **`Graphics`** methods .

Common Programming Error 11.1

Spelling any **`static Color`** *class constant with an initial capital letter is a syntax error.*

Two **`Color`** constructors are shown in Fig. 11.4—one that takes three **`int`** arguments, and one that takes three **`float`** arguments, with each argument specifying the amount of red, green and blue, respectively. The int values must be between 0 and 255 and the **`float`** values must be between 0.0 and 1.0. The new **`Color`** object will have the specified amounts of red, green and blue. **`Color`** methods **`getRed`**, **`getGreen`** and **`getBlue`** return integer values from 0 to 255 representing the amount of red, green and blue, respectively. **`Graphics`** method **`getColor`** returns a **`Color`** object representing the current drawing color. **`Graphics`** method **`setColor`** sets the current drawing color.

The application of Fig. 11.5 demonstrates several methods from Fig. 11.4 by drawing filled rectangles and strings in several different colors.

```
// Fig. 11.5: ShowColors.java
// Demonstrating Colors.

// Java core packages
import java.awt.*;
import java.awt.event.*;

// Java extension packages
import javax.swing.*;

public class ShowColors extends JFrame {

   // constructor sets window's title bar string and dimensions
   public ShowColors()
   {
      super( "Using colors" );

      setSize( 400, 130 );
      setVisible( true );
   }

   // draw rectangles and Strings in different colors
   public void paint( Graphics g )
   {
      // call superclass's paint method
      super.paint( g );

      // set new drawing color using integers
      g.setColor( new Color( 255, 0, 0 ) );
      g.fillRect( 25, 25, 100, 20 );
      g.drawString( "Current RGB: " + g.getColor(), 130, 40 );

      // set new drawing color using floats
      g.setColor( new Color( 0.0f, 1.0f, 0.0f ) );
      g.fillRect( 25, 50, 100, 20 );
      g.drawString( "Current RGB: " + g.getColor(), 130, 65 );
```

Fig. 11.5 Demonstrating setting and getting a **`Color`** (part 1 of 2).

```
37
38          // set new drawing color using static Color objects
39          g.setColor( Color.blue );
40          g.fillRect( 25, 75, 100, 20 );
41          g.drawString( "Current RGB: " + g.getColor(), 130, 90 );
42
43          // display individual RGB values
44          Color color = Color.magenta;
45          g.setColor( color );
46          g.fillRect( 25, 100, 100, 20 );
47          g.drawString( "RGB values: " + color.getRed() + ", " +
48             color.getGreen() + ", " + color.getBlue(), 130, 115 );
49       }
50
51       // execute application
52       public static void main( String args[] )
53       {
54          ShowColors application = new ShowColors();
55
56          application.setDefaultCloseOperation(
57             JFrame.EXIT_ON_CLOSE );
58       }
59
60    }  // end class ShowColors
```

Using colors

Current RGB: java.awt.Color[r=255,g=0,b=0]

Current RGB: java.awt.Color[r=0,g=255,b=0]

Current RGB: java.awt.Color[r=0,g=0,b=255]

RGB values: 255, 0, 255

Fig. 11.5 Demonstrating setting and getting a **Color** (part 2 of 2).

When the application begins execution, class **ShowColors**'s **paint** method (lines 23–49) is called to paint the window. Line 29 uses **Graphics** method **setColor** to set the current drawing color. Method **setColor** receives a **Color** object. The expression **new Color(255, 0, 0)** creates a new **Color** object that represents red (red value **255**, and **0** for the green and blue values). Line 30 uses **Graphics** method **fillRect** to draw a filled rectangle in the current color. Method **fillRect** receives the same parameters as method **drawRect** (discussed in Chapter 3). Line 31uses **Graphics** method **drawString** to draw a **String** in the current color. The expression **g.getColor()** retrieves the current color from the **Graphics** object. The returned **Color** is concatenated with string **"Current RGB: "**, resulting in an implicit call to class **Color**'s **toString** method. Notice that the **String** representation of the **Color** object contains the class name and package (**java.awt.Color**), and the red, green and blue values.

Lines 34–36 and lines 39–41 perform the same tasks again. Line 34 uses the **Color** constructor with three **float** arguments to create the color green (**0.0f** for red, **1.0f** for green and **0.0f** for blue). Note the syntax of the constants. The letter **f** appended to a floating-point constant indicates that the constant should be treated as type **float**. Normally, floating-point constants are treated as type **double**.

Line 39 sets the current drawing color to one of the predefined **Color** constants (**Color.blue**). Note that the new operator is not needed to create the constant. The **Color** constants are **static**, so they are defined when class **Color** is loaded into memory at execution time.

The statement at lines 47–48 demonstrates **Color** methods **getRed**, **getGreen** and **getBlue** on the predefined **Color.magenta** object.

Notice lines 56–57 in **main**. **JFrame** method **setDefaultCloseOperation** specifies the default action to take when the user clicks the close box on an application window. In this case, we specify ***JFrame.EXIT_ON_CLOSE*** to indicate that the program should terminate when the user clicks the close box. Other options are **DO_NOTHING_ON_CLOSE** (to ignore the window-closing event), **HIDE_ON_CLOSE** (to hide the window, such that it can be redisplayed later) and **DISPOSE_ON_CLOSE** (to dispose of the window, such that it cannot be redisplayed later). From this point forward, we implement our own **WindowListener** only if the program should perform additional tasks when the user clicks the window's close box. Otherwise, we use method **setDefaultCloseOperation** to specify that the program should terminate when the user clicks the close box.

Software Engineering Observation 11.2

*To change the color, you must create a new **Color** object (or use one of the predefined **Color** constants); there are no set methods in class **Color** to change the characteristics of the current color.*

One of the newer features of Java is the predefined GUI component ***JColorChooser*** (package **javax.swing**) for selecting colors. The application of Fig. 11.6 enables you to press a button to display a **JColorChooser** dialog. When you select a color and press the dialog's **OK** button, the background color of the application window changes colors.

```
// Fig. 11.6: ShowColors2.java
// Demonstrating JColorChooser.

// Java core packages
import java.awt.*;
import java.awt.event.*;

// Java extension packages
import javax.swing.*;

public class ShowColors2 extends JFrame {
   private JButton changeColorButton;
   private Color color = Color.lightGray;
   private Container container;

   // set up GUI
   public ShowColors2()
   {
      super( "Using JColorChooser" );

```

Fig. 11.6 Demonstrating the **JColorChooser** dialog (part 1 of 3).

```
      container = getContentPane();
      container.setLayout( new FlowLayout() );

      // set up changeColorButton and register its event handler
      changeColorButton = new JButton( "Change Color" );

      changeColorButton.addActionListener(

         // anonymous inner class
         new ActionListener() {

            // display JColorChooser when user clicks button
            public void actionPerformed( ActionEvent event )
            {
               color = JColorChooser.showDialog(
                  ShowColors2.this, "Choose a color", color );

               // set default color, if no color is returned
               if ( color == null )
                  color = Color.lightGray;

               // change content pane's background color
               container.setBackground( color );
            }

         }  // end anonymous inner class

      ); // end call to addActionListener

      container.add( changeColorButton );

      setSize( 400, 130 );
      setVisible( true );
   }

   // execute application
   public static void main( String args[] )
   {
      ShowColors2 application = new ShowColors2();

      application.setDefaultCloseOperation(
         JFrame.EXIT_ON_CLOSE );
   }

}  // end class ShowColors2
```

Fig. 11.6 Demonstrating the **JColorChooser** dialog (part 2 of 3).

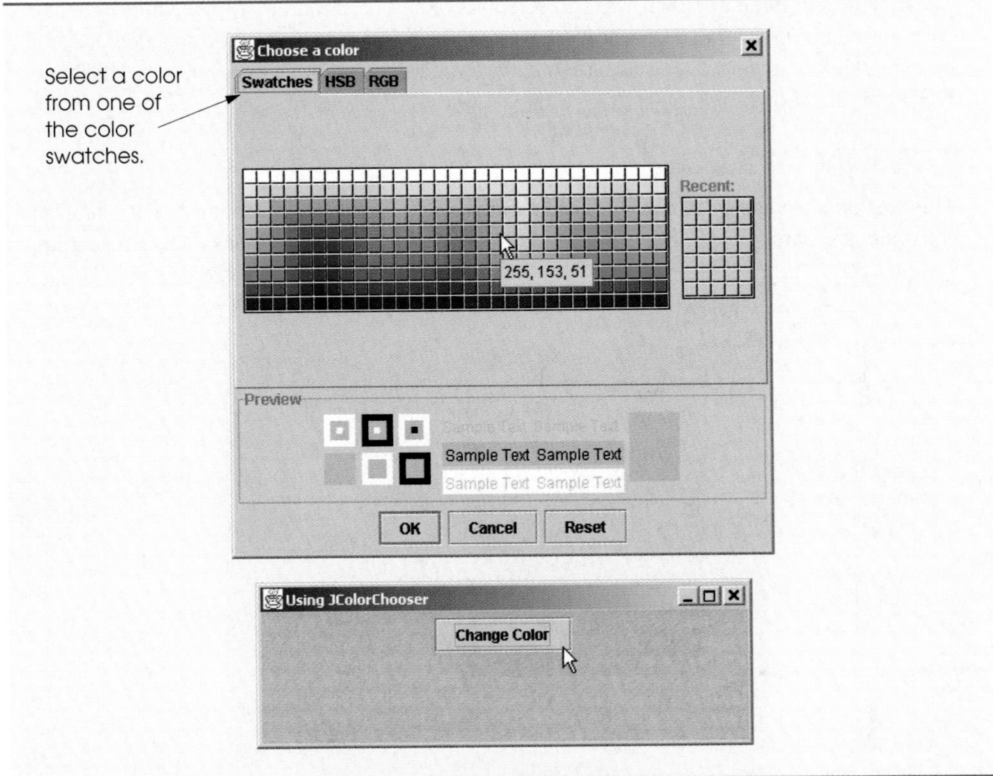

Fig. 11.6 Demonstrating the **`JColorChooser`** dialog (part 3 of 3).

Lines 35–36 (from method **`actionPerformed`** for **`changeColor`**) use **`static`** method ***`showDialog`*** of class **`JColorChooser`** to display the color chooser dialog. This method returns the selected **`Color`** object (**`null`**, if the user presses **Cancel** or closes the dialog without pressing **OK**).

Method **`showDialog`** takes three arguments—a reference to its parent **`Component`**, a **`String`** to display in the title bar of the dialog and the initial selected **`Color`** for the dialog. The parent component is the window from which the dialog is displayed. While the color chooser dialog is on the screen, the user cannot interact with the parent component. This type of dialog is called a *modal dialog* and is discussed in Chapter 13. Notice the special syntax **`ShowColors2.this`** used in the preceding statement. When using an inner class, you can access the outer class object's **`this`** reference by qualifying **`this`** with the name of the outer class and the dot (**`.`**) operator.

After the user selects a color, lines 39–40 determine whether **`color`** is **`null`**, and, if so, set **`color`** to the default **`Color.lightGray`**. Line 43 uses method **`setBackground`** to change the background color of the content pane (represented by **`container`** in this program). Method **`setBackground`** is one of the many **`Component`** methods that can be used on most GUI components.

The second screen capture of Fig. 11.6 demonstrates the default **`JColorChooser`** dialog that allows the user to select a color from a variety of *color swatches*. Notice that there are actually three tabs across the top of the dialog—***Swatches***, ***HSB*** and ***RGB***.

These represent three different ways to select a color. The **HSB** tab allows you to select a color based on *hue*, *saturation* and *brightness*. The **RGB** tab allows you to select a color by using sliders to select the red, green and blue components of the color. The **HSB** and **RGB** tabs are shown in Fig. 11.7.

11.4 Font Control

This section introduces methods and constants for font control. Most font methods and font constants are part of class Font. Some methods of class **`Font`** and class **`Graphics`** are summarized in Fig. 11.8.

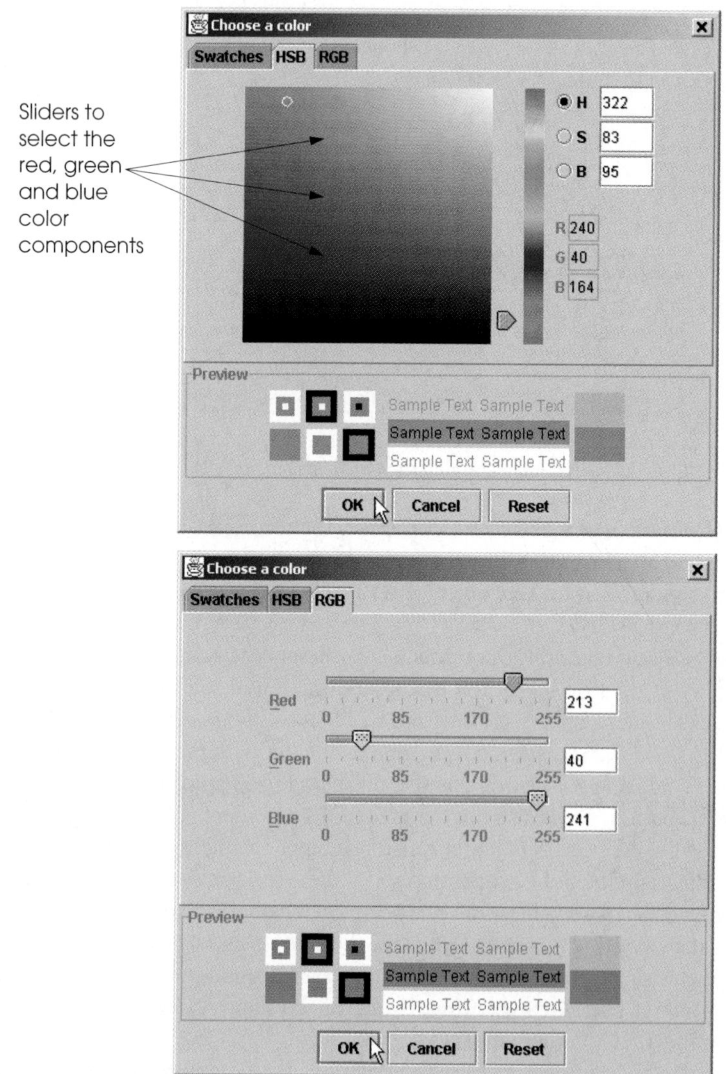

Fig. 11.7 The **HSB** and **RGB** tabs of the **`JColorChooser`** dialog.

Method or constant	Description
`public final static int PLAIN // Font class`	
	A constant representing a plain font style.
`public final static int BOLD // Font class`	
	A constant representing a bold font style.
`public final static int ITALIC // Font class`	
	A constant representing an italic font style.
`public Font( String name, int style, int size )`	
	Creates a **Font** object with the specified font, style and size.
`public int getStyle() // Font class`	
	Returns an integer value indicating the current font style.
`public int getSize() // Font class`	
	Returns an integer value indicating the current font size.
`public String getName() // Font class`	
	Returns the current font name as a string.
`public String getFamily() // Font class`	
	Returns the font's family name as a string.
`public boolean isPlain() // Font class`	
	Tests a font for a plain font style. Returns **true** if the font is plain.
`public boolean isBold() // Font class`	
	Tests a font for a bold font style. Returns **true** if the font is bold.
`public boolean isItalic() // Font class`	
	Tests a font for an italic font style. Returns **true** if the font is italic.
`public Font getFont() // Graphics class`	
	Returns a **Font** object reference representing the current font.
`public void setFont( Font f ) // Graphics class`	
	Sets the current font to the font, style and size specified by the **Font** object reference **f**.

Fig. 11.8 **Font** methods, constants and font-related **Graphics** methods .

Class **Font**'s constructor takes three arguments—the *font name, font style* and *font size*. The font name is any font currently supported by the system where the program is running, such as standard Java fonts **Monospaced**, **SansSerif** and **Serif**. The font style is **Font.PLAIN**, **Font.ITALIC** or **Font.BOLD** (**static** constants of class **Font**). Font styles can be used in combination (e.g., **Font.ITALIC + Font.BOLD**). The font size is measured in points. A *point* is 1/72 of an inch. **Graphics** method **setFont** sets the current drawing font—the font in which text will be displayed—to its **Font** argument.

Portability Tip 11.2

The number of fonts varies greatly across systems. The J2SDK guarantees that the fonts **`Serif`**, **`Monospaced`**, **`SansSerif`**, **`Dialog`** *and* **`DialogInput`** *will be available.*

Common Programming Error 11.2

Specifying a font that is not available on a system is a logic error. Java will substitute that system's default font.

The program of Fig. 11.9 displays text in four different fonts, with each font in a different size. The program uses the **`Font`** constructor to initialize **`Font`** objects on lines 30, 35, 40 and 47 (each in a call to **`Graphics`** method **`setFont`** to change the drawing font). Each call to the Font constructor passes a font name (**`Serif`**, **`Monospaced`** or **`SansSerif`**) as a **`String`**, a font style (**`Font.PLAIN`**, **`Font.ITALIC`** or **`Font.BOLD`**) and a font size. Once **`Graphics`** method setFont is invoked, all text displayed following the call will appear in the new font until the font is changed. Note that line 35 changes the drawing color to red, so the next string displayed appears in red.

```
1  // Fig. 11.9: Fonts.java
2  // Using fonts
3
4  // Java core packages
5  import java.awt.*;
6  import java.awt.event.*;
7
8  // Java extension packages
9  import javax.swing.*;
10
11 public class Fonts extends JFrame {
12
13    // set window's title bar and dimensions
14    public Fonts()
15    {
16       super( "Using fonts" );
17
18       setSize( 420, 125 );
19       setVisible( true );
20    }
21
22    // display Strings in different fonts and colors
23    public void paint( Graphics g )
24    {
25       // call superclass's paint method
26       super.paint( g );
27
28       // set current font to Serif (Times), bold, 12pt
29       // and draw a string
30       g.setFont( new Font( "Serif", Font.BOLD, 12 ) );
31       g.drawString( "Serif 12 point bold.", 20, 50 );
32
```

Fig. 11.9 Using **`Graphics`** method **`setFont`** to change **`Font`**s (part 1 of 2).

```
      // set current font to Monospaced (Courier),
      // italic, 24pt and draw a string
      g.setFont( new Font( "Monospaced", Font.ITALIC, 24 ) );
      g.drawString( "Monospaced 24 point italic.", 20, 70 );

      // set current font to SansSerif (Helvetica),
      // plain, 14pt and draw a string
      g.setFont( new Font( "SansSerif", Font.PLAIN, 14 ) );
      g.drawString( "SansSerif 14 point plain.", 20, 90 );

      // set current font to Serif (times), bold/italic,
      // 18pt and draw a string
      g.setColor( Color.red );
      g.setFont(
         new Font( "Serif", Font.BOLD + Font.ITALIC, 18 ) );
      g.drawString( g.getFont().getName() + " " +
         g.getFont().getSize() +
         " point bold italic.", 20, 110 );
   }

   // execute application
   public static void main( String args[] )
   {
      Fonts application = new Fonts();

      application.setDefaultCloseOperation(
         JFrame.EXIT_ON_CLOSE );
   }

}  // end class Fonts
```

Using fonts

Serif 12 point bold.

Monospaced 24 point italic.

SansSerif 14 point plain.

Serif 18 point bold italic.

Fig. 11.9 Using **Graphics** method **setFont** to change **Font**s (part 2 of 2).

Software Engineering Observation 11.3

To change the font, you must create a new **Font** *object; there are no* set *methods in class* **Font** *to change the characteristics of the current font.*

Often, it is necessary to get information about the current font, such as the font name, the font style and the font size. Several **Font** methods used to get font information are summarized in Fig. 11.8. Method **getStyle** returns an integer value representing the current style. The integer value returned is either **Font.PLAIN**, **Font.ITALIC**, **Font.BOLD** or any combination of **Font.PLAIN**, **Font.ITALIC** and **Font.BOLD**.

Method **getSize** returns the font size in points. Method **getName** returns the current font name as a **String**. Method **getFamily** returns the name of the font family to which the current font belongs. The name of the font family is platform specific.

Portability Tip 11.3

Java provides several standardized font names and maps these into system-specific font names for portability. This is transparent to the programmer.

Font methods are also available to test the style of the current font and are summarized in Fig. 11.8. The **isPlain** method returns **true** if the current font style is plain. The **isBold** method returns **true** if the current font style is bold. The **isItalic** method returns **true** if the current font style is italic.

Sometimes precise information about a font's metrics must be known—such as *height*, *descent* (the amount a character dips below the baseline), *ascent* (the amount a character rises above the baseline) and *leading* (the difference between the descent of one line of text and the ascent of the line of text below it—i.e., the interline spacing). Figure 11.10 illustrates some of the common *font metrics*. Note that the coordinate passed to **drawString** corresponds to the lower-left corner of the baseline of the font.

Class ***FontMetrics*** defines several methods for obtaining font metrics. These methods and **Graphics** method ***getFontMetrics*** are summarized in Fig. 11.11.

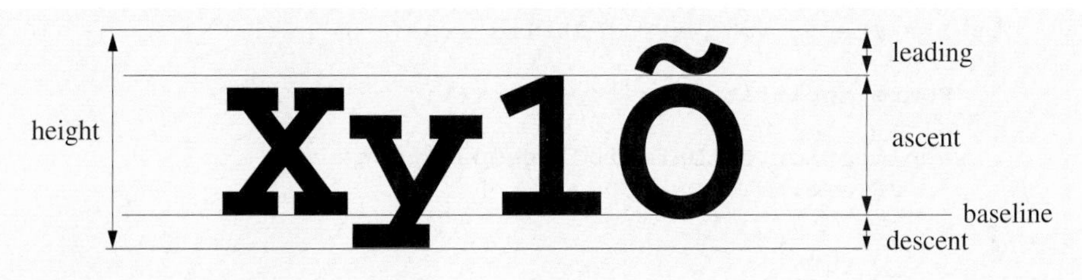

Fig. 11.10 Font metrics.

Method	Description
`public int getAscent()   // FontMetrics class`	
	Returns a value representing the ascent of a font in points.
`public int getDescent()   // FontMetrics class`	
	Returns a value representing the descent of a font in points.
`public int getLeading()   // FontMetrics class`	
	Returns a value representing the leading of a font in points.
`public int getHeight()   // FontMetrics class`	
	Returns a value representing the height of a font in points.
`public FontMetrics getFontMetrics()   // Graphics class`	
	Returns the **FontMetrics** object for the current drawing **Font**.
`public FontMetrics getFontMetrics( Font f ) // Graphics class`	
	Returns the **FontMetrics** object for the specified **Font** argument.

Fig. 11.11 **FontMetrics** and **Graphics** methods for obtaining font metrics.

The program of Fig. 11.12 uses the methods of Fig. 11.11 to obtain font metric information for two fonts.

```
// Fig. 11.12: Metrics.java
// Demonstrating methods of class FontMetrics and
// class Graphics useful for obtaining font metrics.

// Java core packages
import java.awt.*;
import java.awt.event.*;

// Java extension packages
import javax.swing.*;

public class Metrics extends JFrame {

   // set window's title bar String and dimensions
   public Metrics()
   {
      super( "Demonstrating FontMetrics" );

      setSize( 510, 210 );
      setVisible( true );
   }

   // display font metrics
   public void paint( Graphics g )
   {
      // call superclass's paint method
      super.paint( g );

      g.setFont( new Font( "SansSerif", Font.BOLD, 12 ) );
      FontMetrics metrics = g.getFontMetrics();
      g.drawString( "Current font: " + g.getFont(), 10, 40 );
      g.drawString( "Ascent: " + metrics.getAscent(), 10, 55 );
      g.drawString( "Descent: " + metrics.getDescent(), 10, 70 );
      g.drawString( "Height: " + metrics.getHeight(), 10, 85 );
      g.drawString( "Leading: " + metrics.getLeading(), 10, 100);

      Font font = new Font( "Serif", Font.ITALIC, 14 );
      metrics = g.getFontMetrics( font );
      g.setFont( font );
      g.drawString( "Current font: " + font, 10, 130 );
      g.drawString( "Ascent: " + metrics.getAscent(), 10, 145 );
      g.drawString( "Descent: " + metrics.getDescent(), 10, 160);
      g.drawString( "Height: " + metrics.getHeight(), 10, 175 );
      g.drawString( "Leading: " + metrics.getLeading(), 10, 190);
   }

   // execute application
   public static void main( String args[] )
   {
      Metrics application = new Metrics();
```

Fig. 11.12 Obtaining font metric information (part 1 of 2).

```
51
52         application.setDefaultCloseOperation(
53            JFrame.EXIT_ON_CLOSE );
54      }
55
56   }  // end class Metrics
```

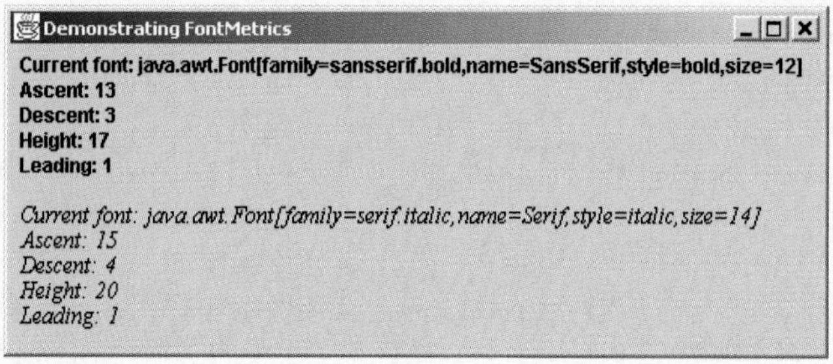

Demonstrating FontMetrics
Current font: java.awt.Font[family=sansserif.bold,name=SansSerif,style=bold,size=12]
Ascent: 13
Descent: 3
Height: 17
Leading: 1

Current font: java.awt.Font[family=serif.italic,name=Serif,style=italic,size=14]
Ascent: 15
Descent: 4
Height: 20
Leading: 1

Fig. 11.12 Obtaining font metric information (part 2 of 2).

Line 29 creates and sets the current drawing font to a **SansSerif**, bold, 12-point font. Line 30 uses **Graphics** method **getFontMetrics** to obtain the **FontMetrics** object for the current font. Line 31 uses an implicit call to class **Font**'s **toString** method to output the string representation of the font. Lines 32–35 use **FontMetric** methods to obtain the ascent, descent, height and leading for the font.

Line 37 creates a new **Serif**, italic, 14-point font. Line 38 uses a second version of **Graphics** method **getFontMetrics**, which receives a **Font** argument and returns a corresponding **FontMetrics** object. Lines 41–44 obtain the ascent, descent, height and leading for the font. Notice that the font metrics are slightly different for the two fonts.

11.5 Drawing Lines, Rectangles and Ovals

This section presents a variety of **Graphics** methods for drawing lines, rectangles and ovals. The methods and their parameters are summarized in Fig. 11.13. For each drawing method that requires a **width** and **height** parameter, the **width** and **height** must be nonnegative values. Otherwise, the shape will not display..

Method	Description
`public void drawLine( int x1, int y1, int x2, int y2 )`	
	Draws a line between the point (**x1**, **y1**) and the point (**x2**, **y2**).
`public void drawRect( int x, int y, int width, int height )`	
	Draws a rectangle of the specified **width** and **height**. The top-left corner of the rectangle has the coordinates (**x**, **y**).

Fig. 11.13 **Graphics** methods that draw lines, rectangles and ovals (part 1 of 2).

Method	Description
`public void fillRect( int x, int y, int width, int height )`	Draws a solid rectangle with the specified **width** and **height**. The top-left corner of the rectangle has the coordinate (**x**, **y**).
`public void clearRect( int x, int y, int width, int height )`	Draws a solid rectangle with the specified **width** and **height** in the current background color. The top-left corner of the rectangle has the coordinate (**x**, **y**).
`public void drawRoundRect( int x, int y, int width, int height, int arcWidth, int arcHeight )`	Draws a rectangle with rounded corners in the current color with the specified **width** and **height**. The **arcWidth** and **arcHeight** determine the rounding of the corners (see Fig. 11.15).
`public void fillRoundRect( int x, int y, int width, int height, int arcWidth, int arcHeight )`	Draws a solid rectangle with rounded corners in the current color with the specified **width** and **height**. The **arcWidth** and **arcHeight** determine the rounding of the corners (see Fig. 11.15).
`public void draw3DRect( int x, int y, int width, int height, boolean b )`	Draws a three-dimensional rectangle in the current color with the specified **width** and **height**. The top-left corner of the rectangle has the coordinates (**x**, **y**). The rectangle appears raised when b is true and is lowered when b is false.
`public void fill3DRect( int x, int y, int width, int height, boolean b )`	Draws a filled three-dimensional rectangle in the current color with the specified **width** and **height**. The top-left corner of the rectangle has the coordinates (**x**, **y**). The rectangle appears raised when b is true and is lowered when b is false.
`public void drawOval( int x, int y, int width, int height )`	Draws an oval in the current color with the specified **width** and **height**. The bounding rectangle's top-left corner is at the coordinates (**x**, **y**). The oval touches all four sides of the bounding rectangle at the center of each side (see Fig. 11.16).
`public void fillOval( int x, int y, int width, int height )`	Draws a filled oval in the current color with the specified **width** and **height**. The bounding rectangle's top-left corner is at the coordinates *(**x**, **y**)*. The oval touches all four sides of the bounding rectangle at the center of each side (see Fig. 11.16).

Fig. 11.13 **Graphics** methods that draw lines, rectangles and ovals (part 2 of 2).

The application of Fig. 11.14 demonstrates drawing a variety of lines, rectangles, 3D rectangles, rounded rectangles and ovals.

```
// Fig. 11.14: LinesRectsOvals.java
// Drawing lines, rectangles and ovals

// Java core packages
import java.awt.*;
import java.awt.event.*;

// Java extension packages
import javax.swing.*;

public class LinesRectsOvals extends JFrame {

   // set window's title bar String and dimensions
   public LinesRectsOvals()
   {
      super( "Drawing lines, rectangles and ovals" );

      setSize( 400, 165 );
      setVisible( true );
   }

   // display various lines, rectangles and ovals
   public void paint( Graphics g )
   {
      // call superclass's paint method
      super.paint( g );

      g.setColor( Color.red );
      g.drawLine( 5, 30, 350, 30 );

      g.setColor( Color.blue );
      g.drawRect( 5, 40, 90, 55 );
      g.fillRect( 100, 40, 90, 55 );

      g.setColor( Color.cyan );
      g.fillRoundRect( 195, 40, 90, 55, 50, 50 );
      g.drawRoundRect( 290, 40, 90, 55, 20, 20 );

      g.setColor( Color.yellow );
      g.draw3DRect( 5, 100, 90, 55, true );
      g.fill3DRect( 100, 100, 90, 55, false );

      g.setColor( Color.magenta );
      g.drawOval( 195, 100, 90, 55 );
      g.fillOval( 290, 100, 90, 55 );
   }

```

Fig. 11.14 Demonstrating **Graphics** method **drawLine** (part 1 of 2).

```
48      // execute application
49      public static void main( String args[] )
50      {
51         LinesRectsOvals application = new LinesRectsOvals();
52
53         application.setDefaultCloseOperation(
54            JFrame.EXIT_ON_CLOSE );
55      }
56
57   }  // end class LinesRectsOvals
```

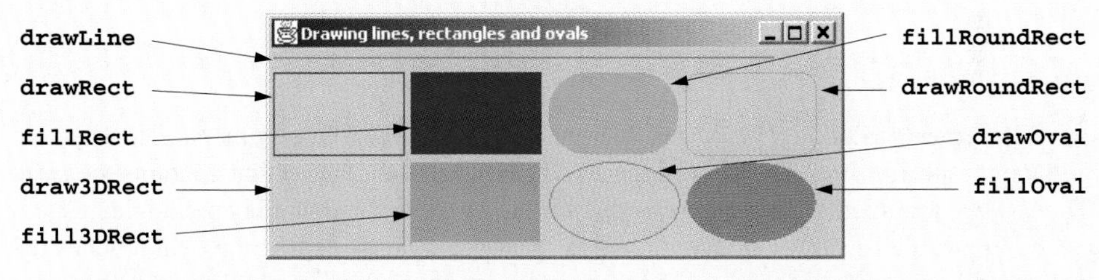

Fig. 11.14 Demonstrating **Graphics** method **drawLine** (part 2 of 2).

Methods **fillRoundRect** (line 36) and **drawRoundRect** (line 37) draw rectangles with rounded corners. Their first two arguments specify the coordinates of the upper-left corner of the *bounding rectangle*—the area in which the rounded rectangle will be drawn. Note that the upper-left corner coordinates are not the edge of the rounded rectangle, but the coordinates where the edge would be if the rectangle had square corners. The third and fourth arguments specify the **width** and **height** of the rectangle. Their last two arguments—**arcWidth** and **arcHeight**—determine the horizontal and vertical diameters of the arcs used to represent the corners.

Methods **draw3DRect** (line 40) and **fill3DRect** (line 41) take the same arguments. The first two arguments specify the top-left corner of the rectangle. The next two arguments specify the **width** and **height** of the rectangle, respectively. The last argument determines whether the rectangle is *raised* (**true**) or *lowered* (**false**). The three-dimensional effect of **draw3DRect** appears as two edges of the rectangle in the original color and two edges in a slightly darker color. The three-dimensional effect of **fill3DRect** appears as two edges of the rectangle in the original drawing color and the fill and other two edges in a slightly darker color. Raised rectangles have the original drawing color edges at the top and left of the rectangle. Lowered rectangles have the original drawing color edges at the bottom and right of the rectangle. The three-dimensional effect is difficult to see in some colors.

Figure 11.15 labels the arc width, arc height, width and height of a rounded rectangle. Using the same value for **arcWidth** and **arcHeight** produces a quarter circle at each corner. When **width**, **height**, **arcWidth** and **arcHeight** have the same values, the result is a circle. If the values for **width** and **height** are the same and the values of **arcWidth** and **arcHeight** are 0, the result is a square.

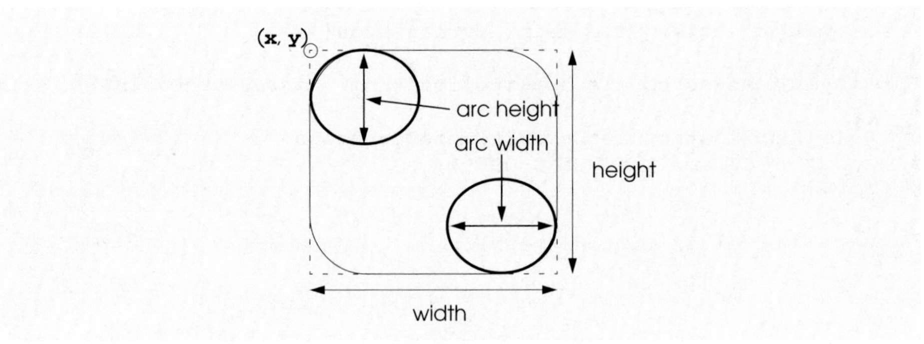

Fig. 11.15 The arc width and arc height for rounded rectangles.

The **drawOval** and **fillOval** methods take the same four arguments. The first two arguments specify the top-left coordinate of the bounding rectangle that contains the oval. The last two arguments specify the **width** and **height** of the bounding rectangle, respectively. Figure 11.16 shows an oval bounded by a rectangle. Note that the oval touches the center of all four sides of the bounding rectangle (the bounding rectangle is not displayed on the screen).

11.6 Drawing Arcs

An *arc* is a portion of a oval. Arc angles are measured in degrees. Arcs *sweep* from a *starting angle* the number of degrees specified by their *arc angle*. The starting angle indicates in degrees where the arc begins. The arc angle specifies the total number of degrees through which the arc sweeps. Figure 11.17 illustrates two arcs. The left set of axes shows an arc sweeping from zero degrees to approximately 110 degrees. Arcs that sweep in a counterclockwise direction are measured in *positive degrees*. The right set of axes shows an arc sweeping from zero degrees to approximately –110 degrees. Arcs that sweep in a clockwise direction are measured in *negative degrees*. Notice the dashed boxes around the arcs in Fig. 11.17. When drawing an arc, we specify a bounding rectangle for an oval. The arc will sweep along part of the oval. The **Graphics** methods ***drawArc*** and ***fillArc*** for drawing arcs are summarized in Fig. 11.18.

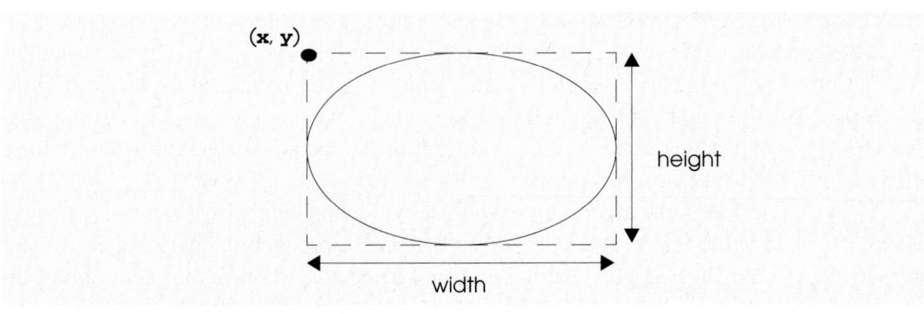

Fig. 11.16 An oval bounded by a rectangle.

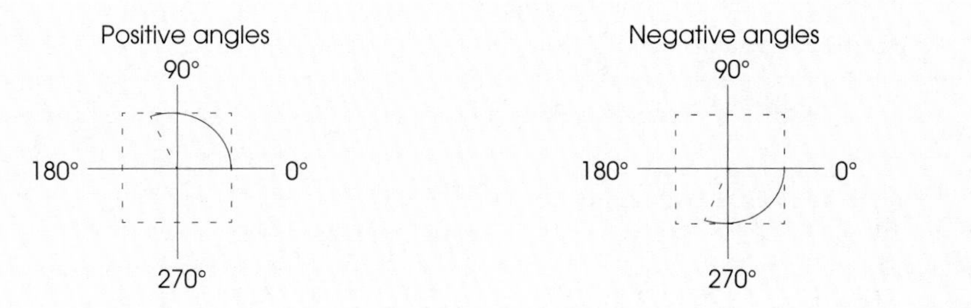

Fig. 11.17 Positive and negative arc angles.

Method	Description
`public void drawArc( int x, int y, int width, int height, int startAngle, int arcAngle )`	Draws an arc relative to the bounding rectangle's top-left coordinates (**x**, **y**) with the specified **width** and **height**. The arc segment is drawn starting at startAngle and sweeps arcAngle degrees.
`public void fillArc( int x, int y, int width, int height, int startAngle, int arcAngle )`	Draws a solid arc (i.e., a sector) relative to the bounding rectangle's top-left coordinates (**x**, **y**) with the specified **width** and **height**. The arc segment is drawn starting at startAngle and sweeps arcAngle degrees.

Fig. 11.18 **Graphics** methods for drawing arcs.

The program of Fig. 11.19 demonstrates the arc methods of Fig. 11.18. The program draws six arcs (three unfilled and three filled). To illustrate the bounding rectangle that helps determine where the arc appears, the first three arcs are displayed inside a yellow rectangle that has the same **x**, **y**, **width** and **height** arguments as the arcs.

```
// Fig. 11.19: DrawArcs.java
// Drawing arcs

// Java core packages
import java.awt.*;
import java.awt.event.*;

// Java extension packages
import javax.swing.*;

public class DrawArcs extends JFrame {

```

Fig. 11.19 Demonstrating **drawArc** and **fillArc** (part 1 of 3).

```
   // set window's title bar String and dimensions
   public DrawArcs()
   {
      super( "Drawing Arcs" );

      setSize( 300, 170 );
      setVisible( true );
   }

   // draw rectangles and arcs
   public void paint( Graphics g )
   {
      // call superclass's paint method
      super.paint( g );

      // start at 0 and sweep 360 degrees
      g.setColor( Color.yellow );
      g.drawRect( 15, 35, 80, 80 );
      g.setColor( Color.black );
      g.drawArc( 15, 35, 80, 80, 0, 360 );

      // start at 0 and sweep 110 degrees
      g.setColor( Color.yellow );
      g.drawRect( 100, 35, 80, 80 );
      g.setColor( Color.black );
      g.drawArc( 100, 35, 80, 80, 0, 110 );

      // start at 0 and sweep -270 degrees
      g.setColor( Color.yellow );
      g.drawRect( 185, 35, 80, 80 );
      g.setColor( Color.black );
      g.drawArc( 185, 35, 80, 80, 0, -270 );

      // start at 0 and sweep 360 degrees
      g.fillArc( 15, 120, 80, 40, 0, 360 );

      // start at 270 and sweep -90 degrees
      g.fillArc( 100, 120, 80, 40, 270, -90 );

      // start at 0 and sweep -270 degrees
      g.fillArc( 185, 120, 80, 40, 0, -270 );
   }

   // execute application
   public static void main( String args[] )
   {
      DrawArcs application = new DrawArcs();

      application.setDefaultCloseOperation(
         JFrame.EXIT_ON_CLOSE );
   }

} // end class DrawArcs
```

Fig. 11.19 Demonstrating **drawArc** and **fillArc** (part 2 of 3).

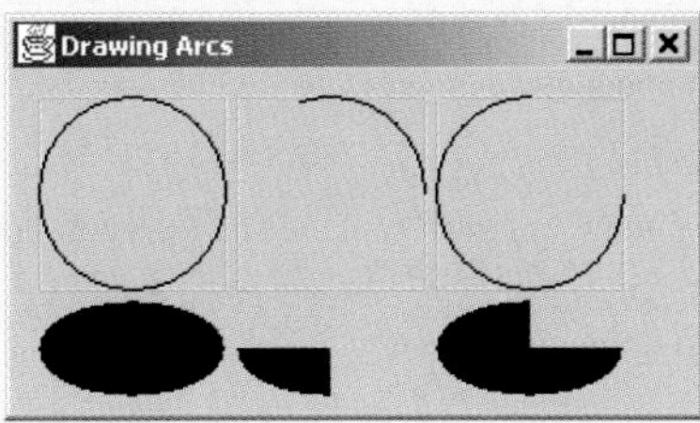

Fig. 11.19 Demonstrating **drawArc** and **fillArc** (part 3 of 3).

11.7 Drawing Polygons and Polylines

Polygons are multisided shapes. *Polylines* are a series of connected points. Graphics methods for drawing polygons and polylines are discussed in Fig. 11.20. Note that some methods require a ***Polygon*** object (package **java.awt**). Class **Polygon**'s constructors are also described in Fig. 11.20.

Method	Description
`public void drawPolygon( int xPoints[], int yPoints[], int points )`	Draws a polygon. The *x*-coordinate of each point is specified in the **xPoints** array and the *y*-coordinate of each point is specified in the **yPoints** array. The last argument specifies the number of **points**. This method draws a closed polygon—even if the last point is different from the first point.
`public void drawPolyline( int xPoints[], int yPoints[], int points )`	Draws a series of connected lines. The *x*-coordinate of each point is specified in the **xPoints** array and the *y*-coordinate of each point is specified in the **yPoints** array. The last argument specifies the number of **points**. If the last point is different from the first point, the polyline is not closed.
`public void drawPolygon( Polygon p )`	Draws the specified closed polygon.
`public void fillPolygon( int xPoints[], int yPoints[], int points )`	Draws a solid polygon. The *x*-coordinate of each point is specified in the **xPoints** array and the *y*-coordinate of each point is specified in the **yPoints** array. The last argument specifies the number of **points**. This method draws a closed polygon—even if the last point is different from the first point.
`public void fillPolygon( Polygon p )`	Draws the specified solid polygon. The polygon is closed.

Fig. 11.20 **Graphics** methods for drawing polygons and class **Polygon** constructors (part 1 of 2).

Method	Description
`public Polygon()` `// Polygon class`	Constructs a new polygon object. The polygon does not contain any points.
`public Polygon( int xValues[], int yValues[], int numberOfPoints )` `// Polygon class`	Constructs a new polygon object. The polygon has **`numberOfPoints`** sides, with each point consisting of an *x*-coordinate from **`xValues`** and a *y*-coordinate from **`yValues`**.

Fig. 11.20 **`Graphics`** methods for drawing polygons and class **`Polygon`** constructors (part 2 of 2).

The program of Fig. 11.21 draws polygons and polylines, using the methods and constructors in Fig. 11.20.

```
// Fig. 11.21: DrawPolygons.java
// Drawing polygons

// Java core packages
import java.awt.*;
import java.awt.event.*;

// Java extension packages
import javax.swing.*;

public class DrawPolygons extends JFrame {

   // set window's title bar String and dimensions
   public DrawPolygons()
   {
      super( "Drawing Polygons" );

      setSize( 275, 230 );
      setVisible( true );
   }

   // draw polygons and polylines
   public void paint( Graphics g )
   {
      // call superclass's paint method
      super.paint( g );

      int xValues[] = { 20, 40, 50, 30, 20, 15 };
      int yValues[] = { 50, 50, 60, 80, 80, 60 };
      Polygon polygon1 = new Polygon( xValues, yValues, 6 );

      g.drawPolygon( polygon1 );
```

Fig. 11.21 Demonstrating **`drawPolygon`** and **`fillPolygon`**.

```
33
34          int xValues2[] = { 70, 90, 100, 80, 70, 65, 60 };
35          int yValues2[] = { 100, 100, 110, 110, 130, 110, 90 };
36
37          g.drawPolyline( xValues2, yValues2, 7 );
38
39          int xValues3[] = { 120, 140, 150, 190 };
40          int yValues3[] = { 40, 70, 80, 60 };
41
42          g.fillPolygon( xValues3, yValues3, 4 );
43
44          Polygon polygon2 = new Polygon();
45          polygon2.addPoint( 165, 135 );
46          polygon2.addPoint( 175, 150 );
47          polygon2.addPoint( 270, 200 );
48          polygon2.addPoint( 200, 220 );
49          polygon2.addPoint( 130, 180 );
50
51          g.fillPolygon( polygon2 );
52       }
53
54       // execute application
55       public static void main( String args[] )
56       {
57          DrawPolygons application = new DrawPolygons();
58
59          application.setDefaultCloseOperation(
60             JFrame.EXIT_ON_CLOSE );
61       }
62
63    }  // end class DrawPloygons
```

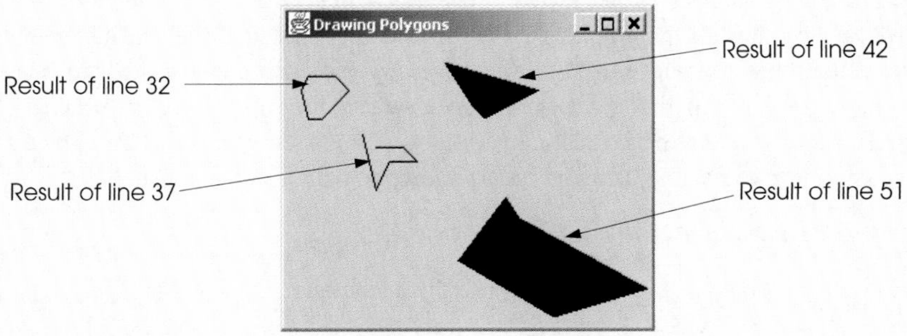

Drawing Polygons

Result of line 32

Result of line 42

Result of line 37

Result of line 51

Fig. 11.21 Demonstrating **drawPolygon** and **fillPolygon**.

Lines 28–29 create two **int** arrays and use them to specify the points for **Polygon polygon1**. The **Polygon** constructor call at line 30 receives array **xValues**, which contains the *x*-coordinate of each point, array **yValues**, which contains the *y*-coordinate of each point, and 6 (the number of points in the polygon). Line 32 displays **polygon1** by passing it as an argument to **Graphics** method **drawPolygon**.

Lines 34–35 create two **int** arrays and use them to specify the points for a series of connected lines. Array **xValues2** contains the *x*-coordinate of each point and array

yValues2 contains the *y*-coordinate of each point. Line 37 uses **Graphics** method **drawPolyline** to display the series of connected lines specified with the arguments **xValues2**, **yValues2** and **7** (the number of points).

Lines 39–40 create two **int** arrays and use them to specify the points of a polygon. Array **xValues3** contains the *x*-coordinate of each point and array **yValues3** contains the *y*-coordinate of each point. Line 42 displays a polygon by passing to **Graphics** method **fillPolygon** the two arrays (**xValues3** and **yValues3**) and the number of points to draw (**4**).

Common Programming Error 11.3

*An **ArrayIndexOutOfBoundsException** is thrown if the number of points specified in the third argument to method **drawPolygon** or method **fillPolygon** is greater than the number of elements in the arrays of coordinates that define the polygon to display.*

Line 44 creates **Polygon polygon2** with no points. Lines 45–49 use **Polygon** method ***addPoint*** to add pairs of *x*- and *y*-coordinates to the **Polygon**. Line 51 displays **Polygon polygon2** by passing it to **Graphics** method **fillPolygon**.

11.8 The Java2D API

The new *Java2D API* provides advanced two-dimensional graphics capabilities for programmers who require detailed and complex graphical manipulations. The API includes features for processing line art, text and images in packages **java.awt**, **java.awt.image**, **java.awt.color**, **java.awt.font**, **java.awt.geom**, **java.awt.print** and **java.awt.image.renderable**. The capabilities of the API are far too broad to cover in this textbook. For an overview of the capabilities, see the Java2D demo (demonstrated in Chapter 3). In this section, we present an overview of several Java2D capabilities.

Drawing with the Java2D API is accomplished with an instance of class ***Graphics2D*** (package **java.awt**). Class **Graphics2D** is a subclass of class **Graphics**, so it has all the graphics capabilities demonstrated earlier in this chapter. In fact, the actual object we have used to draw in every **paint** method is a **Graphics2D** object that is passed to method **paint** and accessed via the superclass **Graphics** reference **g**. To access the **Graphics2D** capabilities, we must downcast the **Graphics** reference passed to **paint** to a **Graphics2D** reference with a statement such as

```
Graphics2D g2d = ( Graphics2D ) g;
```

The programs of the next several sections use this technique.

11.9 Java2D Shapes

Next, we present several Java2D shapes from package **java.awt.geom**, including ***Ellipse2D.Double***, ***Rectangle2D.Double***, ***RoundRectangle2D.Double***, ***Arc2D.Double*** and ***Line2D.Double***. Note the syntax of each class name. Each of these classes represents a shape with dimensions specified as double-precision floating-point values. There is a separate version of each represented with single-precision floating-point values (such as ***Ellipse2D.Float***). In each case, **Double** is a **static** inner class of the class to the left of the dot operator (e.g., **Ellipse2D**). To use the **static** inner class, we simply qualify its name with the outer class name.

The program of Fig. 11.22 demonstrates several Java2D shapes and drawing characteristics, such as thickening lines, filling shapes with patterns and drawing dashed lines. These are just a few of the many capabilities provided by Java2D.

```
// Fig. 11.22: Shapes.java
// Demonstrating some Java2D shapes

// Java core packages
import java.awt.*;
import java.awt.event.*;
import java.awt.geom.*;
import java.awt.image.*;

// Java extension packages
import javax.swing.*;

public class Shapes extends JFrame {

   // set window's title bar String and dimensions
   public Shapes()
   {
      super( "Drawing 2D shapes" );

      setSize( 425, 160 );
      setVisible( true );
   }

   // draw shapes with Java2D API
   public void paint( Graphics g )
   {
      // call superclass's paint method
      super.paint( g );

      // create 2D by casting g to Graphics2D
      Graphics2D g2d = ( Graphics2D ) g;

      // draw 2D ellipse filled with a blue-yellow gradient
      g2d.setPaint( new GradientPaint( 5, 30, Color.blue, 35,
         100, Color.yellow, true ) );
      g2d.fill( new Ellipse2D.Double( 5, 30, 65, 100 ) );

      // draw 2D rectangle in red
      g2d.setPaint( Color.red );
      g2d.setStroke( new BasicStroke( 10.0f ) );
      g2d.draw( new Rectangle2D.Double( 80, 30, 65, 100 ) );

      // draw 2D rounded rectangle with a buffered background
      BufferedImage buffImage = new BufferedImage(
         10, 10, BufferedImage.TYPE_INT_RGB );

      Graphics2D gg = buffImage.createGraphics();
      gg.setColor( Color.yellow ); // draw in yellow
```

Fig. 11.22 Demonstrating some Java2D shapes.

```
      gg.fillRect( 0, 0, 10, 10 ); // draw a filled rectangle
      gg.setColor( Color.black );  // draw in black
      gg.drawRect( 1, 1, 6, 6 );   // draw a rectangle
      gg.setColor( Color.blue );   // draw in blue
      gg.fillRect( 1, 1, 3, 3 );   // draw a filled rectangle
      gg.setColor( Color.red );    // draw in red
      gg.fillRect( 4, 4, 3, 3 );   // draw a filled rectangle

      // paint buffImage onto the JFrame
      g2d.setPaint( new TexturePaint(
         buffImage, new Rectangle( 10, 10 ) ) );
      g2d.fill( new RoundRectangle2D.Double(
         155, 30, 75, 100, 50, 50 ) );

      // draw 2D pie-shaped arc in white
      g2d.setPaint( Color.white );
      g2d.setStroke( new BasicStroke( 6.0f ) );
      g2d.draw( new Arc2D.Double(
         240, 30, 75, 100, 0, 270, Arc2D.PIE ) );

      // draw 2D lines in green and yellow
      g2d.setPaint( Color.green );
      g2d.draw( new Line2D.Double( 395, 30, 320, 150 ) );

      float dashes[] = { 10 };

      g2d.setPaint( Color.yellow );
      g2d.setStroke( new BasicStroke( 4, BasicStroke.CAP_ROUND,
         BasicStroke.JOIN_ROUND, 10, dashes, 0 ) );
      g2d.draw( new Line2D.Double( 320, 30, 395, 150 ) );
   }

   // execute application
   public static void main( String args[] )
   {
      Shapes application = new Shapes();

      application.setDefaultCloseOperation(
         JFrame.EXIT_ON_CLOSE );
   }

}  // end class Shapes
```

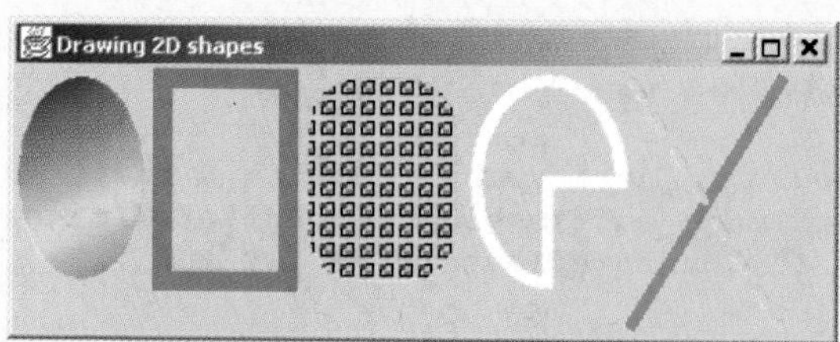

Fig. 11.22 Demonstrating some Java2D shapes.

Line 31 casts the **Graphics** reference received by **paint** to a **Graphics2D** reference and assigns it to **g2d** to allow access to the **Java2D** features.

The first shape we draw is an oval filled with gradually changing colors. Lines 34–35 invoke **Graphics2D** method ***setPaint*** to set the ***Paint*** object that determines the color for the shape to display. A **Paint** object is an object of any class that implements interface **java.awt.Paint**. The **Paint** object can be something as simple as one of the predefined **Color** objects introduced in Section 11.3 (class **Color** implements **Paint**), or the **Paint** object can be an instance of the Java2D API's ***GradientPaint***, ***SystemColor*** or ***TexturePaint*** classes. In this case, we use a **GradientPaint** object.

Class **GradientPaint** helps draw a shape in a gradually changing colors—called a *gradient*. The **GradientPaint** constructor used here requires seven arguments. The first two arguments specify the starting coordinate for the gradient. The third argument specifies the starting **Color** for the gradient. The fourth and fifth arguments specify the ending coordinate for the gradient. The sixth argument specifies the ending **Color** for the gradient. The last argument specifies if the gradient is cyclic (**true**) or acyclic (**false**). The two coordinates determine the direction of the gradient. Because the second coordinate *(35, 100)* is down and to the right of the first coordinate *(5, 30)*, the gradient goes down and to the right at an angle. Because this gradient is cyclic (**true**), the color starts with blue, gradually becomes yellow, then gradually returns to blue. If the gradient is acyclic, the color transitions from the first color specified (e.g., blue) to the second color (e.g., yellow).

Line 36 uses **Graphics2D** method ***fill*** to draw a filled ***Shape*** object. The **Shape** object is an instance of any class that implements interface **Shape** (package **java.awt**)—in this case, an instance of class **Ellipse2D.Double**. The **Ellipse2D.Double** constructor receives four arguments specifying the bounding rectangle for the ellipse to display.

Next we draw a red rectangle with a thick border. Line 39 uses **setPaint** to set the **Paint** object to **Color.red**. Line 40 uses **Graphics2D** method ***setStroke*** to set the characteristics of the rectangle's border (or the lines for any other shape). Method **setStroke** requires a ***Stroke*** object as its argument. The **Stroke** object is an instance of any class that implements interface **Stroke** (package **java.awt**)—in this case, an instance of class ***BasicStroke***. Class **BasicStroke** provides a variety of constructors to specify the width of the line, how the line ends (called the *end caps*), how lines join together (called *line joins*) and the dash attributes of the line (if it is a dashed line). The constructor here specifies that the line should be 10 pixels wide.

Line 41uses **Graphics2D** method ***draw*** to draw a ***Shape*** object—in this case, an instance of class **Rectangle2D.Double**. The **Rectangle2D.Double** constructor receives four arguments specifying the upper-left *x*-coordinate, upper-left *y*-coordinate, width and height of the rectangle.

Next we draw a rounded rectangle filled with a pattern created in a ***BufferedImage*** (package **java.awt.image**) object. Lines 44–45 create the **BufferedImage** object. Class **BufferedImage** can be used to produce images in color and gray scale. This particular **BufferedImage** is 10 pixels wide and 10 pixels tall. The third constructor argument **BufferedImage.TYPE_INT_RGB** indicates that the image is stored in color using the RGB color scheme.

To create the fill pattern for the rounded rectangle, we must first draw into the **BufferedImage**. Line 47 creates a **Graphics2D** object that can be used to draw into the **BufferedImage**. Lines 48–55 use methods **setColor**, **fillRect** and **drawRect** (discussed earlier in this chapter) to create the pattern.

Lines 58–59 set the **Paint** object to a new **TexturePaint** (package **java.awt**) object. A **TexturePaint** object uses the image stored in its associated **BufferedImage** as the fill texture for a filled-in shape. The second argument specifies the **Rectangle** area from the **BufferedImage** that will be replicated through the texture. In this case, the **Rectangle** is the same size as the **BufferedImage**. However, a smaller portion of the **BufferedImage** can be used.

Lines 60–61use **Graphics2D** method **fill** to draw a filled **Shape** object—in this case, an instance of class ***RoundRectangle2D.Double***. The constructor for class **RoundRectangle2D.Double** receives six arguments specifying the rectangle dimensions and the arc width and arc height used to determine the rounding of the corners.

Next we draw a pie-shaped arc with a thick white line. Line 64 sets the **Paint** object to **Color.white**. Line 65 sets the **Stroke** object to a new **BasicStroke** for a line 6 pixels wide. Lines 66–67 use **Graphics2D** method **draw** to draw a **Shape** object—in this case, an **Arc2D.Double**. The **Arc2D.Double** constructor's first four arguments specifying the upper-left *x*-coordinate, upper-left *y*-coordinate, width and height of the bounding rectangle for the arc. The fifth argument specifies the start angle. The sixth argument specifies the arc angle. The last argument specifies the how the arc is closed. Constant ***Arc2D.PIE*** indicates that the arc is closed by drawing two lines. One line from the arc's starting point to the center of the bounding rectangle and one line from the center of the bounding rectangle to the ending point. Class **Arc2D** provides two other **static** constants for specifying how the arc is closed. Constant ***Arc2D.CHORD*** draws a line from the starting point to the ending point. Constant ***Arc2D.OPEN*** specifies that the arc is not closed.

Finally, we draw two lines using ***Line2D*** objects—one solid and one dashed. Line 70 sets the **Paint** object to **Color.green**. Line 71 uses **Graphics2D** method **draw** to draw a **Shape** object—in this case, an instance of class **Line2D.Double**. The **Line2D.Double** constructor's arguments specify starting coordinates and ending coordinates of the line.

Line 73 defines a one-element **float** array containing the value 10. This array will be used to describe the dashes in the dashed line. In this case, each dash will be 10 pixels long. To create dashes of different lengths in a pattern, simply provide the lengths of each dash as an element in the array. Line 75 sets the **Paint** object to **Color.yellow**. Lines 76–77 set the **Stroke** object to a new **BasicStroke**. The line will be **4** pixels wide and will have rounded ends (**BasicStroke.CAP_ROUND**). If lines join together (as in a rectangle at the corners), the joining of the lines will be rounded (**BasicStroke.JOIN_ROUND**). The **dashes** argument specifies the dash lengths for the line. The last argument indicates the starting subscript in the **dashes** array for the first dash in the pattern. Line 78 then draws a line with the current **Stroke**.

Next we present a general path—a shape constructed from straight lines and complex curves. A general path is represented with an object of class ***GeneralPath*** (package **java.awt.geom**). The program of Fig. 11.23 demonstrates drawing a general path in the shape of a five-pointed star.

```
// Fig. 11.23: Shapes2.java
// Demonstrating a general path

// Java core packages
import java.awt.*;
import java.awt.event.*;
import java.awt.geom.*;

// Java extension packages
import javax.swing.*;

public class Shapes2 extends JFrame {

   // set window's title bar String, background color
   // and dimensions
   public Shapes2()
   {
      super( "Drawing 2D Shapes" );

      getContentPane().setBackground( Color.yellow );
      setSize( 400, 400 );
      setVisible( true );
   }

   // draw general paths
   public void paint( Graphics g )
   {
      // call superclass's paint method
      super.paint( g );

      int xPoints[] =
         { 55, 67, 109, 73, 83, 55, 27, 37, 1, 43 };
      int yPoints[] =
         { 0, 36, 36, 54, 96, 72, 96, 54, 36, 36 };

      Graphics2D g2d = ( Graphics2D ) g;

      // create a star from a series of points
      GeneralPath star = new GeneralPath();

      // set the initial coordinate of the General Path
      star.moveTo( xPoints[ 0 ], yPoints[ 0 ] );

      // create the star--this does not draw the star
      for ( int count = 1; count < xPoints.length; count++ )
         star.lineTo( xPoints[ count ], yPoints[ count ] );

      // close the shape
      star.closePath();

      // translate the origin to (200, 200)
      g2d.translate( 200, 200 );
```

Fig. 11.23 Demonstrating some Java2D shapes

```
53
54      // rotate around origin and draw stars in random colors
55      for ( int count = 1; count <= 20; count++ ) {
56
57         // rotate coordinate system
58         g2d.rotate( Math.PI / 10.0 );
59
60         // set random drawing color
61         g2d.setColor( new Color(
62            ( int ) ( Math.random() * 256 ),
63            ( int ) ( Math.random() * 256 ),
64            ( int ) ( Math.random() * 256 ) ) );
65
66         // draw filled star
67         g2d.fill( star );
68      }
69
70   } // end method paint
71
72   // execute application
73   public static void main( String args[] )
74   {
75      Shapes2 application = new Shapes2();
76
77      application.setDefaultCloseOperation(
78         JFrame.EXIT_ON_CLOSE );
79   }
80
81 } // end class Shapes2
```

Fig. 11.23 Demonstrating some Java2D shapes

Lines 31–34 define two **int** arrays representing the *x*- and *y*-coordinates of the points in the star. Line 39 defines **GeneralPath** object **star**.

Line 42 uses **GeneralPath** method ***moveTo*** to specify the first point in the **star**. The **for** structure at lines 45–46 use **GeneralPath** method ***lineTo*** to draw a line to the next point in the **star**. Each new call to **lineTo** draws a line from the previous point to the current point. Line 49 uses **GeneralPath** method ***closePath*** to draw a line from the last point to the point specified in the last call to **moveTo**. This completes the general path.

Line 52 uses **Graphics2D** method ***translate*** to move the drawing origin to location *(200, 200)*. All drawing operations now use location *(200, 200)* as *(0, 0)*.

The **for** structure at line 55–68 draws the **star** 20 times by rotating it around the new origin point. Line 58 uses **Graphics2D** method ***rotate*** to rotate the next displayed shape. The argument specifies the rotation angle in radians (with 360° = 2π radians). Line 67 uses **Graphics2D** method **fill** to draw a filled version of the **star**.

11.10 (Optional Case Study) Thinking About Objects: Designing Interfaces with the UML

In Section 10.22, we incorporated event handling into our simulation by modifying the collaboration diagram that deals with passengers entering and exiting the elevator. We included both event handling and inheritance in that diagram. The **Elevator** informs its **Door** of the **Elevator**'s arrival. This **Door** opens the arrival **Floor**'s **Door** by obtaining its handle through a **Location** object (which was included in the arrival event), and potentially two **Person** objects exit and enter the **Elevator** after both **Door**s open. We also discussed listener interfaces. In this section, we represent our listener interface with the UML.

Realizations

The UML expresses the relationship between a class and an interface through a *realization*. A class *realizes*, or implements, the behaviors of an interface. A class diagram can show a realization between classes and interfaces. As mentioned in "Thinking About Objects" Section 3.8, the UML provides two notations to draw a class diagram—the complete diagram and the elided (condensed) diagram. Figure 11.24 shows the complete class diagram that models the realization between class **Person** and interface **DoorListener**. The diagram is similar to the generalization diagram, except that the arrow expressing the relationship is dashed instead of solid. Note that the middle compartment in interface **DoorListener** is empty, because interfaces do not contain variables—interfaces can contain constants, but interface **DoorListener** does not contain any constants. Lastly, note the word "interface" placed in guillemets (« ») located in the first compartment of interface **DoorListener**. This notation distinguishes interface **DoorListener** as an interface in our system. Items placed in guillemets are called *stereotypes* in the UML. A stereotype indicates an element's role—or purpose—in a UML diagram.

Figure 11.25 shows the alternate way to represent the realization of class **Person** and interface **DoorListener** in the UML. Figure 11.25 is the elided diagram of Fig. 11.24. The small circle represents the interface, and the solid line represents the realization. By hiding its operations, we condense the interface, making it easier to read; however, in doing so, we sacrifice the information about its behaviors. When constructing an elided diagram, common practice is to place the information regarding any behavior in a separate diagram—for example, we place the full **DoorListener** class in the class diagram of Fig. 11.28.

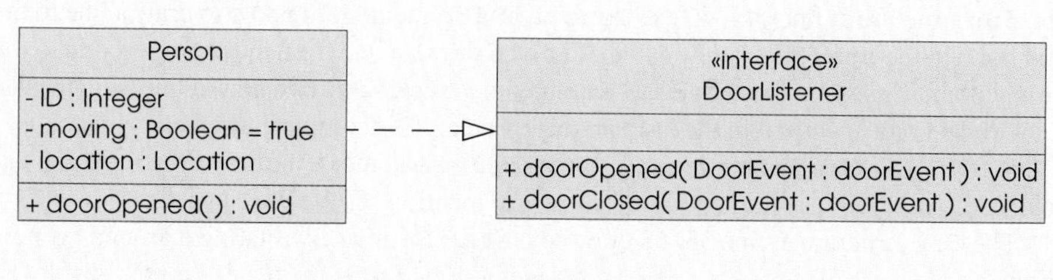

Fig. 11.24 Class diagram that models class **`Person`** realizing interface **`DoorListener`**.

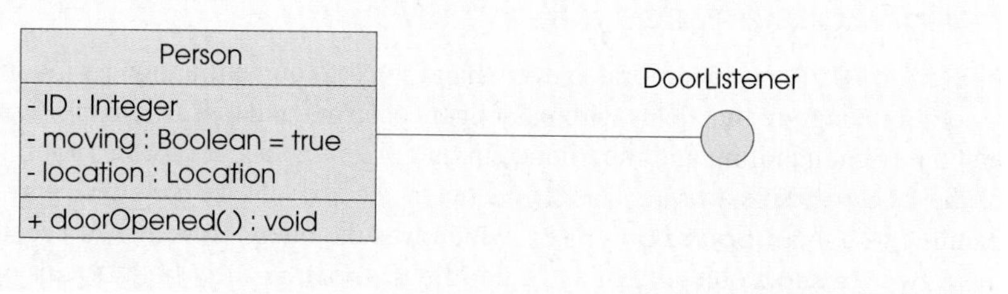

Fig. 11.25 Elided class diagram that models class **`Person`** realizing interface **`DoorListener`**.

Forward engineering from the UML to implemented Java code benefits from well-constructed realization diagrams. When declaring any class, specify the realization between that class and its interface—that class will "implement" the interface and override the interface's methods. For example, we use Fig. 11.24 to begin constructing **`Person.java`**:

```
public class Person implements DoorListener {

   // constructor
   public Person() {}

   // methods of DoorListener
   public void doorOpened( DoorEvent doorEvent ) {}
   public void doorClosed( DoorEvent doorEvent ) {}
}
```

Figure 11.26 shows the Java complete implementation for Fig. 11.24. Lines 6–8 and lines 14–15 include the attributes and operations of **`Person`**, respectively—in this case, the **`doorOpened`** operation (line 14) was already included when we implemented the **`DoorListener`** interface, so we include only the attributes of **`Person`**:

```
1  // Person.java
2  // Generated from Fig. 11.24
3  public class Person implements DoorListener {
```

Fig. 11.26 Class **`Person`** is generated from Fig. 11.24 (part 1 of 2).

```

   // attributes
   private int ID;
   private boolean moving = true;
   private Location location;

   // constructor
   public Person() {}

   // methods of DoorListener
   public void doorOpened( DoorEvent doorEvent ) {}
   public void doorClosed( DoorEvent doorEvent ) {}
}
```

Fig. 11.26 Class **`Person`** is generated from Fig. 11.24 (part 2 of 2).

When a **`Door`** opens or closes, that **`Door`** invokes only those methods declared in interface **`DoorListener`**, but only if the **`Person`** has registered with that **`Door`** to receive **`DoorEvent`**s. Finally, we present the elided class diagram that models the realizations in our elevator model in Fig. 11.27—the elided diagram does not contain any interface methods (making the diagram easier to read), so we present the class diagram for interfaces in Fig. 11.28, which shows all interface methods. Refer to these diagrams when studying the elevator simulation implementation in Appendices G, H and I.

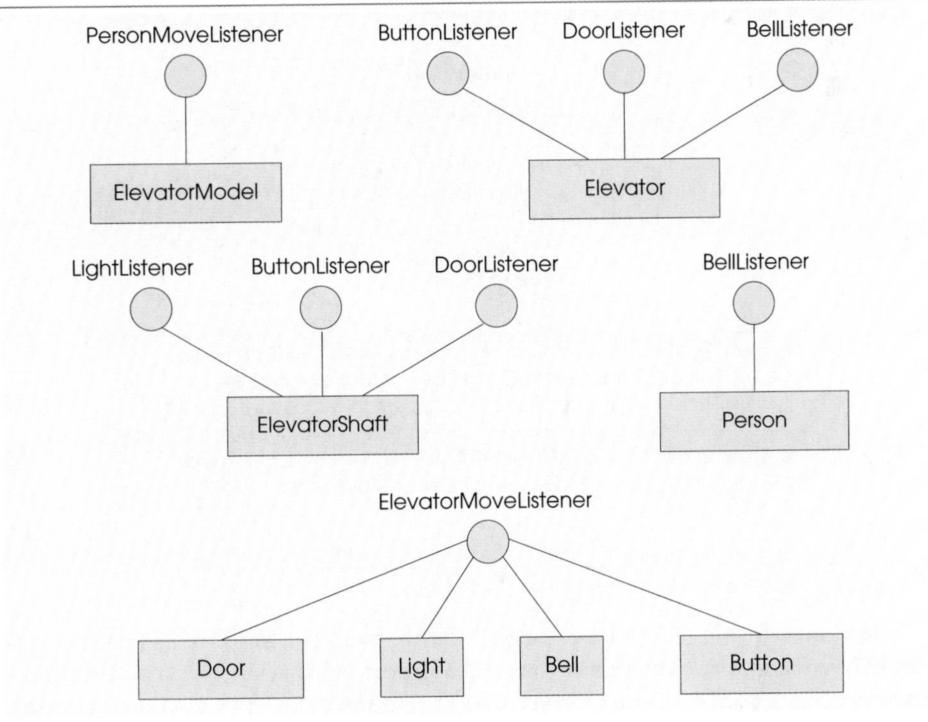

Fig. 11.27 Class diagram that models realizations in the elevator model.

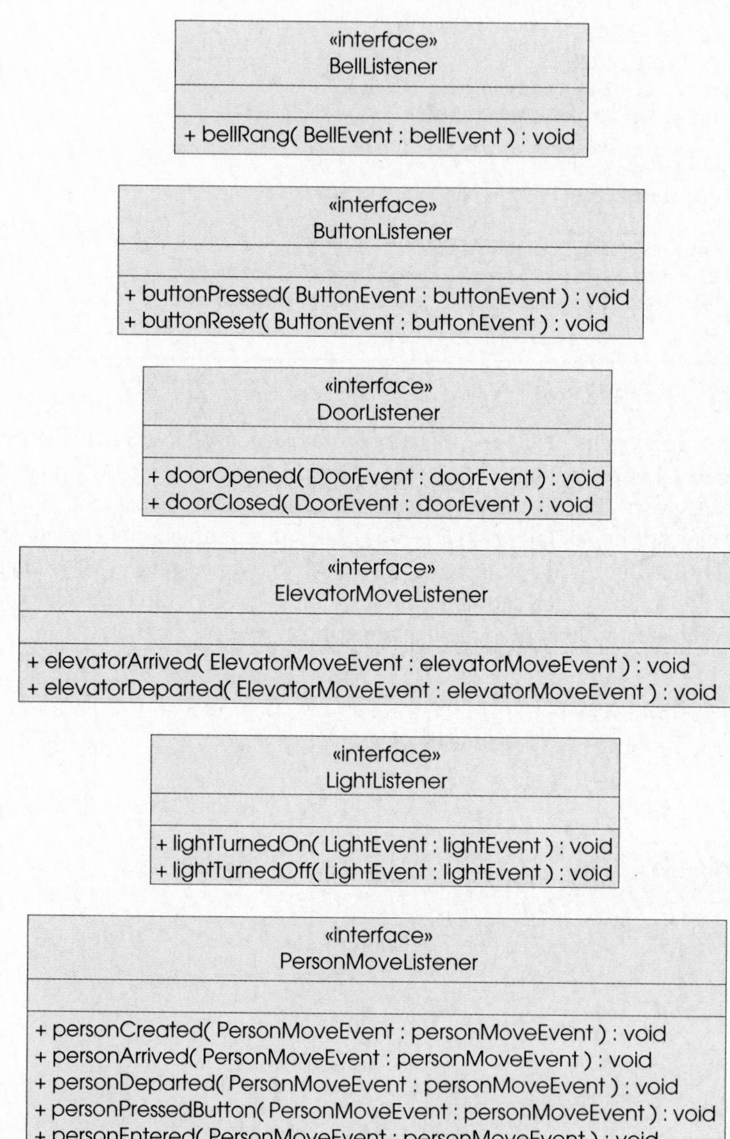

Fig. 11.28 Class diagram for listener interfaces.

According to Fig. 11.27, classes **`Door`**, **`Light`**, **`Bell`** and **`Button`** implement interface **`ElevatorMoveListener`**. Class **`Elevator`** implements interfaces **`ButtonListener`**, **`DoorListener`** and **`BellListener`**. Class **`ElevatorModel`** implements interface **`PersonMoveListener`**. Class **`ElevatorShaft`** implements interfaces **`LightListener`**, **`ButtonListener`** and **`DoorListener`**. Lastly, class

Person implements interface **DoorListener**. We reexamine Fig. 11.27 in Appendix H when we begin coding our model.

In this section we showed how to represent interfaces and realizations with the UML. We also presented class diagrams showing the listener interfaces and their realizations for our elevator simulation. In "Thinking About Objects" Section 12.16, we model how the user interacts with our simulation.

SUMMARY

- A coordinate system is a scheme for identifying every possible point on the screen.
- The upper-left corner of a GUI component has the coordinates *(0, 0)*. A coordinate pair is composed of an x-coordinate (the horizontal coordinate) and a y-coordinate (the vertical coordinate).
- Coordinate units are measured in pixels. A pixel is a display monitor's smallest unit of resolution.
- A graphics context enables drawing on the screen in Java. A Graphics object manages a graphics context by controlling how information is drawn.
- **Graphics** objects contain methods for drawing, font manipulation, color manipulation and so on.
- Method **paint** is normally called in response to an *event*, such as uncovering a window.
- Method **repaint** requests a call to **Component** method **update** as soon as possible to clear the **Component**'s background of any previous drawing, then **update** calls **paint** directly.
- Class **Color** defines methods and constants for manipulating colors in a Java program.
- Java uses RGB colors in which the red, green and blue color components are integers in the range from 0 to 255 or floating-point values in the range from 0.0 to 1.0. The larger the RGB value, the greater the amount of that particular color.
- **Color** methods **getRed**, **getGreen** and **getBlue** return integer values from 0 to 255 representing the amount of red, green and blue in a **Color**.
- Class **Color** provides 13 predefined **Color** objects.
- **Graphics** method getColor returns a **Color** object representing the current drawing color. **Graphics** method setColor sets the current drawing color.
- Java provides class **JColorChooser** to display a dialog for selecting colors.
- **static** method **showDialog** of class **JColorChooser** displays a color chooser dialog. This method returns the selected **Color** object (**null**, if none is selected).
- The default **JColorChooser** dialog allows you to select a color from a variety of color swatches. The **HSB** tab allows you to select a color based on hue, saturation and brightness. The **RGB** tab allows you to select a color by using sliders for the red, green and blue components of the color.
- **Component** method **setBackground** (one of the many **Component** methods that can be used on most GUI components) changes the background color of a component.
- Class **Font**'s constructor takes three arguments—the font name, the font style and the font size. The font name is any font currently supported by the system. The font style is **Font.PLAIN**, **Font.ITALIC** or **Font.BOLD**. The font size is measured in points.
- **Graphics** method **setFont** sets the drawing font.
- Class **FontMetrics** defines several methods for obtaining font metrics.
- **Graphics** method **getFontMetrics** with no arguments obtains the **FontMetrics** object for the current font. **Graphics** method **getFontMetrics** that receives a **Font** argument returns a corresponding **FontMetrics** object.

- Methods **draw3DRect** and **fill3DRect** take five arguments specifying the top-left corner of the rectangle, the **width** and **height** of the rectangle and whether the rectangle is raised (**true**) or lowered (**false**).
- Methods **drawRoundRect** and **fillRoundRect** draw rectangles with rounded corners. Their first two arguments specify the upper-left corner, the third and fourth arguments specify the **width** and **height**, and the last two arguments—**arcWidth** and **arcHeight**—determine the horizontal and vertical diameters of the arcs used to represent the corners.
- Methods **drawOval** and **fillOval** take the same arguments—the top-left coordinate and the **width** and the **height** of the bounding rectangle that contains the oval.
- An arc is a portion of an oval. Arcs sweep from a starting angle the number of degrees specified by their arc angle. The starting angle specifies where the arc begins and the arc angle specifies the total number of degrees through which the arc sweeps. Arcs that sweep counterclockwise are measured in positive degrees and arcs that sweep clockwise are measured in negative degrees.
- Methods **drawArc** and **fillArc** take the same arguments—the top-left coordinate, the **width** and the **height** of the bounding rectangle that contains the arc and the **startAngle** and **arcAngle** that define the sweep of the arc.
- Polygons are multisided shapes. Polylines are a series of connected points.
- One **Polygon** constructor receives an array containing the *x*-coordinate of each point, an array containing the *y*-coordinate of each point and the number of points in the polygon.
- One version of **Graphics** method **drawPolygon** displays a **Polygon** object. Another version receives an array containing the x-coordinate of each point, an array containing the y-coordinate of each point and the number of points in the polygon and displays the corresponding polygon.
- **Graphics** method **drawPolyline** displays a series of connected lines specified by its arguments (an array containing the x-coordinate of each point, an array containing the y-coordinate of each point and the number of points).
- **Polygon** method **addPoint** adds pairs of x- and y-coordinates to a **Polygon**.
- The Java2D API provides advanced two-dimensional graphics capabilities for processing line art, text and images.
- To access the **Graphics2D** capabilities, downcast the **Graphics** reference passed to **paint** to a **Graphics2d** reference.
- **Graphics2D** method **setPaint** sets the **Paint** object that determines the color and texture for the shape to display. A **Paint** object is an object of any class that implements interface **java.awt.Paint**. The **Paint** object can be a **Color** or an instance of the Java2D API's **GradientPaint**, **SystemColor** or **TexturePaint** classes.
- Class **GradientPaint** draws a shape in a gradually changing color called a gradient.
- **Graphics2D** method **fill** draws a filled **Shape** object. The **Shape** object is an instance of any class that implements interface **Shape**.
- The **Ellipse2D.Double** constructor receives four arguments specifying the bounding rectangle for the ellipse to display.
- **Graphics2D** method **setStroke** sets the characteristics of the lines used to draw a shape. Method **setStroke** requires a **Stroke** object as its argument. The **Stroke** object is an instance of any class that implements interface **Stroke**, such as a **BasicStroke**.
- **Graphics2D** method **draw** draws a **Shape** object. The **Shape** object is an instance of any class that implements interface **Shape**.
- The **Rectangle2D.Double** constructor receives four arguments specifying the upper-left *x*-coordinate, upper-left *y*-coordinate, width and height of the rectangle.

- Class **BufferedImage** can be used to produce images in color and gray scale.
- A **TexturePaint** object uses the image stored in its associated **BufferedImage** as the fill texture for a filled-in shape.
- The **RoundRectangle2D.Double** constructor receives six arguments specifying the rectangle's dimensions and the arc width and arc height used to determine the rounding of the corners.
- The **Arc2D.Double** constructor's first four arguments specify the upper-left *x*-coordinate, upper-left *y*-coordinate, width and height of the bounding rectangle for the arc. The fifth argument specifies the start angle. The sixth argument specifies the end angle. The last argument specifies the type of arc (**Arc2D.PIE**, **Arc2D.CHORD** or **Arc2D.OPEN**).
- The **Line2D.Double** constructor's arguments specify starting and ending line coordinates.
- A general path is a shape constructed from straight lines and complex curves represented with an object of class **GeneralPath** (package **java.awt.geom**).
- **GeneralPath** method **moveTo** specifies the first point in a general path. **GeneralPath** method **lineTo** draws a line to the next point in the general path. Each new call to **lineTo** draws a line from the previous point to the current point. **GeneralPath** method **closePath** draws a line from the last point to the point specified in the last call to **moveTo**.
- **Graphics2D** method **translate** moves the drawing origin to a new location. All drawing operations now use that location as *(0, 0)*.
- **Graphics2D** method **rotate** to rotate the next that is displayed. Its argument specifies the rotation angle in radians (with 360° = 2π radians).

TERMINOLOGY

addPoint method
angle
arc bounded by a rectangle
arc height
arc sweeping through an angle
arc width
Arc2D.Double class
ascent
background color
baseline
bounding rectangle
BufferedImage class
closed polygon
closePath method
Color class
Component class
coordinate
coordinate system
degree
descent
draw an arc
draw method
draw3DRect method
drawArc method
drawLine method
drawOval method
drawPolygon method
drawPolyline method
drawRect method
drawRoundRect method
Ellipse2D.Double class
event
event-driven process
fill method
fill3DRect method
fillArc method
filled polygon
fillOval method
fillPolygon method
fillRect method
fillRoundRect method
font
Font class
font metrics
font name
font style
FontMetrics class
GeneralPath class
getAscent method
getBlue method
getDescent method
getFamily method

getFont method
getFontList method
getFontMetrics method
getGreen method
getHeight method
getLeading method
getName method
getRed method
getSize method
getStyle method
GradientPaint class
Graphics class
graphics context
graphics object
Graphics2D class
isBold method
isItalic method
isPlain method
Java2D API
leading
Line2D.Double class
lineTo method
Monospaced font
moveTo method
negative degrees
Paint interface
paint method
pixel
point
polygon
Polygon class
positive degrees
Rectangle2D.Double class
repaint method
RGB value
rotate method
RoundRectangle2D.Double class
SansSerif font
Serif font
setColor method
setFont method
setPaint method
setStroke method
Shape interface
Stroke interface
SystemColor class
TexturePaint class
translate method
update method
vertical component
x-axis
x-coordinate
y-axis
y-coordinate

SELF-REVIEW EXERCISES

11.1 Fill in the blanks in each of the following statements:

a) In Java2D, method __________ of class __________ sets the characteristics of a line used to draw a shape.
b) Class __________ helps define the fill for a shape such that the fill gradually changes from one color to another.
c) The __________ method of class **Graphics** draws a line between two points.
d) RGB is short for __________, __________ and __________.
e) Font sizes are measured in units called __________.
f) Class __________ helps define the fill for a shape using a pattern drawn in a **BufferedImage**.

11.2 State whether each of the following is *true* or *false*. If *false*, explain why.

a) The first two arguments of **Graphics** method drawOval specify the center coordinate of the oval.
b) In the Java coordinate system, *x* values increase from left to right.
c) Method **fillPolygon** draws a solid polygon in the current color.
d) Method **drawArc** allows negative angles.
e) Method **getSize** returns the size of the current font in centimeters.
f) Pixel coordinate *(0, 0)* is located at the exact center of the monitor.

11.3 Find the error(s) in each of the following and explain how to correct the error(s). Assume that **g** is a **Graphics** object.

a) `g.setFont( "SansSerif" );`
b) `g.erase( x, y, w, h );     // clear rectangle at (x, y)`
c) `Font f = new Font( "Serif", Font.BOLDITALIC, 12 );`
d) `g.setColor( Color.Yellow );  // change color to yellow`

ANSWERS TO SELF-REVIEW EXERCISES

11.1 a) **setStroke**, **Graphics2D**. b) **GradientPaint**. c) **drawLine**. d) red, green, blue. e) points. f) **TexturePaint**.

11.2 a) False. The first two arguments specify the upper-left corner of the bounding rectangle.
b) True.
c) True.
d) True.
e) False. Font sizes are measured in points.
f) False. The coordinate *(0,0)* corresponds to the upper-left corner of a GUI component on which drawing occurs.

11.3 a) The **setFont** method takes a **Font** object as an argument—not a **String**.
b) The **Graphics** class does not have an **erase** method. The **clearRect** method should be used.
c) **Font.BOLDITALIC** is not a valid font style. To get a bold italic font, use **Font.BOLD + Font.ITALIC**.
d) **Yellow** should begin with a lowercase letter: **g.setColor(Color.yellow);**.

EXERCISES

11.4 Fill in the blanks in each of the following statements:
a) Class _________ of the Java2D API is used to define ovals.
b) Methods **draw** and **fill** of class **Graphics2D** require an object of type _________ as their argument.
c) The three constants that specify font style are _________, _________ and _________.
d) **Graphics2D** method _________ sets the painting color for Java2D shapes.

11.5 State whether each of the following is *true* or *false*. If *false*, explain why.
a) The **drawPolygon** method automatically connects the endpoints of the polygon.
b) The **drawLine** method draws a line between two points.
c) The **fillArc** method uses degrees to specify the angle.
d) In the Java coordinate system, *y* values increase from top to bottom.
e) The **Graphics** class inherits directly from class **Object**.
f) The **Graphics** class is an **abstract** class.
g) The **Font** class inherits directly from class **Graphics**.

11.6 Write a program that draws a series of eight concentric circles. The circles should be separated by 10 pixels. Use the **drawOval** method of class **Graphics**.

11.7 Write a program that draws a series of eight concentric circles. The circles should be separated by 10 pixels. Use the **drawArc** method.

11.8 Modify your solution to Exercise 11.6 to draw the ovals by using instances of class **Ellipse2D.Double** and method **draw** of class **Graphics2D**.

11.9 Write a program that draws lines of random lengths in random colors.

11.10 Modify your solution to Exercise 11.9 to draw random lines, in random colors and random line thicknesses. Use class **Line2D.Double** and method **draw** of class **Graphics2D** to draw the lines.

11.11 Write a program that displays randomly generated triangles in different colors. Each triangle should be filled with a different color. Use class **GeneralPath** and method **fill** of class **Graphics2D** to draw the triangles.

11.12 Write a program that randomly draws characters in different font sizes and colors.

11.13 Write a program that draws an 8-by-8 grid. Use the **drawLine** method.

11.14 Modify your solution to Exercise 11.13 to draw the grid using instances of class **Line2D.Double** and method **draw** of class **Graphics2D**.

11.15 Write a program that draws a 10-by-10 grid. Use the **drawRect** method.

11.16 Modify your solution to Exercise 11.15 to draw the grid by using instances of class **Rectangle2D.Double** and method **draw** of class **Graphics2D**.

11.17 Write a program that draws a tetrahedron (a pyramid). Use class **GeneralPath** and method **draw** of class **Graphics2D**.

11.18 Write a program that draws a cube. Use class **GeneralPath** and method **draw** of class **Graphics2D**.

11.19 In Exercise 3.9, you wrote an applet that input the radius of a circle from the user and displayed the circle's diameter, circumference and area. Modify your solution to Exercise 3.9 to read a set of coordinates in addition to the radius. Then draw the circle and display the circle's diameter, circumference and area, using an **Ellipse2D.Double** object to represent the circle and method **draw** of class **Graphics2D** to display the circle.

11.20 Write an application that simulates a screen saver. The application should randomly draw lines using method **drawLine** of class **Graphics**. After drawing 100 lines, the application should clear itself and start drawing lines again. To allow the program to draw continuously, place a call to **repaint** as the last line in method **paint**. Do you notice any problems with this on your system?

11.21 Here is a peek ahead. Package **javax.swing** contains a class called ***Timer*** that is capable of calling method **actionPerformed** of interface **ActionListener** at a fixed time interval (specified in milliseconds). Modify your solution to Exercise 11.20 to remove the call to **repaint** from method **paint**. Define your class so it implements **ActionListener**. (The **actionPerformed** method should simply call **repaint**.) Define an instance variable of type **Timer** called **timer** in your class. In the constructor for your class, write the following statements:

```
timer = new Timer( 1000, this );
timer.start();
```

This creates an instance of class **Timer** that will call **this** object's **actionPerformed** method every **1000** milliseconds (i.e., every second).

11.22 Modify your solution to Exercise 11.21 to enable the user to enter the number of random lines that should be drawn before the application clears itself and starts drawing lines again. Use a **JTextField** to obtain the value. The user should be able to type a new number into the **JTextField** at any time during the program's execution. Use an inner class definition to perform event handling for the **JTextField**.

11.23 Modify your solution to Exercise 11.21 such that it uses random number generation to choose different shapes to display (use methods of class **Graphics**).]

11.24 Modify your solution to Exercise 11.23 to use classes and drawing capabilities of the Java2D API. For shapes such as rectangles and ellipses, draw them with randomly generated gradients (use class **GradientPaint** to generate the gradient).

11.25 Write a graphical version of your solution to Exercise 6.37—the *Towers of Hanoi*. After studying Chapter 18, you will be able to implement a version of this exercise using Java's image, animation and audio capabilities.

11.26 Modify the die-rolling program of Fig. 7.8 so that it updates the counts for each side of the die after each roll. Convert the application into a windowed application (i.e., a subclass of **`JFrame`**) and use **`Graphics`** method **`drawString`** to output the totals.

11.27 Modify your solution to Exercise 7.21—*Turtle Graphics*—to add a graphical user interface using **`JTextField`**s and **`JButton`**s. Also, draw lines rather than drawing asterisks (**`*`**). When the turtle graphics program specifies a move, translate the number of positions into a number of pixels on the screen by multiplying the number of positions by 10 (or any value you choose). Implement the drawing with Java2D API features.

11.28 Produce a graphical version of the Knight's Tour problem (Exercises 7.22, 7.23 and 7.26). As each move is made, the appropriate cell of the chessboard should be updated with the proper move number. If the result of the program is a *full tour* or a *closed tour*, the program should display an appropriate message. If you would like, use class **`Timer`** (see Exercise 11.24) to help animate the Knight's Tour. Every second, the next move should be made.

11.29 Produce a graphical version of the *Tortoise and the Hare* simulation (Exercise 7.41). Simulate the mountain by drawing an arc that extends from the bottom-left of the window to the top-right of the window. The tortoise and the hare should race up the mountain. Implement the graphical output so the tortoise and the hare are actually printed on the arc every move. [Note: Extend the length of the race from 70 to 300 to allow yourself a larger graphics area.]

11.30 Produce a graphical version of the *Maze Traversal* problem (Exercises 7.38-7.40). Use the mazes you produced as guides for creating the graphical versions. While the maze is being solved, a small circle should be displayed in the maze indicating the current position. If you would like, use class **`Timer`** (see Exercise 11.24) to help animate the traversal of the maze. Every second, the next move should be made.

11.31 Produce a graphical version of the *Bucket Sort* (Exercise 7.28) that shows each value being placed into the appropriate bucket and eventually being copied back to the original array.

11.32 Write a program that uses method **`drawPolyline`** to draw a spiral.

11.33 Write a program that inputs four numbers and graphs the numbers as a pie chart. Use class **`Arc2D.Double`** and method **`fill`** of class **`Graphics2D`** to perform the drawing. Draw each piece of the pie in a separate color.

11.34 Write an applet that inputs four numbers and graphs the numbers as a bar graph. Use class **`Rectangle2D.Double`** and method **`fill`** of class **`Graphics2D`** to perform the drawing. Draw each bar in a different color.

12

Graphical User Interface Components: Part 1

Objectives

- To understand the design principles of graphical user interfaces (GUI).
- To be able to build graphical user interfaces.
- To understand the packages containing GUI components and event-handling classes and interfaces.
- To be able to create and manipulate buttons, labels, lists, text fields and panels.
- To understand mouse events and keyboard events.
- To understand and be able to use layout managers.

... the wisest prophets make sure of the event first.
Horace Walpole

Do you think I can listen all day to such stuff?
Lewis Carroll

Speak the affirmative; emphasize your choice by utter ignoring of all that you reject.
Ralph Waldo Emerson

You pays your money and you takes your choice.
Punch

Guess if you can, choose if you dare.
Pierre Corneille

All hope abandon, ye who enter here!
Dante Alighieri

Exit, pursued by a bear.
William Shakespeare

Outline

12.1 Introduction
12.2 Swing Overview
12.3 `JLabel`
12.4 Event-Handling Model
12.5 `JTextField` and `JPasswordField`
12.5.1 How Event Handling Works
12.6 `JButton`
12.7 `JCheckBox` and `JRadioButton`
12.8 `JComboBox`
12.9 `JList`
12.10 Multiple-Selection Lists
12.11 Mouse Event Handling
12.12 Adapter Classes
12.13 Keyboard Event Handling
12.14 Layout Managers
12.14.1 `FlowLayout`
12.14.2 `BorderLayout`
12.14.3 `GridLayout`
12.15 Panels
12.16 (Optional Case Study) Thinking About Objects: Use Cases

Summary • Terminology • Self-Review Exercises • Answers to Self-Review Exercises • Exercises

12.1 Introduction

A *graphical user interface* (*GUI*) presents a pictorial interface to a program. A GUI (pronounced "GOO-EE") gives a program a distinctive "look" and "feel." Providing different programs with a consistent set of intuitive user interface components provides users with a basic level of familiarity with each program before they ever use it. In turn, this reduces the time users require to learn a program and increases their ability to use the program in a productive manner.

Look-and-Feel Observation 12.1

Consistent user interfaces enable a user to learn new applications faster.

As an example of a GUI, Fig. 12.1 contains a Netscape Navigator window with some of its GUI components labeled. In the window, there is a *menu bar* containing *menus* (**File**, **Edit**, **View** etc.). Below the menu bar there is a set of *buttons* that each have a defined task in Netscape Navigator. To the right of the buttons there is a *text field* in which the user can type the name of the World Wide Web site to visit. The menus, buttons and text fields are part of Netscape Navigator's GUI. They enable you to interact with the Navigator program.

In this chapter and the next, we demonstrate many GUI components that enable users to interact with your programs.

GUIs are built from *GUI components* (sometimes called *controls* or *widgets*—shorthand notation for *window gadgets*). A GUI component is an object with which the user interacts via the mouse, the keyboard or another form of input, such as voice recognition. Several common GUI components are listed in Figure 12.2. In the sections that follow, we discuss each of these GUI components in detail. In the next chapter, we discuss more advanced GUI components.

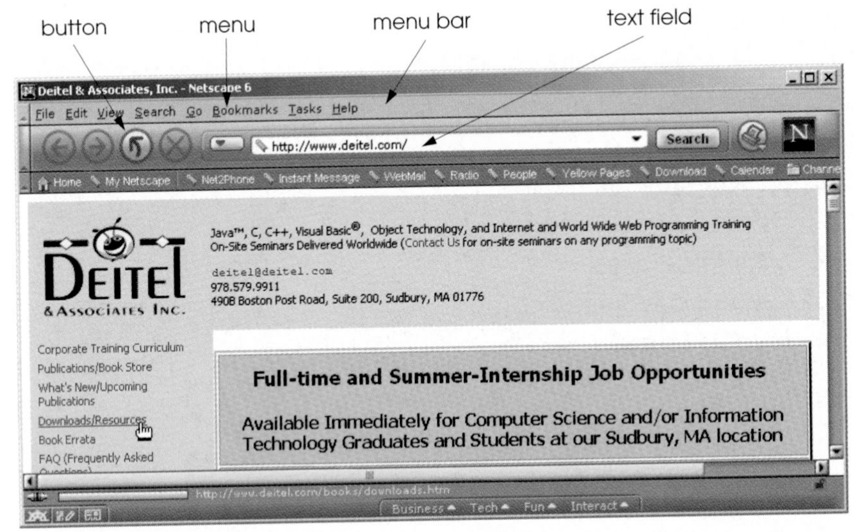

Fig. 12.1 A sample Netscape Navigator window with GUI components.

Component	Description
`JLabel`	An area where uneditable text or icons can be displayed.
`JTextField`	An area in which the user inputs data from the keyboard. The area can also display information.
`JButton`	An area that triggers an event when clicked.
`JCheckBox`	A GUI component that is either selected or not selected.
`JComboBox`	A drop-down list of items from which the user can make a selection by clicking an item in the list or possibly by typing into the box.
`JList`	An area where a list of items is displayed from which the user can make a selection by clicking once on any element in the list. Double-clicking an element in the list generates an action event. Multiple elements can be selected.
`JPanel`	A container in which components can be placed.

Fig. 12.2 Some basic GUI components.

12.2 Swing Overview

The classes that create the GUI components of Fig. 12.2 are part of the *Swing GUI components* from package **javax.swing**. These GUI components became standard in Java with the release of the Java 2 platform version 1.2. Most *Swing components* (as they are commonly called) are written, manipulated and displayed completely in Java (so-called *pure Java* components).

The original GUI components from the *Abstract Windowing Toolkit* package **java.awt** (also called the *AWT*) are tied directly to the local platform's graphical user interface capabilities. When a Java program with an AWT GUI executes on different Java platforms, the program's GUI components display differently on each platform. Consider a program that displays an object of type **Button** (package **java.awt**). On a computer running the Microsoft Windows operating system, the **Button** will have the same look and feel as the buttons in other Windows applications. Similarly, on a computer running the Apple Macintosh operating system, the **Button** will have the same look and feel as the buttons in other Macintosh applications. In addition to the differences in appearance, sometimes the manner in which a user interacts with a particular AWT component differs between platforms.

Together, the appearance and how the user interacts with the program are known as that program's *look and feel*. The Swing components allow the programmer to specify a uniform look and feel across all platforms. In addition, Swing enables programs to provide a custom look and feel for each platform or even to change the look and feel while the program is running. For example, a program could enable users to choose their preferred look and feel.

Look-and-Feel Observation 12.2

Swing components are written in Java, so they provide a greater level of portability and flexibility than the original Java GUI components from package **java.awt**.

Swing components are often referred to as *lightweight components*—they are written completely in Java so they are not "weighed down" by the complex GUI capabilities of the platform on which they are used. AWT components (many of which parallel the Swing components) that are tied to the local platform are correspondingly called *heavyweight components*—they rely on the local platform's *windowing system* to determine their functionality and their look and feel. Each heavyweight component has a *peer* (from package **java.awt.peer**) that is responsible for the interactions between the component and the local platform that display and manipulate the component. Several Swing components are still heavyweight components. In particular, subclasses of **java.awt.Window** (such as **JFrame** used in several previous chapters) that display windows on the screen and subclasses of **java.applet.Applet** (such as **JApplet**) still require direct interaction with the local windowing system. As such, heavyweight Swing GUI components are less flexible than many of the lightweight components we will demonstrate.

Portability Tip 12.1

The look of a GUI defined with heavyweight GUI components from package **java.awt** *may vary across platforms. Heavyweight components "tie" into the "local" platform GUI, which varies from platform to platform.*

Figure 12.3 shows an inheritance hierarchy of the classes that define attributes and behaviors that are common to most Swing components. Each class is displayed with its fully qualified package name and class name. Much of each GUI component's functionality is derived from these classes. A class that inherits from the **`Component`** class *is a* **`Component`**. For example, class **`Container`** inherits from class **`Component`**, and class **`Component`** inherits from **`Object`**. Thus, a **`Container`** *is a* **`Component`** and *is an* **`Object`**, and a **`Component`** *is an* **`Object`**. A class that inherits from class **`Container`** *is a* **`Container`**. Thus, a **`JComponent`** *is a* **`Container`**.

Software Engineering Observation 12.1

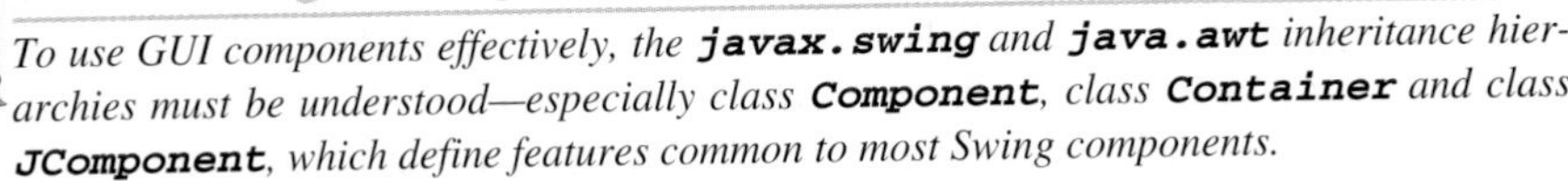

To use GUI components effectively, the **`javax.swing`** *and* **`java.awt`** *inheritance hierarchies must be understood—especially class* **`Component`**, *class* **`Container`** *and class* **`JComponent`**, *which define features common to most Swing components.*

Class **`Component`** defines the common attributes and behaviors of all subclasses of **`Component`**. With few exceptions, most GUI components extend class **`Component`** directly or indirectly. One method that originates in class **`Component`** that has been used frequently to this point is **`paint`**. Other methods discussed previously that originated in Component are **`repaint`** and **`update`**. It is important to understand the methods of class **`Component`** because much of the functionality inherited by every subclass of **`Component`** is defined by the **`Component`** class originally. Operations common to most GUI components (both Swing and AWT) are found in class **`Component`**.

Good Programming Practice 12.1

Study the methods of class **`Component`** *in the Java 2 SDK on-line documentation to learn the capabilities common to most GUI components.*

A **`Container`** is a collection of related components. In applications with **`JFrame`**s and in applets, we attach components to the content pane, which is an object of class **`Container`**. Class **`Container`** defines the common attributes and behaviors for all subclasses of **`Container`**. One method that originates in class **`Container`** is **`add`** for adding components to a **`Container`**. Another method that originates in class **`Container`** is **`setLayout`**, which enables a program to specify the layout manager that helps a **`Container`** position and size its components.

Good Programming Practice 12.2

Study the methods of class **`Container`** *in the Java 2 SDK on-line documentation to learn the capabilities common to every container for GUI components.*

Class **`JComponent`** is the superclass to most Swing components. This class defines the common attributes and behaviors of all subclasses of **`JComponent`**.

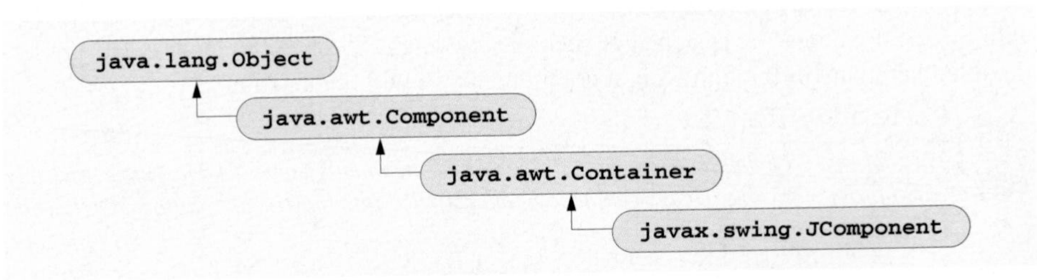

Fig. 12.3 Common superclasses of many of the Swing components.

Good Programming Practice 12.3

Study the methods of class **`JComponent`** *in the Java 2 SDK on-line documentation to learn the capabilities common to every container for GUI components.*

Swing components that subclass **`JComponent`** have many features, including:

1. A *pluggable look and feel* that can be used to customize the look and feel when the program executes on different platforms.
2. Shortcut keys (called *mnemonics*) for direct access to GUI components through the keyboard.
3. Common event-handling capabilities for cases where several GUI components initiate the same actions in a program.
4. Brief descriptions of a GUI component's purpose (called *tool tips*) that are displayed when the mouse cursor is positioned over the component for a short time.
5. Support for assistive technologies such as braille screen readers for blind people.
6. Support for user interface *localization*—customizing the user interface for display in different languages and cultural conventions.

These are just some of the many features of the Swing components. We discuss several of these features here and in Chapter 13.

12.3 JLabel

Labels provide text instructions or information on a GUI. Labels are defined with class ***`JLabel`***—a subclass of **`JComponent`**. A label displays a single line of *read-only text*, an image or both text and an image. Programs rarely change a label's contents after creating it. The application of Figure 12.4 demonstrates several **`JLabel`** features.

```
// Fig. 12.4: LabelTest.java
// Demonstrating the JLabel class.

// Java core packages
import java.awt.*;
import java.awt.event.*;

// Java extension packages
import javax.swing.*;

public class LabelTest extends JFrame {
   private JLabel label1, label2, label3;

   // set up GUI
   public LabelTest()
   {
      super( "Testing JLabel" );

```

Fig. 12.4 Demonstrating class **`JLabel`** (part 1 of 2).

```
      // get content pane and set its layout
      Container container = getContentPane();
      container.setLayout( new FlowLayout() );

      // JLabel constructor with a string argument
      label1 = new JLabel( "Label with text" );
      label1.setToolTipText( "This is label1" );
      container.add( label1 );

      // JLabel constructor with string, Icon and
      // alignment arguments
      Icon bug = new ImageIcon( "bug1.gif" );
      label2 = new JLabel( "Label with text and icon",
         bug, SwingConstants.LEFT );
      label2.setToolTipText( "This is label2" );
      container.add( label2 );

      // JLabel constructor no arguments
      label3 = new JLabel();
      label3.setText( "Label with icon and text at bottom" );
      label3.setIcon( bug );
      label3.setHorizontalTextPosition( SwingConstants.CENTER );
      label3.setVerticalTextPosition( SwingConstants.BOTTOM );
      label3.setToolTipText( "This is label3" );
      container.add( label3 );

      setSize( 275, 170 );
      setVisible( true );
   }

   // execute application
   public static void main( String args[] )
   {
      LabelTest application = new LabelTest();

      application.setDefaultCloseOperation(
         JFrame.EXIT_ON_CLOSE );
   }

}  // end class LabelTest
```

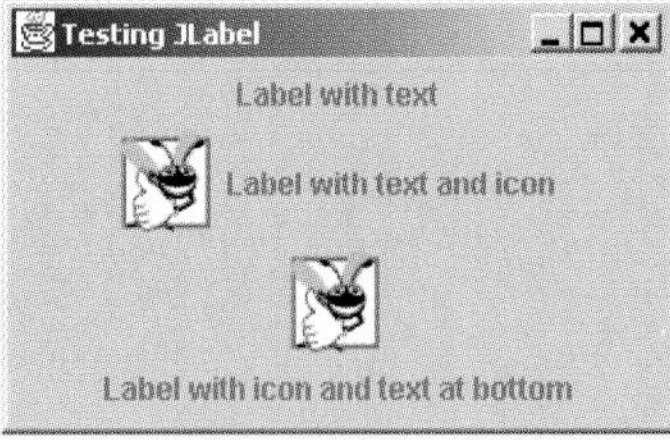

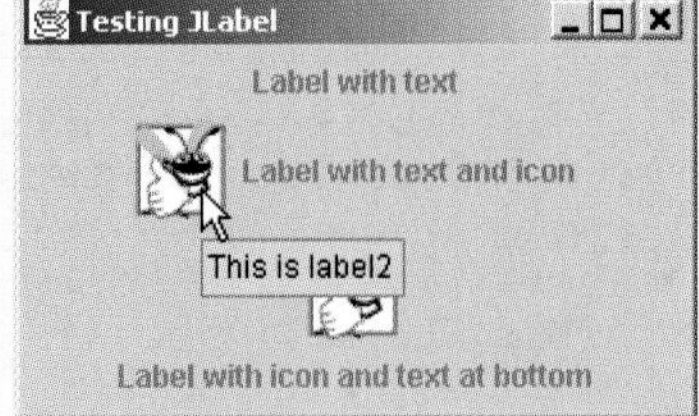

Fig. 12.4 Demonstrating class **JLabel** (part 2 of 2).

Good Programming Practice 12.4

Study the methods of class **javax.swing.JLabel** *in the Java 2 SDK on-line documentation to learn the complete capabilities of the class before using it.*

The program declares three **JLabel**s at line 12. The **JLabel** objects are instantiated in the **LabelTest** constructor (line 15–47). Line 24 creates a **JLabel** object with the text **"Label with text"**. The label displays this text when the label appears on the screen (i.e., when the window is displayed in this program).

Line 25 uses method ***setToolTipText*** (inherited into class **JLabel** from class **JComponent**) to specify the tool tip (see the second screen capture in Fig. 12.4) that is displayed automatically when the user positions the mouse cursor over the label in the GUI. When you execute this program, try positioning the mouse over each label to see its tool tip. Line 26 adds **label1** to the content pane.

Look-and-Feel Observation 12.3

Use tool tips (set with **JComponent** *method* **setToolTipText***) to add descriptive text to your GUI components. This text helps the user determine the GUI component's purpose in the user interface.*

Several Swing components can display images by specifying an ***Icon*** as an argument to their constructor or by using a method that is normally called ***setIcon***. An **Icon** is an object of any class that implements interface ***Icon*** (package **javax.swing**). One such class is ***ImageIcon*** (package **javax.swing**), which supports several image formats, including *Graphics Interchange Format (GIF)*, *Portable Network Graphics (PNG)* and *Joint Photographic Experts Group (JPEG)*. File names for each of these types typically end with **.gif**, **.png** or **.jpg** (or **.jpeg**), respectively. We discuss images in more detail in Chapter 18, Multimedia. Line 30 defines an **ImageIcon** object. The file **bug1.gif** contains the image to load and store in the **ImageIcon** object. This file is assumed to be in the same directory as the program (we will discuss locating the file elsewhere in Chapter 18). The **ImageIcon** object is assigned to **Icon** reference **bug**. Remember, class **ImageIcon** implements interface **Icon**, therefore an **ImageIcon** *is an* **Icon**.

Class **JLabel** supports the display of **Icon**s. Lines 31–32 use another **JLabel** constructor to create a label that displays the text **"Label with text and icon"** and the **Icon** to which **bug** refers and is *left justified* or *left aligned* (i.e., the icon and text are at the left side of the label's area on the screen). Interface ***SwingConstants*** (package **javax.swing**) defines a set of common integer constants (such as **SwingConstants.LEFT**) that are used with many Swing components. By default, the text appears to the right of the image when a label contains both text and an image. The horizontal and vertical alignments of a label can be set with methods ***setHorizontalAlignment*** and ***setVerticalAlignment***, respectively. Line 33 specifies the tool tip text for **label2**. Line 34 adds **label2** to the content pane.

Common Programming Error 12.1

If you do not explicitly add a GUI component to a container, the GUI component will not be displayed when the container appears on the screen.

Common Programming Error 12.2

Adding to a container a component that has not been instantiated throws a ***NullPointerException***.

Class **JLabel** provides many methods to configure a label after it has been instantiated. Line 37 creates a **JLabel** and invokes the no-argument (default constructor). Such a label has no text or **Icon**. Line 38 uses **JLabel** method ***setText*** to set the text displayed on the label. A corresponding method ***getText*** retrieves the current text displayed on a label. Line 39 uses **JLabel** method ***setIcon*** to set the **Icon** displayed on the label. A corresponding method ***getIcon*** retrieves the current **Icon** displayed on a label. Lines 40–41 use **JLabel** methods ***setHorizontalTextPosition*** and ***setVertical-TextPosition*** to specify the text position in the label. In this case, the text will be centered horizontally and will appear at the bottom of the label. Thus, the **Icon** will appear above the text. Line 42 sets the tool tip text for the **label3**. Line 43 adds **label3** to the content pane.

12.4 Event-Handling Model

In the preceding section, we did not discuss event handling because there are no specific events for **JLabel** objects. GUIs are *event driven* (i.e., they generate *events* when the user of the program interacts with the GUI). Some common interactions are moving the mouse, clicking the mouse, clicking a button, typing in a text field, selecting an item from a menu, closing a window, etc. When a user interaction occurs, an event is sent to the program. GUI event information is stored in an object of a class that extends **AWTEvent**. Figure 12.5 illustrates a hierarchy containing many of the event classes we use from package **java.awt.event**. Many of these event classes are discussed throughout this chapter and Chapter 13. The event types from package ***java.awt.event*** are used with both AWT and Swing components. Additional event types have also been added that are specific to several types of Swing components. New Swing-component event types are defined in package ***javax.swing.event***.

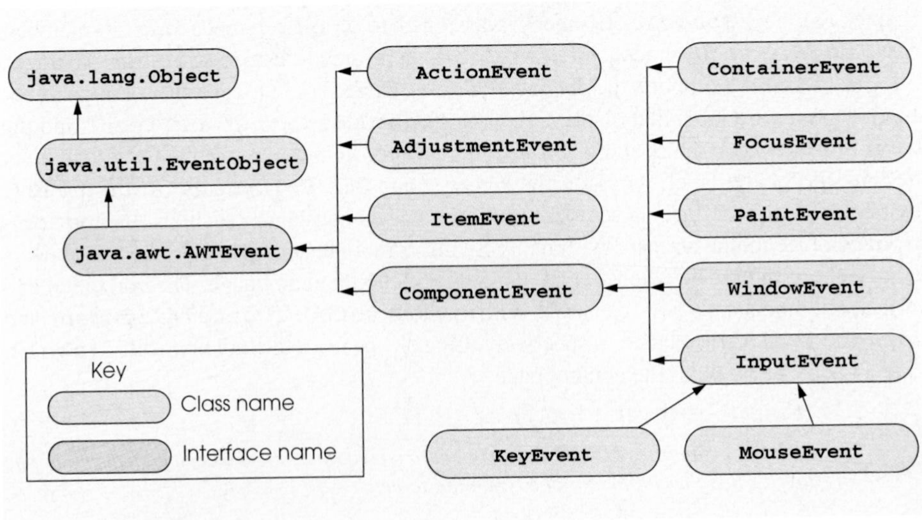

Fig. 12.5 Some event classes of package **java.awt.event**.

There are three parts to the event-handling mechanism—the *event source*, the *event object* and the *event listener*. The event source is the particular GUI component with which the user interacts. The event object encapsulates information about the event that occurred. This information includes a reference to the event source and any event-specific information that may be required by the event listener to handle the event. The event listener is an object that is notified by the event source when an event occurs. The event listener receives an event object when it is notified of the event, then uses the object to respond to the event. The event source is required to provide methods that enable listeners to be registered and unregistered. The event source also is required to maintain a list of its registered listeners and be able to notify its listeners when an event occurs.

The programmer must perform two key tasks to process a graphical user interface event in a program—register an *event listener* for the GUI component that is expected to generate the event, and implement an *event handling method* (or set of event-handling methods). Commonly, event-handling methods are called *event handlers*. An event listener for a GUI event is an object of a class that implements one or more of the event-listener interfaces from package **java.awt.event** and package **javax.swing.event**. Many of the event-listener types are common to both Swing and AWT components. Such types are defined in package **java.awt.event**, and many of these are shown in Fig. 12.6. Additional event-listener types that are specific to Swing components are defined in package **javax.swing.event**.

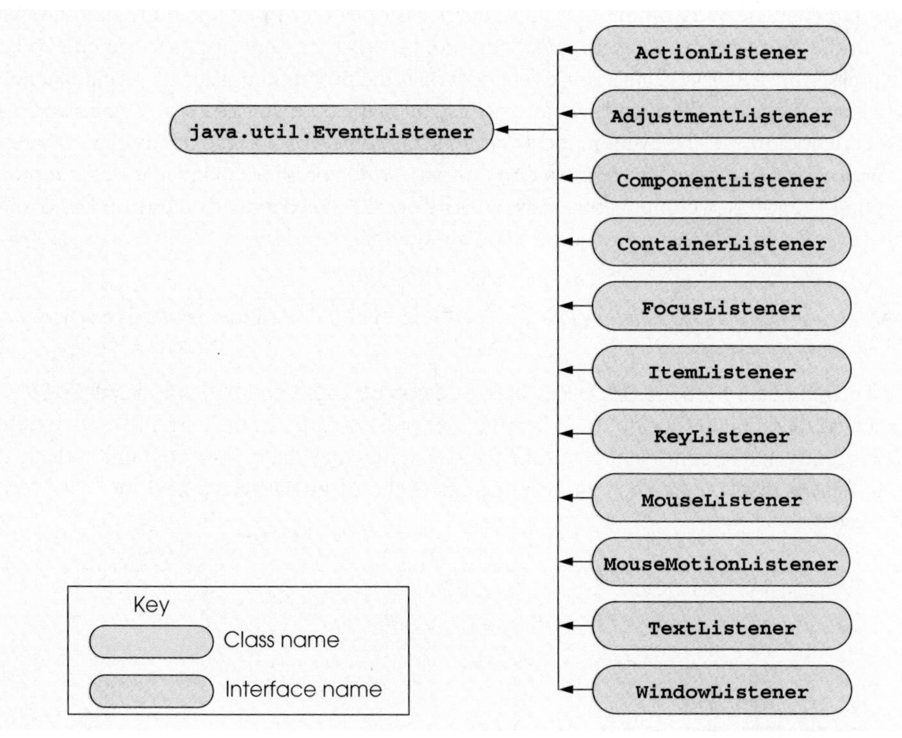

Fig. 12.6 Event-listener interfaces of package **java.awt.event**.

An event listener object "listens" for specific types of events generated by event sources (normally GUI components) in a program. An event handler is a method that is called in response to a particular type of event. Each event-listener interface specifies one or more event-handling methods that *must* be defined in the class that implements the event-listener interface. Remember that interfaces define **abstract** methods. Any class that implements an interface must define all the methods of that interface; otherwise, the class is an **abstract** class and cannot be used to create objects. The use of event listeners in event handling is known as the *delegation event model*—the processing of an event is delegated to a particular object (the listener) in the program.

When an event occurs, the GUI component with which the user interacted notifies its registered listeners by calling each listener's appropriate event handling method. For example, when the user presses the *Enter* key in a **JTextField**, the registered listener's **actionPerformed** method is called. How did the event handler get registered? How does the GUI component know to call **actionPerformed** as opposed to some other event handling method? We answer these questions and diagram the interaction as part of the next example.

12.5 JTextField and JPasswordField

JTextFields and ***JPasswordFields*** (package **javax.swing**) are single-line areas in which text can be entered by the user from the keyboard or text can simply be displayed. A **JPasswordField** shows that a character was typed as the user enters characters, but hides the characters, assuming that they represent a password that should remain known only to the user. When the user types data into a **JTextField** or **JPasswordField** and presses the *Enter* key, an action event occurs. If the program registers an event listener, the listener processes the event and can use the data in the **JTextField** or **JPasswordField** at the time of the event in the program. Class **JTextField** extends class ***JTextComponent*** (package **javax.swing.text**), which provides many features common to Swing's text-based components. Class **JPasswordField** extends **JTextField** and adds several methods that are specific to processing passwords.

Common Programming Error 12.3

*Using a lowercase **f** in the class names **JTextField** or **JPasswordField** is a syntax error.*

The application of Fig. 12.7 uses classes **JTextField** and **JPasswordField** to create and manipulate four fields. When the user presses *Enter* in the currently active field (the currently active component "has the *focus*"), a message dialog box containing the text in the field is displayed. When an event occurs in the **JPasswordField**, the password is revealed.

```
// Fig. 12.7: TextFieldTest.java
// Demonstrating the JTextField class.

// Java core packages
import java.awt.*;
import java.awt.event.*;
```

Fig. 12.7 Demonstrating **JTextFields** and **JPasswordFields** (part 1 of 4).

```
// Java extension packages
import javax.swing.*;

public class TextFieldTest extends JFrame {
   private JTextField textField1, textField2, textField3;
   private JPasswordField passwordField;

   // set up GUI
   public TextFieldTest()
   {
      super( "Testing JTextField and JPasswordField" );

      Container container = getContentPane();
      container.setLayout( new FlowLayout() );

      // construct textfield with default sizing
      textField1 = new JTextField( 10 );
      container.add( textField1 );

      // construct textfield with default text
      textField2 = new JTextField( "Enter text here" );
      container.add( textField2 );

      // construct textfield with default text and
      // 20 visible elements and no event handler
      textField3 = new JTextField( "Uneditable text field", 20 );
      textField3.setEditable( false );
      container.add( textField3 );

      // construct textfield with default text
      passwordField = new JPasswordField( "Hidden text" );
      container.add( passwordField );

      // register event handlers
      TextFieldHandler handler = new TextFieldHandler();
      textField1.addActionListener( handler );
      textField2.addActionListener( handler );
      textField3.addActionListener( handler );
      passwordField.addActionListener( handler );

      setSize( 325, 100 );
      setVisible( true );
   }

   // execute application
   public static void main( String args[] )
   {
      TextFieldTest application = new TextFieldTest();

      application.setDefaultCloseOperation(
         JFrame.EXIT_ON_CLOSE );
   }
```

Fig. 12.7 Demonstrating **JTextField**s and **JPasswordField**s (part 2 of 4).

```

   // private inner class for event handling
   private class TextFieldHandler implements ActionListener {

      // process text field events
      public void actionPerformed( ActionEvent event )
      {
         String string = "";

         // user pressed Enter in JTextField textField1
         if ( event.getSource() == textField1 )
            string = "textField1: " + event.getActionCommand();

         // user pressed Enter in JTextField textField2
         else if ( event.getSource() == textField2 )
            string = "textField2: " + event.getActionCommand();

         // user pressed Enter in JTextField textField3
         else if ( event.getSource() == textField3 )
            string = "textField3: " + event.getActionCommand();

         // user pressed Enter in JTextField passwordField
         else if ( event.getSource() == passwordField ) {
            JPasswordField pwd =
               ( JPasswordField ) event.getSource();
            string = "passwordField: " +
               new String( passwordField.getPassword() );
         }

         JOptionPane.showMessageDialog( null, string );
      }

   } // end private inner class TextFieldHandler

} // end class TextFieldTest
```

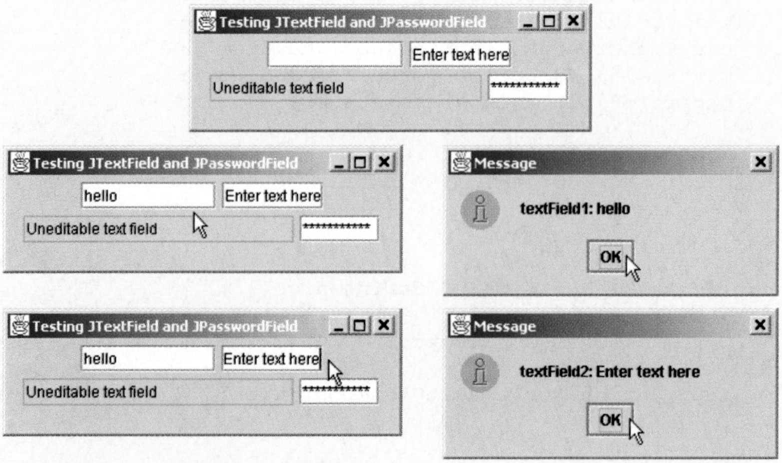

Fig. 12.7 Demonstrating **JTextField**s and **JPasswordField**s (part 3 of 4).

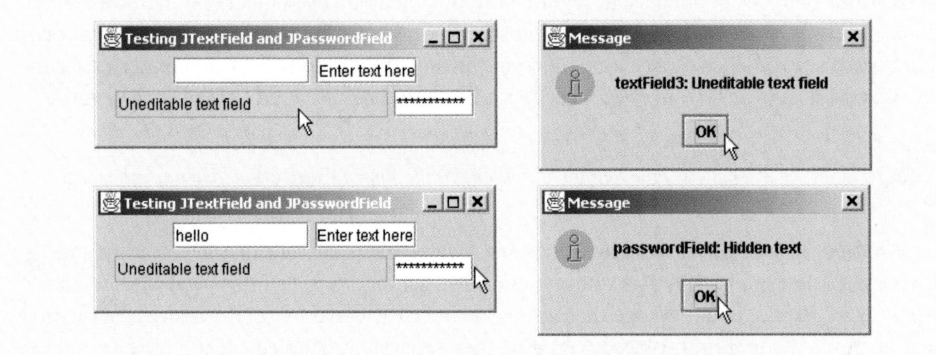

Fig. 12.7 Demonstrating **JTextField**s and **JPasswordField**s (part 4 of 4).

Lines 12–13 declare three references for **JTextField**s (**textField1**, **textField2** and **textField3**) and a **JPasswordField** (**passwordField**). Each of these is instantiated in the constructor (line 16–50). Line 24 defines **JTextField textField1** with **10** columns of text. The width of the text field will be the width in pixels of the average character in the text field's current font multiplied by 10. Line 25 adds **textField1** to the content pane.

Line 28 defines **textField2** with the initial text **"Enter text here"** to display in the text field. The width of the text field is determined by the text. Line 29 adds **textField2** to the content pane.

Line 33 defines **textField3** and call the **JTextField** constructor with two arguments—the default text **"Uneditable text field"** to display in the text field and the number of columns (**20**). The width of the text field is determined by the number of columns specified. Line 34 uses method ***setEditable*** (inherited into **JTextField** from class **JTextComponent**) to indicate that the user cannot modify the text in the text field. Line 35 adds **textField3** to the content pane.

Line 38 defines **JPasswordField passwordField** with the text **"Hidden text"** to display in the text field. The width of the text field is determined by the text. Notice that the text is displayed as a string of asterisks when the program executes. Line 39 adds **passwordField** to the content pane.

For the event-handling in this example, we defined inner class **TextFieldHandler** (lines 62–92), which implements interface **ActionListener** (class **TextFieldHandler** is discussed shortly). Thus, every instance of class **TextFieldHandler** *is an* **ActionListener**. Line 42 defines an instance of class **TextFieldHandler** and assigns it to reference **handler**. This one instance will be used as the event-listener object for the **JTextField**s and the **JPasswordField** in this example.

Lines 43–46 are the event registration statements that specify the event listener object for each of the three **JTextField**s and for the **JPasswordField**. After these statements execute, the object to which **handler** refers is *listening for events* (i.e., it will be notified when an event occurs) on these four objects. The program calls **JTextField** method **addActionListener** to register the event for each component. Method **addActionListener** receives as its argument an **ActionListener** object. Thus, any object of a class that implements interface **ActionListener** (i.e., any object that *is an* **Action-**

Listener) can be supplied as an argument to this method. The object to which **handler** refers *is an* **ActionListener** because its class implements interface **ActionListener**. Now, when the user presses *Enter* in any of these four fields, method **actionPerformed** (line 65–90) in class **TextFieldHandler** is called to handle the event.

The event listener for an event must implement the appropriate event-listener interface.

Method **actionPerformed** uses its **ActionEvent** argument's method **getSource** to determine the GUI component with which the user interacted and creates a **String** to display in a message dialog box. **ActionEvent** method **getActionCommand** returns the text in the **JTextField** that generated the event. If the user interacted with the **JPasswordField**, lines 83–84 cast the **Component** reference returned by **event.getSource()** to a **JPasswordField** reference so that lines 85–86 can use **JPasswordField** method ***getPassword*** to obtain the password and create the **String** to display. Method **getPassword** returns the password as an array of type **char** that is used as an argument to a **String** constructor to create a **String**. Line 89 displays a message box indicating the GUI component reference name and the text the user typed in the field.

Note that even an uneditable **JTextField** can generate an event. Simply click the text field, then press *Enter*. Also note that the actual text of the password is displayed when you press *Enter* in the **JPasswordField** (of course, you would normally not do this!).

Common Programming Error 12.4

Forgetting to register an event handler object for a particular GUI component's event type results in no events being handled for that component for that event type.

Using a separate class to define an event listener is a common programming practice for separating the GUI interface from the implementation of its event handler. For the remainder of this chapter and Chapter 13, many programs use separate event-listener classes to process GUI events.

12.5.1 How Event Handling Works

Let us illustrate how the event-handling mechanism works using **textField1** from the preceding example. We have two remaining open questions from Section 12.4:

1. How did the event handler get registered?
2. How does the GUI component know to call **actionPerformed** as opposed to some other event handling method?

The first question is answered by the event registration performed in lines 43–46 of the program. Figure 12.8 diagrams **JTextField** reference **textField1**, the **JTextField** object to which it refers and the listener object that is registered to handle the **JTextField**'s event.

Every **JComponent** has an object of class ***EventListenerList*** (package **javax.swing.event**) called ***listenerList*** as an instance variable. All registered listeners are stored in the **listenerList** (diagramed as an array in Figure 12.8). When the statement

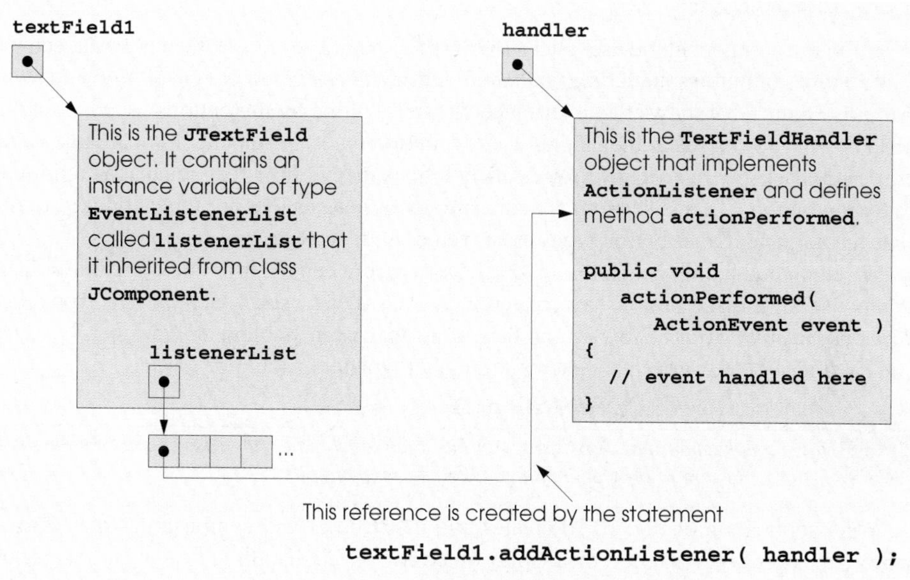
textField1
handler
This is the JTextField object. It contains an instance variable of type EventListenerList called listenerList that it inherited from class JComponent.
listenerList
This is the TextFieldHandler object that implements ActionListener and defines method actionPerformed.
public void
actionPerformed(
ActionEvent event)
{
// event handled here
}
This reference is created by the statement
textField1.addActionListener(handler);

Fig. 12.8 Event registration for **JTextField textField1**.

```
textField1.addActionListener( handler );
```

executes in Fig. 12.7, a new entry is placed in the **listenerList** for **JTextField textField1**, indicating both the reference to the listener object and the type of listener (in this case **ActionListener**).

The type is important in answering the second question—how does the GUI component know to call **actionPerformed** rather than another event handling method? Every **JComponent** actually supports several different event types, including *mouse events*, *key events* and others. When an event occurs, the event is *dispatched* only to the event listeners of the appropriate type. The dispatching of an event is simply calling the event handling method for each registered listener for that event type.

Each event type has a corresponding event-listener interface. For example, **ActionEvent**s are handled by **ActionListener**s, ***MouseEvent**s* are handled by ***MouseListener**s* (and ***MouseMotionListener**s* as we will see) and ***KeyEvent**s* are handled by ***KeyListener**s*. When an event is generated by a user interaction with a component, the component is handed a unique *event ID* specifying the event type that occurred. The GUI component uses the event ID to decide the type of listener to which the event should be dispatched and the method to call. In the case of an **ActionEvent**, the event is dispatched to every registered **ActionListener**'s **actionPerformed** method (the only method in interface **ActionListener**). In the case of a **MouseEvent**, the event is dispatched to every registered **MouseListener** (or **MouseMotionListener**, depending on the event that occurs). The event ID of the **MouseEvent** determines which of the seven different mouse event handling methods are called. All of this decision logic is handled for you by the GUI components. We discuss other event types and event-listener interfaces as they are needed with each new component we cover.

12.6 JButton

A *button* is a component the user clicks to trigger a specific action. A Java program can use several types of buttons, including *command buttons*, *check boxes*, *toggle buttons* and *radio buttons*. Figure 12.9 shows the inheritance hierarchy of the Swing buttons we cover in this chapter. As you can see in the diagram, all the button types are subclasses of ***AbstractButton*** (package **javax.swing**), which defines many of the features that are common to Swing buttons. In this section, we concentrate on buttons that are typically used to initiate a command. Other button types are covered in the next several sections.

A command button generates an **ActionEvent** when the user clicks the button with the mouse. Command buttons are created with class ***JButton***, which inherits from class **AbstractButton**. The text on the face of a **JButton** is called a *button label*. A GUI can have many **JButton**s, but each button label typically should be unique.

Look-and-Feel Observation 12.4

*Having more than one **JButton** with the same label makes the **JButton**s ambiguous to the user. Be sure to provide a unique label for each button.*

The application of Fig. 12.10 creates two **JButton**s and demonstrates that **JButton**s (like **JLabel**s) support the display of **Icon**s. Event handling for the buttons is performed by a single instance of inner class **ButtonHandler** (defined at lines 53–62).

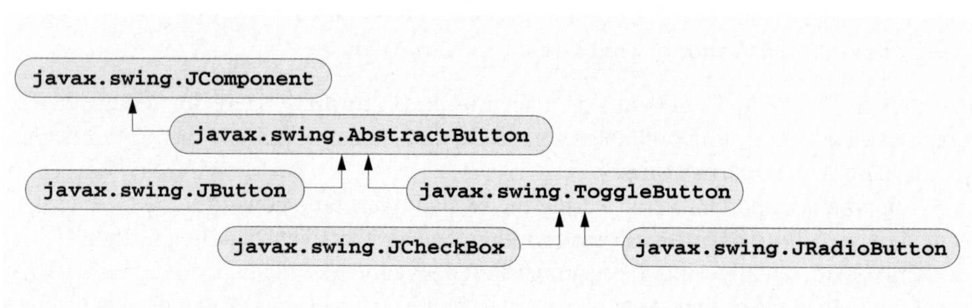

Fig. 12.9 The button hierarchy.

```
1  // Fig. 12.10: ButtonTest.java
2  // Creating JButtons.
3
4  // Java core packages
5  import java.awt.*;
6  import java.awt.event.*;
7
8  // Java extension packages
9  import javax.swing.*;
10
11 public class ButtonTest extends JFrame {
12    private JButton plainButton, fancyButton;
```

Fig. 12.10 Demonstrating command buttons and action events (part 1 of 3).

```

   // set up GUI
   public ButtonTest()
   {
      super( "Testing Buttons" );

      // get content pane and set its layout
      Container container = getContentPane();
      container.setLayout( new FlowLayout() );

      // create buttons
      plainButton = new JButton( "Plain Button" );
      container.add( plainButton );

      Icon bug1 = new ImageIcon( "bug1.gif" );
      Icon bug2 = new ImageIcon( "bug2.gif" );
      fancyButton = new JButton( "Fancy Button", bug1 );
      fancyButton.setRolloverIcon( bug2 );
      container.add( fancyButton );

      // create an instance of inner class ButtonHandler
      // to use for button event handling
      ButtonHandler handler = new ButtonHandler();
      fancyButton.addActionListener( handler );
      plainButton.addActionListener( handler );

      setSize( 275, 100 );
      setVisible( true );
   }

   // execute application
   public static void main( String args[] )
   {
      ButtonTest application = new ButtonTest();

      application.setDefaultCloseOperation(
         JFrame.EXIT_ON_CLOSE );
   }

   // inner class for button event handling
   private class ButtonHandler implements ActionListener {

      // handle button event
      public void actionPerformed( ActionEvent event )
      {
         JOptionPane.showMessageDialog( null,
            "You pressed: " + event.getActionCommand() );
      }

   }  // end private inner class ButtonHandler

}  // end class ButtonTest
```

Fig. 12.10 Demonstrating command buttons and action events (part 2 of 3).

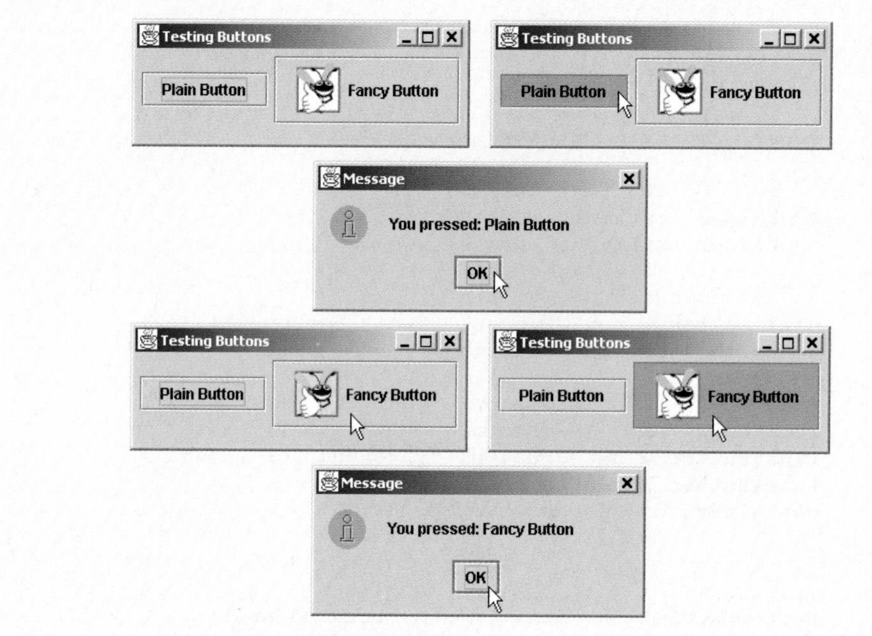

Fig. 12.10 Demonstrating command buttons and action events (part 3 of 3).

Line 12 declares two references to instances of class **JButton**—**plainButton** and **fancyButton**—that are instantiated in the constructor.

Line 24 creates **plainButton** with the button label **"Plain Button"**. Line 25 adds the button to the content pane.

A **JButton** can display **Icon**s. To provide the user with an extra level of visual interactivity with the GUI, a **JButton** can also have a *rollover* **Icon**—an **Icon** that is displayed when the mouse is positioned over the button. The icon on the button changes as the mouse moves in and out of the button's area on the screen. Lines 27–28 create two **ImageIcon** objects that represent the default **Icon** and rollover **Icon** for the **JButton** created at line 29. Both statements assume the image files are stored in the same directory as the program (this is commonly the case for applications that use images).

Line 29 creates **fancyButton** with default text **"Fancy Button"** and the **Icon** **bug1**. By default, the text is displayed to the right of the icon. Line 30 uses method ***setRolloverIcon*** (inherited from class **AbstractButton** into class **JButton**) to specify the image displayed on the button when the user positions the mouse over the button. Line 31 adds the button to the content pane.

Look-and-Feel Observation 12.5

*Using rollover icons for **JButton**s provides the user with visual feedback indicating that if they click the mouse, the button's action will occur.*

JButtons (like **JTextField**s) generate **ActionEvent**s. As mentioned previously, an **ActionEvent** can be processed by any **ActionListener** object. Lines 35–37 register an **ActionListener** object for each **JButton**. Inner class **ButtonHandler** (lines 53–62) defines **actionPerformed** to display a message dialog box containing the label for the button that was pressed by the user. **ActionEvent** method **getActionCommand** returns the label on the button that generated the event.

12.7 JCheckBox and JRadioButton

The Swing GUI components contain three types of *state buttons*—***JToggleButton***, ***JCheckBox*** and ***JRadioButton***—that have on/off or true/false values. **JToggleButton**s are frequently used with *toolbars* (sets of small buttons typically located on a bar across the top of a window) and are covered in Chapter 13. Classes **JCheckBox** and **JRadioButton** are subclasses of **JToggleButton**. A **JRadioButton** is different from a **JCheckBox** in that there are normally several **JRadioButton**s that are grouped together and only one of the **JRadioButton**s in the group can be selected (true) at any time. We first discuss class **JCheckBox**.

Look-and-Feel Observation 12.6

Because class ***AbstractButton*** *supports displaying text and images on a button, all subclasses of* ***AbstractButton*** *also support displaying text and images.*

The application of Fig. 12.11 uses two **JCheckBox** objects to change the font style of the text displayed in a **JTextField**. One **JCheckBox** applies a bold style when selected and the other applies an italic style when selected. If both are selected, the style of the font is bold and italic. When the program initially executes, neither **JCheckBox** is checked (**true**).

```
// Fig. 12.11: CheckBoxTest.java
// Creating Checkbox buttons.

// Java core packages
import java.awt.*;
import java.awt.event.*;

// Java extension packages
import javax.swing.*;

public class CheckBoxTest extends JFrame {
   private JTextField field;
   private JCheckBox bold, italic;

   // set up GUI
   public CheckBoxTest()
   {
      super( "JCheckBox Test" );

      // get content pane and set its layout
      Container container = getContentPane();
      container.setLayout( new FlowLayout() );

      // set up JTextField and set its font
      field =
         new JTextField( "Watch the font style change", 20 );
```

Fig. 12.11 Program that creates two **JCheckBox** buttons (part 1 of 3).

```
      field.setFont( new Font( "Serif", Font.PLAIN, 14 ) );
      container.add( field );

      // create checkbox objects
      bold = new JCheckBox( "Bold" );
      container.add( bold );

      italic = new JCheckBox( "Italic" );
      container.add( italic );

      // register listeners for JCheckBoxes
      CheckBoxHandler handler = new CheckBoxHandler();
      bold.addItemListener( handler );
      italic.addItemListener( handler );

      setSize( 275, 100 );
      setVisible( true );
   }

   // execute application
   public static void main( String args[] )
   {
      CheckBoxTest application = new CheckBoxTest();

      application.setDefaultCloseOperation(
         JFrame.EXIT_ON_CLOSE );
   }

   // private inner class for ItemListener event handling
   private class CheckBoxHandler implements ItemListener {
      private int valBold = Font.PLAIN;
      private int valItalic = Font.PLAIN;

      // respond to checkbox events
      public void itemStateChanged( ItemEvent event )
      {
         // process bold checkbox events
         if ( event.getSource() == bold )

            if ( event.getStateChange() == ItemEvent.SELECTED )
               valBold = Font.BOLD;
            else
               valBold = Font.PLAIN;

         // process italic checkbox events
         if ( event.getSource() == italic )

            if ( event.getStateChange() == ItemEvent.SELECTED )
               valItalic = Font.ITALIC;
            else
               valItalic = Font.PLAIN;

```

Fig. 12.11 Program that creates two **JCheckBox** buttons (part 2 of 3).

```
79          // set text field font
80          field.setFont(
81             new Font( "Serif", valBold + valItalic, 14 ) );
82       }
83
84    }  // end private inner class CheckBoxHandler
85
86 }  // end class CheckBoxTest
```

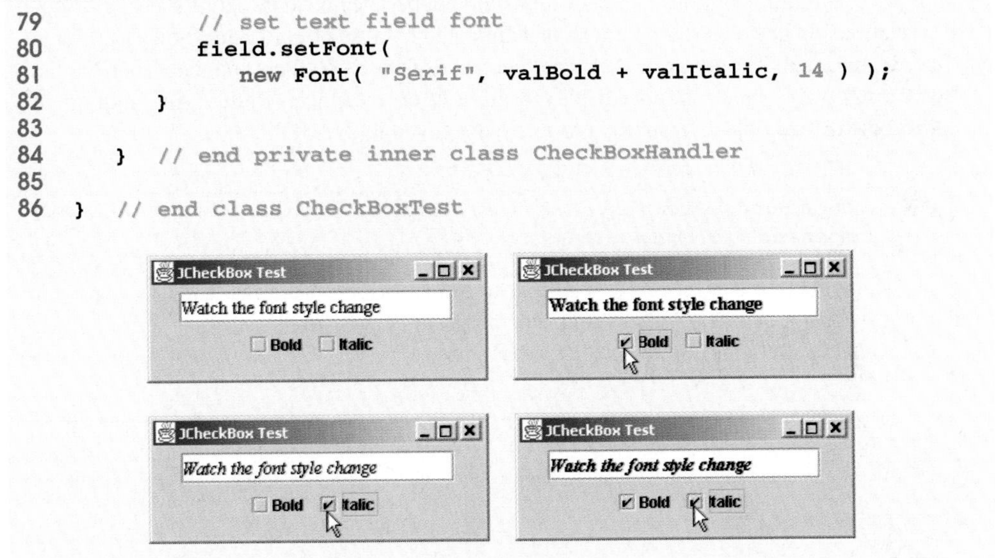

Fig. 12.11 Program that creates two **JCheckBox** buttons (part 3 of 3).

After the **JTextField** is created and initialized, line 27 sets the font of the **JTextField** to **Serif**, **PLAIN** style and **14**-point size. Next, the constructor creates two **JCheckBox** objects with lines 31 and 34. The **String** passed to the constructor is the *check box label* that appears to the right of the **JCheckBox** by default.

When the user clicks a **JCheckBox**, an **ItemEvent** occurs that can be handled by an **ItemListener** (any object of a class that implements interface **ItemListener**). An **ItemListener** must define method ***itemStateChanged***. In this example, the event handling is performed by an instance of inner class **CheckBoxHandler** (lines 56–84). Lines 38–40 create an instance of class **CheckBoxHandler** and register it with method ***addItemListener*** as the **ItemListener** for both the **bold** and **italic** **JCheckBox**es.

Method **itemStateChanged** (lines 61–82) is called when the user clicks either the **bold** or the **italic** checkbox. The method uses **event.getSource()** to determine which **JCheckBox** was clicked. If it was **JCheckBox bold**, the **if/else** structure at lines 66–69 uses **ItemEvent** method ***getStateChange*** to determine the state of the button (**ItemEvent.SELECTED** or **ItemEvent.DESELECTED**). If the state is selected, integer **valBold** is assigned **Font.BOLD**; otherwise, **valBold** is assigned **Font.PLAIN**. A similar **if/else** structure is executed if **JCheckBox italic** is clicked. If the **italic** state is selected, integer **valItalic** is assigned **Font.ITALIC**; otherwise, **valItalic** is assigned **Font.PLAIN**. The sum of **valBold** and **valItalic** is used at lines 80–81 as the style of the new font for the **JTextField**.

Radio buttons (defined with class ***JRadioButton***) are similar to check boxes in that they have two states—*selected* and *not selected* (also called *deselected*). However, radio buttons normally appear as a *group* in which only one radio button can be selected at a time. Selecting a different radio button in the group automatically forces all other radio buttons in the group to be deselected. Radio buttons are used to represent a set of *mutually exclusive* options (i.e., multiple options in the group would not be selected at the same time). The logical relationship between radio buttons is maintained by a ***ButtonGroup*** object (package **javax.swing**). The **ButtonGroup** object itself is not a GUI component. Therefore, a **ButtonGroup** object is not displayed in a user interface. Rather, the individual **JRadioButton** objects from the group are displayed in the GUI.

Common Programming Error 12.5

*Adding a **ButtonGroup** object (or an object of any other class that does not derive from **Component**) to a container is a syntax error.*

The application of Fig. 12.12 is similar to the preceding program. The user can alter the font style of a **JTextField**'s text. The program uses radio buttons that permit only a single font style in the group to be selected at a time.

```
// Fig. 12.12: RadioButtonTest.java
// Creating radio buttons using ButtonGroup and JRadioButton.

// Java core packages
import java.awt.*;
import java.awt.event.*;

// Java extension packages
import javax.swing.*;

public class RadioButtonTest extends JFrame {
   private JTextField field;
   private Font plainFont, boldFont, italicFont, boldItalicFont;
   private JRadioButton plainButton, boldButton, italicButton,
      boldItalicButton;
   private ButtonGroup radioGroup;

   // create GUI and fonts
   public RadioButtonTest()
   {
      super( "RadioButton Test" );

      // get content pane and set its layout
      Container container = getContentPane();
      container.setLayout( new FlowLayout() );

      // set up JTextField
      field =
         new JTextField( "Watch the font style change", 25 );
      container.add( field );

      // create radio buttons
      plainButton = new JRadioButton( "Plain", true );
      container.add( plainButton );

      boldButton = new JRadioButton( "Bold", false);
      container.add( boldButton );
```

Fig. 12.12 Creating and manipulating radio button (part 1 of 3).

```

      italicButton = new JRadioButton( "Italic", false );
      container.add( italicButton );

      boldItalicButton = new JRadioButton(
         "Bold/Italic", false );
      container.add( boldItalicButton );

      // register events for JRadioButtons
      RadioButtonHandler handler = new RadioButtonHandler();
      plainButton.addItemListener( handler );
      boldButton.addItemListener( handler );
      italicButton.addItemListener( handler );
      boldItalicButton.addItemListener( handler );

      // create logical relationship between JRadioButtons
      radioGroup = new ButtonGroup();
      radioGroup.add( plainButton );
      radioGroup.add( boldButton );
      radioGroup.add( italicButton );
      radioGroup.add( boldItalicButton );

      // create font objects
      plainFont = new Font( "Serif", Font.PLAIN, 14 );
      boldFont = new Font( "Serif", Font.BOLD, 14 );
      italicFont = new Font( "Serif", Font.ITALIC, 14 );
      boldItalicFont =
         new Font( "Serif", Font.BOLD + Font.ITALIC, 14 );
      field.setFont( plainFont );

      setSize( 300, 100 );
      setVisible( true );
   }

   // execute application
   public static void main( String args[] )
   {
      RadioButtonTest application = new RadioButtonTest();

      application.setDefaultCloseOperation(
         JFrame.EXIT_ON_CLOSE );
   }

   // private inner class to handle radio button events
   private class RadioButtonHandler implements ItemListener {

      // handle radio button events
      public void itemStateChanged( ItemEvent event )
      {
         // user clicked plainButton
         if ( event.getSource() == plainButton )
            field.setFont( plainFont );

```

Fig. 12.12 Creating and manipulating radio button (part 2 of 3).

```
91             // user clicked boldButton
92             else if ( event.getSource() == boldButton )
93                field.setFont( boldFont );
94
95             // user clicked italicButton
96             else if ( event.getSource() == italicButton )
97                field.setFont( italicFont );
98
99             // user clicked boldItalicButton
100            else if ( event.getSource() == boldItalicButton )
101               field.setFont( boldItalicFont );
102         }
103
104      } // end private inner class RadioButtonHandler
105
106   } // end class RadioButtonTest
```

Fig. 12.12 Creating and manipulating radio button (part 3 of 3).

Lines 33–44 in the constructor define each **JRadioButton** object and add it to the application window's content pane. Each **JRadioButton** is initialized with a constructor call like line 33. This constructor supplies the label that appears to the right of the **JRadioButton** by default and the initial state of the **JRadioButton**. A **true** second argument indicates that the **JRadioButton** should appear selected when it is displayed.

JRadioButtons, like **JCheckBox**es, generate **ItemEvent**s when they are clicked. Lines 47–51 create an instance of inner class **RadioButtonHandler** (defined at lines 82–104) and register it to handle the **ItemEvent** generated when the user clicks any one of the **JRadioButton**s.

Line 54 instantiates a **ButtonGroup** object and assigns it to reference **radioGroup**. This object is the "glue" that binds the four **JRadioButton** objects together to form the logical relationship that allows only one of the four buttons to be selected at a time. Lines 55–58 use **ButtonGroup** method ***add*** to associate each of the **JRadioButton**s with **radioGroup**. If more than one selected **JRadioButton** object is added to the group, the first selected **JRadioButton** added will be selected when the GUI is displayed.

Class **RadioButtonHandler** (line 82–104) implements interface **ItemListener** so it can handle item events generated by the **JRadioButton**s. Each **JRadioButton** in the program has an instance of this class (**handler**) registered as its **ItemListener**. When the user clicks a **JRadioButton**, **radioGroup** turns off the previously selected **JRadioButton** and method **itemStateChanged** (line 85–102) executes. The method determines which **JRadioButton** was clicked using method **getSource** (inherited indirectly from **EventObject** into **ItemEvent**), then sets the font in the **JTextField** to one of the **Font** objects created in the constructor.

12.8 JComboBox

A *combo box* (sometimes called a *drop-down list*) provides a list of items from which the user can make a selection. Combo boxes are implemented with class ***JComboBox***, which inherits from class **JComponent**. **JComboBox**es generate **ItemEvent**s like **JCheckBox**es and **JRadioButton**s.

The application of Fig. 12.13 uses a **JComboBox** to provide a list of four image file names. When an image file name is selected, the corresponding image is displayed as an **Icon** on a **JLabel**. The screen captures for this program show the **JComboBox** list after the selection was made to illustrate which image file name was selected.

Lines 17–19 declare and initialize array icons with four new **ImageIcon** objects. **String** array **names** (defined on lines 15–16) contains the names of the four image files that are stored in the same directory as the application.

Line 31 creates a **JComboBox** object, using the **String**s in array **names** as the elements in the list. A numeric *index* keeps track of the ordering of items in the **JComboBox**. The first item is added at index 0; the next item is added at index 1, and so forth. The first item added to a **JComboBox** appears as the currently selected item when the **JComboBox** is displayed. Other items are selected by clicking the **JComboBox**. When clicked, the **JComboBox** expands into a list from which the user can make a selection.

Line 32 uses **JComboBox** method ***setMaximumRowCount*** to set the maximum number of elements that are displayed when the user clicks the **JComboBox**. If there are more items in the **JComboBox** than the maximum number of elements that are displayed, the **JComboBox** automatically provides a *scrollbar* (see the first screen capture) that allows the user to view all the elements in the list. The user can click the *scroll arrows* at the top and bottom of the scrollbar to move up and down through the list one element at a time, or the user can drag the *scroll box* in the middle of the scrollbar up and down to move through the list. To drag the scroll box, hold the mouse button down with the mouse cursor on the scroll box and move the mouse.

```
1  // Fig. 12.13: ComboBoxTest.java
2  // Using a JComboBox to select an image to display.
3
4  // Java core packages
5  import java.awt.*;
6  import java.awt.event.*;
7
8  // Java extension packages
9  import javax.swing.*;
10
11 public class ComboBoxTest extends JFrame {
12    private JComboBox imagesComboBox;
13    private JLabel label;
14
```

Fig. 12.13 Program that uses a **JComboBox** to select an icon (part 1 of 3).

```
   private String names[] =
      { "bug1.gif", "bug2.gif",  "travelbug.gif", "buganim.gif" };
   private Icon icons[] = { new ImageIcon( names[ 0 ] ),
      new ImageIcon( names[ 1 ] ), new ImageIcon( names[ 2 ] ),
      new ImageIcon( names[ 3 ] ) };

   // set up GUI
   public ComboBoxTest()
   {
      super( "Testing JComboBox" );

      // get content pane and set its layout
      Container container = getContentPane();
      container.setLayout( new FlowLayout() );

      // set up JComboBox and register its event handler
      imagesComboBox = new JComboBox( names );
      imagesComboBox.setMaximumRowCount( 3 );

      imagesComboBox.addItemListener(

         // anonymous inner class to handle JComboBox events
         new ItemListener() {

            // handle JComboBox event
            public void itemStateChanged( ItemEvent event )
            {
               // determine whether check box selected
               if ( event.getStateChange() == ItemEvent.SELECTED )
                  label.setIcon( icons[
                     imagesComboBox.getSelectedIndex() ] );
            }

         }  // end anonymous inner class

      ); // end call to addItemListener

      container.add( imagesComboBox );

      // set up JLabel to display ImageIcons
      label = new JLabel( icons[ 0 ] );
      container.add( label );

      setSize( 350, 100 );
      setVisible( true );
   }

   // execute application
   public static void main( String args[] )
   {
      ComboBoxTest application = new ComboBoxTest();

```

Fig. 12.13 Program that uses a **JComboBox** to select an icon (part 2 of 3).

```
67          application.setDefaultCloseOperation(
68             JFrame.EXIT_ON_CLOSE );
69       }
70
71    }  // end class ComboBoxTest
```

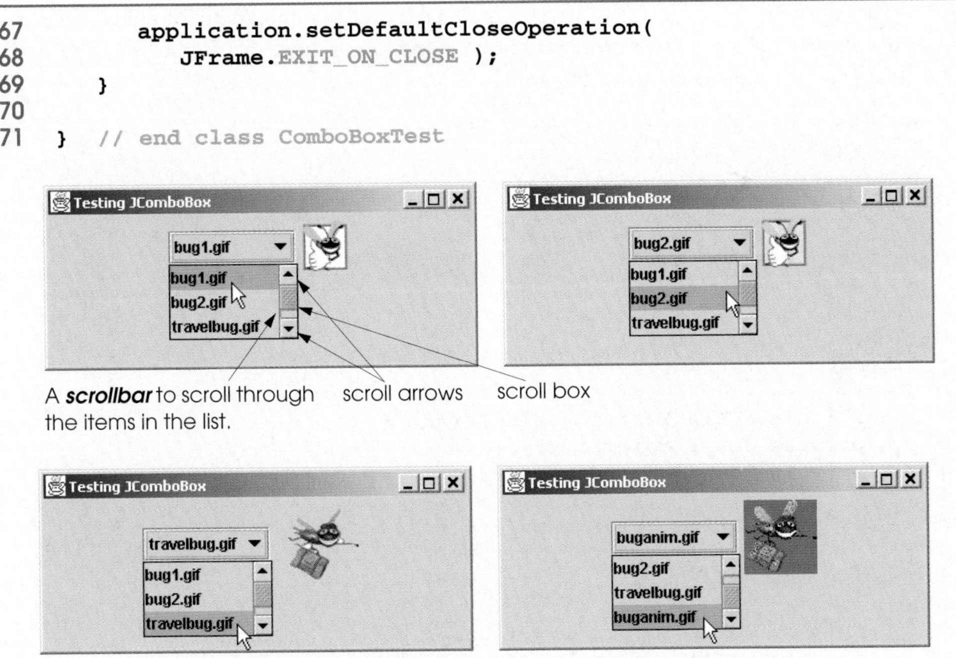

Fig. 12.13 Program that uses a **JComboBox** to select an icon (part 3 of 3).

Look-and-Feel Observation 12.7

Set the maximum row count for a **JComboBox** *to a number of rows that prevents the list from expanding outside the bounds of the window or applet in which it is used. This will ensure that the list displays correctly when it is expanded by the user.*

Lines 34–50 register an instance of an anonymous inner class that implements **ItemListener** as the listener for **JComboBox images**. When the user makes a selection from **images**, method **itemStateChanged** (line 40–46) sets the **Icon** for **label**. The **Icon** is selected from array **icons** by determining the index number of the selected item in the **JComboBox** with method ***getSelectedIndex*** in line 45. Note that line 43 changes the icon only for a selected item. The reason for the **if** structure here is that for each item that is selected from a **JComboBox**, another item is deselected. Thus, two events occur for each item selected. We wish to display only the icon for the item the user just selected.

12.9 JList

A *list* displays a series of items from which the user may select one or more items. Lists are created with class **JList**, which inherits from class **JComponent**. Class **JList** supports *single-selection lists* (i.e., lists that allow only one item to be selected at a time) and *multiple-selection lists* (lists that allow any number of items to be selected). In this section, we discuss single-selection lists.

The application of Fig. 12.14 creates a **JList** of 13 colors. When a color name is clicked in the **JList**, a ***ListSelectionEvent*** occurs and the application window content pane's background color changes.

```
// Fig. 12.14: ListTest.java
// Selecting colors from a JList.

// Java core packages
import java.awt.*;

// Java extension packages
import javax.swing.*;
import javax.swing.event.*;

public class ListTest extends JFrame {
   private JList colorList;
   private Container container;

   private String colorNames[] = { "Black", "Blue", "Cyan",
      "Dark Gray", "Gray", "Green", "Light Gray", "Magenta",
      "Orange", "Pink", "Red", "White", "Yellow" };

   private Color colors[] = { Color.black, Color.blue,
      Color.cyan, Color.darkGray, Color.gray, Color.green,
      Color.lightGray, Color.magenta, Color.orange, Color.pink,
      Color.red, Color.white, Color.yellow };

   // set up GUI
   public ListTest()
   {
      super( "List Test" );

      // get content pane and set its layout
      container = getContentPane();
      container.setLayout( new FlowLayout() );

      // create a list with items in colorNames array
      colorList = new JList( colorNames );
      colorList.setVisibleRowCount( 5 );

      // do not allow multiple selections
      colorList.setSelectionMode(
         ListSelectionModel.SINGLE_SELECTION );

      // add a JScrollPane containing JList to content pane
      container.add( new JScrollPane( colorList ) );

      // set up event handler
      colorList.addListSelectionListener(

         // anonymous inner class for list selection events
         new ListSelectionListener() {
```

Fig. 12.14 Selecting colors from a **JList** (part 1 of 2).

```
49
50             // handle list selection events
51             public void valueChanged( ListSelectionEvent event )
52             {
53                container.setBackground(
54                   colors[ colorList.getSelectedIndex() ] );
55             }
56
57          }  // end anonymous inner class
58
59       ); // end call to addListSelectionListener
60
61       setSize( 350, 150 );
62       setVisible( true );
63    }
64
65    // execute application
66    public static void main( String args[] )
67    {
68       ListTest application = new ListTest();
69
70       application.setDefaultCloseOperation(
71          JFrame.EXIT_ON_CLOSE );
72    }
73
74 }  // end class ListTest
```

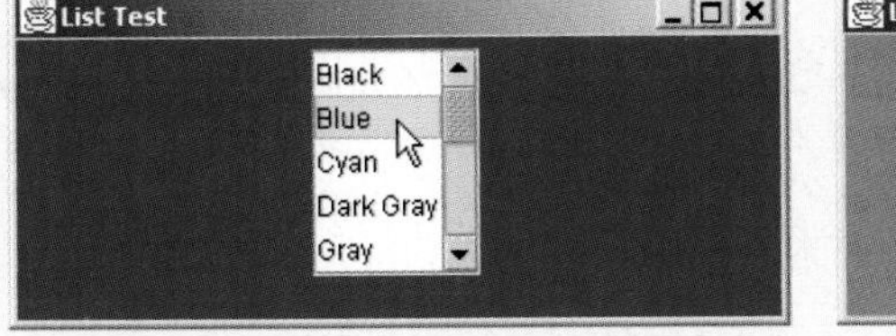

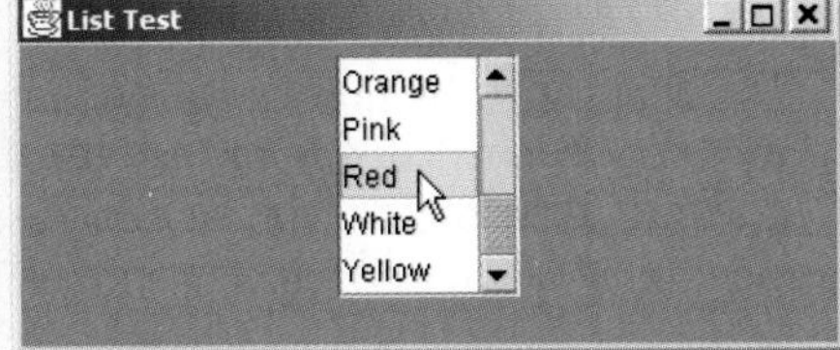

Fig. 12.14 Selecting colors from a **JList** (part 2 of 2).

A **JList** object is instantiated at line 34 and assigned to reference **colorList** in the constructor. The argument to the **JList** constructor is the array of **Object**s (in this case **String**s) to display in the list. Line 35 uses **JList** method ***setVisibleRowCount*** to determine the number of items that are visible in the list.

Lines 38–39 use **JList** method ***setSelectionMode*** to specify the list *selection mode*. Class ***ListSelectionModel*** (package **javax.swing**) defines constants ***SINGLE_SELECTION***, ***SINGLE_INTERVAL_SELECTION*** and ***MULTIPLE_INTERVAL_SELECTION*** to specify a **JList**'s selection mode. A **SINGLE_SELECTION** list allows only one item to be selected at a time. A **SINGLE_INTERVAL_SELECTION** list is a multiple-selection list that allows several items in a contiguous range in the list to be selected. A **MULTIPLE_INTERVAL_SELECTION** list is a multiple-selection list that does not restrict the items that can be selected.

Unlike **JComboBox**, **JList**s *do not* provide a scrollbar if there are more items in the list than the number of visible rows. In this case, a ***JScrollPane*** object is used to provide the automatic scrolling capability for the **JList**. Line 42 adds a new instance of class ***JScrollPane*** to the content pane. The **JScrollPane** constructor receives as its argument the **JComponent** for which it will provide automatic scrolling functionality (in this case **JList colorList**). Notice in the screen captures that a scrollbar created by the **JScrollPane** appears at the right side of the **JList**. By default, the scrollbar appears only when the number of items in the **JList** exceeds the number of visible items.

Lines 45–59 use **JList** method ***addListSelectionListener*** to register an instance of an anonymous inner class that implements ***ListSelectionListener*** (defined in package **javax.swing.event**) as the listener for **JList colorList**. When the user makes a selection from **colorList**, method ***valueChanged*** (line 51–55) executes and sets the background color of the content pane with method ***setBackground*** (inherited from class **Component** into class **Container**). The color is selected from the array **colors** with the selected item's index in the list that is returned by **JList** method **getSelectedIndex** (as with arrays, **JList** indexing is zero based).

12.10 Multiple-Selection Lists

A *multiple-selection list* enables the user to select many items from a **JList**. A **SINGLE_INTERVAL_SELECTION** list allows selection of a contiguous range of items in the list by clicking the first item, then holding the *Shift* key while clicking the last item to select in the range. A **MULTIPLE_INTERVAL_SELECTION** list allows continuous range selection as described for a **SINGLE_INTERVAL_SELECTION** list and allows miscellaneous items to be selected by holding the *Ctrl* key (sometimes called to *Control* key)while clicking each item to select. To deselect an item, hold the *Ctrl* key while clicking the item a second time.

The application of Fig. 12.15 uses multiple-selection lists to copy items from one **JList** to another. One list is a **MULTIPLE_INTERVAL_SELECTION** list and the other is a **SINGLE_INTERVAL_SELECTION** list. When you execute the program, try using the selection techniques described above to select items in both lists.

```java
// Fig. 12.15: MultipleSelection.java
// Copying items from one List to another.

// Java core packages
import java.awt.*;
import java.awt.event.*;

// Java extension packages
import javax.swing.*;

public class MultipleSelection extends JFrame {
   private JList colorList, copyList;
   private JButton copyButton;

   private String colorNames[] = { "Black", "Blue", "Cyan",
      "Dark Gray", "Gray", "Green", "Light Gray",
      "Magenta", "Orange", "Pink", "Red", "White", "Yellow" };
```

Fig. 12.15 Using a multiple-selection **JList** (part 1 of 3).

```

   // set up GUI
   public MultipleSelection()
   {
      super( "Multiple Selection Lists" );

      // get content pane and set its layout
      Container container = getContentPane();
      container.setLayout( new FlowLayout() );

      // set up JList colorList
      colorList = new JList( colorNames );
      colorList.setVisibleRowCount( 5 );
      colorList.setFixedCellHeight( 15 );
      colorList.setSelectionMode(
         ListSelectionModel.MULTIPLE_INTERVAL_SELECTION );
      container.add( new JScrollPane( colorList ) );

      // create copy button and register its listener
      copyButton = new JButton( "Copy >>>" );

      copyButton.addActionListener(

         // anonymous inner class for button event
         new ActionListener() {

            // handle button event
            public void actionPerformed( ActionEvent event )
            {
               // place selected values in copyList
               copyList.setListData(
                  colorList.getSelectedValues() );
            }

         }  // end anonymous inner class

      ); // end call to addActionListener

      container.add( copyButton );

      // set up JList copyList
      copyList = new JList( );
      copyList.setVisibleRowCount( 5 );
      copyList.setFixedCellWidth( 100 );
      copyList.setFixedCellHeight( 15 );
      copyList.setSelectionMode(
         ListSelectionModel.SINGLE_INTERVAL_SELECTION );
      container.add( new JScrollPane( copyList ) );

      setSize( 300, 120 );
      setVisible( true );
   }

```

Fig. 12.15 Using a multiple-selection **JList** (part 2 of 3).

```
71      // execute application
72      public static void main( String args[] )
73      {
74         MultipleSelection application = new MultipleSelection();
75
76         application.setDefaultCloseOperation(
77            JFrame.EXIT_ON_CLOSE );
78      }
79
80   }  // end class MultipleSelection
```

Fig. 12.15 Using a multiple-selection **JList** (part 3 of 3).

Line 29 creates **JList colorList** and initializes it with the **String**s in the array **colorNames**. Line 30 sets the number of visible rows in **colorList** to **5**. Line 31 uses **JList** method ***setFixedCellHeight*** to specify the height in pixels of each item in the **JList**. We do this to ensure that the rows in both **JLists** in the example have the same height. Lines 32–33 specify that **colorList** is a **MULTIPLE_INTERVAL_SELECTION** list. Line 34 adds a new **JScrollPane** containing **colorList** to the content pane. Lines 59–65 perform similar tasks for **JList copyList**, which is defined as a **SINGLE_INTERVAL_SELECTION** list. Line 61 uses **JList** method ***setFixedCellWidth*** to set **copyList**'s width to 100 pixels.

A multiple-selection list does not have a specific event associated with making multiple selections. Normally, an event generated by another GUI component (known as an *external event*) specifies when the multiple selections in a **JList** should be processed. In this example, the user clicks **JButton copyButton** to trigger the event that copies the selected items in **colorList** to **copyList**.

When the user clicks **copyButton**, method **actionPerformed** (line 45–50) is called. Lines 48–49 use **JList** method ***setListData*** to set the items displayed in **copyList**. Line 49 calls **colorList**'s method ***getSelectedValues***, which returns an array of **Object**s representing the selected items in **colorList**. In this example, the returned array is passed as the argument to **copyList**'s **setListData** method.

Many students ask how reference **copyList** can be used in line 48, when the program does not create the object to which it refers until Line 59. Remember that method **actionPerformed** at lines 45–50 does not execute until the user presses the **copyButton**, which cannot occur until after the call to the constructor completes. At that point in the program's execution, line 59 already has initialized **copyList** with a new **JList** object.

12.11 Mouse Event Handling

This section presents the ***MouseListener*** and ***MouseMotionListener*** event-listener interfaces for handling *mouse events*. Mouse events can be trapped for any GUI component that derives from **java.awt.Component**. The methods of interfaces **MouseListener** and **MouseMotionListener** are summarized in Figure 12.16.

Each of the mouse event handling methods takes a ***MouseEvent*** object as its argument. A **MouseEvent** object contains information about the mouse event that occurred, including the *x*- and *y*-coordinates of the location where the event occurred. The **MouseListener** and **MouseMotionListener** methods are called automatically when the mouse interacts with a **Component** if listener objects are registered for a particular **Component**. Method ***mousePressed*** is called when a mouse button is pressed with the mouse cursor over a component. Using methods and constants of class ***InputEvent*** (the superclass of **MouseEvent**), a program can determine which mouse button the user clicked. Method ***mouseClicked*** is called whenever a mouse button is released without moving the mouse after a **mousePressed** operation. Method ***mouseReleased*** is called whenever a mouse button is released. Method ***mouseEntered*** is called when the mouse cursor enters the physical boundaries of a **Component**. Method ***mouseExited*** is called when the mouse cursor leaves the physical boundaries of a **Component**. Method ***mouseDragged*** is called when the mouse button is pressed and held, and the mouse is moved (a process known as *dragging*). The **mouseDragged** event is preceded by a **mousePressed** event and followed by a **mouseReleased** event. Method ***mouseMoved*** is called when the mouse is moved with the mouse cursor over a component (and no mouse buttons pressed).

MouseListener and MouseMotionListener interface methods

Methods of interface ***MouseListener***

public void mousePressed(MouseEvent event)

Called when a mouse button is pressed with the mouse cursor on a component.

public void mouseClicked(MouseEvent event)

Called when a mouse button is pressed and released on a component without moving the mouse cursor.

public void mouseReleased(MouseEvent event)

Called when a mouse button is released after being pressed. This event is always preceded by a **mousePressed** event.

public void mouseEntered(MouseEvent event)

Called when the mouse cursor enters the bounds of a component.

public void mouseExited(MouseEvent event)

Called when the mouse cursor leaves the bounds of a component.

Methods of interface ***MouseMotionListener***

public void mouseDragged(MouseEvent event)

Called when the mouse button is pressed with the mouse cursor on a component and the mouse is moved. This event is always preceded by a call to **mousePressed**.

public void mouseMoved(MouseEvent event)

Called when the mouse is moved with the mouse cursor on a component.

Fig. 12.16 **MouseListener** and **MouseMotionListener** interface methods.

Look-and-Feel Observation 12.8

Method calls to **mouseDragged** *are sent to the* **MouseMotionListener** *for the* **Component** *on which the drag operation started. Similarly, the* **mouseReleased** *method call is sent to the* **MouseListener** *for the* **Component** *on which the drag operation started.*

The **MouseTracker** application (Fig. 12.17) demonstrates the **MouseListener** and **MouseMotionListener** methods. The application class implements both interfaces so it can listen for its own mouse events. Note that all seven methods from these two interfaces must be defined by the programmer when a class implements both interfaces. The message dialog box in the sample output windows appears when the user moves the mouse into the application window.

```
// Fig. 12.17: MouseTracker.java
// Demonstrating mouse events.

// Java core packages
import java.awt.*;
import java.awt.event.*;

// Java extension packages
import javax.swing.*;

public class MouseTracker extends JFrame
   implements MouseListener, MouseMotionListener {

   private JLabel statusBar;

   // set up GUI and register mouse event handlers
   public MouseTracker()
   {
      super( "Demonstrating Mouse Events" );

      statusBar = new JLabel();
      getContentPane().add( statusBar, BorderLayout.SOUTH );

      // application listens to its own mouse events
      addMouseListener( this );
      addMouseMotionListener( this );

      setSize( 275, 100 );
      setVisible( true );
   }

   // MouseListener event handlers

   // handle event when mouse released immediately after press
   public void mouseClicked( MouseEvent event )
   {
      statusBar.setText( "Clicked at [" + event.getX() +
         ", " + event.getY() + "]" );
   }
```

Fig. 12.17 Demonstrating mouse event handling (part 1 of 3).

```

   // handle event when mouse pressed
   public void mousePressed( MouseEvent event )
   {
      statusBar.setText( "Pressed at [" + event.getX() +
         ", " + event.getY() + "]" );
   }

   // handle event when mouse released after dragging
   public void mouseReleased( MouseEvent event )
   {
      statusBar.setText( "Released at [" + event.getX() +
         ", " + event.getY() + "]" );
   }

   // handle event when mouse enters area
   public void mouseEntered( MouseEvent event )
   {
      JOptionPane.showMessageDialog( null, "Mouse in window" );
   }

   // handle event when mouse exits area
   public void mouseExited( MouseEvent event )
   {
      statusBar.setText( "Mouse outside window" );
   }

   // MouseMotionListener event handlers

   // handle event when user drags mouse with button pressed
   public void mouseDragged( MouseEvent event )
   {
      statusBar.setText( "Dragged at [" + event.getX() +
         ", " + event.getY() + "]" );
   }

   // handle event when user moves mouse
   public void mouseMoved( MouseEvent event )
   {
      statusBar.setText( "Moved at [" + event.getX() +
         ", " + event.getY() + "]" );
   }

   // execute application
   public static void main( String args[] )
   {
      MouseTracker application = new MouseTracker();

      application.setDefaultCloseOperation(
         JFrame.EXIT_ON_CLOSE );
   }

}  // end class MouseTracker
```

Fig. 12.17 Demonstrating mouse event handling (part 2 of 3).

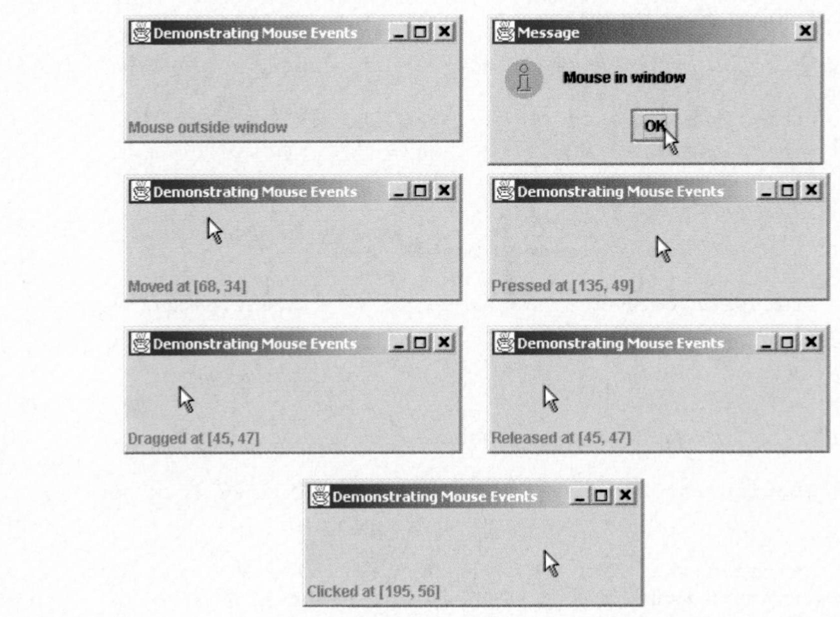

Fig. 12.17 Demonstrating mouse event handling (part 3 of 3).

Each mouse event results in a **`String`** displayed in **`JLabel statusBar`** at the bottom of the window.

Lines 21–22 in the constructor define **`JLabel statusBar`** and attach it to the content pane. Until now, each time we used the content pane, method **`setLayout`** was called to set the content pane's layout manager to a **`FlowLayout`**. This allowed the content pane to display the GUI components we attached to it from left to right. If the GUI components do not fit on one line, the **`FlowLayout`** creates additional lines to continue displaying the GUI components. Actually, the default layout manager is a ***`BorderLayout`*** that divides the content pane's area into five regions—north, south, east, west and center. Line 22 uses a new version of **`Container`** method **`add`** to attach **`statusBar`** to the region ***`BorderLayout.SOUTH`***, which extends across the entire bottom of the content pane. We discuss **`BorderLayout`** and several other layout managers in detail later in this chapter.

Lines 25–26 in the constructor register the **`MouseTracker`** window object as the listener for its own mouse events. Methods ***`addMouseListener`*** and ***`addMouseMotionListener`*** are **`Component`** methods that can be used to register mouse event listeners for an object of any class that extends **`Component`**.

When the mouse enters or exits the application area, method **`mouseEntered`** (lines 56–59) and method **`mouseExited`** (lines 62–65) are called, respectively. Method **`mouseExited`** displays a message in **`statusBar`** indicating that the mouse is outside the application (see the first sample output window). Method **`mouseEntered`** displays a message dialog box indicating that the mouse entered the application window. [Note: Be sure to press *Enter* to dismiss the message dialog, rather than using the mouse. If you use the mouse to dismiss the dialog, when you move the mouse over the window again, **`mouseEntered`** redisplays the dialog. This will prevent you from trying the other mouse events.]

When any of the other five events occur, they display a message in **statusBar** that includes a **String** that represents the event that occurred and the coordinates where the mouse event occurred. The *x* and *y* coordinates of the mouse when the event occurred are obtained with **MouseEvent** methods ***getX*** and ***getY***, respectively.

12.12 Adapter Classes

Many of the event-listener interfaces provide multiple methods; **MouseListener** and **MouseMotionListener** are examples. It is not always desirable to define every method in an event-listener interface. For example, a program may only need the **mouseClicked** handler from interface **MouseListener** or the **mouseDragged** handler from **MouseMotionListener**. In our windowed applications (subclasses of **JFrame**) terminating the application has been handled with **windowClosing** from interface **WindowListener**, which actually specifies seven window-event-handling methods. For many of the listener interfaces that contain multiple methods, package **java.awt.event** and package **javax.swing.event** provide event-listener *adapter classes*. An adapter class implements an interface and provides a default implementation (with an empty method body) of every method in the interface. The **java.awt.event** adapter classes are shown in Fig. 12.18 along with the interfaces they implement.

The programmer can extend the adapter class to inherit the default implementation of every method, then override the method(s) needed for event handling. The default implementation of each method in the adapter class has an empty body. This is exactly what we have been doing in each application example that extends **JFrame** and defines method **windowClosing** to handle the closing of the window and termination of the application.

Software Engineering Observation 12.3

When a class implements an interface, the class has an "is a" relationship with that interface. All direct and indirect subclasses of that class inherit this relationship. Thus, an object of a class that extends an event adapter class is an *object of the corresponding event listener type (e.g., an object of a subclass of* ***MouseAdapter*** is a ***MouseListener****).*

Event adapter class	Implements interface
`ComponentAdapter`	`ComponentListener`
`ContainerAdapter`	`ContainerListener`
`FocusAdapter`	`FocusListener`
`KeyAdapter`	`KeyListener`
`MouseAdapter`	`MouseListener`
`MouseMotionAdapter`	`MouseMotionListener`
`WindowAdapter`	`WindowListener`

Fig. 12.18 Event adapter classes and the interfaces they implement.

The **Painter** application of Fig. 12.19 uses the **mouseDragged** event handler to create a simple drawing program. The user can draw pictures with the mouse by dragging the mouse on the background of the window. This example does not use method **mouseMoved**, so our **MouseMotionListener** is defined as a subclass of **MouseMotionAdapter**. This class already defines both **mouseMoved** and **mouseDragged**, so we can simply override **mouseDragged** to provide the drawing functionality.

```
// Fig. 12.19: Painter.java
// Using class MouseMotionAdapter.

// Java core packages
import java.awt.*;
import java.awt.event.*;

// Java extension packages
import javax.swing.*;

public class Painter extends JFrame {
   private int xValue = -10, yValue = -10;

   // set up GUI and register mouse event handler
   public Painter()
   {
      super( "A simple paint program" );

      // create a label and place it in SOUTH of BorderLayout
      getContentPane().add(
         new Label( "Drag the mouse to draw" ),
         BorderLayout.SOUTH );

      addMouseMotionListener(

         // anonymous inner class
         new MouseMotionAdapter() {

            // store drag coordinates and repaint
            public void mouseDragged( MouseEvent event )
            {
               xValue = event.getX();
               yValue = event.getY();
               repaint();
            }

         } // end anonymous inner class

      ); // end call to addMouseMotionListener

      setSize( 300, 150 );
      setVisible( true );
   }

```

Fig. 12.19 Program that demonstrates adapter classes (part 1 of 2).

```
45       // draw oval in a 4-by-4 bounding box at the specified
46       // location on the window
47       public void paint( Graphics g )
48       {
49          // we purposely did not call super.paint( g ) here to
50          // prevent repainting
51
52          g.fillOval( xValue, yValue, 4, 4 );
53       }
54
55       // execute application
56       public static void main( String args[] )
57       {
58          Painter application = new Painter();
59
60          application.addWindowListener(
61
62             // adapter to handle only windowClosing event
63             new WindowAdapter() {
64
65                public void windowClosing( WindowEvent event )
66                {
67                   System.exit( 0 );
68                }
69
70             }  // end anonymous inner class
71
72          ); // end call to addWindowListener
73       }
74
75    }  // end class Painter
```

Fig. 12.19 Program that demonstrates adapter classes (part 2 of 2).

The instance variables **xValue** and **yValue** store the coordinates of the **mouseDragged** event. Initially, the coordinates are set outside the window area to prevent an oval from drawing on the background area in the first call to **paint** when the window is displayed. Lines 24–39 register a **MouseMotionListener** to listen for the window's mouse motion events (remember that a call to a method that is not preceded by a reference and a dot operator is really preceded by "**this.**", indicating that the method is called for the current instance of the class at execution time). Lines 27–37 define an anonymous inner class that extends class **MouseMotionAdapter** (which implements **MouseMotionListener**). The anonymous inner class inherits a default implementation of both method **mouseMoved** and method **mouseDragged**. Thus, the anonymous inner class already satisfies the requirement that in all methods an interface must be implemented. However, the default methods do nothing when they are called. So, we override method **mouseDragged** at lines 30–35 to capture the *x*- and *y*-coordinates of the mouse-dragged event and store them in instance variables **xValue** and **yValue**, then call **repaint** to initiate drawing the next oval on the background (performed by method **paint** at lines 47–53). Note that **paint** does not call the superclass version of **paint** inherited from **JFrame**. The superclass version normally clears the background of the window. Not calling the superclass version enables our program to keep all the ovals on the window at once. However, notice that if you cover the window with another window, only the last oval displayed still appears, because our program does not keep track of all the ovals displayed previously.

Lines 60–72 register a **WindowListener** to listen for the application window's window events (such as closing the window). Lines 63–70 define an anonymous inner class that extends class **WindowAdapter** (which implements **WindowListener**). The anonymous inner class inherits a default implementation of seven different window-event-handler methods. Thus, the anonymous inner class already satisfies the requirement that in all methods an interface must be implemented. However, the default methods do nothing when they are called. So, we override method **windowClosing** at lines 65–68 to terminate the application when the user clicks the application window's close box.

The **MouseDetails** application of Fig. 12.20 demonstrates how to determine the number of mouse clicks (i.e., the click count) and how to distinguish between the different mouse buttons. The event listener in this program is an object of inner class **MouseClickHandler** (lines 47–75) that extends **MouseAdapter** so we can define just the **mouseClicked** method we need in this example.

```
1  // Fig. 12.20: MouseDetails.java
2  // Demonstrating mouse clicks and
3  // distinguishing between mouse buttons.
4
5  // Java core packages
6  import java.awt.*;
7  import java.awt.event.*;
8
9  // Java extension packages
10 import javax.swing.*;
11
12 public class MouseDetails extends JFrame {
13    private int xPos, yPos;
14
15    // set title bar String, register mouse listener and size
16    // and show window
17    public MouseDetails()
18    {
19       super( "Mouse clicks and buttons" );
20
21       addMouseListener( new MouseClickHandler() );
22
23       setSize( 350, 150 );
24       setVisible( true );
25    }
```

Fig. 12.20 Distinguishing among left, center and right mouse-button clicks (part 1 of 3).

```

   // draw String at location where mouse was clicked
   public void paint( Graphics g )
   {
      // call superclass's paint method
      super.paint( g );

      g.drawString( "Clicked @ [" + xPos + ", " + yPos + "]",
         xPos, yPos );
   }

   // execute application
   public static void main( String args[] )
   {
      MouseDetails application = new MouseDetails();

      application.setDefaultCloseOperation(
         JFrame.EXIT_ON_CLOSE );
   }

   // inner class to handle mouse events
   private class MouseClickHandler extends MouseAdapter {

      // handle mouse click event and determine which mouse
      // button was pressed
      public void mouseClicked( MouseEvent event )
      {
         xPos = event.getX();
         yPos = event.getY();

         String title =
            "Clicked " + event.getClickCount() + " time(s)";

         // right mouse button
         if ( event.isMetaDown() )
            title += " with right mouse button";

         // middle mouse button
         else if ( event.isAltDown() )
            title += " with center mouse button";

         // left mouse button
         else
            title += " with left mouse button";

         setTitle( title );  // set title bar of window
         repaint();
      }

   }  // end private inner class MouseClickHandler

}  // end class MouseDetails
```

Fig. 12.20 Distinguishing among left, center and right mouse-button clicks (part 2 of 3).

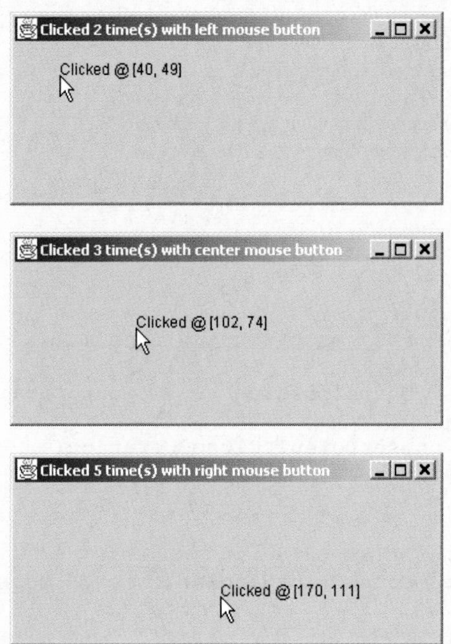

Fig. 12.20 Distinguishing among left, center and right mouse-button clicks (part 3 of 3).

A user of a Java program may be on a system with a one-, two- or three-button mouse. Java provides a mechanism to distinguish among mouse buttons. Class **`MouseEvent`** inherits several methods from class **`InputEvent`** that can distinguish between mouse buttons on a multi-button mouse or can mimic a multi-button mouse with a combined keystroke and mouse-button click. Figure 12.21 shows the **`InputEvent`** methods used to distinguish between mouse-button clicks. Java assumes that every mouse contains a left mouse button. Thus, it is simple to test for a left-mouse-button click. However, users with a one- or two-button mouse must use a combination of pressing keys on the keyboard and clicking the mouse at the same time to simulate the missing buttons on the mouse. In the case of a one- or two-button mouse, this program assumes that the center mouse button is clicked if the user holds the *Alt* key and clicks the left mouse button on a two-button mouse or the only mouse button on a one-button mouse. In the case of a one-button mouse, this program assumes that the right mouse button is clicked if the user holds the *Meta* key and clicks the mouse button.

Method **`mouseClicked`** (lines 51–73) first captures the coordinates where the event occurred and stores them in instance variables **`xPos`** and **`yPos`** of class **`MouseDetails`**. Lines 56–57 create a string containing the number of mouse clicks (as returned by **`MouseEvent`** method ***`getClickCount`*** at line 57). The nested **`if`** structure at lines 60–69 uses methods **`isMetaDown`** and **`isAltDown`** to determine which mouse button the user clicked and appends an appropriate string to **`title`** in each case. The resulting string is displayed in the title bar of the window with method ***`setTitle`*** (inherited into class **`JFrame`** from class **`Frame`**) at line 71. Line 72 calls **`repaint`** to initiate a call to **`paint`** to draw a string at the location where the user clicked the mouse.

`InputEvent` method	**Description**
`isMetaDown()`	This method returns **`true`** when the user clicks the right mouse button on a mouse with two or three buttons. To simulate a right-mouse-button click on a one-button mouse, the user can press the *Meta* key on the keyboard and click the mouse button.
`isAltDown()`	This method returns **`true`** when the user clicks the middle mouse button on a mouse with three buttons. To simulate a middle-mouse-button click on a one- or two-button mouse, the user can press the *Alt* key on the keyboard and click the mouse button.

Fig. 12.21 **`InputEvent`** methods that help distinguish among left-, center- and right-mouse-button clicks .

12.13 Keyboard Event Handling

This section presents the **`KeyListener`** event-listener interface for handling *key events*. Key events are generated when keys on the keyboard are pressed and released. A class that implements **`KeyListener`** must provide definitions for methods ***`keyPressed`***, ***`keyReleased`*** and ***`keyTyped`***, each of which receives a ***`KeyEvent`*** as its argument. Class **`KeyEvent`** is a subclass of **`InputEvent`**. Method **`keyPressed`** is called in response to pressing any key. Method **`keyTyped`** is called in response to pressing any key that is not an *action key* (e.g., an arrow key, *Home*, *End*, *Page Up*, *Page Down*, a function key, *Num Lock*, *Print Screen*, *Scroll Lock*, *Caps Lock* and *Pause*). Method **`keyReleased`** is called when the key is released after any **`keyPressed`** or **`keyTyped`** event.

Figure 12.22 demonstrates the **`KeyListener`** methods. Class **`KeyDemo`** implements the **`KeyListener`** interface, so all three methods are defined in the application.

```
// Fig. 12.22: KeyDemo.java
// Demonstrating keystroke events.

// Java core packages
import java.awt.*;
import java.awt.event.*;

// Java extension packages
import javax.swing.*;

public class KeyDemo extends JFrame implements KeyListener {
   private String line1 = "", line2 = "";
   private String line3 = "";
   private JTextArea textArea;

   // set up GUI
   public KeyDemo()
   {
      super( "Demonstrating Keystroke Events" );
```

Fig. 12.22 Demonstrating key event-handling (part 1 of 3).

```java

      // set up JTextArea
      textArea = new JTextArea( 10, 15 );
      textArea.setText( "Press any key on the keyboard..." );
      textArea.setEnabled( false );
      getContentPane().add( textArea );

      // allow frame to process Key events
      addKeyListener( this );

      setSize( 350, 100 );
      setVisible( true );
   }

   // handle press of any key
   public void keyPressed( KeyEvent event )
   {
      line1 = "Key pressed: " +
         event.getKeyText( event.getKeyCode() );
      setLines2and3( event );
   }

   // handle release of any key
   public void keyReleased( KeyEvent event )
   {
      line1 = "Key released: " +
         event.getKeyText( event.getKeyCode() );
      setLines2and3( event );
   }

   // handle press of an action key
   public void keyTyped( KeyEvent event )
   {
      line1 = "Key typed: " + event.getKeyChar();
      setLines2and3( event );
   }

   // set second and third lines of output
   private void setLines2and3( KeyEvent event )
   {
      line2 = "This key is " +
         ( event.isActionKey() ? "" : "not " ) +
         "an action key";

      String temp =
         event.getKeyModifiersText( event.getModifiers() );

      line3 = "Modifier keys pressed: " +
         ( temp.equals( "" ) ? "none" : temp );

      textArea.setText(
         line1 + "\n" + line2 + "\n" + line3 + "\n" );
   }
```

Fig. 12.22 Demonstrating key event-handling (part 2 of 3).

```
73
74     // execute application
75     public static void main( String args[] )
76     {
77        KeyDemo application = new KeyDemo();
78
79        application.setDefaultCloseOperation(
80           JFrame.EXIT_ON_CLOSE );
81     }
82
83  }  // end class KeyDemo
```

Fig. 12.22 Demonstrating key event-handling (part 3 of 3).

The constructor (lines 17–32) registers the application to handle its own key events with method ***addKeyListener*** at line 28. Method **addKeyListener** is defined in class **Component**, so every subclass of **Component** can notify **KeyListener**s of key events for that **Component**.

Line 25 in the constructor adds **JTextArea textArea** (where the program's output is displayed) to the content pane. Notice, in the screen captures, that **textArea** occupies the entire window. This is due to the content pane's default **BorderLayout** (discussed in Section 12.14.2 and demonstrated in Fig. 12.25). When a single **Component** is added to a **BorderLayout**, the **Component** occupies the entire **Container**.

Methods **keyPressed** (lines 35–40) and **keyReleased** (lines 43–48) use **KeyEvent** method ***getKeyCode*** to get the *virtual key code* of the key that was pressed. Class **KeyEvent** maintains a set of constants—the virtual key code constants—that represent every key on the keyboard. These constants can be compared with the return value of **getKeyCode** to test for individual keys on the keyboard. The value returned by **getKeyCode** is passed to **KeyEvent** method ***getKeyText***, which returns a **String** containing the name of the key that was pressed. For a complete list of virtual key constants, see the on-line documentation for class **KeyEvent** (package **java.awt.event**). Method **keyTyped** (lines 51–55) uses **KeyEvent** method ***getKeyChar*** to get the Unicode value of the character typed.

All three event handling methods finish by calling method **setLines2and3** (lines 58–72) and passing it the **KeyEvent** object. This method uses **KeyEvent** method ***isActionKey*** to determine if the key in the event was an action key. Also, **InputEvent** method ***getModifiers*** is called to determine if any modifier keys (such as *Shift*, *Alt* and *Ctrl*) were pressed when the key event occurred. The result of this method is passed to **KeyEvent** method ***getKeyModifiersText***, which produces a string containing the names of the pressed modifier keys.

[Note: If you need to test for a specific key on the keyboard, class **KeyEvent** provides a *key constant* for every key on the keyboard. These constants can be used from the key event handlers to determine if a particular key was pressed. Also, to determine whether the *Alt*, *Ctrl*, *Meta* and *Shift* keys are pressed individually, **InputEvent** methods **isAltDown**, ***isControlDown***, **isMetaDown** and ***isShiftDown*** each return a **boolean** indicating if the particular key was pressed during the key event.]

12.14 Layout Managers

Layout managers are provided to arrange GUI components on a container for presentation purposes. The layout managers provide basic layout capabilities that are easier to use than determining the exact position and size of every GUI component. This enables the programmer to concentrate on the basic "look and feel" and lets the layout managers process most of the layout details.

Look-and-Feel Observation 12.9

Most Java programming environments provide GUI design tools that help a programmer graphically design a GUI, then automatically write Java code to create the GUI.

Some GUI designers also allow the programmer to use the layout managers described here and in Chapter 13. Figure 12.23 summarizes the layout managers presented in this chapter. Other layout managers are discussed in Chapter 13.

Layout manager	Description
FlowLayout	Default for **java.awt.Applet**, **java.awt.Panel** and **javax.swing.JPanel**. Places components sequentially (left to right) in the order they were added. It is also possible to specify the order of the components using the **Container** method **add** that takes a **Component** and an integer index position as arguments.
BorderLayout	Default for the content panes of **JFrame**s (and other windows) and **JApplet**s. Arranges the components into five areas: North, South, East, West and Center.
GridLayout	Arranges the components into rows and columns.

Fig. 12.23 Layout managers.

Most previous applet and application examples in which we created our own GUI used layout manager ***`FlowLayout`***. Class **`FlowLayout`** inherits from class **`Object`** and implements interface ***`LayoutManager`***, which defines the methods a layout manager uses to arrange and size GUI components on a container.

12.14.1 `FlowLayout`

FlowLayout is the most basic layout manager. GUI components are placed on a container from left to right in the order in which they are added to the container. When the edge of the container is reached, components are continued on the next line. Class **`FlowLayout`** allows GUI components to be *left-aligned*, *centered* (the default) and *right-aligned*.

The application of Fig. 12.24 creates three **`JButton`** objects and adds them to the application, using a **`FlowLayout`** layout manager. The components are automatically center-aligned. When the user clicks **Left**, the alignment for the layout manager is changed to a left-aligned **`FlowLayout`**. When the user clicks **Right**, the alignment for the layout manager is changed to a right-aligned **`FlowLayout`**. When the user clicks **Center**, the alignment for the layout manager is changed to a center-aligned **`FlowLayout`**. Each button has its own event handler that is defined with an inner class that implements **`ActionListener`**. The sample output windows show each of the **`FlowLayout`** alignments. Also, the last sample output window shows the centered alignment after the window has been resized to a smaller width. Notice that the button **Right** now appears on a new line.

```
// Fig. 12.24: FlowLayoutDemo.java
// Demonstrating FlowLayout alignments.

// Java core packages
import java.awt.*;
import java.awt.event.*;

// Java extension packages
import javax.swing.*;

public class FlowLayoutDemo extends JFrame {
   private JButton leftButton, centerButton, rightButton;
   private Container container;
   private FlowLayout layout;

   // set up GUI and register button listeners
   public FlowLayoutDemo()
   {
      super( "FlowLayout Demo" );

      layout = new FlowLayout();

      // get content pane and set its layout
      container = getContentPane();
      container.setLayout( layout );

```

Fig. 12.24 Program that demonstrates components in **`FlowLayout`** (part 1 of 3).

```
      // set up leftButton and register listener
      leftButton = new JButton( "Left" );

      leftButton.addActionListener(

         // anonymous inner class
         new ActionListener() {

            // process leftButton event
            public void actionPerformed( ActionEvent event )
            {
               layout.setAlignment( FlowLayout.LEFT );

               // re-align attached components
               layout.layoutContainer( container );
            }

         }  // end anonymous inner class

      ); // end call to addActionListener

      container.add( leftButton );

      // set up centerButton and register listener
      centerButton = new JButton( "Center" );

      centerButton.addActionListener(

         // anonymous inner class
         new ActionListener() {

            // process centerButton event
            public void actionPerformed( ActionEvent event )
            {
               layout.setAlignment( FlowLayout.CENTER );

               // re-align attached components
               layout.layoutContainer( container );
            }
         }
      );

      container.add( centerButton );

      // set up rightButton and register listener
      rightButton = new JButton( "Right" );

      rightButton.addActionListener(

         // anonymous inner class
         new ActionListener() {

```

Fig. 12.24 Program that demonstrates components in **FlowLayout** (part 2 of 3).

```
79              // process rightButton event
80              public void actionPerformed( ActionEvent event )
81              {
82                 layout.setAlignment( FlowLayout.RIGHT );
83
84                 // re-align attached components
85                 layout.layoutContainer( container );
86              }
87           }
88        );
89
90        container.add( rightButton );
91
92        setSize( 300, 75 );
93        setVisible( true );
94     }
95
96     // execute application
97     public static void main( String args[] )
98     {
99        FlowLayoutDemo application = new FlowLayoutDemo();
100
101       application.setDefaultCloseOperation(
102          JFrame.EXIT_ON_CLOSE );
103    }
104
105 }  // end class FlowLayoutDemo
```

Fig. 12.24 Program that demonstrates components in **`FlowLayout`** (part 3 of 3).

As seen previously, a container's layout is set with method ***`setLayout`*** of class **`Container`**. Line 25 sets the content pane's layout manager to the **`FlowLayout`** defined at line 21. Normally, the layout is set before any GUI components are added to a container.

Look-and-Feel Observation 12.10

Each container can have only one layout manager at a time. (Separate containers in the same program can have different layout managers.)

Each button's **actionPerformed** event handler executes two statements. For example, line 38 in method **actionPerformed** for button **left** uses **FlowLayout** method ***setAlignment*** to change the alignment for the **FlowLayout** to a left-aligned (***FlowLayout.LEFT***) **FlowLayout**. Line 41 uses **LayoutManager** interface method ***layoutContainer*** to specify that the content pane should be rearranged based on the adjusted layout.

According to which button was clicked, the **actionPerformed** method for each button sets the **FlowLayout**'s alignment to ***FlowLayout.LEFT***, ***FlowLayout.CENTER*** or ***FlowLayout.RIGHT***.

12.14.2 BorderLayout

The ***BorderLayout*** layout manager (the default layout manager for the content pane) arranges components into five regions: ***NORTH***, ***SOUTH***, ***EAST***, ***WEST*** and ***CENTER*** (North corresponds to the top of the container). Class **BorderLayout** inherits from **Object** and implements interface ***LayoutManager2*** (a subinterface of **LayoutManager** that adds several methods for enhanced layout processing).

Up to five components can be added directly to a **BorderLayout**—one for each region. The component placed in each region can be a container to which other components are attached. The components placed in the **NORTH** and **SOUTH** regions extend horizontally to the sides of the container and are as tall as the components placed in those regions. The **EAST** and **WEST** regions expand vertically between the **NORTH** and **SOUTH** regions and are as wide as the components placed in those regions. The component placed in the **CENTER** region expands to take all remaining space in the layout (this is the reason the **JTextArea** in Fig. 12.22 occupies the entire window). If all five regions are occupied, the entire container's space is covered by GUI components. If the **NORTH** or **SOUTH** region is not occupied, the GUI components in the **EAST**, **CENTER** and **WEST** regions expand vertically to fill the remaining space. If the **EAST** or **WEST** region is not occupied, the GUI component in the **CENTER** region expands horizontally to fill the remaining space. If the **CENTER** region is not occupied, the area is left empty—the other GUI components do not expand to fill the remaining space.

The application of Fig. 12.25 demonstrates the **BorderLayout** layout manager by using five **JButton**s.

```
// Fig. 12.25: BorderLayoutDemo.java
// Demonstrating BorderLayout.

// Java core packages
import java.awt.*;
import java.awt.event.*;

// Java extension packages
import javax.swing.*;

public class BorderLayoutDemo extends JFrame
   implements ActionListener {

```

Fig. 12.25 Demonstrating components in **BorderLayout** (part 1 of 3).

```
    private JButton buttons[];
    private String names[] = { "Hide North", "Hide South",
       "Hide East", "Hide West", "Hide Center" };
    private BorderLayout layout;

    // set up GUI and event handling
    public BorderLayoutDemo()
    {
       super( "BorderLayout Demo" );

       layout = new BorderLayout( 5, 5 );

       // get content pane and set its layout
       Container container = getContentPane();
       container.setLayout( layout );

       // instantiate button objects
       buttons = new JButton[ names.length ];

       for ( int count = 0; count < names.length; count++ ) {
          buttons[ count ] = new JButton( names[ count ] );
          buttons[ count ].addActionListener( this );
       }

       // place buttons in BorderLayout; order not important
       container.add( buttons[ 0 ], BorderLayout.NORTH );
       container.add( buttons[ 1 ], BorderLayout.SOUTH );
       container.add( buttons[ 2 ], BorderLayout.EAST );
       container.add( buttons[ 3 ], BorderLayout.WEST );
       container.add( buttons[ 4 ], BorderLayout.CENTER );

       setSize( 300, 200 );
       setVisible( true );
    }

    // handle button events
    public void actionPerformed( ActionEvent event )
    {
       for ( int count = 0; count < buttons.length; count++ )

          if ( event.getSource() == buttons[ count ] )
             buttons[ count ].setVisible( false );
          else
             buttons[ count ].setVisible( true );

       // re-layout the content pane
       layout.layoutContainer( getContentPane() );
    }

    // execute application
    public static void main( String args[] )
    {
       BorderLayoutDemo application = new BorderLayoutDemo();
```

Fig. 12.25 Demonstrating components in **BorderLayout** (part 2 of 3).

```
67
68         application.setDefaultCloseOperation(
69            JFrame.EXIT_ON_CLOSE );
70      }
71
72   }  // end class BorderLayoutDemo
```

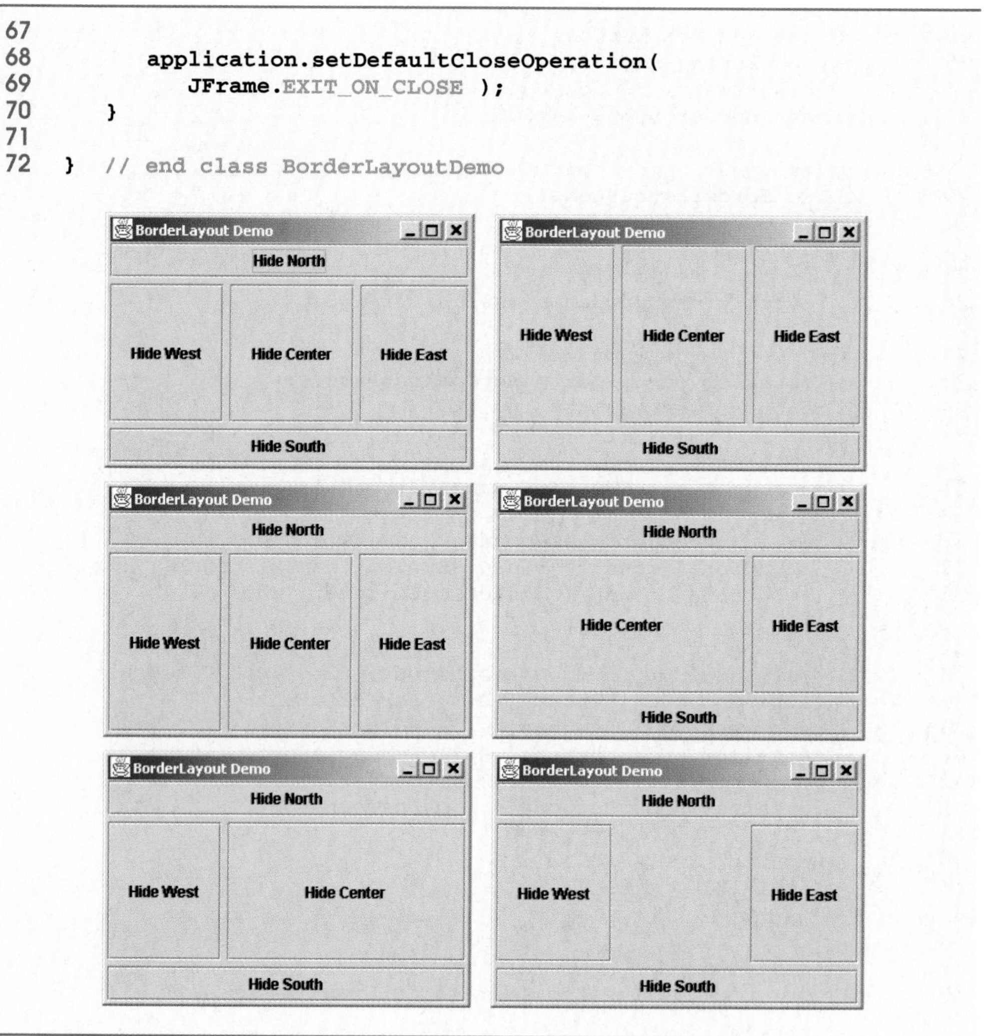

Fig. 12.25 Demonstrating components in **`BorderLayout`** (part 3 of 3).

Line 24 in the constructor defines a **`BorderLayout`**. The arguments specify the number of pixels between components that are arranged horizontally (*horizontal gap space*) and the number of pixels between components that are arranged vertically (*vertical gap space*), respectively. The default **`BorderLayout`** constructor supplies 0 pixels of gap space horizontally and vertically. Line 28 uses method **`setLayout`** to set the content pane's layout to **`layout`**.

Adding **`Component`**s to a **`BorderLayout`** requires a different add method from class **`Container`**, which takes two arguments—the **`Component`** to add and the region in which the **`Component`** will be placed. For example, line 39 specifies that the **`buttons[ 0 ]`** should appear in the **`NORTH`** position. The components can be added in any order, but only one component can be added to each region.

Look-and-Feel Observation 12.11

If no region is specified when adding a **Component** *to a* **BorderLayout**, *it is assumed that the* **Component** *should be added to region* **BorderLayout.CENTER**

Common Programming Error 12.6

Adding more than one component to a particular region in a **BorderLayout** *results in only the last component added being displayed. There is no error message to indicate this problem.*

When the user clicks on a particular **JButton** in the layout, method **actionPerformed** (lines 50–61) executes. The **for** loop at lines 52–57 uses an **if/else** structure to hide the particular **JButton** that generated the event. Method ***setVisible*** (inherited into **JButton** from class **Component**) is called with a **false** argument to hide the **JButton**. If the current **JButton** in the array is not the one that generated the event, method **setVisible** is called with a **true** argument to ensure that the **JButton** is displayed on the screen. Line 60 uses **LayoutManager** method **layoutContainer** to recalculate the layout of the content pane. Notice in the screen captures of Fig. 12.25 that certain regions in the **BorderLayout** change shape as **JButton**s are hidden and displayed in other regions. Try resizing the application window to see how the various regions resize based on the width and height of the window.

12.14.3 GridLayout

The ***GridLayout*** layout manager divides the container into a grid so that components can be placed in rows and columns. Class **GridLayout** inherits directly from class **Object** and implements interface **LayoutManager**. Every **Component** in a **GridLayout** has the same width and height. Components are added to a **GridLayout** starting at the top-left cell of the grid and proceeding left-to-right until the row is full. Then the process continues left-to-right on the next row of the grid, etc. Figure 12.26 demonstrates the **GridLayout** layout manager using six **JButton**s.

```
// Fig. 12.26: GridLayoutDemo.java
// Demonstrating GridLayout.

// Java core packages
import java.awt.*;
import java.awt.event.*;

// Java extension packages
import javax.swing.*;

public class GridLayoutDemo extends JFrame
   implements ActionListener {

   private JButton buttons[];
   private String names[] =
      { "one", "two", "three", "four", "five", "six" };
   private boolean toggle = true;
```

Fig. 12.26 Program that demonstrates components in **GridLayout**.

```
   private Container container;
   private GridLayout grid1, grid2;

   // set up GUI
   public GridLayoutDemo()
   {
      super( "GridLayout Demo" );

      // set up layouts
      grid1 = new GridLayout( 2, 3, 5, 5 );
      grid2 = new GridLayout( 3, 2 );

      // get content pane and set its layout
      container = getContentPane();
      container.setLayout( grid1 );

      // create and add buttons
      buttons = new JButton[ names.length ];

      for ( int count = 0; count < names.length; count++ ) {
         buttons[ count ] = new JButton( names[ count ] );
         buttons[ count ].addActionListener( this );
         container.add( buttons[ count ] );
      }

      setSize( 300, 150 );
      setVisible( true );
   }

   // handle button events by toggling between layouts
   public void actionPerformed( ActionEvent event )
   {
      if ( toggle )
         container.setLayout( grid2 );
      else
         container.setLayout( grid1 );

      toggle = !toggle;   // set toggle to opposite value
      container.validate();
   }

   // execute application
   public static void main( String args[] )
   {
      GridLayoutDemo application = new GridLayoutDemo();

      application.setDefaultCloseOperation(
         JFrame.EXIT_ON_CLOSE );
   }

}  // end class GridLayoutDemo
```

Fig. 12.26 Program that demonstrates components in **GridLayout**.

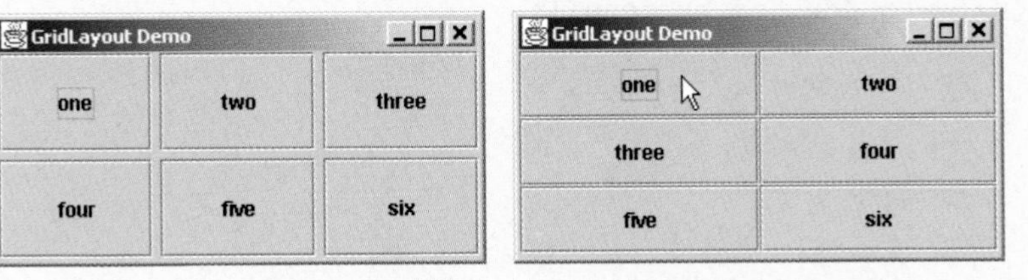

Fig. 12.26 Program that demonstrates components in **GridLayout**.

Lines 27–28 in the constructor define two **GridLayout** objects. The **GridLayout** constructor used at line 27 specifies a **GridLayout** with **2** rows, **3** columns, **5** pixels of horizontal-gap space between **Component**s in the grid and **5** pixels of vertical-gap space between **Component**s in the grid. The **GridLayout** constructor used at line 28 specifies a **GridLayout** with **3** rows, **2** columns and no gap space.

The **JButton** objects in this example initially are arranged using **grid1** (set for the content pane at line 32 with method **setLayout**). The first component is added to the first column of the first row. The next component is added to the second column of the first row, and so on. When a **JButton** is pressed, method **actionPerformed** (lines 48–57) is called. Every call to **actionPerformed** toggles the layout between **grid2** and **grid1**.

Line 56 illustrates another way to relayout a container for which the layout has changed. **Container** method ***validate*** recomputes the container's layout based on the current layout manager for the **Container** and the current set of displayed GUI components.

12.15 Panels

Complex GUIs (like Fig. 12.1) require that each component be placed in an exact location. They often consist of multiple *panels* with each panel's components arranged in a specific layout. Panels are created with class ***JPanel***—a subclass of **JComponent**. Class **JComponent** inherits from class **java.awt.Container**, so every **JPanel** is a **Container**. Thus **JPanel**s may have components, including other panels, added to them.

The program of Fig. 12.27 demonstrates how a **JPanel** can be used to create a more complex layout for **Component**s.

```
// Fig. 12.27: PanelDemo.java
// Using a JPanel to help lay out components.

// Java core packages
import java.awt.*;
import java.awt.event.*;

// Java extension packages
import javax.swing.*;

public class PanelDemo extends JFrame {
   private JPanel buttonPanel;
```

Fig. 12.27 A **JPanel** with five **JButton**s in a **GridLayout** attached to the **SOUTH** region of a **BorderLayout** (part 1 of 2).

```
   private JButton buttons[];

   // set up GUI
   public PanelDemo()
   {
      super( "Panel Demo" );

      // get content pane
      Container container = getContentPane();

      // create buttons array
      buttons = new JButton[ 5 ];

      // set up panel and set its layout
      buttonPanel = new JPanel();
      buttonPanel.setLayout(
         new GridLayout( 1, buttons.length ) );

      // create and add buttons
      for ( int count = 0; count < buttons.length; count++ ) {
         buttons[ count ] =
            new JButton( "Button " + ( count + 1 ) );
         buttonPanel.add( buttons[ count ] );
      }

      container.add( buttonPanel, BorderLayout.SOUTH );

      setSize( 425, 150 );
      setVisible( true );
   }

   // execute application
   public static void main( String args[] )
   {
      PanelDemo application = new PanelDemo();

      application.setDefaultCloseOperation(
         JFrame.EXIT_ON_CLOSE );
   }

}  // end class PanelDemo
```

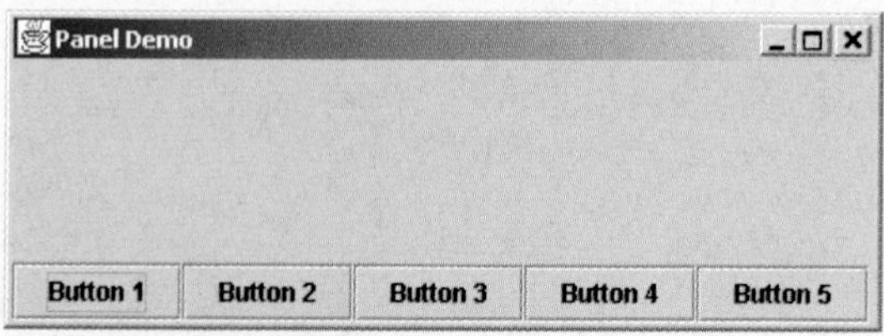

Fig. 12.27 A **JPanel** with five **JButton**s in a **GridLayout** attached to the **SOUTH** region of a **BorderLayout** (part 2 of 2).

After **JPanel buttonPanel** is created at line 27, lines 28–29 set **buttonPanel**'s layout to a **GridLayout** of one row and five columns (there are five **JButton**s in array **buttons**). The five **JButton**s in array **buttons** are added to the **JPanel** in the loop with line 35. Notice that the buttons are added directly to the **JPanel**—class **JPanel** does not have a content pane like an applet or a **JFrame**. Line 38 uses the content pane's default **BorderLayout** to add **buttonPanel** to the **SOUTH** region. Note that the **SOUTH** region is as tall as the buttons on **buttonPanel**. A **JPanel** is sized to the components it contains. As more components are added, the **JPanel** grows (according to the restrictions of its layout manager) to accommodate the components. Resize the window to see how the layout manager affects the size of the **JButton**s.

12.16 (Optional Case Study) Thinking About Objects: Use Cases

The previous eight "Thinking About Objects" sections have concentrated on the elevator-simulation model. We have identified and honed the structure and behavior of our system. In this section, we model the interaction between the user and our elevator simulation through the UML use-case diagram, which describes the sets of scenarios that occur between the user and the system.

Use-Case Diagrams

When developers begin a project, they rarely start with as detailed a problem statement as the one we provided in Section 2.9. This document and others are the result of the *object-oriented analysis* (OOA) phase. In this phase you meet with the people who want you to build a system and with the people who will eventually use that system. You use the information gained in these meetings to compile a list of *system requirements*. These requirements guide you and your fellow developers as you design the system. In our case study, the problem statement described the requirements of our elevator simulation in sufficient detail that you did not need to go through an analysis phase. The analysis phase is enormously important—you should consult the references we provide in Section 2.9 to learn more about object-oriented analysis.

The UML provides the *use-case diagram* to facilitate requirements gathering. This diagram models the interactions between the system's external clients and the *use cases* of the system. Each use case represents a different capability that the system provides to clients. For example, automated teller machines typically have several use cases, including "Deposit Money," "Withdraw Money" and "Transfer Funds."

In larger systems, use-case diagrams are indispensable tools that help system designers remain focused on satisfying the users' needs. The goal of the use-case diagram is to show the kinds of interactions users have with a system without providing the details of those interactions: those details are, of course, provided in other UML diagrams.

Figure 12.28 shows the use-case diagram for our elevator simulation. The stick figure represents an *actor*, which, in turn, represents a set of roles that an *external entity*—such as a person or another system—can play. Consider again our automated teller machine example. The actor is a **BankCustomer** who can deposit, withdraw and transfer funds from the ATM. In this sense, **BankCustomer** is more like a class rather than an object—it is not an actual person, but rather describes the roles that a real person—when playing the part of a **BankCustomer**—can perform while interacting with the ATM (deposit, withdraw and transfer funds). A person is an external entity that can play the part of a **BankCustomer**. In the same manner as an object is an instance of a class, a person playing the part of a **BankCustomer** performing one of its roles (such as making a deposit) is an *instance of actor* **BankCustomer**. For example, when a person named Mary plays the part of a **BankCustomer** making a deposit, Mary—in the role of the depositor—becomes an instance of actor **BankCustomer**. Later in that day, another person named Jon can be another instance of actor **BankCustomer**. In the course of a day, several hundred people might use the ATM machine—some are "depositors", some are "withdrawers" and some are "transferrers," but all of these people are instances of actor **BankCustomer**.

The problem statement in our elevator simulation supplies the actors—"The user requires the ability to create a person in the simulation and situate that person on a given floor." Therefore, the actor of our system is the user who controls the simulation (i.e., the user who clicks the buttons to create new **Person**s in the simulation). An external entity—a real person—plays the part of the user to control the simulation. In our system, the use case is "Create Person," which encompasses creating a **Person** object, then placing that **Person** on either the first or second **Floor**. Figure 12.28 models one actor called "User." The actor's *name* appears underneath the actor.

The *system box* (i.e., the enclosing rectangle in the figure) contains the use cases for the system. Notice that the box is labeled "Elevator Simulation." This title shows that this use-case model focuses on the one use case that our simulation provides to users (i.e., "Create Person"). The UML models each use case as an oval. The system box for a system with multiple use cases would have one oval per use case.

There is a reasonable alternate view of the use case of our elevator simulation. The problem statement from Section 2.9 mentioned that the company requested the elevator simulation to "determine whether the elevator will meet the company's needs." We are designing a simulation of a real-world scenario—the **Person** object in the simulation represents an actual human being using an actual elevator. Thus, we may view the user of the elevator simulation as the user of the elevator. Therefore, specifying a use case from the **Person** object's perspective helps model how a real person uses a real elevator system. We offer the use case of Fig. 12.29, titled "Relocate Person." This use case describes the **Person** moving (relocating) to the other **Floor**. (The **Person** travels to the second **Floor** if starting on the first **Floor** and to the first **Floor** if starting on the second **Floor**.) This use case encompasses all actions that the **Person** performs along his or her journey, such as walking across a **Floor** to the **Elevator**, pressing **Button**s and riding the **Elevator** to the other **Floor**.

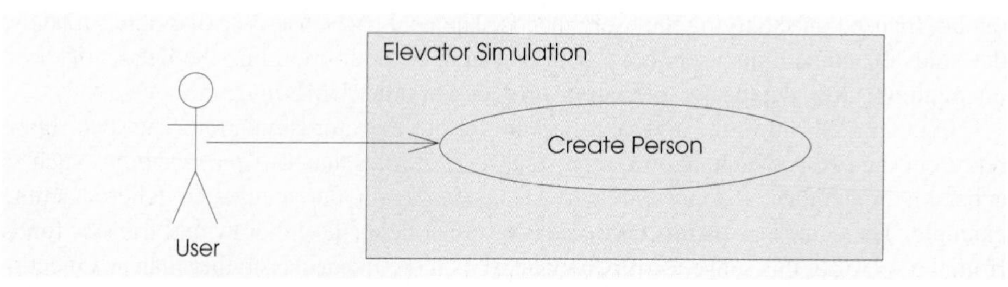

Fig. 12.28 Use-case diagram for elevator simulation from user's perspective.

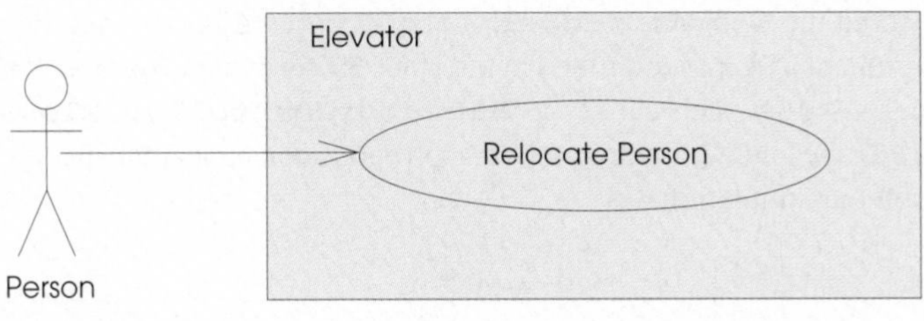

Fig. 12.29 Use-case diagram from the perspective of a **`Person`**.

We must ensure that our use cases do not model interactions that are too specific between the external client and the system. For example, we do not subdivide each use case into two separate use cases—such as "Create Person on first Floor" and "Create Person on second Floor," or "Relocate Person to first Floor" and "Relocate Person to second Floor"—because the functionality of such use cases is repetitive (i.e., these seemingly alternative use cases are really the same). Improper and repetitive subdivision of use cases can create problems during implementation. For example, if the designer of an automated teller machine separated its "Withdraw Money" use case into "Withdraw Specific Amounts" use cases (e.g., "Withdraw $1.00," "Withdraw $2.00," etc.), there could exist an enormous number of use cases for the system. This would make the implementation tedious. (Our elevator system contains only two floors—separating the use case into two would not cause that much extra work; if our system contained 100 floors, however, creating 100 use cases would be unwieldy.)

Constructing the Graphical User Interface

Our simulation implements both the "Create Person" and "Relocate Person" use cases. We have studied the "Relocate Person" use case through the activity diagram of the **`Person`** in Fig. 5.29—we implement this use case and the activity diagram in Appendix H when we create class **`Person`**. We implement the "Create Person" use case through a graphical user interface (GUI). We implement our GUI in class **`ElevatorController`** (Fig. 12.30, line 17), which is a **`JPanel`** subclass containing two **`JButton`** objects—**`firstControllerButton`** (line 21) and **`secondControllerButton`** (line 22). Each **`JButton`** corresponds to a **`Floor`** on which to place a **`Person`**.[1] Lines 33–38 instantiate these **`JButton`**s and add them to the **`ElevatorController`**.

We discuss in Section 13.17 how class **`ElevatorModel`** ties together all objects composing our elevator simulation model. Line 25 of class **`ElevatorController`** declares a reference to the **`ElevatorModel`**, because the **`ElevatorController`** allows the user to interact with the model. Lines 42–56 and 60–74 declare two anonymous **`ActionListener`** objects and register them with **`firstFloorControllerButton`** and **`secondFloorControllerButton`**, respectively, for **`ActionEvent`**s. When the user presses either **`JButton`**, lines 49–50 and 67–68 of methods **`actionPer-`**

1. This approach is feasible with only two **`Floor`**s. If the building had 100 **`Floor`**s, we might have opted for the user to specify the desired **`Floor`** in a **`JTextField`** and press a **`JButton`** to process the request.

formed call the **ElevatorModel**'s method **addPerson**, which instantiates a **Person** object in the **ElevatorModel** on the specified **Floor**. Method **addPerson** takes as an argument a **String** defined in interface **ElevatorConstants** (Fig. 12.31). This interface—used by such classes as **ElevatorController**, **ElevatorModel**, **Elevator**, **Floor** and **ElevatorView**—provides constants that specify the names of **Location**s in our simulation.

```
// ElevatorController.java
// Controller for Elevator Simulation
package com.deitel.jhtp4.elevator.controller;

// Java core packages
import java.awt.*;
import java.awt.event.*;

// Java extension packages
import javax.swing.*;

// Deitel packages
import com.deitel.jhtp4.elevator.model.*;
import com.deitel.jhtp4.elevator.event.*;
import com.deitel.jhtp4.elevator.ElevatorConstants;

public class ElevatorController extends JPanel
   implements ElevatorConstants {

   // controller contains two JButtons
   private JButton firstControllerButton;
   private JButton secondControllerButton;

   // reference to model
   private ElevatorModel elevatorModel;

   public ElevatorController( ElevatorModel model )
   {
      elevatorModel = model;
      setBackground( Color.white );

      // add first button to controller
      firstControllerButton = new JButton( "First Floor" );
      add( firstControllerButton );

      // add second button to controller
      secondControllerButton = new JButton( "Second Floor" );
      add( secondControllerButton );

      // anonymous inner class registers to receive ActionEvents
      // from first Controller JButton
      firstControllerButton.addActionListener(
         new ActionListener() {

```

Fig. 12.30 Class **ElevatorController** processes user input (part 1 of 3).

```
            // invoked when a JButton has been pressed
            public void actionPerformed( ActionEvent event )
            {
               // place Person on first Floor
               elevatorModel.addPerson(
                  FIRST_FLOOR_NAME );

               // disable user input
               firstControllerButton.setEnabled( false );
            }
         } // end anonymous inner class
      );

      // anonymous inner class registers to receive ActionEvents
      // from second Controller JButton
      secondControllerButton.addActionListener(
         new ActionListener() {

            // invoked when a JButton has been pressed
            public void actionPerformed( ActionEvent event )
            {
               // place Person on second Floor
               elevatorModel.addPerson(
                  SECOND_FLOOR_NAME );

               // disable user input
               secondControllerButton.setEnabled( false );
            }
         } // end anonymous inner class
      );

      // anonymous inner class enables user input on Floor if
      // Person enters Elevator on that Floor
      elevatorModel.addPersonMoveListener(
         new PersonMoveListener() {

            // invoked when Person has entered Elevator
            public void personEntered(
               PersonMoveEvent event )
            {
               // get Floor of departure
               String location =
                  event.getLocation().getLocationName();

               // enable first JButton if first Floor departure
               if ( location.equals( FIRST_FLOOR_NAME ) )
                  firstControllerButton.setEnabled( true );

               // enable second JButton if second Floor
               else
                  secondControllerButton.setEnabled( true );

            } // end method personEntered
```

Fig. 12.30 Class **ElevatorController** processes user input (part 2 of 3).

```
98
99                  // other methods implementing PersonMoveListener
100                 public void personCreated(
101                    PersonMoveEvent event ) {}
102
103                 public void personArrived(
104                    PersonMoveEvent event ) {}
105
106                 public void personExited(
107                    PersonMoveEvent event ) {}
108
109                 public void personDeparted(
110                    PersonMoveEvent event ) {}
111
112                 public void personPressedButton(
113                    PersonMoveEvent event ) {}
114
115              } // end anonymous inner class
116           );
117        } // end ElevatorController constructor
118     }
```

Fig. 12.30 Class **ElevatorController** processes user input (part 3 of 3).

Lines 53 and 71 of methods **actionPerformed** disable the respective **JButton**s to prevent the user from creating more than one **Person** per **Floor**. Lines 78–116 of class **ElevatorController** declare an anonymous **PersonMoveListener** that registers with the **ElevatorModel** to reenable the **JButton**s. Method **personEntered** (lines 82–97) of the **PersonMoveListener** reenables the **JButton** associated with the **Floor** that the **Elevator** services—after the **Person** has entered the **Elevator**, the user may place another **Person** on the **Floor**.

We mentioned in Section 9.23 that classes **Elevator** and **Floor** inherited attribute **capacity** from superclass **Location**—in Appendix H, we were going to use this attribute to prevent more than one **Person** from occupying a **Location**. However, the **PersonMoveListener**'s method **personEntered** in class **ElevatorController** prevents the user from creating more than one **Person** per **Floor**. Therefore, we have negated the need for attribute **capacity** in class **Location**. Figure 12.32 is the modified class diagram of Fig. 9.18 removing this attribute.

```
// ElevatorConstants.java
// Constants used between ElevatorModel and ElevatorView
package com.deitel.jhtp4.elevator;

public interface ElevatorConstants {

   public static final String FIRST_FLOOR_NAME = "firstFloor";
   public static final String SECOND_FLOOR_NAME = "secondFloor";
   public static final String ELEVATOR_NAME = "elevator";
}
```

Fig. 12.31 Interface **ElevatorConstants** provides **Location** name constants.

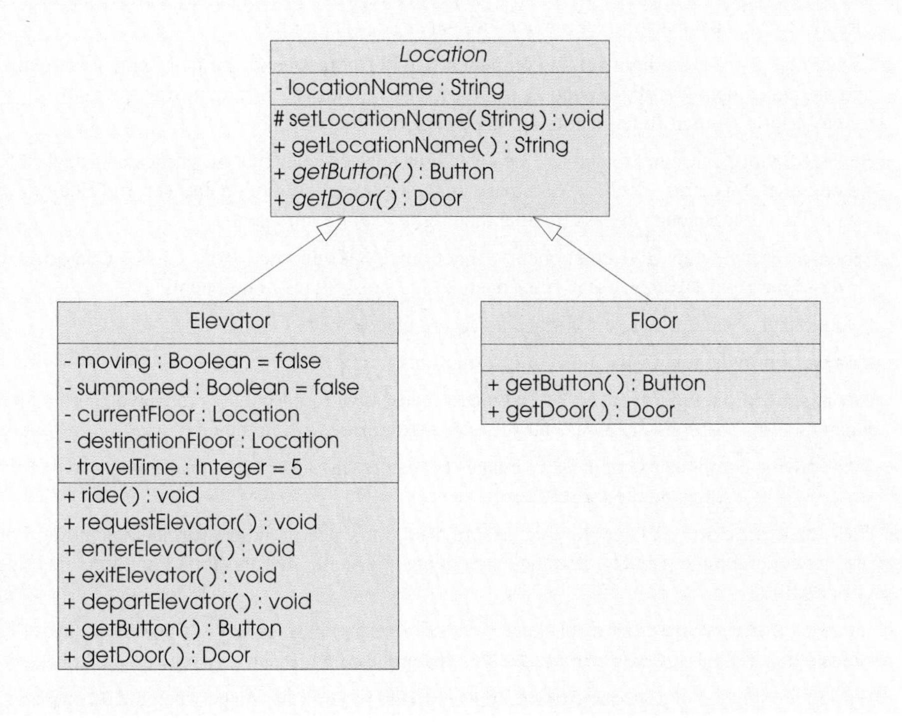

Fig. 12.32 Modified class diagram showing generalization of superclass **`Location`** and subclasses **`Elevator`** and **`Floor`**.

In this section we mentioned that the goal of object-oriented ananlysis is to produce a system-requirements document. We introduced the UML use-case diagram that facilitates gathering system requirements, and we examined the two use cases in our elevator simulation. We implemented our simulator's Graphical User Interface in Java.

This section concludes the discussion on the interaction between the user and the simulation model. In "Thinking About Objects" Section 13.17, we integrate class **`ElevatorController`** with the rest of the simulation. We also introduce the UML Component diagram, which models the **`.class`**, **`.java`**, image and sound files that comprise our system.

SUMMARY

- A graphical user interface (GUI) presents a pictorial interface to a program. A GUI (pronounced "GOO-EE") gives a program a distinctive "look" and "feel."
- By providing different applications with a consistent set of intuitive user interface components, GUIs allow the user to spend more time using the program in a productive manner.
- GUIs are built from GUI components (sometimes called controls or widgets). A GUI component is a visual object with which the user interacts via the mouse or the keyboard.
- Swing GUI components are defined in package **`javax.swing`**. Swing components are written, manipulated and displayed completely in Java.

- The original GUI components from the Abstract Windowing Toolkit package **java.awt** are tied directly to the local platform's graphical user interface capabilities.
- Swing components are lightweight components. AWT components are tied to the local platform and are called heavyweight components—they must rely on the local platform's windowing system to determine their functionality and their look and feel.
- Several Swing GUI components are heavyweight GUI components: in particular, subclasses of **java.awt.Window** (such as **JFrame**) that display windows on the screen. Heavyweight Swing GUI components are less flexible than lightweight components.
- Much of each Swing GUI component's functionality is inherited from classes **Component, Container** and **JComponent** (the superclass to most Swing components).
- A Container is an area where components can be placed.
- **JLabel**s provide text instructions or information on a GUI.
- **JComponent** method **setToolTipText** specifies the tool tip that is displayed automatically when the user positions the mouse cursor over a **JComponent** in the GUI.
- Many Swing components can display images by specifying an **Icon** as an argument to their constructor or by using a method **setIcon**.
- Class **ImageIcon** (package **javax.swing**) supports several image formats, including Portable Network Graphics (PNG), Graphics Interchange Format (GIF) and Joint Photographic Experts Group (JPEG).
- Interface **SwingConstants** (package **javax.swing**) defines a set of common integer constants (such as **SwingConstants.LEFT**) that are used with many Swing components.
- By default, the text of a **JComponent** appears to the right of the image when the **JComponent** contains both text and an image.
- The horizontal and vertical alignments of a **JLabel** can be set with methods **setHorizontal-Alignment** and **setVerticalAlignment**. Method **setText** sets the text displayed on the label. Method **getText** retrieves the current text displayed on a label. Methods **setHorizon-talTextPosition** and **setVerticalTextPosition** specify the text position in a label.
- **JComponent** method **setIcon** sets the **Icon** displayed on a **JComponent**. Method **get-Icon** retrieves the current **Icon** displayed on a **JComponent**.
- GUIs generate events when the user interacts with the GUI. Information about a GUI event is stored in an object of a class that extends **AWTEvent**.
- To process an event, the programmer must register an event listener and implement one or more event handlers.
- The use of event listeners in event handling is known as the delegation event model—the processing of an event is delegated to a particular object in the program.
- When an event occurs, the GUI component with which the user interacted notifies its registered listeners by calling each listener's appropriate event handling method.
- **JTextFields** and **JPasswordFields** are single-line areas in which text can be entered by the user from the keyboard or text can simply be displayed. A **JPasswordField** shows that a character was typed as the user enters characters, but automatically hides the characters.
- When the user types data into a **JTextField** or **JPasswordField** and presses the Enter key, an **ActionEvent** occurs.
- **JTextComponent** method **setEditable** determines whether the user can modify the text in a **JTextComponent**.
- **JPasswordField** method **getPassword** returns the password as an array of type **char**.

- Every **JComponent** contains an object of class **EventListenerList** (package **javax.swing.event**) called **listenerList** in which all registered listeners are stored.
- Every **JComponent** supports several different event types, including mouse events, key events and others. When an event occurs, the event is dispatched only to the event listeners of the appropriate type. Each event type has a corresponding event-listener interface.
- When an event is generated by a user interaction with a component, the component is handed a unique event ID specifying the event type. The GUI component uses the event ID to decide the type of listener to which the event should be dispatched and the event handler method to call.
- A **JButton** generates an **ActionEvent** when the user clicks the button with the mouse.
- An **AbstractButton** can have a rollover **Icon** that is displayed when the mouse is positioned over the button. The icon changes as the mouse moves in and out of the button's area on the screen. **AbstractButton** method **setRolloverIcon** specifies the image displayed on a button when the user positions the mouse over the button.
- The Swing GUI components contain three state button types—**JToggleButton**, **JCheckBox** and **JRadioButton**—that have on/off or true/false values. Classes **JCheckBox** and **JRadioButton** are subclasses of **JToggleButton**.
- When the user clicks a **JCheckBox**, an **ItemEvent** is generated that can be handled by an **ItemListener**. **ItemListener**s must define method **itemStateChanged**. **ItemEvent** method **getStateChange** determines the state of a **JToggleButton**.
- **JRadioButtons** are similar to **JCheckBox**es in that they have two states—selected and not selected (also called deselected). **JRadioButtons** normally appear as a group in which only one radio button can be selected at a time.
- The logical relationship between radio buttons is maintained by a **ButtonGroup** object.
- The **JRadioButton** constructor supplies the label that appears to the right of the **JRadioButton** by default and the initial state of the **JRadioButton**. A **true** second argument indicates that the **JRadioButton** should appear selected when it is displayed.
- **JRadioButton**s generate **ItemEvent**s when they are clicked.
- **ButtonGroup** method **add** associates a **JRadioButton** with a **ButtonGroup**. If more than one selected **JRadioButton** object is added to the group, the last selected **JRadioButton** added will be selected when the GUI is displayed.
- A **JComboBox** (sometimes called a drop-down list) provides a list of items from which the user can make a selection. **JComboBox**es generate **ItemEvent**s. A numeric index keeps track of the ordering of items in a JComboBox. The first item is added at index 0, the next item is added at index 1 and so forth. The first item added to a JComboBox appears as the currently selected item when the JComboBox is displayed. **JComboBox** method **getSelectedIndex** returns the index number of the selected item.
- A **JList** displays a series of items from which the user may select one or more items. Class **JList** supports single- and multiple-selection lists. When an item is clicked in a **JList**, a **ListSelectionEvent** occurs.
- **JList** method **setVisibleRowCount** determines the number of items that are visible in the list. Method **setSelectionMode** specifies the selection mode for the list.
- Class **JList** does *not* automatically provide a scrollbar if there are more items in the list than the number of visible rows. A **JScrollPane** object is used to provide the automatic scrolling capability for a **JList**.
- A **SINGLE_INTERVAL_SELECTION** list allows selection of a contiguous range of items by clicking the first item, then holding the Shift key while clicking the last item to select in the range.

- A **MULTIPLE_INTERVAL_SELECTION** list allows continuous range selection as described for a **SINGLE_INTERVAL_SELECTION** list and allows miscellaneous items to be selected by holding the Ctrl key while clicking each item to select.
- **JList** method **setFixedCellHeight** specifies the height in pixels of each item in a **JList**. Method **setFixedCellWidth** sets the width in pixels of a **JList**.
- Normally, an event generated by another GUI component (known as an external event) specifies when the multiple selections in a **JList** should be processed.
- **JList** method **setListData** sets the items displayed in a **JList**. Method **getSelectedValues** returns the selected items as an array of **Object**s.
- Mouse events can be trapped for any GUI component that derives from **java.awt.Component** using **MouseListener**s and **MouseMotionListener**s.
- Each mouse event handling method takes as its argument a **MouseEvent** object containing information about the mouse event and the location where the event occurred.
- Methods **addMouseListener** and **addMouseMotionListener** are **Component** methods used to register mouse event listeners for an object of any class that extends **Component**.
- Many of the event-listener interfaces provide multiple methods. For each, there is a corresponding event-listener adapter class that provides a default implementation of every method in the interface. The programmer can extend the adapter class to inherit the default implementation of every method and simply override the method or methods needed for event handling in the program.
- **MouseEvent** method **getClickCount** returns the number of mouse clicks.
- **InputEvent** methods **isMetaDown** and **isAltDown** are used to determine which mouse button the user clicked.
- **KeyListener**s handle key events that are generated when keys on the keyboard are pressed and released. A **KeyListener** must provide definitions for methods **keyPressed**, **keyReleased** and **keyTyped**, each of which receives a **KeyEvent** as its argument.
- Method **keyPressed** is called in response to pressing any key. Method **keyTyped** is called in response to pressing any key that is not an action key (i.e., an arrow key, *Home*, *End*, *Page Up*, *Page Down*, a function key, *Num Lock*, *Print Screen*, *Scroll Lock*, *Caps Lock* and *Pause*). Method **keyReleased** is called when the key is released after any **keyPressed** or **keyTyped** event.
- **KeyEvent** method **getKeyCode** gets the virtual key code of the key that was pressed. Class **KeyEvent** maintains a set of virtual key code constants that represent every key on the keyboard.
- **KeyEvent** method **getKeyText** returns a **String** containing the name of the key that corresponds to its virtual key code argument. Method **getKeyChar** gets the Unicode value of the character typed. Method **isActionKey** determines if the key in the event was an action key.
- **InputEvent** method **getModifiers** determines if any modifier keys (such as Shift, Alt and Ctrl) were pressed when the key event occurred. **KeyEvent** method **getKeyModifiersText** produces a string containing the names of the pressed modifier keys.
- Layout managers arrange GUI components on a container for presentation purposes.
- **FlowLayout** lays out components from left to right in the order in which they are added to the container. When the edge of the container is reached, components are continued on the next line.
- **FlowLayout** method **setAlignment** changes the alignment for the **FlowLayout** to **FlowLayout.LEFT**, **FlowLayout.CENTER** or **FlowLayout.RIGHT**.
- The **BorderLayout** layout manager arranges components into five regions: North, South, East, West and Center. One component can be added to each region.

- **LayoutManager** method **layoutContainer** recalculates the layout of its **Container** argument.
- The **GridLayout** layout manager divides the container into a grid of rows and columns. Components are added to a **GridLayout** starting at the top-left cell and proceeding from left to right until the row is full. Then the process continues from left to right on the next row of the grid, and so on.
- **Container** method **validate** recomputes the container's layout based on the current layout manager for the **Container** and the current set of displayed GUI components.
- Panels are created with class **JPanel**, which inherits from class JComponent. JPanels may have components, including other panels, added to them.

TERMINOLOGY

.gif file name extension
.jpg file name extension
"listen" for an event
Abstract Windowing Toolkit
AbstractButton class
ActionEvent class
ActionListener interface
actionPerformed method
adapter class
add method of **ButtonGroup**
add method of class **Container**
addItemListener method
addKeyListener method
addListSelectionListener method
addMouseListener method
addMouseMotionListener method
assistive technologies
BorderLayout class
BorderLayout.CENTER
BorderLayout.EAST
BorderLayout.NORTH
BorderLayout.SOUTH
BorderLayout.WEST
button
button label
ButtonGroup class
centered
check box
check box label
command button
Component class
ComponentAdapter class
ComponentListener interface
Container class
ContainerAdapter class
ContainerListener interface
control
delegation event model
dispatch an event
dragging
drop-down list
event
event driven
event handler
event ID
event listener
event-listener interface
EventListenerList class
EventObject class
FlowLayout class
FlowLayout.CENTER
FlowLayout.LEFT
FlowLayout.RIGHT
focus
FocusAdapter class
FocusListener interface
Font.BOLD
Font.ITALIC
Font.PLAIN
getActionCommand method
getClickCount method
getIcon method
getKeyChar method of **KeyEvent**
getKeyCode method of **KeyEvent**
getKeyModifiersText method
getKeyText method of **KeyEvent**
getModifiers method of **InputEvent**
getPassword method of **JPasswordField**
getSelectedIndex method of **JComboBox**
getSelectedIndex method of **JList**
getSelectedValues method of **JList**
getSource method of **ActionEvent**
getStateChange method of **ItemEvent**
getText method of **JLabel**
getX method of **MouseEvent**
getY method of **MouseEvent**

Graphics Interchange Format (GIF)
GridLayout class
GUI component
heavyweight component
horizontal gap space
Icon interface
ImageIcon class
InputEvent class
isActionKey method of **KeyEvent**
isAltDown method of **InputEvent**
isMetaDown method of **InputEvent**
ItemEvent class
ItemEvent.DESELECTED
ItemEvent.SELECTED
ItemListener interface
itemStateChanged method
java.awt package
java.awt.event package
javax.swing package
javax.swing.event package
JButton class
JCheckBox class
JComboBox class
JComponent class
JLabel class
JList class
Joint Photographic Experts Group (JPEG)
JPanel class
JPasswordField class
JRadioButton class
JScrollPane class
JTextComponent class
JTextField class
JToggleButton class
KeyAdapter class
KeyEvent class
KeyListener interface
keyPressed method of **KeyListener**
keyReleased method of **KeyListener**
keyTyped method of **KeyListener**
label
layout manager
layoutContainer method
LayoutManger interface
left aligned
left justified
lightweight component
ListSelectionEvent class
ListSelectionListener interface
ListSelectionModel interface
look and feel
menu
menu bar
MouseAdapter class
mouseClicked method
mouseDragged method
mouseEntered method
MouseEvent class
mouseExited method
MouseListener interface
MouseMotionAdapter class
MouseMotionListener interface
mouseMoved method
mousePressed method
mouseReleased method
multiple-selection list
password
pluggable look and feel
radio button
read-only text
register an event listener
right-aligned
rollover icon
scroll arrow
scroll box
scrollbar
selection mode
setAlignment method
setBackground method
setEditable method
setFixedCellHeight method
setFixedCellWidth method
setHorizontalAlignment method
setHorizontalTextPosition method
setIcon method
setLayout method of class **Container**
setListData method of **JList**
setMaximumRowCount method
setRolloverIcon method
setSelectionMode method
setToolTipText method
setVerticalAlignment method
setVerticalTextPosition method
setVisible method
setVisibleRowCount method
shortcut key (mnemonics)
single-selection list
SwingConstants interface
tool tips
toolbar

user interface localization
validate method
valueChanged method
vertical gap space
widget (window gadget)
window
WindowAdapter class
windowClosing method
windowing system
WindowListener interface

SELF-REVIEW EXERCISES

12.1 Fill in the blanks in each of the following statements:

a) Method __________ is called when the mouse is moved and an event listener is registered to handle the event.
b) Text that cannot be modified by the user is called __________ text.
c) A __________ arranges GUI components on a **Container**.
d) The **add** method for attaching GUI components is a __________ class method.
e) GUI is an acronym for __________.
f) Method __________ is used to set the layout manager for a container.
g) A **mouseDragged** method call is preceded by a __________ method call and followed by a __________ method call.

12.2 State whether each of the following is *true* or *false*. If *false*, explain why.

a) **BorderLayout** is the default layout manager for a content pane.
b) When the mouse cursor is moved into the bounds of a GUI component, method **mouseOver** is called.
c) A **JPanel** cannot be added to another **JPanel**.
d) In a **BorderLayout**, two buttons added to the **NORTH** region will be placed side by side.
e) When one is using **BorderLayout**, a maximum of five components may be used.

12.3 Find the error(s) in each of the following and explain how to correct it (them).

a) `buttonName = JButton( "Caption" );`
b) `JLabel aLabel, JLabel;       // create references`
c) `txtField = new JTextField( 50, "Default Text" );`
d)
```
Container container = getContentPane();
setLayout( new BorderLayout() );
button1 = new JButton( "North Star" );
button2 = new JButton( "South Pole" );
container.add( button1 );
container.add( button2 );
```

ANSWERS TO SELF-REVIEW EXERCISES

12.1 a) **mouseMoved**. b) uneditable (read-only). c) layout manager. d) **Container**. e) graphical user interface. f) **setLayout**. g) **mousePressed**, **mouseReleased**.

12.2 a) True.
b) False. Method **mouseEntered** is called.
c) False. A **JPanel** can be added to another **JPanel** because **JPanel** derives indirectly from **Component**. Therefore, a **JPanel** is a **Component**. Any **Component** can be added to a **Container**.
d) False. Only the last button added will be displayed. Remember that only one component can be added to each region in a **BorderLayout**.
e) True.

12.3 a) **new** is needed to instantiate the object.
b) JLabel is a class name and cannot be used as a variable name.

c) The arguments passed to the constructor are reversed. The **String** must be passed first.

d) **BorderLayout** has been set and components are being added without specifying the region. Proper **add** statements might be

```
container.add( button1, BorderLayout.NORTH );
container.add( button2, BorderLayout.SOUTH );
```

EXERCISES

12.4 Fill in the blanks in each of the following statements:

a) The **JTextField** class inherits directly from __________.

b) The layout managers discussed in this chapter are __________, __________ and __________.

c) **Container** method __________ attaches a GUI component to a container.

d) Method __________ is called when a mouse button is released (without moving the mouse).

e) The __________ class is used to create a group of **JRadioButton**s.

12.5 State whether each of the following is *true* or *false*. If *false*, explain why.

a) Only one layout manager can be used per **Container**.

b) GUI components can be added to a **Container** in any order in a **BorderLayout**.

c) **JRadioButton**s provide a series of mutually exclusive options (only one can be **true** at a time).

d) **Graphics** method **setFont** is used to set the font for text fields.

e) A **JList** displays a scrollbar if there are more items in the list than can be displayed.

f) A **Mouse** object contains a method called **mouseDragged**.

12.6 State whether each of the following is *true* or *false*. If *false*, explain why.

a) A **JApplet** does not have a content pane.

b) A **JPanel** is a **JComponent**.

c) A **JPanel** is a **Component**.

d) A **JLabel** is a **Container**.

e) A **JList** is a **JPanel**.

f) An **AbstractButton** is a **JButton**.

g) A **JTextField** is an **Object**.

h) **ButtonGroup** inherits from JComponent.

12.7 Find any error(s) in each of the following and explain how to correct it (them).

a) `import javax.swing.*        // include swing package`

b) `panelObject.GridLayout( 8, 8 ); // set GridLayout`

c)
```
container.setLayout(
    new FlowLayout( FlowLayout.DEFAULT ) );
```

d) `container.add( eastButton, EAST );   // BorderLayout`

12.8 Create the following GUI. You do not have to provide any functionality.

12.9 Create the following GUI. You do not have to provide any functionality.

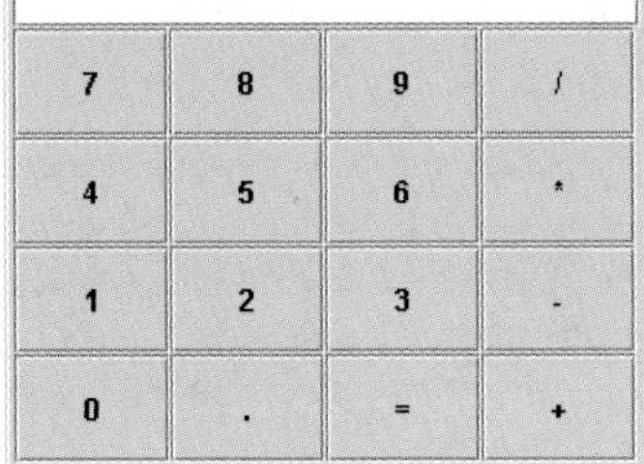

12.10 Create the following GUI. You do not have to provide any functionality.

12.11 Create the following GUI. You do not have to provide any functionality.

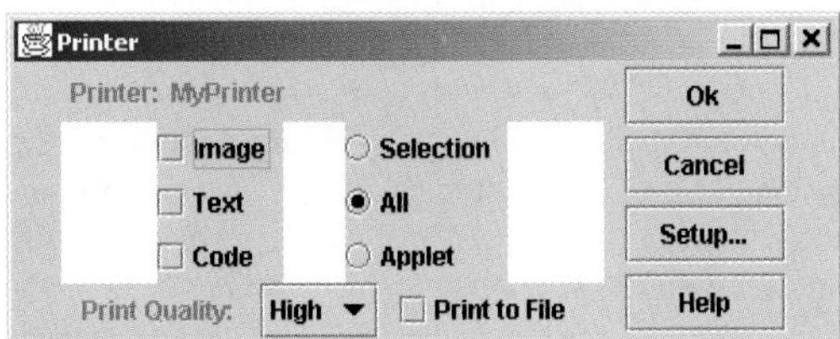

12.12 Write a temperature conversion program that converts from Fahrenheit to Celsius. The Fahrenheit temperature should be entered from the keyboard (via a **`JTextField`**). A **`JLabel`** should be used to display the converted temperature. Use the following formula for the conversion:

$$Celsius = 5 / 9 \times (Fahrenheit - 32)$$

12.13 Enhance the temperature conversion program of Exercise 12.12 by adding the Kelvin temperature scale. The program should also allow the user to make conversions between any two scales. Use the following formula for the conversion between Kelvin and Celsius (in addition to the formula in Exercise 12.12):

$$Kelvin = Celsius + 273$$

12.14 Write an application that allows the user to draw a rectangle by dragging the mouse on the application window. The upper-left coordinate should be the location where the user presses the mouse button, and the lower-right coordinate should be the location where the user releases the mouse button. Also display the area of the rectangle in a **`JLabel`** in the **`SOUTH`** region of a **`BorderLayout`**. Use the following formula for the area:

$$area = width \times height$$

12.15 Modify the program of Exercise 12.14 to draw different shapes. The user should be allowed to choose from an oval, an arc, a line, a rectangle with rounded corners and a predefined polygon. Also display the mouse coordinates in the status bar.

12.16 Write a program that will allow the user to draw a shape with the mouse. The shape to draw should be determined by a **KeyEvent** using the following keys: *c* draws a circle, *o* draws an oval, *r* draws a rectangle and *l* draws a line. The size and placement of the shape should be determined by the **mousePressed** and **mouseReleased** events. Display the name of the current shape in a **JLabel** in the **SOUTH** region of a **BorderLayout**. The initial shape should default to a circle.

12.17 Create an application that enables the user to paint a picture. The user should be able to choose the shape to draw, the color in which the shape should appear and whether the shape should be filled with color. Use the graphical user interface components we discussed in this chapter, such as **JComboBox**es, **JRadioButton**s and **JCheckBox**es, to allow the user to select various options. The program should provide a **JButton** object that allows the user to erase the window.

12.18 Write a program that uses **System.out.println** statements to print out events as they occur. Provide a **JComboBox** with a minimum of four items. The user should be able to choose an event to "monitor" from the **JComboBox**. When that particular event occurs, display information about the event in a message dialog box. Use method **toString** on the event object to convert it to a string representation.

12.19 Write a program that draws a square. As the mouse moves over the drawing area, repaint the square with the upper-left corner of the square following the exact path of the mouse cursor.

12.20 Modify the program of Fig. 12.19 to incorporate colors. In a separate window, provide a "toolbar" of **JRadioButton** objects that lists the following six colors: red, black, magenta, blue, green and yellow. The toolbar should be implemented as a subclass of **JFrame** called **ToolBarWindow** and should consist of six buttons, each with the appropriate color name. When a new color is selected, drawing should occur in the new color. Determine the currently selected color in the **mousePressed** event handler of the main window by calling a public method **getCurrentColor** on the **ToolBarWindow**. [Note: In Chapter 13, we discuss how to combine GUI components and drawing, using separate **JPanel**s for each. This provides programs with more flexibility in laying out the components and drawing.]

12.21 Write a program that plays "guess the number" as follows: Your program chooses the number to be guessed by selecting an integer at random in the range 1–1000. The program then displays in a label:

```
I have a number between 1 and 1000 can you guess my number?
Please enter your first guess.
```

A **JTextField** should be used to input the guess. As each guess is input the background color should change to either red or blue. Red indicates that the user is getting "warmer" and blue indicates that the user is getting "colder." A **JLabel** should display either "**Too High**" or "**Too Low**" to help the user zero in on the correct answer. When the user gets the correct answer, "**Correct!**" should be displayed and the **JTextField** used for input should be changed to uneditable. A **JButton** should be provided to allow the user to play the game again. When the **JButton** is clicked, a new random number should be generated and the input **JTextField** changed to editable.

12.22 It is often useful to display the events that occur during the execution of a program to help understand when the events occur and how they are generated. Write a program that enables the user to generate and process every event discussed in this chapter. The program should provide methods from the **ActionListener**, **ItemListener**, **ListSelectionListener**, **MouseListener**, **MouseMotionListener** and **KeyListener** interfaces to display messages when the events occur. Use method **toString** to convert the event objects received in each event handler into a **String** that can be displayed. Method **toString** creates a **String** containing all the information in the event object.

12.23 Modify your solution to Exercise 12.17 to enable the user to select a font and a font size, then type text into a **JTextField**. When the user presses *Enter*, the text should be displayed on the background in the chosen font and size. Modify the program further to allow the user to specify the exact position at which the text should be displayed.

12.24 Write a program that allows the user to select a shape from a **JComboBox**, then draws that shape 20 times with random locations and dimensions in method **paint**. The first item in the **JComboBox** should be the default shape that is displayed the first time **paint** is called.

12.25 Modify Exercise 12.24 to draw each of the 20 randomly sized shapes in a randomly selected color. Use all 13 predefined **Color** objects in an array of **Color**s.

12.26 Modify Exercise 12.25 to allow the user to select the color in which shapes should be drawn from a **JColorChooser** dialog.

12.27 Write a program using methods from interface **MouseListener** that allows the user to press the mouse button, drag the mouse and release the mouse button. When the mouse is released, draw a rectangle with the appropriate upper-left corner, width and height. (*Hint*: The **mousePressed** method should capture the set of coordinates at which the user presses and holds the mouse button initially, and the **mouseReleased** method should capture the set of coordinates at which the user releases the mouse button. Both methods should store the appropriate coordinate values. All calculations of the width, height and upper-left corner should be performed by the **paint** method before the shape is drawn.)

12.28 Modify Exercise 12.27 to provided a "rubber-banding" effect. As the user drags the mouse, the user should be able to see the current size of the rectangle to know exactly what the rectangle will look like when the mouse button is released. (*Hint*: Method **mouseDragged** should perform the same tasks as **mouseReleased**.)

12.29 Modify Exercise 12.28 to allow the user to select which shape to draw. A **JComboBox** should provide options including at least rectangle, oval, line and rounded rectangle.

12.30 Modify Exercise 12.29 to allow the user to select the drawing color from a **JColorChooser** dialog box.

12.31 Modify Exercise 12.30 to allow the user to specify whether a shape should be filled or empty when it is drawn. The user should click a **JCheckBox** to indicate filled or empty.

12.32 *(Painting program)* Using the techniques of Exercise 9.28–Exercise 9.29 and Exercise 12.27–Exercise 12.30 and the graphics techniques of Chapter 11, rewrite Exercise 12.31 to allow the user to draw multiple shapes and store each shape in an array of shapes. (If you feel ambitious, investigate the capabilities of class **Vector** in Chapter 20.) For this program, create your own classes (like those in the class hierarchy described in Exercise 9.28–Exercise 9.29) from which objects will be created to store each shape the user draws. The classes should store the location, dimensions and color of each shape and should indicate whether the shape is filled or unfilled. Your classes should all derive from a class called **MyShape** that has all the common features of every shape type. Every subclass of **MyShape** should have its own method **draw**, which returns **void** and receives a **Graphics** object as its argument. When the application window's **paint** method is called, it should walk through the array of shapes and display each shape by polymorphically calling the shape's **draw** method (passing the **Graphics** object as an argument). Each shape's **draw** method should know how to draw the shape. As a minimum, your program should provide the following classes: **MyLine**, **MyOval**, **MyRect**, **MyRoundRect**. Design the class hierarchy for maximum software reuse, and place all your classes in the package **shapes**. Import this package into your program.

12.33 Modify Exercise 12.32 to provide an **Undo** button that can be used repeatedly to undo the last painting operation. If there are no shapes in the array of shapes, the Undo button should be disabled.

13

Graphical User Interface Components: Part 2

Objectives

- To create and manipulate text areas, sliders, menus, popup menus and windows.
- To be able to create customized **JPanel** objects.
- To be able to create a program that can execute as either an applet or an application.
- To be able to change the look-and-feel of a GUI, using Swing's pluggable look-and-feel (PLAF).
- To be able to create a multiple document interface with **JDesktopPane** and **JInternalFrame**.
- To be able to use advanced layout managers.

I claim not to have controlled events, but confess plainly that events have controlled me.
Abraham Lincoln

A good symbol is the best argument, and is a missionary to persuade thousands.
Ralph Waldo Emerson

Capture its reality in paint!
Paul Cézanne

Outline

13.1 Introduction
13.2 `JTextArea`
13.3 Creating a Customized Subclass of `JPanel`
13.4 Creating a Self-Contained Subclass of `JPanel`
13.5 `JSlider`
13.6 Windows
13.7 Designing Programs that Execute as Applets or Applications
13.8 Using Menus with Frames
13.9 Using `JPopupMenus`
13.10 Pluggable Look-and-Feel
13.11 Using `JDesktopPane` and `JInternalFrame`
13.12 Layout Managers
13.13 `BoxLayout` Layout Manager
13.14 `CardLayout` Layout Manager
13.15 `GridBagLayout` Layout Manager
13.16 `GridBagConstraints` Constants `RELATIVE` and `REMAINDER`
13.17 (Optional Case Study) Thinking About Objects: Model-View-Controller
13.18 (Optional) Discovering Design Patterns: Design Patterns Used in Packages `java.awt` and `javax.swing`
13.18.1 Creational Design Patterns
13.18.2 Structural Design Patterns
13.18.3 Behavioral Design Patterns
13.18.4 Conclusion

Summary • Terminology • Self-Review Exercises • Answers to Self-Review Exercises • Exercises

13.1 Introduction

In this chapter, we continue our study of GUIs. We discuss more advanced components and layout managers and lay the groundwork for building complex GUIs.

We begin our discussion with another text-based GUI component—***JTextArea***—which allows multiple lines of text to be displayed or input. We continue with two examples of *customizing class* ***JPanel*** in which we discuss issues that relate to painting on Swing GUI components. Next, we illustrate how to design a Java program that can execute as both an applet and an application. An important aspect of any complete GUI is a system of *menus* that enable the user to effectively perform tasks in the program. The next two examples discuss how to create and use menus. The look-and-feel of a Swing GUI can be uniform across all platforms on which the Java program is executed, or the GUI can be customized by using Swing's *pluggable look-and-feel (PLAF).* The next example illustrates how to change between Swing's default *metal look-and-feel,* a look-and-feel that simulates *Motif* (a popular UNIX look-and-feel) and one that simulates Microsoft's Windows look-and-feel. Many of today's applications use a *multiple document interface (MDI),* [i.e., a main window (often called the *parent window*) containing other windows (often called *child windows*) to manage several open *documents* in parallel. For example, many e-mail programs allow you to have several e-mail windows open at the same time so you can compose and/or read multiple e-mail messages. The next example discusses Swing's classes that provide support for creating multiple document interfaces. Finally, the chapter finishes with a series of examples discussing several advanced layout managers for organizing graphical user interfaces.

Swing is a large and complex topic. There are many more GUI components and capabilities than can be presented here. Several more Swing GUI components are introduced in the remaining chapters of this book as they are needed. Our book *Advanced Java 2 Platform How to Program* discusses other, more advanced Swing components and capabilities.

13.2 JTextArea

JTextArea**s* provide an area for manipulating multiple lines of text. Like class **JTextField**, class **JTextArea** inherits from ***JTextComponent, which defines common methods for **JTextField**s, **JTextArea**s and several other text-based GUI components.

The application of Fig. 13.1 demonstrates **JTextArea**s. One **JTextArea** displays text that the user can select. The other **JTextArea** is uneditable. Its purpose is to display the text the user selected in the first **JTextArea**. **JTextArea**s do not have action events like **JTextField**s. Often, an *external event*—an event generated by a different GUI component—indicates when to process the text in a **JTextArea**. For example, when typing an e-mail message, you often click a **Send** button to take the text of the message and send it to the recipient. Similarly, when editing a document in a word processor, you normally save the file by selecting a menu item called **Save** or **Save As...**. In this program, the button **Copy >>>** generates the external event that copies the selected text in the left **JTextArea** and displays it in the right **JTextArea**.

```
// Fig. 13.1: TextAreaDemo.java
// Copying selected text from one text area to another.

// Java core packages
import java.awt.*;
import java.awt.event.*;

// Java extension packages
import javax.swing.*;

public class TextAreaDemo extends JFrame {
   private JTextArea textArea1, textArea2;
   private JButton copyButton;

```

Fig. 13.1 Copying selected text from one text area to another (part 1 of 3).

```
   // set up GUI
   public TextAreaDemo()
   {
      super( "TextArea Demo" );

      Box box = Box.createHorizontalBox();

      String string = "This is a demo string to\n" +
         "illustrate copying text\n" +
         "from one TextArea to \n" +
         "another TextArea using an\n" + "external event\n";

      // set up textArea1
      textArea1 = new JTextArea( string, 10, 15 );
      box.add( new JScrollPane( textArea1 ) );

      // set up copyButton
      copyButton = new JButton( "Copy >>>" );
      copyButton.addActionListener(

         // anonymous inner class to handle copyButton event
         new ActionListener() {

            // set text in textArea2 to selected
            // text from textArea1
            public void actionPerformed( ActionEvent event )
            {
               textArea2.setText( textArea1.getSelectedText() );
            }

         }  // end anonymous inner class

      ); // end call to addActionListener

      box.add( copyButton );

      // set up textArea2
      textArea2 = new JTextArea( 10, 15 );
      textArea2.setEditable( false );
      box.add( new JScrollPane( textArea2 ) );

      // add box to content pane
      Container container = getContentPane();
      container.add( box );   // place in BorderLayout.CENTER

      setSize( 425, 200 );
      setVisible( true );
   }

   // execute application
   public static void main( String args[] )
   {
      TextAreaDemo application = new TextAreaDemo();
```

Fig. 13.1 Copying selected text from one text area to another (part 2 of 3).

```
68
69          application.setDefaultCloseOperation(
70             JFrame.EXIT_ON_CLOSE );
71       }
72
73    }  // end class TextAreaDemo
```

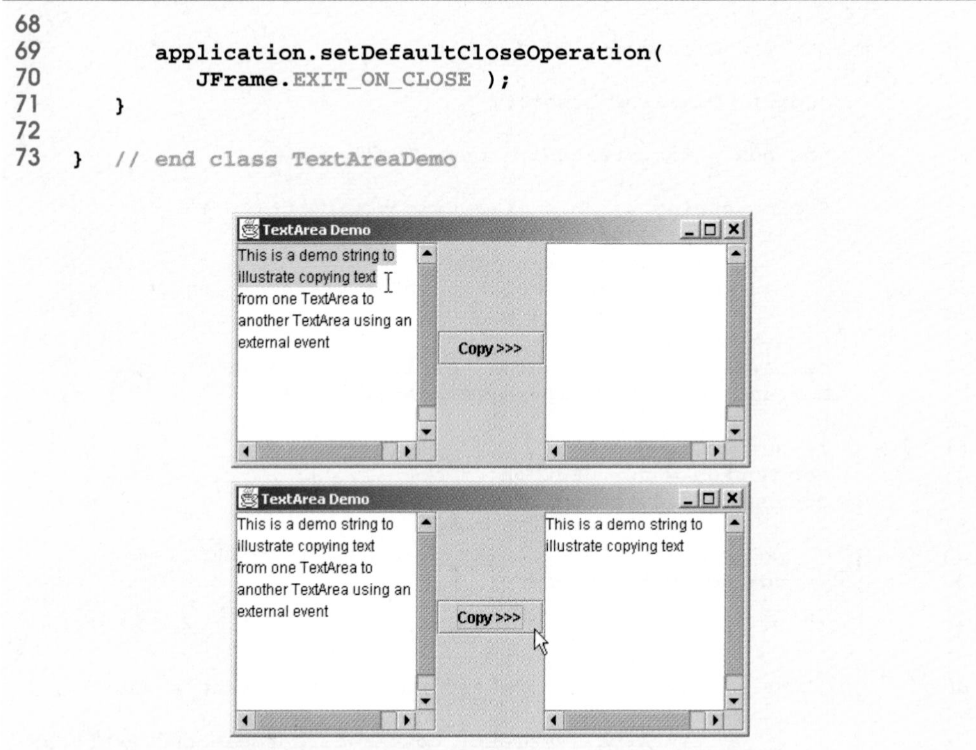

Fig. 13.1 Copying selected text from one text area to another (part 3 of 3).

Look-and-Feel Observation 13.1

Often an external event determines when the text in a **JTextArea** *should be processed.*

In the constructor method (lines 16–62), line 20 creates a ***Box*** *container* (package **javax.swing**) for organizing the GUI components. Class **Box** is a subclass of **Container** that uses a ***BoxLayout*** layout manager to arrange the GUI components either horizontally or vertically. Section 13.13 discusses **BoxLayout** in detail. Class **Box** provides static method ***createHorizontalBox*** to create a **Box** that arranges components from left to right in the order that the components are attached.

The application instantiates **JTextArea** objects **textArea1** (line 28) and **textArea2** (line 52). Each **JTextArea** has **10** visible rows and **15** visible columns. Line 28 specifies that **string** should be displayed as the default **JTextArea** content. A **JTextArea** does not provide scrollbars if it cannot display its complete contents. For this reason, line 29 creates a **JScrollPane** object, initializes it with **textArea1** and attaches it to container **box**. By default, horizontal and vertical scrollbars will appear as necessary.

Lines 32–49 instantiate **JButton** object **copyButton** with the label "**Copy >>>**," create an anonymous inner class to handle **copyButton**'s **ActionEvent** and add **copyButton** to container **box**. This button provides the external event that determines when the program should copy the selected text in **textArea1** to **textArea2**. When the user clicks **copyButton**, line 42 in **actionPerformed** indicates that method

getSelectedText (inherited into **JTextArea** from **JTextComponent**) should return the *selected text* from **textArea1**. The user selects text by dragging the mouse over the desired text to highlight it. Method **setText** changes the text in **textArea2** to the **String** that method **getSelectedText** returns.

Lines 52–54 create **textArea2** and add it to container **box**. Lines 57–58 obtain the content pane for the window and add **box** to the content pane. Remember that the default layout of the content pane is a **BorderLayout** and that the add method attaches its argument to the **CENTER** of the **BorderLayout** if method **add** does not specify the region.

It is sometimes desirable when text reaches the right side of a **JTextArea** to have the text wrap to the next line. This is referred to as *automatic word wrap*.

Look-and-Feel Observation 13.2

*To provide automatic word wrap functionality for a **JTextArea**, invoke **JTextArea** method **setLineWrap** with a **true** argument.*

This example uses a **JScrollPane** to provide scrolling functionality for a **JTextArea**. By default, **JScrollPane** provides scrollbars only if they are required. You can set the horizontal and vertical *scrollbar policies* for the **JScrollPane** when a **JScrollPane** is constructed or with methods ***setHorizontalScrollBarPolicy*** and ***setVerticalScrollBarPolicy*** of class **JScrollPane** at any time. Class **JScrollPane** provides the constants

```
JScrollPane.VERTICAL_SCROLLBAR_ALWAYS
JScrollPane.HORIZONTAL_SCROLLBAR_ALWAYS
```

to indicate that a scrollbar should always appear, constants

```
JScrollPane.VERTICAL_SCROLLBAR_AS_NEEDED
JScrollPane.HORIZONTAL_SCROLLBAR_AS_NEEDED
```

to indicate that a scrollbar should appear only if necessary, and constants

```
JScrollPane.VERTICAL_SCROLLBAR_NEVER
JScrollPane.HORIZONTAL_SCROLLBAR_NEVER
```

to indicate that a scrollbar should never appear. If the horizontal scrollbar policy is set to **JScrollPane.HORIZONTAL_SCROLLBAR_NEVER**, a **JTextArea** attached to the **JScrollPane** will exhibit automatic word wrap behavior.

13.3 Creating a Customized Subclass of JPanel

In Chapter 12, we saw that **JPanel**s can aggregate a set of GUI components for layout purposes. **JPanel**s are quite flexible. Some of their many uses include creating *dedicated drawing areas* and creating areas that receive mouse events. Programs often extend class **JPanel** to create new components. Our next example uses a **JPanel** to create a dedicated drawing area. Dedicated drawing areas help separate drawing from the rest of your graphical user interface. This can be beneficial in Swing graphical user interfaces. If graphics and Swing GUI components are not displayed in the correct order, it is possible that the GUI components will not display correctly. For example, to ensure that graphics and GUI both display correctly, we can separate the GUI and the graphics by creating dedicated drawing areas as subclasses of **JPanel**.

Look-and-Feel Observation 13.3

Combining graphics and Swing GUI components can lead to incorrect display of the graphics, the GUI components or both. Using **JPanel***s for drawing can eliminate this problem by providing a dedicated area for graphics.*

Swing components that inherit from class **JComponent** contain method ***paintComponent*** that helps them draw properly in the context of a Swing GUI. When customizing a **JPanel** for use as a dedicated drawing area, the subclass should override method **paintComponent** and call the superclass version of **paintComponent** as the first statement in the body of the overridden method. This ensures that painting occurs in the proper order and that Swing's painting mechanism remains intact. An important part of this mechanism is that subclasses of **JComponent** support *transparency*, which can be set with method ***setOpaque*** (a **false** argument indicates the component is transparent). To paint a component correctly, the program must determine whether the component is transparent. The code that performs this check is in the superclass version of **paintComponent**. When a component is transparent, **paintComponent** will not clear the component's background when the program paints the component. When a component is *opaque*, **paintComponent** clears the background before continuing the painting operation. If the superclass version of **paintComponent** is not called, an opaque GUI component typically will not display correctly on the user interface. Also, if the superclass version is called after performing the customized drawing statements, the results typically will be erased.

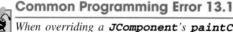

Look-and-Feel Observation 13.4

When overriding a **JComponent***'s* **paintComponent** *method, the first statement in the body should always be a call to the superclass's original version of the method.*

Common Programming Error 13.1

When overriding a **JComponent***'s* **paintComponent** *method, not calling the superclass's original version of* **paintComponent** *might prevent the GUI component from displaying properly on the GUI.*

Common Programming Error 13.2

When overriding a **JComponent***'s* **paintComponent** *method, calling the superclass's* **paintComponent** *method after other drawing is performed erases the other drawings.*

Classes **JFrame** and **JApplet** are not subclasses of **JComponent**; therefore, they do not contain method **paintComponent**. To draw directly on subclasses of **JFrame** and **JApplet**, override method **paint**.

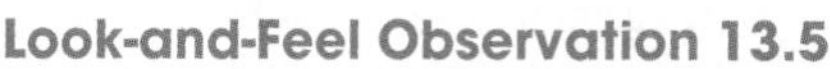

Look-and-Feel Observation 13.5

Calling **repaint** *for a Swing GUI component indicates that the component should be painted as soon as possible. The background of the GUI component is cleared only if the component is opaque. Most Swing components are transparent by default.* **JComponent** *method* **setOpaque** *can be passed a* **boolean** *argument indicating whether the component is opaque (***true***) or transparent (***false***). The GUI components of package* **java.awt** *are different from Swing components, in that* **repaint** *results in a call to* **Component** *method* **update** *(which clears the component's background) and* **update** *calls method* **paint** *(rather than* **paintComponent***).*

The program of Fig. 13.2 and Fig. 13.3 demonstrates a customized subclass of **JPanel**. Class **CustomPanel** (Fig. 13.2) has its own **paintComponent** method that draws a circle or a square, depending on the value passed to **CustomPanel**'s **draw** method. For this purpose, **CustomPanel** line 11 defines constants that enable the program to specify the shape a **CustomPanel** draws on itself with each call to its **paintComponent** method. Class **CustomPanelTest** (Fig. 13.3) creates a **CustomPanel** and a GUI that enable the user to choose which shape to draw.

Class **CustomPanel** contains one instance variable, **shape**, that stores an integer representing the shape to draw. Method **paintComponent** (lines 15–23) draws a shape on the panel. If **shape** is **CIRCLE**, **Graphics** method **fillOval** draws a solid circle. If **shape** is **SQUARE**, **Graphics** method **fillRect** draws a solid square. Method **draw** (lines 26–30) sets instance variable **shape** and calls **repaint** to refresh the **CustomPanel** object. Note that calling **repaint** (which is really **this.repaint()**) for the **CustomPanel** schedules a painting operation for the **CustomPanel**. Method **paintComponent** will be called to repaint the **CustomPanel** and draw the appropriate shape.

```
1  // Fig. 13.2: CustomPanel.java
2  // A customized JPanel class.
3
4  // Java core packages
5  import java.awt.*;
6
7  // Java extension packages
8  import javax.swing.*;
9
10 public class CustomPanel extends JPanel {
11    public final static int CIRCLE = 1, SQUARE = 2;
12    private int shape;
13
14    // use shape to draw an oval or rectangle
15    public void paintComponent( Graphics g )
16    {
17       super.paintComponent( g );
18
19       if ( shape == CIRCLE )
20          g.fillOval( 50, 10, 60, 60 );
21       else if ( shape == SQUARE )
22          g.fillRect( 50, 10, 60, 60 );
23    }
24
25    // set shape value and repaint CustomPanel
26    public void draw( int shapeToDraw )
27    {
28       shape = shapeToDraw;
29       repaint();
30    }
31
32 }  // end class CustomPanel
```

Fig. 13.2 Defining a custom drawing area by subclassing **JPanel**.

Class **CustomPanelTest** (Fig. 13.3) instantiates a **CustomPanel** object (line 22 of its constructor) and sets its background color to green, so the **CustomPanel** area is visible on the application. Next, the constructor instantiates **JButton** objects **squareButton** and **circleButton**. Lines 27–40 register an event handler for **squareButton**'s **ActionEvent**. Lines 43–56 register an event handler for **circleButton**'s **ActionEvent**. Lines 35 and 51 each call **CustomPanel** method **draw**. In each case, the appropriate constant (**CustomPanel.SQUARE** or **CustomPanel.CIRCLE**) is passed as an argument to indicate which shape to draw.

```
1  // Fig. 13.3: CustomPanelTest.java
2  // Using a customized Panel object.
3
4  // Java core packages
5  import java.awt.*;
6  import java.awt.event.*;
7
8  // Java extension packages
9  import javax.swing.*;
10
11 public class CustomPanelTest extends JFrame {
12    private JPanel buttonPanel;
13    private CustomPanel myPanel;
14    private JButton circleButton, squareButton;
15
16    // set up GUI
17    public CustomPanelTest()
18    {
19       super( "CustomPanel Test" );
20
21       // create custom drawing area
22       myPanel = new CustomPanel();
23       myPanel.setBackground( Color.green );
24
25       // set up squareButton
26       squareButton = new JButton( "Square" );
27       squareButton.addActionListener(
28
29          // anonymous inner class to handle squareButton events
30          new ActionListener() {
31
32             // draw a square
33             public void actionPerformed( ActionEvent event )
34             {
35                myPanel.draw( CustomPanel.SQUARE );
36             }
37
38          }  // end anonymous inner class
39
40       ); // end call to addActionListener
41
42       circleButton = new JButton( "Circle" );
```

Fig. 13.3 Drawing on a customized subclass of class **JPanel** (part 1 of 2).

```
43          circleButton.addActionListener(
44
45             // anonymous inner class to handle circleButton events
46             new ActionListener() {
47
48                // draw a circle
49                public void actionPerformed( ActionEvent event )
50                {
51                   myPanel.draw( CustomPanel.CIRCLE );
52                }
53
54             }  // end anonymous inner class
55
56          ); // end call to addActionListener
57
58          // set up panel containing buttons
59          buttonPanel = new JPanel();
60          buttonPanel.setLayout( new GridLayout( 1, 2 ) );
61          buttonPanel.add( circleButton );
62          buttonPanel.add( squareButton );
63
64          // attach button panel & custom drawing area to content pane
65          Container container = getContentPane();
66          container.add( myPanel, BorderLayout.CENTER );
67          container.add( buttonPanel, BorderLayout.SOUTH );
68
69          setSize( 300, 150 );
70          setVisible( true );
71       }
72
73       // execute application
74       public static void main( String args[] )
75       {
76          CustomPanelTest application = new CustomPanelTest();
77
78          application.setDefaultCloseOperation(
79             JFrame.EXIT_ON_CLOSE );
80       }
81
82    }  // end class CustomPanelTest
```

Fig. 13.3 Drawing on a customized subclass of class **JPanel** (part 2 of 2).

For layout of the buttons, **CustomPanelTest** creates **JPanel buttonPanel** with a **GridLayout** of one row and two columns (lines 59–60), then attaches the buttons to the panel (lines 61–62). Finally, **CustomPanelTest** adds **myPanel** to the **CENTER** region of the content pane and adds **buttonPanel** to the **SOUTH** region of the content pane. Note that the **BorderLayout** expands **myPanel** to fill the center region.

13.4 Creating a Self-Contained Subclass of JPanel

JPanels do not support conventional events supported by other GUI components, like buttons, text fields and windows. However, **JPanel**s are capable of recognizing such lower-level events as mouse events and key events. The program of Fig. 13.4 and Fig. 13.5 allows the user to draw an oval on a subclass of **JPanel** by dragging the mouse across the panel. Class **SelfContainedPanel** (Fig. 13.4) listens for its own mouse events and draws an oval on itself in response to those mouse events. The location and size of the oval are determined from the coordinates of the mouse events. The coordinates at which the user presses the mouse button specify the starting point for the oval's bounding box. As the user drags the mouse, the coordinates of the mouse pointer specify another point. Together, the program uses these points to calculate the upper-left *x-y* coordinate, the width and the height of the oval's bounding box. The size of the oval changes continuously while the user drags the mouse. When the user releases the mouse button, the program calculates the final bounding box for the oval and draws the oval. Line 4 of Fig. 13.4 indicates that class **SelfContainedPanel** is in package **com.deitel.jhtp4.ch13** for future reuse. Class **SelfContainedPanelTest** imports **SelfContainedPanel** at line 13 of Fig. 13.5.

```
1   // Fig. 13.4: SelfContainedPanel.java
2   // A self-contained JPanel class that
3   // handles its own mouse events.
4   package com.deitel.jhtp4.ch13;
5
6   // Java core packages
7   import java.awt.*;
8   import java.awt.event.*;
9
10  // Java extension packages
11  import javax.swing.*;
12
13  public class SelfContainedPanel extends JPanel {
14     private int x1, y1, x2, y2;
15
16     // set up mouse event handling for SelfContainedPanel
17     public SelfContainedPanel()
18     {
19        // set up mouse listener
20        addMouseListener(
21
22           // anonymous inner class for mouse pressed and
23           // released event handling
24           new MouseAdapter() {
25
26              // handle mouse press event
27              public void mousePressed( MouseEvent event )
28              {
29                 x1 = event.getX();
```

Fig. 13.4 Customized subclass of **JPanel** that processes mouse events (part 1 of 2).

```
               y1 = event.getY();
            }

            // handle mouse release event
            public void mouseReleased( MouseEvent event )
            {
               x2 = event.getX();
               y2 = event.getY();
               repaint();
            }

         } // end anonymous inner class

      ); // end call to addMouseListener

      // set up mouse motion listener
      addMouseMotionListener(

         // anonymous inner class to handle mouse drag events
         new MouseMotionAdapter() {

            // handle mouse drag event
            public void mouseDragged( MouseEvent event )
            {
               x2 = event.getX();
               y2 = event.getY();
               repaint();
            }

         }  // end anonymous inner class

      ); // end call to addMouseMotionListener

   }  // end constructor

   // return preferred width and height of SelfContainedPanel
   public Dimension getPreferredSize()
   {
      return new Dimension( 150, 100 );
   }

   // paint an oval at the specified coordinates
   public void paintComponent( Graphics g )
   {
      super.paintComponent( g );

      g.drawOval( Math.min( x1, x2 ), Math.min( y1, y2 ),
         Math.abs( x1 - x2 ), Math.abs( y1 - y2 ) );
   }

}  // end class SelfContainedPanel
```

Fig. 13.4 Customized subclass of **JPanel** that processes mouse events (part 2 of 2).

Class **SelfContainedPanel** (Fig. 13.4) extends class **JPanel**. Instance variables **x1** and **y1** store the initial coordinates where the **mousePressed** event occurs on the **SelfContainedPanel**. Instance variables **x2** and **y2** store the coordinates where the user drags the mouse or releases the mouse button. All the coordinates are with respect to the upper-left corner of the **SelfContainedPanel**.

Look-and-Feel Observation 13.6

Drawing on any GUI component is performed with coordinates that are measured from the upper-left corner (0, 0) of that GUI component.

The **SelfContainedPanel** constructor (lines 17–63) uses methods **addMouseListener** and **addMouseMotionListener** to register anonymous inner-class objects to handle mouse events and mouse motion events for the **SelfContainedPanel**. Only **mousePressed** (lines 27–31), **mouseReleased** (lines 34–39) and **mouseDragged** (lines 52–57) are overridden to perform tasks. The other mouse event-handling methods are inherited by the anonymous inner classes from the adapter classes **MouseAdapter** and **MouseMotionAdapter**.

By extending class **JPanel**, we are actually creating a new GUI component. Layout managers often use a GUI component's ***getPreferredSize*** method (inherited from class **java.awt.Component**) to determine the preferred width and height of a component when laying out that component as part of a GUI. If a new component has a preferred width and height, it should override method **getPreferredSize** (lines 66–69) to return that width and height as an object of class ***Dimension*** (package **java.awt**).

Look-and-Feel Observation 13.7

*The default size of a **JPanel** object is 10 pixels wide and 10 pixels tall.*

Look-and-Feel Observation 13.8

*When subclassing **JPanel** (or any other **JComponent**), override method **getPreferredSize** if the new component should have a specific preferred width and height.*

Method **paintComponent** (lines 72–78) draws an oval, using the current values of instance variables **x1**, **y1**, **x2** and **y2**. The width, height and upper-left corner are determined by the pressing and holding of the mouse button, the dragging of the mouse and releasingof the mouse button on the **SelfContainedPanel** drawing area.

The initial coordinates **x1** and **y1** on the **SelfContainedPanel** drawing area are captured in method **mousePressed** (lines 27–31). As the user drags the mouse after the initial **mousePressed** operation, the program generates a series of calls to **mouseDragged** (lines 52–57) while the user continues to hold the mouse button and move the mouse. Each call captures in variables **x2** and **y2** the current location of the mouse with respect to the upper-left corner of the **SelfContainedPanel** and calls **repaint** to draw the current version of the oval. Drawing is strictly confined to the **SelfContainedPanel**, even if the user drags outside the **SelfContainedPanel** drawing area. Anything drawn off the **SelfContainedPanel** is *clipped*—pixels are not displayed outside the bounds of the **SelfContainedPanel**.

The calculations provided in method **paintComponent** determine the proper upper-left corner, using method **Math.min** twice to find the smaller *x* coordinate and *y* coordinate. The oval's width and height must be positive values or the oval is not displayed.

Method **Math.abs** gets the absolute value of the subtractions **x1 - x2** and **y1 - y2** that determine the width and height of the oval's bounding rectangle, respectively. When the calculations are complete, **paintComponent** draws the oval. The call to the superclass version of **paintComponent** at the beginning of the method guarantees that the previous oval displayed on the **SelfContainedPanel** is erased before the new one is displayed.

Look-and-Feel Observation 13.9

Most Swing GUI components can be transparent or opaque. If a Swing GUI component is opaque, when its **paintComponent** *method is called, its background will be cleared. Otherwise, its background will not be cleared. Only opaque components can display a customized background color.*

Look-and-Feel Observation 13.10

JPanel *objects are opaque by default.*

When the user releases the mouse button, method **mouseReleased** (lines 34–39) captures in variables **x2** and **y2** the final location of the mouse and invokes **repaint** to draw the final version of the oval.

Class **SelfContainedPanelTest**'s constructor (lines 21–57 of Fig. 13.5) creates an instance of class **SelfContainedPanel** (line 24) and sets the background color (line 25) of the **SelfContainedPanel** to yellow so that its area is visible against the background of the application window.

```
1  // Fig. 13.5: SelfContainedPanelTest.java
2  // Creating a self-contained subclass of JPanel
3  // that processes its own mouse events.
4
5  // Java core packages
6  import java.awt.*;
7  import java.awt.event.*;
8
9  // Java extension packages
10 import javax.swing.*;
11
12 // Deitel packages
13 import com.deitel.jhtp4.ch13.SelfContainedPanel;
14
15 public class SelfContainedPanelTest extends JFrame {
16    private SelfContainedPanel myPanel;
17
18
19    // set up GUI and mouse motion event handlers for
20    // application window
21    public SelfContainedPanelTest()
22    {
23       // set up a SelfContainedPanel
24       myPanel = new SelfContainedPanel();
25       myPanel.setBackground( Color.yellow );
26
27       Container container = getContentPane();
```

Fig. 13.5 Capturing mouse events with a **JPanel** (part 1 of 3).

```
      container.setLayout( new FlowLayout() );
      container.add( myPanel );

      // set up mouse motion event handling
      addMouseMotionListener(

         // anonymous inner class for mouse motion event handling
         new MouseMotionListener() {

            // handle mouse drag event
            public void mouseDragged( MouseEvent event )
            {
               setTitle( "Dragging: x=" + event.getX() +
                  "; y=" + event.getY() );
            }

            // handle mouse move event
            public void mouseMoved( MouseEvent event )
            {
               setTitle( "Moving: x=" + event.getX() +
                  "; y=" + event.getY() );
            }

         }  // end anonymous inner class

      ); // end call to addMouseMotionListener

      setSize( 300, 200 );
      setVisible( true );
   }

   // execute application
   public static void main( String args[] )
   {
      SelfContainedPanelTest application =
         new SelfContainedPanelTest();

      application.setDefaultCloseOperation(
         JFrame.EXIT_ON_CLOSE );
   }

}  // end class SelfContainedPanelTest
```

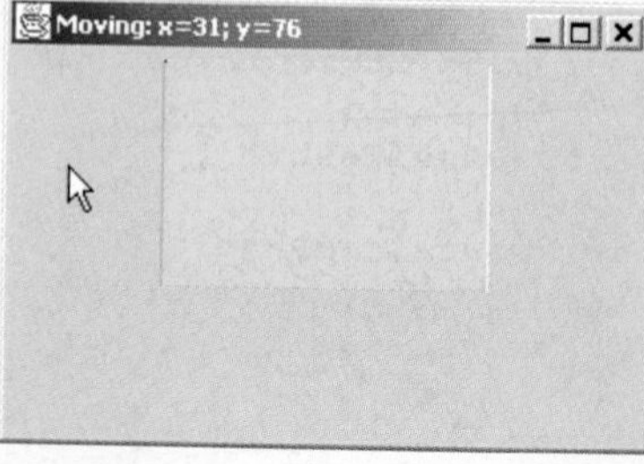

Fig. 13.5 Capturing mouse events with a **JPanel** (part 2 of 3).

Fig. 13.5 Capturing mouse events with a **JPanel** (part 3 of 3).

We would like this program to distinguish between mouse motion events on the **SelfContainedPanel** and mouse motion events on the application window, so lines 32–53 register an object of an anonymous inner class to handle the application's mouse motion events. Event handlers **mouseDragged** (lines 38–42) and **mouseMoved** (lines 45–49) use method **setTitle** (inherited from class **java.awt.Frame**) to display a **String** in the window's title bar indicating the *x-y* coordinate where the mouse motion event occurred.

When executing this program, try dragging from the background of the application window into the **SelfContainedPanel** area to see that the drag events are sent to the application window rather than the **SelfContainedPanel**. Then, start a new drag operation in the **SelfContainedPanel** area and drag out to the background of the application window to see that the drag events are sent to the **SelfContainedPanel** rather than to the application window.

Look-and-Feel Observation 13.11

A mouse drag operation begins with a mouse-pressed event. All subsequent mouse drag events (until the user releases the mouse button) are sent to the GUI component that received the original mouse-pressed event.

13.5 JSlider

JSlider*s** enable the user to select from a range of integer values. Class ***JSlider inherits from **JComponent**. Figure 13.6 shows a horizontal **JSlider** with *tick marks* and the *thumb* that allows the user to select a value. **JSlider**s are highly customizable in that they can display *major tick marks*, *minor tick marks* and labels for the tick marks. They also support *snap-to ticks* where positioning the thumb between two tick marks causes the thumb to *snap* to the closest tick mark.

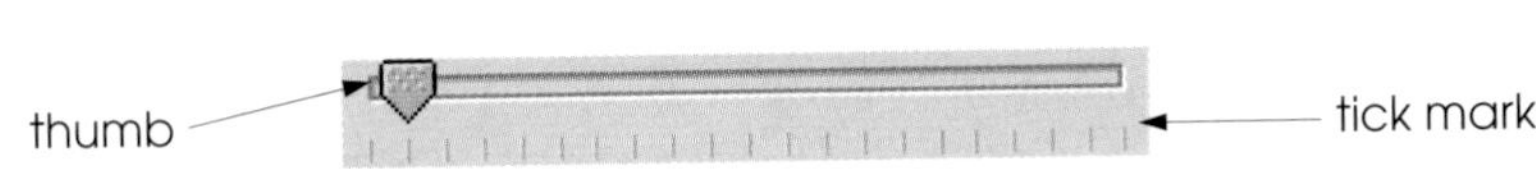

Fig. 13.6 Horizontal **JSlider** component.

Most Swing GUI components support user interactions through the mouse and the keyboard. For example, if a **JSlider** has the *focus* (i.e., it is the currently selected GUI component in the user interface), the *left arrow key* and *right arrow key* cause the thumb of the **JSlider** to decrease or increase by 1, respectively. The *down arrow key* and *up arrow key* also cause the thumb of the **JSlider** to decrease or increase by 1, respectively. The *PgDn key* (page down) and *PgUp key* (page up) cause the thumb of the **JSlider** to decrease or increase by *block increments* of one-tenth of the range of values, respectively. The *Home key* moves the thumb to the minimum value of the **JSlider** and the *End key* moves the thumb to the maximum value of the **JSlider**.

Look-and-Feel Observation 13.12

Most Swing components support user interactions through the mouse and the keyboard.

JSliders have either a *horizontal orientation* or a *vertical orientation*. For a horizontal **JSlider**, the minimum value is at the extreme left and the maximum value is at the extreme right of the **JSlider**. For a vertical **JSlider**, the minimum value is at the extreme bottom and the maximum value is at the extreme top of the **JSlider**. The relative position of the thumb indicates the current value of the **JSlider**.

Look-and-Feel Observation 13.13

The minimum and maximum value positions on a **JSlider** *can be switched by calling the* **JSlider** *method* **setInverted** *with boolean argument* **true**.

The program of Fig. 13.7 and Fig. 13.8 allows the user to size a circle drawn on a subclass of **JPanel** called **OvalPanel** (Fig. 13.7). The user specifies the diameter of the circle with a horizontal **JSlider**. Application class **SliderDemo** (Fig. 13.8) creates the **JSlider** that controls the diameter of the circle. Class **OvalPanel** is a subclass of **JPanel** that knows how to draw a circle on itself, using its own instance variable **diameter** to determine the diameter of the circle—the **diameter** is used as the width and height of the bounding box in which the circle is displayed. The **diameter** value is set when the user interacts with the **JSlider**. The event handler calls method **setDiameter** in class **OvalPanel** to set the **diameter** and calls **repaint** to draw the new circle. The **repaint** call results in a call to **OvalPanel**'s **paintComponent** method.

Class **OvalPanel** (Fig. 13.7) contains a **paintComponent** method (lines 14–19) that draws a filled oval (a circle in this example), a **setDiameter** method (lines 22–28) that changes the **diameter** of the circle and **repaint**s the **OvalPanel**, a **getPreferredSize** method (lines 31–34) that defines the preferred width and height of an **OvalPanel** and a **getMinimumSize** method (lines 37–40) that defines the minimum width and height of an **OvalPanel**.

Look-and-Feel Observation 13.14

If a new GUI component has a minimum width and height (i.e., smaller dimensions would render the component ineffective on the display), override method **getMinimumSize** *to return the minimum width and height as an instance of class* **Dimension**.

Look-and-Feel Observation 13.15

For many GUI components, method **getMinimumSize** *is defined to return the result of a call to that component's* **getPreferredSize** *method.*

```
// Fig. 13.7: OvalPanel.java
// A customized JPanel class.

// Java core packages
import java.awt.*;

// Java extension packages
import javax.swing.*;

public class OvalPanel extends JPanel {
   private int diameter = 10;

   // draw an oval of the specified diameter
   public void paintComponent( Graphics g )
   {
      super.paintComponent( g );

      g.fillOval( 10, 10, diameter, diameter );
   }

   // validate and set diameter, then repaint
   public void setDiameter( int newDiameter )
   {
      // if diameter invalid, default to 10
      diameter = ( newDiameter >= 0 ? newDiameter : 10 );

      repaint();
   }

   // used by layout manager to determine preferred size
   public Dimension getPreferredSize()
   {
      return new Dimension( 200, 200 );
   }

   // used by layout manager to determine minimum size
   public Dimension getMinimumSize()
   {
      return getPreferredSize();
   }

} // end class OvalPanel
```

Fig. 13.7 Custom subclass of **JPanel** for drawing circles of a specified diameter.

Class **SliderDemo**'s constructor (lines 17–54 of Fig. 13.8) instantiates **OvalPanel** object **myPanel** and sets its background color (lines 22–23). Lines 26–27 instantiate **JSlider** object **diameterSlider** to control the diameter of the circle drawn on the **OvalPanel**. The orientation of **diameterSlider** is **HORIZONTAL** (a constant in interface **SwingConstants**). The second and third constructor arguments to the **JSlider** constructor indicate the minimum and maximum integer values in the range of values for this **JSlider**. The last constructor argument indicates that the initial value of the **JSlider** (i.e., where the thumb is displayed) should be **10**.

```
// Fig. 13.8: SliderDemo.java
// Using JSliders to size an oval.

// Java core packages
import java.awt.*;
import java.awt.event.*;

// Java extension packages
import javax.swing.*;
import javax.swing.event.*;

public class SliderDemo extends JFrame {
   private JSlider diameterSlider;
   private OvalPanel myPanel;

   // set up GUI
   public SliderDemo()
   {
      super( "Slider Demo" );

      // set up OvalPanel
      myPanel = new OvalPanel();
      myPanel.setBackground( Color.yellow );

      // set up JSlider to control diameter value
      diameterSlider =
         new JSlider( SwingConstants.HORIZONTAL, 0, 200, 10 );
      diameterSlider.setMajorTickSpacing( 10 );
      diameterSlider.setPaintTicks( true );

      // register JSlider event listener
      diameterSlider.addChangeListener(

         // anonymous inner class to handle JSlider events
         new ChangeListener() {

            // handle change in slider value
            public void stateChanged( ChangeEvent e )
            {
               myPanel.setDiameter( diameterSlider.getValue() );
            }

         }  // end anonymous inner class

      ); // end call to addChangeListener

      // attach components to content pane
      Container container = getContentPane();
      container.add( diameterSlider, BorderLayout.SOUTH );
      container.add( myPanel, BorderLayout.CENTER );

      setSize( 220, 270 );
```

Fig. 13.8 Using a **JSlider** to determine the diameter of a circle (part 1 of 2).

```
53         setVisible( true );
54     }
55
56     // execute application
57     public static void main( String args[] )
58     {
59        SliderDemo application = new SliderDemo();
60
61        application.setDefaultCloseOperation(
62           JFrame.EXIT_ON_CLOSE );
63     }
64
65  } // end class SliderDemo
```

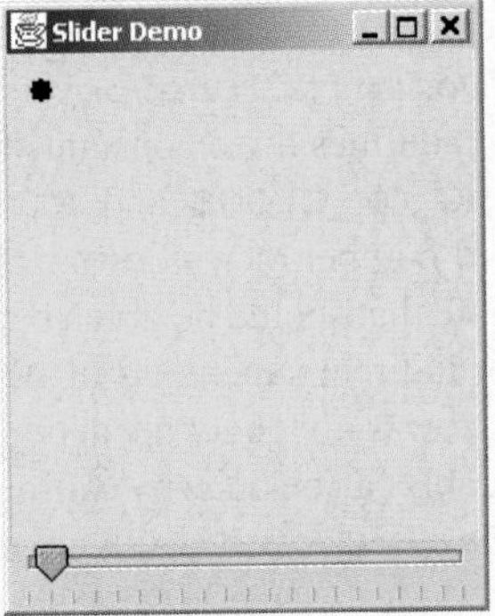

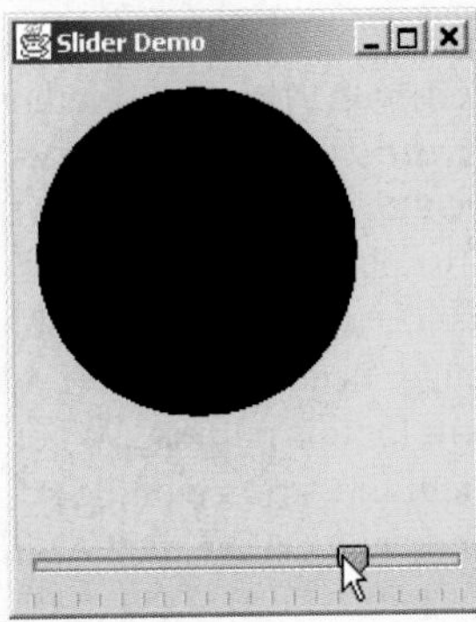

Fig. 13.8 Using a **JSlider** to determine the diameter of a circle (part 2 of 2).

Lines 28–29 customize the appearance of the **JSlider**. Method ***setMajorTickSpacing*** indicates that each tick mark represents 10 values in the range of values supported by the **JSlider**. Method ***setPaintTicks*** with a **true** argument indicates that the tick marks should be displayed (they are not displayed by default). See the **JSlider** on-line documentation for more information on methods that are used to customize a **JSlider**'s appearance.

JSliders generate ***ChangeEvent**s* (package **javax.swing.event**) when the user interacts with a **JSlider**. An object of a class that implements interface ***ChangeListener*** (package **javax.swing.event**) and defines method ***stateChanged*** can respond to **ChangeEvent**s. Lines 32–45 register an object of an anonymous inner class that implements **ChangeListener** to handle **diameterSlider**'s events. When method **stateChanged** is called in response to a user interaction, it calls **myPanel**'s **setDiameter** method and passes the current value of the **JSlider** as an argument. Method ***getValue*** of class ***JSlider*** returns the current thumb position.

13.6 Windows

From Chapter 9 to this chapter, most applications have used an instance of a subclass of **JFrame** as the application window. In this section, we discuss several important issues regarding **JFrame**s.

A **`JFrame`** is a *window* with a *title bar* and a *border*. Class **`JFrame`** is a subclass of ***`java.awt.Frame`*** (which is a subclass of **`java.awt.Window`**). As such, **`JFrame`** is one of the few Swing GUI components that is not a lightweight GUI component. Unlike most Swing components, **`JFrame`** is not written completely in Java. In fact, when you display a window from a Java program, the window is provided by the local platform's set of GUI components—the window will look like all other windows displayed on that platform. When a Java program executes on a Macintosh and displays a window, the window's title bar and borders will look like other Macintosh applications. When a Java program executes on Microsoft Windows and displays a window, the window's title bar and borders will look like other Microsoft Windows applications. And when a Java program executes on a Unix platform and displays a window, the window's title bar and borders will look like other Unix applications on that platform.

Class **`JFrame`** supports three operations when the user closes the window. By default, a window is hidden (i.e., removed from the screen) when the user closes a window. This can be controlled with **`JFrame`** method ***`setDefaultCloseOperation`***. Interface ***`WindowConstants`*** (package **`javax.swing`**) defines three constants for use with this method—**`DISPOSE_ON_CLOSE`**, **`DO_NOTHING_ON_CLOSE`** and **`HIDE_ON_CLOSE`** (the default). Most platforms only allow a limited number of windows to be displayed on the screen. As such, a window is a valuable resource that should be given back to the system when it is no longer needed. Class **`Window`** (an indirect superclass of **`JFrame`**) defines method ***`dispose`*** for this purpose. When a **`Window`** is no longer needed in an application, you should explicitly **`dispose`** of the **`Window`**. This can be done by calling the **`Window`**'s **`dispose`** method or by calling method **`setDefaultCloseOperation`** with the argument **`WindowConstants.DISPOSE_ON_CLOSE`**. Also, terminating an application will return window resources to the system. Setting the default close operation to **`DO_NOTHING_ON_CLOSE`** indicates that you will determine what to do when the user indicates that the window should be closed.

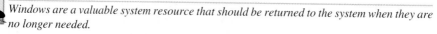

Software Engineering Observation 13.1

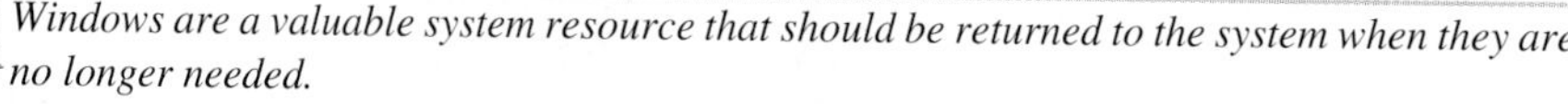

Windows are a valuable system resource that should be returned to the system when they are no longer needed.

By default, a window is not displayed on the screen until the program invokes the window's ***`setVisible`*** method (inherited from class **`java.awt.Component`**) with a **`true`** argument or invokes the window's ***`show`*** method, which takes no arguments. Also, a window's size should be set with a call to method ***`setSize`*** (inherited from class **`java.awt.Component`**). The position of a window when it appears on the screen is specified with method ***`setLocation`*** (inherited from class **`java.awt.Component`**).

Common Programming Error 13.3

*Forgetting to call method **`show`** or method **`setVisible`** on a window is a run-time logic error; the window is not displayed.*

Common Programming Error 13.4

*Forgetting to call the **`setSize`** method on a window is a run-time logic error—only the title bar appears.*

All windows generate *window events* when the user manipulates the window. Event listeners are registered for window events with method ***`addWindowListener`*** of class

Window. Interface ***WindowListener*** (implemented by window event listeners) provides seven methods for handling window events—***windowActivated*** (called when the user makes a window the active window), ***windowClosed*** (called after the window is closed), ***windowClosing*** (called when the user initiates closing of the window), ***windowDeactivated*** (called when the user makes another window the active window), ***windowIconified*** (called when the user minimizes a window), ***windowDeiconified*** (called when the user restores a window from being minimized) and ***windowOpened*** (called when a program first displays a window on the screen).

Most windows have an icon at the top-left or top-right corner that enables a user to close the window and terminate a program. Most windows also have an icon in the upper-left corner of the window that displays a menu when the user clicks the icon. This menu normally contains a **Close** option to close the window and several other options for manipulating the window.

13.7 Designing Programs that Execute as Applets or Applications

It is sometimes desirable to design a Java program that can execute both as a stand-alone application and as an applet in a Web browser. Such a program can be used to provide the same functionality to users worldwide by making the applet available for download via Web and can be installed on a computer as a stand-alone application. The next example discusses how to create a small program that can execute both as an applet and as an application. [*Note*: In Chapter 16 and Chapter 17, we discuss several issues that make applets different from applications and security restrictions placed on applets that prevent certain application features from working in an applet.]

Frequently, programs use **JFrame**s to create *GUI-based applications*. The **JFrame** provides the space in which the application GUI appears. When the user closes the **JFrame**, the application terminates. In this section, we demonstrate how to convert an applet into a GUI-based application. The program of Fig. 13.9 presents an applet that also can be executed as an application.

Software Engineering Observation 13.2

When designing a program to execute as both an applet and an application, begin by defining it as an applet, because applets have limitations due to security restrictions imposed on them by Web browsers. If the program executes properly as an applet, it can be made to work properly as an application. However, the reverse is not always true.

Our applet class **DrawShapes** presents the user with three buttons which, when pressed, cause an instance of class **DrawPanel** (lines 121–126) to draw a random line, rectangle or oval (depending on which button is pressed). The applet does not contain any new features as far as GUI components, layouts or drawing are concerned. The only new feature is that the **DrawShapes** class now also contains a **main** method (lines 60–99) that can be used to execute the program as an application. We discuss this method in detail below.

The HTML document that loads the applet into the **appletviewer** or a Web browser specifies the applet's width and height as 300 and 200, respectively. When the program executes as an application with the **java** interpreter, you can supply arguments to the program (called *command-line arguments*) that specify the width and height of the application window. For example, the command

```
java DrawShapes 600 400
```

contains two command-line arguments—600 and 400—that specify the width and height of the application window. Java passes the command-line arguments to **main** as the array of **String**s called ***args***, which we have declared in the parameter list of every application's **main** method, but not used until this point. The first argument after the application class name is the first **String** in the array **args**, and the length of the array is the total number of command-line arguments. Line 60 begins the definition of **main** and declares array **args** as an array of **String**s that allows the application to access the command-line arguments. Line 62 defines variables **width** and **height** that are used to specify the size of the application window.

```
1  // Fig. 13.9: DrawShapes\.java
2  // Draw random lines, rectangles and ovals
3
4  // Java core packages
5  import java.awt.*;
6  import java.awt.event.*;
7
8  // Java extension packages
9  import javax.swing.*;
10
11 public class DrawShapes extends JApplet {
12    private JButton choices[];
13    private String names[] = { "Line", "Rectangle", "Oval" };
14    private JPanel buttonPanel;
15    private DrawPanel drawingPanel;
16    private int width = 300, height = 200;
17
18    // initialize applet; set up GUI
19    public void init()
20    {
21       // set up DrawPanel
22       drawingPanel = new DrawPanel( width, height );
23
24       // create array of buttons
25       choices = new JButton[ names.length ];
26
27       // set up panel for buttons
28       buttonPanel = new JPanel();
29       buttonPanel.setLayout(
30          new GridLayout( 1, choices.length ) );
31
32       // set up buttons and register their listeners
33       ButtonHandler handler = new ButtonHandler();
34
35       for ( int count = 0; count < choices.length; count++ ) {
36          choices[ count ] = new JButton( names[ count ] );
37          buttonPanel.add( choices[ count ] );
38          choices[ count ].addActionListener( handler );
39       }
```

Fig. 13.9 Creating a GUI-based application from an applet (part 1 of 4).

```

      // attach components to content pane
      Container container = getContentPane();
      container.add( buttonPanel, BorderLayout.NORTH );
      container.add( drawingPanel, BorderLayout.CENTER );
   }

   // enables application to specify width of drawing area
   public void setWidth( int newWidth )
   {
      width = ( newWidth >= 0 ? newWidth : 300 );
   }

   // enables application to specify height of drawing area
   public void setHeight( int newHeight )
   {
      height = ( newHeight >= 0 ? newHeight : 200 );
   }

   // execute applet as an application
   public static void main( String args[] )
   {
      int width, height;

      // check for command-line arguments
      if ( args.length != 2 ) {
         width = 300;
         height = 200;
      }
      else {
         width = Integer.parseInt( args[ 0 ] );
         height = Integer.parseInt( args[ 1 ] );
      }

      // create window in which applet will execute
      JFrame applicationWindow =
         new JFrame( "An applet running as an application" );

      applicationWindow.setDefaultCloseOperation(
         JFrame.EXIT_ON_CLOSE );

      // create one applet instance
      DrawShapes appletObject = new DrawShapes();
      appletObject.setWidth( width );
      appletObject.setHeight( height );

      // call applet's init and start methods
      appletObject.init();
      appletObject.start();

      // attach applet to center of window
      applicationWindow.getContentPane().add( appletObject );

```

Fig. 13.9 Creating a GUI-based application from an applet (part 2 of 4).

```
      // set the window's size
      applicationWindow.setSize( width, height );

      // showing the window causes all GUI components
      // attached to the window to be painted
      applicationWindow.setVisible( true );
   }

   // private inner class to handle button events
   private class ButtonHandler implements ActionListener {

      // determine button user pressed and set drawing area's
      // current choice
      public void actionPerformed( ActionEvent event )
      {
         for ( int count = 0; count < choices.length; count++ )

            if ( event.getSource() == choices[ count ] ) {
               drawingPanel.setCurrentChoice( count );
               break;
            }
      }

   }  // end private inner class ButtonHandler

}  // end class DrawShapes

// subclass of JPanel to allow drawing in a separate area
class DrawPanel extends JPanel {
   private int currentChoice = -1;  // don't draw first time
   private int width = 100, height = 100;

   // initialize width and height of DrawPanel
   public DrawPanel( int newWidth, int newHeight )
   {
      width = ( newWidth >= 0 ? newWidth : 100 );
      height = ( newHeight >= 0 ? newHeight : 100 );
   }

   // draw line, rectangle or oval based on user's choice
   public void paintComponent( Graphics g )
   {
      super.paintComponent( g );

      switch( currentChoice ) {

         case 0:
            g.drawLine( randomX(), randomY(),
               randomX(), randomY() );
            break;

```

Fig. 13.9 Creating a GUI-based application from an applet (part 3 of 4).

```
144             case 1:
145                g.drawRect( randomX(), randomY(),
146                   randomX(), randomY() );
147                break;
148
149             case 2:
150                g.drawOval( randomX(), randomY(),
151                   randomX(), randomY() );
152                break;
153          }
154
155       }  // end method paintComponent
156
157       // specify current shape choice and repaint
158       public void setCurrentChoice( int choice )
159       {
160          currentChoice = choice;
161          repaint();
162       }
163
164       // pick random x coordinate
165       private int randomX()
166       {
167          return ( int ) ( Math.random() * width );
168       }
169
170       // pick random y coordinate
171       private int randomY()
172       {
173          return ( int ) ( Math.random() * height );
174       }
175
176    }  // end class DrawPanel
```

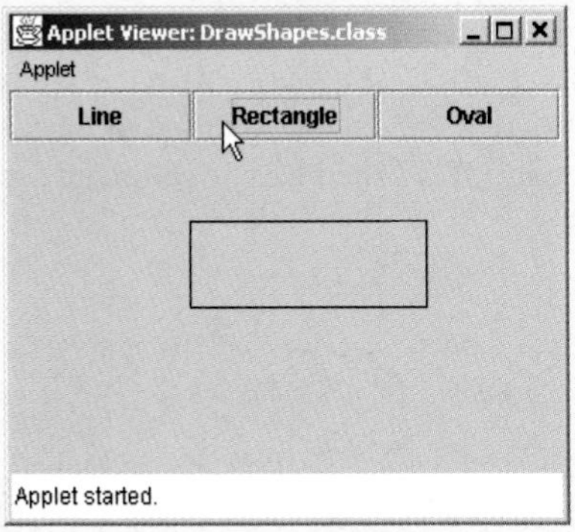

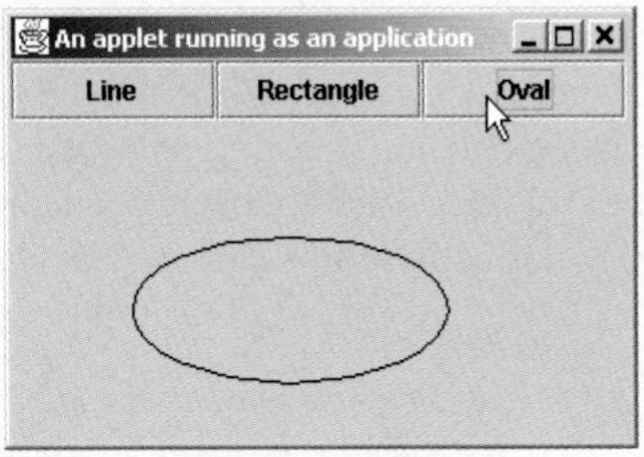

Fig. 13.9 Creating a GUI-based application from an applet (part 4 of 4).

Lines 65–72 determine the initial width and height of the application window. The **`if`** condition determines the length of array **`args`**. If the number of elements is not 2, the **`width`** and **`height`** are set to 300 and 200 by default. Otherwise, lines 70–71 convert the command-line arguments from **`String`**s to **`int`** values with **`parseInt`** and use them as the **`width`** and **height**. [*Note*: This program assumes that the user inputs whole-number values for the command-line arguments; if not, an exception will occur. In Chapter 14, we discuss how to make our programs more robust by dealing with improper values when they occur.]

When an applet executes, the window in which it executes is supplied by the applet container (i.e., the **appletviewer** or browser). When a program executes as an application, the application must create its own window (if one is required). Lines 75–76 create the **JFrame** to which the program will attach the applet. As with any **JFrame** that is used as the application's primary window, you should provide a mechanism to terminate the application. Lines 78–79 specify that the application should terminate when the user closes the window.

Software Engineering Observation 13.3

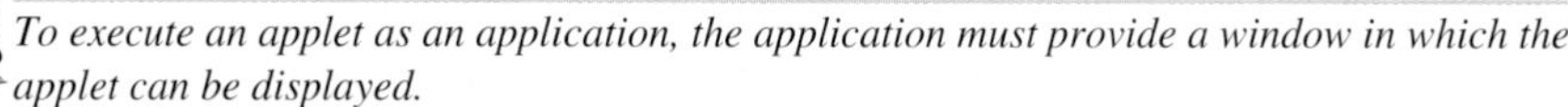

To execute an applet as an application, the application must provide a window in which the applet can be displayed.

When an applet executes in an applet container, the container creates one object of the applet class to execute the applet's tasks. In an application, objects are not created unless the application explicitly contains statements that create objects. Line 82 defines one instance of applet class **DrawShapes**. Notice the call to the no-argument constructor. We did not define a constructor in class **DrawShapes** (applet classes typically do not define constructors). Remember that the compiler provides a default constructor for a class that does not define any constructors. Lines 83–84 call **DrawShapes** methods **setWidth** and **setHeight** to validate the values for **width** and **height** (improper values are set to 300 and 200, respectively).

Software Engineering Observation 13.4

To execute an applet as an application, the application must create an instance of the applet class to execute.

When an applet executes in an applet container, the container guarantees that methods **init**, **start** and **paint** will be called to begin the applet's execution. However, these methods are not special to an application. Method **init** and **start** are not invoked automatically or required by an application. (Method paint is part of any window and will be called when it is necessary to repaint the window.) Lines 87–88 invoke **appletObject**'s **init** method to initialize the applet and set up its GUI, then invoke method **start**. [*Note*: In our example, we did not override method **start**. It is called here to mimic the start-up sequence normally followed for an applet.]

Software Engineering Observation 13.5

When executing an applet as an application, the application must call **init** *and* **start** *explicitly to simulate the normal applet start-up sequence of method calls.*

When an applet executes in an applet container, the applet is normally attached to the applet container's window. An application must explicitly attach an applet object to the application window. Line 91 obtains a reference to the **applicationWindow**'s content pane and adds the **appletObject** to the default **CENTER** of the content pane's **BorderLayout**. The **appletObject** will occupy the entire window.

Software Engineering Observation 13.6

When one is executing an applet as an application, the application must attach the applet object to its window.

Finally, the application window must be sized and displayed on the screen. Line 94 sets the application window's size, and line 98 displays the window. When a Java program displays any window, all the components attached to the window receive calls to their **paint** methods (if they are heavyweight components) or their **paintComponent** methods (if they are lightweight components). Thus, displaying the application window results in a call to the applet's **paint** method to complete the normal start-up sequence for the applet.

Try executing this program as an applet and as an application to see that it has the same functionality when executed.

13.8 Using Menus with Frames

Menus are an integral part of GUIs. Menus allow the user to perform actions without unnecessarily "cluttering" a graphical user interface with extra GUI components. In Swing GUIs, menus can be attached only to objects of the classes that provide method **setJMenuBar**. Two such classes are **JFrame** and **JApplet**. The classes used to define menus are ***JMenuBar***, ***JMenuItem***, ***JMenu***, ***JCheckBoxMenuItem*** and class ***JRadioButtonMenuItem***.

Look-and-Feel Observation 13.16

Menus simplify GUIs by reducing the number of components the user views.

Class **JMenuBar** (a subclass of **JComponent**) contains the methods necessary to manage a *menu bar*, which is a container for menus.

Class **JMenuItem** (a subclass of **javax.swing.AbstractButton**) contains the methods necessary to manage *menu items*. A menu item is a GUI component inside a menu that, when selected, causes an action to be performed. A menu item can be used to initiate an action or it can be a *submenu* that provides more menu items from which the user can select. Submenus are useful for grouping related menu items in a menu.

Class **JMenu** (a subclass of **javax.swing.JMenuItem**) contains the methods necessary for managing *menus*. Menus contain menu items and are added to menu bars or to other menus as submenus. When a menu is clicked, the menu expands to show its list of menu items. Clicking a menu item generates an action event.

Class **JCheckBoxMenuItem** (a subclass of **javax.swing.JMenuItem**) contains the methods necessary to manage menu items that can be toggled on or off. When a **JCheckBoxMenuItem** is selected, a check appears to the left of the menu item. When the **JCheckBoxMenuItem** is selected again, the check to the left of the menu item is removed.

Class **JRadioButtonMenuItem** (a subclass of **javax.swing.JMenuItem**) contains the methods necessary to manage menu items that can be toggled on or off like **JCheckBoxMenuItem**s. When multiple **JRadioButtonMenuItem**s are maintained as part of a **ButtonGroup**, only one item in the group can be selected at a given time. When a **JRadioButtonMenuItem** is selected, a filled circle appears to the left of the menu item. When another **JRadioButtonMenuItem** is selected, the filled circle to the left of the previously selected menu item is removed.

The application of Fig. 13.10 demonstrates various types of menu items. The program also demonstrates how to specify special characters called mnemonics that can provide quick access to a menu or menu item from the keyboard. Mnemonics can be used with objects of all classes that have subclass **javax.swing.AbstractButton**.

```
// Fig. 13.10: MenuTest.java
// Demonstrating menus

// Java core packages
import java.awt.*;
import java.awt.event.*;

// Java extension packages
import javax.swing.*;

public class MenuTest extends JFrame {
   private Color colorValues[] =
      { Color.black, Color.blue, Color.red, Color.green };

   private JRadioButtonMenuItem colorItems[], fonts[];
   private JCheckBoxMenuItem styleItems[];
   private JLabel displayLabel;
   private ButtonGroup fontGroup, colorGroup;
   private int style;

   // set up GUI
   public MenuTest()
   {
      super( "Using JMenus" );

      // set up File menu and its menu items
      JMenu fileMenu = new JMenu( "File" );
      fileMenu.setMnemonic( 'F' );

      // set up About... menu item
      JMenuItem aboutItem = new JMenuItem( "About..." );
      aboutItem.setMnemonic( 'A' );

      aboutItem.addActionListener(

         // anonymous inner class to handle menu item event
         new ActionListener() {

            // display message dialog when user selects About...
            public void actionPerformed( ActionEvent event )
            {
               JOptionPane.showMessageDialog( MenuTest.this,
                  "This is an example\nof using menus",
                  "About", JOptionPane.PLAIN_MESSAGE );
            }

         }  // end anonymous inner class

      ); // end call to addActionListener

      fileMenu.add( aboutItem );

```

Fig. 13.10 Using **JMenus** and mnemonics (part 1 of 5).

```
      // set up Exit menu item
      JMenuItem exitItem = new JMenuItem( "Exit" );
      exitItem.setMnemonic( 'x' );

      exitItem.addActionListener(

         // anonymous inner class to handle exitItem event
         new ActionListener() {

            // terminate application when user clicks exitItem
            public void actionPerformed( ActionEvent event )
            {
               System.exit( 0 );
            }

         }  // end anonymous inner class

      ); // end call to addActionListener

      fileMenu.add( exitItem );

      // create menu bar and attach it to MenuTest window
      JMenuBar bar = new JMenuBar();
      setJMenuBar( bar );
      bar.add( fileMenu );

      // create Format menu, its submenus and menu items
      JMenu formatMenu = new JMenu( "Format" );
      formatMenu.setMnemonic( 'r' );

      // create Color submenu
      String colors[] = { "Black", "Blue", "Red", "Green" };

      JMenu colorMenu = new JMenu( "Color" );
      colorMenu.setMnemonic( 'C' );

      colorItems = new JRadioButtonMenuItem[ colors.length ];
      colorGroup = new ButtonGroup();
      ItemHandler itemHandler = new ItemHandler();

      // create color radio button menu items
      for ( int count = 0; count < colors.length; count++ ) {
         colorItems[ count ] =
            new JRadioButtonMenuItem( colors[ count ] );

         colorMenu.add( colorItems[ count ] );
         colorGroup.add( colorItems[ count ] );

         colorItems[ count ].addActionListener( itemHandler );
      }

      // select first Color menu item
      colorItems[ 0 ].setSelected( true );
```

Fig. 13.10 Using **JMenu**s and mnemonics (part 2 of 5).

```

      // add format menu to menu bar
      formatMenu.add( colorMenu );
      formatMenu.addSeparator();

      // create Font submenu
      String fontNames[] = { "Serif", "Monospaced", "SansSerif" };

      JMenu fontMenu = new JMenu( "Font" );
      fontMenu.setMnemonic( 'n' );

      fonts = new JRadioButtonMenuItem[ fontNames.length ];
      fontGroup = new ButtonGroup();

      // create Font radio button menu items
      for ( int count = 0; count < fonts.length; count++ ) {
         fonts[ count ] =
            new JRadioButtonMenuItem( fontNames[ count ] );

         fontMenu.add( fonts[ count ] );
         fontGroup.add( fonts[ count ] );

         fonts[ count ].addActionListener( itemHandler );
      }

      // select first Font menu item
      fonts[ 0 ].setSelected( true );

      fontMenu.addSeparator();

      // set up style menu items
      String styleNames[] = { "Bold", "Italic" };

      styleItems = new JCheckBoxMenuItem[ styleNames.length ];
      StyleHandler styleHandler = new StyleHandler();

      // create style checkbox menu items
      for ( int count = 0; count < styleNames.length; count++ ) {
         styleItems[ count ] =
            new JCheckBoxMenuItem( styleNames[ count ] );

         fontMenu.add( styleItems[ count ] );

         styleItems[ count ].addItemListener( styleHandler );
      }

      // put Font menu in Format menu
      formatMenu.add( fontMenu );

      // add Format menu to menu bar
      bar.add( formatMenu );

```

Fig. 13.10 Using **JMenu**s and mnemonics (part 3 of 5).

```
      // set up label to display text
      displayLabel = new JLabel(
         "Sample Text", SwingConstants.CENTER );
      displayLabel.setForeground( colorValues[ 0 ] );
      displayLabel.setFont(
         new Font( "TimesRoman", Font.PLAIN, 72 ) );

      getContentPane().setBackground( Color.cyan );
      getContentPane().add( displayLabel, BorderLayout.CENTER );

      setSize( 500, 200 );
      setVisible( true );

   } // end constructor

   // execute application
   public static void main( String args[] )
   {
      MenuTest application = new MenuTest();

      application.setDefaultCloseOperation(
         JFrame.EXIT_ON_CLOSE );
   }

   // inner class to handle action events from menu items
   private class ItemHandler implements ActionListener {

      // process color and font selections
      public void actionPerformed( ActionEvent event )
      {
         // process color selection
         for ( int count = 0; count < colorItems.length; count++ )

            if ( colorItems[ count ].isSelected() ) {
               displayLabel.setForeground( colorValues[ count ] );
               break;
            }

         // process font selection
         for ( int count = 0; count < fonts.length; count++ )

            if ( event.getSource() == fonts[ count ] ) {
               displayLabel.setFont( new Font(
                  fonts[ count ].getText(), style, 72 ) );
               break;
            }

         repaint();
      }

   } // end class ItemHandler

```

Fig. 13.10 Using **JMenu**s and mnemonics (part 4 of 5).

```
210    // inner class to handle item events from check box menu items
211    private class StyleHandler implements ItemListener {
212
213       // process font style selections
214       public void itemStateChanged( ItemEvent e )
215       {
216          style = 0;
217
218          // check for bold selection
219          if ( styleItems[ 0 ].isSelected() )
220             style += Font.BOLD;
221
222          // check for italic selection
223          if ( styleItems[ 1 ].isSelected() )
224             style += Font.ITALIC;
225
226          displayLabel.setFont( new Font(
227             displayLabel.getFont().getName(), style, 72 ) );
228
229          repaint();
230       }
231
232    }  // end class StyleHandler
233
234 }  // end class MenuTest
```

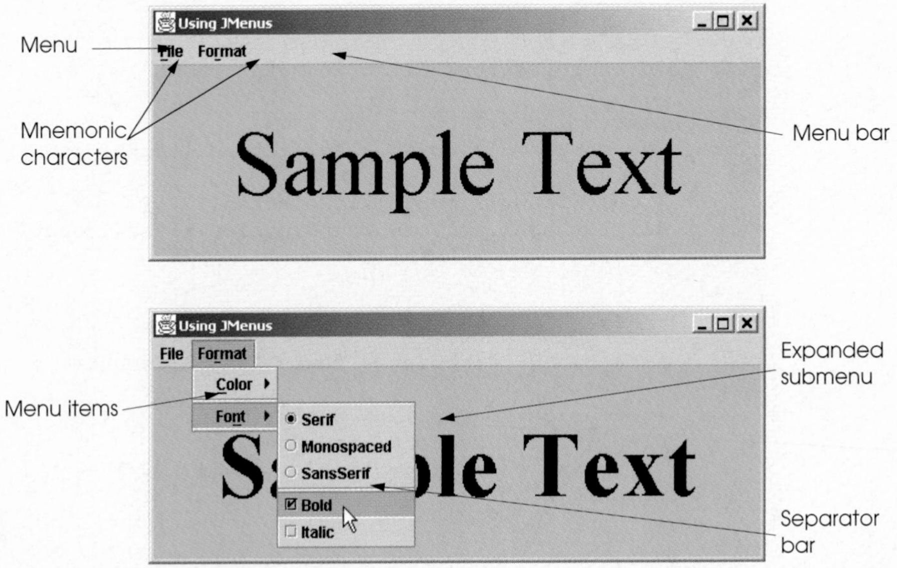

Fig. 13.10 Using **JMenu**s and mnemonics (part 5 of 5).

Class **MenuTest** (line 11) is a completely self-contained class—it defines all the GUI components and event handling for the menu items. Most of the code for this application appears in the class's constructor (lines 22–171).

Lines 27–72 set up the **File** menu and attach it to the menu bar. The **File** menu contains an **About...** menu item that displays a message dialog when the menu item is selected and an **Exit** menu item that can be selected to terminate the application.

Line 27 creates **fileMenu** and passes to the constructor the string "**File**" as the name of the menu. Line 28 uses **AbstractButton** method ***setMnemonic*** (inherited into class **JMenu**) to indicate that **F** is the *mnemonic* for this menu. Pressing the *Alt* key and the letter *F* opens the menu, just as clicking the menu name with the mouse would. In the GUI, the mnemonic character in the menu's name is displayed with an underline (see the screen captures).

Look-and-Feel Observation 13.17

Mnemonics provide quick access to menu commands and button commands through the keyboard.

Look-and-Feel Observation 13.18

Different mnemonics should be used for each button or menu item. Normally, the first letter in the label on the menu item or button is used as the mnemonic. If multiple buttons or menu items start with the same letter, choose the next most prominent letter in the name (e.g., ***x*** *is commonly chosen for a button or menu item called* ***Exit****).*

Lines 31–32 define **JMenuItem aboutItem** with the name "**About...**" and set its mnemonic to the letter **A**. This menu item is added to **fileMenu** at line 51. To access the **About...** item through the keyboard, press the *Alt* key and letter *F* to open the **File** menu, then press *A* to select the **About...** menu item. Lines 34–49 create an **ActionListener** to process **aboutItem**'s action event. Lines 42–44 display a message dialog box. In most prior uses of **showMessageDialog**, the first argument has been **null**. The purpose of the first argument is to specify the *parent window* for the dialog box. The parent window helps determine where the dialog box will be displayed. If the parent window is specified as **null**, the dialog box appears in the center of the screen. If the parent window is not **null**, the dialog box appears centered over the specified parent window. In this example, the program specifies the parent window with **MenuTest.this**—the **this** reference of class **MenuTest**. When using the **this** reference in an inner class, specifying **this** by itself refers to the inner-class object. To reference the outer-class object's **this** reference, qualify **this** with the outer-class name and a dot operator (**.**).

Dialog boxes can be either *modal* or *modeless*. A *modal dialog box* does not allow any other window in the application to be accessed until the dialog box is dismissed. A *modeless dialog box* allows other windows to be accessed while the dialog is displayed. By default, the dialogs displayed with class **JOptionPane** are modal dialogs. Class ***JDialog*** can be used to create your own modeless or modal dialogs.

Lines 54–72 define menu item **exitItem**, set its mnemonic to **x**, register an **ActionListener** that terminates the application when the user selects **exitItem** and add **exitItem** to the **fileMenu**.

Lines 75–77 create the **JMenuBar**, attach it to the application window with **JFrame** method ***setJMenuBar*** and use **JMenuBar** method ***add*** to attach the **fileMenu** to the menu bar.

Common Programming Error 13.5

Forgetting to set the menu bar with ***JFrame*** *method* ***setJMenuBar*** *results in the menu bar not being displayed on the* ***JFrame****.*

Look-and-Feel Observation 13.19

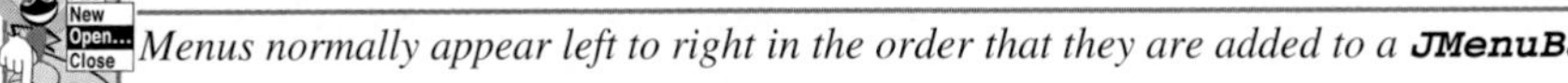

Menus normally appear left to right in the order that they are added to a **`JMenuBar`**.

Lines 80–81 create menu **`formatMenu`** and set its mnemonic to **`r`** (**`F`** is not used because that is the **File** menu's mnemonic).

Lines 86–87 create menu **`colorMenu`** (this will be a submenu in the **Format** menu) and set its mnemonic to **`C`**. Line 89 creates **`JRadioButtonMenuItem`** array **`colorItems`** that refers to the menu items in **`colorMenu`**. Line 90 creates the **`ButtonGroup colorGroup`**, which ensures that only one of the menu items in the **Color** submenu is selected at a time. Line 91 defines an instance of inner class **`ItemHandler`** (defined at lines 183–208) that responds to selections from the **Color** submenu and the **Font** submenu (discussed shortly). The **`for`** structure at lines 94–102 creates each **`JRadioButtonMenuItem`** in array **`colorItems`**, adds each menu item to **`colorMenu`**, adds each menu item to **`colorGroup`** and registers the **`ActionListener`** for each menu item.

Line 105 uses **`AbstractButton`** method ***`setSelected`*** to select the first element in the **`colorItems`** array. Line 108 adds the **`colorMenu`** as a submenu of the **`formatMenu`**.

Look-and-Feel Observation 13.20

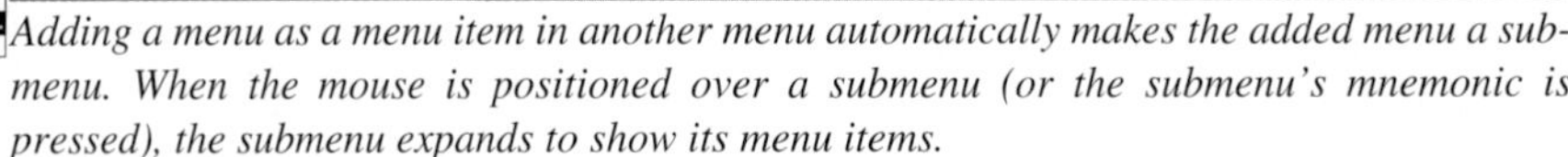

Adding a menu as a menu item in another menu automatically makes the added menu a submenu. When the mouse is positioned over a submenu (or the submenu's mnemonic is pressed), the submenu expands to show its menu items.

Line 109 adds a *separator* line to the menu. The separator appears as a horizontal line in the menu.

Look-and-Feel Observation 13.21

Separators can be added to a menu to group menu items logically.

Look-and-Feel Observation 13.22

Any lightweight GUI component (i.e., a component that subclasses **`JComponent`***) can be added to a* **`JMenu`** *or to a* **`JMenuBar`**.

Lines 114–132 create the **Font** submenu and several **`JRadioButtonMenuItem`**s and select the first element of **`JRadioButtonMenuItem`** array **`fonts`**. Line 139 creates a **`JCheckBoxMenuItem`** array to represent the menu items for specifying bold and italic styles for the fonts. Line 140 defines an instance of inner class **`StyleHandler`** (defined at lines 211–232) to respond to the **`JCheckBoxMenuItem`** events. The **`for`** structure at lines 143–150 creates each **`JCheckBoxMenuItem`**, adds each menu item to **`fontMenu`** and registers the **`ItemListener`** for each menu item. Line 153 adds **`fontMenu`** as a submenu of **`formatMenu`**. Line 156 adds the **`formatMenu`** to **`bar`**.

Lines 159–163 create a **`JLabel`** for which the **Format** menu items control the font, font color and font style. The initial foreground color is set to the first element of array **`colorValues`** (**`Color.black`**) and the initial font is set to **`TimesRoman`** with **`PLAIN`** style and **`72`**-point size. Line 165 sets the background color of the window's content pane to **`Color.cyan`**, and line 166 attaches the **`JLabel`** to the **`CENTER`** of the content pane's **`BorderLayout`**.

Method **actionPerformed** of class **ItemHandler** (lines 186–206) uses two **for** structures to determine which font or color menu item generated the event and sets the font or color of the **JLabel display**, respectively. The **if** condition at line 191 uses **AbstractButton** method ***isSelected*** to determine the selected **JRadioButton-MenuItem**. The **if** condition at line 199 uses **EventSource** method **getSource** to get a reference to the **JRadioButtonMenuItem** that generated the event. Line 201 uses **AbstractButton** method **getText** to obtain the name of the font from the menu item.

The program calls method **itemStateChanged** of class **StyleHandler** (lines 214–230) if the user selects a **JCheckBoxMenuItem** in the **fontMenu**. Lines 219 and 223 determine whether either or both of the **JCheckBoxMenuItem**s are selected and use their combined state to determine the new style of the font.

13.9 Using JPopupMenus

Many of today's computer applications provide so-called *context-sensitive popup menus*. In Swing, such menus are created with class **JPopupMenu** (a subclass of **JComponent**). These menus provide options that are specific to the component for which the *popup trigger event* was generated. On most systems, the popup trigger event occurs when the user presses and releases the right mouse button.

Look-and-Feel Observation 13.23

The popup trigger event is platform specific. On most platforms that use a mouse with multiple mouse buttons, the popup trigger event occurs when the user clicks the right mouse button.

Figure 13.11 creates a **JPopupMenu** that allows the user to select one of three colors and change the background color of the window. When the user clicks the right mouse button on the **PopupTest** window's background, a **JPopupMenu** containing colors appears. If the user clicks one of the **JRadioButtonMenuItem**s that represents a color, method **actionPerformed** of class **ItemHandler** changes the background color of the window's content pane.

```
// Fig. 13.11: PopupTest.java
// Demonstrating JPopupMenus

// Java core packages
import java.awt.*;
import java.awt.event.*;

// Java extension packages
import javax.swing.*;

public class PopupTest extends JFrame {

   private JRadioButtonMenuItem items[];
   private Color colorValues[] =
      { Color.blue, Color.yellow, Color.red };

   private JPopupMenu popupMenu;

```

Fig. 13.11 Using a **PopupMenu** object (part 1 of 3).

```
   // set up GUI
   public PopupTest()
   {
      super( "Using JPopupMenus" );

      ItemHandler handler = new ItemHandler();
      String colors[] = { "Blue", "Yellow", "Red" };

      // set up popup menu and its items
      ButtonGroup colorGroup = new ButtonGroup();
      popupMenu = new JPopupMenu();
      items = new JRadioButtonMenuItem[ 3 ];

      // construct each menu item and add to popup menu; also
      // enable event handling for each menu item
      for ( int count = 0; count < items.length; count++ ) {
         items[ count ] =
            new JRadioButtonMenuItem( colors[ count ] );

         popupMenu.add( items[ count ] );
         colorGroup.add( items[ count ] );

         items[ count ].addActionListener( handler );
      }

      getContentPane().setBackground( Color.white );

      // define a MouseListener for the window that displays
      // a JPopupMenu when the popup trigger event occurs
      addMouseListener(

         // anonymous inner class to handle mouse events
         new MouseAdapter() {

            // handle mouse press event
            public void mousePressed( MouseEvent event )
            {
               checkForTriggerEvent( event );
            }

            // handle mouse release event
            public void mouseReleased( MouseEvent event )
            {
               checkForTriggerEvent( event );
            }

            // determine whether event should trigger popup menu
            private void checkForTriggerEvent( MouseEvent event )
            {
               if ( event.isPopupTrigger() )
                  popupMenu.show( event.getComponent(),
                     event.getX(), event.getY() );
            }
```

Fig. 13.11 Using a **PopupMenu** object (part 2 of 3).

```
72
73          }  // end anonymous inner clas
74
75       ); // end call to addMouseListener
76
77       setSize( 300, 200 );
78       setVisible( true );
79    }
80
81    // execute application
82    public static void main( String args[] )
83    {
84       PopupTest application = new PopupTest();
85
86       application.setDefaultCloseOperation(
87          JFrame.EXIT_ON_CLOSE );
88    }
89
90    // private inner class to handle menu item events
91    private class ItemHandler implements ActionListener {
92
93       // process menu item selections
94       public void actionPerformed( ActionEvent event )
95       {
96          // determine which menu item was selected
97          for ( int i = 0; i < items.length; i++ )
98             if ( event.getSource() == items[ i ] ) {
99                getContentPane().setBackground(
100                  colorValues[ i ] );
101               repaint();
102               return;
103            }
104      }
105
106   }  // end private inner class ItemHandler
107
108 }  // end class PopupTest
```

Fig. 13.11 Using a **PopupMenu** object (part 3 of 3).

The constructor for class **PopupTest** (lines 20–79) defines the **JPopupMenu** at line 29. The **for** structure at lines 34–42 creates **JRadioButtonMenuItems** to add to the **JPopupMenu**, adds them to the **JPopupMenu** (line 38), adds them to **ButtonGroup**

colorGroup (to maintain one selected **JRadioButtonMenuItem** at a time) and registers an **ActionListener** for each menu item.

Lines 48–75 register an instance of an anonymous inner class that extends **MouseAdapter** to handle the mouse events of the application window. Methods **mousePressed** (lines 54–57) and **mouseReleased** (lines 60–63) check for the popup-trigger event. Each method calls **private** utility method **checkForTriggerEvent** (lines 66–71) to determine whether the popup-trigger event occurred. **MouseEvent** method ***isPopupTrigger*** returns **true** if the popup-trigger event occurred. If so, method ***show*** of class **JPopupMenu** displays the **JPopupMenu**. The first argument to method **show** specifies the *origin component,* whose position helps determine where the **JPopupMenu** will appear on the screen. The last two arguments are the *x-y* coordinate from the origin component's upper-left corner at which the **JPopupMenu** should appear.

Look-and-Feel Observation 13.24

Displaying a ***JPopupMenu*** *for the popup-trigger event of multiple different GUI components requires registering mouse event handlers to check for the popup-trigger event for each of those GUI components.*

When the user selects a menu item from the popup menu, class **ItemHandler**'s (lines 91–106) method **actionPerformed** (lines 94–104) determines which **JRadioButtonMenuItem** the user selected, then sets the background color of the window's content pane.

13.10 Pluggable Look-and-Feel

A program that uses Java's Abstract Windowing Toolkit GUI components (package ***java.awt***) takes on the look-and-feel of the platform on which the program executes. A Java program running on a Macintosh looks like other programs running on a Macintosh. A Java program running on Microsoft Windows looks like other programs running on Microsoft Windows. A Java program running on a UNIX platform looks like other programs running on that UNIX platform. This could be desirable, because it allows users of the program on each platform to use the GUI components with which they are already familiar. However, this also introduces interesting portability issues.

Portability Tip 13.1

Programs that use Java's Abstract Windowing Toolkit GUI components (package ***java.awt****) take on the look-and-feel of the platform on which they execute.*

Portability Tip 13.2

GUI components on each platform have different looks that can require different amounts of space to display. This could change the layout and alignments of GUI components.

Portability Tip 13.3

GUI components on each platform have different default functionality (e.g., some platforms allow a button with the focus to be "pressed" with the space bar, and some do not).

Swing's lightweight GUI components eliminate many of these issues by providing uniform functionality across platforms and by defining a uniform cross-platform look-and-feel (known as the metal look-and-feel). Swing also provides the flexibility to customize the look-and-feel to appear as a Microsoft Windows-style look-and-feel or a Motif-style (UNIX) look-and-feel.

The program of Fig. 13.12 demonstrates how to change the look-and-feel of a Swing GUI. The program creates several GUI components so you can see the change in the look-and-feel of several GUI components at the same time. The first output window shows the standard metal look-and-feel, the second output window shows the Motif look-and-feel, and the third output window shows the Windows look-and-feel.

```
// Fig. 13.12: LookAndFeelDemo.java
// Changing the look and feel.

// Java core packages
import java.awt.*;
import java.awt.event.*;

// Java extension packages
import javax.swing.*;

public class LookAndFeelDemo extends JFrame {

   private String strings[] = { "Metal", "Motif", "Windows" };
   private UIManager.LookAndFeelInfo looks[];
   private JRadioButton radio[];
   private ButtonGroup group;
   private JButton button;
   private JLabel label;
   private JComboBox comboBox;

   // set up GUI
   public LookAndFeelDemo()
   {
      super( "Look and Feel Demo" );

      Container container = getContentPane();

      // set up panel for NORTH of BorderLayout
      JPanel northPanel = new JPanel();
      northPanel.setLayout( new GridLayout( 3, 1, 0, 5 ) );

      // set up label for NORTH panel
      label = new JLabel( "This is a Metal look-and-feel",
         SwingConstants.CENTER );
      northPanel.add( label );

      // set up button for NORTH panel
      button = new JButton( "JButton" );
      northPanel.add( button );

      // set up combo box for NORTH panel
      comboBox = new JComboBox( strings );
      northPanel.add( comboBox );
```

Fig. 13.12 Changing the look-and-feel of a Swing-based GUI (part 1 of 3).

```
      // attach NORTH panel to content pane
      container.add( northPanel, BorderLayout.NORTH );

      // create array for radio buttons
      radio = new JRadioButton[ strings.length ];

      // set up panel for SOUTH of BorderLayout
      JPanel southPanel = new JPanel();
      southPanel.setLayout(
         new GridLayout( 1, radio.length ) );

      // set up radio buttons for SOUTH panel
      group = new ButtonGroup();
      ItemHandler handler = new ItemHandler();

      for ( int count = 0; count < radio.length; count++ ) {
         radio[ count ] = new JRadioButton( strings[ count ] );
         radio[ count ].addItemListener( handler );
         group.add( radio[ count ] );
         southPanel.add( radio[ count ] );
      }

      // attach SOUTH panel to content pane
      container.add( southPanel, BorderLayout.SOUTH );

      // get installed look-and-feel information
      looks = UIManager.getInstalledLookAndFeels();

      setSize( 300, 200 );
      setVisible( true );

      radio[ 0 ].setSelected( true );
   }

   // use UIManager to change look-and-feel of GUI
   private void changeTheLookAndFeel( int value )
   {
      // change look and feel
      try {
         UIManager.setLookAndFeel(
            looks[ value ].getClassName() );
         SwingUtilities.updateComponentTreeUI( this );
      }

      // process problems changing look and feel
      catch ( Exception exception ) {
         exception.printStackTrace();
      }
   }

```

Fig. 13.12 Changing the look-and-feel of a Swing-based GUI (part 2 of 3).

```
   // execute application
   public static void main( String args[] )
   {
      LookAndFeelDemo application = new LookAndFeelDemo();

      application.setDefaultCloseOperation(
         JFrame.EXIT_ON_CLOSE );
   }

   // private inner class to handle radio button events
   private class ItemHandler implements ItemListener {

      // process user's look-and-feel selection
      public void itemStateChanged( ItemEvent event )
      {
         for ( int count = 0; count < radio.length; count++ )

            if ( radio[ count ].isSelected() ) {
               label.setText( "This is a " +
                  strings[ count ] + " look-and-feel" );
               comboBox.setSelectedIndex( count );

               changeTheLookAndFeel( count );
            }
      }

   } // end private inner class ItemHandler

} // end class LookAndFeelDemo
```

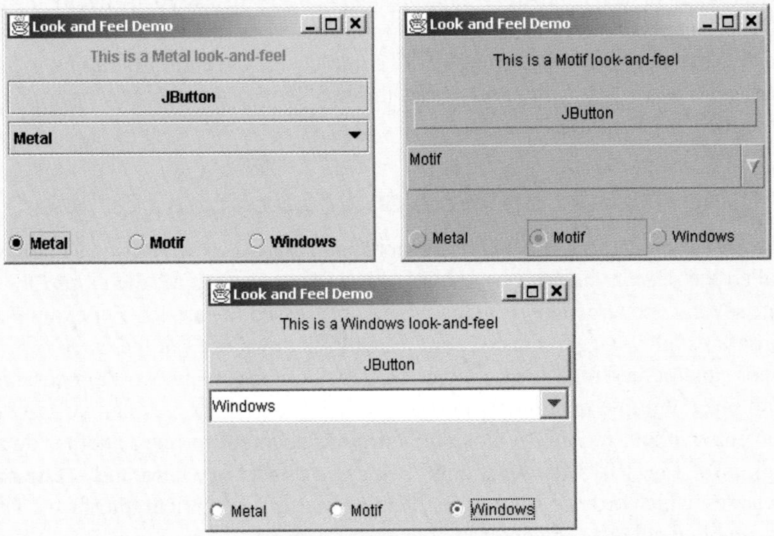

Fig. 13.12 Changing the look-and-feel of a Swing-based GUI (part 3 of 3).

All the GUI components and event handling in this example have been covered before, so we concentrate on the mechanism for changing the look-and-feel in this example.

Class ***UIManager*** (package ***javax.swing***) contains **public static** inner class ***LookAndFeelInfo*** that is used to maintain information about a look-and-feel. Line 14 declares an array of type **UIManager.LookAndFeelInfo** (notice the syntax used to access the inner class **LookAndFeelInfo**). Line 71 uses **static** method ***getInstalledLookAndFeels*** of class **UIManager** to get the array of **UIManager.LookAndFeelInfo** objects that describe the installed look-and-feels.

Performance Tip 13.1

Each look-and-feel is represented by a Java class. ***UIManager*** *method* ***getInstalledLookAndFeels*** *does not load each class. Rather, it provides access to the names of each look-and-feel, so a choice of look-and-feel can be made (presumably one time at program startup). This reduces the overhead of loading additional classes that the program will not use.*

Utility method **changeTheLookAndFeel** (lines 80–93) is called by the event handler (defined in **private** inner class **ItemHandler** at lines 105–121) for the **JRadioButton**s at the bottom of the user interface. The event handler passes an integer representing the element in array **looks** that should be used to change the look-and-feel. Lines 84–85 use **static** method ***setLookAndFeel*** of class **UIManager** to change the look-and-feel. Method ***getClassName*** of class **UIManager.LookAndFeelInfo** determines the name of the look-and-feel class that corresponds to the **UIManager.LookAndFeelInfo**. If the look-and-feel class is not already loaded, it will be loaded as part of the call to **setLookAndFeel**. Line 86 uses **static** method ***updateComponentTreeUI*** of class ***SwingUtilities*** (package **javax.swing**) to change the look-and-feel of every component attached to its argument (this instance of class **LookAndFeelDemo**) to the new look-and-feel.

The preceding two statements appear in a special block of code called a ***try*** *block*. This code is part of the *exception-handling mechanism* discussed in detail in the next chapter. This code is required in case lines 84–85 attempt to change the look-and-feel to a look-and-feel that does not exist. Lines 90–92 complete the exception-handling mechanism with a ***catch*** *handler* that simply processes this problem (if it occurs) by printing an error message at the command line.

13.11 Using JDesktopPane and JInternalFrame

Many of today's applications use a *multiple document interface (MDI)* [i.e., a main window (often called the *parent window*) containing other windows (often called *child windows*)] to manage several open *documents* that are being processed in parallel. For example, many e-mail programs allow you to have several e-mail windows open at the same time so you can compose and/or read multiple e-mail messages. Similarly, many word processors allow the user to open multiple documents in separate windows so the user can switch between the documents without having to close the current document to open another document. The program of Fig. 13.13 demonstrates Swing's ***JDesktopPane*** and ***JInternalFrame*** classes, which provide support for creating multiple document interfaces. The child windows simply display an image of the cover of this book.

Lines 20–27 define a **JMenuBar**, a **JMenu** and a **JMenuItem**, add the **JMenuItem** to the **JMenu**, add the **JMenu** to the **JMenuBar** and set the **JMenuBar** for the application window. When the user selects the **JMenuItem newFrame**, the program creates and displays a new **JInternalFrame**.

```
// Fig. 13.13: DesktopTest.java
// Demonstrating JDesktopPane.

// Java core packages
import java.awt.*;
import java.awt.event.*;

// Java extension packages
import javax.swing.*;

public class DesktopTest extends JFrame {
   private JDesktopPane theDesktop;

   // set up GUI
   public DesktopTest()
   {
      super( "Using a JDesktopPane" );

      // create menu bar, menu and menu item
      JMenuBar bar = new JMenuBar();
      JMenu addMenu = new JMenu( "Add" );
      JMenuItem newFrame = new JMenuItem( "Internal Frame" );

      addMenu.add( newFrame );
      bar.add( addMenu );

      setJMenuBar( bar );

      // set up desktop
      theDesktop = new JDesktopPane();
      getContentPane().add( theDesktop );

      // set up listener for newFrame menu item
      newFrame.addActionListener(

         // anonymous inner class to handle menu item event
         new ActionListener() {

            // display new internal window
            public void actionPerformed( ActionEvent event ) {

               // create internal frame
               JInternalFrame frame = new JInternalFrame(
                  "Internal Frame", true, true, true, true );

               // attach panel to internal frame content pane
               Container container = frame.getContentPane();
               MyJPanel panel = new MyJPanel();
               container.add( panel, BorderLayout.CENTER );

               // set size internal frame to size of its contents
               frame.pack();

```

Fig. 13.13 Creating a multiple document interface (part 1 of 3).

```
               // attach internal frame to desktop and show it
               theDesktop.add( frame );
               frame.setVisible( true );
            }

         } // end anonymous inner class

      ); // end call to addActionListener

      setSize( 600, 440 );
      setVisible( true );

   } // end constructor

   // execute application
   public static void main( String args[] )
   {
      DesktopTest application = new DesktopTest();

      application.setDefaultCloseOperation(
         JFrame.EXIT_ON_CLOSE );
   }

} // end class DesktopTest

// class to display an ImageIcon on a panel
class MyJPanel extends JPanel {
   private ImageIcon imageIcon;

   // load image
   public MyJPanel()
   {
      imageIcon = new ImageIcon( "jhtp4.png" );
   }

   // display imageIcon on panel
   public void paintComponent( Graphics g )
   {
      // call superclass paintComponent method
      super.paintComponent( g );

      // display icon
      imageIcon.paintIcon( this, g, 0, 0 );
   }

   // return image dimensions
   public Dimension getPreferredSize()
   {
      return new Dimension( imageIcon.getIconWidth(),
         imageIcon.getIconHeight() );
   }

} // end class MyJPanel
```

Fig. 13.13 Creating a multiple document interface (part 2 of 3).

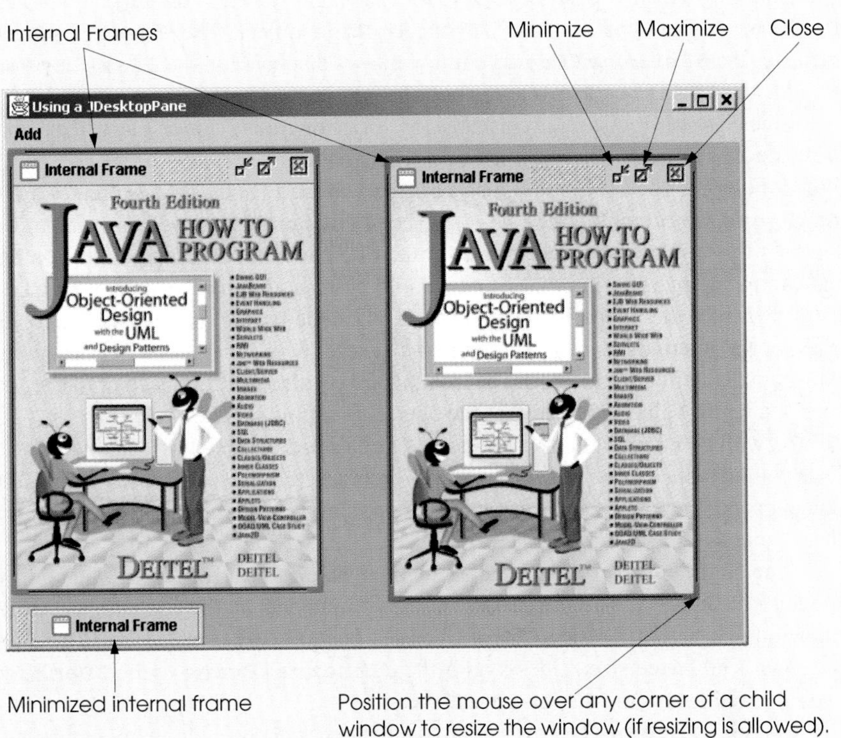

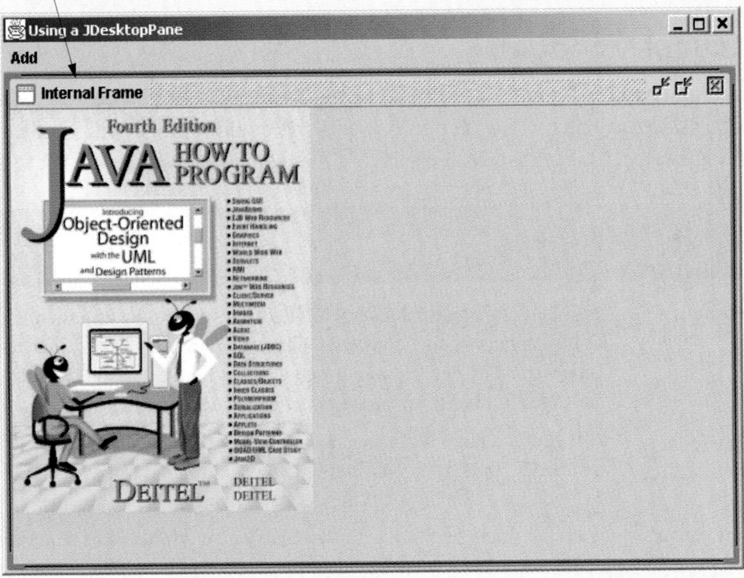

Fig. 13.13 Creating a multiple document interface (part 3 of 3).

Line 30 creates ***JDesktopPane*** (package **javax.swing**) reference **theDesktop** and assigns it a new **JDesktopPane** object. The **JDesktopPane** object manages the **JInternalFrame** child windows displayed in the **JDesktopPane**. Line 31 adds the **JDesktopPane** to the application window's content pane.

Lines 34–61 register an instance of an anonymous inner class that implements **ActionListener** to handle the event when the user selects the **newFrame** menu item. When the event occurs, method **actionPerformed** (lines 40–57) creates a **JInternalFrame** object with lines 43–44. The **JInternalFrame** constructor used here requires five arguments—a **String** for the title bar of the internal window, a **boolean** indicating whether the internal frame should be resizable by the user, a **boolean** indicating whether the internal frame should be closable by the user, a **boolean** indicating whether the internal frame should be maximizable by the user and a **boolean** indicating whether the internal frame should be minimizable by the user. For each of the boolean arguments, a **true** value indicates that the operation should be allowed.

As with **JFrame**s and **JApplet**s, a **JInternalFrame** has a content pane to which GUI components can be attached. Line 47 gets a reference to the **JInternalFrame**'s content pane. Line 48 creates an instance of our class **MyJPanel** (defined at lines 80–106) that is added to the **JInternalFrame**'s content pane at line 49.

Line 52 uses **JInternalFrame** method ***pack*** to set the size of the child window. Method **pack** uses the preferred sizes of the components on the content pane to determine the window's size. Class **MyJPanel** defines method **getPreferredSize** to specify the panel's preferred size. Line 55 adds the **JInternalFrame** to the **JDesktopPane**, and line 56 displays the **JInternalFrame**.

Classes **JInternalFrame** and **JDesktopPane** provide many methods for managing child windows. See the on-line API documentation for a complete list of these methods.

13.12 Layout Managers

In the preceding chapter, we introduced three layout managers—**FlowLayout**, **BorderLayout** and **GridLayout**. This section presents three additional layout managers (summarized in Figure 13.14). We discuss these layout managers in the sections that follow.

Layout Manager	Description
BoxLayout	A layout manager that allows GUI components to be arranged left-to-right or top-to-bottom in a container. Class ***Box*** defines a container with **BoxLayout** as its default layout manager and provides static methods to create a **Box** with a horizontal or vertical **BoxLayout**.
CardLayout	A layout manager that stacks components like a deck of cards. If a component in the deck is a container, it can use any layout manager. Only the component at the "top" of the deck is visible.
GridBagLayout	A layout manager similar to **GridLayout**. Unlike **GridLayout**, each component size can vary and components can be added in any order.

Fig. 13.14 Additional layout managers.

13.13 BoxLayout Layout Manager

The **BoxLayout** *layout manager* arranges GUI components horizontally along the *x*-axis or vertically along the *y*-axis of a container. The program of Fig. 13.15 demonstrates **BoxLayout** and the container class **Box** that uses **BoxLayout** as its default layout manager.

In the constructor for class **BoxLayoutDemo**, lines 19–20 obtain a reference to the content pane and set its layout to a **BorderLayout** with 30 pixels of horizontal and 30 pixels of vertical gap space between components. The space is to help isolate each of the containers with **BoxLayout** in this example.

Lines 23–28 define an array of **Box** container references called **boxes** and initialize each element of the array with **Box** objects. Elements 0 and 2 of the array are initialized with **static** method ***createHorizontalBox*** of class **Box**, which returns a **Box** container with a horizontal **BoxLayout** (GUI components are arranged left-to-right). Elements 1 and 3 of the array are initialized with **static** method ***createVerticalBox*** of class **Box**, which returns a **Box** container with a vertical **BoxLayout** (GUI components are arranged top-to-bottom).

```
1   // Fig. 13.15: BoxLayoutDemo.java
2   // Demonstrating BoxLayout.
3
4   // Java core packages
5   import java.awt.*;
6   import java.awt.event.*;
7
8   // Java extension packages
9   import javax.swing.*;
10
11  public class BoxLayoutDemo extends JFrame {
12
13     // set up GUI
14     public BoxLayoutDemo()
15     {
16        super( "Demostrating BoxLayout" );
17        final int SIZE = 3;
18
19        Container container = getContentPane();
20        container.setLayout( new BorderLayout( 30, 30 ) );
21
22        // create Box containers with BoxLayout
23        Box boxes[] = new Box[ 4 ];
24
25        boxes[ 0 ] = Box.createHorizontalBox();
26        boxes[ 1 ] = Box.createVerticalBox();
27        boxes[ 2 ] = Box.createHorizontalBox();
28        boxes[ 3 ] = Box.createVerticalBox();
29
30        // add buttons to boxes[ 0 ]
31        for ( int count = 0; count < SIZE; count++ )
32           boxes[ 0 ].add( new JButton( "boxes[0]: " + count ) );
```

Fig. 13.15 Demonstrating the **BoxLayout** layout manager (part 1 of 3).

```

      // create strut and add buttons to boxes[ 1 ]
      for ( int count = 0; count < SIZE; count++ ) {
         boxes[ 1 ].add( Box.createVerticalStrut( 25 ) );
         boxes[ 1 ].add( new JButton( "boxes[1]: " + count ) );
      }

      // create horizontal glue and add buttons to boxes[ 2 ]
      for ( int count = 0; count < SIZE; count++ ) {
         boxes[ 2 ].add( Box.createHorizontalGlue() );
         boxes[ 2 ].add( new JButton( "boxes[2]: " + count ) );
      }

      // create rigid area and add buttons to boxes[ 3 ]
      for ( int count = 0; count < SIZE; count++ ) {
         boxes[ 3 ].add(
            Box.createRigidArea( new Dimension( 12, 8 ) ) );
         boxes[ 3 ].add( new JButton( "boxes[3]: " + count ) );
      }

      // create vertical glue and add buttons to panel
      JPanel panel = new JPanel();
      panel.setLayout(
         new BoxLayout( panel, BoxLayout.Y_AXIS ) );

      for ( int count = 0; count < SIZE; count++ ) {
         panel.add( Box.createGlue() );
         panel.add( new JButton( "panel: " + count ) );
      }

      // place panels on frame
      container.add( boxes[ 0 ], BorderLayout.NORTH );
      container.add( boxes[ 1 ], BorderLayout.EAST );
      container.add( boxes[ 2 ], BorderLayout.SOUTH );
      container.add( boxes[ 3 ], BorderLayout.WEST );
      container.add( panel, BorderLayout.CENTER );

      setSize( 350, 300 );
      setVisible( true );

   } // end constructor

   // execute application
   public static void main( String args[] )
   {
      BoxLayoutDemo application = new BoxLayoutDemo();

      application.setDefaultCloseOperation(
         JFrame.EXIT_ON_CLOSE );
   }

} // end class BoxLayoutDemo
```

Fig. 13.15 Demonstrating the **BoxLayout** layout manager (part 2 of 3).

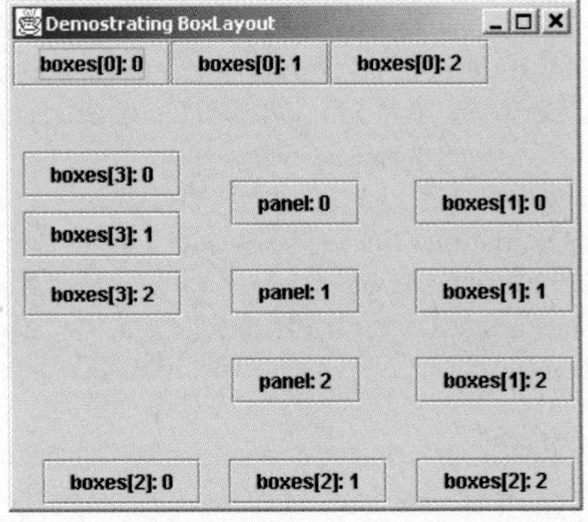

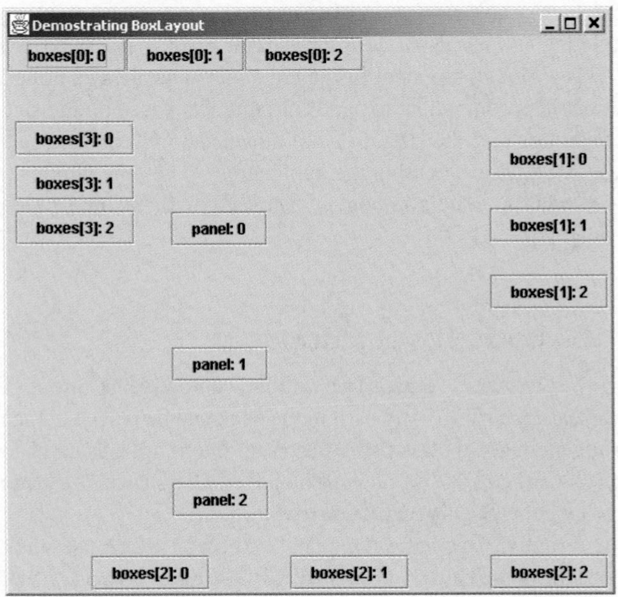

Fig. 13.15 Demonstrating the **`BoxLayout`** layout manager (part 3 of 3).

The **`for`** structure at lines 31–32 adds three **`JButton`**s to **`boxes[ 0 ]`** (a horizontal **`Box`**). The **`for`** structure at lines 35–38 adds three **`JButton`**s to **`boxes[ 1 ]`** (a vertical **`Box`**). Before adding each button, line 36 adds a *vertical strut* to the container with **`static`** method ***`createVerticalStrut`*** of class **`Box`**. A vertical strut is an invisible GUI component that has a fixed pixel height and is used to guarantee a fixed amount of space between GUI components. The argument to method **`createVerticalStrut`** determines the height of the strut in pixels. Class **`Box`** also defines method ***`createHorizontalStrut`*** for horizontal **`BoxLayout`**s.

The **`for`** structure at lines 41–44 adds three **`JButton`**s to **`boxes[ 2 ]`** (a horizontal **`Box`**). Before adding each button, line 42 adds *horizontal glue* to the container with **`static`** method ***`createHorizontalGlue`*** of class **`Box`**. Horizontal glue is an invisible GUI component that can be used between fixed-size GUI components to occupy additional space. Normally, extra space appears to the right of the last horizontal GUI component or below the last vertical GUI component in a **BoxLayout**. Glue allows the extra space to be placed between GUI components. Class **Box** also defines method ***createVerticalGlue*** for vertical **BoxLayout**s.

The **for** structure at lines 47–51 adds three **JButton**s to **boxes[3]** (a vertical **Box**). Before adding each button, lines 48–49 add a *rigid area* to the container with **static** method ***createRigidArea*** of class **Box**. A rigid area is an invisible GUI component that always has a fixed pixel width and height. The argument to method **createRigidArea** is a **Dimension** object that specifies the width and height of the rigid area.

Lines 54–56 create a **JPanel** object and set its layout in the conventional manner, using **Container** method **setLayout**. The **BoxLayout** constructor receives a reference to the container for which it controls the layout and a constant indicating whether the layout is horizontal (***BoxLayout.X_AXIS***) or vertical (***BoxLayout.Y_AXIS***).

The **for** structure at lines 58–61 adds three **JButton**s to **panel**.Before adding each button, line 59 adds a glue component to the container with **static** method ***createGlue*** of class **Box**. This component expands or contracts based on the size of the **Box**.

The **Box** containers and the **JPanel** are attached to the content pane's **BorderLayout** at lines 64–68. Try executing the application. When the window appears, resize the window to see how the glue components, strut components and rigid area affect the layout in each container.

13.14 CardLayout Layout Manager

The ***CardLayout layout manager*** arranges components into a "deck" of cards where only the top card is visible. Any card in the deck can be placed at the top of the deck at any time by using methods of class **CardLayout**. Each card is usually a container, such as a panel, and each card can use any layout manager. Class **CardLayout** inherits from **Object** and implements the **LayoutManager2** interface.

The program of Fig. 13.16 creates five panels. **JPanel deck** uses the **CardLayout** layout manager to control the card that is displayed. **JPanel**s **card1**, **card2** and **card3** are the individual cards in **deck**. **JPanel buttons** contains four buttons (with labels **First card**, **Next card**, **Previous card** and **Last card**) that enable the user to manipulate the deck. When the user clicks the **First card** button, the first card in **deck** (i.e., **card1**) is displayed. When the user clicks the **Last card** button, the last card (i.e., **card3**) in **deck** is displayed. Each time the user clicks the **Previous card** button, the previous card in **deck** is displayed. Each time the user clicks the **Next card** button, the next card in **deck** is displayed. Clicking the **Previous card** button or the **Next card** button repeatedly allows the user to cycle through the **deck** of cards. Application class **CardDeck** implements **ActionListener**, so the action events generated by the **JButton**s on **JPanel buttons** are handled by the application in its **actionPerformed** method.

Class **CardDeck** declares a reference of type **CardLayout** called **cardManager** (line 13). This reference is used to invoke **CardLayout** methods that manipulate the cards in the deck.

```
// Fig. 13.16: CardDeck.java
// Demonstrating CardLayout.

// Java core packages
import java.awt.*;
import java.awt.event.*;

// Java extension packages
import javax.swing.*;

public class CardDeck extends JFrame implements ActionListener {

   private CardLayout cardManager;
   private JPanel deck;
   private JButton controls[];
   private String names[] = { "First card", "Next card",
      "Previous card", "Last card" };

   // set up GUI
   public CardDeck()
   {
      super( "CardLayout " );

      Container container = getContentPane();

      // create the JPanel with CardLayout
      deck = new JPanel();
      cardManager = new CardLayout();
      deck.setLayout( cardManager );

      // set up card1 and add it to JPanel deck
      JLabel label1 =
         new JLabel( "card one", SwingConstants.CENTER );
      JPanel card1 = new JPanel();
      card1.add( label1 );
      deck.add( card1, label1.getText() ); // add card to deck

      // set up card2 and add it to JPanel deck
      JLabel label2 =
         new JLabel( "card two", SwingConstants.CENTER );
      JPanel card2 = new JPanel();
      card2.setBackground( Color.yellow );
      card2.add( label2 );
      deck.add( card2, label2.getText() ); // add card to deck

      // set up card3 and add it to JPanel deck
      JLabel label3 = new JLabel( "card three" );
      JPanel card3 = new JPanel();
      card3.setLayout( new BorderLayout() );
      card3.add( new JButton( "North" ), BorderLayout.NORTH );
      card3.add( new JButton( "West" ), BorderLayout.WEST );
      card3.add( new JButton( "East" ), BorderLayout.EAST );
      card3.add( new JButton( "South" ), BorderLayout.SOUTH );
```

Fig. 13.16 Demonstrating the **CardLayout** layout manager (part 1 of 3).

```
      card3.add( label3, BorderLayout.CENTER );
      deck.add( card3, label3.getText() ); // add card to deck

      // create and layout buttons that will control deck
      JPanel buttons = new JPanel();
      buttons.setLayout( new GridLayout( 2, 2 ) );
      controls = new JButton[ names.length ];

      for ( int count = 0; count < controls.length; count++ ) {
         controls[ count ] = new JButton( names[ count ] );
         controls[ count ].addActionListener( this );
         buttons.add( controls[ count ] );
      }

      // add JPanel deck and JPanel buttons to the applet
      container.add( buttons, BorderLayout.WEST );
      container.add( deck, BorderLayout.EAST );

      setSize( 450, 200 );
      setVisible( true );

   }  // end constructor

   // handle button events by switching cards
   public void actionPerformed( ActionEvent event )
   {
      // show first card
      if ( event.getSource() == controls[ 0 ] )
         cardManager.first( deck );

      // show next card
      else if ( event.getSource() == controls[ 1 ] )
         cardManager.next( deck );

      // show previous card
      else if ( event.getSource() == controls[ 2 ] )
         cardManager.previous( deck );

      // show last card
      else if ( event.getSource() == controls[ 3 ] )
         cardManager.last( deck );
   }

   // execute application
   public static void main( String args[] )
   {
      CardDeck cardDeckDemo = new CardDeck();

      cardDeckDemo.setDefaultCloseOperation(
         JFrame.EXIT_ON_CLOSE );
   }

}  // end class CardDeck
```

Fig. 13.16 Demonstrating the **CardLayout** layout manager (part 2 of 3).

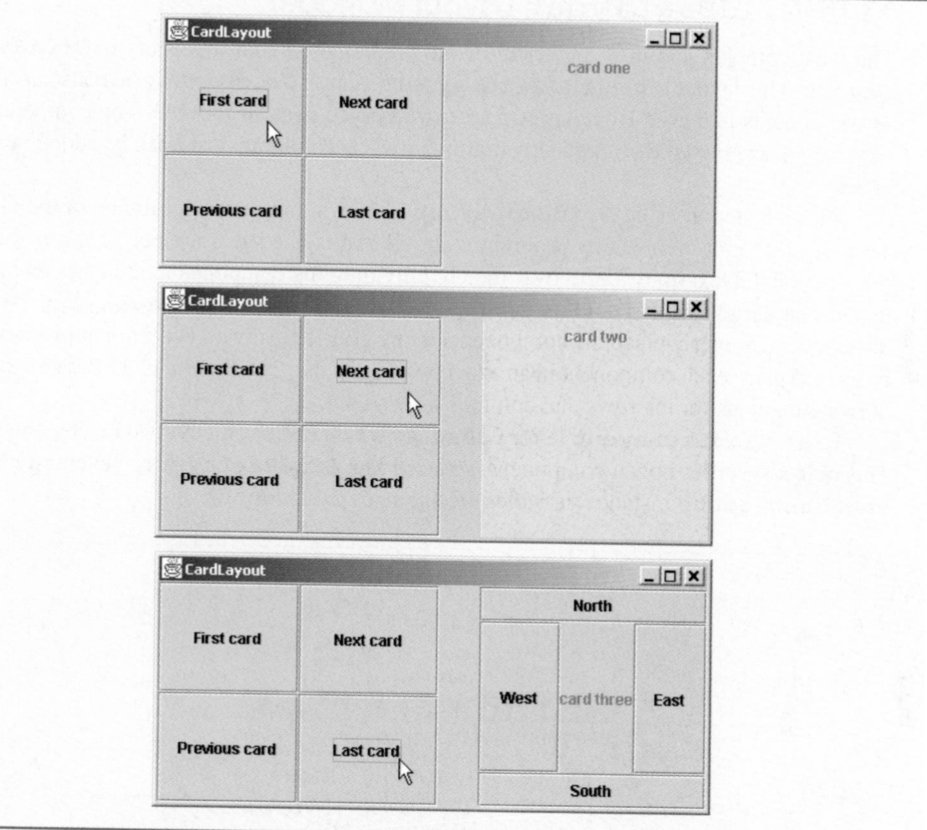

Fig. 13.16 Demonstrating the **CardLayout** layout manager (part 3 of 3).

The constructor method (lines 20–75) builds the GUI. Lines 27–29 create **JPanel deck**, create **CardLayout** object **cardManager** and set the layout manager for **deck** to **cardManager**. Next, the constructor creates the **JPanel**s **card1**, **card2**, and **card3** and their GUI components. As we set up each card, we add the card to **deck**, using **Container** method **add** with two arguments—a **Component** and a **String**. The **Component** is the **JPanel** object that represents the card. The **String** argument identifies the card. For example, line 36 adds **JPanel card1** to deck and uses **JLabel label1**'s label as the **String** identifier for the card. **JPanel**s **card2** and **card3** are added to **deck** at lines 44–55. Next, the constructor creates the **JPanel buttons** and its **JButton** objects (lines 58–66). Line 64 registers the **ActionListener** for each **JButton**. Finally, **buttons** and **deck** are added to the content pane's **WEST** and **EAST** regions, respectively.

Method **actionPerformed** (lines 78–95) determines which **JButton** generated the event by using **EventObject** method **getSource**. **CardLayout** methods ***first***, ***previous***, ***next*** and ***last*** are used to display the particular card corresponding to which **JButton** the user pressed. Method **first** displays the first card added to the deck. Method **previous** displays the previous card in the deck. Method **next** displays the next card in the deck. Method **last** displays the last card in the deck. Note that **deck** is passed to each of these methods.

13.15 `GridBagLayout` Layout Manager

The most complex and most powerful of the predefined layout managers is ***`GridBagLayout`***. This layout is similar to **`GridLayout`** because **`GridBagLayout`** also arranges components in a grid. However, **`GridBagLayout`** is more flexible. The components can vary in size (i.e., they can occupy multiple rows and columns) and can be added in any order.

The first step in using **`GridBagLayout`** is determining the appearance of the GUI. This step does not involve any programming; all that is needed is a piece of paper. First, draw the GUI. Next draw a grid over the GUI dividing the components into rows and columns. The initial row and column numbers should be 0 so the **`GridBagLayout`** layout manager can properly place the components in the grid. The row and column numbers will be used to place each component in an exact position in the grid. Figure 13.17 demonstrates drawing the lines for the rows and columns over a GUI.

To use **`GridBagLayout`**, a ***`GridBagConstraints`*** object must be constructed. This object specifies how a component is placed in a **`GridBagLayout`**. Several **`GridBagConstraints`** instance variables are summarized in Fig. 13.18.

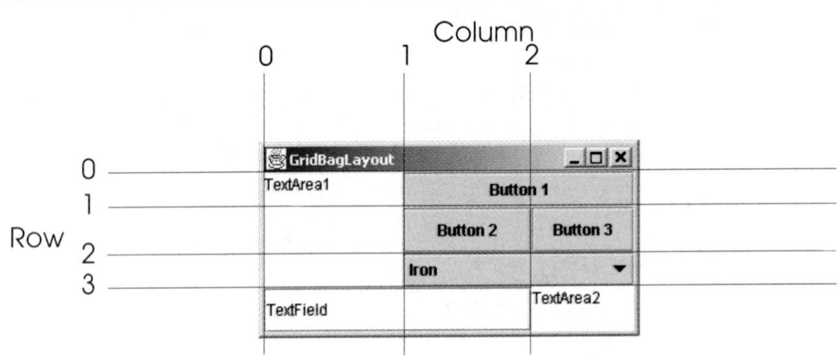

Fig. 13.17 Designing a GUI that will use **`GridBagLayout`**.

`GridBagConstraints` Instance Variable	Description
`gridx`	The column in which the component will be placed.
`gridy`	The row in which the component will be placed.
`gridwidth`	The number of columns the component occupies.
`gridheight`	The number of rows the component occupies.
`weightx`	The portion of extra space to allocate horizontally. The components can become wider when extra space is available.
`weighty`	The portion of extra space to allocate vertically. The components can become taller when extra space is available.

Fig. 13.18 **`GridBagConstraints`** instance variables.

Variables ***gridx*** and ***gridy*** specify the row and column where the upper-left corner of the component is placed in the grid. Variable **gridx** corresponds to the column and the variable **gridy** corresponds to the row. In Fig. 13.17, the **JComboBox** (displaying "**Iron**") has a **gridx** value of 1 and a **gridy** value of 2.

Variable ***gridwidth*** specifies the number of columns a component occupies. In Fig. 13.17, the **JComboBox** button occupies two columns. Variable ***gridheight*** specifies the number of rows a component occupies. In Fig. 13.17, the **JTextArea** on the left side of the window occupies three rows.

Variable ***weightx*** specifies how to distribute extra horizontal space to components in a **GridBagLayout** when the container is resized. A zero value indicates that the component does not grow horizontally on its own. However, if the component spans a column containing a component with nonzero **weightx** value, the component with zero **weightx** value will grow horizontally in the same proportion as the other component(s) in the same column. This is because each component must be maintained in the same row and column in which it was originally placed.

Variable ***weighty*** specifies how to distribute extra vertical space to components in a **GridBagLayout** when the container is resized. A zero value indicates that the component does not grow vertically on its own. However, if the component spans a row containing a component with nonzero **weighty** value, the component with zero **weighty** value grows vertically in the same proportion as the other component(s) in the same row.

In Fig. 13.17, the effects of **weighty** and **weightx** cannot easily be seen until the container is resized and additional space becomes available. Components with larger weight values occupy more of the additional space than components with smaller weight values. The exercises explore the effects of varying **weightx** and **weighty**.

Components should be given nonzero positive weight values—otherwise the components will "huddle" together in the middle of the container. Figure 13.19 shows the GUI of Fig. 13.17—where all weights have been set to zero.

Common Programming Error 13.6

Using a negative value for either ***weightx*** *or* ***weighty*** *is a logic error.*

GridBagConstraints instance variable ***fill*** specifies how much of the component's area (the number of rows and columns the component occupies in the grid) is occupied. The variable **fill** is assigned one of the following **GridBagConstraints** constants: ***NONE***, ***VERTICAL***, ***HORIZONTAL*** or ***BOTH***. The default value is **NONE**, which indicates that the component will not grow in either direction. **VERTICAL** indicates that the component will grow vertically. **HORIZONTAL** indicates that the component will grow horizontally. **BOTH** indicates that the component will grow in both directions.

GridBagConstraints instance variable ***anchor*** specifies the location of the component in the area when the component does not fill the entire area. The variable **anchor** is assigned one of the following **GridBagConstraints** constants: ***NORTH***, ***NORTHEAST***, ***EAST***, ***SOUTHEAST***, ***SOUTH***, ***SOUTHWEST***, ***WEST***, ***NORTHWEST*** or ***CENTER***. The default value is **CENTER**.

The program of Fig. 13.20 uses the **GridBagLayout** layout manager to arrange the components in the GUI of Fig. 13.17. The program does nothing other than demonstrate how to use **GridBagLayout**.

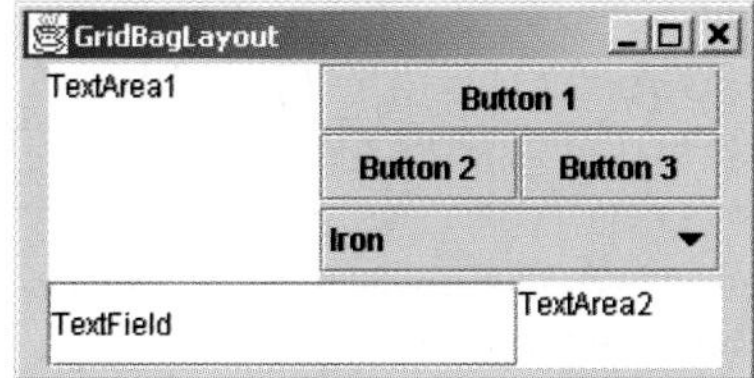

Fig. 13.19 **`GridBagLayout`** with the weights set to zero.

```
// Fig. 13.20: GridBagDemo.java
// Demonstrating GridBagLayout.

// Java core packages
import java.awt.*;
import java.awt.event.*;

// Java extension packages
import javax.swing.*;

public class GridBagDemo extends JFrame {
   private Container container;
   private GridBagLayout layout;
   private GridBagConstraints constraints;

   // set up GUI
   public GridBagDemo()
   {
      super( "GridBagLayout" );

      container = getContentPane();
      layout = new GridBagLayout();
      container.setLayout( layout );

      // instantiate gridbag constraints
      constraints = new GridBagConstraints();

      // create GUI components
      JTextArea textArea1 = new JTextArea( "TextArea1", 5, 10 );
      JTextArea textArea2 = new JTextArea( "TextArea2", 2, 2 );

      String names[] = { "Iron", "Steel", "Brass" };
      JComboBox comboBox = new JComboBox( names );

      JTextField textField = new JTextField( "TextField" );
      JButton button1 = new JButton( "Button 1" );
      JButton button2 = new JButton( "Button 2" );
      JButton button3 = new JButton( "Button 3" );
```

Fig. 13.20 Demonstrating the **`GridBagLayout`** layout manager (part 1 of 3).

```

      // textArea1
      // weightx and weighty are both 0: the default
      // anchor for all components is CENTER: the default
      constraints.fill = GridBagConstraints.BOTH;
      addComponent( textArea1, 0, 0, 1, 3 );

      // button1
      // weightx and weighty are both 0: the default
      constraints.fill = GridBagConstraints.HORIZONTAL;
      addComponent( button1, 0, 1, 2, 1 );

      // comboBox
      // weightx and weighty are both 0: the default
      // fill is HORIZONTAL
      addComponent( comboBox, 2, 1, 2, 1 );

      // button2
      constraints.weightx = 1000;  // can grow wider
      constraints.weighty = 1;     // can grow taller
      constraints.fill = GridBagConstraints.BOTH;
      addComponent( button2, 1, 1, 1, 1 );

      // button3
      // fill is BOTH
      constraints.weightx = 0;
      constraints.weighty = 0;
      addComponent( button3, 1, 2, 1, 1 );

      // textField
      // weightx and weighty are both 0, fill is BOTH
      addComponent( textField, 3, 0, 2, 1 );

      // textArea2
      // weightx and weighty are both 0, fill is BOTH
      addComponent( textArea2, 3, 2, 1, 1 );

      setSize( 300, 150 );
      setVisible( true );
   }

   // method to set constraints on
   private void addComponent( Component component,
      int row, int column, int width, int height )
   {
      // set gridx and gridy
      constraints.gridx = column;
      constraints.gridy = row;

      // set gridwidth and gridheight
      constraints.gridwidth = width;
      constraints.gridheight = height;

```

Fig. 13.20 Demonstrating the **GridBagLayout** layout manager (part 2 of 3).

```
92          // set constraints and add component
93          layout.setConstraints( component, constraints );
94          container.add( component );
95       }
96
97       // execute application
98       public static void main( String args[] )
99       {
100         GridBagDemo application = new GridBagDemo();
101
102         application.setDefaultCloseOperation(
103            JFrame.EXIT_ON_CLOSE );
104      }
105
106   }  // end class GridBagDemo
```

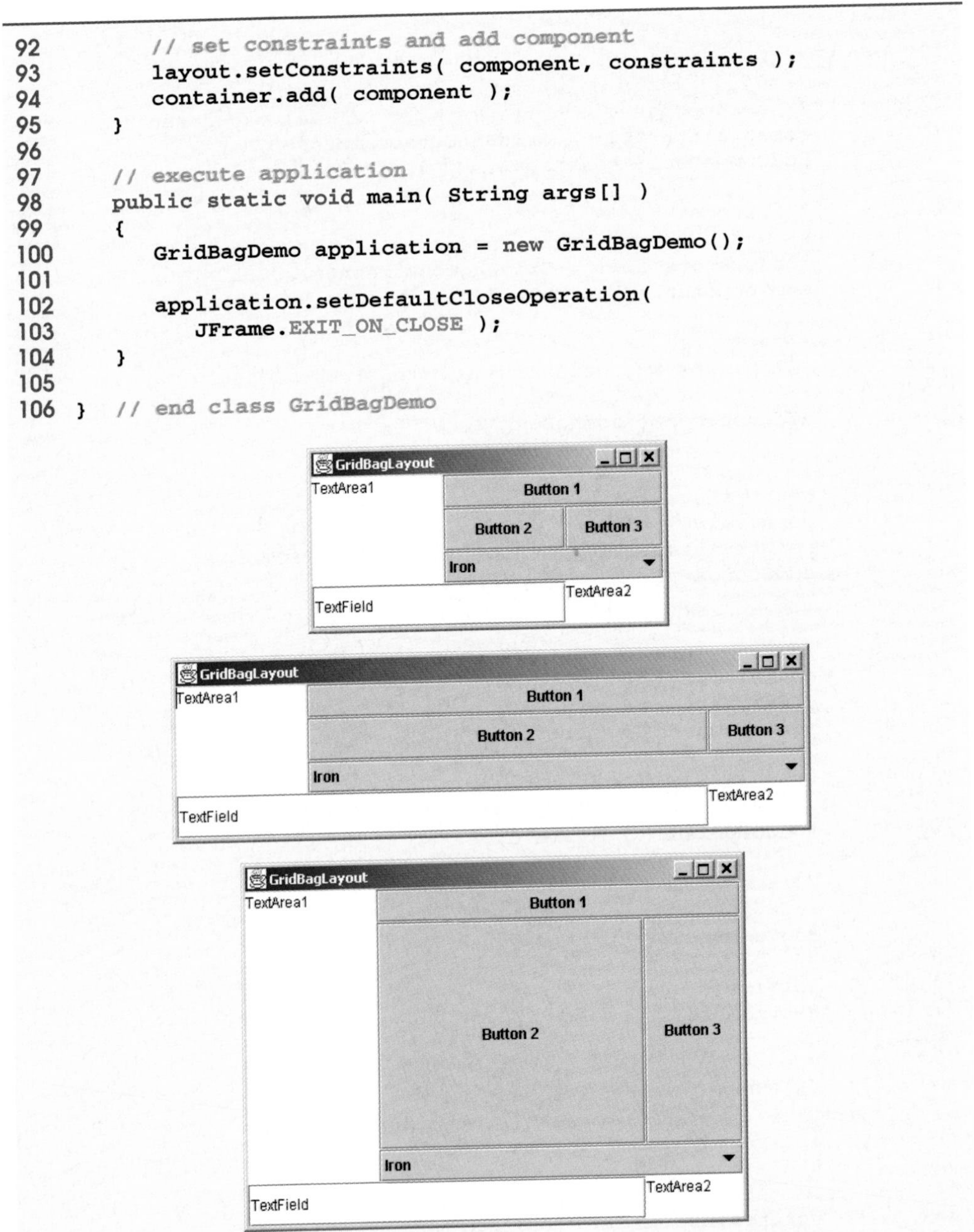

Fig. 13.20 Demonstrating the **`GridBagLayout`** layout manager (part 3 of 3).

The GUI consists of three **`JButton`**s, two **`JTextArea`**s, a **`JComboBox`** and a **`JTextField`**. The layout manager for the content pane is **`GridBagLayout`**. Lines 22–23 instantiate the **`GridBagLayout`** object and set the layout manager for the content pane to **`layout`**. The **`GridBagConstraints`** object used to determine the location and size of each component in the grid is instantiated with line 26. Lines 23 through 30 instantiate each of the GUI components that will be added to the content pane.

JTextArea textArea1 is the first component added to the **GridBagLayout** (line 44). The values for **weightx** and **weighty** values are not specified in **gbConstraints**, so each has the value zero by default. Thus, the **JTextArea** will not resize itself even if space is available. However, the **JTextArea** spans multiple rows, so the vertical size is subject to the **weighty** values of **JButton**s **button2** and **button3**. When either **button2** or **button3** is resized vertically based on its **weighty** value, the **JTextArea** is also resized.

Line 43 sets variable **fill** in **constraints** to **GridBagConstraints.BOTH**, causing the **JTextArea** to always fill its entire allocated area in the grid. An **anchor** value is not specified in **constraints**, so the default **CENTER** is used. We do not use variable **anchor** in this program, so all components will use the default. Line 36 calls our utility method ***addComponent*** method (defined at lines 81–95). The **JTextArea** object, the row, the column, the number of columns to span and the number of rows to span are passed as arguments.

Method **addComponent**'s parameters are a **Component** reference **component** and integers **row**, **column**, **width** and **height**. Lines 85–86 set the **GridBagConstraints** variables **gridx** and **gridy**. The **gridx** variable is assigned the column in which the **Component** will be placed, and the **gridy** value is assigned the row in which the **Component** will be placed. Lines 89–90 set the **GridBagConstraints** variables **gridwidth** and **gridheight**. The **gridwidth** variable specifies the number of columns the **Component** will span in the grid and the **gridheight** variable specifies the number of rows the **Component** will span in the grid. Line 93 sets the **GridBagConstraints** for a component in the **GridBagLayout**. Method ***setConstraints*** of class **GridBagLayout** takes a **Component** argument and a **GridBagConstraints** argument. Method **add** (line 94) is used to add the component to the content pane.

JButton object **button1** is the next component added (lines 48–49). The values of **weightx** and **weighty** are still zero. The **fill** variable is set to **HORIZONTAL**—the component will always fill its area in the horizontal direction. The vertical direction is not filled. The **weighty** value is zero, so the button will become taller only if another component in the same row has a nonzero **weighty** value. **JButton b1** is located at row 0, column 1. One row and two columns are occupied.

JComboBox comboBox is the next component added (line 54). The **weightx** and **weighty** values are zero, and the **fill** variable is set to **HORIZONTAL**. The **JComboBox** button will grow only in the horizontal direction. Note that the **weightx**, **weighty** and **fill** variables remain set in **gbConstraints** until they are changed. The **JComboBox** button is placed at row 2, column 1. One row and two columns are occupied.

JButton object **button2** is the next component added (lines 57–60). **JButton button2** is given a **weightx** value of **1000** and a **weighty** value of **1**. The area occupied by the button is capable of growing in the vertical and horizontal directions. The **fill** variable is set to **BOTH**, which specifies that the button will always fill the entire area. When the window is resized, **b2** will grow. The button is placed at row 1, column 1. One row and one column are occupied.

JButton button3 is added next (lines 64–66). Both the **weightx** value and **weighty** value are set to zero, and the value of **fill** is **BOTH**. **JButton button3** will grow if the window is resized; it is affected by the weight values of **button2**. Note that the **weightx** value for **button2** is much larger than **button3**. When resizing occurs, **button2** will occupy a larger percentage of the new space. The button is placed at row 1, column 2. One row and one column are occupied.

Both the **JTextField** (line 70) and **JTextArea textArea2** (line 74) have a **weightx** value 0 and a **weighty** value 0. The value of **fill** is **BOTH**. The **JTextField** is placed at row 3, column 0, and the **JTextArea** is placed at row 3, column 2. The **JTextField** occupies one row and two columns. The **JTextArea** occupies one row and one column.

When you execute this application, try resizing the window to see how the constraints for each GUI component affect its position and size in the window.

13.16 GridBagConstraints Constants RELATIVE and REMAINDER

A variation of **GridBagLayout** does not use **gridx** and **gridy**. Rather, **GridbagConstraints** constants ***RELATIVE*** and ***REMAINDER*** are used in their place. **RELATIVE** specifies that the next-to-last component in a particular row should be placed to the right of the previous component in that row. **REMAINDER** specifies that a component is the last component in a row. Any component that is not the second-to-last or last component on a row must specify values for **GridbagConstraints** variables **gridwidth** and **gridheight**. Class **GridBagDemo2** in Fig. 13.21 arranges components in **GridBagLayout**, using these constants.

```
// Fig. 13.21: GridBagDemo2.java
// Demonstrating GridBagLayout constants.

// Java core packages
import java.awt.*;
import java.awt.event.*;

// Java extension packages
import javax.swing.*;

public class GridBagDemo2 extends JFrame {
   private GridBagLayout layout;
   private GridBagConstraints constraints;
   private Container container;

   // set up GUI
   public GridBagDemo2()
   {
      super( "GridBagLayout" );

      container = getContentPane();
      layout = new GridBagLayout();
      container.setLayout( layout );

```

Fig. 13.21 Demonstrating the **GridBagConstraints** constants **RELATIVE** and **REMAINDER** (part 1 of 3).

```
      // instantiate gridbag constraints
      constraints = new GridBagConstraints();

      // create GUI components
      String metals[] = { "Copper", "Aluminum", "Silver" };
      JComboBox comboBox = new JComboBox( metals );

      JTextField textField = new JTextField( "TextField" );

      String fonts[] = { "Serif", "Monospaced" };
      JList list = new JList( fonts );

      String names[] =
         { "zero", "one", "two", "three", "four" };
      JButton buttons[] = new JButton[ names.length ];

      for ( int count = 0; count < buttons.length; count++ )
         buttons[ count ] = new JButton( names[ count ] );

      // define GUI component constraints
      // textField
      constraints.weightx = 1;
      constraints.weighty = 1;
      constraints.fill = GridBagConstraints.BOTH;
      constraints.gridwidth = GridBagConstraints.REMAINDER;
      addComponent( textField );

      // buttons[0] -- weightx and weighty are 1: fill is BOTH
      constraints.gridwidth = 1;
      addComponent( buttons[ 0 ] );

      // buttons[1] -- weightx and weighty are 1: fill is BOTH
      constraints.gridwidth = GridBagConstraints.RELATIVE;
      addComponent( buttons[ 1 ] );

      // buttons[2] -- weightx and weighty are 1: fill is BOTH
      constraints.gridwidth = GridBagConstraints.REMAINDER;
      addComponent( buttons[ 2 ] );

      // comboBox -- weightx is 1: fill is BOTH
      constraints.weighty = 0;
      constraints.gridwidth = GridBagConstraints.REMAINDER;
      addComponent( comboBox );

      // buttons[3] -- weightx is 1: fill is BOTH
      constraints.weighty = 1;
      constraints.gridwidth = GridBagConstraints.REMAINDER;
      addComponent( buttons[ 3 ] );

      // buttons[4] -- weightx and weighty are 1: fill is BOTH
      constraints.gridwidth = GridBagConstraints.RELATIVE;
      addComponent( buttons[ 4 ] );
```

Fig. 13.21 Demonstrating the **GridBagConstraints** constants **RELATIVE** and **REMAINDER** (part 2 of 3).

```
77
78        // list -- weightx and weighty are 1: fill is BOTH
79        constraints.gridwidth = GridBagConstraints.REMAINDER;
80        addComponent( list );
81
82        setSize( 300, 200 );
83        setVisible( true );
84
85     }  // end constructor
86
87     // addComponent is programmer-defined
88     private void addComponent( Component component )
89     {
90        layout.setConstraints( component, constraints );
91        container.add( component );      // add component
92     }
93
94     // execute application
95     public static void main( String args[] )
96     {
97        GridBagDemo2 application = new GridBagDemo2();
98
99        application.setDefaultCloseOperation(
100          JFrame.EXIT_ON_CLOSE );
101    }
102
103 }  // end class GridBagDemo2
```

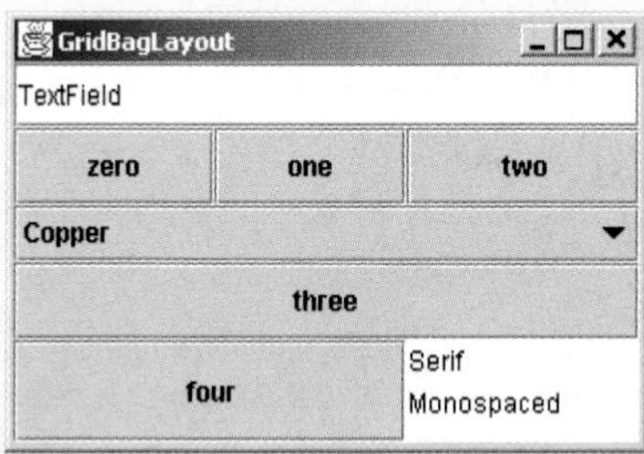

Fig. 13.21 Demonstrating the **GridBagConstraints** constants **RELATIVE** and **REMAINDER** (part 3 of 3).

Lines 22–23 construct a **GridBagLayout** and set the content pane's layout manager to **GridBagLayout**. The components that are placed in **GridBagLayout** are each constructed (lines 29–42). The components are five **JButton**s, one **JTextField**, one **JList** and one **JComboBox**.

The **JTextField** is added first (lines 46–50). The **weightx** and **weighty** values are set to 1. The **fill** variable is set to **BOTH**. Line 49 specifies that the **JTextField** is the last component on the line. The **JTextField** is added to the content pane with a call to our utility method **addComponent** (defined at lines 88–92). Method **addComponent** takes a **Component** argument and uses **GridBagLayout** method **setConstraints** to set the constraints for the **Component**. Method **add** attaches the component to the content pane.

JButton buttons[0] (lines 53–54) has **weightx** and **weighty** values of 1. The **fill** variable is **BOTH**. Because **buttons[0]** is not one of the last two components on the row, it is given a **gridwidth** of 1 so it will occupy one column. The **JButton** is added to the content pane with a call to utility method **addComponent**.

JButton buttons[1] (lines 57–58) has **weightx** and **weighty** values of 1. The **fill** variable is **BOTH**. Line 57 specifies that the **JButton** is to be placed relative to the previous component. The **Button** is added to the **JFrame** with a call to **addComponent**.

JButton buttons[2] (lines 61–62) has **weightx** and **weighty** values of 1. The **fill** variable is **BOTH**. This **JButton** is the last component on the line, so **REMAINDER** is used. The **JButton** is added to the content pane with a call to utility method **addComponent**.

The **JComboBox** button (lines 65–67) has a **weightx** 1 and a **weighty** 0. The **JComboBox** will not grow in the vertical direction. The **JComboBox** is the only component on the line, so **REMAINDER** is used. The **JComboBox** is added to the content pane with a call to utility method **addComponent**.

JButton buttons[3] (lines 70–72) has **weightx** and **weighty** values of 1. The **fill** variable is **BOTH**. This **JButton** is the only component on the line, so **REMAINDER** is used. The **JButton** is added to the content pane with a call to utility method **addComponent**.

JButton buttons[4] (lines 75–76) has **weightx** and **weighty** values of 1. The **fill** variable is **BOTH**. This **JButton** is the next-to-last component on the line, so **RELATIVE** is used. The **JButton** is added to the content pane with a call to utility method **addComponent**.

The **JList** component (lines 79–80) has **weightx** and **weighty** values of 1. The **fill** variable is **BOTH**. The **JList** is added to the content pane with a call to utility method **addComponent**.

13.17 (Optional Case Study) Thinking About Objects: Model-View-Controller

Design patterns describe proven strategies for building reliable object-oriented software systems. Our case study adheres to the *Model-View-Controller* (MVC) architecture, which uses several design patterns.[1] MVC divides system responsibilities into three parts:

1. the *model*, which contains all program data and logic;
2. the *view*, which provides a visual presentation of the model and
3. the *controller*, which defines the system behavior by sending user input to the model.

Using the controller, the user changes the data in the model. The model then informs the view of the change in data. The view changes its visual presentation to reflect the changes in the model.

For example, in our simulation, the user adds a **Person** to the model by pressing either the **First Floor** or **Second Floor** **JButton** in the controller (see Fig. 2.22–

1. For those readers who seek further study in design patterns and MVC architecture, we encourage you to read our "Discovering Design Patterns" material in Sections 1.16, 9.24, 13.18, 15.13, 17.11 and 21.12

Fig. 2.24). The model then notifies the view of the **Person**'s creation. The view, in response to this notification, displays a **Person** on a **Floor**. The model is unaware of how the view displays the **Person**, and the view is unaware of how or why the model created the **Person**.

The MVC architecture helps construct reliable and easily modifiable systems. If we desire text-based output rather than graphical output for the elevator simulation, we may create an alternate view to produce text-based output, without altering the model or the controller. We could also provide a three-dimensional view that uses a first-person perspective to allow the user to "take part" in the simulation; such views are commonly employed in virtual-reality-based systems.

Elevator-Simulation MVC

We now apply the MVC architecture to our elevator simulation. Every UML diagram we have provided to this point (with the exception of the use-case diagram) relates to the model of our elevator system. We provide a "higher-level" class diagram of the simulation in Fig. 13.22. Class **ElevatorSimulation**—a **JFrame** subclass—aggregates one instance each of classes **ElevatorModel**, **ElevatorView** and **ElevatorController** to create the **ElevatorSimulation** application. As mentioned in "Thinking About Objects" Section 10.22, the rectangle with the upper-right corner "folded over" represents a note in the UML. In this case, each note points to a specific class (through a dotted line) to describe that class' role in the system. Classes **ElevatorModel**, **ElevatorView** and **ElevatorController** encapsulate all objects comprising the model, view and controller portions of our simulation, respectively.

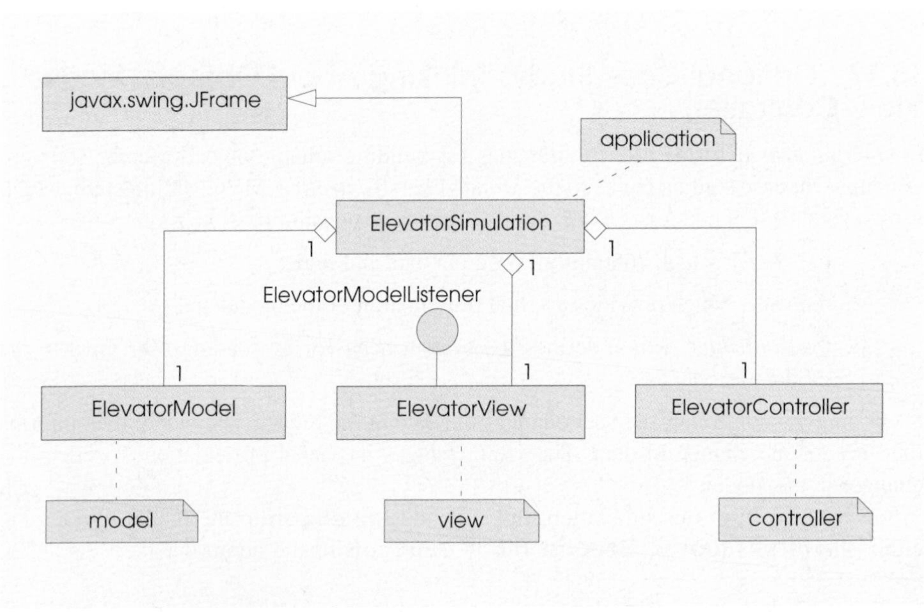

Fig. 13.22 Class diagram of the elevator simulation.

We showed in Fig. 9.38 that class **ElevatorModel** is an aggregation of several classes. To save space, we do not repeat this aggregation in Fig. 13.22. Class **ElevatorView** is also an aggregation of several classes—we expand the class diagram of **ElevatorView** in "Thinking About Objects" Section 22.9 to show these additional classes. Class **ElevatorController**, as described in Section 12.16, represents the simulation controller. Note that class **ElevatorView** implements interface **ElevatorModelListener**, which implements all interfaces used in our simulation, so the **ElevatorView** can receive all events from the model.

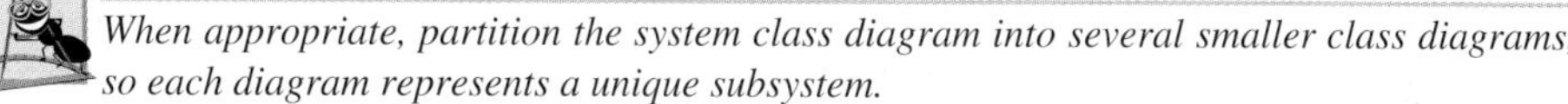

Software Engineering Observation 13.7

When appropriate, partition the system class diagram into several smaller class diagrams, so each diagram represents a unique subsystem.

Class **ElevatorSimulation** contains no attributes other than its references to an **ElevatorModel** object, an **ElevatorView** object and an **ElevatorController** object. The only behavior for class **ElevatorSimulation** is to start the program—therefore, in Java, class **ElevatorSimulation** contains a **static main** method that calls the constructor, which instantiates the **ElevatorModel**, **ElevatorView** and **ElevatorController** objects. We implement class **ElevatorSimulation** in Java later in this section.

Component Diagrams

Figure 13.22 helps us construct another diagram of the UML that we use to design our system—the *component diagram*. The component diagram models the "pieces"—called *components*—that the system needs to perform its tasks. These pieces include binary executables, compiled **.class** files, **.java** files, images, packages, resources, etc. We present the component diagram for our simulation in Fig. 13.23.

In Fig. 13.23, each box that contains the two small white boxes overlapping its left side is a *component*. A component in the UML is drawn similar to a plug (the two overlapping boxes represent the plug's prongs)—a component may be "plugged-in" to other systems without having to change the component. Our system contains five components: **ElevatorSimulation.class**, **ElevatorSimulation.java**, **ElevatorModel.java**, **ElevatorView.java** and **ElevatorController.java**.

In Fig. 13.23, the graphics that resemble folders (boxes with tabs in their upper-left corners) represent *packages* in the UML. We can group classes, objects, components, use cases, etc., in a package. In this diagram (and in the remainder of our case study), the UML packages refer to Java packages (introduced in Section 8.5). In our discussion, we use lower-case bold-face Courier type for package names. The packages in our system are **model**, **view** and **controller**. Component **ElevatorSimulation.java** contains one instance each of all components in these packages. Currently, each package contains only one component—a **.java** file. The **model** package contains **ElevatorModel.java**, the **view** package contains **ElevatorView.java** and the **controller** package contains **ElevatorController.java**. We add components to each package in the appendices, when we implement each class from our class diagrams into a component (**.java** file).

The dotted arrows in Fig. 13.23 indicate a *dependency* between two components—the direction of the arrow indicates the "depends on" relationship. A dependency describes the relationship between components in which changes in one component affect another component. For example, component **ElevatorSimulation.class** depends on component **ElevatorSimulation.java**, because a change in **ElevatorSimulation.java** affects **ElevatorSimulation.class** when **ElevatorSimulation.java** is compiled. Section 12.16 mentioned that the **ElevatorController** object contains a reference to the **ElevatorModel** object (to place **Person**s on **Floor**s). Therefore, **ElevatorController.java** depends on **ElevatorModel.java**.

Software Engineering Observation 13.8

A component diagram's dependencies help designers group components for reuse in future systems. For example, in our simulation, designers can reuse **ElevatorModel.java** *in other systems without having to reuse* **ElevatorView.java** *(and vice versa), because these components do not depend on each other. However, if a designer wanted to reuse* **ElevatorController.java***, the designer would have to reuse* **ElevatorModel.java***.*

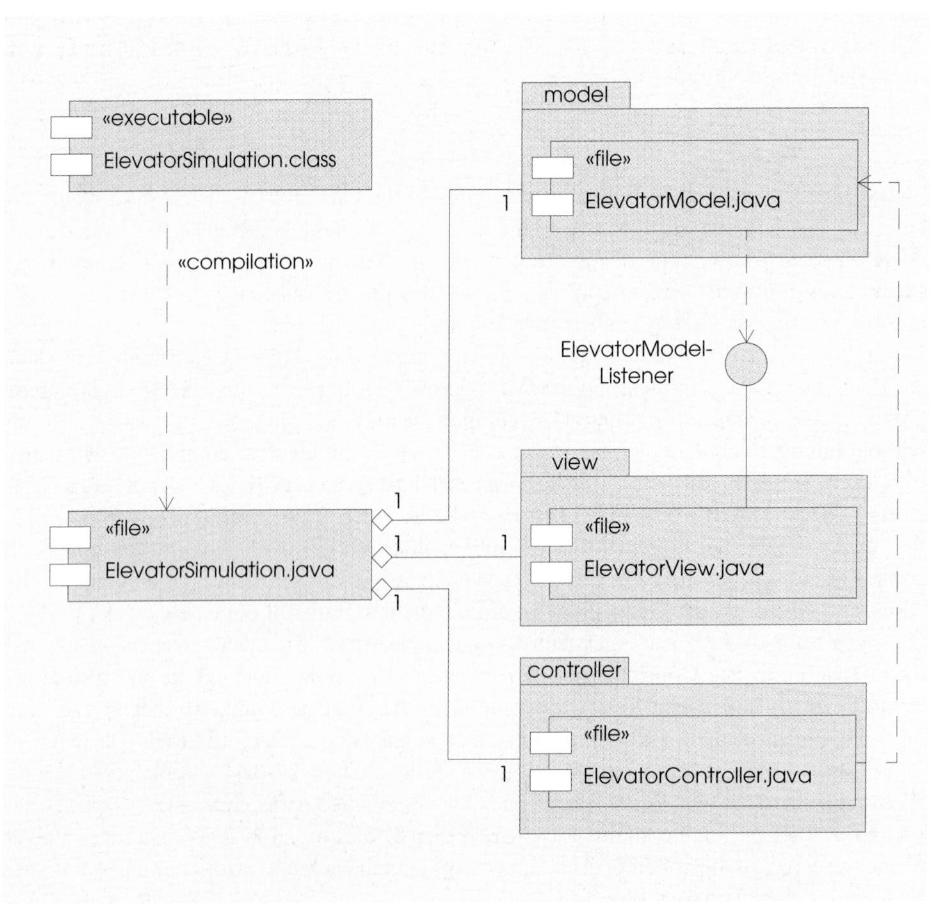

Fig. 13.23 Component diagram for elevator simulation.

According to Fig. 13.23, **ElevatorModel.java** and **ElevatorView.java** do not depend on each other—they communicate through interface **ElevatorModelListener**, which implements all interfaces in the simulation. **ElevatorView.java** realizes interface **ElevatorModelListener**, and **ElevatorModel.java** depends on interface **ElevatorModelListener**.

Figure 13.23 contains several *stereotypes*—words placed in *guillemets* (« ») indicating an element's role. We mentioned the «interface» stereotype in "Thinking About Objects" Section 11.10. The «compilation» stereotype describes the dependency between **ElevatorSimulation.class** and **ElevatorSimulation.java**—**ElevatorSimulation.java** compiles to **ElevatorSimulation.class**. The «executable» stereotype specifies that a component is an application, and the «file» stereotype specifies that a component is a file containing source code for the executable.

Implementation: ***ElevatorSimulation.java***

We use the component diagram of Fig. 13.23, the class diagram of Fig. 13.22 and the use-case diagram of Fig. 12.28 to implement **ElevatorSimulation.java** (Fig. 13.24). Lines 12–14 import packages **model**, **view** and **controller** as specified in Fig. 13.23.

```
1  // ElevatorSimulation.java
2  // Application with Elevator Model, View, and Controller (MVC)
3  package com.deitel.jhtp4.elevator;
4
5  // Java core packages
6  import java.awt.*;
7
8  // Java extension packages
9  import javax.swing.*;
10
11 // Deitel packages
12 import com.deitel.jhtp4.elevator.model.*;
13 import com.deitel.jhtp4.elevator.view.*;
14 import com.deitel.jhtp4.elevator.controller.*;
15
16 public class ElevatorSimulation extends JFrame {
17
18    // model, view and controller
19    private ElevatorModel model;
20    private ElevatorView view;
21    private ElevatorController controller;
22
23    // constructor instantiates model, view, and controller
24    public ElevatorSimulation()
25    {
26       super( "Deitel Elevator Simulation" );
27
28       // instantiate model, view and controller
29       model = new ElevatorModel();
30       view = new ElevatorView();
31       controller = new ElevatorController( model );
```

Fig. 13.24 Class **ElevatorSimulation** is the application for the elevator simulation (part 1 of 2).

```
32
33       // register View for Model events
34       model.setElevatorModelListener( view );
35
36       // add view and controller to ElevatorSimulation
37       getContentPane().add( view, BorderLayout.CENTER );
38       getContentPane().add( controller, BorderLayout.SOUTH );
39
40    } // end ElevatorSimulation constructor
41
42    // main method starts program
43    public static void main( String args[] )
44    {
45       // instantiate ElevatorSimulation
46       ElevatorSimulation simulation = new ElevatorSimulation();
47       simulation.setDefaultCloseOperation( EXIT_ON_CLOSE );
48       simulation.pack();
49       simulation.setVisible( true );
50    }
51 }
```

Fig. 13.24 Class **ElevatorSimulation** is the application for the elevator simulation (part 2 of 2).

The class diagram of Fig. 13.22 specifies that class **ElevatorSimulation** is a subclass of **javax.swing.JFrame**—line 16 declares class **ElevatorSimulation** as a **public** class extending class **JFrame**. Lines 19–21 implement class **ElevatorSimulation**'s aggregation of class **ElevatorModel**, the **ElevatorView** and the **ElevatorController** (shown in Fig. 13.22) by declaring one object from each class. Lines 29–31 of the **ElevatorSimulation** constructor initialize these objects.

Figure 13.22 and Fig. 13.23 specify that the **ElevatorView** is an **ElevatorModelListener** for the **ElevatorModel**. Line 34 registers the **ElevatorView** as a listener for **ElevatorModelEvent**s, so the **ElevatorView** can receive events from the **ElevatorModel** and properly represent the state of the model. Lines 37–38 add the **ElevatorView** and the **ElevatorController** to the **ElevatorSimulation**. According to the stereotypes in Fig. 13.23, **ElevatorSimulation.java** compiles to **ElevatorSimulation.class**, which is executable—lines 43–50 provide method **main** that runs the application.

We have completed the design of the components of our system. "Thinking About Objects" Section 15.12 concludes the design of the model by solving the interaction problems encountered in Fig. 10.25. Finally, Section 22.9 completes the design of the view and describes in greater detail how the **ElevatorView** receives events from the **ElevatorModel**. These last two sections will prepare you for the walkthrough of our elevator-simulation implementation in Appendices G, H and I.

13.18 (Optional) Discovering Design Patterns: Design Patterns Used in Packages `java.awt` and `javax.swing`

We continue our discussion from Section 9.24 on design patterns. This section introduces those design patterns associated with Java GUI components. After reading this section, you should understand better how these components take advantage of design patterns and how developers integrate design patterns with Java GUI applications.

13.18.1 Creational Design Patterns

Now, we continue our treatment of creational design patterns, which provide ways to instantiate objects in a system.

Factory Method

Suppose we are designing a system that opens an image from a specified file. Several different image formats exist, such as GIF and JPEG. We can use method **createImage** of class **java.awt.Component** to create an **Image** object. For example, to create a JPEG and GIF image in an object of a **Component** subclass—such as a **JPanel** object, we pass the name of the image file to method **createImage**, which returns an **Image** object that stores the image data. We can create two **Image** objects, each which contains data for two images having entirely different structures. For example, a JPEG image can hold up to 16.7 million colors, whereas a GIF image can hold up to only 256. Also, a GIF image can contain transparent pixels that are not rendered on screen, whereas a JPEG image cannot contain transparent pixels.

Class **Image** is an abstract class that represents an image we can display on screen. Using the parameter passed by the programmer, method **createImage** determines the specific **Image** subclass from which to instantiate the **Image** object. We can design systems to allow the user to specify which image to create, and method **createImage** will determine the subclass from which to instantiate the **Image**. If the parameter passed to method **createImage** references a JPEG file, method **createImage** instantiates and returns an object of an **Image** subclass suitable for JPEG images. If the parameter references a GIF file, **createImage** instantiates and returns an object of an **Image** subclass suitable for GIF images.

Method **createImage** is an example of the *Factory Method design pattern*. The sole purpose of this *factory method* is to create objects by allowing the system to determine which class to instantiate at run time. We can design a system that allows a user to specify what type of image to create at run time. Class **Component** might not be able to determine which **Image** subclass to instantiate until the user specifies the image to load. For more information on method **createImage**, visit

www.java.sun.com/j2se/1.3/docs/api/java/awt/Component.html#createImage(java.awt.image.ImageProducer)

13.18.2 Structural Design Patterns

We now discuss three more structural design patterns. The Adapter design pattern helps objects with incompatible interfaces collaborate with one another. The Bridge design pattern helps designers enhance platform independence in their systems. The Composite design pattern provides a way for designers to organize and manipulate objects.

Adapter

The *Adapter design pattern* provides an object with a new interface that *adapts* to another object's interface, allowing both objects to collaborate with one another. The adapter in this pattern is similar to an adapter for a plug on an electrical device—electrical sockets in Europe are different from those in the United States, so an adapter is needed to plug an American device into a European electrical socket and vice versa.

Java provides several classes that use the Adapter design pattern. Objects of these classes act as adapters between objects that generate certain events and those objects that handle these events. For example, a **MouseAdapter**, which we explained in Section 12.12, adapts an object that generates **MouseEvent**s to an object that handles **MouseEvent**s.

Bridge

Suppose we are designing class **Button** for both the Windows and Macintosh operating systems. Class **Button** contains specific button information such as an **ActionListener** and a **String** label. We design classes **Win32Button** and **MacButton** to extend class **Button**. Class **Win32Button** contains "look-and-feel" information on how to display a **Button** on the Windows operating system and class **MacButton** contains "look-and-feel" information on how to display a **Button** on the Macintosh operating system.

Two problems arise from this approach. First, if we create new **Button** subclasses, we must create corresponding **Win32Button** and **MacButton** subclasses. For example, if we create class **ImageButton** (a **Button** with an overlapping **Image**) that extends class **Button**, we must create additional subclasses **Win32ImageButton** and **MacImageButton**. In fact, we must create **Button** subclasses for every operating system we wish to support, which increases development time. The second problem is that when a new operating system enters the market, we must create additional **Button** subclasses specific to that operating system.

The *Bridge design pattern* avoids these problems by separating an abstraction (e.g., a **Button**) and its implementations (e.g., **Win32Button**, **MacButton**, etc.) into different class hierarchies. For example, the Java AWT classes use the Bridge design pattern to enable designers to create AWT **Button** subclasses without needing to create corresponding subclasses for each operating system. Each AWT **Button** maintains a reference to a **ButtonPeer**, which is the superclass for platform-specific implementations, such as **Win32ButtonPeer**, **MacButtonPeer**, etc. When a programmer creates a **Button** object, class **Button** calls factory method **createButton** of class **Toolkit** to create the platform-specific **ButtonPeer** object. The **Button** object stores a reference to its **ButtonPeer**—this reference is the "bridge" in the Bridge design pattern. When the programmer invokes methods on the **Button** object, the **Button** object invokes the appropriate method on its **ButtonPeer** to fulfill the request. If a designer creates a **Button** subclass called **ImageButton**, the designer does not need to create a corresponding **Win32ImageButton** or **MacImageButton** with platform-specific image-drawing capabilities. An **ImageButton** "is a" **Button**. Therefore, when an **ImageButton** needs to display its image, the **ImageButton** uses its **ButtonPeer**'s **Graphics** object to render the image on each platform. This design pattern enables designers to create new cross-platform GUI components using a "bridge" to hide platform-specific details.

Portability Tip 13.2

Designers often use the Bridge design pattern to enhance the platform independence of their systems. This design pattern enables designers to create new cross-platform components using a "bridge" to hide platform-specific details.

Composite

Designers often organize components into hierarchical structures (e.g., a hierarchy of directories and files on a hard drive)—each node in the structure represents a component (e.g., a file or directory). Each node can contain references to other nodes. A node is called a *branch* if it contains a reference to one or more nodes (e.g., a directory containing files). A node is called a *leaf* if it does not contain a reference to another node (e.g., a file). Occasionally, a structure contains objects from several different classes (e.g., a directory can contain files and directories). When an object—called a *client*—wants to traverse the structure, the client must determine the particular class for each node. Making this determination can be time consuming, and the structure can become hard to maintain.

In the *Composite design pattern*, each component in a hierarchical structure implements the same interface or extends a common superclass. This polymorphism (introduced in Section 9.10) ensures that clients can traverse all elements—branch or leaf—uniformly in the structure. Using this pattern, a client traversing the structure does not have to determine each component type, because all components implement the same interface or extend the same superclass.

Java GUI components use the Composite design pattern. Consider the Swing component class **JPanel**, which extends class **JComponent**. Class **JComponent** extends class **java.awt.Container**, which extends class **java.awt.Component** (Fig. 13.25). Class **Container** provides method **add**, which appends a **Component** object (or **Component** subclass object) to that **Container** object. Therefore, a **JPanel** object may be added to any object of a **Component** subclass, and any object from a **Component** subclass may be added to that **JPanel** object. A **JPanel** object can contain any GUI component while remaining unaware of that component's specific type.

A client, such as a **JPanel** object, can traverse all components uniformly in the hierarchy. For example, if the **JPanel** object calls method **repaint** of superclass **Container**, method **repaint** displays the **JPanel** object and all components added to the **JPanel** object. Method **repaint** does not have to determine each component's type, because all components inherit from superclass **Container**, which contains method **repaint**.

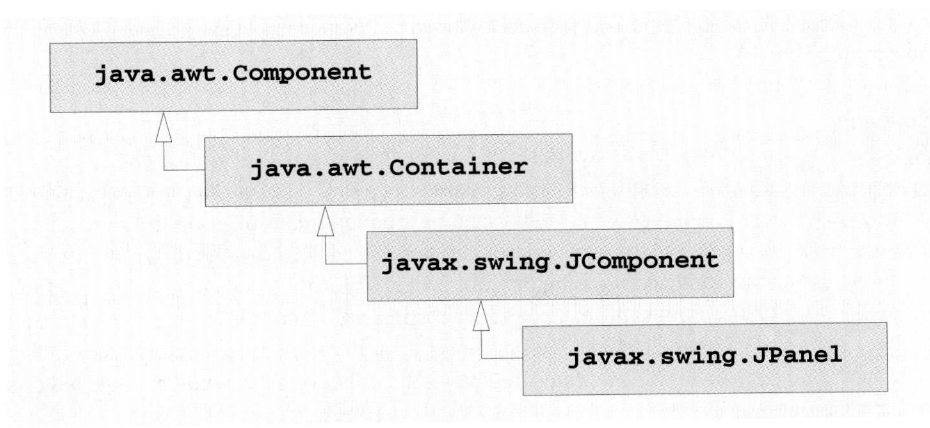

Fig. 13.25 Inheritance hierarchy for class **JPanel**.

13.18.3 Behavioral Design Patterns

In this section, we continue our discussion on behavioral design patterns. We discuss the Chain-of-Responsibility, Command, Observer, Strategy and Template Method design patterns.

Chain-of-Responsibility

In object-oriented systems, objects interact by sending messages to one another. Often, a system needs to determine at run time the object that will handle a particular message. For example, consider the design of a three-line office phone system. When a person calls the office, the first line handles the call—if the first line is busy, the second line handles the call, and if the second line is busy, the third line handles the call. If all lines in the system are busy, an automated speaker instructs that person to wait for the next available line—when a line becomes available, that line handles the call.

The *Chain-of-Responsibility design pattern* enables a system to determine at run time the object that will handle a message. This pattern allows an object to send a message to several objects in a *chain* of objects. Each object in the chain either may handle the message or pass the message to the next object in the chain. For instance, the first line in the phone system is the first object in the chain of responsibility, the second line is the second object, the third line is the third object, and the automated speaker is the fourth object. Note that this mechanism is not the final object in the chain—the next available line handles the message, and that line is the final object in the chain. The chain is created dynamically in response to the presence or absence of specific message handlers.

Several Java AWT GUI components use the Chain-of-Responsibility design pattern to handle certain events. For example, class **java.awt.Button** overrides method **processEvent** of class **java.awt.Component** to process **AWTEvent** objects. Method **processEvent** attempts to handle the **AWTEvent** upon receiving this event as an argument. If method **processEvent** determines that the **AWTEvent** is an **ActionEvent** (i.e., the **Button** has been pressed), the method handles the event by invoking method **processActionEvent**, which informs any **ActionListener** registered with the **Button** that the **Button** has been pressed. If method **processEvent** determines that the **AWTEvent** is not an **ActionEvent**, the method is unable to handle the event and passes the **AWTEvent** to method **processEvent** of superclass **Component** (the next object in the chain).

Command

Applications often provide users with several ways to perform a given task. For example, in a word processor there might be an **Edit** menu with menu items for cutting, copying and pasting text. There could also be a toolbar and/or a popup menu offering the same items. The functionality the application provides is the same in each case—the different interface components for invoking the functionality are provided for the user's convenience. However, the same GUI component instance (e.g., **JButton**) cannot be used for menus and toolbars and popup menus, so the developer must code the same functionality three times. If there were many such interface items, repeating this functionality would become tedious and error-prone.

The *Command design pattern* solves this problem by enabling developers to specify the desired functionality (e.g., copying text) once in a reusable object; that functionality can then be added to a menu, toolbar, popup menu or other mechanisms. This design pattern is called Command because it defines a user command, or instruction. This pattern allows a designer to encapsulate a command, so that the command may be used among several objects.

Observer

Suppose we want to design a program for viewing bank account information. This system includes class **BankStatementData** to store data pertaining to bank statements, and classes **TextDisplay**, **BarGraphDisplay** and **PieChartDisplay** to display the data.[2] Figure 13.26 shows the design for our system. Class **TextDisplay** displays the data in text format, class **BarGraphDisplay** displays the data in bar-graph format and class **PieChartDisplay** displays the data as a pie chart. We want to design the system so that the **BankStatementData** object notifies the objects displaying the data of a change in the data. We also want to design the system to loosen *coupling*—the degree to which classes depend on each other in a system.

Software Engineering Observation 13.9

Loosely-coupled classes are easier to reuse and modify than are tightly-coupled classes, which depend heavily on each other. A modification in a class in a tightly-coupled system usually results in modifying other classes in that system. A modification to one of a group of loosely-coupled classes would require little or no modification to the other classes in the group.

The *Observer design pattern* is appropriate for systems like that of Fig. 13.26. This pattern promotes loose coupling between a *subject* object and *observer* objects—a subject notifies the observers when the subject changes state. When notified by the subject, the observers change in response to the change in the subject. In our example, the **BankStatementData** object is the subject, and the objects displaying the data are the observers. A subject can notify several observers; therefore, the subject contains a one-to-many relationship with the observers.

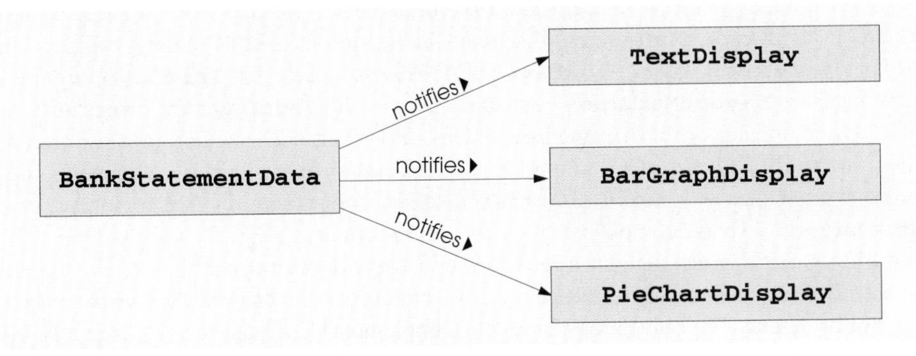

Fig. 13.26 Basis for the Observer design pattern.

2. This approach is the basis for the Model-View-Controller architecture pattern, discussed in Sections 13.17 and 17.11.

The Java API contains classes that use the Observer design pattern. Class **java.util.Observable** represents a subject. Class **Observable** provides method **addObserver**, which takes a **java.util.Observer** argument. Interface **Observer** allows the **Observable** object to notify the **Observer** when the **Observable** objects changes state. The **Observer** can be an instance of any class that implements interface **Observer**; because the **Observable** object invokes methods defined in interface **Observer**, the objects remain loosely coupled. If a developer changes the way in which a particular **Observer** responds to changes in the **Observable** object, the developer does not need to change the **Observable** object. The **Observable** object interacts with its **Observer**s only through interface **Observer**, which enables the loose coupling.

The optional elevator simulation case study in the "Thinking About Objects" sections uses the Observer design pattern to allow the **ElevatorModel** object (the subject) to notify the **ElevatorView** object (the observer) of changes in the **ElevatorModel**. The simulation does not use class **Observable** and interface **Observer** from the Java library—rather, it uses a custom interface **ElevatorModelListener** that provides functionality similar to that of interface **Observable**.

The Swing GUI components use the Observer design pattern. GUI components collaborate with their listeners to respond to user interactions. For example, an **ActionListener** observes state changes in a **JButton** (the subject) by registering to handle that **JButton**'s events. When pressed by the user, the **JButton** notifies its **ActionListener** objects (the observers) that the **JButton**'s state has changed (i.e., the **JButton** has been pressed).

Strategy

The *Strategy design pattern* is similar to the State design pattern (discussed in Section 9.24.3). We mentioned that the State design pattern contains a state object, which encapsulates the state of a context object. The Strategy design pattern contains a *strategy object*, which is analogous to the State design pattern's state object. The key difference between a state object and a strategy object is that the strategy object encapsulates an *algorithm* rather than state information.

For example, **java.awt.Container** components implement the Strategy design pattern using **LayoutManager**s (discussed in Section 12.14) as strategy objects. In package **java.awt**, classes **FlowLayout**, **BorderLayout** and **GridLayout** implement interface **LayoutManager**. Each class uses method **addLayoutComponent** to add GUI components to a **Container** object—however, each method uses a different algorithm to display these GUI components: a **FlowLayout** displays components in a left-to-right sequence; a **BorderLayout** displays components in five regions; and a **GridLayout** displays components in row-column format.

Class **Container** contains a reference to a **LayoutManager** object (the strategy object). Because an interface reference (i.e., the reference to the **LayoutManager** object) can hold references to objects of classes that implement that interface (i.e., the **FlowLayout**, **BorderLayout** or **GridLayout** objects), the **LayoutManager** object can reference a **FlowLayout**, **BorderLayout** or **GridLayout** at any one time. Class **Container** can change this reference through method **setLayout** to select different layouts at run time.

Class **FlowLayoutDemo** (Fig. 12.24) demonstrates the application of the Strategy pattern—line 16 declares a new **FlowLayout** object and line 19 invokes the **Con-**

tainer object's method **setLayout** to assign the **FlowLayout** object to the **Container** object. In this example, the **FlowLayout** provides the strategy for laying out the components.

Template Method

The *Template Method design pattern* also deals with algorithms. The Strategy design pattern allows several objects to contain distinct algorithms. However, the Template Method design pattern requires all objects to share a single algorithm defined by a superclass.

For example, consider the design of Fig. 13.26, which we mentioned in the Observer design pattern discussion. Objects of classes **TextDisplay**, **BarGraphDisplay** and **PieChartDisplay** use the same basic algorithm for acquiring and displaying the data—get all statements from the **BankStatementData** object, parse the statements then display the statements. The Template Method design pattern allows us to create an abstract superclass called **BankStatementDisplay** that provides the central algorithm for displaying the data. In this example, the algorithm comprises abstract methods **getData**, **parseData** and **displayData** comprise the algorithm. Classes **TextDisplay**, **BarGraphDisplay** and **PieChartDisplay** extend class **BankStatementDisplay** to inherit the algorithm, so each object can use the same algorithm. Each **BankStatementDisplay** subclass then overrides each method in a way specific to that subclass, because each class implements the algorithm differently from one another. For example, classes **TextDisplay**, **BarGraphDisplay** and **PieChartDisplay** might get and parse the data identically, but each class displays that data differently.

The Template Method design pattern allows us to extend the algorithm to other **BankStatementDisplay** subclasses—e.g., we could create classes, such as **LineGraphDisplay** or class **3DimensionalDisplay**, that use the same algorithm inherited from class **BankStatementDisplay**.

13.18.4 Conclusion

In this "Discovering Design Patterns" section, we discussed how Swing components take advantage of design patterns and how developers can integrate design patterns with GUI applications in Java. In "Discovering Design Patterns" Section 15.13, we discuss concurrency design patterns, which are particularly useful for developing multithreaded systems.

SUMMARY

- **JTextAreas** provide an area for manipulating multiple lines of text. Like class **JTextField**, class **JTextArea** inherits from **JTextComponent**.
- An external event (i.e., an event generated by a different GUI component) normally indicates when the text in a **JTextArea** should be processed.
- Scrollbars are provided for a **JTextArea** by attaching it to a **JScrollPane** object.
- Method **getSelectedText** returns the selected text from a **JTextArea**. Text is selected by dragging the mouse over the desired text to highlight it.
- Method **setText** sets the text in a **JTextArea**.
- To provide automatic word wrap in a **JTextArea**, attach it to a **JScrollPane** with horizontal scrollbar policy **JScrollPane.HORIZONTAL_SCROLLBAR_NEVER**.

- The horizontal and vertical scrollbar policies for a **JScrollPane** are set when a **JScrollPane** is constructed or with methods **setHorizontalScrollBarPolicy** and **setVerticalScrollBarPolicy** of class **JScrollPane**.
- A **JPanel** can be used as a dedicated drawing area that can receive mouse events and is often extended to create new GUI components.
- Swing components that inherit from class **JComponent** contain method **paintComponent**, which helps them draw properly in the context of a Swing GUI. **JComponent** method **paintComponent** should be overridden to call to the superclass version of **paintComponent** as the first statement in its body.
- Classes **JFrame** and **JApplet** are not subclasses of **JComponent**; therefore, they do not contain method **paintComponent** (they have method **paint**).
- Calling **repaint** for a Swing GUI component indicates that the component should be painted as soon as possible. The background of the GUI component is cleared only if the component is opaque. Most Swing components are transparent by default. **JComponent** method **setOpaque** can be passed a **boolean** argument indicating whether the component is opaque (**true**) or transparent (**false**). The GUI components of package **java.awt** are different from Swing components in that **repaint** results in a call to **Component** method **update** (which clears the component's background) and **update** calls method **paint** (rather than **paintComponent**).
- Method **setTitle** displays a **String** in a window's title bar.
- Drawing on any GUI component is performed with coordinates that are measured from the upper-left corner (0, 0) of that GUI component.
- Layout managers often use a GUI component's **getPreferredSize** method to determine the preferred width and height of a component when laying out that component as part of a GUI. If a new component has a preferred width and height, it should override method **getPreferredSize** to return that width and height as an object of class **Dimension** (package **java.awt**).
- The default size of a **JPanel** object is 0 pixels wide and 0 pixels tall.
- A mouse drag operation begins with a mouse-pressed event. All subsequent mouse drag events (for which **mouseDragged** will be called) are sent to the GUI component that received the original mouse-pressed event.
- **JSlider**s enable the user to select from a range of integer values. **JSlider**s can display major tick marks, minor tick marks and labels for the tick marks. They also support snap-to ticks, where positioning the thumb between two tick marks causes the thumb to *snap* to the closest tick mark.
- Most Swing GUI components support user interactions through both the mouse and the keyboard.
- If a **JSlider** has the focus, the left arrow key and right arrow key cause the thumb of the **JSlider** to decrease or increase by 1. The down arrow key and up arrow key also cause the thumb of the **JSlider** to decrease or increase by 1, respectively. The *PgDn key* (page down) and *PgUp key* (page up) cause the thumb of the **JSlider** to decrease or increase by block increments of one-tenth of the range of values, respectively. The *Home key* moves the thumb to the minimum value of the **JSlider** and the *End key* moves the thumb to the maximum value of the **JSlider**.
- **JSlider**s have either a horizontal orientation or a vertical orientation. For a horizontal **JSlider**, the minimum value is at the extreme left and the maximum value is at the extreme right of the **JSlider**. For a vertical **JSlider**, the minimum value is at the extreme bottom and the maximum value is at the extreme top of the **JSlider**. The relative position of the thumb indicates the current value of the **JSlider**.
- Method **setMajorTickSpacing** of class **JSlider** sets the spacing for tick marks on a **JSlider**. Method **setPaintTicks** with a **true** argument indicates that the tick marks should be displayed.

- **JSlider**s generate **ChangeEvents** (package **javax.swing.event**) when the user interacts with a **JSlider**. A **ChangeListener** (package **javax.swing.event**) defines method **stateChanged** that can respond to **ChangeEvent**s.
- Method **getValue** of class **JSlider** returns the current thumb position.
- A **JFrame** is a window with a title bar and a border. Class **JFrame** is a subclass of **java.awt.Frame** (which is a subclass of **java.awt.Window**).
- Class **JFrame** supports three operations when the user closes the window. By default, a **JFrame** is hidden when the user closes a window. This can be controlled with **JFrame** method **setDefaultCloseOperation**. Interface **WindowConstants** (package **javax.swing**) defines three constants for use with this method—**DISPOSE_ON_CLOSE**, **DO_NOTHING_ON_CLOSE** and **HIDE_ON_CLOSE** (the default).
- By default, a window is not displayed on the screen until its **setVisible** method is called with **true** as an argument. A window can also be displayed by calling its **show** method.
- A window's size should be set with a call to method **setSize**. The position of a window when it appears on the screen is specified with method **setLocation**.
- All windows generate window events when the user manipulates the window. Event listeners are registered for window events with method **addWindowListener** of class **Window**. The **WindowListener** interface provides seven methods for handling window events—**windowActivated** (called when the window is made active by clicking the window), **windowClosed** (called after the window is closed), **windowClosing** (called when the user initiates closing of the window), **windowDeactivated** (called when another window is made active), **windowIconified** (called when the user minimizes a window), **windowDeiconified** (called when a window is restored from being minimized) and **windowOpened** (called when a window is first displayed on the screen).
- The command-line arguments are automatically passed to **main** as the array of **String**s called **args**. The first argument after the application class name is the first **String** in the array **args**, and the length of the array is the total number of command-line arguments.
- *Menus* are an integral part of GUIs. Menus allow the user to perform actions without unnecessarily "cluttering" a graphical user interface with extra GUI components.
- In Swing GUIs, menus can be attached only to objects of the classes that provide method **setJMenuBar**. Two such classes are **JFrame** and **JApplet**.
- The classes used to define menus are **JMenuBar**, **JMenuItem**, **JMenu**, **JCheckBoxMenuItem** and class **JRadioButtonMenuItem**.
- A **JMenuBar** is a container for menus.
- A **JMenuItem** is a GUI component inside a menu that, when selected, causes an action to be performed. A **JMenuItem** can be used to initiate an action or it can be a *submenu* that provides more menu items from which the user can select.
- A **JMenu** contains menu items and can be added to a **JMenuBar** or to other **JMenu**s as submenus. When a menu is clicked, the menu expands to show its list of menu items.
- When a **JCheckBoxMenuItem** is selected, a check appears to the left of the menu item. When the **JCheckBoxMenuItem** is selected again, the check to the left of the menu item is removed.
- When multiple **JRadioButtonMenuItem**s are maintained as part of a **ButtonGroup**, only one item in the group can be selected at a given time. When a **JRadioButtonMenuItem** is selected, a filled circle appears to the left of the menu item. When another **JRadioButtonMenuItem** is selected, the filled circle to the left of the previously selected menu item is removed.
- **JFrame** method **setJMenuBar** attaches a menu bar to a **JFrame**.

- **AbstractButton** method **setMnemonic** (inherited into class **JMenu**) specifies the mnemonic for an **AbstractButton** object. Pressing the *Alt* key and the mnemonic performs the **AbstractButton**'s action (in the case of a menu, it opens the menu).
- Mnemonic characters are normally displayed with an underline.
- Dialog boxes can be either modal or modeless. A modal dialog box does not allow any other window in the application to be accessed until the dialog box is dismissed. A modeless dialog box allows other windows to be accessed while the dialog is displayed. By default, the dialogs displayed with class **JOptionPane** are modal dialogs. Class **JDialog** can be used to create your own modeless or modal dialogs.
- **JMenu** method **addSeparator** adds a separator line to a menu.
- Context-sensitive popup menus are created with class **JPopupMenu**. These menus provide options that are specific to the component for which the popup-trigger event was generated. On most systems, the popup-trigger event occurs when the user presses and releases the right mouse button.
- **MouseEvent** method **isPopupTrigger** returns **true** if the popup-trigger event occurred.
- Method **show** of class **JPopupMenu** displays a **JPopupMenu**. The first argument to method **show** specifies the origin component, whose position helps determine where the **JPopupMenu** will appear on the screen. The last two arguments are the x and y coordinates from the origin component's upper-left corner at which the **JPopupMenu** should appear.
- Class **UIManager** contains a **public static** inner class called **LookAndFeelInfo** that is used to maintain information about a look-and-feel.
- **UIManager static** method **getInstalledLookAndFeels** gets an array of **UIManager.LookAndFeelInfo** objects that describe the installed look-and-feels.
- **UIManager static** method **setLookAndFeel** changes the look-and-feel.
- **SwingUtilities static** method **updateComponentTreeUI** changes the look-and-feel of every component attached to its **Component** argument to the new look-and-feel.
- Many of today's applications use a multiple document interface (MDI) [i.e., a main window (often called the parent window) containing other windows (often called child windows)] to manage several open documents that are being processed in parallel.
- Swing's **JDesktopPane** and **JInternalFrame** classes provide support for creating multiple document interfaces.
- **BoxLayout** is a layout manager that allows GUI components to be arranged left-to-right or top-to-bottom in a container. Class **Box** defines a container with **BoxLayout** as its default layout manager and provides static methods to create a **Box** with a horizontal or vertical **BoxLayout**.
- **CardLayout** is a layout manager that stacks components like a deck of cards. Each container in the stack can use any layout manager. Only the container at the "top" of the deck is visible.
- **GridBagLayout** is a layout manager similar to **GridLayout**. Unlike with **GridLayout**, each component size can vary, and components can be added in any order.
- **Box static** method **createHorizontalBox** returns a **Box** container with a horizontal **BoxLayout**. **Box static** method **createVerticalBox** of class **Box** returns a **Box** container with a vertical **BoxLayout**.
- **Box static** method **createVerticalStrut** adds a *vertical strut* to a container. A vertical strut is an invisible GUI component that has a fixed pixel height and is used to guarantee a fixed amount of space between GUI components. Class **Box** also defines method **createHorizontalStrut** for horizontal **BoxLayout**s.
- **Box static** method **createHorizontalGlue** adds horizontal glue to a container. Horizontal glue is an invisible GUI component that can be used between fixed-size GUI components to

occupy additional space. Class **Box** also defines method **createVerticalGlue** for vertical **BoxLayout**s.

- **Box static** method **createRigidArea** adds a rigid area to a container. A rigid area is an invisible GUI component that always has a fixed pixel width and height.
- The **BoxLayout** constructor receives a reference to the container for which it controls the layout and a constant indicating whether the layout is horizontal (**BoxLayout.X_AXIS**) or vertical (**BoxLayout.Y_AXIS**).
- **CardLayout** methods **first**, **previous**, **next** and **last** are used to display a particular card. Method **first** displays the first card. Method **previous** displays the previous card. Method **next** displays the next card. Method **last** displays the last card.
- To use **GridBagLayout**, a **GridBagConstraints** object must be used to specify how a component is placed in a **GridBagLayout**.
- Method **setConstraints** of class **GridBagLayout** takes a **Component** argument and a **GridBagConstraints** argument and sets the constraints of the **Component**.

TERMINOLOGY

addSeparator method of class **JMenu**
addWindowListener method of **Window**
anchor variable of **GridBagConstraints**
automatic word wrap
Box class
BoxLayout layout manager
BoxLayout.X_AXIS
BoxLayout.Y_AXIS
CardLayout layout manager
ChangeEvent class
ChangeListener interface
child window
command-line arguments
context-sensitive popup menu
createHorizontalBox method of **Box**
createHorizontalGlue method of **Box**
createHorizontalStrut method of **Box**
createRigidArea method of **Box**
createVerticalBox method of **Box**
createVerticalGlue method of **Box**
createVerticalStrut method of **Box**
dedicated drawing area
Dimension class
dispose method of class **Window**
external event
fill variable of **GridBagConstraints**
first method of **CardLayout**
getClassName method
getInstalledLookAndFeels method
getMinimumSize method of **Component**
getPreferredSize method of **Component**
getSelectedText method
getValue method of class **JSlider**
GridBagConstraints class
GridBagConstraints.BOTH
GridBagConstraints.CENTER
GridBagConstraints.EAST
GridBagConstraints.HORIZONTAL
GridBagConstraints.NONE
GridBagConstraints.NORTH
GridBagConstraints.NORTHEAST
GridBagConstraints.NORTHWEST
GridBagConstraints.RELATIVE
GridBagConstraints.REMAINDER
GridBagConstraints.SOUTH
GridBagConstraints.SOUTHEAST
GridBagConstraints.SOUTHWEST
GridBagConstraints.VERTICAL
GridBagConstraints.WEST
GridBagLayout layout manager
gridheight variable
gridwidth variable
gridx variable of **GridBagConstraints**
gridy variable of **GridBagConstraints**
isPopupTrigger method of **MouseEvent**
JCheckBoxMenuItem class
JDesktopPane class
JInternalFrame class
JMenu class
JMenuBar class
JMenuItem class
JPopupMenu class
JRadioButtonMenuItem class
JSlider class
JTextArea class
JTextComponent class

labels for tick marks
last method of class **CardLayout**
major tick mark
menu
menu bar
menu item
metal look-and-feel
method **setMnemonic** of **AbstractButton**
minor tick mark
mnemonic
modal dialog
modeless dialog
Motif look-and-feel
multiple document interface (MDI)
next method of class **CardLayout**
paintComponent method of **JComponent**
parent window
pluggable look-and-feel (PLAF)
previous method of class **CardLayout**
scrollbar policies for a **JScrollPane**
setConstraints method
setDefaultCloseOperation method
setHorizontalScrollBarPolicy method
setJMenuBar method
setLookAndFeel method
setMajorTickSpacing method
setOpaque method of class **JComponent**
setPaintTicks method of class **JSlider**
setSelected method of **AbstractButton**
setTitle method of class **Frame**
setVerticalScrollBarPolicy method
show method of class **JPopupMenu**
snap-to ticks
submenu
super.paintComponent(g);
SwingConstants.HORIZONTAL
SwingConstants.VERTICAL
thumb of a **JSlider**
tick mark
UIManager class
UIManager.LookAndFeelInfo class
updateComponentTreeUI method
vertical strut
weightx variable of **GridBagConstraints**
weighty variable of **GridBagConstraints**
windowActivated method
windowClosed method
windowClosing method
WindowConstants.DISPOSE_ON_CLOSE
windowDeactivated method
windowDeiconified method
windowIconified method
WindowListener interface
windowOpened method
Windows look-and-feel

SELF-REVIEW EXERCISES

13.1 Fill in the blanks in each of the following statements:

a) The __________ class is used to create a menu object.
b) The __________ method places a separator bar in a menu.
c) Passing **false** to a **TextArea**'s __________ method prevents its text from being modified by the user.
d) **JSlider** events are handled by the __________ method of interface __________.
e) The **GridBagConstraints** instance variable __________ is set to **CENTER** by default.

13.2 State whether each of the following is *true* or *false*. If *false*, explain why.

a) When the programmer creates a **JFrame**, a minimum of one menu must be created and added to the **JFrame**.
b) The variable **fill** belongs to the **GridBagLayout** class.
c) **JFrame**s and applets cannot be used together in the same program.
d) The top-left corner of a **JFrame** or applet has a coordinate of (0, 0).
e) A **JTextArea**'s text is always read-only.
f) Class **JTextArea** is a direct subclass of class **Component**.
g) The default layout for a **Box** is **BoxLayout**.

13.3 Find the error(s) in each of the following and explain how to correct the error(s).

a) **JMenubar b;**
b) **mySlider = JSlider(1000, 222, 100, 450);**

c) `gbc.fill = GridBagConstraints.NORTHWEST;    // set fill`

d)
```
// override to paint on a customized Swing component
public void paintcomponent( Graphics g )
{
   g.drawString( "HELLO", 50, 50 );
}
```

e)
```
// create a JFrame and display it
JFrame f = new JFrame( "A Window" );
f.setVisible( true );
```

ANSWERS TO SELF-REVIEW EXERCISES

13.1 a) **JMenu**. b) **addSeparator**. c) **setEditable**. d) **stateChanged**, **ChangeListener**. e) **anchor**.

13.2
a) False. A **JFrame** does not require any menus.
b) False. The variable **fill** belongs to the **GridBagConstraints** class.
c) False. They can be used together.
d) True.
e) False. **JTextArea**s are editable by default.
f) False. **JTextArea** derives from class **JTextComponent**.
g) True.

13.3
a) **JMenubar** should be **JMenuBar**.
b) The first argument to the constructor should be either **SwingConstants.HORIZONTAL** or **SwingConstants.VERTICAL**, and the **new** operator must be used after the = operator.
c) The constant should be either **BOTH**, **HORIZONTAL**, **VERTICAL** or **NONE**.
d) **paintcomponent** should be **paintComponent** and the method should call **super.paintComponent(g)** as its first statement.
e) The **JFrame**'s **setSize** method must also be called to determine the size of the window.

EXERCISES

13.4 Fill in the blanks in each of the following statements:
a) A dedicated drawing area can be defined as a subclass of ________.
b) A **JMenuItem** that is a **JMenu** is called a ________
c) Both **JTextField**s and **JTextArea**s inherit directly from class ________.
d) The ________ method attaches a **JMenuBar** to a **JFrame**.
e) Container class ________ has a default **BoxLayout**.
f) A ________ manages a set of child windows defined with class **JInternalFrame**.

13.5 State whether each of the following is *true* or *false*. If *false*, explain why.
a) Menus require a **JMenuBar** object so they can be attached to a **JFrame**.
b) A **JPanel** object is capable of receiving mouse events.
c) **CardLayout** is the default layout manager for a **JFrame**.
d) Method **setEditable** is a **JTextComponent** method.
e) The **GridBagLayout** layout manager implements **LayoutManager**.
f) **JPanel** objects are containers to which other GUI components can be attached.
g) Class **JFrame** inherits directly from class **Container**.
h) **JApplet**s can contain menus.

13.6 Find the error(s) in each of the following. Explain how to correct the error(s).
a) `x.add( new JMenuItem( "Submenu Color" ) ); // create submenu`

b) **container.setLayout(m = new GridbagLayout());**
c) **String s = JTextArea.getText();**

13.7 Write a program that displays a circle of random size and calculates and displays the area, radius, diameter and circumference. Use the following equations: $diameter = 2 \infty radius$, $area = \pi \infty radius^2$, $circumference = 2 \infty \pi \infty radius$. Use the constant **Math.PI** for pi (π). All drawing should be done on a subclass of **JPanel**, and the results of the calculations should be displayed in a read-only **JTextArea**.

13.8 Enhance the program of Exercise 13.7 by allowing the user to alter the radius with a **JSlider**. The program should work for all radii in the range from 100 to 200. As the radius changes, the diameter, area and circumference should be updated and displayed. The initial radius should be 150. Use the equations of Exercise 13.7. All drawing should be done on a subclass of **JPanel**, and the results of the calculations should be displayed in a read-only **JTextArea**.

13.9 Explore the effects of varying the **weightx** and **weighty** values of the program of Fig. 13.20. What happens when a component has a nonzero weight, but is not allowed to fill the whole area (i.e., the **fill** value is not **BOTH**)?

13.10 Write a program that uses the **paintComponent** method to draw the current value of a **JSlider** on a subclass of **JPanel**. In addition, provide a **JTextField** where a specific value can be entered. The **JTextField** should display the current value of the **JSlider** at all times. A **JLabel** should be used to identify the **JTextField**. The **JSlider** methods **setValue** and **getValue** should be used. [Note: The **setValue** method is a **public** method that does not return a value and takes one integer argument—the **JSlider** value, which determines the position of the thumb.]

13.11 Modify the program of Fig. 13.16 to use a single **JComboBox** instead of the four separate **JButton**s. Each "card" should not be modified.

13.12 Modify the program of Fig. 13.16 by adding a minimum of two new "cards" to the deck.

13.13 Define a subclass of **JPanel** called **MyColorChooser** that provides three **JSlider** objects and three **JTextField** objects. Each **JSlider** represents the values from 0 to 255 for the red, green and blue parts of a color. Use the red, green and blue values as the arguments to the **Color** constructor to create a new **Color** object. Display the current value of each **JSlider** in the corresponding **JTextField**. When the user changes the value of the **JSlider**, the **JTextField** should be changed accordingly. Define class **MyColorChooser** so it can be reused in other applications or applets. Use your new GUI component as part of an applet that displays the current **Color** value by drawing a filled rectangle.

13.14 Modify the **MyColorChooser** class of Exercise 13.13 to allow the user to type an integer value into a **JTextField** to set the red, green or blue value. When the user presses *Enter* in the **JTextField**, the corresponding **JSlider** should be set to the appropriate value.

13.15 Modify the applet of Exercise 13.14 to draw the current color as a rectangle on an instance of a subclass of **JPanel** called **DrawPanel**. Class **DrawPanel** should provide its own **paintComponent** method to draw the rectangle and should provide *set* methods to set the red, green and blue values for the current color. When any *set* method is invoked for the class **DrawPanel**, the object should automatically **repaint** itself.

13.16 Modify the applet of Exercise 13.15 to allow the user to drag the mouse across the **DrawPanel** to draw a shape in the current color. Enable the user to choose what shape to draw.

13.17 Modify the program of Exercise 13.16 to enable the program to run as an application. The existing applet's code should be modified only by adding a **main** method to launch the application in its own **JFrame**. Provide the user with the ability to terminate the application by clicking the close box on the window that is displayed and by selecting **Exit** from a **File** menu. Use the techniques shown in Fig. 13.9.

13.18 *(Complete Drawing Application)* Using the techniques developed in Exercise 12.27–Exercise 12.33 and Exercise 13.13–Exercise 13.17, create a complete drawing program that can execute as both an applet and an application. The program should use the GUI components of Chapter 12 and Chapter 13 to enable the user to select the shape, color and fill characteristics. Each shape should be stored in an array of **MyShape** objects, where **MyShape** is the superclass in your hierarchy of shape classes (see Exercise 9.28 and Exercise 9.29). Use a **JDesktopPane** and **JInternalFrame**s to allow the user to create multiple separate drawings in separate child windows. Create the user interface as a separate child window containing all the GUI components that allow the user to determine the characteristics of the shape to be drawn. The user can then click in any **JInternalFrame** to draw the shape.

13.19 A company pays its employees as managers (who receive a fixed weekly salary), hourly workers (who receive a fixed hourly wage for up to the first 40 hours they work and "time-and-a-half," i.e., 1.5 times their hourly wage, for overtime hours worked), commission workers (who receive $250 plus 5.7% of their gross weekly sales) or pieceworkers (who receive a fixed amount of money per item for each of the items they produce—each pieceworker in this company works on only one type of item). Write an application to compute the weekly pay for each employee. Each type of employee has its own pay code: Managers have paycode 1, hourly workers have code 2, commission workers have code 3 and pieceworkers have code 4. Use a **switch** to compute each employee's pay based on that employee's paycode. Use a **CardLayout** to display the appropriate GUI components that allow the user to enter the facts your program needs to calculate each employee's pay based on that employee's paycode.

14

Exception Handling

Objectives

- To understand exception and error handling.
- To be able to use **`try`** blocks to delineate code in which an exception may occur.
- To be able to **`throw`** exceptions.
- To use **`catch`** blocks to specify exception handlers.
- To use the **`finally`** block to release resources.
- To understand the Java exception hierarchy.
- To create programmer-defined exceptions.

It is common sense to take a method and try it. If it fails, admit it frankly and try another. But above all, try something.
Franklin Delano Roosevelt

O! throw away the worser part of it,
And live the purer with the other half.
William Shakespeare

If they're running and they don't look where they're going
I have to come out from somewhere and catch them.
Jerome David Salinger

And oftentimes excusing of a fault
Doth make the fault the worse by the excuse.
William Shakespeare

I never forget a face, but in your case I'll make an exception.
Groucho (Julius Henry) Marx

Outline

14.1 Introduction
14.2 When Exception Handling Should Be Used
14.3 Other Error-Handling Techniques
14.4 Basics of Java Exception Handling
14.5 `try` Blocks
14.6 Throwing an Exception
14.7 Catching an Exception
14.8 Exception-Handling Example: Divide by Zero
14.9 Rethrowing an Exception
14.10 `throws` Clause
14.11 Constructors, Finalizers and Exception Handling
14.12 Exceptions and Inheritance
14.13 `finally` Block
14.14 Using `printStackTrace` and `getMessage`

Summary • Terminology • Self-Review Exercises • Answers to Self-Review Exercises • Exercises

14.1 Introduction

In this chapter, we introduce *exception handling*. An *exception* is an indication that a problem occurred during the program's execution. The extensibility of Java can increase the number and types of errors that can occur. Every new class can add its own error possibilities. The features presented here enable programmers to write clearer, more robust, more fault-tolerant programs. We also consider when exception handling should not be used.

The style and details of exception handling in Java as presented in this chapter are based in part on the work of Andrew Koenig and Bjarne Stroustrup as presented in their paper, "Exception Handling for C++ (revised)," published in the *Proceedings of the USENIX C++ Conference* held in San Francisco in April 1990. Their work forms the basis of C++ exception handling. Java's designers chose to implement an exception handling mechanism similar to that used in C++.

Error-handling code varies in nature and quantity among software systems depending on the application and whether the software is a product for release. Products tend to contain far more error-handling code than does "casual" software.

There are many popular means for dealing with errors. Most commonly, error-handling code is interspersed throughout a system's code. Errors are dealt with at the places in the code where the errors can occur. The advantage to this approach is that a programmer reading code can see the error processing in the immediate vicinity of the code and determine if the proper error checking has been implemented.

The problem with this scheme is that the code can become "polluted" with the error processing. It becomes more difficult for a programmer concerned with the application itself to read the code and determine if it is functioning correctly. This can make understanding and maintaining the application difficult.

Some common examples of exceptions are an out-of-bounds array subscript, arithmetic overflow (i.e., a value outside the representable range of values), division by zero, invalid method parameters and memory exhaustion.

Good Programming Practice 14.1

Using Java exception handling enables the programmer to remove the error-handling code from the "main line" of the program's execution. This improves program clarity and enhances modifiability.

Exception handling is provided to enable programs to catch and handle errors rather than letting them occur and suffering the consequences. Exception handling is designed for dealing with *synchronous errors* such as an attempt to divide by zero (that occurs as the program executes the divide instruction). Exception handling is not designed to deal with *asynchronous* events such as disk I/O completions, network message arrivals, mouse clicks, keystrokes and the like; these are best handled through other means, such as Java event listeners.

Java exception handling enables a program to catch all exceptions, all exceptions of a certain type or all exceptions of related types. This flexibility makes programs more robust by reducing the likelihood that programs will not process problems during program execution.

Exception handling is used in situations in which the system can recover from the malfunction that caused the exception. The recovery procedure is called an *exception handler*. The exception handler can be defined in the method that may cause an exception or in a calling method.

Software Engineering Observation 14.1

Use exceptions for malfunctions that must be processed in a different method from where they are detected. Use conventional error-handling techniques for local error processing in which a method is able to deal with its own exceptions.

Exception handling is designed to process exceptional conditions—problems that do not happen frequently, but *can* happen. It is possible that the exception-handling code may not be optimized to the same performance levels as other language elements.

Performance Tip 14.1

When an exception does not occur, little or no overhead is imposed by the presence of exception handling code. When exceptions happen, they do incur execution-time overhead.

Testing and Debugging Tip 14.1

Exception handling helps improve a program's fault tolerance.

Good Programming Practice 14.2

Using Java's standardized exception handling rather than having programmers use a diversity of "home-grown" techniques improves program clarity on large projects.

We will see that exceptions are objects of classes derived from superclass **`Exception`**. We will show how to deal with "uncaught" exceptions. We will consider how unexpected exceptions are handled by Java. We will show how related exception types can be represented by exception subclasses that are derived from a common exception superclass.

Exception handling can be viewed as another means of returning control from a method or exiting a block of code. Normally, when an exception occurs, the exception is handled by a caller of the method generating the exception, by a caller of that caller, or however far back in the call stack it becomes necessary to go to find a handler for that exception.

Software Engineering Observation 14.2

Exception handling is particularly well-suited to systems of separately developed components. Such systems are typical of real-world software. Exception handling makes it easier to combine the components and have them work together effectively.

Software Engineering Observation 14.3

With other programming languages that do not support exception handling, programmers often delay writing error-processing code, and sometimes programmers simply forget to include it. This results in less-robust, and thus inferior, software products. Java forces the programmer to deal with exception handling from the inception of a project. Still, the programmer must put considerable effort into incorporating an exception-handling strategy into software projects.

Software Engineering Observation 14.4

It is best to incorporate your exception-handling strategy into a system from the inception of the design process. It is difficult to add effective exception handling after a system has been implemented.

14.2 When Exception Handling Should Be Used

Exception handling should be used

- to process exceptional situations where a method is unable to complete its task for reasons it cannot control,
- to process exceptions from program components that are not geared to handling those exceptions directly, or
- on large projects to handle exceptions in a uniform manner project wide.

Software Engineering Observation 14.5

The client of a library class will likely have unique error processing in mind for an exception generated in the library class. It is unlikely that a library class will perform error processing that would meet the unique needs of all clients. Exceptions are an appropriate means for dealing with errors produced by library classes.

14.3 Other Error-Handling Techniques

We have presented various ways of dealing with exceptional situations prior to this chapter. A program can ignore some exception types. This can be devastating for software products released to the general public, or for special-purpose software needed for mission-critical situations. But for software developed for your own purposes, it is common to ignore many kinds of errors. A program could be directed to abort upon encountering an exceptional situation. This prevents a program from running to completion and producing incorrect results. For many types of errors this is a good strategy. Such a strategy is inappropriate for mission-critical applications. Resource issues also are important here. If a program obtains a resource, the program should return that resource before program termination.

Common Programming Error 14.1

Aborting a program could leave a resource in a state in which other programs would not be able to acquire the resource; hence, we would have a so-called "resource leak."

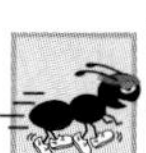

Good Programming Practice 14.3

If your method is capable of handling a given type of exception, then handle it rather than passing the exception on to other regions of your program. This makes programs clearer.

Performance Tip 14.2

If an error can be processed locally instead of throwing an exception, do so. This will improve program execution speed. Exception handling is slow compared to local processing.

14.4 Basics of Java Exception Handling

In this section, we overview the Java exception-handling process. Throughout the chapter, we present detailed discussions of the steps discussed here.

Java exception handling is geared to situations in which the method that detects an error is unable to deal with it. Such a method will *throw an exception*. There is no guarantee that there will be "anything out there" (i.e., an *exception handler*—code that executes when the program detects an exception) to process that kind of exception. If there is, the exception will be *caught* and *handled*. The following *Testing and Debugging Tip* describes what happens if no appropriate exception handler can be found.

Testing and Debugging Tip 14.2

All Java applets and certain Java applications are GUI-based. Some Java applications are not GUI-based; these are often called command-line applications (or console applications). When an exception is not caught in a command-line application, the program terminates (i.e., Java exits) after the default exception handler runs. When an exception is not caught in an applet or a GUI-based application, the GUI remains displayed and the user can continue using the applet or application even after the default exception handler runs. However, the program may be in an inconsistent state and may produce incorrect results.

The programmer encloses in a ***try*** *block* the code that may generate an exception and any code that should not execute if an exception occurs. The **try** block is followed by zero or more ***catch*** *blocks*. Each **catch** block specifies the type of exception it can catch and contains an exception handler. After the last **catch** block, an optional **finally** block provides code that always executes, regardless of whether an exception occurs. As we will see, the **finally** block is an ideal location for code that releases resources to prevent "resource leaks." The **try** block must be followed by a **catch** block or a **finally** block.

When a method throws an exception, program control leaves the **try** block and continues execution at the first **catch** block. The program searches the **catch** blocks in order looking for an appropriate handler. (We will soon discuss what makes a handler "appropriate".) If the type of the thrown exception matches the parameter type in one of the **catch** blocks, the code for that **catch** block executes. If a **try** block completes successfully without throwing any exceptions, the program skips the exception handlers for that block and resumes execution after the last **catch** block. If a **finally** block appears after the last **catch** block, the **finally** block executes regardless of whether an exception occurs.

In a method definition, a ***throws*** *clause* specifies the exceptions the method throws. This clause appears after the parameter list and before the method body. The clause contains a comma-separated list of potential exceptions the method will throw if a problem occurs while the method executes. Such exceptions may by thrown be statements in the method's body, or they may be thrown by methods called in the body. The point at which the **throw** occurs is called the *throw point*.

When an exception occurs, the block in which the exception occurred expires (terminates)—program control cannot return directly to the throw point. Java uses the *termination model of exception handling* rather than the *resumption model of exception handling*. In the resumption model, control would return to the point at which the exception occurred and resume execution.

When an exception occurs, it is possible to communicate information to the exception handler from the vicinity in which the exception occurred. That information is the type of thrown exception object or information harvested from the vicinity in which the exception occurred and placed into the thrown object.

14.5 try Blocks

An exception that occurs in a **try** block normally is caught by an exception handler specified by a **catch** block immediately following that **try** block as in

```
try {
    statements that may throw an exception
}
catch( ExceptionType exceptionReference ) {
    statements to process an exception
}
```

A **try** block can be followed by zero or more **catch** blocks. If a **try** block executes and no exceptions are thrown, all the exception handlers are skipped and control resumes with the first statement after the last exception handler. If a **finally** block (presented in Section 14.13) follows the last **catch** block, the code in the **finally** block executes regardless of whether an exception is thrown. Note that an exception handler cannot access objects defined in the corresponding **try** block, because the **try** block expires before the handler begins executing.

Common Programming Error 14.2

It is a syntax error to separate with other code the **catch** *handlers that correspond to a particular* **try** *block.*

14.6 Throwing an Exception

The ***throw*** statement is executed to indicate that an exception has occurred (i.e., a method could not complete successfully). This is called *throwing an exception*. A **throw** statement specifies an object to be thrown. The operand of a **throw** can be of any class derived from class **Throwable** (package **java.lang**) The two immediate subclasses of class **Throwable** are **Exception** and **Error**. **Error**s are particularly serious system problems that generally should not be caught. **Exception**s are caused by problems that should be caught and processed during program execution to make a program more robust. If the operand of the **throw** is an object of class **Exception**, it is called an *exception object*.

Testing and Debugging Tip 14.3

*When **toString** is invoked on any **Throwable** object, its resulting **String** includes the descriptive **String** that was supplied to the constructor, or simply the class name if no **String** was supplied.*

Testing and Debugging Tip 14.4

An object can be thrown without containing information about the problem that occurred. In this case, simple knowledge that an exception of a particular type occurred may provide sufficient information for the handler to process the problem correctly.

When an exception is thrown, control exits the current **try** block and proceeds to an appropriate **catch** handler (if one exists) after that **try** block. It is possible that the **throw** point could be in a deeply nested scope within a **try** block; control will still proceed to the **catch** handler. It is also possible that the **throw** point could be in a deeply nested method call; still, control will proceed to the **catch** handler.

A **try** block may appear to contain no error checking and include no **throw** statements, but methods called from the **try** block may throw exceptions. Also, statements in a **try** block that do not invoke methods may cause exceptions. For example, a statement that performs array subscripting on an array object throws an **ArrayIndexOutOfBoundsException** if the statement specifies an invalid array subscript. Any method call can invoke code that might **throw** an exception or call another method that throws an exception.

14.7 Catching an Exception

Exception handlers are contained in **catch** blocks. Each **catch** block starts with the keyword **catch** followed by parentheses containing a class name (specifying the type of exception to be caught) and a parameter name. The handler can reference the thrown object through this parameter. This is followed by a block delineating the exception-handling code. When a handler catches an exception, the code in the **catch** block executes.

Common Programming Error 14.3

*Logic errors can occur if you assume that after an exception is processed, control will return to the first statement after the **throw**. Program control continues with the first statement after the **catch** handlers.*

Common Programming Error 14.4

*Specifying a comma-separated list of **catch** parameters is a syntax error. A **catch** can have only a single parameter.*

Common Programming Error 14.5

*It is a syntax error to **catch** the same type in two different **catch** blocks associated with a particular **try** block.*

A **catch** that catches a **Throwable** object

```
catch( Throwable throwable )
```

catches all exceptions and errors. Similarly, a **catch** that catches an **Exception** object

```
catch( Exception exception )
```

catches all exceptions. In general, programs do not define exception handlers for type Throwable, because **Error**s normally should not be caught in a program.

Common Programming Error 14.6

Placing **catch(Exception exception)** *before other* **catch** *blocks that catch specific types of exceptions would prevent those blocks from executing; an exception handler that catches type* **Exception** *must be placed last in the list of exception handlers following a* **try** *block, or a syntax error occurs.*

It is possible that a **try** block will not have a corresponding **catch** handler that matches a particular thrown object. This causes the search for a matching **catch** handler to continue in the next enclosing **try** block. As this process continues, eventually the program may determine that there is no handler on the execution stack that matches the type of the thrown object. In this case, a non-GUI-based application terminates—applets and GUI-based applications return to their regular event processing. Although applets and GUI-based applications continue to execute, they may execute incorrectly.

Software Engineering Observation 14.6

If you know that a method may throw an exception, include appropriate exception-handling code in your program. This will make your program more robust.

Good Programming Practice 14.4

Read the online API documentation for a method before using that method in a program. The documentation specifies the exceptions thrown by the method (if any) and indicates reasons why such exceptions may occur.

Good Programming Practice 14.5

Read the online API documentation for an exception class before writing exception-handling code for that type of exception. The documentation for an exception class typically contains potential reasons that such exceptions may occur during program execution.

It is possible that several exception handlers will provide an acceptable match to the type of the exception. This can happen for several reasons: There can be a "catch-all" handler **catch(Exception exception)** that will catch any exception. Also, inheritance relationships enable a subclass object to be caught either by a handler specifying the subclass type, or by handlers specifying the types of any of that class's superclasses. The first exception handler that matches the exception type executes—all other exception handlers for the corresponding **try** block are ignored.

Software Engineering Observation 14.7

If several handlers match the type of an exception, and if each of these handles the exception differently, then the order of the handlers will affect the manner in which the exception is handled.

Common Programming Error 14.7

It is a syntax error if a **catch** *that catches a superclass object is placed before a* **catch** *for that class's subclass types.*

Sometimes a program may process many closely related types of exceptions. Instead of providing separate **catch** handlers for each, a programmer can provide a single **catch** handler for a group of exceptions.

What happens when an exception occurs in an exception handler? The **try** block that noticed the exception expires before the exception handler begins running, so exceptions occurring in an exception handler are processed by **catch** handlers for an enclosing **try** block. The enclosing **try** block watches for errors occurring in the original **try** block's **catch** handlers. An enclosing **try** block is either a **try** block that contains a complete **try/catch** sequence or a **try** block in a calling method.

Exception handlers can be written a variety of ways. They can rethrow an exception (as we will see in Section 14.9). They can convert one type of exception into another by throwing a different type of exception. They can perform any necessary recovery and resume execution after the last exception handler. They can look at the situation causing the error, remove the cause of the error and retry by calling the original method that caused an exception. They can return a status value to their environment, etc.

It is not possible to return to the **throw** point by issuing a **return** statement in a **catch** handler. Such a **return** simply returns control to the method that called the method containing the **catch** block. Again, the **throw** point is in a block that has expired, so returning to that point via a **return** statement would not make sense.

Software Engineering Observation 14.8

Another reason not to use exceptions for conventional flow of control is that these "additional" exceptions can "get in the way" of genuine error-type exceptions. It becomes more difficult for the programmer to keep track of the larger number of exception cases. Exceptional situations should be rare, not commonplace.

Common Programming Error 14.8

Assuming that an exception thrown from a **catch** *handler will be processed by that handler or any other handler associated with the same* **try** *block can lead to logic errors.*

14.8 Exception-Handling Example: Divide by Zero

Now let us consider a simple example of exception handling. The application of Fig. 14.1 and Fig. 14.2 uses **try**, **throw** and **catch** to detect, indicate and handle exceptions. The application displays two **JTextField**s in which the user can type integers. When the user presses the *Enter* key in the second **JTextField**, the program calls method **actionPerformed** to read the two integers from the **JTextField**s and pass the integers to method **quotient**, which calculates the quotient of the two values and returns a **double** result. If the user types 0 in the second **JTextField**, the program uses an exception to indicate that the user is attempting to divide by zero. Also, if the user types a noninteger value in either **JTextField**, a **NumberFormatException** occurs. In prior examples that read numeric values from the user, we simply assumed that the user would input a proper integer value. However, users sometimes make mistakes. This program demonstrates how to catch the **NumberFormatException** that occurs when a program attempts to convert a **String** that does not represent an integer value to an **int** value with **Integer** method **parseInt**.

Before we discuss the program, consider the sample executions shown in the five output windows of Fig. 14.2. The first window shows a successful execution. The user typed the values 100 and 7. The third **JTextField** shows the result of the division performed by method **quotient**. In the second output window, the user entered the string "hello" in the second **JTextField**. When the user presses *Enter* in the second **JText-**

Field, an error-message dialog is displayed indicating that an integer must be entered. In the last two windows, a zero denominator is entered and the program detects the problem, throws an exception and issues an appropriate diagnostic message.

Now let's discuss the program beginning with class **DivideByZeroException** of Fig. 14.1. Java can test for division by zero when the values in the division are both integers. If Java discovers an attempt to divide by zero in integer arithmetic, Java throws an ***ArithmeticException***. However, our program performs a floating-point division of two integers by casting the first integer to a **double** before performing the calculation. Java allows floating-point division by zero. The result is positive or negative infinity. (Classes **Float** and **Double** of package **java.lang** each provide constants that represent these values.) Even though Java allows floating-point division by zero, we would like to use exception handling in this example to indicate to the user of our program that they are attempting to divide by zero.

As we will see, method **quotient** throws an exception when it receives zero as its second argument. A method can throw an exception of any existing type in the Java API or of a type specific to the program. In this example, we demonstrate defining a new exception type. Actually, we could use class **ArithmeticException** (package **java.lang**) with a customized error message in this program.

Good Programming Practice 14.6

Associating each type of serious execution-time malfunction with an appropriately named ***Exception*** *class improves program clarity.*

Software Engineering Observation 14.9

If possible, use an existing exception type, rather than creating a new class. The Java API contains many exception types that may be suitable for your program.

```
// Fig. 14.1: DivideByZeroException.java
// Definition of class DivideByZeroException.
// Used to throw an exception when a
// divide-by-zero is attempted.
public class DivideByZeroException extends ArithmeticException {

   // no-argument constructor specifies default error message
   public DivideByZeroException()
   {
      super( "Attempted to divide by zero" );
   }

   // constructor to allow customized error message
   public DivideByZeroException( String message )
   {
      super( message );
   }

}  // end class DivideByZeroException
```

Fig. 14.1 Exception class **DivideByZeroException**.

Class **DivideByZeroException** extends class **ArithmeticException**. We chose to extend class **ArithmeticException** because dividing by zero occurs during arithmetic. Like any other class, an exception class can contain instance variables and methods. A typical exception class contains only two constructors—one that takes no arguments and specifies a default exception message and one that receives a customized exception message as a **String**. The default constructor (lines 8–11) specifies the string **"Attempted to divide by zero"** as the exception message that indicates what went wrong. This string is passed to the superclass constructor to initialize the error message associated with the exception object. The other constructor (lines 14–17) passes its argument—a customized error-message string—to the superclass constructor.

Software Engineering Observation 14.10

When defining your own exception type, subclass an existing related exception type in the Java API. This requires you to investigate the existing exceptions in the Java API. If the existing types are not appropriate for subclassing, the new exception class should extend **Exception** *if the client of your code should be required to handle the exception, or should extend* **RuntimeException** *if the client of your code should have the option of ignoring the exception.*

Now consider the **DivideByZeroTest** application (Fig. 14.2). The application's constructor (lines 21–51) builds a graphical user interface with three **JLabel**s (all right aligned) and three **JTextField**s and registers the **DivideByZeroTest** object as the **ActionListener** for **JTextField inputField2**.

```
1  // Fig. 14.2: DivideByZeroTest.java
2  // A simple exception handling example.
3  // Checking for a divide-by-zero-error.
4
5  // Java core packages
6  import java.awt.*;
7  import java.awt.event.*;
8  import java.text.DecimalFormat;
9
10 // Java extension packages
11 import javax.swing.*;
12
13 public class DivideByZeroTest extends JFrame
14    implements ActionListener {
15
16    private JTextField inputField1, inputField2, outputField;
17    private int number1, number2;
18    private double result;
19
20    // set up GUI
21    public DivideByZeroTest()
22    {
23       super( "Demonstrating Exceptions" );
24
```

Fig. 14.2 A simple exception-handling example with divide by zero (part 1 of 3).

```
      // get content pane and set its layout
      Container container = getContentPane();
      container.setLayout( new GridLayout( 3, 2 ) );

      // set up label and inputField1
      container.add(
         new JLabel( "Enter numerator ", SwingConstants.RIGHT ) );
      inputField1 = new JTextField( 10 );
      container.add( inputField1 );

      // set up label and inputField2; register listener
      container.add(
         new JLabel( "Enter denominator and press Enter ",
            SwingConstants.RIGHT ) );
      inputField2 = new JTextField( 10 );
      container.add( inputField2 );
      inputField2.addActionListener( this );

      // set up label and outputField
      container.add(
         new JLabel( "RESULT ", SwingConstants.RIGHT ) );
      outputField = new JTextField();
      container.add( outputField );

      setSize( 425, 100 );
      setVisible( true );
   }

   // process GUI events
   public void actionPerformed( ActionEvent event )
   {
      DecimalFormat precision3 = new DecimalFormat( "0.000" );

      outputField.setText( "" );   // clear outputField

      // read two numbers and calculate quotient
      try {
         number1 = Integer.parseInt( inputField1.getText() );
         number2 = Integer.parseInt( inputField2.getText() );

         result = quotient( number1, number2 );
         outputField.setText( precision3.format( result ) );
      }

      // process improperly formatted input
      catch ( NumberFormatException numberFormatException ) {
         JOptionPane.showMessageDialog( this,
            "You must enter two integers",
            "Invalid Number Format",
            JOptionPane.ERROR_MESSAGE );
      }

```

Fig. 14.2 A simple exception-handling example with divide by zero (part 2 of 3).

```
      // process attempts to divide by zero
      catch ( ArithmeticException arithmeticException ) {
         JOptionPane.showMessageDialog( this,
            arithmeticException.toString(),
            "Arithmetic Exception",
            JOptionPane.ERROR_MESSAGE );
      }
   }

   // method quotient demonstrated throwing an exception
   // when a divide-by-zero error occurs
   public double quotient( int numerator, int denominator )
      throws DivideByZeroException
   {
      if ( denominator == 0 )
         throw new DivideByZeroException();

      return ( double ) numerator / denominator;
   }

   // execute application
   public static void main( String args[] )
   {
      DivideByZeroTest application = new DivideByZeroTest();

      application.setDefaultCloseOperation(
         JFrame.EXIT_ON_CLOSE );
   }

}  // end class DivideByZeroTest
```

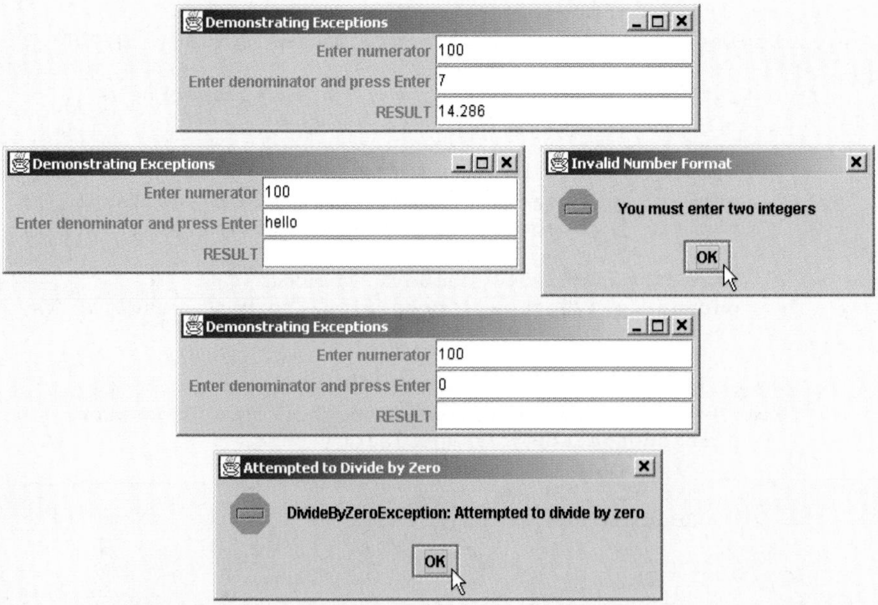

Demonstrating Exceptions
Enter numerator 100
Enter denominator and press Enter 7
RESULT 14.286

Demonstrating Exceptions
Enter numerator 100
Enter denominator and press Enter hello
RESULT

Invalid Number Format
You must enter two integers
OK

Demonstrating Exceptions
Enter numerator 100
Enter denominator and press Enter 0
RESULT

Attempted to Divide by Zero
DivideByZeroException: Attempted to divide by zero
OK

Fig. 14.2 A simple exception-handling example with divide by zero (part 3 of 3).

When the user inputs the denominator and presses the *Enter* key, the program calls method **actionPerformed** (lines 54–84). Next, method **actionPerformed** proceeds with a **try** block (lines 61–67), which encloses the code that may **throw** an exception and any code that should not be executed if an exception occurs. The statements that read the integers from the **JTextField**s (lines 62–63) each use method **Integer.parseInt** to convert **String**s to **int** values. Method **parseInt** throws a **NumberFormatException** if its **String** argument is not a valid integer. The division that can cause the divide-by-zero error is not performed explicitly in the **try** block. Rather, the call to method **quotient** (line 65) invokes the code that attempts the division. Method **quotient** (lines 89–96) **throw**s the **DivideByZeroException** object, as we will see momentarily. In general, errors may surface through explicitly mentioned code in a **try** block, through calls to a method or even through deeply nested method calls initiated by code in a **try** block.

The **try** block in this example is followed by two **catch** blocks—lines 70–75 contain the exception handler for the **NumberFormatException** and lines 78–83 contain the exception handler for the **DivideByZeroException**. In general, when the program detects an exception while executing a **try** block, the program catches the exception in a **catch** block that specifies an appropriate exception type (i.e., the type in the **catch** matches the thrown exception type exactly or is a superclass of the thrown exception type). In Fig. 14.2, the first **catch** block specifies that it will catch exception objects of type **NumberFormatException** (this type matches the exception object type thrown in method **Integer.parseInt**) and the second **catch** block specifies that it will catch exception objects of type **ArithmeticException** (this type is a superclass of the exception object type thrown in method **quotient**). Only the matching **catch** handler executes when an exception occurs. Both our exception handlers simply display an error-message dialog, but exception handlers can be more elaborate than this. After executing an exception handler, program control proceeds to the first statement after the last **catch** block (or in the **finally** block, if one is present).

If the code in the **try** block does not **throw** an exception, then the **catch** handlers are skipped and execution resumes with the first line of code after the **catch** handlers (or in the **finally** block, if one is present). In Fig. 14.2, method **actionPerformed** simply returns, but the program could continue executing more statements after the **catch** blocks.

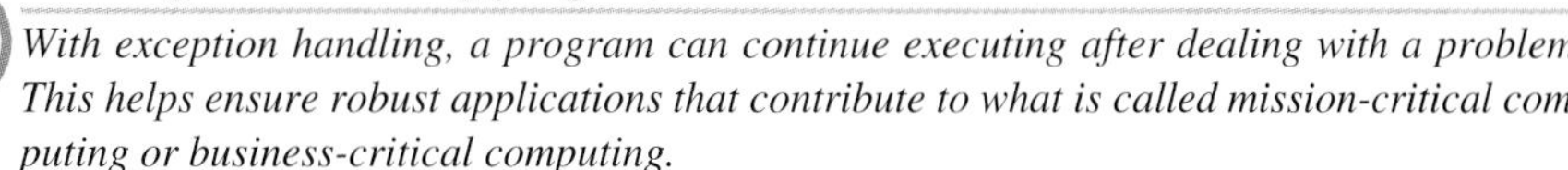

Testing and Debugging Tip 14.5

With exception handling, a program can continue executing after dealing with a problem. This helps ensure robust applications that contribute to what is called mission-critical computing or business-critical computing.

Now let us examine method **quotient** (lines 89–96). When the **if** structure determines that **denominator** is zero, the body of the **if** executes a **throw** statement that creates and **throw**s a new **DivideByZeroException** object. This object will be caught by the **catch** block (lines 78–83) specifying type **ArithmeticException** after the **try** block. The **catch** block specifies parameter name **arithmeticException** to receive the thrown exception object. The **ArithmeticException** handler converts the exception to a **String** via **toString** and passes this **String** as the message to display in an error-message dialog.

If **denominator** is not zero, **quotient** does not throw an exception. Rather, **quotient** performs the division and returns the result of the division to the point of invocation of method **quotient** in the **try** block (line 65). Line 66 displays the result of the calculation in the third **JTextField**. In this case, the **try** block completes successfully, so the program skips the **catch** blocks and the **actionPerformed** method completes execution normally.

Note that when **quotient** throws the **DivideByZeroException**, **quotient**'s block expires (i.e., the method terminates). This would cause any of its local variables to be destroyed—objects that were referenced by local variables in the block would have their reference counts decremented accordingly (and are possibly marked for garbage collection). Also, the **try** block from which the method was called expires before line 66 can execute. Here, too, if there were local variables created in the **try** block prior to the exception being thrown, these variables would be destroyed.

If a **NumberFormatException** is generated by lines 62–63, the **try** block expires and execution continues with the exception handler at line 70, which displays an error message to tell the user to input integers. Then the **actionPerformed** method continues with the next valid statement after the **catch** blocks (i.e., the method terminates in this example).

14.9 Rethrowing an Exception

It is possible that the **catch** handler that catches an exception may decide it cannot process the exception, or it may want to let some other **catch** handler handle the exception. In this case, the handler that received the exception can rethrow the exception with the statement

```
throw exceptionReference;
```

where *exceptionReference* is the parameter name for the exception in the **catch** handler. Such a **throw** rethrows the exception to the next enclosing **try** block.

Even if a handler can process an exception, and regardless of whether it does any processing on that exception, the handler still can rethrow the exception for further processing outside the handler. A rethrown exception is detected by the next enclosing **try** block and is handled by an exception handler listed after that enclosing **try** block.

14.10 throws Clause

A **throws** clause lists the exceptions that can be thrown by a method as in

```
int functionName( parameterList )
   throws ExceptionType1, ExceptionType2, ExceptionType3, ...
{
   // method body
}
```

The types of exceptions that are thrown by a method are specified in the method definition with a comma-separated list in the **throws** clause. A method can **throw** objects of the indicated classes, or it can **throw** objects of their subclasses.

Some exceptions can occur at any point during the execution of the program. Many of these exceptions can be avoided by coding properly. These are run-time exceptions, and they derive from class ***RuntimeException***. For example, if your program attempts to access an out-of-range array subscript, an exception of type **ArrayIndexOutOfBoundsException** (derived from **RuntimeException**) occurs. Your program clearly can avoid such a problem; hence, it is a run-time exception.

Another run-time exception occurs when your program creates an object reference, but has not yet created an object and assigned it to the reference. Attempting to use such a **null** reference causes a **NullPointerException** to be thrown. Clearly, your program can avoid this circumstance; hence, it is a run-time exception. Another run-time exception is an invalid cast, which throws a **ClassCastException**.

There are a variety of exceptions that are not **RuntimeException**s. Two of the most common are **InterruptedException**s (see Chapter 15, "Multithreading") and **IOException**s (see Chapter 16, "Files and Streams").

Not all errors and exceptions that can be thrown from a method are required to be listed in the **throws** clause. **Error**s do not need to be listed, nor do **RuntimeException**s (avoidable exceptions). **Error**s are serious system problems that can occur almost anywhere, and most programs will not be able to recover from them. Methods should process **RuntimeException**s caught in their bodies directly rather than passing them on to other program components. If a method throws any non-**RuntimeException**s, it *must* specify those exception types in its **throws** clause.

Software Engineering Observation 14.11

*If a non-**RuntimeException** is thrown by a method, or if that method calls methods that throw non-**RuntimeException**s, each of those exceptions must be declared in the **throws** clause of that method or caught in a **try/catch** in that method.*

Java distinguishes *checked* **Exception**s versus *unchecked* ***RuntimeExceptions*** and **Error**s. A method's checked exceptions need to be listed in that method's **throws** clause. **Error**s and **RuntimeException**s can be thrown from almost any method, so it would be cumbersome for programmers to be required to list them for every method definition. Such exceptions and errors are not required to be listed in a method's **throw**s clause and, hence, are said to be "unchecked" by the compiler. All non-**RuntimeException**s a method can **throw** must be listed in that method's **throws** clause and, hence, are said to be "checked" by the compiler. If a non-**RuntimeException** is not listed in the throws clause, the compiler will issue an error message indicating that the exception must be caught (with a **try/catch** in the body of the method) or declared (with a **throws** clause).

Common Programming Error 14.9

*It is a syntax error if a method throws a checked exception not in that method's **throws** clause.*

Common Programming Error 14.10

*Attempting to throw a checked exception from a method that has no **throws** clause is a syntax error.*

Software Engineering Observation 14.12

*If your method calls other methods that explicitly **throw** checked exceptions, those exceptions must be listed in the **throws** clause of your method, unless your method catches those exceptions. This is Java's "**catch**-or-declare" requirement.*

Common Programming Error 14.11

*If a subclass method overrides a superclass method, it is an error for the subclass method to list more exceptions in its **throws** list than the overridden superclass method does. A subclass's **throws** list can contain a subset of a superclass's **throws** list.*

Java's ***catch**-or-declare requirement* demands that the programmer either **catch** each checked exception or place it in the **throws** clause of a method. Of course, placing a checked exception in the **throws** clause would force other methods to process the checked exception as well. If a programmer feels a particular checked exception is unlikely to occur, the programmer might elect to catch that checked exception and do nothing with it to avoid being forced to deal with it later. This can of course come back to haunt you, because as a program evolves, it may become important to deal with this checked exception.

Testing and Debugging Tip 14.6

*Do not try to circumvent Java's **catch**-or-declare requirement by simply catching exceptions and doing nothing with them. Exceptions are generally of a serious enough nature that they need to be processed rather than suppressed.*

Testing and Debugging Tip 14.7

*The Java compiler, through the **throws** clause used with exception handling, forces programmers to process the exceptions that can be thrown from each method a program calls. This helps avoid bugs that arise in programs when programmers ignore the fact that problems occur and make no provisions for these problems.*

Software Engineering Observation 14.13

*Subclass methods that do not override their corresponding superclass methods exhibit the same exception-handling behavior of the inherited superclass methods. The **throws** clause of a subclass method that overrides a superclass method may contain the same list of exceptions as the overridden superclass method or a subset of that list.*

Common Programming Error 14.12

*The Java compiler requires that a method either catch any checked exceptions thrown in the method (either directly from the method's body or indirectly through called methods) or declare checked **Exception**s the method can **throw** to other methods; otherwise, the Java compiler issues a syntax error.*

Testing and Debugging Tip 14.8

*Suppose a method **throws** all subclasses of a particular exception superclass. You may be tempted to list only the superclass in the **throws** clause. Instead, explicitly list all the subclasses. This focuses the programmer's attention on the specific **Exception**s that may occur and will often help avoid bugs caused by performing general processing for a category of exception types.*

Figure 14.3–Fig. 14.8 list many of Java's **Error**s and **Exception**s hierarchically for the packages **java.lang**, **java.util**, **java.io**, **java.awt** and **java.net**. In these tables, a class indented under another class is a subclass. The exception and error classes for the other packages of the Java API can be found in the Java online documentation. The online documentation for each method in the API specifies whether that method throws exceptions and what the exceptions are that can be thrown. We show a portion of Java's **Error** hierarchy in Fig. 14.3. Most Java programmers ignore **Error**s. They are serious but rare events.

Figure 14.4 is particularly important because it lists many of Java's **Runtime-Exception**s. Although Java programmers are not required to declare these exceptions in **throws** clauses, these are the exceptions that commonly will be caught and handled in Java applications.

The `java.lang` package errors

```
Error (all in java.lang except for AWTError, which is in java.awt)
   LinkageError
      ClassCircularityError
      ClassFormatError
      ExceptionInInitializerError
      IncompatibleClassChangeError
         AbstractMethodError
         IllegalAccessError
         InstantiationError
         NoSuchFieldError
         NoSuchMethodError
      NoClassDefFoundError
      UnsatisfiedLinkError
      VerifyError
   ThreadDeath
   VirtualMachineError (Abstract class)
      InternalError
      OutOfMemoryError
      StackOverflowError
      UnknownError
   AWTError (package java.awt)
```

Fig. 14.3 The `java.lang` package errors .

The `java.lang` package exceptions

```
Exception
   ClassNotFoundException
   CloneNotSupportedException
   IllegalAccessException
   InstantiationException
   InterruptedException
   NoSuchFieldException
   NoSuchMethodException
```

Fig. 14.4 The `java.lang` package exceptions (part 1 of 2).

The `java.lang` package exceptions

```
RuntimeException
    ArithmeticException
    ArrayStoreException
    ClassCastException
    IllegalArgumentException
        IllegalThreadStateException
        NumberFormatException
    IllegalMonitorStateException
    IllegalStateException
    IndexOutOfBoundsException
        ArrayIndexOutOfBoundsException
        StringIndexOutOfBoundsException
    NegativeArraySizeException
    NullPointerException
    SecurityException
```

Fig. 14.4 The **java.lang** package exceptions (part 2 of 2).

Figure 14.5 lists Java's other three **RuntimeException**s data types. We will encounter these exceptions in Chapter 20 when we study the **Vector** class. A **Vector** is a dynamic array that can grow and shrink to accommodate a program's varying storage requirements.

Figure 14.6 lists Java's **IOException**s. These are all checked exceptions that can occur during input/output and file processing.

Figure 14.7 lists the **java.awt** package's only checked **Exception**, the **AWTException**. This is a checked exception that is thrown by various abstract windowing toolkit methods.

The `java.util` package exceptions

```
Exception
    RuntimeException
        EmptyStackException
        MissingResourceException
        NoSuchElementException
    TooManyListenersException
```

Fig. 14.5 The **java.util** package exceptions.

The `java.io` package exceptions

```
Exception
   IOException
      CharConversionException
      EOFException
      FileNotFoundException
      InterruptedIOException
      ObjectStreamException
         InvalidClassException
         InvalidObjectException
         NotActiveException
         NotSerializableException
         OptionalDataException
         StreamCorruptedException
         WriteAbortedException
      SyncFailedException
      UnsupportedCodingException
      UTFDataFormatException
```

Fig. 14.6 The **`java.io`** package exceptions .

The `java.awt` package exceptions

```
Exception
   AWTException
   RuntimeException
      IllegalStateException
         IllegalComponentStateException
```

Fig. 14.7 The **`java.awt`** package exceptions .

Figure 14.8 lists the **`IOException`**s of the **`java.net`** package. These are all checked **`Exception`**s that indicate various networking problems.

Most packages in the Java API define **`Exception`**s and **`Error`**s specific to the package. For a complete list of these types, see the online API documentation for the package.

The `java.net` package exceptions

```
Exception
   IOException
      BindException
      MalformedURLException
      ProtocolException
      SocketException
         ConnectException
         NoRouteToHostException
      UnknownHostException
      UnknownServiceException
```

Fig. 14.8 The **`java.net`** package exceptions.

14.11 Constructors, Finalizers and Exception Handling

First, let us deal with an issue we have mentioned, but that has yet to be resolved satisfactorily. What happens when an error is detected in a constructor? The problem is that a constructor cannot return a value, so how do we let the program know that an object has not been constructed properly? One scheme is to return the improperly constructed object and hope that anyone using the object would perform appropriate tests to determine that the object is in fact bad. However, this directly contradicts discussions in Chapter 8 in which we indicated that you should maintain an object in a consistent state at all times. Another scheme is to set some instance variable with an error indicator outside the constructor, but this is a poor programming practice. In Java, the typical (and proper) mechanism is to throw an exception from the constructor to the code creating the object. The thrown object contains the information about the failed constructor call and the caller is responsible for handling the failure.

When an exception occurs in a constructor, other objects created by that constructor are marked for eventual garbage collection. Before each object is garbage collected, its **`finalize`** method will be called.

14.12 Exceptions and Inheritance

Various exception classes can be derived from a common superclass. If a **`catch`** is written to catch exception objects of a superclass type, it can also catch all objects of subclasses of that superclass. This can allow for polymorphic processing of related exceptions.

Using inheritance with exceptions enables an exception handler to catch related errors with a concise notation. One could certainly catch each subclass exception object individually if those exceptions require different processing, but it is more concise to catch the superclass exception object. Of course, this makes sense only if the handling behavior would be the same for all subclasses. Otherwise, catch each subclass exception individually.

Testing and Debugging Tip 14.9

Catching subclass exception objects individually is subject to error if the programmer forgets to test for one or more of the subclass types explicitly; catching the superclass guarantees that objects of all subclasses will be caught. Often, a catch of the superclass type follows all other subclass exception handlers to ensure that all exceptions are processed properly.

14.13 `finally` Block

Programs that obtain certain types of resources must return those resources to the system explicitly to avoid so-called *resource leaks.* In programming languages like C and C++, the most common kind of resource leak is a memory leak. Java performs automatic garbage collection of memory no longer used by programs, thus avoiding most memory leaks. However, other types of resource leaks can occur in Java.

Software Engineering Observation 14.14

A **`finally`** *block typically contains code to release resources acquired in its corresponding* **`try`** *block; this is an effective way to eliminate resource leaks. For example, the* **`finally`** *block should close any files opened in the* **`try`** *block.*

Testing and Debugging Tip 14.10

Actually, Java does not eliminate memory leaks completely. There is a subtle issue here. Java will not garbage collect an object until there are no more references to the object. Thus, memory leaks can occur, but only if programmers erroneously keep references to unwanted objects. Most memory leak problems are solved by Java's garbage collection.

The **`finally`** block is optional. If it is present, it is placed after the last of a **`try`** block's **`catch`** blocks, as follows:

```
try {
    statements
    resource-acquisition statements
}
catch ( AKindOfException exception1 ) {
    exception-handling statements
}
catch ( AnotherKindOfException exception2 ) {
    exception-handling statements
}
finally {
    statements
    resource-release statements
}
```

Java guarantees that a **`finally`** block (if one is present) will execute regardless of whether any exception is thrown in the corresponding **`try`** block or any of its corresponding **`catch`** blocks. Java also guarantees that a **`finally`** block (if one is present) will execute if a **`try`** block exits via a **`return`**, **`break`** or **`continue`** statement.

Resource-release code is placed in a **`finally`** block. Suppose a resource is allocated in a **`try`** block. If no exception occurs, the **`catch`** handlers are skipped and control proceeds to the **`finally`** block, which frees the resource. Control then proceeds to the first statement after the **`finally`** block.

If an exception occurs, the program skips the rest of the **try** block. If the program catches the exception in one of the **catch** handlers, the program processes the exception. Then the **finally** block releases the resource, and control then proceeds to the first statement after the **finally** block.

If an exception that occurs in the **try** block cannot be caught by one of the **catch** handlers, the program skips the rest of the **try** block and control proceeds to the **finally** block, which releases the resource. Then the program passes the exception up the call chain until some calling method chooses to **catch** it. If no method chooses to deal with it, a non-GUI-based application terminates.

If a **catch** handler throws an exception, the **finally** block still executes. Then the exception is passed up the call chain for a calling method to **catch** and handle.

The Java application of Fig. 14.9 demonstrates that the **finally** block (if one is present) executes even if an exception is not thrown in the corresponding **try** block. The program contains methods **main** (lines 7–21), **throwException** (lines 24–50) and **doesNotThrowException** (lines 53–75). Methods **throwException** and **doesNotThrowException** are declared **static** so **main** (another **static** method) can call them directly.

Method **main** begins executing, enters its **try** block and immediately calls **throwException** (line 11). Method **throwException** throws an **Exception** (line 29), catches it (line 33) and rethrows it (line 37). The rethrown exception will be handled in **main**, but first the **finally** block (lines 44–47) executes. Method **main** detects the rethrown exception in the **try** block in **main** (lines 10–12) and handles it by the **catch** block (lines 15–18). Next, **main** calls method **doesNotThrowException** (line 20). No exception is thrown in **doesNotThrowException**'s **try** block, so the program skips the **catch** block (lines 61–64), but the **finally** block (lines 68–61) nevertheless executes. Control proceeds to the statement after the **finally** block. Then control returns to **main** and the program terminates.

```
1  // Fig. 14.9: UsingExceptions.java
2  // Demonstration of the try-catch-finally
3  // exception handling mechanism.
4  public class UsingExceptions {
5
6     // execute application
7     public static void main( String args[] )
8     {
9        // call method throwException
10       try {
11          throwException();
12       }
13
14       // catch Exceptions thrown by method throwException
15       catch ( Exception exception )
16       {
17          System.err.println( "Exception handled in main" );
18       }
19
```

Fig. 14.9 Demonstration of the **try-catch-finally** exception-handling mechanism (part 1 of 3).

```
         doesNotThrowException();
      }

      // demonstrate try/catch/finally
      public static void throwException() throws Exception
      {
         // throw an exception and immediately catch it
         try {
            System.out.println( "Method throwException" );
            throw new Exception();  // generate exception
         }

         // catch exception thrown in try block
         catch ( Exception exception )
         {
            System.err.println(
               "Exception handled in method throwException" );
            throw exception;  // rethrow for further processing

            // any code here would not be reached
         }

         // this block executes regardless of what occurs in
         // try/catch
         finally {
            System.err.println(
               "Finally executed in throwException" );
         }

         // any code here would not be reached
      }

      // demonstrate finally when no exception occurs
      public static void doesNotThrowException()
      {
         // try block does not throw an exception
         try {
            System.out.println( "Method doesNotThrowException" );
         }

         // catch does not execute, because no exception thrown
         catch( Exception exception )
         {
            System.err.println( exception.toString() );
         }

         // this block executes regardless of what occurs in
         // try/catch
         finally {
            System.err.println(
               "Finally executed in doesNotThrowException" );
         }
```

Fig. 14.9 Demonstration of the `try-catch-finally` exception-handling mechanism (part 2 of 3).

```

         System.out.println(
            "End of method doesNotThrowException" );
      }

   }  // end class UsingExceptions
```

```
Method throwException
Exception handled in method throwException
Finally executed in throwException
Exception handled in main
Method doesNotThrowException
Finally executed in doesNotThrowException
End of method doesNotThrowException
```

Fig. 14.9 Demonstration of the **try-catch-finally** exception-handling mechanism (part 3 of 3).

The Java application in Fig. 14.10 demonstrates that when an exception thrown in a **try** block is *not* caught in a corresponding **catch** block, the exception will be detected in the next outer **try** block and handled by an appropriate **catch** block (if one is present) associated with that outer **try** block.

```
// Fig. 14.10: UsingExceptions.java
// Demonstration of stack unwinding.
public class UsingExceptions {

   // execute application
   public static void main( String args[] )
   {
      // call throwException to demonstrate stack unwinding
      try {
         throwException();
      }

      // catch exception thrown in throwException
      catch ( Exception exception ) {
         System.err.println( "Exception handled in main" );
      }
   }

   // throwException throws an exception that is not caught in
   // the body of this method
   public static void throwException() throws Exception
   {
      // throw an exception and catch it in main
      try {
         System.out.println( "Method throwException" );
         throw new Exception();       // generate exception
      }
```

Fig. 14.10 Demonstration of stack unwinding (part 1 of 2).

```
28
29         // catch is incorrect type, so Exception not caught
30         catch( RuntimeException runtimeException ) {
31            System.err.println(
32               "Exception handled in method throwException" );
33         }
34
35         // finally block always executes
36         finally {
37            System.err.println( "Finally is always executed" );
38         }
39      }
40
41   }  // end class UsingExceptions
```

```
Method throwException
Finally is always executed
Exception handled in main
```

Fig. 14.10 Demonstration of stack unwinding (part 2 of 2).

When method **main** executes, line 10 in the **try** block calls **throwException** (lines 21–39). In the **try** block of method **throwException**, line 26 throws an **Exception**. This terminates the **try** block immediately and control proceeds to the **catch** handler at line 30. The type being caught (**RuntimeException**) is not an exact match with the thrown type (**Exception**) and is not a superclass of the thrown type, so the exception is not caught in method **throwException**. The exception must be handled before normal program execution can continue. Therefore, method **throwException** terminates (but not until its **finally** block executes) and returns control to the point from which it was called in the program (line 10). Line 10 is in the enclosing **try** block. If the exception has not yet been handled, the **try** block terminates and an attempt is made to catch the exception at line 14. The type being caught (**Exception**) matches the thrown type. Therefore, the **catch** handler processes the exception and the program terminates at the end of **main**.

As we have seen, a **finally** block executes for a variety of reasons, such as a **try** completing successfully, handling of an exception in a local **catch**, an exception being thrown for which no local **catch** is available or execution of a program control statement like a **return**, **break** or **continue**. Normally, the **finally** block executes, then behaves appropriately (we will call this **finally**'s "continuation action") depending on the reason program control entered the block. For example, if an exception is thrown in the **finally** block, the continuation action will be for *that* exception to be processed in the next enclosing **try** block. Unfortunately, if there was an exception that had not yet been caught, that exception is lost and the more recent exception is processed. This is dangerous.

Common Programming Error 14.13

If an exception is thrown for which no local **catch** *is available, when control enters the local* **finally** *block, the* **finally** *block could also* **throw** *an exception. If this happens, the first exception will be lost.*

Testing and Debugging Tip 14.11

Avoid placing code that can **`throw`** *an exception in a* **`finally`** *block. If such code is required, enclose the code in a* **`try/catch`** *within the* **`finally`** *block.*

Good Programming Practice 14.7

Java's exception-handling mechanism is intended to remove error-processing code from the main line of a program's code to improve program clarity. Do not place **`try/catch/finally`** *around every statement that may throw an exception. This makes programs difficult to read. Rather, place one* **`try`** *block around a significant portion of your code, follow that* **`try`** *block with* **`catch`** *blocks that handle each possible exception and follow the* **`catch`** *blocks with a single* **`finally`** *block (if one is required).*

Performance Tip 14.3

As a rule, resources should be released as soon as it is apparent that they are no longer needed. This makes these resources immediately available for reuse and can improve program performance.

Software Engineering Observation 14.15

If a **`try`** *block has a corresponding* **`finally`** *block, the* **`finally`** *block will execute even if the* **`try`** *block exits with* **`return`**, **`break`** *or* **`continue`**; *then the effect of the* **`return`**, **`break`** *or* **`continue`** *will occur.*

14.14 Using `printStackTrace` and `getMessage`

Exceptions derive from class **`Throwable`**. Class **`Throwable`** offers a **`printStackTrace`** method that prints the method call stack. By calling this method for a **`Throwable`** object that has been caught, a program can print the method call stack. Often, this is helpful in testing and debugging. Two other overloaded versions of **`printStackTrace`** enable the program to direct the stack trace to a **`PrintStream`** or **`PrintWriter`** stream. In this section, we consider an example that exercises the **`printStackTrace`** method and another useful method, **`getMessage`**.

Testing and Debugging Tip 14.12

All **`Throwable`** *objects contain a* **`printStackTrace`** *method that prints a stack trace for the object.*

Testing and Debugging Tip 14.13

An exception that is not caught eventually causes Java's default exception handler to run. This displays the name of the exception, the optional character string that was supplied when the exception was constructed and a complete execution stack trace. The stack trace shows the complete method call stack. This lets the programmer see the path of execution that led to the exception file-by-file (and thus class-by-class) and method-by-method. This information is helpful in debugging a program.

There are two constructors for class **`Throwable`**. The first constructor

```
public Throwable()
```

takes no arguments. The second constructor

```
public Throwable( String informationString )
```

takes the argument **informationString**, which is descriptive information about the **Throwable** object. The **informationString** stored in the **Throwable** object may be obtained with method **getMessage**.

***Throwable** classes have a constructor that accepts a **String** argument. Using this form of the constructor is helpful in determining the source of the exception via method **getMessage**.*

Figure 14.11 demonstrates **getMessage** and **printStackTrace**. Method **getMessage** returns the descriptive **String** stored in an exception. Method **printStackTrace** outputs to the standard error stream (normally, the command line or console) an error message with the class name of the exception, the descriptive **String** stored in the exception and a list of the methods that had not completed execution when the exception was thrown (i.e., all methods currently residing on the method call stack).

In the program, **main** invokes **method1**, **method1** invokes **method2** and **method2** invokes **method3**. At this point, the method call stack for the program is

```
method3
method2
method1
main
```

with the last method called (**method3**) at the top and the first method called (**main**) at the bottom. When **method3** throws an **Exception** (line 36), a stack-trace message is generated and stored in the **Exception** object. The stack trace reflects the throw point in the code (i.e., line 36). Then, the stack unwinds to the first method in the method call stack in which the exception can be caught (i.e., **main** because it contains a **catch** handler for **Exception**). The **catch** handler then uses **getMessage** and **printStackTrace** on the **Exception** object **exception** to produce the output. Notice that the line numbers in the output window correspond to the line numbers in the program.

```
1  // Fig. 14.11: UsingExceptions.java
2  // Demonstrating the getMessage and printStackTrace
3  // methods inherited into all exception classes.
4  public class UsingExceptions {
5
6     // execute application
7     public static void main( String args[] )
8     {
9        // call method1
10       try {
11          method1();
12       }
13
14       // catch Exceptions thrown from method1
15       catch ( Exception exception ) {
16          System.err.println( exception.getMessage() + "\n" );
17          exception.printStackTrace();
18       }
19    }
```

Fig. 14.11 Using **getMessage** and **printStackTrace** (part 1 of 2).

```
    // call method2; throw exceptions back to main
    public static void method1() throws Exception
    {
       method2();
    }

    // call method3; throw exceptions back to method1
    public static void method2() throws Exception
    {
       method3();
    }

    // throw Exception back to method2
    public static void method3() throws Exception
    {
       throw new Exception( "Exception thrown in method3" );
    }

 }  // end class Using Exceptions
```

```
Exception thrown in method3

java.lang.Exception: Exception thrown in method3
        at UsingExceptions.method3(UsingExceptions.java:36)
        at UsingExceptions.method2(UsingExceptions.java:30)
        at UsingExceptions.method1(UsingExceptions.java:24)
        at UsingExceptions.main(UsingExceptions.java:11))
```

Fig. 14.11 Using **getMessage** and **printStackTrace** (part 2 of 2).

SUMMARY

- Some common examples of exceptions are memory exhaustion, an out-of-bounds array subscript, arithmetic overflow, division by zero and invalid method parameters.
- Exception handling is designed for dealing with synchronous malfunctions (i.e., those that occur as the result of a program's execution).
- Exception handling is used in situations in which a malfunction will be dealt with in a different scope from that which detected the malfunction.
- Exception handling should be used to process exceptions from software components such as methods, libraries and classes that are likely to be widely used and where it does not make sense for those components to handle their own exceptions.
- Exception handling should be used on large projects to handle error processing in a standardized manner for the entire project.
- Java exception handling is geared to situations in which the method that detects an error is unable to deal with it. Such a method will **throw** an exception. If the exception matches the type of the parameter in one of the **catch** blocks, the code for that **catch** block executes.
- The programmer encloses in a **try** block the code that may generate an exception. The **try** block is followed by one or more **catch** blocks. Each **catch** block specifies the type of exception it can catch and handle. Each **catch** block is an exception handler.

- If no exceptions are thrown in the **try** block, the exception handlers for that block are skipped. Then the program resumes execution after the last **catch** block, after executing a **finally** block if one is provided.
- Exceptions are thrown in a **try** block in a method or from a method called directly or indirectly from the **try** block.
- The operand of a **throw** can be of any class derived from **Throwable**. The immediate subclasses of **Throwable** are **Error** and **Exception**.
- **RuntimeException**s and **Error**s are said to be "unchecked." Non-**RuntimeException**s are said to be "checked." The checked exceptions thrown by a particular method must be specified in that method's **throws** clause.
- Exceptions are caught by the closest exception handler (for the **try** block from which the exception was thrown) specifying an appropriate type.
- An exception terminates the block in which the exception occurred.
- A handler may rethrow the object to an outer **try** block.
- **catch(Exception exception)** catches all **Exception**s.
- **catch(Throwable throwable)** catches all **Exception**s and **Error**s.
- If no handler matches a particular thrown object, the search for a match continues in an enclosing **try** block.
- Exception handlers are searched in order for an appropriate match based on type. The first handler that matches is executed. When that handler finishes executing, control resumes with the first statement after the last **catch** block.
- The order of the exception handlers affects how an exception is handled.
- A subclass object can be caught either by a handler specifying that subclass type or by handlers specifying the types of any direct or indirect superclasses of that subclass.
- If no handler is found for an exception, a non-GUI-based application terminates; an applet or a GUI-based application will return to its regular event handling.
- An exception handler cannot access variables in the scope of its **try** block because by the time the exception handler begins executing, the **try** block has expired. Information the handler needs is normally passed in the thrown object.
- Exception handlers can rethrow an exception. They can convert one type of exception into another by throwing a different exception. They can perform any necessary recovery and resume execution after the last exception handler. They can look at the situation causing the error, remove the cause of the error and retry by calling the original method that caused an exception. They can simply return some status value to their environment.
- A handler that catches a subclass object should be placed before a handler that catches a superclass object. If the superclass handler were first, it would catch superclass objects and the objects of subclasses of that superclass.
- When an exception is caught, it is possible that resources may have been allocated, but not yet released in the **try** block. A **finally** block should release these resources.
- It is possible that the handler that catches an exception may decide it cannot process the exception. In this case, the handler can simply rethrow the exception. A **throw** followed by the exception object name rethrows the exception.
- Even if a handler can process an exception, and regardless of whether it does any processing on that exception, the handler can rethrow the exception for further processing outside the handler. A rethrown exception is detected by the next enclosing **try** block (normally in a calling method) and is

handled by an appropriate exception handler (if there is one) listed after that enclosing **try** block.

- A **throws** clause lists the checked exceptions that may be thrown from a method. A method may **throw** the indicated exceptions, or it may **throw** subclass types. If a checked exception not listed in the **throws** clause is thrown, a syntax error occurs.
- A powerful reason for using inheritance with exceptions is to **catch** a variety of related errors easily with concise notation. One could certainly **catch** each type of subclass exception object individually, but it is more concise to simply **catch** the superclass exception object.

TERMINOLOGY

ArithmeticException
array exceptions
ArrayIndexOutOfBoundsException
business-critical computing
catch a group of exceptions
catch all exceptions
catch an exception
catch block
catch(Exception e)
catch-or-declare requirement
checked **Exception**s
ClassCastException
declare exceptions that can be thrown
default exception handler
EmptyStackException
Error class
Error class hierarchy
error handling
exception
Exception class
Exception class hierarchy
exception handler
exception handling
exception object
fault tolerance
FileNotFoundException
finally block
getMessage method of **Throwable** class
handle an exception
IllegalAccessException
IncompatibleClassChangeException
instanceof operator
InstantiationException
InternalException
InterruptedException
IOException
library exception classes
memory exhaustion
mission-critical computing
NegativeArraySizeException
NoClassDefFoundException
non-run-time exception
null reference
NullPointerException
OutOfMemoryError
printStackTrace method (**Throwable**)
resource leak
resumption model of exception handling
rethrow an exception
RuntimeException
stack unwinding
synchronous error
termination model of exception handling
throw an exception
throw point
throw statement
Throwable class
throws clause
try block
unchecked **Exception**s
UnsatisfiedLinkException

SELF-REVIEW EXERCISES

14.1 List five common examples of exceptions.

14.2 Why should exception-handling techniques not be used for conventional program control?

14.3 Why are exceptions particularly appropriate for dealing with errors produced by library classes and methods?

14.4 What is a “resource leak?”

14.5 If no exceptions are thrown in a **try** block, where does control proceed to when the **try** block completes execution?

14.6 What happens if an exception occurs and an appropriate exception handler cannot be found?

14.7 Give a key advantage of using **catch(Exception e)**.

14.8 Should a conventional applet or application catch **Error** objects?

14.9 What happens if several handlers match the type of the thrown object?

14.10 Why would a programmer specify a superclass type as the type of a **catch** handler, then throw objects of subclass types?

14.11 How might a **catch** handler be written to process related types of errors without using inheritance among exception classes?

14.12 What is the key reason for using **finally** blocks?

14.13 Does throwing an **Exception** have to cause program termination?

14.14 What happens when a **catch** handler throws an **Exception**?

14.15 What happens to a local reference in a **try** block when that block throws an **Exception**?

ANSWERS TO SELF-REVIEW EXERCISES

14.1 Memory exhaustion, array subscript out of bounds, arithmetic overflow, division by zero, invalid method parameters.

14.2 (a) **Exception** handling is designed to handle infrequently occurring situations that often result in program termination, so compiler writers are not required to implement exception handling to perform optimally. (b) Flow of control with conventional control structures is generally clearer and more efficient than with exceptions. (c) Problems can occur because the stack is unwound when an exception occurs and resources allocated prior to the exception may not be freed. (d) The "additional" exceptions can get in the way of genuine error-type exceptions. It becomes more difficult for the programmer to keep track of the larger number of exception cases.

14.3 It is unlikely that library classes and methods could perform error processing that would meet the unique needs of all users.

14.4 A resource leak occurs when an executing program does not properly release a resource when the resource is no longer needed. If the program attempts to use the resource again in the future, the program may not be able to access the resource.

14.5 The exception handlers (in the **catch** blocks) for that **try** block are skipped, and the program resumes execution after the last **catch** block. If there is a **finally** block, it is executed and the program resumes execution after the **finally** block.

14.6 A non-GUI-based application terminates; an applet or a GUI-based application resumes regular event processing.

14.7 The form **catch(Exception e)** catches any type of exception thrown in a **try** block. An advantage is that no thrown **Exception** can slip by.

14.8 **Error**s are usually serious problems with the underlying Java system; most programs will not want to catch **Error**s.

14.9 The first matching **Exception** handler after the **try** block is executed.

14.10 This is a nice way to catch related types of exceptions, but it should be used carefully.

14.11 Provide a single `Exception` subclass and `catch` handler for a group of exceptions. As each exception occurs, the exception object can be created with different instance data. The `catch` handler can examine this data to distinguish the type of the `Exception`.

14.12 The `finally` block is the preferred means for preventing resource leaks.

14.13 No, but it does terminate the block in which the `Exception` is thrown.

14.14 The exception will be processed by a `catch` handler (if one exists) associated with the `try` block (if one exists) enclosing the `catch` handler that caused the exception.

14.15 The reference is removed from memory, and the reference count for the referenced object is decremented. If the reference count is zero, the object is marked for garbage collection.

EXERCISES

14.16 Under what circumstances would you use the following `catch` handler?

```
catch ( Exception exception ) {
   throw exception;
}
```

14.17 List the benefits of exception handling over conventional means of error processing.

14.18 Describe an object-oriented technique for handling related exceptions.

14.19 Until this chapter, we have found that dealing with errors detected by constructors is a bit awkward. Explain why exception handling is an effective means for dealing with constructor failure.

14.20 Suppose a program throws an exception and the appropriate exception handler begins executing. Now suppose that the exception handler itself throws the same exception. Does this create an infinite recursion? Explain your answer.

14.21 Use inheritance to create an exception superclass and various exception subclasses. Write a program to demonstrate that the `catch` specifying the superclass catches subclass exceptions.

14.22 Write a Java program that shows that not all finalizers for objects constructed in a block are necessarily called after an exception is thrown from that block.

14.23 Write a Java program that demonstrates how various exceptions are caught with

```
catch ( Exception exception )
```

14.24 Write a Java program that shows that the order of exception handlers is important. If you try to catch a superclass exception type before a subclass type, the compiler should generate errors. Explain why these errors occur.

14.25 Write a Java program that shows a constructor passing information about constructor failure to an exception handler after a `try` block.

14.26 Write a Java program that illustrates rethrowing an exception.

14.27 Write a Java program that shows that a method with its own `try` block does not have to catch every possible error generated within the `try`. Some exceptions can slip through to, and be handled in, other scopes.

15

Multithreading

Objectives

- To understand the notion of multithreading.
- To appreciate how multithreading can improve performance.
- To understand how to create, manage and destroy threads.
- To understand the life cycle of a thread.
- To study several examples of thread synchronization.
- To understand thread priorities and scheduling.
- To understand daemon threads and thread groups.

The spider's touch, how exquisitely fine!
Feels at each thread, and lives along the line.
Alexander Pope

A person with one watch knows what time it is; a person with two watches is never sure.
Proverb

Conversation is but carving!
Give no more to every guest,
Than he's able to digest.
Jonathan Swift

Learn to labor and to wait.
Henry Wadsworth Longfellow

The most general definition of beauty...Multeity in Unity.
Samuel Taylor Coleridge

Outline

15.1 Introduction
15.2 Class `Thread`: An Overview of the `Thread` Methods
15.3 Thread States: Life Cycle of a Thread
15.4 Thread Priorities and Thread Scheduling
15.5 Thread Synchronization
15.6 Producer/Consumer Relationship without Thread Synchronization
15.7 Producer/Consumer Relationship with Thread Synchronization
15.8 Producer/Consumer Relationship: The Circular Buffer
15.9 Daemon Threads
15.10 `Runnable` Interface
15.11 Thread Groups
15.12 (Optional Case Study) Thinking About Objects: Multithreading
15.13 (Optional) Discovering Design Patterns: Concurrent Design Patterns

Summary • Terminology • Self-Review Exercises • Answers to Self-Review Exercises • Exercises

15.1 Introduction

It would be nice if we could "do one thing at a time" and "do it well," but that is simply not how the world works. The human body performs a great variety of operations *in parallel,* or as we will say throughout this chapter, *concurrently.* Respiration, blood circulation and digestion, for example, can occur concurrently. All of the senses—seeing, touching, smelling, tasting and hearing—can all occur concurrently. An automobile can be accelerating, turning, air conditioning and playing music concurrently. Computers, too, perform operations concurrently. It is common today for desktop personal computers to be compiling a program, printing a file and receiving e-mail messages over a network concurrently.

Concurrency is important in our lives. Ironically, though, most programming languages do not enable programmers to specify concurrent activities. Rather, programming languages generally provide only a simple set of control structures that enable programmers to perform one action at a time then proceed to the next action after the previous one is finished. The kind of concurrency that computers perform today normally is implemented as operating systems "primitives" available only to highly experienced "systems programmers."

The Ada programming language developed by the United States Department of Defense made concurrency primitives widely available to defense contractors building command and control systems. But Ada has not been widely used in universities and commercial industry.

Java is unique among popular general-purpose programming languages in that it makes concurrency primitives available to the applications programmer. The programmer specifies that applications contain threads of execution, each thread designating a portion of a program that may execute concurrently with other threads. This capability, called *multithreading,* gives the Java programmer powerful capabilities not available in C and C++, the languages on which Java is based. C and C++ are called single-threaded languages.

[*Note*: On many computer platforms, C and C++ programs can perform multithreading by using system specific code libraries.]

Software Engineering Observation 15.1

Unlike many languages that do not have built-in multithreading (such as C and C++) and must therefore make calls to operating system multithreading primitives, Java includes multithreading primitives as part of the language itself (actually in classes **`Thread`**, **`ThreadGroup`**, **`ThreadLocal`** *and* **`ThreadDeath`** *of the* **`java.lang`** *package). This encourages the use of multithreading among a larger part of the applications-programming community.*

We will discuss many applications of concurrent programming. When programs download large files such as audio clips or video clips from the World Wide Web, we do not want to wait until an entire clip is downloaded before starting the playback. So we can put multiple threads to work: One that downloads a clip and another that plays the clip so that these activities, or tasks, may proceed concurrently. To avoid choppy playback, we will coordinate the threads so that the player thread does not begin until there is a sufficient amount of the clip in memory to keep the player thread busy.

Another example of multithreading is Java's automatic garbage collection. In C and C++, the programmer is responsible for reclaiming dynamically allocated memory. Java provides a garbage collector thread that reclaims dynamically allocated memory that the program no longer needs.

Testing and Debugging Tip 15.1

In C and C++, programmers must provide explicit statements that reclaim dynamically allocated memory. When memory is not reclaimed (because a programmer forgets to do so, because of a logic error or because an exception diverts program control), this results in an all-too-common error called a memory leak that can eventually exhaust the supply of free memory and may cause premature program termination. Java's automatic garbage collection eliminates the vast majority of memory leaks, that is, those that are due to orphaned (unreferenced) objects.

Java's garbage collector runs as a low-priority thread. When Java determines that there are no longer any references to an object, it marks the object for eventual garbage collection. The garbage-collector thread runs when processor time is available and when there are no higher priority runnable threads. However, the garbage collector will run immediately when the system is out of memory.

Performance Tip 15.1

Setting an object reference to **`null`** *marks that object for eventual garbage collection (if there are no other references to the object). This can help conserve memory in a system in which a local variable that refers to an object does not go out of scope because the method in which it appears executes for a lengthy period.*

Writing multithreaded programs can be tricky. Although the human mind can perform many functions concurrently, humans find it difficult to jump between parallel "trains of thought." To see why multithreading can be difficult to program and understand, try the following experiment: open three books to page 1. Now try reading the books concurrently. Read a few words from the first book, then read a few words from the second book, then read a few words from the third book, then loop back and read the next few words from the first book, and so on. After a brief time, you will appreciate the challenges of multithreading: switching between books, reading briefly, remembering your place in each book, moving the book you are reading closer so you can see it, pushing books you are not reading aside, and amidst all this chaos, trying to comprehend the content of the books!

Performance Tip 15.2

A problem with single-threaded applications is that lengthy activities must complete before other activities can begin. In a multithreaded application, threads can share a processor (or set of processors), so that multiple tasks are performed in parallel.

Although Java is perhaps the world's most portable programming language, certain portions of the language are nevertheless platform dependent. In particular, there are differences among the first three Java platforms implemented, namely the Solaris implementation and the Win32 implementations (i.e., Windows-based implementations for Windows 95 and Windows NT).

The Solaris Java platform runs a thread of a given priority to completion or until a higher priority thread becomes ready. At that point preemption occurs (i.e., the processor is given to the higher priority thread while the previously running thread must wait).

In the 32-bit Java implementations for Windows 95 and Windows NT, threads are timesliced. This means that each thread is given a limited amount of time (called a time *quantum*) to execute on a processor, and when that time expires the thread is made to wait while all other threads of equal priority get their chances to use their quantum in round-robin fashion. Then the original thread resumes execution. Thus, on Windows 95 and Windows NT, a running thread can be preempted by a thread of equal priority; whereas, on the Solaris implementation, a running Java thread can only be preempted by a higher priority thread. Future Solaris Java systems are expected to perform timeslicing as well.

Portability Tip 15.1

Java multithreading is platform dependent. Thus, a multithreaded application could behave differently on different Java implementations.

15.2 Class `Thread`: An Overview of the `Thread` Methods

In this section, we overview the various thread-related methods in the Java API. We use many of these methods in live-code examples throughout the chapter. The reader should refer to the Java API directly for more details on using each method, especially the exceptions thrown by each method.

Class **`Thread`** (package **`java.lang`**) has several constructors. The constructor

```
public Thread( String threadName )
```

constructs a **`Thread`** object whose name is **`threadName`**. The constructor

```
public Thread()
```

constructs a **`Thread`** whose name is **`"Thread-"`** concatenated with a number, like **`Thread-1`**, **`Thread-2`**, and so on.

The code that "does the real work" of a thread is placed in its ***`run`*** method. The **`run`** method can be overridden in a subclass of **`Thread`** or it may be implemented in a ***`Runnable`*** object; **`Runnable`** is an important Java interface that we study in Section 15.10.

A program launches a thread's execution by calling the thread's ***`start`*** method, which, in turn, calls method **`run`**. After **`start`** launches the thread, **`start`** returns to its caller immediately. The caller then executes concurrently with the launched thread. The **start** method throws an ***IllegalThreadStateException*** if the thread it is trying to start has already been started.

The **static** method ***sleep*** is called with an argument specifying how long the currently executing thread should sleep (in milliseconds); while a thread sleeps, it does not contend for the processor, so other threads can execute. This can give lower priority threads a chance to run.

The ***interrupt*** method is called to interrupt a thread. The **static** method ***interrupted*** returns **true** if the current thread has been interrupted and **false** otherwise. A program can invoke a specific thread's ***isInterrupted*** method to determine whether that thread has been interrupted.

Method ***isAlive*** returns **true** if **start** has been called for a given thread and the thread is not dead (i.e., its controlling **run** method has not completed execution).

Method ***setName*** sets a **Thread**'s name. Method ***getName*** returns the name of the **Thread**. Method ***toString*** returns a **String** consisting of the name of the thread, the priority of the thread and the thread's ***ThreadGroup*** (discussed in Section 15.11).

The **static** method ***currentThread*** returns a reference to the currently executing **Thread**.

Method ***join*** waits for the **Thread** to which the message is sent to die before the calling **Thread** can proceed; no argument or an argument of 0 milliseconds to method **join** indicates that the current **Thread** will wait forever for the target **Thread** to die before the calling **Thread** proceeds. Such waiting can be dangerous; it can lead to two particularly serious problems called *deadlock* and *indefinite postponement.* We will discuss these momentarily.

Testing and Debugging Tip 15.2

Method **dumpStack** *is useful for debugging multithreaded applications. A program calls* **static** *method* **dumpStack** *to print a method-call stack trace for the current* **Thread***.*

15.3 Thread States: Life Cycle of a Thread

At any time, a thread is said to be in one of several *thread states* (illustrated in Fig. 15.1). Let us say that a thread that was just created is in the *born* state. The thread remains in this state until the program calls the thread's **start** method, which causes the thread to enter the *ready* state (also known as the *runnable* state). The highest priority *ready* thread enters the *running state* (i.e., the thread begins executing), when the system assigns a processor to the thread. A thread enters the *dead* state when its **run** method completes or terminates for any reason—a *dead* thread eventually will be disposed of by the system.

One common way for a *running* thread to enter the blocked state is when the thread issues an input/output request. In this case, a blocked thread becomes ready when the I/O for which it is waiting completes. A blocked thread cannot use a processor even if one is available.

When the program calls method **sleep** in a running thread, that thread enters the sleeping state. A sleeping thread becomes ready after the designated sleep time expires. A sleeping thread cannot use a processor even if one is available. If the program calls method **interrupt** on a sleeping thread, that thread exits the sleeping state and becomes ready to execute.

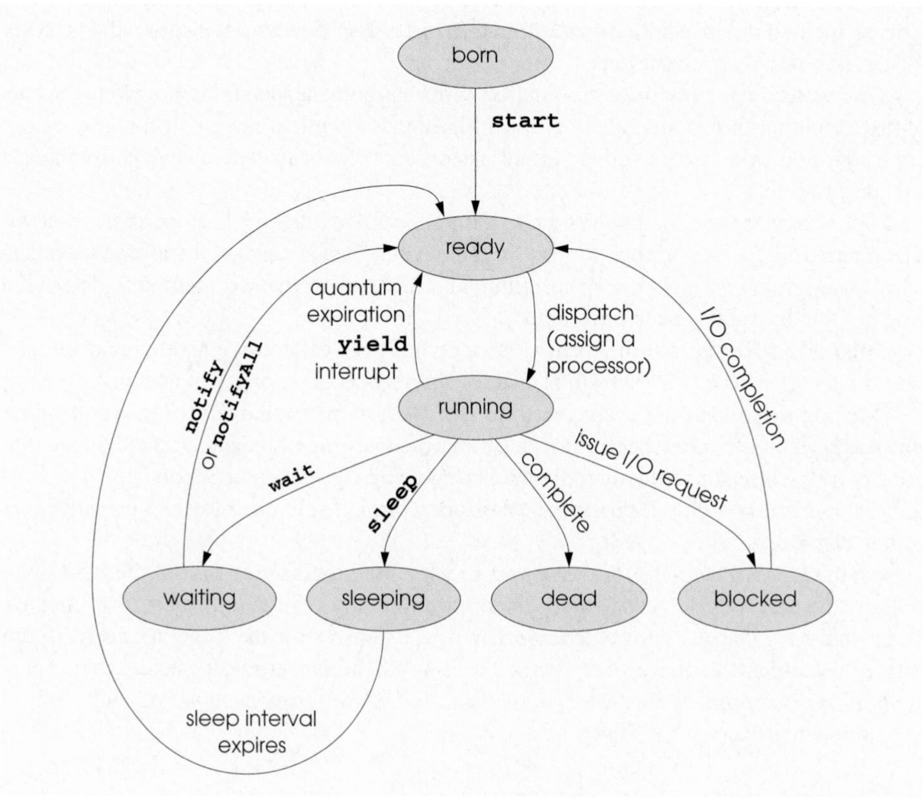

Fig. 15.1 State diagram showing the Life cycle of a thread.

When a running thread calls **`wait`**, the thread enters a waiting state for the particular object on which **`wait`** was called. One thread in the waiting state for a particular object becomes ready on a call to **`notify`** issued by another thread associated with that object. Every thread in the waiting state for a given object becomes ready on a call to **`notifyAll`** by another thread associated with that object. The **`wait`**, **`notify`** and **`notifyAll`** methods will be discussed in more depth shortly, when we consider monitors.

A thread enters the *dead state* when its **`run`** method either completes or throws an uncaught exception.

15.4 Thread Priorities and Thread Scheduling

Every Java applet or application is multithreaded. Every Java thread has a priority in the range **`Thread.MIN_PRIORITY`** (a constant of 1) and **`Thread.MAX_PRIORITY`** (a constant of 10). By default, each thread is given priority **`Thread.NORM_PRIORITY`** (a constant of 5). Each new thread inherits the priority of the thread that creates it.

Some Java platforms support a concept called *timeslicing* and some do not. Without timeslicing, each thread in a set of equal-priority threads runs to completion (unless the thread leaves the running state and enters the waiting, sleeping or blocked state, or the thread gets interrupted by a higher priority thread) before that thread's peers get a chance to execute. With timeslicing, each thread receives a brief burst of processor time called a *quantum* during which that thread can execute. At the completion of the quantum, even if that thread has not finished executing, the operating system takes the processor away from that thread and gives it to the next thread of equal priority (if one is available).

The job of the Java scheduler is to keep the highest priority thread running at all times, and if timeslicing is available, to ensure that several equally high-priority threads each execute for a quantum in round-robin fashion (i.e., these threads can be timesliced). Figure 15.2 illustrates Java's multilevel priority queue for threads. In the figure, threads A and B each execute for a quantum in round-robin fashion until both threads complete execution. Next, thread C runs to completion. Then, threads D, E and F each execute for a quantum in round-robin fashion until they all complete execution. This process continues until all threads run to completion. Note that new higher-priority threads could postpone—possibly indefinitely—the execution of lower priority threads. Such *indefinite postponement* often is referred to more colorfully as *starvation*.

A thread's priority can be adjusted with method ***setPriority***, which takes an **int** argument. If the argument is not in the range 1 through 10, **setPriority** throws an **IllegalArgumentException**. Method ***getPriority*** returns the thread's priority.

A thread can call the **yield** method to give other threads a chance to execute. Actually, whenever a higher priority thread becomes ready, the operating system preempts the current thread. So, a thread cannot **yield** to a higher priority thread, because the first thread would have been preempted when the higher priority thread became ready. Similarly, **yield** always allows the highest priority-*ready* thread to run, so if only lower priority threads are ready at the time of a **yield** call, the current thread will be the highest priority thread and will continue executing. Therefore, a thread **yield**s to give threads of an equal priority a chance to run. On a timesliced system this is unnecessary, because threads of equal priority will each execute for their quantum (or until they lose the processor for some other reason), and other threads of equal priority will execute in round-robin fashion. Thus **yield** is appropriate for nontimesliced systems in which a thread would ordinarily run to completion before another thread of equal priority would have an opportunity to run.

Performance Tip 15.3

On nontimesliced systems, cooperating threads of equal priority should periodically call **yield** *to enable their peers to proceed smoothly.*

Portability Tip 15.2

Java applets and applications should be programmed to work on all Java platforms to realize Java's goal of true portability. When designing applets and applications that use threads, you must consider the threading capabilities of all the platforms on which the applets and applications will execute.

A thread executes unless it dies, it becomes blocked by the operating system for input/output (or some other reason), it calls **sleep**, it calls **wait**, it calls **yield**, it is preempted by a thread of higher priority or its quantum expires. A thread with a higher priority than the running thread can become ready (and hence preempt the running thread) if a sleeping thread finishes sleeping, if I/O completes for a thread waiting for that I/O or if either **notify** or **notifyAll** is called on a thread that has called **wait**.

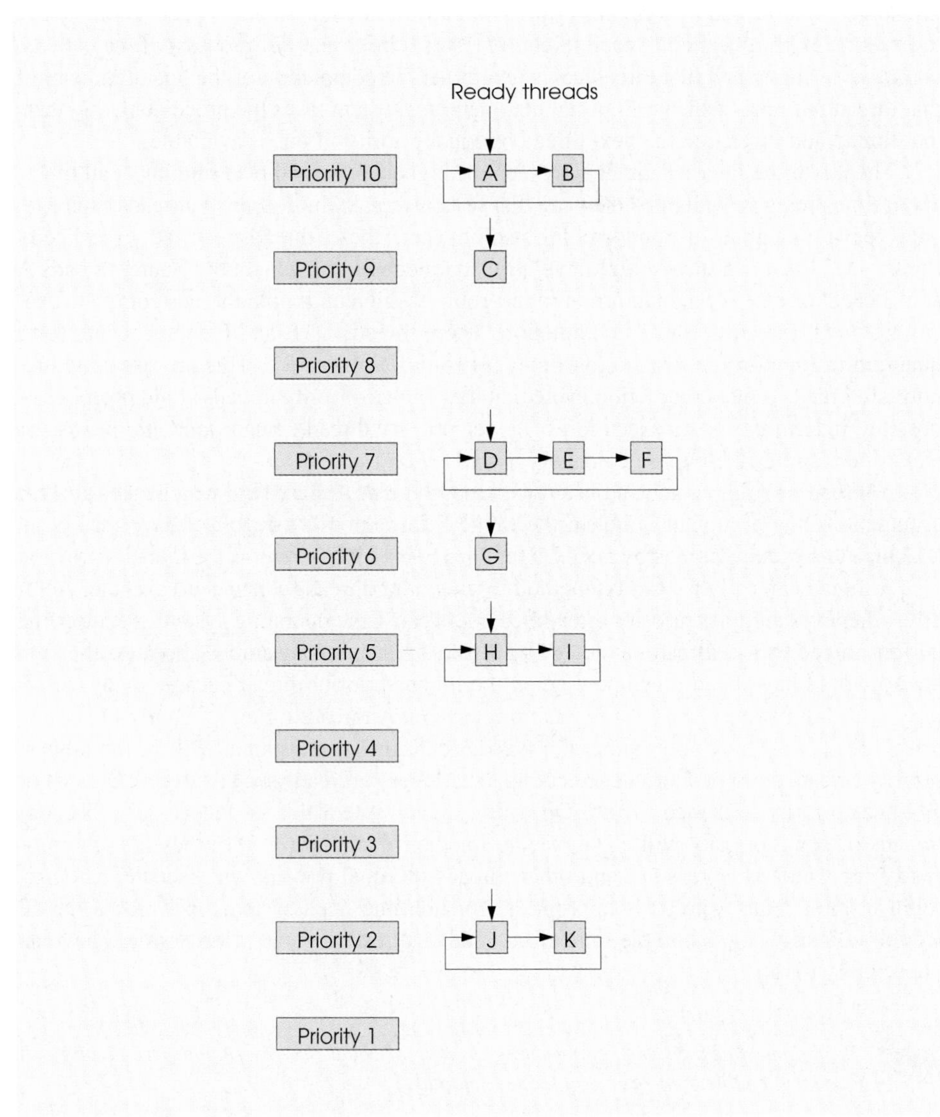

Fig. 15.2 Java thread priority scheduling.

The application of Fig. 15.3 demonstrates basic threading techniques, including creation of a class derived from **Thread**, construction of a **Thread** and using the **Thread** class **sleep** method. Each thread of execution we create in the program displays its name after sleeping for a random amount of time between 0 and 5 seconds. You will see that the **main** method (i.e., the ***main** thread of execution*) terminates before the application terminates. The program consists of two classes—**ThreadTester** (lines 4–28) and **PrintThread** (lines 33–71).

Class **PrintThread** inherits from **Thread**, so that each object of the class can execute in parallel. The class consists of instance variable **sleepTime**, a constructor and a

run method. Variable **sleepTime** stores a random integer value chosen when the program creates a **PrintThread** object. Each **PrintThread** object sleeps for the amount of time specified by its **sleepTime**, then outputs its name.

The **PrintThread** constructor (lines 38–48) initializes **sleepTime** to a random integer between 0 and 4999 (0 to 4.999 seconds). Then, the constructor outputs the name of the thread and the value of **sleepTime** to show the values for the particular **PrintThread** being constructed. The name of each thread is specified as a **String** argument to the **PrintThread** constructor and is passed to the superclass constructor at line 40. [*Note*: It is possible to allow class **Thread** to choose a name for your thread by using the **Thread** class's default constructor.

```
1  // Fig. 15.3: ThreadTester.java
2  // Show multiple threads printing at different intervals.
3
4  public class ThreadTester {
5
6     // create and start threads
7     public static void main( String args[] )
8     {
9        PrintThread thread1, thread2, thread3, thread4;
10
11       // create four PrintThread objects
12       thread1 = new PrintThread( "thread1" );
13       thread2 = new PrintThread( "thread2" );
14       thread3 = new PrintThread( "thread3" );
15       thread4 = new PrintThread( "thread4" );
16
17       System.err.println( "\nStarting threads" );
18
19       // start executing PrintThreads
20       thread1.start();
21       thread2.start();
22       thread3.start();
23       thread4.start();
24
25       System.err.println( "Threads started\n" );
26    }
27
28 }  // end class ThreadTester
29
30 // Each object of this class picks a random sleep interval.
31 // When a PrintThread executes, it prints its name, sleeps,
32 // prints its name again and terminates.
33 class PrintThread extends Thread {
34    private int sleepTime;
35
36    // PrintThread constructor assigns name to thread
37    // by calling superclass Thread constructor
```

Fig. 15.3 Multiple threads printing at random intervals (part 1 of 3).

```
    public PrintThread( String name )
    {
       super( name );

       // sleep between 0 and 5 seconds
       sleepTime = (int) ( Math.random() * 5000 );

       // display name and sleepTime
       System.err.println(
          "Name: " + getName() + ";  sleep: " + sleepTime );
    }

    // control thread's execution
    public void run()
    {
       // put thread to sleep for a random interval
       try {
          System.err.println( getName() + " going to sleep" );

          // put thread to sleep
          Thread.sleep( sleepTime );
       }

       // if thread interrupted during sleep, catch exception
       // and display error message
       catch ( InterruptedException interruptedException ) {
          System.err.println( interruptedException.toString() );
       }

       // print thread name
       System.err.println( getName() + " done sleeping" );
    }

 }  // end class PrintThread
```

```
Name: thread1;  sleep: 3593
Name: thread2;  sleep: 2653
Name: thread3;  sleep: 4465
Name: thread4;  sleep: 1318

Starting threads
Threads started

thread1 going to sleep
thread2 going to sleep
thread3 going to sleep
thread4 going to sleep
thread4 done sleeping
thread2 done sleeping
thread1 done sleeping
thread3 done sleeping
```

Fig. 15.3 Multiple threads printing at random intervals (part 2 of 3).

```
Name: thread1;  sleep: 2753
Name: thread2;  sleep: 3199
Name: thread3;  sleep: 2797
Name: thread4;  sleep: 4639

Starting threads
Threads started

thread1 going to sleep
thread2 going to sleep
thread3 going to sleep
thread4 going to sleep
thread1 done sleeping
thread3 done sleeping
thread2 done sleeping
thread4 done sleeping
```

Fig. 15.3 Multiple threads printing at random intervals (part 3 of 3).

When the program invokes a **PrintThread**'s **start** method (inherited from **Thread**), the **PrintThread** object enters the *ready* state. When the system assigns a processor to the **PrintThread** object, it enters the *running* state and its **run** method begins execution. Method **run** (lines 51–69) prints a **String** in the command window indicating that the thread is going to sleep (line 55), then invokes the **sleep** method (line 58) to place the thread into a *sleeping* state. At this point, the thread loses the processor, and the system allows another thread to execute. When the thread awakens, it is placed in a *ready* state again until the system assigns to the thread. When the **PrintThread** object enters the *running* state again, line 68 outputs the thread's name (indicating that the thread is done sleeping), the **run** method terminates and the thread object enters the *dead* state. Note that method **sleep** can throw a checked **InterruptedException** (if another thread invokes the sleeping thread's **interrupt** method); therefore, **sleep** must be called in a **try** block (in this example, we simply output the **String** representation of the exception if one occurs). Note that this example uses **System.err** rather than **System.out** to output lines of text. **System.err** represents the standard error object, which outputs error messages (normally to the command window). **System.out** performs buffered output—it is possible that a message output with **System.out** will not be output immediately. On the other hand, **System.err** uses unbuffered output—messages appear immediately when they are output. Using **System.err** in a multithreaded program helps ensure that the messages from our program are output in the correct order.

Class **ThreadTester**'s **main** method (lines 7–26) creates four objects of class **PrintThread** (lines 12–15) and invokes the **Thread** class **start** method on each one (lines 20–23) to place all four **PrintThread** objects in a *ready* state. Note that the program terminates execution when the last **PrintThread** awakens and prints its name. Also, note that the **main** method (i.e., the **main** thread of execution) terminates after starting the four **PrintThread**s, but the application does not terminate until the last thread dies.

15.5 Thread Synchronization

Java uses *monitors* (as discussed by C.A.R. Hoare in his 1974 paper cited in Exercise 15.24) to perform synchronization. Every object with **synchronized** methods has a monitor. The monitor allows one thread at a time to execute a **synchronized** method on the object. This is accomplished by *locking* the object when the program invokes the **synchronized** method—also known as *obtaining the lock*. If there are several **synchronized** methods, only one **synchronized** method may be active on an object at once; all other threads attempting to invoke **synchronized** methods must wait. When a **synchronized** method finishes executing, the lock on the object is released and the monitor lets the highest priority-*ready* thread attempting to invoke a **synchronized** method proceed. [*Note*: Java also has ***synchronized*** *blocks* of code, which are discussed in the example of Section 15.10].

A thread executing in a **synchronized** method may determine that it cannot proceed, so the thread voluntarily calls **wait**. This removes the thread from contention for the processor and from contention for the monitor object. The thread now waits in the *waiting* state while other threads try to enter the monitor object. When a thread executing a **synchronized** method completes or satisfies the condition on which another thread may be waiting, the thread can **notify** a waiting thread to become *ready* again. At this point, the original thread can attempt to reacquire the lock on the monitor object and execute. The **notify** acts as a signal to the waiting thread that the condition for which the waiting thread has been waiting is now satisfied, so the waiting thread can reenter the monitor. If a thread calls **notifyAll**, then all threads waiting for the monitor become eligible to reenter the monitor (that is, they are all placed in a *ready* state). Remember that only one of those threads can obtain the lock on the object at a time—other threads that attempt to acquire the same lock will be *blocked* by the operating system until the lock becomes available again. Methods **wait**, **notify** and **notifyAll** are inherited by all classes from class **Object**. So any object may have a monitor.

Common Programming Error 15.1

Threads in the waiting state for a monitor object must be awakened explicitly with a ***notify*** *(or* ***interrupt****) or the thread will wait forever. This may cause deadlock. [Note: There are versions of method* ***wait*** *that receive arguments indicating the maximum wait time. If the thread is not notified in the specified amount of time, the thread becomes ready to execute.]*

Testing and Debugging Tip 15.3

Be sure that every call to ***wait*** *has a corresponding call to* ***notify*** *that eventually will end the waiting or call* ***notifyAll*** *as a safeguard.*

Performance Tip 15.4

Synchronization to achieve correct multithreaded behavior can make programs run more slowly due to the monitor overhead and frequently moving threads between the running, waiting and ready states. However, there is not much to say for highly efficient, incorrect multithreaded programs!

Testing and Debugging Tip 15.4

The locking that occurs with the execution of ***synchronized*** *methods could lead to deadlock if the locks are never released. When exceptions occur, Java's exception mechanism coordinates with Java's synchronization mechanism to release appropriate synchronization locks to avoid these kinds of deadlocks.*

Monitor objects maintain a list of all threads waiting to enter the monitor object to execute **synchronized** methods. A thread is inserted in the list and waits for the object if that thread calls a **synchronized** method of the object while another thread is already executing in a **synchronized** method of that object. A thread also is inserted in the list if the thread calls **wait** while operating inside the object. However, it is important to distinguish between waiting threads that blocked because the monitor was busy and threads that explicitly called **wait** inside the monitor. Upon completion of a **synchronized** method, outside threads that blocked because the monitor was busy can proceed to enter the object. Threads that explicitly invoked **wait** can proceed only when notified via a call by another thread to **notify** or **notifyAll**. When it is acceptable for a waiting thread to proceed, the scheduler selects the thread with the highest priority.

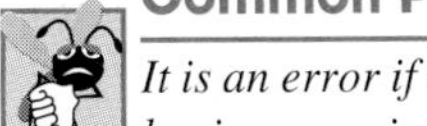

Common Programming Error 15.2

It is an error if a thread issues a **wait**, *a* **notify** *or a* **notifyAll** *on an object without having acquired a lock for the object. This causes an* **IllegalMonitorStateException**.

15.6 Producer/Consumer Relationship without Thread Synchronization

In a producer/consumer relationship, a *producer thread* calling a *produce* method may see that the consumer thread has not read the last message from a shared region of memory called a *buffer*, so the producer thread will call **wait**. When a *consumer thread* reads the message, it will call **notify** to allow a waiting producer to proceed. When a consumer thread enters the monitor and finds the buffer empty, it calls **wait**. A producer finding the buffer empty writes to the buffer, then calls **notify** so a waiting consumer can proceed.

Shared data can get corrupted if we do not synchronize access among multiple threads. Consider a producer/consumer relationship in which a producer thread deposits a sequence of numbers (we use 1, 2, 3, …) into a slot of shared memory. The consumer thread reads this data from the shared memory and prints it. We print what the producer produces as it produces it and what the consumer consumes as it consumes it. The program of Fig. 15.4–Fig. 15.7 demonstrates a producer and a consumer accessing a single shared cell of memory (**int** variable **sharedInt** in Fig. 15.6) without any synchronization. The threads are not synchronized, so data can be lost if the producer places new data into the slot before the consumer consumes the previous data. Also, data can be "doubled" if the consumer consumes data again before the producer produces the next item. To show these possibilities, the consumer thread in this example keeps a total of all the values it reads. The producer thread produces values from 1 to 10. If the consumer reads each value produced only once, the total would be 55. However, if you execute this program several times, you will see that the total is rarely, if ever, 55.

The program consists of four classes—**ProduceInteger** (Fig. 15.4), **ConsumeInteger** (Fig. 15.5), **HoldIntegerUnsynchronized** (Fig. 15.6) and **SharedCell** (Fig. 15.7).

Class **ProduceInteger** (Fig. 15.4)—a subclass of **Thread**—consists of instance variable **sharedObject** (line 4), a constructor (lines 7–11) and a **run** method (lines 15–37). The constructor initializes instance variable **sharedObject** (line 10) to refer to the

HoldIntegerUnsynchronized object **shared**, which was passed as an argument. Class **ProduceInteger**'s **run** method (lines 15–37) consists of a **for** structure that loops 10 times. Each iteration of the loop first invokes method **sleep** to put the **ProduceInteger** object into the sleeping state for a random time interval between 0 and 3 seconds. When the thread awakens, line 31 calls class **HoldIntegerUnsynchronized**'s **setSharedInt** method and passes the value of control variable **count** to set the shared object's instance variable **sharedInt**. When the loop completes, lines 34–36 display a line of text in the command window indicating that the thread finished producing data and that the thread is terminating, then the thread terminates (i.e., the thread dies).

```
1  // Fig. 15.4: ProduceInteger.java
2  // Definition of threaded class ProduceInteger
3  public class ProduceInteger extends Thread {
4     private HoldIntegerUnsynchronized sharedObject;
5
6     // initialize ProduceInteger thread object
7     public ProduceInteger( HoldIntegerUnsynchronized shared )
8     {
9        super( "ProduceInteger" );
10       sharedObject = shared;
11    }
12
13    // ProduceInteger thread loops 10 times and calls
14    // sharedObject's setSharedInt method each time
15    public void run()
16    {
17       for ( int count = 1; count <= 10; count++ ) {
18
19          // sleep for a random interval
20          try {
21             Thread.sleep( ( int ) ( Math.random() * 3000 ) );
22          }
23
24          // process InterruptedException during sleep
25          catch( InterruptedException exception ) {
26             System.err.println( exception.toString() );
27          }
28
29          // call sharedObject method from this
30          // thread of execution
31          sharedObject.setSharedInt( count );
32       }
33
34       System.err.println(
35          getName() + " finished producing values" +
36          "\nTerminating " + getName() );
37    }
38
39 }  // end class ProduceInteger
```

Fig. 15.4 Class **ProduceInteger** represents the producer in a producer/consumer relationship.

Class **ConsumeInteger** (Fig. 15.5)—a subclass of **Thread**—consists of instance variable **sharedObject** (line 4), a constructor (lines 7–11) and a **run** method (lines 15–39). The constructor initializes instance variable **sharedObject** (line 10) to refer to the **HoldIntegerUnsynchronized** object **shared** that was passed as an argument. Class **ConsumeInteger**'s **run** method (lines 15–39) consists of a **do/while** structure that loops until the value 10 is read from the **HoldIntegerUnsynchronized** object to which **sharedObject** refers. Each iteration of the loop invokes method **sleep** to put the **ConsumeInteger** object into the sleeping state for a random time interval between 0 and 3 seconds. Next, line 31 invokes class **HoldIntegerUnsynchronized**'s **getSharedInt** method to get the value of the shared object's instance variable **sharedInt**. Then, line 32 adds the value returned by **getSharedInt** to the variable **sum**. When the loop completes, the **ConsumeInteger** thread displays a line in the command window indicating that it has finished consuming data and terminates (i.e., the thread dies).

```
1  // Fig. 15.5: ConsumeInteger.java
2  // Definition of threaded class ConsumeInteger
3  public class ConsumeInteger extends Thread {
4     private HoldIntegerUnsynchronized sharedObject;
5
6     // initialize ConsumerInteger thread object
7     public ConsumeInteger( HoldIntegerUnsynchronized shared )
8     {
9        super( "ConsumeInteger" );
10       sharedObject = shared;
11    }
12
13    // ConsumeInteger thread loops until it receives 10
14    // from sharedObject's getSharedInt method
15    public void run()
16    {
17       int value, sum = 0;
18
19       do {
20
21          // sleep for a random interval
22          try {
23             Thread.sleep( (int) ( Math.random() * 3000 ) );
24          }
25
26          // process InterruptedException during sleep
27          catch( InterruptedException exception ) {
28             System.err.println( exception.toString() );
29          }
30
31          value = sharedObject.getSharedInt();
32          sum += value;
33
34       } while ( value != 10 );
35
```

Fig. 15.5 Class **ConsumeInteger** represents the consumer in a producer/consumer relationship (part 1 of 2).

```
         System.err.println(
            getName() + " retrieved values totaling: " + sum +
            "\nTerminating " + getName() );
      }

   } // end class ConsumeInteger
```

Fig. 15.5 Class **ConsumeInteger** represents the consumer in a producer/consumer relationship (part 2 of 2).

Class **HoldIntegerUnsynchronized** consists of instance variable **sharedInt** (line 4), method **setSharedInt** (lines 7–13) and method **getSharedInt** (lines 16–22). Methods **setSharedInt** and **getSharedInt** do not synchronize access to instance variable **sharedInt**. Note that each method uses **static Thread** method **currentThread** to obtain a reference to the currently executing thread, then use **Thread** method **getName** to obtain the thread's name.

Class **SharedCell**'s **main** method (lines 6–20) instantiates the shared **HoldIntegerUnsynchronized** object **sharedObject** and uses it as the argument to the constructors for the **ProduceInteger** object **producer** and the **ConsumeInteger** object **consumer**. The **sharedObject** contains the data that will be shared between the two threads. Next, method **main** invokes the **Thread** class **start** method on the **producer** and **consumer** threads to place them in the *ready* state. This launches these threads.

```
1   // Fig. 15.6: HoldIntegerUnsynchronized.java
2   // Definition of class HoldIntegerUnsynchronized.
3   public class HoldIntegerUnsynchronized {
4      private int sharedInt = -1;
5
6      // unsynchronized method to place value in sharedInt
7      public void setSharedInt( int value )
8      {
9         System.err.println( Thread.currentThread().getName() +
10           " setting sharedInt to " + value );
11
12        sharedInt = value;
13     }
14
15     // unsynchronized method return sharedInt's value
16     public int getSharedInt()
17     {
18        System.err.println( Thread.currentThread().getName() +
19           " retrieving sharedInt value " + sharedInt );
20
21        return sharedInt;
22     }
23
24  } // end class HoldIntegerUnsynchronized
```

Fig. 15.6 Class **HoldIntegerUnsynchronized** maintains the data shared between the producer and consumer threads.

```java
// Fig. 15.7: SharedCell.java
// Show multiple threads modifying shared object.
public class SharedCell {

   // execute application
   public static void main( String args[] )
   {
      HoldIntegerUnsynchronized sharedObject =
         new HoldIntegerUnsynchronized();

      // create threads
      ProduceInteger producer =
         new ProduceInteger( sharedObject );
      ConsumeInteger consumer =
         new ConsumeInteger( sharedObject );

      // start threads
      producer.start();
      consumer.start();
   }

} // end class SharedCell
```

```
ConsumeInteger retrieving sharedInt value -1
ConsumeInteger retrieving sharedInt value -1
ProduceInteger setting sharedInt to 1
ProduceInteger setting sharedInt to 2
ConsumeInteger retrieving sharedInt value 2
ProduceInteger setting sharedInt to 3
ProduceInteger setting sharedInt to 4
ProduceInteger setting sharedInt to 5
ConsumeInteger retrieving sharedInt value 5
ProduceInteger setting sharedInt to 6
ProduceInteger setting sharedInt to 7
ProduceInteger setting sharedInt to 8
ConsumeInteger retrieving sharedInt value 8
ConsumeInteger retrieving sharedInt value 8
ProduceInteger setting sharedInt to 9
ConsumeInteger retrieving sharedInt value 9
ConsumeInteger retrieving sharedInt value 9
ProduceInteger setting sharedInt to 10
ProduceInteger finished producing values
Terminating ProduceInteger
ConsumeInteger retrieving sharedInt value 10
ConsumeInteger retrieved values totaling: 49
Terminating ConsumeInteger
```

Fig. 15.7 Threads modifying a shared object without synchronization.

Ideally, we would like every value produced by the **ProduceInteger** object to be consumed exactly once by the **ConsumeInteger** object. However, when we study the output of Fig. 15.7, we see that the values 1, 3, 4, 6 and 7 are lost (i.e., never seen by the consumer) and that the values 8 and 9 are incorrectly retrieved more than once by the consumer. Also, notice that the consumer twice retrieved value –1 (the default value of **sharedInt** set at line 5 of Fig. 15.6) before the producer ever assigned 1 to the **sharedInt** variable. This example clearly demonstrates that access to shared data by concurrent threads must be controlled carefully or a program may produce incorrect results.

To solve the problems of lost data and doubled data in the previous example, we will synchronize access of the concurrent producer and consumer threads to the shared data. Each method used by a producer or consumer to access the shared data is declared with the **synchronized** keyword. When a method declared **synchronized** is running in an object, the object is *locked* so no other **synchronized** method can run in that object at the same time.

15.7 Producer/Consumer Relationship with Thread Synchronization

The application in Fig. 15.8 demonstrates a producer and a consumer accessing a shared cell of memory with synchronization so that the consumer only consumes after the producer produces a value. Classes **ProduceInteger** (Fig. 15.8), **ConsumeInteger** (Fig. 15.9) and **SharedCell** (Fig. 15.11) are identical to Fig. 15.4, Fig. 15.5 and Fig. 15.7 except that they use the new class **HoldIntegerSynchronized** in this example.

Class **HoldIntegerSynchronized** (Fig. 15.10) contains two instance variables—**sharedInt** (line 6) and **writeable** (line 7). Also, method **setSharedInt** (lines 12–39) and method **getSharedInt** (lines 44–70) are now **synchronized** methods. Objects of class **HoldIntegerSynchronized** have monitors, because **HoldIntegerSynchronized** contains **synchronized** methods. Instance variable **writeable** is known as the monitor's *condition variable*—is a **boolean** used by methods **setSharedInt** and **getSharedInt** of class **HoldIntegerSynchronized**. If **writeable** is **true**, **setSharedInt** can place a value into variable **sharedInt**, because the variable currently does not contain information. However, this means **getSharedInt** currently cannot read the value of **sharedInt**. If **writeable** is **false**, **getSharedInt** can read a value from variable **sharedInt** because the variable currently does contain information. However, this means **setSharedInt** currently cannot place a value into **sharedInt**.

```
// Fig. 15.8: ProduceInteger.java
// Definition of threaded class ProduceInteger
public class ProduceInteger extends Thread {
   private HoldIntegerSynchronized sharedObject;

   // initialize ProduceInteger thread object
   public ProduceInteger( HoldIntegerSynchronized shared )
   {
      super( "ProduceInteger" );
      sharedObject = shared;
   }

```

Fig. 15.8 Class **ProduceInteger** represents the producer in a producer/consumer relationship (part 1 of 2).

```
   // ProduceInteger thread loops 10 times and calls
   // sharedObject's setSharedInt method each time
   public void run()
   {
      for ( int count = 1; count <= 10; count++ ) {

         // sleep for a random interval
         try {
            Thread.sleep( ( int ) ( Math.random() * 3000 ) );
         }

         // process InterruptedException during sleep
         catch( InterruptedException exception ) {
            System.err.println( exception.toString() );
         }

         // call sharedObject method from this
         // thread of execution
         sharedObject.setSharedInt( count );
      }

      System.err.println(
         getName() + " finished producing values" +
         "\nTerminating " + getName() );
   }

}  // end class ProduceInteger
```

Fig. 15.8 Class **ProduceInteger** represents the producer in a producer/consumer relationship (part 2 of 2).

```
// Fig. 15.9: ConsumeInteger.java
// Definition of threaded class ConsumeInteger
public class ConsumeInteger extends Thread {
   private HoldIntegerSynchronized sharedObject;

   // initialize ConsumerInteger thread object
   public ConsumeInteger( HoldIntegerSynchronized shared )
   {
      super( "ConsumeInteger" );
      sharedObject = shared;
   }

   // ConsumeInteger thread loops until it receives 10
   // from sharedObject's getSharedInt method
   public void run()
   {
      int value, sum = 0;

```

Fig. 15.9 Class **ConsumeInteger** represents the consumer in a producer/consumer relationship (part 1 of 2).

```
      do {

         // sleep for a random interval
         try {
            Thread.sleep( (int) ( Math.random() * 3000 ) );
         }

         // process InterruptedException during sleep
         catch( InterruptedException exception ) {
            System.err.println( exception.toString() );
         }

         value = sharedObject.getSharedInt();
         sum += value;

      } while ( value != 10 );

      System.err.println(
         getName() + " retrieved values totaling: " + sum +
         "\nTerminating " + getName() );
   }

}  // end class ConsumeInteger
```

Fig. 15.9 Class **ConsumeInteger** represents the consumer in a producer/consumer relationship (part 2 of 2).

When the **ProduceInteger** thread object invokes synchronized method **setSharedInt** (line 31 of Fig. 15.8), the thread acquires a lock on the **HoldIntegerSynchronized** monitor object. The **while** structure in **HoldIntegerSynchronized** at lines 14–25 tests the **writeable** variable with the condition **!writeable**. If this condition is **true**, the thread invokes method **wait**. This places the **ProduceInteger** thread object that called method **setSharedInt** into the waiting state for the **HoldIntegerSynchronized** object and *releases the lock* on it. Now another thread can invoke a **synchronized** method on the **HoldIntegerSynchronized** object.

The **ProduceInteger** object remains in the waiting state until it is *notified* that it may proceed—at which point it enters the *ready* state and waits for the system to assign a processor to it. When the **ProduceInteger** object reenters the *running* state, it reacquires the lock on the **HoldIntegerSynchronized** object implicitly and the **setSharedInt** method continues executing in the **while** structure with the next statement after **wait**. There are no more statements, so the program reevaluates the **while** condition. If the condition is **false**, the program outputs a line to the command window indicating that the producer is setting **sharedInt** to a new value, assigns **value** to **sharedInt**, sets **writeable** to **false** to indicate that the shared memory is now full (i.e., a consumer can read the value and a producer cannot put another value there yet) and invokes method **notify**. If there are any waiting threads, one of those waiting threads enters the *ready* state, indicating that the thread can now attempt its task again (as soon as it is assigned a processor). The **notify** method returns immediately and method **setSharedInt** returns to its caller.

```
// Fig. 15.10: HoldIntegerSynchronized.java
// Definition of class HoldIntegerSynchronized that
// uses thread synchronization to ensure that both
// threads access sharedInt at the proper times.
public class HoldIntegerSynchronized {
   private int sharedInt = -1;
   private boolean writeable = true;  // condition variable

   // synchronized method allows only one thread at a time to
   // invoke this method to set the value for a particular
   // HoldIntegerSynchronized object
   public synchronized void setSharedInt( int value )
   {
      while ( !writeable ) {  // not the producer's turn

         // thread that called this method must wait
         try {
            wait();
         }

         // process Interrupted exception while thread waiting
         catch ( InterruptedException exception ) {
            exception.printStackTrace();
         }
      }

      System.err.println( Thread.currentThread().getName() +
         " setting sharedInt to " + value );

      // set new sharedInt value
      sharedInt = value;

      // indicate that producer cannot store another value until
      // a consumer retrieve current sharedInt value
      writeable = false;

      // tell a waiting thread to become ready
      notify();
   }

   // synchronized method allows only one thread at a time to
   // invoke this method to get the value for a particular
   // HoldIntegerSynchronized object
   public synchronized int getSharedInt()
   {
      while ( writeable ) {   // not the consumer's turn

         // thread that called this method must wait
         try {
            wait();
         }

```

Fig. 15.10 Class **HoldIntegerSynchronized** monitors access to a shared integer (part 1 of 2).

```
53          // process Interrupted exception while thread waiting
54          catch ( InterruptedException exception ) {
55             exception.printStackTrace();
56          }
57       }
58
59       // indicate that producer cant store another value
60       // because a consumer just retrieved sharedInt value
61       writeable = true;
62
63       // tell a waiting thread to become ready
64       notify();
65
66       System.err.println( Thread.currentThread().getName() +
67          " retrieving sharedInt value " + sharedInt );
68
69       return sharedInt;
70    }
71
72 }  // end class HoldIntegerSynchronized
```

Fig. 15.10 Class **HoldIntegerSynchronized** monitors access to a shared integer (part 2 of 2).

Methods **getSharedInt** and **setSharedInt** are implemented similarly. When the **ConsumeInteger** object invokes method **getSharedInt**, the calling thread acquires a lock on the **HoldIntegerSynchronized** object. The **while** structure at lines 46–57 tests the **writeable** variable. If **writeable** is **true** (i.e., there is nothing to consume), the thread invokes method **wait**. This places the **ConsumeInteger** thread object that called method **getSharedInt** into the waiting state for the **HoldIntegerSynchronized** object and releases the lock on it so other **synchronized** methods can be invoked on the object. The **ConsumeInteger** object remains in the waiting state until it is *notified* that it may proceed—at which point it enters the *ready* state and waits to be assigned a processor. When the **ConsumeInteger** object reenters the running state, the thread reacquires the lock on the **HoldIntegerSynchronized** object and the **getSharedInt** method continues executing in the **while** structure with the next statement after **wait**. There are no more statements, so the program tests the **while** condition again. If the condition is **false**, the program sets **writeable** to **true** to indicate that the shared memory is now empty and invokes method **notify**. If there are any waiting threads, one of those waiting threads enters the *ready* state, indicating that the thread can now attempt its task again (as soon as it is assigned a processor). The **notify** method returns immediately. Then, **getSharedInt** outputs a line to the command window indicating that the consumer is retrieving **sharedInt**, then returns the value of **sharedInt** to **getSharedInt**'s caller.

Study the output in Fig. 15.11. Observe that every integer produced is consumed once—no values are lost and no values are doubled. Also, the consumer cannot read a value until the producer produces a value.

```
// Fig. 15.11: SharedCell.java
// Show multiple threads modifying shared object.
public class SharedCell {

   // execute application
   public static void main( String args[] )
   {
      HoldIntegerSynchronized sharedObject =
         new HoldIntegerSynchronized();

      // create threads
      ProduceInteger producer =
         new ProduceInteger( sharedObject );
      ConsumeInteger consumer =
         new ConsumeInteger( sharedObject );

      // start threads
      producer.start();
      consumer.start();
   }

}  // end class SharedCell
```

```
ProduceInteger setting sharedInt to 1
ConsumeInteger retrieving sharedInt value 1
ProduceInteger setting sharedInt to 2
ConsumeInteger retrieving sharedInt value 2
ProduceInteger setting sharedInt to 3
ConsumeInteger retrieving sharedInt value 3
ProduceInteger setting sharedInt to 4
ConsumeInteger retrieving sharedInt value 4
ProduceInteger setting sharedInt to 5
ConsumeInteger retrieving sharedInt value 5
ProduceInteger setting sharedInt to 6
ConsumeInteger retrieving sharedInt value 6
ProduceInteger setting sharedInt to 7
ConsumeInteger retrieving sharedInt value 7
ProduceInteger setting sharedInt to 8
ConsumeInteger retrieving sharedInt value 8
ProduceInteger setting sharedInt to 9
ConsumeInteger retrieving sharedInt value 9
ProduceInteger setting sharedInt to 10
ProduceInteger finished producing values
Terminating ProduceInteger
ConsumeInteger retrieving sharedInt value 10
ConsumeInteger retrieved values totaling: 55
Terminating ConsumeInteger
```

Fig. 15.11 Threads modifying a shared object with synchronization.

15.8 Producer/Consumer Relationship: The Circular Buffer

The program of Fig. 15.8–Fig. 15.11 does access the shared data correctly, but it may not perform optimally. Because the threads are running asynchronously, we cannot predict their relative speeds. If the producer wants to produce faster than the consumer can consume, it cannot do so. To enable the producer to continue producing, we can use a circular buffer that has enough extra cells to handle the "extra" production. The program of Fig. 15.12–Fig. 15.16 demonstrates a producer and a consumer accessing a circular buffer (in this case, a shared array of five cells) with synchronization so that the consumer only consumes a value when there are one or more values in the array, and the producer only produces a value when there are one or more available cells in the array. This program is implemented as a windowed application that sends its output to a **JTextArea**. Class **SharedCell**'s constructor creates the **HoldIntegerSynchronized**, **ProduceInteger** and **ConsumeInteger** objects. The **HoldIntegerSynchronized** object **sharedObject**'s constructor receives a reference to a **JTextArea** object in which the program's output will appear.

This is the first program in which we use separate threads to modify the content displayed in Swing GUI components. The nature of multithreaded programming prevents the programmer from knowing exactly when a thread will execute. Swing components are not thread-safe—if multiple threads access a Swing GUI component, the results may not be correct. All interactions with Swing GUI components should be performed from one thread at a time. Normally, this thread is the *event-dispatch thread* (also known as the *event-handling thread*). Class ***SwingUtilities*** (package **javax.swing**) provides **static** method ***invokeLater*** to help with this process. Method **invokeLater** receives a **Runnable** argument. We will see in the next section that **Runnable** objects have a **run** method. In fact, class **Thread** implements interface **Runnable**, so all **Thread**s have a **run** method. The threads in this example pass objects of class **UpdateThread** (Fig. 15.12) to method **invokeLater**. Each **UpdateThread** object receives a reference to the **JTextArea** in which to append the output and the message to display. Method **run** of class **UpdateThread** appends the message to the **JTextArea**. When the program calls **invokeLater**, the GUI component update will be queued for execution in the event-dispatch thread. The **run** method will then be invoked as part of the event-dispatch thread, ensuring that the GUI component updates in a thread-safe manner.

Common Programming Error 15.3

Interactions with Swing GUI components that change or obtain property values of the components may have incorrect results if the interactions are performed from multiple threads.

Software Engineering Observation 15.2

Use ***SwingUtilities static*** *method* ***invokeLater*** *to ensure that all GUI interactions are performed from the event-dispatch thread.*

Class **ProduceInteger** (Fig. 15.13) has been modified slightly from the version presented in Fig. 15.8. The new version places its output in a **JTextArea**. **ProduceInteger** receives a reference to the **JTextArea** when the program calls the **ProduceInteger** constructor. Note the use of **SwingUtilities** method **invokeLater** in lines 42–44 to ensure that the GUI updates properly.

```
// Fig. 15.12: UpdateThread.java
// Class for updating JTextArea with output.

// Java extension packages
import javax.swing.*;

public class UpdateThread extends Thread {
   private JTextArea outputArea;
   private String messageToOutput;

   // initialize outputArea and message
   public UpdateThread( JTextArea output, String message )
   {
      outputArea = output;
      messageToOutput = message;
   }

   // method called to update outputArea
   public void run()
   {
      outputArea.append( messageToOutput );
   }

}  // end class UpdateThread
```

Fig. 15.12 **UpdateThread** used by **SwingUtilities** method **invokeLater** to ensure GUI updates properly.

```
// Fig. 15.13: ProduceInteger.java
// Definition of threaded class ProduceInteger

// Java extension packages
import javax.swing.*;

public class ProduceInteger extends Thread {
   private HoldIntegerSynchronized sharedObject;
   private JTextArea outputArea;

   // initialize ProduceInteger
   public ProduceInteger( HoldIntegerSynchronized shared,
      JTextArea output )
   {
      super( "ProduceInteger" );

      sharedObject = shared;
      outputArea = output;
   }

   // ProduceInteger thread loops 10 times and calls
   // sharedObject's setSharedInt method each time
```

Fig. 15.13 Class **ProduceInteger** represents the producer in a producer/consumer relationship (part 1 of 2).

```
      public void run()
      {
         for ( int count = 1; count <= 10; count++ ) {

            // sleep for a random interval
            // Note: Interval shortened purposely to fill buffer
            try {
               Thread.sleep( (int) ( Math.random() * 500 ) );
            }

            // process InterruptedException during sleep
            catch( InterruptedException exception ) {
               System.err.println( exception.toString() );
            }

            sharedObject.setSharedInt( count );
         }

         // update Swing GUI component
         SwingUtilities.invokeLater( new UpdateThread( outputArea,
            "\n" + getName() + " finished producing values" +
            "\nTerminating " + getName() + "\n" ) );
      }

   } // end class ProduceInteger
```

Fig. 15.13 Class **ProduceInteger** represents the producer in a producer/consumer relationship (part 2 of 2).

Class **ConsumeInteger** (Fig. 15.14) has been modified slightly from the version presented in Fig. 15.9. The new version places its output in a **JTextArea**. **ConsumeInteger** receives a reference to the **JTextArea** when the program calls the **ConsumeInteger** constructor. Note the use of **SwingUtilities** method **invokeLater** in lines 45–47 to ensure that the GUI updates properly.

```
1  // Fig. 15.14: ConsumeInteger.java
2  // Definition of threaded class ConsumeInteger
3
4  // Java extension packages
5  import javax.swing.*;
6
7  public class ConsumeInteger extends Thread {
8     private HoldIntegerSynchronized sharedObject;
9     private JTextArea outputArea;
10
11    // initialize ConsumeInteger
12    public ConsumeInteger( HoldIntegerSynchronized shared,
13       JTextArea output )
14    {
15       super( "ConsumeInteger" );
```

Fig. 15.14 Class **ConsumeInteger** represents the consumer in a producer/consumer relationship (part 1 of 2).

```

      sharedObject = shared;
      outputArea = output;
   }

   // ConsumeInteger thread loops until it receives 10
   // from sharedObject's getSharedInt method
   public void run()
   {
      int value, sum = 0;

      do {

         // sleep for a random interval
         try {
            Thread.sleep( (int) ( Math.random() * 3000 ) );
         }

         // process InterruptedException during sleep
         catch( InterruptedException exception ) {
            System.err.println( exception.toString() );
         }

         value = sharedObject.getSharedInt();
         sum += value;

      } while ( value != 10 );

      // update Swing GUI component
      SwingUtilities.invokeLater( new UpdateThread( outputArea,
         "\n" + getName() + " retrieved values totaling: " +
         sum + "\nTerminating " + getName() + "\n" ) );
   }

}  // end class ConsumeInteger
```

Fig. 15.14 Class **ConsumeInteger** represents the consumer in a producer/consumer relationship (part 2 of 2).

Once again, the primary changes in this example are in the definition of class **HoldIntegerSynchronized** (Fig. 15.15). The class now contains six instance variables—**sharedInt** is a five-element integer array that is used as the circular buffer, **writeable** indicates if a producer can write into the circular buffer, **readable** indicates if a consumer can read from the circular buffer, **readLocation** indicates the current position from which the consumer can read the next value, **writeLocation** indicates the next location in which the producer can place a value and **outputArea** is the **JTextArea** used by the threads in this program to display output.

```
// Fig. 15.15: HoldIntegerSynchronized.java
// Definition of class HoldIntegerSynchronized that
```

Fig. 15.15 Class **HoldIntegerSynchronized** monitors access to a shared array of integers (part 1 of 5).

```
// uses thread synchronization to ensure that both
// threads access sharedInt at the proper times.

// Java core packages
import java.text.DecimalFormat;

// Java extension packages
import javax.swing.*;

public class HoldIntegerSynchronized {

   // array of shared locations
   private int sharedInt[] = { -1, -1, -1, -1, -1 };

   // variables to maintain buffer information
   private boolean writeable = true;
   private boolean readable = false;
   private int readLocation = 0, writeLocation = 0;

   // GUI component to display output
   private JTextArea outputArea;

   // initialize HoldIntegerSynchronized
   public HoldIntegerSynchronized( JTextArea output )
   {
      outputArea = output;
   }

   // synchronized method allows only one thread at a time to
   // invoke this method to set a value in a particular
   // HoldIntegerSynchronized object
   public synchronized void setSharedInt( int value )
   {
      while ( !writeable ) {

         // thread that called this method must wait
         try {

            // update Swing GUI component
            SwingUtilities.invokeLater( new UpdateThread(
               outputArea, " WAITING TO PRODUCE " + value ) );

            wait();
         }

         // process InterrupteException while thread waiting
         catch ( InterruptedException exception ) {
            System.err.println( exception.toString() );
         }
      }

```

Fig. 15.15 Class **HoldIntegerSynchronized** monitors access to a shared array of integers (part 2 of 5).

```
      // place value in writeLocation
      sharedInt[ writeLocation ] = value;

      // indicate that consumer can read a value
      readable = true;

      // update Swing GUI component
      SwingUtilities.invokeLater( new UpdateThread( outputArea,
         "\nProduced " + value + " into cell " +
         writeLocation ) );

      // update writeLocation for future write operation
      writeLocation = ( writeLocation + 1 ) % 5;

      // update Swing GUI component
      SwingUtilities.invokeLater( new UpdateThread( outputArea,
         "\twrite " + writeLocation + "\tread " +
         readLocation ) );

      displayBuffer( outputArea, sharedInt );

      // test if buffer is full
      if ( writeLocation == readLocation ) {
         writeable = false;

         // update Swing GUI component
         SwingUtilities.invokeLater( new UpdateThread( outputArea,
            "\nBUFFER FULL" ) );
      }

      // tell a waiting thread to become ready
      notify();

   }  // end method setSharedInt

   // synchronized method allows only one thread at a time to
   // invoke this method to get a value from a particular
   // HoldIntegerSynchronized object
   public synchronized int getSharedInt()
   {
      int value;

      while ( !readable ) {

         // thread that called this method must wait
         try {

            // update Swing GUI component
            SwingUtilities.invokeLater( new UpdateThread(
               outputArea, " WAITING TO CONSUME" ) );

```

Fig. 15.15 Class **HoldIntegerSynchronized** monitors access to a shared array of integers (part 3 of 5).

```
            wait();
         }

         // process InterrupteException while thread waiting
         catch ( InterruptedException exception ) {
            System.err.println( exception.toString() );
         }
      }

      // indicate that producer can write a value
      writeable = true;

      // obtain value at current readLocation
      value = sharedInt[ readLocation ];

      // update Swing GUI component
      SwingUtilities.invokeLater( new UpdateThread( outputArea,
         "\nConsumed " + value + " from cell " +
         readLocation ) );

      // update read location for future read operation
      readLocation = ( readLocation + 1 ) % 5;

      // update Swing GUI component
      SwingUtilities.invokeLater( new UpdateThread( outputArea,
         "\twrite " + writeLocation + "\tread " +
         readLocation ) );

      displayBuffer( outputArea, sharedInt );

      // test if buffer is empty
      if ( readLocation == writeLocation ) {
         readable = false;

         // update Swing GUI component
         SwingUtilities.invokeLater( new UpdateThread(
            outputArea, "\nBUFFER EMPTY" ) );
      }

      // tell a waiting thread to become ready
      notify();

      return value;

   } // end method getSharedInt

   // diplay contents of shared buffer
   public void displayBuffer( JTextArea outputArea,
      int buffer[] )
   {
      DecimalFormat formatNumber = new DecimalFormat( " #;-#" );
      StringBuffer outputBuffer = new StringBuffer();
```

Fig. 15.15 Class **HoldIntegerSynchronized** monitors access to a shared array of integers (part 4 of 5).

```
157
158         // place buffer elements in outputBuffer
159         for ( int count = 0; count < buffer.length; count++ )
160            outputBuffer.append(
161               " " + formatNumber.format( buffer[ count ] ) );
162
163         // update Swing GUI component
164         SwingUtilities.invokeLater( new UpdateThread( outputArea,
165            "\tbuffer: " + outputBuffer ) );
166      }
167
168   }  // end class HoldIntegerSynchronized
```

Fig. 15.15 Class **HoldIntegerSynchronized** monitors access to a shared array of integers (part 5 of 5).

Method **setSharedInt** (lines 34–87) performs the same tasks as it did in Fig. 15.10, with a few modifications. When execution continues at line 55 after the **while** loop, **setSharedInt** places the produced value in the circular buffer at location **writeLocation**. Next, **readable** is set to **true** (line 58), because there is at least one value in the buffer that the client can read. Lines 61–63 use **SwingUtilities** method **invokeLater** to append the value produced and the cell where the value was placed to the **JTextArea** (method **run** of class **UpdateThread** performs the actual append operation). Then, line 66 updates **writeLocation** for the next call to **setSharedInt**. The output continues with the current **writeLocation** and **readLocation** values and the values in the circular buffer (lines 69–73). If the **writeLocation** is equal to the **readLocation**, the circular buffer is currently full, so **writeable** is set to **false** (line 77) and the program displays the string **BUFFER FULL** (lines 80–81). Finally, line 85 invokes method **notify** to indicate that a waiting thread should move to the ready state.

Method **getSharedInt** (lines 92–149) also performs the same tasks in this example as it did in Fig. 15.10, with a few minor modifications. When execution continues at line 115 after the **while** loop, **writeable** is set to **true** because there will be at least one open position in the buffer in which the producer can place a value. Next, line 118 assigns **value** the value at **readLocation** in the circular buffer. Lines 121–123 append to the **JTextArea** the value consumed and the cell from which the value was read. Then, line 126 updates **readLocation** for the next call to method **getSharedInt**. Lines 129–131 continue the output in the **JTextArea** with the current **writeLocation** and **readLocation** values and the current values in the circular buffer. If the **readLocation** is equal to the **writeLocation**, the circular buffer is currently empty, so **readable** is set to **false** (line 137), and lines 140–141 display the string **BUFFER EMPTY**. Finally, line 145 invokes method **notify** to place the next waiting thread into the *ready* state, and line 147 returns the retrieved value to the calling method.

In this version of the program, the outputs include the current **writeLocation** and **readLocation** values and the current contents of the buffer **sharedInt**. The elements of the **sharedInt** array were initialized to –1 for output purposes so that you can see each value inserted in the buffer. Notice that after the program places the fifth value in the fifth element of the buffer, the program inserts the sixth value at the beginning of the array—thus providing the *circular buffer* effect. Method **displayBuffer** (lines 152–166) uses a **DecimalFormat** object to format the contents of the array **buffer**. The format control string **" #;-#"** indicates a positive number format and a negative number format—the formats are separated by a semicolon (**;**). The format specifies that positive values should be preceded by a space and negative values should be preceded by a minus sign.

```
// Fig. 15.16: SharedCell.java
// Show multiple threads modifying shared object.

// Java core packages
import java.awt.*;
import java.awt.event.*;
import java.text.DecimalFormat;

// Java extension packages
import javax.swing.*;

public class SharedCell extends JFrame {

   // set up GUI
   public SharedCell()
   {
      super( "Demonstrating Thread Synchronization" );

      JTextArea outputArea = new JTextArea( 20, 30 );
      getContentPane().add( new JScrollPane( outputArea ) );

      setSize( 500, 500 );
      show();

      // set up threads
      HoldIntegerSynchronized sharedObject =
         new HoldIntegerSynchronized( outputArea );

      ProduceInteger producer =
         new ProduceInteger( sharedObject, outputArea );

      ConsumeInteger consumer =
         new ConsumeInteger( sharedObject, outputArea );

      // start threads
      producer.start();
      consumer.start();
   }

   // execute application
   public static void main( String args[] )
   {
      SharedCell application = new SharedCell();

      application.setDefaultCloseOperation(
         JFrame.EXIT_ON_CLOSE );
   }
```

Fig. 15.16 Threads modifying a shared array of cells (part 1 of 2).

```
}  // end class SharedCell
```

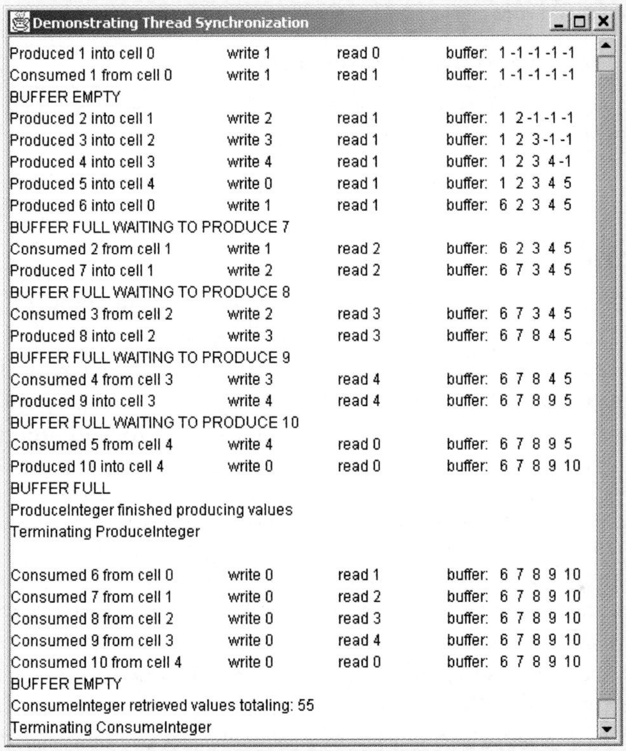

```
Demonstrating Thread Synchronization
Produced 1 into cell 0        write 1    read 0    buffer:  1 -1 -1 -1 -1
Consumed 1 from cell 0        write 1    read 1    buffer:  1 -1 -1 -1 -1
BUFFER EMPTY
Produced 2 into cell 1        write 2    read 1    buffer:  1  2 -1 -1 -1
Produced 3 into cell 2        write 3    read 1    buffer:  1  2  3 -1 -1
Produced 4 into cell 3        write 4    read 1    buffer:  1  2  3  4 -1
Produced 5 into cell 4        write 0    read 1    buffer:  1  2  3  4  5
Produced 6 into cell 0        write 1    read 1    buffer:  6  2  3  4  5
BUFFER FULL WAITING TO PRODUCE 7
Consumed 2 from cell 1        write 1    read 2    buffer:  6  2  3  4  5
Produced 7 into cell 1        write 2    read 2    buffer:  6  7  3  4  5
BUFFER FULL WAITING TO PRODUCE 8
Consumed 3 from cell 2        write 2    read 3    buffer:  6  7  3  4  5
Produced 8 into cell 2        write 3    read 3    buffer:  6  7  8  4  5
BUFFER FULL WAITING TO PRODUCE 9
Consumed 4 from cell 3        write 3    read 4    buffer:  6  7  8  4  5
Produced 9 into cell 3        write 4    read 4    buffer:  6  7  8  9  5
BUFFER FULL WAITING TO PRODUCE 10
Consumed 5 from cell 4        write 4    read 0    buffer:  6  7  8  9  5
Produced 10 into cell 4       write 0    read 0    buffer:  6  7  8  9  10
BUFFER FULL
ProduceInteger finished producing values
Terminating ProduceInteger

Consumed 6 from cell 0        write 0    read 1    buffer:  6  7  8  9  10
Consumed 7 from cell 1        write 0    read 2    buffer:  6  7  8  9  10
Consumed 8 from cell 2        write 0    read 3    buffer:  6  7  8  9  10
Consumed 9 from cell 3        write 0    read 4    buffer:  6  7  8  9  10
Consumed 10 from cell 4       write 0    read 0    buffer:  6  7  8  9  10
BUFFER EMPTY
ConsumeInteger retrieved values totaling: 55
Terminating ConsumeInteger
```

Fig. 15.16 Threads modifying a shared array of cells (part 2 of 2).

15.9 Daemon Threads

A daemon thread is a thread that runs for the benefit of other threads. Unlike conventional user threads (i.e., any non-daemon thread in a program), daemon threads do not prevent a program from terminating. The garbage collector is a daemon thread. Nondaemon threads are conventional user threads or threads such as the event-dispatch thread used to process GUI events. We designate a thread as a daemon with the method call

```
setDaemon( true );
```

A **`false`** argument means that the thread is not a daemon thread. A program can include a mixture of daemon threads and nondaemon threads. When only daemon threads remain in a program, the program exits. If a thread is to be a daemon, it must be set as such before its **`start`** method is called or an **`IllegalThreadStateException`** is thrown. Method **`isDaemon`** returns **`true`** if a thread is a daemon thread and **`false`** otherwise.

Common Programming Error 15.4

Starting a thread, then attempting to make the thread a daemon thread, causes an ***`IllegalThreadStateException`***.

Software Engineering Observation 15.3

The event-dispatch thread is an infinite loop and is not a daemon thread. As such, the event-dispatch thread will not terminate in a windowed application until the application calls **`System`** *method* **`exit`**.

Good Programming Practice 15.1

Do not assign critical tasks to a daemon thread. They are terminated without warning, which may prevent those tasks from completing properly.

15.10 `Runnable` Interface

Until now, we extended class **`Thread`** to create new classes that support multithreading. We overrode the **`run`** method to specify the tasks to be performed concurrently. However, if we want multithreading support in a class that already extends a class other than **`Thread`**, we must implement the ***`Runnable`*** *interface* in that class, because Java does not allow a class to extend more than one class at a time. Class **`Thread`** itself implements the **`Runnable`** interface (package **`java.lang`**) as expressed in the class header

```
public class Thread extends Object implements Runnable
```

Implementing the **`Runnable`** interface in a class enables a program to manipulate objects of that class as **`Runnable`** objects. As with deriving from the **`Thread`** class, the code that controls the thread is placed in method **`run`**.

A program that uses a **`Runnable`** object creates a **`Thread`** object and associates the Runnable object with that **`Thread`**. Class **`Thread`** provides four constructors that can receive references to **`Runnable`** objects as arguments. For example, the constructor

```
public Thread( Runnable runnableObject )
```

registers method **`run`** of **`runnableObject`** as the method to be invoked when the thread begins execution. The constructor

```
public Thread( Runnable runnableObject, String threadName )
```

constructs a **`Thread`** with the name **`threadName`** and registers method **`run`** of its **`runnableObject`** argument as the method to be invoked when the thread begins execution. As always, the thread object's **`start`** method must be called to begin the thread's execution.

Figure 15.17 demonstrates an applet with a **`private`** inner class and an anonymous inner class that each implement interface **`Runnable`**. The example also demonstrates how to suspend a thread (i.e., temporarily prevent it from executing), how to resume a suspended thread and how to terminate a thread that executes until a condition becomes false. Each of these techniques is important because **`Thread`** methods **`suspend`**, **`resume`** and **`stop`** were deprecated (i.e., they should no longer be used in Java programs) with the introduction of the Java 2 Platform. Because these methods are deprecated, we must code our own mechanisms for suspending, resuming and stopping threads. As we will demonstrate, these mechanisms rely on **`synchronized`** blocks of code, loops and **`boolean`** flag variables.

The applet class **RandomCharacters** displays three **JLabel**s and three **JCheckBox**es. A separate thread of execution is associated with each **JLabel** and button pair. Each thread randomly displays letters from the alphabet in its corresponding **JLabel** object. The applet defines the **String alphabet** (line 16) containing the letters from A to Z. This string is shared among the three threads. The applet's **start** method (lines 52–65) instantiates three **Thread** objects (lines 59–60) and initializes each with an instance of class **RunnableObject**, which implements interface **Runnable**. Line 63 invokes the **Thread** class **start** method on each **Thread**, placing the threads in the *ready* state.

Class **RunnableObject** is defined at lines 115–185. Its **run** method (line 120) defines two local variables. Line 123 uses **static** method **currentThread** of class **Thread** to determine the currently executing **Thread** object. Line 125 calls the applet's utility method **getIndex** (defined at lines 68–76) to determine the index of the currently executing thread in the array **threads**. The current thread displays a random character in the **JLabel** object with the same **index** in array **outputs**.

```
1   // Fig. 15.17: RandomCharacters.java
2   // Demonstrating the Runnable interface.
3
4   // Java core packages
5   import java.awt.*;
6   import java.awt.event.*;
7
8   // Java extension packages
9   import javax.swing.*;
10
11  public class RandomCharacters extends JApplet
12     implements ActionListener {
13
14     // declare variables used by applet and
15     // inner class RunnableObject
16     private String alphabet = "ABCDEFGHIJKLMNOPQRSTUVWXYZ";
17     private final static int SIZE = 3;
18
19     private JLabel outputs[];
20     private JCheckBox checkboxes[];
21
22     private Thread threads[];
23     private boolean suspended[];
24
25     // set up GUI and arrays
26     public void init()
27     {
28        outputs = new JLabel[ SIZE ];
29        checkboxes = new JCheckBox[ SIZE ];
30        threads = new Thread[ SIZE ];
31        suspended = new boolean[ SIZE ];
32
33        Container container = getContentPane();
34        container.setLayout( new GridLayout( SIZE, 2, 5, 5 ) );
```

Fig. 15.17 Demonstrating the **Runnable** interface, suspending threads and resuming threads (part 1 of 5).

```
      // create GUI components, register listeners and attach
      // components to content pane
      for ( int count = 0; count < SIZE; count++ ) {
         outputs[ count ] = new JLabel();
         outputs[ count ].setBackground( Color.green );
         outputs[ count ].setOpaque( true );
         container.add( outputs[ count ] );

         checkboxes[ count ] = new JCheckBox( "Suspended" );
         checkboxes[ count ].addActionListener( this );
         container.add( checkboxes[ count ] );
      }
   }

   // Create and start threads. This method called after init
   // and when user revists Web page containing this applet
   public void start()
   {
      // create threads and start every time start is called
      for ( int count = 0; count < threads.length; count++ ) {

         // create Thread and initialize it with object that
         // implements Runnable
         threads[ count ] = new Thread( new RunnableObject(),
            "Thread " + ( count + 1 ) );

         // begin executing Thread
         threads[ count ].start();
      }
   }

   // determine thread location in threads array
   private int getIndex( Thread current )
   {
      for ( int count = 0; count < threads.length; count++ )

         if ( current == threads[ count ] )
            return count;

      return -1;
   }

   // called when user switches Web pages; stops all threads
   public synchronized void stop()
   {
      // Indicate that each thread should terminate. Setting
      // these references to null causes each thread's run
      // method to complete execution.
      for ( int count = 0; count < threads.length; count++ )
         threads[ count ] = null;

```

Fig. 15.17 Demonstrating the **Runnable** interface, suspending threads and resuming threads (part 2 of 5).

```
      // make all waiting threads ready to execute, so they
      // can terminate themselves
      notifyAll();
   }

   // handle button events
   public synchronized void actionPerformed( ActionEvent event )
   {
      for ( int count = 0; count < checkboxes.length; count++ ) {

         if ( event.getSource() == checkboxes[ count ] ) {
            suspended[ count ] = !suspended[ count ];

            // change label color on suspend/resume
            outputs[ count ].setBackground(
               !suspended[ count ] ? Color.green : Color.red );

            // if thread resumed, make sure it starts executing
            if ( !suspended[ count ] )
               notifyAll();

            return;
         }
      }
   }

   // private inner class that implements Runnable so objects
   // of this class can control threads
   private class RunnableObject implements Runnable {

      // Place random characters in GUI. Local variables
      // currentThread and index are declared final so
      // they can be used in an anonymous inner class.
      public void run()
      {
         // get reference to executing thread
         final Thread currentThread = Thread.currentThread();

         // determine thread's position in array
         final int index = getIndex( currentThread );

         // loop condition determines when thread should stop
         while ( threads[ index ] == currentThread ) {

            // sleep from 0 to 1 second
            try {
               Thread.sleep( ( int ) ( Math.random() * 1000 ) );

               // Determine whether thread should suspend
               // execution. Use applet as monitor.
               synchronized( RandomCharacters.this ) {

```

Fig. 15.17 Demonstrating the **Runnable** interface, suspending threads and resuming threads (part 3 of 5).

```
                  while ( suspended[ index ] &&
                     threads[ index ] == currentThread ) {

                     // Temporarily stop thread execution. Use
                     // applet as monitor.
                     RandomCharacters.this.wait();
                  }

               } // end synchronized block
            }

            // process InterruptedExceptions during sleep or wait
            catch ( InterruptedException interruptedException ) {
               System.err.println( "sleep interrupted" );
            }

            // display character on corresponding label
            SwingUtilities.invokeLater(

               // anonymous inner class used by SwingUtilities
               // method invokeLater to ensure GUI
               // updates properly
               new Runnable() {

                  // updates Swing GUI component
                  public void run()
                  {
                     // pick random character
                     char displayChar = alphabet.charAt(
                        ( int ) ( Math.random() * 26 ) );

                     outputs[ index ].setText(
                        currentThread.getName() + ": " +
                        displayChar );
                  }

               } // end anonymous inner class

            ); // end call to SwingUtilities.invokeLater

         } // end while

         System.err.println(
            currentThread.getName() + " terminating" );
      }

   } // end private inner class RunnableObject

} // end class RandomCharacters
```

Fig. 15.17 Demonstrating the **Runnable** interface, suspending threads and resuming threads (part 4 of 5).

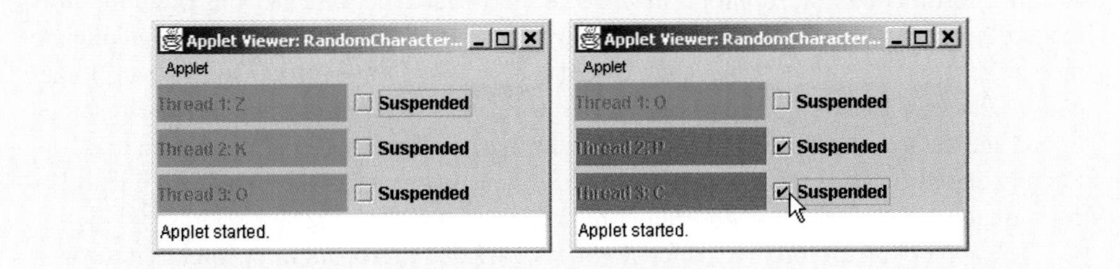

Fig. 15.17 Demonstrating the **Runnable** interface, suspending threads and resuming threads (part 5 of 5).

The **while** loop at lines 129–179 continues to execute as long as the specified **Thread** reference is equal to the reference to the currently executing thread (**currentThread**). In each iteration of the loop, the thread sleeps for a random interval from 0 to 1 second.

When the user clicks the **JCheckBox** to the right of a particular **JLabel**, the corresponding **Thread** should be *suspended* (temporarily prevented from executing) or *resumed* (allowed to continue executing). In previous versions of Java, methods **suspend** and **resume** of class **Thread** were provided to suspend and resume a thread's execution. These methods are now deprecated (i.e., they should no longer be used) because they introduce the possibility of deadlock in a program if they are not used correctly. Suspending and resuming of a thread can be implemented using thread synchronization and methods **wait** and **notify** of class **Object**. Lines 137–147 define a ***synchronized** block* of code (also called a ***synchronized** statement*) that helps suspend the currently executing **Thread**. When the **Thread** reaches the **synchronized** block, the applet object (referenced with **RandomCharacters.this**) is locked and the **while** structure tests **suspended[index]** to determine if the **Thread** should be suspended (i.e., **true**). If so, line 144 invokes method **wait** on the applet object to place the **Thread** in the waiting state. [Note the use of **RandomCharacters.this** to access the applet class's **this** reference from the private inner class **RunnableObject**.] When the **Thread** should resume, the program tells all waiting threads to become ready to execute (we will discuss this shortly). However, only the resumed thread will get a chance to execute. The other suspended thread(s) will reenter the waiting state. Lines 156–177 use **SwingUtilities** method **invokeLater** to update the **JLabel** for the appropriate thread. This example uses an anonymous inner class to implement the **Runnable** interface (lines 161–175) and passes the anonymous inner class object to **invokeLater**. Lines 167–168 choose a random character from the **alphabet** string. Lines 170–172 display the character on the appropriate **JLabel** object.

Software Engineering Observation 15.4

*An inner class can reference its outer class's **this** reference by preceding the **this** reference with the outer class name and a dot operator.*

If the user clicks the **Suspended** check box next to a particular **JLabel**, the program invokes method **actionPerformed** (lines 93–111). The method determines which checkbox received the event. Using the index of that checkbox in array **outputs**, line 98 toggles the corresponding **boolean** in array **suspended**. Lines 101–102 set the background color of the **JLabel** to red if the thread is being suspended and green if the thread is being resumed. If the appropriate **boolean** variable is **false**, the program calls method **notifyAll** (line 106) to move all waiting threads into the ready state and prepare them to resume execution. When each thread is dispatched to the processor to resume execution, the **while** condition at lines 139–140 in the **run** method fails for the resumed thread and the loop terminates. Execution of the **run** method then continues from line 156. For any other threads that became ready, but still are suspended, the condition at lines 139–140 remains true and the threads reenter the waiting state.

The applet's **stop** method (lines 79–90) is provided to stop all three threads if the user leaves the Web page on which this applet resides (you can simulate this by selecting **Stop** from the **appletviewer**'s **Applet** menu). The **for** loop at lines 84–85 sets each **Thread** reference in array **threads** to **null**. Line 89 invokes **Object** method **notifyAll** to ensure that all waiting threads get ready to execute. When the program encounters the **while** loop condition at line 129 for each thread, the condition fails and the **run** method terminates. Thus, each thread dies. If the user returns to the Web page, the applet container calls the applet's **start** method to instantiate and start three new threads.

Performance Tip 15.5

Stopping applet threads when leaving a Web page is a polite programming practice because it prevents your applet from using processor time (which can reduce performance) on the browser's machine when the applet is not being viewed. The threads can be restarted from the applet's **start** *method, which is invoked by the browser when the Web page is revisited by the user.*

15.11 Thread Groups

Sometimes it is useful to identify various threads as belonging to a *thread group*; class **ThreadGroup** contains methods for creating and manipulating thread groups. At constructor time, the group is given a unique name via a **String** argument.

The threads in a thread group can be manipulated as a group. It may, for example, be desirable to **interrupt** all the threads in a group. A thread group can be the *parent thread group* to a *child thread group*. Method calls sent to a parent thread group are also sent to all the threads in that parent's child thread groups.

Class **ThreadGroup** provides two constructors. The constructor

```
public ThreadGroup( String stringName )
```

constructs a **ThreadGroup** with name **stringName**. The constructor

```
public ThreadGroup( ThreadGroup parentThreadGroup,
   String stringName )
```

constructs a child **ThreadGroup** of **parentThreadGroup** called **stringName**.

Class **Thread** provides three constructors that enable the programmer to instantiate a **Thread** and associate it with a **ThreadGroup**. The constructor

```
public Thread( ThreadGroup threadGroup, String stringName )
```

constructs a **Thread** that belongs to **threadGroup** and has the name **stringName**. This constructor is normally invoked for derived classes of **Thread** whose objects should be associated with a **ThreadGroup**.

The constructor

```
public Thread( ThreadGroup threadGroup,
   Runnable runnableObject )
```

constructs a **Thread** that belongs to **threadGroup** and that invokes the **run** method of **runnableObject** when the thread is assigned a processor to begin execution.

The constructor

```
public Thread( ThreadGroup threadGroup,
   Runnable runnableObject, String stringName )
```

constructs a **Thread** that belongs to **threadGroup** and that invokes the **run** method of **runnableObject** when the thread is assigned a processor to begin execution. The name of this **Thread** is indicated by **stringName**.

Class **ThreadGroup** contains many methods for processing groups of threads. Some of these methods are summarized here. For more information on these methods, see the Java API documentation.

1. Method **activeCount** reports the number of active threads in a thread group plus the number of active threads in all its child thread groups.
2. Method **enumerate** has four versions. Two versions copy into an array of **Thread** references the active threads in the **ThreadGroup** (one of these also allows you to recursively get copies of all the active threads in child **ThreadGroup**). Two versions copy into an array of **ThreadGroup** references the active child thread groups in the **ThreadGroup** (one of these also allows you to recursively get copies of all the active thread groups in all the child **ThreadGroups**).
3. Method **getMaxPriority** returns the maximum priority of a **ThreadGroup**. Method **setMaxPriority** sets a new maximum priority for a **ThreadGroup**.
4. Method **getName** returns as a **String** the **ThreadGroup**'s name.
5. Method **getParent** determines the parent of a thread group.
6. Method **parentOf** returns **true** if the **ThreadGroup** to which the message is sent is the parent of, or the same as, the **ThreadGroup** supplied as an argument and returns **false** otherwise.

Testing and Debugging Tip 15.5

*Method **list** lists the **ThreadGroup**. This can help in debugging.*

15.12 (Optional Case Study) Thinking About Objects: Multithreading

Real-world objects perform their operations independently of one another and concurrently (in parallel). As you learned in this chapter, Java is a multithreaded programming language that facilitates the implementation of concurrent activities. The UML also contains support for designing concurrent models, as we will see shortly. In this section, we discuss how our simulation benefits from multithreading.

In "Thinking About Objects" Section 10.25, we encountered a problem with the collaboration diagram of Fig. 10.25—the **waitingPassenger** (the **Person** waiting to ride the **Elevator**) always enters the **Elevator** before the **ridingPassenger** (the **Person** riding the **Elevator**) exits. Proper use of multithreading in Java avoids this problem by guaranteeing that the **waitingPassenger** must wait for the **ridingPassenger** to exit the **Elevator**—as would happen in real life. In our collaboration diagrams, objects pass messages to other objects by calling methods of those other objects—a sending object may proceed only after a method returns. Java refers to such a message pass as a *synchronous call*. However, the synchronous call is not *synchronized*, because several objects may access the method at the same time—the synchronous call cannot guarantee exclusivity to one object. This poses a problem when we model our elevator simulation, because according to Fig. 10.25, the **waitingPassenger** and the **ridingPassenger** may occupy the **Elevator** at the same time, which violates the "capacity-of-one" requirement specified in the problem statement. In this section, we use a **synchronized** method to guarantee that only one **Person** may occupy the **Elevator** at a time.

Threads, Active Classes and Synchronized Methods

Java uses threads—flows of program control independent of other flows—to represent independent, concurrent activities. The UML provides the notion of an *active class* to represent a thread. Classes **Elevator** and **Person** are active classes (threads), because their objects must be able to operate concurrently and independently of one another and of other objects in the system. For example, the **Elevator** must be able to move between **Floor**s while a **Person** is walking on a **Floor**. Figure 15.18 updates the collaboration diagram of Fig. 10.25 to support active classes, which are denoted by a thick black border in the diagram. To ensure that **Person**s enter and exit the **Elevator** in the proper order, we require a specific order in which to send messages—the **Elevator** must send message **3.3.1** (**ridingPassenger** exits) before sending message **3.2.1.1** (**waitingPassenger** enters the **Elevator**). The UML provides a notation to allow synchronization in collaboration diagrams—if we have two messages **A** and **B**, the notation **B/A** indicates that message **A** must wait for **B** to complete before message **A** occurs. For example, the **3.3.1/3.2.1.1** notation before the **enterElevator** message indicates that **waitingPassenger** must wait for **ridingPassenger** to exit the **Elevator** (message **3.3.1**) before entering (message **3.2.1.1**).

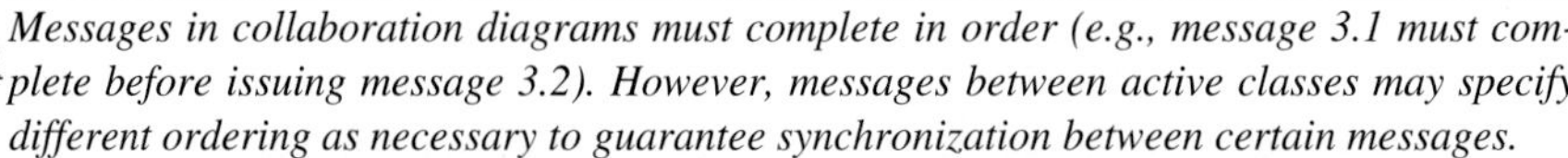

Messages in collaboration diagrams must complete in order (e.g., message 3.1 must complete before issuing message 3.2). However, messages between active classes may specify different ordering as necessary to guarantee synchronization between certain messages.

A **Person** must synchronize with the **Elevator** when traveling to guarantee that only one **Person** occupies the **Elevator** at a time. In Fig. 15.18, we include the **ride** message (**3.2.1.2**) to represent the **Person** riding the **Elevator** to the other **Floor**. The {concurrent} keyword placed after the **ride** message indicates that method **ride** is **synchronized** when we implement our design in Java. The **Elevator** contains method **ride** for the **Person** to allow the synchronization.

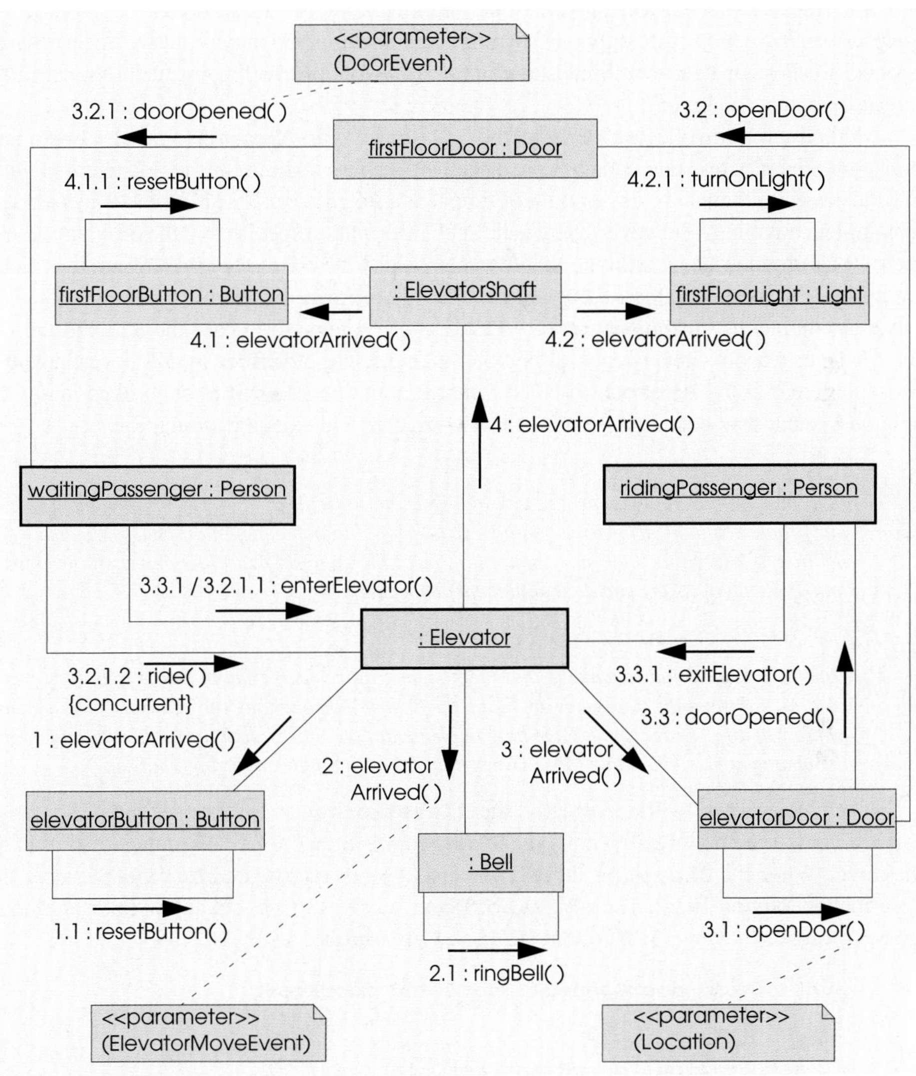

Fig. 15.18 Modified collaboration diagram with active classes for passengers entering and exiting the **Elevator**.

```
public synchronized void ride()
{
   try {
      Thread.sleep( maxTravelTime );
   }

   catch ( InterruptedException interruptedException ) {
      // method doorOpened in Person interrupts method sleep;
      // Person has finished riding Elevator
   }
}
```

Method **ride** guarantees that only one **Person** may ride the **Elevator** at a time—as described in Section 15.5, only one **synchronized** method may be active on an object at once, so all other **Person** threads attempting to invoke **ride** must wait for the current thread to exit method **ride**.

Method **ride** invokes **static** method **sleep** of class **Thread** to put the **Person** thread into the **sleep** state, which represents the **Person** waiting for the ride to complete. We must specify the maximum amount of time that a **Person** will wait for the **Elevator** to complete traveling—however, there is no such information specified in the problem statement. We introduce a new attribute that represents this time—**maxTravelTime**, to which we arbitrarily assign a value of **10** minutes (i.e., a **Person** will wait **10** minutes for the travel to complete). Attribute **maxTravelTime** is a safeguard in case the **Elevator**—for whatever reason—never reaches the other **Floor**. The **Person** should never have to wait this long—if the **Person** waits **10** minutes, then the **Elevator** is broken, and we assume that our **Person** crawls out of the **Elevator** and exits the simulation.

Software Engineering Observation 15.6

In a software-development process, the analysis phase yields a requirements document (e.g., our problem statement). As we continue the design and implementation phase, we discover additional issues that were not apparent to us at the analysis phase. As designers, we must anticipate these issues and deal with them accordingly.

Software Engineering Observation 15.7

One false assumption to make is that the system requirements remain stable (i.e., they provide all information necessary to build the system) throughout the analysis and design phases. In large systems that have long implementation phases, requirements can, and often do, change to accommodate those issues that were not apparent during analysis.

If our **Elevator** works correctly, the **Elevator** travels for five seconds—specifically, invoking method **sleep** halts the **Elevator**'s thread for five seconds to simulate the travel. When the **Elevator** thread awakens, it sends **elevatorArrived** events as described in Section 10.22. The **elevatorDoor** receives this event and invokes method **doorOpened** (message **3.3**) of the **ridingPassenger**, as in:

```
public void doorOpened( DoorEvent doorEvent )
{
   // set Person on Floor where Door opened
   setLocation( doorEvent.getLocation() );

   // interrupt Person's sleep method in run method and
   // Elevator's ride method
   interrupt();
}
```

Method **doorOpened** sets the **ridingPassenger**'s **Location** to the **Floor** at which the **Elevator** arrived, then calls the **ridingPassenger** thread's **interrupt** method. The **interrupt** method terminates the **sleep** method invoked in method **ride**, method **ride** terminates, and the **ridingPassenger** leaves the **Elevator**, then exits the simulation. When the **ridingPassenger** exits the **Elevator**, the **ridingPassenger** releases the monitor on the **Elevator** object, which allows the **waitingPassenger** to invoke the **ride** method and obtain the monitor. Now, the **waitingPassenger** may invoke method **ride** to ride the **Elevator**.

The **ridingPassenger** does not need to send the **exitElevator** message (message **3.3.1**) to the **Elevator**, because the **waitingPassenger** cannot invoke **ride** until the **ridingPassenger** releases the **Elevator**'s monitor—the **ridingPassenger** releases the monitor when the **ridingPassenger** thread exits method **ride** after calling its **interrupt** method. Therefore, the **Person** thread's **interrupt** method is equivalent to the **exitElevator** method (except that the **Person** sends itself the **interrupt** message), and we can substitute method **interrupt** for method **exitElevator**. Also, we can combine methods **ride** and **enterElevator** to handle both entering and riding the **Elevator**—our system needs only method **ride**, which allows a **Person** to obtain a monitor on the **Elevator**. As we implement our model in Appendix H, we use our collaboration diagram to help generate code in Java—however, we will make subtle "Java-specific" adjustments to our code to guarantee that the **Person**s enter and exit the **Elevator** correctly.

Sequence Diagrams

We now present the other type of interaction diagram, called a *sequence diagram*. Like the collaboration diagram, the sequence diagram shows interactions among objects; however, the sequence diagram emphasizes how messages are sent between objects *over time*. Both diagrams model interactions in a system. Collaboration diagrams emphasize what objects interact in a system, and sequence diagrams emphasize when these interactions occur.

Figure 15.19 is the sequence diagram for a **Person** changing floors. A rectangle enclosing the name of an object represents that object. We write object names in sequence diagrams using the same convention we have been using with collaboration diagrams. The dotted line extending down from an object's rectangle is that object's *lifeline*, which represents the progression of time. Actions occur along an object's lifeline in chronological order from top to bottom—an action near the top of a lifeline happens before an action near the bottom. We provide several notes in this diagram to clarify where the **Person** exists in the simulation. Note that the diagram includes several dashed arrows. These arrows represent "return messages," or the return of control to the sending object. Every message ultimately yields a return message. Showing return messages is not mandatory in a sequence diagram—we show return messages for clarity.

Message passing in sequence diagrams is similar to that in collaboration diagrams. An arrow extending from the object sending the message to the object receiving the message represents a message between two objects. The arrowhead points to the rectangle on the receiving object's lifeline. As previously mentioned, when an object returns control, a return message—represented as a dashed line with an arrowhead—extends from the object returning control to the object that initially sent the message.

The sequence in Fig. 15.19 begins when a **Person** presses a **Button** on a **Floor** by sending message **pressButton** to that **Button**. The **Button** then requests the **Elevator** by sending message **requestElevator** to the **Elevator**.

The **Person** must wait for the **Elevator** to process this message before continuing. However, the **Person** does not need to wait for the **Elevator**'s arrival before proceeding with other actions. In our simulation, we force the **Person** to wait, but we could have had the **Person** perform other actions, such as read a newspaper, sway back and forth or place a call on a cell phone as the **Elevator** travels to the **Floor** of the **Person**.

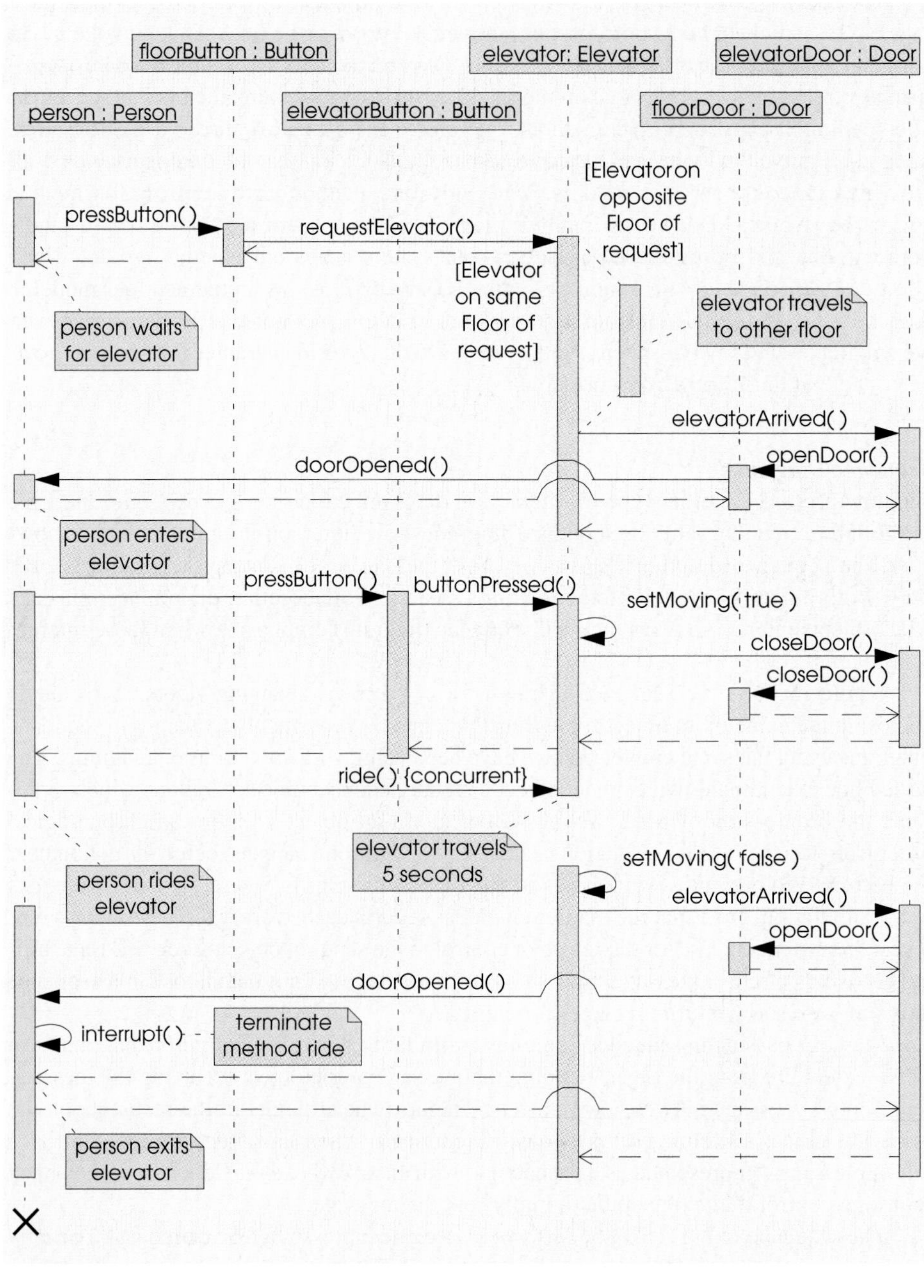

Fig. 15.19 Sequence diagram for a single **`Person`** changing floors in system.

Note the split in flow for the **`Elevator`** after being requested; the flow of execution depends on which **`Floor`** generated the request. If the **`Elevator`** is on a different **`Floor`** than the request, the **Elevator** must move to the **Floor** on which the **Person** is waiting. To save space, the note informing that the **Elevator** moves to the other **Floor** represents this sequence (We will construct this sequence momentarily when we discuss how the **Person** rides the **Elevator** to the other **Floor**.) When the **Elevator** travels to the other **Floor**, the branched sequence merges with the original sequence in the **Elevator**'s lifeline, and the **elevatorDoor** sends an **elevatorArrived** message to the **elevatorDoor** upon arrival.

If the **Elevator** is on the same **Floor** as the request, the **elevatorDoor** immediately sends an **elevatorArrived** message to the **elevatorDoor** upon arrival. The **elevatorDoor** receives the arrival message and opens the **Door** on the arrival **Floor**. This door sends a **doorOpened** message to the **Person**—that **Person** then enters the **Elevator**.

The **Person** then presses the **elevatorButton**, which sends a **buttonPressed** event to the **Elevator**. The **Elevator** gets ready to leave by calling its **private** method **setMoving**, which changes the **Elevator**'s **boolean** attribute **moving** to **true**. The **Elevator** then closes the **elevatorDoor**, which closes the **Door** on that **Floor**. The **Person** then rides the **Elevator** by invoking the **Elevator**'s **synchronized** method **ride**. As in the collaboration diagram, the {concurrent} keyword placed after method **ride** indicates the method is **synchronized**, when implemented in Java.

The remainder of the diagram shows the sequence after the **Elevator**'s arrival at the destination **Floor** (also described in Fig. 15.19). Upon arrival, the **Elevator** stops moving by calling **private** method **setMoving**, which sets attribute **moving** to **false**. The **Elevator** then sends an **elevatorArrived** message to the **elevatorDoor**, which opens the **Door** on that **Floor** and sends the **Person** a **doorOpened** message. Method **doorOpened** wakes the sleeping **Person**'s thread by invoking method **interrupt**, causing method **ride** to terminate and return the **Person**'s thread to the "ready" state. The **Person** exits the simulation shortly afterwards. Note the large "**X**" at the bottom of the **Person**'s lifeline. In a sequence diagram, this "**X**" indicates that the associated object destroys itself (in Java, the **Person** object is marked for garbage collection).

Our Final Class Diagram

The integration of multithreading in our elevator model concludes the design of the model. We implement this model in Appendix H. Figure 15.20 presents the complete class diagram we use when implementing the model. Note that the major difference between the class diagrams of Fig. 15.20 and Fig. 10.30 is the presence of active classes in Fig. 15.20. We have established that classes **Elevator** and **Person** are active classes. However, the problem statement mentioned that "if a person neither enters nor requests the elevator, the elevator closes its door." Having discussed multithreading, we believe that a better requirement would be for the **Door**s to close automatically (using a thread) if they have been open for more than a brief period (e.g., three seconds). In addition, although not mentioned in the problem statement, the **Light**s should turn off automatically—currently, the **Light**s turn off only when the **Elevator** departs from a **Floor**. We mark the **Door**s and **Light**s as active classes to handle this change. We implement this change in Appendix H.

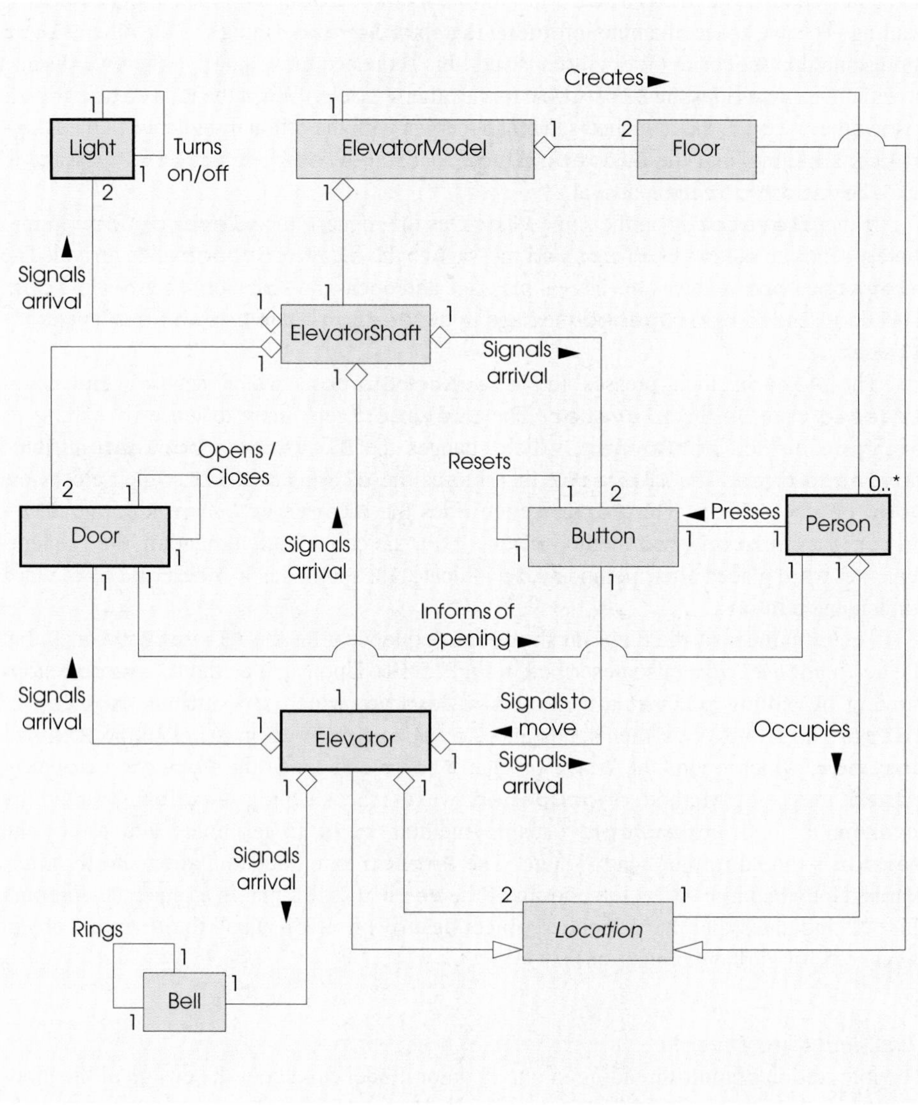

Fig. 15.20 Final class diagram of the elevator simulation

Figure 15.21 presents the attributes and operations for all classes in Fig. 15.20. We use both diagrams to implement the model. We have omitted method **enterElevator** and **exitElevator** from class **Elevator**, because as discussed in the interaction diagrams, method **ride** appears to handle the **Person**'s entering, riding and exiting the **Elevator**. In addition, we have replaced method **departElevator** with **private** method **setMoving**, because according to Fig. 15.19, method **setMoving** provides the service that allows the **Elevator** to depart from a **Floor**. We also include **private** attribute **maxTravelTime**, which represents the maximum time the **Person** will wait to ride the **Elevator**, to class **Person**. We assign **maxTravelTime** a value of **10** minutes (**10** * **60** seconds). We will use these class diagrams to implement our Java code in Appendix H, but we will continue making subtle "Java-specific" adjustments to code. In the appendices, for each class, we create methods that access object references and implement interface methods.

In "Thinking About Objects" Section 22.9, we design the view—the display of our model. When we implement this display in Appendix I, we will have a fully functional 3,594-line elevator simulation.

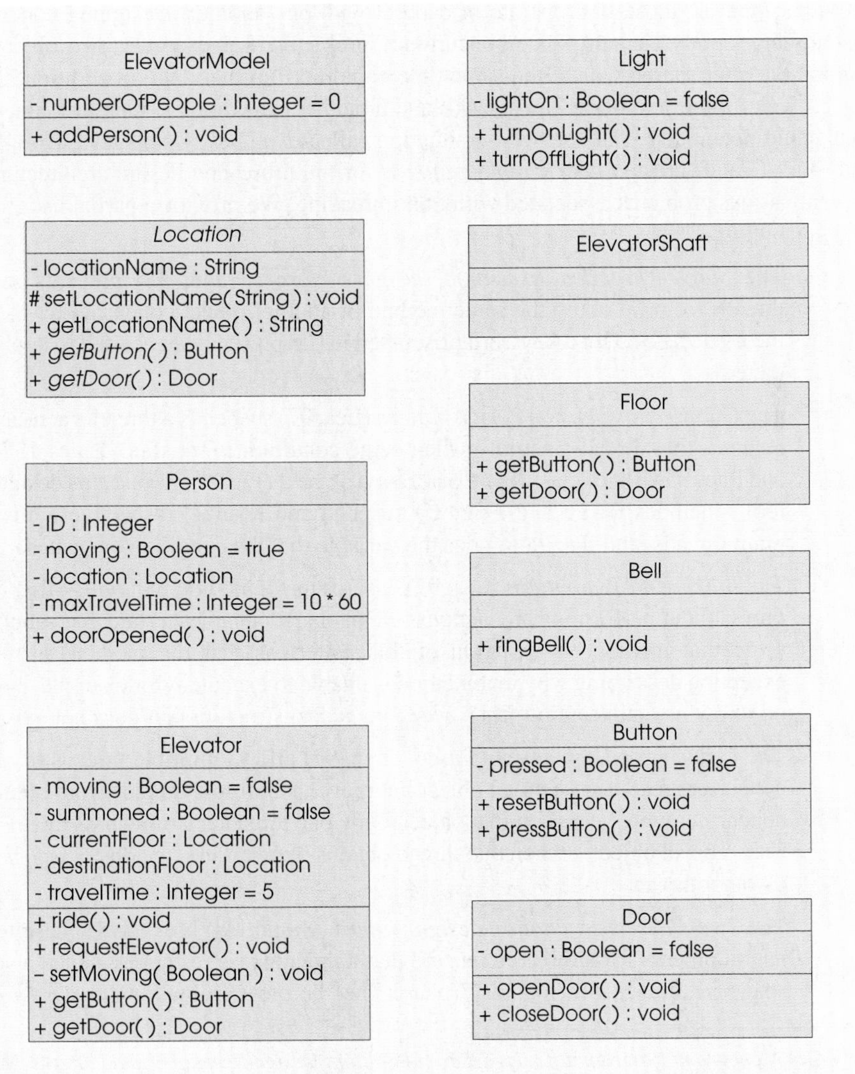

Fig. 15.21 Final class diagram with attributes and operations.

15.13 (Optional) Discovering Design Patterns: Concurrent Design Patterns

Many additional design patterns have been created since the publication of the gang-of-four book, which introduced patterns involving object-oriented systems. Some of these new patterns involve specific object-oriented systems, such as concurrent, distributed or parallel systems. In this section, we discuss concurrency patterns to conclude our discussion of multithreaded programming.

Concurrency Design Patterns

Multithreaded programming languages such as Java allow designers to specify concurrent activities—that is, those that operate in parallel with one another. Designing concurrent systems improperly can introduce concurrency problems. For example, two objects attempting to alter shared data at the same time could corrupt that data. In addition, if two objects wait for one another to finish tasks, and if neither can complete their task, these objects could potentially wait forever—a situation called *deadlock*. Using Java, Doug Lea[1] and Mark Grand[2] created *concurrency patterns* for multithreaded design architectures to prevent various problems associated with multithreading. We provide a partial list of these design patterns:

- The *Single-Threaded Execution design pattern* (Grand, 98) prevents several threads from invoking the same method of another object concurrently. In Java, the **synchronized** keyword (discussed in Chapter 15) can be used to apply this pattern.
- The *Guarded Suspension design pattern* (Lea, 97) suspends a thread's activity and resumes that thread's activity when some condition is satisfied. Lines 137–147 and lines 95–109 of class **RandomCharacters** (Fig. 15.17) use this design pattern—methods **wait** and **notify** suspend and resume, respectively, the program threads, and line 98 toggles the variable that the condition evaluates.
- The *Balking design pattern* (Lea, 97) ensures that a method will *balk*—that is, return without performing any actions—if an object occupies a state that cannot execute that method. A variation of this pattern is that the method throws an exception describing why that method is unable to execute—for example, a method throwing an exception when accessing a data structure that does not exist.
- The *Read/Write Lock design pattern* (Lea, 97) allows multiple threads to obtain concurrent read access on an object but prevents multiple threads from obtaining concurrent write access on that object. Only one thread at a time may obtain write access on an object—when that thread obtains write access, the object is *locked* to all other threads.
- The *Two-Phase Termination design pattern* (Grand, 98) uses a two-phase termination process for a thread to ensure that a thread frees resources—such as other spawned threads—in memory (phase one) before termination (phase two). In

1. D. Lea, *Concurrent Programing in Java, Second Edition: Design Principles and Patterns*. Massachusetts: Addison-Wesley. November 1999.
2. M. Grand, *Patterns in Java; A Catalog of Reusable Design Patterns Illustrated with UML*. New York: John Wiley and Sons, 1998.

Java, a **Thread** object can use this pattern in method **run**. For instance, method **run** can contain an infinite loop that is terminated by some state change—upon termination, method **run** can invoke a **private** method responsible for stopping any other spawned threads (phase one). The thread then terminates after method **run** terminates (phase two).

In "Discovering Design Patterns" Section 17.10, we return to the gang-of-four design patterns. Using the material introduced in Chapters 16 and 17, we identify those classes in package **java.io** and **java.net** that use design patterns.

SUMMARY

- Computers perform operations concurrently, such as compiling a program, printing a file and receiving e-mail messages over a network.
- Programming languages generally provide only a simple set of control structures that enable programmers to perform one action at a time, then proceed to the next action after the previous one is finished.
- The concurrency that computers perform today is normally implemented as operating system "primitives" available only to highly experienced "systems programmers."
- Java makes concurrency primitives available to the programmer.
- Applications contain threads of execution, each thread designating a portion of a program that may execute concurrently with other threads. This capability is called multithreading.
- Java provides a low-priority garbage collector thread that reclaims dynamically allocated memory that is no longer needed. The garbage collector runs when processor time is available and there are no higher priority runnable threads. The garbage collector runs immediately when the system is out of memory to try to reclaim memory.
- Method **run** contains the code that controls a thread's execution.
- A program launches a thread's execution by calling the thread's **start** method, which, in turn, calls method **run**.
- Method **interrupt** is called to interrupt a thread.
- Method **isAlive** returns **true** if **start** has been called for a given thread and the thread is not dead (i.e., the **run** method has not completed execution).
- Method **setName** sets the name of the **Thread**. Method **getName** returns the name of the **Thread**. Method **toString** returns a **String** consisting of the name of the thread, the priority of the thread and the thread's group.
- **Thread static** method **currentThread** returns a reference to the executing **Thread**.
- Method **join** waits for the **Thread** on which **join** is called to die before the current **Thread** can proceed.
- Waiting can be dangerous; it can lead to two serious problems called deadlock and indefinite postponement. Indefinite postponement is also called starvation.
- A thread that was just created is in the born state. The thread remains in this state until the thread's **start** method is called; this causes the thread to enter the ready state.
- A highest priority-ready thread enters the *running state* when the system assigns a processor to the thread.
- A thread enters the dead state when its **run** method completes or terminates for any reason. The system eventually will dispose of a dead thread.

- A *running* thread enters the blocked state when the thread issues an input/output request. A blocked thread becomes ready when the I/O it is waiting for completes. A blocked thread cannot use a processor even if one is available.
- When a running method calls **wait**, the thread enters a waiting state for the particular object in which the thread was running. A thread in the waiting state for a particular object becomes ready on a call to **notify** issued by another thread associated with that object.
- Every thread in the waiting state for a given object becomes ready on a call to **notifyAll** by another thread associated with that object.
- Every Java thread has a priority in the range **Thread.MIN_PRIORITY** (a constant of 1) and **Thread.MAX_PRIORITY** (a constant of 10). By default, each thread is given priority **Thread.NORM_PRIORITY** (a constant of 5).
- Some Java platforms support a concept called timeslicing and some do not. Without timeslicing, threads of equal priority run to completion before their peers get a chance to execute. With timeslicing, each thread receives a brief burst of processor time called a quantum during which that thread can execute. At the completion of the quantum, even if that thread has not finished executing, the processor is taken away from that thread and given to the next thread of equal priority, if one is available.
- The job of the Java scheduler is to keep a highest priority thread running at all times and, if timeslicing is available, to ensure that several equally high-priority threads each execute for a quantum in round-robin fashion.
- A thread's priority can be adjusted with the **setPriority** method. Method **getPriority** returns the thread's priority.
- A thread can call the **yield** method to give other threads a chance to execute.
- Every object that has **synchronized** methods has a monitor. The monitor lets only one thread at a time execute a **synchronized** method on the object.
- A thread executing in a **synchronized** method may determine that it cannot proceed, so the thread voluntarily calls **wait**. This removes the thread from contention for the processor and from contention for the object.
- A thread that has called **wait** is awakened by a thread that calls **notify**. The **notify** acts as a signal to the waiting thread that the condition the waiting thread has been waiting for is now (or could be) satisfied, so it is acceptable for that thread to reenter the monitor.
- A daemon thread serves other threads. When only daemon threads remain in a program, Java will exit. If a thread is to be a daemon, it must be set as such before its **start** method is called.
- To support multithreading in a class derived from some class other than **Thread**, implement the **Runnable** interface in that class.
- Implementing the **Runnable** interface gives us the ability to treat the new class as a **Runnable** object (just like inheriting from a class allows us to treat our subclass as an object of its superclass). As with deriving from the **Thread** class, the code that controls the thread is placed in the **run** method.
- A thread with a **Runnable** class is created by passing to the **Thread** class constructor a reference to an object of the class that implements the **Runnable** interface. The **Thread** constructor registers the **run** method of the **Runnable** object as the method to be invoked when the thread begins execution.
- Class **ThreadGroup** contains the methods for creating and manipulating groups of related threads in a program.

TERMINOLOGY

asynchronous threads
blocked (state of a thread)
blocked on I/O
busy wait
child thread group
circular buffer
concurrent execution of threads
condition variable
consumer
consumer thread
context
currentThread method
daemon thread
dead (state of a thread)
deadlock
destroy method
dumpStack method
Error class **ThreadDeath**
execution context
fixed-priority scheduling
garbage collection by a low-priority thread
getName method
getParent method of **ThreadGroup** class
highest priority runnable thread
I/O completion
IllegalArgumentException
IllegalMonitorStateException
IllegalThreadStateException
indefinite postponement
inherit thread priority
interrupt method
interrupted method
InterruptedException
InterruptedException class
interthread communication
isAlive method
isDaemon method
isInterrupted method
join method
kill a thread
MAX_PRIORITY(10)
memory leak
MIN_PRIORITY(1)
monitor
multiple inheritance
multiprocessing
multithreaded program
multithreaded server
multithreading
new (state of a thread)
nonpreemptive scheduling
NORM_PRIORITY(5)
notify method
notifyAll method
parallelism
parent thread
parent thread group
preemptive scheduling
priority of a thread
producer thread
producer/consumer relationship
programmer-defined thread
quantum
round-robin scheduling
run method
Runnable interface (in **java.lang** package)
runnable state (of a thread)
running (thread state)
scheduler
scheduling a thread
setDaemon method
setName method
setPriority method
shared objects
single-threaded language
single-threaded program
sleep method of **Thread** class
sleeping state (of a thread)
start method
starvation
synchronization
synchronized method
thread
Thread class (in **java.lang** package)
thread group
thread priority
thread safe
thread states
thread synchronization
Thread.MAX_PRIORITY
Thread.MIN_PRIORITY
Thread.NORM_PRIORITY
Thread.sleep()
ThreadDeath exception
ThreadGroup class
timeslicing
wait method
yield method

SELF-REVIEW EXERCISES

15.1 Fill in the blanks in each of the following statements:

a) C and C++ are __________-threaded languages whereas Java is a __________-threaded language.
b) Java provides a __________ thread that reclaims dynamically allocated memory.
c) Java eliminates most __________ errors that occur commonly in languages like C and C++ when dynamically allocated memory is not explicitly reclaimed by the program.
d) Three reasons a thread that is alive could be not runnable (i.e., blocked) are __________, __________ and __________.
e) A thread enters the dead state when __________.
f) A thread's priority can be changed with the __________ method.
g) A thread may give up the processor to a thread of the same priority by calling the method.
h) To wait for a designated number of milliseconds and resume execution, a thread should call the __________ method.
i) The __________ method moves a thread in the object's *waiting* state to the ready state.

15.2 State whether each of the following is *true* or *false*. If *false*, explain why.

a) A thread is not runnable if it is dead.
b) In Java, a higher priority runnable thread will preempt threads of lower priority.
c) The Windows and Windows NT Java systems use timeslicing. Therefore, they can enable threads to preempt threads of the same priority.
d) Threads may **`yield`** to threads of lower priority.

ANSWERS TO SELF-REVIEW EXERCISES

15.1 a) single, multi. b) garbage collector. c) memory leak. d) waiting, sleeping, blocked for input/output. e) its **`run`** method terminates. f) **`setPriority`**. g) **`yield`**. h) **`sleep`**. i) **`notify`**.

15.2 a) True. b) True. c) False. Timeslicing allows a thread to execute until its timeslice (or quantum) expires. Then other threads of equal priority can execute. d) False. Threads can only yield to threads of equal priority.

EXERCISES

15.3 State whether each of the following is *true* or *false*. If *false*, explain why.

a) The **`sleep`** method does not consume processor time while a thread sleeps.
b) Declaring a method **`synchronized`** guarantees that deadlock cannot occur.
c) Java provides a powerful capability called multiple inheritance.
d) **`Thread`** methods **`suspend`** and **`resume`** are deprecated.

15.4 Define each of the following terms.

a) thread
b) multithreading
c) ready state
d) blocked state
e) preemptive scheduling
f) **`Runnable`** interface
g) monitor
h) **`notify`** method
i) producer/consumer relationship

15.5 a) List each of the reasons stated in this chapter for using multithreading.
b) List additional reasons for using multithreading.

15.6 List each of the three reasons given in the text for entering the blocked state. For each of these, describe how the program will normally leave the blocked state and enter the runnable state.

15.7 Distinguish between preemptive scheduling and nonpreemptive scheduling. Which does Java use?

15.8 What is timeslicing? Give a fundamental difference in how scheduling is performed on Java systems that support timeslicing vs. scheduling on Java systems that do not support timeslicing.

15.9 Why would a thread ever want to call **`yield`**?

15.10 What aspects of developing Java applets for the World Wide Web encourage applet designers to use **`yield`** and **`sleep`** abundantly?

15.11 If you choose to write your own **`start`** method, what must you be sure to do to ensure that your threads start up properly?

15.12 Distinguish among each of the following means of pausing threads:
- a) busy wait
- b) sleep
- c) blocking I/O

15.13 Write a Java statement that tests if a thread is alive.

15.14
- a) What is multiple inheritance?
- b) Explain why Java does not offer multiple inheritance.
- c) What feature does Java offer instead of multiple inheritance?
- d) Explain the typical use of this feature.
- e) How does this feature differ from **`abstract`** classes?

15.15 Distinguish between the notions of **`extends`** and **`implements`**.

15.16 Discuss each of the following terms in the context of monitors:
- a) monitor
- b) producer
- c) consumer
- d) **`wait`**
- e) **`notify`**
- f) **`InterruptedException`**
- g) **`synchronized`**

15.17 (Tortoise and the Hare) In the Chapter 7 exercises, you were asked to simulate the legendary race of the tortoise and the hare. Implement a new version of that simulation, this time placing each of the animals in a separate thread. At the start of the race call the **`start`** methods for each of the threads. Use **`wait`**, **`notify`** and **`notifyAll`** to synchronize the animals' activities.

15.18 (Multithreaded, Networked, Collaborative Applications) In Chapter 17, we cover networking in Java. A multithreaded Java application can communicate concurrently with several host computers. This creates the possibility of being able to build some interesting kinds of collaborative applications. In anticipation of studying networking in Chapter 17, develop proposals for several possible multithreaded networked applications. After studying Chapter 17, implement some of those applications.

15.19 Write a Java program to demonstrate that as a high-priority thread executes, it will delay the execution of all lower priority threads.

15.20 If your system supports timeslicing, write a Java program that demonstrates timeslicing among several equal-priority threads. Show that a lower priority thread's execution is deferred by the timeslicing of the higher-priority threads.

15.21 Write a Java program that demonstrates a high priority thread using **`sleep`** to give lower priority threads a chance to run.

15.22 If your system does not support timeslicing, write a Java program that demonstrates two threads using **`yield`** to enable one another to execute.

15.23 Two problems that can occur in systems like Java, that allow threads to wait, are deadlock, in which one or more threads will wait forever for an event that cannot occur, and indefinite postponement, in which one or more threads will be delayed for some unpredictably long time. Give an example of how each of these problems can occur in a multithreaded Java program.

15.24 (Readers and Writers) This exercise asks you to develop a Java monitor to solve a famous problem in concurrency control. This problem was first discussed and solved by P. J. Courtois, F. Heymans and D. L. Parnas in their research paper, "Concurrent Control with Readers and Writers," *Communications of the ACM*, Vol. 14, No. 10, October 1971, pp. 667–668. The interested student might also want to read C. A. R. Hoare's seminal research paper on monitors, "Monitors: An Operating System Structuring Concept," *Communications of the ACM*, Vol. 17, No. 10, October 1974, pp. 549–557. Corrigendum, *Communications of the ACM*, Vol. 18, No. 2, February 1975, p. 95. [The readers and writers problem is discussed at length in Chapter 5 of the author's book: Deitel, H. M., *Operating Systems*, Reading, MA: Addison-Wesley, 1990.]

a) With multithreading, many threads can access shared data; as we have seen, access to shared data needs to be synchronized carefully to avoid corrupting the data.
b) Consider an airline-reservation system in which many clients are attempting to book seats on particular flights between particular cities. All of the information about flights and seats is stored in a common database in memory. The database consists of many entries, each representing a seat on a particular flight for a particular day between particular cities. In a typical airline-reservation scenario, the client will probe around in the database looking for the "optimal" flight to meet that client's needs. So a client may probe the database many times before deciding to book a particular flight. A seat that was available during this probing phase could easily be booked by someone else before the client has a chance to book it. In that case, when the client attempts to make the reservation, the client will discover that the data has changed and the flight is no longer available.
c) The client probing around the database is called a reader. The client attempting to book the flight is called a writer. Clearly, any number of readers can be probing shared data at once, but each writer needs exclusive access to the shared data to prevent the data from being corrupted.
d) Write a multithreaded Java program that launches multiple reader threads and multiple writer threads, each attempting to access a single reservation record. A writer thread has two possible transactions, **`makeReservation`** and **`cancelReservation`**. A reader has one possible transaction, **`queryReservation`**.
e) First implement a version of your program that allows unsynchronized access to the reservation record. Show how the integrity of the database can be corrupted. Next implement a version of your program that uses Java monitor synchronization with **`wait`** and **`notify`** to enforce a disciplined protocol for readers and writers accessing the shared reservation data. In particular, your program should allow multiple readers to access the shared data simultaneously when no writer is active. But if a writer is active, then no readers should be allowed to access the shared data.
f) Be careful. This problem has many subtleties. For example, what happens when there are several active readers and a writer wants to write? If we allow a steady stream of readers to arrive and share the data, they could indefinitely postpone the writer (who may become tired of waiting and take his or her business elsewhere). To solve this problem, you might decide to favor writers over readers. But here, too, there is a trap, because a steady stream of writers could then indefinitely postpone the waiting readers, and they, too, might choose to take their business elsewhere! Implement your monitor with the following methods: **`startReading`**, which is called by any reader who wants to begin accessing

a reservation; **stopReading** to be called by any reader who has finished reading a reservation; **startWriting** to be called by any writer who wants to make a reservation and **stopWriting** to be called by any writer who has finished making a reservation.

15.25 Write a program that bounces a blue ball inside an applet. The ball should be initiated with a **mousePressed** event. When the ball hits the edge of the applet, the ball should bounce off the edge and continue in the opposite direction.

15.26 Modify the program of Exercise 15.25 to add a new ball each time the user clicks the mouse. Provide for a minimum of 20 balls. Randomly choose the color for each new ball.

15.27 Modify the program of Exercise 15.26 to add shadows. As a ball moves, draw a solid black oval at the bottom of the applet. You may consider adding a 3-D effect by increasing or decreasing the size of each ball when a ball hits the edge of the applet.

15.28 Modify the program of Exercise 15.25 or 15.26 to bounce the balls off each other when they collide.

16

Files and Streams

Objectives

- To be able to create, read, write and update files.
- To understand the Java streams class hierarchy.
- To be able to use the **`FileInputStream`** and **`FileOutputStream`** classes.
- To be able to use the **`ObjectInputStream`** and **`ObjectOutputStream`** classes.
- To be able to use class **`RandomAccessFile`**.
- To be able to use a **`JFileChooser`** dialog to access files and directories.
- To become familiar with sequential-access and random-access file processing.
- To be able to use class **`File`**.

I can only assume that a "Do Not File" document is filed in a "Do Not File" file.
Senator Frank Church
Senate Intelligence Subcommittee Hearing, 1975

Consciousness ... does not appear to itself chopped up in bits. ... A "river" or a "stream" are the metaphors by which it is most naturally described.
William James

I read part of it all the way through.
Samuel Goldwyn

It is quite a three-pipe problem.
Sir Arthur Conan Doyle

Outline

16.1 Introduction
16.2 Data Hierarchy
16.3 Files and Streams
16.4 Creating a Sequential-Access File
16.5 Reading Data from a Sequential-Access File
16.6 Updating Sequential-Access Files
16.7 Random-Access Files
16.8 Creating a Random-Access File
16.9 Writing Data Randomly to a Random-Access File
16.10 Reading Data Sequentially from a Random-Access File
16.11 Example: A Transaction-Processing Program
16.12 Class `File`

Summary • Terminology • Self-Review Exercises • Answers to Self-Review Exercises • Exercises

16.1 Introduction

Storage of data in variables and arrays is temporary—the data is lost when a local variable "goes out of scope" or when the program terminates. Programs use *files* for long-term retention of large amounts of data, even after programs that create the data terminate. We refer to data maintained in files as *persistent data*, because the data exists beyond the duration of program execution. Computers store files on *secondary storage devices* such as magnetic disks, optical disks and magnetic tapes. In this chapter, we explain how Java programs create, update and process data files. We consider both "sequential-access" files and "random-access" files and discuss typical applications for each.

File processing is one of the most important capabilities a language must have to support commercial applications that typically process massive amounts of persistent data. In this chapter, we discuss Java's powerful file-processing and stream input/output features. File processing is a subset of Java's stream-processing capabilities that enable a program to read and write bytes in memory, in files and over network connections. We have two goals in this chapter—to introduce file-processing paradigms and to provide the reader with sufficient stream-processing capabilities to support the networking features introduced in Chapter 17.

It would be dangerous to enable applets arriving from anywhere on the World Wide Web to be able to read and write files on the client system. By default, Web browsers prevent applets from performing file processing on the client system. Therefore, file-processing programs generally are implemented as Java applications.

16.2 Data Hierarchy

Ultimately, a computer processes all data items as combinations of zeros and ones, because it is simple and economical for engineers to build electronic devices that can assume two stable states—one state represents `0`, the other state represents `1`. It is remarkable that the impressive functions performed by computers involve only the most fundamental manipulations of **0**s and **1**s.

The smallest data item in a computer can assume the value **0** or the value **1**. Such a data item is called a *bit* (short for "*b*inary dig*it*"—a digit that can assume one of two values). Computer circuitry performs various simple bit manipulations, such as examining the value of a bit, setting the value of a bit and reversing a bit (from **1** to **0** or from **0** to **1**).

It is cumbersome for programmers to work with data in the low-level form of bits. Instead, programmers prefer to work with data in such forms as *decimal digits* (0–9), *letters* (A–Z and a–z), and *special symbols* (e.g., $, @, %, &, *, (,), -, +, ", :, ?, / and many others). Digits, letters and special symbols are known as *characters*. The computer's *character set* is the set of all characters used to write programs and represent data items. Computers can process only **1**s and **0**s, so a computer's character set represents every character as a pattern of **1**s and **0**s. Characters in Java are *Unicode* characters composed of 2 *bytes*. Bytes are most commonly composed of eight bits. Programmers create programs and data items with characters. Computers manipulate and process these characters as patterns of bits. See Appendix K for more information on Unicode.

Just as characters are composed of bits, *fields* are composed of characters or bytes. A field is a group of characters or bytes that conveys meaning. For example, a field consisting of uppercase and lowercase letters can be used to represent a person's name.

Data items processed by computers form a *data hierarchy* in which data items become larger and more complex in structure as we progress from bits, to characters, to fields, etc.

Typically, several fields (called instance variables in Java) compose a *record* (implemented as a **class** in Java). In a payroll system, for example, a record for a particular employee might consist of the following fields (possible data types for these fields are shown in parentheses following each field):

- Employee identification number (**int**)
- Name (**String**)
- Address (**String**)
- Hourly pay rate (**double**)
- Number of exemptions claimed (**int**)
- Year-to-date earnings (**int** or **double**)
- Amount of taxes withheld (**int** or **double**)

Thus, a record is a group of related fields. In the preceding example, each of the fields belongs to the same employee. Of course, a particular company might have many employees and will have a payroll record for each employee. A *file* is a group of related records.[1] A company's payroll file normally contains one record for each employee. Thus, a payroll file for a small company might contain only 22 records, whereas a payroll file for a large company might contain 100,000 records. It is not unusual for a company to have many files, some containing millions, or even billions, of characters of information. Figure 16.1 illustrates the *data hierarchy*.

---

1. More generally, a file can contain arbitrary data in arbitrary formats. In some operating systems, a file is viewed as nothing more than a collection of bytes. In such an operating system, any organization of the bytes in a file (such as organizing the data into records) is a view created by the applications programmer.

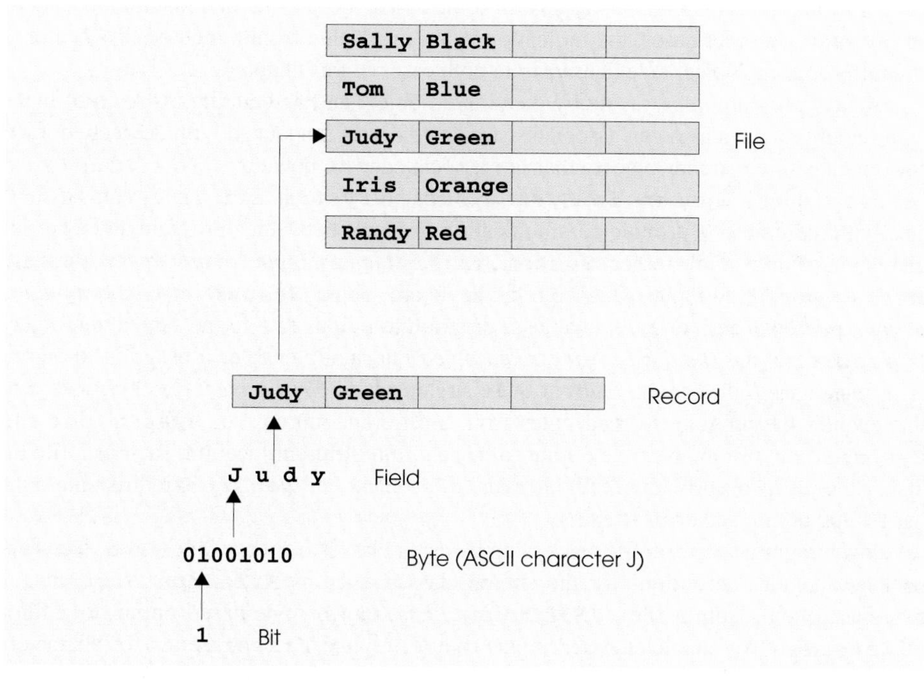

Fig. 16.1 The data hierarchy.

To facilitate the retrieval of specific records from a file, at least one field in each record is chosen as a *record key*. A record key identifies a record as belonging to a particular person or entity that is unique from all other records. In the payroll record described previously, the employee identification number normally would be chosen as the record key.

There are many ways to organize records in a file. The most common organization is called a *sequential file* in which records are stored in order by the record-key field. In a payroll file, records are placed in order by employee identification number. The first employee record in the file contains the lowest employee identification number, and subsequent records contain increasingly higher employee identification numbers.

Most businesses store data in many different files. For example, companies might have payroll files, accounts receivable files (listing money due from clients), accounts payable files (listing money due to suppliers), inventory files (listing facts about all the items handled by the business) and many other file types. Often, a group of related files is called a *database*. A collection of programs designed to create and manage databases is called a *database management system* (DBMS).

16.3 Files and Streams

Java views each file as a sequential *stream* of bytes (Fig. 16.2). Each file ends either with an *end-of-file marker* or at a specific byte number recorded in a system-maintained administrative data structure. Java abstracts this concept from the programmer. A Java program processing a stream of bytes simply receives an indication from the system when the program reaches the end of the stream—the program does not need to know how the underlying platform represents files or streams. In some cases, the end-of-file indication occurs as an exception. In other cases, the indication is a return value from a method invoked on a stream-processing object. We demonstrate both cases in this chapter.

A Java program *opens* a file by creating an object and associating a stream of bytes with the object. Java also can associates streams of bytes associated with devices. In fact, Java creates three stream objects that are associated with devices when a Java program begins executing—***System.in***, ***System.out*** and ***System.err***. The streams associated with these objects provide communication channels between a program and a particular device. For example, object **System.in** (the *standard input stream object*) normally enables a program to input bytes from the keyboard, object **System.out** (the *standard output stream object*) normally enables a program to output data to the screen and object **System.err** (the *standard error stream object*) normally enables a program to output error messages to the screen. Each of these streams can be *redirected*. For **System.in**, this enables the program to read bytes from a different source. For **System.out** and **System.err**, this enables the output to be sent to a different location, such as a file on disk. Class **System** provides methods ***setIn***, ***setOut*** and ***setErr*** to redirect the standard input, output and error streams.

Java programs perform file processing by using classes from package ***java.io***. This package includes definitions for the stream classes, such as ***FileInputStream*** (for byte-based input from a file), ***FileOutputStream*** (for byte-based output to a file), ***FileReader*** (for character-based input from a file) and ***FileWriter*** (for character-based output to a file). Files are opened by creating objects of these stream classes that inherit from classes **InputStream**, **OutputStream**, **Reader** and **Writer**, respectively. Thus, the methods of these stream classes can all be applied to file streams as well. To perform input and output of data types, objects of class **ObjectInputStream**, **DataInputStream**, **ObjectOutputStream** and **DataOutputStream** will be used together with the byte-based file stream classes **FileInputStream** and **File-OutputStream**. Figure 16.3 summarizes the inheritance relationships of many of the Java I/O classes (**abstract** classes are shown in italic font). The following discussion overviews the capabilities of each of the classes in Fig. 16.3.

Java offers many classes for performing input/output. This section briefly overviews many of these classes and explains how they relate to one another. In the rest of the chapter, we use several of these stream classes as we implement a variety of file-processing programs that create, manipulate and destroy sequential-access files and random-access files. We also include a detailed example on class **File**, which is useful for obtaining information about files and directories. In Chapter 17, Networking, we use stream classes extensively to implement networking applications.

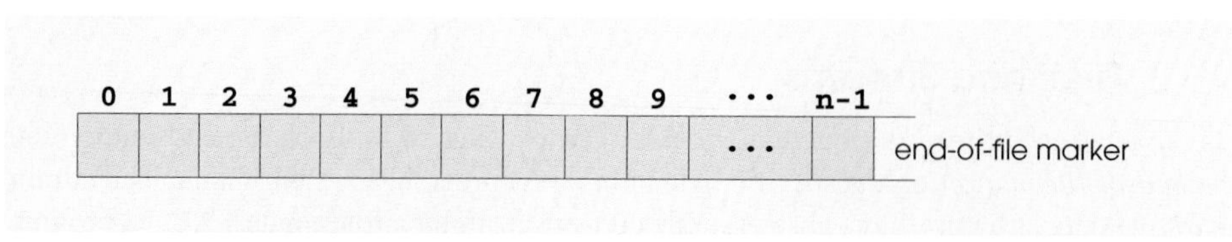

Fig. 16.2 Java's view of a file of *n* bytes.

A portion of the class hierarchy of the `java.io` package

```
java.lang.Object
   File
   FileDescriptor
   InputStream
      ByteArrayInputStream
      FileInputStream
      FilterInputStream
         BufferedInputStream
         DataInputStream
         PushbackInputStream
      ObjectInputStream
      PipedInputStream
      SequenceInputStream
   OutputStream
      ByteArrayOutputStream
      FileOutputStream
      FilterOutputStream
         BufferedOutputStream
         DataOutputStream
         PrintStream
      ObjectOutputStream
      PipedOutputStream
   RandomAccessFile
   Reader
      BufferedReader
         LineNumberReader
      CharArrayReader
      FilterReader
         PushbackReader
      InputStreamReader
         FileReader
      PipedReader
      StringReader
```

Fig. 16.3 A portion of the class hierarchy of the `java.io` package (part 1 of 2).

A portion of the class hierarchy of the `java.io` package

```
Writer
   BufferedWriter
   CharArrayWriter
   FilterWriter
   OutputStreamWriter
      FileWriter
   PipedWriter
   PrintWriter
   StringWriter
```

Fig. 16.3 A portion of the class hierarchy of the **java.io** package (part 2 of 2).

InputStream and ***OutputStream*** (subclasses of **Object**) are **abstract** classes that define methods for performing byte-based input and output, respectively.

Programs perform byte-based file input/output with ***FileInputStream*** (a subclass of **InputStream**) and ***FileOutputStream*** (a subclass of **OutputStream**). We use these classes extensively in the examples in this chapter.

Pipes are synchronized communication channels between threads or processes. Java provides ***PipedOutputStream*** (a subclass of **OutputStream**) and ***PipedInputStream*** (a subclass of **InputStream**) to establish pipes between two threads. One thread sends data to another by writing to a **PipedOutputStream**. The target thread reads information from the pipe via a **PipedInputStream**.

A ***PrintStream*** (a subclass of **FilterOutputStream**) performs text output to the specified stream. Actually, we have been using **PrintStream** output throughout the text to this point—**System.out** is a **PrintStream**, as is **System.err**.

A **FilterInputStream** *filters* an **InputStream**, and a **FilterOutStream** filters an **OutputStream**; filtering simply means that the filter stream provides additional functionality, such as buffering, monitoring line numbers or aggregating data bytes into meaningful primitive-data-type units. **FilterInputStream** and **FilterOutputStream** are **abstract** classes, so additional functionality is provided by their subclasses.

Reading data as raw bytes is fast but crude. Usually programs read data as aggregates of bytes that form an **int**, a **float**, a **double** and so on. Java programs can use several classes to input and output data in aggregate form.

A ***RandomAccessFile*** is useful for direct-access applications, such as transaction-processing applications like airline-reservations systems and point-of-sale systems. With a sequential-access file, each successive input/output request reads or writes the next consecutive set of data in the file. With a random-access file, each successive input/output request could be directed to any part of the file—perhaps one widely separated from the part of the file referenced in the previous request. Direct-access applications provide rapid access to specific data items in large files; often, such applications are used in applications that require users to wait for answers—these answers must be made available quickly, or the people might become impatient and "take their business elsewhere."

The **DataInput** interface is implemented by class **DataInputStream** and class **RandomAccessFile** (discussed later in the chapter); each needs to read primitive data types from a stream. **DataInputStream**s enable a program to read binary data from an **InputStream**. The **DataInput** interface includes methods **read** (for **byte** arrays), **readBoolean**, **readByte**, **readChar**, **readDouble**, **readFloat**, **readFully** (for **byte** arrays), **readInt**, **readLong**, **readShort**, **readUnsignedByte**, **readUnsignedShort**, **readUTF** (for strings) and **skipBytes**.

The **DataOutput** interface is implemented by class **DataOutputStream** (a subclass of **FilterOutputStream**) and class **RandomAccessFile**; each needs to write primitive data types to an **OutputStream**. **DataOutputStream**s enable a program to write binary data to an **OutputStream**. The **DataOutput** interface includes methods **flush**, **size**, **write** (for a **byte**), **write** (for a **byte** array), **writeBoolean**, **writeByte**, **writeBytes**, **writeChar**, **writeChars** (for Unicode **String**s), **writeDouble**, **writeFloat**, **writeInt**, **writeLong**, **writeShort** and **writeUTF**.

Buffering is an I/O-performance-enhancement technique. With a ***BufferedOutputStream*** (a subclass of class **FilterOutputStream**), each output statement does not necessarily result in an actual physical transfer of data to the output device. Rather, each output operation is directed to a region in memory called a buffer that is large enough to hold the data of many output operations. Then, actual transfer to the output device is performed in one large *physical output operation* each time the buffer fills. The output operations directed to the output buffer in memory are often called *logical output operations*. With a **BufferedOutputStream**, a partially filled buffer can be forced out to the device at any time by invoking the stream object's **flush** method.

Performance Tip 16.1

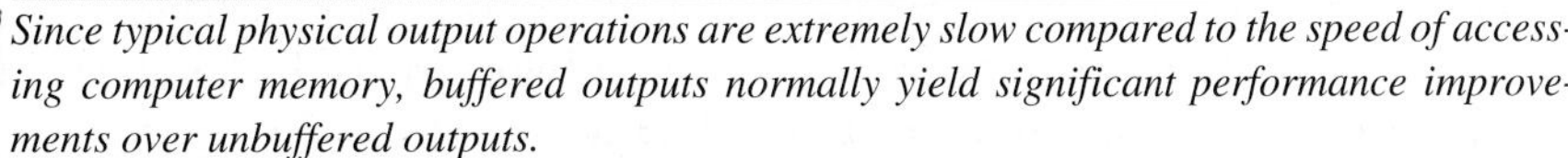

Since typical physical output operations are extremely slow compared to the speed of accessing computer memory, buffered outputs normally yield significant performance improvements over unbuffered outputs.

With a ***BufferedInputStream*** (a subclass of class **FilterInputStream**), many "logical" chunks of data from a file are read as one large *physical input operation* into a memory buffer. As a program requests each new chunk of data, it is taken from the buffer (this is sometimes referred to as a *logical input operation*). When the buffer is empty, the next actual physical input operation from the input device is performed to read in the next group of "logical" chunks of data. Thus, the number of actual physical input operations is small compared with the number of read requests issued by the program.

Performance Tip 16.2

Since typical input operations are extremely slow compared to the speed of accessing computer memory, buffered inputs normally yield significant performance improvements over unbuffered inputs.

A ***PushbackInputStream*** (a subclass of class **FilterInputStream**) is for applications more exotic than those most programmers require. Essentially, the application reading a **PushbackInputStream** reads bytes from the stream and forms aggregates consisting of several bytes. Sometimes, to determine that one aggregate is complete, the application must read the first character "past the end" of the first aggregate. Once the program determines that the current aggregate is complete, the extra character is "pushed back" onto the stream. **PushbackInputStream**s are used by programs (like compilers) that parse their inputs—that is, break them into meaningful units (such as the keywords, identifiers and operators that the compiler must recognize).

When object instance variables are output to a disk file, in a sense we lose the object's type information. We have only data, not type information, on a disk. If the program that is going to read this data knows what object type it corresponds to, then the data is simply read into objects of that type. Sometimes, we would like to read or write an entire object to a file. The ***ObjectInputStream*** and ***ObjectOutputStream*** classes, which respectively implement the ***ObjectInput*** and ***ObjectOutput*** interfaces, enable an entire object to be read from or written to a file (or other stream type). We often chain **ObjectInputStream**s to **FileInputStream**s. (We also chain **ObjectOutputStream**s to **FileOutputStream**s.) The **ObjectOutput** interface contains method **writeObject**, which takes an **Object** that implements interface ***Serializable*** as an argument and writes its information to the **OutputStream**. Correspondingly, the **ObjectInput** interface requires method **readObject**, which reads and returns an **Object** from an **InputStream**. After the reading of an object, it can be cast to the desired type. Additionally, these interfaces include other **Object**-centric methods as well as the same methods as **DataInput** and **DataOutput** for reading and writing primitive data types.

Java stream I/O includes capabilities for inputting from **byte** arrays in memory and outputting to **byte** arrays in memory. A **ByteArrayInputStream** (a subclass of **InputStream**) reads from a **byte** array in memory. A **ByteArrayOutputStream** (a subclass of **OutputStream**) outputs to a **byte** array in memory. One application of **byte**-array I/O is data validation. A program can input an entire line at a time from the input stream into a **byte** array. Then, a validation routine can scrutinize the contents of the **byte** array and correct the data, if necessary. Then, the program can proceed to input from the **byte** array, knowing that the input data is in the proper format. Outputting to a **byte** array is a nice way to take advantage of the powerful output-formatting capabilities of Java streams. For example, data can be prepared in a **byte** array, using the same formatting that will be displayed at a later time, then output to a disk file to preserve the screen image.

A **SequenceInputStream** (a subclass of **InputStream**) enables concatenation of several **InputStream**s, so that the program sees the group as one continuous **InputStream**. As the program reaches the end of an input stream, that stream closes and the next stream in the sequence opens.

In addition to the byte based streams, Java provides ***Reader*** and ***Writer*** classes, which are Unicode, two-byte, character based streams. Most of the byte-based streams have corresponding character-based **Reader** or **Writer** classes.

Class ***BufferedReader*** (a subclass of **abstract** class **Reader**) and class ***BufferedWriter*** (a subclass of **abstract** class **Writer**) enable efficient buffering for character-based streams. Character-based streams use Unicode characters—such streams can process data in any language that the Unicode character set represents.

Class ***CharArrayReader*** and class ***CharArrayWriter*** read and write a stream of characters to a character array.

A ***PushbackReader*** (a subclass of **abstract** class ***FilterReader***) enables characters to be pushed back on a character stream. A ***LineNumberReader*** (a subclass of ***BufferedReader***) is a buffered character-stream that keeps track of line numbers (i.e., a newline, a return or a carriage-return line-feed combination).

Class **FileReader** (a subclass of **InputStreamReader**) and class **FileWriter** (a subclass of **OutputStreamWriter**) read characters from and write characters to a file, respectively. Class **PipedReader** and class **PipedWriter** implement piped-character streams that can be used to transfer information between threads. Class **StringReader** and **StringWriter** read and write characters to **String**s. A **PrintWriter** writes characters to a stream.

Class **File** enables programs to obtain information about a file or directory. We discuss class **File** extensively in Section 16.12.

16.4 Creating a Sequential-Access File

Java imposes no structure on a file. Notions like "record" do not exist in Java files. Therefore, the programmer must structure files to meet the requirements of applications. In the following example, we see how the programmer can impose a simple record structure on a file. First we present the program, then we analyze it in detail.

The program of Fig. 16.4–Fig. 16.6 creates a simple sequential-access file that might be used in an accounts receivable system to help manage the money owed by a company's credit clients. For each client, the program obtains an account number, the client's first name, the client's last name and the client's balance (i.e., the amount the client still owes the company for goods and services received in the past). The data obtained for each client constitutes a record for that client. The program uses the account number as the record key; that is, the file will be created and maintained in account-number order. [*Note*: This program assumes the user enters the records in account-number order. In a comprehensive accounts receivable system, a sorting capability would be provided so the user could enter the records in any order—the records would then be sorted and written to the file.]

Most of the programs in this chapter have a similar GUI, so this program defines class **BankUI** (Fig. 16.4) to encapsulate the GUI. (See the second sample output screen in Fig. 16.6.) Also, the program defines class **AccountRecord** (Fig. 16.5) to encapsulate the client record information (i.e., account, first name, etc.) used by the examples in this chapter. For reuse, classes **BankUI** and **AccountRecord** are defined in package **com.deitel.jhtp4.ch16**.

[*Note*: Most of the programs in this chapter use classes **BankUI** and **AccountRecord**. When you compile these classes, or any others that will be reused in this chapter, you should place the classes in a common directory. When you compile classes that use **BankUI** and **AccountRecord**, be sure to specify the **-classpath** command line argument to both **javac** and **java**, as in

```
javac -classpath .;packageLocation ClassName.java
java -classpath .;packageLocation ClassName
```

where *packageLocation* represents the common directory in which the classes of the package **com.deitel.jhtp4.ch16** reside and *ClassName* represents the class to compile or execute. Be sure to include the current directory (specified with **.**) in the class path. [Note: If your packaged classes are in a JAR file, the *packageLocation* should include the location and name of the actual JAR file.] Also, the path separator shown (**;**, which is used in Microsoft Windows) should be appropriate for your platform (such as **:** on UNIX/Linux).]

Class **BankUI** (Fig. 16.4) contains two **JButton**s and arrays of **JLabel**s and **JTextField**s. The number of **JLabel**s and **JTextField**s is set with the constructor defined at lines 34–75. Methods **getFieldValues** (lines 116–124), **setFieldValues** (lines 104–113) and **clearFields** (lines 96–100) manipulate the text of the **JTextField**s. Methods **getFields** (lines 90–93), **getDoTask1Button** (lines 78–81) and **getDoTask2Button** (lines 84–87) return individual GUI components, so that a client program can add **ActionListener**s (for example).

```
1  // Fig. 16.4: BankUI.java
2  // A reusable GUI for the examples in this chapter.
3  package com.deitel.jhtp4.ch16;
4
5  // Java core packages
6  import java.awt.*;
7
8  // Java extension packages
9  import javax.swing.*;
10
11 public class BankUI extends JPanel {
12
13    // label text for GUI
14    protected final static String names[] = { "Account number",
15       "First name", "Last name", "Balance",
16       "Transaction Amount" };
17
18    // GUI components; protected for future subclass access
19    protected JLabel labels[];
20    protected JTextField fields[];
21    protected JButton doTask1, doTask2;
22    protected JPanel innerPanelCenter, innerPanelSouth;
23
24    // number of text fields in GUI
25    protected int size;
26
27    // constants representing text fields in GUI
28    public static final int ACCOUNT = 0, FIRSTNAME = 1,
29       LASTNAME = 2, BALANCE = 3, TRANSACTION = 4;
30
31    // Set up GUI. Constructor argument of 4 creates four rows
32    // of GUI components. Constructor argument of 5 (used in a
33    // later program) creates five rows of GUI components.
34    public BankUI( int mySize )
35    {
36       size = mySize;
37       labels = new JLabel[ size ];
38       fields = new JTextField[ size ];
39
40       // create labels
41       for ( int count = 0; count < labels.length; count++ )
42          labels[ count ] = new JLabel( names[ count ] );
43
44       // create text fields
45       for ( int count = 0; count < fields.length; count++ )
46          fields[ count ] = new JTextField();
```

Fig. 16.4 **BankUI** contains a reusable GUI for several programs (part 1 of 3).

```

      // create panel to lay out labels and fields
      innerPanelCenter = new JPanel();
      innerPanelCenter.setLayout( new GridLayout( size, 2 ) );

      // attach labels and fields to innerPanelCenter
      for ( int count = 0; count < size; count++ ) {
         innerPanelCenter.add( labels[ count ] );
         innerPanelCenter.add( fields[ count ] );
      }

      // create generic buttons; no labels or event handlers
      doTask1 = new JButton();
      doTask2 = new JButton();

      // create panel to lay out buttons and attach buttons
      innerPanelSouth = new JPanel();
      innerPanelSouth.add( doTask1 );
      innerPanelSouth.add( doTask2 );

      // set layout of this container and attach panels to it
      setLayout( new BorderLayout() );
      add( innerPanelCenter, BorderLayout.CENTER );
      add( innerPanelSouth, BorderLayout.SOUTH );

      // validate layout
      validate();

   }  // end constructor

   // return reference to generic task button doTask1
   public JButton getDoTask1Button()
   {
      return doTask1;
   }

   // return reference to generic task button doTask2
   public JButton getDoTask2Button()
   {
      return doTask2;
   }

   // return reference to fields array of JTextFields
   public JTextField[] getFields()
   {
      return fields;
   }

   // clear content of text fields
   public void clearFields()
   {
      for ( int count = 0; count < size; count++ )
         fields[ count ].setText( "" );
```

Fig. 16.4 **BankUI** contains a reusable GUI for several programs (part 2 of 3).

```
   }

   // set text field values; throw IllegalArgumentException if
   // incorrect number of Strings in argument
   public void setFieldValues( String strings[] )
      throws IllegalArgumentException
   {
      if ( strings.length != size )
         throw new IllegalArgumentException( "There must be " +
            size + " Strings in the array" );

      for ( int count = 0; count < size; count++ )
         fields[ count ].setText( strings[ count ] );
   }

   // get array of Strings with current text field contents
   public String[] getFieldValues()
   {
      String values[] = new String[ size ];

      for ( int count = 0; count < size; count++ )
         values[ count ] = fields[ count ].getText();

      return values;
   }

}  // end class BankUI
```

Fig. 16.4 **BankUI** contains a reusable GUI for several programs (part 3 of 3).

Class **AccountRecord** (Fig. 16.5) implements interface ***Serializable***, which allows objects of **AccountRecord** to be used with **ObjectInputStream**s and **ObjectOutputStream**s. Interface **Serializable** is known as a *tagging interface*. Such an interface contains no methods. A class that implements this interface is *tagged* as being a **Serializable** object, which is important because an **ObjectOutputStream** will not output an object unless it *is a* **Serializable** object. In a class that implements **Serializable**, the programmer must ensure that every instance variable of the class is a **Serializable** type, or must declare particular instance variables as ***transient*** to indicate that those variables are not Serializable and they should be ignored during the serialization process. By default, all primitive type variables are transient. For non-primitive types, you must check the definition of the class (and possibly its superclasses) to ensure that the type is **Serializable**. Class **AccountRecord** contains **private** data members **account**, **firstName**, **lastName** and **balance**. This class also provides **public** "get" and "set" methods for accessing the **private** data members.

```
// Fig. 16.5: AccountRecord.java
// A class that represents one record of information.
package com.deitel.jhtp4.ch16;
```

Fig. 16.5 Class **AccountRecord** maintains information for one account (part 1 of 3).

```java

// Java core packages
import java.io.Serializable;

public class AccountRecord implements Serializable {
   private int account;
   private String firstName;
   private String lastName;
   private double balance;

   // no-argument constructor calls other constructor with
   // default values
   public AccountRecord()
   {
      this( 0, "", "", 0.0 );
   }

   // initialize a record
   public AccountRecord( int acct, String first,
      String last, double bal )
   {
      setAccount( acct );
      setFirstName( first );
      setLastName( last );
      setBalance( bal );
   }

   // set account number
   public void setAccount( int acct )
   {
      account = acct;
   }

   // get account number
   public int getAccount()
   {
      return account;
   }

   // set first name
   public void setFirstName( String first )
   {
      firstName = first;
   }

   // get first name
   public String getFirstName()
   {
      return firstName;
   }

```

Fig. 16.5 Class **AccountRecord** maintains information for one account (part 2 of 3).

```
   // set last name
   public void setLastName( String last )
   {
      lastName = last;
   }

   // get last name
   public String getLastName()
   {
      return lastName;
   }

   // set balance
   public void setBalance( double bal )
   {
      balance = bal;
   }

   // get balance
   public double getBalance()
   {
      return balance;
   }

}  // end class AccountRecord
```

Fig. 16.5 Class **AccountRecord** maintains information for one account (part 3 of 3).

Now, let us discuss the code that creates the sequential-access file (Fig. 16.6). In this example, we introduce class ***JFileChooser*** (package **javax.swing**) for selecting files (as on the second screen in Fig. 16.6). Line 103 constructs a **JFileChooser** instance and assigns it to reference **fileChooser**. Lines 104–105 call method ***setFileSelectionMode*** to specify what the user can select from the **fileChooser**. For this program, we use **JFileChooser static** constant ***FILES_ONLY*** to indicate that only files can be selected. Other **static** constants include ***FILES_AND_DIRECTORIES*** and ***DIRECTORIES_ONLY***.

```
1  // Fig. 16.6: CreateSequentialFile.java
2  // Demonstrating object output with class ObjectOutputStream.
3  // The objects are written sequentially to a file.
4
5  // Java core packages
6  import java.io.*;
7  import java.awt.*;
8  import java.awt.event.*;
9
10 // Java extension packages
11 import javax.swing.*;
12
```

Fig. 16.6 Creating a sequential file (part 1 of 6).

```
// Deitel packages
import com.deitel.jhtp4.ch16.BankUI;
import com.deitel.jhtp4.ch16.AccountRecord;

public class CreateSequentialFile extends JFrame {
   private ObjectOutputStream output;
   private BankUI userInterface;
   private JButton enterButton, openButton;

   // set up GUI
   public CreateSequentialFile()
   {
      super( "Creating a Sequential File of Objects" );

      // create instance of reusable user interface
      userInterface = new BankUI( 4 );  // four textfields
      getContentPane().add(
         userInterface, BorderLayout.CENTER );

      // get reference to generic task button doTask1 in BankUI
      // and configure button for use in this program
      openButton = userInterface.getDoTask1Button();
      openButton.setText( "Save into File ..." );

      // register listener to call openFile when button pressed
      openButton.addActionListener(

         // anonymous inner class to handle openButton event
         new ActionListener() {

            // call openFile when button pressed
            public void actionPerformed( ActionEvent event )
            {
               openFile();
            }

         }  // end anonymous inner class

      ); // end call to addActionListener

      // get reference to generic task button doTask2 in BankUI
      // and configure button for use in this program
      enterButton = userInterface.getDoTask2Button();
      enterButton.setText( "Enter" );
      enterButton.setEnabled( false );  // disable button

      // register listener to call addRecord when button pressed
      enterButton.addActionListener(

         // anonymous inner class to handle enterButton event
         new ActionListener() {

```

Fig. 16.6 Creating a sequential file (part 2 of 6).

```
            // call addRecord when button pressed
            public void actionPerformed( ActionEvent event )
            {
               addRecord();
            }

         }  // end anonymous inner class

      ); // end call to addActionListener

      // register window listener to handle window closing event
      addWindowListener(

         // anonymous inner class to handle windowClosing event
         new WindowAdapter() {

            // add current record in GUI to file, then close file
            public void windowClosing( WindowEvent event )
            {
               if ( output != null )
                  addRecord();

               closeFile();
            }

         }  // end anonymous inner class

      ); // end call to addWindowListener

      setSize( 300, 200 );
      show();

   }  // end CreateSequentialFile constructor

   // allow user to specify file name
   private void openFile()
   {
      // display file dialog, so user can choose file to open
      JFileChooser fileChooser = new JFileChooser();
      fileChooser.setFileSelectionMode(
         JFileChooser.FILES_ONLY );

      int result = fileChooser.showSaveDialog( this );

      // if user clicked Cancel button on dialog, return
      if ( result == JFileChooser.CANCEL_OPTION )
         return;

      // get selected file
      File fileName = fileChooser.getSelectedFile();

```

Fig. 16.6 Creating a sequential file (part 3 of 6).

```
      // display error if invalid
      if ( fileName == null ||
         fileName.getName().equals( "" ) )
         JOptionPane.showMessageDialog( this,
            "Invalid File Name", "Invalid File Name",
            JOptionPane.ERROR_MESSAGE );

      else {

         // open file
         try {
            output = new ObjectOutputStream(
               new FileOutputStream( fileName ) );

            openButton.setEnabled( false );
            enterButton.setEnabled( true );
         }

         // process exceptions from opening file
         catch ( IOException ioException ) {
            JOptionPane.showMessageDialog( this,
               "Error Opening File", "Error",
               JOptionPane.ERROR_MESSAGE );
         }
      }

   } // end method openFile

   // close file and terminate application
   private void closeFile()
   {
      // close file
      try {
         output.close();

         System.exit( 0 );
      }

      // process exceptions from closing file
      catch( IOException ioException ) {
         JOptionPane.showMessageDialog( this,
            "Error closing file", "Error",
            JOptionPane.ERROR_MESSAGE );
         System.exit( 1 );
      }
   }

   // add record to file
   public void addRecord()
   {
      int accountNumber = 0;
      AccountRecord record;
      String fieldValues[] = userInterface.getFieldValues();
```

Fig. 16.6 Creating a sequential file (part 4 of 6).

```

      // if account field value is not empty
      if ( ! fieldValues[ BankUI.ACCOUNT ].equals( "" ) ) {

         // output values to file
         try {
            accountNumber = Integer.parseInt(
               fieldValues[ BankUI.ACCOUNT ] );

            if ( accountNumber > 0 ) {

               // create new record
               record = new AccountRecord( accountNumber,
                  fieldValues[ BankUI.FIRSTNAME ],
                  fieldValues[ BankUI.LASTNAME ],
                  Double.parseDouble(
                     fieldValues[ BankUI.BALANCE ] ) );

               // output record and flush buffer
               output.writeObject( record );
               output.flush();
            }

            // clear textfields
            userInterface.clearFields();
         }

         // process invalid account number or balance format
         catch ( NumberFormatException formatException ) {
            JOptionPane.showMessageDialog( this,
               "Bad account number or balance",
               "Invalid Number Format",
               JOptionPane.ERROR_MESSAGE );
         }

         // process exceptions from file output
         catch ( IOException ioException ) {
            closeFile();
         }

      } // end if

   } // end method addRecord

   // execute application; CreateSequentialFile constructor
   // displays window
   public static void main( String args[] )
   {
      new CreateSequentialFile();
   }

} // end class CreateSequentialFile
```

Fig. 16.6 Creating a sequential file (part 5 of 6).

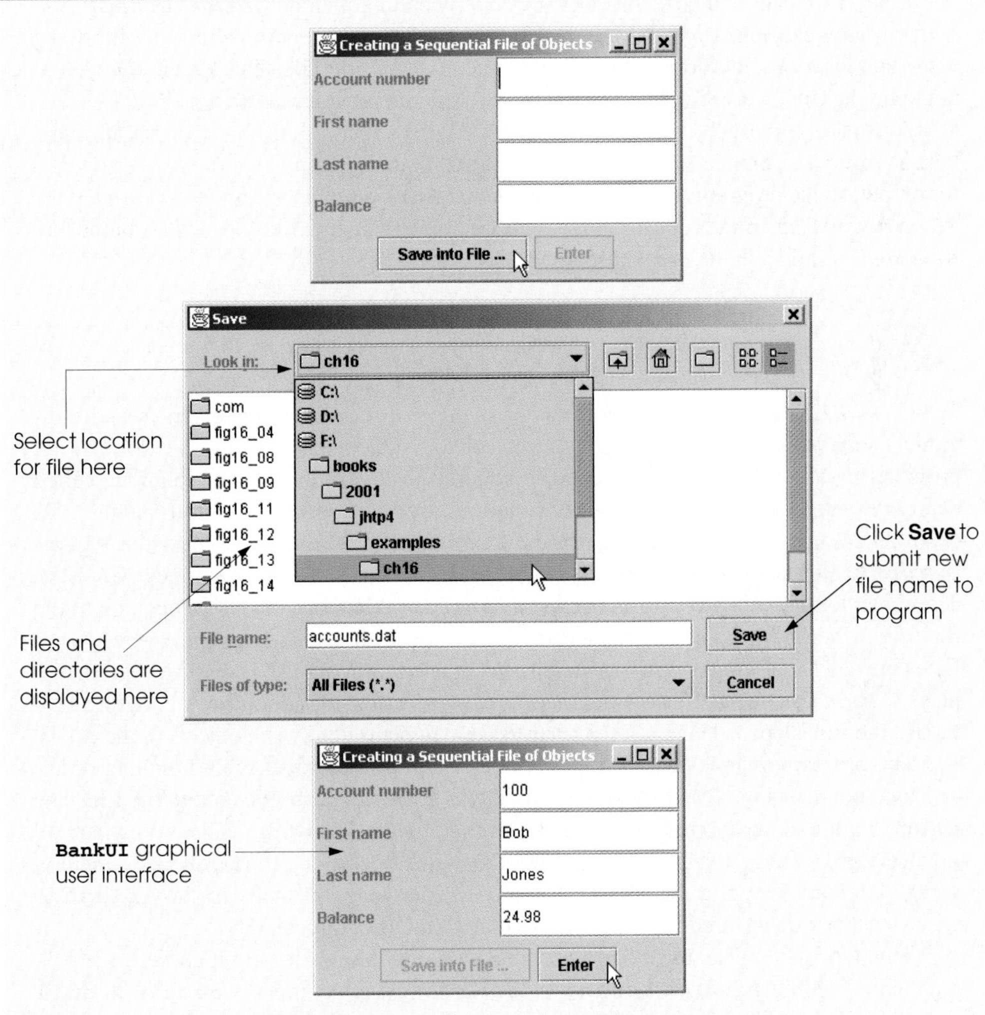

Fig. 16.6 Creating a sequential file (part 6 of 6).

Line 107 calls method ***showSaveDialog*** to display the **JFileChooser** dialog titled **Save**. Argument **this** specifies the **JFileChooser** dialog's *parent* window, which determines the position of the dialog on the screen. If **null** is passed, the dialog is displayed in the center of the window; otherwise, the dialog is centered over the application window. When displayed, a **JFileChooser** dialog does not allow the user to interact with any other program window until the user closes the **JFileChooser** dialog by clicking **Save** or **Cancel**. Dialogs that behave in this fashion are called *modal* dialogs. The user selects the drive, directory and file name, then clicks **Save**. Method **showSaveDialog** returns an integer specifying which button the user clicked (**Save** or **Cancel**) to close the dialog. Line 110 tests whether the user clicked **Cancel** by comparing **result** to **static** constant ***CANCEL_OPTION***. If so, the method returns.

Line 114 retrieves the file the user selected by calling method ***getSelectedFile***, which returns an object of type **File** that encapsulates information about the file (e.g., name and location), but does not represent the contents of the file. This **File** object does not open the file. We assign this **File** object to the reference **fileName**.

As stated previously, a program opens a file by creating an object of stream class **FileInputStream** or **FileOutputStream**. In this example, the file is to be opened for output, so the program creates a **FileOutputStream**. One argument is passed to the **FileOutputStream**'s constructor—a **File** object. Existing files opened for output are *truncated*—all data in the file is discarded.

Common Programming Error 16.1

It is a logic error to open an existing file for output when, in fact, the user wants to preserve the file. The contents of the file are discarded without warning.

Class **FileOutputStream** provides methods for writing **byte** arrays and individual **byte**s to a file. For this program, we need to write objects to a file—a capability not provided by **FileOutputStream**. The solution to this problem is a technique called *chaining of stream objects*—the ability to add the services of one stream to another. To chain an **ObjectOutputStream** to the **FileOutputStream**, we pass the **FileOutputStream** object to the **ObjectOutputStream**'s constructor (lines 127–128). The constructor could throw an ***IOException*** if a problem occurs during opening of the file (e.g., when a file is opened for writing on a drive with insufficient space, a read-only file is opened for writing or a nonexistent file is opened for reading). If so, the program displays a **JOptionPane**. If construction of the two streams does not throw an **IOException**, the file is open. Then, reference **output** can be used to write objects to the file.

The program assumes data is input correctly and in the proper record number order. The user populates the **JTextField**s and clicks **Enter** to write the data to the file. The **Enter** button's **actionPerformed** method (lines 66–69) calls our method **addRecord** (lines 164–211) to perform the write operation. Line 188 calls method ***writeObject*** to write the **record** object to file. Line 189 calls method ***flush*** to ensure that any data stored in memory is written to the file immediately.

When the user clicks the close box (the **X** in the window's top-right corner), the program calls method **windowClosing** (lines 82–88), which compares **output** to **null** (line 84). If **output** is not **null**, the stream is open and methods **addRecord** and **closeFile** (lines 145–161) are called. Method **closeFile** calls method ***close*** for **output** to close the file.

Performance Tip 16.3

Always release resources explicitly and at the earliest possible moment at which it is determined that the resource is no longer needed. This makes the resource immediately available to be reused by your program or by another program, thus improving resource utilization.

When using chained stream objects, the outermost object (the **ObjectOutputStream** in this example) should be used to close the file.

Performance Tip 16.4

Explicitly close each file as soon as it is known that the program will not reference the file again. This can reduce resource usage in a program that will continue executing long after it no longer needs to be referencing a particular file. This practice also improves program clarity.

In the sample execution for the program of Fig. 16.6, we entered information for five accounts (see Fig. 16.7). The program does not show how the data records actually appear in the file. To verify that the file has been created successfully, in the next section we create a program to read the file.

16.5 Reading Data from a Sequential-Access File

Data are stored in files so that they may be retrieved for processing when needed. The previous section demonstrated how to create a file for sequential access. In this section, we discuss how to read data sequentially from a file.

The program of Fig. 16.8 reads records from a file created by the program of Fig. 16.6 and displays the contents of the records. The program opens the file for input by creating a **`FileInputStream`** object. The program specifies the name of the file to open as an argument to the **`FileInputStream`** constructor. In Fig. 16.6, we wrote objects to the file, using an **`ObjectOutputStream`** object. Data must be read from the file in the same format in which it was written to the file. Therefore, we use an **`ObjectInputStream`** chained to a **`FileInputStream`** in this program. Note that the third sample screen capture shows the GUI displaying the last record in the file.

Sample Data			
100	Bob	Jones	24.98
200	Steve	Doe	-345.67
300	Pam	White	0.00
400	Sam	Stone	-42.16
500	Sue	Rich	224.62

Fig. 16.7 Sample data for the program of Fig. 16.6.

```java
// Fig. 16.8: ReadSequentialFile.java
// This program reads a file of objects sequentially
// and displays each record.

// Java core packages
import java.io.*;
import java.awt.*;
import java.awt.event.*;

// Java extension packages
import javax.swing.*;

// Deitel packages
import com.deitel.jhtp4.ch16.*;

public class ReadSequentialFile extends JFrame {
   private ObjectInputStream input;
```

Fig. 16.8 Reading a sequential file (part 1 of 6).

```
   private BankUI userInterface;
   private JButton nextButton, openButton;

   // Constructor -- initialize the Frame
   public ReadSequentialFile()
   {
      super( "Reading a Sequential File of Objects" );

      // create instance of reusable user interface
      userInterface = new BankUI( 4 );  // four textfields
      getContentPane().add(
         userInterface, BorderLayout.CENTER );

      // get reference to generic task button doTask1 from BankUI
      openButton = userInterface.getDoTask1Button();
      openButton.setText( "Open File" );

      // register listener to call openFile when button pressed
      openButton.addActionListener(

         // anonymous inner class to handle openButton event
         new ActionListener() {

            // close file and terminate application
            public void actionPerformed( ActionEvent event )
            {
               openFile();
            }

         }  // end anonymous inner class

      ); // end call to addActionListener

      // register window listener for window closing event
      addWindowListener(

         // anonymous inner class to handle windowClosing event
         new WindowAdapter() {

            // close file and terminate application
            public void windowClosing( WindowEvent event )
            {
               if ( input != null )
                  closeFile();

               System.exit( 0 );
            }

         }  // end anonymous inner class

      ); // end call to addWindowListener

```

Fig. 16.8 Reading a sequential file (part 2 of 6).

```
      // get reference to generic task button doTask2 from BankUI
      nextButton = userInterface.getDoTask2Button();
      nextButton.setText( "Next Record" );
      nextButton.setEnabled( false );

      // register listener to call readRecord when button pressed
      nextButton.addActionListener(

         // anonymous inner class to handle nextRecord event
         new ActionListener() {

            // call readRecord when user clicks nextRecord
            public void actionPerformed( ActionEvent event )
            {
               readRecord();
            }

         }  // end anonymous inner class

      ); // end call to addActionListener

      pack();
      setSize( 300, 200 );
      show();

   }  // end ReadSequentialFile constructor

   // enable user to select file to open
   private void openFile()
   {
      // display file dialog so user can select file to open
      JFileChooser fileChooser = new JFileChooser();
      fileChooser.setFileSelectionMode(
         JFileChooser.FILES_ONLY );

      int result = fileChooser.showOpenDialog( this );

      // if user clicked Cancel button on dialog, return
      if ( result == JFileChooser.CANCEL_OPTION )
         return;

      // obtain selected file
      File fileName = fileChooser.getSelectedFile();

      // display error if file name invalid
      if ( fileName == null ||
           fileName.getName().equals( "" ) )
         JOptionPane.showMessageDialog( this,
            "Invalid File Name", "Invalid File Name",
            JOptionPane.ERROR_MESSAGE );

      else {

```

Fig. 16.8 Reading a sequential file (part 3 of 6).

```
         // open file
         try {
            input = new ObjectInputStream(
               new FileInputStream( fileName ) );

            openButton.setEnabled( false );
            nextButton.setEnabled( true );
         }

         // process exceptions opening file
         catch ( IOException ioException ) {
            JOptionPane.showMessageDialog( this,
               "Error Opening File", "Error",
               JOptionPane.ERROR_MESSAGE );
         }

      } // end else

   } // end method openFile

   // read record from file
   public void readRecord()
   {
      AccountRecord record;

      // input the values from the file
      try {
         record = ( AccountRecord ) input.readObject();

         // create array of Strings to display in GUI
         String values[] = {
            String.valueOf( record.getAccount() ),
            record.getFirstName(),
            record.getLastName(),
            String.valueOf( record.getBalance() ) };

         // display record contents
         userInterface.setFieldValues( values );
      }

      // display message when end-of-file reached
      catch ( EOFException endOfFileException ) {
         nextButton.setEnabled( false );

         JOptionPane.showMessageDialog( this,
            "No more records in file",
            "End of File", JOptionPane.ERROR_MESSAGE );
      }

      // display error message if cannot read object
      // because class not found
      catch ( ClassNotFoundException classNotFoundException ) {
         JOptionPane.showMessageDialog( this,
```

Fig. 16.8 Reading a sequential file (part 4 of 6).

```
                "Unable to create object",
                "Class Not Found", JOptionPane.ERROR_MESSAGE );
        }

        // display error message if cannot read
        // due to problem with file
        catch ( IOException ioException ) {
            JOptionPane.showMessageDialog( this,
                "Error during read from file",
                "Read Error", JOptionPane.ERROR_MESSAGE );
        }
    }

    // close file and terminate application
    private void closeFile()
    {
        // close file and exit
        try {
            input.close();
            System.exit( 0 );
        }

        // process exception while closing file
        catch ( IOException ioException ) {
            JOptionPane.showMessageDialog( this,
                "Error closing file",
                "Error", JOptionPane.ERROR_MESSAGE );

            System.exit( 1 );
        }
    }

    // execute application; ReadSequentialFile constructor
    // displays window
    public static void main( String args[] )
    {
        new ReadSequentialFile();
    }

}  // end class ReadSequentialFile
```

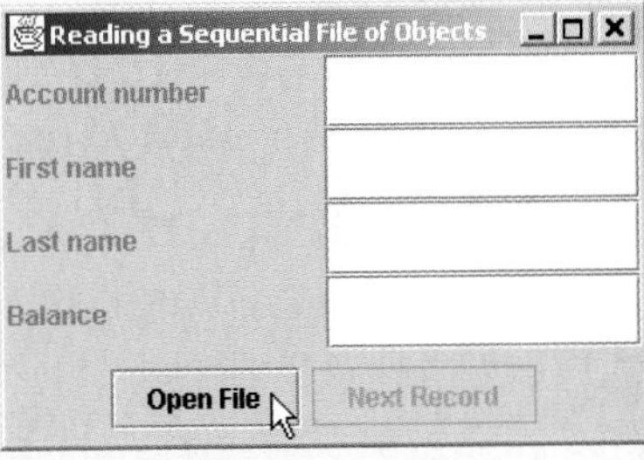

Fig. 16.8 Reading a sequential file (part 5 of 6).

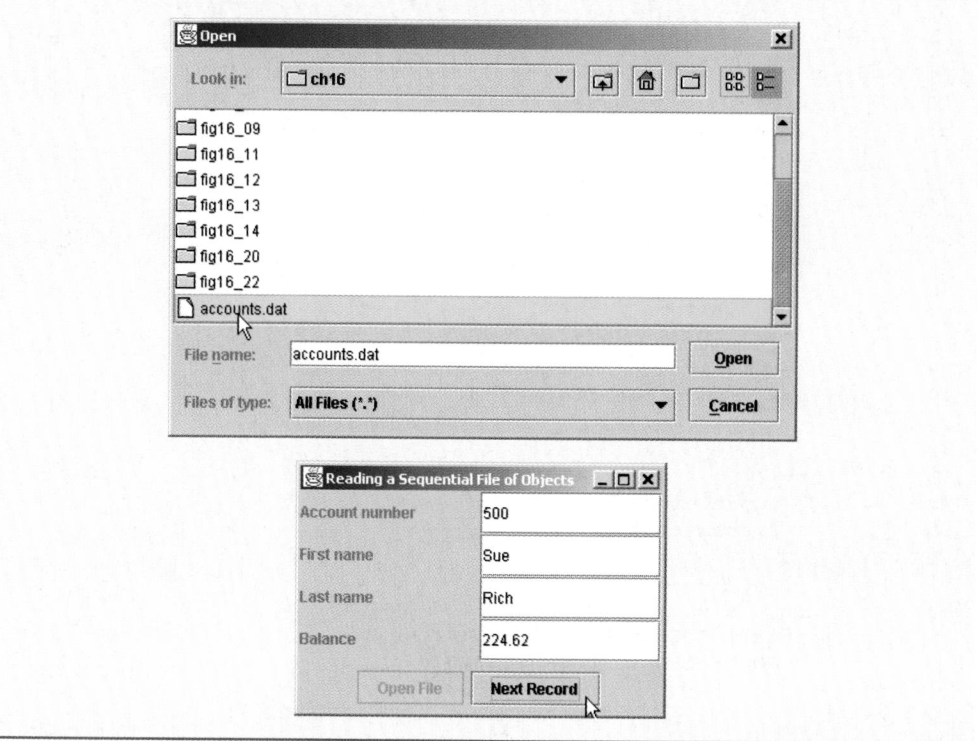

Fig. 16.8 Reading a sequential file (part 6 of 6).

Most of the code in this example is similar to Fig. 16.6, so we discuss only the key lines of code that are different. Line 105 calls **`JFileChooser`** method ***`showOpenDialog`*** to display the **Open** dialog (second screen capture in Fig. 16.8). The behavior and GUI are the same as the dialog displayed by **`showSaveDialog`**, except that the title of the dialog and the **Save** button are both replaced with **Open**.

Lines 125–126 create a **`ObjectInputStream`** object and assign it to **`input`**. The **`File fileName`** is passed to the **`FileInputStream`** constructor to open the file.

The program reads a record from the file each time the user clicks the **Next Record** button. Line 84 in **Next Record**'s **`actionPerformed`** method calls method **`readRecord`** (lines 144–187) to read one record from the file. Line 150 calls method ***`readObject`*** to read an **`Object`** from the **`ObjectInputStream`**. To use **`AccountRecord`** specific methods, we cast the returned **`Object`** to type **`AccountRecord`**. If the end-of-file marker is reached during reading, **`readObject`** throws an ***`EndOfFileException`***.

To retrieve data sequentially from a file, programs normally start reading from the beginning of the file and read all the data consecutively until the desired data are found. It might be necessary to process the file sequentially several times (from the beginning of the file) during the execution of a program. Class **`FileInputStream`** does not provide the ability to reposition to the beginning of the file to read the file again unless the program closes the file and reopens it. Class **`RandomAccessFile`** objects can reposition to the beginning of the file. Class **`RandomAccessFile`** provides all the capabilities of the classes **FileInputStream**, **FileOutputStream**, **DataInputStream** and **DataOutputStream** and adds several other methods, including a ***seek*** that repositions the *file-position pointer* (the byte number of the next byte in the file to be read or written) to any position in the file. However, class **RandomAccessFile** cannot read and write entire objects.

Performance Tip 16.5

The process of closing and reopening a file for the purpose of positioning the file-position pointer back to the beginning of a file is a time-consuming task for the computer. If this is done frequently, it can slow the performance of your program.

The program of Fig. 16.9 enables a credit manager to display the account information for those customers with zero balances (i.e., customers who do not owe the company any money), credit balances (i.e., customers to whom the company owes money) and debit balances (i.e., customers who owe the company money for goods and services received in the past).

The program displays buttons that allow a credit manager to obtain credit information. The **Credit balances** button produces a list of accounts with credit balances. The **Debit balances** button produces a list of accounts with debit balances. The **Zero balances** button produces a list of accounts with zero balances.

Records are displayed in a **JTextArea** called **recordDisplayArea**. The record information is collected by reading through the entire file and determining, for each record, whether it satisfies the criteria for the account type selected by the credit manager. Clicking one of the balance buttons sets variable **accountType** (line 274) to the clicked button's text (e.g., **Zero balances**) and invokes method **readRecords** (191–238), which loops through the file and reads every record. Line 208 of method **readRecords** calls method **shouldDisplay** (241–259) to determine whether the current record satisfies the account type requested. If **shouldDisplay** returns **true**, the program appends the account information for the current record to the **JTextArea recordDisplay**. When the end-of-file marker is reached, line 219 calls method **closeFile** to close the file.

```
1  // Fig. 16.9: CreditInquiry.java
2  // This program reads a file sequentially and displays the
3  // contents in a text area based on the type of account the
4  // user requests (credit balance, debit balance or
5  // zero balance).
6
7  // Java core packages
8  import java.io.*;
9  import java.awt.*;
10 import java.awt.event.*;
11 import java.text.DecimalFormat;
12
13 // Java extension packages
14 import javax.swing.*;
15
16 // Deitel packages
17 import com.deitel.jhtp4.ch16.AccountRecord;
```

Fig. 16.9 Credit inquiry program (part 1 of 7).

```

public class CreditInquiry extends JFrame {
   private JTextArea recordDisplayArea;
   private JButton openButton,
      creditButton, debitButton, zeroButton;
   private JPanel buttonPanel;

   private ObjectInputStream input;
   private FileInputStream fileInput;
   private File fileName;
   private String accountType;

   // set up GUI
   public CreditInquiry()
   {
      super( "Credit Inquiry Program" );

      Container container = getContentPane();

      // set up panel for buttons
      buttonPanel = new JPanel();

      // create and configure button to open file
      openButton = new JButton( "Open File" );
      buttonPanel.add( openButton );

      // register openButton listener
      openButton.addActionListener(

         // anonymous inner class to handle openButton event
         new ActionListener() {

            // open file for processing
            public void actionPerformed( ActionEvent event )
            {
               openFile( true );
            }

         }  // end anonymous inner class

      ); // end call to addActionListener

      // create and configure button to get
      // accounts with credit balances
      creditButton = new JButton( "Credit balances" );
      buttonPanel.add( creditButton );
      creditButton.addActionListener( new ButtonHandler() );

      // create and configure button to get
      // accounts with debit balances
      debitButton = new JButton( "Debit balances" );
      buttonPanel.add( debitButton );
      debitButton.addActionListener( new ButtonHandler() );
```

Fig. 16.9 Credit inquiry program (part 2 of 7).

```

      // create and configure button to get
      // accounts with credit balances
      zeroButton = new JButton( "Zero balances" );
      buttonPanel.add( zeroButton );
      zeroButton.addActionListener( new ButtonHandler() );

      // set up display area
      recordDisplayArea = new JTextArea();
      JScrollPane scroller =
         new JScrollPane( recordDisplayArea );

      // attach components to content pane
      container.add( scroller, BorderLayout.CENTER );
      container.add( buttonPanel, BorderLayout.SOUTH );

      // disable creditButton, debitButton and zeroButton
      creditButton.setEnabled( false );
      debitButton.setEnabled( false );
      zeroButton.setEnabled( false );

      // register window listener
      addWindowListener(

         // anonymous inner class for windowClosing event
         new WindowAdapter() {

            // close file and terminate program
            public void windowClosing( WindowEvent event )
            {
               closeFile();
               System.exit( 0 );
            }

         }  // end anonymous inner class

      ); // end call to addWindowListener

      // pack components and display window
      pack();
      setSize( 600, 250 );
      show();

   }  // end CreditInquiry constructor

   // enable user to choose file to open first time;
   // otherwise, reopen chosen file
   private void openFile( boolean firstTime )
   {
      if ( firstTime ) {

         // display dialog, so user can choose file
         JFileChooser fileChooser = new JFileChooser();
```

Fig. 16.9 Credit inquiry program (part 3 of 7).

```
         fileChooser.setFileSelectionMode(
            JFileChooser.FILES_ONLY );

         int result = fileChooser.showOpenDialog( this );

         // if user clicked Cancel button on dialog, return
         if ( result == JFileChooser.CANCEL_OPTION )
            return;

         // obtain selected file
         fileName = fileChooser.getSelectedFile();
      }

      // display error if file name invalid
      if ( fileName == null ||
         fileName.getName().equals( "" ) )
         JOptionPane.showMessageDialog( this,
            "Invalid File Name", "Invalid File Name",
            JOptionPane.ERROR_MESSAGE );

      else {

         // open file
         try {

            // close file from previous operation
            if ( input != null )
               input.close();

            fileInput = new FileInputStream( fileName );
            input = new ObjectInputStream( fileInput );
            openButton.setEnabled( false );
            creditButton.setEnabled( true );
            debitButton.setEnabled( true );
            zeroButton.setEnabled( true );
         }

         // catch problems manipulating file
         catch ( IOException ioException ) {
            JOptionPane.showMessageDialog( this,
               "File does not exist", "Invalid File Name",
               JOptionPane.ERROR_MESSAGE );
         }
      }

   } // end method openFile

   // close file before application terminates
   private void closeFile()
   {
      // close file
      try {
         input.close();
```

Fig. 16.9 Credit inquiry program (part 4 of 7).

```
      }

      // process exception from closing file
      catch ( IOException ioException ) {
         JOptionPane.showMessageDialog( this,
            "Error closing file",
            "Error", JOptionPane.ERROR_MESSAGE );

         System.exit( 1 );
      }
   }

   // read records from file and display only records of
   // appropriate type
   private void readRecords()
   {
      AccountRecord record;
      DecimalFormat twoDigits = new DecimalFormat( "0.00" );
      openFile( false );

      // read records
      try {
         recordDisplayArea.setText( "The accounts are:\n" );

         // input the values from the file
         while ( true ) {

            // read one AccountRecord
            record = ( AccountRecord ) input.readObject();

            // if proper acount type, display record
            if ( shouldDisplay( record.getBalance() ) )
               recordDisplayArea.append( record.getAccount() +
                  "\t" + record.getFirstName() + "\t" +
                  record.getLastName() + "\t" +
                  twoDigits.format( record.getBalance() ) +
                  "\n" );
         }
      }

      // close file when end-of-file reached
      catch ( EOFException eofException ) {
         closeFile();
      }

      // display error if cannot read object
      // because class not found
      catch ( ClassNotFoundException classNotFound ) {
         JOptionPane.showMessageDialog( this,
            "Unable to create object",
            "Class Not Found", JOptionPane.ERROR_MESSAGE );
      }

```

Fig. 16.9 Credit inquiry program (part 5 of 7).

```
      // display error if cannot read
      // because problem with file
      catch ( IOException ioException ) {
         JOptionPane.showMessageDialog( this,
            "Error reading from file",
            "Error", JOptionPane.ERROR_MESSAGE );
      }

   }  // end method readRecords

   // uses record ty to determine if a record should be displayed
   private boolean shouldDisplay( double balance )
   {
      if ( accountType.equals( "Credit balances" ) &&
         balance < 0 )

         return true;

      else if ( accountType.equals( "Debit balances" ) &&
         balance > 0 )

         return true;

      else if ( accountType.equals( "Zero balances" ) &&
         balance == 0 )

         return true;

      return false;
   }

   // execute application
   public static void main( String args[] )
   {
      new CreditInquiry();
   }

   // private inner class for creditButton, debitButton and
   // zeroButton event handling
   private class ButtonHandler implements ActionListener {

      // read records from file
      public void actionPerformed( ActionEvent event )
      {
         accountType = event.getActionCommand();
         readRecords();
      }

   }  // end class ButtonHandler

}  // end class CreditInquiry
```

Fig. 16.9 Credit inquiry program (part 6 of 7).

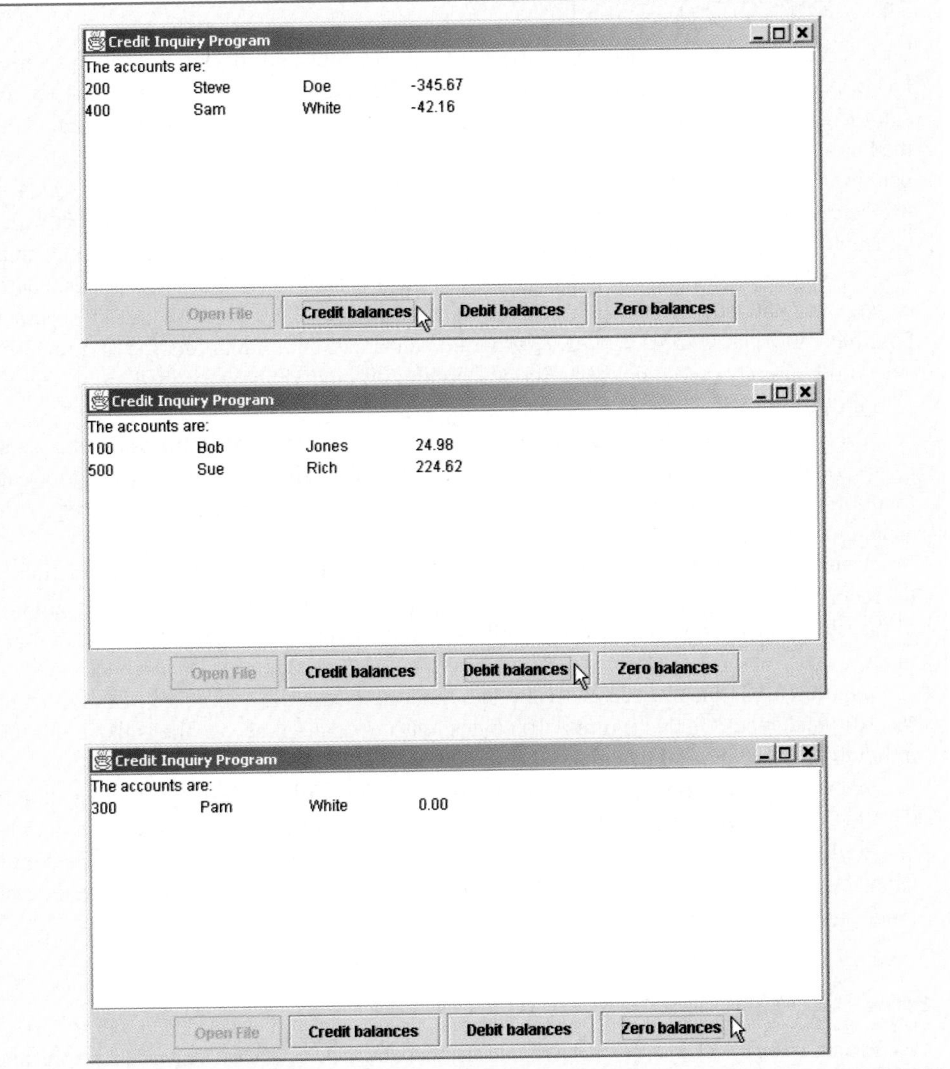

Fig. 16.9 Credit inquiry program (part 7 of 7).

16.6 Updating Sequential-Access Files

Data that is formatted and written to a sequential-access file as shown in Section 16.4 cannot be modified without reading and writing all the data in the file. For example, if the name **`White`** needed to be changed to **`Worthington`**, the old name cannot simply be overwritten. Such updating can be done, but it is awkward. To make the preceding name change, the records before **`White`** in a sequential-access file could be copied to a new file, the updated record would then be written to the new file, and the records after **`White`** would be copied to the new file. This requires processing every record in the file to update one record. If many records are being updated in one pass of the file, this technique can be acceptable.

16.7 Random-Access Files

So far, we have seen how to create sequential-access files and to search through them to locate particular information. Sequential-access files are inappropriate for so-called "*instant-access" applications*, in which a particular record of information must be located immediately. Some popular instant-access applications are airline reservation systems, banking systems, point-of-sale systems, automated-teller machines and other kinds of *transaction-processing systems* that require rapid access to specific data. The bank at which you have your account might have hundreds of thousands or even millions of other customers, yet, when you use an automated teller machine, the bank determines in seconds whether your account has sufficient funds for the transaction. This kind of instant access is possible with *random-access files*. A program can access individual records of a random-access file directly (and quickly) without searching through other records. Random-access files are sometimes called *direct-access files*.

As we have said, Java does not impose structure on a file, so an application that wants to use random-access files must create them. Several techniques can be used to create random-access files. Perhaps the simplest is to require that all records in a file be of the same fixed length.

Using fixed-length records makes it easy for a program to calculate (as a function of the record size and the record key) the exact location of any record relative to the beginning of the file. We will soon see how this facilitates immediate access to specific records, even in large files.

Figure 16.10 illustrates Java's view of a random-access file composed of fixed-length records (each record in this figure is 100 bytes long). A random-access file is like a railroad train with many cars—some empty, some with contents.

A program can insert data in a random-access file without destroying other data in the file. Also, a program can update or delete data stored previously without rewriting the entire file. In the following sections, we explain how to create a random-access file, enter data, read the data both sequentially and randomly, update the data and delete data no longer needed.

16.8 Creating a Random-Access File

`RandomAccessFile` objects have all the capabilities of **`DataInputStream`** and **`DataOutputStream`** objects discussed earlier. When a program associates an object of class **`RandomAccessFile`** with a file, the program reads or writes data beginning at the location in the file specified by the *file-position pointer* and manipulates all data as primitive data types. When writing an **`int`** value, 4 bytes are output to the file. When reading a **`double`** value, 8 bytes are input from the file. The size of the data types is guaranteed, because Java has fixed sizes for all primitive data types regardless of the computing platform.

Random-access file-processing programs rarely write a single field to a file. Normally, they write one object at a time, as we show in the following examples.

Consider the following problem statement:

> *Create a transaction-processing program capable of storing up to 100 fixed-length records for a company that can have up to 100 customers. Each record should consist of an account number that will be used as the record key, a last name, a first name and a balance. The program should be able to update an account, insert a new account and delete an account.*

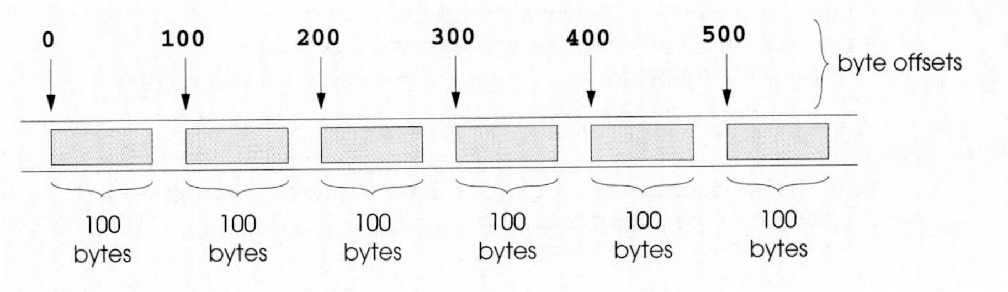

Fig. 16.10 Java's view of a random-access file.

The next several sections introduce the techniques necessary to create this credit-processing program. Figure 16.11 contains the **RandomAccessAccountRecord** class that is used by the next four programs for both reading records from and writing records to a file.

```
// Fig. 16.11: RandomAccessAccountRecord.java
// Subclass of AccountRecord for random access file programs.
package com.deitel.jhtp4.ch16;

// Java core packages
import java.io.*;

public class RandomAccessAccountRecord extends AccountRecord {

   // no-argument constructor calls other constructor
   // with default values
   public RandomAccessAccountRecord()
   {
      this( 0, "", "", 0.0 );
   }

   // initialize a RandomAccessAccountRecord
   public RandomAccessAccountRecord( int account,
      String firstName, String lastName, double balance )
   {
      super( account, firstName, lastName, balance );
   }

   // read a record from specified RandomAccessFile
   public void read( RandomAccessFile file ) throws IOException
   {
      setAccount( file.readInt() );
      setFirstName( padName( file ) );
      setLastName( padName( file ) );
      setBalance( file.readDouble() );
   }

```

Fig. 16.11 **RandomAccessAccountRecord** class used in the random-access file programs (part 1 of 2).

```java
   // ensure that name is proper length
   private String padName( RandomAccessFile file )
      throws IOException
   {
      char name[] = new char[ 15 ], temp;

      for ( int count = 0; count < name.length; count++ ) {
         temp = file.readChar();
         name[ count ] = temp;
      }

      return new String( name ).replace( '\0', ' ' );
   }

   // write a record to specified RandomAccessFile
   public void write( RandomAccessFile file ) throws IOException
   {
      file.writeInt( getAccount() );
      writeName( file, getFirstName() );
      writeName( file, getLastName() );
      file.writeDouble( getBalance() );
   }

   // write a name to file; maximum of 15 characters
   private void writeName( RandomAccessFile file, String name )
      throws IOException
   {
      StringBuffer buffer = null;

      if ( name != null )
         buffer = new StringBuffer( name );
      else
         buffer = new StringBuffer( 15 );

      buffer.setLength( 15 );
      file.writeChars( buffer.toString() );
   }

   // NOTE: This method contains a hard coded value for the
   // size of a record of information.
   public static int size()
   {
      return 72;
   }

}  // end class RandomAccessAccountRecord
```

Fig. 16.11 **RandomAccessAccountRecord** class used in the random-access file programs (part 2 of 2).

Class **RandomAccessAccountRecord** inherits **AccountRecord**'s (Fig. 16.5) implementation, which includes **private** instance variables—**account**, **lastName**, **firstName** and **balance**—as well as their **public** *set* and *get* methods.

Method **read** (lines 25–31) reads one record from the **RandomAccessFile** object passed as an argument. Methods ***readInt*** (line 27) and ***readDouble*** (line 30) read the **account** and **balance**, respectively. Method **read** calls **private** method **padName** (lines 34–45) twice to obtain the first and last names. Method **padName** reads fifteen characters from the **RandomAccessFile** and returns a **String**. If a name is shorter than 15 characters, the program fills each extra character with a null byte (**'\0'**). Swing components, such as **JTextField**s, cannot display null byte characters (which are displayed instead as rectangles). Line 44 solves this problem by replacing null bytes with spaces.

Method **write** (48–54) outputs one record to the **RandomAccessFile** object passed in as an argument. This method uses method ***writeInt*** to output the integer **account**, method ***writeChars*** (called from utility method **writeName**) to output the **firstName** and **lastName** character arrays and method ***writeDouble*** to output the **double balance**. [*Note*: In order to ensure that all records in the **RandomAccess-File** have the same size, we write exactly 15 characters for the first name and exactly 15 characters for the last name.] Method **writeName** (lines 57–69) performs the write operations for the first and last name.

Figure 16.12 illustrates opening a random-access file and writing data to the disk. This program writes 100 **RandomAccessAccountRecord**s, using method **write** (Fig. 16.11). Each **RandomAccessAccountRecord** object contains **0** for the account number, **null** for the last name, **null** for the first name and **0.0** for the balance. The file is initialized to create the proper amount of "empty" space in which the account data will be stored and to enable us to determine in subsequent programs whether each record is empty or contains data.

```
// Fig. 16.12: CreateRandomFile.java
// This program creates a random access file sequentially
// by writing 100 empty records to disk.

// Java core packages
import java.io.*;

// Java extension packages
import javax.swing.*;

// Deitel packages
import com.deitel.jhtp4.ch16.RandomAccessAccountRecord;

public class CreateRandomFile {

   // enable user to select file to open
   private void createFile()
   {
      // display dialog so user can choose file
      JFileChooser fileChooser = new JFileChooser();
      fileChooser.setFileSelectionMode(
         JFileChooser.FILES_ONLY );

      int result = fileChooser.showSaveDialog( null );
```

Fig. 16.12 Creating a random-access file sequentially (part 1 of 3).

```java

      // if user clicked Cancel button on dialog, return
      if ( result == JFileChooser.CANCEL_OPTION )
         return;

      // obtain selected file
      File fileName = fileChooser.getSelectedFile();

      // display error if file name invalid
      if ( fileName == null ||
           fileName.getName().equals( "" ) )
         JOptionPane.showMessageDialog( null,
            "Invalid File Name", "Invalid File Name",
            JOptionPane.ERROR_MESSAGE );

      else {

         // open file
         try {
            RandomAccessFile file =
               new RandomAccessFile( fileName, "rw" );

            RandomAccessAccountRecord blankRecord =
               new RandomAccessAccountRecord();

            // write 100 blank records
            for ( int count = 0; count < 100; count++ )
               blankRecord.write( file );

            // close file
            file.close();

            // display message that file was created
            JOptionPane.showMessageDialog( null,
               "Created file " + fileName, "Status",
               JOptionPane.INFORMATION_MESSAGE );

            System.exit( 0 );  // terminate program
         }

         // process exceptions during open, write or
         // close file operations
         catch ( IOException ioException ) {
            JOptionPane.showMessageDialog( null,
               "Error processing file", "Error processing file",
               JOptionPane.ERROR_MESSAGE );

            System.exit( 1 );
         }
      }

   }  // end method openFile

```

Fig. 16.12 Creating a random-access file sequentially (part 2 of 3).

```
78     // execute application to create file user specifies
79     public static void main( String args[] )
80     {
81        CreateRandomFile application = new CreateRandomFile();
82
83        application.createFile();
84     }
85
86  }  // end class CreateRandomFile
```

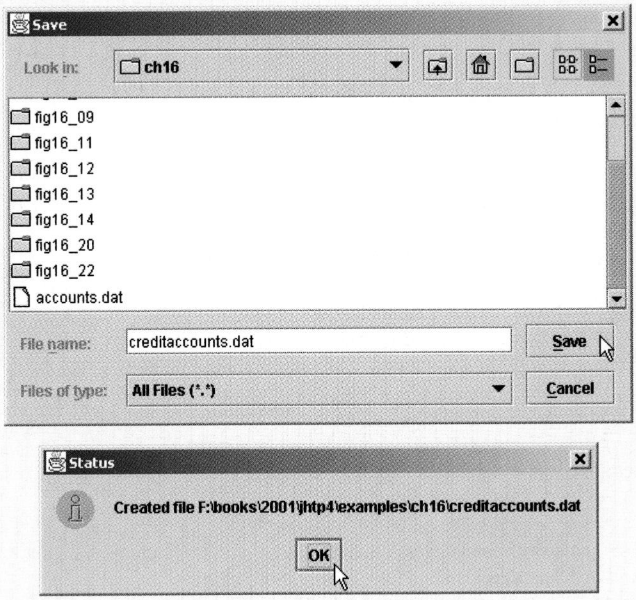

Fig. 16.12 Creating a random-access file sequentially (part 3 of 3).

Lines 44–45 attempt to open a **RandomAccessFile** for use in this program. The **RandomAccessFile** constructor receives two arguments—the file name and the *file open mode*. The file open mode for a **RandomAccessFile** is either **"r"** to open the file for reading or **"rw"** to open the file for reading and writing.

If an **IOException** occurs during the open process, the program displays a message dialog and terminates. If the file opens properly, the program uses a **for** structure (lines 51–52) to invoke **RandomAccessAccountRecord** method **write** 100 times. This statement causes the data members of object **blankRecord** to be written to the file associated with **RandomAccessFile** object **file**.

16.9 Writing Data Randomly to a Random-Access File

Figure 16.13 writes data to a file that is opened with the **"rw"** mode for reading and writing. It uses the **RandomAccessFile** method ***seek*** to determine the exact location in the file at which a record of information is stored. Method **seek** sets the file-position pointer to a specific position in the file relative to the beginning of the file, and the **RandomAccessAccountRecord** class method **write** outputs the data. This program assumes the user does not enter duplicate account numbers and that the user enters appropriate data in each **JTextField**.

```
// Fig. 16.13: WriteRandomFile.java
// This program uses textfields to get information from the
// user at the keyboard and writes the information to a
// random-access file.

// Java core packages
import java.awt.*;
import java.awt.event.*;
import java.io.*;

// Java extension packages
import javax.swing.*;

// Deitel packages
import com.deitel.jhtp4.ch16.*;

public class WriteRandomFile extends JFrame {
   private RandomAccessFile output;
   private BankUI userInterface;
   private JButton enterButton, openButton;

   // set up GUI
   public WriteRandomFile()
   {
      super( "Write to random access file" );

      // create instance of reusable user interface BankUI
      userInterface = new BankUI( 4 );  // four textfields
      getContentPane().add( userInterface,
         BorderLayout.CENTER );

      // get reference to generic task button doTask1 in BankUI
      openButton = userInterface.getDoTask1Button();
      openButton.setText( "Open..." );

      // register listener to call openFile when button pressed
      openButton.addActionListener(

         // anonymous inner class to handle openButton event
         new ActionListener() {

            // allow user to select file to open
            public void actionPerformed( ActionEvent event )
            {
               openFile();
            }

         }  // end anonymous inner class

      ); // end call to addActionListener
```

Fig. 16.13 Writing data randomly to a random-access file (part 1 of 5).

```

      // register window listener for window closing event
      addWindowListener(

         // anonymous inner class to handle windowClosing event
         new WindowAdapter() {

            // add record in GUI, then close file
            public void windowClosing( WindowEvent event )
            {
               if ( output != null )
                  addRecord();

               closeFile();
            }

         }  // end anonymous inner class

      ); // end call to addWindowListener

      // get reference to generic task button doTask2 in BankUI
      enterButton = userInterface.getDoTask2Button();
      enterButton.setText( "Enter" );
      enterButton.setEnabled( false );

      // register listener to call addRecord when button pressed
      enterButton.addActionListener(

         // anonymous inner class to handle enterButton event
         new ActionListener() {

            // add record to file
            public void actionPerformed( ActionEvent event )
            {
               addRecord();
            }

         }  // end anonymous inner class

      ); // end call to addActionListener

      setSize( 300, 150 );
      show();
   }

   // enable user to choose file to open
   private void openFile()
   {
      // display file dialog so user can select file
      JFileChooser fileChooser = new JFileChooser();
      fileChooser.setFileSelectionMode(
         JFileChooser.FILES_ONLY );

```

Fig. 16.13 Writing data randomly to a random-access file (part 2 of 5).

```
      int result = fileChooser.showOpenDialog( this );

      // if user clicked Cancel button on dialog, return
      if ( result == JFileChooser.CANCEL_OPTION )
         return;

      // obtain selected file
      File fileName = fileChooser.getSelectedFile();

      // display error if file name invalid
      if ( fileName == null ||
           fileName.getName().equals( "" ) )
         JOptionPane.showMessageDialog( this,
            "Invalid File Name", "Invalid File Name",
            JOptionPane.ERROR_MESSAGE );

      else {

         // open file
         try {
            output = new RandomAccessFile( fileName, "rw" );
            enterButton.setEnabled( true );
            openButton.setEnabled( false );
         }

         // process exception while opening file
         catch ( IOException ioException ) {
            JOptionPane.showMessageDialog( this,
               "File does not exist",
               "Invalid File Name",
               JOptionPane.ERROR_MESSAGE );
         }
      }

   }  // end method openFile

   // close file and terminate application
   private void closeFile()
   {
      // close file and exit
      try {
         if ( output != null )
            output.close();

         System.exit( 0 );
      }

      // process exception while closing file
      catch( IOException ioException ) {
         JOptionPane.showMessageDialog( this,
            "Error closing file",
            "Error", JOptionPane.ERROR_MESSAGE );

```

Fig. 16.13 Writing data randomly to a random-access file (part 3 of 5).

```
            System.exit( 1 );
        }
    }

    // add one record to file
    public void addRecord()
    {
        int accountNumber = 0;
        String fields[] = userInterface.getFieldValues();
        RandomAccessAccountRecord record =
            new RandomAccessAccountRecord();

        // ensure account field has a value
        if ( ! fields[ BankUI.ACCOUNT ].equals( "" ) ) {

            // output values to file
            try {
                accountNumber =
                    Integer.parseInt( fields[ BankUI.ACCOUNT ] );

                if ( accountNumber > 0 && accountNumber <= 100 ) {
                    record.setAccount( accountNumber );

                    record.setFirstName( fields[ BankUI.FIRSTNAME ] );
                    record.setLastName( fields[ BankUI.LASTNAME ] );
                    record.setBalance( Double.parseDouble(
                        fields[ BankUI.BALANCE ] ) );

                    output.seek( ( accountNumber - 1 ) *
                        RandomAccessAccountRecord.size() );
                    record.write( output );
                }

                userInterface.clearFields();  // clear TextFields
            }

            // process improper account number or balance format
            catch ( NumberFormatException formatException ) {
                    JOptionPane.showMessageDialog( this,
                        "Bad account number or balance",
                        "Invalid Number Format",
                        JOptionPane.ERROR_MESSAGE );
            }

            // process exceptions while writing to file
            catch ( IOException ioException ) {
                closeFile();
            }
        }

    } // end method addRecord

```

Fig. 16.13 Writing data randomly to a random-access file (part 4 of 5).

```
   // execute application
   public static void main( String args[] )
   {
      new WriteRandomFile();
   }

}  // end class WriteRandomFile
```

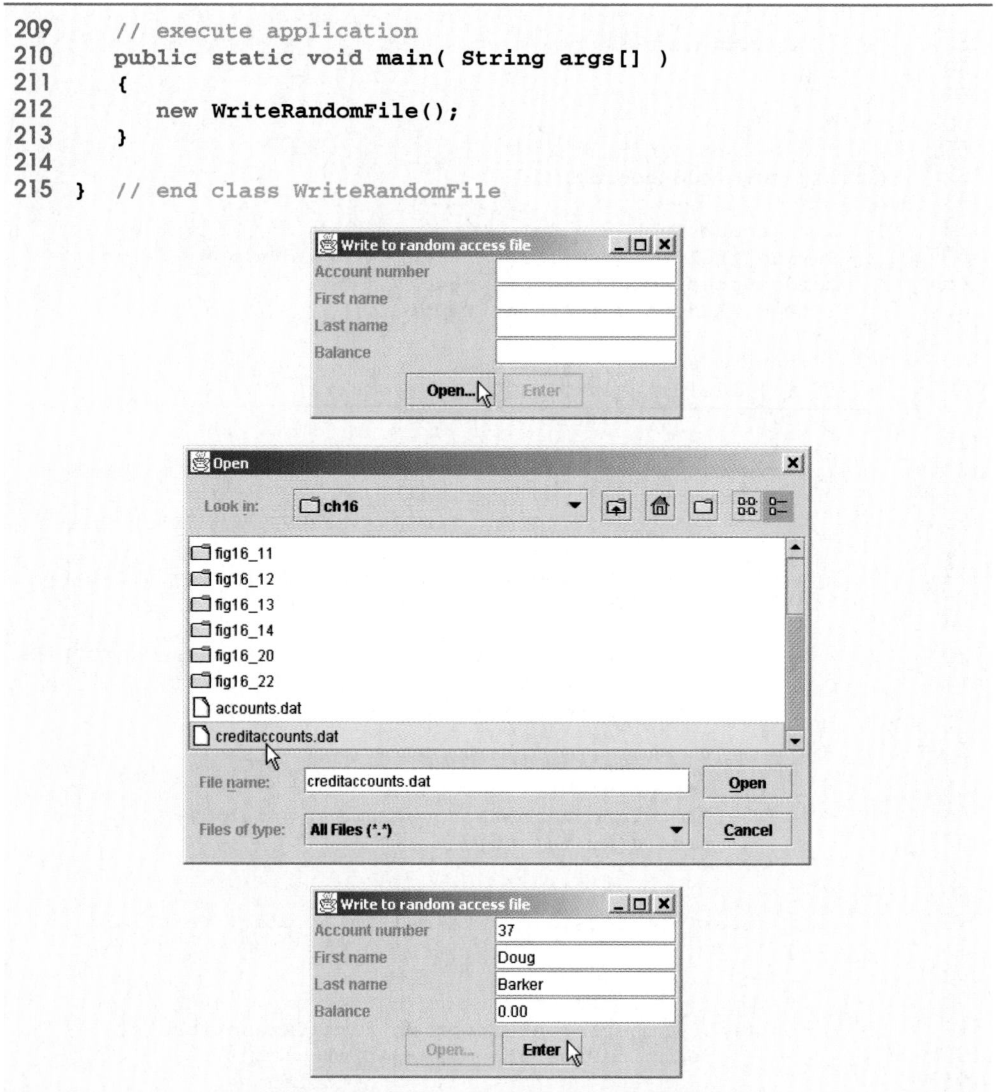

Fig. 16.13 Writing data randomly to a random-access file (part 5 of 5).

The user enters values for the account number, first name, last name and balance. When the user clicks the **Enter** button, the program calls method **addRecord** (162–207) of class **WriteRandomFile** to retrieve the data from the **BankAccountUI**'s **JTextFields**, store the data in **RandomAccessAccountRecord** class object **record** and call the **write** method of class **RandomAccessAccountRecord** to output the data.

Lines 185–186 call **RandomAccessFile** method ***seek*** to position the file-position pointer for object **output** to the byte location calculated by **(accountNumber - 1) * RandomAccessAccountRecord.size()**. Account numbers in this program should be between 1 and 100. We subtract 1 from the account number when calculating the byte location of the record. Thus, for record 1, the file-position pointer is set to byte 0 of the file.

When the user closes the window, the program attempts to add the last record to the file (if there is one in the GUI waiting to be output), closes the file and terminates.

16.10 Reading Data Sequentially from a Random-Access File

In the previous sections, we created a random-access file and wrote data to that file. In this section, we develop a program (Fig. 16.14) that opens a **RandomAccessFile** for reading with the **"r"** file open mode, reads through the file sequentially and displays only those records containing data. This program produces an additional benefit. See whether you can determine what it is; we will reveal it at the end of this section.

Good Programming Practice 16.1

Open a file with the **"r"** *file open mode for input if the contents of the file should not be modified. This prevents unintentional modification of the file's contents. This is another example of the principle of least privilege.*

```
// Fig. 16.14: ReadRandomFile.java
// This program reads a random-access file sequentially and
// displays the contents one record at a time in text fields.

// Java core packages
import java.awt.*;
import java.awt.event.*;
import java.io.*;
import java.text.DecimalFormat;

// Java extension packages
import javax.swing.*;

// Deitel packages
import com.deitel.jhtp4.ch16.*;

public class ReadRandomFile extends JFrame {
   private BankUI userInterface;
   private RandomAccessFile input;
   private JButton nextButton, openButton;

   // set up GUI
   public ReadRandomFile()
   {
      super( "Read Client File" );

      // create reusable user interface instance
      userInterface = new BankUI( 4 );  // four textfields
      getContentPane().add( userInterface );

      // configure generic doTask1 button from BankUI
      openButton = userInterface.getDoTask1Button();
      openButton.setText( "Open File for Reading..." );

```

Fig. 16.14 Reading a random-access file sequentially (part 1 of 5).

```
      // register listener to call openFile when button pressed
      openButton.addActionListener(

         // anonymous inner class to handle openButton event
         new ActionListener() {

            // enable user to select file to open
            public void actionPerformed( ActionEvent event )
            {
               openFile();
            }

         } // end anonymous inner class

      ); // end call to addActionListener

      // configure generic doTask2 button from BankUI
      nextButton = userInterface.getDoTask2Button();
      nextButton.setText( "Next" );
      nextButton.setEnabled( false );

      // register listener to call readRecord when button pressed
      nextButton.addActionListener(

         // anonymous inner class to handle nextButton event
         new ActionListener() {

            // read a record when user clicks nextButton
            public void actionPerformed( ActionEvent event )
            {
               readRecord();
            }

         } // end anonymous inner class

      ); // end call to addActionListener

      // register listener for window closing event
      addWindowListener(

         // anonymous inner class to handle windowClosing event
         new WindowAdapter() {

            // close file and terminate application
            public void windowClosing( WindowEvent event )
            {
               closeFile();
            }

         } // end anonymous inner class

      ); // end call to addWindowListener

```

Fig. 16.14 Reading a random-access file sequentially (part 2 of 5).

```
      setSize( 300, 150 );
      show();
   }

   // enable user to select file to open
   private void openFile()
   {
      // display file dialog so user can select file
      JFileChooser fileChooser = new JFileChooser();
      fileChooser.setFileSelectionMode(
         JFileChooser.FILES_ONLY );

      int result = fileChooser.showOpenDialog( this );

      // if user clicked Cancel button on dialog, return
      if ( result == JFileChooser.CANCEL_OPTION )
         return;

      // obtain selected file
      File fileName = fileChooser.getSelectedFile();

      // display error is file name invalid
      if ( fileName == null ||
           fileName.getName().equals( "" ) )
         JOptionPane.showMessageDialog( this,
            "Invalid File Name", "Invalid File Name",
            JOptionPane.ERROR_MESSAGE );

      else {

         // open file
         try {
            input = new RandomAccessFile( fileName, "r" );
            nextButton.setEnabled( true );
            openButton.setEnabled( false );
         }

         // catch exception while opening file
         catch ( IOException ioException ) {
            JOptionPane.showMessageDialog( this,
               "File does not exist", "Invalid File Name",
               JOptionPane.ERROR_MESSAGE );
         }
      }

   } // end method openFile

   // read one record
   public void readRecord()
   {
      DecimalFormat twoDigits = new DecimalFormat( "0.00" );
      RandomAccessAccountRecord record =
         new RandomAccessAccountRecord();
```

Fig. 16.14 Reading a random-access file sequentially (part 3 of 5).

```java

      // read a record and display
      try {

         do {
            record.read( input );
         } while ( record.getAccount() == 0 );

         String values[] = {
            String.valueOf( record.getAccount() ),
            record.getFirstName(),
            record.getLastName(),
            String.valueOf( record.getBalance() ) };
         userInterface.setFieldValues( values );
      }

      // close file when end-of-file reached
      catch ( EOFException eofException ) {
         JOptionPane.showMessageDialog( this, "No more records",
            "End-of-file reached",
            JOptionPane.INFORMATION_MESSAGE );
         closeFile();
      }

      // process exceptions from problem with file
      catch ( IOException ioException ) {
         JOptionPane.showMessageDialog( this,
            "Error Reading File", "Error",
            JOptionPane.ERROR_MESSAGE );

         System.exit( 1 );
      }

   }  // end method readRecord

   // close file and terminate application
   private void closeFile()
   {
      // close file and exit
      try {
         if ( input != null )
            input.close();

         System.exit( 0 );
      }

      // process exception closing file
      catch( IOException ioException ) {
         JOptionPane.showMessageDialog( this,
            "Error closing file",
            "Error", JOptionPane.ERROR_MESSAGE );

         System.exit( 1 );
```

Fig. 16.14 Reading a random-access file sequentially (part 4 of 5).

```
194          }
195       }
196
197       // execute application
198       public static void main( String args[] )
199       {
200          new ReadRandomFile();
201       }
202
203    }  // end class ReadRandomFile
```

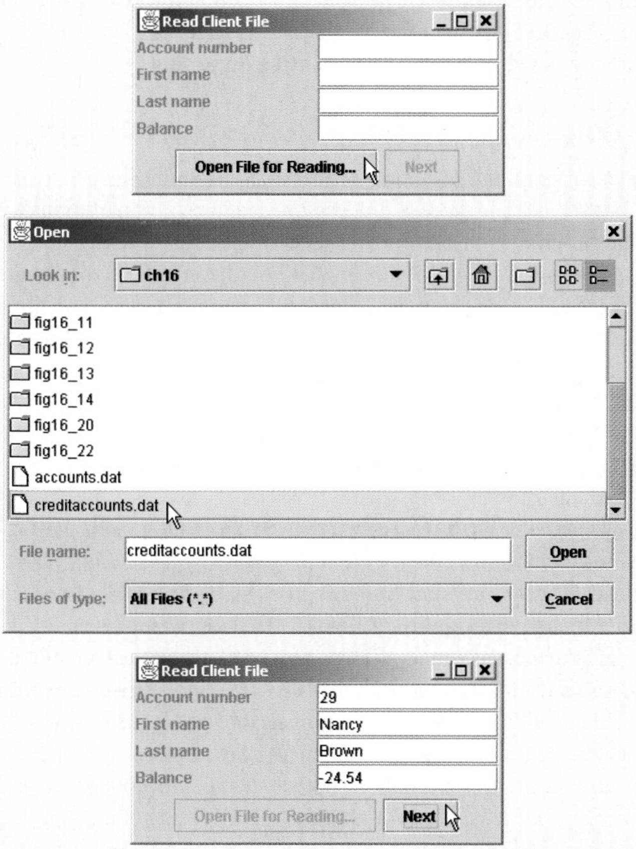

Fig. 16.14 Reading a random-access file sequentially (part 5 of 5).

When the user clicks the **Next** button to read the next record in the file, the program invokes class **ReadRandomFile**'s **readRecord** method (lines 136–174). This method invokes class **RandomAccessAccountRecord**'s **read** method (line 146) to read the data into **RandomAccessAccountRecord** class object **record**. Method **readRecord** reads from the file until it encounters a record with a nonzero account number (zero is the initial value for the account). When **readRecord** encounters a valid account number (i.e., a nonzero value), the loop terminates, and **readRecord** displays the record data in the text fields. When the user clicks the **Done** button or when the end-of-file marker is encountered while reading, method **closeFile** is invoked to close the file and terminate the program.

What about that additional benefit we promised? If you examine the GUI as the program executes, you will notice that the records are displayed in sorted order (by account number)! This is a simple consequence of the way we stored these records in the file, using direct-access techniques. Compared to the bubble sort we have seen (Chapter 7), sorting with direct-access techniques is blazingly fast. The speed is achieved by making the file large enough to hold every possible record that might be created, which enables the program to insert a record between other records without having to reorganize the file. This, of course, means that the file could be sparsely occupied most of the time, a waste of storage. So this is another example of the space/time trade-off. By using large amounts of space, we are able to develop a much faster sorting algorithm.

16.11 Example: A Transaction-Processing Program

We now present a substantial transaction-processing program (Fig. 16.20), using a random-access file to achieve "instant" access processing. The program maintains a bank's account information. The program updates existing accounts, adds new accounts and deletes accounts. We assume that the program of Fig. 16.12 has been executed to create a file and that the program of Fig. 16.13 has been executed to insert initial data. The techniques used in this example have been presented in the earlier **RandomAccessFile** examples.

This program GUI consists of a window with a menu bar containing a **File** menu and internal frames that enable the user to perform insert, update and delete record operations on the file. The internal frames are subclasses of **JInternalFrame** that are managed by a **JDesktopPane** (as discussed in Chapter 13). The **File** menu has five menu items to select various tasks, as shown in Fig. 16.15.

When the user selects **Update Record** from the **File** menu, the **Update Record** internal frame (Fig. 16.16) allows the user to update an existing account. The code that implements the **Update Record** internal frame is in class **UpdateDialog** (lines 238–458 of Fig. 16.20). In the first screen capture of Fig. 16.16, the user inputs an account number and presses *Enter* to invoke the account textfield's **actionPerformed** method (lines 345–360 of Fig. 16.20). This reads the account from the file with method **getRecord** (lines 371–418 of Fig. 16.20), which validates the account number, then reads the record with **RandomAccessAccountRecord** method **read**. Next, **getRecord** compares the account number with zero (i.e., no record) to determine whether the record contains information. If not, **getRecord** displays a message stating that the record does not exist; otherwise, it returns the record. Lines 350–357 of the account textfield's **actionPerformed** method extract the account information from the record and display the account information in the internal frame (as shown in the second screen capture of Fig. 16.16). The **Transaction amount** textfield initially contains the string **charge (+) or payment (–)**. The user should select this text and type the transaction amount (a positive value for a charge or a negative value for a payment), then press *Enter* to invoke the transaction textfield's **actionPerformed** method (lines 295–330 of Fig. 16.20). Method **addRecord** (lines 421–456 of Fig. 16.20) takes the transaction amount, adds it to the current balance and calls **RandomAccessAccountRecord** method **setBalance** to update the display. Clicking **Save Changes** writes the updated record to disk; clicking **Cancel** closes the internal frame without writing the record to disk. The windows in Fig. 16.17 show a sample of a transaction being input.

When the user selects **New Record** from the **File** menu, the **New Record** internal frame in Fig. 16.18 allows the user to add a new record. The code that implements the **New Record** internal frame is in class **`NewDialog`** (lines 461–615 of Fig. 16.20). The user enters data in the **`JTextField`**s and clicks **Save Changes** to write the record to disk. If the account number already exists, the program displays an error message and does not attempt to write the record. Clicking **Cancel** closes the internal frame without attempting to write the record.

Selecting **Delete Record** from the **File** menu displays the **Delete Record** internal frame in Fig. 16.19, which allows the user to delete a record from the file. The code that implements the **Delete Record** internal frame is in class **`DeleteDialog`** (lines 618–774 of Fig. 16.20). The user enters the account number in the **`JTextField`** and presses *Enter*. Only an existing record can be deleted, so, if the specified account is empty, the program displays an error message. This enables the user to check whether the record exists before deleting the record. Clicking the **Delete Record** button in the internal frame sets the record's account number to 0 (which this application considers to be an empty record). Clicking **Cancel** closes the internal frame without deleting the record.

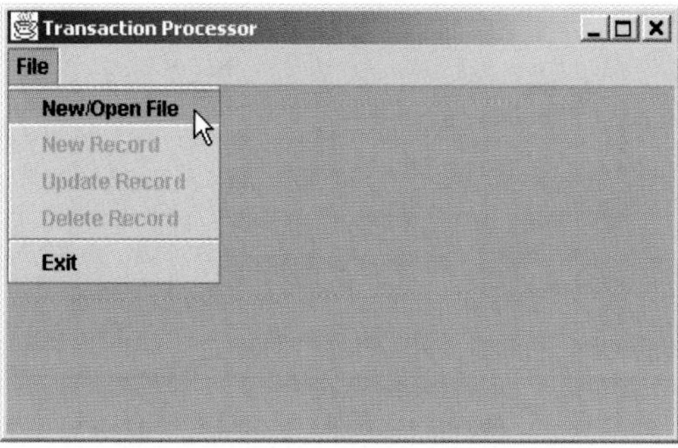

Fig. 16.15 The initial **Transaction Processor** window.

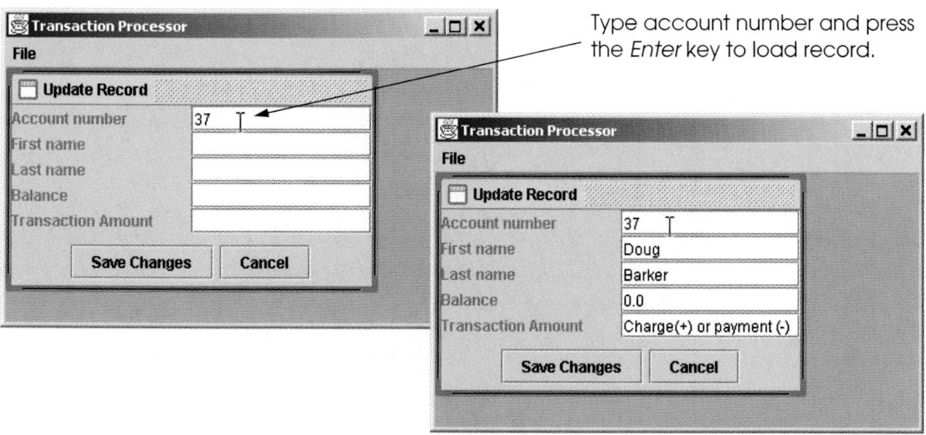

Fig. 16.16 Loading a record into the **Update Record** internal frame.

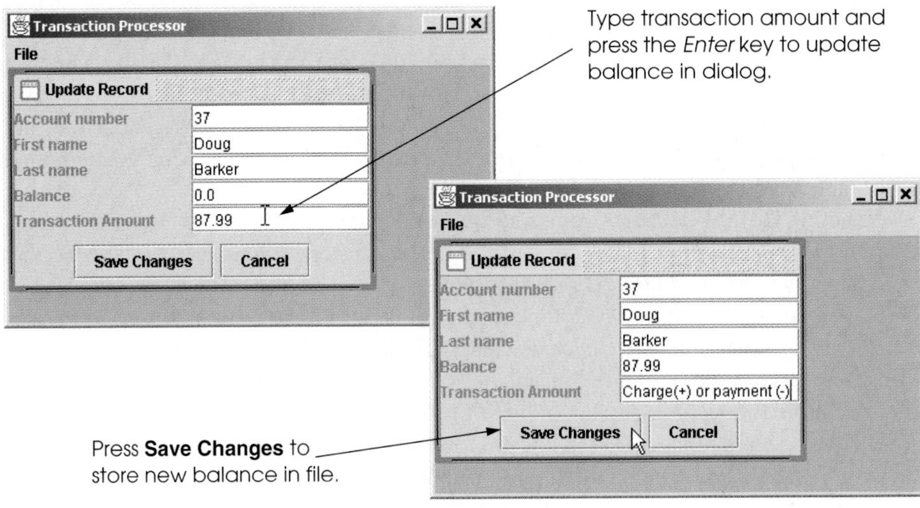

Fig. 16.17 Inputting a transaction in the **Update Record** internal frame.

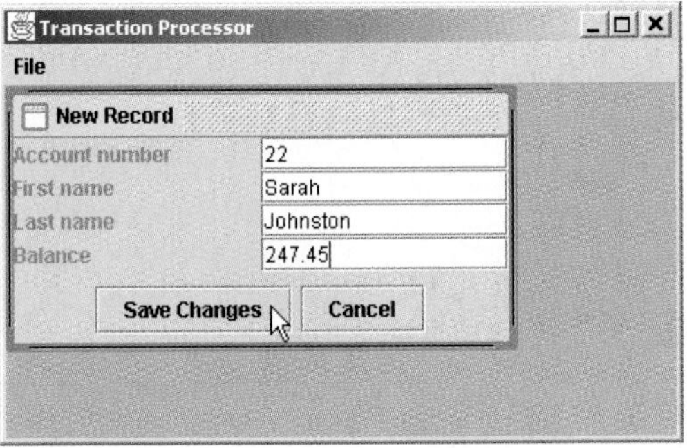

Fig. 16.18 **New Record** internal frame.

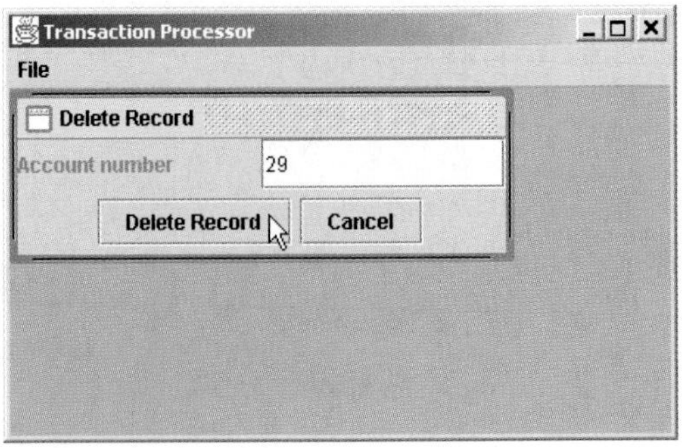

Fig. 16.19 **Delete Record** internal frame.

The **`TransactionProcessor`** program appears in Fig. 16.20. The program opens the file with file open mode **`"rw"`** (reading and writing).

```
// Transaction processing program using RandomAccessFiles.
// This program reads a random-access file sequentially,
// updates records already written to the file, creates new
// records to be placed in the file and deletes data
// already in the file.

// Java core packages
import java.awt.*;
import java.awt.event.*;
import java.io.*;
import java.text.DecimalFormat;

// Java extension packages
import javax.swing.*;

// Deitel packages
import com.deitel.jhtp4.ch16.*;

public class TransactionProcessor extends JFrame {
   private UpdateDialog updateDialog;
   private NewDialog newDialog;
   private DeleteDialog deleteDialog;
   private JMenuItem newItem, updateItem, deleteItem,
      openItem, exitItem;
   private JDesktopPane desktop;
   private RandomAccessFile file;
   private RandomAccessAccountRecord record;

   // set up GUI
   public TransactionProcessor()
   {
      super( "Transaction Processor" );

      // set up desktop, menu bar and File menu
      desktop = new JDesktopPane();
      getContentPane().add( desktop );

      JMenuBar menuBar = new JMenuBar();
      setJMenuBar( menuBar );

      JMenu fileMenu = new JMenu( "File" );
      menuBar.add( fileMenu );

      // set up menu item for adding a record
      newItem = new JMenuItem( "New Record" );
      newItem.setEnabled( false );

```

Fig. 16.20 Transaction-processing program (part 1 of 15).

```
      // display new record dialog when user selects New Record
      newItem.addActionListener(

         new ActionListener() {

            public void actionPerformed( ActionEvent event )
            {
               newDialog.setVisible( true );
            }
         }
      );

      // set up menu item for updating a record
      updateItem = new JMenuItem( "Update Record" );
      updateItem.setEnabled( false );

      // display update dialog when user selects Update Record
      updateItem.addActionListener(

         new ActionListener() {

            public void actionPerformed( ActionEvent event )
            {
               updateDialog.setVisible( true );
            }
         }
      );

      // set up menu item for deleting a record
      deleteItem = new JMenuItem( "Delete Record" );
      deleteItem.setEnabled( false );

      // display delete dialog when user selects Delete Record
      deleteItem.addActionListener(

         new ActionListener() {

            public void actionPerformed( ActionEvent event )
            {
               deleteDialog.setVisible( true );
            }
         }
      );

      // set up button for opening file
      openItem = new JMenuItem( "New/Open File" );

      // enable user to select file to open, then set up
      // dialog boxes
      openItem.addActionListener(

         new ActionListener() {

```

Fig. 16.20 Transaction-processing program (part 2 of 15).

```
            public void actionPerformed( ActionEvent event )
            {
               boolean opened = openFile();

               if ( !opened )
                  return;

               openItem.setEnabled( false );

               // set up internal frames for record processing
               updateDialog = new UpdateDialog( file );
               desktop.add( updateDialog );

               deleteDialog = new DeleteDialog( file );
               desktop.add ( deleteDialog );

               newDialog = new NewDialog( file );
               desktop.add( newDialog );
            }

         }  // end anonymous inner class

      ); // end call to addActionListener

      // set up menu item for exiting program
      exitItem = new JMenuItem( "Exit" );
      exitItem.setEnabled( true );

      // teminate application
      exitItem.addActionListener(

         new ActionListener() {

            public void actionPerformed( ActionEvent event )
            {
               closeFile();
            }
         }
      );

      // attach menu items to File menu
      fileMenu.add( openItem );
      fileMenu.add( newItem );
      fileMenu.add( updateItem );
      fileMenu.add( deleteItem );
      fileMenu.addSeparator();
      fileMenu.add( exitItem );

      // configure window
      setDefaultCloseOperation(
         WindowConstants.DO_NOTHING_ON_CLOSE );

      setSize( 400, 250  );
```

Fig. 16.20 Transaction-processing program (part 3 of 15).

```
      setVisible( true );

   } // end TransactionProcessor constructor

   // enable user to select file to open
   private boolean openFile()
   {
      // display dialog so user can select file
      JFileChooser fileChooser = new JFileChooser();
      fileChooser.setFileSelectionMode(
         JFileChooser.FILES_ONLY );

      int result = fileChooser.showOpenDialog( this );

      // if user clicked Cancel button on dialog, return
      if ( result == JFileChooser.CANCEL_OPTION )
         return false;

      // obtain selected file
      File fileName = fileChooser.getSelectedFile();

      // display error if file name invalid
      if ( fileName == null ||
           fileName.getName().equals( "" ) ) {
         JOptionPane.showMessageDialog( this,
            "Invalid File Name", "Invalid File Name",
            JOptionPane.ERROR_MESSAGE );

         return false;
      }

      else {

         // open file
         try {
            file = new RandomAccessFile( fileName, "rw" );
            openItem.setEnabled( false );
            newItem.setEnabled( true );
            updateItem.setEnabled( true );
            deleteItem.setEnabled( true );
         }

         // process problems opening file
         catch ( IOException ioException ) {
            JOptionPane.showMessageDialog( this,
               "File does not exist", "Invalid File Name",
               JOptionPane.ERROR_MESSAGE );

            return false;
         }
      }

      return true;  // file opened
```

Fig. 16.20 Transaction-processing program (part 4 of 15).

```
    }

    // close file and terminate application
    private void closeFile()
    {
       // close file and exit
       try {
          if ( file != null )
             file.close();

          System.exit( 0 );
       }

       // process exceptions closing file
       catch( IOException ioException ) {
          JOptionPane.showMessageDialog( this,
             "Error closing file",
             "Error", JOptionPane.ERROR_MESSAGE );
          System.exit( 1 );
       }
    }

    // execute application
    public static void main( String args[] )
    {
       new TransactionProcessor();
    }

} // end class TransactionProcessor

// class for udpating records
class UpdateDialog extends JInternalFrame {
    private RandomAccessFile file;
    private BankUI userInterface;

    // set up GUI
    public UpdateDialog( RandomAccessFile updateFile )
    {
       super( "Update Record" );

       file = updateFile;

       // set up GUI components
       userInterface = new BankUI( 5 );
       getContentPane().add( userInterface,
          BorderLayout.CENTER );

       // set up Save Changes button and register listener
       JButton saveButton = userInterface.getDoTask1Button();
       saveButton.setText( "Save Changes" );

       saveButton.addActionListener(

```

Fig. 16.20 Transaction-processing program (part 5 of 15).

```
            new ActionListener() {

               public void actionPerformed( ActionEvent event )
               {
                  addRecord( getRecord() );
                  setVisible( false );
                  userInterface.clearFields();
               }
            }
         );

         // set up Cancel button and register listener
         JButton cancelButton = userInterface.getDoTask2Button();
         cancelButton.setText( "Cancel" );

         cancelButton.addActionListener(

            new ActionListener() {

               public void actionPerformed( ActionEvent event )
               {
                  setVisible( false );
                  userInterface.clearFields();
               }
            }
         );

         // set up listener for transaction textfield
         JTextField transactionField =
            userInterface.getFields()[ BankUI.TRANSACTION ];

         transactionField.addActionListener(

            new ActionListener() {

               public void actionPerformed( ActionEvent event )
               {
                  // add transaction amount to balance
                  try {
                     RandomAccessAccountRecord record = getRecord();

                     // get textfield values from userInterface
                     String fieldValues[] =
                        userInterface.getFieldValues();

                     // get transaction amount
                     double change = Double.parseDouble(
                        fieldValues[ BankUI.TRANSACTION ] );

                     // specify Strings to display in GUI
                     String[] values = {
                        String.valueOf( record.getAccount() ),
                        record.getFirstName(),
```

Fig. 16.20 Transaction-processing program (part 6 of 15).

```
                        record.getLastName(),
                        String.valueOf( record.getBalance()
                           + change ),
                        "Charge(+) or payment (-)" };

                     // display Strings in GUI
                     userInterface.setFieldValues( values );
                  }

                  // process invalid number in transaction field
                  catch ( NumberFormatException numberFormat ) {
                     JOptionPane.showMessageDialog( null,
                        "Invalid Transaction",
                        "Invalid Number Format",
                        JOptionPane.ERROR_MESSAGE );
                  }

               } // end method actionPerformed

            } // end anonymous inner class

         ); // end call to addActionListener

         // set up listener for account text field
         JTextField accountField =
            userInterface.getFields()[ BankUI.ACCOUNT ];

         accountField.addActionListener(

            new ActionListener() {

               // get record and display contents in GUI
               public void actionPerformed( ActionEvent event )
               {
                  RandomAccessAccountRecord record = getRecord();

                  if ( record.getAccount() != 0 )  {
                     String values[] = {
                        String.valueOf( record.getAccount() ),
                        record.getFirstName(),
                        record.getLastName(),
                        String.valueOf( record.getBalance() ),
                        "Charge(+) or payment (-)" };

                     userInterface.setFieldValues( values );
                  }

               } // end method actionPerformed

            } // end anonymous inner class

         ); // end call to addActionListener

```

Fig. 16.20 Transaction-processing program (part 7 of 15).

```
      setSize( 300, 175 );
      setVisible( false );
   }

   // get record from file
   private RandomAccessAccountRecord getRecord()
   {
      RandomAccessAccountRecord record =
         new RandomAccessAccountRecord();

      // get record from file
      try {
         JTextField accountField =
            userInterface.getFields()[ BankUI.ACCOUNT ];

         int accountNumber =
            Integer.parseInt( accountField.getText() );

         if ( accountNumber < 1 || accountNumber > 100 ) {
            JOptionPane.showMessageDialog( this,
               "Account Does Not Exist",
               "Error", JOptionPane.ERROR_MESSAGE );
            return record;
         }

         // seek to appropriate record location in file
         file.seek( ( accountNumber - 1 ) *
            RandomAccessAccountRecord.size() );
         record.read( file );

         if ( record.getAccount() == 0 )
            JOptionPane.showMessageDialog( this,
               "Account Does Not Exist",
               "Error", JOptionPane.ERROR_MESSAGE );
      }

      // process invalid account number format
      catch ( NumberFormatException numberFormat ) {
         JOptionPane.showMessageDialog( this,
            "Invalid Account", "Invalid Number Format",
            JOptionPane.ERROR_MESSAGE );
      }

      // process file processing problems
      catch ( IOException ioException ) {
         JOptionPane.showMessageDialog( this,
            "Error Reading File",
            "Error", JOptionPane.ERROR_MESSAGE );
      }

      return record;

   } // end method getRecord
```

Fig. 16.20 Transaction-processing program (part 8 of 15).

```

   // add record to file
   public void addRecord( RandomAccessAccountRecord record )
   {
      // update record in file
      try {
         int accountNumber = record.getAccount();

         file.seek( ( accountNumber - 1 ) *
            RandomAccessAccountRecord.size() );

         String[] values = userInterface.getFieldValues();

         // set firstName, lastName and balance in record
         record.setFirstName( values[ BankUI.FIRSTNAME ] );
         record.setLastName( values[ BankUI.LASTNAME ] );
         record.setBalance(
            Double.parseDouble( values[ BankUI.BALANCE ]  ) );

         // rewrite record to file
         record.write( file );
      }

      // process file processing problems
      catch ( IOException ioException ) {
         JOptionPane.showMessageDialog( this,
            "Error Writing To File",
            "Error", JOptionPane.ERROR_MESSAGE );
      }

      // process invalid balance value
      catch ( NumberFormatException numberFormat ) {
         JOptionPane.showMessageDialog( this,
         "Bad Balance", "Invalid Number Format",
         JOptionPane.ERROR_MESSAGE );
      }

   }  // end method addRecord

}  // end class UpdateDialog

// class for creating new records
class NewDialog extends JInternalFrame {
   private RandomAccessFile file;
   private BankUI userInterface;

   // set up GUI
   public NewDialog( RandomAccessFile newFile )
   {
      super( "New Record" );

      file = newFile;

```

Fig. 16.20 Transaction-processing program (part 9 of 15).

```
         // attach user interface to dialog
         userInterface = new BankUI( 4 );
         getContentPane().add( userInterface,
            BorderLayout.CENTER );

         // set up Save Changes button and register listener
         JButton saveButton = userInterface.getDoTask1Button();
         saveButton.setText( "Save Changes" );

         saveButton.addActionListener(

            new ActionListener() {

               // add new record to file
               public void actionPerformed( ActionEvent event )
               {
                  addRecord( getRecord() );
                  setVisible( false );
                  userInterface.clearFields();
               }

            }  // end anonymous inner class

         ); // end call to addActionListener

         JButton cancelButton = userInterface.getDoTask2Button();
         cancelButton.setText( "Cancel" );

         cancelButton.addActionListener(

            new ActionListener() {

               // dismiss dialog without storing new record
               public void actionPerformed( ActionEvent event )
               {
                 setVisible( false );
                 userInterface.clearFields();
               }

            }  // end anonymous inner class

         ); // end call to addActionListener

         setSize( 300, 150 );
         setVisible( false );

      }  // end constructor

      // get record from file
      private RandomAccessAccountRecord getRecord()
      {
         RandomAccessAccountRecord record =
            new RandomAccessAccountRecord();
```

Fig. 16.20 Transaction-processing program (part 10 of 15).

```

      // get record from file
      try {
         JTextField accountField =
            userInterface.getFields()[ BankUI.ACCOUNT ];

         int accountNumber =
            Integer.parseInt( accountField.getText() );

         if ( accountNumber < 1 || accountNumber > 100 ) {
            JOptionPane.showMessageDialog( this,
               "Account Does Not Exist",
               "Error", JOptionPane.ERROR_MESSAGE );
            return record;
         }

         // seek to record location
         file.seek( ( accountNumber - 1 ) *
            RandomAccessAccountRecord.size() );

         // read record from file
         record.read( file );
      }

      // process invalid account number format
      catch ( NumberFormatException numberFormat ) {
         JOptionPane.showMessageDialog( this,
            "Account Does Not Exist", "Invalid Number Format",
            JOptionPane.ERROR_MESSAGE );
      }

      // process file processing problems
      catch ( IOException ioException ) {
         JOptionPane.showMessageDialog( this,
            "Error Reading File",
            "Error", JOptionPane.ERROR_MESSAGE );
      }

      return record;

   }  // end method getRecord

   // add record to file
   public void addRecord( RandomAccessAccountRecord record )
   {
      String[] fields = userInterface.getFieldValues();

      if ( record.getAccount() != 0 ) {
         JOptionPane.showMessageDialog( this,
            "Record Already Exists",
            "Error", JOptionPane.ERROR_MESSAGE );
         return;
      }
```

Fig. 16.20 Transaction-processing program (part 11 of 15).

```java

      // output the values to the file
      try {

         // set account, first name, last name and balance
         // for record
         record.setAccount( Integer.parseInt(
            fields[ BankUI.ACCOUNT ] ) );
         record.setFirstName( fields[ BankUI.FIRSTNAME ] );
         record.setLastName( fields[ BankUI.LASTNAME ] );
         record.setBalance( Double.parseDouble(
            fields[ BankUI.BALANCE ] ) );

         // seek to record location
         file.seek( ( record.getAccount() - 1 ) *
            RandomAccessAccountRecord.size() );

         // write record
         record.write( file );
      }

      // process invalid account or balance format
      catch ( NumberFormatException numberFormat ) {
         JOptionPane.showMessageDialog( this,
            "Invalid Balance", "Invalid Number Format",
            JOptionPane.ERROR_MESSAGE );
      }

      // process file processing problems
      catch ( IOException ioException ) {
         JOptionPane.showMessageDialog( this,
            "Error Writing To File",
            "Error", JOptionPane.ERROR_MESSAGE );
      }

   }  // end method addRecord

}  // end class NewDialog

// class for deleting records
class DeleteDialog extends JInternalFrame {
   private RandomAccessFile file;  // file for output
   private BankUI userInterface;

   // set up GUI
   public DeleteDialog( RandomAccessFile deleteFile )
   {
      super( "Delete Record" );

      file = deleteFile;

      // create BankUI with only account field
      userInterface = new BankUI( 1 );
```

Fig. 16.20 Transaction-processing program (part 12 of 15).

```

      getContentPane().add( userInterface,
         BorderLayout.CENTER );

      // set up Delete Record button and register listener
      JButton deleteButton = userInterface.getDoTask1Button();
      deleteButton.setText( "Delete Record" );

      deleteButton.addActionListener(

         new ActionListener() {

            // overwrite existing record
            public void actionPerformed( ActionEvent event )
            {
               addRecord( getRecord() );
               setVisible( false );
               userInterface.clearFields();
            }

         }  // end anonymous inner class

      ); // end call to addActionListener

      // set up Cancel button and register listener
      JButton cancelButton = userInterface.getDoTask2Button();
      cancelButton.setText( "Cancel" );

      cancelButton.addActionListener(

         new ActionListener() {

            // cancel delete operation by hiding dialog
            public void actionPerformed( ActionEvent event )
            {
               setVisible( false );
            }

         }  // end anonymous inner class

      ); // end call to addActionListener

      // set up listener for account text field
      JTextField accountField =
         userInterface.getFields()[ BankUI.ACCOUNT ];

      accountField.addActionListener(

         new ActionListener() {

            public void actionPerformed( ActionEvent event )
            {
               RandomAccessAccountRecord record = getRecord();
```

Fig. 16.20 Transaction-processing program (part 13 of 15).

```
         }

      }  // end anonymous inner class

   ); // end call to addActionListener

   setSize( 300, 100 );
   setVisible( false );

}  // end constructor

// get record from file
private RandomAccessAccountRecord getRecord()
{
   RandomAccessAccountRecord record =
      new RandomAccessAccountRecord();

   // get record from file
   try {
      JTextField accountField =
         userInterface.getFields()[ BankUI.ACCOUNT ];

      int accountNumber =
         Integer.parseInt( accountField.getText() );

      if ( accountNumber < 1 || accountNumber > 100 ) {
         JOptionPane.showMessageDialog( this,
            "Account Does Not Exist",
            "Error", JOptionPane.ERROR_MESSAGE );
         return( record );
      }

      // seek to record location and read record
      file.seek( ( accountNumber - 1 ) *
         RandomAccessAccountRecord.size() );
      record.read( file );

      if ( record.getAccount() == 0 )
         JOptionPane.showMessageDialog( this,
            "Account Does Not Exist",
            "Error", JOptionPane.ERROR_MESSAGE );
   }

   // process invalid account number format
   catch ( NumberFormatException numberFormat ) {
      JOptionPane.showMessageDialog( this,
         "Account Does Not Exist",
         "Invalid Number Format",
         JOptionPane.ERROR_MESSAGE );
   }

   // process file processing problems
   catch ( IOException ioException ) {
```

Fig. 16.20 Transaction-processing program (part 14 of 15).

```
         JOptionPane.showMessageDialog( this,
            "Error Reading File",
            "Error", JOptionPane.ERROR_MESSAGE );
      }

      return record;

   } // end method getRecord

   // add record to file
   public void addRecord( RandomAccessAccountRecord record )
   {
      if ( record.getAccount() == 0 )
         return;

      // delete record by setting account number to 0
      try {
         int accountNumber = record.getAccount();

         // seek to record position
         file.seek( ( accountNumber - 1 ) *
            RandomAccessAccountRecord.size() );

         // set account to 0 and overwrite record
         record.setAccount( 0 );
         record.write( file );
      }

      // process file processing problems
      catch ( IOException ioException ) {
         JOptionPane.showMessageDialog( this,
            "Error Writing To File",
            "Error", JOptionPane.ERROR_MESSAGE );
      }

   } // end method addRecord

} // end class DeleteDialog
```

Fig. 16.20 Transaction-processing program (part 15 of 15).

16.12 Class `File`

As we stated at the beginning of this chapter, the **`java.io`** package contains an abundance of classes for processing input and output. We concentrated on the classes for processing sequential files (**`FileInputStream`** and **`FileOutputStream`**), for processing object streams (**`ObjectInputStream`** and **`ObjectOutputStream`**) and for processing random-access files (**`RandomAccessFile`**). In this section, we discuss class **`File`**, which is particularly useful for retrieving information about a file or a directory from a disk. Objects of class **`File`** do not open files or provide any file-processing capabilities.

One application of a **`File`** object is to determine whether a file exists before attempting to open the file. In *Common Programming Error 16.1*, we warned that opening an existing file for output by using a **`FileOutputStream`** object discards the contents of that file *without warning*. If a program using a **File** determines that a file already exists, the program can warn that the user is about to discard the original file's contents.

Good Programming Practice 16.2

Use a **File** *object to determine whether a file exists before opening the file with a* **File-OutputStream** *object.*

Class **File** provides three constructors. The constructor

```
public File( String name )
```

stores the **String** argument **name** in the object. The **name** can contain *path information* as well as a file or directory name. A file or directory's path specifies the location of the file or directory on disk. The path includes some or all of the directories leading to the file or directory. An *absolute path* contains all the directories, starting with the *root directory* that lead to a specific file or directory. Every file or directory on a particular disk drive has the same root directory in its path. A *relative path* contains a subset of the directories leading to a specific file or directory. Relative paths normally start from the directory in which the application began executing.

The constructor

```
public File( String pathToName, String name )
```

uses argument **pathToName** (an absolute or relative path) to locate the file or directory specified by **name**.

The constructor

```
public File( File directory, String name )
```

uses an existing **File** object **directory** (an absolute or relative path) to locate the file or directory specified by **name**.

Figure 16.21 discusses some common **File** methods. See the Java API for other **File** methods.

Method	Description
`boolean canRead()`	Returns **true** if a file is readable; **false** otherwise.
`boolean canWrite()`	Returns **true** if a file is writable; **false** otherwise.
`boolean exists()`	Returns **true** if the name specified as the argument to the **File** constructor is a file or directory in the specified path; **false** otherwise.
`boolean isFile()`	Returns **true** if the name specified as the argument to the **File** constructor is a file; **false** otherwise.
`boolean isDirectory()`	Returns **true** if the name specified as the argument to the **File** constructor is a directory; **false** otherwise.
`boolean isAbsolute()`	Returns **true** if the arguments specified to the **File** constructor indicate an absolute path to a file or directory; **false** otherwise.

Fig. 16.21 Some commonly used **File** methods (part 1 of 2).

Method	Description
`String getAbsolutePath()`	Returns a **`String`** with the absolute path of the file or directory.
`String getName()`	Returns a **`String`** with the name of the file or directory.
`String getPath()`	Returns a **`String`** with the path of the file or directory.
`String getParent()`	Returns a **`String`** with the parent directory of the file or directory—that is, the directory in which the file or directory can be found.
`long length()`	Returns the length of the file in bytes. If the **`File`** object represents a directory, **`0`** is returned.
`long lastModified()`	Returns a platform-dependent representation of the time at which the file or directory was last modified. The value returned is only useful for comparison with other values returned by this method.
`String[] list()`	Returns an array of **`String`**s representing the contents of a directory.

Fig. 16.21 Some commonly used **`File`** methods (part 2 of 2).

Good Programming Practice 16.3

*Use **`File`** method **`isFile`** to determine that a **`File`** object represents a file (not a directory) before attempting to open a file.*

Good Programming Practice 16.4

*Before attempting to open a file for reading, use **`File`** method **`canRead`** to determine whether the file is readable.*

Good Programming Practice 16.5

*Before attempting to open a file for writing, use **`File`** method **`canWrite`** to determine whether the file is writable.*

Figure 16.22 demonstrates class **`File`**. The **`FileTest`** application creates a GUI containing a **`JTextField`** for entering a file name or directory name and a **`JTextArea`** for displaying information about the file name or directory name input.

```
// Fig. 16.22: FileTest.java
// Demonstrating the File class.

// Java core packages
import java.awt.*;
import java.awt.event.*;
import java.io.*;

```

Fig. 16.22 Demonstrating class **`File`** (part 1 of 4).

```
// Java extension packages
import javax.swing.*;

public class FileTest extends JFrame
   implements ActionListener {

   private JTextField enterField;
   private JTextArea outputArea;

   // set up GUI
   public FileTest()
   {
      super( "Testing class File" );

      enterField = new JTextField(
         "Enter file or directory name here" );
      enterField.addActionListener( this );
      outputArea = new JTextArea();

      ScrollPane scrollPane = new ScrollPane();
      scrollPane.add( outputArea );

      Container container = getContentPane();
      container.add( enterField, BorderLayout.NORTH );
      container.add( scrollPane, BorderLayout.CENTER );

      setSize( 400, 400 );
      show();
   }

   // display information about file user specifies
   public void actionPerformed( ActionEvent actionEvent )
   {
      File name = new File( actionEvent.getActionCommand() );

      // if name exists, output information about it
      if ( name.exists() ) {
         outputArea.setText(
            name.getName() + " exists\n" +
            ( name.isFile() ?
               "is a file\n" : "is not a file\n" ) +
            ( name.isDirectory() ?
               "is a directory\n" : "is not a directory\n" ) +
            ( name.isAbsolute() ? "is absolute path\n" :
               "is not absolute path\n" ) +
            "Last modified: " + name.lastModified() +
            "\nLength: " + name.length() +
            "\nPath: " + name.getPath() +
            "\nAbsolute path: " + name.getAbsolutePath() +
            "\nParent: " + name.getParent() );

         // output information if name is a file
         if ( name.isFile() ) {
```

Fig. 16.22 Demonstrating class **File** (part 2 of 4).

```java

         // append contents of file to outputArea
         try {
            BufferedReader input = new BufferedReader(
               new FileReader( name ) );
            StringBuffer buffer = new StringBuffer();
            String text;
            outputArea.append( "\n\n" );

            while ( ( text = input.readLine() ) != null )
               buffer.append( text + "\n" );

            outputArea.append( buffer.toString() );
         }

         // process file processing problems
         catch( IOException ioException ) {
            JOptionPane.showMessageDialog( this,
               "FILE ERROR",
               "FILE ERROR", JOptionPane.ERROR_MESSAGE );
         }
      }

      // output directory listing
      else if ( name.isDirectory() ) {
         String directory[] = name.list();

         outputArea.append( "\n\nDirectory contents:\n");

         for ( int i = 0; i < directory.length; i++ )
            outputArea.append( directory[ i ] + "\n" );
      }
   }

   // not file or directory, output error message
   else {
      JOptionPane.showMessageDialog( this,
         actionEvent.getActionCommand() + " Does Not Exist",
         "ERROR", JOptionPane.ERROR_MESSAGE );
   }

} // end method actionPerformed

// execute application
public static void main( String args[] )
{
   FileTest application = new FileTest();

   application.setDefaultCloseOperation(
      JFrame.EXIT_ON_CLOSE );
}

} // end class FileTest
```

Fig. 16.22 Demonstrating class **File** (part 3 of 4).

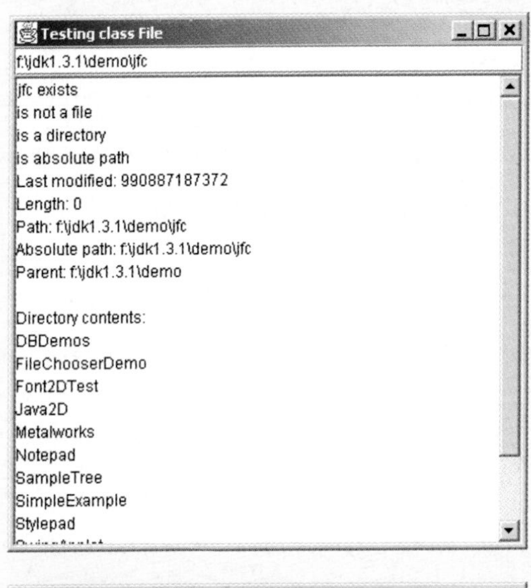

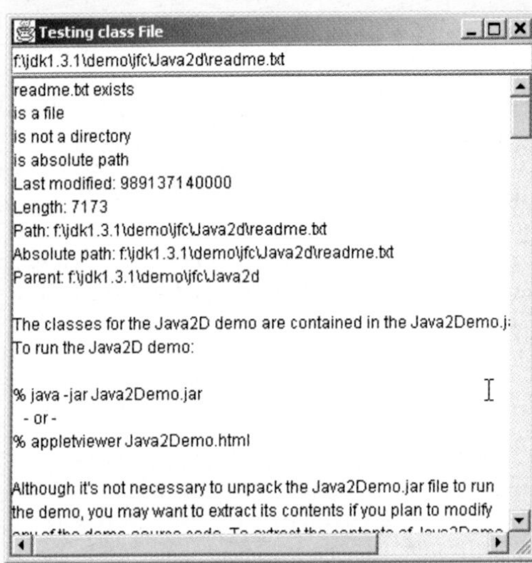

Fig. 16.22 Demonstrating class **File** (part 4 of 4).

The user types a file name or directory name into the text field and presses the *Enter* key to invoke method **actionPerformed** (lines 40–103), which creates a new **File** object (line 42) and assigns it to **name**. Line 45 invokes **File** method **exists** to determine whether the name input by the user exists (either as a file or as a directory) on the disk. If the name input by the user does not exist, the **actionPerformed** method proceeds to lines 97–101 and displays a message dialog containing the name the user typed, followed by "**Does Not Exist**." Otherwise, the body of the **if** structure (lines 45–94) executes. The program outputs the name of the file or directory, then outputs the results of testing the **File** object with **isFile** (line 48), **isDirectory** (line 50) and **isAbsolute** (line 52). Next, the program displays the values returned by **lastModified** (line 54),

length (line 55), **getPath** (line 56), **getAbsolutePath** (line 57) and **getParent** (line 58).

If the **File** object represents a file (line 61), the program reads the contents of the file and displays the contents in the **JTextArea**. The program uses a **BufferedReader** object chained to a **FileReader** object (lines 65–66) to open the file for reading and to read the file one line at a time with method **readLine** (line 71). Note that the **FileReader** object was initialized with the **File** object **name** (line 66).

If the **File** object represents a directory (line 86), the program reads the contents of the directory into the program by using **File** method **list**, then displays the directory contents in the **JTextArea**.

The first output demonstrates a **File** object associated with the **jfc** directory from the Java 2 Software Development Kit. The second output of this program demonstrates a **File** object associated with the **readme.txt** file from the Java 2 Software Development Kit. In both cases, we specified an absolute path on our personal computer.

Note that the **** *separator character* is used to separate directories and files in the path. On a UNIX workstation, the separator character would be the **/** character. Java processes both characters identically in a path name. So, if we specified the path

```
c:\java/readme.txt
```

which uses one of each separator character, Java still processes the file properly.

Common Programming Error 16.2

Using **** *as a directory separator rather than* **** *in a string literal is a logic error. A single* **** *indicates that the* **** *and the next character represent an escape sequence. To insert a* **** *in a string literal, you must use* ****.

Good Programming Practice 16.6

When building ***String****s that represent path information, use* ***File.separatorChar*** *to obtain the local computer's proper separator character, rather than explicitly using* **/** *or* ****.

SUMMARY

- All data items processed by a computer are reduced to combinations of zeros and ones.
- The smallest data item in a computer (a bit) can assume the value **0** or the value **1**.
- Digits, letters and special symbols are called characters. The set of all characters used to write programs and represent data items on a particular computer is called that computer's character set. Every character in a computer's character set is represented as a pattern of **1**s and **0**s. (Characters in Java are Unicode characters composed of 2 bytes.)
- A field is a group of characters (or bytes) that conveys meaning.
- A record is a group of related fields.
- At least one field in a record is chosen as a record key to identify a record as belonging to a particular person or entity that is unique from all other records in the file.
- Java imposes no structure on a file. Notions like "record" do not exist in Java. The programmer must structure a file appropriately to meet the requirements of an application.
- A collection of programs designed to create and manage databases is called a database management system (DBMS).
- Java views each file as a sequential stream of bytes.

- Each file ends in some machine-dependent form of end-of-file marker.
- Streams provide communication channels between programs and files, memory or other programs across a network.
- Programs use classes from package **java.io** to perform Java file I/O. This package includes the definitions for the stream classes, such as **FileInputStream**, **FileOutputStream**, **DataInputStream** and **DataOutputStream**.
- Files are opened by instantiating objects of stream classes **FileInputStream**, **FileOutputStream**, **RandomAccessFile**, **FileReader** and **FileWriter**.
- **InputStream** (a subclass of **Object**) and **OutputStream** (a subclass of **Object**) are **abstract** classes that define methods for performing input and output, respectively.
- File input/output is done with **FileInputStream** (a subclass of **InputStream**) and **FileOutputStream** (a subclass of **OutputStream**).
- Pipes are synchronized communication channels between threads. A pipe is established between two threads. One thread sends data to another by writing to a **PipedOutputStream** (a subclass of **OutputStream)**. The target thread reads information from the pipe via a **PipedInputStream** (a subclass of **InputStream**).
- A **PrintStream** (a subclass of **FilterOutputStream**) performs output to the screen (or the "standard output" as defined by your local operating system). **System.out** is a **PrintStream** (as is **System.err**).
- A **FilterInputStream** filters an **InputStream**; a **FilterOutStream** filters an **OutputStream**. Filtering means simply that the filter stream provides additional functionality, such as buffering, monitoring of line numbers or aggregating of data bytes into meaningful primitive-data-type units.
- Reading data as raw bytes is fast but crude. Usually, programs read data as aggregates of bytes that form an **int**, a **float**, a **double**, and so on. To accomplish this, we use a **DataInputStream** (a subclass of class **FilterInputStream**).
- Interface **DataInput** is implemented by class **DataInputStream** and class **RandomAccessFile**; each needs to read primitive data types from a stream.
- **DataInputStream**s enable a program to read binary data from an **InputStream**.
- The **DataInput** interface includes methods **read** (for **byte** arrays), **readBoolean**, **readByte**, **readChar**, **readDouble**, **readFloat**, **readFully** (for **byte** arrays), **readInt**, **readLine**, **readLong**, **readShort**, **readUnsignedByte**, **readUnsignedShort**, **readUTF** (for Unicode) and **skipBytes**.
- The **DataOutput** interface is implemented by class **DataOutputStream** (a subclass of class **FilterOutputStream**) and class **RandomAccessFile**; each needs to write primitive data types to an **OutputStream**.
- **DataOutputStream**s enable a program to write binary data to an **OutputStream**. The **DataOutput** interface includes methods **flush**, **size**, **write** (for a byte), **write** (for a **byte** array), **writeBoolean**, **writeByte**, **writeBytes**, **writeChar**, **writeChars** (for Unicode **String**s), **writeDouble**, **writeFloat**, **writeInt**, **writeLong**, **writeShort** and **writeUTF**.
- Buffering is an I/O-performance-enhancement technique.
- With a **BufferedOutputStream** (a subclass of class **FilterOutputStream**), each output statement does not necessarily result in an actual physical transfer of data to the output device. Rather, each output operation is directed to a region in memory called a buffer that is large enough to hold the data of many output operations. Then, actual output to the output device is performed

in one large physical output operation each time the buffer fills. The output operations directed to the output buffer in memory are often called logical output operations.

- With a **BufferedInputStream**, many "logical" chunks of data from a file are read as one large physical input operation into a memory buffer. As a program requests each new chunk of data, it is taken from the buffer (this is sometimes referred to as a logical input operation). When the buffer is empty, the next physical input operation from the input device is performed to read in the next group of "logical" chunks of data. Thus, the number of physical input operations is small compared with the number of read requests issued by the program.
- With a **BufferedOutputStream** a partially filled buffer can be forced out to the device at any time with an explicit **flush**.
- The **ObjectInput** interface is similar to the **DataInput** interface, but includes additional methods to read **Object**s from **InputStream**s.
- The **ObjectOutput** interface is similar to the **DataOutput** interface, but includes additional methods to write **Object**s to **OutputStream**s.
- The **ObjectInputStream** and **ObjectOutputStream** classes implement the **ObjectInput** and **ObjectOutput** interfaces, respectively.
- A **PushbackInputStream** is a subclass of class **FilterInputStream**. The application reading a **PushbackInputStream** reads bytes from the stream and forms aggregates consisting of several bytes. Sometimes, to determine that one aggregate is complete, the application must read the first character "past the end" of the first aggregate. Once the program has determined that the current aggregate is complete, the extra character is "pushed back" onto the stream.
- **PushbackInputStream**s are used by programs, like compilers, that parse their inputs—that is, break them into meaningful units (such as the keywords, identifiers and operators that the Java compiler must recognize).
- A **RandomAccessFile** (a subclass of **Object**) is useful for such direct-access applications as transaction-processing applications, like airline-reservations systems and point-of-sale systems.
- With a sequential-access file, each successive input/output request reads or writes the next consecutive set of data in the file.
- With a random-access file, each successive input/output request might be directed to any part of the file, perhaps one widely separated from the part of the file referenced in the previous request.
- Direct-access applications provide rapid access to specific data items in large files; such applications are often used while people are waiting for answers—these answers must be made available quickly, or the people might become impatient and "take their business elsewhere."
- A **ByteArrayInputStream** (a subclass of **abstract** class **InputStream**) performs its inputs from a **byte** array in memory.
- A **ByteArrayOutputStream** (a subclass of **abstract** class **OutputStream**) outputs to a **byte** array in memory.
- An application of **byte**-array input/output is data validation. A program can input an entire line at a time from the input stream into a **byte** array. Then, a validation routine can scrutinize the contents of the **byte** array and correct the data, if necessary. The program can now proceed to input from the **byte** array, knowing that the input data is in the proper format.
- A **StringBufferInputStream** (a subclass of **abstract** class **InputStream**) inputs from a **StringBuffer** object.
- A **SequenceInputStream** (a subclass of **abstract** class **InputStream**) enables several **InputStream**s to be concatenated so that the program will see the group as one continuous **InputStream**. As the end of each input stream is reached, the stream is closed, and the next stream in the sequence is opened.

- Class **BufferedReader** and class **BufferedWriter** enable efficient buffering for character-based streams.
- Class **CharArrayReader** and class **CharArrayWriter** read and write a stream of characters to a character array.
- A **PushbackReader** (a subclass of **abstract** class **FilterReader**) enables characters to be placed back on a character stream. A **LineNumberReader** (a subclass of **BufferedReader**) is a buffered character-stream that keeps track of line numbers (e.g., a newline, a return or a carriage-return line-feed combination).
- Class **FileReader** (a subclass of **InputStreamReader**) and class **FileWriter** (a subclass of **OutputStreamWriter**) read and write characters to a file. Class **PipedReader** and class **PipedWriter** are piped-character streams. Class **StringReader** and **StringWriter** read and write characters to **String**s. A **PrintWriter** writes characters to a stream.
- Class **File** enables programs to obtain information about a file or directory.
- Files are opened for output by creating a **FileOutputStream** class object. One argument is passed to the constructor—the filename. Existing files are truncated, and all data in the file is lost. Nonexistent files are created.
- A program can process no files, one file or several files. Each file has a unique name and is associated with an appropriate file stream object. All file-processing methods must refer to a file with the appropriate object.
- A file-position pointer indicates the position in the file from which the next input is to occur or at which the next output is to be placed.
- A convenient way to implement random-access files is by using only fixed-length records. Using this technique, a program can quickly calculate the exact location of a record relative to the beginning of the file.
- Data can be inserted in a random-access file without destroying other data in the file. Data can be updated or deleted without rewriting the entire file.
- The **RandomAccessFile** class has the same capabilities for input and output as the **DataInputStream** and **DataOutputStream** classes and also supports seeking to a specific byte position in the file, with method **seek**.

TERMINOLOGY

absolute path
alphabetic field
alphanumeric field
binary digit
bit
buffer
BufferedInputStream class
BufferedOutputStream class
BufferedReader class
BufferedWriter class
buffering
byte
ByteArrayInputStream class
ByteArrayOutputStream class
CANCEL_OPTION constant
canRead method of **File** class
canWrite method of **File** class
chaining stream objects
character field
character set
CharArrayReader class
CharArrayWriter class
close a file
close method
data hierarchy
data validation
database
database management system (DBMS)
DataInput interface
DataOutput interface
decimal digit
direct-access applications

DIRECTORIES_ONLY constant
directory
end-of-file
end-of-file marker
EndOfFileException
exists method of **File** class
field
file
File class
file name
FileInputStream class
FileOutputStream class
file-position pointer
FileReader class
FILES_AND_DIRECTORIES constant
FILES_ONLY constant
FileWriter class
FilterInputStream class
FilterOutputStream class
FilterReader class
flush
getAbsolutePath method of **File** class
getName method of **File** class
getParent method of **File** class
getPath method of **File** class
getSelectedFile method
input stream
InputStream class
InputStreamReader class
instant-access application
IOException
isAbsolute method of **File** class
isDirectory method of **File** class
isFile method of **File** class
JFileChooser class
lastModified method of **File** class
length method of **File** class
LineNumberReader class
list method of **File** class
logical input operation
logical output operation
memory buffer
modal dialog
numeric field
ObjectInput interface
ObjectInputStream class
ObjectOutput interface
ObjectOutputStream class
open a file
output stream
OutputStream class
OutputStreamWriter class
partially filled buffer
persistent data
physical input operation
physical output operation
pipe
PipedInputStream class
PipedOutputStream class
PipedReader class
PipedWriter class
PrintStream class
PrintWriter class
PushbackInputStream class
PushbackReader class
r file open mode
random-access file
RandomAccessFile class
read method
readBoolean method
readByte method
readChar method
readDouble method
Reader class
readFloat method
readFully method
readInt method
readLong method
readObject method
readShort method
readUnsignedByte method
readUnsignedShort method
record
record key
relative path
root directory
rw file open mode
seek method
SequenceInputStream class
sequential-access file
Serializable interface
setFileSelectionMode method
showOpenDialog method
showSaveDialog method
standard output
StringReader class
StringWriter class
System.err (standard error stream)
System.in (standard input stream)
System.out (standard output stream)

transaction-processing systems
truncate an existing file
Unicode character set
write method
writeBoolean method
writeByte method
writeBytes method
writeChar method
writeChars method
writeDouble method
writeFloat method
writeInt method
writeLong method
writeObject method
Writer class
writeShort method

SELF-REVIEW EXERCISES

16.1 Fill in the blanks in each of the following statements:

a) Ultimately, all data items processed by a computer are reduced to combinations of __________ and __________.
b) The smallest data item a computer can process is called a __________.
c) A __________ is a group of related records.
d) Digits, letters and special symbols are referred to as __________.
e) A group of related files is called a __________.
f) Method __________ of the file stream classes **FileOutputStream**, **FileInputStream**, and **RandomAccessFile** closes a file.
g) **RandomAccessFile** method __________ reads an integer from the specified stream.
h) **RandomAccessFile** method __________ reads a line of text from the specified stream.
i) **RandomAccessFile** method __________ sets the file-position pointer to a specific location in a file for input or output.

16.2 State which of the following are *true* and which are *false*. If *false*, explain why.

a) The programmer must explicitly create the **System.in**, **System.out** and **System.err** objects.
b) If the file-position pointer points to a location in a sequential file other than the beginning of the file, the file must be closed and reopened to read from the beginning of the file.
c) It is not necessary to search through all the records in a random-access file to find a specific record.
d) Records in random-access files must be of uniform length.
e) Method **seek** must seek relative to the beginning of a file.

16.3 Assume that each of the following statements applies to the same program.

a) Write a statement that opens file **"oldmast.dat"** for input; use **ObjectInputStream** object **inOldMaster** chained to a **FileInputStream** object.
b) Write a statement that opens file **"trans.dat"** for input; use **ObjectInputStream** object **inTransaction** chained to a **FileInputStream** object.
c) Write a statement that opens file **"newmast.dat"** for output (and creation); use **ObjectOutputStream** object **outNewMaster** chained to a **FileOutputStream**.
d) Write a set of statements that read a record from the file **"oldmast.dat"**. The record consists of integer **accountNumber**, string **name** and floating-point **currentBalance**; use **ObjectInputStream** object **inOldMaster**.
e) Write a set of statements that read a record from the file **"trans.dat"**. The record consists of integer **accountNumber** and floating-point **dollarAmount**; use **ObjectInputStream** object **inTransaction**.
f) Write a set of statements that outputs a record to the file **"newmast.dat"**. The record consists of integer **accountNumber**, string **name** and floating point **currentBalance**; use **DataOutputStream** object **outNewMaster**.

16.4 Find the error and show how to correct it in each of the following.

a) Assume **account**, **company** and **amount** are declared.

```
ObjectOutputStream outputStream;

outputStream.writeInt( account );
outputStream.writeChars( company );
outputStream.writeDouble( amount );
```

b) The following statement should read a record from the file **"payables.dat"**. The **ObjectInputStream** object **inPayable** refers to this file, and **FileInputStream** object **inReceivable** refers to the file **"receivables.dat"**.

```
account = inReceivable.readInt();
companyID = inReceivable.readLong();
amount = inReceivable.readDouble();
```

ANSWERS TO SELF-REVIEW EXERCISES

16.1 a) 1s, 0s. b) bit. c) file. d) characters. e) database. f) **close**. g) **readInt**. h) **readLine**. i) **seek**.

16.2 a) False. These three streams are created automatically for the programmer.
b) True.
c) True.
d) False. Records in a random-access file are normally of uniform length.
e) True.

16.3 a)
```
ObjectInputStream inOldMaster;
inOldMaster = new ObjectInputStream(
   new FileInputStream( "oldmast.dat" ) );
```
b)
```
ObjectInputStream inTransaction;
inTransaction = new ObjectInputStream(
   new FileInputStream( "trans.dat" ) );
```
c)
```
ObjectOutputStream outNewMaster;
outNewMaster = new ObjectOutputStream(
   new FileOutputStream( "newmast.dat" ) );
```
d)
```
accountNumber = inOldMaster.readInt();
name = inOldMaster.readUTF();
currentBalance = inOldMaster.readDouble();
```
e)
```
accountNumber = inTransaction.readInt();
dollarAmount = inTransaction.readDouble();
```
f)
```
outNewMaster.writeInt( accountNumber );
outNewMaster.writeUTF( name );
outNewMaster.writeDouble( currentBalance );
```

16.4 a) Error: The file has not been opened before the attempt is made to output data to the stream.
Correction: Create a new **ObjectOutputStream** object chained to a **FileOutputStream** object to open the file for output.

b) Error: The incorrect **FileInputStream** object is being used to read a record from file **"payables.dat"**.
Correction: Use object **inPayable** to refer to **"payables.dat"**.

EXERCISES

16.5 Fill in the blanks in each of the following:

a) Computers store large amounts of data on secondary storage devices as ________.
b) A ________ is composed of several fields.
c) A field that may contain only digits, letters and blanks is called an ________ field.
d) To facilitate the retrieval of specific records from a file, one field in each record is chosen as a ________.
e) The vast majority of information stored in computer systems is stored in ________ files.
f) The standard stream objects are ________, ________ and ________.

16.6 State which of the following are *true* and which are *false*. If *false*, explain why.

a) The impressive functions performed by computers essentially involve the manipulation of zeros and ones.
b) People specify programs and data items as characters; computers then manipulate and process these characters as groups of zeros and ones.
c) A person's 5-digit zip code is an example of a numeric field.
d) A person's street address is generally considered to be an alphabetic field.
e) Data items represented in computers form a data hierarchy in which data items become larger and more complex as we progress from fields to characters to bits, etc.
f) A record key identifies a record as belonging to a particular field.
g) Companies store all their information in a single file to facilitate computer processing.
h) When a program creates a file, the file is automatically retained by the computer for future reference.

16.7 Exercise 16.3 asked the reader to write a series of single statements. Actually, these statements form the core of an important type of file-processing program, namely, a file-matching program. In commercial data processing, it is common to have several files in each application system. In an accounts receivable system, for example, there is generally a master file containing detailed information about each customer, such as the customer's name, address, telephone number, outstanding balance, credit limit, discount terms, contract arrangements and possibly a condensed history of recent purchases and cash payments.

a) As transactions occur (i.e., sales are made and cash payments arrive in the mail), they are entered into a file. At the end of each business period (i.e., a month for some companies, a week for others, and a day in some cases) the file of transactions (called `"trans.dat"` in Exercise 16.3) is applied to the master file (called `"oldmast.dat"` in Exercise 16.3), thus updating each account's record of purchases and payments. During an updating run, the master file is rewritten as a new file (`"newmast.dat"`), which is then used at the end of the next business period to begin the updating process again.
b) File-matching programs must deal with certain problems that do not exist in single-file programs. For example, a match does not always occur. A customer on the master file might not have made any purchases or cash payments in the current business period; therefore, no record for this customer will appear on the transaction file. Similarly, a customer who did make some purchases or cash payments could have just moved to this community, and the company might not have had a chance to create a master record for this customer.
c) Use the statements in Exercise 16.3 as a basis for writing a complete file-matching accounts receivable program. Use the account number on each file as the record key for matching purposes. Assume that each file is a sequential file with records stored in increasing account-number order.
d) When a match occurs (i.e., records with the same account number appear on both the master file and the transaction file), add the dollar amount on the transaction file to the

current balance on the master file, and write the **"newmast.dat"** record. (Assume that purchases are indicated by positive amounts on the transaction file, payments by negative amounts.) When there is a master record for a particular account but no corresponding transaction record, merely write the master record to **"newmast.dat"**. When there is a transaction record but no corresponding master record, print the message **"Unmatched transaction record for account number ..."** (fill in the account number from the transaction record).

16.8 After writing the program of Exercise 16.7, write a simple program to create some test data for checking out the program. Use the sample account data in Fig. 16.23 and Fig. 16.24. Run the program of Exercise 16.7, using the files of test data created in this exercise. Print the new master file. Check that the accounts have been updated correctly.

16.9 It is possible (actually common) to have several transaction records with the same record key. This occurs because a particular customer might make several purchases and cash payments during a business period. Rewrite your accounts receivable file-matching program of Exercise 16.7 to provide for the possibility of handling several transaction records with the same record key. Modify the test data of Exercise 16.8 to include the additional transaction records in Fig. 16.25.

Master file Account number	Name	Balance
100	Alan Jones	348.17
300	Mary Smith	27.19
500	Sam Sharp	0.00
700	Suzy Green	-14.22

Fig. 16.23 Sample data for master file.

Transaction file Account number	Transaction amount
100	27.14
300	62.11
400	100.56
900	82.17

Fig. 16.24 Sample data for transaction file.

Account number	Dollar amount
300	83.89
700	80.78
700	1.53

Fig. 16.25 Additional transaction records.

16.10 You are the owner of a hardware store and need to keep an inventory that can tell you what different tools you have, how many of each you have on hand and the cost of each one. Write a program that initializes the random-access file **"hardware.dat"** to one hundred empty records, lets you input the data concerning each tool, enables you to list all your tools, lets you delete a record for a tool that you no longer have and lets you update *any* information in the file. The tool identification number should be the record number. Use the information in Fig. 16.26 to start your file.

16.11 *(Telephone Number Word Generator)* Standard telephone keypads contain the digits 0 through 9. The numbers 2 through 9 each have three letters associated with them (see Fig. 16.27).

Many people find it difficult to memorize phone numbers, so they use the correspondence between digits and letters to develop seven-letter words that correspond to their phone numbers. For example, a person whose telephone number is 686-2377 might use the correspondence indicated in Fig. 16.27 to develop the seven-letter word "NUMBERS." Each seven-letter word corresponds to exactly one seven-digit telephone number. The restaurant wishing to increase its takeout business could surely do so with the number 825-3688 (i.e., "TAKEOUT").

Record #	Tool name	Quantity	Cost
3	Electric sander	18	35.99
19	Hammer	128	10.00
26	Jig saw	16	14.25
39	Lawn mower	10	79.50
56	Power saw	8	89.99
76	Screwdriver	236	4.99
81	Sledge hammer	32	19.75
88	Wrench	65	6.48

Fig. 16.26 Data for Exercise 16.10.

Digit	Letters
2	**A B C**
3	**D E F**
4	**G H I**
5	**J K L**
6	**M N O**
7	**P R S**
8	**T U V**
9	**W X Y**

Fig. 16.27 Telephone keypad digits and letters.

Each seven-letter phone number corresponds to many separate seven-letter words. Unfortunately, most of these represent unrecognizable juxtapositions of letters. It is possible, however, that the owner of a barber shop would be pleased to know that the shop's telephone number, 424-7288, corresponds to "HAIRCUT." The owner of a liquor store would, no doubt, be delighted to find that the store's number, 233-7226, corresponds to "BEERCAN." A veterinarian with the phone number 738-2273 would be pleased to know that the number corresponds to the letters "PETCARE." An automotive dealership would be pleased to know that the dealership number, 639-2277, corresponds to "NEWCARS."

Write a program that, given a seven-digit number, writes to a file every possible seven-letter word combination corresponding to that number. There are 2187 (3^7) such combinations. Avoid phone numbers with the digits 0 and 1.

17

Networking

Objectives

- To understand Java networking with URIs, sockets and datagrams.
- To implement Java networking applications by using sockets and datagrams.
- To understand how to implement Java clients and servers that communicate with one another.
- To understand how to implement network-based collaborative applications.
- To construct a multithreaded server.

If the presence of electricity can be made visible in any part of a circuit, I see no reason why intelligence may not be transmitted instantaneously by electricity.
Samuel F. B. Morse

Mr. Watson, come here, I want you.
Alexander Graham Bell

What networks of railroads, highways and canals were in another age, the networks of telecommunications, information and computerization … are today.
Bruno Kreisky, Austrian Chancellor

Science may never come up with a better office-communication system than the coffee break.
Earl Wilson

It's currently a problem of access to gigabits through punybaud.
J. C. R. Licklider

Outline

17.1 Introduction
17.2 Manipulating URIs
17.3 Reading a File on a Web Server
17.4 Establishing a Simple Server Using Stream Sockets
17.5 Establishing a Simple Client Using Stream Sockets
17.6 Client/Server Interaction with Stream Socket Connections
17.7 Connectionless Client/Server Interaction with Datagrams
17.8 Client/Server Tic-Tac-Toe Using a Multithreaded Server
17.9 Security and the Network
17.10 DeitelMessenger Chat Server and Client
17.10.1 DeitelMessengerServer and Supporting Classes
17.10.2 DeitelMessenger Client and Supporting Classes
17.11 (Optional) Discovering Design Patterns: Design Patterns Used in Packages `java.io` and `java.net`
17.11.1 Creational Design Patterns
17.11.2 Structural Design Patterns
17.11.3 Architectural Patterns
17.11.4 Conclusion

Summary • Terminology • Self-Review Exercises • Answers to Self-Review Exercises • Exercises

17.1 Introduction

There is much excitement over the Internet and the World Wide Web. The Internet ties the "information world" together. The World Wide Web makes the Internet easy to use and gives it the flair and sizzle of multimedia. Organizations see the Internet and the Web as crucial to their information-systems strategies. Java provides a number of built-in networking capabilities that make it easy to develop Internet-based and Web-based applications. Not only can Java specify parallelism through multithreading, but it can enable programs to search the world for information and to collaborate with programs running on other computers internationally, nationally or just within an organization. Java can enable applets and applications to communicate with one another (subject to security constraints).

Networking is a massive and complex topic. Computer science and computer engineering students will typically take a full-semester, upper level course in computer networking and continue with further study at the graduate level. Java provides a rich complement of networking capabilities and will likely be used as an implementation vehicle in computer networking courses. In *Java How to Program, Fourth Edition*, we introduce a portion of Java's networking concepts and capabilities. For more advanced networking capabilities, refer to our book *Advanced Java 2 Platform How to Program.*

Java's networking capabilities are grouped into several packages. The fundamental networking capabilities are defined by classes and interfaces of package **`java.net`**, through which Java offers *socket-based communications* that enable applications to view networking as streams of data. The classes and interfaces of package **`java.net`** also offer *packet-based communications* that enable individual *packets* of information to be transmitted—this is commonly used to transmit audio and video over the Internet. In this chapter, we show how to create and manipulate sockets and how to communicate with packets of data.

Our discussion of networking focuses on both sides of a *client-server relationship*. The *client* requests that some action be performed, and the *server* performs the action and responds to the client. A common implementation of the request-response model is between World Wide Web browsers and World Wide Web servers. When a user selects a Web site to browse through a browser (the client application), a request is sent to the appropriate Web server (the server application). The server normally responds to the client by sending an appropriate HTML Web page.

We demonstrate the Swing GUI component ***`JEditorPane`*** and its ability to render an HTML document downloaded from the World Wide Web. We also introduce Java's a *socket-based communications,* which enable applications to view networking as if it were file I/O—a program can read from a *socket* or write to a socket as simply as reading from a file or writing to a file. We show how to create and manipulate sockets.

Java provides *stream sockets* and *datagram sockets.* With *stream sockets*, a process establishes a *connection* to another process. While the connection is in place, data flows between the processes in continuous *streams*. Stream sockets are said to provide a *connection-oriented service*. The protocol used for transmission is the popular *TCP (Transmission Control Protocol).*

With *datagram sockets*, individual *packets* of information are transmitted. This is not the right protocol for everyday users, because, unlike TCP, the protocol used—*UDP*, the *User Datagram Protocol*—is a *connectionless service*, and it does not guarantee that packets arrive in any particular order. In fact, packets can be lost, can be duplicated and can even arrive out of sequence. So, with UDP, significant extra programming is required on the user's part to deal with these problems (if the user chooses to do so). UDP is most appropriate for network applications that do not require the error checking and reliability of TCP. Stream sockets and the TCP protocol will be the most desirable for the vast majority of Java programmers.

Performance Tip 17.1

Connectionless services generally offer greater performance, but less reliability than connection-oriented services.

Portability Tip 17.1

The TCP protocol and its related set of protocols enable a great variety of heterogeneous computer systems (i.e., computer systems with different processors and different operating systems) to intercommunicate.

The chapter ends with a case study in which we implement a client/server chat application similar to the instant-messaging services popular on the Web today. The program incorporates many networking techniques introduced in this chapter. The program also introduces *multicasting*, in which a server can *publish* information and clients can *subscribe* to that information. Each time the server publishes more information, all subscribers receive that information. Throughout the examples of this chapter, we will see that many of the networking details are handled by the Java classes we use.

17.2 Manipulating URIs

The Internet offers many protocols. The *HyperText Transfer Protocol* (*HTTP*) that forms the basis of the World Wide Web uses *URIs* (*Uniform Resource Identifiers*) to locate data on the Internet. URIs frequently are called *URLs* (*Uniform Resource Locators*). Actually, a URL is a type of URI. Common URIs refer to files or directories and can reference objects that perform complex tasks, such as database lookups and Internet searches. If you know the URI of publicly available HTML files anywhere on the World Wide Web, you can access that data through HTTP. Java makes it easy to manipulate URIs. Using a URI that refers to the exact location of a resource (such as a Web page) as an argument to the ***showDocument*** method of interface ***AppletContext*** causes the browser in which the applet is executing to display the resource at the specified URI. The applet of Fig. 17.1 and Fig. 17.2 enables the user to select a Web page from a **JList** and causes the browser to display the corresponding page.

This applet takes advantage of *applet parameters* specified in the HTML document that invokes the applet. When browsing the World Wide Web, often you will come across applets that are in the public domain—you can use them free of charge on your own Web pages (normally in exchange for crediting the applet's creator). One common feature of such applets is the ability to customize the applet via parameters that are supplied from the HTML file that invokes the applet. For example, Fig. 17.1 contains the HTML that invokes the applet **SiteSelector** in Fig. 17.2. The HTML document contains eight parameters specified with the ***param*** *element*—these lines must appear between the starting and ending **applet** tags. The applet can read these values and use them to customize itself. Any number of **param** tags can appear between the starting and ending **applet** tags. Each parameter has a ***name*** and a ***value***. **Applet** method ***getParameter*** retrieves the **value** associated with a specific parameter and returns the **value** as a **String**. The argument passed to **getParameter** is a **String** containing the name of the parameter in the **param** tag. In this example, parameters represent the title of each Web site the user can select and the location of each site. Any number of parameters can be specified. However, these parameters must be named **title***#*, where the value of *#* starts at **0** and increments by one for each new title. Each title should have a corresponding location parameter of the form **location***#*, where the value of *#* starts at **0** and increments by one for each new location. The statement

```
<html>
<title>Site Selector</title>
<body>
   <applet code = "SiteSelector.class" width = "300" height = "75">
      <param name = "title0" value = "Java Home Page">
      <param name = "location0" value = "http://java.sun.com/">
      <param name = "title1" value = "Deitel">
      <param name = "location1" value = "http://www.deitel.com/">
      <param name = "title2" value = "JGuru">
      <param name = "location2" value = "http://www.jGuru.com/">
      <param name = "title3" value = "JavaWorld">
     <param name = "location3" value = "http://www.javaworld.com/">
   </applet>
</body>
</html>
```

Fig. 17.1 HTML document to load **SiteSelector** applet.

```
String title = getParameter( "title0" );
```

gets the value associated with the **"title0"** parameter and assigns it to **String** reference **title**. If there is not a **param** tag containing the specified parameter, **getParameter** returns **null**.

The applet (Fig. 17.2) obtains from the HTML document (Fig. 17.1) the choices that will be displayed in the applet's **JList**. Class **SiteSelector** uses a ***Hashtable*** (package ***java.util***) to store the World Wide Web site names and URIs. A **Hashtable** stores *key/value pairs*. The program uses the *key* to store and retrieve the associated *value* in the **Hashtable**. In this example, the *key* is the **String** in the **JList** that represents the Web site name, and the value is a **URL** object that stores the URI of the Web site to display in the browser. Class **Hashtable** provides two methods of importance in this example—***put*** and ***get***. Method **put** takes two arguments—a key and its associated value—and places the value in the **Hashtable** at a location determined by the key. Method **get** takes one argument—a key—and retrieves the value (as an **Object** reference) associated with the key. Class **SiteSelector** also contains a **Vector** (package **java.util**) in which the site names are placed so they can be used to initialize the **JList** (one version of the **JList** constructor receives a **Vector** object). A **Vector** is a dynamically resizable array of **Object**s. Class **Vector** provides method ***add*** to add a new element to the end of the **Vector**. Classes **Hashtable** and **Vector** are discussed in detail in Chapter 20.

Lines 23–24 in method **init** (lines 20–63) create the **Hashtable** and **Vector** objects. Line 27 calls our utility method **getSitesFromHTMLParameters** (lines 66–108) to obtain the HTML parameters from the HTML document that invoked the applet.

In method **getSitesFromHTMLParameters**, line 75 uses **Applet** method **getParameter** to obtain a Web site title. If the **title** is not **null**, the loop at lines 78–106 begins executing. Line 81 uses **Applet** method **getParameter** to obtain the corresponding location. Line 87 uses the **location** as the initial value of a new **URL** object. The **URL** constructor determines whether the **String** passed as an argument represents a valid Uniform Resource Identifier. If not, the **URL** constructor throws a ***MalformedURLException***. Notice that the **URL** constructor must be called in a **try** block. If the **URL** constructor generates a **MalformedURLException**, the call to **printStackTrace** (line 98) causes the program to display a stack trace. Then the program attempts to obtain the next Web site title. The program does not add the site for the invalid URI to the **Hashtable**, so the title will not be displayed in the **JList**.

Common Programming Error 17.1

*A **MalformedURLException** is thrown when a **String** that is not in proper URI format is passed to a **URL** constructor.*

For a proper **URL**, line 90 places the **title** and **URL** into the **Hashtable**, and line 93 adds the **title** to the **Vector**. Line 104 gets the next title from the HTML document. When the call to **getParameter** at line 104 returns **null**, the loop terminates.

When method **getSitesFromHTMLParameters** returns to **init**, lines 30–61 construct the applet's GUI. Lines 31–32 add the **JLabel** "**Choose a site to browse**" to the **NORTH** of the content pane's **BorderLayout**. Lines 36–58 register an instance of an anonymous inner class that implements **ListSelectionListener** to handle the **siteChooser**'s events. Lines 60–61 add **siteChooser** to the **CENTER** of the content pane's **BorderLayout**.

```java
// Fig. 17.2: SiteSelector.java
// This program uses a button to load a document from a URL.

// Java core packages
import java.net.*;
import java.util.*;
import java.awt.*;
import java.applet.AppletContext;

// Java extension packages
import javax.swing.*;
import javax.swing.event.*;

public class SiteSelector extends JApplet {
   private Hashtable sites;     // site names and URLs
   private Vector siteNames;    // site names
   private JList siteChooser;   // list of sites to choose from

   // read HTML parameters and set up GUI
   public void init()
   {
      // create Hashtable and Vector
      sites = new Hashtable();
      siteNames = new Vector();

      // obtain parameters from HTML document
      getSitesFromHTMLParameters();

      // create GUI components and layout interface
      Container container = getContentPane();
      container.add( new JLabel( "Choose a site to browse" ),
         BorderLayout.NORTH );

      siteChooser = new JList( siteNames );

      siteChooser.addListSelectionListener(

         new ListSelectionListener() {

            // go to site user selected
            public void valueChanged( ListSelectionEvent event )
            {
               // get selected site name
               Object object = siteChooser.getSelectedValue();

               // use site name to locate corresponding URL
               URL newDocument = ( URL ) sites.get( object );

               // get reference to applet container
               AppletContext browser = getAppletContext();

               // tell applet container to change pages
               browser.showDocument( newDocument );
```

Fig. 17.2 Loading a document from a URL into a browser (part 1 of 3).

```
            }  // end method valueChanged

         }  // end anonymous inner class

      ); // end call to addListSelectionListener

      container.add( new JScrollPane( siteChooser ),
         BorderLayout.CENTER );

   }  // end method init

   // obtain parameters from HTML document
   private void getSitesFromHTMLParameters()
   {
      // look for applet parameters in the HTML document
      // and add sites to Hashtable
      String title, location;
      URL url;
      int counter = 0;

      // obtain first site title
      title = getParameter( "title" + counter );

      // loop until no more parameters in HTML document
      while ( title != null ) {

         // obtain site location
         location = getParameter( "location" + counter );

         // place title/URL in Hashtable and title in Vector
         try {

            // convert location to URL
            url = new URL( location );

            // put title/URL in Hashtable
            sites.put( title, url );

               // put title in Vector
            siteNames.add( title );
         }

         // process invalid URL format
         catch ( MalformedURLException urlException ) {
            urlException.printStackTrace();
         }

         ++counter;

         // obtain next site title
         title = getParameter( "title" + counter );

      }  // end while
```

Fig. 17.2 Loading a document from a URL into a browser (part 2 of 3).

```
107
108     } // end method getSitesFromHTMLParameters
109
110 } // end class SiteSelector
```

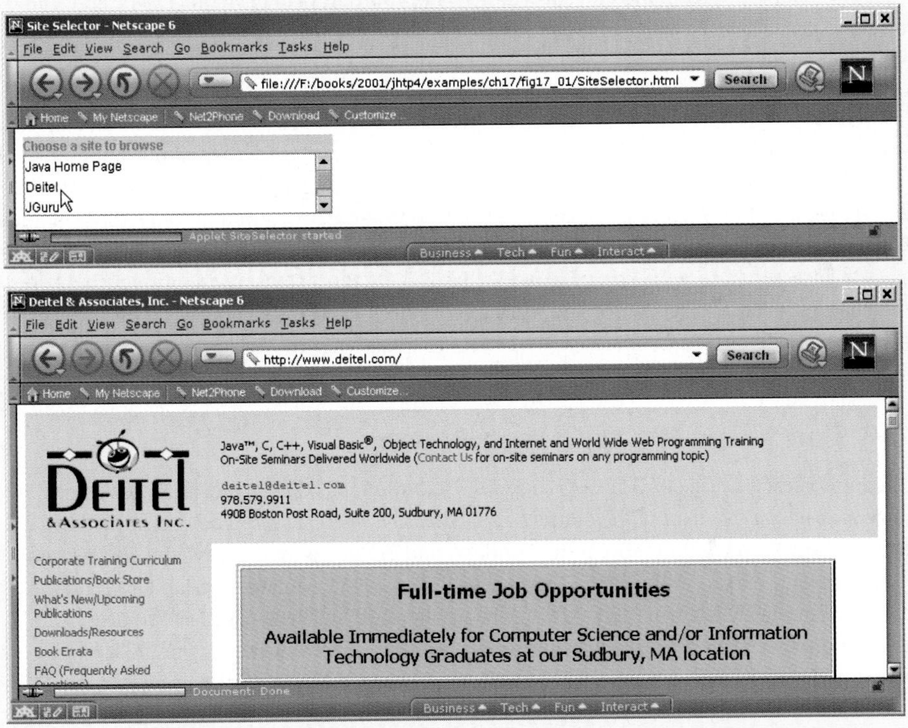

Fig. 17.2 Loading a document from a URL into a browser (part 3 of 3).

When the user selects one of the Web sites in **siteChooser**, the program calls method **valueChanged** (lines 41–54). Line 44 obtains the selected site name from the **JList**. Line 47 passes the selected site name (the *key*) to **Hashtable** method **get**, which locates and returns an **Object** reference to the corresponding **URL** object (the *value*). The **URL** cast operator converts the reference to a **URL** that can be assigned to reference **newDocument**.

Line 50 uses **Applet** method **getAppletContext** to get a reference to an **AppletContext** object that represents the applet container. Line 53 uses the **AppletContext** reference **browser** to invoke **AppletContext** method ***showDocument***, which receives a **URL** object as an argument and passes it to the **AppletContext** (i.e., the browser). The browser displays in the current browser window the World Wide Web resource associated with that **URL**. In this example, all the resources are HTML documents.

For programmers familiar with *HTML frames*, there is a second version of **AppletContext** method **showDocument** that enables an applet to specify the so-called *target frame* in which to display the World Wide Web resource. The second version of **showDocument** takes two arguments—a **URL** object specifying the resource to display and a **String** representing the target frame. There are some special target frames that can be used as the second argument. The target frame ***_blank*** results in a new Web browser window to display the content from the specified URI. The target frame **_self** specifies that the content from the specified URI should be displayed in the same frame as the applet (the applet's HTML page is replaced in this case). The target frame **_top** specifies that the browser should remove the current frames in the browser window, then display the content from the specified URI in the current window. For more information on HTML and frames, see the *World Wide Web Consortium (W3C)* Web site

http://www.w3.org

[Note: This applet must be run from a World Wide Web browser, such as Netscape *Navigator* or Microsoft *Internet Explorer*, to see the results of displaying another Web page. The **appletviewer** is capable only of executing applets—it ignores all other HTML tags. If the Web sites in the program contained Java applets, only those applets would appear in the **appletviewer** when the user selects a Web site. Each applet would execute in a separate **appletviewer** window. Of the browsers mentioned here, only Netscape Navigator 6 currently supports the features of Java 2. You will need to use the Java Plug-in (discussed in Chapter 3) to execute this applet in Microsoft *Internet Explorer* or older versions of Netscape *Navigator*.]

17.3 Reading a File on a Web Server

The application of Fig. 17.3 uses Swing GUI component ***JEditorPane*** (from package **javax.swing**) to display the contents of a file on a Web server. The user inputs the URI in the **JTextField** at the top of the window, and the program displays the corresponding document (if it exists) in the **JEditorPane**. Class **JEditorPane** is able to render both plain text and HTML-formatted text, so this application acts as a simple Web browser. The application also demonstrates how to process ***HyperlinkEvent****s* when the user clicks a hyperlink in the HTML document. The screen captures in Fig. 17.3 illustrate that the **JEditorPane** can display both simple text (the first screen) and HTML text (the second screen). The techniques shown in this example also can be used in applets. However, applets are allowed to read files only on the server from which the applet was downloaded.

```
// Fig. 17.3: ReadServerFile.java
// This program uses a JEditorPane to display the
// contents of a file on a Web server.

// Java core packages
import java.awt.*;
import java.awt.event.*;
import java.net.*;
import java.io.*;

// Java extension packages
import javax.swing.*;
import javax.swing.event.*;

public class ReadServerFile extends JFrame {
   private JTextField enterField;
   private JEditorPane contentsArea;
```

Fig. 17.3 Reading a file by opening a connection through a **URL** (part 1 of 4)

```

   // set up GUI
   public ReadServerFile()
   {
      super( "Simple Web Browser" );

      Container container = getContentPane();

      // create enterField and register its listener
      enterField = new JTextField( "Enter file URL here" );

      enterField.addActionListener(

         new ActionListener() {

            // get document specified by user
            public void actionPerformed( ActionEvent event )
            {
               getThePage( event.getActionCommand() );
            }

         }  // end anonymous inner class

      ); // end call to addActionListener

      container.add( enterField, BorderLayout.NORTH );

      // create contentsArea and register HyperlinkEvent listener
      contentsArea = new JEditorPane();
      contentsArea.setEditable( false );

      contentsArea.addHyperlinkListener(

         new HyperlinkListener() {

            // if user clicked hyperlink, go to specified page
            public void hyperlinkUpdate( HyperlinkEvent event )
            {
               if ( event.getEventType() ==
                     HyperlinkEvent.EventType.ACTIVATED )
                  getThePage( event.getURL().toString() );
            }

         }  // end anonymous inner class

      ); // end call to addHyperlinkListener

      container.add( new JScrollPane( contentsArea ),
         BorderLayout.CENTER );

      setSize( 400, 300 );
      setVisible( true );
   }
```

Fig. 17.3 Reading a file by opening a connection through a **URL** (part 2 of 4)

```

   // load document; change mouse cursor to indicate status
   private void getThePage( String location )
   {
      // change mouse cursor to WAIT_CURSOR
      setCursor( Cursor.getPredefinedCursor(
         Cursor.WAIT_CURSOR ) );

      // load document into contentsArea and display location in
      // enterField
      try {
         contentsArea.setPage( location );
         enterField.setText( location );
      }

      // process problems loading document
      catch ( IOException ioException ) {
         JOptionPane.showMessageDialog( this,
            "Error retrieving specified URL",
            "Bad URL", JOptionPane.ERROR_MESSAGE );
      }

      setCursor( Cursor.getPredefinedCursor(
         Cursor.DEFAULT_CURSOR ) );
   }

   // begin application execution
   public static void main( String args[] )
   {
      ReadServerFile application = new ReadServerFile();

      application.setDefaultCloseOperation(
         JFrame.EXIT_ON_CLOSE );
   }

}  // end class ReadServerFile
```

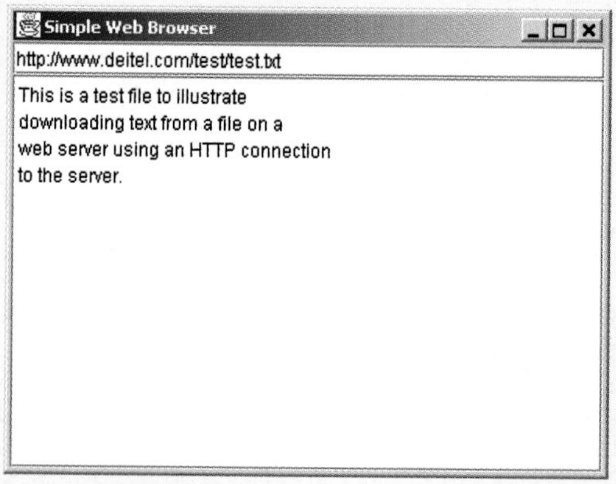

Simple Web Browser

http://www.deitel.com/test/test.txt

This is a test file to illustrate
downloading text from a file on a
web server using an HTTP connection
to the server.

Fig. 17.3 Reading a file by opening a connection through a **URL** (part 3 of 4)

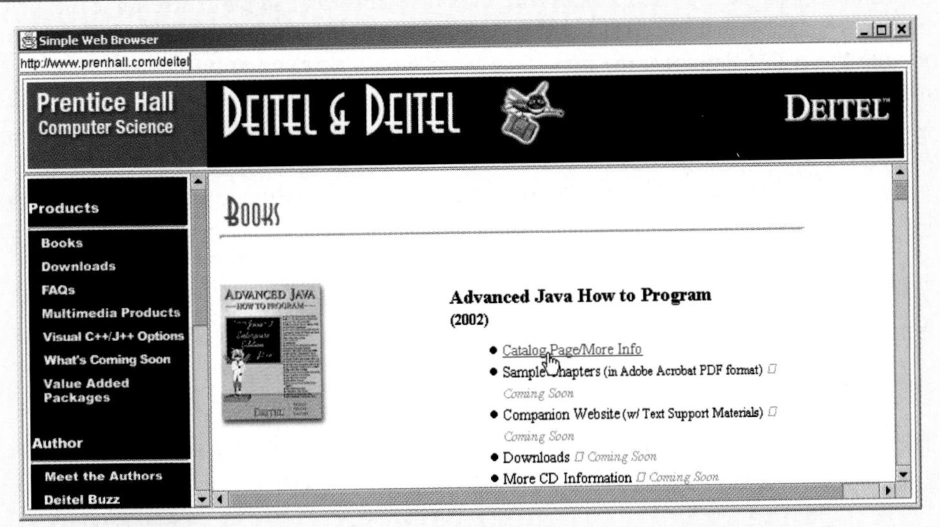

Fig. 17.3 Reading a file by opening a connection through a **URL** (part 4 of 4)

The application class **ReadServerFile** contains **JTextField enterField**, in which the user enters the URI of the file to read and **JEditorPane contentsArea** to display the contents of the file. When the user presses the *Enter* key in the **JTextField**, the program calls method **actionPerformed** (lines 34–37). Line 36 uses **ActionEvent** method **getActionCommand** to get the **String** the user input in the **JTextField** and passes that string to utility method **getThePage** (lines 73–95).

Lines 76–77 in method **getThePage** use method ***setCursor*** (inherited into class **JFrame** from class **Component**) to change the mouse cursor to the *wait cursor* (normally, an hourglass or a watch). If the file being downloaded is large, the wait cursor indicates to the user that the program is performing a task and that the user should wait for the task to complete. The **static Cursor** method ***getPredefinedCursor*** receives an integer indicating the cursor type (***Cursor.WAIT_CURSOR*** in this case). See the API documentation for class **Cursor** for a complete list of cursors.

Line 82 uses **JEditorPane** method ***setPage*** to download the document specified by **location** and display it in the **JEditorPane contents**. If there is an error downloading the document, method **setPage** throws an **IOException**. Also, if an invalid URL is specified, a **MalformedURLException** (a sublcass of **IOException**) occurs. If the document loads successfully, line 83 displays the current location in **enterField**.

Lines 93–94 sets the **Cursor** back to ***Cursor.DEFAULT_CURSOR*** (the default **Cursor**) to indicate that the document download is complete.

Typically, an HTML document contains *hyperlinks*—text, images or GUI components which, when clicked, provide quick access to another document on the Web. If a **JEditorPane** contains an HTML document and the user clicks a hyperlink, the **JEditorPane** generates a ***HyperlinkEvent*** (package **javax.swing.event**) and notifies all registered ***HyperlinkListeners*** (package **javax.swing.event**) of that event. Lines 49–63 register a **HyperlinkListener** to handle **HyperlinkEvent**s. When a **HyperlinkEvent** occurs, the program calls method **hyperlinkUpdate** (lines 54–

59). Lines 56–57 use **HyperlinkEvent** method ***getEventType*** to determine the type of the **HyperlinkEvent**. Class **HyperlinkEvent** contains **public** inner class ***EventType*** that defines three hyperlink event types: ***ACTIVATED*** (the user clicked a hyperlink to change Web pages), ***ENTERED*** (the user moved the mouse over a hyperlink) and ***EXITED*** (the user moved the mouse away from a hyperlink). If a hyperlink was **ACTIVATED**, line 58 uses **HyperlinkEvent** method ***getURL*** to obtain the **URL** represented by the hyperlink. Method **toString** converts the returned **URL** to a **String** format that can be passed to utility method **getThePage**.

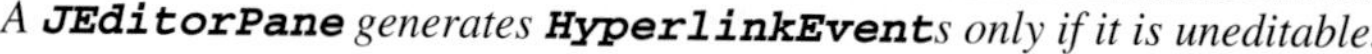

*A **JEditorPane** generates **HyperlinkEvent**s only if it is uneditable.*

17.4 Establishing a Simple Server Using Stream Sockets

The two examples discussed so far use high-level Java networking capabilities to communicate between applications. In those examples, it was not the Java programmer's responsibility to establish the connection between a client and a server. The first program relied on the Web browser to communicate with a Web server. The second program relied on a **JEditorPane** to perform the connection. This section begins our discussion of creating your own applications that can communicate with one another.

Establishing a simple server in Java requires five steps. Step 1 is to create a ***ServerSocket*** object. A call to the **ServerSocket** constructor such as

```
ServerSocket server = new ServerSocket( port, queueLength );
```

registers an available *port number* and specifies a maximum number of clients that can wait to connect to the server (i.e., the *queueLength*). The port number is used by clients to located the server application on the server computer. This often is called the *handshake point*. If the queue is full, the server refuses client connections. The preceding statement establishes the port where the server waits for connections from clients (a process known as *binding the server to the port*). Each client will ask to connect to the server on this *port*.

Programs manage each client connection with a ***Socket*** object. After binding the server to a port with a **ServerSocket** (Step 2), the server listens indefinitely (or *blocks*) for an attempt by a client to connect. To listen for a client, the program calls **ServerSocket** method **accept**, as in

```
Socket connection = server.accept();
```

This statement returns a **Socket** object when a connection with a client is established.

Step 3 is to get the **OutputStream** and **InputStream** objects that enable the server to communicate with the client by sending and receiving bytes. The server sends information to the client via an **OutputStream** object. The server receives information from the client via an **InputStream** object. To obtain the streams, the server invokes method **getOutputStream** on the **Socket** to get a reference to the **OutputStream** associated with the **Socket** and invokes method **getInputStream** on the **Socket** to get a reference to the **InputStream** associated with the **Socket**.

The **OutputStream** and **InputStream** objects can be used to send or receive individual bytes or sets of bytes with the **OutputStream** method **write** and the **InputStream** method **read**, respectively. Often it is useful to send or receive values of primitive data types (such as **int** and **double**) or **Serializable** class data types (such as **String**) rather than sending bytes. In this case, we can use the techniques of Chapter 16 to *chain* other stream types (such as **ObjectOutputStream** and **ObjectInputStream**) to the **OutputStream** and **InputStream** associated with the **Socket**. For example,

```
ObjectInputStream input =
   new ObjectInputStream( connection.getInputStream() );

ObjectOutputStream output =
   new ObjectOutputStream( connection.getOutputStream() );
```

The beauty of establishing these relationships is that whatever the server writes to the **ObjectOutputStream** is sent via the **OutputStream** and is available at the client's **InputStream** and whatever the client writes to its **OutputStream** (with a corresponding **ObjectOutputStream**) is available via the server's **InputStream**.

Step 4 is the *processing* phase, in which the server and the client communicate via the **InputStream** and **OutputStream** objects. In Step 5, when the transmission is complete, the server closes the connection by invoking the **close** method on the **Socket** and on the corresponding streams.

Software Engineering Observation 17.2

With sockets, network I/O appears to Java programs to be identical to sequential file I/O. Sockets hide much of the complexity of network programming from the programmer.

Software Engineering Observation 17.3

With Java's multithreading, we can create multithreaded servers that can manage many simultaneous connections with many clients; this multithreaded-server architecture is precisely what popular network servers use.

Software Engineering Observation 17.4

A multithreaded server can take the **Socket** *returned by each call to* **accept** *and create a new thread that manages network I/O across that* **Socket**, *or a multithreaded server can maintain a pool of threads (a set of already existing threads) ready to manage network I/O across the new* **Socket**s *as they are created.*

Performance Tip 17.2

In high-performance systems in which memory is abundant, a multithreaded server can be implemented to create a pool of threads that can be assigned quickly to handle network I/O across each new **Socket** *as it is created. Thus, when the server receives a connection, the server need not incur the overhead of thread creation.*

17.5 Establishing a Simple Client Using Stream Sockets

Establishing a simple client in Java requires four steps. In Step 1, we create a **Socket** to connect to the server. The **Socket** constructor establishes the connection to the server. For example, the statement

```
Socket connection = new Socket( serverAddress, port );
```

uses the **Socket** constructor with two arguments—the server's Internet address (*serverAddress*) and the *port* number. If the connection attempt is successful, this statement returns a **Socket**. A connection attempt that fails throws an instance of a subclass of **IOException**, so many programs simply catch **IOException**. An ***UnknownHostException*** occurs when a server address indicated by a client cannot be resolved. A ***ConnectException*** is thrown when an error occurs while attempting to connect to a server.

In Step 2, the client uses **Socket** methods **getInputStream** and **getOutputStream** to obtain references to the **Socket**'s **InputStream** and **OutputStream**. As we mentioned in the preceding section, often it is useful to send or receive values of primitive data types (such as **int** and **double**) or class data types (such as **String** and **Employee**) rather than sending bytes. If the server is sending information in the form of actual data types, the client should receive the information in the same format. Thus, if the server sends values with an **ObjectOutputStream**, the client should read those values with an **ObjectInputStream**.

Step 3 is the processing phase in which the client and the server communicate via the **InputStream** and **OutputStream** objects. In Step 4, the client closes the connection when the transmission is complete by invoking the **close** method on the **Socket** and the corresponding streams. When processing information sent by a server, the client must determine when the server is finished sending information so the client can call **close** to close the **Socket** connection. For example, the **InputStream** method **read** returns the value –1 when it detects end-of-stream (also called EOF—end-of-file). If an **ObjectInputStream** is used to read information from the server, an **EOFException** occurs when the client attempts to read a value from a stream on which end-of-stream is detected.

17.6 Client/Server Interaction with Stream Socket Connections

The applications of Fig. 17.4 and Fig. 17.5 use *stream sockets* to demonstrate a simple *client/server chat application*. The server waits for a client connection attempt. When a client application connects to the server, the server application sends a **String** object (remember that **String**s are **Serializable**) indicating that the connection was successful to the client. Then the client displays the message. Both the client and the server applications contain **JTextField**s, which allow the user to type a message and send it to the other application. When the client or the server sends the **String** "**TERMINATE**", the connection between the client and the server terminates. Then the server waits for the next client to connect. The definition of class **Server** appears in Fig. 17.4. The definition of class **Client** appears in Fig. 17.5. The screen captures showing the execution between the client and the server are shown as part of Fig. 17.5.

Class **Server**'s constructor (lines 25–58) creates the GUI of the application (a **JTextField** and a **JTextArea**). The **Server** object displays its output in a **JTextArea**. When the **main** method (lines 186–194) executes, it creates an instance of class **Server**, specifies the window's default close operation and calls method **runServer** (defined at lines 61–97).

Method **runServer** does the work of setting up the server to receive a connection and processing the connection when it occurs. The method creates a **ServerSocket** called **server** (line 68) to wait for connections. The **ServerSocket** is set up to listen for a connection from a client at port **5000**. The second argument to the constructor is the number of connections that can wait in a queue to connect to the server (**100** in this example). If the queue is full when a client attempts to connect, the server refuses the connection.

```
// Fig. 17.4: Server.java
// Set up a Server that will receive a connection
// from a client, send a string to the client,
// and close the connection.

// Java core packages
import java.io.*;
import java.net.*;
import java.awt.*;
import java.awt.event.*;

// Java extension packages
import javax.swing.*;

public class Server extends JFrame {
   private JTextField enterField;
   private JTextArea displayArea;
   private ObjectOutputStream output;
   private ObjectInputStream input;
   private ServerSocket server;
   private Socket connection;
   private int counter = 1;

   // set up GUI
   public Server()
   {
      super( "Server" );

      Container container = getContentPane();

      // create enterField and register listener
      enterField = new JTextField();
      enterField.setEnabled( false );

      enterField.addActionListener(

         new ActionListener() {

            // send message to client
            public void actionPerformed( ActionEvent event )
            {
               sendData( event.getActionCommand() );
            }

         }  // end anonymous inner class

      ); // end call to addActionListener

      container.add( enterField, BorderLayout.NORTH );

      // create displayArea
      displayArea = new JTextArea();
```

Fig. 17.4 Server portion of a client/server stream-socket connection (part 1 of 4).

```
      container.add( new JScrollPane( displayArea ),
         BorderLayout.CENTER );

      setSize( 300, 150 );
      setVisible( true );
   }

   // set up and run server
   public void runServer()
   {
      // set up server to receive connections;
      // process connections
      try {

         // Step 1: Create a ServerSocket.
         server = new ServerSocket( 5000, 100 );

         while ( true ) {

            // Step 2: Wait for a connection.
            waitForConnection();

            // Step 3: Get input and output streams.
            getStreams();

            // Step 4: Process connection.
            processConnection();

            // Step 5: Close connection.
            closeConnection();

            ++counter;
         }
      }

      // process EOFException when client closes connection
      catch ( EOFException eofException ) {
         System.out.println( "Client terminated connection" );
      }

      // process problems with I/O
      catch ( IOException ioException ) {
         ioException.printStackTrace();
      }
   }

   // wait for connection to arrive, then display connection info
   private void waitForConnection() throws IOException
   {
      displayArea.setText( "Waiting for connection\n" );

      // allow server to accept a connection
      connection = server.accept();
```

Fig. 17.4 Server portion of a client/server stream-socket connection (part 2 of 4).

```

      displayArea.append( "Connection " + counter +
         " received from: " +
         connection.getInetAddress().getHostName() );
   }

   // get streams to send and receive data
   private void getStreams() throws IOException
   {
      // set up output stream for objects
      output = new ObjectOutputStream(
         connection.getOutputStream() );

      // flush output buffer to send header information
      output.flush();

      // set up input stream for objects
      input = new ObjectInputStream(
         connection.getInputStream() );

      displayArea.append( "\nGot I/O streams\n" );
   }

   // process connection with client
   private void processConnection() throws IOException
   {
      // send connection successful message to client
      String message = "SERVER>>> Connection successful";
      output.writeObject( message );
      output.flush();

      // enable enterField so server user can send messages
      enterField.setEnabled( true );

      // process messages sent from client
      do {

         // read message and display it
         try {
            message = ( String ) input.readObject();
            displayArea.append( "\n" + message );
            displayArea.setCaretPosition(
               displayArea.getText().length() );
         }

         // catch problems reading from client
         catch ( ClassNotFoundException classNotFoundException ) {
            displayArea.append( "\nUnknown object type received" );
         }

      } while ( !message.equals( "CLIENT>>> TERMINATE" ) );
   }

```

Fig. 17.4 Server portion of a client/server stream-socket connection (part 3 of 4).

```
159     // close streams and socket
160     private void closeConnection() throws IOException
161     {
162        displayArea.append( "\nUser terminated connection" );
163        enterField.setEnabled( false );
164        output.close();
165        input.close();
166        connection.close();
167     }
168
169     // send message to client
170     private void sendData( String message )
171     {
172        // send object to client
173        try {
174           output.writeObject( "SERVER>>> " + message );
175           output.flush();
176           displayArea.append( "\nSERVER>>>" + message );
177        }
178
179        // process problems sending object
180        catch ( IOException ioException ) {
181           displayArea.append( "\nError writing object" );
182        }
183     }
184
185     // execute application
186     public static void main( String args[] )
187     {
188        Server application = new Server();
189
190        application.setDefaultCloseOperation(
191           JFrame.EXIT_ON_CLOSE );
192
193        application.runServer();
194     }
195
196  }  // end class Server
```

Fig. 17.4 Server portion of a client/server stream-socket connection (part 4 of 4).

Software Engineering Observation 17.5

Port numbers can be between 0 and 65,535. Many operating systems reserve port numbers below 1024 for system services (such as e-mail and World Wide Web servers). Generally, these ports should not be specified as connection ports in user programs. In fact, some operating systems require special access privileges to use port numbers below 1024.

Line 73 calls method **waitForConnection** (lines 100–110) to wait for a client connection. After the connection is established, line 76 calls method **getStreams** (lines 113–127) to obtain references to the **InputStream** and **OutputStream** for the connection. Line 79 calls method **processConnection** to send the initial connection message to the client and to process all messages received from the client. Line 82 calls method **closeConnection** to terminate the connection with the client.

In method **waitForConnection** (lines 100–110), line 105 uses **ServerSocket** method **accept** to wait for a connection from a client and assigns the resulting **Socket** to **connection**. This method blocks until a connection is received (i.e., the thread in which **accept** is called stops executing until a client connects). Lines 107–109 output the host name of the computer that made the connection. **Socket** method **getInetAddress** returns an **InetAddress** object (package **java.net**) containing information about the client computer. **InetAddress** method ***getHostName*** returns the host name of the client computer. For example, if the Internet address of the computer is **127.0.0.1**, the corresponding host name would be **localhost**.

Method **getStreams** (lines 113–127) obtains references to the **InputStream** and **OutputStream** of the **Socket** and uses them to initialize an **ObjectInputStream** and an **ObjectOutputStream**, respectively. Notice the call to **ObjectOutputStream** method **flush** at line 120. This statement causes the **ObjectOutputStream** on the server to send a *stream header* to the corresponding client's **ObjectInputStream**. The stream header contains information such as the version of object serialization being used to send objects. This information is required by the **ObjectInputStream** so it can prepare to receive those objects correctly.

Software Engineering Observation 17.6

*When using an **ObjectOutputStream** and **ObjectInputStream** to send and receive objects over a network connection, always create the **ObjectOutputStream** first and **flush** the stream so the client's **ObjectInputStream** can prepare to receive the data. This is required only for applications that communicate using **ObjectOutputStream** and **ObjectInputStream***

Line 134 of method **processConnection** (lines 130–157) uses **ObjectOutputStream** method **writeObject** to send the string "**SERVER>>> Connection successful**" to the client. Line 135 flushes the output stream to ensure that the object is sent immediately; otherwise, the object could be held in an output buffer until more information is available to send.

Performance Tip 17.3

Output buffers typically are used to increase the efficiency of an application by sending larger amounts of data fewer times. The input and output components of a computer are typically much slower than the memory of the computer.

The **do/while** structure at lines 141–156 loops until the server receives the message "**CLIENT>>> TERMINATE**." Line 145 uses **ObjectInputStream** method **readObject** to read a **String** from the client. Line 146 displays the message in the **JTextArea**. Lines 147–148 use **JTextComponent** method ***setCaretPosition*** to position the input cursor in the **JTextArea** after the last character in the **JTextArea**. This scrolls the **JTextArea** as text is appended to it.

When the transmission is complete, method **processConnection** returns and the program calls method **closeConnection** (lines 160–167) to close the streams associated with the **Socket** and close the **Socket**. Next, the server waits for the next connection attempt from a client by continuing with line 73 at the beginning of the **while** loop.

When the user of the server application enters a **String** in the **JTextField** and presses the *Enter* key, the program calls method **actionPerformed** (lines 40–43), reads the **String** from the **JTextField** and calls utility method **sendData** (lines 170–183).

Method **sendData** sends the **String** object to the client, flushes the output buffer and appends the same **String** to the **JTextArea** in the server window.

Notice that the **Server** receives a connection, processes the connection, closes the connection and waits for the next connection. A more likely scenario would be a **Server** that receives a connection, sets up that connection to be processed as a separate thread of execution, and waits for new connections. The separate threads that process existing connections can continue to execute while the **Server** concentrates on new connection requests.

Like class **Server**, class **Client**'s (Fig. 17.5) constructor creates the GUI of the application (a **JTextField** and a **JTextArea**). The **Client** object displays its output in a **JTextArea**. When the **main** method (line 175–188) executes, it creates an instance of class **Client**, specifies the window's default close operation and calls method **runClient** (defined at lines 63–90). In this example, you can execute the client from any computer on the Internet and specify the Internet address or host name of the server computer as a command-line argument to the program. For example,

```
java Client 192.168.1.15
```

connects to the **Server** on the computer with Internet address **192.168.1.15**.

```
1   // Fig. 17.5: Client.java
2   // Set up a Client that will read information sent
3   // from a Server and display the information.
4
5   // Java core packages
6   import java.io.*;
7   import java.net.*;
8   import java.awt.*;
9   import java.awt.event.*;
10
11  // Java extension packages
12  import javax.swing.*;
13
14  public class Client extends JFrame {
15     private JTextField enterField;
16     private JTextArea displayArea;
17     private ObjectOutputStream output;
18     private ObjectInputStream input;
19     private String message = "";
20     private String chatServer;
21     private Socket client;
22
23     // initialize chatServer and set up GUI
24     public Client( String host )
25     {
26        super( "Client" );
27
28        // set server to which this client connects
29        chatServer = host;
```

Fig. 17.5 Demonstrating the client portion of a stream-socket connection between a client and a server (part 1 of 5).

```

      Container container = getContentPane();

      // create enterField and register listener
      enterField = new JTextField();
      enterField.setEnabled( false );

      enterField.addActionListener(

         new ActionListener() {

            // send message to server
            public void actionPerformed( ActionEvent event )
            {
               sendData( event.getActionCommand() );
            }

         }  // end anonymous inner class

      ); // end call to addActionListener

      container.add( enterField, BorderLayout.NORTH );

      // create displayArea
      displayArea = new JTextArea();
      container.add( new JScrollPane( displayArea ),
         BorderLayout.CENTER );

      setSize( 300, 150 );
      setVisible( true );
   }

   // connect to server and process messages from server
   public void runClient()
   {
      // connect to server, get streams, process connection
      try {

         // Step 1: Create a Socket to make connection
         connectToServer();

         // Step 2: Get the input and output streams
         getStreams();

         // Step 3: Process connection
         processConnection();

         // Step 4: Close connection
         closeConnection();
      }

```

Fig. 17.5 Demonstrating the client portion of a stream-socket connection between a client and a server (part 2 of 5).

```
         // server closed connection
         catch ( EOFException eofException ) {
            System.out.println( "Server terminated connection" );
         }

         // process problems communicating with server
         catch ( IOException ioException ) {
            ioException.printStackTrace();
         }
      }

      // get streams to send and receive data
      private void getStreams() throws IOException
      {
         // set up output stream for objects
         output = new ObjectOutputStream(
            client.getOutputStream() );

         // flush output buffer to send header information
         output.flush();

         // set up input stream for objects
         input = new ObjectInputStream(
            client.getInputStream() );

         displayArea.append( "\nGot I/O streams\n" );
      }

      // connect to server
      private void connectToServer() throws IOException
      {
         displayArea.setText( "Attempting connection\n" );

         // create Socket to make connection to server
         client = new Socket(
            InetAddress.getByName( chatServer ), 5000 );

         // display connection information
         displayArea.append( "Connected to: " +
            client.getInetAddress().getHostName() );
      }

      // process connection with server
      private void processConnection() throws IOException
      {
         // enable enterField so client user can send messages
         enterField.setEnabled( true );

         // process messages sent from server
         do {

```

Fig. 17.5 Demonstrating the client portion of a stream-socket connection between a client and a server (part 3 of 5).

```
         // read message and display it
         try {
            message = ( String ) input.readObject();
            displayArea.append( "\n" + message );
            displayArea.setCaretPosition(
               displayArea.getText().length() );
         }

         // catch problems reading from server
         catch ( ClassNotFoundException classNotFoundException ) {
            displayArea.append( "\nUnknown object type received" );
         }

      } while ( !message.equals( "SERVER>>> TERMINATE" ) );

   } // end method process connection

   // close streams and socket
   private void closeConnection() throws IOException
   {
      displayArea.append( "\nClosing connection" );
      output.close();
      input.close();
      client.close();
   }

   // send message to server
   private void sendData( String message )
   {
      // send object to server
      try {
         output.writeObject( "CLIENT>>> " + message );
         output.flush();
         displayArea.append( "\nCLIENT>>>" + message );
      }

      // process problems sending object
      catch ( IOException ioException ) {
         displayArea.append( "\nError writing object" );
      }
   }

   // execute application
   public static void main( String args[] )
   {
      Client application;

      if ( args.length == 0 )
         application = new Client( "127.0.0.1" );
      else
         application = new Client( args[ 0 ] );

```

Fig. 17.5 Demonstrating the client portion of a stream-socket connection between a client and a server (part 4 of 5).

```
184         application.setDefaultCloseOperation(
185            JFrame.EXIT_ON_CLOSE );
186
187         application.runClient();
188      }
189
190   }  // end class Client
```

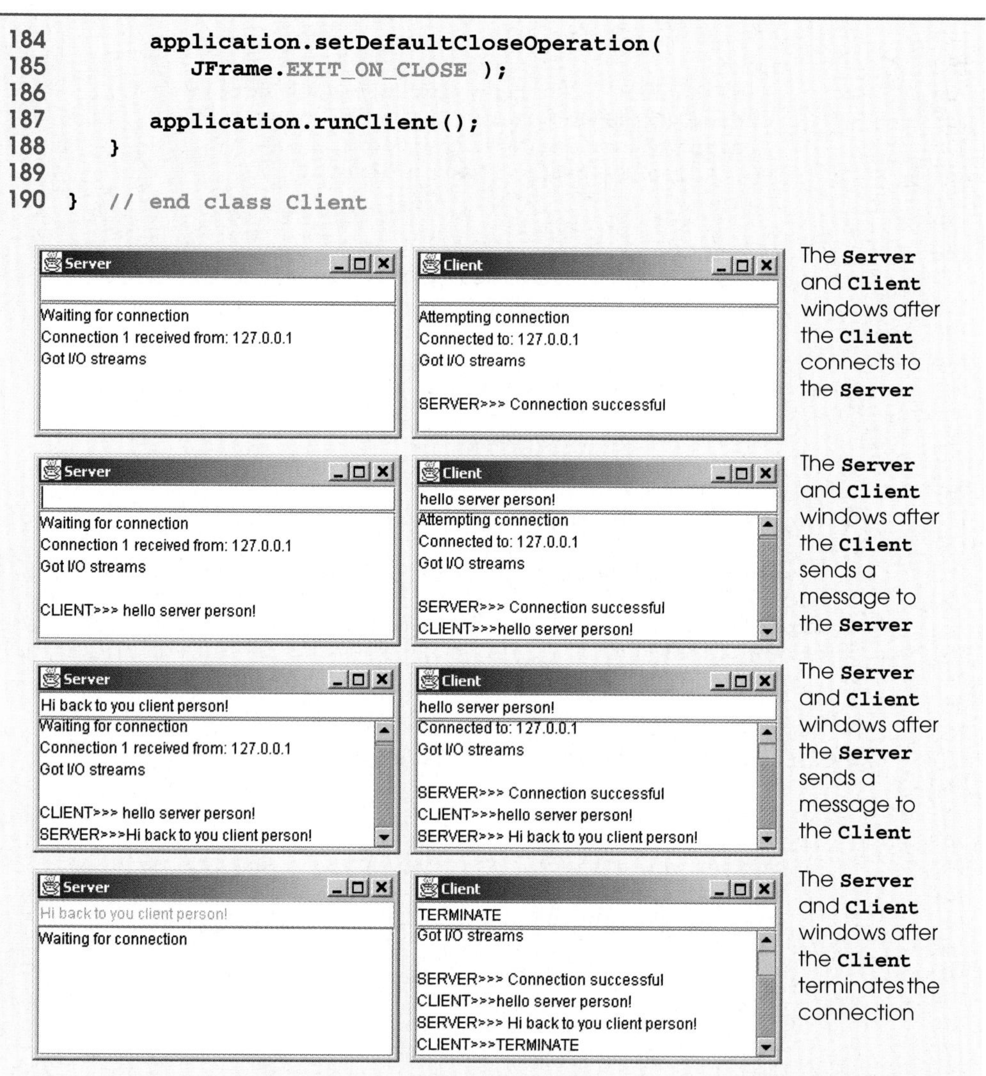

The **Server** and **Client** windows after the **Client** connects to the **Server**

The **Server** and **Client** windows after the **Client** sends a message to the **Server**

The **Server** and **Client** windows after the **Server** sends a message to the **Client**

The **Server** and **Client** windows after the **Client** terminates the connection

Fig. 17.5 Demonstrating the client portion of a stream-socket connection between a client and a server (part 5 of 5).

Client method **runClient** (lines 63–90) performs the work necessary to connect to the **Server**, to receive data from the **Server** and to send data to the **Server**. Line 69 calls method **connectToServer** (lines 110–121) to perform the connection. After connecting, line 72 calls method **getStreams** (lines 93–107) to obtain references to the **Socket**'s **InputStream** and **OutputStream** objects. Then line 75 calls method **processConnection** (124–147) to handle messages sent from the server. When the connection terminates, line 78 calls **closeConnection** to close the streams and the **Socket**.

Method **connectToServer** (lines 110–121) creates a **Socket** called **client** (lines 115–116) to establish a connection. The method passes two arguments to the

Socket constructor—the Internet address of the server computer and the port number (5000) where that computer is awaiting client connections. The call to **InetAddress static** method **getByName** in the first argument returns an **InetAddress** object containing the Internet address specified as a command-line argument to the application (or **127.0.0.1** if no command-line arguments are specified). Method **getByName** can receive a **String** containing either the actual Internet address or the host name of the server. The first argument also could have been written other ways. For the localhost address 127.0.0.1, the first argument could be

```
InetAddress.getByName( "localhost" )
```

or

```
InetAddress.getLocalHost()
```

Also, there are versions of the **Socket** constructor that receive a **String** for the Internet address or host name. The first argument could have been specified as **"127.0.0.1"** or **"localhost"**. [*Note*: We chose to demonstrate the client/server relationship by connecting between programs executing on the same computer (**localhost**). Normally, this first argument would be the Internet address of another computer. The **InetAddress** object for another computer can be obtained by specifying the Internet address or host name of the other computer as the **String** argument to **InetAddress.getByName**.]

The **Socket** constructor's second argument is the server port number. This number must match the port number at which the server is waiting for connections (called the handshake point). Once the connection is made, a message is displayed in the **JTextArea** (lines 119–120) indicating the name of the server computer to which the client connected.

The **Client** uses an **ObjectOutputStream** to send data to the server and an **ObjectInputStream** to receive data from the server. Method **getStreams** (lines 93–107) creates the **ObjectOutputStream** and **ObjectInputStream** objects that use the **OutputStream** and **InputStream** objects associated with **client**.

Method **processConnection** (lines 124–147) contains a **do/while** structure that loops until the client receives the message "**SERVER>>> TERMINATE**." Line 134 uses **ObjectInputStream** method **readObject** to read a **String** from the server. Line 135 displays the message in the **JTextArea**. Lines 136–137 use **JTextComponent** method **setCaretPosition** to position the input cursor in the **JTextArea** after the last character in the **JTextArea**.

When the transmission is complete, method **closeConnection** (lines 150–156) closes the streams and the **Socket**.

When the user of the client application enters a **String** in the **JTextField** and presses the *Enter* key, the program calls method **actionPerformed** (lines 42–45) to read the **String** from the **JTextField** and invoke utility method **sendData** (159–172). Method **sendData** sends the **String** object to server client, flushes the output buffer and appends the same **String** to the **JTextArea** in the client window.

17.7 Connectionless Client/Server Interaction with Datagrams

We have been discussing *connection-oriented, streams-based transmission*. Now we consider *connectionless transmission with datagrams*.

Connection-oriented transmission is like the telephone system in which you dial and are given a *connection* to the telephone of the person with whom you wish to communicate. The connection is maintained for the duration of your phone call, even when you are not talking.

Connectionless transmission with *datagrams* is more like the way mail is carried via the postal service. If a large message will not fit in one envelope, you break it into separate message pieces that you place in separate, sequentially numbered envelopes. Each of the letters is then mailed at the same time. The letters could arrive in order, out of order or not at all (although the last case is rare, it does happen). The person at the receiving end reassembles the message pieces into sequential order before attempting to make sense of the message. If your message is small enough to fit in one envelope, you do not have to worry about the "out-of-sequence" problem, but it is still possible that your message might not arrive. One difference between datagrams and postal mail is that duplicates of datagrams can arrive on the receiving computer.

The programs of Fig. 17.6 and Fig. 17.7 use datagrams to send packets of information between a client application and a server application. In the **Client** application (Fig. 17.7), the user types a message into a **JTextField** and presses *Enter*. The program converts the message into a **byte** array and places it in a datagram packet that is sent to the server. The **Server** (Fig. 17.6) receives the packet and displays the information in the packet, then *echoes* the packet back to the client. When the client receives the packet, the client displays the information in the packet. In this example, the **Client** and **Server** classes are implemented similarly.

Class **Server** (Fig. 17.6) defines two **DatagramPacket**s that the server uses to send and receive information and one **DatagramSocket** that sends and receives these packets. The constructor for class **Server** (lines 20–41) creates the graphical user interface where the packets of information will be displayed. Next the constructor creates the **DatagramSocket** in a **try** block. Line 32 uses the **DatagramSocket** constructor that takes an integer port number argument (**5000**) to bind the server to a port where the server can receive packets from clients. **Client**s sending packets to this **Server** specify port **5000** in the packets they send. The **DatagramSocket** constructor throws a ***SocketException*** if it fails to bind the **DatagramSocket** to a port.

Common Programming Error 17.2

Specifying a port that is already in use or specifying an invalid port number when creating a ***DatagramSocket*** *results in a* ***BindException****.*

```
1  // Fig. 17.6: Server.java
2  // Set up a Server that will receive packets from a
3  // client and send packets to a client.
4
5  // Java core packages
6  import java.io.*;
7  import java.net.*;
8  import java.awt.*;
9  import java.awt.event.*;
10
```

Fig. 17.6 Demonstrating the server side of connectionless client/server computing with datagrams (part 1 of 4).

```
// Java extension packages
import javax.swing.*;

public class Server extends JFrame {
   private JTextArea displayArea;
   private DatagramPacket sendPacket, receivePacket;
   private DatagramSocket socket;

   // set up GUI and DatagramSocket
   public Server()
   {
      super( "Server" );

      displayArea = new JTextArea();
      getContentPane().add( new JScrollPane( displayArea ),
         BorderLayout.CENTER );
      setSize( 400, 300 );
      setVisible( true );

      // create DatagramSocket for sending and receiving packets
      try {
         socket = new DatagramSocket( 5000 );
      }

      // process problems creating DatagramSocket
      catch( SocketException socketException ) {
         socketException.printStackTrace();
         System.exit( 1 );
      }

   }  // end Server constructor

   // wait for packets to arrive, then display data and echo
   // packet to client
   public void waitForPackets()
   {
      // loop forever
      while ( true ) {

         // receive packet, display contents, echo to client
         try {

            // set up packet
            byte data[] = new byte[ 100 ];
            receivePacket =
               new DatagramPacket( data, data.length );

            // wait for packet
            socket.receive( receivePacket );

            // process packet
            displayPacket();
```

Fig. 17.6 Demonstrating the server side of connectionless client/server computing with datagrams (part 2 of 4).

```

            // echo information from packet back to client
            sendPacketToClient();
         }

         // process problems manipulating packet
         catch( IOException ioException ) {
            displayArea.append( ioException.toString() + "\n" );
            ioException.printStackTrace();
         }

      } // end while

   } // end method waitForPackets

   // display packet contents
   private void displayPacket()
   {
      displayArea.append( "\nPacket received:" +
         "\nFrom host: " + receivePacket.getAddress() +
         "\nHost port: " + receivePacket.getPort() +
         "\nLength: " + receivePacket.getLength() +
         "\nContaining:\n\t" +
         new String( receivePacket.getData(), 0,
            receivePacket.getLength() ) );
   }

   // echo packet to client
   private void sendPacketToClient() throws IOException
   {
      displayArea.append( "\n\nEcho data to client..." );

      // create packet to send
      sendPacket = new DatagramPacket( receivePacket.getData(),
         receivePacket.getLength(), receivePacket.getAddress(),
         receivePacket.getPort() );

      // send packet
      socket.send( sendPacket );

      displayArea.append( "Packet sent\n" );
      displayArea.setCaretPosition(
         displayArea.getText().length() );
   }

   // execute application
   public static void main( String args[] )
   {
      Server application = new Server();

      application.setDefaultCloseOperation(
         JFrame.EXIT_ON_CLOSE );
```

Fig. 17.6 Demonstrating the server side of connectionless client/server computing with datagrams (part 3 of 4).

```
115
116             application.waitForPackets();
117         }
118
119 }  // end class Server
```

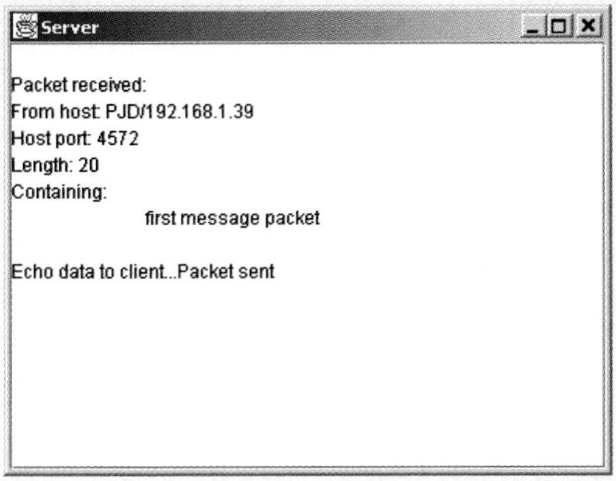

Server

Packet received:
From host: PJD/192.168.1.39
Host port: 4572
Length: 20
Containing:
first message packet

Echo data to client...Packet sent

The **Server** window after the client sends a packet of data

Fig. 17.6 Demonstrating the server side of connectionless client/server computing with datagrams (part 4 of 4).

Server method **waitForPackets** (lines 45–76) uses an infinite loop to wait for packets to arrive at the **Server**. Lines 54–56 create a **DatagramPacket** in which a received packet of information can be stored. The **DatagramPacket** constructor for this purpose receives two arguments—a **byte** array containing the data and the length of the **byte** array. Line 59 waits for a packet to arrive at the **Server**. Method ***receive*** blocks until a packet arrives, then stores the packet in its **DatagramPacket** argument. Method **receive** throws an **IOException** if an error occurs receiving a packet.

When a packet arrives, the program calls method **displayPacket** (lines 79–88) to append the packet's contents to **displayArea**. **DatagramPacket** method ***getAddress*** (line 82) returns an **InetAddress** object containing the host name of the computer from which the packet was sent. Method ***getPort*** (line 83) returns an integer specifying the port number through which the host computer sent the packet. Method ***getLength*** (line 84) returns an integer representing the number of bytes of data that were sent. Method ***getData*** (line 86) returns a **byte** array containing the data that was sent. The program uses the **byte** array to initialize a **String** object so the data can be output to the **JTextArea**.

After displaying a packet, the program calls method **sendPacketToClient** (line 65) to create a new packet and send it to the client. Lines 96–98 create **sendPacket** and pass four arguments to the **DatagramPacket** constructor. The first argument specifies the **byte** array to send. The second argument specifies the number of bytes to send. The third argument specifies the client computer's Internet address, to which the packet will be sent. The fourth argument specifies the port where the client is waiting to receive packets. Line 101 sends the packet over the network. Method ***send*** throws an **IOException** if an error occurs sending a packet.

Class **Client** (Fig. 17.7) works similarly to class **Server**, except that the **Client** sends packets only when the user types a message in a **JTextField** and presses the *Enter* key. When this occurs, the program calls method **actionPerformed** (lines 34–67), which converts the **String** the user entered in the **JTextField** into a **byte** array (line 45). Lines 48–50 create a **DatagramPacket** and initialize it with the **byte** array, the length of the **String** that was entered by the user, the Internet address to which the packet is to be sent (**InetAddress.getLocalHost()** in this example) and the port number at which the **Server** is waiting for packets. Line 53 sends the packet. Note that the client in this example must know that the server is receiving packets at port 5000; otherwise, the server will not receive the packets.

```
1   // Fig. 17.7: Client.java
2   // Set up a Client that will send packets to a
3   // server and receive packets from a server.
4
5   // Java core packages
6   import java.io.*;
7   import java.net.*;
8   import java.awt.*;
9   import java.awt.event.*;
10
11  // Java extension packages
12  import javax.swing.*;
13
14  public class Client extends JFrame {
15     private JTextField enterField;
16     private JTextArea displayArea;
17     private DatagramPacket sendPacket, receivePacket;
18     private DatagramSocket socket;
19
20     // set up GUI and DatagramSocket
21     public Client()
22     {
23        super( "Client" );
24
25        Container container = getContentPane();
26
27        enterField = new JTextField( "Type message here" );
28
29        enterField.addActionListener(
30
31           new ActionListener() {
32
33              // create and send a packet
34              public void actionPerformed( ActionEvent event )
35              {
36                 // create and send packet
37                 try {
38                    displayArea.append(
39                       "\nSending packet containing: " +
40                       event.getActionCommand() + "\n" );
41
```

Fig. 17.7 Demonstrating the client side of connectionless client/server computing with datagrams (part 1 of 4).

```
                  // get message from textfield and convert to
                  // array of bytes
                  String message = event.getActionCommand();
                  byte data[] = message.getBytes();

                  // create sendPacket
                  sendPacket = new DatagramPacket(
                     data, data.length,
                     InetAddress.getLocalHost(), 5000 );

                  // send packet
                  socket.send( sendPacket );

                  displayArea.append( "Packet sent\n" );
                  displayArea.setCaretPosition(
                     displayArea.getText().length() );
               }

               // process problems creating or sending packet
               catch ( IOException ioException ) {
                  displayArea.append(
                     ioException.toString() + "\n" );
                  ioException.printStackTrace();
               }

            } // end actionPerformed

         } // end anonymous inner class

      ); // end call to addActionListener

      container.add( enterField, BorderLayout.NORTH );

      displayArea = new JTextArea();
      container.add( new JScrollPane( displayArea ),
         BorderLayout.CENTER );

      setSize( 400, 300 );
      setVisible( true );

      // create DatagramSocket for sending and receiving packets
      try {
         socket = new DatagramSocket();
      }

      // catch problems creating DatagramSocket
      catch( SocketException socketException ) {
         socketException.printStackTrace();
         System.exit( 1 );
      }

   } // end Client constructor
```

Fig. 17.7 Demonstrating the client side of connectionless client/server computing with datagrams (part 2 of 4).

```

   // wait for packets to arrive from Server,
   // then display packet contents
   public void waitForPackets()
   {
      // loop forever
      while ( true ) {

         // receive packet and display contents
         try {

            // set up packet
            byte data[] = new byte[ 100 ];
            receivePacket =
               new DatagramPacket( data, data.length );

            // wait for packet
            socket.receive( receivePacket );

            // display packet contents
            displayPacket();
         }

         // process problems receiving or displaying packet
         catch( IOException exception ) {
            displayArea.append( exception.toString() + "\n" );
            exception.printStackTrace();
         }

      } // end while

   } // end method waitForPackets

   // display contents of receivePacket
   private void displayPacket()
   {
      displayArea.append( "\nPacket received:" +
         "\nFrom host: " + receivePacket.getAddress() +
         "\nHost port: " + receivePacket.getPort() +
         "\nLength: " + receivePacket.getLength() +
         "\nContaining:\n\t" +
         new String( receivePacket.getData(), 0,
            receivePacket.getLength() ) );

      displayArea.setCaretPosition(
         displayArea.getText().length() );
   }

   // execute application
   public static void main( String args[] )
   {
      Client application = new Client();
```

Fig. 17.7 Demonstrating the client side of connectionless client/server computing with datagrams (part 3 of 4).

```
146
147          application.setDefaultCloseOperation(
148             JFrame.EXIT_ON_CLOSE );
149
150          application.waitForPackets();
151       }
152
153    }  // end class Client
```

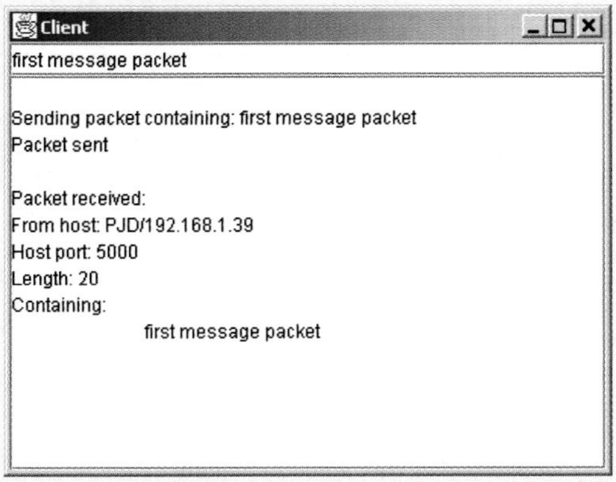

Client

first message packet

Sending packet containing: first message packet
Packet sent

Packet received:
From host: PJD/192.168.1.39
Host port: 5000
Length: 20
Containing:
first message packet

The **Client** window after sending a packet to the server and receiving the packet back from the server

Fig. 17.7 Demonstrating the client side of connectionless client/server computing with datagrams (part 4 of 4).

Notice that the **DatagramSocket** constructor call (line 84) in this application does not specify any arguments. This constructor allows the computer to select the next available port number for the **DatagramSocket**. The client does not need a specific port number, because the server receives the client's port number as part of each **DatagramPacket** sent by the client. Thus, the server can send packets back to the same computer and port number from which the server receives a packet of information.

Client method **waitForPackets** (lines 97–125) uses an infinite loop to wait for packets from the server. Line 111 blocks until a packet arrives. Note that this does not prevent the user from sending a packet, because the GUI events are handled in the event dispatch thread. It only prevents the **while** loop from continuing until a packet arrives at the **Client**. When a packet arrives, line 111 stores the packet in **receivePacket**, and line 114 calls method **displayPacket** (128–140) to display the packet's contents in the **JTextArea**.

17.8 Client/Server Tic-Tac-Toe Using a Multithreaded Server

In this section, we present the popular game Tic-Tac-Toe implemented by using client/server techniques with stream sockets. The program consists of a **TicTacToeServer** application (Fig. 17.8) that allows two **TicTacToeClient** applets (Fig. 17.9) to connect to the server and play Tic-Tac-Toe (outputs shown in Fig. 17.10). As the server receives each client connection, it creates an instance of inner class **Player** (lines 158–279 of Fig. 17.8) to process the client in a separate thread. These threads enable the clients to play the game independently. The server assigns Xs to the first client to connect (X makes the first move) and assigns

Os to the second client to connect. The server maintains the information about the board so it can determine whether a player's move is a valid or invalid move. Each **TicTacToe-Client** applet (Fig. 17.9) maintains its own GUI version of the Tic-Tac-Toe board on which it displays the state of the game. The clients can place a mark only in an empty square on the board. Class **Square** (lines 212–270 of Fig. 17.9) implements each of the nine squares on the board. Class **TicTacToeServer** and class **Player** are implemented in file **TicTac-ToeServer.java** (Fig. 17.8). Class **TicTacToeClient** and class **Square** are implemented in file **TicTacToeClient.java** (Fig. 17.9).

```
// Fig. 17.8: TicTacToeServer.java
// This class maintains a game of Tic-Tac-Toe for two
// client applets.

// Java core packages
import java.awt.*;
import java.awt.event.*;
import java.net.*;
import java.io.*;

// Java extension packages
import javax.swing.*;

public class TicTacToeServer extends JFrame {
   private byte board[];
   private JTextArea outputArea;
   private Player players[];
   private ServerSocket server;
   private int currentPlayer;

   // set up tic-tac-toe server and GUI that displays messages
   public TicTacToeServer()
   {
      super( "Tic-Tac-Toe Server" );

      board = new byte[ 9 ];
      players = new Player[ 2 ];
      currentPlayer = 0;

      // set up ServerSocket
      try {
         server = new ServerSocket( 5000, 2 );
      }

      // process problems creating ServerSocket
      catch( IOException ioException ) {
         ioException.printStackTrace();
         System.exit( 1 );
      }

      // set up JTextArea to display messages during execution
      outputArea = new JTextArea();
```

Fig. 17.8 Server side of client/server Tic-Tac-Toe program (part 1 of 6).

```
      getContentPane().add( outputArea, BorderLayout.CENTER );
      outputArea.setText( "Server awaiting connections\n" );

      setSize( 300, 300 );
      setVisible( true );
   }

   // wait for two connections so game can be played
   public void execute()
   {
      // wait for each client to connect
      for ( int i = 0; i < players.length; i++ ) {

         // wait for connection, create Player, start thread
         try {
            players[ i ] = new Player( server.accept(), i );
            players[ i ].start();
         }

         // process problems receiving connection from client
         catch( IOException ioException ) {
            ioException.printStackTrace();
            System.exit( 1 );
         }
      }

      // Player X is suspended until Player O connects.
      // Resume player X now.
      synchronized ( players[ 0 ] ) {
         players[ 0 ].setSuspended( false );
         players[ 0 ].notify();
      }

   }  // end method execute

   // display a message in outputArea
   public void display( String message )
   {
      outputArea.append( message + "\n" );
   }

   // Determine if a move is valid.
   // This method is synchronized because only one move can be
   // made at a time.
   public synchronized boolean validMove(
      int location, int player )
   {
      boolean moveDone = false;

      // while not current player, must wait for turn
      while ( player != currentPlayer ) {

```

Fig. 17.8 Server side of client/server Tic-Tac-Toe program (part 2 of 6).

```
         // wait for turn
         try {
            wait();
         }

         // catch wait interruptions
         catch( InterruptedException interruptedException ) {
            interruptedException.printStackTrace();
         }
      }

      // if location not occupied, make move
      if ( !isOccupied( location ) ) {

         // set move in board array
         board[ location ] =
            ( byte ) ( currentPlayer == 0 ? 'X' : 'O' );

         // change current player
         currentPlayer = ( currentPlayer + 1 ) % 2;

         // let new current player know that move occurred
         players[ currentPlayer ].otherPlayerMoved( location );

         // tell waiting player to continue
         notify();

         // tell player that made move that the move was valid
         return true;
      }

      // tell player that made move that the move was not valid
      else
         return false;
   }

   // determine whether location is occupied
   public boolean isOccupied( int location )
   {
      if ( board[ location ] == 'X' || board [ location ] == 'O' )
          return true;
      else
          return false;
   }

   // place code in this method to determine whether game over
   public boolean gameOver()
   {
      return false;
   }

```

Fig. 17.8 Server side of client/server Tic-Tac-Toe program (part 3 of 6).

```
   // execute application
   public static void main( String args[] )
   {
      TicTacToeServer application = new TicTacToeServer();

      application.setDefaultCloseOperation(
         JFrame.EXIT_ON_CLOSE );

      application.execute();
   }

   // private inner class Player manages each Player as a thread
   private class Player extends Thread {
      private Socket connection;
      private DataInputStream input;
      private DataOutputStream output;
      private int playerNumber;
      private char mark;
      protected boolean suspended = true;

      // set up Player thread
      public Player( Socket socket, int number )
      {
         playerNumber = number;

         // specify player's mark
         mark = ( playerNumber == 0 ? 'X' : 'O' );

         connection = socket;

         // obtain streams from Socket
         try {
            input = new DataInputStream(
               connection.getInputStream() );
            output = new DataOutputStream(
               connection.getOutputStream() );
         }

         // process problems getting streams
         catch( IOException ioException ) {
            ioException.printStackTrace();
            System.exit( 1 );
         }
      }

      // send message that other player moved; message contains
      // a String followed by an int
      public void otherPlayerMoved( int location )
      {
         // send message indicating move
         try {
            output.writeUTF( "Opponent moved" );
```

Fig. 17.8 Server side of client/server Tic-Tac-Toe program (part 4 of 6).

```
            output.writeInt( location );
         }

         // process problems sending message
         catch ( IOException ioException ) {
            ioException.printStackTrace();
         }
      }

      // control thread's execution
      public void run()
      {
         // send client message indicating its mark (X or O),
         // process messages from client
         try {
            display( "Player " + ( playerNumber == 0 ?
               'X' : 'O' ) + " connected" );

            // send player's mark
            output.writeChar( mark );

            // send message indicating connection
            output.writeUTF( "Player " +
               ( playerNumber == 0 ? "X connected\n" :
                  "O connected, please wait\n" ) );

            // if player X, wait for another player to arrive
            if ( mark == 'X' ) {
               output.writeUTF( "Waiting for another player" );

               // wait for player O
               try {
                  synchronized( this ) {
                     while ( suspended )
                        wait();
                  }
               }

               // process interruptions while waiting
               catch ( InterruptedException exception ) {
                  exception.printStackTrace();
               }

               // send message that other player connected and
               // player X can make a move
               output.writeUTF(
                  "Other player connected. Your move." );
            }

            // while game not over
            while ( ! gameOver() ) {

```

Fig. 17.8 Server side of client/server Tic-Tac-Toe program (part 5 of 6).

```
250                 // get move location from client
251                 int location = input.readInt();
252 
253                 // check for valid move
254                 if ( validMove( location, playerNumber ) ) {
255                    display( "loc: " + location );
256                    output.writeUTF( "Valid move." );
257                 }
258                 else
259                    output.writeUTF( "Invalid move, try again" );
260              }
261 
262              // close connection to client
263              connection.close();
264           }
265 
266           // process problems communicating with client
267           catch( IOException ioException ) {
268              ioException.printStackTrace();
269              System.exit( 1 );
270           }
271        }
272 
273        // set whether or not thread is suspended
274        public void setSuspended( boolean status )
275        {
276           suspended = status;
277        }
278 
279     } // end class Player
280 
281  } // end class TicTacToeServer
```

Tic-Tac-Toe Server
Server awaiting connections
Player X connected
Player O connected
loc: 0
loc: 4
loc: 3
loc: 5
loc: 6
loc: 8
loc: 7
loc: 1
loc: 2

Fig. 17.8 Server side of client/server Tic-Tac-Toe program (part 6 of 6).

We begin with a discussion of the server side of the Tic-Tac-Toe game. When the **`TicTacToeServer`** application executes, the **`main`** method (lines 147–155) creates a **`TicTacToeServer`** object called **`application`**. The constructor (lines 22–48) attempts to set up a **`ServerSocket`**. If successful, the program displays the server window, and **main** invokes the **TicTacToeServer** method **execute** (lines 51–76). Method **execute** loops twice, blocking at line 58 each time while waiting for a client connection. When a client connects, line 58 creates a new **Player** object to manage the connection as a separate thread, and line 59 calls that object's **start** method to begin executing the thread.

When the **TicTacToeServer** creates a **Player**, the **Player** constructor (lines 167–189) receives the **Socket** object representing the connection to the client and gets the associated input and output streams. The **Player**'s **run** method (lines 208–271) controls the information that is sent to the client and the information that is received from the client. First, it tells the client that the client's connection has been made (lines 213–214), then it passes to the client the character that the client will place on the board when a move is made (line 217). Lines 230–233 suspend each **Player** thread as it starts executing, because neither player is allowed to make a move when it first connects. Player X can move only when player O connects, and player O can make a move only after player X.

At this point, the game can be played, and the **run** method begins executing its **while** structure (lines 248–260). Each iteration of this **while** structure reads an integer (line 253) representing the location where the client wants to place a mark, and line 254 invokes the **TicTacToeServer** method **validMove** (lines 87–129) to check the move. Lines 254–259 send a message to the client indicating whether the move was valid. The program maintains board locations as numbers from 0 to 8 (0 through 2 for the first row, 3 through 5 for the second row and 6 through 8 for the third row).

Method **validMove** (lines 87–129 in class **TicTacToeServer**) is a **synchronized** method that allows only one player at a time to move. Synchronizing **validMove** prevents both players from modifying the state information of the game simultaneously. If the **Player** attempting to validate a move is not the current player (i.e., the one allowed to make a move), the **Player** is placed in a *wait* state until it is that **Player**'s turn to move. If the position for the move being validated is already occupied on the board, **validMove** returns **false**. Otherwise, the server places a mark for the player in its local representation of the board (lines 110–111), notifies the other **Player** object (line 117) that a move has been made (so the client can be sent a message), invokes method **notify** (line 120) so the waiting **Player** (if there is one) can validate a move and returns **true** (line 123) to indicate that the move is valid.

When a **TicTacToeClient** (Fig. 17.9) applet begins execution, it creates a **JTextArea** in which messages from the server and a representation of the board using nine **Square** objects are displayed. The applet's **start** method (lines 80–104) opens a connection to the server and gets the associated input and output streams from the **Socket** object. Class **TicTacToeClient** implements interface **Runnable** so that a separate thread can read messages from the server. This approach enables the user to interact with the board (in the event-dispatch thread) while waiting for messages from the server. After establishing the connection to the server, line 102 creates **Thread** object **outputThread** and initializes it with the **Runnable** applet, then line 103 calls the thread's **start** method. The applet's **run** method (lines 108–137) controls the separate thread of execution. The method first reads the mark character (X or O) from the server (line 112), then loops continually (lines 123–135) and reads messages from the server (line 127). Each message is passed to the applet's **processMessage** method (lines 140–211) for processing.

```
// Fig. 17.9: TicTacToeClient.java
// Client for the TicTacToe program

// Java core packages
import java.awt.*;
import java.awt.event.*;
import java.net.*;
import java.io.*;

// Java extension packages
import javax.swing.*;

// Client class to let a user play Tic-Tac-Toe with
// another user across a network.
public class TicTacToeClient extends JApplet
   implements Runnable {

   private JTextField idField;
   private JTextArea displayArea;
   private JPanel boardPanel, panel2;
   private Square board[][], currentSquare;
   private Socket connection;
   private DataInputStream input;
   private DataOutputStream output;
   private Thread outputThread;
   private char myMark;
   private boolean myTurn;

   // Set up user-interface and board
   public void init()
   {
      Container container = getContentPane();

      // set up JTextArea to display messages to user
      displayArea = new JTextArea( 4, 30 );
      displayArea.setEditable( false );
      container.add( new JScrollPane( displayArea ),
         BorderLayout.SOUTH );

      // set up panel for squares in board
      boardPanel = new JPanel();
      boardPanel.setLayout( new GridLayout( 3, 3, 0, 0 ) );

      // create board
      board = new Square[ 3 ][ 3 ];

      // When creating a Square, the location argument to the
      // constructor is a value from 0 to 8 indicating the
      // position of the Square on the board. Values 0, 1,
      // and 2 are the first row, values 3, 4, and 5 are the
      // second row. Values 6, 7, and 8 are the third row.
      for ( int row = 0; row < board.length; row++ ) {

```

Fig. 17.9 Client side of client/server Tic-Tac-Toe program (part 1 of 6).

```
            for ( int column = 0;
                     column < board[ row ].length; column++ ) {

               // create Square
               board[ row ][ column ] =
                  new Square( ' ', row * 3 + column );

               boardPanel.add( board[ row ][ column ] );
            }

         }

         // textfield to display player's mark
         idField = new JTextField();
         idField.setEditable( false );
         container.add( idField, BorderLayout.NORTH );

         // set up panel to contain boardPanel (for layout purposes)
         panel2 = new JPanel();
         panel2.add( boardPanel, BorderLayout.CENTER );
         container.add( panel2, BorderLayout.CENTER );
      }

      // Make connection to server and get associated streams.
      // Start separate thread to allow this applet to
      // continually update its output in text area display.
      public void start()
      {
         // connect to server, get streams and start outputThread
         try {

            // make connection
            connection = new Socket(
               InetAddress.getByName( "127.0.0.1" ), 5000 );

            // get streams
            input = new DataInputStream(
               connection.getInputStream() );
            output = new DataOutputStream(
               connection.getOutputStream() );
         }

         // catch problems setting up connection and streams
         catch ( IOException ioException ) {
            ioException.printStackTrace();
         }

         // create and start output thread
         outputThread = new Thread( this );
         outputThread.start();
      }

```

Fig. 17.9 Client side of client/server Tic-Tac-Toe program (part 2 of 6).

```
   // control thread that allows continuous update of the
   // text area displayArea
   public void run()
   {
      // get player's mark (X or O)
      try {
         myMark = input.readChar();
         idField.setText( "You are player \"" + myMark + "\"" );
         myTurn = ( myMark == 'X' ? true : false );
      }

      // process problems communicating with server
      catch ( IOException ioException ) {
         ioException.printStackTrace();
      }

      // receive messages sent to client and output them
      while ( true ) {

         // read message from server and process message
         try {
            String message = input.readUTF();
            processMessage( message );
         }

         // process problems communicating with server
         catch ( IOException ioException ) {
            ioException.printStackTrace();
         }
      }

   } // end method run

   // process messages received by client
   public void processMessage( String message )
   {
      // valid move occurred
      if ( message.equals( "Valid move." ) ) {
         displayArea.append( "Valid move, please wait.\n" );

         // set mark in square from event-dispatch thread
         SwingUtilities.invokeLater(

            new Runnable() {

               public void run()
               {
                  currentSquare.setMark( myMark );
               }

            }

```

Fig. 17.9 Client side of client/server Tic-Tac-Toe program (part 3 of 6).

```
         ); // end call to invokeLater
      }

      // invalid move occurred
      else if ( message.equals( "Invalid move, try again" ) ) {
         displayArea.append( message + "\n" );
         myTurn = true;
      }

      // opponent moved
      else if ( message.equals( "Opponent moved" ) ) {

         // get move location and update board
         try {
            final int location = input.readInt();

            // set mark in square from event-dispatch thread
            SwingUtilities.invokeLater(

               new Runnable() {

                  public void run()
                  {
                     int row = location / 3;
                     int column = location % 3;

                     board[ row ][ column ].setMark(
                        ( myMark == 'X' ? 'O' : 'X' ) );
                     displayArea.append(
                        "Opponent moved. Your turn.\n" );
                  }

               }

            ); // end call to invokeLater

            myTurn = true;
         }

         // process problems communicating with server
         catch ( IOException ioException ) {
            ioException.printStackTrace();
         }

      }

      // simply display message
      else
         displayArea.append( message + "\n" );

      displayArea.setCaretPosition(
         displayArea.getText().length() );
```

Fig. 17.9 Client side of client/server Tic-Tac-Toe program (part 4 of 6).

```java

   } // end method processMessage

   // send message to server indicating clicked square
   public void sendClickedSquare( int location )
   {
      if ( myTurn ) {

         // send location to server
         try {
            output.writeInt( location );
            myTurn = false;
         }

         // process problems communicating with server
         catch ( IOException ioException ) {
            ioException.printStackTrace();
         }
      }
   }

   // set current Square
   public void setCurrentSquare( Square square )
   {
      currentSquare = square;
   }

   // private class for the sqaures on the board
   private class Square extends JPanel {
      private char mark;
      private int location;

      public Square( char squareMark, int squareLocation )
      {
         mark = squareMark;
         location = squareLocation;

         addMouseListener(

            new MouseAdapter() {

               public void mouseReleased( MouseEvent e )
               {
                  setCurrentSquare( Square.this );
                  sendClickedSquare( getSquareLocation() );
               }

            } // end anonymous inner class

         ); // end call to addMouseListener

      } // end Square constructor
```

Fig. 17.9 Client side of client/server Tic-Tac-Toe program (part 5 of 6).

```
262
263         // return preferred size of Square
264         public Dimension getPreferredSize()
265         {
266            return new Dimension( 30, 30 );
267         }
268
269         // return minimum size of Square
270         public Dimension getMinimumSize()
271         {
272            return getPreferredSize();
273         }
274
275         // set mark for Square
276         public void setMark( char newMark )
277         {
278            mark = newMark;
279            repaint();
280         }
281
282         // return Square location
283         public int getSquareLocation()
284         {
285            return location;
286         }
287
288         // draw Square
289         public void paintComponent( Graphics g )
290         {
291            super.paintComponent( g );
292
293            g.drawRect( 0, 0, 29, 29 );
294            g.drawString( String.valueOf( mark ), 11, 20 );
295         }
296
297      }  // end class Square
298
299   }  // end class TicTacToeClient
```

Fig. 17.9 Client side of client/server Tic-Tac-Toe program (part 6 of 6).

If the message received is **`Valid move.`**, lines 143–159 display the message **`Valid move, please wait.`** and call class **`Square`**'s **`setMark`** method to set the client's mark in the current square (the one in which the user clicked) using **`SwingUtilities`** method **`invokeLater`** to ensure that the GUI updates occur in the event dispatch thread. If the message received is **`Invalid move, try again.`**, lines 162–165 display the message so the user can click a different square. If the message received is **`Opponent moved.`**, lines 168–195 read an integer from the server indicating where the opponent moved and place a mark in that square of the board (again using **`SwingUtilities`** method **`invokeLater`** to ensure that the GUI updates occur in the event dispatch thread). If any other message is received, line 206 simply displays the message.

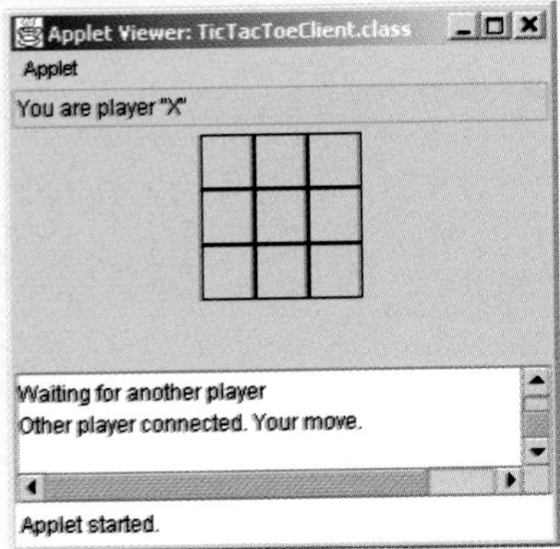

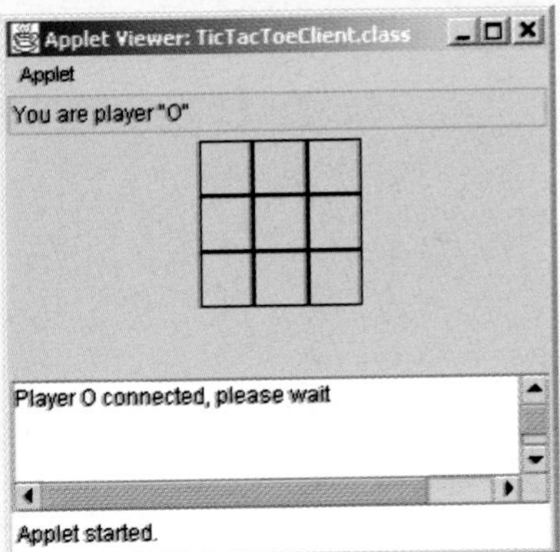

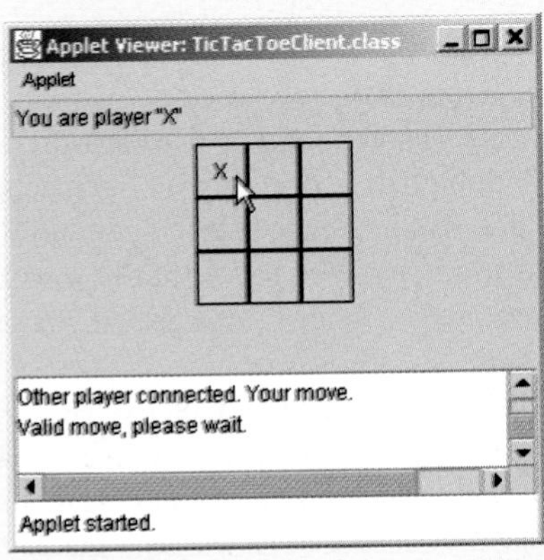

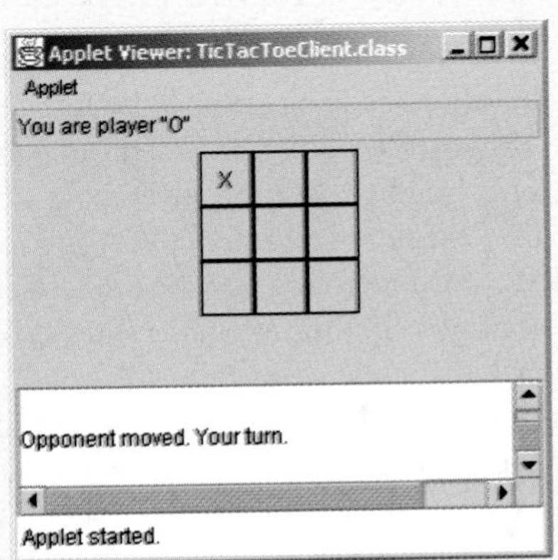

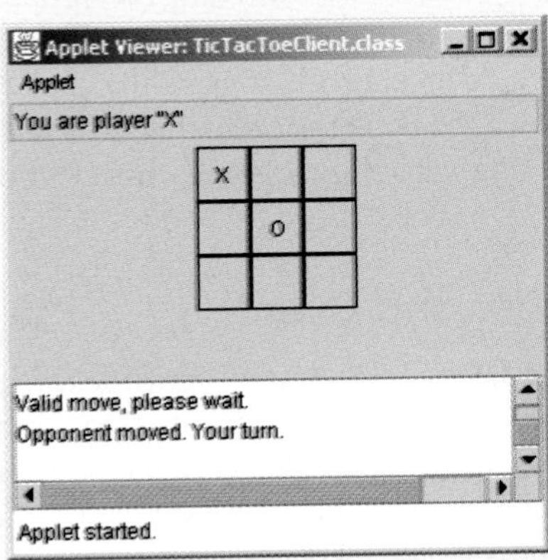

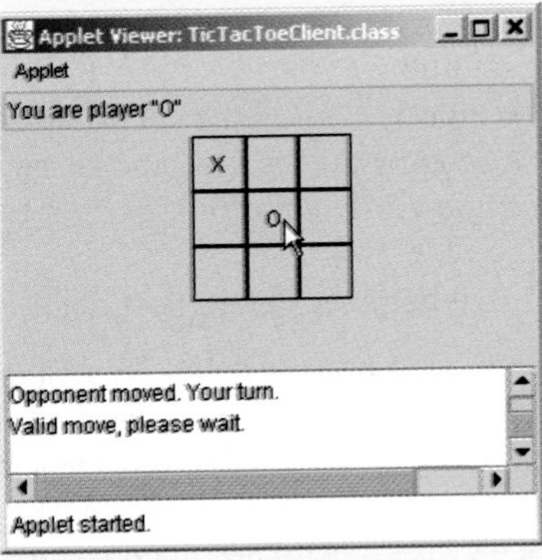

Fig. 17.10 Sample outputs from the client/server Tic-Tac-Toe program (part 1 of 2).

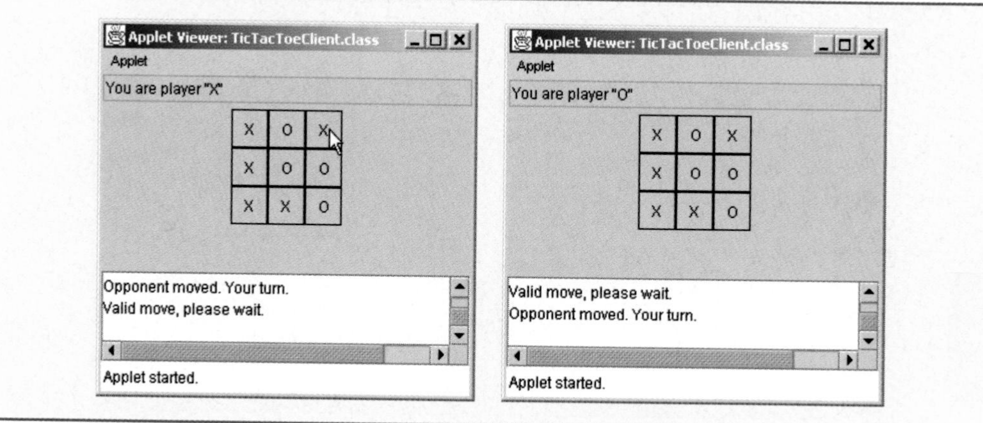

Fig. 17.10 Sample outputs from the client/server Tic-Tac-Toe program (part 2 of 2).

17.9 Security and the Network

As much as we look forward to writing a great variety of powerful network-based applications, our efforts may be crimped by limitations imposed on Java because of security concerns.c Many Web browsers, such as Netscape *Communicator* and Microsoft *Internet Explorer*, by default prohibit Java applets from doing file processing on the machines on which they execute. Think about it. A Java applet is designed to be sent to your browser via an HTML document that could be downloaded from any Web server in the world. Often you will know very little about the sources of Java applets that will execute on your system. To allow these applets free rein with your files could be disastrous.

A more subtle situation occurs with limiting the machines to which executing applets can connect. To build truly collaborative applications, we would ideally like to have our applets communicate with machines almost anywhere. The Java security manager in a Web browser often restricts an applet so that it can communicate only with the machine from which it was originally downloaded.

These restrictions might seem too harsh. However, the Java Security API now provides capabilities for signed applets that will enable browsers to determine whether an applet is downloaded from a *trusted source*. In cases where an applet is trusted, the applet can be given additional access to the computer on which the applet is executing. The features of the Java Security API and additional networking capabilities are discussed in our text *Advanced Java 2 Platform How to Program.*

17.10 DeitelMessenger Chat Server and Client

Chat rooms have become quite common on the Internet. Chat rooms provide a central location where users can chat with each other through short text messages. Each participant in a chat room can see all messages that other users post, and each user can post messages in the chat room. This section presents our capstone networking case study that integrates many of the Java networking, multithreading and Swing GUI features we have learned thus far to build an online chat system. We also introduce *multicast*, which enables an application to send **DatagramPacket**s to groups of clients. After reading this section, you will be able to build significant networking applications.

17.10.1 DeitelMessengerServer and Supporting Classes

The **DeitelMessengerServer** (Fig. 17.11) is the heart of the online chat system. Chat clients can participate in a chat by connecting to the **DeitelMessengerServer**. Method **startServer** (lines 19–54) launches **DeitelMessengerServer**. Lines 25–26 create a **ServerSocket** to accept incoming network connections. Recall that the **ServerSocket** constructor takes as its first argument the port on which the server should listen for incoming connections. Interface **SocketMessengerConstants** (Fig. 17.12) defines the port value as the constant **SERVER_PORT** to ensure that the server and the clients uses the correct port number. Class **DeitelMessengerServer** implements interface **SocketMessengerConstants** to facilitate referencing the constants defined in that interface.

```
1  // DeitelMessengerServer.java
2  // DeitelMessengerServer is a multi-threaded, socket- and
3  // packet-based chat server.
4  package com.deitel.messenger.sockets.server;
5
6  // Java core packages
7  import java.util.*;
8  import java.net.*;
9  import java.io.*;
10
11 // Deitel packages
12 import com.deitel.messenger.*;
13 import com.deitel.messenger.sockets.*;
14
15 public class DeitelMessengerServer implements MessageListener,
16    SocketMessengerConstants {
17
18    // start chat server
19    public void startServer()
20    {
21       // create server and manage new clients
22       try {
23
24          // create ServerSocket for incoming connections
25          ServerSocket serverSocket =
26             new ServerSocket( SERVER_PORT, 100 );
27
28          System.out.println( "Server listening on port " +
29             SERVER_PORT + " ..." );
30
31          // listen for clients constantly
32          while ( true ) {
33
34             // accept new client connection
35             Socket clientSocket = serverSocket.accept();
36
37             // create new ReceivingThread for receiving
38             // messages from client
```

Fig. 17.11 **DeitelMessengerServer** application for managing a chat room (part 1 of 2).

```
39             new ReceivingThread( this, clientSocket ).start();
40 
41             // print connection information
42             System.out.println( "Connection received from: " +
43                clientSocket.getInetAddress() );
44 
45          } // end while
46 
47       } // end try
48 
49       // handle exception creating server and connecting clients
50       catch ( IOException ioException ) {
51          ioException.printStackTrace();
52       }
53 
54    } // end method startServer
55 
56    // when new message is received, broadcast message to clients
57    public void messageReceived( String from, String message )
58    {
59       // create String containing entire message
60       String completeMessage = from + MESSAGE_SEPARATOR + message;
61 
62       // create and start MulticastSendingThread to broadcast
63       // new messages to all clients
64       new MulticastSendingThread(
65          completeMessage.getBytes() ).start();
66    }
67 
68    // start the server
69    public static void main ( String args[] )
70    {
71       new DeitelMessengerServer().startServer();
72    }
73 }
```

```
Server listening on port 5000 ...
Connection received from: SEANSANTRY/XXX.XXX.XXX.XXX
Connection received from: PJD/XXX.XXX.XXX.XXX
```

Fig. 17.11 **DeitelMessengerServer** application for managing a chat room (part 2 of 2).

Lines 32–45 listen continuously for new client connections. Line 35 invokes method **accept** of class **ServerSocket** to wait for and accept a new client connection. Line 39 creates and starts a new **ReceivingThread** for the client. Class **ReceivingThread** (Fig. 17.14) is a **Thread** subclass that listens for new incoming messages from a particular client. The first argument to the **ReceivingThread** constructor is a **MessageListener** (Fig. 17.13), to which messages from the client should be delivered. Class **DeitelMessengerServer** implements interface **MessageListener** (line 15) and therefore can pass the **this** reference to the **ReceivingThread** constructor.

Method **messageReceived** (lines 57–66) is required by interface **MessageListener**. When each **ReceivingThread** receives a new message from a client, the **ReceivingThread** passes the message to a **MessageListener** through method **messageReceived**. Line 60 concatenates the **from String** with the separator **>>>** and the message body. Lines 64–65 create and **start** a new **MulticastSendingThread** to deliver **completeMessage** to all listening clients. Class **MulticastSendingThread** (Fig. 17.15) uses *multicast* as an efficient mechanism for sending one message to multiple clients. We discuss the details of multicasting shortly. Method **main** (lines 69–72) creates a new **DeitelMessengerServer** instance and starts the server.

Interface **SocketMessengerConstants** (Fig. 17.12) declares constants for use in the various classes that make up the Deitel messenger system. Classes can access these **static** constants either by referencing the constants through interface **SocketMessengerConstants** (e.g., **SocketMessengerConstants.SERVER_PORT**) or by implementing the interface and referencing the constants directly.

Line 9 defines the **String** constant **MULTICAST_ADDRESS**, which contains the address to which a **MulticastSendingThread** (Fig. 17.15) should send messages. This address is one of the addresses reserved for multicast, which we will describe soon. Line 12 defines the integer constant **MULTICAST_LISTENING_PORT**—the port on which clients should listen for new messages. Line 15 defines the integer constant **MULTICAST_SENDING_PORT**—the port to which a **MulticastSendingThread** should post new messages at the **MULTICAST_ADDRESS**. Line 18 defines the integer constant **SERVER_PORT**—the port on which **DeitelMessengerServer** listens for incoming client connections. Line 21 defines **String** constant **DISCONNECT_STRING**, which is the **String** that a client sends to **DeitelMessengerServer** when the user wishes to leave the chat room. Line 24 defines **String** constant **MESSAGE_SEPARATOR**, which separates the user name from the message body. Line 27 specifies the maximum message size in bytes.

```
1  // SocketMessengerConstants.java
2  // SocketMessengerConstants defines constants for the port numbers
3  // and multicast address in DeitelMessenger
4  package com.deitel.messenger.sockets;
5
6  public interface SocketMessengerConstants {
7
8     // address for multicast datagrams
9     public static final String MULTICAST_ADDRESS = "230.0.0.1";
10
11    // port for listening for multicast datagrams
12    public static final int MULTICAST_LISTENING_PORT = 5555;
13
14    // port for sending multicast datagrams
15    public static final int MULTICAST_SENDING_PORT = 5554;
16
17    // port for Socket connections to DeitelMessengerServer
18    public static final int SERVER_PORT = 5000;
```

Fig. 17.12 **SocketMessengerConstants** declares constants for use throughout the **DeitelMessengerServer** and **DeitelMessenger** applications (part 1 of 2).

```

    // String that indicates disconnect
    public static final String DISCONNECT_STRING = "DISCONNECT";

    // String that separates the user name from the message body
    public static final String MESSAGE_SEPARATOR = ">>>";

    // message size (in bytes)
    public static final int MESSAGE_SIZE = 512;
}
```

Fig. 17.12 **SocketMessengerConstants** declares constants for use throughout the **DeitelMessengerServer** and **DeitelMessenger** applications (part 2 of 2).

Many different classes in the Deitel messenger system receive messages. For example, **DeitelMessengerServer** receives messages from clients and delivers those messages to all chat room participants. As we will see, the user interface for each client also receives messages and displays those messages to the users. Each of the classes that receives messages implements interface **MessageListener** (Fig. 17.13). The interface declares method **messageReceived**, which allows an implementing class to receive chat messages. Method **messageReceived** takes two **String** arguments representing the name of the user who sent the message and the message body, respectively.

DeitelMessengerServer uses instances of class **ReceivingThread** (Fig. 17.14) to listen for new messages from each client. Class **ReceivingThread** extends class **Thread**. This enables **DeitelMessengerServer** to create an object of class **ReceivingThread** for each client, to handle messages from multiple clients at once. When **DeitelMessengerServer** receives a new client connection, **DeitelMessengerServer** creates a new **ReceivingThread** for the client, then continues listening for new client connections. The **ReceivingThread** listens for new messages from a single client and passes those messages back to the **DeitelMessengerServer** through method **messageReceived**.

```
// MessageListener.java
// MessageListener is an interface for classes that wish to
// receive new chat messages.
package com.deitel.messenger;

public interface MessageListener {

   // receive new chat message
   public void messageReceived( String from, String message );
}
```

Fig. 17.13 **MessageListener** interface that defines method **messageReceived** for receiving new chat messages.

```
// ReceivingThread.java
// ReceivingThread is a Thread that listens for messages
// from a particular client and delivers messages to a
// MessageListener.
package com.deitel.messenger.sockets.server;

// Java core packages
import java.io.*;
import java.net.*;
import java.util.StringTokenizer;

// Deitel packages
import com.deitel.messenger.*;
import com.deitel.messenger.sockets.*;

public class ReceivingThread extends Thread implements
   SocketMessengerConstants {

   private BufferedReader input;
   private MessageListener messageListener;
   private boolean keepListening = true;

   // ReceivingThread constructor
   public ReceivingThread( MessageListener listener,
      Socket clientSocket )
   {
      // invoke superclass constructor to name Thread
      super( "ReceivingThread: " + clientSocket );

      // set listener to which new messages should be sent
      messageListener = listener;

      // set timeout for reading from clientSocket and create
      // BufferedReader for reading incoming messages
      try {
         clientSocket.setSoTimeout( 5000 );

         input = new BufferedReader( new InputStreamReader(
            clientSocket.getInputStream() ) );
      }

      // handle exception creating BufferedReader
      catch ( IOException ioException ) {
         ioException.printStackTrace();
      }

   } // end ReceivingThread constructor

   // listen for new messages and deliver them to MessageListener
   public void run()
   {
      String message;
```

Fig. 17.14 **ReceivingThread** for listening for new messages from **DeitelMessengerServer** clients in separate **Thread**s (part 1 of 3).

```
         // listen for messages until stopped
         while ( keepListening ) {

            // read message from BufferedReader
            try {
               message = input.readLine();
            }

            // handle exception if read times out
            catch ( InterruptedIOException interruptedIOException ) {

               // continue to next iteration to keep listening
               continue;
            }

            // handle exception reading message
            catch ( IOException ioException ) {
               ioException.printStackTrace();
               break;
            }

            // ensure non-null message
            if ( message != null ) {

               // tokenize message to retrieve user name
               // and message body
               StringTokenizer tokenizer =
                  new StringTokenizer( message, MESSAGE_SEPARATOR );

               // ignore messages that do not contain a user
               // name and message body
               if ( tokenizer.countTokens() == 2 ) {

                  // send message to MessageListener
                  messageListener.messageReceived(
                     tokenizer.nextToken(),    // user name
                     tokenizer.nextToken() ); // message body
               }

               else

                  // if disconnect message received, stop listening
                  if ( message.equalsIgnoreCase( MESSAGE_SEPARATOR +
                     DISCONNECT_STRING ) ) {

                     stopListening();
                  }

            } // end if

         } // end while
```

Fig. 17.14 **ReceivingThread** for listening for new messages from **DeitelMessengerServer** clients in separate **Thread**s (part 2 of 3).

```
105
106          // close BufferedReader (also closes Socket)
107          try {
108             input.close();
109          }
110
111          // handle exception closing BufferedReader
112          catch ( IOException ioException ) {
113             ioException.printStackTrace();
114          }
115
116       } // end method run
117
118       // stop listening for incoming messages
119       public void stopListening()
120       {
121          keepListening = false;
122       }
123 }
```

Fig. 17.14 **ReceivingThread** for listening for new messages from **DeitelMessengerServer** clients in separate **Thread**s (part 3 of 3).

The **ReceivingThread** constructor (lines 24–47) takes as its first argument a **MessageListener**. The **ReceivingThread** will deliver new messages to this **MessageListener** by invoking method **messageReceived** of interface **MessageListener**. The **Socket** argument to the **ReceivingThread** constructor is the connection to a particular client. Line 28 invokes the **Thread** constructor to provide a unique name for each **ReceivingThread** instance. Naming the **ReceivingThread** this way can be useful when debugging the application. Line 31 sets the **MessageListener** to which the **ReceivingThread** should deliver new messages. Line 36 invokes method **setSoTimeout** of class **Socket** with an integer argument of **5000** milliseconds. Reading data from a **Socket** is a *blocking call*—the current thread is put in the blocked state (Fig. 15.1) while the thread waits for the read operation to complete. Method **setSoTimeout** specifies that, if no data is received in the given number of milliseconds, the **Socket** should issue an **InterruptedIOException**, which the current thread can catch, then continue executing. This technique prevents the current thread from deadlocking if no more data is available from the **Socket**. Lines 38–39 create a new **BufferedReader** for the **clientSocket**'s **InputStream**. The **ReceivingThread** uses this **BufferedReader** to read new messages from the client.

Method **run** (lines 50–116) listens continuously for new messages from the client. Lines 55–104 loop as long as the **boolean** variable **keepListening** is **true**. Line 59 invokes **BufferedReader** method **readLine** to read a line of data from the client. If more than **5000** milliseconds pass without reading any data, method **readLine** throws an **InterruptedIOException**, which indicates that the timeout set on line 36 has expired. Line 66 uses keyword **continue** to go to the next iteration of the **while** loop to continue listening for messages. Lines 70–73 catch an **IOException**, which indicates a more severe problem from method **readLine**. Line 71 prints a stack trace to aid in debugging the application, and line 72 uses keyword **break** to terminate the **while** loop.

When a client sends a message to the server, the client separates the user's name from the message body with the String **MESSAGE_SEPARATOR**. If there are no exceptions thrown when reading data from the client and the message is not **null** (line 76), lines 80–81 create a new **StringTokenizer**. This **StringTokenizer** separates each message into two tokens delimited by **MESSAGE_SEPARATOR**. The first token is the sender's user name; the second token is the message. Line 85 checks for the proper number of tokens, and lines 88–90 invoke method **messageReceived** of interface **MessageListener** to deliver the new message to the registered **MessageListener**. If the **StringTokenizer** does not produce two tokens, lines 96–97 check the message to see whether it matches the constant **DISCONNECT_STRING**, which would indicate that the user wishes to leave the chat room. If the **String**s match, line 99 invokes **ReceivingThread** method **stopListening** to terminate the **ReceivingThread**.

Method **stopListening** (lines 119–122) sets boolean variable **keepListening** to **false**. This causes the **while** loop condition on line 55 to fail and causes the **ReceivingThread** to close the client **Socket** (line 108). Then, method **run** returns, which terminates the **ReceivingThread**'s execution.

MulticastSendingThread (Fig. 17.15) delivers **DatagramPacket**s containing chat messages to a group of clients. Multicast is an efficient way to send data to many clients without the overhead of broadcasting that data to every host on the Internet. To understand multicast, let us look at a real-world analogy—the relationship between a magazine publisher and that magazine's subscribers. The magazine publisher produces a magazine and provides the magazine to a distributor. Customers interested in that magazine obtain a subscription and begin receiving the magazine in the mail from the distributor. This communication is quite different from a television broadcast. When a television station produces a television program, the station broadcasts that television show throughout a geographical region or perhaps throughout the world by using satellites. Broadcasting a television show for 10,000 viewers is no more expensive to the television station than broadcasting a television show for 100 viewers—the radio signal carrying the broadcast reaches a wide area. However, printing and delivering a magazine to 10,000 readers would be much more expensive than printing and delivering the magazine to 100 readers. Most magazine publishers could not stay in business if they had to broadcast their magazines to everyone, so magazine publishers multicast their magazines to a group of subscribers instead.

Using multicast, an application can "publish" **DatagramPacket**s to be delivered to other applications—the "subscribers." An application multicasts **DatagramPacket**s by sending the **DatagramPacket**s to a *multicast address*, which is an IP address reserved for multicast in the range from **224.0.0.0** to **239.255.255.255**. Clients that wish to receive these **DatagramPacket**s can connect to the appropriate multicast address to join the group of subscribers—the *multicast group*. When an application sends a **DatagramPacket** to the multicast address, each client in the multicast group receives the **DatagramPacket**. Multicast **DatagramPacket**s, like unicast **DatagramPacket**s (Fig. 17.7), are not reliable—packets are not guaranteed to reach any destination. Also, the order in which the particular clients receive the datagrams is not guaranteed.

Class **MulticastSendingThread** extends class **Thread** to enable **DeitelMessengerServer** to send multicast messages in a separate thread. Each time **DeitelMessengerServer** needs to multicast a message, the server creates a new **MulticastSendingThread** with the contents of the message and starts the thread.

The **MulticastSendingThread** constructor (lines 20–26) takes as an argument an array of **byte**s containing the message.

```
1  // MulticastSendingThread.java
2  // MulticastSendingThread is a Thread that broadcasts a chat
3  // message using a multicast datagram.
4  package com.deitel.messenger.sockets.server;
5
6  // Java core packages
7  import java.io.*;
8  import java.net.*;
9
10 // Deitel packages
11 import com.deitel.messenger.sockets.*;
12
13 public class MulticastSendingThread extends Thread
14    implements SocketMessengerConstants {
15
16    // message data
17    private byte[] messageBytes;
18
19    // MulticastSendingThread constructor
20    public MulticastSendingThread( byte[] bytes )
21    {
22       // invoke superclass constructor to name Thread
23       super( "MulticastSendingThread" );
24
25       messageBytes = bytes;
26    }
27
28    // deliver message to MULTICAST_ADDRESS over DatagramSocket
29    public void run()
30    {
31       // deliver message
32       try {
33
34          // create DatagramSocket for sending message
35          DatagramSocket socket =
36             new DatagramSocket( MULTICAST_SENDING_PORT );
37
38          // use InetAddress reserved for multicast group
39          InetAddress group = InetAddress.getByName(
40             MULTICAST_ADDRESS );
41
42          // create DatagramPacket containing message
43          DatagramPacket packet = new DatagramPacket(
44             messageBytes, messageBytes.length, group,
45             MULTICAST_LISTENING_PORT );
46
47          // send packet to multicast group and close socket
48          socket.send( packet );
```

Fig. 17.15 **MulticastSendingThread** for delivering outgoing messages to a multicast group via **DatagramPacket**s.

```
49             socket.close();
50         }
51 
52         // handle exception delivering message
53         catch ( IOException ioException ) {
54             ioException.printStackTrace();
55         }
56 
57     } // end method run
58 }
```

Fig. 17.15 **MulticastSendingThread** for delivering outgoing messages to a multicast group via **DatagramPacket**s.

Method **run** (lines 29–57) delivers the message to the multicast address. Lines 35–36 create a new **DatagramSocket**. Recall from the packet-networking example that we used **DatagramSocket**s to send *unicast* **DatagramPacket**s—packets sent from one host directly to another host. Delivering **DatagramPacket**s by using multicast is exactly the same, except the address to which the **DatagramPacket**s are sent is a multicast address in the range from **224.0.0.0** to **239.255.255.255**. Lines 39–40 create an **InetAddress** object for the multicast address, which is defined as a constant in interface **SocketMessengerConstants**. Lines 43–45 create the **DatagramPacket** containing the message. The first argument to the **DatagramPacket** constructor is the **byte** array containing the message. The second argument is the length of the **byte** array. The third argument specifies the **InetAddress** to which the packet should be sent, and the last argument specifies the port number through which the packet should be delivered to the multicast address. Line 48 invokes method **send** of class **DatagramSocket** to send the **DatagramPacket**. When the **DatagramPacket** is delivered to the multicast address, all clients listening to that multicast address on the proper port receive the **DatagramPacket**. Line 49 closes the **DatagramSocket**, and the run method returns, terminating the **MulticastSendingThread**.

17.10.2 DeitelMessenger Client and Supporting Classes

The client for the **DeitelMessengerServer** consists of several pieces. A class that implements interface **MessageManager** (Fig. 17.16) manages communication with the server. A **Thread** subclass listens for messages at **DeitelMessengerServer**'s multicast address. Another **Thread** subclass sends messages from the client to **DeitelMessengerServer**. A **JFrame** subclass provides a GUI for the client.

Interface **MessageManager** (Fig. 17.16) defines methods for managing communication with **DeitelMessengerServer**. We define this interface to abstract the base functionality a client needs to interact with a chat server from the underlying communication mechanism needed to communicate with that chat server. This abstraction enables us to provide **MessageManager** implementations that use other network protocols to implement the communication details. For example, if we want to connect to a different chat server that does not use multicast **DatagramPacket**s, we could implement the **MessageManager** interface with the appropriate network protocols for this alternate messaging server. We would not need to modify any other code in the client, because the other components of the client refer only to interface **MessageManager**, and not to some particular **MessageManager** implementation. Likewise, the **MessageManager** interface methods refer to other components of the client only through interface **MessageListener**. Therefore, other components of the client can change without requiring changes in the **MessageManager** or its implementations.Method **connect** (line 10) connects **MessageManager** to **DeitelMessengerServer** and routes incoming messages to the appropriate **MessageListener**. Method **disconnect** (line 14) disconnects the **MessageManager** from the **DeitelMessengerServer** and stops delivering messages to the given **MessageListener**. Method **sendMessage** (line 17) sends a new message to **DeitelMessengerServer**.

Class **SocketMessageManager** (Fig. 17.17) implements interface **MessageManager** (line 16), using **Socket**s and **MulticastSocket**s to communicate with **DeitelMessengerServer** and receive incoming messages. Line 20 declares the **Socket** that **SocketMessageManager** uses to connect and send messages to **DeitelMessengerServer**. Line 26 declares the **PacketReceivingThread** (Fig. 17.19) that listens for new incoming messages. The **boolean** flag **connected** (line 29) indicates whether the **SocketMessageManager** is connected to **DeitelMessengerServer**.\

```
1  // MessageManager.java
2  // MessageManager is an interface for objects capable of managing
3  // communications with a message server.
4  package com.deitel.messenger;
5
6  public interface MessageManager {
7
8     // connect to message server and route incoming messages
9     // to given MessageListener
10    public void connect( MessageListener listener );
11
12    // disconnect from message server and stop routing
13    // incoming messages to given MessageListener
14    public void disconnect( MessageListener listener );
15
16    // send message to message server
17    public void sendMessage( String from, String message );
18 }
```

Fig. 17.16 **MessageManager** interface that defines methods for communicating with a **DeitelMessengerServer**.

```
1  // SocketMessageManager.java
2  // SocketMessageManager is a MessageManager implementation for
3  // communicating with a DeitelMessengerServer using Sockets
4  // and MulticastSockets.
5  package com.deitel.messenger.sockets.client;
6
```

Fig. 17.17 **SocketMessageManager** implementation of interface **MessageManager** for communicating via **Socket**s and multicast **DatagramPacket**s (part 1 of 4).

```
// Java core packages
import java.util.*;
import java.net.*;
import java.io.*;

// Deitel packages
import com.deitel.messenger.*;
import com.deitel.messenger.sockets.*;

public class SocketMessageManager implements MessageManager,
   SocketMessengerConstants {

   // Socket for outgoing messages
   private Socket clientSocket;

   // DeitelMessengerServer address
   private String serverAddress;

   // Thread for receiving multicast messages
   private PacketReceivingThread receivingThread;

   // flag indicating connection status
   private boolean connected = false;

   // SocketMessageManager constructor
   public SocketMessageManager( String address )
   {
      serverAddress = address;
   }

   // connect to server and send messages to given MessageListener
   public void connect( MessageListener listener )
   {
      // if already connected, return immediately
      if ( connected )
         return;

      // open Socket connection to DeitelMessengerServer
      try {
         clientSocket = new Socket(
            InetAddress.getByName( serverAddress ), SERVER_PORT );

         // create Thread for receiving incoming messages
         receivingThread = new PacketReceivingThread( listener );
         receivingThread.start();

         // update connected flag
         connected = true;

      } // end try

```

Fig. 17.17 **SocketMessageManager** implementation of interface **MessageManager** for communicating via **Socket**s and multicast **DatagramPacket**s (part 2 of 4).

```
      // handle exception connecting to server
      catch ( IOException ioException ) {
         ioException.printStackTrace();
      }

   } // end method connect

   // disconnect from server and unregister given MessageListener
   public void disconnect( MessageListener listener )
   {
      // if not connected, return immediately
      if ( !connected )
         return;

      // stop listening thread and disconnect from server
      try {

         // notify server that client is disconnecting
         Thread disconnectThread = new SendingThread(
            clientSocket, "", DISCONNECT_STRING );
         disconnectThread.start();

         // wait 10 seconds for disconnect message to be sent
         disconnectThread.join( 10000 );

         // stop receivingThread and remove given MessageListener
         receivingThread.stopListening();

         // close outgoing Socket
         clientSocket.close();

      } // end try

      // handle exception disconnecting from server
      catch ( IOException ioException ) {
         ioException.printStackTrace();
      }

      // handle exception joining disconnectThread
      catch ( InterruptedException interruptedException ) {
         interruptedException.printStackTrace();
      }

      // update connected flag
      connected = false;

   } // end method disconnect

   // send message to server
   public void sendMessage( String from, String message )
   {
```

Fig. 17.17 **SocketMessageManager** implementation of interface **MessageManager** for communicating via **Socket**s and multicast **DatagramPacket**s (part 3 of 4).

```
109         // if not connected, return immediately
110         if ( !connected )
111             return;
112
113         // create and start new SendingThread to deliver message
114         new SendingThread( clientSocket, from, message).start();
115     }
116 }
```

Fig. 17.17 **SocketMessageManager** implementation of interface **MessageManager** for communicating via **Socket**s and multicast **DatagramPacket**s (part 4 of 4).

The **SocketMessageManager** constructor (lines 32–35) receives the address of the **DeitelMessengerServer** to which **SocketMessageManager** should connect. Method **connect** (lines 38–63) connects **SocketMessageManager** to **DeitelMessengerServer**. If **SocketMessageManager** was connected previously, line 42 returns from method **connect**. Lines 46–47 create a new **Socket** to communicate with **DeitelMessengerServer**. Line 47 creates an **InetAddress** object for the server's address and uses the constant **SERVER_PORT** to specify the port on which the client should connect. Line 50 creates a new **PacketReceivingThread**, which listens for incoming multicast messages from **DeitelMessengerServer**. Line 51 starts **PacketReceivingThread**. Line 54 updates **boolean** variable **connected** to indicate that **SocketMessageManager** is connected to the server.

Method **disconnect** (lines 66–104) terminates the **SocketMessageManager**'s connection to **DeitelMessengerServer**. If **SocketMessageManager** is not connected, line 70 returns from method **disconnect**. Lines 76–77 create a new **SendingThread** (Fig. 17.18) to send **DISCONNECT_STRING** to **DeitelMessengerServer**. Class **SendingThread** delivers a message to **DeitelMessengerServer** over the **SocketMessageManager**'s **Socket** connection. Line 78 starts the **SendingThread** to deliver the message. Line 81 invokes **SendingThread** method **join** (inherited from **Thread**) to wait for the disconnect message to be delivered. The integer argument **10000** specifies that the current thread should wait only 10 seconds to **join** the **SendingThread** before continuing. Once the disconnect message has been delivered, line 84 invokes method **stopListening** of class **PacketReceivingThread** to stop receiving incoming chat messages. Line 87 closes the **Socket** connection to **DeitelMessengerServer**.

Method **sendMessage** (lines 107–115) sends an outgoing message to **DeitelMessengerServer**. If **SocketMessageManager** is not connected, line 111 returns from method **sendMessage**. Line 114 creates and starts a new **SendingThread** instance (Fig. 17.18) to deliver the new message in a separate thread of execution.

Class **SendingThread** (Fig. 17.18) extends class **Thread** to deliver outgoing messages to the **DeitelMessengerServer** in a separate thread of execution. **SendingThread**'s constructor (lines 21–31) takes as arguments the **Socket** over which to send the message, the **userName** from whom the message came and the **message** body. Line 30 concatenates **userName**, **MESSAGE_SEPARATOR** and **message** to build **messageToSend**. Constant **MESSAGE_SEPARATOR** enables the message recipient to parse the message into two parts—the sending user's name and the message body—by using a **StringTokenizer**.

```
// SendingThread.java
// SendingThread sends a message to the chat server in a
// separate Thread.
package com.deitel.messenger.sockets.client;

// Java core packages
import java.io.*;
import java.net.*;

// Deitel packages
import com.deitel.messenger.sockets.*;

public class SendingThread extends Thread
   implements SocketMessengerConstants {

   // Socket over which to send message
   private Socket clientSocket;
   private String messageToSend;

   // SendingThread constructor
   public SendingThread( Socket socket, String userName,
      String message )
   {
      // invoke superclass constructor to name Thread
      super( "SendingThread: " + socket );

      clientSocket = socket;

      // build the message to be sent
      messageToSend = userName + MESSAGE_SEPARATOR + message;
   }

   // send message and exit Thread
   public void run()
   {
      // send message and flush PrintWriter
      try {
         PrintWriter writer =
            new PrintWriter( clientSocket.getOutputStream() );
         writer.println( messageToSend );
         writer.flush();
      }

      // handle exception sending message
      catch ( IOException ioException ) {
         ioException.printStackTrace();
      }

   } // end method run
}
```

Fig. 17.18 **SendingThread** for delivering outgoing messages to **DeitelMessengerServer**.

Method **run** (lines 34–49) delivers the complete message to **DeitelMessengerServer**, using the **Socket** provided to the **SendingThread** constructor. Lines 38–39 create a new **PrintWriter** for the **clientSocket**'s **OutputStream**. Line 40 invokes method **println** of class **PrintWriter** to send the message. Line 41 invokes method **flush** of class **PrintWriter** to ensure that the message is sent immediately. Note that class **SendingThread** does not close the **clientSocket**. Class **SocketMessageManager** uses a new instance of class **SendingThread** for each message the client sends, so the **clientSocket** must remain open until the user disconnects from **DeitelMessengerServer**.

Class **PacketReceivingThread** extends class **Thread** to enable **SocketMessageManager** to listen for incoming messages in a separate thread of execution. Line 19 declares the **MessageListener** to which **PacketReceivingThread** will deliver incoming messages. Line 22 declares a **MulticastSocket**, which enables **PacketReceivingThread** to receive multicast **DatagramPacket**s. Line 25 declares an **InetAddress** reference for the multicast address to which **DeitelMessengerServer** posts new chat messages. The **MulticastSocket** connects to this **InetAddress** to listen for incoming chat messages.

```
1  // PacketReceivingThread.java
2  // PacketReceivingThread listens for DatagramPackets containing
3  // messages from a DeitelMessengerServer.
4  package com.deitel.messenger.sockets.client;
5
6  // Java core packages
7  import java.io.*;
8  import java.net.*;
9  import java.util.*;
10
11 // Deitel packages
12 import com.deitel.messenger.*;
13 import com.deitel.messenger.sockets.*;
14
15 public class PacketReceivingThread extends Thread
16    implements SocketMessengerConstants {
17
18    // MessageListener to whom messages should be delivered
19    private MessageListener messageListener;
20
21    // MulticastSocket for receiving broadcast messages
22    private MulticastSocket multicastSocket;
23
24    // InetAddress of group for messages
25    private InetAddress multicastGroup;
26
27    // flag for terminating PacketReceivingThread
28    private boolean keepListening = true;
29
```

Fig. 17.19 **PacketReceivingThread** for listening for new multicast messages from **DeitelMessengerServer** in a separate **Thread** (part 1 of 4).

```
   // PacketReceivingThread constructor
   public PacketReceivingThread( MessageListener listener )
   {
      // invoke superclass constructor to name Thread
      super( "PacketReceivingThread" );

      // set MessageListener
      messageListener = listener;

      // connect MulticastSocket to multicast address and port
      try {
         multicastSocket =
            new MulticastSocket( MULTICAST_LISTENING_PORT );

         multicastGroup =
            InetAddress.getByName( MULTICAST_ADDRESS );

         // join multicast group to receive messages
         multicastSocket.joinGroup( multicastGroup );

         // set 5 second time-out when waiting for new packets
         multicastSocket.setSoTimeout( 5000 );
      }

      // handle exception connecting to multicast address
      catch ( IOException ioException ) {
         ioException.printStackTrace();
      }

   } // end PacketReceivingThread constructor

   // listen for messages from multicast group
   public void run()
   {
      // listen for messages until stopped
      while ( keepListening ) {

         // create buffer for incoming message
         byte[] buffer = new byte[ MESSAGE_SIZE ];

         // create DatagramPacket for incoming message
         DatagramPacket packet = new DatagramPacket( buffer,
            MESSAGE_SIZE );

         // receive new DatagramPacket (blocking call)
         try {
            multicastSocket.receive( packet );
         }

         // handle exception when receive times out
         catch ( InterruptedIOException interruptedIOException ) {

```

Fig. 17.19 **PacketReceivingThread** for listening for new multicast messages from **DeitelMessengerServer** in a separate **Thread** (part 2 of 4).

```
            // continue to next iteration to keep listening
            continue;
         }

         // handle exception reading packet from multicast group
         catch ( IOException ioException ) {
            ioException.printStackTrace();
            break;
         }

         // put message data in a String
         String message = new String( packet.getData() );

         // ensure non-null message
         if ( message != null ) {

            // trim extra whitespace from end of message
            message = message.trim();

            // tokenize message to retrieve user name
            // and message body
            StringTokenizer tokenizer =
               new StringTokenizer( message, MESSAGE_SEPARATOR );

            // ignore messages that do not contain a user
            // name and message body
            if ( tokenizer.countTokens() == 2 ) {

               // send message to MessageListener
               messageListener.messageReceived(
                  tokenizer.nextToken(),    // user name
                  tokenizer.nextToken() ); // message body
            }

         } // end if

      } // end while

      // leave multicast group and close MulticastSocket
      try {
         multicastSocket.leaveGroup( multicastGroup );
         multicastSocket.close();
      }

      // handle exception reading packet from multicast group
      catch ( IOException ioException ) {
         ioException.printStackTrace();
      }

   } // end method run

```

Fig. 17.19 **PacketReceivingThread** for listening for new multicast messages from **DeitelMessengerServer** in a separate **Thread** (part 3 of 4).

```
133    // stop listening for new messages
134    public void stopListening()
135    {
136       // terminate Thread
137       keepListening = false;
138    }
139 }
```

Fig. 17.19 **PacketReceivingThread** for listening for new multicast messages from **DeitelMessengerServer** in a separate **Thread** (part 4 of 4).

The **PacketReceivingThread** constructor (lines 31–59) takes as an argument the **MessageListener** to which the **PacketReceivingThread** should deliver incoming messages. Recall that interface **MessageListener** defines a single method **messageReceived**. When the **PacketReceivingThread** receives a new chat message over the **MulticastSocket**, **PacketReceivingThread** invokes method **messageReceived** to deliver the new message to the **MessageListener**.

Lines 41–42 create a new **MulticastSocket** and pass to the **MulticastSocket** constructor the constant **MULTICAST_LISTENING_PORT** from interface **SocketMessengerConstants**. This argument specifies the port on which the **MulticastSocket** should listen for incoming chat messages. Lines 44–45 create an **InetAddress** object for the **MULTICAST_ADDRESS**, to which **DeitelMessengerServer** multicasts new chat messages. Line 48 invokes method **joinGroup** of class **MulticastSocket** to register the **MulticastSocket** to receive messages sent to **MULTICAST_ADDRESS**. Line 51 invokes **MulticastSocket** method **setSoTime-out** to specify that, if no data is received in **5000** milliseconds, the **MulticastSocket** should issue an **InterruptedIOException**, which the current thread can catch, then continue executing. This approach prevents **PacketReceivingThread** from deadlocking when waiting for incoming data. Also, if the **MulticastSocket** did not ever time out, the **while** loop would not be able to check the **keepListening** variable and would therefore prevent **PacketReceivingThread** from stopping if **keepListening** were set to **false**.

Method **run** (lines 62–131) listens for incoming multicast messages. Line 68 creates a **byte** array in which to store the incoming **DatagramPacket** data. Lines 71–72 create a **DatagramPacket** to store the incoming message. Line 76 invokes method **receive** of class **MulticastSocket** with the **DatagramPacket** packet as an argument. This is a blocking call that reads an incoming packet from the multicast address. If **5000** milliseconds pass without receipt of a packet, method **receive** throws an **InterruptedIOException**, because we previously set a **5000** millisecond time-out (line 51). Line 83 uses keyword **continue** to proceed to the next **while** loop iteration to continue listening for incoming messages. For other **IOException**s, line 89 **break**s the **while** loop to terminate the **PacketReceivingThread**.

Line 93 invokes method **getData** of class **DatagramPacket** to retrieve the message data. Line 99 invokes method **trim** of class **String** to remove extra whitespace from the end of the message. Recall that **DatagramPacket**s are a fixed size—**512** bytes in this example—so, if the message is shorter than **512** bytes, there will be extra whitespace after the message. Lines 103–104 create a **StringTokenizer** to separate the message body from the name of the user who sent the message. Line 108 checks for the correct number of tokens. Lines 111–113 invoke method **messageReceived** of interface **MessageListener** to deliver the incoming message to the **PacketReceivingThread**'s **MessageListener**.

If the program invokes method **stopListening** (lines 134–138), the **while** loop in method **run** (lines 62–118) terminates. Line 122 invokes method **leaveGroup** of class **MulticastSocket** to stop receiving messages from the multicast address. Line 123 invokes method **close** of class **MulticastSocket** to close the **MulticastSocket**. **PacketReceivingThread** then terminates when method **run** returns.

Class **ClientGUI** (Fig. 17.20) extends class **JFrame** to create a GUI for a user to send and receive chat messages. The GUI consists of a **JTextArea** for displaying incoming messages (line 22), a **JTextArea** for entering new messages (line 23), **JButton**s and **JMenuItem**s for connecting to and disconnecting from the server (lines 26–29) and a **JButton** for sending messages (line 32). The GUI also contains a **JLabel** that displays whether the client is connected or disconnected.

```
1   // ClientGUI.java
2   // ClientGUI provides a user interface for sending and receiving
3   // messages to and from the DeitelMessengerServer.
4   package com.deitel.messenger;
5
6   // Java core packages
7   import java.io.*;
8   import java.net.*;
9   import java.awt.*;
10  import java.awt.event.*;
11
12  // Java standard extensions
13  import javax.swing.*;
14  import javax.swing.border.*;
15
16  public class ClientGUI extends JFrame {
17
18     // JMenu for connecting/disconnecting server
19     private JMenu serverMenu;
20
21     // JTextAreas for displaying and inputting messages
22     private JTextArea messageArea;
23     private JTextArea inputArea;
24
25     // JButtons and JMenuItems for connecting and disconnecting
26     private JButton connectButton;
27     private JMenuItem connectMenuItem;
28     private JButton disconnectButton;
29     private JMenuItem disconnectMenuItem;
30
31     // JButton for sending messages
32     private JButton sendButton;
33
34     // JLabel for displaying connection status
35     private JLabel statusBar;
```

Fig. 17.20 **ClientGUI** subclass of **JFrame** for presenting a GUI for viewing and sending chat messages (part 1 of 6).

```
   // userName to add to outgoing messages
   private String userName;

   // MessageManager for communicating with server
   private MessageManager messageManager;

   // MessageListener for receiving incoming messages
   private MessageListener messageListener;

   // ClientGUI constructor
   public ClientGUI( MessageManager manager )
   {
      super( "Deitel Messenger" );

      // set the MessageManager
      messageManager = manager;

      // create MyMessageListener for receiving messages
      messageListener = new MyMessageListener();

      // create File JMenu
      serverMenu = new JMenu ( "Server" );
      serverMenu.setMnemonic( 'S' );
      JMenuBar menuBar = new JMenuBar();
      menuBar.add( serverMenu );
      setJMenuBar( menuBar );

      // create ImageIcon for connect buttons
      Icon connectIcon = new ImageIcon(
         getClass().getResource( "images/Connect.gif" ) );

      // create connectButton and connectMenuItem
      connectButton = new JButton( "Connect", connectIcon );
      connectMenuItem = new JMenuItem( "Connect", connectIcon );
      connectMenuItem.setMnemonic( 'C' );

      // create ConnectListener for connect buttons
      ActionListener connectListener = new ConnectListener();
      connectButton.addActionListener( connectListener );
      connectMenuItem.addActionListener( connectListener );

      // create ImageIcon for disconnect buttons
      Icon disconnectIcon = new ImageIcon(
         getClass().getResource( "images/Disconnect.gif" ) );

      // create disconnectButton and disconnectMenuItem
      disconnectButton = new JButton( "Disconnect",
         disconnectIcon );
      disconnectMenuItem = new JMenuItem( "Disconnect",
         disconnectIcon );
      disconnectMenuItem.setMnemonic( 'D' );
```

Fig. 17.20 **ClientGUI** subclass of **JFrame** for presenting a GUI for viewing and sending chat messages (part 2 of 6).

```

         // disable disconnect buttons
         disconnectButton.setEnabled( false );
         disconnectMenuItem.setEnabled( false );

         // create DisconnectListener for disconnect buttons
         ActionListener disconnectListener =
            new DisconnectListener();
         disconnectButton.addActionListener( disconnectListener );
         disconnectMenuItem.addActionListener( disconnectListener );

         // add connect and disconnect JMenuItems to fileMenu
         serverMenu.add( connectMenuItem );
         serverMenu.add( disconnectMenuItem );

         // add connect and disconnect JButtons to buttonPanel
         JPanel buttonPanel = new JPanel();
         buttonPanel.add( connectButton );
         buttonPanel.add( disconnectButton );

         // create JTextArea for displaying messages
         messageArea = new JTextArea();

         // disable editing and wrap words at end of line
         messageArea.setEditable( false );
         messageArea.setWrapStyleWord( true );
         messageArea.setLineWrap( true );

         // put messageArea in JScrollPane to enable scrolling
         JPanel messagePanel = new JPanel();
         messagePanel.setLayout( new BorderLayout( 10, 10 ) );
         messagePanel.add( new JScrollPane( messageArea ),
            BorderLayout.CENTER );

         // create JTextArea for entering new messages
         inputArea = new JTextArea( 4, 20 );
         inputArea.setWrapStyleWord( true );
         inputArea.setLineWrap( true );
         inputArea.setEditable( false );

         // create Icon for sendButton
         Icon sendIcon = new ImageIcon(
            getClass().getResource( "images/Send.gif" ) );

         // create sendButton and disable it
         sendButton = new JButton( "Send", sendIcon );
         sendButton.setEnabled( false );

         // create ActionListener for sendButton
         sendButton.addActionListener(
            new ActionListener() {

```

Fig. 17.20 **ClientGUI** subclass of **JFrame** for presenting a GUI for viewing and sending chat messages (part 3 of 6).

```java
            // send new message when user activates sendButton
            public void actionPerformed( ActionEvent event )
            {
               messageManager.sendMessage( userName,
                  inputArea.getText());

               // clear inputArea
               inputArea.setText( "" );
            }
         } // end ActionListener
      );

      // lay out inputArea and sendButton in BoxLayout and
      // add Box to messagePanel
      Box box = new Box( BoxLayout.X_AXIS );
      box.add( new JScrollPane( inputArea ) );
      box.add( sendButton );
      messagePanel.add( box, BorderLayout.SOUTH );

      // create JLabel for statusBar with a recessed border
      statusBar = new JLabel( "Not Connected" );
      statusBar.setBorder(
         new BevelBorder( BevelBorder.LOWERED ) );

      // lay out components in JFrame
      Container container = getContentPane();
      container.add( buttonPanel, BorderLayout.NORTH );
      container.add( messagePanel, BorderLayout.CENTER );
      container.add( statusBar, BorderLayout.SOUTH );

      // add WindowListener to disconnect when user quits
      addWindowListener (
         new WindowAdapter () {

            // disconnect from server and exit application
            public void windowClosing ( WindowEvent event )
            {
               messageManager.disconnect( messageListener );
               System.exit( 0 );
            }
         }
      );

   } // end ClientGUI constructor

   // ConnectListener listens for user requests to connect to
   // DeitelMessengerSever
   private class ConnectListener implements ActionListener {

      // connect to server and enable/disable GUI components
      public void actionPerformed( ActionEvent event )
      {
```

Fig. 17.20 **ClientGUI** subclass of **JFrame** for presenting a GUI for viewing and sending chat messages (part 4 of 6).

```
        // connect to server and route messages to
        // messageListener
        messageManager.connect( messageListener );

        // prompt for userName
        userName = JOptionPane.showInputDialog(
           ClientGUI.this, "Enter user name:" );

        // clear messageArea
        messageArea.setText( "" );

        // update GUI components
        connectButton.setEnabled( false );
        connectMenuItem.setEnabled( false );
        disconnectButton.setEnabled( true );
        disconnectMenuItem.setEnabled( true );
        sendButton.setEnabled( true );
        inputArea.setEditable( true );
        inputArea.requestFocus();
        statusBar.setText( "Connected: " + userName );
     }

  } // end ConnectListener inner class

  // DisconnectListener listens for user requests to disconnect
  // from DeitelMessengerServer
  private class DisconnectListener implements ActionListener {

     // disconnect from server and enable/disable GUI components
     public void actionPerformed( ActionEvent event )
     {
        // disconnect from server and stop routing messages
        // to messageListener
        messageManager.disconnect( messageListener );

        // update GUI componets
        sendButton.setEnabled( false );
        disconnectButton.setEnabled( false );
        disconnectMenuItem.setEnabled( false );
        inputArea.setEditable( false );
        connectButton.setEnabled( true );
        connectMenuItem.setEnabled( true );
        statusBar.setText( "Not Connected" );
     }

  } // end DisconnectListener inner class

  // MyMessageListener listens for new messages from the
  // MessageManager and displays the messages in messageArea
  // using a MessageDisplayer.
  private class MyMessageListener implements MessageListener {

```

Fig. 17.20 **ClientGUI** subclass of **JFrame** for presenting a GUI for viewing and sending chat messages (part 5 of 6).

```
244        // when received, display new messages in messageArea
245        public void messageReceived( String from, String message )
246        {
247           // append message using MessageDisplayer and
248           // invokeLater, ensuring thread-safe access messageArea
249           SwingUtilities.invokeLater(
250              new MessageDisplayer( from, message ) );
251
252        } // end method messageReceived
253
254     }  // end MyMessageListener inner class
255
256     // MessageDisplayer displays a new messaage by
257     // appending the message to the messageArea JTextArea. This
258     // Runnable object should be executed only on the Event
259     // thread, because it modifies a live Swing component.
260     private class MessageDisplayer implements Runnable {
261
262        private String fromUser;
263        private String messageBody;
264
265        // MessageDisplayer constructor
266        public MessageDisplayer( String from, String body )
267        {
268           fromUser = from;
269           messageBody = body;
270        }
271
272        // display new message in messageArea
273        public void run()
274        {
275           // append new message
276           messageArea.append( "\n" + fromUser + "> " +
277              messageBody );
278
279           // move caret to end of messageArea to ensure new
280           // message is visible on screen
281           messageArea.setCaretPosition(
282              messageArea.getText().length() );
283        }
284
285     } // end MessageDisplayer inner class
286  }
```

Fig. 17.20 **ClientGUI** subclass of **JFrame** for presenting a GUI for viewing and sending chat messages (part 6 of 6).

ClientGUI uses a **MessageManager** (line 41) to handle all communication with the chat server. Recall that **MessageManager** is an interface and therefore allows **ClientGUI** to use any **MessageManager** implementation without the need to change any code in **ClientGUI**. Class **ClientGUI** also uses a **MessageListener** (line 44) to receive incoming messages from the **MessageManager**.

The **ClientGUI** constructor (lines 47–183) takes as an argument the **MessageManager** for communicating with **DeitelMessengerServer**. Line 52 sets the **Cli-**

entGUI's **MessageManager**. Line 55 creates an instance of **MyMessageListener**, which implements interface **MessageListener**. Lines 58–62 create a **Server** menu that contains **JMenuItem**s for connecting to and disconnecting from the chat server. Lines 65–66 create an **ImageIcon** for **connectButton** and **connectMenuItem**.

Line 66 invokes method **getClass** (inherited from class **Object**) to retrieve the **Class** object that represents the **ClientGUI** class definition. Line 66 then invokes method ***getResource*** of class **Class** to load the connect image. The Java virtual machine loads class definitions into memory, using a *class loader*. Method **getResource** of **Class** uses the **Class** object's class loader to specify the location of a resource, such as an image file. Specifying resource locations in this manner enables programs to avoid hard-coded or absolute paths, which can make programs more difficult to deploy. Using the techniques described here enables an applet or application to load files from locations that are relative to the location of the **.class** file for a given class.

Lines 69–70 create **connectButton** and **connectMenuItem**, each with the label **"Connect"** and the **Icon connectIcon**. Line 71 invokes method **setMnemonic** of class **JMenuItem** to set the mnemonic character for keyboard access to **connectMenuItem**. Line 74 creates an instance of **private** inner class **ConnectListener**, which implements interface **ActionListener** to handle **ActionEvent**s from **connectButton** and **connectMenuItem**. Lines 75–76 add **connectListener** as an **ActionListener** for **connectButton** and **connectMenuItem**.

Lines 79–80 create an **ImageIcon** for the **disconnectButton** and **disconnectMenuItem** components. Lines 83–86 create **disconnectButton** and **disconnectMenuItem**, each with the label **"Disconnect"** and the **Icon disconnectIcon**. Line 87 invokes method **setMnemonic** of class **JMenuItem** to enable keyboard access to **disconnectMenuItem**. Lines 90–91 invoke method **setEnabled** of class **JButton** and class **JMenuItem** with a **false** argument to disable **disconnectButton** and **disconnectMenuItem**. This prevents the user from attempting to disconnect from the server because the client is not yet connected. Lines 94–95 create an instance of **private** inner class **DisconnectListener**, which implements interface **ActionListener** to handle **ActionEvent**s from **disconnectButton** and **disconnectMenuItem**. Lines 96–97 add **disconnectListener** as an **ActionListener** for the **disconnectButton** and **disconnectMenuItem** components.

Lines 100–101 add **connectMenuItem** and **disconnectMenuItem** to the **Server JMenu**. Lines 104–106 create a **JPanel** and add **connectButton** and **disconnectButton** to that **JPanel**. Line 109 creates the **JTextArea messageArea**, in which the client displays incoming messages. Line 112 invokes method **setEnabled** with a **false** argument, to disable editing ot the text in **messageArea**. Lines 113–114 invoke methods **setWrapStyleWord** and **setLineWrap** of class **JTextArea** to enable word wrapping in **messageArea**. If a message is longer than the width of the **messageArea**, the **messageArea** will wrap the text after the last word that fits on each line, making longer messages easier to read. Lines 117–120 create a **JPanel** for the **messageArea** and add the **messageArea** to the **JPanel** in a **JScrollPane**. The **JScrollPane** adds scroll bars to the **messageArea** to enable the user to scroll through messages that exceed the size of **messageArea**.

Line 123 creates the **inputArea JTextArea** for entering new messages. The arguments to the **JTextArea** constructor specify a four-line **JTextArea** that is twenty characters wide. Lines 124–125 enable word and line wrapping, and line 126 disables editing the **inputArea**. When the client connects to the chat server, **ConnectListener** enables the **inputArea** to allow the user to type new messages.

Line 129 creates an **ImageIcon** for **sendButton**. Line 133 creates **sendButton**, which the user can click to send a message the user has typed. Line 134 disables **sendButton**; the **ConnectListener** enables the **sendButton** when the client connects to the chat server. Lines 137–150 add an **ActionListener** to **sendButton**. Lines 143–144 invoke method **sendMessage** of interface **MessageManager** with the **userName** and **inputArea** text as arguments. This statement sends the user's name and whatever text the user entered in **inputArea** to **DeitelMessengerServer** as a new chat message. Line 147 invokes method **setText** of class **JTextArea** with an empty **String** argument to clear the **inputArea** for the next message.

Lines 154–157 use a **BoxLayout** to arrange the **inputArea** and **sendButton**. Line 155 places **inputArea** in a **JScrollPane** to enable scrolling of long messages. Line 157 adds the **Box** containing **inputArea** and **sendButton** to the **SOUTH** region of **messagePanel**. Lines 160–162 create the **statusBar JLabel**. This **JLabel** displays whether the client is connected to or disconnected from the chat server. Lines 161–162 invoke method **setBorder** of class **JLabel** and create a new **BevelBorder** of type **BevelBorder.LOWERED**. This border makes the **JLabel** appear recessed, as is common with status bars in many applications. Lines 165–168 lay out **buttonPanel**, **messagePanel** and **statusBar** in the **ClientGUI JFrame**.

Lines 171–181 add a **WindowListener** to the **ClientGUI JFrame**. Line 177 invokes method **disconnect** of interface **MessageManager** to disconnect from the chat server in case the user quits while still connected.

Inner class **ConnectListener** (lines 187–214) handles events from **connectButton** and **connectMenuItem**. Line 194 invokes method connect of class **MessageManager** to connect to the chat server. Line 194 passes as an argument to method **connect** the **MessageListener** to which new messages should be delivered. Lines 197-198 prompt the user for a user name, and line 201 clears the **messageArea JTextArea**. Lines 204–209 enable the components for disconnecting from the server and for sending messages and disable components for connecting to the server. Line 210 invokes method **requestFocus** of class **JTextArea** to place the text-input cursor in the **inputArea** so the user can begin typing a message more easily.

Inner class **DisconnectListener** (lines 218–237) handles events from **disconnectButton** and **disconnectMenuItem**. Line 225 invokes method **disconnect** of class **MessageManager** to disconnect from the chat server. Lines 228–234 disable the components for sending messages and the components for disconnecting then enable the components for connecting to the chat server.

Inner class **MyMessageListener** (lines 242–254) implements interface **MessageListener** to receive incoming messages from the **MessageManager**. When a new message is received, the program invokes method **messageReceived** (lines 242–252) with the user name of the sender and the message body. Lines 249–250 invoke **static** method **invokeLater** of class **SwingUtilties** with a new instance of **MessageDisplayer** to append the new message to **messageArea**. Recall, from Chapter 15, that Swing components should be accessed only from the event dispatching thread. Method **messageReceived** is invoked by the **PacketReceivingThread** in class **SocketMessageManager** and therefore cannot append the message text to **messageArea** directly, as this would occur in **PacketReceivingThread**, not the event-dispatch thread.

Inner class **MessageDisplayer** (lines 260–285) implements interface **Runnable** to provide a thread-safe way to append text to the **messageArea JTextArea**. The **MessageDisplayer** constructor (lines 266–270) takes as arguments the user name and message to send. Method **run** (lines 273–283) appends the user name, **"> "** and **messageBody** to **messageArea**. Lines 281–282 invoke method **setCaretPosition** of class **JTextArea** to scroll **messageArea** to the bottom to display the most recently received message. Instances of class **MessageDisplayer** should execute only as part of the event-dispatching thread, to ensure thread-safe access to the **messageArea** Swing component.

Class **DeitelMessenger** (Fig. 17.21) launches the client for the **DeitelMessengerServer**. Lines 18–21 create a new **SocketMessageManager** to connect to the **DeitelMessengerServer** with the IP address specified as a command-line argument to the application. Lines 24–27 create a **ClientGUI** for the **MessageManager**, set the **ClientGUI** size and make the **ClientGUI** visible.

```
1  // DeitelMessenger.java
2  // DeitelMessenger is a chat application that uses a ClientGUI
3  // and SocketMessageManager to communicate with
4  // DeitelMessengerServer.
5  package com.deitel.messenger.sockets.client;
6
7  // Deitel packages
8  import com.deitel.messenger.*;
9
10 public class DeitelMessenger {
11
12    // execute application
13    public static void main( String args[] )
14    {
15       MessageManager messageManager;
16
17       // create new DeitelMessenger
18       if ( args.length == 0 )
19          messageManager = new SocketMessageManager( "localhost" );
20       else
21          messageManager = new SocketMessageManager( args[ 0 ] );
22
23       // create GUI for SocketMessageManager
24       ClientGUI clientGUI = new ClientGUI( messageManager );
25       clientGUI.setSize( 300, 400 );
26       clientGUI.setResizable( false );
27       clientGUI.setVisible( true );
28    }
29 }
```

Fig. 17.21 **DeitelMessenger** application for participating in a **DeitelMessengerServer** chat session (part 1 of 3).

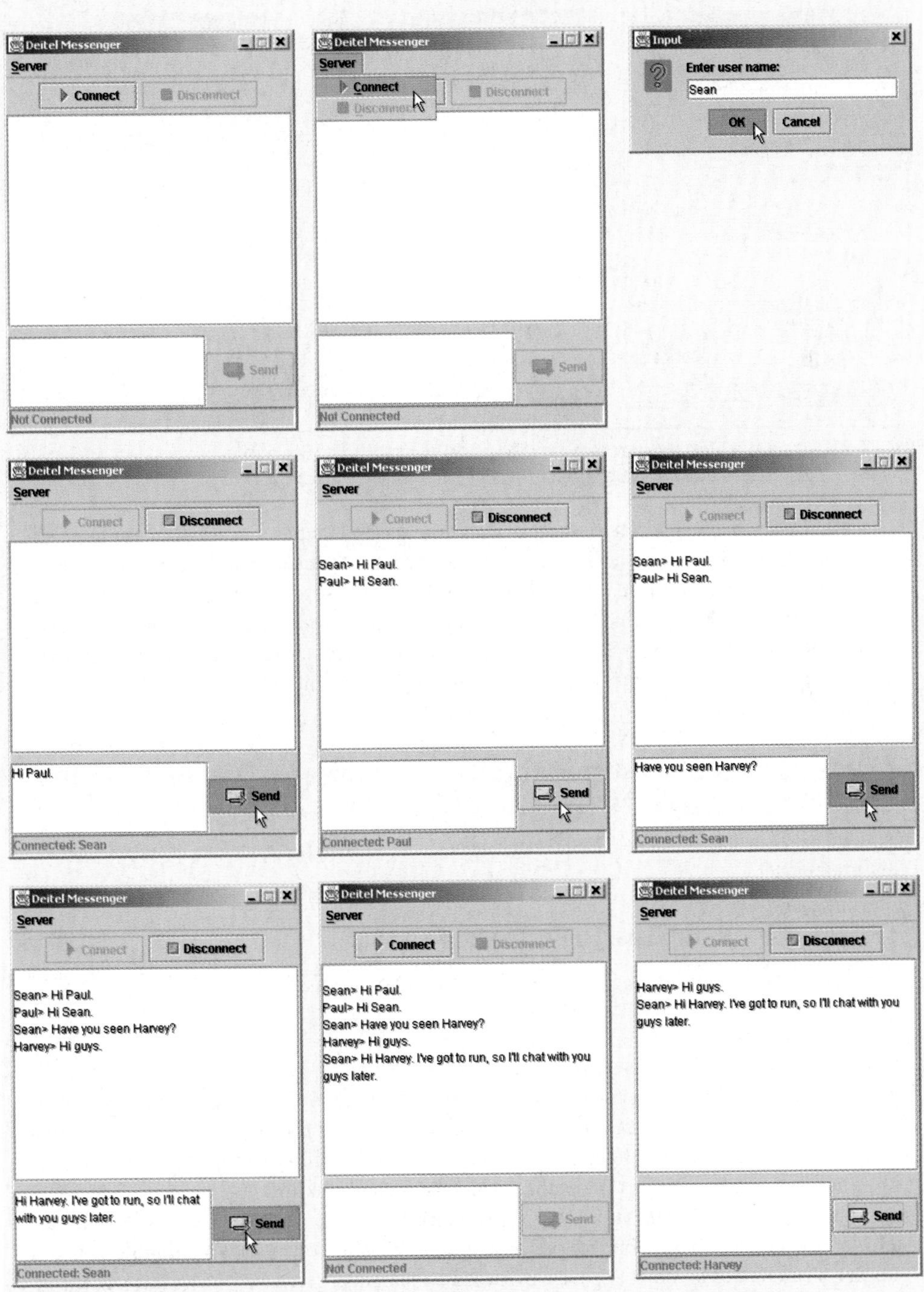

Fig. 17.21 **`DeitelMessenger`** application for participating in a **`DeitelMessengerServer`** chat session (part 2 of 3).

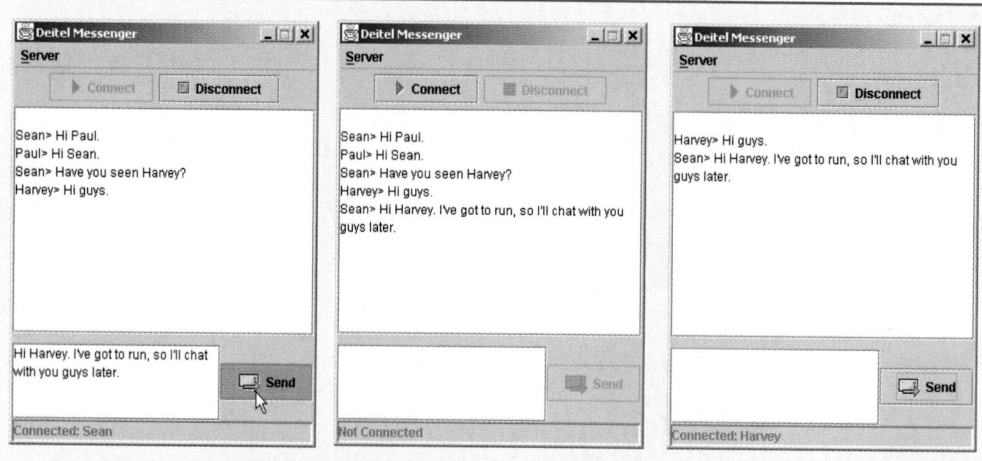

Fig. 17.21 **DeitelMessenger** application for participating in a **DeitelMessengerServer** chat session (part 3 of 3).

The Deitel messenger case study is a significant application that uses many intermediate Java features, such as networking with **Socket**s, **DatagramPacket**s and **MulticastSocket**s, multithreading and Swing GUI. The case study also demonstrates good software engineering practices by separating interface from implementation, enabling developers to build **MessageManager**s for different network protocols and **MessageListener**s that provide different user interfaces. You should now be able to apply these techniques to your own, more complex, Java projects.

17.11 (Optional) Discovering Design Patterns: Design Patterns Used in Packages java.io and java.net

This section introduces those design patterns associated with the Java file, streams and networking packages.

17.11.1 Creational Design Patterns

We now continue our discussion of creational design patterns.

Abstract Factory

Like the Factory Method design pattern, the *Abstract Factory design pattern* allows a system to determine the subclass from which to instantiate an object at run time. Often, this subclass is unknown during development. However, Abstract Factory uses an object known as a *factory* that uses an interface to instantiate objects. A factory creates a product; in this case, that product is an object of a subclass determined at run time.

The Java socket library in package **java.net** uses the Abstract Factory design pattern. A socket describes a connection, or a stream of data, between two computers. Class **Socket** references an object of a **SocketImpl** subclass (Section 17.5). Class **Socket** also contains a **static** reference to an object implementing interface **SocketImplFactory**. The **Socket** constructor invokes method **createSocketImpl** of interface **SocketFactory** to create the **SocketImpl** object. The object that implements interface **SocketFactory** is the factory, and an object of a **SocketImpl** subclass is the product of that factory. The system cannot specify the **SocketImpl** subclass from which to instantiate until run time, because the system has no knowledge of what type of **Socket** implementation is required (e.g., a socket configured to the local network's security requirements). Method **createSocketImpl** decides the **SocketImpl** subclass from which to instantiate the object at run time.

17.11.2 Structural Design Patterns

This section concludes our discussion of structural design patterns.

Decorator

Let us reexamine class **CreateSequentialFile** (Fig. 16.6). Lines 127–128 of this class allow an **ObjectOutputStream** object, which writes objects to a file, to gain the responsibilities of a **FileOutputStream** object, which provides methods for writing **byte**s to files. Class **CreateSequentialFile** appears to "chain" objects—a **FileOutputStream** object is the argument to the **ObjectOutputStream**'s constructor. The fact that the **ObjectOutputStream** object can gain the behavior of a **FileOutputStream** dynamically prevents the need for creating a separate class called **ObjectFileOutputStream**, which would implement the behaviors of both classes.

Lines 127–128 of class **CreateSequentialFile** show an example of the *Decorator design pattern*, which allows an object to gain additional responsibilities dynamically. Using this pattern, designers do not have to create separate, unnecessary classes to add responsibilities to objects of a given class.

Let us consider a more complex example to discover how the Decorator design pattern can simplify a system's structure. Suppose we wanted to enhance the I/O-performance of the previous example by using a **BufferedOutputStream**. Using the Decorator design pattern, we would write

```
output = new ObjectOutputStream(
   new BufferedOutputStream(
      new FileOutputStream( fileName ) ) );
```

We can chain objects in this manner, because **ObjectOutputStream**, **BufferedOutputStream** and **FileOutputStream** extend abstract superclass **OutputStream**, and each subclass constructor takes an **OutputStream** object as a parameter. If the stream objects in package **java.io** did not use the Decorator pattern (i.e., did not satisfy these two requirements), package **java.io** would have to provide classes **BufferedFileOutputStream**, **ObjectBufferedOutputStream**, **ObjectBufferedFileOutputStream** and **ObjectFileOutputStream**. Consider how many classes we would have to create if we chained even more stream objects without applying the Decorator pattern.

Facade

When driving a car, you know that pressing the gas pedal accelerates your car, but you are unaware of exactly how the gas pedal causes your car to accelerate. This principle is the foundation of the *Facade design pattern*, which allows an object—called a *facade object*—to provide a simple interface for the behaviors of a *subsystem*—an aggregate of objects that comprise collectively a major system responsibility. The gas pedal, for example, is the facade object for the car's acceleration subsystem, the steering wheel is the facade object for the car's steering subsystem and the brake is the facade object for the car's deceleration subsystem. A *client object* uses the facade object to access the objects behind the facade. The client remains unaware of how the objects behind the facade fulfill responsibilities, so the subsystem complexity is hidden from the client. When you press the gas pedal you act as a client object. The Facade design pattern reduces system complexity, because a client interacts with only one object (the facade). This pattern shields applications developers from subsystem complexities. Developers need to be familiar with only the operations of the facade object, rather than with the more detailed operations of the entire subsystem.

In package **`java.net`**, an object of class **`URL`** is a facade object. This object contains a reference to an **`InetAddress`** object that specifies the host computer's IP address. The URL facade object also references an object from class **`URLStreamHandler`**, which opens the URL connection. The client object that uses the **`URL`** facade object accesses the **`InetAddress`** object and the **`URLStreamHandler`** object through the facade object. However, the client object does not know how the objects behind the **`URL`** facade object accomplish their responsibilities.

17.11.3 Architectural Patterns

Design patterns allow developers to design specific parts of systems, such as abstracting object instantiations or aggregating classes into larger structures. Design patterns also promote loose coupling among objects. *Architectural patterns* promote loose coupling among subsystems. These patterns specify all subsystems in the system and how they interact with each other.[1] We introduce the popular Model-View-Controller and Layers architectural patterns.

MVC

Consider the design of a simple text editor. In this program, the user inputs text from the keyboard and formats this text using the mouse. Our program stores this text and format information into a series of data structures, then displays this information on screen for the user to read what has been inputted.

This program adheres to the *Model-View-Controller* (MVC) *architectural pattern*, which separates application data (contained in the *model*) from graphical presentation components (the *view*) and input-processing logic (the *controller*).[2] Figure 17.22 shows the relationships between components in MVC.

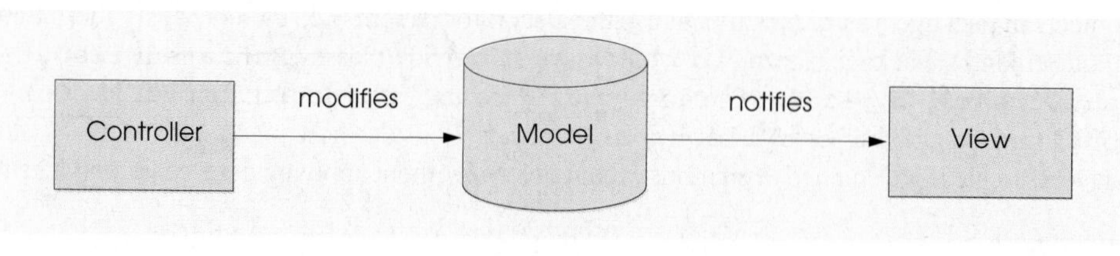

Fig. 17.22 Model-View-Controller Architecture.

1. R. Hartman. "Building on Patterns." *Application Development Trends* May 2001: 19–26.
2. Section 13.17 also discussed Model-View-Controller architecture and its relevance to the elevator simulation case study.

The controller implements logic for processing user inputs. The model contains application data, and the view presents the data stored in the model. When a user provides some input, the controller modifies the model with the given input. The model contains the application data. With regards to the text-editor example, the model might contain only the characters that make up the document. When the model changes, it notifies the view of the change so the view can update its presentation with the changed data. The view in a word processor might display characters using a particular font, with a particular size, etc.

MVC does not restrict an application to a single view and a single controller. In a more sophisticated program (e.g., a word processor), there might be two views of a document model. One view might display an outline of the document and the other might display the complete document. The word processor also might implement multiple controllers—one for handling keyboard input and another for handling mouse selections. If either controller makes a change in the model, both the outline view and the print-preview window will show the change immediately when the model notifies all views of changes.

Another key benefit to the MVC architectural pattern is that developers can modify each component individually without having to modify the other components. For example, developers could modify the view that displays the document outline, but the developers would not have to modify either the model or other views or controllers.

Layers

Consider the design in Fig. 17.23, which presents the basic structure of a *three-tier application*, in which each tier contains a unique system component.

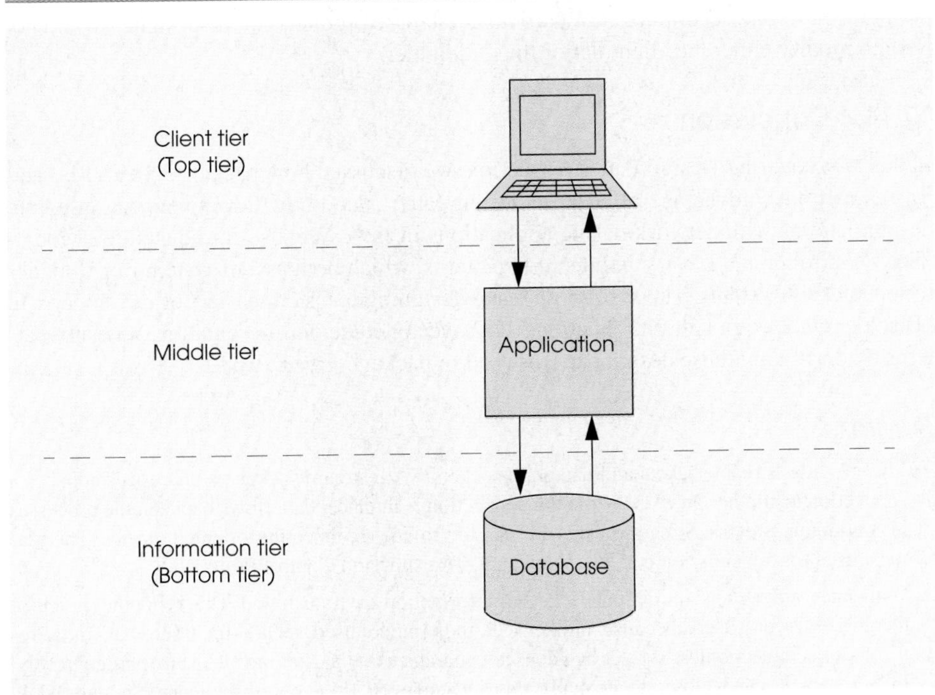

Fig. 17.23 Three-tier application model.

The *information tier* (also called the "bottom tier") maintains data for the application, typically storing the data in a database. The information tier for an online store may contain product information, such as descriptions, prices and quantities in stock and customer information, such as user names, billing addresses and credit-card numbers.

The *middle tier* acts as an intermediary between the information tier and the client tier. The middle tier processes client-tier requests, reads data from and writes data to the database. The middle tier then processes data from the information tier and presents the content to the client tier. This processing is the application's *business logic*, which handles such tasks as retrieving data from the information tier, ensuring that data is reliable before updating the database and presenting data to the client tier. For example, the business logic associated with the middle tier for the online store can verify a customer's credit card with the credit-card issuer before the warehouse ships the customer's order. This business logic could then store (or retrieve) the credit information in the database and notify the client tier that the verification was successful.

The *client tier* (also called the "top tier") is the application's user interface, such as a standard Web browser. Users interact directly with the application through the user interface. The client tier interacts with the middle tier to make requests and retrieve data from the information tier. The client tier then displays data retrieved from the middle tier.

Figure 17.23 is an implementation of the *Layers architectural pattern*, which divides functionality into separate *layers*. Each layer contains a set of system responsibilities and depends on the services of only the next lower layer. In Fig. 17.23, each tier corresponds to a layer. This architectural pattern is useful, because a designer can modify one layer without having to modify the other layers. For example, a designer could modify the information tier in Fig. 17.23 to accommodate a particular database product, but the designer would not have to modify either the client tier or the middle tier.

17.11.4 Conclusion

In this "Discovering Design Patterns" section, we discussed how packages **`java.io`** and **`java.net`** take advantage of specific design patterns and how developers can integrate design patterns with networking/file applications in Java. We also introduced the Model-View-Controller and Layers architectural patterns, which both assign system functionality to separate subsystems. These patterns make designing a system easier for developers. In "Discovering Design Patterns" Section 21.12, we conclude our presentation of design patterns by discussing those design patterns used in package **`java.util`**.

SUMMARY

- Java provides stream sockets and datagram sockets. With stream sockets, a process establishes a connection to another process. While the connection is in place, data flows between the processes in continuous streams. Stream sockets are said to provide a connection-oriented service. The protocol used for transmission is the popular TCP (Transmission Control Protocol).
- With datagram sockets, individual packets of information are transmitted. This is not the right protocol for everyday users, because, unlike TCP, the protocol used, UDP—the User Datagram Protocol—is a connectionless service and does not guarantee that packets arrive in any particular way. In fact, packets can be lost, can be duplicated and can even arrive out of sequence. So, with UDP, significant extra programming is required on the user's part to deal with these problems (if the user chooses to do so).

- The HTTP protocol (Hypertext Transfer Protocol) that forms the basis of the World Wide Web uses URIs (Uniform Resource Identifiers, also called URLs or Uniform Resource Locators) to locate data on the Internet. Common URIs represent files or directories and can represent complex tasks such as database lookups and Internet searches.
- Web browsers often restrict an applet so that it can communicate only with the machine from which it was originally downloaded.
- A **Hashtable** stores key/value pairs. A program uses a key to store and retrieve an associated value in the **Hashtable**. **Hashtable** method **put** takes two arguments—a key and its associated value—and places the value in the **Hashtable** at a location determined by the key. **Hashtable** method **get** takes one argument—a key—and retrieves the value (as an **Object** reference) associated with the key.
- A **Vector** is a dynamically resizable array of **Object**s. **Vector** method **addElement** adds a new element to the end of the **Vector**.
- **Applet** method **getAppletContext** returns a reference to an **AppletContext** object that represents the applet's environment (i.e., the browser in which the applet is executing).
- **AppletContext** method **showDocument** receives a **URL** object as an argument and passes it to the **AppletContext** (i.e., the browser), which displays the World Wide Web resource associated with that **URL**.
- A second version of **AppletContext** method **showDocument** enables an applet to specify the target frame in which Web resource should be displayed. Special target frames include **_blank** (display the content from the specified URI in a new Web browser window), **_self** (display the content from the specified URI in the same frame as the applet) and **_top** (the browser should remove the current frames, then display the content from the specified URI in the current window).
- **Component** method **setCursor** changes the mouse cursor when the cursor is positioned over a specific GUI component. The **Cursor** constructor receives an integer indicating the cursor type (such as **Cursor.WAIT_CURSOR** or **Cursor.DEFAULT_CURSOR**).
- **JEditorPane** method **setPage** downloads the document specified by its argument and displays it in the **JEditorPane**.
- Typically, an HTML document contains hyperlinks—text, images or GUI components that, when clicked, link to another document on the Web. If an HTML document is displayed in a **JEditorPane** and the user clicks a hyperlink, the **JEditorPane** generates a **HyperlinkEvent** (package **javax.swing.event**) and notifies all registered **HyperlinkListener**s (package **javax.swing.event**) of that event.
- **HyperlinkEvent** method **getEventType** determines the type of the **HyperlinkEvent**. Class **HyperlinkEvent** contains **public static** inner class **EventType**, which defines three hyperlink event types: **ACTIVATED** (user clicked a hyperlink), **ENTERED** (user moved the mouse over a hyperlink) and EXITED (user moved the mouse away from a hyperlink).
- **HyperlinkEvent** method **getURL** obtains the **URL** represented by the hyperlink.
- Stream-based connections are managed with **Socket** objects.
- A **ServerSocket** object establishes the port where a server waits for connections from clients. The second argument to the **ServerSocket** constructor specifies the number of clients that can wait for a connection and be processed by the server. If the queue of clients is full, client connections are refused. The **ServerSocket** method **accept** waits indefinitely (i.e., blocks) for a connection from a client and returns a **Socket** object when a connection is established.
- **Socket** method **getOutputStream** gets a reference to the **OutputStream** associated with a **Socket**. **Socket** method **getInputStream** gets a reference to the **InputStream** associated with the **Socket**.

- When transmission over a **Socket** connection is complete, the server closes the connection by invoking the **Socket**'s **close** method.
- A **Socket** object connects a client to a server by specifying the server name and port number when creating the **Socket** object. A failed connection attempt throws an **IOException**.
- When the **InputStream** method **read** returns **-1**, the stream detects that the end-of-stream has been reached.
- An **EOFException** occurs when a **ObjectInputStream** attempts to read a value from a stream on which end-of-stream is detected.
- **InetAddress** method **getByName** returns an **InetAddress** object containing the host name of the computer for which the **String** host name or **String** Internet address is specified as an argument.
- **InetAddress** method **getLocalHost** returns an **InetAddress** object containing the host name of the local computer executing the program.
- The port at which a client connects to a server is sometimes called the handshake point.
- Connection-oriented transmission is like the telephone system—you dial and are given a connection to the telephone of the person with whom you wish to communicate. The connection is maintained for the duration of your phone call, even when you are not talking.
- Connectionless transmission with datagrams is similar to mail carried via the postal service. A large message that will not fit in one envelope can be broken into separate message pieces that are placed in separate, sequentially numbered envelopes. Each of the letters is then mailed at once. The letters could arrive in order, out of order or not at all.
- **DatagramPacket** objects store packets of data for sending or store packets of data received by an application. **DatagramSocket**s send and receive **DatagramPacket**s.
- The **DatagramSocket** constructor that takes no arguments binds the application to a port chosen by the computer on which the program executes. The **DatagramSocket** constructor that takes an integer port number argument binds the application to the specified port. If a **DatagramSocket** constructor fails to bind the application to a port, a **SocketException** occurs.
- **DatagramSocket** method **receive** blocks (waits) until a packet arrives, then stores the packet in its argument.
- **DatagramPacket** method **getAddress** returns an **InetAddress** object containing information about the host computer from which the packet was sent.
- **DatagramPacket** method **getPort** returns an integer specifying the port number through which the host computer sent the **DatagramPacket**.
- **DatagramPacket** method **getLength** returns an integer representing the number of bytes of data in a **DatagramPacket**.
- **DatagramPacket** method **getData** returns a byte array containing the data in a **DatagramPacket**.
- The **DatagramPacket** constructor for a packet to be sent takes four arguments—the byte array to be sent, the number of bytes to be sent, the client address to which the packet will be sent and the port number where the client is waiting to receive packets.
- **DatagramSocket** method send sends a **DatagramPacket** out over the network.
- If an error occurs when receiving or sending a **DatagramPacket**, an **IOException** occurs.
- Reading data from a **Socket** is a blocking call—the current thread is put in the blocked state while the thread waits for the read operation to complete. Method **setSoTimeout** specifies that, if no data is received in the given number of milliseconds, the **Socket** should issue an **Inter-**

ruptedIOException, which the current thread can catch, then continue executing. This prevents the current thread from deadlocking if there is no more data available from the **Socket**.

- Multicast is an efficient way to send data to many clients without the overhead of broadcasting that data to every host on the Internet.
- Using multicast, an application can "publish" **DatagramPacket**s to be delivered to other applications—the "subscribers."
- An application multicasts **DatagramPacket**s by sending the **DatagramPacket**s to a multicast address—an IP address in the range from 224.0.0.0 to 239.255.255.255, reserved for multicast.
- Clients that wish to receive **DatagramPacket**s can connect to the multicast address to join the multicast group that will receive the published **DatagramPacket**s.
- Multicast **DatagramPacket**s are not reliable—packets are not guaranteed to reach any destination. Also, the order in which clients receive the datagrams is not guaranteed.
- The **MulticastSocket** constructor takes as an argument the port to which the **MulticastSocket** should connect to receive incoming **DatagramPacket**s. Method **joinGroup** of class **MulticastSocket** takes as an argument the **InetAddress** of the multicast group to join.
- Method receive of class **MulticastSocket** reads an incoming **DatagramPacket** from a multicast address.

TERMINOLOGY

accept a connection
accept method of **ServerSocket** class
addElement method of class **Vector**
AppletContext interface
bind to a port
BindException class
client
client connects to a server
client/server relationship
client-side socket
close a connection
close method of class **Socket**
collaborative computing
computer networking
connect to a port
connect to a World Wide Web site
ConnectException class
connection
connection request
connectionless service
connectionless transmission with datagrams
connection-oriented service
Cursor class
Cursor.DEFAULT_CURSOR
Cursor.WAIT_CURSOR
datagram
datagram socket
DatagramPacket class
DatagramSocket class
deny a connection
duplicated packets
get method of class **Hashtable**
getAddress method of **DatagramPacket**
getAppletContext method of class **Applet**
getByName method of **InetAddress**
getData method of class **DatagramPacket**
getEventType method
getInputStream method of class **Socket**
getLength method of **DatagramPacket**
getLocalHost method
getLocalHost method of **InetAddress**
getOutputStream method of class **Socket**
getPort method of class **DatagramPacket**
getPredefinedCursor method of Cursor
getURL method of class **HyperlinkEvent**
handshake point
Hashtable class
heterogeneous computer systems
host
Hyperlink.EventType class
Hyperlink.EventType.ACTIVATED
Hyperlink.EventType.ENTERED
Hyperlink.EventType.EXITED
HyperlinkEvent class
HyperlinkListener interface
hyperlinkUpdate method
InetAddress class
Internet

Internet address
InterruptedIOException class
IOException class
Java Security API
java.net package
JEditorPane class
joinGroup method of **MulticastSocket**
key/value pair
leaveGroup method of **MulticastSocket**
lost packets
MalformedURLException class
multicast
multicast address
multicast group
MulticastSocket class
multithreaded server
network programming
networking
open a socket
out-of-sequence packets
packet
packet length
port
port number on a server
put method of class **Hashtable**
read from a socket
receive method of class **DatagramSocket**
register an available port number
send method of class **DatagramSocket**
server
server-side socket
ServerSocket class
setCursor method of class **Component**
setPage method of class **JEditorPane**
setSoTimeout method of class **Socket**
showDocument method of **AppletContext**
socket
Socket class
socket-based communications
SocketException
stream socket
TCP (Transmission Control Protocol)
UDP (User Datagram Protocol)
UnknownHostException
URI (Uniform Resource Identifier)
URL (Uniform Resource Locator)
URL class
Vector class
wait for a connection
wait for a packet
Web browser
Web server
World Wide Web

SELF-REVIEW EXERCISES

17.1 Fill in the blanks in each of the following statements:

a) Exception _________ occurs when an input/output error occurs when closing a socket.
b) Exception _________ occurs when a server address indicated by a client cannot be resolved.
c) If a **DatagramSocket** constructor fails to set up a **DatagramSocket** properly, an exception of type _________ occurs.
d) Many of Java's networking classes are contained in package _________.
e) Class _________ binds the application to a port for datagram transmission.
f) An object of class _________ contains an Internet address.
g) The two types of sockets we discussed in this chapter are _________ sockets and _________ sockets.
h) The acronym URL stands for _________.
i) The acronym URI stands for _________.
j) The key protocol that forms the basis of the World Wide Web is _________.
k) **AppletContext** method _________ receives a **URL** object as an argument and displays in a browser the World Wide Web resource associated with that **URL**.
l) **InetAddress** method **getLocalHost** returns an _________ object containing the local host name of the computer on which the program is executing.
m) Method _________ of class **MulticastSocket** subscribes the **MulticastSocket** to a multicast group.

n) The **URL** constructor determines whether the **String** passed as an argument represents a valid Uniform Resource Identifier. If so, the **URL** object is initialized to contain the URI; otherwise, an exception of type ________ occurs.

17.2 State whether each of the following is *true or false*. *If* false, explain why.

a) An application that uses multicast broadcasts **DatagramPacket**s to every host on the Internet.
b) UDP is a connection-oriented protocol.
c) With stream sockets a process establishes a connection to another process.
d) A server waits at a port for connections from a client.
e) Datagram packet transmission over a network is reliable—packets are guaranteed to arrive in sequence.
f) For security reasons, many Web browsers such as Netscape *Communicator* allow Java applets to do file processing only on the machines on which they execute.
g) Web browsers often restrict an applet so that it can only communicate with the machine from which it was originally downloaded.
h) IP addresses in the range from **224.0.0.0** to **239.255.255.255** are reserved for multicast.

ANSWERS TO SELF-REVIEW EXERCISES

17.1 a) **IOException**. b) **UnknownHostException**. c) **SocketException**. d) **java.net**. e) **DatagramSocket**. f) **InetAddress**. g) stream, datagram. h) Uniform Resource Locator. i) Universal Resource Identifier. j) **http**. k) **showDocument**. l) **InetAddress**. m) **joinGroup**. n) **MalformedURLException**.

17.2 a) False; multicast sends **DatagramPacket**s only to hosts that have joined the multicast group. b) False; UDP is a connectionless protocol and TCP is a connection-oriented protocol. c) True. d) True. e) False; packets could be lost and packets can arrive out of order. f) False; most browsers prevent applets from doing file processing on the client machine. g) True. h) True.

EXERCISES

17.3 Distinguish between connection-oriented and connectionless network services.

17.4 How does a client determine the host name of the client computer?

17.5 Under what circumstances would a **SocketException** be thrown?

17.6 How can a client get a line of text from a server?

17.7 Describe how a client connects to a server.

17.8 Describe how a server sends data to a client.

17.9 Describe how to prepare a server to receive a stream-based connection request from a single client.

17.10 Describe how to prepare a server to receive connection requests from multiple clients if each client that connects should be processed in parallel with all other connected clients.

17.11 How does a server listen for connections at a port?

17.12 What determines how many connect requests from clients can wait in a queue to connect to a server?

17.13 As described in the text, what reasons might cause a server to refuse a connection request from a client?

17.14 Use a socket connection to allow a client to specify a file name and have the server send the contents of the file or indicate that the file does not exist.

17.15 Modify Exercise 17.14 to allow the client to modify the contents of the file and send the file back to the server for storage. The user can edit the file in a **`JTextArea`**, then click a *save changes* button to send the file back to the server.

17.16 Modify program of Fig. 17.2 to allow users to add their own sites to the list and remove sites from the list.

17.17 Multithreaded servers are quite popular today, especially because of the increasing use of multiprocessing servers. Modify the simple server application presented in Section 17.6 to be a multithreaded server. Then use several client applications and have each of them connect to the server simultaneously. Use a **`Vector`** to store the client threads. **`Vector`** provides several methods of use in this exercise. Method **`size`** determines the number of elements in a **`Vector`**. Method **`elementAt`** returns the element in the specified location (as an **`Object`** reference). Method **`add`** places a new element at the end of the **`Vector`**. Method **`remove`** deletes its argument from the **`Vector`**. Method **`lastElement`** returns an **`Object`** reference to the last object you inserted in the **`Vector`**.

17.18 In the text, we presented a tic-tac-toe program controlled by a multithreaded server. Develop a checkers program modeled after the tic-tac-toe program. The two users should alternate making moves. Your program should mediate the players' moves, determining whose turn it is and allowing only valid moves. The players themselves will determine when the game is over.

17.19 Develop a chess-playing program modeled after the checkers program in the Exercise 17.18.

17.20 Develop a Blackjack card game program in which the server application deals cards to each of the client applets. The server should deal additional cards (as per the rules of the game) to each player as requested.

17.21 Develop a Poker card game in which the server application deals cards to each of the client applets. The server should deal additional cards (as per the rules of the game) to each player as requested.

17.22 *(Modifications to the Multithreaded Tic-Tac-Toe Program)* The programs of Fig. 17.8 and Fig. 17.9 implemented a multithreaded, client/server version of the game Tic-Tac-Toe. Our goal in developing this game was to demonstrate a multithreaded server that could process multiple connections from clients at the same time. The server in the example is really a mediator between the two client applets—it makes sure that each move is valid and that each client moves in the proper order. The server does not determine who won or lost or if there was a draw. Also, there is no capability to allow a new game to be played or to terminate an existing game.

The following is a list of suggested modifications to the multithreaded Tic-Tac-Toe application and applet.

a) Modify the **`TicTacToeServer`** class to test for a win, loss or draw on each move in the game. Send a message to each client applet that indicates the result of the game when the game is over.
b) Modify the **`TicTacToeClient`** class to display a button that when clicked allows the client to play another game. The button should be enabled only when a game completes. Note that both class **`TicTacToeClient`** and class **`TicTacToeServer`** must be modified to reset the board and all state information. Also, the other **`TicTacToeClient`** should be notified that a new game is about to begin so its board and state can be reset.
c) Modify the **`TicTacToeClient`** class to provide a button that allows a client to terminate the program at any time. When the user clicks the button, the server and the other client should be notified. The server should then wait for a connection from another client so a new game can begin.
d) Modify the **`TicTacToeClient`** class and the **`TicTacToeServer`** class so the winner of a game can choose game piece X or O for the next game. Remember: X always goes first.

e) If you would like to be ambitious, allow a client to play against the server while the server waits for a connection from another client.

17.23 *(3-D Multithreaded Tic-Tac-Toe)* Modify the multithreaded, client/server Tic-Tac-Toe program to implement a three-dimensional 4-by-4-by-4 version of the game. Implement the server application to mediate between the two clients. Display the three-dimensional board as four boards containing four rows and four columns each. If you would like to be ambitious, try the following modifications:

a) Draw the board in a three-dimensional manner.
b) Allow the server to test for a win, loss or draw. Beware! There are many possible ways to win on a 4-by-4-by-4 board!

17.24 *(Networked Morse Code)* Modify your solution to Exercise 10.27 to enable two applets to send Morse Code messages to each other through a multithreaded server application. Each applet should allow the user to type normal characters in **JTextArea**s, translate the characters into Morse Code and send the coded message through the server to the other client. When messages are received, they should be decoded and displayed as normal characters and as Morse Code. The applet should have two **JTextArea**s: one for displaying the other client's messages and one for typing.

18

Multimedia: Images, Animation, Audio and Video

Objectives

- To understand how to get and display images.
- To create animations from sequences of images.
- To customize an animation applet with applet parameters specified in the applet's HTML document.
- To create image maps.
- To be able to get, play, loop and stop sounds using an **`AudioClip`**.

The wheel that squeaks the loudest … gets the grease.
John Billings (Henry Wheeler Shaw)

We'll use a signal I have tried and found far-reaching and easy to yell. Waa-hoo!
Zane Grey

There is a natural hootchy-kootchy motion to a goldfish.
Walt Disney

Between the motion and the act falls the shadow.
Thomas Stearns Eliot, *The Hollow Men*

Outline

18.1 Introduction
18.2 Loading, Displaying and Scaling Images
18.3 Animating a Series of Images
18.4 Customizing `LogoAnimator` via Applet Parameters
18.5 Image Maps
18.6 Loading and Playing Audio Clips
18.7 Internet and World Wide Web Resources

Summary • Terminology • Self-Review Exercises • Answers to Self-Review Exercises • Exercises

18.1 Introduction

Welcome to what may be the largest revolution in the history of the computer industry. Those of us who entered the field decades ago were interested in using computers primarily to perform arithmetic calculations at high speed. As the computer field evolves, we are beginning to realize that the data-manipulation capabilities of computers are now equally important. The "sizzle" of Java is *multimedia*, the use of *sound*, *images*, *graphics* and *video* to make applications "come alive." Today, many people consider two-dimensional color video to be the "ultimate" in multimedia. Within the decade, we expect all kinds of exciting new three-dimensional applications. Java programmers already can use the *Java3D API* to create substantial 3D graphics applications. We discuss the Java3D API in our book *Advanced Java 2 Platform How to Program.*

Multimedia programming offers many new challenges. The field is already enormous and will grow rapidly. People are rushing to equip their computers for multimedia. Most new computers sold today are "multimedia ready," with CD or DVD drives, audio boards and sometimes with special video capabilities.

Among users who want graphics, two-dimensional graphics no longer suffice. Many people now want three-dimensional, high-resolution, color graphics. True three-dimensional imaging may become available within the next decade. Imagine having ultra-high-resolution, "theater-in-the-round," three-dimensional television. Sporting and entertainment events will seem to take place on your living room floor! Medical students worldwide will see operations being performed thousands of miles away, as if they were occurring in the same room. People will be able to learn how to drive with extremely realistic driving simulators in their homes before they get behind the wheel. The possibilities are exciting and endless.

Multimedia demands extraordinary computing power. Until recently, affordable computers with this kind of power were not available. Today's ultrafast processors, like the SPARC Ultra from Sun Microsystems, the Pentium and Itanium from Intel, the Alpha from Compaq Computer Corporation and the processors from MIPS/Silicon Graphics (among others) make effective multimedia possible. The computer and communications industries will be primary beneficiaries of the multimedia revolution. Users will be willing to pay for the faster processors, larger memories and wider communications bandwidths that support demanding multimedia applications. Ironically, users may not have to pay more as fierce competition in these industries drives prices down.

We need programming languages that make creating multimedia applications easy. Most programming languages do not have built-in multimedia capabilities. However, Java provides extensive multimedia facilities that enable you to start developing powerful multimedia applications immediately.

This chapter presents a series of "live-code" examples that cover several interesting multimedia features you will need to build useful applications, including:

1. the basics of manipulating images
2. creating smooth animations
3. customizing an animation applet via parameters supplied from the HTML file that invokes an applet
4. playing audio files with the **AudioClip** interface
5. creating image maps that can sense when the cursor is over them even without a mouse click

We will continue our coverage of Java's multimedia capabilities in Chapter 22, where we discuss the *Java Media Framework* (*JMF*) and the *Java Sound APIs*. JMF and Java Sound enable Java programs to play and record audio and video. The JMF even enables Java programs to send audio and video streams—so-called *streaming media*—across a network or the Internet. The chapter exercises for this chapter and Chapter 22 suggest dozens of challenging and interesting projects and even mention some "million-dollar" ideas that could help you make your fortune! When we were creating these exercises, it seemed that the ideas just kept flowing. Multimedia seems to leverage creativity in ways that we have not experienced with "conventional" computer capabilities.

18.2 Loading, Displaying and Scaling Images

Java's multimedia capabilities include graphics, images, animations, sounds and video. We begin our multimedia discussion with images.

The applet of Fig. 18.1 demonstrates loading an ***Image*** (package **java.awt**) and loading an ***ImageIcon*** (package **javax.swing**). The applet displays the **Image** in its original size and scaled to a larger size, using two versions of **Graphics** method ***drawImage***. The applet also draws the **ImageIcon** using its method ***paintIcon***. Class **ImageIcon** is easier than **Image** to use, because its constructor can receive arguments of several different formats, including a **byte** array containing the bytes of an image, an **Image** already loaded in memory, a **String** representing the location of an image and a **URL** representing the location of an image.

```
// Fig. 18.1: LoadImageAndScale.java
// Load an image and display it in its original size
// and scale it to twice its original width and height.
// Load and display the same image as an ImageIcon.

// Java core packages
import java.applet.Applet;
import java.awt.*;
```

Fig. 18.1 Loading and displaying an image in an applet (part 1 of 2).

```

// Java extension packages
import javax.swing.*;

public class LoadImageAndScale extends JApplet {
   private Image logo1;
   private ImageIcon logo2;

   // load image when applet is loaded
   public void init()
   {
      logo1 = getImage( getDocumentBase(), "logo.gif" );
      logo2 = new ImageIcon( "logo.gif" );
   }

   // display image
   public void paint( Graphics g )
   {
      // draw original image
      g.drawImage( logo1, 0, 0, this );

      // draw image scaled to fit width of applet
      // and height of applet minus 120 pixels
      g.drawImage( logo1, 0, 120,
         getWidth(), getHeight() - 120, this );

      // draw icon using its paintIcon method
      logo2.paintIcon( this, g, 180, 0 );
   }

} // end class LoadImageAndScale
```

Fig. 18.1 Loading and displaying an image in an applet (part 2 of 2).

Lines 14 and 15 declare an **Image** reference and an **ImageIcon** reference, respectively. Class **Image** is an **abstract** class; therefore, the applet cannot create an object of class **Image** directly. Rather, the applet must call a method that causes the applet container to load and return the **Image** for use in the program. Class **Applet** (the superclass of **JApplet**) provides a method that does just that. Line 20 in method **init** uses **Applet** method ***getImage*** to load an **Image** into the applet. This version of **getImage** takes two arguments—the location of the image file and the file name of the image. In the first argument, **Applet** method **getDocumentBase** returns a **URL** representing the location of the image on the Internet (or on your computer if the applet was loaded from your computer). The program assumes that the image is stored in the same directory as the HTML file that invoked the applet. Method **getDocumentBase** returns the location of the HTML file on the Internet as an object of class **URL**. The second argument specifies an image file name. Java supports several image formats, including *Graphics Interchange Format (GIF)*, *Joint Photographic Experts Group (JPEG)* and *Portable Network Graphics (PNG)*. File names for each of these types end with **.gif**, **.jpg** (or **.jpeg**) and **.png**, respectively.

Portability Tip 18.1

*Class **Image** is an **abstract** class and, as a result, programs cannot instantiate **Image** objects. To achieve platform independence, the Java implementation on each platform provides its own subclass of **Image** to store image information.*

When line 20 invokes method **getImage** to set up loading of the image from the local computer (or downloading of the image from the Internet). When the image is required by the program, the image is loaded in a separate thread of execution. This enables the program to continue execution while the image loads. [*Note:* If the requested file is not available, method **getImage** does not indicate an error.]

Class **ImageIcon** is not an **abstract** class; therefore, a program can create an **ImageIcon** object. Line 21 in method **init** creates an **ImageIcon** object that loads the same **logo.gif** image. Class **ImageIcon** provides several constructors that enable programs to initialize **ImageIcon** objects with images from the local computer or with images stored on the Internet.

The applet's **paint** method (lines 25–37) displays the images. Line 28 uses **Graphics** method **drawImage** to display an **Image**. Method **drawImage** receives four arguments. The first argument is a reference to the **Image** object to display (**logo1**). The second and third arguments are the *x*- and *y*-coordinates at which to display the image on the applet; the coordinates indicate the upper-left corner of the image. The last argument is a reference to an ***ImageObserver*** object. Normally, the **ImageObserver** is the object on which the program displays the image. An **ImageObserver** can be any object that implements interface **ImageObserver**. Class **Component** (one of class **Applet**'s indirect superclasses) implements interface **ImageObserver**. Therefore, all **Component**s (including our applet) are **ImageObserver**s. The **ImageObserver** argument is important when displaying large images that require a long time to download from the Internet. It is possible that a program will execute the code that displays the image before the image downloads completely. The **ImageObserver** is notified to update the displayed image as the remainder of the image loads. When executing this applet, watch carefully as pieces of the image display while the image loads. [*Note*: On faster computers, you might not notice this effect.]

Lines 32–33 use another version of **Graphics** method **drawImage** to output a *scaled* version of the image. The fourth and fifth arguments specify the *width* and *height* of the image for display purposes. Method **drawImage** scales the image to fit the specified width and height. In this example, the fourth argument indicates that the width of the scaled image should be the width of the applet, and the fifth argument indicates that the height should be 120 pixels less than the height of the applet. Line 33 determines the width and height of the applet by calling methods **getWidth** and **getHeight** (inherited from class **Component**).

Line 36 uses **ImageIcon** method ***paintIcon*** to display the image. The method requires four arguments—a reference to the **Component** on which to display the image, a reference to the **Graphics** object that will render the image, the *x*-coordinate of the upper-left corner of the image and the *y*-coordinate of the upper-left corner of the image.

If you compare the two techniques for loading and displaying images in this example, you can see that using **ImageIcon** is simpler. You can create objects of class **ImageIcon** directly, and there is no need to use an **ImageObserver** reference when displaying the image. For this reason, we use class **ImageIcon** for the remainder of the chapter. [*Note*: Class **ImageIcon**'s **paintIcon** method does not allow scaling of an image. However, the class provides method **getImage**, which returns an **Image** reference that **Graphics** method **drawImage** can use to display a scaled image.]

18.3 Animating a Series of Images

The next example demonstrates animating a series of images that are stored in an array. The application uses the same techniques to load and display **ImageIcon**s as shown in Fig. 18.1. The animation presented in Fig. 18.2 is designed as a subclass of **JPanel** (called **LogoAnimator**) that can be attached to an application window or possibly to a **JApplet**. Class **LogoAnimator** also defines a **main** method (defined at lines 96–117) to execute the animation as an application. Method **main** defines an instance of class **JFrame** and attaches a **LogoAnimator** object to the **JFrame** to display the animation.

```
1  // Fig. 18.2: LogoAnimator.java
2  // Animation a series of images
3
4  // Java core packages
5  import java.awt.*;
6  import java.awt.event.*;
7
8  // Java extension packages
9  import javax.swing.*;
10
11 public class LogoAnimator extends JPanel
12    implements ActionListener {
13
14    protected ImageIcon images[];        // array of images
15
16    protected int totalImages = 30,      // number of images
17                  currentImage = 0,      // current image index
18                  animationDelay = 50,   // millisecond delay
19                  width,                 // image width
20                  height;                // image height
```

Fig. 18.2 Animating a series of images (part 1 of 3).

```

   protected String imageName = "deitel";  // base image name
   protected Timer animationTimer;  // Timer drives animation

   // initialize LogoAnimator by loading images
   public LogoAnimator()
   {
      initializeAnimation();
   }

   // initialize animation
   protected void initializeAnimation()
   {
      images = new ImageIcon[ totalImages ];

      // load images
      for ( int count = 0; count < images.length; ++count )
         images[ count ] = new ImageIcon( getClass().getResource(
            "images/" + imageName + count + ".gif" ) );

      width = images[ 0 ].getIconWidth();   // get icon width
      height = images[ 0 ].getIconHeight(); // get icon height
   }

   // display current image
   public void paintComponent( Graphics g )
   {
      super.paintComponent( g );

      images[ currentImage ].paintIcon( this, g, 0, 0 );
      currentImage = ( currentImage + 1 ) % totalImages;
   }

   // respond to Timer's event
   public void actionPerformed( ActionEvent actionEvent )
   {
      repaint();  // repaint animator
   }

   // start or restart animation
   public void startAnimation()
   {
      if ( animationTimer == null ) {
         currentImage = 0;
         animationTimer = new Timer( animationDelay, this );
         animationTimer.start();
      }
      else  // continue from last image displayed
         if ( ! animationTimer.isRunning() )
            animationTimer.restart();
   }

```

Fig. 18.2 Animating a series of images (part 2 of 3).

```
   // stop animation timer
   public void stopAnimation()
   {
      animationTimer.stop();
   }

   // return minimum size of animation
   public Dimension getMinimumSize()
   {
      return getPreferredSize();
   }

   // return preferred size of animation
   public Dimension getPreferredSize()
   {
      return new Dimension( width, height );
   }

   // execute animation in a JFrame
   public static void main( String args[] )
   {
      // create LogoAnimator
      LogoAnimator animation = new LogoAnimator();

      // set up window
      JFrame window = new JFrame( "Animator test" );

      Container container = window.getContentPane();
      container.add( animation );

      window.setDefaultCloseOperation( JFrame.EXIT_ON_CLOSE );

      // size and display window
      window.pack();
      Insets insets = window.getInsets();

      window.setSize( animation.getPreferredSize().width +
         insets.left + insets.right,
         animation.getPreferredSize().height +
         insets.top + insets.bottom );

      window.setVisible( true );
      animation.startAnimation();  // begin animation

   }  // end method main

}  // end class LogoAnimator
```

Fig. 18.2 Animating a series of images (part 3 of 3).

Class **LogoAnimator** maintains an array of **ImageIcon**s that are loaded in method **initializeAnimation** (lines 32–43), which is called from the constructor. As the **for** structure (lines 37–39) creates each **ImageIcon** object, the **ImageIcon** constructor loads one of the animation's 30 images. The constructor argument uses **String** concatenation to assemble the file name from the pieces **"images/"**, **imageName**, **count** and **".gif"**. Each of the images in the animation is in a file called **deitel#.gif**, where # is a value in the range 0–29 specified by the loop's control variable **count**. Lines 41–42 determine the width and height of the animation from the size of the first image in array **images**.

Performance Tip 18.1

It is more efficient to load the frames of the animation as one image than to load each image separately. (A painting program can be used to combine the frames of the animation into one image. If the images are being loaded from the Web, every image loaded requires a separate connection to the site containing the images.

Performance Tip 18.2

Loading all the frames of an animation as one large image can force your program to wait to begin displaying the animation.

After the **LogoAnimator** constructor loads the images, method **main** sets up the window in which the animation will appear and calls **startAnimation** (defined at lines 61–71) to begin the animation. The animation is driven by an instance of class ***Timer*** (package **javax.swing**). A **Timer** generates **ActionEvent**s at a fixed interval in milliseconds (normally specified as an argument to the **Timer**'s constructor) and notifies all of its **ActionListener**s that the event occurred. Lines 63–67 determine whether the **Timer** reference **animationTimer** is **null**. If so, line 64 sets **currentImage** to 0, to indicate that the animation should begin with the image in the first element of array **images**. Line 65 assigns a new **Timer** object to **animationTimer**. The **Timer** constructor receives two arguments—the delay in milliseconds (**animationDelay** is 50 in this example) and the **ActionListener** that will respond to the **Timer**'s **ActionEvent**s. Class **LogoAnimator** implements **ActionListener** so line 65 specifies **this** as the listener. Line 66 starts the **Timer** object. Once started, **animationTimer** will generate an **ActionEvent** every 50 milliseconds. Lines 69–70 enable a program to restart an animation that the program stopped previously. For example, to make an animation "browser friendly" in an applet, the animation should stop when the user switches Web pages. If the user returns to the Web page with the animation, method **startAnimation** can be called to restart the animation. The **if** condition at line 73 uses **Timer** method **isRunning** to determine whether the **Timer** is running (i.e., generating events). If it is not running, line 70 calls **Timer** method **restart** to indicate that the **Timer** should start generating events again.

In response to every **Timer** event in this example, the program calls method **actionPerformed** (lines 55–58). Line 57 calls **LogoAnimator**'s **repaint** method to schedule a call to the **LogoAnimator**'s **update** method (inherited from class **JPanel**) which, in turn, calls **LogoAnimator**'s **paintComponent** method (lines 46–52). Remember that any subclass of **JComponent** that performs drawing should do so in its **paintComponent** method. As mentioned in Chapter 13, the first statement in any **paintComponent** method should be a call to the superclass's **paintComponent** method to ensure that Swing components are displayed correctly.

Lines 50–51 paint the **ImageIcon** at element **currentImage** in the array and prepare for the next image to be displayed by incrementing **currentImage** by 1. Notice the modulus calculation to ensure that the value of **currentImage** is set to 0 when it is incremented past 29 (the last element subscript in the array).

Method **stopAnimation** (lines 74–77) stops the animation with line 76, which calls **Timer** method ***stop*** to indicate that the **Timer** should stop generating events. This prevents **actionPerformed** from calling **repaint** to initiate the painting of the next image in the array.

Software Engineering Observation 18.1

When creating an animation for use in an applet, provide a mechanism for disabling the animation when the user browses a new Web page separate from the page on which the animation applet resides.

Methods **getMinimumSize** (lines 80–83) and **getPreferredSize** (lines 86–89) override the corresponding methods inherited from class **Component** and enable layout managers to determine the appropriate size of a **LogoAnimator** in a layout. In this example, the images are 160 pixels wide and 80 pixels tall, so method **getPreferredSize** returns a **Dimension** object containing the numbers 160 and 80. Method **getMinimumSize** simply calls **getPreferredSize** (a common programming practice).

Lines 107–112 of **main** size the application window based on the **LogoAnimator**'s preferred size and the window's *insets*. The insets specify the number of pixels for the window's top, bottom, left and right borders. Using the insets of the window ensures that the window's *client area* is large enough to display the **LogoAnimator** correctly. The client area is the part of a window in which the window displays GUI components. The program obtains the window's insets by calling method ***getInsets*** at line 107. The method returns an ***Insets*** object that contains **public** data members ***top***, ***bottom***, ***left*** and ***right***.

18.4 Customizing LogoAnimator via Applet Parameters

When browsing the World Wide Web, you often will come across applets that are in the public domain—you can use them free of charge on your own Web pages (normally in exchange for crediting the applet's creator). One common feature of such applets is the ability to be customized via parameters that are supplied from the HTML file that invokes the applet. For example, the HTML

```
<html>
<applet code = "LogoApplet.class" width = 400 height = 400>
<param name = "totalimages" value = "30">
<param name = "imagename" value = "deitel">
<param name = "animationdelay" value = "200">
</applet>
</html>
```

from file **LogoApplet.html**, invokes the applet **LogoApplet** (Fig. 18.4) and specifies three parameters. The ***param*** *tag* lines must appear between the starting and ending **applet** tags. Each parameter has a ***name*** and a ***value***. **Applet** method ***getParameter*** returns a **String** representing the **value** associated with a specific parameter **name**. The argument to **getParameter** is a **String** containing the name of the parameter in the **param** tag. For example, the statement

```
parameter = getParameter( "animationdelay" );
```

gets the value 200 associated with parameter **animationdelay** and assigns it to **String** reference **parameter**. If there is not a **param** tag containing the specified parameter name, **getParameter** returns **null**.

Class **LogoAnimator2** (Fig. 18.3) extends class **LogoAnimator** and adds a constructor that takes three arguments—the total number of images in the animation, the delay between displaying images and the base image name. Class **LogoApplet** (Fig. 18.4) allows Web page designers to customize the animation to use their own images. Three parameters are provided in the applet's HTML document. Parameter **animationdelay** is the number of milliseconds to sleep between displaying images. This value will be converted to an integer and used as the value for instance variable **sleepTime**. Parameter **imagename** is the base name of the images to be loaded. This **String** will be assigned to instance variable **imageName**. The applet assumes that the images are in a subdirectory named **images** that can be found in the same directory as the applet. The applet also assumes that the image file names are numbered from 0 (as in Fig. 18.2). Parameter **totalimages** represents the total number of images in the animation. Its value will be converted to an integer and assigned to instance variable **totalImages**.

```
// Fig. 18.3: LogoAnimator2.java
// Animating a series of images

// Java core packages
import java.awt.*;

// Java extension packages
import javax.swing.*;

public class LogoAnimator2 extends LogoAnimator {

   // default constructor
   public LogoAnimator2()
   {
      super();
   }

   // new constructor to support customization
   public LogoAnimator2( int count, int delay, String name )
   {
      totalImages = count;
      animationDelay = delay;
      imageName = name;

      initializeAnimation();
   }

```

Fig. 18.3 **LogoAnimator2** subclass of **LogoAnimator** (Fig. 18.2) adds a constructor for customizing the number of images, animation delay and base image name (part 1 of 2).

```
   // start animation as application in its own window
   public static void main( String args[] )
   {
      // create LogoAnimator
      LogoAnimator2 animation = new LogoAnimator2();

      // set up window
      JFrame window = new JFrame( "Animator test" );

      Container container = window.getContentPane();
      container.add( animation );

      window.setDefaultCloseOperation( JFrame.EXIT_ON_CLOSE );

      // size and display window
      window.pack();
      Insets insets = window.getInsets();

      window.setSize( animation.getPreferredSize().width +
         insets.left + insets.right,
         animation.getPreferredSize().height +
         insets.top + insets.bottom );

      window.setVisible( true );
      animation.startAnimation();  // begin animation

   }  // end method main

}  // end class LogoAnimator2
```

Fig. 18.3 **`LogoAnimator2`** subclass of **`LogoAnimator`** (Fig. 18.2) adds a constructor for customizing the number of images, animation delay and base image name (part 2 of 2).

```
// Fig. 18.4: LogoApplet.java
// Customizing an applet via HTML parameters.
//
// HTML parameter "animationdelay" is an int indicating
// milliseconds to sleep between images (default 50).
//
// HTML parameter "imagename" is the base name of the images
// that will be displayed (i.e., "deitel" is the base name
// for images "deitel0.gif," "deitel1.gif," etc.). The applet
// assumes that images are in an "images" subdirectory of
// the directory in which the applet resides.
//
// HTML parameter "totalimages" is an integer representing the
// total number of images in the animation. The applet assumes
// images are numbered from 0 to totalimages - 1 (default 30).

// Java core packages
import java.awt.*;
```

Fig. 18.4 Customizing an animation applet via the **`param`** HTML tag (part 1 of 2).

```java

// Java extension packages
import javax.swing.*;

public class LogoApplet extends JApplet {

   // obtain parameters from HTML and customize applet
   public void init()
   {
      String parameter;

      // get animation delay from HTML document
      parameter = getParameter( "animationdelay" );

      int animationDelay = ( parameter == null ?
         50 : Integer.parseInt( parameter ) );

      // get base image name from HTML document
      String imageName = getParameter( "imagename" );

      // get total number of images from HTML document
      parameter = getParameter( "totalimages" );

      int totalImages = ( parameter == null ?
         0 : Integer.parseInt( parameter ) );

      // create instance of LogoAnimator
      LogoAnimator2 animator;

      if ( imageName == null || totalImages == 0 )
         animator = new LogoAnimator2();
      else
         animator = new LogoAnimator2( totalImages,
            animationDelay, imageName );

      // attach animator to applet and start animation
      getContentPane().add( animator );
      animator.startAnimation();

   }  // end method init

}  // end class LogoApplet
```

Fig. 18.4 Customizing an animation applet via the **`param`** HTML tag (part 2 of 2).

Class **LogoApplet** (Fig. 18.4) defines an **init** method in which the three HTML parameters are read with **Applet** method **getParameter** (lines 31, 37 and 40). After the applet reads these parameters and the two integer parameters are converted to **int** values, the **if/else** structure at lines 48 through 51 creates a **LogoAnimator2** and calls its three-argument constructor. If the **imageName** is **null** or **totalImages** is **0**, the applet calls the default **LogoAnimator2** constructor and uses the default animation. Otherwise, the applet passes **totalImages**, **animationDelay** and **imageName** to the three-argument **LogoAnimator2** constructor, and the constructor uses those arguments to customize the animation. **LogoAnimator2**'s three-argument constructor invokes **LogoAnimator**'s **initalizeAnimation** method to load the images and determine the width and height of the animation.

18.5 Image Maps

Image maps are a common technique used to create interactive Web pages. An image map is an image that has *hot areas* that the user can click to accomplish a task, such as loading a different Web page into a browser. When the user positions the mouse pointer over a hot area, normally a descriptive message appears in the status area of the browser or in a pop-up window.

Figure 18.5 loads an image containing several of the common tip icons used throughout this book. The program allows the user to position the mouse pointer over an icon and display a descriptive message for the icon. Event handler **mouseMoved** (lines 42–46) takes the mouse coordinates and passes them to method **translateLocation** (lines 63–76). Method **translateLocation** tests the coordinates to determine the icon over which the mouse was positioned when the **mouseMoved** event occurred. Method **translateLocation** then returns a message indicating what the icon represents. This message is displayed in the **appletviewer**'s (or browser's) status bar.

```
1  // Fig. 18.5: ImageMap.java
2  // Demonstrating an image map.
3
4  // Java core packages
5  import java.awt.*;
6  import java.awt.event.*;
7
8  // Java extension packages
9  import javax.swing.*;
10
11 public class ImageMap extends JApplet {
12    private ImageIcon mapImage;
13
14    private String captions[] = { "Common Programming Error",
15       "Good Programming Practice",
16       "Graphical User Interface Tip", "Performance Tip",
17       "Portability Tip", "Software Engineering Observation",
18       "Testing and Debugging Tip" };
19
```

Fig. 18.5 Demonstrating an image map (part 1 of 4).

```
   // set up mouse listeners
   public void init()
   {
      addMouseListener(

         new MouseAdapter() {

            // indicate when mouse pointer exits applet area
            public void mouseExited( MouseEvent event )
            {
               showStatus( "Pointer outside applet" );
            }

         } // end anonymous inner class

      ); // end addMouseListener method call

      addMouseMotionListener(

         new MouseMotionAdapter() {

            // determine icon over which mouse appears
            public void mouseMoved( MouseEvent event )
            {
               showStatus( translateLocation(
                  event.getX(), event.getY() ) );
            }

         } // end anonymous inner class

      ); // end addMouseMotionListener method call

      mapImage = new ImageIcon( "icons.png" );

   } // end method init

   // display mapImage
   public void paint( Graphics g )
   {
      mapImage.paintIcon( this, g, 0, 0 );
   }

   // return tip caption based on mouse coordinates
   public String translateLocation( int x, int y )
   {
      // if coordinates outside image, return immediately
      if ( x >= mapImage.getIconWidth() ||
           y >= mapImage.getIconHeight() )
         return "";

      // determine icon number (0 - 6)
      int iconWidth = mapImage.getIconWidth() / 7;
      int iconNumber = x / iconWidth;
```

Fig. 18.5 Demonstrating an image map (part 2 of 4).

```

      // return appropriate icon caption
      return captions[ iconNumber ];
   }

}  // end class ImageMap
```

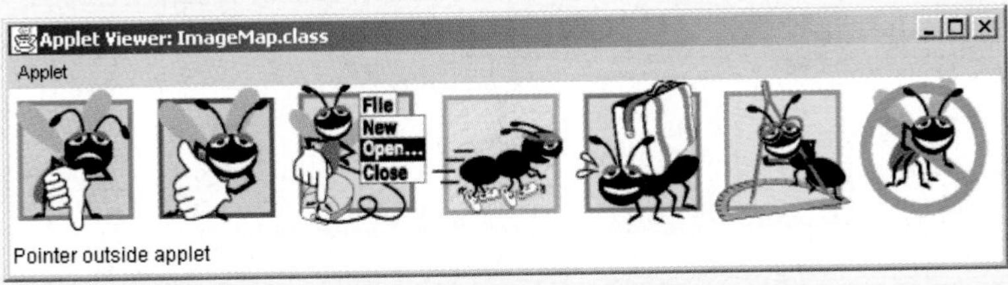

Fig. 18.5 Demonstrating an image map (part 3 of 4).

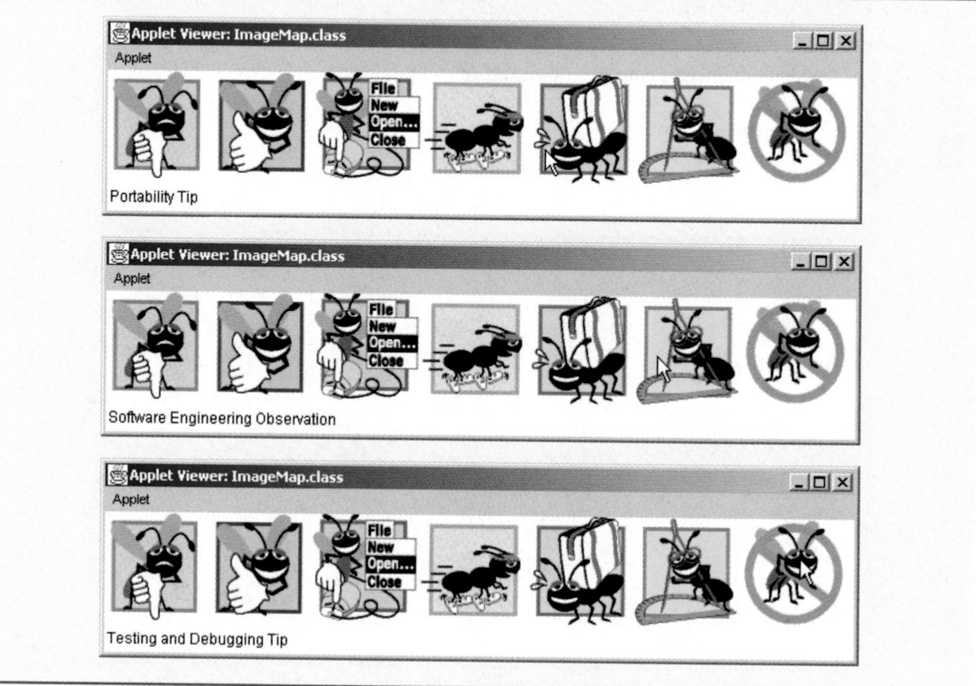

Fig. 18.5 Demonstrating an image map (part 4 of 4).

Clicking in this applet will not cause any action. In Chapter 17, Networking, we discussed the techniques required to load another Web page into a browser via **URL**s and the **AppletContext** interface. Using those techniques, this applet could associate each icon with a **URL** that the browser would display when the user clicks the icon.

18.6 Loading and Playing Audio Clips

Java programs can manipulate and play *audio clips*. It is easy for users to capture their own audio clips, and there are many clips available in software products and over the Internet. Your system needs to be equipped with audio hardware (speakers and a sound board) to be able to play the audio clips.

Java provides several mechanisms for playing sounds in an applet. The two simplest methods are the **Applet**'s ***play*** method and the ***play*** method from the ***AudioClip*** interface. Additional audio capabilities are discussed in Chapter 22. If you would like to play a sound once in a program, the **Applet** method **play** loads the sound and plays it once; the sound is marked for garbage collection after it plays. The **Applet** method **play** has two forms:

```
public void play( URL location, String soundFileName );
public void play( URL soundURL );
```

The first version loads the audio clip stored in file **soundFileName** from **location** and plays the sound. The first argument is normally a call to the applet's **getDocument-**

Base or ***getCodeBase*** method. Method **getDocumentBase** indicates the location of the HTML file that loaded the applet (if the applet is in a package, this indicates the location of the package or JAR file containing the package). Method **getCodeBase** indicates the location of the applet's **.class** file. The second version of method **play** takes a **URL** that contains the location and the file name of the audio clip. The statement

```
play( getDocumentBase(), "hi.au" );
```

loads the audio clip in file **hi.au** and plays it once.

The *sound engine* that plays the audio clips supports several audio file formats, including *Sun Audio file format* (**.au** *extension*), *Windows Wave file format* (**.wav** *extension*), *Macintosh AIFF file format* (**.aif** *or* **.aiff** *extension*) and *Musical Instrument Digital Interface* (*MIDI*) *file format* (**.mid** *or* **.rmi** *extensions*). The Java Media Framework (JMF) and Java Sound APIs support additional formats.

The program of Fig. 18.6 demonstrates loading and playing an ***AudioClip*** (package **java.applet**). This technique is more flexible than **Applet** method **play**. An applet can use an AudioClip to store audio for repeated use throughout the program's execution. **Applet** method ***getAudioClip*** has two forms that take the same arguments as method **play** described previously. Method **getAudioClip** returns a reference to an **AudioClip**. An **AudioClip** has three methods—***play***, ***loop*** and ***stop***. Method **play** plays the audio once. Method **loop** continuously loops the audio clip in the background. Method **stop** terminates an audio clip that is currently playing. In the program, each of these methods is associated with a button on the applet.

Lines 62–63 in the applet's **init** method use **getAudioClip** to load two audio files—a Windows Wave file (**welcome.wav**) and a Sun Audio file (**hi.au**). The user can select which audio clip to play from **JComboBox chooseSound**. Notice that the applet's **stop** method is overridden at lines 69–72. When the user switches Web pages, the applet container calls the applet's **stop** method. This enables the applet to stop playing the audio clip. Otherwise, the audio clip continues to play in the background—even if the applet is not displayed in the browser. This is not really a problem, but it can be annoying to the user if the audio clip is looping. The **stop** method is provided here as a convenience to the user.

Good Programming Practice 18.1

When playing audio clips in an applet or application, provide a mechanism for the user to disable the audio.

```
1  // Fig. 18.6: LoadAudioAndPlay.java
2  // Load an audio clip and play it.
3
4  // Java core packages
5  import java.applet.*;
6  import java.awt.*;
7  import java.awt.event.*;
8
9  // Java extension packages
10 import javax.swing.*;
```

Fig. 18.6 Loading and playing an **AudioClip** (part 1 of 3).

```

public class LoadAudioAndPlay extends JApplet {
   private AudioClip sound1, sound2, currentSound;
   private JButton playSound, loopSound, stopSound;
   private JComboBox chooseSound;

   // load the image when the applet begins executing
   public void init()
   {
      Container container = getContentPane();
      container.setLayout( new FlowLayout() );

      String choices[] = { "Welcome", "Hi" };
      chooseSound = new JComboBox( choices );

      chooseSound.addItemListener(

         new ItemListener() {

            // stop sound and change to sound to user's selection
            public void itemStateChanged( ItemEvent e )
            {
               currentSound.stop();

               currentSound =
                  chooseSound.getSelectedIndex() == 0 ?
                     sound1 : sound2;
            }

         }  // end anonymous inner class

      ); // end addItemListener method call

      container.add( chooseSound );

      // set up button event handler and buttons
      ButtonHandler handler = new ButtonHandler();

      playSound = new JButton( "Play" );
      playSound.addActionListener( handler );
      container.add( playSound );

      loopSound = new JButton( "Loop" );
      loopSound.addActionListener( handler );
      container.add( loopSound );

      stopSound = new JButton( "Stop" );
      stopSound.addActionListener( handler );
      container.add( stopSound );

      // load sounds and set currentSound
      sound1 = getAudioClip( getDocumentBase(), "welcome.wav" );
      sound2 = getAudioClip( getDocumentBase(), "hi.au" );
```

Fig. 18.6 Loading and playing an **AudioClip** (part 2 of 3).

```
         currentSound = sound1;

   } // end method init

   // stop the sound when the user switches Web pages
   public void stop()
   {
      currentSound.stop();
   }

   // private inner class to handle button events
   private class ButtonHandler implements ActionListener {

      // process play, loop and stop button events
      public void actionPerformed( ActionEvent actionEvent )
      {
         if ( actionEvent.getSource() == playSound )
            currentSound.play();

         else if ( actionEvent.getSource() == loopSound )
            currentSound.loop();

         else if ( actionEvent.getSource() == stopSound )
            currentSound.stop();
      }
   }

} // end class LoadAudioAndPlay
```

Fig. 18.6 Loading and playing an **AudioClip** (part 3 of 3).

18.7 Internet and World Wide Web Resources

This section presents several Internet and Web resources for multimedia-related sites. (Additional resources are provided in Chapter 22.)

www.nasa.gov/gallery/index.html
The *NASA multimedia gallery* contains a wide variety of images, audio clips and video clips that you can download and use to test your Java multimedia programs.

sunsite.sut.ac.jp/multimed/
The *Sunsite Japan Multimedia Collection* also provides a wide variety of images, audio clips and video clips that you can download for educational purposes.

www.anbg.gov.au/anbg/index.html
The *Australian National Botanic Gardens* Web site provides links to sounds of many animals. Try, for example, the *Common Birds* link.

www.thefreesite.com
TheFreeSite.com has links to free sounds and clip art.

www.soundcentral.com
SoundCentral provides audio clips in WAV, AU, AIFF and MIDI formats.

www.animationfactory.com
The *Animation Factory* provides thousands of free GIF animations for personal use.

www.clipart.com
ClipArt.com contains links to Web sites that provide free art.

www.pngart.com
PNGART.com provides over 50,000 free images in PNG format, in an effort to help this newer image format gain popularity.

developer.java.sun.com/developer/techDocs/hi/repository
The *Java Look-and-Feel Graphics Repository* provides standard images for use in a Swing GUI.

SUMMARY

- **Applet** method **getImage** loads an **Image**. One version of **getImage** takes two arguments—a location where the image is stored, and the file name of the image.
- **Applet** method **getDocumentBase** returns the location of the applet's HTML file on the Internet as an object of class **URL** (package **java.net**).
- Java supports several image formats, including Graphics Interchange Format (GIF), Joint Photographic Experts Group (JPEG) and Portable Network Graphics (PNG). File names for each of these types end with **.gif**, **.jpg** (or **.jpeg**) or **.png**, respectively.
- Class **ImageIcon** provides constructors that allow an **ImageIcon** object to be initialized with an image from the local computer or with an image stored on a Web server on the Internet.
- **Graphics** method **drawImage** receives four arguments—a reference to the **Image** object in which the image is stored, the *x*- and *y*-coordinates where the image should be displayed and a reference to an **ImageObserver** object.
- Another version of **Graphics** method **drawImage** outputs a *scaled* image. The fourth and fifth arguments specify the width and height of the image for display purposes.
- Interface **ImageObserver** is implemented by class **Component** (an indirect superclass of **Applet**). **ImageObserver**s are notified to update an image that was displayed as the remainder of the image is loaded.
- **ImageIcon** method **paintIcon** displays the **ImageIcon**'s image. The method requires four arguments—a reference to the **Component** on which the image will be displayed, a reference to the **Graphics** object used to render the image, the *x*-coordinate of the upper-left corner of the image and the *y*-coordinate of the upper-left corner of the image.
- Class **ImageIcon**'s **paintIcon** method does not allow scaling of an image. The class provides method **getImage**, which returns an **Image** reference that can be used with **Graphics** method **drawImage** to display a scaled version of an image.
- **Timer** objects generate **ActionEvent**s at fixed intervals in milliseconds and notify their registered **ActionListener**s that the events occurred. The **Timer** constructor receives two arguments—the delay in milliseconds and the **ActionListener**. **Timer** method **start** indicates that the **Timer** should start generating events. **Timer** method **stop** indicates that the **Timer** should stop generating events. **Timer** method **restart** indicates that the **Timer** should start generating events again.

- Applets can be customized via parameters (the **<param>** tag) that are supplied from the HTML file that invokes the applet. The **<param>** tag lines must appear between the starting **applet** tag and the ending **applet** tag. Each parameter has a **name** and a **value**.
- **Applet** method **getParameter** gets the **value** associated with a specific parameter and returns the **value** as a **String**. The argument passed to **getParameter** is a **String** containing the name of the parameter in the **param** tag. If there is no **param** tag containing the specified parameter, **getParameter** returns **null**.
- An image map is an image that has hot areas that the user can click to accomplish a task, such as loading a different Web page into a browser.
- **Applet** method **play** has two forms:

```
public void play( URL location, String soundFileName );
public void play( URL soundURL );
```

- One version loads the audio clip stored in file **soundFileName** from **location** and plays the sound; the other takes a **URL** that contains the location and the file name of the audio clip.
- **Applet** method **getDocumentBase** indicates the location of the HTML file that loaded the applet. Method **getCodeBase** indicates where the **.class** file for an applet is located.
- The sound engine that plays audio clips supports several audio file formats, including Sun Audio file format (**.au** extension), Windows Wave file format (**.wav** extension), Macintosh AIFF file format (**.aif** or **.aiff** extension) and Musical Instrument Digital Interface (MIDI) file format (**.mid** or **.rmi** extensions). The Java Media Framework (JMF) supports other additional formats.
- **Applet** method **getAudioClip** has two forms that take the same arguments as the **play** method. Method **getAudioClip** returns a reference to an **AudioClip**. **AudioClip**s have three methods—**play**, **loop** and **stop**. Method **play** plays the audio once. Method **loop** continuously loops the audio clip. Method **stop** terminates an audio clip that is currently playing.

TERMINOLOGY

.aif file name extension
.aiff file name extension
.au file name extension
.gif file name extension
.jpeg file name extension
.jpg file name extension
.mid file name extension
.rmi file name extension
.wav file name extension
animating a series of images
animation
audio clip
customize an applet
drawImage method of **Graphics**
getAudioClip method of **Applet**
getCodeBase method of **Applet**
getDocumentBase method of **Applet**
getHeight method of **Component**
getIconHeight method of **ImageIcon**
getIconWidth method of **ImageIcon**
getImage method of **Applet**
getImage method of **ImageIcon**
getParameter method of **Applet**
getWidth method of **Component**
graphics
Graphics Interchange Format (GIF)
height of an image
hot area of an image map
Image class
image map
ImageIcon class
ImageObserver interface
images
information button
Joint Photographic Experts Group (JPEG)
loop method of interface **AudioClip**
Macintosh AIFF file (**.aif** or **.aiff**)
multimedia
Musical Instrument Digital Interface (MIDI)
mute button
name attribute of **param** tag
paintIcon method of class **ImageIcon**

param tag
play method of class **Applet**
play method of interface **AudioClip**
restart method of class **Timer**
scaling an image
sound
sound engine
space/time trade-off
start method of class **Timer**
stop method of class **Timer**
stop method of interface **AudioClip**
Sun Audio file format (**.au**)
Timer class
update method of class **Component**
value attribute of **param** tag
volume control
width of an image
Windows Wave file (**.wav**)

SELF-REVIEW EXERCISES

18.1 Fill in the blanks in each of the following statements:

a) **Applet** method ________ loads an image into an applet.
b) **Applet** method ________ returns as an object of class **URL** the location on the Internet of the HTML file that invoked the applet.
c) **Graphics** method ________ displays an image on an applet.
d) Java provides two mechanisms for playing sounds in an applet—the **Applet**'s **play** method and the **play** method from the ________ interface.
e) An ________ is an image that has *hot areas* that the user can click to accomplish a task such as loading a different Web page.
f) Method ________ of class **ImageIcon** displays the **ImageIcon**'s image.
g) Java supports several image formats, including ________, ________ and ________.

18.2 State whether each of the following is true or false. If false, explain why.

a) A sound will be garbage collected as soon as it has finished playing.
b) Class **ImageIcon** provides constructors that allow an **ImageIcon** object to be initialized only with an image from the local computer.
c) **Applet** method **getParameter** gets the **value** associated with a specific HTML parameter and returns the **value** as a **String**.

ANSWERS TO SELF-REVIEW EXERCISES

18.1 a) **getImage**. b) **getDocumentBase**. c) **drawImage**. d) **AudioClip**. e) image map. f) **paintIcon**. g) Graphics Interchange Format (GIF), Joint Photographic Experts Group (JPEG) Portable Network Graphics (PNG).

18.2 a) False. The sound will be marked for garbage collection (if it is not referenced by an **AudioClip**) and will be garbage collected when the garbage collector is able to run. b) False. **ImageIcon** can load images from the Internet as well. c) True.

EXERCISES

18.3 Describe how to make an animation "browser friendly."

18.4 Describe the Java methods for playing and manipulating audio clips.

18.5 How can Java applets be customized with information from an HTML file?

18.6 Explain how image maps are used. List 10 examples in which image maps are used.

18.7 *(Randomly Erasing an Image)* Suppose an image is displayed in a rectangular screen area. One way to erase the image is simply to set every pixel to the same color immediately, but this is a dull visual effect. Write a Java program that displays an image and then erases it by using random-number generation to select individual pixels to erase. After most of the image is erased, erase all of the remaining pixels at once. You can refer to individual pixels by having a line that starts and ends at the same point. You might try several variants of this problem. For example, you might display lines randomly or display shapes randomly to erase regions of the screen.

18.8 *(Text Flasher)* Create a Java program that repeatedly flashes text on the screen. Do this by alternating the text with a plain background-color image. Allow the user to control the "blink speed" and the background color or pattern.

18.9 *(Image Flasher)* Create a Java program that repeatedly flashes an image on the screen. Do this by alternating the image with a plain background-color image.

18.10 *(Digital Clock)* Implement a program that displays a digital clock on the screen. You might add options to scale the clock; display day, month and year; issue an alarm; play certain audios at designated times and the like.

18.11 *(Calling Attention to an Image)* If you want to emphasize an image, you might place a row of simulated light bulbs around your image. You can let the light bulbs flash in unison, or you can let them fire on and off in sequence one after the other.

18.12 *(Image Zooming)* Create a program that enables you to zoom in on, or away from, an image.

SPECIAL SECTION: CHALLENGING MULTIMEDIA PROJECTS

The preceding exercises are keyed to the text and designed to test the reader's understanding of fundamental multimedia concepts. This section includes a collection of advanced multimedia projects. The reader should find these problems challenging, yet entertaining. The problems vary considerably in difficulty. Some require an hour or two of program writing and implementation. Others are useful for lab assignments that might require two or three weeks of study and implementation. Some are challenging term projects. [*Note*: Solutions are not provided for these exercises.].

18.13 *(Animation)* Create a a general purpose Java animation program. Your program should allow the user to specify the sequence of frames to be displayed, the speed at which the images are displayed, audios that should be played while the animation is running and so on.

18.14 *(Limericks)* Modify the limerick-writing program you wrote in Exercise 10.10 to sing the limericks your program creates.

18.15 *(Random Inter-Image Transition)* This provides a nice visual effect. If you are displaying one image in a given area on the screen and you would like to transition to another image in the same screen area, store the new screen image in an off-screen buffer and randomly copy pixels from the new image to the display area, overlaying the previous pixels at those locations. When the vast majority of the pixels have been copied, copy the entire new image to the display area to be sure you are displaying the complete new image. To implement this program, you may need to use the **`PixelGrabber`** and **`MemoryImageSource`** classes (see the Java API documentation for descriptions of these classes). You might try several variants of this problem. For example, try selecting all the pixels in a randomly selected straight line or shape in the new image, and overlay those pixels above the corresponding positions of the old image.

18.16 *(Background Audio)* Add background audio to one of your favorite applications by using the **`loop`** method of class **`AudioClip`** to play the sound in the background while you interact with your application in the normal way.

18.17 *(Scrolling Marquee Sign)* Create a Java program that scrolls dotted characters from right to left (or from left to right if that is appropriate for your language) across a Marquee-like display sign. As an option, display the text in a continuous loop, so that after the text disappears at one end it reappears at the other end.

18.18 *(Scrolling Image Marquee)* Create a Java program that scrolls an image across a Marquee screen.

18.19 *(Analog Clock)* Create a Java program that displays an analog clock with hour, minute and second hands that move appropriately as the time changes.

18.20 *(Dynamic Audio and Graphical Kaleidoscope)* Write a kaleidoscope program that displays reflected graphics to simulate the popular children's toy. Incorporate audio effects that "mirror" your program's dynamically changing graphics.

18.21 *(Automatic Jigsaw Puzzle Generator)* Create a Java jigsaw puzzle generator and manipulator. Your user specifies an image. Your program loads and displays the image. Your program then breaks the image into randomly selected shapes and shuffles the shapes. The user then uses the mouse to move the puzzle pieces around to solve the puzzle. Add appropriate audio sounds as the pieces are being moved around and snapped back into place. You might keep tabs on each piece and where it really belongs and then use audio effects to help the user get the pieces into the correct positions.

18.22 *(Maze Generator and Walker)* Develop a multimedia-based maze generator and traverser program based on the maze programs you wrote in Exercise 7.38–Exercise 7.40. Let the user customize the maze by specifying the number of rows and columns and by indicating the level of difficulty. Have an animated mouse walk the maze. Use audio to dramatize the movement of your mouse character.

18.23 *(One-Armed Bandit)* Develop a multimedia simulation of a one-armed bandit. Have three spinning wheels. Place various fruits and symbols on each wheel. Use true random-number generation to simulate the spinning of each wheel and the stopping of each wheel on a symbol.

18.24 *(Horse Race)* Create a Java simulation of a horse race. Have multiple contenders. Use audios for a race announcer. Play the appropriate audios to indicate the correct status of each of the contenders throughout the race. Use audios to announce the final results. You might try to simulate the kinds of horse-racing games that are often played at carnivals. The players get turns at the mouse and have to perform some skill-oriented manipulation with the mouse to advance their horses.

18.25 *(Shuffleboard)* Develop a multimedia-based simulation of the game of shuffleboard. Use appropriate audio and visual effects.

18.26 *(Game of Pool)* Create a multimedia-based simulation of the game of pool. Each player takes turns using the mouse to position a pool stick and to hit the stick against the ball at the appropriate angle to try to get the pool balls to fall into the pockets. Your program should keep score.

18.27 *(Artist)* Design a Java art program that will give an artist a great variety of capabilities to draw, use images, use animations, etc., to create a dynamic multimedia art display.

18.28 *(Fireworks Designer)* Create a Java program that someone might use to create a fireworks display. Create a variety of fireworks demonstrations. Then orchestrate the firing of the fireworks for maximum effect.

18.29 *(Floor Planner)* Develop a Java program that will help someone arrange furniture in his or her home. Add features that enable the person to achieve the best possible arrangement.

18.30 *(Crossword)* Crossword puzzles are among the most popular pastimes. Develop a multimedia-based crossword-puzzle program. Your program should enable the player to place and erase words easily. Tie your program to a large computerized dictionary. Your program also should be able to suggest words based on which letters have already been filled in. Provide other features that will make the crossword-puzzle enthusiast's job easier.

18.31 *(15 Puzzle)* Write a multimedia-based Java program that enables the user to play the game of 15. There is a 4-by-4 board for a total of 16 slots. One of the slots is empty. The other slots are occupied by 15 tiles numbered 1 through 15. Any tile next to the currently empty slot can be moved into that slot by clicking on the tile. Your program should create the board with the tiles out of order. The goal is to arrange the tiles into sequential order, row by row.

18.32 *(Reaction Time/Reaction Precision Tester)* Create a Java program that moves a randomly created shape around the screen. The user moves the mouse to catch and click on the shape. The shape's speed and size can be varied. Keep statistics on how much time the user typically takes to catch a shape of a given size. The user will probably have more difficulty catching faster moving, smaller shapes.

18.33 *(Calendar/Tickler File)* Using both audio and images create a general purpose calendar and "tickler" file. For example, the program should sing "Happy Birthday" when you use it on your birthday. Have the program display images and play audios associated with important events. Also, have the program remind you in advance of these important events. It would be nice, for example, to have the program give you a week's notice so you can pick up an appropriate greeting card for that special person.

18.34 *(Rotating Images)* Create a Java program that lets you rotate an image through some number of degrees (out of a maximum of 360 degrees). The program should let you specify that you want to spin the image continuously. The program should let you adjust the spin speed dynamically.

18.35 *(Coloring Black and White Photographs and Images)* Create a Java program that lets you paint a black and white photograph with color. Provide a color palette for selecting colors. Your program should let you apply different colors to different regions of the image.

18.36 *(Multimedia-Based Simpletron Simulator)* Modify the Simpletron simulator that you developed in the exercises in the previous chapters to include multimedia features. Add computer-like sounds to indicate that the Simpletron is executing instructions. Add a breaking glass sound when a fatal error occurs. Use flashing lights to indicate which cells of memory and/or which registers are currently being manipulated. Use other multimedia techniques, as appropriate, to make your Simpletron simulator more valuable to its users as an educational tool.

19

Data Structures

Objectives

- To be able to form linked data structures using references, self-referential classes and recursion.
- To be able to create and manipulate dynamic data structures, such as linked lists, queues, stacks and binary trees.
- To understand various important applications of linked data structures.
- To understand how to create reusable data structures with classes, inheritance and composition.

Much that I bound, I could not free;
Much that I freed returned to me.
Lee Wilson Dodd

'Will you walk a little faster?' said a whiting to a snail,
'There's a porpoise close behind us, and he's treading on my tail.'
Lewis Carroll

There is always room at the top.
Daniel Webster

Push on—keep moving.
Thomas Morton

I think that I shall never see
A poem lovely as a tree.
Joyce Kilmer

Outline

19.1 Introduction
19.2 Self-Referential Classes
19.3 Dynamic Memory Allocation
19.4 Linked Lists
19.5 Stacks
19.6 Queues
19.7 Trees

Summary • Terminology • Self-Review Exercises • Answers to Self-Review Exercises • Exercises • Special Section: Building Your Own Compiler

19.1 Introduction

We have studied such fixed-size *data structures* as single- and double-subscripted arrays. This chapter introduces *dynamic data structures* that grow and shrink at execution time. *Linked lists* are collections of data items "lined up in a row"—insertions and deletions can be made anywhere in a linked list. *Stacks* are important in compilers and operating systems; insertions and deletions are made only at one end of a stack—its *top*. *Queues* represent waiting lines; insertions are made at the back (also referred to as the *tail*) of a queue and deletions are made from the front (also referred to as the *head*) of a queue. *Binary trees* facilitate high-speed searching and sorting of data, eliminating of duplicate data items efficiently, representing file system directories, compiling expressions into machine language and many other interesting applications.

We will discuss each of the major types of data structures and implement programs that create and manipulate them. We use classes, inheritance and composition to create and package these data structures for reusability and maintainability. In Chapter 20, "Java Utilities Package and Bit Manipulation," and Chapter 21, "Collections," we discuss Java's predefined classes that implement the data structures discussed in this chapter.

The chapter examples are practical programs that can be used in more advanced courses and in industrial applications. The exercises include a rich collection of useful applications.

We encourage you to attempt the major project described in the special section entitled *Building Your Own Compiler*. You have been using a Java compiler to translate your Java programs to bytecodes so that you could execute these programs on your computer. In this project, you will actually build your own compiler. It will read a file of statements written in a simple, yet powerful high-level language similar to early versions of the popular language Basic. Your compiler will translate these statements into a file of Simpletron Machine Language (SML) instructions—SML is the language you learned in the Chapter 7 special section, *Building Your Own Computer*. Your Simpletron Simulator program will then execute the SML program produced by your compiler! Implementing this project by using an object-oriented approach will give you a wonderful opportunity to exercise most of what you have learned in this book. The special section carefully walks you through the specifications of the high-level language and describes the algorithms you will need to convert each type of high-level language statement into machine language instructions. If you enjoy being challenged, you might attempt the many enhancements to both the compiler and the Simpletron Simulator suggested in the exercises.

19.2 Self-Referential Classes

A *self-referential class* contains an instance variable that refers to another object of the same class type. For example, the definition

```
class Node {
   private int data;
   private Node nextNode;

   public Node( int data )            { /* constructor body */ }
   public void setData( int data )  { /* method body */ }
   public int getData()               { /* method body */ }
   public void setNext( Node next ) { /* method body */ }
   public Node getNext()              { /* method body */ }
}
```

defines class **Node**. This type has two **private** instance variables—integer **data** and **Node** reference **nextNode**. Member **nextNode** references an object of type **Node**, an object of the same type as the one being declared here—hence, the term "self-referential class." Member **nextNode** is a *link*—**nextNode** "links" an object of type **Node** to another object of the same type. Type **Node** also has five methods: a constructor that receives an integer to initialize **data**, a **setData** method to set the value **data**, a **getData** method to return the value of **data**, a **setNext** method to set the value of **nextNode** and a **getNext** method to return the value of member **nextNode**.

Programs can link self-referential objects together to form such useful data structures as lists, queues, stacks and trees. Figure 19.1 illustrates two self-referential objects linked together to form a list. A backslash—representing a **null** reference—is placed in the link member of the second self-referential object to indicate that the link does not refer to another object. The backslash is for illustration purposes; it does not correspond to the backslash character in Java. Normally, a **null** reference indicates the end of a data structure.

Common Programming Error 19.1

Not setting the link in the last node of a list to **null** *is a logic error.*

19.3 Dynamic Memory Allocation

Creating and maintaining dynamic data structures requires *dynamic memory allocation*—the ability for a program to obtain more memory space at execution time to hold new nodes and to release space no longer needed. As we have already learned, Java programs do not explicitly release dynamically allocated memory. Rather, Java performs automatic garbage collection on objects that are no longer referenced in a program.

The limit for dynamic memory allocation can be as large as the amount of available physical memory in the computer or the amount of available disk space in a virtual-memory system. Often, the limits are much smaller, because the computer's available memory must be shared among many applications.

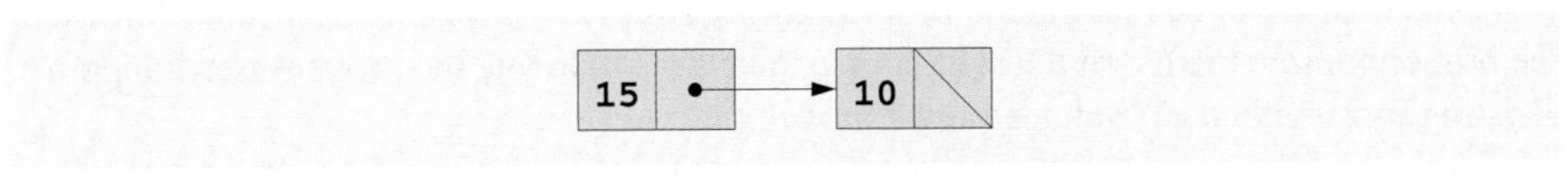

Fig. 19.1 Two self-referential class objects linked together.

Operator **new** is essential to dynamic memory allocation. Operator **new** takes as an operand the type of the object being dynamically allocated and returns a reference to a newly created object of that type. For example, the statement

```
Node nodeToAdd = new Node( 10 );
```

allocates the appropriate amount of memory to store a **Node** object and places a reference to this object in **nodeToAdd**. If no memory is available, **new** throws an **OutOfMemory-Error**. The 10 is the **Node** object's data.

The following sections discuss lists, stacks, queues and trees that use dynamic memory allocation and self-referential classes to create dynamic data structures.

19.4 Linked Lists

A *linked list* is a linear collection (i.e., a sequence) of self-referential class objects, called *nodes,* connected by reference *links*—hence, the term "linked" list. A program accesses a linked list via a reference to the first node of the list. The program accesses each subsequent node via the link reference stored in the previous node. By convention, the link reference in the last node of a list is set to **null** to mark the end of the list. Data are stored in a linked list dynamically—the list creates each node as necessary. A node can contain data of any type, including objects of other classes. Stacks and queues are also linear data structures and, as we will see, are constrained versions of linked lists. Trees are nonlinear data structures.

Lists of data can be stored in arrays, but linked lists provide several advantages. A linked list is appropriate when the number of data elements to be represented in the data structure is unpredictable. Linked lists are dynamic, so the length of a list can increase or decrease as necessary. The size of a "conventional" Java array, however, cannot be altered, because the array size is fixed at the time the program creates the array. "Conventional" arrays can become full. Linked lists become full only when the system has insufficient memory to satisfy dynamic storage allocation requests. Package **java.util** contains class **LinkedList** for implementing and manipulating linked lists that grow and shrink during program execution. We discuss class **LinkedList** in Chapter 21, "Collections."

Performance Tip 19.1

An array can be declared to contain more elements than the number of items expected, but this can waste memory. Linked lists can provide better memory utilization in these situations. Linked lists allow the program to adapt at runtime.

Performance Tip 19.2

Insertion into a linked list is fast—only two references have to be modified (after you have located the place to do the insertion). All existing nodes remain at their current locations in memory.

Linked lists can be maintained in sorted order simply by inserting each new element at the proper point in the list (it does, of course, take time to locate the proper insertion point). Existing list elements do not need to be moved.

Linked list nodes normally are not stored contiguously in memory. Rather, they are logically contiguous. Figure 19.2 illustrates a linked list with several nodes. This diagram presents a *singly-linked list*—each node contains one reference to the next node in the list. Often, linked lists are implemented as doubly-linked lists—each node contains a reference to the next node in the list and a reference to the previous node in the list. Java's **LinkedList** class (see Chapter 21) is a doubly-linked list implementation.

Performance Tip 19.3

Insertion and deletion in a sorted array can be time consuming—all the elements following the inserted or deleted element must be shifted appropriately.

Performance Tip 19.4

The elements of an array are stored contiguously in memory. This allows immediate access to any array element, because the address of any element can be calculated directly as its offset from the beginning of the array. Linked lists do not afford such immediate access to their elements—an element can be accessed only by traversing the list from the front.

Performance Tip 19.5

Using dynamic memory allocation (instead of arrays) for data structures that grow and shrink at execution time can save memory. Keep in mind, however, that references occupy space, and that dynamic memory allocation incurs the overhead of method calls.

The program of Fig. 19.3–Fig. 19.5 uses a **List** class to manipulate a list of miscellaneous object types. The **main** method of class **ListTest** (Fig. 19.5) creates a list of objects, inserts objects at the beginning of the list using method **insertAtFront**, inserts objects at the end of the list using method **insertAtBack**, deletes objects from the front of the list using method **removeFromFront** and deletes objects from the end of the list using method **removeFromBack**. After each insert and remove operation, **ListTest** calls **List** method **print** to display the current list contents. A detailed discussion of the program follows. If an attempt is made to remove an item from an empty list, an **EmptyListException** (Fig. 19.4) occurs.

The program of Fig. 19.3–Fig. 19.5 consists of four classes—**ListNode** (Fig. 19.3), **List** (Fig. 19.3), **EmptyListException** (Fig. 19.4) and **ListTest** (Fig. 19.5). The **List** and **ListNode** classes are placed in package **com.deitel.jhtp4.ch19**, so they can be reused throughout this chapter. Encapsulated in each **List** object is a linked list of **ListNode** objects. The **ListNode** class (lines 6–38 of Fig. 19.3) consists of package-access members **data** and **nextNode**. **ListNode** member **data** can refer to any **Object**. **ListNode** member **nextNode** stores a reference to the next **ListNode** object in the linked list.

[*Note*: Many of the classes in this chapter are defined in the package **com.deitel.jhtp4.ch19**. Each such class should be compiled with the **-d** command-line option to **javac**. When compiling the classes that are not in this package and when running the programs, be sure to use the **-classpath** option to **javac** and **java**, respectively.]

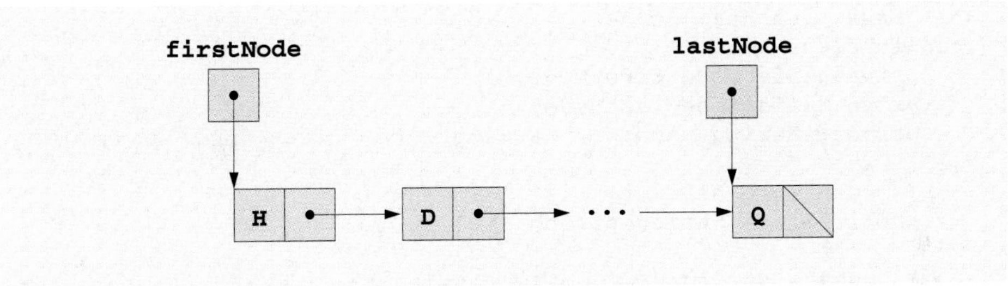

Fig. 19.2 A graphical representation of a linked list.

```
// Fig. 19.3: List.java
// Class ListNode and class List definitions
package com.deitel.jhtp4.ch19;

// class to represent one node in a list
class ListNode {

   // package access members; List can access these directly
   Object data;
   ListNode nextNode;

   // constructor to create a ListNode that refers to object
   ListNode( Object object )
   {
      this( object, null );
   }

   // constructor to create ListNode that refers to Object
   // and to next ListNode in List
   ListNode( Object object, ListNode node )
   {
      data = object;
      nextNode = node;
   }

   // return Object in this node
   Object getObject()
   {
      return data;
   }

   // get next node
   ListNode getNext()
   {
      return nextNode;
   }

}  // end class ListNode

```

Fig. 19.3 Definitions of class **ListNode** and class **List** (part 1 of 4).

```
// class List definition
public class List {
   private ListNode firstNode;
   private ListNode lastNode;
   private String name;  // String like "list" used in printing

   // construct an empty List with a name
   public List( String string )
   {
      name = string;
      firstNode = lastNode = null;
   }

   // construct empty List with "list" as the name
   public List()
   {
      this( "list" );
   }

   // Insert Object at front of List. If List is empty,
   // firstNode and lastNode will refer to same object.
   // Otherwise, firstNode refers to new node.
   public synchronized void insertAtFront( Object insertItem )
   {
      if ( isEmpty() )
         firstNode = lastNode = new ListNode( insertItem );

      else
         firstNode = new ListNode( insertItem, firstNode );
   }

   // Insert Object at end of List. If List is empty,
   // firstNode and lastNode will refer to same Object.
   // Otherwise, lastNode's nextNode refers to new node.
   public synchronized void insertAtBack( Object insertItem )
   {
      if ( isEmpty() )
         firstNode = lastNode = new ListNode( insertItem );

      else
         lastNode = lastNode.nextNode =
            new ListNode( insertItem );
   }

   // remove first node from List
   public synchronized Object removeFromFront()
      throws EmptyListException
   {
      Object removeItem = null;

      // throw exception if List is empty
      if ( isEmpty() )
         throw new EmptyListException( name );
```

Fig. 19.3 Definitions of class **ListNode** and class **List** (part 2 of 4).

```
      // retrieve data being removed
      removeItem = firstNode.data;

      // reset the firstNode and lastNode references
      if ( firstNode == lastNode )
         firstNode = lastNode = null;

      else
         firstNode = firstNode.nextNode;

      // return removed node data
      return removeItem;
   }

   // Remove last node from List
   public synchronized Object removeFromBack()
      throws EmptyListException
   {
      Object removeItem = null;

      // throw exception if List is empty
      if ( isEmpty() )
         throw new EmptyListException( name );

      // retrieve data being removed
      removeItem = lastNode.data;

      // reset firstNode and lastNode references
      if ( firstNode == lastNode )
         firstNode = lastNode = null;

      else {

         // locate new last node
         ListNode current = firstNode;

         // loop while current node does not refer to lastNode
         while ( current.nextNode != lastNode )
            current = current.nextNode;

         // current is new lastNode
         lastNode = current;
         current.nextNode = null;
      }

      // return removed node data
      return removeItem;
   }

   // return true if List is empty
   public synchronized boolean isEmpty()
   {
```

Fig. 19.3 Definitions of class **ListNode** and class **List** (part 3 of 4).

```
146         return firstNode == null;
147     }
148
149     // output List contents
150     public synchronized void print()
151     {
152         if ( isEmpty() ) {
153             System.out.println( "Empty " + name );
154             return;
155         }
156
157         System.out.print( "The " + name + " is: " );
158
159         ListNode current = firstNode;
160
161         // while not at end of list, output current node's data
162         while ( current != null ) {
163             System.out.print( current.data.toString() + " " );
164             current = current.nextNode;
165         }
166
167         System.out.println( "\n" );
168     }
169
170 }   // end class List
```

Fig. 19.3 Definitions of class **ListNode** and class **List** (part 4 of 4).

Class **List** contains **private** members **firstNode** (a reference to the first **ListNode** in a **List**) and **lastNode** (a reference to the last **ListNode** in a **List**). The constructors (lines 47–51 and 54–57) initialize both references to **null**. The most important methods of class **List** are the **synchronized** methods **insertAtFront** (lines 62–69), **insertAtBack** (lines 74–82), **removeFromFront** (lines 85–106) and **removeFromBack** (lines 109–141). These methods are declared **synchronized** so **List** objects can be *multithread safe* when used in a multithreaded program. If one thread is modifying the contents of a **List**, no other thread can modify the same **List** object at the same time. Method **isEmpty** (lines 144–147) is a *predicate method* that determines whether the list is empty (i.e., the reference to the first node of the list is **null**). Predicate methods typically test a condition and do not modify the object on which they are called. If the list is empty, method **isEmpty** returns **true**; otherwise, it returns **false**. Method **print** (lines 150–168) displays the list's contents. Both **isEmpty** and **print** are also **synchronized** methods.

```
// Fig. 19.4: EmptyListException.java
// Class EmptyListException definition
package com.deitel.jhtp4.ch19;

public class EmptyListException extends RuntimeException {

```

Fig. 19.4 Definition of class **EmptyListException** (part 1 of 2).

```
    // initialize an EmptyListException
    public EmptyListException( String name )
    {
       super( "The " + name + " is empty" );
    }

 }  // end class EmptyListException
```

Fig. 19.4 Definition of class **EmptyListException** (part 2 of 2).

```
// Fig. 19.5: ListTest.java
// Class ListTest

// Deitel packages
import com.deitel.jhtp4.ch19.List;
import com.deitel.jhtp4.ch19.EmptyListException;

public class ListTest {

   // test class List
   public static void main( String args[] )
   {
      List list = new List();  // create the List container

      // create objects to store in List
      Boolean bool = Boolean.TRUE;
      Character character = new Character( '$' );
      Integer integer = new Integer( 34567 );
      String string = "hello";

      // use List insert methods
      list.insertAtFront( bool );
      list.print();
      list.insertAtFront( character );
      list.print();
      list.insertAtBack( integer );
      list.print();
      list.insertAtBack( string );
      list.print();

      // use List remove methods
      Object removedObject;

      // remove objects from list; print after each removal
      try {
         removedObject = list.removeFromFront();
         System.out.println(
            removedObject.toString() + " removed" );
         list.print();

```

Fig. 19.5 Manipulating a linked list.

```
         removedObject = list.removeFromFront();
         System.out.println(
            removedObject.toString() + " removed" );
         list.print();

         removedObject = list.removeFromBack();
         System.out.println(
            removedObject.toString() + " removed" );
         list.print();

         removedObject = list.removeFromBack();
         System.out.println(
            removedObject.toString() + " removed" );
         list.print();
      }

      // process exception if List is empty when attempt is
      // made to remove an item
      catch ( EmptyListException emptyListException ) {
         emptyListException.printStackTrace();
      }

   } // end method main

} // end class ListTest
```

```
The list is: true

The list is: $ true

The list is: $ true 34567

The list is: $ true 34567 hello

$ removed
The list is: true 34567 hello

true removed
The list is: 34567 hello

hello removed
The list is: 34567

34567 removed
Empty list
```

Fig. 19.5 Manipulating a linked list.

Over the next several pages, we discuss each of the methods of class **`List`** (Fig. 19.3) in detail. Method **`insertAtFront`** (lines 62–69 of Fig. 19.3) places a new node at the front of the list. The method consists of several steps (Fig. 19.6 illustrates the operation):

1. Call **`isEmpty`** to determine whether the list is empty (line 64).

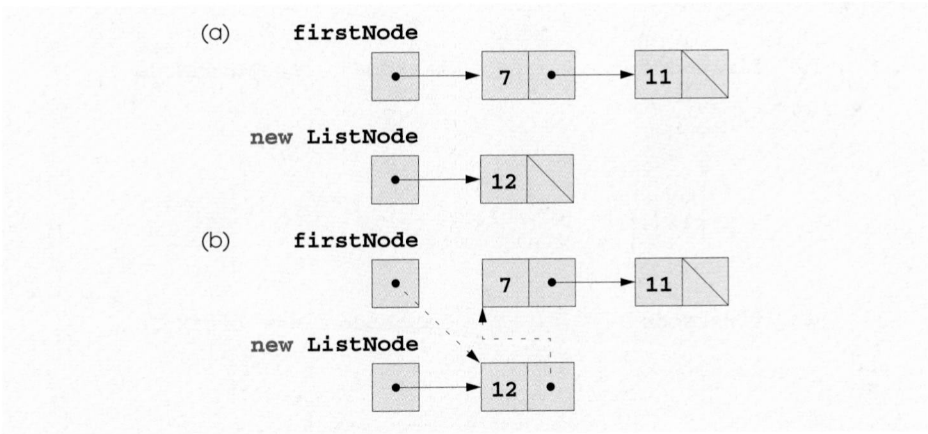

Fig. 19.6 The **insertAtFront** operation.

2. If the list is empty, both **firstNode** and **lastNode** are set to the **ListNode** allocated with **new** and initialized with **insertItem** (line 65). The **ListNode** constructor at lines 13–16 calls the **ListNode** constructor at lines 20–24 to set instance variable **data** to refer to the **insertItem** passed as an argument and to set reference **nextNode** to **null**.
3. If the list is not empty, the new node is "threaded" (not to be confused with multithreading) or "linked" into the list by setting **firstNode** to a new **ListNode** object and initializing that object with **insertItem** and **firstNode** (line 68). When the **ListNode** constructor (lines 20–24) executes, it sets instance variable **data** to refer to the **insertItem** passed as an argument and performs the insertion by setting the **nextNode** reference to the **ListNode** passed as an argument.

In Fig. 19.6, part (a) shows the list and the new node during the **insertAtFront** operation and before the program threads the new node into the list. The dotted arrows in part (b) illustrate step 3 of the **insertAtFront** operation that enables the node containing **12** to become the new list front.

Method **insertAtBack** (lines 74–82 of Fig. 19.3) places a new node at the back of the list. The method consists of several steps (Fig. 19.7 illustrates the operation):

1. Call **isEmpty** to determine whether the list is empty (line 76).
2. If the list is empty, both **firstNode** and **lastNode** are set to the **ListNode** allocated with **new** and initialized with **insertItem** (line 77). The **ListNode** constructor at lines 13–16 calls the **ListNode** constructor at lines 20–24 to set instance variable **data** to refer to the **insertItem** passed as an argument and to set reference **nextNode** to **null**.
3. If the list is not empty, the new node is threaded into the list by setting **LastNode** and **lastNode.nextNode** to the **ListNode** that was allocated with **new** and initialized with **insertItem** (lines 80–81). When the **ListNode** constructor (lines 13–16) executes, it sets instance variable **data** to refer to the **insertItem** passed as an argument and sets reference **nextNode** to **null**.

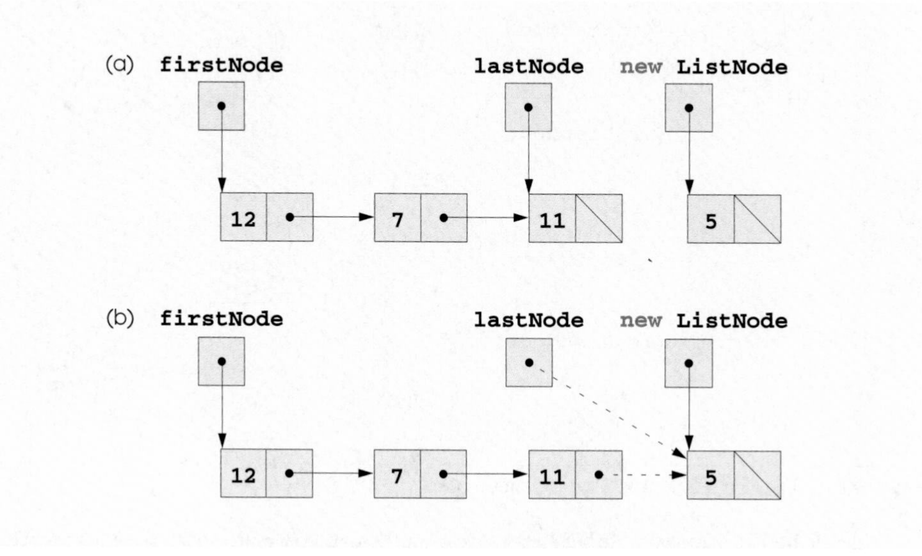

Fig. 19.7 A graphical representation of the **insertAtBack** operation.

In Fig. 19.7, part (a) shows the list and the new node during the **insertAtBack** operation and before the program threads the new node into the list. The dotted arrows in part (b) illustrate the steps of method **insertAtBack** that enable a new node to be added to the end of a list that is not empty.

Method **removeFromFront** (lines 85–106 of Fig. 19.3) removes the front node of the list and returns a reference to the removed data. The method throws an **EmptyList-Exception** (lines 91–92) if the list is empty when the program calls this method. Otherwise, the method returns a reference to the removed data. The method consists of several steps (illustrated in Fig. 19.8):

1. Assign **firstNode.data** (the data being removed from the list) to reference **removeItem** (line 95).
2. If the objects to which **firstNode** and **lastNode** refer are equal (line 98), the list has only one element prior to the removal attempt. In this case, the method sets **firstNode** and **lastNode** to **null** (line 99) to "dethread" (remove) the node from the list (leaving the list empty).
3. If the list has more than one node prior to removal, then the method leaves reference **lastNode** as is and simply assigns **firstNode.nextNode** to reference **firstNode** (line 102). Thus, **firstNode** references the node that was the second node prior to the **removeFromFront** call.
4. Return the **removeItem** reference (line 105).

In Fig. 19.8, part (a) illustrates the list before the removal operation. Part (b) shows actual reference manipulations.

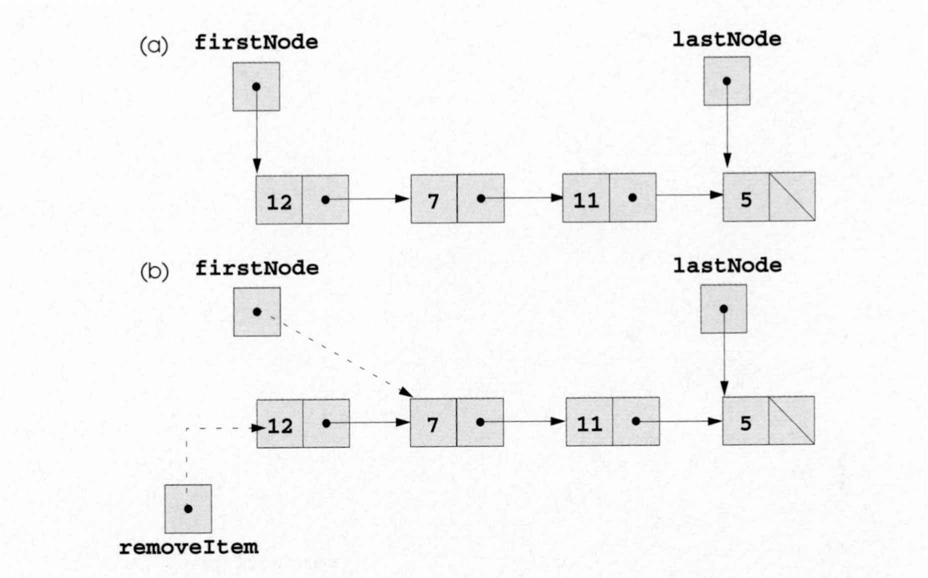

Fig. 19.8 A graphical representation of the **`removeFromFront`** operation.

Method **`removeFromBack`** (lines 109–141 of Fig. 19.3) removes the last node of a list and returns a reference to the removed data. The method throws an **`EmptyListException`** (lines 94 and 95) if the list is empty when the program calls this method. The method consists of several steps (Fig. 19.9 illustrates the operation):

1. Assign **`lastNode.data`** (the data being removed from the list) to reference **`removeItem`** (line 119).
2. If the objects to which **`firstNode`** and **`lastNode`** refer are equal (line 122), the list has only one element prior to the removal attempt. In this case, the method sets **`firstNode`** and **`lastNode`** to **`null`** (line 123) to dethread (remove) that node from the list (leaving the list empty).
3. If the list has more than one node prior to removal, then create the **`ListNode`** reference **`current`** and assign it **`firstNode`**.
4. Now "walk the list" with **`current`** until it references the node before the last node. The **`while`** loop (lines 131–132) assigns **`current.nextNode`** to **`current`** as long as **`current.nextNode`** is not **`lastNode`**.
5. After locating the second-to-last node, assign **`current`** to **`lastNode`** (line 135) to dethread the last node from the list.
6. Set the **`current.nextNode`** to **`null`** (line 136) to terminate the list at the current node.
7. Return the **`removeItem`** reference (liner 140).

In Fig. 19.9, part (a) illustrates the list before the removal operation. Part (b) shows the actual reference manipulations.

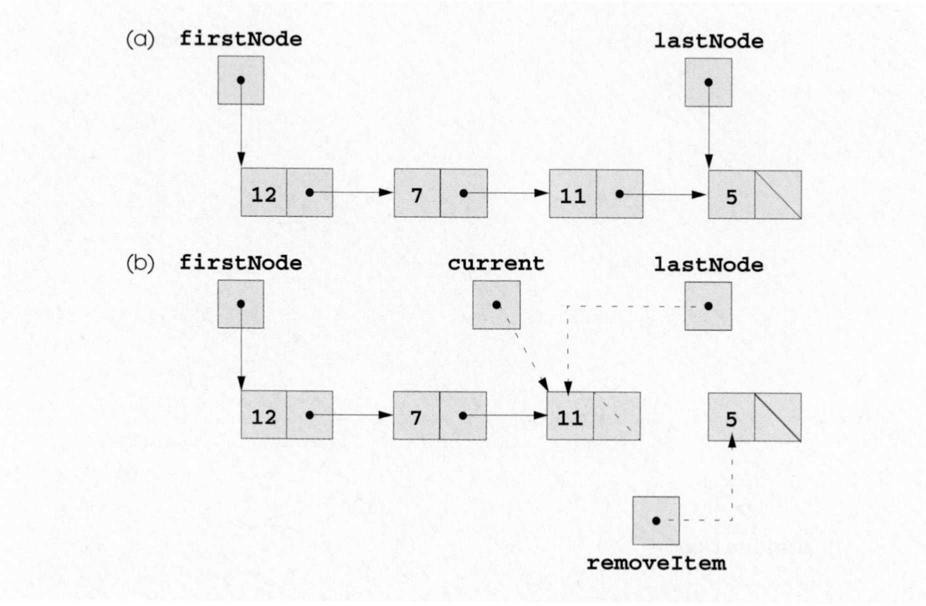

Fig. 19.9 A graphical representation of the **removeFromBack** operation.

Method **print** (lines 150–168) first determines whether the list is empty (lines 152–155). If so, **print** displays a message indicating that the list is empty and returns control to the calling method. Otherwise, **print** outputs the data in the list. Line 159 creates **ListNode** reference **current** and initializes it with **firstNode**. While **current** is not **null**, there are more items in the list. therefore, line 163 outputs a **String** representation of **current.data**. Line 164 moves to the next node in the list by assigning the value of **current.nextNode** to **current**. This printing algorithm is identical for linked lists, stacks and queues.

19.5 Stacks

A *stack* is a constrained version of a linked list—new nodes can be added to a stack and removed from a stack only at the top. For this reason, a stack is referred to as a *last-in, first-out* (*LIFO*) data structure. The link member in the bottom (i.e., last) node of the stack is set to **null** to indicate the bottom of the stack.

Common Programming Error 19.2

Not setting the link in the bottom node of a stack to **null** *is a common logic error.*

The primary methods used to manipulate a stack are ***push*** and ***pop***. Method **push** adds a new node to the top of the stack. Method **pop** removes a node from the top of the stack and returns the data from the popped node.

Stacks have many interesting applications. For example, when a program calls a method, the called method must know how to return to its caller, so the return address of the calling method is pushed onto the *program execution stack*. If a series of method calls occurs, the successive return addresses are pushed onto the stack in last-in, first-out order so that each method can return to its caller. Stacks support recursive method calls in the same manner as they do conventional nonrecursive method calls.

The program execution stack contains the memory for local variables on each invocation of a method during a program's execution. When the method returns to its caller, the memory for that method's local variables is popped off the stack and those variables are no longer known to the program.

Compilers use stacks to evaluate arithmetic expressions and generate machine language code to process the expressions. The exercises in this chapter explore several applications of stacks, including using them to develop a complete working compiler. The **java.util** package of the Java API contains class **Stack** for implementing and manipulating stacks that can grow and shrink during program execution. We will discuss class **Stack** in Chapter 20.

We take advantage of the close relationship between lists and stacks to implement a stack class by reusing a list class. We demonstrate two different forms of reusability. First, we implement the stack class by extending class **List** of Fig. 19.3. Then we implement an identically performing stack class through composition by including a **List** object as a **private** member of a stack class. The list, stack and queue data structures in this chapter are implemented to store **Object** references to encourage further reusability. Thus, any object type can be stored in a list, stack or queue.

The application of Fig. 19.10 and Fig. 19.11 creates a stack class by extending class **List** of Fig. 19.3. We want the stack to have methods **push**, **pop**, **isEmpty** and **print**. Essentially, these are the methods **insertAtFront**, **removeFromFront**, **isEmpty** and **print** of class **List**. Of course, class **List** contains other methods (such as **insertAtBack** and **removeFromBack**) that we would rather not make accessible through the **public** interface to the stack class. It is important to remember that all methods in the **public** interface of class **List** class also are **public** methods of the subclass **StackInheritance** (Fig. 19.10). When we implement the stack's methods, we have each **StackInheritance** method call the appropriate **List** method—method **push** calls **insertAtFront** and method **pop** calls **removeFromFront**. Class **StackInheritance** is defined as part of package **com.deitel.jhtp4.ch19** for reuse purposes. Note that **StackInheritance** does not import **List**, because both classes are in the same package.

```java
// Fig. 19.10: StackInheritance.java
// Derived from class List
package com.deitel.jhtp4.ch19;

public class StackInheritance extends List {

   // construct stack
   public StackInheritance()
   {
      super( "stack" );
   }

```

Fig. 19.10 Class **StackInheritance** extends class **List** (part 1 of 2).

```
    // add object to stack
    public synchronized void push( Object object )
    {
       insertAtFront( object );
    }

    // remove object from stack
    public synchronized Object pop() throws EmptyListException
    {
       return removeFromFront();
    }

} // end class StackInheritance
```

Fig. 19.10 Class **StackInheritance** extends class **List** (part 2 of 2).

Class **StackInheritanceTest**'s method **main** (Fig. 19.11) uses class **StackInheritance** to instantiate a stack of **Object**s called **stack**. The program pushes onto the stack (lines 22, 24, 26 and 28) a **Boolean** object containing **true**, a **Character** object containing **$**, an **Integer** object containing **34567** and a **String** object containing **hello**, then popped off **stack**. Lines 37–42 pop the objects from the stack in an infinite **while** loop. When there are no objects left to pop, an method **pop** throws an **EmptyListException**, and the program displays the exception's stack trace, which shows the methods on the program execution stack at the time the exception occurred. Note that the program uses method **print** (inherited from **List**) to output the contents of the stack.

```
1  // Fig. 19.11: StackInheritanceTest.java
2  // Class StackInheritanceTest
3
4  // Deitel packages
5  import com.deitel.jhtp4.ch19.StackInheritance;
6  import com.deitel.jhtp4.ch19.EmptyListException;
7
8  public class StackInheritanceTest {
9
10    // test class StackInheritance
11    public static void main( String args[] )
12    {
13       StackInheritance stack = new StackInheritance();
14
15       // create objects to store in the stack
16       Boolean bool = Boolean.TRUE;
17       Character character = new Character( '$' );
18       Integer integer = new Integer( 34567 );
19       String string = "hello";
20
21       // use push method
22       stack.push( bool );
23       stack.print();
24       stack.push( character );
```

Fig. 19.11 A simple stack program (part 1 of 2).

```
      stack.print();
      stack.push( integer );
      stack.print();
      stack.push( string );
      stack.print();

      // remove items from stack
      try {

         // use pop method
         Object removedObject = null;

         while ( true ) {
            removedObject = stack.pop();
            System.out.println( removedObject.toString() +
               " popped" );
            stack.print();
         }
      }

      // catch exception if stack empty when item popped
      catch ( EmptyListException emptyListException ) {
         emptyListException.printStackTrace();
      }

   }  // end method main

}  // end class StackInheritanceTest
```

```
The stack is: true

The stack is: $ true

The stack is: 34567 $ true

The stack is: hello 34567 $ true

hello popped
The stack is: 34567 $ true

34567 popped
The stack is: $ true

$ popped
The stack is: true

true popped
Empty stack
com.deitel.jhtp4.ch19.EmptyListException: The stack is empty
        at com.deitel.jhtp4.ch19.List.removeFromFront(List.java:92)
        at com.deitel.jhtp4.ch19.StackInheritance.pop(
           StackInheritance.java:22)
        at StackInheritanceTest.main(StackInheritanceTest.java:38)
```

Fig. 19.11 A simple stack program (part 2 of 2).

Another way to implement a stack class is by reusing a list class through composition. The class in Fig. 19.12 uses a **private** object of class **List** (line 6) in the definition of class **StackComposition**. Composition enables us to hide the methods of class **List** that should not be in our stack's **public** interface by providing **public** interface methods only to the required **List** methods. This technique of implementing each stack method as a call to a **List** method is called *delegating*—the stack method invoked *delegates* the call to the appropriate **List** method. In particular, **StackComposition** delegates calls to **List** methods **insertAtFront**, **removeFromFront**, **isEmpty** and **print**. In this example, we do not show class **StackCompositionTest**, because the only difference in this example is that we change the type of the stack from **Stack-Inheritance** to **StackComposition**. If you execute the application from the code on the CD that accompanies this book, you will see that the output is identical.

```
1  // Fig. 19.12: StackComposition.java
2  // Class StackComposition definition with composed List object
3  package com.deitel.jhtp4.ch19;
4
5  public class StackComposition {
6     private List stackList;
7
8     // construct stack
9     public StackComposition()
10    {
11       stackList = new List( "stack" );
12    }
13
14    // add object to stack
15    public synchronized void push( Object object )
16    {
17       stackList.insertAtFront( object );
18    }
19
20    // remove object from stack
21    public synchronized Object pop() throws EmptyListException
22    {
23       return stackList.removeFromFront();
24    }
25
26    // determine if stack is empty
27    public synchronized boolean isEmpty()
28    {
29       return stackList.isEmpty();
30    }
31
32    // output stack contents
33    public synchronized void print()
34    {
35       stackList.print();
36    }
37
38 }  // end class StackComposition
```

Fig. 19.12 A simple stack class using composition.

19.6 Queues

Another common data structure is the *queue.* A queue is similar to a checkout line in a supermarket—the cashier services the person at the beginning of the line first. Other customers enter the line only at the end and wait for service. Queue nodes are removed only from the *head* (or front) of the queue and are inserted only at the *tail* (or end) of the queue. For this reason, a queue is a *first-in, first-out (FIFO)* data structure. The insert and remove operations are known as ***enqueue*** and ***dequeue***.

Queues have many applications in computer systems. Most computers have only a single processor, so only one application at a time can be serviced. Entries for the other applications are placed in a queue. The entry at the front of the queue is the next to receive service. Each entry gradually advances to the front of the queue as applications receive service.

Queues are also used to support print spooling. A multiuser environment may have only a single printer. Many users may send print jobs to the printer. Even when the printer is busy, other people may still send print jobs. These are "spooled" to disk (much as thread is wound onto a spool) where they wait in a queue until the printer becomes available.

Information packets also wait in queues in computer networks. Each time a packet arrives at a network node, it must be routed to the next node on the network along the path to the packet's final destination. The routing node routes one packet at a time, so additional packets are enqueued until the router can route them.

A file server in a computer network handles file-access requests from many clients throughout the network. Servers have a limited capacity to service requests from clients. When that capacity is exceeded, client requests wait in queues.

The application of Fig. 19.13 and Fig. 19.14 creates a queue by extending class **List** (Fig. 19.3). We want class **QueueInheritance** (Fig. 19.13) to have methods **enqueue** and **dequeue**, **isEmpty** and **print**. Note that these are essentially the **List** methods **insertAtBack** and **removeFromFront**. Of course, class **List** contains other methods (i.e., **insertAtFront** and **removeFromBack**) that we would rather not make accessible through the **public** interface of the queue. Remember that all methods in the **public** interface of the **List** class are also **public** methods of the subclass **QueueInheritance**. In the queue's implementation, each method of class **QueueInheritance** calls the appropriate **List** method—method **enqueue** calls **insertAtBack** and method **dequeue** calls **removeFromFront**. Class **QueueInheritance** is defined in package **com.deitel.jhtp4.ch19** for reuse purposes.

Common Programming Error 19.3

Not setting the link in the last node of a queue to **null** *is a common logic error.*

```
// Fig. 19.13: QueueInheritance.java
// Class QueueInheritance extends class List

// Deitel packages
package com.deitel.jhtp4.ch19;

public class QueueInheritance extends List {

```

Fig. 19.13 Class **QueueInheritance** extends class **List** (part 1 of 2).

```
    // construct queue
    public QueueInheritance()
    {
       super( "queue" );
    }

    // add object to queue
    public synchronized void enqueue( Object object )
    {
       insertAtBack( object );
    }

    // remove object from queue
    public synchronized Object dequeue() throws EmptyListException
    {
       return removeFromFront();
    }

 }  // end class QueueInheritance
```

Fig. 19.13 Class **QueueInheritance** extends class **List** (part 2 of 2).

Class **QueueInheritanceTest** method **main** (Fig. 19.14) uses class **QueueInheritance** to instantiate a queue of **Object**s called **queue**. Lines 22, 24, 26 and 28 enqueue a **Boolean** object containing **true**, a **Character** object containing **$**, an **Integer** object containing **34567** and a **String** object containing **hello**. Lines 37–42 use an infinite **while** loop to dequeue the objects in first-in, first-out order. When there are no objects left to dequeue, method dequeue throws an **EmptyListException**, and the program displays the exception's stack trace.

```
1  // Fig. 19.14: QueueInheritanceTest.java
2  // Class QueueInheritanceTest
3
4  // Deitel packages
5  import com.deitel.jhtp4.ch19.QueueInheritance;
6  import com.deitel.jhtp4.ch19.EmptyListException;
7
8  public class QueueInheritanceTest {
9
10    // test class QueueInheritance
11    public static void main( String args[] )
12    {
13       QueueInheritance queue = new QueueInheritance();
14
15       // create objects to store in queue
16       Boolean bool = Boolean.TRUE;
17       Character character = new Character( '$' );
18       Integer integer = new Integer( 34567 );
19       String string = "hello";
```

Fig. 19.14 Processing a queue (part 1 of 3).

```

      // use enqueue method
      queue.enqueue( bool );
      queue.print();
      queue.enqueue( character );
      queue.print();
      queue.enqueue( integer );
      queue.print();
      queue.enqueue( string );
      queue.print();

      // remove objects from queue
      try {

         // use dequeue method
         Object removedObject = null;

         while ( true ) {
            removedObject = queue.dequeue();
            System.out.println( removedObject.toString() +
               " dequeued" );
            queue.print();
         }
      }

      // process exception if queue empty when item removed
      catch ( EmptyListException emptyListException ) {
         emptyListException.printStackTrace();
      }

   }  // end method main

}  // end class QueueInheritanceTest
```

```
The queue is: true

The queue is: true $

The queue is: true $ 34567

The queue is: true $ 34567 hello

true dequeued
The queue is: $ 34567 hello

$ dequeued
The queue is: 34567 hello

34567 dequeued
The queue is: hello

hello dequeued
Empty queue
```

(continued on next page)

Fig. 19.14 Processing a queue (part 2 of 3).

(continued from previous page)

```
com.deitel.jhtp4.ch19.EmptyListException: The queue is empty
        at com.deitel.jhtp4.ch19.List.removeFromFront(List.java:92)
        at com.deitel.jhtp4.ch19.QueueInheritance.dequeue(
           QueueInheritance.java:24)
        at QueueInheritanceTest.main(QueueInheritanceTest.java:38)
```

Fig. 19.14 Processing a queue (part 3 of 3).

19.7 Trees

Linked lists, stacks and queues are *linear data structures* (i.e., *sequences*). A tree is a non-linear, two-dimensional data structure with special properties. Tree nodes contain two or more links. This section discusses *binary trees* (Fig. 19.15)—trees whose nodes all contain two links (none, one or both of which may be **null**). The *root node* is the first node in a tree. Each link in the root node refers to a *child.* The *left child* is the first node in the *left subtree,* and the *right child* is the first node in the *right subtree.* The children of a specific node are called *siblings.* A node with no children is called a *leaf node.* Computer scientists normally draw trees from the root node down—exactly the opposite of the way most trees grow in nature.

Common Programming Error 19.4

Not setting to **null** *the links in leaf nodes of a tree is a common logic error.*

In our binary tree example, we create a special binary tree called a *binary search tree.* A binary search tree (with no duplicate node values) has the characteristic that the values in any left subtree are less than the value in the subtree's parent node, and the values in any right subtree are greater than the value in the subtree's parent node. Figure 19.16 illustrates a binary search tree with 12 integer values. Note that the shape of the binary search tree that corresponds to a set of data can vary, depending on the order in which the values are inserted into the tree.

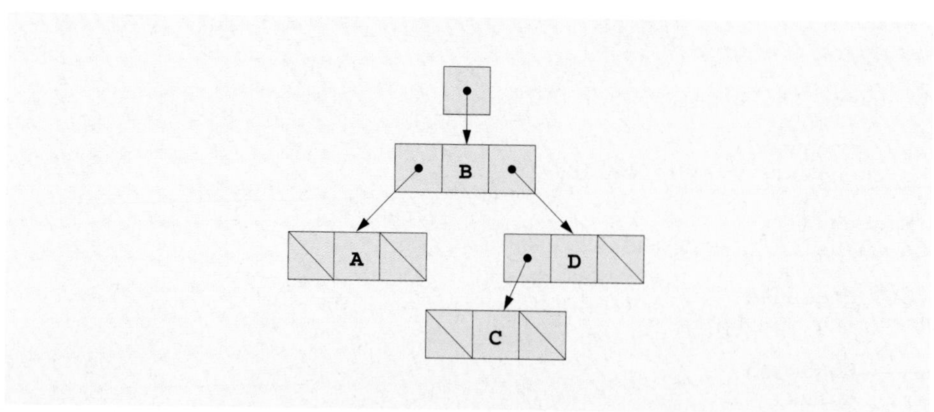

Fig. 19.15 A graphical representation of a binary tree.

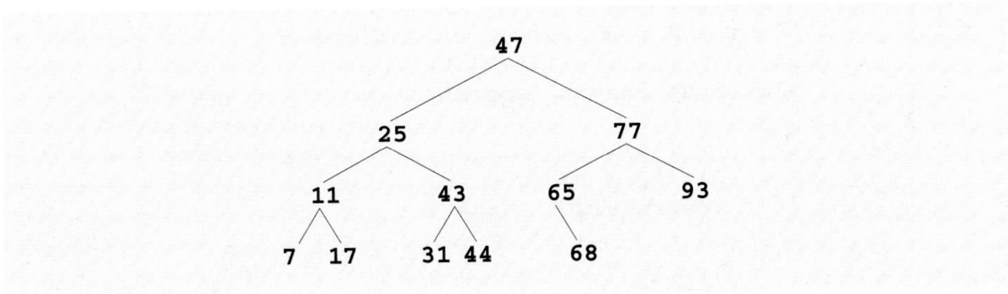

Fig. 19.16 A binary search tree containing 12 values.

The application of Fig. 19.17 and Fig. 19.18 creates a binary search tree of integers and traverses it (i.e., walks through all its nodes) three ways—using recursive *inorder, preorder* and *postorder traversals*. The program generates 10 random numbers and inserts each into the tree. Class **Tree** is defined in package **com.deitel.jhtp4.ch19** for reuse purposes.

```
// Fig. 19.17: Tree.java
// Definition of class TreeNode and class Tree.

// Deitel packages
package com.deitel.jhtp4.ch19;

// class TreeNode definition
class TreeNode {

   // package access members
   TreeNode leftNode;
   int data;
   TreeNode rightNode;

   // initialize data and make this a leaf node
   public TreeNode( int nodeData )
   {
      data = nodeData;
      leftNode = rightNode = null;  // node has no children
   }

   // insert TreeNode into Tree that contains nodes;
   // ignore duplicate values
   public synchronized void insert( int insertValue )
   {
      // insert in left subtree
      if ( insertValue < data ) {

         // insert new TreeNode
         if ( leftNode == null )
            leftNode = new TreeNode( insertValue );

```

Fig. 19.17 Definitions of **TreeNode** and **Tree** for a binary search tree (part 1 of 4).

```
            // continue traversing left subtree
            else
               leftNode.insert( insertValue );
         }

         // insert in right subtree
         else if ( insertValue > data ) {

            // insert new TreeNode
            if ( rightNode == null )
               rightNode = new TreeNode( insertValue );

            // continue traversing right subtree
            else
               rightNode.insert( insertValue );
         }

      }  // end method insert

   }  // end class TreeNode

   // class Tree definition
   public class Tree {
      private TreeNode root;

      // construct an empty Tree of integers
      public Tree()
      {
         root = null;
      }

      // Insert a new node in the binary search tree.
      // If the root node is null, create the root node here.
      // Otherwise, call the insert method of class TreeNode.
      public synchronized void insertNode( int insertValue )
      {
         if ( root == null )
            root = new TreeNode( insertValue );

         else
            root.insert( insertValue );
      }

      // begin preorder traversal
      public synchronized void preorderTraversal()
      {
         preorderHelper( root );
      }

      // recursive method to perform preorder traversal
      private void preorderHelper( TreeNode node )
      {
```

Fig. 19.17 Definitions of **TreeNode** and **Tree** for a binary search tree (part 2 of 4).

```
         if ( node == null )
            return;

         // output node data
         System.out.print( node.data + " " );

         // traverse left subtree
         preorderHelper( node.leftNode );

         // traverse right subtree
         preorderHelper( node.rightNode );
      }

      // begin inorder traversal
      public synchronized void inorderTraversal()
      {
         inorderHelper( root );
      }

      // recursive method to perform inorder traversal
      private void inorderHelper( TreeNode node )
      {
         if ( node == null )
            return;

         // traverse left subtree
         inorderHelper( node.leftNode );

         // output node data
         System.out.print( node.data + " " );

         // traverse right subtree
         inorderHelper( node.rightNode );
      }

      // begin postorder traversal
      public synchronized void postorderTraversal()
      {
         postorderHelper( root );
      }

      // recursive method to perform postorder traversal
      private void postorderHelper( TreeNode node )
      {
         if ( node == null )
            return;

         // traverse left subtree
         postorderHelper( node.leftNode );

         // traverse right subtree
         postorderHelper( node.rightNode );

```

Fig. 19.17 Definitions of **TreeNode** and **Tree** for a binary search tree (part 3 of 4).

```
         // output node data
         System.out.print( node.data + " " );
      }

}  // end class Tree
```

Fig. 19.17 Definitions of **TreeNode** and **Tree** for a binary search tree (part 4 of 4).

Let us walk through the binary tree program. Method **main** of class **TreeTest** (Fig. 19.18) begins by instantiating an empty **Tree** object and storing it in reference **tree** (line 11). The program randomly generates 10 integers, each of which is inserted into the binary tree through a call to **synchronized** method **insertNode** (line 21). The program then performs preorder, inorder and postorder traversals (these will be explained shortly) of **tree**.

```
1  // Fig. 19.18: TreeTest.java
2  // This program tests class Tree.
3  import com.deitel.jhtp4.ch19.Tree;
4
5  // Class TreeTest definition
6  public class TreeTest {
7
8     // test class Tree
9     public static void main( String args[] )
10    {
11       Tree tree = new Tree();
12       int value;
13
14       System.out.println( "Inserting the following values: " );
15
16       // insert 10 random integers from 0-99 in tree
17       for ( int i = 1; i <= 10; i++ ) {
18          value = ( int ) ( Math.random() * 100 );
19          System.out.print( value + " " );
20
21          tree.insertNode( value );
22       }
23
24       // perform preorder traveral of tree
25       System.out.println ( "\n\nPreorder traversal" );
26       tree.preorderTraversal();
27
28       // perform inorder traveral of tree
29       System.out.println ( "\n\nInorder traversal" );
30       tree.inorderTraversal();
31
32       // perform postorder traveral of tree
33       System.out.println ( "\n\nPostorder traversal" );
34       tree.postorderTraversal();
35       System.out.println();
36    }
```

Fig. 19.18 Creating and traversing a binary tree (part 1 of 2).

```java

}  // end class TreeTest
```

```
Inserting the following values:
39 69 94 47 50 72 55 41 97 73

Preorder traversal
39 69 47 41 50 55 94 72 73 97

Inorder traversal
39 41 47 50 55 69 72 73 94 97

Postorder traversal
41 55 50 47 73 72 97 94 69 39
```

Fig. 19.18 Creating and traversing a binary tree (part 2 of 2).

Class **Tree** (lines 55–142 of Fig. 19.17) has as **private** data **root**—a reference to the root node of the tree. The class contains **public** method **insertNode** (lines 67–74) to insert a new node in the tree and **public** methods **preorderTraversal** (lines 77–80), **inorderTraversal** (lines 99–102) and **postorderTraversal** (lines 121–124) to begin traversals of the tree. Each of these methods calls a separate recursive utility method to perform the traversal operations on the internal representation of the tree. The **Tree** constructor (lines 59–62) initializes **root** to **null** to indicate that the tree is empty.

The **Tree** class's **synchronized** method **insertNode** (lines 67–74) first determines if the tree is empty. If so, it allocates a new **TreeNode**, initializes the node with the integer being inserted in the tree and assigns the new node to the **root** reference (line 70). If the tree is not empty, insertNode calls **TreeNode** method **insert** (lines 24–52). This method uses recursion to determine the location for the new node in the tree and inserts the node at that location. *A node can be inserted only as a leaf node in a binary search tree.*

The **TreeNode** method **insert** compares the value to insert with the **data** value in the root node. If the insert value is less than the root node data, the program determines if the left subtree is empty (line 30). If so, line 31 allocates a new **TreeNode**, initializes it with the integer being inserted and assigns the new node to reference **leftNode**. Otherwise, line 35 recursively calls **insert** for the left subtree to insert the value into the left subtree. If the insert value is greater than the root node data, the program determines if the right subtree is empty (line 42). If so, line 43 allocates a new **TreeNode**, initializes it with the integer being inserted and assigns the new node to reference **rightNode**. Otherwise, line 47 recursively calls **insert** for the right subtree to insert the value in the right subtree.

Methods **inorderTraversal**, **preorderTraversal** and **postorderTraversal** call helper methods **inorderHelper** (lines 105–118), **preorderHelper** (lines 83–96) and **postorderHelper** (lines 127–140), respectively, to traverse the tree (Fig. 19.19) and print the node values. The purpose of the helper methods in class **Tree** is to allow the programmer to start a traversal without the need to obtain a reference to the **root** node first, then call the recursive method with that reference. Methods **inorderTraversal**, **preorderTraversal** and **postorderTraversal** simply take the **private root** reference and pass it to the appropriate helper method to initiate a traversal of the tree.

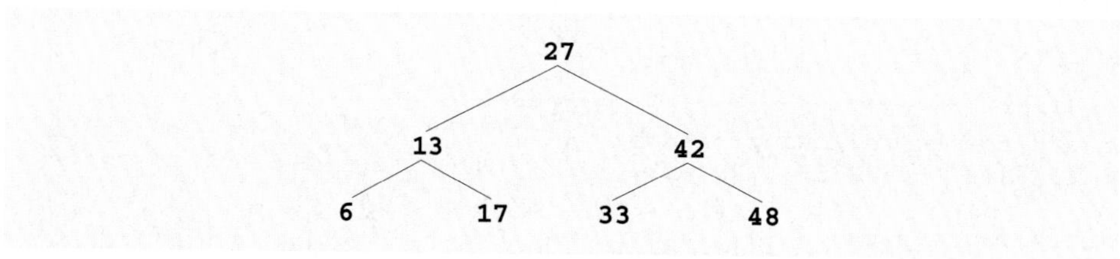

Fig. 19.19 A binary search tree.

Method **inorderHelper** (lines 105–118) defines the steps for an inorder traversal. Those steps are as follows:

1. Traverse the left subtree with a call to **inorderHelper** (line 111).
2. Process the value in the node (line 114).
3. Traverse the right subtree with a call to **inorderHelper** (line 117).

The inorder traversal does not process the value in a node until the values in that node's left subtree are processed. The inorder traversal of the tree in Fig. 19.19 is

```
6 13 17 27 33 42 48
```

Note that the inorder traversal of a binary search tree prints the node values in ascending order. The process of creating a binary search tree actually sorts the data—and thus, this process is called the *binary tree sort*.

Method **preorderHelper** (lines 83–96) defines the steps for a preorder traversal. Those steps are as follows:

1. Process the value in the node (line 89).
2. Traverse the left subtree with a call to **preorderHelper** (line 92).
3. Traverse the right subtree with a call to **preorderHelper** (line 95).

The preorder traversal processes the value in each node as the node is visited. After processing the value in a given node, the preorder traversal processes the values in the left subtree, then the values in the right subtree. The preorder traversal of the tree in Fig. 19.19 is

```
27 13 6 17 42 33 48
```

Method **postorderHelper** (lines 127–140) defines the steps for a postorder traversal. Those steps are as follows:

1. Traverse the left subtree with a **postorderHelper** (line 133).
2. Traverse the right subtree with a **postorderHelper** (line 136).
3. Process the value in the node (line 139).

The postorder traversal processes the value in each node after the values of all that node's children are processed. The **postorderTraversal** of the tree in Fig. 19.19 is

```
6 17 13 33 48 42 27
```

The binary search tree facilitates *duplicate elimination*. While building a tree, the insertion operation recognizes attempts to insert a duplicate value, because a duplicate follows the same "go left" or "go right" decisions on each comparison as the original value did. Thus, the insertion operation eventually compares the duplicate with a node containing the same value. At this point, the insertion operation might simply discard the duplicate value.

Searching a binary tree for a value that matches a key value is fast, especially for *tightly packed* trees. In a tightly packed tree, each level contains about twice as many elements as the previous level. Figure 19.19 is a tightly packed binary tree. A binary search tree with n elements has a minimum of $\log_2 n$ levels. Thus, at most $\log_2 n$ comparisons are required either to find a match or to determine that no match exists. Searching a (tightly packed) 1000-element binary search tree requires at most 10 comparisons, because $2^{10} > 1000$. Searching a (tightly packed) 1,000,000-element binary search tree requires at most 20 comparisons, because $2^{20} > 1,000,000$.

The chapter exercises present algorithms for several other binary tree operations, such as deleting an item from a binary tree, printing a binary tree in a two-dimensional tree format and performing a *level-order traversal of a binary tree*. The level-order traversal of a binary tree visits the nodes of the tree row-by-row, starting at the root node level. On each level of the tree, a level-order traversal visits the nodes from left to right. Other binary tree exercises include allowing a binary search tree to contain duplicate values, inserting string values in a binary tree and determining how many levels are contained in a binary tree.

SUMMARY

- Dynamic data structures can grow and shrink at execution time.
- Linked lists are collections of data items "lined up in a row"—insertions and deletions can be made anywhere in a linked list.
- Stacks are important in compilers and operating systems—insertions and deletions are made only at one end of a stack, its top.
- Queues represent waiting lines; insertions are made at the back (also referred to as the tail) of a queue and deletions are made from the front (also referred to as the head) of a queue.
- Binary trees facilitate high-speed searching and sorting of data, eliminating duplicate data items efficiently, representing file system directories and compiling expressions into machine language.
- A self-referential class contains a reference that refers to another object of the same class type. Self-referential objects can be linked together to form useful data structures such as lists, queues, stacks and trees.
- Creating and maintaining dynamic data structures requires dynamic memory allocation—the ability for a program to obtain more memory space at execution time to hold new nodes and to release space no longer needed.
- The limit for dynamic memory allocation can be as large as the available physical memory in the computer or the amount of available disk space in a virtual-memory system. Often, the limits are much smaller because the computer's available memory must be shared among many users.
- Operator **`new`** takes as an operand the type of the object being dynamically allocated and returns a reference to a newly created object of that type. If no memory is available, **`new`** throws an **`OutOfMemoryError`**.
- A linked list is a linear collection (i.e., a sequence) of self-referential class objects, called nodes, connected by reference links.
- A linked list is accessed via a reference to the first node of the list. Each subsequent node is accessed via the link-reference member stored in the previous node.

- By convention, the link reference in the last node of a list is set to **`null`** to mark the end of the list.
- A node can contain data of any type, including objects of other classes.
- Trees are nonlinear data structures.
- A linked list is appropriate when the number of data elements to be represented in the data structure is unpredictable. Linked lists are dynamic, so the length of a list can increase or decrease as necessary.
- The size of a "conventional" Java array cannot be altered—the size is fixed at creation time.
- Linked lists can be maintained in sorted order simply by inserting each new element at the proper point in the list.
- List nodes are normally not stored contiguously in memory. Rather, they are logically contiguous.
- Methods that manipulate the contents of a list should be declared **`synchronized`** so list objects can be *multithread safe* when used in a multithreaded program. If one thread is modifying the contents of a list, no other thread is allowed to modify the same list at the same time.
- A stack is a constrained version of a linked list—new nodes can be added to a stack and removed from a stack only at the top. A stack is referred to as a last-in, first-out (LIFO) data structure.
- The primary methods used to manipulate a stack are **`push`** and **`pop`**. Method **`push`** adds a new node to the top of the stack. Method **`pop`** removes a node from the top of the stack and returns the **`data`** object from the popped node.
- Stacks have many interesting applications. When a method call is made, the called method must know how to return to its caller, so the return address is pushed onto the program execution stack. If a series of method calls occurs, the successive return values are pushed onto the stack in last-in, first-out order so that each method can return to its caller.
- The program execution stack contains the space created for local variables on each invocation of a method. When the method returns to its caller, the space for that method's local variables is popped off the stack, and those variables are no longer known to the program.
- Stacks are also used by compilers in the process of evaluating arithmetic expressions and generating machine language code to process the expressions.
- The technique of implementing each stack method as a call to a **`List`** method is called delegating—the stack method invoked delegates the call to the appropriate **`List`** method.
- A queue is a constrained version of a list.
- A queue is similar to a checkout line in a supermarket—the first person in line is serviced first, and other customers enter the line only at the end and wait to be serviced.
- Queue nodes are removed only from the head of the queue and are inserted only at the tail of the queue. For this reason, a queue is referred to as a first-in, first-out (FIFO) data structure.
- The insert and remove operations for a queue are known as **`enqueue`** and **`dequeue`**.
- Queues have many applications in computer systems. Most computers have only a single processor, so only one user at a time can be serviced. Entries for the other users are placed in a queue. The entry at the front of the queue is the next to receive service. Each entry gradually advances to the front of the queue as users receive service.
- Queues are also used to support print spooling. A multiuser environment might have only a single printer. Many users may be generating outputs to be printed. If the printer is busy, other outputs may still be generated. These are "spooled" to disk (much as thread is wound onto a spool) where they wait in a queue until the printer becomes available.
- Information packets also wait in queues in computer networks. Each time a packet arrives at a network node, it must be routed to the next node on the network along the path to the packet's final

destination. The routing node routes one packet at a time, so additional packets are enqueued until the router can route them.

- A file server in a computer network handles file-access requests from many clients throughout the network. Servers have a limited capacity to service requests from clients. When that capacity is exceeded, client requests wait in queues.
- A tree is a nonlinear, two-dimensional data structure.
- Tree nodes contain two or more links.
- A binary tree is a tree whose nodes all contain two links. The root node is the first node in a tree.
- Each link in the root node refers to a child. The left child is the first node in the left subtree, and the right child is the first node in the right subtree.
- The children of a node are called siblings. A node with no children is called a leaf node.
- Computer scientists normally draw trees from the root node down.
- A binary search tree (with no duplicate node values) has the characteristic that the values in any left subtree are less than the value in its parent node, and the values in any right subtree are greater than the value in its parent node.
- A node can be inserted only as a leaf node in a binary search tree.
- An inorder traversal of a binary search tree processes the node values in ascending order.
- The process of creating a binary search tree actually sorts the data—and thus this process is called the binary tree sort.
- In a preorder traversal, the value in each node is processed as the node is visited. After the value in a given node is processed, the values in the left subtree are processed, then the values in the right subtree are processed.
- In a postorder traversal, the value in each node is processed after the values of its children.
- The binary search tree facilitates duplicate elimination. As the tree is created, attempts to insert a duplicate value are recognized because a duplicate follows the same "go left" or "go right" decisions on each comparison as the original value did. Thus, the duplicate eventually is compared with a node containing the same value. The duplicate value could simply be discarded at this point.
- Searching a binary tree for a value that matches a key value is also fast, especially for tightly packed trees. In a tightly packed tree, each level contains about twice as many elements as the previous level. So a binary search tree with n elements has a minimum of $\log_2 n$ levels, and thus at most $\log_2 n$, comparisons would have to be made either to find a match or to determine that no match exists. Searching a (tightly packed) 1000-element binary search tree requires at most 10 comparisons, because $2^{10} > 1000$. Searching a (tightly packed) 1,000,000-element binary search tree requires at most 20 comparisons, because $2^{20} > 1{,}000{,}000$.

TERMINOLOGY

binary search tree
binary tree
binary tree sort
child node
children
delegating
deleting a node
dequeue
duplicate elimination
dynamic data structures
enqueue
FIFO (first-in, first-out)
head of a queue
inorder traversal of a binary tree
inserting a node
leaf node
left child
left subtree
level-order traversal of a binary tree
LIFO (last-in, first-out)

linear data structure
linked list
node
nonlinear data structure
`null` reference
`OutOfMemoryError`
parent node
pop
postorder traversal of a binary tree
predicate method
preorder traversal of a binary tree
program execution stack
push
queue
recursive tree traversal algorithms
right child
right subtree
root node
self-referential class
stack
subtree
tail of a queue
top of a stack
traversal
tree
visiting a node

SELF-REVIEW EXERCISES

19.1 Fill in the blanks in each of the following statements:

a) A self-__________ class is used to form dynamic data structures that can grow and shrink at execution time.
b) Operator __________ dynamically allocates memory; this operator returns a reference to the allocated memory.
c) A __________ is a constrained version of a linked list in which nodes can be inserted and deleted only from the start of the list; this data structure returns node values in last-in, first-out order.
d) A method that does not alter a linked list, but simply looks at the list to determine whether it is empty is referred to as a __________ method.
e) A queue is referred to as a __________ data structure because the first nodes inserted are the first nodes removed.
f) The reference to the next node in a linked list is referred to as a __________.
g) Automatically reclaiming dynamically allocated memory in Java is called __________.
h) A __________ is a constrained version of a linked list in which nodes can be inserted only at the end of the list and deleted only from the start of the list.
i) A __________ is a nonlinear, two-dimensional data structure that contains nodes with two or more links.
j) A stack is referred to as a __________ data structure because the last node inserted is the first node removed.
k) The nodes of a __________ tree contain two link members.
l) The first node of a tree is the __________ node.
m) Each link in a tree node refers to a __________ or __________ of that node.
n) A tree node that has no children is called a __________ node.
o) The four traversal algorithms we mentioned in the text for binary search trees are __________, __________, __________ and __________.

19.2 What are the differences between a linked list and a stack?

19.3 What are the differences between a stack and a queue?

19.4 Perhaps a more appropriate title for this chapter would have been "Reusable Data Structures." Comment on how each of the following entities or concepts contributes to the reusability of data structures:

a) classes
b) inheritance
c) composition

19.5 Manually provide the inorder, preorder and postorder traversals of the binary search tree of Fig. 19.20.

ANSWERS TO SELF-REVIEW EXERCISES

19.1 a) referential. b) **`new`**. c) stack. d) predicate. e) first-in, first-out (FIFO). f) link. g) garbage collection. h) queue. i) tree j) last-in, first-out (LIFO). k) binary. l) root. m) child or subtree. n) leaf. o) inorder, preorder, postorder, level order.

19.2 It is possible to insert a node anywhere in a linked list and remove a node from anywhere in a linked list. Nodes in a stack may only be inserted at the top of the stack and removed from the top of a stack.

19.3 A queue is a FIFO data structure that has references to both its head and its tail so that nodes may be inserted at the tail and deleted from the head. A stack is a LIFO data structure that has a single reference to the top of the stack where both insertion and deletion of nodes are performed.

19.4
a) Classes allow us to instantiate as many data structure objects of a certain type (i.e., class) as we wish.
b) Inheritance enables us to reuse code from a superclass in a subclass so that the derived class data structure is also a base-class data structure.
c) Composition enables us to reuse code by making a class object data structure a member of a composed class; if we make the class object a **`private`** member of the composed class, then the class object's public methods are not available through the composed object's interface.

19.5 The inorder traversal is

```
11 18 19 28 32 40 44 49 69 71 72 83 92 97 99
```

The preorder traversal is

```
49 28 18 11 19 40 32 44 83 71 69 72 97 92 99
```

The postorder traversal is

```
11 19 18 32 44 40 28 69 72 71 92 99 97 83 49
```

EXERCISES

19.6 Write a program that concatenates two linked-list objects of characters. Class **`ListConcatenate`** should include a method **`concatenate`** that takes references to both list objects as arguments and concatenates the second list to the first list.

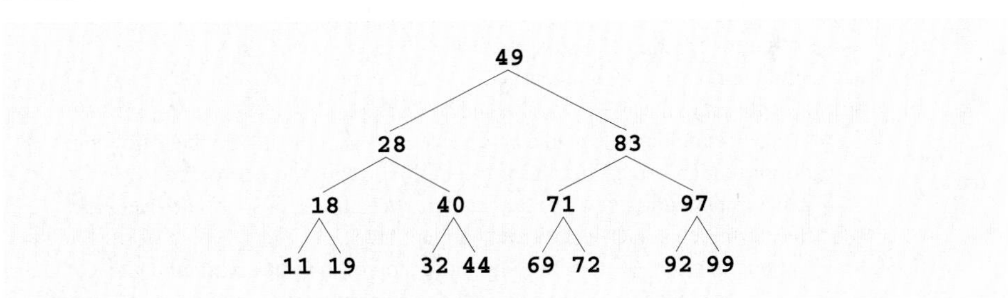

Fig. 19.20 A 15-node binary search tree.

19.7 Write a program that merges two ordered-list objects of integers into a single ordered list object of integers. Method **merge** of class **ListMerge** should receive references to each of the list objects to be merged and should return a reference to the merged list object.

19.8 Write a program that inserts 25 random integers from 0 to 100 in order into a linked list object. The program should calculate the sum of the elements and the floating-point average of the elements.

19.9 Write a program that creates a linked list object of 10 characters, then creates a second list object containing a copy of the first list, but in reverse order.

19.10 Write a program that inputs a line of text and uses a stack object to print the words of the line in reverse order.

19.11 Write a program that uses a stack to determine whether a string is a palindrome (i.e., the string is spelled identically backward and forward). The program should ignore spaces and punctuation.

19.12 Stacks are used by compilers to help in the process of evaluating expressions and generating machine language code. In this and the next exercise, we investigate how compilers evaluate arithmetic expressions consisting only of constants, operators and parentheses.

Humans generally write expressions like **3 + 4** and **7 / 9** in which the operator (**+** or **/** here) is written between its operands—this is called *infix notation*. Computers "prefer" *postfix notation*, in which the operator is written to the right of its two operands. The preceding infix expressions would appear in postfix notation as **3 4 +** and **7 9 /**, respectively.

To evaluate a complex infix expression, a compiler would first convert the expression to postfix notation and evaluate the postfix version of the expression. Each of these algorithms requires only a single left-to-right pass of the expression. Each algorithm uses a stack object in support of its operation, and in each algorithm, the stack is used for a different purpose.

In this exercise, you will write a Java version of the infix-to-postfix conversion algorithm. In the next exercise, you will write a Java version of the postfix expression evaluation algorithm. In a later exercise, you will discover that code you write in this exercise can help you implement a complete working compiler.

Write class **InfixToPostfixConverter** to convert an ordinary infix arithmetic expression (assume a valid expression is entered) with single-digit integers such as

```
(6 + 2) * 5 - 8 / 4
```

to a postfix expression. The postfix version of the preceding infix expression is (note that no parenthesis are needed)

```
6 2 + 5 * 8 4 / -
```

The program should read the expression into **StringBuffer infix** and use one of the stack classes implemented in this chapter to help create the postfix expression in **StringBuffer postfix**. The algorithm for creating a postfix expression is as follows:

a) Push a left parenthesis **'('** on the stack.
b) Append a right parenthesis **')'** to the end of **infix**.
c) While the stack is not empty, read **infix** from left to right and do the following:
    If the current character in **infix** is a digit, append it to **postfix**.
    If the current character in **infix** is a left parenthesis, push it onto the stack.
    If the current character in **infix** is an operator:
        Pop operators (if there are any) at the top of the stack while they have equal or higher precedence than the current operator, and append the popped operators to **postfix**.
        Push the current character in **infix** onto the stack.

If the current character in **infix** is a right parenthesis:
Pop operators from the top of the stack and append them to **postfix** until a left parenthesis is at the top of the stack.
Pop (and discard) the left parenthesis from the stack.

The following arithmetic operations are allowed in an expression:

+ addition
- subtraction
***** multiplication
/ division
^ exponentiation
% modulus

The stack should be maintained with stack nodes that each contain an instance variable and a reference to the next stack node. Some of the methods you may want to provide are as follows:

a) Method **convertToPostfix**, which converts the infix expression to postfix notation.
b) Method **isOperator**, which determines whether **c** is an operator.
c) Method **precedence**, which determines if the precedence of **operator1** (from the infix expression) is less than, equal to or greater than the precedence of **operator2** (from the stack). The method returns **true** if **operator1** has lower precedence than **operator2**. Otherwise, **false** is returned.
d) Method **stackTop** (this should be added to the stack class), which returns the top value of the stack without popping the stack.

19.13 Write class **PostfixEvaluator**, which evaluates a postfix expression (assume it is valid) such as

```
6 2 + 5 * 8 4 / -
```

The program should read a postfix expression consisting of digits and operators into a **StringBuffer**. Using modified versions of the stack methods implemented earlier in this chapter, the program should scan the expression and evaluate it. The algorithm is as follows:

a) Append a right parenthesis (**')'**) to the end of the postfix expression. When the right-parenthesis character is encountered, no further processing is necessary.
b) When the right-parenthesis character has not been encountered, read the expression from left to right.
If the current character is a digit do the following:
Push its integer value on the stack (the integer value of a digit character is its value in the computer's character set minus the value of **'0'** in Unicode).
Otherwise, if the current character is an *operator*:
Pop the two top elements of the stack into variables **x** and **y**.
Calculate **y** *operator* **x**.
Push the result of the calculation onto the stack.
c) When the right parenthesis is encountered in the expression, pop the top value of the stack. This is the result of the postfix expression.

[*Note*: In b) above (based on the sample expression at the beginning of this exercises), if the operator is **'/'**, the top of the stack is **2** and the next element in the stack is **8**, then pop **2** into **x**, pop **8** into **y**, evaluate **8 / 2** and push the result, **4**, back on the stack. This note also applies to operator **'-'**.]
The arithmetic operations allowed in an expression are:

+ addition
- subtraction
***** multiplication
/ division

`^` exponentiation
`%` modulus

The stack should be maintained with one of the stack classes introduced in this chapter. You may want to provide the following methods:

a) Method **`evaluatePostfixExpression`**, which evaluates the postfix expression.
b) Method **`calculate`**, which evaluates the expression **`op1 operator op2`**.
c) Method **`push`**, which pushes a value onto the stack.
d) Method **`pop`**, which pops a value off the stack.
e) Method **`isEmpty`**, which determines whether the stack is empty.
f) Method **`printStack`**, which prints the stack.

19.14 Modify the postfix evaluator program of Exercise 19.13 so that it can process integer operands larger than 9.

19.15 *(Supermarket Simulation)* Write a program that simulates a checkout line at a supermarket. The line is a queue object. Customers (i.e., customer objects) arrive in random integer intervals of from 1 to 4 minutes. Also, each customer is serviced in random integer intervals of from 1 to 4 minutes. Obviously, the rates need to be balanced. If the average arrival rate is larger than the average service rate, the queue will grow infinitely. Even with "balanced" rates, randomness can still cause long lines. Run the supermarket simulation for a 12-hour day (720 minutes), using the following algorithm:

a) Choose a random integer between 1 and 4 to determine the minute at which the first customer arrives.
b) At the first customer's arrival time, do the following:
   Determine customer's service time (random integer from 1 to 4).
   Begin servicing the customer.
   Schedule the arrival time of the next customer (random integer 1 to 4 added to the current time).
c) For each minute of the day, consider the following:
   If the next customer arrives, proceed as follows:
      Say so.
      Enqueue the customer.
      Schedule the arrival time of the next customer.
   If service was completed for the last customer, do the following:
      Say so.
      Dequeue next customer to be serviced.
      Determine customer's service completion time (random integer from 1 to 4 added to the current time).

Now run your simulation for 720 minutes and answer each of the following:

a) What is the maximum number of customers in the queue at any time?
b) What is the longest wait any one customer experiences?
c) What happens if the arrival interval is changed from 1 to 4 minutes to 1 to 3 minutes?

19.16 Modify the program of Fig. 19.17 and Fig. 19.18 to allow the binary tree to contain duplicates.

19.17 Write a program based on the program of Fig. 19.17 and Fig. 19.18 that inputs a line of text, tokenizes the sentence into separate words (you might want to use the **`StreamTokenizer`** class from the **`java.io`** package), inserts the words in a binary search tree and prints the inorder, preorder and post-order traversals of the tree.

19.18 In this chapter, we saw that duplicate elimination is straightforward when creating a binary search tree. Describe how you would perform duplicate elimination when using only a single-subscripted array. Compare the performance of array-based duplicate elimination with the performance of binary-search-tree-based duplicate elimination.

19.19 Write a method **`depth`** that receives a binary tree and determines how many levels it has.

19.20 (*Recursively Print a List Backwards*) Write a method **`printListBackwards`** that recursively outputs the items in a linked list object in reverse order. Write a test program that creates a sorted list of integers and prints the list in reverse order.

19.21 (*Recursively Search a List*) Write a method **`searchList`** that recursively searches a linked list object for a specified value. Method **`searchList`** should return a reference to the value if it is found; otherwise, null should be returned. Use your method in a test program that creates a list of integers. The program should prompt the user for a value to locate in the list.

19.22 (*Binary Tree Delete*) In this exercise, we discuss deleting items from binary search trees. The deletion algorithm is not as straightforward as the insertion algorithm. There are three cases that are encountered when deleting an item—the item is contained in a leaf node (i.e., it has no children), the item is contained in a node that has one child or the item is contained in a node that has two children.

If the item to be deleted is contained in a leaf node, the node is deleted and the reference in the parent node is set to null.

If the item to be deleted is contained in a node with one child, the reference in the parent node is set to reference the child node and the node containing the data item is deleted. This causes the child node to take the place of the deleted node in the tree.

The last case is the most difficult. When a node with two children is deleted, another node in the tree must take its place. However, the reference in the parent node cannot simply be assigned to reference one of the children of the node to be deleted. In most cases, the resulting binary search tree would not adhere to the following characteristic of binary search trees (with no duplicate values): *The values in any left subtree are less than the value in the parent node, and the values in any right subtree are greater than the value in the parent node.*

Which node is used as a *replacement node* to maintain this characteristic? It is either the node containing the largest value in the tree less than the value in the node being deleted, or the node containing the smallest value in the tree greater than the value in the node being deleted. Let us consider the node with the smaller value. In a binary search tree, the largest value less than a parent's value is located in the left subtree of the parent node and is guaranteed to be contained in the rightmost node of the subtree. This node is located by walking down the left subtree to the right until the reference to the right child of the current node is null. We are now referencing the replacement node, which is either a leaf node or a node with one child to its left. If the replacement node is a leaf node, the steps to perform the deletion are as follows:

a) Store the reference to the node to be deleted in a temporary reference variable.
b) Set the reference in the parent of the node being deleted to reference the replacement node.
c) Set the reference in the parent of the replacement node to null.
d) Set the reference to the right subtree in the replacement node to reference the right subtree of the node to be deleted.
e) Set the reference to the left subtree in the replacement node to reference the left subtree of the node to be deleted.

The deletion steps for a replacement node with a left child are similar to those for a replacement node with no children, but the algorithm also must move the child into the replacement node's position in the tree. If the replacement node is a node with a left child, the steps to perform the deletion are as follows:

a) Store the reference to the node to be deleted in a temporary reference variable.
b) Set the reference in the parent of the node being deleted to reference the replacement node.
c) Set the reference in the parent of the replacement node reference to the left child of the replacement node.

d) Set the reference to the right subtree in the replacement node reference to the right subtree of the node to be deleted.
e) Set the reference to the left subtree in the replacement node to reference the left subtree of the node to be deleted.

Write method **deleteNode**, which takes as its argument the value to be deleted. Method **deleteNode** should locate in the tree the node containing the value to be deleted and use the algorithms discussed here to delete the node. If the value is not found in the tree, the method should print a message that indicates whether the value is deleted. Modify the program of Fig. 19.17 and Fig. 19.18 to use this method. After deleting an item, call the methods **inorderTraversal**, **preorderTraversal** and **postorderTraversal** to confirm that the delete operation was performed correctly.

19.23 (*Binary Tree Search*) Write method **binaryTreeSearch**, which attempts to locate a specified value in a binary search tree object. The method should take as an argument a search key to be located. If the node containing the search key is found, the method should return a reference to that node; otherwise, the method should return a null reference.

19.24 (*Level-Order Binary Tree Traversal*) The program of Fig. 19.17 and Fig. 19.18 illustrated three recursive methods of traversing a binary tree—inorder, preorder and postorder traversals. This exercise presents the *level-order traversal* of a binary tree, in which the node values are printed level-by-level, starting at the root node level. The nodes on each level are printed from left to right. The level-order traversal is not a recursive algorithm. It uses a queue object to control the output of the nodes. The algorithm is as follows:

a) Insert the root node in the queue.
b) While there are nodes left in the queue, do the following:
    Get the next node in the queue.
    Print the node's value.
    If the reference to the left child of the node is not null:
        Insert the left child node in the queue.
    If the reference to the right child of the node is not null:
        Insert the right child node in the queue.

Write method **levelOrder** to perform a level-order traversal of a binary tree object. Modify the program of Fig. 19.17 and Fig. 19.18 to use this method. [*Note*: You will also need to use queue-processing methods of Fig. 19.13 in this program.]

19.25 (*Printing Trees*) Write a recursive method **outputTree** to display a binary tree object on the screen. The method should output the tree row-by-row, with the top of the tree at the left of the screen and the bottom of the tree toward the right of the screen. Each row is output vertically. For example, the binary tree illustrated in Fig. 19.20 is output as shown in Fig. 19.21.

Note that the rightmost leaf node appears at the top of the output in the rightmost column and the root node appears at the left of the output. Each column of output starts five spaces to the right of the preceding column. Method **outputTree** should receive an argument **totalSpaces** representing the number of spaces preceding the value to be output. (This variable should start at zero so the root node is output at the left of the screen.) The method uses a modified inorder traversal to output the tree—it starts at the rightmost node in the tree and works back to the left. The algorithm is as follows:

While the reference to the current node is not null, perform the following:
    Recursively call **outputTree** with the right subtree of the current node and
        totalSpaces + 5.
    Use a **for** structure to count from 1 to **totalSpaces** and output spaces.
    Output the value in the current node.
    Set the reference to the current node to refer to the left subtree of the current node.
    Increment **totalSpaces** by 5.

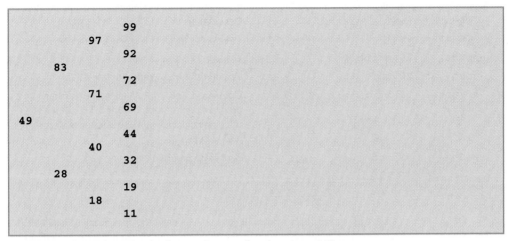

```
            99
        97
            92
    83
            72
        71
            69
49
            44
        40
            32
    28
            19
        18
            11
```

Fig. 19.21 Sample output of recursive method **outputTree**.

SPECIAL SECTION: BUILDING YOUR OWN COMPILER

In Exercise 7.42 and Exercise 7.43, we introduced Simpletron Machine Language (SML), and you implemented a Simpletron computer simulator to execute programs written in SML. In this section, we build a compiler that converts programs written in a high-level programming language to SML. This section "ties" together the entire programming process. You will write programs in this new high-level language, compile these programs on the compiler you build and run the programs on the simulator you built in Exercise 7.43. You should make every effort to implement your compiler in an object-oriented manner.

19.26 (*The Simple Language*) Before we begin building the compiler, we discuss a simple, yet powerful high-level language similar to early versions of the popular language Basic. We call the language *Simple*. Every Simple *statement* consists of a *line number* and a Simple *instruction*. Line numbers must appear in ascending order. Each instruction begins with one of the following Simple *commands*: **rem**, **input**, **let**, **print**, **goto**, **if/goto** or **end** (see Fig. 19.22). All commands except **end** can be used repeatedly. Simple evaluates only integer expressions using the **+**, **-**, ***** and **/** operators. These operators have the same precedence as in Java. Parentheses can be used to change the order of evaluation of an expression.

Command	Example statement	Description
rem	**50 rem this is a remark**	Any text following the command **rem** is for documentation purposes only and is ignored by the compiler.
input	**30 input x**	Display a question mark to prompt the user to enter an integer. Read that integer from the keyboard and store the integer in **x**.
let	**80 let u = 4 * (j - 56)**	Assign **u** the value of **4 * (j - 56)**. Note that an arbitrarily complex expression can appear to the right of the equal sign.

Fig. 19.22 Simple commands (part 1 of 2).

Command	Example statement	Description
print	**10 print w**	Display the value of **w**.
goto	**70 goto 45**	Transfer program control to line **45**.
if/goto	**35 if i == z goto 80**	Compare **i** and **z** for equality and transfer program control to line **80** if the condition is true; otherwise, continue execution with the next statement.
end	**99 end**	Terminate program execution.

Fig. 19.22 Simple commands (part 2 of 2).

Our Simple compiler recognizes only lowercase letters. All characters in a Simple file should be lowercase. (Uppercase letters result in a syntax error unless they appear in a **rem** statement, in which case they are ignored.) A *variable name* is a single letter. Simple does not allow descriptive variable names, so variables should be explained in remarks to indicate their use in a program. Simple uses only integer variables. Simple does not have variable declarations—merely mentioning a variable name in a program causes the variable to be declared and initialized to zero. The syntax of Simple does not allow string manipulation (reading a string, writing a string, comparing strings etc.). If a string is encountered in a Simple program (after a command other than **rem**), the compiler generates a syntax error. The first version of our compiler assumes that Simple programs are entered correctly. Exercise 19.29 asks the reader to modify the compiler to perform syntax error checking.

Simple uses the conditional **if/goto** and unconditional **goto** statements to alter the flow of control during program execution. If the condition in the **if/goto** statement is true, control is transferred to a specific line of the program. The following relational and equality operators are valid in an **if/goto** statement: **<**, **>**, **<=**, **>=**, **==** or **!=**. The precedence of these operators is the same as in Java.

Let us now consider several programs that demonstrate Simple's features. The first program (Fig. 19.23) reads two integers from the keyboard, stores the values in variables **a** and **b** and computes and prints their sum (stored in variable **c**).

The program of Fig. 19.24 determines and prints the larger of two integers. The integers are input from the keyboard and stored in **s** and **t**. The **if/goto** statement tests the condition **s >= t**. If the condition is true, control is transferred to line **90** and **s** is output; otherwise, **t** is output and control is transferred to the **end** statement in line **99**, where the program terminates.

```
10 rem   determine and print the sum of two integers
15 rem
20 rem   input the two integers
30 input a
40 input b
45 rem
50 rem   add integers and store result in c
60 let c = a + b
65 rem
70 rem   print the result
80 print c
90 rem   terminate program execution
99 end
```

Fig. 19.23 Simple program that determines the sum of two integers.

Simple does not provide a repetition structure (such as Java's **for**, **while** or **do/while**). However, Simple can simulate each of Java's repetition structures by using the **if/goto** and **goto** statements. Figure 19.25 uses a sentinel-controlled loop to calculate the squares of several integers. Each integer is input from the keyboard and stored in variable **j**. If the value entered is the sentinel value **-9999**, control is transferred to line **99**, where the program terminates. Otherwise, **k** is assigned the square of **j**, **k** is output to the screen and control is passed to line **20**, where the next integer is input.

Using the sample programs of Fig. 19.23–Fig. 19.25 as your guide, write a Simple program to accomplish each of the following:

a) Input three integers, determine their average and print the result.
b) Use a sentinel-controlled loop to input 10 integers and compute and print their sum.
c) Use a counter-controlled loop to input 7 integers, some positive and some negative, and compute and print their average.
d) Input a series of integers and determine and print the largest. The first integer input indicates how many numbers should be processed.
e) Input 10 integers and print the smallest.
f) Calculate and print the sum of the even integers from 2 to 30.
g) Calculate and print the product of the odd integers from 1 to 9.

```
10 rem   determine and print the larger of two integers
20 input s
30 input t
32 rem
35 rem   test if s >= t
40 if s >= t goto 90
45 rem
50 rem   t is greater than s, so print t
60 print t
70 goto 99
75 rem
80 rem   s is greater than or equal to t, so print s
90 print s
99 end
```

Fig. 19.24 Simple program that finds the larger of two integers.

```
10 rem   calculate the squares of several integers
20 input j
23 rem
25 rem   test for sentinel value
30 if j == -9999 goto 99
33 rem
35 rem   calculate square of j and assign result to k
40 let k = j * j
50 print k
53 rem
55 rem   loop to get next j
60 goto 20
99 end
```

Fig. 19.25 Calculate the squares of several integers.

19.27 (*Building A Compiler; Prerequisite: Complete Exercise 7.42, Exercise 7.43, Exercise 19.12, Exercise 19.13 and Exercise 19.26*) Now that the Simple language has been presented (Exercise 19.26), we discuss how to build a Simple compiler. First, we consider the process by which a Simple program is converted to SML and executed by the Simpletron simulator (see Fig. 19.26). A file containing a Simple program is read by the compiler and converted to SML code. The SML code is output to a file on disk, in which SML instructions appear one per line. The SML file is then loaded into the Simpletron simulator, and the results are sent to a file on disk and to the screen. Note that the Simpletron program developed in Exercise 7.43 took its input from the keyboard. It must be modified to read from a file so it can run the programs produced by our compiler.

The Simple compiler performs two *passes* of the Simple program to convert it to SML. The first pass constructs a *symbol table* (object) in which every *line number* (object), *variable name* (object) and *constant* (object) of the Simple program is stored with its type and corresponding location in the final SML code (the symbol table is discussed in detail below). The first pass also produces the corresponding SML instruction object(s) for each of the Simple statements (object, etc.). If the Simple program contains statements that transfer control to a line later in the program, the first pass results in an SML program containing some "unfinished" instructions. The second pass of the compiler locates and completes the unfinished instructions and outputs the SML program to a file.

First Pass

The compiler begins by reading one statement of the Simple program into memory. The line must be separated into its individual *tokens* (i.e., "pieces" of a statement) for processing and compilation. (The **StreamTokenizer** class from the **java.io** package can be used.) Recall that every statement begins with a line number followed by a command. As the compiler breaks a statement into tokens, if the token is a line number, a variable or a constant, it is placed in the symbol table. A line number is placed in the symbol table only if it is the first token in a statement. The **symbolTable** object is an array of **tableEntry** objects representing each symbol in the program. There is no restriction on the number of symbols that can appear in the program. Therefore, the **symbolTable** for a particular program could be large. Make the **symbolTable** a 100-element array for now. You can increase or decrease its size once the program is working.

Each **tableEntry** object contains three members. Member **symbol** is an integer containing the Unicode representation of a variable (remember that variable names are single characters), a line number or a constant. Member **type** is one of the following characters indicating the symbol's type: **'C'** for constant, **'L'** for line number or **'V'** for variable. Member **location** contains the Simpletron memory location (**00** to **99**) to which the symbol refers. Simpletron memory is an array of 100 integers in which SML instructions and data are stored. For a line number, the location is the element in the Simpletron memory array at which the SML instructions for the Simple statement begin. For a variable or constant, the location is the element in the Simpletron memory array in which the variable or constant is stored. Variables and constants are allocated from the end of Simpletron's memory backwards. The first variable or constant is stored at location **99**, the next at location **98**, etc.

The symbol table plays an integral part in converting Simple programs to SML. We learned in Chapter 7 that an SML instruction is a four-digit integer comprised of two parts—the *operation code* and the *operand*. The operation code is determined by commands in Simple. For example, the simple command **input** corresponds to SML operation code **10** (read), and the Simple command **print** corresponds to SML operation code **11** (write). The operand is a memory location containing the data on which the operation code performs its task (e.g., operation code **10** reads a value from the keyboard and stores it in the memory location specified by the operand). The compiler searches **symbolTable** to determine the Simpletron memory location for each symbol, so the corresponding location can be used to complete the SML instructions.

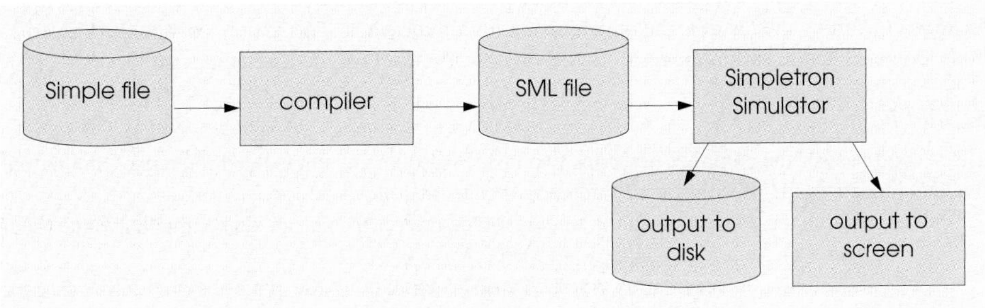

Fig. 19.26 Writing, compiling and executing a Simple language program.

The compilation of each Simple statement is based on its command. For example, after the line number in a **rem** statement is inserted in the symbol table, the remainder of the statement is ignored by the compiler because a remark is for documentation purposes only. The **input**, **print**, **goto** and **end** statements correspond to the SML *read, write, branch (*to a specific location) and *halt* instructions. Statements containing these Simple commands are converted directly to SML. (*Note*: A **goto** statement may contain an unresolved reference if the specified line number refers to a statement further into the Simple program file; this is sometimes called a forward reference.)

When a **goto** statement is compiled with an unresolved reference, the SML instruction must be *flagged* to indicate that the second pass of the compiler must complete the instruction. The flags are stored in a 100-element array **flags** of type **int** in which each element is initialized to **-1**. If the memory location to which a line number in the Simple program refers is not yet known (i.e., it is not in the symbol table), the line number is stored in array **flags** in the element with the same subscript as the incomplete instruction. The operand of the incomplete instruction is set to **00** temporarily. For example, an unconditional branch instruction (making a forward reference) is left as **+4000** until the second pass of the compiler. The second pass of the compiler will be described shortly.

Compilation of **if/goto** and **let** statements is more complicated than other statements—they are the only statements that produce more than one SML instruction. For an **if/goto** statement, the compiler produces code to test the condition and to branch to another line if necessary. The result of the branch could be an unresolved reference. Each of the relational and equality operators can be simulated by using SML's *branch zero* and *branch negative* instructions (or possibly a combination of both).

For a **let** statement, the compiler produces code to evaluate an arbitrarily complex arithmetic expression consisting of integer variables and/or constants. Expressions should separate each operand and operator with spaces. Exercise 19.12 and Exercise 19.13 presented the infix-to-postfix conversion algorithm and the postfix evaluation algorithm used by compilers to evaluate expressions. Before proceeding with your compiler, you should complete each of these exercises. When a compiler encounters an expression, it converts the expression from infix notation to postfix notation, then evaluates the postfix expression.

How is it that the compiler produces the machine language to evaluate an expression containing variables? The postfix evaluation algorithm contains a "hook" where the compiler can generate SML instructions rather than actually evaluating the expression. To enable this "hook" in the compiler, the postfix evaluation algorithm must be modified to search the symbol table for each symbol it encounters (and possibly insert it), determine the symbol's corresponding memory location and *push the memory location on the stack (instead of the symbol).* When an operator is encountered in the postfix expression, the two memory locations at the top of the stack are popped, and machine language for effecting the operation is produced by using the memory locations as operands. The result of each subexpression is stored in a temporary location in memory and pushed back onto the stack so the evaluation of the postfix expression can continue. When postfix evaluation is complete, the memory location containing the result is the only location left on the stack. This is popped, and SML instructions are generated to assign the result to the variable at the left of the **let** statement.

Second Pass

The second pass of the compiler performs two tasks: Resolve any unresolved references and output the SML code to a file. Resolution of references occurs as follows:

a) Search the **flags** array for an unresolved reference (i.e., an element with a value other than **-1**).
b) Locate the object in array **symbolTable** containing the symbol stored in the **flags** array (be sure that the type of the symbol is **'L'** for line number).
c) Insert the memory location from member **location** into the instruction with the unresolved reference (remember that an instruction containing an unresolved reference has operand **00**).
d) Repeat steps (a), (b) and (c) until the end of the **flags** array is reached.

After the resolution process is complete, the entire array containing the SML code is output to a disk file with one SML instruction per line. This file can be read by the Simpletron for execution (after the simulator is modified to read its input from a file). Compiling your first Simple program into an SML file and executing that file should give you a real sense of personal accomplishment.

A Complete Example

The following example illustrates complete conversion of a Simple program to SML as it will be performed by the Simple compiler. Consider a Simple program that inputs an integer and sums the values from 1 to that integer. The program and the SML instructions produced by the first pass of the Simple compiler are illustrated in Fig. 19.27. The symbol table constructed by the first pass is shown in Fig. 19.28.

Simple program	SML location and instruction	Description
5 rem sum 1 to x	*none*	**rem** ignored
10 input x	**00 +1099**	read **x** into location **99**
15 rem check y == x	*none*	**rem** ignored
20 if y == x goto 60	**01 +2098**	load **y** (**98**) into accumulator
	02 +3199	sub **x** (**99**) from accumulator
	03 +4200	branch zero to unresolved location
25 rem increment y	*none*	**rem** ignored
30 let y = y + 1	**04 +2098**	load **y** into accumulator
	05 +3097	add **1** (**97**) to accumulator
	06 +2196	store in temporary location **96**
	07 +2096	load from temporary location **96**
	08 +2198	store accumulator in **y**
35 rem add y to total	*none*	**rem** ignored

Fig. 19.27 SML instructions produced after the compiler's first pass (part 1 of 2).

Simple program	SML location and instruction	Description
`40 let t = t + y`	`09 +2095`	load **`t`** (**`95`**) into accumulator
	`10 +3098`	add **`y`** to accumulator
	`11 +2194`	store in temporary location **`94`**
	`12 +2094`	load from temporary location **`94`**
	`13 +2195`	store accumulator in **`t`**
`45 rem loop y`	*none*	**`rem`** ignored
`50 goto 20`	`14 +4001`	branch to location **`01`**
`55 rem output result`	*none*	**`rem`** ignored
`60 print t`	`15 +1195`	output **`t`** to screen
`99 end`	`16 +4300`	terminate execution

Fig. 19.27 SML instructions produced after the compiler's first pass (part 2 of 2).

Symbol	Type	Location
`5`	`L`	`00`
`10`	`L`	`00`
`'x'`	`V`	`99`
`15`	`L`	`01`
`20`	`L`	`01`
`'y'`	`V`	`98`
`25`	`L`	`04`
`30`	`L`	`04`
`1`	`C`	`97`
`35`	`L`	`09`
`40`	`L`	`09`
`'t'`	`V`	`95`
`45`	`L`	`14`
`50`	`L`	`14`
`55`	`L`	`15`
`60`	`L`	`15`
`99`	`L`	`16`

Fig. 19.28 Symbol table for program of Fig. 19.27.

Most Simple statements convert directly to single SML instructions. The exceptions in this program are remarks, the **`if/goto`** statement in line **`20`** and the **`let`** statements. Remarks do not translate into machine language. However, the line number for a remark is placed in the symbol table in case the line number is referenced in a **goto** statement or an **if/goto** statement. Line **20** of the program specifies that, if the condition **y == x** is true, program control is transferred to line **60**. Since line **60** appears later in the program, the first pass of the compiler has not as yet placed **60** in the symbol table. (Statement line numbers are placed in the symbol table only when they appear as the first token in a statement.) Therefore, it is not possible at this time to determine the operand of the SML *branch zero* instruction at location **03** in the array of SML instructions. The compiler places **60** in location **03** of the **flags** array to indicate that the second pass completes this instruction.

We must keep track of the next instruction location in the SML array because there is not a one-to-one correspondence between Simple statements and SML instructions. For example, the **if/goto** statement of line **20** compiles into three SML instructions. Each time an instruction is produced, we must increment the *instruction counter* to the next location in the SML array. Note that the size of Simpletron's memory could present a problem for Simple programs with many statements, variables and constants. It is conceivable that the compiler will run out of memory. To test for this case, your program should contain a *data counter* to keep track of the location at which the next variable or constant will be stored in the SML array. If the value of the instruction counter is larger than the value of the data counter, the SML array is full. In this case, the compilation process should terminate, and the compiler should print an error message indicating that it ran out of memory during compilation. This serves to emphasize that, although the programmer is freed from the burdens of managing memory by the compiler, the compiler itself must carefully determine the placement of instructions and data in memory and must check for such errors as memory being exhausted during the compilation process.

A Step-by-Step View of the Compilation Process

Let us now walk through the compilation process for the Simple program in Fig. 19.27. The compiler reads the first line of the program

```
5 rem sum 1 to x
```

into memory. The first token in the statement (the line number) is determined using the **StreamTokenizer** class (see Chapter 10 for a discussion of Java's string manipulation methods). The token returned by the **StreamTokenizer** is converted to an integer by using **static** method **Integer.parseInt()**, so the symbol **5** can be located in the symbol table. If the symbol is not found, it is inserted in the symbol table.

We are at the beginning of the program and this is the first line, and no symbols are in the table yet. Therefore, **5** is inserted into the symbol table as type **L** (line number) and assigned the first location in SML array (**00**). Although this line is a remark, a space in the symbol table is still allocated for the line number (in case it is referenced by a **goto** or an **if/goto**). No SML instruction is generated for a **rem** statement, so the instruction counter is not incremented.

```
10 input x
```

is tokenized next. The line number **10** is placed in the symbol table as type **L** and assigned the first location in the SML array (**00** because a remark began the program, so the instruction counter is currently **00**). The command **input** indicates that the next token is a variable (only a variable can appear in an **input** statement). **input** corresponds directly to an SML operation code; therefore, the compiler simply has to determine the location of **x** in the SML array. Symbol **x** is not found in the symbol table. So, it is inserted into the symbol table as the Unicode representation of **x**, given type **V** and assigned location **99** in the SML array (data storage begins at **99** and is allocated backwards). SML code can now be generated for this statement. Operation code **10** (the SML read operation code) is multiplied by 100, and the location of **x** (as determined in the symbol table) is added to complete the instruction. The instruction is then stored in the SML array at location **00**. The instruction counter is incremented by one, because a single SML instruction was produced.

The statement

```
15 rem   check y == x
```

is tokenized next. The symbol table is searched for line number **15** (which is not found). The line number is inserted as type **L** and assigned the next location in the array, **01**. (Remember that **rem** statements do not produce code, so the instruction counter is not incremented.)

The statement

```
20 if y == x goto 60
```

is tokenized next. Line number **20** is inserted in the symbol table and given type **L** at the next location in the SML array **01**. The command **if** indicates that a condition is to be evaluated. The variable **y** is not found in the symbol table, so it is inserted and given the type **V** and the SML location **98**. Next, SML instructions are generated to evaluate the condition. There is no direct equivalent in SML for the **if/goto**; it must be simulated by performing a calculation using **x** and **y** and branching according to the result. If **y** is equal to **x**, the result of subtracting **x** from **y** is zero, so the *branch zero* instruction can be used with the result of the calculation to simulate the **if/goto** statement. The first step requires that **y** be loaded (from SML location **98**) into the accumulator. This produces the instruction **01 +2098**. Next, **x** is subtracted from the accumulator. This produces the instruction **02 +3199**. The value in the accumulator may be zero, positive or negative. The operator is **==**, so we want to *branch zero*. First, the symbol table is searched for the branch location (**60** in this case), which is not found. So, **60** is placed in the **flags** array at location **03**, and the instruction **03 +4200** is generated. (We cannot add the branch location because we have not yet assigned a location to line **60** in the SML array.) The instruction counter is incremented to **04**.

The compiler proceeds to the statement

```
25 rem   increment y
```

The line number **25** is inserted in the symbol table as type **L** and assigned SML location **04**. The instruction counter is not incremented.

When the statement

```
30 let y = y + 1
```

is tokenized, the line number **30** is inserted in the symbol table as type **L** and assigned SML location **04**. Command **let** indicates that the line is an assignment statement. First, all the symbols on the line are inserted in the symbol table (if they are not already there). The integer **1** is added to the symbol table as type **C** and assigned SML location **97**. Next, the right side of the assignment is converted from infix to postfix notation. Then the postfix expression (**y 1 +**) is evaluated. Symbol **y** is located in the symbol table, and its corresponding memory location is pushed onto the stack. Symbol **1** is also located in the symbol table, and its corresponding memory location is pushed onto the stack. When the operator **+** is encountered, the postfix evaluator pops the stack into the right operand of the operator and pops the stack again into the left operand of the operator, then produces the SML instructions

```
04 +2098    (load y)
05 +3097    (add 1)
```

The result of the expression is stored in a temporary location in memory (**96**) with instruction

```
06 +2196    (store temporary)
```

and the temporary location is pushed onto the stack. Now that the expression has been evaluated, the result must be stored in **y** (i.e., the variable on the left side of **=**). So, the temporary location is loaded into the accumulator and the accumulator is stored in **y** with the instructions

```
07 +2096    (load temporary)
08 +2198    (store y)
```

The reader will immediately notice that SML instructions appear to be redundant. We will discuss this issue shortly.

When the statement

```
35 rem   add y to total
```

is tokenized, line number **35** is inserted in the symbol table as type **L** and assigned location **09**.

The statement

```
40 let t = t + y
```

is similar to line **30**. The variable **t** is inserted in the symbol table as type **V** and assigned SML location **95**. The instructions follow the same logic and format as line **30**, and the instructions **09 +2095**, **10 +3098**, **11 +2194**, **12 +2094** and **13 +2195** are generated. Note that the result of **t + y** is assigned to temporary location **94** before being assigned to **t** (**95**). Once again, the reader will note that the instructions in memory locations **11** and **12** appear to be redundant. Again, we will discuss this shortly.

The statement

```
45 rem   loop y
```

is a remark, so line **45** is added to the symbol table as type **L** and assigned SML location **14**.

The statement

```
50 goto 20
```

transfers control to line **20**. Line number **50** is inserted in the symbol table as type **L** and assigned SML location **14**. The equivalent of **goto** in SML is the *unconditional branch* (**40**) instruction that transfers control to a specific SML location. The compiler searches the symbol table for line **20** and finds that it corresponds to SML location **01**. The operation code (**40**) is multiplied by 100, and location **01** is added to it to produce the instruction **14 +4001**.

The statement

```
55 rem   output result
```

is a remark, so line **55** is inserted in the symbol table as type **L** and assigned SML location **15**.

The statement

```
60 print t
```

is an output statement. Line number **60** is inserted in the symbol table as type **L** and assigned SML location **15**. The equivalent of **print** in SML is operation code **11** (*write*). The location of **t** is determined from the symbol table and added to the result of the operation code multiplied by 100.

The statement

```
99 end
```

is the final line of the program. Line number **99** is stored in the symbol table as type **L** and assigned SML location **16**. The **end** command produces the SML instruction **+4300** (**43** is *halt* in SML), which is written as the final instruction in the SML memory array.

This completes the first pass of the compiler. We now consider the second pass. The **flags** array is searched for values other than **-1**. Location **03** contains **60**, so the compiler knows that instruction **03** is incomplete. The compiler completes the instruction by searching the symbol table for **60**, determining its location and adding the location to the incomplete instruction. In this case, the search determines that line **60** corresponds to SML location **15**, so the completed instruction **03 +4215** is produced, replacing **03 +4200**. The Simple program has now been compiled successfully.

To build the compiler, you will have to perform each of the following tasks:

a) Modify the Simpletron simulator program you wrote in Exercise 7.43 to take its input from a file specified by the user (see Chapter 16). The simulator should output its results to a disk file in the same format as the screen output. Convert the simulator to be an object-oriented program. In particular, make each part of the hardware an object. Arrange the instruction types into a class hierarchy using inheritance. Then execute the program polymorphically simply by telling each instruction to execute itself with an **executeInstruction** message.

b) Modify the infix-to-postfix evaluation algorithm of Exercise 19.12 to process multidigit integer operands and single-letter variable name operands. (*Hint*: Class **StreamTokenizer** can be used to locate each constant and variable in an expression, and constants can be converted from strings to integers by using **Integer** class method **parseInt**.) [*Note*: The data representation of the postfix expression must be altered to support variable names and integer constants.]

c) Modify the postfix evaluation algorithm to process multidigit integer operands and variable name operands. Also, the algorithm should now implement the "hook" discussed earlier so that SML instructions are produced rather than directly evaluating the expression. (*Hint*: Class **StreamTokenizer** can be used to locate each constant and variable in an expression, and constants can be converted from strings to integers by using **Integer** class method **parseInt**.) [*Note*: The data representation of the postfix expression must be altered to support variable names and integer constants.]

d) Build the compiler. Incorporate parts b) and c) for evaluating expressions in **let** statements. Your program should contain a method that performs the first pass of the compiler and a method that performs the second pass of the compiler. Both methods can call other methods to accomplish their tasks. Make your compiler as object oriented as possible.

19.28 (*Optimizing the Simple Compiler*) When a program is compiled and converted into SML, a set of instructions is generated. Certain combinations of instructions often repeat themselves, usually in triplets called *productions*. A production normally consists of three instructions, such as *load*, *add* and *store*. For example, Fig. 19.29 illustrates five of the SML instructions that were produced in the compilation of the program in Fig. 19.27. The first three instructions are the production that adds **1** to **y**. Note that instructions **06** and **07** store the accumulator value in temporary location **96**, then load the value back into the accumulator so instruction **08** can store the value in location **98**. Often a production is followed by a load instruction for the same location that was just stored. This code can be *optimized* by eliminating the store instruction and the subsequent load instruction that operate on the same memory location, thus enabling the Simpletron to execute the program faster. Figure 19.30 illustrates the optimized SML for the program of Fig. 19.27. Note that there are four fewer instructions in the optimized code—a memory-space savings of 25%.

```
04    +2098   (load)
05    +3097   (add)
06    +2196   (store)
07    +2096   (load)
08    +2198   (store)
```

Fig. 19.29 Unoptimized code from the program of Fig. 19.25.

Simple program	SML location and instruction	Description
`5 rem sum 1 to x`	*none*	**`rem`** ignored
`10 input x`	`00 +1099`	read **`x`** into location **`99`**
`15 rem check y == x`	*none*	**`rem`** ignored
`20 if y == x goto 60`	`01 +2098`	load **`y`** (**`98`**) into accumulator
	`02 +3199`	sub **`x`** (**`99`**) from accumulator
	`03 +4211`	branch to location **`11`** if zero
`25 rem increment y`	*none*	**`rem`** ignored
`30 let y = y + 1`	`04 +2098`	load **`y`** into accumulator
	`05 +3097`	add **`1`** (**`97`**) to accumulator
	`06 +2198`	store accumulator in **`y`** (**`98`**)
`35 rem add y to total`	*none*	**`rem`** ignored
`40 let t = t + y`	`07 +2096`	load **`t`** from location (**`96`**)
	`08 +3098`	add **`y`** (**`98`**) accumulator
	`09 +2196`	store accumulator in **`t`** (**`96`**)
`45 rem loop y`	*none*	**`rem`** ignored
`50 goto 20`	`10 +4001`	branch to location **`01`**
`55 rem output result`	*none*	**`rem`** ignored
`60 print t`	`11 +1196`	output **`t`** (**`96`**) to screen
`99 end`	`12 +4300`	terminate execution

Fig. 19.30 Optimized code for the program of Fig. 19.27.

19.29 (*Modifications to the Simple Compiler*) Perform the following modifications to the Simple compiler. Some of these modifications might also require modifications to the Simpletron simulator program written in Exercise 7.43.

a) Allow the modulus operator (**`%`**) to be used in **`let`** statements. Simpletron Machine Language must be modified to include a modulus instruction.
b) Allow exponentiation in a **`let`** statement using **`^`** as the exponentiation operator. Simpletron Machine Language must be modified to include an exponentiation instruction.
c) Allow the compiler to recognize uppercase and lowercase letters in Simple statements (e.g., **`'A'`** is equivalent to **`'a'`**). No modifications to the Simpletron simulator are required.
d) Allow **`input`** statements to read values for multiple variables such as **`input x, y`**. No modifications to the Simpletron simulator are required to perform this enhancement to the Simple compiler.
e) Allow the compiler to output multiple values from a single **`print`** statement, such as **`print a, b, c`**. No modifications to the Simpletron simulator are required to perform this enhancement.
f) Add syntax-checking capabilities to the compiler so error messages are output when syntax errors are encountered in a Simple program. No modifications to the Simpletron simulator are required.

g) Allow arrays of integers. No modifications to the Simpletron simulator are required to perform this enhancement.

h) Allow subroutines specified by the Simple commands **gosub** and **return**. Command **gosub** passes program control to a subroutine and command **return** passes control back to the statement after the **gosub**. This is similar to a method call in Java. The same subroutine can be called from many **gosub** commands distributed throughout a program. No modifications to the Simpletron simulator are required.

i) Allow repetition structures of the form

```
for x = 2 to 10 step 2
    Simple statements
next
```

This **for** statement loops from **2** to **10** with an increment of **2**. The **next** line marks the end of the body of the **for** line. No modifications to the Simpletron simulator are required.

j) Allow repetition structures of the form

```
for x = 2 to 10
    Simple statements
next
```

This **for** statement loops from **2** to **10** with a default increment of **1**. No modifications to the Simpletron simulator are required.

k) Allow the compiler to process string input and output. This requires the Simpletron simulator to be modified to process and store string values. [*Hint*: Each Simpletron word (i.e., memory location) can be divided into two groups, each holding a two-digit integer. Each two-digit integer represents the Unicode decimal equivalent of a character. Add a machine-language instruction that will print a string beginning at a certain Simpletron memory location. The first half of the Simpletron word at that location is a count of the number of characters in the string (i.e., the length of the string). Each succeeding half word contains one Unicode character expressed as two decimal digits. The machine language instruction checks the length and prints the string by translating each two-digit number into its equivalent character.]

l) Allow the compiler to process floating-point values in addition to integers. The Simpletron Simulator must also be modified to process floating-point values.

19.30 (*A Simple Interpreter*) An interpreter is a program that reads a high-level language program statement, determines the operation to be performed by the statement and executes the operation immediately. The high-level language program is not converted into machine language first. Interpreters execute more slowly than compilers do, because each statement encountered in the program being interpreted must first be deciphered at execution time. If statements are contained in a loop, the statements are deciphered each time they are encountered in the loop. Early versions of the Basic programming language were implemented as interpreters. Most Java programs are run interpretively.

Write an interpreter for the Simple language discussed in Exercise 19.26. The program should use the infix-to-postfix converter developed in Exercise 19.12 and the postfix evaluator developed in Exercise 19.13 to evaluate expressions in a **let** statement. The same restrictions placed on the Simple language in Exercise 19.26 should be adhered to in this program. Test the interpreter with the Simple programs written in Exercise 19.26. Compare the results of running these programs in the interpreter with the results of compiling the Simple programs and running them in the Simpletron simulator built in Exercise 7.43.

19.31 (*Insert/Delete Anywhere in a Linked List*) Our linked-list class allowed insertions and deletions at only the front and the back of the linked list. These capabilities were convenient for us when we used inheritance or composition to produce a stack class and a queue class with a minimal amount of code simply by reusing the list class. Linked lists are normally more general than those we provided. Modify the linked-list class we developed in this chapter to handle insertions and deletions anywhere in the list.

19.32 *(Lists and Queues without Tail References)* Our implementation of a linked list (Fig. 19.3) used both a **firstNode** and a **lastNode**. The **lastNode** was useful for the **insertAtBack** and **removeFromBack** methods of the **List** class. The **insertAtBack** method corresponds to the **enqueue** method of the **Queue** class.

Rewrite the **List** class so that it does not use a **lastNode**. Thus, any operations on the tail of a list must begin searching the list from the front. Does this affect our implementation of the **Queue** class (Fig. 19.13)?

19.33 *(Performance of Binary Tree Sorting and Searching)* One problem with the binary tree sort is that the order in which the data is inserted affects the shape of the tree—for the same collection of data, different orderings can yield binary trees of dramatically different shapes. The performance of the binary tree sorting and searching algorithms is sensitive to the shape of the binary tree. What shape would a binary tree have if its data were inserted in increasing order? in decreasing order? What shape should the tree have to achieve maximal searching performance?

19.34 *(Indexed Lists)* As presented in the text, linked lists must be searched sequentially. For large lists, this can result in poor performance. A common technique for improving list-searching performance is to create and maintain an index to the list. An index is a set of references to key places in the list. For example, an application that searches a large list of names could improve performance by creating an index with 26 entries—one for each letter of the alphabet. A search operation for a last name beginning with 'Y' would then first search the index to determine where the 'Y' entries begin, then "jump into" the list at that point and search linearly until the desired name is found. This would be much faster than searching the linked list from the beginning. Use the **List** class of Fig. 19.3 as the basis of an **IndexedList** class.

Write a program that demonstrates the operation of indexed lists. Be sure to include methods **insertInIndexedList**, **searchIndexedList** and **deleteFromIndexedList**.

20

Java Utilities Package and Bit Manipulation

Objectives

- To understand containers, such as classes **`Vector`** and **`Stack`**, and the **`Enumeration`** interface.
- To be able to create **`Hashtable`** objects and persistent hash tables called **`Properties`** objects.
- To understand random number generation with instances of class **`Random`**.
- To use bit manipulation and **`BitSet`** objects.

Nothing can have value without being an object of utility.
Karl Marx

I've been in Who's Who, and I know what's what, but this is the first time I ever made the dictionary.
Mae West

O! many a shaft at sent
Finds mark the archer little meant!
Sir Walter Scott

There was the Door to which I found no Key;
There was the Veil through which I might not see.
Edward FitzGerald, The Rubáiyát of Omar Khayyám, st. 32

"It's a poor sort of memory that only works backwards," the Queen remarked.
Lewis Carroll [Charles Lutwidge Dodgson]

Not by age but by capacity is wisdom acquired.
Titus Maccius Plautus, Trinummus, act II, sc. ii, l.88

Outline

20.1 Introduction
20.2 **Vector** Class and **Enumeration** Interface
20.3 **Stack** Class
20.4 **Dictionary** Class
20.5 **Hashtable** Class
20.6 **Properties** Class
20.7 **Random** Class
20.8 Bit Manipulation and the Bitwise Operators
20.9 **BitSet** Class

Summary • Terminology • Self-Review Exercises • Answers to Self-Review Exercises • Exercises

20.1 Introduction

This chapter discusses several utility classes and interfaces in package **java.util**, including class ***Vector***, interface ***Enumeration***, class ***Stack***, class ***Dictionary***, class ***Hashtable***, class ***Properties***, class ***Random*** and class ***BitSet***.

Programs use class **Vector** to create array-like objects that can grow and shrink dynamically as a program's data storage requirements change. We consider interface **Enumeration**, which enables a program to iterate through the elements of a container such as a **Vector**.

Class **Stack** offers conventional stack operations **push** and **pop**, as well as others we did not consider in Chapter 19.

Class **Dictionary** is an **abstract** class that provides a framework for storing keyed data in tables and retrieving that data. The chapter explains the theory of "hashing," a technique for rapidly storing and retrieving information from tables, and demonstrates the construction and manipulation of hash tables with Java's **Hashtable** class. Also, the chapter considers class **Properties**, which provides support for persistent hash tables—hash tables that can be written to a file with an output stream and read from a file with an input stream.

Class **Random** provides a richer collection of random number capabilities than is available with static method **random** of class **Math**.

The chapter presents an extensive discussion of bit manipulation operators, followed by a discussion of class **BitSet** that enables the creation of bit-array-like objects for setting and getting individual bit values.

Chapter 21, Collections, introduces a framework for manipulating groups of objects called *collections*. Objects of type **Vector**, **Stack** and **Hashtable** are collections.

20.2 **Vector** Class and **Enumeration** Interface

In most programming languages, including Java, conventional arrays are fixed in size—they cannot grow or shrink in response to an application's changing storage requirements. Java class ***Vector*** provides the capabilities of array-like data structures that can resize themselves dynamically.

At any time, the **Vector** contains a certain number of elements less than or equal to its *capacity*. The capacity is the space that has been reserved for the **Vector**'s elements. If a **Vector** requires additional capacity, it grows by a *capacity increment* that you specify or by a default assumed by the system. If you do not specify a capacity increment, the system will double the size of the **Vector** each time additional capacity is needed.

Performance Tip 20.1

Inserting additional elements into a **Vector** *whose current size is less than its capacity is a relatively fast operation.*

Performance Tip 20.2

It is a relatively slow operation to insert an element into a **Vector** *that needs to grow larger to accommodate the new element.*

Performance Tip 20.3

The default capacity increment doubles the size of the **Vector**. *This may seem a waste of storage, but it is actually an efficient way for many* **Vector***s to grow quickly to be "about the right size." This is much more efficient time-wise than growing the* **Vector** *each time by only as much space as it takes to hold a single element. This disadvantage is that the* **Vector** *might occupy more space than it requires.*

Performance Tip 20.4

If storage is at a premium, use **Vector** *method* **trimToSize** *to trim a* **Vector***'s capacity to the* **Vector***'s exact size. This optimizes a* **Vector***'s use of storage. However, adding another element to the* **Vector** *will force the* **Vector** *to grow dynamically—trimming leaves no room for growth.*

Vectors store references to **Object**s. Thus, a program can store references to any objects in a **Vector**. To store values of primitive data types in **Vector**s, use the type-wrapper classes (e.g., **Integer**, **Long**, **Float**) from package **java.lang** to create objects containing the primitive data type values.

Figure 20.1 demonstrates class **Vector** and several of its methods. The program provides a **JButton** that enables the user to test each of the methods. The user can type a **String** into the provided **JTextField**, and then press a button to see what the method does. Each operation displays a message in a **JLabel** to indicate the results of the operation.

```
// Fig. 20.1: VectorTest.java
// Testing the Vector class of the java.util package

// Java core packages
import java.util.*;
import java.awt.*;
import java.awt.event.*;

// Java extension packages
import javax.swing.*;

public class VectorTest extends JFrame {
   private JLabel statusLabel;
```

Fig. 20.1 Demonstrating class **Vector** of package **java.util** (part 1 of 6).

```
    private Vector vector;
    private JTextField inputField;

    // set up GUI to test Vector methods
    public VectorTest()
    {
        super( "Vector Example" );

        Container container = getContentPane();
        container.setLayout( new FlowLayout() );

        statusLabel = new JLabel();
        vector = new Vector( 1 );

        container.add( new JLabel( "Enter a string" ) );

        inputField = new JTextField( 10 );
        container.add( inputField );

        // button to add element to vector
        JButton addButton = new JButton( "Add" );

        addButton.addActionListener(

            new ActionListener() {

                public void actionPerformed( ActionEvent event )
                {
                    // add an element to vector
                    vector.addElement( inputField.getText() );
                    statusLabel.setText( "Added to end: " +
                        inputField.getText() );
                    inputField.setText( "" );
                }
            }
        ); // end call to addActionListener

        container.add( addButton );

        // button to remove element from vector
        JButton removeButton = new JButton( "Remove" );

        removeButton.addActionListener(

            new ActionListener() {

                public void actionPerformed( ActionEvent event )
                {
                    // remove element from vector
                    if ( vector.removeElement( inputField.getText() ) )
                        statusLabel.setText( "Removed: " +
                            inputField.getText() );
```

Fig. 20.1 Demonstrating class **Vector** of package **java.util** (part 2 of 6).

```
            else
               statusLabel.setText( inputField.getText() +
                  " not in vector" );
         }
      }
   ); // end call to addActionListener

   container.add( removeButton );

   // button to get first element of vector
   JButton firstButton = new JButton( "First" );

   firstButton.addActionListener(

      new ActionListener() {

         public void actionPerformed( ActionEvent event )
         {
            // return first element of vector
            try {
               statusLabel.setText(
                  "First element: " + vector.firstElement() );
            }

            // catch exception if Vector empty
            catch ( NoSuchElementException exception ) {
               statusLabel.setText( exception.toString() );
            }
         }
      }
   ); // end call to addActionListener

   container.add( firstButton );

   // button to get last element of vector
   JButton lastButton = new JButton( "Last" );

   lastButton.addActionListener(

      new ActionListener() {

         public void actionPerformed( ActionEvent event )
         {
            // return last element of vector
            try {
               statusLabel.setText(
                  "Last element: " + vector.lastElement() );
            }

            // catch exception if Vector empty
            catch ( NoSuchElementException exception ) {
               statusLabel.setText( exception.toString() );
            }
```

Fig. 20.1 Demonstrating class **Vector** of package **java.util** (part 3 of 6).

```
            }
         }
      ); // end call to addActionListener

      container.add( lastButton );

      // button to determine whether vector is empty
      JButton emptyButton = new JButton( "Is Empty?" );

      emptyButton.addActionListener(

         new ActionListener() {

            public void actionPerformed( ActionEvent event )
            {
               // determine if Vector is empty
               statusLabel.setText( vector.isEmpty() ?
                  "Vector is empty" : "Vector is not empty" );
            }
         }
      ); // end call to addActionListener

      container.add( emptyButton );

      // button to determine whether vector contains search key
      JButton containsButton = new JButton( "Contains" );

      containsButton.addActionListener(

         new ActionListener() {

            public void actionPerformed( ActionEvent event )
            {
               String searchKey = inputField.getText();

               // determine if Vector contains searchKey
               if ( vector.contains( searchKey ) )
                  statusLabel.setText(
                     "Vector contains " + searchKey );
               else
                  statusLabel.setText(
                     "Vector does not contain " + searchKey );
            }
         }
      ); // end call to addActionListener

      container.add( containsButton );

      // button to determine location of value in vector
      JButton locationButton = new JButton( "Location" );

      locationButton.addActionListener(

```

Fig. 20.1 Demonstrating class **Vector** of package **java.util** (part 4 of 6).

```
         new ActionListener() {

            public void actionPerformed( ActionEvent event )
            {
               // get location of an object in Vector
               statusLabel.setText( "Element is at location " +
                  vector.indexOf( inputField.getText() ) );
            }
         }
      ); // end call to addActionListener

      container.add( locationButton );

      // button to trim vector size
      JButton trimButton = new JButton( "Trim" );

      trimButton.addActionListener(

         new ActionListener() {

            public void actionPerformed( ActionEvent event )
            {
               // remove unoccupied elements to save memory
               vector.trimToSize();
               statusLabel.setText( "Vector trimmed to size" );
            }
         }
      );

      container.add( trimButton );

      // button to display vector size and capacity
      JButton statsButton = new JButton( "Statistics" );

      statsButton.addActionListener(

         new ActionListener() {

            public void actionPerformed( ActionEvent event )
            {
               // get size and capacity of Vector
               statusLabel.setText( "Size = " + vector.size() +
                  "; capacity = " + vector.capacity() );
            }
         }
      ); // end call to addActionListener

      container.add( statsButton );

      // button to display vector contents
      JButton displayButton = new JButton( "Display" );

      displayButton.addActionListener(
```

Fig. 20.1 Demonstrating class **Vector** of package **java.util** (part 5 of 6).

```
225
226          new ActionListener() {
227
228             public void actionPerformed( ActionEvent event )
229             {
230                // use Enumeration to output Vector contents
231                Enumeration enum = vector.elements();
232                StringBuffer buf = new StringBuffer();
233
234                while ( enum.hasMoreElements() )
235                   buf.append( enum.nextElement() ).append( "  " );
236
237                JOptionPane.showMessageDialog( null,
238                   buf.toString(), "Display",
239                   JOptionPane.PLAIN_MESSAGE );
240             }
241          }
242       ); // end call to addActionListener
243
244       container.add( displayButton );
245       container.add( statusLabel );
246
247       setSize( 300, 200 );
248       setVisible( true );
249
250    } // end VectorTest constructor
251
252    // execute application
253    public static void main( String args[] )
254    {
255       VectorTest application = new VectorTest();
256
257       application.setDefaultCloseOperation(
258          JFrame.EXIT_ON_CLOSE );
259    }
260
261 } // end class VectorTest
```

Fig. 20.1 Demonstrating class **`Vector`** of package **`java.util`** (part 6 of 6).

The application's constructor creates a **`Vector`** (line 26) with an initial capacity of one element. This **`Vector`** will double in size each time it needs to grow to accommodate more elements. Class **`Vector`** provides three other constructors. The no-argument constructor creates an empty **`Vector`** with an *initial capacity* of 10 elements. The constructor that takes two arguments creates a **Vector** with an *initial capacity* specified by the first argument and a *capacity increment* specified by the second argument. Each time the **Vector** needs to grow, it will add space for the specified number of elements in the capacity increment. The constructor that takes a **Collection** allows creates a copy of a collection's elements and stores them in the **Vector**. In Chapter 21, we discuss **Collection**s.

Line 43 calls **Vector** method ***addElement*** to add its argument to the end of the **Vector**. If necessary, the **Vector** increases its capacity to accommodate the new element. Class **Vector** also provides method ***insertElementAt*** to insert an element at a specified position in the **Vector** and method ***setElementAt*** to set the element at a specific position in the **Vector**. Method **insertElementAt** makes room for the new element by shifting elements. Method **setElementAt** replaces the element at the specified position with its argument.

Line 63 calls **Vector** method ***removeElement*** to remove the first occurrence of its argument from the **Vector**. The method returns **true** if it finds the element in the **Vector**; otherwise, the method returns **false**. If the element is removed, all elements after that element in the **Vector** shift one position toward the beginning of the **Vector** to fill in the position of the removed element. Class **Vector** also provides method **removeAllElements** to remove every element from the **Vector** and method **removeElementAt** to remove the element at a specified index.

Line 87 calls **Vector** method ***firstElement*** to return a reference to the first element in the **Vector**. This method throws a **NoSuchElementException** if there are no elements currently in the **Vector**. Line 112 calls **Vector** method ***lastElement*** to return a reference to the last element in the **Vector**. This method throws a **NoSuchElementException** if there are no elements currently in the **Vector**.

Line 135 calls **Vector** method ***isEmpty*** to determine whether the **Vector** is empty. The method returns **true** if there are no elements in the **Vector**; otherwise, the method returns **false**.

Line 155 calls **Vector** method ***contains*** to determine whether the **Vector** contains the **searchKey** specified as an argument. Method **contains** returns **true** if **searchKey** is in the **Vector**; otherwise, the method returns **false**. Method **contains** uses **Object** method **equals** to determine whether the **searchKey** is equal to one of the **Vector**'s elements. Many classes override method **equals** to perform the comparisons in a manner specific to those classes. For example, class **String** defines **equals** to compare the individual characters in the two **String**s being compared. If method **equals** is not overridden, the original version from class **Object** is used. This version performs comparisons using operator **==** to determine whether two references refer to the same object in memory.

Line 178 calls **Vector** method ***indexOf*** to determine the index of the first location in the **Vector** containing the argument. The method returns **-1** if the argument is not found in the **Vector**. An overloaded version of this method takes a second argument specifying the index in the **Vector** at which the search should begin.

Performance Tip 20.5

Vector *methods* ***contains*** *and* ***indexOf*** *perform linear searches of a* ***Vector****'s contents, which are inefficient for large* ***Vector****s. If a program frequently searches for elements in a collection, consider using a* ***Hashtable*** *(see Section 20.5) or one of the Java Collection API's* ***Map*** *implementations (see Chapter 21).*

Line 195 calls **Vector** method ***trimToSize*** to reduce the capacity of the **Vector** to the current number of elements in the **Vector** (i.e., the **Vector**'s current size).

Lines 213–214 use **Vector** methods ***size*** and ***capacity*** to determine the number of elements currently in the **Vector** and the number of elements that can be stored in the **Vector** without allocating more memory, respectively.

Line 231 calls **Vector** method ***elements*** to return an ***Enumeration*** that enables the program to iterate through the **Vector**'s elements. An **Enumeration** provides two methods—***hasMoreElements*** and ***nextElement***. In line 234, method **hasMoreElements** returns **true** if there are more elements in the **Vector**. In line 235, method **nextElement** returns a reference to the next element in the **Vector**. If there are no more elements, method **nextElement** throws a **NoSuchElementException**.

For complete information on class **Vector** and its other methods, see the online Java API documentation.

20.3 Stack Class

In Chapter 19, Data Structures, we learned how to build such fundamental data structures as linked lists, stacks, queues and trees. In a world of software reuse, instead of building data structures as we need them, often we can take advantage of existing data structures. In this section, we investigate class ***Stack*** in the Java utilities package (**java.util**).

In Section 20.2, we discussed class **Vector**, which implements a dynamically resizable array. Class **Stack** extends class **Vector** to implement a stack data structure. As does **Vector**, class **Stack** stores references to **Object**s. To store primitive data types, use the appropriate type-wrapper class to create an object containing the primitive value (**Boolean**, **Byte**, **Character**, **Short**, **Integer**, **Long**, **Float** or **Double**). Figure 20.2 provides a GUI that enables the user to test each of the **Stack** methods.

```
// Fig. 20.2: StackTest.java
// Testing the Stack class of the java.util package

// Java core packages
import java.awt.*;
import java.awt.event.*;
import java.util.*;

// Java extension packages
import javax.swing.*;

public class StackTest extends JFrame {
   private JLabel statusLabel;
   private JTextField inputField;
   private Stack stack;

   // create GUI to manipulate a Stack
   public StackTest()
   {
      super( "Stacks" );

```

Fig. 20.2 Demonstrating class **Stack** of package **java.util** (part 1 of 5).

```
      Container container = getContentPane();

      statusLabel = new JLabel();
      stack = new Stack();

      container.setLayout( new FlowLayout() );
      container.add( new JLabel( "Enter a string" ) );
      inputField = new JTextField( 10 );
      container.add( inputField );

      // button to place object on stack
      JButton pushButton = new JButton( "Push" );

      pushButton.addActionListener(

         new ActionListener() {

            public void actionPerformed( ActionEvent event )
            {
               // put object on Stack
               statusLabel.setText( "Pushed: " +
                  stack.push( inputField.getText() ) );
            }
         }
      );

      container.add( pushButton );

      // button to remove top object on stack
      JButton popButton = new JButton( "Pop" );

      popButton.addActionListener(

         new ActionListener() {

            public void actionPerformed( ActionEvent event )
            {
               // remove element from Stack
               try {
                  statusLabel.setText( "Popped: " + stack.pop() );
               }

               // process exception if Stack empty
               catch ( EmptyStackException exception ) {
                  statusLabel.setText( exception.toString() );
               }
            }
         }
      );

      container.add( popButton );

```

Fig. 20.2 Demonstrating class **Stack** of package **java.util** (part 2 of 5).

```
      // button to look at top element of stack
      JButton peekButton = new JButton( "Peek" );

      peekButton.addActionListener(

         new ActionListener() {

            public void actionPerformed( ActionEvent event )
            {
               // look at top object on Stack
               try {
                  statusLabel.setText( "Top: " + stack.peek() );
               }

               // process exception if Stack empty
               catch ( EmptyStackException exception ) {
                  statusLabel.setText( exception.toString() );
               }
            }
         }
      );

      container.add( peekButton );

      // button to determine whether stack is empty
      JButton emptyButton = new JButton( "Is Empty?" );

      emptyButton.addActionListener(

         new ActionListener() {

            public void actionPerformed( ActionEvent event )
            {
               // determine if Stack is empty
               statusLabel.setText( stack.empty() ?
                  "Stack is empty" : "Stack is not empty" );
            }
         }
      );

      container.add( emptyButton );

      // button to determine whether search key is in stack
      JButton searchButton = new JButton( "Search" );

      searchButton.addActionListener(

         new ActionListener() {

            public void actionPerformed( ActionEvent event )
            {
               // search Stack for specified object
               String searchKey = inputField.getText();
```

Fig. 20.2 Demonstrating class **Stack** of package **java.util** (part 3 of 5).

```
               int result = stack.search( searchKey );

               if ( result == -1 )
                  statusLabel.setText( searchKey + " not found" );
               else
                  statusLabel.setText( searchKey +
                     " found at element " + result );
            }
         }
      );

      container.add( searchButton );

      // button to display stack contents
      JButton displayButton = new JButton( "Display" );

      displayButton.addActionListener(

         new ActionListener() {

            public void actionPerformed( ActionEvent event )
            {
               // output Stack contents
               Enumeration enumeration = stack.elements();
               StringBuffer buffer = new StringBuffer();

               while ( enumeration.hasMoreElements() )
                  buffer.append(
                     enumeration.nextElement() ).append( " " );

               JOptionPane.showMessageDialog( null,
                   buffer.toString(), "Display",
                   JOptionPane.PLAIN_MESSAGE );
            }
         }
      );

      container.add( displayButton );
      container.add( statusLabel );

      setSize( 675, 100 );
      setVisible( true );
   }

   // execute application
   public static void main( String args[] )
   {
      StackTest application = new StackTest();

      application.setDefaultCloseOperation(
         JFrame.EXIT_ON_CLOSE );
   }

```

Fig. 20.2 Demonstrating class **Stack** of package **java.util** (part 4 of 5).

```
180 }  // end class StackTest
```

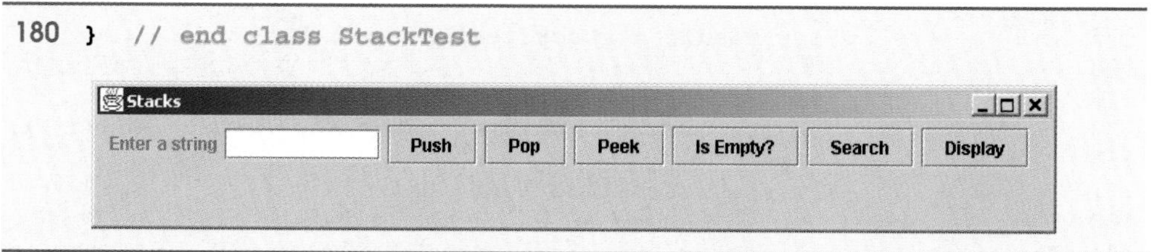

Fig. 20.2 Demonstrating class **Stack** of package **java.util** (part 5 of 5).

Line 25 creates an empty **Stack**. Line 43 calls **Stack** method ***push*** to add its argument to the top of the stack. The method returns an **Object** reference to its argument.

Line 61 calls **Stack** method ***pop*** to remove the top element of the stack. The method returns an **Object** reference to the removed element. If there are no elements in the **Stack**, method **pop** throws an ***EmptyStackException***.

Line 85 calls **Stack** method ***peek*** to view the top element of the stack without removing the element. Method **peek** returns an **Object** reference to the element.

Line 108 calls **Stack** method ***empty*** to determine whether the stack is empty. If it is empty, the method returns **true**; otherwise, the method returns **false**.

Line 127 calls **Stack** method ***search*** to determine whether its argument is in the stack. If so, the method returns the position of the element in the stack. *Note that the top element is position 1.* If the element is not in the stack, **-1** is returned.

The entire **public** interface of class **Vector** is actually part of class **Stack**, because **Stack** inherits from **Vector**. To prove this, our example provides a button to display the contents of the stack. This button invokes method **elements** to get an **Enumeration** of the stack; it then uses the **Enumeration** to walk through the stack elements.

Testing and Debugging Tip 20.1

Stack *extends* ***Vector****, so the user may perform operations on* ***Stack*** *objects that are ordinarily not allowed on conventional stack data structures. This could "corrupt" the elements of the* ***Stack*** *and destroy the integrity of the* ***Stack****.*

20.4 Dictionary Class

A ***Dictionary*** maps *keys* to *values*. When searching a **Dictionary** for a value, the program provides a key and the **Dictionary** returns the corresponding value. **Dictionary** is an **abstract** class. In particular, it is the superclass of class **Hashtable**, which we discuss in Section 20.5. Class **Dictionary** provides the **public** interface methods required to maintain a table of *key–value pairs* where the keys help store and retrieve the values in the table. Each key in the table is unique. The data structure is similar to a dictionary of words and definitions—the word is the *key* that is used to look up the definition (i.e., the *value*).

Dictionary method **size** returns the number of key–value pairs in a **Dictionary** object. Method ***isEmpty*** returns **true** if a **Dictionary** is empty, and **false** otherwise. Method ***keys*** returns an **Enumeration** that a program can use to iterate through a **Dictionary**'s keys. Method **elements** returns an **Enumeration** that a program can use to iterate through a **Dictionary**'s values. Method ***get*** returns the object that corresponds to a given key value. Method ***put*** puts an object associated with a given key into the table. Method ***remove*** removes an element corresponding to a given key and returns a reference to it.

20.5 `Hashtable` Class

Object-oriented programming languages facilitate creating new data types. When a program creates objects of new or existing types, the program then needs to manage those objects efficiently. This includes storing and retrieving objects. Storing and retrieving information with arrays is efficient if some aspect of your data directly matches the key value and if those keys are unique and tightly packed. If you have 100 employees with 9-digit Social Security numbers and you want to store and retrieve employee data by using the Social Security number as a key, it would nominally require an array with 999,999,999 elements, because there are 999,999,999 unique 9-digit numbers. This is impractical for virtually all applications that use Social Security numbers as keys. If the program could have an array that large, the program could get high performance for both storing and retrieving employee records by simply using the Social Security number as the array index.

There are numerous applications that have this problem, namely, that either the keys are of the wrong type (i.e., not nonnegative integers), or they may be of the right type, but sparsely spread over a huge range.

What is needed is a high-speed scheme for converting keys such as Social Security numbers, inventory part numbers and the like into unique array subscripts. Then, when an application needs to store something, the scheme could convert the application key rapidly into a subscript and the record of information could be stored at that slot in the array. Retrieval is accomplished the same way: Once the application has a key for which it wants to retrieve the data record, the application simply applies the conversion to the key—this produces the array subscript where the data is stored and the data is retrieved.

The scheme we describe here is the basis of a technique called *hashing*. Why the name? When we convert a key into an array subscript, we literally scramble the bits, forming a kind of "mishmashed" number. The number actually has no real significance beyond its usefulness in storing and retrieving this particular number data record.

A glitch in the scheme occurs when *collisions* occur (i.e., when two different keys "hash into" the same cell (or element) in the array). We cannot store two different data records in the same space, so we need to find an alternative home for all records beyond the first that hash to a particular array subscript. There are many schemes for doing this. One is to "hash again" (i.e., to reapply the hashing transformation to the key to provide a next candidate cell in the array). The hashing process is designed to distribute the values throughout the table, so the assumption is that with just a few hashes an available cell will be found.

Another scheme uses one hash to locate the first candidate cell. If that cell is occupied, successive cells are searched linearly until an available cell is found. Retrieval works the same way: The key is hashed once to determine the initial location to check to see whether it contains the desired data. If it does, the search is finished. If it does not, successive cells are searched linearly until the desired data is found.

The most popular solution to hash table collisions is to have each cell of the table be a hash "bucket," typically a linked list of all the key–value pairs that hash to that cell. This is the solution that Java's ***`Hashtable`*** class (from package **`java.util`**) implements.

One factor that affects the performance of hashing schemes is called the *load factor*. This is the ratio of the number of occupied cells in the hash table to the size of the hash table. The closer this ratio gets to 1.0, the greater the chance of collisions.

Performance Tip 20.6

The load factor in a hash table is a classic example of a space–time trade-off: By increasing the load factor, we get better memory utilization, but the program runs slower, due to increased hashing collisions. By decreasing the load factor, we get better program speed, because of reduced hashing collisions, but we get poorer memory utilization, because a larger portion of the hash table remains empty.

The complexity of programming hash tables properly is too much for most casual programmers. Computer science students study hashing schemes thoroughly in courses called "Data Structures" or "Algorithms." Recognizing the value of hashing to most programmers, Java provides class **Hashtable** and some related features to enable programmers to use hashing without having to implement the messy details.

Actually, the preceding sentence is profoundly important in our study of object-oriented programming. As discussed in earlier chapters, classes encapsulate and hide complexity (i.e., implementation details) and offer user-friendly interfaces. Crafting classes to do this properly is one of the most valued skills in the field of object-oriented programming.

Figure 20.3 provides a GUI that enables you to test several **Hashtable** methods. Line 25 creates an empty **Hashtable** with a default capacity of 101 elements and a default load factor of .75. When the number of occupied slots in the **Hashtable** becomes more than the capacity times the load factor, the table grows larger. Class **Hashtable** also provides a constructor that takes one argument specifying the capacity and a constructor that takes two arguments, specifying the capacity and load factor, respectively.

```
1  // Fig. 20.3: HashtableTest.java
2  // Demonstrates class Hashtable of the java.util package.
3
4  // Java core packages
5  import java.awt.*;
6  import java.awt.event.*;
7  import java.util.*;
8
9  // Java extensions packages
10 import javax.swing.*;
11
12 public class HashtableTest extends JFrame {
13    private JLabel statusLabel;
14    private Hashtable table;
15    private JTextArea displayArea;
16    private JTextField lastNameField;
17    private JTextField firstNameField;
18
19    // set up GUI to demonstrate Hashtable features
20    public HashtableTest()
21    {
22       super( "Hashtable Example" );
23
24       statusLabel = new JLabel();
25       table = new Hashtable();
26       displayArea = new JTextArea( 4, 20 );
```

Fig. 20.3 Demonstrating class **Hashtable** (part 1 of 6).

```
      displayArea.setEditable( false );

      JPanel northSubPanel = new JPanel();

      northSubPanel.add( new JLabel( "First name" ) );
      firstNameField = new JTextField( 8 );
      northSubPanel.add( firstNameField );

      northSubPanel.add( new JLabel( "Last name (key)" ) );
      lastNameField = new JTextField( 8 );
      northSubPanel.add( lastNameField );

      JPanel northPanel = new JPanel();
      northPanel.setLayout( new BorderLayout() );
      northPanel.add( northSubPanel, BorderLayout.NORTH );
      northPanel.add( statusLabel, BorderLayout.SOUTH );

      JPanel southPanel = new JPanel();
      southPanel.setLayout( new GridLayout( 2, 5 ) );
      JButton putButton = new JButton( "Put" );

      putButton.addActionListener(

         new ActionListener() {

            // add new key/value pair to hash table
            public void actionPerformed( ActionEvent event )
            {
               Employee employee = new Employee(
                  firstNameField.getText(),
                  lastNameField.getText() );

               Object value =
                  table.put( lastNameField.getText(), employee );

               // first time this key was added
               if ( value == null )
                  statusLabel.setText(
                     "Put: " + employee.toString() );

               // replaced previous value for this key
               else
                  statusLabel.setText(
                     "Put: " + employee.toString() +
                     "; Replaced: " + value.toString() );
            }
         }
      );

      southPanel.add( putButton );

      // button to get value for specific key
      JButton getButton = new JButton( "Get" );
```

Fig. 20.3 Demonstrating class **Hashtable** (part 2 of 6).

```

      getButton.addActionListener(

         new ActionListener() {

            // get value for specific key
            public void actionPerformed( ActionEvent event )
            {
               Object value = table.get( lastNameField.getText() );

               // value found for key
               if ( value != null )
                  statusLabel.setText(
                     "Get: " + value.toString() );

               // value not found for key
               else
                  statusLabel.setText(
                     "Get: " + lastNameField.getText() +
                     " not in table" );
            }
         }
      );

      southPanel.add( getButton );

      // button to remove key/value pair from table
      JButton removeButton = new JButton( "Remove" );

      removeButton.addActionListener(

         new ActionListener() {

            // remove key/value pair
            public void actionPerformed( ActionEvent event )
            {
               Object value =
                  table.remove( lastNameField.getText() );

               // key found
               if ( value != null )
                  statusLabel.setText( "Remove: " +
                     value.toString() );

               // key not found
               else
                  statusLabel.setText( "Remove: " +
                     lastNameField.getText() + " not in table" );
            }
         }
      );

      southPanel.add( removeButton );
```

Fig. 20.3 Demonstrating class **Hashtable** (part 3 of 6).

```

      // button to detetmine whether hash table is empty
      JButton emptyButton = new JButton( "Empty" );

      emptyButton.addActionListener(

         new ActionListener() {

            // determine whether hash table is empty
            public void actionPerformed( ActionEvent event )
            {
               statusLabel.setText( "Empty: " + table.isEmpty() );
            }
         }
      );

      southPanel.add( emptyButton );

      // button to determine whether hash table contains key
      JButton containsKeyButton = new JButton( "Contains key" );

      containsKeyButton.addActionListener(

         new ActionListener() {

            // determine whether hash table contains key
            public void actionPerformed( ActionEvent event )
            {
               statusLabel.setText( "Contains key: " +
                  table.containsKey( lastNameField.getText() ) );
            }
         }
      );

      southPanel.add( containsKeyButton );

      // button to clear all hash table contents
      JButton clearButton = new JButton( "Clear table" );

      clearButton.addActionListener(

         new ActionListener() {

            // clear hash table contents
            public void actionPerformed( ActionEvent event )
            {
               table.clear();
               statusLabel.setText( "Clear: Table is now empty" );
            }
         }
      );

      southPanel.add( clearButton );
```

Fig. 20.3 Demonstrating class **Hashtable** (part 4 of 6).

```java

      // button to display hash table elements
      JButton listElementsButton = new JButton( "List objects" );

      listElementsButton.addActionListener(

         new ActionListener() {

            // display hash table elements
            public void actionPerformed( ActionEvent event )
            {
               StringBuffer buffer = new StringBuffer();

               for ( Enumeration enumeration = table.elements();
                     enumeration.hasMoreElements(); )
                  buffer.append(
                     enumeration.nextElement() ).append( '\n' );

               displayArea.setText( buffer.toString() );
            }
         }
      );

      southPanel.add( listElementsButton );

      // button to display hash table keys
      JButton listKeysButton = new JButton( "List keys" );

      listKeysButton.addActionListener(

         new ActionListener() {

            // display hash table KEYS
            public void actionPerformed( ActionEvent event )
            {
               StringBuffer buffer = new StringBuffer();

               for ( Enumeration enumeration = table.keys();
                     enumeration.hasMoreElements(); )
                  buffer.append(
                     enumeration.nextElement() ).append( '\n' );

                  JOptionPane.showMessageDialog( null,
                     buffer.toString(), "Display",
                     JOptionPane.PLAIN_MESSAGE );
            }
         }
      );

      southPanel.add( listKeysButton );

      Container container = getContentPane();
      container.add( northPanel, BorderLayout.NORTH );
```

Fig. 20.3 Demonstrating class **Hashtable** (part 5 of 6).

```
      container.add( new JScrollPane( displayArea ),
         BorderLayout.CENTER );
      container.add( southPanel, BorderLayout.SOUTH );

      setSize( 540, 300 );
      setVisible( true );
   }

   // execute application
   public static void main( String args[] )
   {
      HashtableTest application = new HashtableTest();

      application.setDefaultCloseOperation(
         JFrame.EXIT_ON_CLOSE );
   }

}  // end class HashtableTest

// Employee class to represent first and last name
class Employee {
   private String first, last;

   // initialize an Employee
   public Employee( String firstName, String lastName )
   {
      first = firstName;
      last = lastName;
   }

   // convert Employee to String representation
   public String toString()
   {
      return first + " " + last;
   }

}  // end class Employee
```

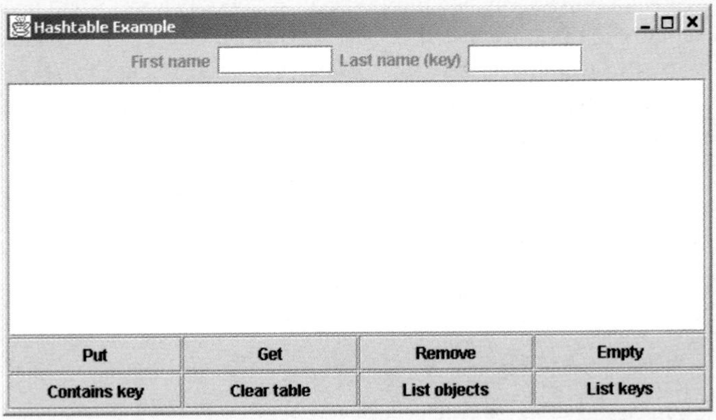

Fig. 20.3 Demonstrating class **Hashtable** (part 6 of 6).

Lines 59–60 call **Hashtable** method ***put*** to add a *key* (the first argument) and a *value* (the second argument) into the **Hashtable**. Method **put** returns **null** if key has not been inserted in the **Hashtable** previously. Otherwise, method **put** returns the original value for that key in the **Hashtable**; this helps the program manage cases in which it intends to replace the value stored for a given key. If either the key or the value is **null**, a **NullPointerException** occurs.

Line 88 calls **Hashtable** method ***get*** to locate the value associated with the key specified as an argument. If the key is present in the table, **get** returns an **Object** reference to the corresponding value; otherwise, the method returns **null**.

Lines 116–117 call **Hashtable** method ***remove*** to remove a key–value pair from the table. The method returns a reference to the removed **Object**. If there is no value mapped to the specified key, the method returns **null**.

Line 144 calls **Hashtable** method **isEmpty**, which returns **true** if the **Hashtable** is empty; otherwise it returns **false**.

Line 162 calls **Hashtable** method ***containsKey*** to determine whether the key specified as an argument is in the **Hashtable** (i.e., a value is associated with that key). If so, the method returns **true**; otherwise, the method returns **false**. Class **Hashtable** also provides method ***contains*** to determine whether the **Object** specified as its argument is in the **Hashtable**.

Line 179 calls **Hashtable** method ***clear*** to empty the **Hashtable** contents. Line 199 calls **Hashtable** method ***elements*** to obtain an **Enumeration** of the values in the **Hashtable**. Line 223 calls **Hashtable** method ***keys*** to obtain an **Enumeration** of the keys in the **Hashtable**.

For more information on class **Hashtable** and its methods, see the online Java API documentation.

20.6 Properties Class

A ***Properties*** object is a persistent **Hashtable** object that normally stores key–value pairs of **String**s—assuming that you use methods ***setProperty*** and ***getProperty*** to manipulate the table rather than **Hashtable** methods **put** and **get**. By persistent, we mean that the **Hashtable** object can be written to an output stream and directed to a file, and read back in through an input stream. In fact, most objects in Java can now be output and input with Java's object serialization (see Chapter 16). The **Properties** class extends class **Hashtable**, so **Properties** objects have the methods we discussed in Fig. 20.3. The keys and values in a **Properties** object must be of type **String**. Class **Properties** provides some additional methods that are demonstrated in Fig. 20.4.

```
// Fig. 20.4: PropertiesTest.java
// Demonstrates class Properties of the java.util package.

// Java core packages
import java.awt.*;
import java.awt.event.*;
import java.io.*;
import java.util.*;
```

Fig. 20.4 Demonstrating class **Properties** (part 1 of 6).

```

// Java extension packages
import javax.swing.*;

public class PropertiesTest extends JFrame {
   private JLabel statusLabel;
   private Properties table;
   private JTextArea displayArea;
   private JTextField valueField, nameField;

   // set up GUI to test Properties table
   public PropertiesTest()
   {
      super( "Properties Test" );

      // create Properties table
      table = new Properties();

      Container container = getContentPane();

      // set up NORTH of window's BorderLayout
      JPanel northSubPanel = new JPanel();

      northSubPanel.add( new JLabel( "Property value" ) );
      valueField = new JTextField( 10 );
      northSubPanel.add( valueField );

      northSubPanel.add( new JLabel( "Property name (key)" ) );
      nameField = new JTextField( 10 );
      northSubPanel.add( nameField );

      JPanel northPanel = new JPanel();
      northPanel.setLayout( new BorderLayout() );
      northPanel.add( northSubPanel, BorderLayout.NORTH );

      statusLabel = new JLabel();
      northPanel.add( statusLabel, BorderLayout.SOUTH );

      container.add( northPanel, BorderLayout.NORTH );

      // set up CENTER of window's BorderLayout
      displayArea = new JTextArea( 4, 35 );
      container.add( new JScrollPane( displayArea ),
         BorderLayout.CENTER );

      // set up SOUTH of window's BorderLayout
      JPanel southPanel = new JPanel();
      southPanel.setLayout( new GridLayout( 1, 5 ) );

      // button to put a name/value pair in Properties table
      JButton putButton = new JButton( "Put" );

```

Fig. 20.4 Demonstrating class **`Properties`** (part 2 of 6).

```
      putButton.addActionListener(

         new ActionListener() {

            // put name/value pair in Properties table
            public void actionPerformed( ActionEvent event )
            {
               Object value = table.setProperty(
                  nameField.getText(), valueField.getText() );

               if ( value == null )
                  showstatus( "Put: " + nameField.getText() +
                     " " + valueField.getText() );

               else
                  showstatus( "Put: " + nameField.getText() +
                     " " + valueField.getText() +
                     "; Replaced: " + value.toString() );

               listProperties();
            }
         }
      ); // end call to addActionListener

      southPanel.add( putButton );

      // button to empty contents of Properties table
      JButton clearButton = new JButton( "Clear" );

      clearButton.addActionListener(

         new ActionListener() {

            // use method clear to empty table
            public void actionPerformed( ActionEvent event )
            {
               table.clear();
               showstatus( "Table in memory cleared" );
               listProperties();
            }
         }
      ); // end call to addActionListener

      southPanel.add( clearButton );

      // button to get value of a property
      JButton getPropertyButton = new JButton( "Get property" );

      getPropertyButton.addActionListener(

         new ActionListener() {

```

Fig. 20.4 Demonstrating class **Properties** (part 3 of 6).

```
         // use method getProperty to obtain a property value
         public void actionPerformed( ActionEvent event )
         {
            Object value = table.getProperty(
               nameField.getText() );

            if ( value != null )
               showstatus( "Get property: " +
                  nameField.getText() + " " +
                  value.toString() );

            else
               showstatus( "Get: " + nameField.getText() +
                  " not in table" );

            listProperties();
         }
      }
   ); // end call to addActionListener

   southPanel.add( getPropertyButton );

   // button to contents of Properties table to file
   JButton saveButton = new JButton( "Save" );

   saveButton.addActionListener(

      new ActionListener() {

         // use method save to place contents in file
         public void actionPerformed( ActionEvent event )
         {
            // save contents of table
            try {
               FileOutputStream output =
                  new FileOutputStream( "props.dat" );

               table.store( output, "Sample Properties" );
               output.close();

               listProperties();
            }

            // process problems with file output
            catch( IOException ioException ) {
               ioException.printStackTrace();
            }
         }
      }
   ); // end call to addActionListener

   southPanel.add( saveButton );

```

Fig. 20.4 Demonstrating class **Properties** (part 4 of 6).

```
      // button to load contents of Properties table from file
      JButton loadButton = new JButton( "Load" );

      loadButton.addActionListener(

         new ActionListener() {

            // use method load to read contents from file
            public void actionPerformed( ActionEvent event )
            {
               // load contents of table
               try {
                  FileInputStream input =
                     new FileInputStream( "props.dat" );

                  table.load( input );
                  input.close();
                  listProperties();
               }

               // process problems with file input
               catch( IOException ioException ) {
                  ioException.printStackTrace();
               }
            }
         }
      ); // end call to addActionListener

      southPanel.add( loadButton );

      container.add( southPanel, BorderLayout.SOUTH );

      setSize( 550, 225 );
      setVisible( true );
   }

   // output property values
   public void listProperties()
   {
      StringBuffer buffer = new StringBuffer();
      String name, value;

      Enumeration enumeration = table.propertyNames();

      while ( enumeration.hasMoreElements() ) {
         name = enumeration.nextElement().toString();
         value = table.getProperty( name );

         buffer.append( name ).append( '\t' );
         buffer.append( value ).append( '\n' );
      }

      displayArea.setText( buffer.toString() );
```

Fig. 20.4 Demonstrating class **Properties** (part 5 of 6).

```
219    }  // end method ListProperties
220
221    // display String in statusLabel label
222    public void showstatus( String s )
223    {
224       statusLabel.setText( s );
225    }
226
227    // execute application
228    public static void main( String args[] )
229    {
230       PropertiesTest application = new PropertiesTest();
231
232       application.setDefaultCloseOperation(
233          JFrame.EXIT_ON_CLOSE );
234    }
235
236 }  // end class PropertiesTest
```

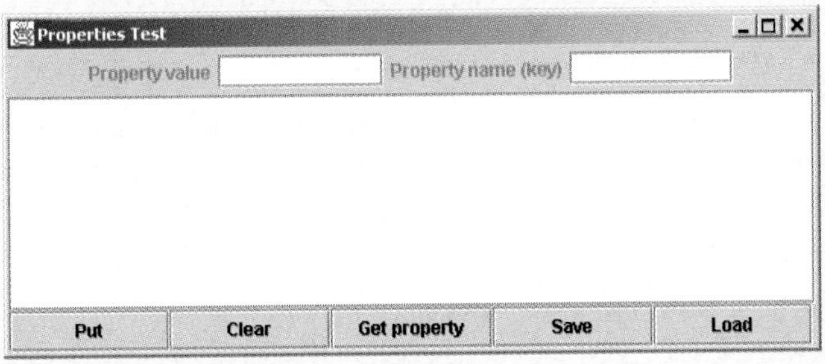

Fig. 20.4 Demonstrating class **Properties** (part 6 of 6).

Line 25 uses the no-argument constructor to create an empty **Properties** table with no default properties. Class **Properties** also provides an overloaded constructor that receives a reference to a **Properties** object containing default property values.

Lines 68–69 call **Properties** method **setProperty** to store a value for the specified key. If the key does not exist in the table, **setProperty** returns **null**; otherwise, it returns the previous value for that key.

Lines 116–117 call **Properties** method ***getProperty*** to locate the value associated with the specified key. If the key is not found in this **Properties** object, **getProperty** uses the one in the default **Properties** object (if there is one). The process continues recursively until there are no more default **Properties** objects (remember that every **Properties** object can be initialized with a default **Properties** object), at which point **getProperty** returns **null**. An overloaded version of this method receives two arguments, the second of which is the default value to return if **getProperty** cannot locate the key.

Line 150 calls **Properties** method ***store*** to save the contents of the **Properties** object to the **OutputStream** object specified as the first argument (in this case, a **FileOutputStream**). The **String** argument is a description of the **Properties** object. Class **Properties** also provides method ***list***, which takes a **PrintStream** argument. This method is useful for displaying the set of properties.

Testing and Debugging Tip 20.2

*Use **`Properties`** method **`list`** to display the contents of a **`Properties`** object for debugging purposes.*

Line 181 calls **`Properties`** method ***`load`*** to restore the contents of the **`Properties`** object from the **`InputStream`** specified as the first argument (in this case, a **`FileInputStream`**).

Line 208 calls **`Properties`** method ***`propertyNames`*** to obtain an **`Enumeration`** of the property names. The value of each property can be determined by using method **`getProperty`**.

20.7 Random Class

We discussed random-number generation in Chapter 6, Methods, where we used **`Math`** class method **`random`**. Java provides extensive additional random number generation capabilities in class ***`Random`***. We briefly walk through the API calls here.

A new random-number generator can be created by using

```
Random r = new Random();
```

This form uses the computer's current time to seed its random-number generator differently during each constructor call and thus generates different sequences of random numbers for each **`Random`** object.

To create a pseudorandom-number generator with "repeatability," use

```
Random r = new Random( seedValue );
```

The **`seedValue`** argument (type **`long`**) is used in the random number calculation to "seed" the random number generator. If the same **`seedValue`** is used every time, the **`Random`** object produces the same sequence of random numbers.

Testing and Debugging Tip 20.3

*While a program is under development, use the form **`Random(seedValue)`** that produces a repeatable sequence of random numbers. If a bug occurs, fix the bug and test with the same **`seedValue`**; this allows you to reconstruct the exact same sequence of random numbers that caused the bug. Once the bugs have been removed, use the form **`Random()`**, which generates a new sequence of random numbers each time the program is run.*

The call

```
r.setSeed( seedValue );
```

resets **`r`**'s seed value at any time.

The calls

```
r.nextInt()
r.nextLong()
```

generate uniformly distributed random integers. You can use **`Math.abs`** to take the absolute value of the number produced by ***`nextInt`***, thus giving a number in the range from zero through approximately 2 billion. Then use the **`%`** operator to scale the number. For example, to roll a six-sided die, if you scale with a 6, you will get a number in the range from

0 through 5. Then simply shift this value by adding 1 to produce a number in the range from 1 through 6. The expression is as follows:

```
Math.abs( r.nextInt() ) % 6 + 1
```

The calls

```
r.nextFloat()
r.nextDouble()
```

generate uniformly distributed values in the range 0.0 <= *x* < 1.0.

The call

```
r.nextGaussian()
```

generates a **double** value with a probability density of a *Gaussian* (i.e., "normal") distribution (mean of 0.0 and standard deviation of 1.0).

20.8 Bit Manipulation and the Bitwise Operators

Java provides extensive bit-manipulation capabilities for programmers who need to get down to the so-called "bits-and-bytes" level. Operating systems, test equipment software, networking software and many other kinds of software require that the programmer communicate "directly with the hardware." In this section and the next, we discuss Java's bit-manipulation capabilities. We introduce Java's bitwise operators, and we demonstrate their use in live-code examples.

Computers represent all data internally as sequences of bits. Each bit can assume the value **0** or the value **1**. On most systems, a sequence of 8 bits forms a byte—the standard storage unit for a variable of type **byte**. Other data types are stored in larger numbers of bytes. The bitwise operators can manipulate the bits of integral operands (i.e., those having type **byte**, **char**, **short**, **int** and **long**).

Note that the bitwise operator discussions in this section show the binary representations of the integer operands. For a detailed explanation of the binary (also called base 2) number system, see Appendix E, Number Systems.

The bitwise operators are *bitwise AND* (**&**), *bitwise inclusive OR* (**|**), *bitwise exclusive OR* (**^**), *left shift* (**<<**), *right shift with sign extension* (**>>**), *right shift with zero extension* (**>>>**) and complement (**~**). The bitwise AND, bitwise inclusive OR and bitwise exclusive OR operators compare their two operands bit by bit. The bitwise AND operator sets each bit in the result to 1 if the corresponding bit in both operands is 1. The bitwise inclusive OR operator sets each bit in the result to 1 if the corresponding bit in either (or both) operand(s) is 1. The bitwise exclusive OR operator sets each bit in the result to 1 if the corresponding bit in exactly one operand is 1. The left shift operator shifts the bits of its left operand to the left by the number of bits specified in its right operand. The right shift operator with sign extension shifts the bits in its left operand to the right by the number of bits specified in its right operand—if the left operand is negative, **1**s are shifted in from the left; otherwise, **0**s are shifted in from the left. The right shift operator with zero extension shifts the bits in its left operand to the right by the number of bits specified in its right operand—**0**s are shifted in from the left. The bitwise complement operator sets all **0** bits in its operand to **1** in the result and sets all **1** bits to **0** in the result. Detailed discussions of each bitwise operator appear in the following examples. The bitwise operators are summarized in Fig. 20.5.

Operator	Name	Description
`&`	bitwise AND	The bits in the result are set to **`1`** if the corresponding bits in the two operands are both **`1`**.
`|`	bitwise inclusive OR	The bits in the result are set to **`1`** if at least one of the corresponding bits in the two operands is **`1`**.
`^`	bitwise exclusive OR	The bits in the result are set to **`1`** if exactly one of the corresponding bits in the two operands is **`1`**.
`<<`	left shift	Shifts the bits of the first operand left by the number of bits specified by the second operand; fill from the right with **`0`** bits.
`>>`	right shift with sign extension	Shifts the bits of the first operand right by the number of bits specified by the second operand. If the first operand is negative, **`1`**s are shifted in from the left; otherwise, **`0`**s are shifted in from the left.
`>>>`	right shift with zero extension	Shifts the bits of the first operand right by the number of bits specified by the second operand; **`0`**s are shifted in from the left.
`~`	one's complement	All **`0`** bits are set to **`1`** and all **`1`** bits are set to **`0`**.

Fig. 20.5 The bitwise operators .

When using the bitwise operators, it is useful to display values in their binary representation to illustrate the effects of these operators. The application of Fig. 20.6 allows the user to enter an integer into a **`JTextField`** and press *Enter*. Method **`actionPerformed`** (lines 32–36) reads the **`String`** from the **`JTextField`**, converts it to an integer and invokes method **`getBits`** (lines 55–80) to obtain a **`String`** representation of the integer in bits. The result is displayed in the output **`JTextField`**. The integer is displayed in its binary representation in groups of eight bits each. Method **`getBits`** uses the bitwise AND operator to combine variable **`value`** with variable **`displayMask`**. Often, the bitwise AND operator is used with an operand called a *mask*—an integer value with specific bits set to **`1`**. Masks are used to hide some bits in a value while selecting other bits. In **`getBits`**, mask variable **`displayMask`** is assigned the value **`1 << 31`** or

```
10000000 00000000 00000000 00000000
```

The left shift operator shifts the value **`1`** from the low-order (rightmost) bit to the high-order (leftmost) bit in **`displayMask`** and fills in **`0`** bits from the right.

```
1  // Fig. 20.6: PrintBits.java
2  // Printing an unsigned integer in bits
3
4  // Java core packages
5  import java.awt.*;
6  import java.awt.event.*;
```

Fig. 20.6 Printing the bits in an integer (part 1 of 3).

```
// Java extension packages
import javax.swing.*;

public class PrintBits extends JFrame {
   private JTextField outputField;

   // set up GUI
   public PrintBits()
   {
      super( "Printing bit representations for numbers" );

      Container container = getContentPane();
      container.setLayout( new FlowLayout() );

      container.add( new JLabel( "Enter an integer " ) );

      // textfield to read value from user
      JTextField inputField = new JTextField( 10 );

      inputField.addActionListener(

         new ActionListener() {

            // read integer and get bitwise representation
            public void actionPerformed( ActionEvent event )
            {
               int value = Integer.parseInt(
                  event.getActionCommand() );
               outputField.setText( getBits( value ) );
            }
         }
      );

      container.add( inputField );

      container.add( new JLabel( "The integer in bits is" ) );

      // textfield to display integer in bitwise form
      outputField = new JTextField( 33 );
      outputField.setEditable( false );
      container.add( outputField );

      setSize( 720, 70 );
      setVisible( true );
   }

   // display bit representation of specified int value
   private String getBits( int value )
   {
      // create int value with 1 in leftmost bit and 0s elsewhere
      int displayMask = 1 << 31;

```

Fig. 20.6 Printing the bits in an integer (part 2 of 3).

```
60          // buffer to build output
61          StringBuffer buffer = new StringBuffer( 35 );
62
63          // for each bit append 0 or 1 to buffer
64          for ( int bit = 1; bit <= 32; bit++ ) {
65
66             // use displayMask to isolate bit and determine whether
67             // bit has value of 0 or 1
68             buffer.append(
69                ( value & displayMask ) == 0 ? '0' : '1' );
70
71             // shift value one position to left
72             value <<= 1;
73
74             // append space to buffer every 8 bits
75             if ( bit % 8 == 0 )
76                buffer.append( ' ' );
77          }
78
79          return buffer.toString();
80       }
81
82       // execute application
83       public static void main( String args[] )
84       {
85          PrintBits application = new PrintBits();
86
87          application.setDefaultCloseOperation(
88             JFrame.EXIT_ON_CLOSE );
89       }
90
91    }  // end class PrintBits
```

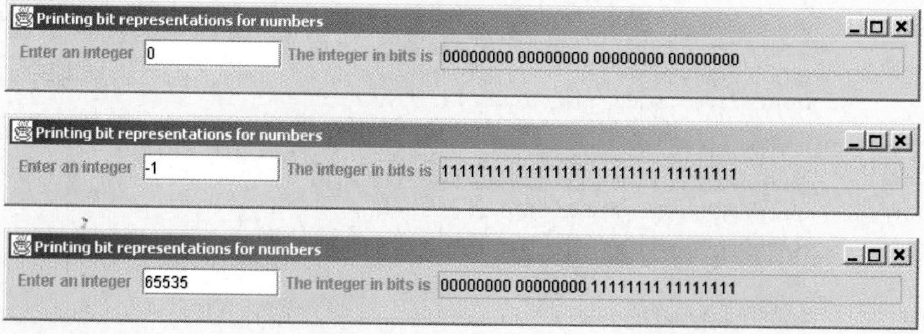

Printing bit representations for numbers
Enter an integer 0 The integer in bits is 00000000 00000000 00000000 00000000

Printing bit representations for numbers
Enter an integer -1 The integer in bits is 11111111 11111111 11111111 11111111

Printing bit representations for numbers
Enter an integer 65535 The integer in bits is 00000000 00000000 11111111 11111111

Fig. 20.6 Printing the bits in an integer (part 3 of 3).

Lines 68–69 append a **1** or a **0** to a **StringBuffer** for the current leftmost bit of variable **value**. Assume that **value** contains **4000000000 (11101110 01101011 00101000 00000000)**. When **value** and **displayMask** are combined using **&**, all the bits except the high-order (leftmost) bit in variable **value** are "masked off" (hidden), because any bit "ANDed" with **0** yields **0**. If the leftmost bit is **1**, **value & displayMask** evaluates to a nonzero value and **1** is appended; otherwise, **0** is appended. Then variable **value** is left shifted one bit by the expression **value <<= 1** (this is equivalent to **value = value << 1**). These steps are repeated for each bit in variable **value**. At the end of method **getBits**, the **StringBuffer** is converted to a **String** in line 79 and returned from the method. Figure 20.7 summarizes the results of combining two bits with the bitwise AND (**&**) operator.

Common Programming Error 20.1

*Using the logical AND operator (**&&**) for the bitwise AND operator (**&**) is a common programming error.*

Figure 20.8 demonstrates the bitwise AND operator, the bitwise inclusive OR operator, the bitwise exclusive OR operator and the bitwise complement operator. The program uses method **getBits** (lines 163–188) to get a **String** representation of the integer values. The program allows the user to enter values into **JTextField**s (for the binary operators, two values must be entered), and then to press the button representing the operation they would like to test. The program displays the result of each operation in both integer and bitwise representations.

The first output window for Fig. 20.8 shows the results of combining the value **65535** and the value **1** with the bitwise AND operator (**&**). All the bits except the low-order bit in the value **65535** are "masked off" (hidden) by "ANDing" with the value **1**.

Bit 1	Bit 2	Bit 1 & Bit 2
0	0	0
1	0	0
0	1	0
1	1	1

Fig. 20.7 Results of combining two bits with the bitwise AND operator (**&**).

```
1  // Fig. 20.8: MiscBitOps.java
2  // Using the bitwise AND, bitwise inclusive OR, bitwise
3  // exclusive OR, and bitwise complement operators.
4
5  // Java core packages
6  import java.awt.*;
7  import java.awt.event.*;
8
9  // Java extension packages
10 import javax.swing.*;
11
12 public class MiscBitOps extends JFrame {
13    private JTextField input1Field, input2Field,
14       bits1Field, bits2Field, bits3Field, resultField;
```

Fig. 20.8 Demonstrating the bitwise AND, bitwise inclusive OR, bitwise exclusive OR and bitwise complement operators (part 1 of 6).

```
   private int value1, value2;

   // set up GUI
   public MiscBitOps()
   {
      super( "Bitwise operators" );

      JPanel inputPanel = new JPanel();
      inputPanel.setLayout( new GridLayout( 4, 2 ) );

      inputPanel.add( new JLabel( "Enter 2 ints" ) );
      inputPanel.add( new JLabel( "" ) );

      inputPanel.add( new JLabel( "Value 1" ) );
      input1Field = new JTextField( 8 );
      inputPanel.add( input1Field );

      inputPanel.add( new JLabel( "Value 2" ) );
      input2Field = new JTextField( 8 );
      inputPanel.add( input2Field );

      inputPanel.add( new JLabel( "Result" ) );
      resultField = new JTextField( 8 );
      resultField.setEditable( false );
      inputPanel.add( resultField );

      JPanel bitsPanel = new JPanel();
      bitsPanel.setLayout( new GridLayout( 4, 1 ) );
      bitsPanel.add( new JLabel( "Bit representations" ) );

      bits1Field = new JTextField( 33 );
      bits1Field.setEditable( false );
      bitsPanel.add( bits1Field );

      bits2Field = new JTextField( 33 );
      bits2Field.setEditable( false );
      bitsPanel.add( bits2Field );

      bits3Field = new JTextField( 33 );
      bits3Field.setEditable( false );
      bitsPanel.add( bits3Field );

      JPanel buttonPanel = new JPanel();

      // button to perform bitwise AND
      JButton andButton = new JButton( "AND" );

      andButton.addActionListener(

         new ActionListener() {

```

Fig. 20.8 Demonstrating the bitwise AND, bitwise inclusive OR, bitwise exclusive OR and bitwise complement operators (part 2 of 6).

```
            // perform bitwise AND and display results
            public void actionPerformed( ActionEvent event )
            {
               setFields();
               resultField.setText(
                  Integer.toString( value1 & value2 ) );
               bits3Field.setText( getBits( value1 & value2 ) );
            }
         }
      );

      buttonPanel.add( andButton );

      // button to perform bitwise inclusive OR
      JButton inclusiveOrButton = new JButton( "Inclusive OR" );

      inclusiveOrButton.addActionListener(

         new ActionListener() {

            // perform bitwise inclusive OR and display results
            public void actionPerformed( ActionEvent event )
            {
               setFields();
               resultField.setText(
                  Integer.toString( value1 | value2 ) );
               bits3Field.setText( getBits( value1 | value2 ) );
            }
         }
      );

      buttonPanel.add( inclusiveOrButton );

      // button to perform bitwise exclusive OR
      JButton exclusiveOrButton = new JButton( "Exclusive OR" );

      exclusiveOrButton.addActionListener(

         new ActionListener() {

            // perform bitwise exclusive OR and display results
            public void actionPerformed( ActionEvent event )
            {
               setFields();
               resultField.setText(
                  Integer.toString( value1 ^ value2 ) );
               bits3Field.setText( getBits( value1 ^ value2 ) );
            }
         }
      );

      buttonPanel.add( exclusiveOrButton );
```

Fig. 20.8 Demonstrating the bitwise AND, bitwise inclusive OR, bitwise exclusive OR and bitwise complement operators (part 3 of 6).

```

      // button to perform bitwise complement
      JButton complementButton = new JButton( "Complement" );

      complementButton.addActionListener(

         new ActionListener() {

            // perform bitwise complement and display results
            public void actionPerformed( ActionEvent event )
            {
               input2Field.setText( "" );
               bits2Field.setText( "" );

               int value = Integer.parseInt( input1Field.getText() );

               resultField.setText( Integer.toString( ~value ) );
               bits1Field.setText( getBits( value ) );
               bits3Field.setText( getBits( ~value ) );
            }
         }
      );

      buttonPanel.add( complementButton );

      Container container = getContentPane();
      container.add( inputPanel, BorderLayout.WEST );
      container.add( bitsPanel, BorderLayout.EAST );
      container.add( buttonPanel, BorderLayout.SOUTH );

      setSize( 600, 150 );
      setVisible( true );
   }

   // display numbers and their bit form
   private void setFields()
   {
      value1 = Integer.parseInt( input1Field.getText() );
      value2 = Integer.parseInt( input2Field.getText() );

      bits1Field.setText( getBits( value1 ) );
      bits2Field.setText( getBits( value2 ) );
   }

   // display bit representation of specified int value
   private String getBits( int value )
   {
      // create int value with 1 in leftmost bit and 0s elsewhere
      int displayMask = 1 << 31;

      // buffer to build output
      StringBuffer buffer = new StringBuffer( 35 );
```

Fig. 20.8 Demonstrating the bitwise AND, bitwise inclusive OR, bitwise exclusive OR and bitwise complement operators (part 4 of 6).

```

      // for each bit append 0 or 1 to buffer
      for ( int bit = 1; bit <= 32; bit++ ) {

         // use displayMask to isolate bit and determine whether
         // bit has value of 0 or 1
         buffer.append(
            ( value & displayMask ) == 0 ? '0' : '1' );

         // shift value one position to left
         value <<= 1;

         // append space to buffer every 8 bits
         if ( bit % 8 == 0 )
            buffer.append( ' ' );
      }

      return buffer.toString();
   }

   // execute application
   public static void main( String args[] )
   {
      MiscBitOps application = new MiscBitOps();

      application.setDefaultCloseOperation(
         JFrame.EXIT_ON_CLOSE );
   }

}  // end class MiscBitOps
```

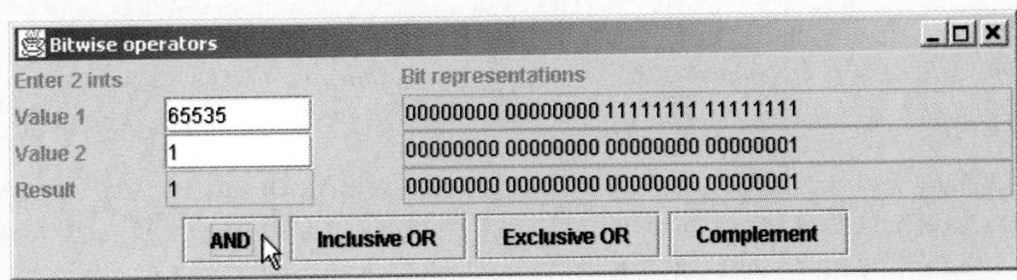

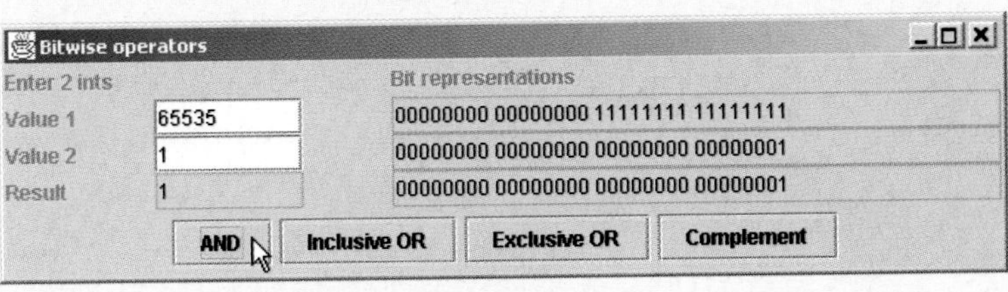

Fig. 20.8 Demonstrating the bitwise AND, bitwise inclusive OR, bitwise exclusive OR and bitwise complement operators (part 5 of 6).

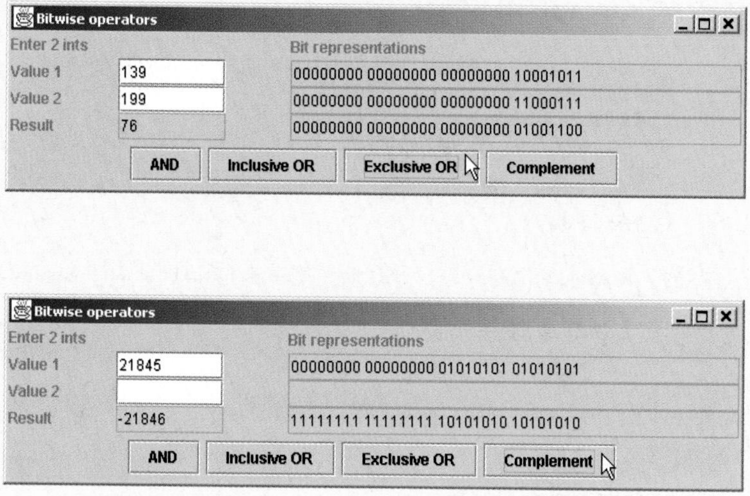

Fig. 20.8 Demonstrating the bitwise AND, bitwise inclusive OR, bitwise exclusive OR and bitwise complement operators (part 6 of 6).

The bitwise inclusive OR operator sets specific bits to 1 in an operand. The second output window for Fig. 20.8 shows the results of combining the value **`15`** and the value **`241`** by using the bitwise OR operator—the result is **`255`**. Figure 20.9 summarizes the results of combining two bits with the bitwise inclusive OR operator.

Common Programming Error 20.2

Using the logical OR operator (**`||`** *) for the bitwise OR operator (* **`|`** *) is a common programming error.*

The bitwise exclusive OR operator (**`^`**) sets each bit in the result to 1 if *exactly* one of the corresponding bits in its two operands is 1. The third output of Fig. 20.8 shows the results of combining the value **`139`** and the value **`199`** by using the exclusive OR operator—the result is **`76`**. Figure 20.10 summarizes the results of combining two bits with the bitwise exclusive OR operator.

Bit 1	Bit 2	Bit 1 | Bit 2
0	0	0
1	0	1
0	1	1
1	1	1

Fig. 20.9 Results of combining two bits with the bitwise inclusive OR operator (**`|`**).

Bit 1	Bit 2	Bit 1 ^ Bit 2
0	0	0
1	0	1
0	1	1
1	1	0

Fig. 20.10 Results of combining two bits with the bitwise exclusive OR operator (**^**).

The *bitwise* complement operator (**~**) sets all **1** bits in its operand to **0** in the result and sets all **0** bits to **1** in the result—otherwise referred to as "taking the *one's complement* of the value." The fourth output window for Fig. 20.8 shows the results of taking the one's complement of the value **21845**. The result is **-21846**.

The program of Fig. 20.11 demonstrates the *left shift operator* (**<<**), the *right shift operator with sign extension* (**>>**) and the *right shift operator with zero extension* (**>>>**). Method **getBits** (lines 113–138) obtains a **String** containing the bit representation of the integer values. The program allows the user to enter an integer into a **JTextField** and press *Enter* to display the bit representation of the integer in a second **JTextField**. The the user can press a button representing a shift operation to perform a 1-bit shift and view the results of the shift in both integer and bitwise representation.

```
1  // Fig. 20.11: BitShift.java
2  // Using the bitwise shift operators.
3
4  // Java core packages
5  import java.awt.*;
6  import java.awt.event.*;
7
8  // Java extension packages
9  import javax.swing.*;
10
11 public class BitShift extends JFrame {
12    private JTextField bitsField;
13    private JTextField valueField;
14
15    // set up GUI
16    public BitShift()
17    {
18       super( "Shifting bits" );
19
20       Container container = getContentPane();
21       container.setLayout( new FlowLayout() );
22
23       container.add( new JLabel( "Integer to shift " ) );
24
25       // textfield for user to input integer
26       valueField = new JTextField( 12 );
```

Fig. 20.11 Demonstrating the bitwise shift operators (part 1 of 5).

```
      container.add( valueField );

      valueField.addActionListener(

         new ActionListener() {

            // read value and display its bitwise representation
            public void actionPerformed( ActionEvent event )
            {
              int value = Integer.parseInt( valueField.getText() );
               bitsField.setText( getBits( value ) );
            }
         }
      );

      // textfield to display bitwise representation of an integer
      bitsField = new JTextField( 33 );
      bitsField.setEditable( false );
      container.add( bitsField );

      // button to shift bits left by one position
      JButton leftButton = new JButton( "<<" );

      leftButton.addActionListener(

         new ActionListener() {

            // left shift one position and display new value
            public void actionPerformed( ActionEvent event )
            {
              int value = Integer.parseInt( valueField.getText() );
               value <<= 1;
               valueField.setText( Integer.toString( value ) );
               bitsField.setText( getBits( value ) );
            }
         }
      );

      container.add( leftButton );

     // button to right shift value one position with sign extension
      JButton rightSignButton = new JButton( ">>" );

      rightSignButton.addActionListener(

         new ActionListener() {

            // right shift one position and display new value
            public void actionPerformed( ActionEvent event )
            {
              int value = Integer.parseInt( valueField.getText() );
               value >>= 1;
               valueField.setText( Integer.toString( value ) );
```

Fig. 20.11 Demonstrating the bitwise shift operators (part 2 of 5).

```
                bitsField.setText( getBits( value ) );
             }
          }
       );

       container.add( rightSignButton );

      // button to right shift value one position with zero extension
       JButton rightZeroButton = new JButton( ">>>" );

       rightZeroButton.addActionListener(

          new ActionListener() {

             // right shift one position and display new value
             public void actionPerformed( ActionEvent event )
             {
                int value = Integer.parseInt( valueField.getText() );
                value >>>= 1;
                valueField.setText( Integer.toString( value ) );

                bitsField.setText( getBits( value ) );
             }
          }
       );

       container.add( rightZeroButton );

       setSize( 400, 120 );
       setVisible( true );
    }

    // display bit representation of specified int value
    private String getBits( int value )
    {
       // create int value with 1 in leftmost bit and 0s elsewhere
       int displayMask = 1 << 31;

       // buffer to build output
       StringBuffer buffer = new StringBuffer( 35 );

       // for each bit append 0 or 1 to buffer
       for ( int bit = 1; bit <= 32; bit++ ) {

          // use displayMask to isolate bit and determine whether
          // bit has value of 0 or 1
          buffer.append(
             ( value & displayMask ) == 0 ? '0' : '1' );

          // shift value one position to left
          value <<= 1;

```

Fig. 20.11 Demonstrating the bitwise shift operators (part 3 of 5).

```
            // append space to buffer every 8 bits
            if ( bit % 8 == 0 )
               buffer.append( ' ' );
         }

         return buffer.toString();
      }

      // execute application
      public static void main( String args[] )
      {
         BitShift application = new BitShift();

         application.setDefaultCloseOperation(
            JFrame.EXIT_ON_CLOSE );
      }

   }  // end class BitShift
```

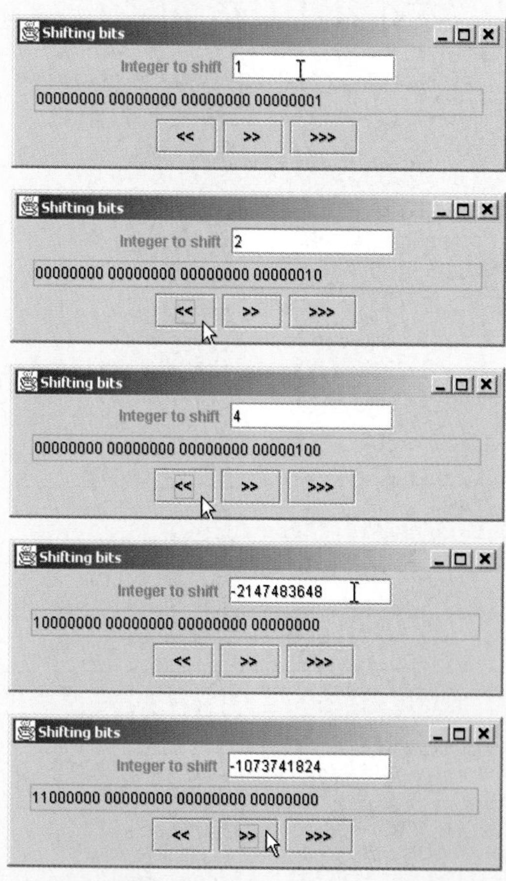

Fig. 20.11 Demonstrating the bitwise shift operators (part 4 of 5).

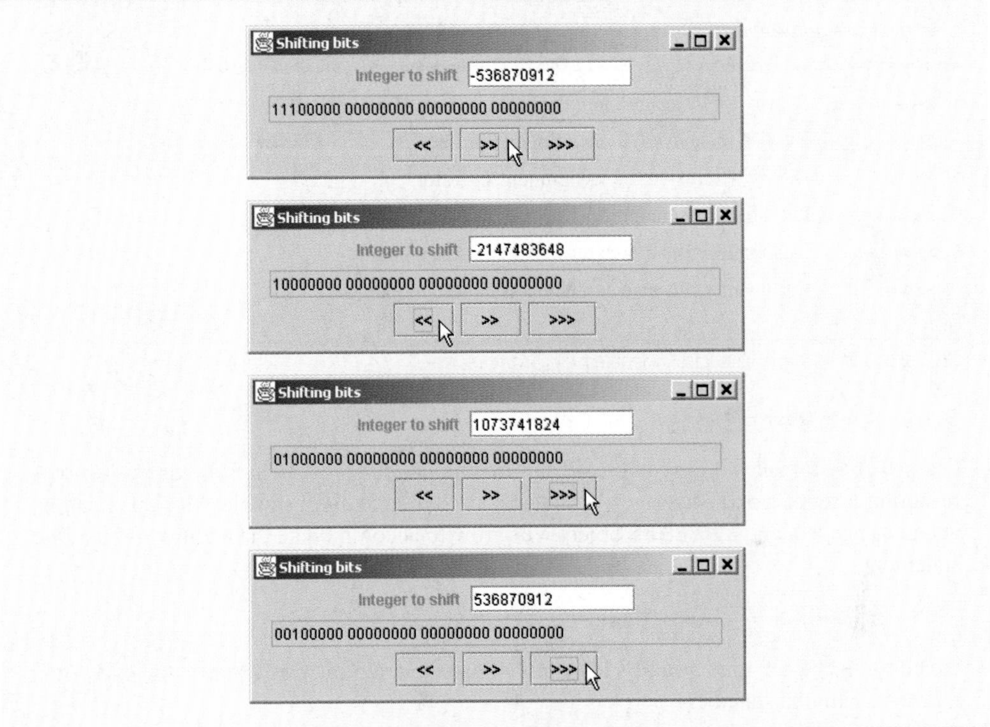

Shifting bits
Integer to shift -536870912
11100000 00000000 00000000 00000000
<< >> >>>

Shifting bits
Integer to shift -2147483648
10000000 00000000 00000000 00000000
<< >> >>>

Shifting bits
Integer to shift 1073741824
01000000 00000000 00000000 00000000
<< >> >>>

Shifting bits
Integer to shift 536870912
00100000 00000000 00000000 00000000
<< >> >>>

Fig. 20.11 Demonstrating the bitwise shift operators (part 5 of 5).

The left shift operator (**<<**) shifts the bits of its left operand to the left by the number of bits specified in its right operand (performed at line 58 in the program). Bits vacated to the right are replaced with **0**s; **1**s shifted off the left are lost. The first four output windows of Fig. 20.11 demonstrate the left shift operator. Starting with the value 1, the left shift button was pressed twice, resulting in the values 2 and 4, respectively. The fourth output window shows the result of **value1** being shifted 31 times. Note that the result is a negative value. That is because a 1 in the high-order bit is used to indicate a negative value in an integer.

The right shift operator with sign extension (**>>**) shifts the bits of its left operand to the right by the number of bits specified in its right operand (performed at line 78 in the program). Performing a right shift causes the vacated bits at the left to be replaced by **0**s if the number is positive or **1**s if the number is negative. Any **1**s shifted off the right are lost. The fifth and sixth output windows show the results of right shifting (with sign extension) the value in the fourth output window two times.

The right shift operator with zero extension (**>>>**) shifts the bits of its left operand to the right by the number of bits specified in its right operand (performed at line 98 in the program). Performing a right shift causes the vacated bits at the left to be replaced by **0**s. Any **1**s shifted off the right are lost. The eighth and ninth output windows show the results of right shifting (with zero extension) the value in the seventh output window two times.

Each bitwise operator (except the bitwise complement operator) has a corresponding assignment operator. These *bitwise assignment operators* are shown in Fig. 20.12.

Bitwise assignment operators	
`&=`	Bitwise AND assignment operator.
`|=`	Bitwise inclusive OR assignment operator.
`^=`	Bitwise exclusive OR assignment operator.
`<<=`	Left shift assignment operator.
`>>=`	Right shift with sign extension assignment operator.
`>>>=`	Right shift with zero extension assignment operator.

Fig. 20.12 The bitwise assignment operators.

20.9 `BitSet` Class

Class ***BitSet*** makes it easy to create and manipulate *bit sets*. Bit sets are useful for representing a set of **boolean** flags. **BitSet**s are dynamically resizable. More bits can be added as needed, and a **BitSet** object will grow to accommodate the additional bits. The statement

```
BitSet b = new BitSet();
```

creates a **BitSet** that initially is empty. Also, a program can specify the size of a **BitSet** with the statement

```
BitSet b = new BitSet( size );
```

which creates a **BitSet** with **size** bits.

The statement

```
b.set( bitNumber );
```

sets bit **bitNumber** "on." This makes the underlying value of that bit 1. Note that bit numbers are zero based, like **Vector**s. The statement

```
b.clear( bitNumber );
```

sets bit **bitNumber** "off." This makes the underlying value of that bit 0. The statement

```
b.get( bitNumber );
```

gets the value of bit **bitNumber**. The result is returned as **true** if the bit is on, **false** if the bit is off.

The statement

```
b.and( b1 );
```

performs a bit-by-bit logical AND between **BitSet**s **b** and **b1**. The result is stored in **b**. Bitwise logical OR and bitwise logical XOR are performed by the statements

```
b.or( b1 );
b.xor( b2 );
```

The expression

```
b.size()
```

returns the size of the **BitSet**. The expression

```
b.equals( b1 )
```

compares the two **BitSet**s for equality. The expression

```
b.toString()
```

creates a **String** representation of the **BitSet** contents. This is helpful for debugging.

Figure 20.13 revisits the Sieve of Eratosthenes for finding prime numbers, which we discussed in Exercise 7.27. This example uses a **BitSet** rather than an array to implement the algorithm. The program displays all the prime numbers from 2 to 1023 in a **JTextArea** and provides a **JTextField** in which the user can type any number from 2 to 1023 to determine whether that number is prime (in which case a message is displayed in a **JLabel**).

```
// Fig. 20.13: BitSetTest.java
// Using a BitSet to demonstrate the Sieve of Eratosthenes.

// Java core packages
import java.awt.*;
import java.awt.event.*;
import java.util.*;

// Java extension packages
import javax.swing.*;

public class BitSetTest extends JFrame {
   private BitSet sieve;
   private JLabel statusLabel;
   private JTextField inputField;

   // set up GUI
   public BitSetTest()
   {
      super( "BitSets" );

      sieve = new BitSet( 1024 );

      Container container = getContentPane();

      statusLabel = new JLabel( "" );
      container.add( statusLabel, BorderLayout.SOUTH );

      JPanel inputPanel = new JPanel();

      inputPanel.add( new JLabel(
         "Enter a value from 2 to 1023" ) );
```

Fig. 20.13 Demonstrating the Sieve of Eratosthenes using a **BitSet** (part 1 of 3).

```

      // textfield for user to input a value from 2 to 1023
      inputField = new JTextField( 10 );

      inputField.addActionListener(

         new ActionListener() {

            // determine whether value is prime number
            public void actionPerformed( ActionEvent event )
            {
              int value = Integer.parseInt( inputField.getText() );

               if ( sieve.get( value ) )
                  statusLabel.setText(
                     value + " is a prime number" );

               else
                  statusLabel.setText( value +
                     " is not a prime number" );
            }
         }
      );

      inputPanel.add( inputField );
      container.add( inputPanel, BorderLayout.NORTH );

      JTextArea primesArea = new JTextArea();

      container.add( new JScrollPane( primesArea ),
         BorderLayout.CENTER );

      // set all bits from 1 to 1023
      int size = sieve.size();

      for ( int i = 2; i < size; i++ )
         sieve.set( i );

      // perform Sieve of Eratosthenes
      int finalBit = ( int ) Math.sqrt( sieve.size() );

      for ( int i = 2; i < finalBit; i++ )

         if ( sieve.get( i ) )

            for ( int j = 2 * i; j < size; j += i )
               sieve.clear( j );

      // display prime numbers from 1 to 1023
      int counter = 0;

```

Fig. 20.13 Demonstrating the Sieve of Eratosthenes using a **BitSet** (part 2 of 3).

```
84         for ( int i = 2; i < size; i++ )
85
86            if ( sieve.get( i ) ) {
87               primesArea.append( String.valueOf( i ) );
88               primesArea.append( ++counter % 7 == 0 ? "\n" : "\t" );
89            }
90
91         setSize( 600, 450 );
92         setVisible( true );
93      }
94
95      // execute application
96      public static void main( String args[] )
97      {
98         BitSetTest application = new BitSetTest();
99
100        application.setDefaultCloseOperation(
101           JFrame.EXIT_ON_CLOSE );
102     }
103
104  }  // end class BitSetTest
```

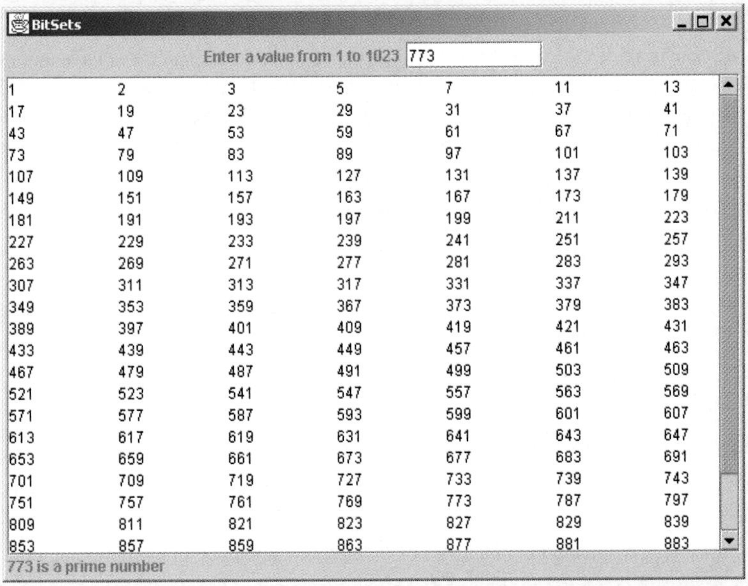

BitSets

Enter a value from 1 to 1023 773

1	2	3	5	7	11	13
17	19	23	29	31	37	41
43	47	53	59	61	67	71
73	79	83	89	97	101	103
107	109	113	127	131	137	139
149	151	157	163	167	173	179
181	191	193	197	199	211	223
227	229	233	239	241	251	257
263	269	271	277	281	283	293
307	311	313	317	331	337	347
349	353	359	367	373	379	383
389	397	401	409	419	421	431
433	439	443	449	457	461	463
467	479	487	491	499	503	509
521	523	541	547	557	563	569
571	577	587	593	599	601	607
613	617	619	631	641	643	647
653	659	661	673	677	683	691
701	709	719	727	733	739	743
751	757	761	769	773	787	797
809	811	821	823	827	829	839
853	857	859	863	877	881	883

773 is a prime number

Fig. 20.13 Demonstrating the Sieve of Eratosthenes using a **BitSet** (part 3 of 3).

Line 22 creates a **BitSet** of 1024 bits. We ignore the bit at index 0 in this program. Lines 68–69 set all the bits in the **BitSet** to on with **BitSet** method **set**. Lines 72–79 determine all the prime numbers from 2 to 1023. The integer **finalBit** specifies when the algorithm is complete. The basic algorithm is that a number is prime if it has no divisors other than 1 and itself. Starting with the number 2, once we know a number is prime, we can eliminate all multiples of that number. The number 2 is only divisible by 1 and itself, so it is prime. Therefore, we can eliminate 4, 6, 8 and so on. Elimination of a value consists of setting its bit to off with **BitSet** method **clear**. The number 3 is divisible by 1 and itself. Therefore, we can eliminate all multiples of 3 (keep in mind that all even numbers have already been eliminated). After the list of primes is displayed, the user can type a value from 2 to 1023 in the textfield and press enter to determine whether the number is prime. Method **actionPerformed** (lines 42–53) uses **BitSet** method **get** (line 46) to determine whether the bit for the number the user entered is set. If so, lines 47–48 display a message indicating that the number is prime. Otherwise, lines 51–52 display a message indicating that the number is not prime.

SUMMARY

- Class **Vector** manages dynamically resizable arrays. At any time the **Vector** contains a certain number of elements which is less than or equal to its capacity. The capacity is the space that has been reserved for the array.
- If a **Vector** needs to grow, it grows by an increment that you specify or by a default assumed by the system. If you do not specify a capacity increment, the system automatically doubles the size of the **Vector** each time additional capacity is required.
- **Vector**s store references to **Object**s. To store values of primitive data types in **Vector**s, use the type-wrapper classes (**Byte**, **Short**, **Integer**, **Long**, **Float**, **Double**, **Boolean** and **Character**) to create objects containing the primitive data type values.
- Class **Vector** provides three constructors. The no-argument constructor creates an empty **Vector**. The constructor that takes one argument creates a **Vector** with an initial capacity specified by the argument. The constructor that takes two arguments creates a **Vector** with an initial capacity specified by the first argument and a capacity increment specified by the second argument.
- **Vector** method **addElement** adds its argument to the end of the **Vector**. Method **insertElementAt** inserts an element at the specified position. Method **setElementAt** sets the element at a specific position.
- **Vector** method **removeElement** removes the first occurrence of its argument. Method **removeAllElements** removes every element from the **Vector**. Method **removeElementAt** removes the element at the specified index.
- **Vector** method **firstElement** returns a reference to the first element. Method **lastElement** returns a reference to the last element.
- **Vector** method **isEmpty** determines whether the **Vector** is empty.
- **Vector** method **contains** determines whether the **Vector** contains the **searchKey** specified as an argument.
- **Vector** method **indexOf** gets the index of the first location of its argument. The method returns **-1** if the argument is not found in the **Vector**.
- **Vector** method **trimToSize** cuts the capacity of the **Vector** to the **Vector**'s size. Methods **size** and **capacity** determine the number of elements currently in the **Vector** and the number of elements that can be stored in the **Vector** without allocating more memory, respectively.
- **Vector** method **elements** returns a reference to an **Enumeration** containing the elements of the **Vector**.
- **Enumeration** method **hasMoreElements** determines whether there are more elements. Method **nextElement** returns a reference to the next element.
- Class **Stack** extends class **Vector**. **Stack** method **push** adds its argument to the top of the stack. Method **pop** removes the top element of the stack. Method **peek** returns an **Object** ref-

erence to the top element of the stack without removing the element. **Stack** method **empty** determines whether the stack is empty.

- A **Dictionary** transforms keys to values.
- Hashing is a high-speed scheme for converting keys into unique array subscripts for storage and retrieval of information.The load factor is the ratio of the number of occupied cells in a hash table to the size of the hash table. The closer this ratio gets to 1.0, the greater the chance of collisions.
- The no-argument **Hashtable** constructor creates a **Hashtable** with a default capacity of 101 elements and a default load factor of .75. The **Hashtable** constructor that takes one argument specifies the initial capacity; the constructor that takes two arguments specifies the initial capacity and load factor, respectively.
- **Hashtable** method **put** adds a key and a value into a **Hashtable**. Method **get** locates the value associated with the specified key. Method **remove** deletes the value associated with the specified key. Method **isEmpty** determines whether the table is empty.
- **Hashtable** method **containsKey** determines whether the key specified as an argument is in the **Hashtable** (i.e., a value is associated with that key). Method **contains** determines whether the **Object** specified as its argument is in the **Hashtable**. Method **clear** empties the **Hashtable**. Method **elements** obtains an **Enumeration** of the values. Method **keys** obtains an **Enumeration** of the keys.
- A **Properties** object is a persistent **Hashtable** object. Class **Properties** extends **Hashtable**. Keys and values in a **Properties** object must be **String**s.
- The **Properties** no-argument constructor creates an empty **Properties** table with no default properties. There is also an overloaded constructor that is passed a reference to a default **Properties** object containing default property values.
- **Properties** method **getProperty** locates the value of the key specified as an argument. Method **store** saves the contents of the **Properties** object to the **OutputStream** object specified as the first argument. Method **load** restores the contents of the **Properties** object from the **InputStream** object specified as the argument. Method **propertyNames** obtains an **Enumeration** of the property names.
- Java provides extensive random-number generation capabilities in class **Random**. Class **Random**'s no-argument constructor uses the time to seed its random-number generator differently each time it is called. To create a pseudorandom-number generator with repeatability, use the **Random** constructor that takes a seed argument.
- **Random** method **setSeed** sets the seed. Methods **nextInt** and **nextLong** generate uniformly distributed random integers. Methods **nextFloat** and **nextDouble** generate uniformly distributed values in the range $0.0 <= x < 1.0$.
- The bitwise AND (**&**) operator sets each bit in the result to 1 if the corresponding bit in both operands is 1.
- The bitwise inclusive OR (**|**) operator sets each bit in the result to 1 if the corresponding bit in either (or both) operand(s) is 1.
- The bitwise exclusive OR (**^**) operator sets each bit in the result to 1 if the corresponding bit in exactly one operand is 1.
- The left shift (**<<**) operator shifts the bits of its left operand to the left by the number of bits specified in its right operand.
- The right shift operator with sign extension (**>>**) shifts the bits in its left operand to the right by the number of bits specified in its right operand—if the left operand is negative, **1**s are shifted in from the left; otherwise, **0**s are shifted in from the left.

- The right shift operator with zero extension (**>>>**) shifts the bits in its left operand to the right by the number of bits specified in its right operand—**0**s are shifted in from the left.
- The bitwise complement (**~**) operator sets all **0** bits in its operand to **1** in the result and sets all **1** bits to **0** in the result.
- Each bitwise operator (except complement) has a corresponding assignment operator.
- The no-argument **BitSet** constructor creates an empty **BitSet**. The one-argument **BitSet** constructor creates a **BitSet** with the number of bits specified by its argument.
- **BitSet** method **set** sets the specified bit "on." Method **clear** sets the specified bit "off." Method **get** returns **true** if the bit is on, **false** if the bit is off.
- **BitSet** method **and** performs a bit-by-bit logical AND between **BitSet**s. The result is stored in the **BitSet** that invoked the method. Similarly, bitwise logical OR and bitwise logical XOR are performed by methods **or** and **xor**.
- **BitSet** method **size** returns the size of a **BitSet**. Method **toString** converts a **BitSet** to a **String**.

TERMINOLOGY

addElement method of class **Vector**
and method of class **BitSet**
bit set
BitSet class
bitwise assignment operators
    &= (bitwise AND)
    ^= (bitwise exclusive OR)
    |= (bitwise inclusive OR)
    <<= (left shift)
    >>= (right shift)
    >>>= (right shift with zero extension)
bitwise manipulation operators
    & bitwise AND
    ^ bitwise exclusive OR
    | bitwise inclusive OR
    ~ one's complement
    << left shift
    >> right shift
    >>> right shift with zero extension
capacity increment of a **Vector**
capacity method of class **Vector**
capacity of a **Vector**
clear method of class **BitSet**
clear method of class **Hashtable**
clone method of class **BitSet**
collision in hashing
contains method of class **Vector**
containsKey method of class **Hashtable**
defaults
Dictionary class
dynamically resizable array
elementAt method of class **Vector**
elements method of class **Dictionary**
elements method of class **Vector**
EmptyStackException class
enumerate successive elements
Enumeration interface
equals method of class **Object**
firstElement method of class **Vector**
get method of class **BitSet**
get method of class **Dictionary**
getProperty method of class **Properties**
hashCode method of class **Object**
hashing
Hashtable class
hasMoreElements method (**Enumeration**)
indexOf method of class **Vector**
initial capacity of a **Vector**
insertElementAt method of class **Vector**
isEmpty method of class **Dictionary**
isEmpty method of class **Vector**
iterate through container elements
java.util package
key in a **Dictionary**
key/value pair
keys method of class **Dictionary**
lastElement method of class **Vector**
list method of class **Properties**
load factor in hashing
load method of class **Properties**
nextDouble method of class **Random**
nextElement method of **Enumeration**
nextFloat method of class **Random**
nextInt method of class **Random**

nextLong method of class **Random**
NoSuchElementException class
NullPointerException
or method of class **BitSet**
peek method of class **Stack**
persistent hash table
pop method of class **Stack**
Properties class
propertyNames method of **Properties**
pseudorandom numbers
push method of class **Stack**
put method of class **Dictionary**
Random class
remove method of class **Dictionary**
removeAllElements method of **Vector**
removeElement method of class **Vector**
removeElementAt method of class **Vector**
search method of class **Stack**
seed of a random-number generator
set method of class **BitSet**
setElementAt method of class **Vector**
setSeed method of class **Random**
setSize method of class **Vector**
size method of class **Dictionary**
size method of class **Vector**
Stack class
store method of class **Properties**
trimToSize method of class **Vector**
Vector class
white-space characters
xor method of class **BitSet**

SELF-REVIEW EXERCISES

20.1 Fill in the blanks in each of the following statements:

a) Java class ________ provides the capabilities of array-like data structures that can resize themselves dynamically.
b) If you do not specify a capacity increment, the system will ________ the size of the **Vector** each time additional capacity is needed.
c) If storage is at a premium, use the ________ method of the **Vector** class to trim a **Vector** to its exact size.

20.2 State whether each of the following is *true* or *false*. If *false*, explain why.

a) Values of primitive data types may be stored directly in a **Vector**.
b) With hashing, as the load factor increases, the chance of collisions decreases.

20.3 Under what circumstances is an **EmptyStackException** thrown?

20.4 Fill in the blanks in each of the following statements:

a) Bits in the result of an expression using operator ________ are set to 1 if the corresponding bits in each operand are set to 1. Otherwise, the bits are set to zero.
b) Bits in the result of an expression using operator ________ are set to 1 if at least one of the corresponding bits in either operand is set to 1. Otherwise, the bits are set to zero.
c) Bits in the result of an expression using operator ________ are set to 1 if exactly one of the corresponding bits in either operand is set to 1. Otherwise, the bits are set to zero.
d) The bitwise AND operator (**&**) is often used to ________ bits, that is, to select certain bits from a bit string while zeroing others.
e) The ________ operator is used to shift the bits of a value to the left.
f) The ________ operator shifts the bits of a value to the right with sign extension, and the ________ operator shifts the bits of a value to the right with zero extension.

ANSWERS TO SELF-REVIEW EXERCISES

20.1 a) **Vector**. b) double. c) **trimToSize**.

20.2 a) False; a **Vector** stores only **Object**s. A program must use the type-wrapper classes (**Byte**, **Short**, **Integer**, **Long**, **Float**, **Double**, **Boolean** and **Character**) from package **java.lang** to create **Object**s containing the primitive data type values. b) False; as the load factor increases, there are fewer available slots relative to the total number of slots, so the chance of selecting an occupied slot (a collision) with a hashing operation increases.

20.3 When a program calls **pop** or **peek** on an empty **Stack** object, an **EmptyStackException** occurs.

20.4 a) bitwise AND (**&**). b) bitwise inclusive OR (**|**). c) bitwise exclusive OR (**^**). d) mask. e) left shift operator (**<<**). f) right shift operator with sign extension (**>>**), right shift operator with zero extension (**>>>**).

EXERCISES

20.5 Define each of the following terms in the context of hashing:

a) key
b) collision
c) hashing transformation
d) load factor
e) space–time trade-off
f) **Hashtable** class
g) capacity of a **Hashtable**

20.6 Explain briefly the operation of each of the following methods of class **Vector**:

a) **addElement**
b) **insertElementAt**
c) **setElementAt**
d) **removeElement**
e) **removeAllElements**
f) **removeElementAt**
g) **firstElement**
h) **lastElement**
i) **isEmpty**
j) **contains**
k) **indexOf**
l) **trimToSize**
m) **size**
n) **capacity**

20.7 Explain why inserting additional elements into a **Vector** object whose current size is less than its capacity is a relatively fast operation and why inserting additional elements into a **Vector** object whose current size is at capacity is a relatively slow operation.

20.8 In the text, we state that the default capacity increment of doubling the size of a **Vector** might seem wasteful of storage, but it is actually an efficient way for **Vector**s to grow quickly to be "about the right size." Explain this statement. Explain the pros and cons of this doubling algorithm. What can a program do when it determines that the doubling is wasting space?

20.9 Explain the use of the **Enumeration** interface with objects of class **Vector**.

20.10 By extending class **Vector**, Java's designers were able to create class **Stack** quickly. What are the negative aspects of this use of inheritance, particularly for class **Stack**?

20.11 Explain briefly the operation of each of the following methods of class **Hashtable**:

a) **put**
b) **get**
c) **remove**
d) **isEmpty**

e) **containsKey**
f) **contains**
g) **clear**
h) **elements**
i) **keys**

20.12 Explain how to use the **Random** class to create pseudorandom numbers with the repeatability required for debugging purposes.

20.13 Use a **Hashtable** to create a reusable class for choosing one of the 13 predefined colors in class **Color**. The name of the color should be used as keys and the predefined **Color** objects should be used as values. Place this class in a package that can be imported into any Java program. Use your new class in an application that allows the user to select a color and draw a shape in that color.

20.14 Modify your solution to Exercise 13.18—the polymorphic painting program—to store every shape the user draws in a **Vector** of **MyShape** objects. For the purpose of this exercise, create your own **Vector** subclass called **ShapeVector** that manipulates only **MyShape** objects. Provide the following capabilities in your program:

a) Allow the user of the program to remove any number of shapes from the **Vector** by clicking an **Undo** button.
b) Allow the user to select any shape on the screen and move it to a new location. This requires the addition of a new method to the **MyShape** hierarchy. The method's first line should be

```
public boolean isInside()
```

This method should be overridden for each subclass of **MyShape** to determine whether the coordinates where the user pressed the mouse button are inside the shape.
c) Allow the user to select any shape on the screen and change its color.
d) Allow the user to select any shape on the screen that can be filled or unfilled and change its fill state.

20.15 What does it mean when we state that a **Properties** object is a "persistent" **Hashtable** object? Explain the operation of each of the following methods of the **Properties** class:

a) **load**
b) **store**
c) **getProperty**
d) **propertyNames**
e) **list**

20.16 Why might you want to use objects of class **BitSet**? Explain the operation of each of the following methods of class **BitSet**:

a) **set**
b) **clear**
c) **get**
d) **and**
e) **or**
f) **xor**
g) **size**
h) **equals**
i) **clone**
j) **toString**
k) **hashCode**

20.17 Write a program that right shifts an integer variable 4 bits with sign extension and then right shifts the same integer variable 4 bits with zero extension. The program should print the integer in bits before and after each shift operation. Run your program once with a positive integer and once with a negative integer.

20.18 Show how shifting an integer left by 1 can be used to simulate multiplication by 2 and how shifting an integer right by 2 can be used to simulate division by 2. Be careful to consider issues related to the sign of an integer.

20.19 Write a program that reverses the order of the bits in an integer value. The program should input the value from the user and call method **`reverseBits`** to print the bits in reverse order. Print the value in bits both before and after the bits are reversed to confirm that the bits are reversed properly. You might want to implement both a recursive and an iterative solution.

20.20 Modify your solution to Exercise 19.10 to use class **`Stack`**.

20.21 Modify your solution to Exercise 19.12 to use class **`Stack`**.

20.22 Modify your solution to Exercise 19.13 to use class **`Stack`**.

21

Collections

Objectives

- To understand what collections are.
- To understand Java 2's new array capabilities.
- To use the collections framework implementations.
- To be able to use collections framework algorithms to manipulate various collections.
- To be able to use the collections framework interfaces to program polymorphically.
- To be able to use iterators to walk through the elements of a collection.
- To understand synchronization wrappers and modifiability wrappers.

I think this is the most extraordinary collection of talent, of human knowledge, that has ever been gathered together at the White House—with the possible exception of when Thomas Jefferson dines alone.
John F. Kennedy

The shapes a bright container can contain!
Theodore Roethke

Journey over all the universe in a map.
Miguel de Cervantes

It is an immutable law in business that words are words, explanations are explanations, promises are promises — but only performance is reality.
Harold S. Green

Outline

21.1 Introduction
21.2 Collections Overview
21.3 Class **Arrays**
21.4 Interface **Collection** and Class **Collections**
21.5 Lists
21.6 Algorithms
21.6.1 Algorithm **sort**
21.6.2 Algorithm **shuffle**
21.6.3 Algorithms **reverse**, **fill**, **copy**, **max** and **min**
21.6.4 Algorithm **binarySearch**
21.7 Sets
21.8 Maps
21.9 Synchronization Wrappers
21.10 Unmodifiable Wrappers
21.11 Abstract Implementations
21.12 (Optional) Discovering Design Patterns: Design Patterns Used in Package **java.util**

Summary • Terminology • Self-Review Exercises • Answers to Self-Review Exercises • Exercises

21.1 Introduction

In Chapter 19, we discussed how to create and manipulate data structures. The discussion was "low level," in the sense that we painstakingly created each element of each data structure dynamically with **new** and modified the data structures by directly manipulating their elements and references to their elements. In this chapter, we consider the Java collections framework, which gives the programmer access to prepackaged data structures, as well as algorithms for manipulating those data structures.

With collections, instead of creating data structures, the programmer simply uses existing data structures, without concern for how the data structures are implemented. This methodology is a marvelous example of code reuse. Programmers can code faster and can expect excellent performance, maximizing execution speed and minimizing memory consumption. We will discuss the interfaces of the collections framework, the implementation classes, the algorithms that process them and the *iterators* that "walk" through them.

Some examples of collections are the cards you hold in a card game, your favorite songs stored in your computer and the real-estate records in your local registry of deeds (which map book numbers and page numbers to property owners). Java 2 provides an entire collections framework, whereas earlier versions of Java provided just a few collection classes, such as **Hashtable**, **Stack** and **Vector** (see Chapter 20), as well as built-in array capabilities. If you know C++, you will be familiar with its collections framework, which is called the Standard Template Library (STL). (See Chapter 20 of *C++ How to Program, Third Edition*, by H. M. Deitel and P. J. Deitel, ©2001, Prentice Hall).

The Java collections framework provides ready-to-go, reusable componentry; you do not need to write your own collection classes. The collections are standardized so applications can share them easily, without having to be concerned with the details of their implementation. These collections are written for broad reuse. They are tuned for rapid execution as well as efficient use of memory. The collections framework encourages further reusability. As new data structures and algorithms are developed that fit this framework, a large base of programmers already will be familiar with the interfaces and algorithms implemented by those data structures.

21.2 Collections Overview

A collection is a data structure—actually, an object—that can hold other objects. The collection interfaces define the operations that a program can perform on each type of collection. The collection implementations execute the operations in particular ways, some more appropriate than others for specific kinds of applications. Thecollection implementations are carefully constructed for rapid execution and efficient use of memory. Collections encourage software reuse by providing convenient functionality.

The collections framework provides interfaces that define the operations to be performed generically on various types of collections. Some of the interfaces are **Collection**, **Set**, **List** and **Map**. Several implementations of these interfaces are provided within the framework. Programmers may also provide implementations specific to their own requirements.

The collections framework includes a number of other features that minimize the amount of coding programmers need to do to create and manipulate collections.

The classes and interfaces that comprise the collections framework are members of package **java.util**. In the next section, we begin our discussion by examining the capabilities that have been added for array manipulation.

21.3 Class Arrays

We begin our discussion of the collections framework by looking at class ***Arrays***, which provides **static** methods for manipulating arrays. In Chapter 7, our discussion of array manipulation was "low level," in the sense that we wrote the actual code to sort and search arrays. Class **Arrays** provides "high-level" methods, such as ***binarySearch*** for searching a sorted array, ***equals*** for comparing arrays, ***fill*** for placing values into an array and ***sort*** for sorting an array. These methods are overloaded for primitive-type arrays and **Object** arrays. Figure 21.1 demonstrates the use of these methods.

```
// Fig. 21.1: UsingArrays.java
// Using Java arrays.

// Java core packages
import java.util.*;
```

Fig. 21.1 Using methods of class **Arrays** (part 1 of 3).

```java

public class UsingArrays {
   private int intValues[] = { 1, 2, 3, 4, 5, 6 };
   private double doubleValues[] = { 8.4, 9.3, 0.2, 7.9, 3.4 };
   private int filledInt[], intValuesCopy[];

   // initialize arrays
   public UsingArrays()
   {
      filledInt = new int[ 10 ];
      intValuesCopy = new int[ intValues.length ];

      Arrays.fill( filledInt, 7 );   // fill with 7s

      Arrays.sort( doubleValues );   // sort doubleValues

      System.arraycopy( intValues, 0, intValuesCopy,
         0, intValues.length );
   }

   // output values in each array
   public void printArrays()
   {
      System.out.print( "doubleValues: " );

      for ( int count = 0; count < doubleValues.length; count++ )
         System.out.print( doubleValues[ count ] + " " );

      System.out.print( "\nintValues: " );

      for ( int count = 0; count < intValues.length; count++ )
         System.out.print( intValues[ count ] + " " );

      System.out.print( "\nfilledInt: " );

      for ( int count = 0; count < filledInt.length; count++ )
         System.out.print( filledInt[ count ] + " " );

      System.out.print( "\nintValuesCopy: " );

      for ( int count = 0; count < intValuesCopy.length; count++ )
         System.out.print( intValuesCopy[ count ] + " " );

      System.out.println();
   }

   // find value in array intValues
   public int searchForInt( int value )
   {
      return Arrays.binarySearch( intValues, value );
   }

```

Fig. 21.1 Using methods of class **Arrays** (part 2 of 3).

```
58      // compare array contents
59      public void printEquality()
60      {
61         boolean b = Arrays.equals( intValues, intValuesCopy );
62
63         System.out.println( "intValues " + ( b ? "==" : "!=" )
64                             + " intValuesCopy" );
65
66         b = Arrays.equals( intValues, filledInt );
67
68         System.out.println( "intValues " + ( b ? "==" : "!=" )
69                             + " filledInt" );
70      }
71
72      // execute application
73      public static void main( String args[] )
74      {
75         UsingArrays usingArrays = new UsingArrays();
76
77         usingArrays.printArrays();
78         usingArrays.printEquality();
79
80         int location = usingArrays.searchForInt( 5 );
81         System.out.println( ( location >= 0 ?
82            "Found 5 at element " + location : "5 not found" ) +
83            " in intValues" );
84
85         location = usingArrays.searchForInt( 8763 );
86         System.out.println( ( location >= 0 ?
87            "Found 8763 at element " + location :
88            "8763 not found" ) + " in intValues" );
89      }
90
91   }  // end class UsingArrays
```

```
doubleValues: 0.2 3.4 7.9 8.4 9.3
intValues: 1 2 3 4 5 6
filledInt: 7 7 7 7 7 7 7 7 7 7
intValuesCopy: 1 2 3 4 5 6
intValues == intValuesCopy
intValues != filledInt
Found 5 at element 4 in intValues
8763 not found in intValues
```

Fig. 21.1 Using methods of class **Arrays** (part 3 of 3).

Line 18 calls **Arrays static** method **fill** to populate all 10 elements of array **filledInt** with **7**s. Overloaded versions of **fill** allow the programmer to populate a specific range of elements with the same value.

Line 20 sorts the elements of array **doubleValues**. Overloaded versions of **sort** allow the programmer to sort a specific range of elements. **Arrays static** method **sort** orders the array's elements in ascending order by default. We discuss how to sort in descending order later in the chapter.

Lines 22–23 copy array **intValues** into array **intValuesCopy**. The first argument (**intValues**) passed to **System static** method ***arraycopy*** is the array from which elements are copied. The second argument (**0**) is the array (i.e., **intValues**) subscript that specifies the starting point in the range of elements to copy. This value can be any valid array subscript. The third argument (**intValuesCopy**) specifies the array that stores the copy. The fourth argument (**0**) specifies the subscript in the destination array (i.e., **intValues-Copy**) where the first copied element is stored. The last argument (**intValues.length**) specifies the number of source-array (i.e., **intValues**) elements to copy.

Line 55 calls **Arrays static** method **binarySearch** to perform a binary search on **intValues**, using **value** as the key. If **value** is found, **binarySearch** returns the subscript location where **value** was found. If **value** is not found, **binarySearch** returns a negative value. The negative value returned is based on the search key's *insertion point*—the index where the key would be inserted in the binary search tree if this were an insert operation. After **binarySearch** determines the insertion point, it changes the insertion point's sign to negative and subtracts **1** to obtain the return value. For example, in Fig. 21.1, the insertion point for the value **8763** is the element with subscript **6** in the array. Method **binarySearch** changes the insertion point to **-6** and subtracts **1** from it, then returns the value **-7**. This return value is useful for adding elements to a sorted array.

Common Programming Error 21.1

Passing an unsorted array to ***binarySearch*** *is a logic error. The value returned by* ***binarySearch*** *is undefined.*

Lines 61 and 66 call method **equals** to determine whether the elements of two arrays are equivalent. If they are equal, method **equals** returns **true**; otherwise, it returns **false**.

One of the most important features of the collection framework is the ability to manipulate the elements of one collection type through a different collection type, regardless of the collection's internal implementation. The **public** set of methods through which collections are manipulated is called a *view*.

Class **Arrays** provides **static** method ***asList*** for viewing an array as a ***List*** collection type (a type that encapsulates behavior similar to that of the linked lists created in Chapter 19; we will say more about **List**s later in the chapter). A **List** view allows the programmer to manipulate the array programmatically as if it were a **List** by calling **List** methods. Any modifications made through the **List** view change the array, and any modifications made to the array change the **List** view. Figure 21.2 demonstrates method **asList**.

```
// Fig. 21.2: UsingAsList.java
// Using method asList

// Java core packages
import java.util.*;

public class UsingAsList {
   private String values[] = { "red", "white", "blue" };
   private List list;

```

Fig. 21.2 Using **static** method **asList** (part 1 of 2).

```
11    // initialize List and set value at location 1
12    public UsingAsList()
13    {
14       list = Arrays.asList( values );   // get List
15       list.set( 1, "green" );           // change a value
16    }
17
18    // output List and array
19    public void printElements()
20    {
21       System.out.print( "List elements : " );
22
23       for ( int count = 0; count < list.size(); count++ )
24          System.out.print( list.get( count ) + " " );
25
26       System.out.print( "\nArray elements: " );
27
28       for ( int count = 0; count < values.length; count++ )
29          System.out.print( values[ count ] + " " );
30
31       System.out.println();
32    }
33
34    // execute application
35    public static void main( String args[] )
36    {
37       new UsingAsList().printElements();
38    }
39
40 }  // end class UsingAsList
```

```
List elements : red green blue
Array elements: red green blue
```

Fig. 21.2 Using **static** method **asList** (part 2 of 2).

Line 9 declares a **List** reference called **list**. Line 14 uses **static Arrays** method **asList** to obtain a fixed-size **List** view of array **values**.

Performance Tip 21.1

Arrays.asList *creates a fixed-size* ***List*** *that operates faster than any of the provided* ***List*** *implementations.*

Common Programming Error 21.2

A ***List*** *created with* ***Arrays.asList*** *is fixed in size; calling methods* ***add*** *or* ***remove*** *throws an* ***UnsupportedOperationException***

Line 15 calls **List** method **set** to change the contents of **List** element **1** to **"green"**. Because the program views the array as a **List**, line 15 changes array element **values[1]** from **"white"** to **"green"**. Any changes made to the **List** view are made to the underlying array object.

Software Engineering Observation 21.1

With the collections framework, there are many methods that apply to **`List`***s and* **`Collection`***s that you would like to be able to use for arrays.* **`Arrays.asList`** *allows you to pass an array into a* **`List`** *or* **`Collection`** *parameter.*

Line 23 calls **`List`** method ***`size`*** to get the number of items in the **`List`**. Line 24 calls **`List`** method ***`get`*** to retrieve an individual item from the **`List`**. Notice that the value returned by **`size`** is equal to the number of elements in array **`values`** and that the items returned by **`get`** are the elements of array **`values`**.

21.4 Interface `Collection` and Class `Collections`

Interface ***`Collection`*** is the root interface in the collections hierarchy from which interfaces **`Set`** (a collection that does not contain duplicates—discussed in Section 21.7) and **`List`** are derived. Interface **`Collection`** contains *bulk operations* (i.e., operations performed on the entire collection) for adding, clearing, comparing and retaining objects (also called *elements*) in the collection. **`Collection`**s can also be converted to arrays. In addition, interface **`Collection`** provides a method that returns an ***`Iterator`***. **`Iterator`**s are similar to the **`Enumeration`**s introduced in Chapter 20. The primary difference between an **`Iterator`** and an **`Enumeration`** is that **`Iterator`**s can remove elements from a collection, whereas **`Enumeration`**s cannot. Other methods of interface **`Collection`** enable a program to determine a collection's size, a collection's hash code and whether a collection is empty.

Software Engineering Observation 21.2

`Collection` *is used commonly as a method parameter type to allow polymorphic processing of all objects that implement interface* **`Collection`**.

Software Engineering Observation 21.3

Most collection implementations provide a constructor that takes a **`Collection`** *argument, thereby allowing one collection type to be treated as another collection type.*

Class ***`Collections`*** provides **`static`** methods that manipulate collections polymorphically. These methods implement algorithms for searching, sorting, and so on. You will learn more about these algorithms in Section 21.6. Other **`Collections`** methods include *wrapper methods* that return new collections. We discuss wrapper methods in Section 21.9 and Section 21.10.

21.5 Lists

A **`List`** is an ordered **`Collection`** that can contain duplicate elements. A **`List`** is sometimes called a *sequence*. Like arrays, **`List`**s are zero based (i.e., the first element's *index* is zero). In addition to the interface methods inherited from **`Collection`**, **`List`** provides methods for manipulating elements via their indices, manipulating a specified range of elements, searching the elements and getting a ***`ListIterator`*** to access the elements.

Interface **`List`** is implemented by classes ***`ArrayList`***, ***`LinkedList`*** and **`Vector`**. Class **`ArrayList`** is a resizable-array implementation of a **`List`**. Class **`ArrayList`**'s behavior and capabilities are similar to those of the **`Vector`** class, introduced in Chapter 20. A **`LinkedList`** is a linked-list implementation of a **`List`**.

Performance Tip 21.2

`ArrayList`s behave like un`synchronized` `Vector`s and therefore execute faster than `Vector`s, because `ArrayList`s are not thread safe.

`LinkedList`s can be used to create stacks, queues, trees and deques (double-ended queues).

Figure 21.3 uses an **`ArrayList`** to demonstrate some of the capabilities of **`Collection`** interfaces. The program places **`String`**s and **`Color`**s in an **`ArrayList`** and uses an **`Iterator`** to remove the **`String`**s from the **`ArrayList`** collection.

```
// Fig. 21.3: CollectionTest.java
// Using the Collection interface

// Java core packages
import java.awt.Color;
import java.util.*;

public class CollectionTest {
   private String colors[] = { "red", "white", "blue" };

   // create ArrayList, add objects to it and manipulate it
   public CollectionTest()
   {
      ArrayList list = new ArrayList();

      // add objects to list
      list.add( Color.magenta );     // add a color object

      for ( int count = 0; count < colors.length; count++ )
         list.add( colors[ count ] );

      list.add( Color.cyan );        // add a color object

      // output list contents
      System.out.println( "\nArrayList: " );

      for ( int count = 0; count < list.size(); count++ )
         System.out.print( list.get( count ) + " " );

      // remove all String objects
      removeStrings( list );

      // output list contents
      System.out.println( "\n\nArrayList after calling" +
         " removeStrings: " );

      for ( int count = 0; count < list.size(); count++ )
         System.out.print( list.get( count ) + " " );
   }
```

Fig. 21.3 Using an **`ArrayList`** to demonstrate interface **`Collection`** (part 1 of 2).

```
40
41     // remove String objects from Collection
42     public void removeStrings( Collection collection )
43     {
44        // get iterator
45        Iterator iterator = collection.iterator();
46
47        // loop while collection has items
48        while ( iterator.hasNext() )
49
50           if ( iterator.next() instanceof String )
51              iterator.remove();  // remove String object
52     }
53
54     // execute application
55     public static void main( String args[] )
56     {
57        new CollectionTest();
58     }
59
60  }  // end class CollectionTest
```

```
ArrayList:
java.awt.Color[r=255,g=0,b=255] red white blue java.awt.Color
[r=0,g=255,b=255]

ArrayList after calling removeStrings:
java.awt.Color[r=255,g=0,b=255] java.awt.Color[r=0,g=255,b=255]
```

Fig. 21.3 Using an **ArrayList** to demonstrate interface **Collection** (part 2 of 2).

Line 14 creates reference **list** and initializes it with an instance of an **ArrayList**. Lines 17–22 populate **list** with **Color** and **String** objects. Lines 25–28 output each element of **list**. Line 27 calls **List** method ***size*** to get the number of **ArrayList** elements. Line 28 uses **List** method ***get*** to retrieve individual element values. Line 31 calls programmer-defined method **removeStrings** (defined on lines 42–52), passing **list** to it as an argument. Method **removeStrings** deletes **String**s from a collection. Lines 34–38 print the elements of **list** after **removeStrings** removes the **String** objects from the list. Notice that the output in Fig. 21.3 contains only **Color**s.

Method **removeStrings** declares one parameter of type **Collection** that allows any **Collection** to be passed as an argument to this method. The method accesses the elements of the **Collection** via an **Iterator**. Line 45 calls method ***iterator*** to get an **Iterator** for the **Collection**. The **while** loop condition on line 48 calls **Iterator** method ***hasNext*** to determine if the **Collection** contains any more elements. Method **hasNext** returns **true** if another element exists and **false** otherwise.

The **if** condition at line 50 calls **Iterator** method ***next*** to obtain a reference to the next element, then uses **instanceof** to determine whether the object is a **String**. If so, line 51 calls **Iterator** method ***remove*** to remove the **String** from the **Collection**.

Common Programming Error 21.3

When iterating through a collection with an **`Iterator`**, *use* **`Iterator`** *method* **`remove`** *to delete an element from the collection. Using the collection's* **`remove`** *method will result in a* **`ConcurrentModificationException`**

Figure 21.4 demonstrates operations on **`LinkedList`**s. The program creates two **`LinkedList`**s that each contain **`String`**s. The elements of one **`List`** are added to the other. Then, all the **`String`**s are converted to uppercase, and a range of elements is deleted.

```
// Fig. 21.4: ListTest.java
// Using LinkLists

// Java core packages
import java.util.*;

public class ListTest {
   private String colors[] = { "black", "yellow", "green",
      "blue", "violet", "silver" };
   private String colors2[] = { "gold", "white", "brown",
      "blue", "gray", "silver" };

   // set up and manipulate LinkedList objects
   public ListTest()
   {
      LinkedList link = new LinkedList();
      LinkedList link2 = new LinkedList();

      // add elements to each list
      for ( int count = 0; count < colors.length; count++ ) {
         link.add( colors[ count ] );
         link2.add( colors2[ count ] );
      }

      link.addAll( link2 );            // concatenate lists
      link2 = null;                    // release resources

      printList( link );

      uppercaseStrings( link );

      printList( link );

      System.out.print( "\nDeleting elements 4 to 6..." );
      removeItems( link, 4, 7 );

      printList( link );
   }

   // output List contents
   public void printList( List list )
   {
      System.out.println( "\nlist: " );
```

Fig. 21.4 Using **`List`**s and **`ListIterator`**s (part 1 of 2).

```
44
45          for ( int count = 0; count < list.size(); count++ )
46             System.out.print( list.get( count ) + " " );
47
48          System.out.println();
49       }
50
51       // locate String objects and convert to uppercase
52       public void uppercaseStrings( List list )
53       {
54          ListIterator iterator = list.listIterator();
55
56          while ( iterator.hasNext() ) {
57             Object object = iterator.next();  // get item
58
59             if ( object instanceof String )   // check for String
60                iterator.set(
61                   ( ( String ) object ).toUpperCase() );
62          }
63       }
64
65       // obtain sublist and use clear method to delete sublist items
66       public void removeItems( List list, int start, int end )
67       {
68          list.subList( start, end ).clear();  // remove items
69       }
70
71       // execute application
72       public static void main( String args[] )
73       {
74          new ListTest();
75       }
76
77    }  // end class ListTest
```

```
list:
black yellow green blue violet silver gold white brown blue gray silver

list:
BLACK YELLOW GREEN BLUE VIOLET SILVER GOLD WHITE BROWN BLUE GRAY SILVER

Deleting elements 4 to 6...
list:
BLACK YELLOW GREEN BLUE WHITE BROWN BLUE GRAY SILVER
```

Fig. 21.4 Using **Lists** and **ListIterators** (part 2 of 2).

Lines 16–17 create **LinkedLists** **link** and **link2**, respectively. Lines 20–23 call method **add** to append elements from arrays **colors** and **colors2** to the end of **LinkedLists** **link** and **link2**, respectively.

Line 25 calls method ***addAll*** to append all elements of **link2** to the end of **link**. Line 26 sets **link2** to **null**, so **LinkedList** can be garbage collected. Line 28 calls programmer-defined method **printList** (lines 41–49) to output the **link**'s contents.

Line 30 calls programmer-defined method **uppercaseStrings** (lines 52–63) to convert the **String** elements to uppercase; then line 32 calls **printList** to display the modified **String**s. Line 34 calls programmer-defined method **removeItems** (lines 66–69) to remove the elements at positions 4 through 6 of the list.

Method **uppercaseStrings** (lines 52–63) changes lowercase **String** elements in the **List** passed to it to uppercase **String**s. Line 54 calls method ***listIterator*** to get a *bidirectional iterator* (i.e., an iterator that can traverse a **List** backward or forward) for the **List**. The **while** condition calls method **hasNext** to determine whether the **List** contains another element. Line 57 gets the next **Object** from the **List** and assigns it to **object**. The **if** condition tests **object** to determine whether it is an **instanceof** class **String**. If so, lines 60–61 cast **object** to a **String**, call method **toUpperCase** to get an uppercase version of the **String** and call method ***set*** to replace the current **String** to which **iterator** refers with the **String** returned by method **toUpperCase**.

Programmer-defined method **removeItems** (lines 66–69) removes a range of items from the list. Line 68 calls method ***subList*** to obtain a portion of the **List** called a *sublist*. The sublist is simply a view into the **List** on which **subList** is called. Method **subList** takes two arguments—the beginning index for the sublist and the ending index for the sublist. Note that the ending index is not part of the range of the sublist. In this example, we pass **4** for the beginning index and **7** for the ending index to **subList**. The sublist returned is the elements with indices **4** through **6**. Next, the program calls method ***clear*** on the sublist to remove the elements of the sublist from the **List**. Any changes made to a sublist are made to the original **List**.

Figure 21.5 uses method ***toArray*** to get an array from a collection (i.e., **LinkedList**). The program adds a series of **String**s to a **LinkedList** and calls method **toArray** to get an array from the **LinkedList**.

```
// Fig. 21.5: UsingToArray.java
// Using method toArray

// Java core packages
import java.util.*;

public class UsingToArray {

   // create LinkedList, add elements and convert to array
   public UsingToArray()
   {
      LinkedList links;
      String colors[] = { "black", "blue", "yellow" };

      links = new LinkedList( Arrays.asList( colors ) );

      links.addLast( "red" );   // add as last item
      links.add( "pink" );      // add to the end
      links.add( 3, "green" );  // add at 3rd index
      links.addFirst( "cyan" ); // add as first item

```

Fig. 21.5 Using method **toArray** (part 1 of 2).

```
22         // get LinkedList elements as an array
23         colors = ( String [] ) links.toArray(
24            new String[ links.size() ] );
25
26         System.out.println( "colors: " );
27
28         for ( int count = 0; count < colors.length; count++ )
29            System.out.println( colors[ count ] );
30      }
31
32      // execute application
33      public static void main( String args[] )
34      {
35         new UsingToArray();
36      }
37
38   }  // end class UsingToArray
```

```
colors:
cyan
black
blue
yellow
green
red
pink
```

Fig. 21.5 Using method **toArray** (part 2 of 2).

Line 15 constructs a **LinkedList** containing the elements of array **colors** and assigns the **LinkedList** to **links**. Line 17 calls method ***addLast*** to add **"red"** to the end of **links**. Lines 18–19 call method ***add*** to add **"pink"** as the last element and **"green"** as the element at index **3** (i.e., the fourth element). Line 20 calls ***addFirst*** to add **"cyan"** as the new first item in the **LinkedList**. [*Note*: When **"cyan"** is added as the first element, **"green"** becomes the fifith element in the **LinkedList**.]

Lines 23–24 call method **toArray** to get a **String** array from **links**. The array is a copy of the list elements—modifying the contents of the array does not modify the **LinkedList**. The array passed to method **toArray** is of the same data type as that returned by **toArray**. If the number of elements in the array is greater than the number of elements in the **LinkedList**, **toArray** copies the list elements into its array argument and returns that array. If the **LinkedList** has more elements than the number of elements in the array passed to **toArray**, **toArray** allocates a new array of the same type it receives as an argument, copies the list elements into the new array and returns the new array.

Common Programming Error 21.4

Passing an array that contains data to **toArray** *can create logic errors. If the number of elements in the array is smaller than the number of elements in the* **Object** *calling* **toArray***, new memory is allocated to store the* **Object***'s elements—without preserving the array's elements. If the number of elements in the array is greater than the number of elements in the* **Object***, the elements of the array (starting at subscript* **0***) are overwritten with the* **Object***'s elements. Array elements that are not overwritten retain their values.*

21.6 Algorithms

The collections framework provides a variety of high-performance algorithms for manipulating collection elements. These algorithms are implemented as **`static`** methods. Algorithms ***`sort`***, ***`binarySearch`***, ***`reverse`***, ***`shuffle`***, ***`fill`*** and ***`copy`*** operate on **`List`**s. Algorithms ***`min`*** and ***`max`*** operate on **`Collection`**s.

Algorithm ***`reverse`*** reverses the elements of a **`List`**, ***`fill`*** sets every **`List`** element to refer to a specified **`Object`** and **`copy`** copies references from one **`List`** into another.

The collections framework algorithms are polymorphic. That is, each algorithm can operate on objects that offer given interfaces without concern to the underlying implementations.

21.6.1 Algorithm `sort`

Algorithm ***`sort`*** sorts the elements of a **`List`**. The order is determined by the natural order of the elements' type. The **`sort`** call may specify as a second argument a ***`Comparator`*** object that specifies how to determine the ordering of the elements.

Algorithm **`sort`** uses a *stable sort* (i.e., a sort that does not reorder equivalent elements while sorting). The **`sort`** algorithm is fast. For readers who have studied some complexity theory in data structures or algorithms courses, this sort runs in n log(n) time. (Readers not familiar with complexity theory, may rest assured that this algorithm is extremely fast .

Software Engineering Observation 21.6

The Java API documentation sometimes provides implementation details. For example, **`sort`** *is implemented as a modified merge sort. Avoid writing code that is dependent on implementation details, because they can change.*

Figure 21.6 uses algorithm **`sort`** to order the elements of an **`ArrayList`** into ascending order (line 21).

```
1   // Fig. 21.6: Sort1.java
2   // Using algorithm sort
3
4   // Java core packages
5   import java.util.*;
6
7   public class Sort1 {
8      private static String suits[] =
9         { "Hearts", "Diamonds", "Clubs", "Spades" };
10
11     // display array elements
12     public void printElements()
13     {
14        // create ArrayList
15        ArrayList list = new ArrayList( Arrays.asList( suits ) );
16
17        // output list
18        System.out.println( "Unsorted array elements:\n" + list );
```

Fig. 21.6 Using algorithm **`sort`** (part 1 of 2).

```

      // sort ArrayList
      Collections.sort( list );

      // output list
      System.out.println( "Sorted array elements:\n" + list );
   }

   // execute application
   public static void main( String args[] )
   {
      new Sort1().printElements();
   }

}  // end class Sort1
```

```
Unsorted array elements:
[Hearts, Diamonds, Clubs, Spades]
Sorted array elements:
[Clubs, Diamonds, Hearts, Spades]
```

Fig. 21.6 Using algorithm **sort** (part 2 of 2).

Figure 21.7 sorts the same **String**s used in Fig. 21.6 into descending order. The example introduces the **Comparator** object, for sorting a **Collection**'s elements in a different order.

```
// Fig. 21.7: Sort2.java
// Using a Comparator object with algorithm sort

// Java core packages
import java.util.*;

public class Sort2 {
   private static String suits[] =
      { "Hearts", "Diamonds", "Clubs", "Spades" };

   // output List elements
   public void printElements()
   {
      // create List
      List list = Arrays.asList( suits );

      // output List elements
      System.out.println( "Unsorted array elements:\n" + list );

      // sort in descending order using a comparator
      Collections.sort( list, Collections.reverseOrder() );

```

Fig. 21.7 Using a **Comparator** object in **sort** (part 1 of 2).

```
23          // output List elements
24          System.out.println( "Sorted list elements:\n" + list );
25       }
26
27       // execute application
28       public static void main( String args[] )
29       {
30          new Sort2().printElements();
31       }
32
33    }  // end class Sort2
```

```
Unsorted array elements:
[Hearts, Diamonds, Clubs, Spades]
Sorted list elements:
[Spades, Hearts, Diamonds, Clubs]
```

Fig. 21.7 Using a **`Comparator`** object in **`sort`** (part 2 of 2).

Line 21 calls **`Collections`**'s method **`sort`** to order the **`List`** view of the array into descending order. The **`static Collections`** method ***`reverseOrder`*** returns a **`Comparator`** object that represents the collection's reverse order. For sorting a **`List`** view of a **`String`** array, the reverse order is a *lexicographical comparison*—the comparator compares the Unicode values that represent each element—in descending order.

21.6.2 Algorithm `shuffle`

Algorithm **`shuffle`** randomly orders a **`List`**'s elements. In Chapter 10, we presented a card shuffling and dealing simulation where we used a loop to shuffle a deck of cards. In Fig. 21.8, we use algorithm **`shuffle`** to shuffle the deck of cards. Much of the code is the same as in Fig. 10.19. The shuffling of the deck occurs on line 63, which calls **`static Collections`** method **`shuffle`** to shuffle the array through the array's **`List`** view.

```
1   // Fig. 21.8: Cards.java
2   // Using algorithm shuffle
3
4   // Java core packages
5   import java.util.*;
6
7   // class to represent a Card in a deck of cards
8   class Card {
9      private String face;
10     private String suit;
11
12     // initialize a Card
13     public Card( String initialface, String initialSuit )
14     {
15        face = initialface;
16        suit = initialSuit;
17     }
```

Fig. 21.8 Card shuffling and dealing example (part 1 of 3).

```java

   // return face of Card
   public String getFace()
   {
      return face;
   }

   // return suit of Card
   public String getSuit()
   {
      return suit;
   }

   // return String representation of Card
   public String toString()
   {
      StringBuffer buffer =
         new StringBuffer( face + " of " + suit );

      buffer.setLength( 20 );

      return buffer.toString();
   }

} // end class Card

// class Cards definition
public class Cards {
   private static String suits[] =
      { "Hearts", "Clubs", "Diamonds", "Spades" };
   private static String faces[] = { "Ace", "Deuce", "Three",
      "Four", "Five", "Six", "Seven", "Eight", "Nine", "Ten",
      "Jack", "Queen", "King" };
   private List list;

   // set up deck of Cards and shuffle
   public Cards()
   {
      Card deck[] = new Card[ 52 ];

      for ( int count = 0; count < deck.length; count++ )
         deck[ count ] = new Card( faces[ count % 13 ],
            suits[ count / 13 ] );

      list = Arrays.asList( deck );   // get List
      Collections.shuffle( list );    // shuffle deck
   }

   // output deck
   public void printCards()
   {
      int half = list.size() / 2 - 1;

```

Fig. 21.8 Card shuffling and dealing example (part 2 of 3).

```
      for ( int i = 0, j = half; i <= half; i++, j++ )
         System.out.println(
            list.get( i ).toString() + list.get( j ) );
   }

   // execute application
   public static void main( String args[] )
   {
      new Cards().printCards();
   }

}  // end class Cards
```

```
King of Diamonds     Ten of Spades
Deuce of Hearts      Five of Spades
King of Clubs        Five of Clubs
Jack of Diamonds     Jack of Spades
King of Spades       Ten of Clubs
Six of Clubs         Three of Clubs
Seven of Clubs       Jack of Clubs
Seven of Hearts      Six of Spades
Eight of Hearts      Six of Diamonds
King of Hearts       Nine of Diamonds
Ace of Hearts        Four of Hearts
Jack of Hearts       Queen of Diamonds
Queen of Clubs       Six of Hearts
Seven of Diamonds    Ace of Spades
Three of Spades      Deuce of Spades
Seven of Spades      Five of Diamonds
Ten of Hearts        Queen of Hearts
Ten of Diamonds      Eight of Clubs
Nine of Spades       Three of Diamonds
Four of Spades       Ace of Clubs
Four of Clubs        Four of Diamonds
Nine of Clubs        Three of Hearts
Eight of Diamonds    Deuce of Diamonds
Deuce of Clubs       Nine of Hearts
Eight of Spades      Five of Hearts
Ten of Spades        Queen of Spades
```

Fig. 21.8 Card shuffling and dealing example (part 3 of 3).

21.6.3 Algorithms `reverse`, `fill`, `copy`, `max` and `min`

Class **`Collections`** provides algorithms for reversing, filling and copying **`List`**s. Algorithm **`reverse`** reverses the order of the elements in a **`List`**, and algorithm **`fill`** overwrites elements in a **`List`** with a specified value. The **`fill`** operation is useful for reinitializing a **`List`**. Algorithm **`copy`** takes two arguments: A destination **`List`** and a source **`List`**. Each source **`List`** element is copied to the destination **`List`**. The destination **`List`** must be at least as long as the source **`List`**: otherwise, an **`IndexOutOfBoundsException`** is thrown. If the destination **`List`** is longer, the elements not overwritten are unchanged.

Each of the algorithms we have seen so far operates on **Lists**. Algorithms **min** and **max** each operate on **Collections**.

Algorithm **min** returns the smallest element in a **List** (remember a **List** is a **Collection**) and algorithm **max** returns the largest element in a **List**. Both of these algorithms can be called with a **Comparator** object as a second argument. Figure 21.9 demonstrates the use of algorithms **reverse**, **fill**, **copy**, **min** and **max**.

```
// Fig. 21.9: Algorithms1.java
// Using algorithms reverse, fill, copy, min and max

// Java core packages
import java.util.*;

public class Algorithms1 {
   private String letters[] = { "P", "C", "M" }, lettersCopy[];
   private List list, copyList;

   // create a List and manipulate it with algorithms from
   // class Collections
   public Algorithms1()
   {
      list = Arrays.asList( letters );      // get List
      lettersCopy = new String[ 3 ];
      copyList = Arrays.asList( lettersCopy );

      System.out.println( "Printing initial statistics: " );
      printStatistics( list );

      Collections.reverse( list );          // reverse order
      System.out.println( "\nPrinting statistics after " +
         "calling reverse: " );
      printStatistics( list );

      Collections.copy( copyList, list );  // copy List
      System.out.println( "\nPrinting statistics after " +
         "copying: " );
      printStatistics( copyList );

      System.out.println( "\nPrinting statistics after " +
         "calling fill: " );
      Collections.fill( list, "R" );
      printStatistics( list );
   }

   // output List information
   private void printStatistics( List listRef )
   {
      System.out.print( "The list is: " );

      for ( int k = 0; k < listRef.size(); k++ )
         System.out.print( listRef.get( k ) + " " );

```

Fig. 21.9 Using algorithms **reverse**, **fill**, **copy**, **max** and **min** (part 1 of 2).

```
46         System.out.print( "\nMax: " + Collections.max( listRef ) );
47         System.out.println(
48            "  Min: " + Collections.min( listRef ) );
49      }
50
51      // execute application
52      public static void main( String args[] )
53      {
54         new Algorithms1();
55      }
56
57   }  // end class Algorithms1
```

```
Printing initial statistics:
The list is: P C M
Max: P  Min: C
Printing statistics after calling reverse:
The list is: M C P
Max: P  Min: C
Printing statistics after copying:
The list is: M C P
Max: P  Min: C
Printing statistics after calling fill:
The list is: R R R
Max: R  Min: R
```

Fig. 21.9 Using algorithms **reverse**, **fill**, **copy**, **max** and **min** (part 2 of 2).

Line 22 calls **Collections** method ***reverse*** to reverse the order of **list**. Method **reverse** takes one **List** argument. (**list** is a **List** view of **String** array **letters**.) Array **letters** now has its elements in reverse order.

Line 27 copies the elements of **list** into **copyList** with **Collections** method **copy**. Changes to **copyList** do not change **letters**—this is a separate **List** that is not a **List** view for **letters**. Method **copy** requires two **List** arguments.

Line 34 calls **Collections** method **fill** to place the **String "R"** in each element of **list**. Because **list** is a **List** view of **letters**, this operation changes each element in **letters** to **"R"**. Method **fill** requires a **List** for the first argument and an **Object** for the second argument.

Lines 46 and 48, call **Collection** methods **max** and **min** to find the largest element and the smallest element, respectively, in **list**.

21.6.4 Algorithm binarySearch

Earlier in this text, we studied the high-speed binary search algorithm. This algorithm is built right into the Java collections framework. The **binarySearch** algorithm locates an **Object** in a **List** (i.e., **LinkedList**, **Vector** or **ArrayList**) If the **Object** is found, the index (position relative to 0) of that **Object** is returned. If the **Object** is not found, **binarySearch** returns a negative value. Algorithm **binarySearch** determines this negative value by first calculating the insertion point and changing the insertion point's sign to negative. Finally, **binarySearch** subtracts one from the insertion point to obtain the return value.

Figure 21.10 uses the **binarySearch** algorithm to search for a series of **String**s in an **ArrayList**.

```
// Fig. 21.10: BinarySearchTest.java
// Using algorithm binarySearch

// Java core packages
import java.util.*;

public class BinarySearchTest {
   private String colors[] = { "red", "white", "blue", "black",
      "yellow", "purple", "tan", "pink" };
   private ArrayList list;          // ArrayList reference

   // create, sort and output list
   public BinarySearchTest()
   {
      list = new ArrayList( Arrays.asList( colors ) );
      Collections.sort( list );    // sort the ArrayList
      System.out.println( "Sorted ArrayList: " + list );
   }

   // search list for various values
   public void printSearchResults()
   {
      printSearchResultsHelper( colors[ 3 ] ); // first item
      printSearchResultsHelper( colors[ 0 ] ); // middle item
      printSearchResultsHelper( colors[ 7 ] ); // last item
      printSearchResultsHelper( "aardvark" );  // below lowest
      printSearchResultsHelper( "goat" );      // does not exist
      printSearchResultsHelper( "zebra" );     // does not exist
   }

   // helper method to perform searches
   private void printSearchResultsHelper( String key )
   {
      int result = 0;

      System.out.println( "\nSearching for: " + key );
      result = Collections.binarySearch( list, key );
      System.out.println(
         ( result >= 0 ? "Found at index " + result :
         "Not Found (" + result + ")" ) );
   }

   // execute application
   public static void main( String args[] )
   {
      new BinarySearchTest().printSearchResults();
   }

}  // end class BinarySearchTest
```

Fig. 21.10 Using algorithm **binarySearch** (part 1 of 2).

```
Sorted ArrayList: black blue pink purple red tan white yellow
Searching for: black
Found at index 0

Searching for: red
Found at index 4

Searching for: pink
Found at index 2

Searching for: aardvark
Not Found (-1)

Searching for: goat
Not Found (-3)

Searching for: zebra
Not Found (-9)
```

Fig. 21.10 Using algorithm **binarySearch** (part 2 of 2).

Line 16 calls **Collections** method **sort** to sort **list** into ascending order. Line 37 calls **Collections** method **binarySearch** to search **list** for the specified **key**. Method **binarySearch** takes a **List** as the first argument and an **Object** as the second argument. An overloaded version of **binarySearch** takes a **Comparator** object as its third argument, to specify how **binarySearch** should compare elements.

If the search key is found, method **binarySearch** returns the **List** index of the element containing the search key. When a search key is found in the **List**, the value returned by **binarySearch** is greater than or equal to zero. If the search key is not found, method **binarySearch** returns a negative number.

Software Engineering Observation 21.7

Java does not guarantee which item will be found first when a **binarySearch** *is performed on a* **List** *containing multiple elements equivalent to the search key.*

21.7 Sets

A ***Set*** is a **Collection** that contains unique elements (i.e., no duplicate elements). The collections framework contains two **Set** implementations: —***HashSet*** and ***TreeSet***. **HashSet** stores its elements in a hash table, and **TreeSet** stores its elements in a tree. Figure 21.11 uses a **HashSet** to remove duplicate **String**s from an **ArrayList**.

Programmer-defined method **printNonDuplicates** (lines 23–35) takes a **Collection** argument. Line 26 constructs a **HashSet** from the **Collection** received as an argument to **printNonDuplicates**. When the **HashSet** is constructed, it removes any duplicates in the **Collection**. By definition, **Set**s do not contain any duplicates. Line 27 gets an **Iterator** for the **HashSet**. The **while** loop (lines 31–32) calls **Iterator** methods **hasNext** and **next** to access the **HashSet** elements.

Interface ***SortedSet*** extends **Set** and maintains its elements in sorted order (i.e., the elements' natural order or an order specified by a **Comparator**). Class **TreeSet** implements **SortedSet**.

```
// Fig. 21.11: SetTest.java
// Using a HashSet to remove duplicates

// Java core packages
import java.util.*;

public class SetTest {
   private String colors[] = { "red", "white", "blue",
      "green", "gray", "orange", "tan", "white", "cyan",
      "peach", "gray", "orange" };

   // create and output ArrayList
   public SetTest()
   {
      ArrayList list;

      list = new ArrayList( Arrays.asList( colors ) );
      System.out.println( "ArrayList: " + list );
      printNonDuplicates( list );
   }

   // create set from array to eliminate duplicates
   public void printNonDuplicates( Collection collection )
   {
      // create a HashSet and obtain its iterator
      HashSet set = new HashSet( collection );
      Iterator iterator = set.iterator();

      System.out.println( "\nNonduplicates are: " );

      while ( iterator.hasNext() )
         System.out.print( iterator.next() + " " );

      System.out.println();
   }

   // execute application
   public static void main( String args[] )
   {
      new SetTest();
   }

}  // end class SetTest
```

```
ArrayList: [red, white, blue, green, gray, orange, tan, white, cyan,
peach, gray, orange]

Nonduplicates are:
orange cyan green tan white blue peach red gray
```

Fig. 21.11 Using a **HashSet** to remove duplicates.

The program of Fig. 21.12 places **Strings** into a **TreeSet**. The **Strings** are sorted automatically when they are added to the **TreeSet**. Also, *range-view methods* (i.e., methods that enable a program to view a portion of a collection) are demonstrated in this example.

```java
// Fig. 21.12: SortedSetTest.java
// Using TreeSet and SortedSet

// Java core packages
import java.util.*;

public class SortedSetTest {
   private static String names[] = { "yellow", "green", "black",
      "tan", "grey", "white", "orange", "red", "green" };

   // create a sorted set with TreeSet, then manipulate it
   public SortedSetTest()
   {
      TreeSet tree = new TreeSet( Arrays.asList( names ) );

      System.out.println( "set: " );
      printSet( tree );

      // get headSet based upon "orange"
      System.out.print( "\nheadSet (\"orange\"):  " );
      printSet( tree.headSet( "orange" ) );

      // get tailSet based upon "orange"
      System.out.print( "tailSet (\"orange\"):  " );
      printSet( tree.tailSet( "orange" ) );

      // get first and last elements
      System.out.println( "first: " + tree.first() );
      System.out.println( "last : " + tree.last() );
   }

   // output set
   public void printSet( SortedSet set )
   {
      Iterator iterator = set.iterator();

      while ( iterator.hasNext() )
         System.out.print( iterator.next() + " " );

      System.out.println();
   }

   // execute application
   public static void main( String args[] )
   {
      new SortedSetTest();
   }
```

Fig. 21.12 Using **SortedSet**s and **TreeSet**s.

```
48
49 }  // end class SortedSetTest
```

```
set:
black green grey orange red tan white yellow

headSet ("orange"):  black green grey
tailSet ("orange"):  orange red tan white yellow
first: black
last : yellow
```

Fig. 21.12 Using **SortedSet**s and **TreeSet**s.

Line 14 constructs a **TreeSet** object containing the elements of **names** and assigns a reference to this object to **tree**. Line 21 calls method ***headSet*** to get a subset of the **TreeSet** less than **"orange"**. Any changes made to the subset are made to the **TreeSet** (i.e., the subset returned is a view of the **TreeSet**). Line 25 calls method ***tailSet*** to get a subset greater than or equal to **"orange"**. Like **headSet**, any changes made through the **tailSet** view are made to the **TreeSet**. Lines 28–29 call methods ***first*** and ***last*** to get the smallest and largest elements, respectively.

Programmer-defined method **printSet** (lines 33–41) takes a **SortedSet** (e.g., a **TreeSet**) as an argument and prints it. Line 35 gets an **Iterator** for the **Set**. The body of the **while** loop prints each element of the **SortedSet**.

21.8 Maps

Map*s* associate keys to values and cannot contain duplicate keys (i.e., each key can map to only one value; this type of mapping is called *one-to-one mapping*). **Map**s differ from **Set**s in that **Map**s contain keys and values, whereas **Set**s contain only keys. Classes ***HashMap*** and ***TreeMap*** implement the **Map** interface. **HashMap**s store elements in **HashTable**s, and **TreeMap**s store elements in trees. Interface ***SortedMap*** extends **Map** and maintains its keys in sorted order (i.e., the elements' natural order or an order, specified by a **Comparator**). Class **TreeMap** implements **SortedMap**.

Figure 21.13 uses a **HashMap** to count the number of **String**s that begin with a given letter. [Note: Unlike class **Hashtable**, class **HashMap** allows a **null** key and **null** values].

```
// Fig. 21.13: MapTest.java
// Using a HashMap to store the number of words that
// begin with a given letter

// Java core packages
import java.util.*;

public class MapTest {
   private static String names[] = { "one", "two", "three",
      "four", "five", "six", "seven", "two", "ten", "four" };
```

Fig. 21.13 Using **HashMap**s and **Map**s (part 1 of 2).

```
11
12    // build a HashMap and output contents
13    public MapTest()
14    {
15       HashMap map = new HashMap();
16       Integer i;
17
18       for ( int count = 0; count < names.length; count++ ) {
19          i = ( Integer ) map.get(
20             new Character( names[ count ].charAt( 0 ) ) );
21
22          // if key is not in map then give it value one
23          // otherwise increment its value by 1
24          if ( i == null )
25             map.put(
26                new Character( names[ count ].charAt( 0 ) ),
27                new Integer( 1 ) );
28          else
29             map.put(
30                new Character( names[ count ].charAt( 0 ) ),
31                new Integer( i.intValue() + 1 ) );
32       }
33
34       System.out.println(
35          "\nnumber of words beginning with each letter:    " );
36       printMap( map );
37    }
38
39    // output map contents
40    public void printMap( Map mapRef )
41    {
42       System.out.println( mapRef.toString() );
43       System.out.println( "size: " + mapRef.size() );
44       System.out.println( "isEmpty: " + mapRef.isEmpty() );
45    }
46
47    // execute application
48    public static void main( String args[] )
49    {
50       new MapTest();
51    }
52
53 }  // end class MapTest
```

```
number of words beginning with each letter:
{t=4, s=2, o=1, f=3}
size: 4
isEmpty: false
```

Fig. 21.13 Using **HashMap**s and **Map**s (part 2 of 2).

Line 15 constructs **HashMap map**. The **for** loop on lines 18–32 uses **map** to store the number of words in array **names** that begin with a given letter. Lines 19–20 call method ***get*** to retrieve a **Character** (the first letter of a **String** in **names**) from the

HashMap. If the **HashMap** does not contain a mapping for the **Character**, **get** returns **null**. If the **HashMap** does contain the mapping for the **Character**, its mapping value is returned as an **Object**. The returned value is cast to **Integer** and assigned to **i**.

If **i** is **null**, the **Character** is not in the **HashMap**, and lines 25–27 call method ***put*** to write an **Integer** containing **1** to the **HashMap**. The **Integer** value stored in the **HashMap** is the number of words beginning with that **Character**.

If the **Character** is in the **HashMap**, lines 29–31 increment the **Integer** counter by one and write the updated counter to the **HashMap**. A **HashMap** cannot contain duplicates, so **put** replaces the previous **Integer** object with the new one.

Programmer-defined method **printMap** takes one **Map** argument and prints it, using method **toString**. Lines 43–44 call methods ***size*** and ***isEmpty*** to get the number of values in the **Map** and a **boolean** indicating whether the **Map** is empty, respectively.

21.9 Synchronization Wrappers

In Chapter 15, we discussed multithreading. The built-in collections are unsynchronized. Concurrent access to a **Collection** by multiple threads could cause indeterminate results or fatal errors. To prevent potential threading problems, synchronization wrappers are used around collection classes that might be accessed by multiple threads. A *wrapper class* receives method calls, adds some functionality for thread safety and delegates the calls to the wrapped class.

The **Collections** API provides a set of **public static** methods for converting collections to synchronized versions. Method headers for the synchronization wrappers are listed in Fig. 21.14.

21.10 Unmodifiable Wrappers

The **Collections** API provides a set of **public static** methods for converting collections to unmodifiable versions (called *unmodifiable wrappers*) of those collections. Method headers for these methods are listed in Fig. 21.15. Unmodifiable wrappers throw **UnsupportedOperationException**s if attempts are made to modify the collection.

Software Engineering Observation 21.8

When creating an unmodifiable wrapper, not holding a reference to the backing collection ensures nonmodifiability.

public static method header
`Collection synchronizedCollection( Collection c )`
`List synchronizedList( List aList )`
`Set synchronizedSet( Set s )`
`SortedSet synchronizedSortedSet( SortedSet s )`
`Map synchronizedMap( Map m )`
`SortedMap synchronizedSortedMap( SortedMap m )`

Fig. 21.14 Synchronization wrapper methods.

public static method header
`Collection unmodifiableCollection( Collection c )`
`List unmodifiableList( List aList )`
`Set unmodifiableSet( Set s )`
`SortedSet unmodifiableSortedSet( SortedSet s )`
`Map unmodifiableMap( Map m )`
`SortedMap unmodifiableSortedMap( SortedMap m )`

Fig. 21.15 Unmodifiable wrapper methods.

Software Engineering Observation 21.9

You can use an unmodifiable wrapper to create a collection that offers read-only access to others, while allowing read–write access to yourself. You do this simply by giving others a reference to the unmodifiable wrapper while you also retain a reference to the wrapped collection itself.

21.11 Abstract Implementations

The collections framework provides various abstract implementations (i.e., "bare bones" implementations of collection interfaces from which the programmer can quickly "flesh out" complete customized implementations). These abstract implementations are a thin **`Collection`** implementation called an ***`AbstractCollection`***, a thin **`List`** implementation with random-access backing called an ***`AbstractList`***, a thin **`Map`** implementation called an ***`AbstractMap`***, a thin **`List`** implementation with sequential-access backing called an ***`AbstractSequentialList`*** and a thin **`Set`** implementation called an ***`AbstractSet`***.

To write a custom implementation, begin by selecting as a base the abstract-implementation class that best meets your needs. Next, implement each of the class's **`abstract`** methods. Then, if your collection is to be modifiable, override any concrete methods that prevent modification.

21.12 (Optional) Discovering Design Patterns: Design Patterns Used in Package `java.util`

In this section, we use the material on data structures and collections discussed in Chapters 19, 20 and 21 to identify classes from package **`java.util`** that use design patterns. This section concludes our treatment of design patterns.

21.12.1 Creational Design Patterns

We conclude the discussion of creational design patterns by discussing the Prototype design pattern.

Prototype

Sometimes, a system must make a copy of an object but will not know that object's class until run time. For example, consider the drawing program design of Exercise

9.28—classes **MyLine**, **MyOval** and **MyRect** represent "shape" classes that extend abstract superclass **MyShape**. We could modify this exercise to allow the user to create, copy and paste new instances of class **MyLine** into the program. The *Prototype design pattern* allows an object—called a *prototype*—to return a copy of that prototype to a requesting object—called a *client*. Every prototype must belong to a class that implements a common interface that allows the prototype to clone itself. For example, the Java API provides method **clone** from class **java.lang.Object** and interface **java.lang.Cloneable**—any object from a class implementing **Cloneable** can use method **clone** to copy itself. Specifically, method **clone** creates a copy of an object, then returns a reference to that object. If we designate class **MyLine** as the prototype for Exercise 9.28, then class **MyLine** must implement interface **Cloneable**. To create a new line in our drawing, we clone the **MyLine** prototype. To copy a preexisting line, we clone that object. Method **clone** also is useful in methods that return a reference to an object, but the developer does not want that object to be altered through that reference—method **clone** returns a reference to the copy of the object instead of returning that object's reference. For more information of interface **Cloneable**, visit

www.java.sun.com/j2se/1.3/docs/api/java/lang/Cloneable.html

21.12.2 Behavioral Design Patterns

We conclude the discussion of behavioral design patterns by discussing the Iterator design pattern.

Iterator

Designers use data structures such as arrays, linked lists and hash tables, to organize data in a program. The *Iterator design pattern* allows objects to access individual objects from any data structure without knowing the data structure's behavior (such as traversing the structure or removing an element from that structure) or how that data structure stores objects. Instructions for traversing the data structure and accessing its elements are stored in a separate object called an *iterator*. Each data structure can create an iterator—each iterator implements methods of a common interface to traverse the data structure and access its data. An object can traverse two differently structured data structures—such as a linked list and a hash table—in the same manner, because both data structures contain an iterator object that belongs to a class implementing a common interface. Java provides interface **Iterator** from package **java.util**, which we discussed in Section 21.5—class **CollectionTest** (Fig 21.3) uses an **Iterator** object.

21.12.3 Conclusion

In our optional "Discovering Design Patterns" sections, we have introduced the importance, usefulness and prevalence of design patterns. We have mentioned that in their book *Design Patterns, Elements of Reusable Object-Oriented Software*, the "gang of four" described 23 design patterns that provide proven strategies for building systems. Each pattern belongs to one of three pattern categories: creational, which address issues related to object creation; structural, which provide ways to organize classes and objects in a system; and behavioral, which offer strategies to model how objects collaborate with one another in a system.

Of the 23 design patterns, we discussed 18 of the more popular ones used by the Java community. In Sections 9.24, 13.18, 15.13, 17.11 and 21.12, we divided the discussion according to how certain Java packages—such as package **java.awt**, **javax.swing**, **java.io**, **java.net** and **java.util**—use these design patterns. We also discussed patterns not described by the "gang of four," such as concurrency patterns, which are useful in multithreaded systems, and architectural patterns, which help designers assign functionality to various subsystems in a system. We have motivated each pattern—that is, explained why that pattern is important and how it may be used. When appropriate, we supplied several examples in the form of real-world analogies (e.g., the adapter in the Adapter design pattern is similar to an adapter for a plug on an electrical device). We also gave examples of how Java packages take advantage of design patterns (e.g., Swing GUI components use the Observer design pattern to collaborate with their listeners to respond to user interactions). We also provided examples of how certain programs in *Java How to Program, Fourth edition* used design patterns (e.g., the elevator-simulation case study in our optional "Thinking About Objects" sections uses the State design pattern to represent a **Person** object's location in the simulation).

We hope that you view our "Discovering Design Patterns" sections as a beginning to further study of design patterns. If you have not done so already, we recommend that you visit the many URLs we have provided in Section 9.24.5, Internet and World-Wide-Web Resources. We recommend that you then read the gang-of-four book. This information will help you build better systems using the collective wisdom of the object-technology industry.

If you have studied the optional sections in this book, you have been introduced to more substantial Java systems. If you have read our optional "Thinking About Objects" Sections, you have immersed yourself in a substantial design and Java implementation experience learning a disciplined approach to object-oriented design with the UML. If you have read our optional "Discovering Design Patterns" Sections, you have raised your awareness of the more advanced topic of design patterns.

We hope you continue your study of design patterns, and we would be most grateful if you would send your comments, criticisms and suggestions for improvement of *Java How to Program* to **deitel@deitel.com**. Good luck!

SUMMARY

- The Java collections framework gives the programmer access to prepackaged data structures, as well as algorithms for manipulating those data structures.
- Java 2 provides an entire collections framework, whereas earlier versions of Java provided just a few collection classes, like **HashTable** and **Vector**, as well as built-in array capabilities.
- A collection is a data structure; actually, it is an object that can hold other objects. The collection interfaces define the operations that can be performed on each type of collection.
- The collections framework includes a number of other features that minimize the amount of work programmers need to do to create and manipulate collections. This structure is an effective implementation of the notion of reuse.
- The classes and interfaces that compose the collections framework are members of the **java.util** package.
- Class **Arrays** provides **static** methods for manipulating arrays. Class **Arrays** methods include **binarySearch** for searching a sorted array, **equals** for comparing arrays, **fill** for placing items in an array, **sort** for sorting an array and **asList**.

- Class **Arrays** provides method **asList** for getting a "**List** view" of the array. A **List** view allows the programmer to programmatically manipulate the array as if it were a **List**. This allows the programmer to treat an array as a collection. Any modifications made through the **List** view change the array, and any modifications to the array change the **List** view.
- Method **size** gets the number of items in a **List**, and method **get** gets an individual **List** element.
- Interface **Collection** is the root interface in the collections hierarchy from which interfaces **Set** and **List** are derived. Interface **Collection** contains bulk operations for adding, clearing, comparing and retaining objects in the collection.
- Interface **Collection** provides a method **iterator** for getting an **Iterator**.
- Class **Collections** provides **static** methods for manipulating collections. Many of the methods are implementations of polymorphic algorithms for searching, sorting and so on.
- A **List** is an ordered **Collection** that can contain duplicate elements. A **List** is sometimes called a *sequence*.
- Interface **List** is implemented by classes **ArrayList**, **LinkedList** and **Vector**. Class **ArrayList** is a resizable-array implementation of a **List**. **ArrayList** behavior and capabilities are similar to those of class **Vector**. A **LinkedList** is a linked-list implementation of a **List**.
- **Iterator** method **hasNext** determines whether a **Collection** contains another element. Method **hasNext** returns **true** if another element exists, **false** otherwise. Method **next** returns the next object in the **Collection** and advances the **Iterator**.
- Method **subList** gets a portion of a **List**, called a *sublist*. Any changes made to a sublist are also made to the **List** (i.e., the sublist is a "list view" of its corresponding **List** elements).
- Method **clear** removes elements from a **List**.
- Method **toArray** returns the contents of a collection as an array.
- Algorithms **sort**, **binarySearch**, **reverse**, **shuffle**, **fill** and **copy** operate on **List**s. Algorithms **min** and **max** operate on **Collections**. Algorithm **reverse** reverses the elements of a **List**, **fill** sets every **List** element to a specified **Object** and **copy** copies elements from one **List** into another **List**. Algorithm **sort** sorts the elements of a **List**.
- Algorithms **min** and **max** find the smallest item and the largest item in a **Collection**.
- The **Comparator** object provides a means of sorting a **Collection**'s elements in an order other than the **Collection**'s natural order.
- Method **reverseOrder** returns a **Comparator** object that represents the reverse order for a collection.
- Algorithm **shuffle** randomly orders the elements of a **List**.
- Algorithm **binarySearch** locates an **Object** in a **List**.
- A **Set** is a **Collection** that contains no duplicate elements. The collections framework contains two **Set** implementations: **HashSet** and **TreeSet**. **HashSet** stores its elements in a hash table; **TreeSet** stores its elements in a tree.
- Interface **SortedSet** extends **Set** and maintains its elements in sorted order. Class **TreeSet** implements **SortedSet**.
- Method **headSet** gets a subset of a **TreeSet** less than a specified element. Any changes made to the subset are made to the **TreeSet**. Method **tailSet** gets a subset greater than or equal to a specified element. Any changes made through the **tailSet** view are made to the **TreeSet**.
- **Map**s map keys to values and cannot contain duplicate keys. **Map**s differ from **Set**s in that **Map**s contain both keys and the values, whereas **Set**s contain only keys. Classes **HashMap** and

TreeMap implement the **Map** interface. **HashMap**s store elements in a **HashTable**, and **TreeMap**s store elements in a tree.

- Interface **SortedMap** extends **Map** and maintains its elements in sorted order. Class **TreeMap** implements **SortedMap**.
- The built-in collections are unsynchronized. Concurrent access to a **Collection** by independent threads could cause indeterminate results. To prevent this, synchronization wrappers are used around classes that might be accessed by multiple threads.
- The **Collections** API provides a set of **public static** methods for converting collections to unmodifiable versions. Unmodifiable wrappers throw **UnsupportedOperationException**s if attempts are made to modify the collection.
- The collections framework provides various abstract implementations (i.e., "bare bones" implementations of collection interfaces from which the programmer can quickly "flesh out" complete customized implementations).

TERMINOLOGY

AbstractCollection class
AbstractList class
AbstractMap class
AbstractSequentialList class
AbstractSet class
add method
addFirst method
addLast method
algorithms
ArrayList
arrays
arrays as collections
Arrays.asList
bidirectional iterator
binarySearch algorithm
clear method
Collection interface
collections
Collections class
collections framework
collections placed in arrays
Comparator object
copy algorithm
data structures
delete an element from a collection
deque
double-ended queue (deque)
duplicate elements
Enumeration interface
fill algorithm
HashMap class
HashSet class
Hashtable class
hashtable implementation
hasNext method
implementation classes
insert an element into a collection
interface
isEmpty method
iterator
Iterator interface
key
lexicographical comparison
LinkedList class
List interface
ListIterator
map
Map collection interface
mapping keys to values
mappings
maps as collections
max algorithm
min algorithm
modifiable collections
natural ordering
next method
one-to-one mapping
ordered collection
ordering
queue
range-view methods
reverse algorithm
reverseOrder method
sequence
Set interface
shuffle algorithm
size method
sort a **List**

sort algorithm
SortedMap collection interface
SortedSet collection interface
stable sort
synchronization wrappers
TreeMap class
TreeSet class
unmodifiable collections
Vector class
view
view an array as a **List**
wrapper class

SELF-REVIEW EXERCISES

21.1 Fill in the blanks in each of the following statements:
a) **Object**s in a collection are called __________.
b) An element in a **List** can be accessed by using the element's __________.
c) **List**s are sometimes called __________.
d) You can use a/an __________ to create a collection that offers only read-only access to others while allowing read–write access to yourself.
e) __________ can be used to create stacks, queues, trees and deques (double-ended queues).

21.2 State whether each of the following is *true* or *false*. If *false*, explain why.
a) A **Set** can contain duplicates.
b) A **Map** can contain duplicate keys.
c) A **LinkedList** can contain duplicates.
d) **Collections** is an **interface**.
e) **Iterator**s can remove elements, while **Enumeration**s cannot.

ANSWERS TO SELF-REVIEW EXERCISES

21.1 a) elements. b) index. c) sequences. d) unmodifiable wrapper. e) ***LinkedList***s.

21.2 a) False. A **Set** cannot contain duplicate values.
b) False. A **Map** cannot contain duplicate keys.
c) True.
d) False. **Collections** is a **class**, and **Collection** is an **interface**.
e) True.

EXERCISES

21.3 Define each of the following terms:
a) **Collection**
b) **Collections**
c) **Comparator**
d) **List**

21.4 Briefly answer the following questions:
a) What is the primary difference between a **Set** and a **Map**?
b) Can a double-subscripted array be passed to **Arrays** method **asList**? If yes, how would an individual element be accessed?
c) What must you do before adding a primitive data type (e.g., **double**) to a collection?

21.5 Explain briefly the operation of each of the following **Iterator**-related methods:
a) **iterator**
b) **hasNext**
c) **next**

21.6 State whether each of the following is *true* or *false*. If *false*, explain why.

a) Elements in a **Collection** must be sorted in ascending order before performing a **binarySearch**.

b) Method **first** gets the first element in a **TreeSet**.

c) A **List** created with **Arrays.asList** is resizable.

d) Class **Arrays** provides static method **sort** for sorting array elements.

21.7 Rewrite method **printList** of Fig. 21.4 to use a **ListIterator**.

21.8 Rewrite lines 16–23 in Fig. 21.4 to be more concise by using the **asList** method and the **LinkedList** constructor that takes a **Collection** argument.

21.9 Write a program that reads in a series of first names and stores them in a **LinkedList**. Do not store duplicate names. Allow the user to search for a first name.

21.10 Modify the program of Fig. 21.13 to count the number of occurrences of all letters (e.g., five occurrences of "o" in the example). Display the results.

21.11 Write a program that determines and prints the number of duplicate words in a sentence. Treat uppercase and lowercase letters the same. Ignore punctuation.

21.12 Rewrite your solution to Exercise 19.8 to use a **LinkedList** collection.

21.13 Rewrite your solution to Exercise 19.9 to use a **LinkedList** collection.

21.14 Write a program that takes a whole-number input from a user and determines if it is prime. If the number is prime, add it to a **JTextArea**. If the number is not prime, display the prime factors of the number in a **JLabel**. Remember that a prime number's factors are only 1 and the prime number itself. Every number that is not prime has a unique prime factorization. For example, consider the number 54. The factors of 54 are 2, 3, 3 and 3. When the values are multiplied together, the result is 54. For the number 54, the prime factors output should be 2 and 3. Use **Set**s as part of your solution.

21.15 Rewrite your solution to Exercise 22.21 to use a **LinkedList**.

21.16 Write a program that tokenizes (using class **StreamTokenizer**) a line of text input by the user and places each token in a tree. Print the elements of the sorted tree.

22

Java Media Framework and Java Sound (on CD)

Objectives

- To understand the capabilities of the Java Media Framework (JMF).
- To understand the capabilities of the Java Sound API.
- To be able to play audio and video media with JMF.
- To be able to stream media over a network.
- To be able to capture, format and save media.
- To be able to play sounds with the Java Sound API.
- To be able to play, record, and synthesize MIDI with the Java Sound API.

Chapter 22 is included on the CD that accompanies this book in printable Adobe® Acrobat® PDF format. The chapter includes pages 1236–1345. In addition to presenting the Java Media Framework and Java Sound APIs, this chapter continues the optional "Thinking About Objects" object-oriented design case study by presenting the multimedia features of the elevator simulator.

Java Demos

A.1 Introduction[1]

In this appendix, we list some of the best Java demos we found on the Web. We began our journey at **software.dev.earthweb.com/java**. This site is an incredible Java resource and has some of the best Java demos including a huge compilation of games. The code ranges from basic to complex. Many of the authors of these games and other resources have provided source code. We hope you enjoy surfing these sites as much as we did.

A.2 The Sites

softwaredev.earthweb.com/java

Gamelan, a site owned by *EarthWeb*, has been a wonderful Java resource since the early days of Java. This site originally was a large Java repository where individuals traded ideas on Java and examples of Java programming. One of its early benefits was the volume of Java source code that was available to the many people learning Java. It is now an all-around Java resource with Java references, free Java downloads, areas where you can ask questions to Java experts, discussion groups on Java, a glossary of Java-related terminology, upcoming Java-related events, directories for specialized industry topics and hundreds of other Java resources.

www.jars.com

Another *EarthWeb* Web site is *JARS*—originally called the *Java Applet Rating Service*. The JARS site calls itself the "#1 Java Review Service." This site originally was a large Java repository for applets. It rated every applet registered at the site as top 1%, top 5% and top 25%, so you could immediately view the best applets on the Web. Early in the development of the Java language, having your applet rated here was a great way to demonstrate your Java programming abilities. JARS is now another all-around resource for Java programmers.

---

1. There are many Java-related Web sites that cover more advanced Java topics such as servlets, JavaServer Pages (JSP), Enterprise Java Beans (EJB), database, Java 2 Enterprise Edition (J2EE), Java 2 Micro Edition (J2ME), Security, XML and many more. These sites are provided in our companion book, *Advanced Java 2 Platform How to Program* (ISBN# 0-13-089560-1).

www.javashareware.com
Java Shareware contains hundreds of Java applications, applets, classes and other Java resources. The site includes a large number of links to other Java developer Web sites.

javaboutique.internet.com
Java Boutique is a great resource for any Java programmer. The site offers applets, applications, forums, tutorials, reviews, glossaries and more.

www.thejmaker.com
The J Maker has numerous live Java demos, including games, menus and animated visual effects. Many of the programs on this site are acclaimed worldwide and some have won awards.

www.demicron.com/gallery/photoalbum2/index.shtml
The PhotoAlbum II has some of the coolest effects we have found on the Web. The effects include a liquid effect, folding an image into a paper airplane and others.

www.blaupunkt.de/simulations/svdef_en.html
The *Sevilla RDM 168* is a simulation, built with Java, of a car Radio and CD player. You can tune into a variety of on-line radio stations or CDs, adjust the volume, clock settings and more.

www.frontiernet.net/~imaging/play_a_piano.html
Play A Piano is a Java applet that allows you to play the piano or watch the sound waves and listen as the piano plays itself.

www.gamesdomain.co.uk/GamesArena/goldmine
Goldmine is a fun game using simple animation.

www.javaonthebrain.com
This site offers many new and original Java games for the Web. Source code for many of the programs is provided.

www.javagamepark.com
If you are looking for games, the *Java Game Park* site has loads of them. All of the games are written in Java. The source code is provided in some cases.

teamball.sdsu.edu/~boyns/java/
This site has interesting games written in Java and includes source code for many of them.

www.cruzio.com/~sabweb/arcade/index.html
SABames Arcade is another source for Java video games. Source code is provided for many of the games. Don't miss the SabBowl bowling game.

dogfeathers.com/java/hyprcube.html
Stereoscopic Animated Hypercube. If you happen to possess the old red and blue 3D glasses, check this site out. The programmer was able to create a 3D image using Java. It isn't really a complicated image, just some cubes, however the idea that you can create images that will jump off your screen is a great concept!

www.npac.syr.edu/projects/vishuman/VisibleHuman.html
This site has won various awards. You can look at cross sections of the human body.

www-groups.dcs.st-and.ac.uk/~history/Java/
Famous Curves Applet Index. Provides graphs of complex curves. Allows the user to alter the parameters to the equations that calculate the curves.

Java Resources

B.1 Resources[1]

java.sun.com

The *Sun Microsystems, Inc. Java Web site* is an essential stop when searching the Web for Java information. Go to this site to download the Java 2 Software Development Kit. This site offers news, information, on-line support, code samples and more.

java.sun.com/docs/codeconv/html/CodeConvTOC.doc.html

This site reviews the *Sun Microsystems, Inc.* code conventions for the Java programming language.

www.softwaredev.earthweb.com

This site provides a wide variety of information on Java and other Internet-related topics. The Java directory page contains links to thousands of Java applets and other Java resources.

softwaredev.earthweb.com/java

The *Gamelan* site has been a wonderful Java resource since the early days of Java. This site originally was a large Java repository where individuals traded ideas on Java and examples of Java programming. One of its early benefits was the volume of Java source code that was available to the many people learning Java. It is now an all-around Java resource with Java references, free Java downloads, areas where you can ask questions of Java experts, discussion groups on Java, a glossary of Java terminology, upcoming Java events, directories for specialized industry topics and hundreds of other Java resources.

www.jars.com

Another *Earthweb.com* Web site is *JARS*—originally called the *Java Applet Rating Service*. The JARS site calls itself the "#1 Java Review Service." This site originated as a large Java repository for applets. Its benefit was that it rated every applet registered at the site as top 1%, top 5% and top 25%, so you could immediately view the best applets on the Web. Early in the development of the Java language, having your applet rated here was a great way to demonstrate your Java programming abilities. JARS is now another all-around resource for Java programmers.

---

1. There are many Java-related Web sites that cover more advanced Java topics such as servlets, JavaServer Pages (JSP), Enterprise Java Beans (EJB), database, Java 2 Enterprise Edition (J2EE), Java 2 Micro Edition (J2ME), Security, XML and many more. These sites are provided in our companion book, *Advanced Java 2 Platform How to Program* (ISBN# 0-13-089560-1).

developer.java.sun.com/developer
On the Sun Microsystems Java Web site, visit the *Java Developer Connection*. The site includes technical support, discussion forums, on-line training courses, technical articles, resources, announcements of new Java features, early access to new Java technologies and links to other important Java Web sites. Even though the site is free, you must register to use it.

www.acme.com/java
This page has several animated Java applets with the source code provided. This site is an excellent resource for information on Java. The page provides software, notes and a list of hyperlinks to other resources. Under software you will find animated applets, utility classes and applications.

www.javaworld.com/index.html
The JavaWorld online magazine provides a collection of Java articles, tips, news and discussions. A questions area of this site addresses both general and specific problems programmers face.

www.nikos.com/javatoys
The *Java Toys* Web site includes links to the latest Java news, Java User Groups (JUGs), FAQs, tools, Java-related mailing lists, books and white papers.

www.java-zone.com
The *Development Exchange Java Zone* site includes Java discussion groups, an "ask the Java Pro" section and some recent Java news.

www.ibiblio.org/javafaq
This site provides the latest Java news. It also has some helpful Java resources including a Java FAQ List, a tutorial called Brewing Java, Java User Groups, Java Links, the Java Book List, Java Trade Shows, Java Training and Exercises.

dir.yahoo.com/Computers_and_Internet/Programming_Languages/Java
Yahoo, a popular World Wide Web search engine, provides a complete Java resource. You can initiate a search using key words or explore the categories listed at the site including games, contests, events, tutorials and documentation, mailing lists, security and more.

www-106.ibm.com/developerworks/java
The *IBM Developers Java Technology Zone* site lists the latest news, tools, code, case studies and events related to IBM and Java.

B.2 Products

java.sun.com/products
Download the Java 2 SDK and other Java products from the *Sun Microsystems Java Products page*.

www.sun.com/forte/ffj/index.cgi
The *NetBeans* IDE is a customizable, platform independent, visual programming development environment.

www.borland.com/jbuilder
The *Borland JBuilder* IDE home page has news, product information and customer support.

www.towerj.com
At this site you will find information on how to enhance the performance of server-side Java applications along with free evaluation copies of native Java compilers.

www.symantec.com/domain/cafe
Visit the *Symantec* site for information on their *Visual Café Integrated Development Environment.*

www-4.ibm.com/software/ad/vajava
Download and read more about the IBM Visual Age for Java development environment.

www.metrowerks.com
The *Metrowerks CodeWarrior* IDE supports a few programming languages, including Java.

B.3 FAQs

www.ibiblio.org/javafaq/javafaq.html
This is a comprehensive resource for both Java language basics and more advanced topics in Java Programming. *Section 6: Language Issues* and *Section 11: Common Errors and Problems* may be particularly useful, as they clarify situations that often are not explained well.

www.afu.com/javafaq.html
This is another FAQ which covers a fairly broad slice of topics in Java. This includes some good code samples and hints for getting projects to compile and run.
www.nikos.com/javatoys/faqs.html
The *Java Toys* Web site includes links to FAQs on a broad range of Java-related topics.

www.jguru.com/faq/index.jsp
This is a thorough compilation of FAQs on Java and related subjects. Questions can be read in order or searched for by subject.

B.4 Tutorials

Several tutorials are on the sites listed in the Resources section.

java.sun.com/docs/books/tutorial/
The *Java Tutorial Site* has a number of tutorials, including sections on JavaBeans, JDBC, RMI, Servlets, Collections and Java Native Interface.

www.ibiblio.org/javafaq/
This site provides the latest Java news. It also has some helpful Java resources including the Java FAQ List, a tutorial called Brewing Java, Java User Groups, Java Links, the Java Book List, Java Conferences, Java Course Notes and Java Seminar Slides.

B.5 Magazines

www.javaworld.com
The *JavaWorld* on-line magazine is an excellent resource for current Java information. You will find news clips, conference information and links to Java-related Web sites.

www.sys-con.com/java
Catch up with the latest Java news at the *Java Developer's Journal* site. This magazine is one of the premier resources for Java news.

www.javareport.com
The *Java Report* is a great resource for Java developers. You will find the latest industry news, sample code, event listings, products and jobs.

www.javapro.com
The *JAVAPro* is an excellent Java developer resource with up-to-the-minute technical articles.

B.6 Java Applets

java.sun.com/applets/index.html
This page contains a variety of Java applet resources, including free applets you can use on your own Web site, the demonstration applets from the J2SDK and a variety of other applets. There is a section entitled "Applets at Work" where you can read about applets in industry.

developer.java.sun.com/developer/
On the Sun Microsystems Java Web site, visit the *Java Developer Connection*. This free site has close to one million members. The site includes technical support, discussion forums, on-line training courses, technical articles, resources, announcements of new Java features, early access to new Java technologies, and links to other important Java Web sites.

www.gamelan.com
Gamelan, a site owned by *EarthWeb*, has been a wonderful Java resource since the early days of Java. This site originally was a large Java repository where individuals traded ideas on Java and examples of Java programming. One of its early benefits was the volume of Java source code that was available to the many people learning Java. It is now an all-around Java resource with Java references, free Java downloads, areas where you can ask questions to Java experts, discussion groups on Java, a glossary of Java-related terminology, upcoming Java-related events, directories for specialized industry topics and hundreds of other Java resources.

www.jars.com
Another *EarthWeb* Web site is *JARS*—originally called the *Java Applet Rating Service*. The JARS site calls itself the "#1 Java Review Service." This site originally was a large Java repository for applets. Its benefit was that it rated every applet registered at the site as top 1%, top 5% and top 25%, so you could immediately view the best applets on the Web. Early in the development of the Java language, having your applet rated here was a great way to demonstrate your Java programming abilities. JARS is now another all-around resource for Java programmers.

B.7 Multimedia

java.sun.com/products/java-media/jmf
This is the *Java Media Framework home page* on the Java Web site. Here you can download the latest Sun implementation of the JMF (see Chapter 22). The site also contains the documentation for the JMF.

www.nasa.gov/gallery/index.html
The *NASA multimedia gallery* contains a wide variety of images, audio clips and video clips that you can download and use to test your Java multimedia programs.

sunsite.sut.ac.jp/multimed
The *Sunsite Japan Multimedia Collection* also provides a wide variety of images, audio clips and video clips that you can download for educational purposes.

www.anbg.gov.au/anbg/index.html
The *Australian National Botanic Gardens* Web site provides links to the audio clips of many animal sounds.

java.sun.com/products/java-media/jmf/index.html
This site provides an HTML-based on-line guide to the Java Media Framework API.

B.8 Newsgroups

Newsgroups are forums on the Internet in which people can post questions, responses, hints and clarifications for other users. Newsgroups can be a valuable resource to anyone learning Java or anyone with questions on specific Java topics. When posting your own questions to a newsgroup, provide specific details of the problem you are trying to solve (such as a problem with a program you are writing). This will enable other people reading the newsgroup to understand your posting and (hopefully) provide a response to you. Be sure to specify a subject heading that clearly states your problem. If you are responding to other people's questions, verify your response before posting it to ensure that the response is correct. Newsgroups should not be used to promote products or services, nor should contact information (such as email addresses for other newsgroup users) be used for unrelated purposes. These are generally not forums for chatting, so posts should be courteous and to the point.

Normally, newsgroup reader software is required for you to interact with a newsgroup. Such software is provided as part of Netscape Navigator and Microsoft Outlook Express, and there are many other newsgroup software programs available. You also can access newsgroups through the Web. If you do not use newsgroups already, try the *Google* site

groups.google.com

Type the name of the group you would like to view (you can also search for newsgroups) and you will be presented with a list of that newsgroup's current topics and questions. Listed below are some Java newsgroups that you may find useful.

news:comp.lang.java.advocacy
This group is an active center of discussion for current Java culture, including the merits of different programming languages.

news:comp.lang.java.announce
This group provides announcements on major additions to Java, new class libraries and conferences.

news:comp.lang.java.api
This groups contains questions about bugs, compile errors, Java specifications and which classes are most appropriate for different situations.

news:comp.lang.java.gui
This group responds to problems encountered working with Java graphical user interfaces. If you are having trouble with a particular component, layout or event, this may be a good place to start.

news:comp.lang.java.help
This group is particularly active. It addresses many language and environment issues. Questions include requests for classes or algorithms that solve a specific problem.

news:comp.lang.java.machine
For people interested in the inner workings of Java, this group focuses on the Java Virtual Machine.

news:comp.lang.java.misc
This group contains everything from job postings to questions about the Java documentation and is mainly for questions that do not fit into other Java newsgroup categories.

news:comp.lang.java.programmer
This group is another extremely active forum that addresses a range of questions. Posts tend to be largely project-oriented and concerned with overall program style and structure.

news:comp.lang.java.softwaretools
This newsgroup is centered around Java software products, their uses, their faults and possible modifications. Some questions about writing effective software are also included here.

news:comp.lang.java.tech
This is a new group devoted to the technical aspects of Java and its inner workings.

Operator Precedence Chart

Operators are shown in decreasing order of precedence from top to bottom.

Operator	Type	Associativity
()	parentheses	left to right
[]	array subscript	
.	member selection	
++	unary postincrement	right to left
--	unary postdecrement	
++	unary preincrement	right to left
--	unary predecrement	
+	unary plus	
-	unary minus	
!	unary logical negation	
~	unary bitwise complement	
(*type*)	unary cast	
*	multiplication	left to right
/	division	
%	modulus	
+	addition	left to right
-	subtraction	
<<	bitwise left shift	left to right
>>	bitwise right shift with sign extension	
>>>	bitwise right shift with zero extension	

Fig. C.1 Operator precedence chart (part 1 of 2).

<table>
<tr><th>Operator</th><th>Type</th><th>Associativity</th></tr>
<tr><td><</td><td>relational less than</td><td>left to right</td></tr>
<tr><td><=</td><td>relational less than or equal to</td><td></td></tr>
<tr><td>></td><td>relational greater than</td><td></td></tr>
<tr><td>>=</td><td>relational greater than or equal to</td><td></td></tr>
<tr><td>instanceof</td><td>type comparison</td><td></td></tr>
<tr><td>==</td><td>relational is equal to</td><td>left to right</td></tr>
<tr><td>!=</td><td>relational is not equal to</td><td></td></tr>
<tr><td>&</td><td>bitwise AND</td><td>left to right</td></tr>
<tr><td>^</td><td>bitwise exclusive OR
boolean logical exclusive OR</td><td>left to right</td></tr>
<tr><td>|</td><td>bitwise inclusive OR
boolean logical inclusive OR</td><td>left to right</td></tr>
<tr><td>&&</td><td>logical AND</td><td>left to right</td></tr>
<tr><td>||</td><td>logical OR</td><td>left to right</td></tr>
<tr><td>?:</td><td>ternary conditional</td><td>right to left</td></tr>
<tr><td>=</td><td>assignment</td><td>right to left</td></tr>
<tr><td>+=</td><td>addition assignment</td><td></td></tr>
<tr><td>-=</td><td>subtraction assignment</td><td></td></tr>
<tr><td>*=</td><td>multiplication assignment</td><td></td></tr>
<tr><td>/=</td><td>division assignment</td><td></td></tr>
<tr><td>%=</td><td>modulus assignment</td><td></td></tr>
<tr><td>&=</td><td>bitwise AND assignment</td><td></td></tr>
<tr><td>^=</td><td>bitwise exclusive OR assignment</td><td></td></tr>
<tr><td>|=</td><td>bitwise inclusive OR assignment</td><td></td></tr>
<tr><td><<=</td><td>bitwise left shift assignment</td><td></td></tr>
<tr><td>>>=</td><td>bitwise right shift with sign extension assignment</td><td></td></tr>
<tr><td>>>>=</td><td>bitwise right shift with zero extension assignment</td><td></td></tr>
</table>

Fig. C.1 Operator precedence chart (part 2 of 2).

ASCII Character Set

	0	1	2	3	4	5	6	7	8	9
0	nul	soh	stx	etx	eot	enq	ack	bel	bs	ht
1	nl	vt	ff	cr	so	si	dle	dc1	dc2	dc3
2	dc4	nak	syn	etb	can	em	sub	esc	fs	gs
3	rs	us	sp	!	"	#	$	%	&	‘
4	(	)	*	+	,	-	.	/	0	1
5	2	3	4	5	6	7	8	9	:	;
6	<	=	>	?	@	A	B	C	D	E
7	F	G	H	I	J	K	L	M	N	O
8	P	Q	R	S	T	U	V	W	X	Y
9	Z	[	\	]	^	_	’	a	b	c
10	d	e	f	g	h	i	j	k	l	m
11	n	o	p	q	r	s	t	u	v	w
12	x	y	z	{	|	}	~	del		

Fig. D.1 ASCII character set.

The digits at the left of the table are the left digits of the decimal equivalent (0-127) of the character code, and the digits at the top of the table are the right digits of the character code. For example, the character code for “F” is 70, and the character code for “&” is 38.

Most users of this book are interested in the ASCII character set used to represent English characters on many computers. The ASCII character set is a subset of the Unicode character set used by Java to represent characters from most of the world’s languages. For more information on the Unicode character set, see Appendix K.

Number Systems (on CD)

Objectives

- To understand basic number systems concepts such as base, positional value, and symbol value.
- To understand how to work with numbers represented in the binary, octal, and hexadecimal number systems
- To be able to abbreviate binary numbers as octal numbers or hexadecimal numbers.
- To be able to convert octal numbers and hexadecimal numbers to binary numbers.
- To be able to covert back and forth between decimal numbers and their binary, octal, and hexadecimal equivalents.
- To understand binary arithmetic, and how negative binary numbers are represented using two's complement notation.

Appendix E is included on the CD that accompanies this book in printable Adobe® Acrobat® PDF format. The appendix includes pages 1356–1368.

Creating HTML Documentation with `javadoc` (on CD)

Objectives

- To introduce the javadoc J2SDK tool.
- To introduce documentation comments.
- To understand javadoc tags.
- To be able to generate HTML API documentation with javadoc.
- To understand javadoc generated documentation files.

Appendix F is included on the CD that accompanies this book in printable Adobe® Acrobat® PDF format. The appendix includes pages 1369–1383.

G

Elevator Events and Listener Interfaces (on CD)

Appendix G is included on the CD that accompanies this book in printable Adobe® Acrobat® PDF format. The appendix includes pages 1384–1392. This appendix is the first of three CD-based appendices that continue our optional "Thinking About Objects" case study. This appendix presents the event classes and event-listener interfaces for the implementation of the object-oriented elevator simulator.

Elevator Model (on CD)

Appendix H is included on the CD that accompanies this book in printable Adobe® Acrobat® PDF format. The appendix includes pages 1393–1437. This appendix is the second of three CD-based appendices that continue our optional "Thinking About Objects" case study. This appendix presents the code for all 10 classes that collectively represent the model and concludes the discussion of the elevator model. We discuss each class separately and in detail.

I

Elevator View (on CD)

Appendix I is included on the CD that accompanies this book in printable Adobe® Acrobat® PDF format. The appendix includes pages 1438–1464. This appendix completes our optional "Thinking About Objects" case study. It contains the implementation for class **ElevatorView**—the largest class in the simulation. We split the discussion of the **ElevatorView** into five topics—*Class Objects*, *Class Constants*, *Class Constructor*, *Event Handling* and *Component Diagrams Revisited*.

J

Career Opportunities (on CD)

Objectives

- To explore the various online career services.
- To examine the advantages and disadvantages of posting and finding jobs online.
- To review the major online career services Web sites available to job seekers.
- To explore the various online services available to employers seeking to build their workforces.

Appendix J is included on the CD that accompanies this book in printable Adobe® Acrobat® PDF format. The appendix includes pages 1465–1488.

Unicode® (on CD)

Objectives

- To become familiar with Unicode.
- To discuss the mission of the Unicode Consortium.
- To discuss the design basis of Unicode.
- To understand the three Unicode encoding forms: UTF-8, UTF-16 and UTF-32.
- To introduce characters and glyphs.
- To discuss the advantages and disadvantages of using Unicode.
- To provide a brief tour of the Unicode Consortium's Web site.

Appendix K is included on the CD that accompanies this book in printable Adobe® Acrobat® PDF format. The appendix includes pages 1489–1500.

Bibliography

Sun Microsystems Resources

Block, J., "Tutorial: Collections", **java.sun.com/docs/books/tutorial/collections/index.html**, 1999

Fisher, M., "The JDBC Tutorial and Reference: Second Edition Chapter 3 Excerpt" **developer.java.sun.com/developer/Books/JDBCTutorial/index.html**, 1999

Gosling, J., and McGilton, H., "The Java Language Environment: a White Paper", **java.sun.com/docs/white/langenv**, 1996

Kluyt, O., "JavaBeans: Unlocking the BeanContext API," **developer.java.sun.com/developer/technicalArticles/Beans/BeanContext/index.html**

Meloan, M.D. "The Science Of Java Sound" **developer.java.sun.com/developer/technicalArticles/Media/JavaSoundAPI/index.html**

Papageorge, J., "Getting Started with JDBC" **developer.java.sun.com/developer/technicalArticles/Interviews/StartJDBC/index.html**, 1999

Sundsted, T., "XML and JAVA Tackle Entries Application Integration" **developer.java.sun.com/developer/technicalArticles/Networking/XMLAndJava/index.html**, 1999

Sun Microsystems, "JavaBeans Specifications and Tutorials", **java.sun.com/beans/docs/spec.html**

Sun Microsystems, "Enterprise JavaBeans Specifications and Tutorials", **java.sun.com/products/ejb/newspec.html**

Sun Microsystems, "Java 2D API Specifications and Tutorials", **java.sun.com/products/java-media/2D/forDevelopers/2Dapi/index.html**

Sun Microsystems, "RMI Specifications and Tutorials", **java.sun.com/products/jdk/1.2/docs/guide/rmi/**

Sun Microsystems, "Java Servlets API Specifications and Tutorials", **java.sun.com/products/servlet/index.html**, 1999

Sun Microsystems, "Java Foundation Classes: White Paper", **java.sun.com/marketing/collateral/foundation_classes.html**, 1999

Sun Microsystems, "The Collections Framework Overview", **java.sun.com/products/jdk/1.2/docs/guide/collections/overview.html**, 1999

Sun Microsystems, "Java Database Connectivity", **java.sun.com/marketing/collateral/jdbc_ds.html**

Sun Microsystems, "Getting Started with Swing", **java.sun.com/docs/books/tutorial/uiswing/start/index.html**

Sun Microsystems "Swing Features and Concepts" **java.sun.com/docs/books/tutorial/uiswing/overview/index.html**

Sun Microsystems "Using Swing Components" **java.sun.com/docs/books/tutorial/uiswing/components/index.html**

Sun Microsystems "Converting to swing" **java.sun.com/docs/books/tutorial/uiswing/converting/index.html**

Sun Microsystems "Laying Out Components within a Container" **java.sun.com/docs/books/tutorial/uiswing/layout/index.html**

Zucowski, J., "Mastering Java 2 Chapter 16: Transferring Data" **developer.java.sun.com/developer/Books/MasteringJava/Ch16/index.html**, 1999

Zucowski, J., "Mastering Java 2 Chapter 17: Java Collections" **developer.java.sun.com/developer/Books/MasteringJava/Ch17/index.html**, 1999

Other Resources

Arnold, K., J. Gosling, and D. Holmes. *The Java™ Programming Language: Third Edition*. Reading, MA: Addison-Wesley, 2000.

Barker, J. *Beginning Java Objects: From Concepts to Code*. Birmingham: Wrox Press, 2000.

Barnebee, J., "Java NT Services: Migrating you Java Server from Unix to an NT Boot-Time Environment," *Java Developer's Journal,* February 1999, pp. 54-56

Bell, D. and Parr, M., *Java for Students Second Edition,* London, UK: Prentice Hall Europe, 1999

Bennet, S., J. Skelton, and K. Lunn. *Schaum's Outline of UML*. New York, NY: McGraw Hill, 2001.

Berg, C.J., *Advanced Java Development for Enterprise Applications,* Upper Saddle River, NJ: Prentice Hall, 1998

Berg, D. and Fritzinger, J.S., *Advanced Techniques for Java Developers,* New York, NY: John Wiley & Sons, Inc., 1997

Bloch, J. *Effective Java™ Programming Language Guide*. Reading, MA: Addison-Wesley, 2001.

Booch, G. *Object-Oriented Analysis and Design with Applications*. Reading, MA; Addison-Wesley, 1994.

Booch, G., J. Rumbaugh, and I. Jacobson. *The Complete UML Training Course*. Reading, MA: Addison-Wesley, 2000.

Brodsky, S. and T. Grose. *Mastering XMI: Java Programming XMI, XML, and UML*. New York, NY: John Wiley & Sons, 2002.

Brogden, B., *Exam Cram: Java 2 Exam 310-025*, Scottsdale, AZ: The Coriolis Group, 1999

Bryson, T., "Exploring the Java 3D API," *Performance Computing,* April 1999, pp. 28-34

Callahan, T., "So You Want a Standalone Database for Java," *Java Developer's Journal,* December 1998, pp. 28-36

Campione, M.; Walrath, K.; Huml, A.; and the Tutorial Team, *The Java Tutorial Continued: The Rest of the JDK*, Reading, MA: Addison-Wesley, 1999

Campione, M., K. Walrath, and A. Huml. *The Java™ Tutorial, Third Edition: A Short Course on the Basics.* Reading, MA: Addison-Wesley, 2000.

Carey, J., B. Carlson, and T. Graser. *San Francisco™ Design Patterns: Blueprint for Business Software*. Reading, MA: Addison-Wesley, 2000.

Catalano, C., "Java Applets", *ComputerWorld,* May 3, 1999, p. 72

Cheesman, J., and J. Daniels. *UML Components: A Simple Process for Specifying Component-Based Software (The Component Software Series)*. Reading, MA: Addison-Wesley, 2000.

Coad, P.; Mayfeild, M.;and Kern, J., *Java Design: Building Better Apps and Applets: Second Edition,* Upper Saddle River, NJ: Yourdon Press, 1999

Coffee, P., "Java, Thin Clients Give Video Provider Tele-'Vision'," *PC Week,* April 12, 1999, p. 55

Cooper, J. *Java Design Patterns; A Tutorial*. Reading, MA: Addition-Wesley, 2000.

Daconta, M. C., E. Monk, J. P. Keller, and K. Bohnenberger. *Java Pitfalls: Time-Saving Solutions and Workarounds to Improve Programs*. New York, NY: John Wiley & Sons, 2000.

Detlefs, D., "Concurrent Coffee," *Performance Computing*, July 1999, pp.25-29

Eckel, B. *Thinking In Java: 2nd Edition*. Upper Saddle River, NJ: Prentice Hall, 2000.

Flynn, J., and B. Clarke, "The World Wakes up to Java!" Computer Technology Review, 1996, pp. 33–37.

Flanagan, D. *Java Examples In A Nutshell*. Sabastopol, CA: O'Reilly and Associates, 2000.

Folwer, M. and K. Scott. *UML Distilled Second Edition; A Brief Guide to the Standard Object Modeling Language*. Reading, MA: Addison-Wesley, 1999.

Gamma, E., R. Helm, R. Johnson, and J. Vlissides. *Design Patterns; Elements of Reusable Object-Oriented Software.* Reading, MA: Addison-Wesley, 1995.

George, J., "Java - Into Its Fourth Year," *Java Developer's Journal,* February 1999, p. 66

Gilbert, S., and McCarty, B., *Object-Oriented Design in Java,* Corte Madera, CA: Waite Group Press, 1998

Grand, M. *Patterns in Java; A Catalog Reusable Design Patterns Illustrated with UML*. New York, NY: John Wiley & Sons, 1998.

Haggar, P., "Effective Exception Handling in Java," *Java Report,* April 1999, pp. 55- 64

Halfhill, T. R. "How to Soup up Java: Part 1," *Byte Magazine*, May 1998, pp. 60-80

Haverlock, K. "Object Serialization, Java, and C++," *Dr. Dobb's Journal,* August 1998, pp. 32-34

Heller, P., and Roberts, S., *Java 2 Developers Handbook,* Alameda, CA: Sybex, Inc., 1999

Hemrajani, A., "Programming with I/O Streams: Part 3," *Java Developer's Journal,* February 1999,pp. 18-22

Hof, R. D., and J. Verity, "Scott McNealy's Rising Sun," Cover Story, Business Week, January 22, 1996, pp. 66–73.

Horstmann, C. S. and G. Cornell. *Core Java2: Volume 1-Fundamentals*. Upper Saddle River, NJ: Prentice Hall, 2001.

Horstmann, C. S. and G. Cornell. *Core Java2: Volume II-Advanced Features*. Upper Saddle River, NJ; Prentice Hall, 2001.

Hunt J., "The Collection API," *Java Report,* April 1999, pp. 17-32

Hunter, J., and Kadel, R., "Everywhere You Look: Enterprise Server-Side Java", *Javaworld,* March 27, 1998, online

Larman, C. *Applying UML and Patterns; An Introduction to Object-Oriented Analysis and Design*. Upper Saddle River, NJ: Prentice Hall, 1998.

Lea, D. *Concurrent Programming in Java™ Second Edition Design Principles and Patterns*. Reading, MA: Addison-Wesley, 2000.

Lauinger, T., "Object-Oriented Software Development in Java," *Java Report,* February 1999, pp. 59-61

Malarvannan, M., "A Multithreaded Server in Java", *Web Techniques,* October 1998, pp. 47-51

Maruyama, H.; Tamura, K.; and Uramoto Naohiko, *XML and JAVA: Developing Web Applications,* Reading, MA: Addison-Wesley Publishing Company, Inc., 1999

Oaks, S., "How Do I Create My Own UI Component?" Java Report, March/April 1996, pp. 64, 63.

Oaks, S., "Two Techniques for Handling Events," *Java Report,* July/August, 1996. p. 80.

Oaks, S. and H. Wong, Java Threads, Sebastopol, CA: O'Reilly & Associates, Inc., 1997.

Page-Jones, M. *Fundamentals of Object-Oriented Design in UML*. Reading, MA: Addison-Wesley, 1999.

Penker, M. and Hans-Erik E. *Business Modeling with UML: Business Patterns At Work*. New York, NY: John Wiley & Sons, 2000.

Pratik P. and Moss, K. *Java Database Programming with JDBC: Second Edition,* Scottsdale, AZ: The Coriolis Group, 1997

RineHart, M., *Java Database Development*, Berkeley, CA: Osborn/McGraw-Hill, 1998

Roberts, Si., P. Heller, M. Ernest, and R. et al. *The Complete Java 2 Certification Study Guide*. Alameda, CA: SYBEX, 2000.

Rodrigues, L., "On JavaBeans Customization", *Java Developer's Journal,* May 1999, pp.-21

Rumbaugh, J., I. Jacobson, and G. Booch. *The Unified Modeling Language Reference Manual*. Reading, MA: Addison-Wesley, 1999.

Rumbaugh, J., I. Jacobson, and G. Booch. *The Unified Modeling Language User Guide*. Reading, MA: Addison-Wesley, 1999.

Rumbaugh, J., I. Jacobson, and G. Booch. *The Unified Software Development Process*. Reading, MA: Addison-Wesley, 1999.

Scott, K. *UML Explained*. Reading, MA: Addison-Wesley, 2001.

Shirazi, J. *Java Performance Tuning*. Sabastopol, CA: O'Reilly and Associates, 2000.

Stevens, P. and R.J. Pooley. *Using UML: Software Engineering with Objects and Components Revised Edition*. Reading, MA: Addison-Wesley, 2000.

Sun Microsystems Inc. *Java™ Look and Feel Design Guidelines, Second Edition.* Reading, MA: Addison-Wesley, 2001.

Tan, E. M., "Java-The Software Design," *Java Developer's Journal,* January 1999, pp. 58-59

Topley, K. *Core Swing: Advanced Programming*. Upper Saddle River, NJ: Prentice Hall, 2000.

Venners, B., *Inside the Java Virtual Machine,* New York, NY: McGraw-Hill, 1998

Vlissides, J. *Pattern Hatching; Design Patterns Applied.* Reading, MA: Addison-Wesley, 1998.

Walsh, A., and Fronckowiak, J., *Java Bible,* Foster City, CA; IDG Books Worldwide, Inc. 1998

Index

Symbols

!, logical NOT 222, 226
!=, not equals 80, 81, 222
%, modulus 77, 78
&&, logical AND 222, 225
&, boolean logical AND 222
( ), parentheses 78
* 57
*, multiplication 77, 78
++, preincrement/postincrement 179
+, addition 77, 78, 384, 560
+=, addition assignment operator 178, 560
--, predecrement/postdecrement 179, 180
-, subtraction 77, 78
.java file name extensionjava file name extension 116
/* */ multiline comment 57
/** */ Java documentation comment 57
/, division 77, 78
//, single-line comment 56, 57, 114
<, less than 80
<=, less than or equal 80, 222
<applet> tag 131, 198, 201
<html> tag 1077
=, assignment 72, 129, 172, 179
==, is equal to 80, 85
>, greater than 80
>= greater than or equal to 80
?:, conditional operator 156, 181
?:, ternary conditional 156, 181
@author 1375
@files 1379
@link 1383
@since 1383
@version 1379
[], array subscript 356
\ separator character 967
\", double-quote escape sequence 64
\, escape character 64
\n, newline escape sequence 64, 122, 209
\r, carriage return escape sequence 64
\t, tab escape sequence 64, 209
^, boolean logical exclusive OR 222
{, left brace 59, 60
|=, boolean logical inclusive OR 222
||, logical OR 222, 224
}, right brace 59, 60

Numerics

15 Puzzle 1092
3D effect 893

A

abbreviating assignment expressions 178
abnormally terminate a program 328
abort on an exceptional situation 807
abs method of Math 250
absolute path 962, 967
absolute value 250
abstract class 474, 475, 476, 487, 494, 515, 519, 526, 1072, 1401, 1402
abstract data type (ADT) 381, 432
Abstract Factory design pattern 521, 1056
abstract Implementations 1229
abstract keyword 152, 474, 1148, 1160
abstract method 477, 486, 487, 516, 519, 656, 1229, 1402
abstract superclass 474, 475, 477, 486
Abstract Windowing Toolkit 758
Abstract Windowing Toolkit (AWT) 649
Abstract Windowing Toolkit Event Package 260
AbstractButton 662, 664, 747, 753
abstraction 22, 448
AbstractList class 1229
AbstractMap class 1229

AbstractSequentialList class 1229
accept 990, 994, 997, 1013
access modifier 515
access shared data 854, 892
access to new Java technologies 135
accessibility heuristic 365
accessor method 383, 389, 400
AccountRecord.java 906
accounts receivable file 975
accumulator 371
accumulator register 374
action 3, 60, 149, 234, 432, 585, 587
action event 272, 648, 722
action key 689
action oriented 380
action-oriented 23
action symbol 152
action/decision model of computing 154, 155
ActionEvent 269, 272, 308, 658, 660, 661, 663, 694, 724, 744, 1076
ActionListener 269, 270, 496, 644, 658, 659, 661, 663, 718, 744, 772, 814
actionPerformed method of **ActionListener** 270, 272, 282, 404, 494, 504, 509, 644, 656, 660, 663, 677, 694, 699, 724, 744, 770, 812, 818
activate a text field 72
ACTIVATED 987, 990
active 128
active class 878, 883, 1407, 1418
activity 42, 92, 234, 238
activity diagram 42, 91, 235, 236, 237, 1435
actor 703, 704
acyclic 631
Ada Lovelace 15
Ada programming language 15, 838
adapter class 512, 683
Adapter design pattern 521, 524, 789
add method of **Container** 251, 271, 650, 652
add method of **JMenuBar** 753
add method of **Vector** 982
addActionListener 272, 404, 504, 506, 659, 663, 677, 694
addComponent 777, 781
addElement 1155
addHyperlinkListener 987
adding components to a content pane 650
addItemListener 666
addition 77
Addition.java 69, 70
AdditionApplet.html 125
AdditionApplet.java 123
addKeyListener 690, 691
addListSelectionListener 674
addMenu 763
addMouseListener 680, 730, 732, 756, 1082
addMouseMotionListener 680, 731, 732, 734, 1082
addPoint 627, 628
addSeparator 750
addTarget 1272
addWindowListener 740
AdjustmentEvent 654
administrative section of the computer 8
ADTs 432
Advanced Java 2 Platform How to Program 6, 16, 45, 722, 1026
Advantage Hiring, Inc. 1473
aggregation 138, 388, 435, 788
.aif or **.aiff** extension 1085, 1237, 1278
Airline Reservation System 892
airline reservation system 892, 900
airline reservations system 361
airlines reservations system 361
algebraic notation 77
algorithm 149, 160, 286, 794, 1202, 1215
Algorithms1.java 1220
alphabetizing 542
ALU 8
America's Job Bank 1471
American National Standards Committee on Computers and Information Processing (X3) 11
American National Standards Institute (ANSI) 5, 433
American Society for Female Entrepreneurs 1473
analysis 24, 90
Analysis.java 176
Analytical Engine 15
and 1189
Andrew Koenig 805
animated shape 112
AnimatedPanel 1317, 1318, 1323, 1326, 1327, 1457, 1458, 1460, 1461, 1463, 1464
AnimatedPanel.java 1323
animating a series of images 1073
animation 4, 6, 44, 112, 292, 605, 645, 1070, 1077, 1091, 1323, 1327
animation speed 112
Animator applet 108
anonymous inner class 501, 507, 508, 511, 673, 685, 708, 724, 735, 739
anonymous **String** object 538, 545
ANSI 5, 11, 433
ANSI C standard document 19
anti-aliasing 112
API 16
append a string 74
append method of **JTextArea** 209
append method of **StringBuffer** 564
Apple Computer, Inc. 9, 1491
Applet 112, 114, 259, 692, 1072, 1329
applet 18, 21, 56, 106, 129, 134, 251, 275, 650, 981, 1072, 1077
applet **.class** file 119
applet arriving from the World Wide Web 895
applet container 106, 117
applet content pane 254, 271, 281
applet display area 119
applet graphics context 604
applet **paint** method 747
applet parameter 981
applet start-up sequence of method calls 746
applet that can also be executed as an application 741
applet width and height 741
AppletContext 981
applets directory 108
Applets hyperlink 134

applets in the public domain 981, 1077
appletviewer 106, 109, 111, 112, 115, 118, 198, 201, 269, 292, 741
appletviewer's **Applet** menu 110
application 18, 56, 59, 87, 88, 106, 133
application class definition 163
application programming interface (API) 13
application service provider (ASP) 1473
application window 735
applications primary window 746
applications programming interface (API) 16
Aquent.com 1478
arc 108, 621
arc angle 622
arc method 623
Arc2D 602
Arc2d.CHORD 632
Arc2D.Double 628, 630, 645
Arc2D.OPEN 632
Arc2d.PIE 630
arcHeight 619, 621
architectural patterns 521, 1058, 1060
archive attribute 410
ArcTest applet 108
arcWidth 619, 621
area of a circle 312
argument 61, 249
argument to a method call 251
arithmetic and logic unit (ALU) 8
arithmetic assignment operators: **+=**, **-=**, ***=**, **/=** and **%=** 188
arithmetic calculation 76
arithmetic mean (average) 78
arithmetic operators 76, 372
arithmetic overflow 806
ArithmeticException 813
array 287, 314, 895, 982, 1230
array allocated with **new** 328
array bounds 328
array declaration 319
arraycopy 1204
ArrayIndexOutOfBound-sException 328, 628, 810, 818
ArrayList 1208, 1209, 1210, 1215, 1221, 1223
Arrays 1203
arrays are Java objects 379
arrays of arrays 343
arrow 146, 214
arrow key 689
arrowhead 881
ascending order 335, 1205, 1223
ascent 616, 618
ASCII 377, 1491
ASCII character set Appendix 1355
asList 1206, 1208, 1215, 1216, 1224, 1234
assembler 10
assembly language 10
assign a value to a variable 72
assigning class objects 383
assigning subclass references to superclass references 452
assignment operator, **=** 72, 73, 81, 129, 172, 179
assignment operators 178
assignment statement 72, 128
associate left to right 86, 181
associate right to left 77, 86, 173, 181
association 24, 42, 138, 139, 435, 436
association name 138, 139
associativity of operators 77, 86, 181, 316
asterisk (*) 125
asynchronous events 806
attribute 23, 42, 183, 184, 186, 234, 237, 238, 434, 435, 436, 513, 517, 518, 636, 885
attribute (data) 115, 137, 141, 380, 382, 464
attribute compartment 186
attribute name 186
attribute type 186
.au 1237, 1278
.au file 1327
.au, Sun Audio file extension 1237, 1278
audio 4, 6, 90, 259, 645, 1277, 1317, 1327
audio clip 1084, 1085, 1087, 1419
audio clips 839, 1316
audio playback 110
audio speaker 8
AudioClip 1084, 1086, 1089, 1327, 1329, 1457, 1459, 1460, 1461
AudioFormat 1282
AudioFormat.Encoding 1282
AudioInputStream 1281
AudioSystem 1281
Australian National Botanic Gardens Web site 1087, 1316
Author
note 1375
-author argument 1379
automated teller machine 703
automatic conversion 74
automatic duration 274
automatic garbage collection 825, 839
automatic scrolling 676
automatic variables must be initialized 274
automatic word wrap 725
automatically initialized 274
average 160, 165, 166
Average1.java 161
Average2.java 169
.avi 1237
.avi (Microsoft Audio/Video Interleave extension) 1237
AWT components 649
AWTEvent 654
AWTException 822

B

B 11
Babbage, Charles 15
background color 609, 611, 718, 733
background of application window 733
backing collection 1228
backslash, \ 64
backwards compatibility 1378
Balking design pattern 521, 886
bandwidth 1069
BankUI.java 904
bar chart 108, 243, 323
bar graph 645
bar of asterisks 323
BarChart applet 108
base 3, 10, 11, 572, 1175
base case 278, 280, 284, 285
base class 115, 382
baseline of the font 616
Basic 14, 1095
Basic Latin 1496
BasicStroke 602, 629, 632
batch file 68

batch processing 8
batches 8
BCPL 11
behavior 23, 42, 293, 464
behavior (method) 115, 380, 382
behavior of the system 235, 238, 352, 703
behavioral design patterns 27, 520, 524, 792, 1230
Bell 879
Bell 137, 139, 141, 185, 187, 293, 294, 295, 353, 435, 436, 518, 587, 637, 884, 885, 1400, 1401, 1419, 1420, 1437, 1456
Bell Laboratories 11
BellEvent 585, 1385, 1392, 1428, 1463
BellListener 637, 638, 1388, 1392, 1400, 1401, 1415, 1419, 1428
Bid4Geeks.com 1477
BigDecimal 281
BigInteger 281
BilingualJobs.com 1473
binary 243
binary (base 2) number system 1357
binary arithmetic operators 172
binary integer 195
binary operator 72, 76, 226
binary search 335, 337, 338, 340
binary search 1221
binary search algorithm 1221
binary search tree 1116, 1121
binary tree 1095, 1122
binary tree delete 1131
binary tree search 1132
binary tree sort 1122
binarySearch 1203, 1204, 1206, 1221, 1222, 1223
BinarySearch.java 338
BinarySearchTest.java 1222
bind the server to a port 1004
BindException 1004
binding the server to the port 990
bit (size of unit) 1491
bit manipulation 1148
BitSet 1190, 1197
BitSetTest.java 1191
BitShift.java 1185
bitwise AND, **&** 1175
bitwise assignment operators 1189
bitwise complement operator, **~** 1185
bitwise exclusive OR operator, **^** 1184, 1185
bitwise exclusive OR, **/** 1184
bitwise exclusive OR, **^** 1175
bitwise inclusive OR, **|** 1175
bitwise operators 1175
bitwise shift operators 1185
Bjarne Stroustrup 805
black box 122
black jack card game 1066
Blackvoices.com 1472
blank line 58, 167
_blank target frame 985
Blink applet 108
blink speed 1091
blinking text 108
block 158, 171, 254, 990, 1007
block is exited 274
block scope 275, 388
block until connection received 997
blocked for input/output 843
blocked state 841
blocking call 1033
blocks nested 275
blueprint 115
Bluetooth 1477
body 59
body of a class definition 382
body of a loop 205
body of a method definition 60
body of an **if** structure 79
Bohm, C. 151, 233
BOLD 613, 666
Booch, Grady 25, 26
Boolean 513
Boolean 1114, 1156
boolean expression 156
boolean logical AND, **&** 225
boolean logical exclusive OR, **^** 226
boolean logical inclusive OR, **|** 225
boolean primitive data type 152, 154, 183
boolean promotions 258
boolean variables initialized to **false** 274
border 740
BorderLayout 680, 691, 692, 696, 725, 746, 754, 760, 766, 768, 770
BorderLayout.CENTER 697, 699, 729
BorderLayout.EAST 697
BorderLayout.NORTH 697, 743, 768, 771
BorderLayout.SOUTH 680, 697, 702, 738
BorderLayout.WEST 697
BorderLayoutDemo.java 696
Borland's JBuilder 16
born state 841
Boss.java 479
BOTH 779, 781, 801
bottom 603
bottom of a loop 217
bouncing ball 1344
bounding box for an oval 147
bounding rectangle 217, 619, 621, 622, 733, 736
Box container 724, 767
BoxLayout 724, 767, 768
BoxLayout.X_AXIS 770
BoxLayout.Y_AXIS 770
BoxLayoutDemo.java 767
braces (**{** and **}**) 126, 158, 171, 202, 216, 220, 253
braces not required 214
braces that delimit a compound statement 158
braces, **{** and **}** 319
brackets, **[** and **]** 316
braille screen reader 651
branch 236, 237, 791
branch point 237
Brassringcampus.com 1480
break 152, 213, 214, 218, 245, 275
BreakLabelTest.java 221
BreakTest.java 218
Bridge design pattern 521, 524, 790
brightness 612
browser 18, 65, 118, 198, 292, 741
browser friendly 1076
browser in which applet executes 116
browsing 981, 1077
browsing the Internet 120
brute force 366
brute force version of Knight's Tour 366
bubble sort 332, 359
improve performance 359
bubble up 1399, 1409, 1416, 1428
BubbleSort.java 333

bucket sort 367
buffer 849, 900, 901, 997, 1263
buffer empty 849
BufferedImage 629, 631
BufferedInputStream 901
BufferedOutputStream 901, 1057
BufferedReader 902, 967, 1033
BufferedWriter 902
Builder design pattern 521
building block approach to creating programs 13, 24
building blocks 149, 198, 231
Building Your Own Compiler 1095, 1136
Building Your Own Computer 371
built-in array capabilities 1202
built-in data types 71, 432
built-in multithreading 839
bulk operation 1208
business-critical computing 817
Button 513, 515, 583, 637, 662, 881, 882, 884, 1400, 1401, 1402, 1404, 1408, 1409, 1415, 1416, 1420, 1428, 1435, 1437
button 66, 68
button label 662
ButtonEvent 585, 1386, 1392, 1409, 1416, 1428, 1462
ButtonGroup 668, 747, 748, 750, 756, 757
ButtonListener 637, 638, 1388, 1389, 1392, 1400, 1401, 1409, 1415, 1416, 1428
ButtonTest.java 662
ButtonText.java 662
Byte 513
Byte 1156
byte 183
byte array 1036
byte offset 929
byte primitive data type 152, 210, 1057, 1175
byte promotions 258
ByteArrayInputStream 902
ByteArrayOutputStream 902
bytecode 16, 17, 21, 61, 118, 1095
bytecode verifier 19

C

C 3, 5, 9, 11, 14, 380, 838
C How to Program 5, 6
C Programming Language 11
C++ 5, 9, 11, 12, 838
C++ How to Program 6
C++-style single-line comments 57
call-by-reference 329
call-by-value 329
call chain 826
call stack 830, 831
called method 248
caller 248
calling a method 200, 248
calling method 329
CampusCareerCenter.com 1480
CANCEL_OPTION 910, 913
CannotRealizeException 1261
canRead 962
canWrite 962
CAP_ROUND 630
capacity 1149
capacity 561, 1156
capacity increment 1149, 1155
capacity of a **StringBuffer** 559
Caps Lock 689
capture device 1239, 1249
captured media 1249
CaptureDevice interface 1260
CaptureDeviceInfo 1260
CaptureDeviceInfo class 1259, 1260
CaptureDeviceManager 1260, 1333
CapturePlayer 1259
CapturePlayer.java 1250
card games 579
card shuffling and dealing simulation 579, 1217
CardDeck.java 771
CardLayout 766, 770, 773
Cards.java 1217
CardTest applet 108
Career.com 1471
CareerLeader.com 1475
CareerPath.com 1471
CareerWeb 1471
caretaker object 525
carriage return 64
carry bit 1364
Cartesian coordinates 442
cascaded method calls 421
Cascading super references 461
case conversion methods of class **Character** 569
case keyword 152
case label 213, 215
case sensitive 58
case-sensitive language 159
case sensitivity 394
cases in a **switch** 214
casino 261, 265
Cast 459
cast 819
cast operator 168, 172, 259, 452
casting a superclass reference to a subclass reference 532
catch all exceptions 810, 811, 831
catch block 808, 809, 810, 817, 818, 826
catch handler 152, 762, 809, 811, 817, 825
catch related errors 824
catch superclass type 811, 824
catch-or-declare requirement 819
cd to change directories 108, 112
ceil method of **Math** 250
Celsius equivalent of a Fahrenheit temperature 308
Celsiuss 717
CENTER 694, 725, 746, 775
center mouse button click 688
centered 693
central processing unit (CPU) 8
chain 991
Chain-of-Responsibility design pattern 521, 524
chained stream object 914
chaining of stream objects 914
Chain-of-Responsibility design pattern 792
chance 261
change directories 108, 112
ChangeEvent 739
ChangeListener 739
changing look-and-feel of a Swing-based GUI 762
char array 540
char keyword 152, 183
char primitive data type 210
char promotions 258
char variable 71
Character 513, 537, 564, 569, 1114, 1156, 1227

character 260, 896, 1492, 1498
Character class **static** conversion methods 572
character constant 538
character set 103, 109, 896, 1491
character string 60
CharArrayReader 902
CharArrayWriter 902
charAt method 563, 1227
charValue method 574
check amount 597
check boxes 662, 667
check protection 597
checkbox 112
checkbox is unchecked 112
checkbox label 667
CheckBoxTest.java 665
checked exception 819, 820
checkerboard 195
checkerboard pattern 102, 147
checkers program 1066
chess-playing program 1066
ChiefMonster 1479
child 1116
child thread group 876
child window 722, 762, 766, 801
choice 111, 112
choppy playback 839
circle 621, 643
circle of random size 802
Circle.java 457, 462, 489, 497
circular buffer 860, 867
circumference 101, 146, 802
CJK Unified Ideographs 1496
clarity 2, 19
Class 1052
class 13, 23, 42, 187, 239, 293, 295, 296, 350, 380, 434, 435
class 896
class average 160
class-average program with counter-controlled repetition 161
class-average program with sentinel-controlled repetition 169
class cannot inherit from a final class 474
class comment 1375
class constructor 435
class declared **final** 474
class definition 58, 59, 70, 115, 126, 291, 382, 452
class diagram 42, 43, 91, 137, 138, 139, 183, 186, 294, 295, 434, 435, 436, 516, 517, 518, 637, 638, 785, 787, 883, 885, 1317, 1318, 1399, 1409, 1420, 1429
.class file 18, 62, 385, 392, 417, 512, 1085
class hierarchies headed by abstract superclasses 473
class hierarchy 476
class keyword 58, 152
class libraries 13, 210, 411, 433, 448, 464
class loader 18, 1052
class name 58, 59, 392, 435
class scope 275, 388
class-scope variable hidden by method-scope variable 388
ClassCastException 452
classes 247
classes to implement abstract data types 433
ClassName.**this** 753, 875
ClassNotFoundException 918, 995, 1001
CLASSPATH 394
-classpath command line argument to **java** 394, 903
-classpath command line argument to **javac** 394, 903
"class-wide" information 427
clear 1190
clearRect method 619
click a button 662
click a tab 113
click count 686
click the mouse 68, 72, 109, 110, 128, 664
click the scroll arrows 671
clicking a button 654
clicking menu item generates action event 747
clicking the close box 802
clicking the mouse 654
client 293, 352, 383
client connections 990
client object 583, 1058
client of a class 432
client of a library 807
client of the object 115
client portion of a stream socket connection 998
client/server computing 9
client tier 1060
client window 1003
Client.java 998, 1008
client/server 1008
client/server chat 992
client's site 21
ClientGUI.java 1046
Clip 1281
Clip method **start** 1282
Clip.LOOP_CONTINUOSLY 1282, 1335
clipped 732
ClipPlayer.java 1278
ClipPlayerTest.java 1283
clock 108, 1092
Clock applet 108
close 914, 924, 936
close a file 921, 937
close a window 506
close method of class **Multi-castSocket** 1046
closed polygons 625
closed tour 366, 645
closePath 633
closing a window 654
closing right brace (**}**) 275
COBOL (COmmon Business Oriented Language) 14
code attribute of **<applet>** tag 119
code reuse 1202
code value 1492, 1496, 1498
coercion of arguments 258
coin tossing 261, 309
collaboration 42, 43, 183, 350, 351, 352, 353, 586, 588, 1404
collaboration diagram 43, 91, 352, 353, 586, 879
collaborative applications 891, 1026
collaborative computing 6
Collection 1155, 1208, 1210, 1224
collection 475
collection 1215
Collection implementation 1228
collection implementation 1203
collection interfaces 1203
Collections 1218, 1220
collections 48, 1148

collections framework 1202, 1208
collections framework algorithm 1215
collections hierarchy 1208
CollectionTest.java 1209
Collegegrads.com 1480
collisions 1161
Color 605, 606, 633
color 111, 602
color chooser dialog 611
Color constant 605, 606, 607, 609
color manipulation 604
color screen 118
color swatches 611
column 343
combo box 111, 112, 671
ComboBoxTest.java 671
comma (**,**) 206
comma in an argument list 67
comma-separated list 71, 84, 203, 254
comma-separated list of arguments 249
command-and-control software system 15
command and control systems 838
command button 662
Command design pattern 521, 524
command design pattern 792
command line 1380
command-line argument 109, 111, 112
command-line application 808
command-line argument 741, 743
command-line output window 462
Command Prompt 18, 60
command window 60, 63, 72, 107, 109, 118, 847, 850, 856
comma-separated list of parameters 254
comment, **//**) 56, 71
commercial applications 14, 895
commercial data processing 974
commission 192, 358
CommissionWorker.java 480
Common Birds link 1316
common interface for the members of a class hierarchy 476
common programming errors 13
Comparator object 1215, 1216, 1217, 1220, 1223, 1226
Comparator object in **sort** 1216
compareTo 543, 545, 593
comparing **String** objects 542
Comparison.java 81
compilation error 61
compilation process 1140
compile 61, 1095
compile a program 16
compile-time error 61
compiled applet class 119
compiled C or C++ code 21
compiler 10, 18
complement, **~** 1175
complete 841
Complete Detailed MIDI 1.0 specification 1285
Complex 440
complex class 440
complex curve 632
complex number 441
complexity 335
complexity theory 286, 1215
Component 604, 611, 648, 679, 732, 740, 779, 789, 791, 1073, 1246
component 4, 23, 24, 44, 92, 259, 678, 785, 788
component diagram 44, 91, 785, 787, 1391, 1436, 1463
component-oriented software development 433
component reuse 786
Component's paint method 605
Component's repaint method 605
ComponentAdapter 683
ComponentEvent 654
ComponentListener 683
components 12
Composite design pattern 521, 524, 791
composition 388, 414, 448, 465
compound interest 207, 242, 243
comprehensive job sites 1466
computational complexity 335
compute-intensive applets 21
computer 7
computer-assisted instruction (CAI) 309
computer dump 375
computer program 7
computer programmer 7
computer simulator 374
computers in education 309
concat 552
concatenate 252, 384
concatenated method calls 421
concatenation 74, 85, 560
concatenation operator, **+** 130, 384
concentric circles 643
concrete class 474, 533
concrete method 516, 1404
concurrency 838
concurrency control 892
concurrency design patterns 886
concurrency problem 886
concurrent 877
concurrent access to a **Collection** by multiple threads 1228
concurrent design patterns 520, 521
concurrent producer and consumer threads 854
concurrent programming 839
concurrent threads 854
ConcurrentModificationException 1407
condition 79
condition variable 854
conditional expression 156, 383
conditional operator, **?:** 156, 181
configureComplete method 1271
ConfigureCompleteEvent 1271
Configuring 1271
Confusing the equality operator **==** with the assignment operator **=** 81
connect method of **DataSource** 1260
connect to server on a port 990
connect to the server 991
connected lines 625
ConnectException 992
connection 980, 1002
connection attempt 991
connection between client and server terminates 992
connection from a client 1018

connection-oriented, streams-based transmission 1003
connection port 996
connection to a server 1018
connectionless client/server computing with datagrams 1004
connectionless service 980
connectionless transmission with datagrams 1003
connector symbol 152
conserve memory 839
consistent state 384, 387, 396, 401
console applications 808
constant integral expression 215
constant strings 560
constant variable 215, 270, 322
constructor 352, 394, 462
constructor failure 836
consume memory 286
ConsumeInteger.java 851, 855
consumer 853, 856, 857
consumer electronic devices 12
consuming data 851
Container 269, 271
Container 251, 252, 269, 603, 650, 652, 692, 701, 791
container 648
container for menus 747
ContainerAdapter 683
ContainerListener 683
contains 1168
Content Descriptor.RAW_RTP 1271
content pane 251, 254, 271, 281, 330, 611, 650, 653, 754
ContentDescriptor 1271
contention for the processor 848
context-sensitive popup menu 755
continue 152, 218, 219, 222, 223, 245, 275, 1033, 1045
ContinueLabelTest.java 223
ContinueTest.java 219
control structure 151, 153, 198, 234, 286
control-structure nesting 153
control-structure stacking 153, 231
control variable 202, 203
Controller 1238, 1246
controller 44, 87, 91, 783, 784, 785, 786, 787
controller (in MVC architecture) 1058, 1059
ControllerAdapter 1247
ControllerEvent 1248, 1249
ControllerListener 1247
controlling expression 213
controls 648
converge on a base case 278
conversion template 133
conversions between number systems 572
convert a binary number to decimal 1362
convert a hexadecimal number to decimal 1362
convert a superclass reference to a subclass reference 452
convert an applet into a GUI-based application 741
convert an integral value to a floating-point value 259
convert an octal number to decimal 1362
convert between classes and built-in types 383
Cooljobs.com 1480
cooperating threads of equal priority 843
coordinate system 602, 604
coordinates 117
coordinates (0, 0) 602
coordinates at which user releases mouse button 719
copy algorithm 1219, 1220, 1233
copy constructor 538
copy of a large object 380
copy text from one text area to another 722
core package 65
corporate culture 1469, 1472
cos method of **Math** 250
cosine 250
counter 161, 167
counter-controlled repetition 161, 170, 174, 176, 198, 199, 201, 202, 286, 373
counter variable 213
countTokens 577
Courier font 342, 750
Courtois, P. J. 892
CPU 8
"craft valuable classes" 24
craps (casino game) 261, 265, 270, 312, 361, 1345
Craps.java 265
create a package 390
create a **Socket** 991
create an inner class object 513
create new classes from existing class definitions 382
create new types 433
createDataSink 1333
createDataSink method of **Manager** 1262
createDataSource method of **Manager** 1260
createGlue 768, 770
createHorizontalBox 724, 767
createHorizontalGlue 768, 769
createHorizontalStrut 769
createPlayer method of **Manager** 1247
createProcessor method of **Manager** 1261
CreateRandomFile.java 931
createRealized-Processor 1333
createRigidArea 768
CreateSequential-File.java 908
createVerticalBox 767
createVerticalGlue 770
createVerticalStrut 769
creating a package 390
creating a reusable class 390
creating an instance 172
creating new data types 432
creational design patterns 27, 520, 789, 1056, 1229
credit inquiry program 921
credit limit on a charge account 191
CreditInquiry.java 921
crossword puzzle generator 600
Cruel World 1475
Ctrl key 676, 692
currentThread 841, 852, 857
Cursor 989
cursor 60, 63
Cursor.DEFAULT_CURSOR 989
Cursor.WAIT_CURSOR 989
curve 109, 632
customizing class **Jpanel** 721
CustomPanel.java 727
CustomPanelTest.java 728
Cyber Classroom 3

Cylinder.java 470, 490, 498

D

-d argument 1379
-d command line 1379
daemon thread 869
dangerous cast 459
dangling-**else** problem 157, 193
Dartmouth College 14
dashed lines 629
data 7, 23
data abstraction 432, 472
data entry 66
data hierarchy 896, 897
data in support of actions 432
data integrity 401
data manipulation 1069
data member 380
data representation of an abstract data type 432
data structure 383, 1095, 1230
data type 71
database 6, 981
database management system (DBMS) 897
datagram 1003
datagram packet 1004
datagram socket 980
DatagramPacket 1005, 1026, 1034, 1036, 1045
DatagramSocket 1004, 1005, 1008
DataInput interface 901, 902
DataInputStream 898, 901, 921, 928, 1015, 1019, 1020
DataLine.Info 1282
DataOutput 901, 902
DataOutputStream 898, 901, 921, 928, 1015, 1019, 1020
DataSink 1250, 1259, 1262, 1264
DataSinkEvent 1262, 1333
DataSinkListener 1262, 1333
dataSinkUpdate method 1262, 1333
DataSource 1249, 1271
DataSource class 1259
date 260
Date.java 414
DBCS (double byte character set) 1493
de facto standards 433
De Morgan's Laws 244
dead 842
dead state 841, 847
dead thread 841
deadlock 841, 848, 875, 886, 892, 1045
dealing 579
debugging 473
debugging multithreaded applications 841
DEC PDP-11 computer 11
decimal (base 10) number system 1357
decimal point 171
DecimalFormat class 171, 341
decision 3, 79, 154, 234
decision symbol 152, 154
DeckOfCards.java 579
declaration 71, 159, 254
declaration and initialization of array combined 317
Decorator design pattern 521, 524, 1057
decreasing order 333
decrement 198
decrement operator, **--** 179, 180
decrypt 196
dedicated drawing area 725
deep hierarchy 532
default capacity 1162
default capacity increment 1149
default case 264
default case 213, 214
default color 111
default constructor 395, 414, 454, 459, 538
default constructor of an anonymous inner class 511
default exception handler 808, 830
default font 614
default implementation of each method in an adapter class 683
default keyword 152
default layout of the content pane 725
default load factor 1162
default package 385
default shape 111
default value 126, 182
DEFAULT_CURSOR 988
define a package of classes for reuse 385
definite repetition 161
degree 622
Deitel & Associates, Inc. 5
Deitel, H. M. 892
deitel@deitel.com 7, 46
DeitelMessenger.java 1054
DeitelMessengerServer.java 1027
delegating 1112
delegation event model 656
delete 566
deleteCharAt 566
deleting an item from a binary tree 1123
delimiter string 576
delimiters 576
demo directory 112
demonstration applets 134
Department of Defense (DOD) 15
dependency 785
dependent condition 225
deployment diagram 91
Deprecated link 1380
Deprecated note 1378
deprecated-list.html 1383
dequeue 1113
dequeue operation 434
derived class 115, 382
descending order 335, 1205
descent 616, 618
descriptive words and phrases 184, 186
DESELECTED 667
deselected 667
design 354, 788
design pattern 26, 27, 45, 520, 522, 523, 525, 783, 789, 791, 792, 793, 794, 886, 887, 1057, 1230
design patterns xxxv
Design Patterns, Elements of Reusable Object-Oriented Software 27
design process 24, 41, 43, 44, 87, 90, 294, 296, 435, 785, 883, 1331
DesktopTest.java 763
destroy method of **JApplet** 292
destroy resources allocated to an applet 292
developer.java.sun.com/developer 135
device 7
device-driver object 477
diacritic 1492

Dialog 614
dialog box 65, 68, 753
DialogInput 614
diameter 101, 146, 802
diamond 152, 160
diamond symbol 138, 146, 152, 154, 160, 205, 214, 244
dice game 265
Dice.com 1476
Dictionary class 1148
die-rolling program 645
digit 71, 570, 572, 1357
digit 571
Digital Clock 1091
digital clock exercise 1091
Digital Equipment Corporation PDP-7 11
Digital multimedia 1237
digits reversed 308
Dimension 732, 736, 764, 768, 1024, 1077
dir command on Windows 108
direct-access application 900
direct-access files 928
direct and indirect superclass 490
Direct Sound 1249
direct superclass 447
DIRECTORIES_ONLY 908
directory 903, 961, 963, 1379
directory name 962
directory structure in the JAR file 410
directory tree 112
discussion forums 135
disk 7, 9, 19, 895
disk drive 107
disk I/O completion 806
disk space 1096
dismiss a dialog 68, 75
dispatch 842
dispatching an event 661
display 1317, 1327
display area 119
display monitor 603
display output 65, 87, 91
displaying data on the screen 133
displaying multiple strings 121
dispose 740
dispose method of **RTPManager** 1272
DISPOSE_ON_CLOSE 740
distributed client/server applications 9
distributed computing 9
dithering 108
DitherTest applet 108
diversity 1472
divide-and-conquer approach 247, 250
divide by zero 19, 167, 433, 812, 813
DivideByZeroException.java 813, 817
DivideByZeroTest.java 814
division 77
do/while flowchart 217
do/while repetition structure 152, 215, 216, 230, 234
DO_NOTHING_ON_CLOSE 740
document 106, 722, 762
document Java code 1370
documentation comment 57, 1370
DOD 15
Dogfriendly.com 1480
dollar signs (**$**) 58
Door 514, 515, 637, 884, 1400, 1401, 1404, 1407, 1408, 1409, 1415, 1416, 1428, 1435, 1437, 1456
DoorEvent 585, 1386, 1392, 1407, 1416, 1428, 1462
DoorListener 635, 637, 638, 1388, 1389, 1392, 1400, 1401, 1407, 1415, 1416, 1428
DOS Edit command 16
dot (**.**) operator 67, 117, 249, 388, 424, 427, 451, 456, 611, 628
dot member selection operator 485
Double 129, 513, 1156
double 71, 123, 126, 129
double-byte character set (DBCS) 1493
double click an element 648
double equals, **==** 81
double-precision floating-point number 123
double primitive data type 152, 168, 172, 183
double promotions 258
double quotes, **"** 60, 63, 64
double selection 234
double-selection structure 152, 174
double-subscripted array 343, 344, 347, 358
DoubleArray.java 347
DoWhileTest.java 216
down arrow key 736
drag event 735
drag operation 735
drag the mouse 111, 679, 719
dragging the mouse 725
drags the scroll box 671
draw 629, 631
draw a shape with the mouse 718
draw arc 108
draw complex curve 109
draw graphics 114, 117
draw lines 200
draw lines and points 109
draw lines and points in different colors 111
draw method 719
draw rectangle 129, 145
draw shapes 602
draw **String** 112
draw3DRect 619, 620
drawArc method 622, 643
DrawArcs.java 623
drawImage method of **Graphics** 1070
drawing 604
Drawing Application 533
drawing areas as subclasses of JPanel 725
drawing color 607, 608
drawing in applications 604
drawing program 18, 443
drawing rectangles, strings and ovals 200
drawLine method of **Graphics** 123, 200, 202, 383, 618, 643, 744
drawOval method of **Graphics** 147, 216, 383, 619, 620, 642, 731, 745
drawPolygon method 625, 626, 627, 628
DrawPolygons.java 626
drawPolyline method 625, 627, 645
drawRect method of **Graphics** 129, 130, 147, 383, 618, 620, 624, 630, 632, 644, 745, 1024
drawRoundRect method of **Graphics** 619, 620, 621
DrawShapes.java 742
drawString method of **Graphics** 117, 120, 121, 127, 130, 194, 383, 560, 607, 645, 1024
DrawTest applet 109, 111

Driveway.com 1475
drop-down list 111, 112, 648, 671
dummy value 166
dump 375
dumpStack 841
duplicate elimination 1122
duplicate key 1226
duplicate names 1234
duplicate of datagram 1004
duplicate **String** 1223
duplicate values 1123
duplicates 1228
duration 274
dynamic array 822
dynamic binding 458, 463, 494
dynamic content 12
dynamic data structures 1095
dynamic memory allocation 172, 1096
dynamic method binding 473, 485
dynamically bound method 485
dynamically resizable array 982, 1156

E

EAST 697, 775
echos a packet back to the client 1004
Edit 647
edit 66
edit a program 16
editable **JTextField** 272
editor 17
editor program 16
efficient (Unicode design basis) 1491, 1498
Eight Queens 366, 368
Eight Queens: Brute Force Approaches 366
eLance.com 1478
element of an array 287, 315
element of chance 261
elements 1208
elements 1156, 1160, 1166
Elevator 137, 138, 139, 141, 185, 187, 235, 237, 293, 294, 350, 351, 353, 435, 436, 514, 515, 516, 517, 518, 583, 587, 588, 637, 709, 878, 879, 881, 882, 884, 885, 1400, 1401, 1402, 1407, 1409, 1416, 1420, 1428, 1429, 1435, 1436, 1437, 1456
elevator 87, 88
elevator simulation 87, 88, 135, 234, 295, 704, 784
elevator system 91, 135, 137, 704
ElevatorButton 137, 139, 141, 185, 187, 235, 293, 294, 351, 353, 435, 436, 513, 515
ElevatorConstants 706
ElevatorController 705, 706, 784, 786, 788
ElevatorDoor 137, 139, 141, 185, 187, 293, 294, 295, 351, 352, 353, 435, 436, 514, 515, 583
ElevatorModel 137, 139, 141, 184, 185, 187, 293, 294, 295, 351, 435, 518, 637, 784, 786, 788, 884, 885, 1393, 1399, 1400, 1401, 1415, 1435, 1437, 1460, 1461, 1462, 1463
ElevatorModelEvent 584, 585, 586, 1384, 1392
ElevatorModelListener 784, 786, 788, 1388, 1391, 1392, 1399, 1400, 1401, 1460
ElevatorMoveEvent 585, 589, 1387, 1392, 1461
ElevatorMoveListener 589, 637, 638, 1388, 1389, 1392, 1400, 1401, 1409, 1415, 1416, 1419, 1420
ElevatorMusic 1317, 1318, 1327, 1331, 1457, 1464
ElevatorMusic.java 1329
ElevatorShaft 137, 139, 141, 185, 186, 187, 293, 294, 295, 350, 351, 353, 435, 515, 518, 587, 637, 879, 884, 885, 1393, 1399, 1400, 1401, 1404, 1409, 1415, 1416, 1418, 1420, 1437, 1456
ElevatorSimulation 784, 785, 786, 787, 788
ElevatorView 784, 786, 788, 1317, 1318, 1323, 1327, 1392, 1415, 1416, 1419, 1435, 1438, 1455, 1457, 1458, 1459, 1460, 1461, 1463, 1464
elided diagram 138, 635, 636, 637
eliminate resource leaks 825
Ellipse2D 602
Ellipse2D.Double 628, 643
Ellipse2D.Float 628
else keyword 152
emacs 16
email 996
email program 18
Employee class hierarchy 478
employee identification number 896
Employee.java 416, 428, 478
employees 463
EmployeeTest.java 416, 429
empty body 683
empty sequence 1295
empty set 443
empty statement (**;**) 159
empty statement (semicolon by itself) 216
empty statement, **;** 85
empty string **""** 84
EmptyListException.java 1098, 1102
EmptyStackException 1157, 1160
enable 463
encapsulation 23, 380, 388, 389, 432, 474
enclosing **try** block 818, 829
encoding 1490
encrypt 196
end caps 631
End key 689
end of data entry 166
end-of-file 992
end-of-file marker 920, 921, 943
end-of-stream 992
end points of a line 123
EndOfFileException 920
endOfMedia method 1272
EndOfMediaEvent 1249, 1272
EndofStreamEvent 1262
endsWith method of **String** 546
English-like abbreviations 10
enqueue 434, 1113
ensureCapacity method of **StringBuffer** 561

Enter (or *Return*) key 60, 109, 111, 112, 281, 336, 375, 656
ENTERED 990
entry point 153
entry point of a control structure 231
Enumeration 1166, 1168, 1174, 1208
Enumeration interface 1148, 1160, 1198
EOF (end-of-file) 992
EOFException 994, 1000
equal likelihood 263
equal-priority threads 890
equality operator **==** to compare **String** objects 543
equals 690, 1191, 1203, 1205
equalsIgnoreCase method of **String** 543, 545, 557
Error 809, 819
error detected in a constructor 824
error-handling code 805, 807
Error hierarchy 820
escape character 64
escape sequence 64, 71, 967, 1496
Euler 363
evaluating expressions 1128
event 43, 44, 269, 270, 272, 583, 586, 587, 605, 654, 1384, 1387, 1391, 1399, 1415, 1418, 1435, 1436
event classes 654
event-dispatch thread 860
event-driven nature of graphics 605
event driven 374, 654
event-driven programming 272
event-driven process 605
event handler 270, 655
event handling 43, 269, 270, 494, 586, 588, 654, 660, 1384, 1460
event handling interfaces 512
event-handling mechanism 512
event handling method 655
event handling methods 272
event-handling thread 860
event ID 661
event listener 586, 589, 655, 656, 683, 741, 806
event-listener adapter class 683
event-listener interface 496, 589, 655, 656, 660, 661, 678, 683, 689
event object 655
event processing 811
event registration 659
event source 655
EventListenerList 660
EventObject 671, 773
EventType 990
eWork® Exchange 1478
examination-results problem 175
Examples
AccountRecord.java 906
Addition.java 69, 70
AdditionApplet.html 125
AdditionApplet.java 123
Algorithms1.java 1220
Analysis.java 176
AnimatedPanel.java 1323
Average1.java 161, 169
BankUI.java 904
BinarySearch.java 338
BinarySearchTest.java 1222
BitSetTest.java 1191
BorderLayoutDemo.java 696
Boss.java 479
BoxLayoutDemo.java 767
BreakLabelTest.java 221
BreakTest.java 218
BubbleSort.java 333
ButtonTest.java 662
ButtonText.java 662
CapturePlayer.java 1250
CardDeck.java 771
Cards.java 1217
CheckBoxTest.java 665
Circle.java 457, 462, 489, 497
Client.java 998, 1008
ClientGUI.java 1046
ClipPlayer plays sampled audio files. 1278
ClipPlayer.java 1278
ClipPlayerTest.java 1283
CollectionTest.java 1209
ComboBoxTest.java 671
CommissionWorker.java 480
Comparison.java 81
ConsumeInteger.java 851, 855
ContinueLabelTest.java 223
ContinueTest.java 219
Craps.java 265
CreateRandomFile.java 931
CreateSequentialFile.java 908
CreditInquiry.java 921
CustomPanel.java 727
CustomPanelTest.java 728
Cylinder.java 470, 490, 498
Date.java 414
DeckOfCards.java 579
DeitelMessenger.java 1054
DeitelMessengerServer.java 1027
DesktopTest.java 763
DivideByZeroException.java 813, 817
DivideByZeroTest.java 814
DoubleArray.java 347
DoWhileTest.java 216
DrawArcs.java 623
DrawPolygons.java 626
DrawShapes.java 742
ElevatorMusic.java 1329
Employee.java 416, 428, 478
EmployeeTest.java 416, 429
EmptyListException.java 1098, 1102
FibonacciTest.java 282
FileTest.java 963
FlowLayoutDemo.java 693
Fonts.java 614
ForCounter.java 201
Formatting and saving media from capture devices 1250
GridBagDemo.java 776, 780
GridBagDemo2.java 780

GridLayoutDemo.java 699
HashtableTest.java 1162
HoldIntegerSynchronized.java 857, 863
HoldIntegerUnsynchronized.java 852
HourlyWorker.java 482
ImageMap.java 1081
ImagePanel.java 1319
Increment.java 412
InitArray.java 318, 319, 321, 344
Interest.java 207
KeyDemo.java 689
LabelTest.java 651
LinearSearch.java 336
LinesRectsOvals.java 620
List.java 1099
ListTest.java 1103, 1211
LoadAudioAndPlay.java 1085
LoadImageAndScale.java 1070
LogicalOperators.java 227
LogoAnimator.java 1073
LogoAnimator2.java 1078
LogoApplet.java 1079
LookAndFeelDemo.java 759
MapTest.java 1226
MenuTest.java 748, 751
MessageListener.java 1030
MessageManager.java 1037
MethodOverload.java 289, 290
Metrics.java 617
MidiData loads MIDI files for playback. 1286
MidiData.java 1286
MidiDemo.java 1300
MidiRecord enables a program to record a MIDI sequence. 1292
MidiRecord.java 1292
MidiSynthesizer can generate notes and send them to another MIDI device. 1295
MidiSynthesizer.java 1295
MiscBitOps.java 1179
MouseDetails.java 686
MouseTracker.java 680
MovingPanel.java 1321
MulticastSendingThread.java 1035
MultipleSelection.java 676
OtherCharMethods.java 574
OvalPanel.java 737
PackageDataTest.java 418
PacketReceivingThread.java 1042
Painter.java 684
PanelDemo.java 668, 701
PassArray.java 330
PieceWorker.java 481
Point.java 453, 460, 465, 488, 495
PopupTest.java 755
PrintBits.java 1176
ProduceInteger.java 850, 854, 861, 862
PropertiesTest.java 1169
QueueInheritance.java 1113
QueueInheritanceTest.java 1114
RadioButtonTest.java 668
RandomAccessAccountRecord.java 929
RandomCharacters.java 871
RandomIntegers.java 262
ReadRandomFile.java 939
ReadSequentialFile.java 915
ReadServerFile.java 986
ReceivingThread.java 1031
RTPServer.java 1264
RTPServerTest.java 1272
Scoping.java 276
SelfContainedPanel.java 730
SelfContainedPanelTest.java 733
SendingThread.java 1041
Server.java 993, 1004
Serving streaming media with RTP session managers. 1264
SetTest.java 1224
Shape.java 487, 495
Shapes.java 629
Shapes2.java 633
SharedCell.java 853, 859, 868
ShowColors.java 607
ShowColors2.java 609
SimplePlayer.java 1239
SiteSelector.html 981
SiteSelector.java 983
SliderDemo.java 738
SocketMessageManager.java 1037
SocketMessengerConstants.java 1029
Sort1.java 1215
Sort2.java 1216
SortedSetTest.java 1225
SoundEffects.java 1328
StackComposition.java 1112
StackInheritance.java 1109
StackInheritanceTest.java 1110
StaticCharMethods.java 569
StaticCharMethods2.java 572
StringBufferAppend.java 565
StringBufferCapLen.java 561
StringBufferChars.java 563
StringBufferConstructors.java 560
StringBufferInsert.java 567
StringConcat.java 552
StringConstructors.java 538
StringHashCode.java 548
StringIntern.java 557

StringMisc.java 541
StringStartEnd.java 546
StringValueOf.java 555
StudentPoll.java 326
SubString.java 551
Sum.java 206
SumArray.java 322
SwitchTest.java 211
Test.java 457, 462, 466, 468, 471, 483
TestFieldTest.java 656
TextAreaDemo.java 722
TextFieldTest.java 656
ThisTest.java 419
ThreadTester.java 845
TicTacToeClient.java 1019
TicTacToeServer.java 1012
Time.java 501
Time1.java 381, 391
Time2.java 396
Time3.java 401
Time4.java 422
TimeTest.java 385
TimeTest2.java 389
TimeTest3.java 393
TimeTest4.java 398
TimeTest5.java 405
TimeTest6.java 425
TimeTestWindow.java 503, 508
TokenTest.java 576
Tree.java 1117
TreeTest.java 1120
UpdateThread.java 861
UsingArrays.java 1203
UsingAsList.java 1206
UsingExceptions.java 826, 828, 831
UsingToArray.java 1213
VectorTest.java 1149
Welcome1.java 57
Welcome2.java 63
Welcome3.java 64, 66
WelcomeApplet.html 119
WelcomeApplet.java 113
WelcomeApplet2.html 121
WelcomeApplet2.java 121
WelcomeLines.htm 122
WelcomeLines.java 122
WhileCounter.java 199
WriteRandomFile.java 934
Exception 806, 809, 810, 825, 827
exception 328, 806
exception handler 806, 808, 817, 824
exception handler itself throws the same exception 836
exception handling 762, 806
exception not caught in a command-line application 808
exception not caught in an applet of a GUI-based application 808
exception object 809
exception occurs in an exception handler 812
exception subclass 806
exception superclass 806
exception superclass and various exception subclasses 836
exception thrown and handled by a local **catch** 829
execute 61
execute both as an applet or as an application 741
executing an applet as an application 746
execution stack 811, 1108
execution-time error 19
exhaust the supply of free memory 839
exhausting memory 281
exists 962
exit method of **System** 68, 162
exit point of a control structure 153, 231
EXITED 990
exp method of **Math** 250
expanded submenu 752
Experience.com 1479
explicit conversion 172
explicit use of this reference 424
exponential "explosion" of calls 286
exponential method 250
exponentiation 76, 377
exponentiation operator 209
extending a class 496
extends 447, 451
extends JApplet 115, 126
extends keyword 115, 152, 269
extensibility 476
extensibility of Java 805
extensible 472
extensible language 281, 384
extension package 65
external event 678, 722, 724

F

Facade design pattern 521, 524, 1057
facade object 1057
factorial 196, 242, 278
factorial method 279
factorial method 279
FactorialTest.java 279
factory 1056
factory method 789
Factory Method design pattern 521, 522, 789
Fahrenheit 717
Fahrenheit equivalent of a Celsius temperature 308
false keyword 152, 154
falsity 79
fatal error 19, 158, 376
fault tolerant 72, 805
fetch 375
fibonacci method 285
Fibonacci series 281, 285, 377
Fibonacci series defined recursively 281
FibonacciTest.java 282
field 896
FIFO 433
FIFO order 434
File 898, 903, 914, 920, 961, 965
file 895, 896
file folder 112
file-matching program 974
file name 59, 116
file-open mode 933
File OutputStream 921
file position 921
file-position pointer 921, 928, 933
file processing 4, 822, 895, 898, 1026
file scope 501
file server 9

FileInputStream 898, 900, 902, 914, 915, 920, 924, 961, 1172, 1174
FileOutputStream 898, 900, 902, 911, 914, 961, 1057, 1171, 1173
FileReader 898, 903, 967
FILES_AND_DIRECT-ORIES 908
FILES_ONLY 908, 910
FileTest.java 963
FileTypeDescriptor 1261
FileWriter 898, 903
filing cabinet 112
fill 629, 630, 631, 632, 634, 635, 645, 1203, 1204, 1215, 1219, 1220
fill texture 632
fill with color 602
fill3DRect 619, 620
fillArc 622, 624
filled-in shape 632
filled rectangle 608
filled three-dimensional rectangle 619
fillOval 619, 620, 622
fillOval method 685
fillPolygon 625, 627, 628
fillRect method of **Graphics** 307, 607, 608, 619, 620, 630, 632
fillRoundRect method of **Graphics** 619, 621
filter stream 900
FilterInputStream 900, 901
FilterOutputStream 900, 901
FilterReader 902
final class 474
final keyword 152, 215, 412, 474
final local variable 507
final value 200
final value of control variable 198, 202, 205
final variable 322
final variable 270
finalize method 387, 426, 429, 459, 460, 462, 824, 836
finally block 152, 808, 809, 825, 829
first 1225
first-in, first-out (FIFO) data structure 433, 434, 1113
first pass 1136
first refinement 166, 174
five-pointed star 632
fixed-length record 928
fixed-width font 342
flag value 166
flight simulator 533, 1344
FlipDog.com 1467
Float 513, 1156
float primitive data type 71, 123, 152, 183
float promotions 258
floating-point division 172
floating-point number 123, 124, 127, 128, 170
floating-point constant 208
Floor 137, 139, 141, 184, 185, 187, 293, 294, 435, 514, 515, 516, 518, 705, 708, 709, 881, 884, 885, 1393, 1399, 1401, 1402, 1404, 1420, 1428, 1429, 1435, 1437, 1456
floor method of **Math** 250, 302
FloorButton 137, 139, 141, 185, 187, 235, 293, 294, 295, 350, 351, 352, 353, 435, 513
FloorDoor 137, 139, 141, 185, 187, 293, 294, 295, 350, 351, 353, 435, 514
flow of control 87, 133, 160, 170
flowchart 151, 154, 236
flowchart of **do/while** repetition structure 217
flowchart of **for** structure 204, 205
flowchart reducible to the simplest flowchart 233
flowchart symbols 230
flowcharting the double-selection **if/else** structure 155
flowcharting the single-selection **if** structure 154
flowcharting the **while** repetition structure 160
FlowLayout 269, 281, 665, 682, 692, 695, 766
FlowLayout.CENTER 694, 696
FlowLayout.LEFT 694, 696
FlowLayout.RIGHT 695
FlowLayoutDemo.java 693
flowline 151
flush 901, 914, 995, 996, 1000, 1001
flush the output buffer 1003
flush the output stream 997
Flyweight design pattern 524
focus 656, 736, 758
FocusAdapter 683
FocusListener 683
Font 342
Font 602, 614, 666
font 602, 612, 617
Font class 339, 342
font control 612
font manipulation 342, 604
font metrics 616
font name 613
font size 613
font style 613, 665
Font.BOLD 342, 613, 614, 617, 666, 752
Font.ITALIC 342, 613, 614, 615, 666, 752
Font.PLAIN 342, 347, 613, 614, 615, 666, 751
FontMetrics 602, 616, 617
Fonts.java 614
for repetition structure 152, 201, 202, 203, 204, 205, 206, 209, 213, 230, 234
ForCounter.java 201
forDigit 572
Format 1259, 1270, 1271
format 383
format control string 384
format flag 171
format method of **DecimalFormat** 209
FormatControl 1259, 1260
formatted floating-point number 171
forming structured programs 231
Forté for Java Community Edition 16
forward engineering 434, 435, 437, 518, 520, 636
Fowler, Martin 26
fractal 109
Fractal applet 109
fractional result 172
Frame 735, 740
frame 1281
frame sequence 1326
frames 1281, 1334
FreeAgent 1478
freeware 13
full package name and class name 125
full tour 645

fully qualified class names 392
function 23
function key 689
functionalization 7
Futurestep.com 1473

G

gambling casino 261
game of craps 273
game playing 261
game-playing program 261
Gamma, Erich 27
"gang of four" 27, 523, 524, 886
gang of four 520
garbage collector 387, 426, 429, 430, 459, 462, 463, 540, 818, 825, 839, 869, 1084
garbage collector thread 839
Gates, Bill 14
Gaussian distribution 1175
gc method of **System** 431, 463
general path 632
generalization 43, 515
generalization diagram 514, 635
GeneralPath 602, 632, 644
generating mazes randomly 370
get 982, 1160, 1190, 1208, 1210, 1227
get method 389, 400, 404
getAbsolutePath 963, 964
getActionCommand 658, 663, 665
getActionCommand method of **ActionEvent** 340
getAddress 1006, 1007
getAppletContext method of **Applet** 985
getAscent method 616
getAudioClip method 1085
getAudioInputStream method 1281
getAvailable-Instruments method 1298
getBlue method 606, 607, 609
getByName 1000
getChannels method 1298
getClass method of **Object** 1052
getClassName method of **UIManager.LookAnd-FeelInfo** 762
getClickCount 687
getCodeBase method 1085
getColor method 606, 608
getCommand method 1291
getComponent 756
getContentPane method 663, 751, 756
getContentPane method of **JApplet** 251, 271, 331, 347
getControl 1262
getControlComponent method of **Control** 1262
getCurrencyInstance method of **NumberFormat** 208
getCurrentTimeMillis method of **System** 286
getData 1006, 1007
getData1 method 1291
getData2 method 1291
getDescent method 616
getDeviceList method of **CaptureDevice-Manager** 1260
getDocumentBase method 1072, 1084
getEventType method of **HyperlinkEvent** 990
getFamily method 613, 615
getFieldValue 937
getFont method 613, 615, 616, 752
getFontMetrics method 616, 617
getFormatControls method 1260
getFrameSize method 1282
getGreen method 606, 607, 609
getHeight method 616, 617, 1089
getHostName method of **InetAddress** 995, 997, 1000
getIconHeight 764
getIconWidth 764
getImage method 1089
getInetAddress 995, 997, 1000
getInputStream 990, 992, 995, 1000, 1015, 1020
getInsets 603
getInstalledLookAnd-Feel 760
getInstalledLookAnd-Feels method of **UIMan-ager** 760, 762
getKeyChar 690, 692
getKeyCode 690, 691
getKeyModifiersText 690, 692
getKeyText 690, 691
getLeading method 616, 617
getLength 1006, 1007
getLine method 1282
getLocalHost 1003, 1008, 1009
getLocator method of **Cap-tureDeviceInfo** 1260
getMaxPriority 877
getMessage 830, 831
getMessage method 1291
getMinimumSize 736, 737, 1024, 1077
getModifiers 690, 692
getName 615, 752, 841, 850, 855, 877, 963
getName method 613
getOutputStream 990, 995, 1000, 1015, 1020
getParameter 981, 984, 1077
getParent 877, 963
getPassword 658
getPath 963
getPort 1006, 1007
getPredefinedCursor 988, 989
getPreferredSize 731, 732, 736, 737, 1024, 1077
getPriority 843
getProperty 1170, 1173
getRed method 606, 607, 609
getResource method of **Class** 1052
getSelectedFile 914, 917, 924, 932, 936, 941
getSelectedIndex 672, 675
getSelectedText 725
getSelectedValues 677, 678, 983
getSequencer method of **MidiSystem** 1290
getSize 613, 615
getSource 308, 404, 660, 666, 667, 697, 755, 772
getStateChange 666, 672
getStyle method 613
getTargetFormats method 1282
getText 755, 1010, 1022, 1170
getTick method 1291
getTracks method 1291
getURL method of **HyperlinkEvent** 990

getValue 739
getX 680, 683, 730, 734, 756
getY 680, 683, 731, 734, 756
GIF 653, 1072
.gif 653, 1072
global 275
glyph 1492
golden mean 281
golden ratio 281
good programming practices 13
Gosling, James 12
goto elimination 151
goto statement 151, 233
gradient 629
GradientPaint 602, 629, 644
Grand, Mark 886
graph 109, 243
graph information 323
graphical representation of a linked list 1099
graphical representation of an algorithm 151
graphical user interface 87
graphical user interface (GUI) 4, 66, 69, 91, 259, 404, 647, 705
graphical user interface (GUI) component 66
Graphics 533, 534, 604, 631, 1069, 1070, 1072
graphics 4, 6, 108, 109, 112, 1318, 1464
Graphics class 114, 117, 123, 125, 127, 200, 201, 217, 292, 383, 443, 628, 719
graphics context 604
graphics demo 112
graphics in a platform-independent manner 604
Graphics Interchange Format (GIF) 653, 1072
Graphics2D 628, 631, 632, 635, 643, 644
GraphicsEnvironment class 342
GraphicsTest applet 109
GraphLayout applet 109
greatest common divisor (GCD) 309, 311
grid 699, 774
GridBagConstraints 774, 775, 776, 779, 780
GridBagConstraints instance variable 774
GridBagCon-straints.BOTH 775, 777
GridBagConstraints.HOR IZONTAL 775
GridBagConstraints.REL ATIVE 781
GridBagConstraints.RE-MAINDER 781
GridBagDemo.java 776
GridBagDemo2.java 780
GridBagLayout 766, 774, 775, 776, 779, 780
gridheight 774, 777, 779
GridLayout 692, 699, 729, 742, 759, 766, 772
GridLayoutDemo.java 699
gridwidth 774, 777, 779
gridx 774, 777
gridy 774, 777
gross pay 192
.gsm (GSM file extension) 1237
guard condition 236
Guarded Suspension design pattern 521, 886
"guess the number" game 310
guess the number game 718
GUI 4, 87, 705
GUI-based application 741
GUI component 108, 209, 647
GUI component that generated an event 404
GUI design tools 271
GUI event handling 401, 494, 496, 507
guillemets (« ») 787

H

half word 377
handle 388
handshake point 990, 1003
hard ware 10
hard ware platform 11
hardcopy printer 19
hardware 3, 7
"has a" relationship 448
hash bucket 1162
hash code 548
hash table 548, 575, 1161, 1223
hash table collisions 1161, 1162
hashCode method 548
hashing 1148, 1161
HashMap class 1226, 1227
HashSet class 1223, 1224
Hashtable 982, 983, 1148, 1162, 1168, 1202, 1230
HashtableTest.java 1162
hasMoreElements 1159, 1166, 1172
hasMoreTokens method of **StringTokenizer** 578, 593
hasNext 1210, 1212, 1213, 1224, 1225
head 1095
head of a queue 1113
Headhunter.net 1475
headSet 1225
heavyweight components 649, 747
height 616, 618
height of a rectangle in pixels 130
height of an applet in pixels 119, 251
Helm, Richard 27
Help link 1380
helpdoc.html 1380
helper method 382, 1121
Helvetica font 342
heuristic 365
hexadecimal (base 16) number system 1357
hexadecimal (base16) number system 243, 377
Heymans, F. 892
hidden 740
"hidden" instance variables 275
hide a dialog 68, 75
hide an instance variable 421
hide an internal data representation 434
hide implementation details 248, 388, 432
HIDE_ON_CLOSE 740
hierarchical boss method/worker method relationship 248
hierarchical structure 248
hierarchies designed for implementation inheritance 487
hierarchy diagram 450
hierarchy of shapes 473, 486
high-level language 10, 15
higher-priority thread 839, 840
highest-priority ready thread 843
highest-priority thread 841
highlighted link 1381
Hire.com 1473
HireAbility.com 1477
Hirediversity.com 1472

histogram 243, 323
Histogram.java 323
Hoare, C. A. R. 848, 892
HoldIntegerSynchronized.java 857, 863
HoldIntegerUnsynchronized.java 852
Home key 689
HORIZONTAL 737, 777
horizontal coordinate 602
horizontal gap space 698
horizontal glue 768
horizontal **JSlider** component 735
horizontal orientation 736
horizontal scrollbar policy 725
horizontal tab 64
HORIZONTAL_SCROLLBAR_ALWAYS 725
HORIZONTAL_SCROLLBAR_AS_NEEDED 725
HORIZONTAL_SCROLLBAR_NEVER 725
host name of a server 1003
hot area 1081
hot spot 109
HotDispatch.com 1477
HotJobs.com 1470, 1475
HotSpot compiler 21
hourglass 989
hourly worker 803
HourlyWorker.java 482
housekeeping 426
HTML (Hyper Text Markup Language) 1370
HTML (Hypertext Markup Language) 105, 106, 118, 119
HTML Converter 131
HTML document 112, 198, 201, 292, 741, 980, 981, 1379, 1380
HTML documentation 1370
HTML file 109, 120, 1379
HTML frame 985
HTML tag 119
HTTP (HyperText Transfer Protocol) 981
hue 612
HugeInteger 442
hybrid language 12
Hyperext Transfer Protocol 981
hyperlink 134, 135, 986, 989, 1376, 1379
HyperlinkEvent 986, 989
HyperlinkListener 987, 989
Hypertext Markup Language (HTML) 18
hypotenuse of a right triangle 306

I

I/O completes 843
I/O completion 842
I/O performance enhancement 901
I/O request 842
IBM 9, 14
IBM Corporation 1491
IBM Personal Computer 9
Icon 652, 672
icon 74
identifier 58, 153
identifier's duration 274
identifier's scope 274
identify the classes 135
IDEs 21
IEEE 754 floating point 183
if single-selection structure 79, 84, 152, 154, 155, 210, 230, 234
if/else double-selection structure 152, 155, 168, 175, 210, 230, 234
ignoring element zero 328
IllegalArgumentException 843, 906
IllegalMonitorStateException 849
IllegalThreadStateException 841, 869
Image 1070, 1072
image 4, 6, 292, 645, 1069, 1070, 1087, 1316
image map 1070, 1081
image with hot spots 109
ImageIcon 652, 663, 672, 1070, 1072, 1076, 1077, 1081, 1326
ImageMap applet 109
ImageMap.java 1081
ImageObserver 1072
ImagePanel 1317, 1318, 1457, 1458, 1460, 1464
ImagePanel.java 1319
imaginary part 440
immutable 429, 540
implement 589, 636, 638
implement many interfaces 496
implementation 388, 1438
implementation classes 1202
implementation-dependent code 388
implementation details 380
implementation inheritance 487
implementation of a class hidden from its clients 387
implementation phase 518, 520, 1332
implementation process 41, 43, 44, 45, 294, 434, 637
implements 152, 496
implements **ActionListener** 272
implements an interface 496
implicit conversion 172
implicit subclass-object-to-superclass-object Conversion 463
import entire package 125
import statement 65, 68, 114, 125, 152, 252, 259, 385, 390, 1375
improve performance of bubble sort 359
inconsistent state 808
increasing order 332
increment 198, 203
increment a control variable 200, 205
increment and decrement operators 179
increment expression 219
increment of a **for** structure 204
increment of control variable 202
increment operator, **++** 179
Increment.java 180, 412
indefinite postponement 841, 843, 892
indefinite repetition 166
indefinitely postpone a writer 892
indent size 59
indentation 60, 133, 153
indentation convention 155
indentation techniques 87
independent software vendor 13
index 315
index.html 1380
index-all.html 1383
indexed lists 1146
indexOf 1155
IndexOutOfBoundsException 1219
indirect base class 605
indirect superclass 450, 490
Inet Address 1003, 1007

InetAddress 1000, 1008, 1020, 1036, 1042, 1058, 1272
infinite loop 159, 171, 203, 216, 281, 1007, 1011
infinite recursion 281, 286
infinite series 243
infix notation 1128
infix-to-postfix conversion algorithm 1128
information hiding 23, 380, 389, 419, 432, 448, 474
information tier 1060
INFORMATION_MESSAGE 417
inherit implementation 532
inherit instance variables 452
inherit interface 474, 532
inherit interface and implementation 486
inheritable interface 486
inheritance 23, 43, 115, 139, 269, 380, 382, 388, 446, 450, 464, 472, 513, 514, 515, 517, 518, 1402
inheritance and exception handling 811
inheritance examples 449
inheritance hierarchy 450, 476, 530
inheritance versus composition 531
inheritance with exceptions 824
inheriting interface versus inheriting implementation 532
init method of **JApplet** 116, 118, 127, 129, 130, 251, 281, 292, 333, 345, 746
InitArray.java 318, 319, 321, 344
initial set of classes 380
initial state 235
initial value 199
initial value of an attribute 186
Initial value of control variable 202, 205
initial value of control variable 198
initialization 199, 203
initialization at the beginning of each repetition 178
initialization of an applet 292
initialization phase 168
initialization section of the **for** structure 207
initialize applet's instance variables 127
initialize counters and totals 163
initialize implicitly to default values 395
initialize instance variables 387
initialize method of **RTP-Manager** 1272
initializer list 319, 343
initializer sublist 343
initializers 395
initializing an array with a declaration 320
initializing class objects 383
initializing double-subscripted arrays in declarations 344
initializing multidimensional arrays 344
initiate an action 747
inlining 474
inner block 275
inner class 501, 568, 611, 667, 673, 685, 687, 735, 739, 754, 762, 990
inner class definition 501
inner class for event handling 501, 568
inner class object 507
innermost parentheses 77
innermost square brackets 327
inorder traversal 1119
inorderTraversal 1120
input cursor 1003
input data from the keyboard 648
input device 8
input dialog 69, 72, 73, 75, 128, 163, 213, 269
input dialog's text field 128
input/output 822, 898
input/output operation 152, 372
input/output package 260
input unit 8
InputEvent 679, 688, 689
InputStream 900, 902, 990, 992, 1033, 1174
inputting data from the keyboard 87, 133
insert an item into a container object 383
insert method of **String-Buffer** 566
insertElementAt 1155
insertion point 1098, 1206, 1221
Insets 603
instance 115, 116
instance of a built-in type 380
instance of a user-defined type 380
instance variable 126, 274, 275, 382, 400, 421, 452, 902
instanceof operator 152, 459
instant-access applications 928
instantiate 23, 352, 1399
instantiate (or create) objects 115, 380
instantiated 474
instantiating an object 172
instruction execution cycle 375, 376
Instrument 1295
instrument program number 1299
int 71
int primitive data type 152, 168, 179, 210
int promotions 258
Integer 73, 129, 164, 508, 1114, 1156, 1227
integer 69
integer array 319
integer division 76, 172
integer mathematics 432
integer quotient 76
integer value 71
integerPower method 306
integral expression 215
integral values 210
integrated development environments (IDEs) 16
Intel 1237
intelligent agent 1467
intelligent consumer electronic devices 12
interaction 184
interaction diagram 352, 881
interactions among objects 350, 352, 353, 432
interest rate 207
Interest.java 207
interface 23, 43, 269, 389, 447, 494, 496, 589, 635, 636, 637, 638, 1384, 1388, 1391, 1399, 1419, 1420, 1428
interface 470, 494, 496
interface **ActionListener** 659
interface inheritance 487
interface **ItemListener** 667
interface keyword 152
interface **LayoutManager** 693
interface **MouseListener** 719

interfaces of the collections framework 1202
intern method of **String** 557, 558
internal data representation 434
internal frame closable 766
internal frame maximizable 766
internal frame minimizable 766
internal frame resizable 766
International Standards Organization (ISO) 5, 11, 433
internationalization 260
Internet 3, 4, 15, 107, 134, 981, 1072
Internet address 1007
Internet address of the server 1003
Internet and Web resources 1087, 1316
Internet and World Wide Web How to Program, Second Edition 18
internet domain name in reverse order 392
Internshipprograms.com 1480
interpreter 18, 20, 21, 56, 60, 165, 206
Interpreter design pattern 524
interrupt 842
interrupt 841, 876, 883
InterruptedException 819, 847, 850, 851, 855, 856, 862, 863, 1014
InterruptedIOException 1033, 1045
intersection of two sets 443
InterviewSmart 1480
invalid array reference 328
invalid array subscript 810
invalid cast 819
InvalidMidiDataException 1290, 1299
InvalidMidiException 1290
InvalidSessionAddressException 1272
invoke 249
invokeLater method of **SwingUtilities** 860, 875, 1053
invoking a method 117
IOException 819, 822, 914, 918, 933, 1000
IOExceptions of the **java.net** package 823
"is a" relationship 448, 458
isAbsolute 962, 964
isActionKey 690
isAlive 841
isAltDown 687, 689
isBold 613, 616
isControlDown 692
isDaemon 869
isDefined method of **Character** 569, 570
isDigit method of **Character** 570, 571
isDirectory 962
isEmpty method 383, 1155, 1160, 1168, 1227
isFile 962, 964
isFull 383
isInterrupted 841
isItalic method 613, 616
isJavaIdentifierPart method of **Character** 570, 571
isJavaIdentifierStart method of **Character** 570, 571
isLetter method of **Character** 570, 571
isLetterOrDigit 570
isLetterOrDigit method of **Character** 571
isLowerCase 570, 571
isMetaDown 687, 689
ISO 5, 11, 433
isPlain method 613, 616
isPopupTriggered 756, 758
isRunning 1076
isSelected 751, 755
isSelected method of **AbstractButton** 755
isShiftDown 692
isUpperCase 571
isUpperCase 570
ITALIC 613
ItemEvent 666, 667, 670, 671
ItemHandler 755
ItemListener 666, 667, 669, 670, 672, 673, 718, 754
ItemStateChanged 667, 669, 673, 755
iteration 286
iteration of a loop 198, 203, 219
iterative 281
Iterator 477, 1224, 1225, 1226
iterator 1202
Iterator design pattern 521, 524, 1230

J

J2RE 131
J2SDK (Java 2 Software Development Kit) 3
Jacobson, Ivar 25, 26
Jacopini, G. 151, 233
JApplet 113, 114, 115, 117, 125, 259, 269, 275, 291, 292, 456, 605, 726, 747, 1072
JAR (Java archive) file 31
jar, Java archive utility 409
JARS site 135
.java file name extension 59
Java 2 2, 87, 342
Java 2 development environment 16
Java 2 Multimedia Cyber Classroom Fourth Edition 3
Java 2 Platform 6, 131, 870
Java 2 Platform, Enterprise Edition 6
Java 2 Platform, Micro Edition 6
Java 2 Platform, Standard Edition 3
Java 2 Runtime Environment (J2RE) 131
Java 2 Software Development Kit 57
Java 2 Software Development Kit (J2SDK) 3, 107, 134, 248
Java 2 Software Development Kit (J2SDK) **demo** directory 112
Java 2 Software Development Kit (J2SDK) install directory 107
Java 2 Software Development Kit (J2SDK) version 107
Java 2 Software Development Kit (J2SDK), Standard Edition 3
Java Abstract Windowing Toolkit Event package 260
Java Abstract Windowing Toolkit Package (AWT) 259
Java API documentation 20, 65, 1370
Java applet 115
Java Applet Package 259
Java applet program 107

Java Applet Rating Service 135
Java applications programming interface (API) 13, 65, 246, 259
Java archive (JAR) file 31
Java archive utility, **jar** 409
Java character set 109
Java class libraries 13
Java class library 65
java core package 62
Java demos Appendix 1346
Java Developer Connection 135
Java development kit 3
Java development tool 107
Java-enabled Web browser 130
Java environment 17
.java file name extension 59, 382, 494
Java Input/Output package 260
Java interpreter 17, 120, 165, 206
java interpreter 56, 60, 61, 741
Java Language Package 260
Java Look-and-Feel Graphics Repository 1088
Java Media Framework (JMF) 1237
Java Media Framework home page 1316
Java Media Framework version 1.1 (JMF 1.1) 1085, 1316
Java Networking package 260
Java Plug-in 106, 119, 120, 131, 986
Java Plug-in 1.3 HTML Converter 131, 133
Java Plug-in HTML Converter 131
Java Security API 1026
Java Sound 1249
Java Sound API 1238, 1278
Java Sound Engine 1278
Java source file 1379
Java Swing Event Package 260
Java Swing GUI Components Package 260
Java Text Package 260
Java Utilities Package 260
java.applet package 114, 259, 1327
java.awt package 113, 114, 121, 122, 125, 251, 259, 269, 342, 494, 603, 604, 625, 628, 649, 726, 732, 758, 820, 1070
java.awt package exceptions 823
java.awt.color package 628
java.awt.event package 260, 269, 494, 512, 654, 655, 683, 692
java.awt.font package 628
java.awt.geom package 628
java.awt.image package 628
java.awt.image.renderable package 628
java.awt.peer package 649
java.awt.print package 628
java.io package 260, 820, 898, 899
java.io package exceptions 823
java.lang package 68, 71, 73, 129, 164, 249, 260, 382, 431, 452, 454, 537, 568, 813, 820, 839, 1230
java.math package 281
java.net package 260, 823, 983
java.net package exceptions 824
java.sun.com 3, 5, 134, 260
java.sun.com/applets 134
java.sun.com/docs/books/tutorial/java/javaOO/final.html 474
java.sun.com/j2se 3
java.sun.com/j2se/1.3/docs.html 20, 65
java.sun.com/j2se/1.3/docs/api 259
java.sun.com/j2se/1.3/docs/api/index.html 20, 65
java.sun.com/j2se/1.3/docs/api/overview-summary.html 260
java.sun.com/products/hotspot/ 21
java.sun.com/products/java-media/jmf 1238, 1264
java.sun.com/products/plugin 131
java.text package 171, 207, 209, 260
java.util package 209, 260, 537, 576, 820, 983, 1097, 1148, 1156
java.util package exceptions 822
Java2D API 112, 602, 603, 628
Java2D applet 112
Java2D directory 112
Java2D shapes 628, 629
javac 16
javac compiler 61, 165
javadoc 1369
javadoc home page 1370
javadoc-style comments 57
javadoc tags 1378
javadoc utility program 57, 1370
javasound
// 1249
javax extension packages 66
javax.media package 1246
javax.media package package 1238
javax.media.control package 1262, 1271
javax.media.format package 1261
javax.media.protocol package 1249, 1259
javax.media.rtp.event package 1272
javax.sound.midi package 1278, 1285, 1291, 1327, 1331
javax.sound.midi.spi package 1278
javax.sound.sampled package 1278
javax.sound.sampled.spi package 1278
javax.swing package 65, 66, 114, 125, 209, 259, 260, 269, 506, 605, 609, 644, 650, 653, 660, 724, 740, 762, 766, 1070
javax.swing.event package 260, 654, 660, 676, 739
JButton 269, 271, 645, 648, 662, 664, 676, 678, 693, 699, 702, 705, 708
JButton events 404
JCheckBox 648, 662, 665, 667, 718, 719
JCheckBoxMenuItem 747, 754
JColorChooser 609, 611, 719

JComboBox 648, 671, 673, 718, 719, 759, 775, 781
JComponent 605, 650, 651, 653, 660, 662, 671, 673, 701, 726, 732, 791
JDesktopPane 762, 763, 803, 944
JDialog 753
JEditorPane 980, 986
jfc directory 108, 112
JFileChooser 908, 917, 920, 923, 931, 935, 941
JFileChooser.CANCEL_OPTION 910, 917, 924, 932, 936
JFileChooser.FILES_ONLY 910, 917, 924, 931, 935, 941
JFrame 503, 506, 533, 535, 645, 649, 650, 699, 726, 728, 739, 741, 743, 784, 788
JFrame.EXIT_ON_CLOSE 609
JInternalFrame 762, 766, 944
JLabel 268, 269, 271, 648, 651, 653, 671, 680, 682, 713, 718, 751, 754
JList 648, 673, 674, 675, 676, 781, 983
JMenu 747, 748, 754, 762, 763
JMenuBar 747, 753, 762, 763
JMenuItem 747, 762, 763
JMF 1085, 1238
JMF (Java Media FrameWork) 1237
JMF 2.1.1 1238
JMF API 1237
job 8
jobfind.com 1470
Jobs.com 1471
JobsOnline.com 1475
Johnson, Ralph 27
join 841
JOIN_ROUND 630
joinGroup method of **MulticastSocket** 1045
Joint Photographic Experts Group (JPEG) 653, 1072
JOptionPane 65, 66, 67, 69, 70, 125, 162, 798
JOptionPane constants for message dialog 75
JOptionPane.ERROR_MESSAGE 75
JOptionPane.INFORMATION_MESSAGE 75, 82, 165, 176
JOptionPane.PLAIN_MESSAGE 69, 74, 75, 102
JOptionPane.QUESTION_MESSAGE 75
JOptionPane.WARNING_MESSAGE 75
JPanel 648, 692, 701, 705, 725, 726, 727, 729, 730, 732, 736, 742, 791, 1073, 1317, 1318, 1455
JPanel objects opaque by default 733
JPasswordField 656, 657, 660
JPEG 653, 1088, 1090
.jpeg 653, 1072
.jpg 653, 1072
JPopupMenu 755, 757
JRadioButton 662, 665, 667, 668, 670, 716, 718, 759
JRadioButtonMenuItem 747, 749, 754, 755, 757
JScrollPane 674, 675, 678, 724, 725
JScrollPane class 227, 229
JScrollPane.HORIZONTAL_SCROLLBAR_ALWAYS 725
JScrollPane.HORIZONTAL_SCROLLBAR_AS_NEEDED 725
JScrollPane.HORIZONTAL_SCROLLBAR_NEVER 725
JScrollPane.VERTICAL_SCROLLBAR_ALWAYS 725
JScrollPane.VERTICAL_SCROLLBAR_AS_NEEDED 725
JScrollPane.VERTICAL_SCROLLBAR_NEVER 725
JSlider 735, 736, 737
JTextArea 689, 691, 696, 722, 723, 724, 775, 779, 1052
JTextArea class 209, 242, 252, 254, 256, 318, 319, 323, 344
JTextComponent 656, 659, 722, 725
JTextField 644, 648, 656, 657, 659, 664, 665, 667, 668, 718, 722, 780
JTextField class 269, 271, 272, 281, 322, 336
JToggleButton 665
JumpingBox 109
just-in-time (JIT) compiler 21
JustCJobs.com 1477
JustComputerJobs.com 1477
JustJavaJobs.com 1466, 1477

K

Kelvin temperature scale 717
Kernihan and Ritchie 11
key 982, 1160, 1168
key constants 692
key events 661, 689, 730
key value 335, 1123
key/value pairs 1160, 1161, 982
KeyAdapter 683
keyboard 7, 69, 163, 167, 648, 688
KeyDemo 689
KeyDemo.java 689
KeyEvent 661, 689, 713
KeyListener 661, 683, 689, 691, 718
KeyListener methods 689
keyPressed 689, 691
keyReleased 689
keys 1160
keystroke 806
keyTyped 689
keyword 58, 153
keywords reserved but not used by Java 153
KIS ("keep it simple") 19
Knight's Tour 363, 645
Knight's Tour Walker 1345
Knight's Tour Walker exercise 1345
Knight's Tour: Brute Force Approach 366
Knight's Tour: Closed Tour Test 366

L

label 220, 647, 651
labeled block 221
labeled **break** statement 220

labeled **continue** statement 222
labeled statement 220, 222
labels for tick marks 735
LabelTest.java 651
Lady Ada Lovelace 15
language package 260
LANs 9
large integers 281
largest and smallest integer 102
largest and smallest integer in a group 146
largest value 192
last 772
last 1225
last-in, first-out (LIFO) data structure 1108
lastElement 1155
lastIndexOf 549
last-in-first-out (LIFO) data structure 432
lastModified 963
late binding 486
Latin World 1473
layered software system 476
Layers architecture pattern 521, 1060
layout manager 271, 692, 701
layout of GUI components 108
LayoutManager 696
LayoutManager interface 693, 696
LayoutManager2 interface 770
Lea, Doug 886
leading 616, 618
leaf 791
leaf node 1116
leaf node in a binary search tree 1121
leaveGroup method of class **MulticastSocket** 1046
left 603
left angle bracket (**<**) 119
left arrow key 736
left brace, **{** 59, 60, 70, 115
left child 1116
left justified 653, 693
left mouse button 110
left-mouse-button click 687, 688
left shift OPERATOR, **<<** 1176, 1189
left subtree 1116, 1121, 1131
left-to-right evaluation 79
legacy C code 4
length 561, 742
length 554, 561, 700, 963, 964, 965
length variable of an array 316
letter 570, 896
level-order binary tree traversal 1123, 1132
levels of nesting 200
levels of refinement 168
lexicographical comparison 545, 1217
lexicographical comparison 544
library classes 13, 807
life cycle of a thread 842
lifetime 274
LIFO 432
Light 137, 139, 141, 185, 187, 235, 293, 294, 295, 350, 353, 435, 518, 587, 637, 884, 885, 1400, 1401, 1409, 1415, 1416, 1418, 1437, 1456
LightEvent 585, 1387, 1392, 1463
LightListener 637, 638, 1388, 1390, 1392, 1400, 1401, 1415
lightweight components 649
lightweight GUI component 740, 754
likelihood 263
Limericks 595
line 109, 114, 116, 602, 618, 627, 628
line joins 631
Line method **close** 1282
Line method **start** 1282
Line.Info 1282
Line2D 602
Line2D.Double 628, 630, 643
linear collection 1097
linear data structure 1116
linear search 335, 337, 338, 368
LinearSearch.java 336
LineEvent 1281, 1282
LineEvent.Type 1282
LineEvent.Type.STOP 1282
LineListener 1281, 1282
LineNumberReader 902
lines of random lengths in random colors 643
LinesRectsOvals.java 620
lineTo 633, 635
LineUnavailableException 1282
link 1096, 1097, 1116, 1371
-link command-line argument 1379, 1380
linked list 383, 1095, 1097, 1206, 1230
LinkedList class 1097, 1221, 1235
links to packages 1371
Linux 10
List 1206, 1208, 1210, 1212, 1217, 1218, 1219, 1223, 1326
list 671
list 963, 1173, 1221
list method of **File** 967
List.java 1099
listen for events 272, 659
listener 638, 806, 1384, 1388, 1391
listener interface 44
listener object 1416, 1429
listenerList 660
ListIterator 1211
Lists and Queues without Tail References 1146
ListSelectionEvent 674, 675, 983
ListSelectionListener 674, 718, 982, 983
ListSelectionModel.SINGLE_INTERVAL_SELECTION 677
ListSelectionModel.SINGLE_SELECTION 674, 677
ListTest.java 1103, 1211
literal 74
live-code™ approach 2
load 1172
load an applet 120
load another Web page into a browser 1081, 1084
load factor 1161
load/store operations 372
LoadAudioAndPlay.java 1085
LoadImageAndScale.java 1070
loading 18
loading a document from a URL into a browser 983
loading and playing an AudioClip 1085
local area networks (LANs) 9
local variable 126, 164, 249, 275, 277, 332, 388, 421

local variables created in the **try** 818
locale 209, 260
Locale class 208
Locale.US 208
localhost 997
localization 651, 1490
Location 515, 516, 519, 584, 586, 706, 880, 884, 1384, 1401, 1402, 1407, 1416, 1429, 1437
location (0, 0) 114
location in computer's memory 75
location of an image on the Internet 1072
lock 856
locking an object 848
log method of **Math** 249
logarithm 250
logic error 72, 158, 166, 167, 202
logical AND, **&&** 222, 225
logical decision 7
logical input operations 901
logical negation, **!** 222, 226
logical operators 222, 226
logical OR, **||** 225
logical output operations 901
logical units 7
LogicalOperators.java 227
Logo language 362
LogoAnimator.java 1073
LogoAnimator2.java 1078
LogoApplet.java 1079
Long 513
long keyword 152, 183
long promotions 258
look and feel 649, 651, 692, 758
look and feel observations 13
LookAndFeelDemo.java 759
LookAndFeelInfo 759, 762
loop 166, 1091, 1282, 1335
loop body 203, 215
loop-continuation condition 200, 202, 203, 206, 213, 215, 216, 217, 219
loop counter 198
loop terminating condition 328
looping 174
Lord Byron 15
low-priority thread 463, 841, 843, 891
lowercase letters 58, 71, 159, 896
lowered rectangles 621
ls command on UNIX 108
lvalue ("left value") 181
lvalue ("left value") 315

M

m-by-n array 343
machine dependent 10
machine language 10
Machine Language Programming 371
Macintosh 60, 604, 740, 758
MacOS 10
Macromedia Flash 2 movies 1237
Magazines 1350
magnetic tape 895
main method 61, 70, 83, 163, 165
maintainability 1095
maintenance 473
major tick marks 735
make your point 265
making decisions 87, 133
MalformedURLException 982, 984
Manager 1247
manager 801
Manager method **createRealizedProcessor** 1261
mangled or decorated names 290
manufacturing section of the computer 8
Map 1203, 1226, 1228
Map interface 1226
MapTest.java 1226
mark an object for garbage collection 429
marked for garbage collection 426, 427
mask 1176
master file 974
Math 249, 454
Math.E 249
Math.PI 101, 146, 249, 302, 454
max algorithm 1215, 1219
max method of **Math** 250, 258
maximize a window 506, 765
maximized internal frame 765
maximum 192
maximum method 256
Maximum.java 256
Maze Traversal 645
maze traversal 369
MBAFreeAgent.com 1478
MBCS (multi-byte character set) 1493
MDI 722, 762
mean (average) 78
MediaLocator 1249
MediaLocator class 1247
Mediator design pattern 525
member access modifier 434
member access modifier **private** 382
member access modifier **public** 382
member access modifiers 382
Memento design pattern 520, 525
memento object 525
memory 7, 8
memory buffer 901
memory consumption 1202
memory exhaustion 806
memory leak 426, 825, 839
memory unit 8
memory utilization 1162
MemoryImageSource 1091
menu 66, 67, 647, 648, 722, 747, 752
menu bar 67, 647, 648, 747, 753
menu item 747, 753
MenuTest.java 748, 751
merge sort 1215
message 23, 60, 109, 117, 127, 234, 350, 352, 353, 354, 583, 586, 587, 878, 881, 1399
message dialog 65, 69, 74, 163, 209, 229, 242, 269, 318
message dialog types 74
message name structure 583
message passing 881
MessageListener.java 1030
MessageManager.java 1037
Meta key 688, 689
metal look-and-feel 722, 758, 759
MetaMessage 1331
MetaMessage class 1291
method 13, 24, 60, 234, 247, 434, 516
method body 254
method call 117, 248, 254
method call chaining 424
method call operator 251
method call overloaded 417
method call stack 830, 831
method-call stack trace 841
method definition 60, 254

method is declared **final** 476
method name 294
method overloading 288, 298, 383
MethodOverload.java 289, 290
methods called automatically during applet's execution 292
methods implicitly **final** 474, 513
Metric Conversion Program 598
metric conversion program 598
Metrics.java 617
Microsoft 14, 1491
Microsoft Audio/Video Interleave files 1237
Microsoft Internet Explorer 65, 106, 1026
Microsoft Windows 604, 740, 758
Microsoft Windows-style look-and-feel 759
.mid 1237
.mid (MIDI file extension) 1085, 1237, 1285
.mid file 1327
middle array element 338
middle mouse button 689
middle tier 1060
MIDI 1085, 1278, 1285
MIDI 1327, 1328, 1459
MIDI channel 1298
MIDI device 1290, 1291
MIDI event 1286, 1291
MIDI event-synchronization 1286
MIDI instruments 1295
MIDI message 1290, 1298
MIDI note generation 1298
MIDI notes 1291
MIDI recording 1291, 1295
MIDI resolution 1314, 1315
MIDI saving 1295
MIDI sequence 1291
MIDI supported file types 1295
MIDI synthesizer 1285
MIDI track 1290
MIDI type 1295, 1335
MIDI volume 1314
MidiChannel 1295
MidiData 1285, 1286, 1290
MidiData.java 1286
MidiDemo 1286, 1299
MidiDemo GUI 1299
MidiDemo.java 1300
MidiDevice 1290, 1291
MidiEvent 1291
MidiMessage 1291, 1299
MidiRecord 1292
MidiRecord 1285, 1291, 1295, 1314
MidiRecord.java 1292
MidiSynthesizer 1285, 1295
MidiSynthesizer.java 1295
MidiSystem 1290
MidiUnavailable-Exception 1290, 1298
mileage obtained by automobiles 191
min algorithm 1215, 1219
min method of **Math** 250
minimal browser 120
minimize a window 506, 741, 765
minimize internal frame 765
minimum value in an array 368
minor tick marks 735
minus sign (**-**) indicating private visibility 434
MiscBitOps.java 1179
MissingResourceExcep-tion 120
mission-critical application 807
mission-critical computing 817
mixed-type expression 258
mnemonic 651, 747, 752, 754
modal dialog 611, 753, 913
model 44, 87, 91, 135, 136, 138, 139, 140, 184, 186, 516, 637, 639, 783, 784, 785, 786, 787, 1391, 1392, 1393, 1399, 1404, 1408, 1418, 1429, 1437
model (in MVC architecture) 1058, 1059
model an interaction 352
Model-View-Controller (MVC) 44, 521, 753, 783, 793, 1058
modifiable strings. 560
modifier key 692
modularizing a program with methods 250
module 247
modules in Java 247
modulus operator, **%** 76, 77, 96, 195, 243
MoleculeViewer applet 109
monetary calculations 210
monitor 848, 880, 881
monitor object 848
monitor's condition variable 854
MonitorControl interface 1262
monolithic program 288
Monospaced 342
Monospaced 613, 614, 781
Monster.com 1466, 1470, 1475, 1478
MorganWorks.com 1473
Morse Code 1067, 1345
Morse code 598, 1345
Motif-style (UNIX) look-and-feel 722, 759
mouse 8, 109, 648
mouse button 110, 679
mouse-button click 688
mouse click 686
mouse cursor 679, 989
mouse drag operation 735
mouse event 534
mouse event handling 679
mouse events 661, 678, 725, 730
mouse events of application window 758
mouse motion events 735
mouse pointer 68, 72, 128
mouse pressed event 735
MouseAdapter 683, 730, 732, 756, 758, 1082
mouseClicked 679, 686, 687
mouseClickHandler 683
MouseDetails.java 686
mouseDragged 679, 681, 684, 685, 735
mouseEntered 679, 681
MouseEvent 661, 679, 684, 730, 734, 758, 1082
mouseExited 681, 1082
MouseListener 661, 678, 756
MouseMotionAdapter 684, 1082
MouseMotionListener 661, 678, 683, 734
mouseMoved 679, 681, 684, 735, 1081
mousePressed 679, 715, 730, 732, 756, 758, 893
mouseReleased 679, 714, 731, 732, 756, 758, 1023
MouseTracker 680
MouseTracker.java 680
.mov 1237, 1332
.mov (QuickTime file extension) 1237

moveTo 633
moving the mouse 111, 654
MovingPanel 1317, 1318, 1321, 1323, 1327, 1460, 1464
MovingPanel.java 1321
.mp3 1237
.mp3 (MPEG Layer 3 extension) 1237
MPEG Layer 3 Audio 1237
MPEG-1 videos 1237
.mpg 1237
.mpeg (MPEG-1 file extension) 1237
.mpg (MPEG-1 file extension) 1237
MS-DOS prompt 18, 108
mulit-byte character set (MBCS) 1493
multi-button mouse 688
multicast 1026, 1029, 1034
multicast address 1034, 1036
multicast group 1034
multicasting 980
MulticastSendingThread.java 1035
MulticastSocket 1042, 1045
multilevel priority 843
multimedia 4, 1069
Multimedia Authoring System 1344
Multimedia Authoring System project exercise 1344
Multimedia Gallery 1316
multiple document interface (MDI) 722, 762
multiple inheritance 23, 447, 530
multiple-line comment 57
multiple selection 152
multiple-selection structure 214, 234
multiple-selection list 673, 675, 676, 678
multiple-subscripted array 343, 344
MULTIPLE_INTERVAL_SELECTION 675, 676, 678
MultipleSelection.java 676
multiplication, * 76, 77
multiplicative operators: *, / and % 173
multiplicity 138, 139
multiprogramming 9
multitasking 15
multithread safe 1102
multithreaded programming language 877
multithreaded server application 1067
multithreaded servers 1066
multithreaded Tic-Tac-Toe Program 1066
multithreaded, networked, collaborative applications 891
multithreading 4, 6, 15, 44, 129, 838, 839, 878, 886
Musical Instrument Digital Interface 1285
Musical Instrument Digital Interface (MIDI) file format 1085
Musical Instrument Digital Interface files 1237
Musical Instrumental Data Interface (MIDI) 1278, 1334
mutator method 389, 400
mutually exclusive options 667
MVC 44, 87, 783, 784, 1058, 1059

N

name 75
name direction 138, 139
name of a control variable 198, 199
name of a param 981
name of an activity 236
name of an operation 294
named constant 270, 322
NASA multimedia gallery 1087, 1316
native code 5
native keyword 152
native machine code 21
natural language of a particular computer 10
natural logarithm 250
navigate a directory structure 394
navigation bar 1381
negative arc angles 623
negative binary numbers 1356
negative degree 622
negative infinity 813
NervousText applet 109
nest 174
nested blocks 275
nested building blocks 233
nested control structures 173, 214, 264
nested **for** structure 220, 323, 344, 345, 346
nested **if/else** structure 157, 158, 338, 448
nested parentheses 77
nested structures 233
nested **switch** structure 214
nesting 155, 200, 234
nesting rule 231
NetBeans 16
Netscape Navigator 65, 66, 106, 133, 647, 1026
network message arrival 806
Networked Morse Code 1067
networked, collaborative applications 891
networking 6, 9, 895
networking package 260
networking problems 823
new operator 152, 171, 317, 318, 384, 395, 426, 1097, 1202
newInstance method of **RTPManager** 1271
newline escape sequence, **\n** 63, 64, 71, 122, 209, 377, 538
next 1210, 1212, 1225
nextDouble 1175
nextElement 1159, 1166, 1172
nextFloat 1175
nextGaussian 1175
nextInt 1174
nextToken 577, 578
no-argument constructor 395, 398, 414, 459
NoDataSinkException class 1262
NoDataSourceException 1260
node 791, 1097
non-**public** methods 383
non-**static** class members 431
non-**static** inner class 513
NONE 775
nonfatal logic error 158
nonfatal run-time error 19
nonlinear data structures 1097
nonrecursive method call 287
NoPlayerException 1247
NoProcessorException 1261
NORTH 697, 775
NORTHEAST 775

NORTHWEST 775
NoSuchElementException 1155, 1156
note in the UML 784
noteOff method 1298
noteOn method 1298
Notepad 16
notify 842, 843, 856, 857, 875, 886
notifyAll 842, 843, 849, 876
noun in a problem statement 24
noun phrase in problem statement 1317
noun phrases in problem statement 135, 136
noun phrases in the problem statement 183
nouns 183
nouns in a system-requirements document 380
null 67, 152, 274, 317, 462, 839, 1096, 1115, 1227
NullPointerException 653, 819, 1168
Num Lock key 689
number systems 572
Number Systems Appendix 1356
NumberFormat class 208
NumberFormatException 812, 815, 817
numeric classes 513

O

Object 382, 452, 513, 1384
object 22, 23, 24, 42, 116, 350, 351, 352
object (or instance) 4, 12, 115, 380
object-based programming (OBP) 380
Object class 382, 530, 650, 920
object diagram 42, 91, 140, 1459
Object Management Group (OMG) 25
object of a subclass 452
object of a subclass is instantiated 459
object of a superclass 452
object orientation 22, 379
object oriented 380
object-oriented analysis and design (OOAD) process 24
object-oriented analysis phase 703
object-oriented operating system 477
object-oriented programming (OOP) 107, 446
object-oriented technique for handling related exceptions 836
object serialization 997, 1168
"object speak" 22, 379
"object think" 22, 379
object to be thrown 809
ObjectInput 902, 906
ObjectInputStream 898, 902, 915, 920, 924, 961, 991, 992, 997, 998
object-oriented design (OOD) 22, 23, 41, 45, 87, 90, 293, 434, 1331
object-oriented language 23
object-oriented programming (OOP) 2, 3, 7, 12, 87, 380
ObjectOutput 902
ObjectOutputStream 898, 902, 906, 908, 961, 991, 993, 995, 997, 998, 1000, 1057, 1173
objects 379
objects constructed "inside out" 462
objects returned by reference 329
Observable class 794
Observer design pattern 521, 525, 793
Observer interface 794
observer object 793
octal (base8) 243
octal number system (base 8) 1357
odd 102
off-by-one error 202, 316
offset 929
OK button 68, 128
OMG 25
on-line training courses 135
one-armed bandit 261
one statement per line 85
one-to-one mapping 1226
one-, two- or three-button mouse 688
one's complement 1185, 1364
ones position 1357
online contracting services 1477
online documentation 650, 820
online recruiting 1468
OOAD 24, 25
OOD 22, 23, 135, 183, 186, 1463
OOP 25, 87, 380, 446
opaque 726
opaque Swing GUI components 733
open a file 898
open method of **Clip** 1282
open method of **DataSink** 1262
open source 13
opened 898
opening left brace (**{**) 275
operand 72, 172, 371
operating 839
operating system multithreading primitive 839
operating systems 8
operation 42, 137, 293, 294, 295, 296, 350, 374, 435, 436, 513, 517, 518, 636, 885
operation code 371
operations of an abstract data type 433
operator 76, 168
operator **==** 557
operator precedence 77, 285
operator precedence chart 173
Operator Precedence Chart Appendix 1353
optical disk 895
optimized code 1143
optimizing compiler 210
Optimizing the Simple Compiler 1143
or 1192
Oracle Corporation 1491
order 149, 150
order in which constructors and finalizers are called 459
order in which statements execute 133
order of exception handlers 836
order of promotion 172
origin component 758
originator object 525
OtherCharMethods.java 574
out-of-bounds array subscript 806, 818
out of memory 839
outer block 275
outer class this reference 875
outer class's this reference 513

outer **try** block 828
OutOfMemoryError 1097
output 60, 64
output buffer 997
output cursor 60, 63
output devices 8
output unit 8
OutputStream 900, 901, 902, 990, 992
OutputStreamWriter 903
oval 114, 117, 146, 152, 618, 622, 717
oval bounded by a rectangle 622
oval filled with gradually changing colors 631
oval symbol 152
oval's bounding box 217
OvalPanel.java 737
overflow 376, 806
overlapped building blocks 233
overload 383, 456
overload constructors 395, 454
overload methods 288, 298, 395
override 455, 515, 516, 519, 636
override (replace or redefine) behavior 116
override a method definition 291
override a superclass method 384, 455, 456
override method **toString** 456
oxymoron 322

P

pack method 766
package 65, 92, 259, 385, 390, 414, 785, 1379
package 1391, 1399, 1463
package access 417, 448, 451
package access members of a superclass 451
package-access methods 417
package access to members of a class 418
package directory names 392
package directory structure 390
package name 125
package naming 392
package statement 390
package statement 1379
PackageDataTest.java 418
package-list.txt 1380
packages of the Java API 259
packet 980, 1004
packet is received 1011
PacketReceiving-Thread.java 1042
Page Down key 689
page layout software 537
Page Up key 689
paint 630, 650, 726, 746
paint method of class **JApplet** 198, 199, 202
paint method of **JApplet** 113, 116, 117, 125, 127, 129, 130, 194, 292
paintComponent 605, 726, 727, 732, 736, 737, 747, 801, 1024, 1076, 1318
Painter.java 684
paintIcon 764, 1070, 1073, 1088
painting on Swing GUI components 721
painting program 719
palindrome 195, 368
Palo Alto Research Center (PARC) 12
panel 701
Panel class 692
PanelDemo.java 701
parallel activities 15
parallelogram 449
param tag 981, 1077
parameter 249, 252, 254
parameter list 117, 254
parameter name 254
parameter type 254
Parameters note 1376
PARC 12
parent directory 963
parent node 1116, 1131
parent thread group 876
parent window 722, 762
parent window for a dialog box 753
parent window specified as null 753
parentheses "on the same level" 78
parentheses force order of evaluation 77
parentheses, **()** 77
parentOf 877
Parnas, D. L. 892
parseDouble method of **Double** 124, 129, 250, 256, 257
parseInt method of **Integer** 69, 73, 75, 84, 171, 176, 250, 255, 812
partition 369
partitioning step 369
Pascal 3, 5, 14
Pascal, Blaise 15
pass 332
pass an array element to a method 330
pass an array to a method 330, 355
pass-by-reference 329
pass-by-value 329, 330, 380
PassArray.java 330
password 656
Patch class 1299
PATH environment variable 110
path information 962
pattern 629
pattern of **1**s and **0**s 896
pay 192
payroll file 896, 897
payroll system 463, 477
PDP-11 11
PDP-7 11
peek 1160
peer 649
Peoplescape.com 1473
perfect number 308
performance of binary tree sorting and searching 1146
Performance Tips 13
performing calculations 87, 133
persistent data 895
persistent **Hashtable** 1168
Person 879
Person 137, 139, 140, 184, 185, 187, 235, 236, 293, 294, 295, 350, 351, 352, 353, 435, 514, 516, 517, 518, 583, 587, 635, 636, 637, 704, 705, 706, 708, 878, 881, 882, 884, 885, 1393, 1399, 1400, 1401, 1402, 1404, 1420, 1429, 1435, 1436, 1437, 1456
personal computing 9
PersonMoveEvent 585, 1387, 1392, 1435, 1461
PersonMoveListener 637, 638, 1388, 1390, 1392, 1401, 1435
personMoveListener 1435
physical input operations 901
physical output operations 901
Physics Demo: Bouncing Ball 1344

Physics Demo: Bouncing Ball exercise 1344
Physics Demo: Kinetics 1344
Physics Demo: Kinetics exercise 1344
PI 146
piano player 1286, 1315
"pick off" each digit 103
PIE 630
pie chart 645
pie shaped arc 632
pieceworker 481
PieceWorker.java 481
Pig Latin 595
Pinball Machine 1345
Pinball Machine exercise 1345
pink 606
pipe 900
PipedInputStream 900
PipedOutputStream 900
PipedReader 903
PipedWriter 903
pitch 1291
pixel ("picture element") 732
pixel ("picture element") 118, 198
pixel ("picture element") 603
pixel coordinates 114, 121
PixelGrabber 1091
PLAIN 613, 666
PLAIN_MESSAGE 69, 74
platform 4
play 1084, 1085
play method from **AudioClip** interface 1084
play method of **Applet** 1084
Player 1247
Player method **stop** 1249
Player interface 1238, 1246, 1247, 1248
Player method 1247, 1248
Player method **start** 1248
Player method **close** 1247
Player method **setMediaTime** 1249
playing an **AudioClip** 1085
plug-in 120
pluggable look-and-feel (PLAF) 722
pluggable look-and-feel package 651
plus sign (**+**) indicating public visibility 434
.png 653
.png file 1327
point 110, 613
point-of-sale system 928
point size 342
Point.java 453, 460, 465, 488, 495
Point2D 1318
poker 594
poker card game 1066
polite programming practice 876
poll analysis program 326
Polygon 602, 625, 627
polygon 627, 717
polylines 625
polymorphic behavior 485
polymorphic processing of collections 1208
polymorphic processing of related errors 824
polymorphic programming 473
polymorphic screen manager 475
polymorphically calling a shape's draw method 719
polymorphically manipulate objects of type-wrapper classes 513
polymorphically process **Shape**s 496
polymorphism 215, 380, 446, 458, 463, 472, 475, 476, 486
polymorphism as an alternative to **switch** logic 532
polymorphism effective for implementing layered software systems 476
polynomial 79, 80
pool of threads 991
pop 432
pop 1148
popping off a stack 432
popup menu 756
popup trigger event 755, 756, 758
PopupTest.java 755
port 1264
port number 991, 996, 1003, 1004, 1011
port number 990
port numbers below 996
portability 19, 604, 1493
Portability Tips 13
portable 4, 11
portable GUIs 260
portable programming language 840
position 1318, 1321
position number 315
position number zero 315
positional notation 1357
positional value 1358
positional values in the decimal number system 1358
positive and negative arc angles 623
positive degrees 622
positive or negative infinity 813
postdecrement 179, 180
postfix expression evaluation algorithm 1128
postfix notation 1128
postincrement 179, 180, 181
postincrementing 204
postorder traversal 1120
postorderTraversal 1120
pow method of **Math** 209, 210, 250, 302
power 250, 308
power method 310
power of 2 larger than 1000 159
prebuilt software components 4
precedence 86, 181, 285
precedence and associativity of operations 316
precedence chart 77, 173
precedence chart Appendix 1353
precedence of arithmetic operators 78
predecrement 179, 180
predefined constant 454
predicate method 383, 1102
preempt 840
preempt a thread 843
preemption 840
prefetchComplete method 1248
PrefetchCompleteEvent 1248
Prefetched 1248
Prefetching 1248
preincrement 179, 180, 181
preincrementing 204
premature program termination 328
preorder traversal 1118
preorderTraversal 1120
prepackaged data structures 1202
press and hold the mouse button 111
press the mouse button 719
preview frame rate 1263
primary memory 8
primary window 746
prime 308, 1192, 1235

prime numbers 366
primitive (or built-in) data type 71, 128, 182, 258, 274, 281
primitive data type variables 127
primitive data type variables always passed by value 329
primitive data type variables returned by value 329
primitive type 186
Princeton Review 1480
principal 207
principle of least privilege 274, 389, 412, 939
print a histogram 323
print a line of text 60
print an array 368
print an array recursively 368
print method of **System.out** 63, 72
print on multiple lines 62, 63
print spooling 1113
PrintBits.java 1176
printing a binary tree in a two-dimensional tree format 1123
Printing Dates in Various Formats 597
Printing Trees 1132
println method of **System.out** 60, 63, 72
printStackTrace 830, 831
PrintStream 900, 1173
PrintWriter 1042
priority scheduling 844
private 434
private class members 388
private data 389, 401
private instance variable 400
private keyword 116, 152
private members of a superclass 451
private method 382
private static class member 427
private visibility 434
probability 261
problem statement 41, 42, 87, 184, 185, 186, 704, 1317
procedural programming language 23
procedural programming languages 380
procedure 149
processing phase 168
processing unit 7
Processor interface 1249, 1259
Processor method 1262, 1271
Processor> method 1271
ProcessorModel class 1261, 1333
ProduceInteger.java 850, 854, 861, 862
producer 854, 856, 857
producer method 849
producer thread 849
producer/consumer relationship 849
product of odd integer 242
products 1349
program construction principles 198
program control 56, 107, 150
program development 56, 107
program development process 432
program development tools 178
program execution stack 1108
program in the general 532
program maintenance 473
program termination 328
programChange method 1299
Examples 1169
programmer-defined classes 58
programmer-defined method 248
programmer-defined type 380
Project: Flight Simulator 1344
Project: Multimedia Authoring System 1344
promotion 172
promotion rules 258
promotions for primitive data types 258
prompt 72, 171
prompt the user to enter a value 128
Properties 1148, 1168, 1173, 1199
PropertiesTest.java 1169
propertyNames 1172
protected access 447
protected access modifier 429
protected access vs. **private** access in superclasses 532
protected instance variable 456, 459, 466
protected keyword 116, 152, 388
protected member 515
protected members of a subclass 451
protected members of a superclass 447, 451
Prototype design pattern 521, 522, 1230
Proxy design pattern 520, 524
pseudo-random-number generator 1174
pseudocode 24, 150, 153, 155, 159, 161, 167, 168, 175
public abstract method 494
public class 59, 116, 381, 391
public data 382
public final static data 494
public interface 383, 467, 477
public keyword 59, 115, 116, 117, 152, 382, 434, 435, 436
public members of a subclass 451
public method 382, 383, 388
public methods inherited into a class 486
public operations encapsulated in an object 387
public service 383
public static class members 427
public static method 427
public visibility 434
pure Java components 649
push 432
push 1148
PushBackInputStream 902
PushbackReader 902
pushing into a stack 432
put 982, 1160, 1227
Pythagorean Triples 244

Q

quantum 840, 843
quantum expiration 842
query method 400
queue 383, 433, 1095, 1113
queue to the server 992
QueueInheritance.java 1113
QueueInheritanceTest.java 1114
quicksort 368
QuickTime files 1237, 1332

Quit from the **appletviewer**'s **Applet** menu 112

R

"**r**" file open mode 933, 939
radians 250, 635, 641
radio buttons 111, 662, 667
RadioButtonHandler 669, 670
RadioButtonTest.java 668
radius 146
radius of a circle 312
radix 572
raised rectangles 621
RAM (random access memory) 8
Random 1148, 1174
random 427, 634
random 1174
random-access file 895, 900, 928, 939
random access memory (RAM) 8
Random class 260
random limericks 595
random method of **Math** 261, 264, 306, 359, 427, 850, 851, 855, 856, 862, 863, 1120
random number 1148
random number generation 579
random number generation to create sentences 595
random number generator 1174
random number processing 260
RandomAccessAccountRecord.java 929
RandomAccessFile 900, 920, 928, 929, 931, 933, 936, 939, 961
RandomCharacters.java 871
RandomIntegers.java 262
randomly generated triangles 644
randomly sized shapes 719
range checking 389
range-view methods 1225
rapid applications development (RAD) 411
ratio of successive Fibonacci numbers 281
Rational 441
Rational 441
Rational Software Corporation 25, 90
Rational Unified Process ™ 90
read 941
read-only variable 270
read-only file 914
read-only text 651
read-only variable 322
Read/Write Lock design pattern 521, 886
readability 56, 58
readable 962
readChar 930, 1021
readDouble 931
Reader 892
Reader 902
reader threads 892
Readers and Writers 892
readers and writers problem in concurrency control 892
reading a random-access file sequentially 939
reading a rile on a web server 986
reading a sequential file 916
readInt 931, 1017, 1022
readLine 965, 1033
readObject 902, 918, 920, 925, 995, 1001
ReadRandomFile.java 939
ReadSequentialFile.java 915
ReadServerFile.java 986
readUTF 1021
ready 841
ready state 841, 852, 856, 871
real number 71, 168
real part 440
Real-Time Transport Protocol 1239, 1264
realization 43, 635, 636
realization diagram 636, 637
realizations 43
realizeComplete method 1248, 1271
Realized 1248, 1271
RealizedCompleteEvent 1248
Realizing 1247
receive 1007
receive a connection 992
receive data from the server 1002
receive method of class **MulticastSocket** 1045
Receiver interface 1292, 1295, 1298, 1299
Receiver method **send** 1299
receiving object 583
receiving section of the computer 8
ReceivingThread.java 1031
reclaim memory 431
reclaiming dynamically allocated memory 839
record 896
record key 897, 928, 974
record size 928
record structure 903
recordEnable method 1295
recover from an error 328
Recruitsoft.com 1473
Rectangle 442
Rectangle 442, 629
rectangle 109, 114, 145, 449, 602, 607, 618, 717
rectangle symbol 151, 152, 154, 160, 205, 214, 231
rectangle with rounded corners 717
Rectangle2D 602
Rectangle2D.Double 628, 629, 630, 644
recursion examples and exercises in the text 287
recursion overhead 286
recursion step 278, 284
recursion vs. iteration 286
recursive call 278, 284, 285
recursive calls to method **fibonacci** 285
recursive evaluation 279
recursive **factorial** method 279
recursive method 278
recursive **power** method 310
recursive program 285
recursive step 368
recursively generating Fibonacci numbers 285
Recursively Print a List Backwards 1131
Recursively Search a List 1131
redirect a stream 898
redundant parentheses 79
Refer.com 1473
reference 127
reference count 818
reference initialization to **null** 274
reference to a new object 384
reference to a subclass object implicitly converted into reference to superclass object 463
reference to an object 417

references to **abstract** superclasses 476
references to an object 839
referring to a subclass object with a subclass reference 463
referring to a subclass object with a superclass reference 463
referring to a superclass object with a subclass reference 463
referring to a superclass object with a superclass reference 463
regionMatches 543, 593
register a **WindowListener** 686
register an **ActionListener** 753
register an event listener 655
registered listener 660
registering an event handler 272
registers a window event listener 512
"reinventing the wheel" 65, 248, 259
reinventing the wheel 13
related exception types 806
RELATIVE 780, 781
relative path 962
release a lock 856
release mouse button 719
release resources 825
Reload from **appletviewer**'s **Applet** menu 110, 112
REMAINDER 780, 781
remainder 76
remote computer 18
remove duplicate **String** 1223
remove method 1160, 1168, 1207, 1210
removeAllElements 1155
removeElement 1155
removeElementAt 1155
removeTargets method 1272
repaint 605, 642, 650, 726, 727, 732, 1077
repaint method of **JApplet** 292
repainted 292
repetition 160, 230, 233, 234
repetition condition 200
repetition structure 151, 159, 167, 286
replace 554
request for proposal 1478
requirements 24, 703
reservations system 361
reserved words 58
resizable array 982
resizable-array implementation of a **List** 1208
resolution 603
resource leak 426, 808, 825
responses to a survey 326
restart method of **Timer** 1088
resume 1467, 1472, 1475
resume 870
resume method of Thread 875
resumed 876
resume-filtering software 1472
resumption model of exception handling 809
rethrow an exception 812, 836
rethrown exception 826
return 248
return keyword 152, 252, 253, 254, 255, 278, 329
return message 881
return type 294, 296
return value type 254
Returns note 1378
reusability 1095
reusable components 449
reusable software components 4, 12, 259
reuse 65
"reuse, reuse, reuse." 24
reverse 563, 1215, 1219, 1220, 1221
reverse engineering 434
reverseOrder 1216
RGB 611
RGB values 606
Richards, Martin 11
right 602
right aligned 693
right angle bracket, **>** 119
right arrow key 736
right brace, **{** 59, 60, 70
right brace, **}** 115, 164, 171
right child 1116
right shift operator with sign extension, **>>** 1176, 1189
right shift operator with zero extension, **>>>** 1185, 1189
right subtree 1116, 1121, 1131
right triangle 196
rigid area 770
Ritchie, Dennis 11
.rmf (Rich Music Format file extension) 1285
RMF files 1290
.rmi 1085
robust 72
robust applications 817
robust programs 805
roll a six-sided die 264, 324
roll a six-sided die 6000 times 263
roll two dice 360
rollDice method of craps program 272
RollDie.java 263, 324
rollover **Icon** 664
root directory 962
root node 1116
rotate 634
Roulette 1345
Roulette exercise 1345
round 173, 210, 250
round a number to a specific decimal place 305
round robin 840, 843
rounded rectangle 235, 620, 631
rounding 76, 305
rounding a value to the nearest integer 305
rounding errors 259
RoundRectangle2D 602
RoundRectangle2D.Double 628, 632
RTP 1239, 1264, 1271
RTPManager 1264, 1271
RTPServer.java 1264
RTPServerTest.java 1272
"rubber-banding" effect 719
rule of thumb 220
rules of operator precedence 77, 285
Rumbaugh, James 25, 26
run method 840, 845, 849, 850, 851, 870, 1018
run-time logic error 72
run-time exceptions 818
Runnable 840, 870, 871, 877, 1018, 1019, 1428
runnable state 841
runnable thread 839
running 841
running state 841, 847
running thread 841
RuntimeException 818, 820, 822, 829, 1102
"rw" file open mode 933, 947
rw" to open the file for reading and writing 933

S

Salary.com 1480
same object 558
same signature 456
sampling rate 1259
SansSerif font 342, 613, 614, 615, 618
saturation 612
savings account 207
scalar 330
scalar quantities 330
scaled random integer 262, 265
scaling 261
scaling an image 1070, 1072, 1090
scaling factor 261, 265
scanning images 8
scheduler 843, 849
scheduling 842
scientific and engineering applications 14
scope 203, 274
scope of an identifier 275
scoping example 276
Scoping.java 276
Scott, Kendall 26
screen 8, 163
screen capture 111, 112
screen cursor 64
screen manager program 475
script 1497
scroll 209, 242, 243, 673, 676
scroll arrow 671
scroll box 229, 671
Scroll Lock key 689
scroll through text 209
scrollbar 229, 671, 675, 725
scrollbar policies 725
search key 335, 1223
searching 335, 1095
second-degree polynomial 79, 80
second pass 1136
second refinement 166, 175
secondary storage devices 895
secondary storage unit 8
sector 623
security 19
SecurityException 1262
See Also note 1375
seek 921, 933, 937, 938
SELECTED 666, 672
selected 667
selected text 722
selecting an item from a menu 654
selection 153, 230, 231, 233, 234
selection mode 675
selection sort 368
selection structure 151, 152, 286
self-documenting 71
self-referential class 1096, 1097
self-referential class objects linked together 1097
_self target frame 986
SelfContainedPanel.java 730
SelfContainedPanelTest.java 733
semicolon, **;** 61, 71, 85, 159
send data to the server 1002
send message 117, 127, 128
send method of class **DatagramSocket** 1036
send method of DatagramSocket 1007
sending a message to an object 200
sending object 583
SendingThread.java 1041
SendStream interface 1271, 1272
sentinel-controlled repetition 165, 167, 168, 169, 171, 243, 373
sentinel value 166, 171
separator bar 752
separator line 754
separatorChar variable of **File** 967
sequence 153, 230, 231, 233, 234, 1116, 1208
Sequence class 1290
sequence diagram 44, 91, 352, 881, 882
sequence of messages 353
sequence structure 151, 166
SequenceInputStream 902
sequencer 1286, 1290, 1331
Sequencer interface 1290, 1291
sequencer recording 1295
sequential-access file 895, 897, 900, 903, 908, 928, 991
sequential code 473
sequential execution 150
Serializable 902, 906, 907, 1380
Serif font 342, 613, 614, 617, 781
Server 1006
server object 583
server port number 1003
server portion of a client/server stream socket connection 993
server-side of connectionless client/server computing with datagrams 1004
server waits for connections from clients 990
Server.java 993, 1004
server's Internet address 991
ServerSocket 990, 992, 993, 1012, 1017, 1027, 1028
service 294, 388, 486
services of a class 429
Set 1203, 1208, 1223, 1226
set 1213
set method 389, 400, 404, 405
set-theoretic intersection 443
set-theoretic union 443
setAlignment method 694
setBackground 610, 611, 633, 675, 728, 738, 751, 756
setBounds method 1299
setCaretPosition 997, 1003, 1010, 1022
setColor method 606, 607, 608, 615, 620, 624, 629, 632, 634
setConstraints 779
setContentDescriptor method 1271
setCurrentChoice 744
setCursor 989
setDaemon 869
setDefaultCloseOperation 740
setEditable 657
setEditable method of **JTextField** 272
setElementAt 1155
setEnabled 690
setErr 898
setFieldValues 918
setFileSelectionMode 908, 917, 924, 931, 935, 941
setFixedCellHeight 677
setFixedCellWidth 677, 678
setFont 613, 614, 617, 666, 751
setFont method of **JTextArea** 342, 347, 356
setForeground 751
setHeight 743

setHorizontalAlignment 653
setHorizontalScroll-BarPolicy 725
setHorizontalTextPosi-tion 652
setIcon 652, 653
setIn 898
setInverted 736
setJMenuBar 747, 749, 753, 763, 797
setJMenuBar method of **JFrame** 753
setLayout 650, 657, 693, 695, 698, 701, 767, 770
setLayout method of **Con-tainer** 271
setLayout method of **JAp-plet** 271
setLength method 930
setLineWrap 725
setLineWrap method of class **JTextArea** 1052
setListData 677
setLocation 740
setLookAndFeel 760, 762
setMajorTickSpacing 738, 739
setMaximumRowCount 672
setMaxPriority 877
setMediaTime method 1249
setMessage 1299
setMnemonic 748, 750, 753
setName 841
setOpaque 726
setOut 898
setPage method of **JEditor-Pane** 989
setPaint 629, 630
setPaintTicks 738, 739
setPriority 843
setRolloverIcon 663
setSeed 1174
setSelected 749
setSelected method of **Ab-stractButton** 754
setSelectionMode 674, 677
setSequence method 1290
setSize 633, 652, 740, 744
setSoTimeout method of class **MulticastSocket** 1045
setSoTimeOut method of class **Socket** 1033
setStroke 629, 631
SetTest.java 1224
setText 580, 652, 725
setText method of **JTextAr-ea** 209, 331
Setting an object reference to **null** 839
setTitle 687, 734
setToolTipText 652
setVerticalAlignment 653
setVerticalScrollBar-Policy 725
setVerticalTextPosi-tion 652
setVisible 697
setVisible method of **Com-ponent** 740
setVisibleRowCount 674, 677
setWidth 743
setWrapStyleWord method of class **JTextArea** 1052
shape 111, 628
Shape class hierarchy 450, 451, 532
shape classes 443
Shape object 631
shape, point, circle, cylinder hierarchy 487
Shape.java 487, 495
shapes 109
Shapes.java 629
Shapes2.java 633
share 9
shared data 849
shared memory 856
shared region of memory 849
SharedCell.java 853, 859, 868
shareware 13
shell 60
shell prompt in UNIX 18
shell script 68
shell tool 60
Shift 692
shift 261
shifted and scaled random integers 262
shifting value 265
shipping section of the computer 8
shopping list 159
Short 513, 1156
short-circuit evaluation 225
short keyword 152
short primitive data type 210
short promotions 258
shorthand name 125
ShortMessage class 1291, 1299
ShortMessage.NOTE_OFF 1316
ShortMessage.NOTE_ON 1299, 1316
ShortMessage.PROG-RAM_CHANGE 1299
show 740, 758
ShowColors.java 607
ShowColors2.java 609
showDialog 610
showDocument 981, 985
showInputDialog method of **JOptionPane** 69, 72, 84, 123, 128, 164, 171, 176, 256
showMessageDialog method of **JOptionPane** 67, 73, 74, 82, 121, 176
showOpenDialog 917, 920, 924
showSaveDialog 913, 931
shuffle a deck of cards 1217
shuffle algorithm 1217
shuffle algorithm 1215
shuffling 579
sibling 1116
side effect 225, 285, 329
Sieve of Eratosthenes 366, 1191
signal value 166
signature 290, 395, 455, 456
signed applets 1026
Silicon Graphics 1237
Simple commands 1133
Simple Compiler 1143
simple condition 222
Simple Interpreter 1145
Simple Language 1133
SimpleGraph applet 109
SimplePlayer 1238
SimplePlayer.java 1239
simplest flowchart 231, 232
Simpletron Machine Language (SML) 371, 1095
Simpletron simulator 374, 376, 1093, 1096
simulate a middle-mouse-button click on a one- or two-button mouse 689
simulate a right-mouse-button click on a one-button mouse 689
simulate coin tossing 309
simulated piano keyboard 1286
simulation 261, 352
Simulation: Tortoise and the Hare 370, 645, 1344
simulator 91, 183, 371

sin method of **Math** 250
Since note 1379
sine 250
single-entry/single-exit control structures 153, 154, 230, 231
single inheritance 447
single-line comment, **//** 57, 61, 71, 114
single-precision floating-point number 123
single quotes 538
single selection 234
single-selection list 673
single-selection structure 152
single-subscripted array 343
Single-Threaded Execution design pattern 521, 886
single-threaded languages 838
single-user batch processing 8
SINGLE_INTERVAL_SELECTION 675, 676, 678
SINGLE_SELECTION 675
Singleton design pattern 520, 522
sink 332
sinking sort 332
SiteSelector.html 981
SiteSelector.java 983
SixFigureJobs 1479
size 75
size 1156, 1160, 1190, 1208, 1210, 1227
size of an array 328
size of the applet's display area 119
SkillsVillage.com 1473
sleep 841, 844, 847, 850, 851, 855, 856, 862
sleep interval expires 842
sleeping 841
sleeping state 841, 847, 850, 851
sleeping thread 841, 843
SliderDemo.java 738
small circle 214
small circle symbol 151, 152, 153
small diamond symbol 236
small methods 255
smallest integer in a group 146
smallest of several integers 242
Smalltalk 12
SML 1095
snap-to ticks 735
Socket 990, 998, 1003, 1015, 1018, 1019, 1040, 1056
socket 980
socket-based communications 980
SocketException 1005
SocketImpl 1056
SocketMessageManager.java 1037
SocketMessengerConstants.java 1029
software 3, 7
software asset 24
software-based simulation 371
software model 374
software reusability 250, 446
software reuse 13, 388, 390, 412, 464
software simulator 87
Solaris 840
solid arc 623
solid circle 236
solid circle with an attached arrowhead 235
solid polygon 625
solid rectangle 619
sort 1203, 1205, 1215, 1216, 1222
sort an array 335
Sort1.java 1215
Sort2.java 1216
SortDemo applet 109
sorted array 1098
sorted order 1223, 1226
SortedMap 1226
SortedSet 1223, 1226
SortedSetTest-.java 1225
SortedSetTest.java 1225
sorting 332, 944, 1095
sorting large arrays 335
sorting techniques 109
sound 44, 292, 1069, 1464
sound bank 1298
sound board 1084
sound engine 1085
SoundBank 1295
SoundEffects 1317, 1318, 1327, 1329, 1457, 1459, 1460, 1464
SoundEffects.java 1328
sounds of many animals 1316
source code 107
source code file containing documentation comments 1371
source of an event 404
SOUTH 680, 775
South 696
SOUTHEAST 775
SOUTHWEST 775
space character 58
space/time trade-off 1162, 944
speaker 1084
speaking to computers 8
special character 63, 71, 538
Special Section
  Advanced String Manipulation Exercises 596
  Building Your Own Compiler 1095
  Building Your Own Computer 1095
Special Section: Building Your Own Computer 371
special symbol 896
Spelling Checker project 599
sphere 302
spiral 281, 645
split a statement 68
spooling 1113
SpreadSheet applet 109
spreadsheet program 18
sqrt method of **Math** 249, 250, 258
square 449, 621
square brackets, **[]** 327, 356
square method 252
square root 250
square root of a negative integer is undefined 433
SquareInt.java 252
stable sort 1215
Stack 1108, 1148, 1160, 1202
stack 310, 383, 432, 811, 828, 831, 1095, 1108
stack trace 841
stack trace message 831
stack unwinding 828
stack unwinds 831
StackComposition.java 1112
stacked building blocks 233
stacking 155, 234
stacking rule 231
StackInheritance.java 1109
StackInheritanceTest.java 1110
StackTest.java 1156
"stand-alone" units 9
standard development process 435
standard error stream object 898
standard input 898

standard output object 60
standard output stream object 898
standard reusable components 449
Standard Template Library (STL) 1203
standard time format 386
standardized exception handling 806
"standardized, interchangeable parts" 24
star 633
start 116, 118, 129, 746, 841, 847, 853, 859, 869, 876, 1018, 1020, 1076
start method of **DataSink** 1262
start method of **JApplet** 292
start method of **SendStream** 1272
start method of **Sequencer** 1290
starting angle 622
startRecording method 1295
startsWith method of **String** 546
starvation 843
state 42, 92, 183, 234, 895
State design pattern 520, 525, 794
state diagram 234
state object 794
state transition 42
stateChanged 739
statechart diagram 42, 91, 234, 235, 236
statement 61, 253
statement terminator (;) 61
static class member 427
static class variable 427, 429
static class variable to maintain a count of the number of objects of a class 429
static class variables have class scope 427
static duration 274
static inner class 513, 628
static keyword 153
static method 67, 129, 253, 273, 880, 1329
static method cannot access non-**static** class members 431
static methods of type-wrapper classes 513
StaticCharMethods.java 569
StaticCharMethods2.java 572
status bar 114, 273, 717
stop 870, 1085, 1087, 1089
stop method of **DataLine** 1282
stop method of **JApplet** 292
Stopped 1263
stopRecording 1295
store 1171
Story Teller 1344
Story Teller exercise 1344
straight line 632
straight-line form 77
strategy 365
Strategy design pattern 521, 525, 794
strategy object 794
stream header 997
stream object 898
stream of bytes 897
stream of inputs 166
stream processing 895
stream socket 980, 992, 1011
Streaming media 1263
streams 980
streams-based transmission 1003
StreamTokenizer 1136
StreamTokenizer 1130, 1235
String 70, 71, 172, 537, 538
string 60, 260
String argument 129
String array 317
String class 117
String class searching methods 549
String comparison methods 595
String comparison performance 557
string concatenation 74, 85, 220, 386
string concatenation operator, **+** 74
string constant 538
String constructors 539
string literal 60, 538
string literals as objects of class **String** 172
string of characters 60, 117
String reference 540
StringBuffer class 537, 540, 559
StringBuffer class **insert** methods 567
StringBuffer constructors 560
StringBufferAppend.java 565
StringBufferCapLen.java 561
StringBufferChars.java 563
StringBufferConstructors.java 560
StringBufferInsert.java 567
StringConcat.java 552
StringConstructors.java 538
StringHashCode.java 548
StringIndexOutOfBoundsException class 552, 563
StringIntern.java 557
StringMisc.java 541
StringReader 903
StringStartEnd.java 546
StringTokenizer 260, 537, 576, 595, 1034, 1040
StringValueOf.java 555
StringWriter 903
Stroke object 631, 632
strongly typed languages 182
Stroustrup, Bjarne 12
structural design patterns 27, 520, 523, 789, 1057
structure of the system 137, 140, 186
structured programming 3, 15, 22, 87, 133, 151, 198, 219, 234, 432
structured techniques 220
student poll analysis program 326
StudentPoll.java 326
subclass 115, 382, 447, 448, 449, 451, 515, 516, 519, 585, 588, 788, 790, 1318, 1384, 1435
subclass constructor 453, 459
subclass-object-is-a-superclass-object relationship 447, 463
subclass-object-to-superclass-object conversion 463
subclass of **Thread** 851
subclass reference 452
subdirectory 109

subject object 793
sublist 1213
submenu 747
subscript 315, 343
substring method of **String** 552
SubString.java 551
subsystem 91, 1057
subtraction 77
sum the elements of an array 322
Sum.java 206
SumArray.java 322
summary of recursion examples and exercises in the book 287
Sun Audio 1237, 1278
Sun Audio file format 1085
Sun Microsystems xxxv, 3, 6, 27, 57
Sun Microsystems, Inc. 1491
Sun's HotSpot compiler 21
Sunsite Japan Multimedia Collection 1316
super 451, 452, 456, 459, 461
super keyword 153
superclass 115, 382, 445, 447, 448, 449, 451, 513, 515, 516, 791, 1384, 1401, 1402, 1420
superclass constructor 453
superclass constructor call syntax 455
superclass default constructor 459
superclass **Exception** 806
superclass **finalize** 459
superclass method is overridden in a subclass 460
superclass objects 452
superclass reference 452, 457, 458, 463, 473, 483
superclass reference to refer to a subclass object 473
superclass's constructor 459
superclass's default constructor 454
superclass's **private** members 451
superclass's **protected** members 451
supercomputer 7
Supermarket Simulation 1130
surface area of the cylinder 486
survey 328
suspend 870, 875
suspend an applet's execution 292
suspended a thread 870
swap 333, 334
sweep 622
sweep counterclockwise 622
.swf 1237
.swf (Flash file extension) 1237, 1332
Swing Event Package 260
Swing GUI components package 259, 260, 649
Swing's painting mechanism 726
SwingConstants 652, 737
SwingConstants.BOTTOM 652
SwingConstants.CENTER 652, 751
SwingConstants.HORIZONTAL 738
SwingConstants.LEFT 652
SwingUtilities 762, 860, 875
SwingUtilties class 1053
switch logic 215, 473
switch multiple-selection structure 152, 153, 210, 213, 214, 230, 234, 264, 448
SwitchTest.java 211
Sybase, Inc. 1491
Symantec Visual Cafe 16
symbol 1490
symbol table 1136
SymbolTest applet 109
synchronization 848, 860, 875, 878, 1315
synchronization wrappers 1228
synchronized 879, 886, 1013, 1016, 1102, 1120, 1228
synchronized block 1407
synchronized block of code 875
synchronized blocks of code 848
synchronized keyword 153, 854
synchronized method 848, 856, 858, 878, 880, 883, 1429, 1436
synchronous call 352, 878
synchronous error 806
syntax error 61, 118, 159
synthesizer 1285, 1295
Synthesizer interface 1295
SysexMessage class 1291
system 41, 42, 44, 45, 91, 235, 293, 350, 435
system behavior 91
system box 704
System class 68
system requirements 703
system responsibilities 91
system service 996
system structure 91
System.err (standard error stream) 898, 900
System.exit(0) 66, 68, 162, 504, 510
System.gc() 430, 462
System.in (standard input stream) 898
System.out (standard output stream) 898, 900
System.out.print method 63, 72
System.out.println method 60, 63, 72
SystemColor 631

T

tab 64, 112
tab characters 58
Tab key 59
tab stops 59, 64
table 343
table element 343
tabular format 318, 319
tag 119
tail of a queue 1113
tailSet 1225
tan method of **Math** 250
tangent 250
target frame 985
task 839
TCP (Transmission Control Protocol) 980
telephone number word generating program 976
Telephone Number Word Generator 976
telephone system 1004
Template File combo box 133
Template Method design pattern 521, 525, 795
temporary 172
terminal 9
terminate a program 66, 68, 944
terminate a thread 870
terminate an application 165, 746, 753
terminate nested looping structure 220
terminate successfully 68

terminating right brace (}) of a block 275
termination 328
termination housekeeping 426
termination model of exception handling 809
termination phase 168
termination test 286
ternary operator 156
Test.java 457, 462, 466, 468, 471, 483
testing 473
Testing and Debugging Tips 13
text analysis 596
text editor 60, 537
text field 66, 67, 72, 647, 648
text file 118
Text Package 260
text that jumps 109
TextAreaDemo.java 722
TextFieldTest.java 656
TexturePaint 602, 630
The Complete 2 Java Training Course
Fourth Edition 3
The Complete UML Training Course 26
The Diversity Directory 1472
The National Business and Disability Council (NBDC) 1473
"The Twelve Days of Christmas" 214, 245
The Unified Modeling Language User Guide 26
thick lines 629
thick white lines 632
this 388
this keyword 153, 272, 291, 419, 431, 513, 680
ThisTest.java 419
Thompson, Ken 11
Thread 839, 840, 844, 847, 849, 868, 869, 871, 875, 877, 1018, 1019, 1028, 1034, 1435
thread 292, 463, 878, 886, 1399, 1407, 1419, 1428, 1429
thread dies 847, 851
thread group 876
thread of execution 838
thread priority scheduling 844
thread safety 1228
thread states 841
thread synchronization 875
Thread.MAX_PRIORITY 842
Thread.MIN_PRIORITY 842
Thread.NORM_PRIORITY 842
ThreadDeath 839
ThreadDeath object 839
ThreadGroup 839, 841, 876
ThreadLocal 839
threads modifying a shared array of cells 868
threads running asynchronously 860
ThreadTester.java 845
three-button mouse 688
3-D Multithreaded Tic-Tac-Toe 1067
three-dimensional shape 109
three-dimensional view 109
three-dimensional application 1069
three-dimensional rectangle 619
three-dimensional, high-resolution, color graphics 1069
ThreeDimensionalShape 532
throughput 9
throw an exception 808, 809, 817
throw checked exception 819
throw keyword 153, 809, 818, 820
throw objects of subclasses 818
throw point 809
throw statement 809, 817
Throwable 809, 830
throws clause 808, 819
throws clause of a subclass method that overrides a superclass method 820
throws keyword 153
thumb 229, 735, 737
thumb position 739
Tic-Tac-Toe 1011
tick marks 735
TicTacToe 442
TicTacToe 442
TicTacToe applet 107, 110
TicTacToeClient 1011, 1018, 1066
TicTacToeClient.java 1019
TicTacToeServer 1011, 1015, 1017, 1066
TicTacToeServer.java 1012
tightly packed binary tree 1123
Time 1249
Time.java 501
Time1.java 381, 391
Time2.java 396
Time3.java 401
Time4.java 422
Timer 644, 1076, 1077, 1315, 1458, 1459
Timer delay 1315
timesharing 9
timeslice 840, 842, 843, 890
TimesRoman font 342
TimeTest.java 385
TimeTest2.java 389
TimeTest3.java 393
TimeTest4.java 398
TimeTest5.java 405
TimeTest6.java 425
TimeTestWindow.java 503, 508
title bar 68, 506, 687, 740
title bar of internal window 766
title bar string 74
toArray 1213
toCharArray method of **String** 368, 554
toggle buttons 662
ToggleButton 662
token 260, 576
tokenization 576
TokenTest.java 576
toLowerCase method of **String** 554, 571
toLowerCaseTokenTest.java method of **String** 570
tool tips 651, 653, 654
toolbars 665
top 166, 174, 432, 1160
top-down, stepwise refinement 7, 166, 168, 173
_top target frame 603, 986
Tortoise and the Hare 370, 645, 891, 1344
toString invoked on any **Throwable** object 810
toString method 382, 383, 384
toString method of **Integer** 273
total 161, 166
toUpperCase method of **String** 554, 570, 571
Towers of Hanoi 310, 645, 1344
Towers of Hanoi exercise 645, 1344

Track class 1291, 1295
Track method **get** 1291
TrackControl interface 1271
trailing white-space characters 555
training course 135
transaction file 974
transaction-processing applications 900, 928
transaction-processing program 928, 944
transaction record 975
transfer of control 150, 373, 374, 375
transient 906
transient keyword 153
transition 235, 236, 237
translate 633
translation 10
translator program 10
Transmitter interface 1291, 1295, 1298
transparency 726
transparent Swing GIF components 733
trapezoid 449
traverse a tree 1121
tree 112, 1116, 1223
Tree link 1380
Tree.java 1117
TreeMap 1226
TreeSet 1223, 1226
TreeTest.java 1120
triangle 195
trigger an event 648
trigonometric cosine 250
trigonometric sine 250
trigonometric tangent 250
trillion-instruction-per-second computers 7
trimmethod of **String-Buffer** 554, 555
trimToSize 1149
true keyword 153
truncate 76, 172, 914
trusted source 1026
truth 79
truth table 224
truth table for operator **!** 226
truth table for operator **&&** 224
truth table for operator **^** 226
truth table for operator **||** 225
try block 808, 809, 817, 847
try completing successfully 829
try keyword 153
Turtle Graphics 362, 645
Tutorials 1350
Twelve Days of Christmas 245
two-dimensional array 343, 344
two-dimensional drawing 112
two-dimensional graphics demo 112
two-dimensional data structure 1116
two-dimensional graphics 628, 1069
two-dimensional shapes 602
two largest values 192
Two-Phase Termination design pattern 521, 886
two's complement 1364
TwoDimensionalShape 532
twos position 1359
type 74
type of the thrown exception 808
type-wrapper class 129, 186, 513, 568, 1149, 1156
TYPE_INT_RGB 629
typeless language 11
typesetting system 537
typing in a text field 654

U

U+yyyy (Unicode notational convention) 1492, 1498
UDP 980
UIManager 760, 762
UIManager.LookAnd-FeelInfo 759
UML 22, 25, 41, 42, 43, 44, 45, 87, 90, 91, 138, 140, 186, 515, 518, 635, 636, 703, 878, 1331, 1393, 1436, 1463
UML 1.3 specifications document 26
UML diagram 91
UML Distilled Second Edition 26
UML notes 586
UML Partners 25
unambiguous (Unicode design basis) 1491, 1498
unary cast operator 172
unary operator 172, 226
uncaught exception 806
unchecked 112
unchecked **RuntimeExcep-tion** and **Error** 819
uncovering an applet 605
Undo button 719
uneditable 272, 722
uneditable **JTextField** 272
uneditable text or icons 648
unicast 1036
Unicode 182, 183, 544, 902, 1217
Unicode character 896
Unicode character set 103, 538, 550, 569
Unicode Consortium 1491, 1498, 1499
Unicode Standard 1490, 1498, 1499
Unicode Standard design basis 1491
Unicode Transformation Format (UTF) 1498
Unicode value of the character typed 692
Unified Modeling Language (UML) 22, 25
uniform (Unicode design basis) 1491, 1498
Uniform Resource Identifier (URI) 981
Uniform Resource Locator (URL) 981
union of two sets 443
universal (Unicode design basis) 1498
universal (Unicode design principle) 1491
universal-time format 382, 386
UNIX 10, 16, 60, 68, 107, 604, 758
UNIX look-and-feel 722
UNIX platform 758
UnknownHostException 992
Unmodifiable Wrapper 1228
unnecessary parentheses 79
unstructured flowchart 233
UnsupportedAudioFile-Exception 1281
UnSupportedFormatEx-ception 1272
UnsupportedOperation-Exception 1207, 1228
update 605, 650, 726, 1282
update method of **JApplet** 293
updateComponentTreeUI method of **SwingUtili-ties** 762
updateComponentTreeUI of **SwingUtilities** 760
UpdateThread.java 861

upper-left corner (0, 0)
coordinates of an applet 114, 118, 119, 123
upper-left corner of a GUI component 602
uppercase letter 58, 71
URI 982
URI (uniform resource identifier) 981
URL 1058, 1072, 1084
URL (Uniform Resource Locator) 981
URLStreamHandler 1058
use case 44, 703, 704, 705
use-case diagram 44, 91, 703, 705
user 293
User Datagram Protocol 980
user-defined classes 58
user-defined type 23, 186, 380
user interface 1060
user-interface 43
user interface event 281
user synthesis 1286
UsingArrays.java 1203
UsingAsList.java 1206
UsingExceptions.java 826, 828, 831
UsingToArray.java 1213
UTF (Unicode Transformation Format) 1498
UTF-16 1491, 1498
UTF-32 1491, 1498
UTF-8 1491, 1498
Utilities Package 260
utility method 382

V

vacated bits 1189
validate 700
validate method of **Container** 701
validity checking 401, 409
value 75, 1168
value of a param 981
value to the nearest integer 305
valueOf 555, 1024
variable 24, 71, 128, 380
variable declaration 126
variable is not modifiable 412
variable name 75
variable scope 203
Vault.com 1469
Vector 314, 719, 822, 982, 983, 1154, 1202, 1208, 1221
VectorTest.java 1149
velocity 1321, 1323
verb in a problem statement 23
verb phrase in a problem statement 350
verb phrase in problem statement 293, 295
verbs in a system-requirements document 380
Version note. 1379
VERTICAL 775
vertical coordinate 602
vertical gap space 698
vertical orientation 736
vertical scrolling 724
vertical spacing 153
vertical strut 769
VERTICAL_SCROLLBAR_ALWAYS 725
VERTICAL_SCROLLBAR_AS_NEEDED 725
VERTICAL_SCROLLBAR_NEVER 725
vi 16
video 4, 1069, 1087
video clips 839, 1316
Video for Windows 1249
video game 261, 427
Video Games 1344
video games exercise 1344
video recording 8
View 647
view 44, 66, 87, 91, 783, 784, 785, 786, 787, 1206, 1317, 1318, 1327, 1391, 1392, 1393, 1399, 1464
view (in MVC architecture) 1058, 1059
view a shape from different angles 109
viewable area 130
virtual key code 691
visibility 434
Visitor design pattern 525
visual feedback 664
Visualizing Recursion 311
Vlissides, John 27
void keyword 60, 117, 153, 254
volatile keyword 153
volume of a sphere 302, 304

W

wait 842, 843, 848, 856, 875, 886, 891
wait cursor 989
wait for a new connection 992
WAIT_CURSOR 988
waitForPackets 1005
waiting 842
waiting consumer 849
waiting line 433, 1095
waiting state 856, 875
waiting thread 856, 857, 858
"walk" past end of an array 328
walk the list 1107
warehouse section of the computer 8
.wav 1237, 1278
.wav (WAVE file extension) 1237, 1278
.wav extension 1085
.wav file 1327
WAVE audio 1237, 1278
Web browser 106, 119, 130, 741, 985
web browser 1380
Web page 876, 1371
Web page with animation 1076
Web resources 1087, 1316
Web server 21, 996
WebHire 1470
weightx 774, 775, 779, 781
weighty 774, 775, 777, 779, 781
Welcome1.java 57
Welcome2.java 63
Welcome3.java 64
Welcome4.java 66
WelcomeApplet.html 119
WelcomeApplet.java 113
WelcomeApplet2.html 121
WelcomeApplet2.java 121
WelcomeLines.htm 122
WelcomeLines.java 122
WEST 697, 775
West 697
while repetition structure 148, 153, 159, 164, 167, 168, 230, 234
while repetition structure condition 170
WhileCounter.java 199
white space 153
white-space characters 58, 60, 86, 555, 576
whole/part relationship 138
widgets 648
width 618
width and height of an applet in pixels 119, 251

width and height of application window 741
width of a rectangle in pixels 129
Win32 840
Window 740
window 739
Window class 649, 740
window-event-handling methods 683
window event listeners 741
window events 740
window gadgets 648
windowActivated 741
WindowAdapter 683
windowClosed 741
windowClosing 510, 741
WindowConstants 740
WindowConstants.DISPOSE_ON_CLOSE 740
windowDeactivated 741
windowDeiconified 741
windowIconified 741
windowing system 649
WindowListener 510, 683, 741
windowOpened 741
Windows 10, 68, 107
Windows 2000 10
Windows 95/98 16, 840
Windows look-and-feel 722, 759
Windows Notepad 16
Windows NT 840
Windows Performance Package 1238
Windows Wave file format 1085
WireFrame applet 109
wireless application protocol (WAP) 1477
WirelessResumes.com 1477
Wirth, Nicklaus 14
WORA (Write Once Run Anywhere) 182
word equivalents of check amount 598
word processor 18, 537, 549
word wrap 725
WorkingSolo.com 1478
workstation 9
World Wide Web 4, 12, 15, 107, 134, 647, 839, 895, 981, 1077
World Wide Web browser 18, 65, 119
World Wide Web Consortium (W3C) 986
World Wide Web site 66
worldwide standardization 433
wrap 725
wrapped class 1228
wrapper class 1228
wrapper methods 1208
write 932, 937
writeable 962
writeBytes 901
writeChar 1016
writeChars 930, 931
writeDouble 930, 931
writeInt 930, 931, 1016, 1023
writeObject 902, 914, 995
Writer 902
writer 892
writer threads 892
WriteRandomFile.java 934
writeUTF 1015, 1017
Writing data randomly to a random access file 934
Writing word equivalents of check amount 598
www.advantagehiring.com 1473
www.advisorteam.net/AT/User/kcs.asp 1474
www.careerpower.com 1480
www.chiefmonster.com 1479
www.deitel.com 3, 7, 46, 66
www.driveway.com 1475
www.etest.net 1474
www.ework.com 1478
www.execunet.com 1479
www.freeagent.com 1478
www.jars.com 135
www.jobfind.com 1471
www.jobtrak.com 1475
www.midi.org 1285
www.mindexchange.com 1472
www.nationjob.com 1479
www.omg.org 26
www.prenhall.com/deitel 7
www.recruitsoft.com/corpoVideo 1473
www.recruitsoft.com/process 1473
www.review.com 1480
www.sixfigurejobs.com 1479
www.unicode.org 1493
www.w3.org 986
www.webhire.com 1470
www.xdrive.com 1475

X

x axis 602
x-coordinate 114, 118, 200, 213, 217, 602, 627
X3J11 technical committee 11
XDrive™ 1475
Xerox's Palo Alto Research Center (PARC) 12
xor 1190

Y

y axis 602
y-coordinate 118, 213, 217, 602, 627
Yahoo! 1471
yield 843, 890

Z

zero-based counting 202, 213, 318
zeroth element 315
zooming 1091

End User License Agreements

SUN MICROSYSTEMS, INC.
BINARY CODE LICENSE AGREEMENT

READ THE TERMS OF THIS AGREEMENT AND ANY PROVIDED SUPPLEMENTAL LICENSE TERMS (COLLECTIVELY "AGREEMENT") CAREFULLY BEFORE OPENING THE SOFTWARE MEDIA PACKAGE. BY OPENING THE SOFTWARE MEDIA PACKAGE, YOU AGREE TO THE TERMS OF THIS AGREEMENT. IF YOU ARE ACCESSING THE SOFTWARE ELECTRONICALLY, INDICATE YOUR ACCEPTANCE OF THESE TERMS BY SELECTING THE "ACCEPT" BUTTON AT THE END OF THIS AGREEMENT. IF YOU DO NOT AGREE TO ALL THESE TERMS, PROMPTLY RETURN THE UNUSED SOFTWARE TO YOUR PLACE OF PURCHASE FOR A REFUND OR, IF THE SOFTWARE IS ACCESSED ELECTRONICALLY, SELECT THE "DECLINE" BUTTON AT THE END OF THIS AGREEMENT.

1. LICENSE TO USE. Sun grants you a non-exclusive and non-transferable license for the internal use only of the accompanying software and documentation and any error corrections provided by Sun (collectively "Software"), by the number of users and the class of computer hardware for which the corresponding fee has been paid.

2. RESTRICTIONS. Software is confidential and copyrighted. Title to Software and all associated intellectual property rights is retained by Sun and/or its licensors. Except as specifically authorized in any Supplemental License Terms, you may not make copies of Software, other than a single copy of Software for archival purposes. Unless enforcement is prohibited by applicable law, you may not modify, decompile, or reverse engineer Software. You acknowledge that Software is not designed, licensed or intended for use in the design, construction, operation or maintenance of any nuclear facility. Sun disclaims any express or implied warranty of fitness for such uses. No right, title or interest in or to any trademark, service mark, logo or trade name of Sun or its licensors is granted under this Agreement.

3. LIMITED WARRANTY. Sun warrants to you that for a period of ninety (90) days from the date of purchase, as evidenced by a copy of the receipt, the media on which Software is furnished (if any) will be free of defects in materials and workmanship under normal use. Except for the foregoing, Software is provided "AS IS". Your exclusive remedy and Sun's entire liability under this limited warranty will be at Sun's option to replace Software media or refund the fee paid for Software.

4. DISCLAIMER OF WARRANTY. UNLESS SPECIFIED IN THIS AGREEMENT, ALL EXPRESS OR IMPLIED CONDITIONS, REPRESENTATIONS AND WARRANTIES, INCLUDING ANY IMPLIED WARRANTY OF MERCHANTABILITY, FITNESS FOR A PARTICULAR PURPOSE OR NON-INFRINGEMENT ARE DISCLAIMED, EXCEPT TO THE EXTENT THAT THESE DISCLAIMERS ARE HELD TO BE LEGALLY INVALID.

5. LIMITATION OF LIABILITY. TO THE EXTENT NOT PROHIBITED BY LAW, IN NO EVENT WILL SUN OR ITS LICENSORS BE LIABLE FOR ANY LOST REVENUE, PROFIT OR DATA, OR FOR SPECIAL, INDIRECT, CONSEQUENTIAL, INCIDENTAL OR PUNITIVE DAMAGES, HOWEVER CAUSED REGARDLESS OF THE THEORY OF LIABILITY, ARISING OUT OF OR RELATED TO THE USE OF OR INABILITY TO USE SOFTWARE, EVEN IF SUN HAS BEEN ADVISED OF THE POSSIBILITY OF SUCH DAMAGES. In no event will Sun's liability to you, whether in contract, tort (including negligence), or otherwise, exceed the amount paid by you for Software under this Agreement. The foregoing limitations will apply even if the above stated warranty fails of its essential purpose.

6. Termination. This Agreement is effective until terminated. You may terminate this Agreement at any time by destroying all copies of Software. This Agreement will terminate immediately without notice from Sun if you fail to comply with any provision of this Agreement. Upon Termination, you must destroy all copies of Software.

7. Export Regulations. All Software and technical data delivered under this Agreement are subject to US export control laws and may be subject to export or import regulations in other countries. You agree to comply strictly with all such laws and regulations and acknowledge that you have the responsibility to obtain such licenses to export, re-export, or import as may be required after delivery to you.

8. U.S. Government Restricted Rights. If Software is being acquired by or on behalf of the U.S. Government or by a U.S. Government prime contractor or subcontractor (at any tier), then the Government's rights in Software and accompanying documentation will be only as set forth in this Agreement; this is in accordance with 48 CFR 227.7201 through 227.7202-4 (for Department of Defense (DOD) acquisitions) and with 48 CFR 2.101 and 12.212 (for non-DOD acquisitions).

9. Governing Law. Any action related to this Agreement will be governed by California law and controlling U.S. federal law. No choice of law rules of any jurisdiction will apply.

10. Severability. If any provision of this Agreement is held to be unenforceable, this Agreement will remain in effect with the provision omitted, unless omission would frustrate the intent of the parties, in which case this Agreement will immediately terminate.

11. Integration. This Agreement is the entire agreement between you and Sun relating to its subject matter. It supersedes all prior or contemporaneous oral or written communications, proposals, representations and warranties and prevails over any conflicting or additional terms of any quote, order, acknowledgment, or other communication between the parties relating to its subject matter during the term of this Agreement. No modification of this Agreement will be binding, unless in writing and signed by an authorized representative of each party.

JAVA™ 2 SOFTWARE DEVELOPMENT KIT (J2SDK), STANDARD EDITION, VERSION 1.3 SUPPLEMENTAL LICENSE TERMS

These supplemental license terms ("Supplemental Terms") add to or modify the terms of the Binary Code License Agreement (collectively, the "Agreement"). Capitalized terms not defined in these Supplemental Terms shall have the same meanings ascribed to them in the Agreement. These Supplemental Terms shall supersede any inconsistent or conflicting terms in the Agreement, or in any license contained within the Software.

1. Software Internal Use and Development License Grant. Subject to the terms and conditions of this Agreement, including, but not limited to Section 4 (Java™ Technology Restrictions) of these Supplemental Terms, Sun grants you a non-exclusive, non-transferable, limited license to reproduce internally and use internally the binary form of the Software complete and unmodified for the sole purpose of designing, developing and testing your Java applets and applications intended to run on the Java platform ("Programs").

2. License to Distribute Software. Subject to the terms and conditions of this Agreement, including, but not limited to Section 4 (Java ™ Technology Restrictions) of these Supplemental Terms, Sun grants you a non-exclusive, non-transferable, limited license to reproduce and distribute the Software in binary code form only, provided that (i) you distribute the Software complete and unmodified and only bundled as part of, and for the sole purpose of running, your Programs, (ii) the Programs add significant and primary functionality to the Software, (iii) you do not distribute additional software intended to replace any component(s) of the Software, (iv) you do not remove or alter any proprietary legends or notices contained in the Software, (v) you only distribute the Software subject to a license agreement that protects Sun's interests consistent with the terms contained in this Agreement, and (vi) you agree to defend and indemnify Sun and its licensors from and against any damages, costs, liabilities, settle-

ment amounts and/or expenses (including attorneys' fees) incurred in connection with any claim, lawsuit or action by any third party that arises or results from the use or distribution of any and all Programs and/or Software.

3. License to Distribute Redistributables. Subject to the terms and conditions of this Agreement, including but not limited to Section 4 (Java Technology Restrictions) of these Supplemental Terms, Sun grants you a non-exclusive, non-transferable, limited license to reproduce and distribute the binary form of those files specifically identified as redistributable in the Software "README" file ("Redistributables") provided that: (i) you distribute the Redistributables complete and unmodified (unless otherwise specified in the applicable README file), and only bundled as part of Programs, (ii) you do not distribute additional software intended to supersede any component(s) of the Redistributables, (iii) you do not remove or alter any proprietary legends or notices contained in or on the Redistributables, (iv) you only distribute the Redistributables pursuant to a license agreement that protects Sun's interests consistent with the terms contained in the Agreement, and (v) you agree to defend and indemnify Sun and its licensors from and against any damages, costs, liabilities, settlement amounts and/or expenses (including attorneys' fees) incurred in connection with any claim, lawsuit or action by any third party that arises or results from the use or distribution of any and all Programs and/or Software.

4. Java Technology Restrictions. You may not modify the Java Platform Interface ("JPI", identified as classes contained within the "java" package or any subpackages of the "java" package), by creating additional classes within the JPI or otherwise causing the addition to or modification of the classes in the JPI. In the event that you create an additional class and associated API(s) which (i) extends the functionality of the Java platform, and (ii) is exposed to third party software developers for the purpose of developing additional software which invokes such additional API, you must promptly publish broadly an accurate specification for such API for free use by all developers. You may not create, or authorize your licensees to create, additional classes, interfaces, or subpackages that are in any way identified as "java", "javax", "sun" or similar convention as specified by Sun in any naming convention designation.

5. Trademarks and Logos. You acknowledge and agree as between you and Sun that Sun owns the SUN, SOLARIS, JAVA, JINI, FORTE, STAROFFICE, STARPORTAL and iPLANET trademarks and all SUN, SOLARIS, JAVA, JINI, FORTE, STAROFFICE, STARPORTAL and iPLANET-related trademarks, service marks, logos and other brand designations ("Sun Marks"), and you agree to comply with the Sun Trademark and Logo Usage Requirements currently located at http://www.sun.com/policies/trademarks. Any use you make of the Sun Marks inures to Sun's benefit.

6. Source Code. Software may contain source code that is provided solely for reference purposes pursuant to the terms of this Agreement. Source code may not be redistributed unless expressly provided for in this Agreement.

7. Termination for Infringement. Either party may terminate this Agreement immediately should any Software become, or in either party's opinion be likely to become, the subject of a claim of infringement of any intellectual property right.

For inquiries please contact: Sun Microsystems, Inc. 901 San Antonio Road, Palo Alto, California 94303 (LFI#83838/Form ID#011801)

JAVA™ MEDIA FRAMEWORK (JMF) 2.1.1 BINARY CODE LICENSE AGREEMENT

READ THE TERMS OF THIS AGREEMENT AND ANY PROVIDED SUPPLEMENTAL LICENSE TERMS (COLLECTIVELY "AGREEMENT") CAREFULLY BEFORE OPENING THE SOFTWARE MEDIA PACKAGE. BY OPENING THE SOFTWARE MEDIA PACKAGE, YOU AGREE TO THE TERMS OF THIS AGREEMENT. IF YOU ARE ACCESSING THE SOFTWARE ELECTRONICALLY, INDICATE YOUR ACCEPTANCE OF THESE TERMS BY SELECTING THE "ACCEPT" BUTTON AT THE END OF THIS AGREEMENT. IF YOU DO NOT AGREE TO ALL THESE TERMS, PROMPTLY RETURN THE UNUSED SOFTWARE TO YOUR PLACE OF PURCHASE FOR A REFUND OR, IF THE SOFTWARE IS ACCESSED ELECTRONICALLY, SELECT THE "DECLINE" BUTTON AT THE END OF THIS AGREEMENT.

1. License to Use. Sun Microsystems, Inc. ("Sun") grants you a non-exclusive and non-transferable license for the internal use only of the accompanying software and documentation and any error corrections provided by Sun (collectively "Software"), by the number of users and the class of computer hardware for which the corresponding fee has been paid.

2. Restrictions. Software is confidential and copyrighted. Title to Software and all associated intellectual property rights is retained by Sun and/or its licensors. Except as specifically authorized in any Supplemental

License Terms, you may not make copies of Software, other than a single copy of Software for archival purposes. Unless enforcement is prohibited by applicable law, you may not modify, decompile, or reverse engineer Software. You acknowledge that Software is not designed or intended for use in the design, construction, operation or maintenance of any nuclear facility. Sun disclaims any express or implied warranty of fitness for such uses. No right, title or interest in or to any trademark, service mark, logo or trade name of Sun or its licensors is granted under this Agreement.

3. Limited Warranty. Sun warrants to you that for a period of ninety (90) days from the date of purchase, as evidenced by a copy of the receipt, the media on which Software is furnished (if any) will be free of defects in materials and workmanship under normal use. Except for the foregoing, Software is provided "AS IS". Your exclusive remedy and Sun's entire liability under this limited warranty will be at Sun's option to replace Software media or refund the fee paid for Software.

4. DISCLAIMER OF WARRANTY. UNLESS SPECIFIED IN THIS AGREEMENT, ALL EXPRESS OR IMPLIED CONDITIONS, REPRESENTATIONS AND WARRANTIES, INCLUDING ANY IMPLIED WARRANTY OF MERCHANTABILITY, FITNESS FOR A PARTICULAR PURPOSE OR NON-INFRINGEMENT ARE DISCLAIMED, EXCEPT TO THE EXTENT THAT THESE DISCLAIMERS ARE HELD TO BE LEGALLY INVALID.

5. LIMITATION OF LIABILITY. TO THE EXTENT NOT PROHIBITED BY LAW, IN NO EVENT WILL SUN OR ITS LICENSORS BE LIABLE FOR ANY LOST REVENUE, PROFIT OR DATA, OR FOR SPECIAL, INDIRECT, CONSEQUENTIAL, INCIDENTAL OR PUNITIVE DAMAGES, HOWEVER CAUSED REGARDLESS OF THE THEORY OF LIABILITY, ARISING OUT OF OR RELATED TO THE USE OF OR INABILITY TO USE SOFTWARE, EVEN IF SUN HAS BEEN ADVISED OF THE POSSIBILITY OF SUCH DAMAGES. In no event will Sun's liability to you, whether in contract, tort (including negligence), or otherwise, exceed the amount paid by you for Software under this Agreement. The foregoing limitations will apply even if the above stated warranty fails of its essential purpose.

6. Termination. This Agreement is effective until terminated. You may terminate this Agreement at any time by destroying all copies of Software. This Agreement will terminate immediately without notice from Sun if you fail to comply with any provision of this Agreement. Upon Termination, you must destroy all copies of Software.

7. Export Regulations. All Software and technical data delivered under this Agreement are subject to US export control laws and may be subject to export or import regulations in other countries. You agree to comply strictly with all such laws and regulations and acknowledge that you have the responsibility to obtain such licenses to export, re-export, or import as may be required after delivery to you.

8. U.S. Government Restricted Rights. If Software is being acquired by or on behalf of the U.S. Government or by a U.S. Government prime contractor or subcontractor (at any tier), then the Government's rights in Software and accompanying documentation will be only as set forth in this Agreement; this is in accordance with 48 C.F.R. 227.7202-4 (for Department of Defense (DOD) acquisitions) and with 48 CFR 2.101 and 12.212 (for non-DOD acquisitions).

9. Governing Law. Any action related to this Agreement will be governed by California law and controlling U.S. federal law. No choice of law rules of any jurisdiction will apply.

10. Severability. If any provision of this Agreement is held to be unenforceable, this Agreement will remain in effect with the provision omitted, unless omission would frustrate the intent of the parties, in which case this Agreement will immediately terminate.

11. Integration. This Agreement is the entire agreement between you and Sun relating to its subject matter. It supersedes all prior or contemporaneous oral or written communications, proposals, representations and warranties and prevails over any conflicting or additional terms of any quote, order, acknowledgment, or other communication between the parties relating to its subject matter during the term of this Agreement. No modification of this Agreement will be binding, unless in writing and signed by an authorized representative of each party.

JAVA™ MEDIA FRAMEWORK (JMF) 2.1.1 SUPPLEMENTAL LICENSE TERMS

These supplemental license terms ("Supplemental Terms") add to or modify the terms of the Binary Code License Agreement (collectively, the "Agreement"). Capitalized terms not defined in these Supplemental Terms shall have the same meanings ascribed to them in the Agreement. These Supplemental Terms shall supersede any inconsistent or conflicting terms in the Agreement, or in any license contained within the Software.

1. Software Internal Use and Development License Grant. Subject to the terms and conditions of this Agreement, including, but not limited to Section 3 (Java™ Technology Restrictions) of these Supplemental Terms, Sun grants you a non-exclusive, non-transferable, limited license to reproduce internally and use internally the binary form of the Software, complete and unmodified, for the sole purpose of designing, developing and testing your Java applets and applications ("Programs").

2. License to Distribute Software. In addition to the license granted in Section 1 (Software Internal Use and Development License Grant) of these Supplemental Terms, subject to the terms and conditions of this Agreement, including but not limited to, Section 3 (Java™ Technology Restrictions) of these Supplemental Terms, Sun grants you a non-exclusive, non-transferable, limited license to reproduce and distribute the Software in binary code form only, provided that you:

i. distribute the Software complete and unmodified, except that you may omit those files specifically identified as "optional" in the Software "README" file, which include samples, documents, and bin files, or that are removable by using the Software customizer tool provided, only as part of and for the sole purpose of running your Program into which the Software is incorporated;

ii. do not distribute additional software intended to replace any components of the Software;

iii. do not remove or alter any proprietary legends or notices contained in the Software;

iv. only distribute the Software subject to a license agreement that protects Sun's interests consistent with the terms contained in this Agreement; and

v. agree to defend and indemnify Sun and its licensors from and against any damages, costs, liabilities, settlement amounts or expenses, including attorneys' fees, incurred in connection with any claim, lawsuit or action by any third party that arises or results from the use or distribution of any and all Programs or Software.

3. Java™ Technology Restrictions. You may not modify the Java Platform Interface ("JPI", identified as classes contained within the "java" package or any subpackages of the "java" package), by creating additional classes within the JPI or otherwise causing the addition to or modification of the classes in the JPI. In the event that you create an additional class and associated API's, which:

i. extends the functionality of the Java platform, and

ii. is exposed to third party software developers for the purpose of developing additional software which invokes such additional API, you must promptly publish broadly an accurate specification for such API for free use by all developers. You may not create, or authorize your licensees to create additional classes, interfaces, packages or subpackages that are in any way identified as "java", "javax", "sun" or similar convention as specified by Sun in any class file naming convention designation.

4. Java™ Runtime Availability. Refer to the appropriate version of the Java™ Runtime Environment binary code license (currently located at http://www.java.sun.com/jdk/index.html) for the availability of runtime code which may be distributed with Java™ applets and applications.

5. Trademarks and Logos. You acknowledge and agree as between you and Sun that Sun owns the SUN, SOLARIS, JAVA, JINI, FORTE, STAROFFICE, STARPORTAL and iPLANET trademarks and all SUN, SOLARIS, JAVA, JINI, FORTE, STAROFFICE, STARPORTAL and IPLANET-related trademarks, service marks, logos and other brand designations ("Sun Marks"), and you agree to comply with the Sun Trademark and Logo Usage Requirements currently located at http://www.sun.com/policies/trademarks. Any use you make of the Sun Marks inures to Sun's benefit.

6. Source Code. Software may contain source code that is provided solely for reference purposes pursuant to the terms of this Agreement. Source code may not be redistributed unless expressly provided for in this Agreement.

7. Termination for Infringement. Either party may terminate this Agreement immediately should any Software become, or in either party's opinion be likely to become, the subject of a claim of infringement of any intellectual property right.

For inquiries please contact: Sun Microsystems, Inc. 901 San Antonio Road, Palo Alto, California 94303

LFI# 81806/Form ID#011801 01/23/2001

JAVA™ PLUG-IN HTML CONVERTER, VERSION 1.3 BINARY CODE LICENSE

SUN MICROSYSTEMS, INC., THROUGH JAVASOFT ("SUN") IS WILLING TO LICENSE THE JAVA™ PLUG-IN HTML CONVERTER AND THE ACCOMPANYING DOCUMENTATION INCLUDING

AUTHORIZED COPIES OF EACH (THE "SOFTWARE") TO LICENSEE ONLY ON THE CONDITION THAT LICENSEE ACCEPTS ALL OF THE TERMS IN THIS AGREEMENT.

PLEASE READ THE TERMS CAREFULLY BEFORE CLICKING ON THE "ACCEPT" BUTTON. BY CLICKING ON THE "ACCEPT" BUTTON, LICENSEE ACKNOWLEDGES THAT LICENSEE HAS READ AND UNDERSTANDS THIS AGREEMENT AND AGREES TO BE BOUND BY ITS TERMS AND CONDITIONS.

IF LICENSEE DOES NOT ACCEPT THESE LICENSE TERMS, SUN DOES NOT GRANT ANY LICENSE TO THE SOFTWARE, AND LICENSEE SHOULD CLICK ON THE "REJECT" BUTTON TO EXIT THIS PAGE.

1. LICENSE GRANT

(A) License To Use

Licensee is granted a non-exclusive and non-transferable no fee license to download, install and internally use the binary Software. Licensee may copy the Software, provided that Licensee reproduces all copyright and other proprietary notices that are on the original copy of the Software.

(B) License to Distribute

Licensee is granted a royalty-free right to reproduce and distribute the Software provided that Licensee: (i) distributes Software complete and unmodified only as part of Licensee's value-added applet or application ("Program"), and for the sole purpose of allowing customers of Licensee to modify HTML pages to access Sun's Java™ Plug-in technology; (ii) does not distribute additional software intended to replace any component(s) of the Software; (iii) agrees to incorporate the most current version of the Software that was available 180 days prior to each production release of the Program; (iv) does not remove or alter any proprietary legends or notices contained in the Software; (v) includes the provisions of Sections 1(C), 1(D), 5, 7, 8, 9 in Licensee's license agreement for the Program; (vi) agrees to indemnify, hold harmless, and defend Sun and its licensors from and against any claims or lawsuits, including attorneys' fees, that arise or result from the use or distribution of the Program.

(C) Java Platform Interface

Licensee may not modify the Java Platform Interface ("JPI", identified as classes contained within the "java" package or any subpackage of the "java" package), by creating additional classes within the JPI or otherwise causing the addition to or modification of the classes in the JPI. In the event that Licensee creates any Java-related API and distributes such API to others for applet or application development, Licensee must promptly publish broadly, an accurate specification for such API for free use by all developers of Java-based software.

(D) License Restrictions

The Software is licensed to Licensee only under the terms of this Agreement, and Sun reserves all rights not expressly granted to Licensee. Licensee may not use, copy, modify, or transfer the Software, or any copy thereof, except as expressly provided for in this Agreement. Except as otherwise provided by law for purposes of decompilation of the Software solely for interoperability, Licensee may not reverse engineer, disassemble, decompile, or translate the Software, or otherwise attempt to derive the source code of the Software. Licensee may not rent, lease, loan, sell, or distribute the Software, or any part of the Software. No right, title, or interest in or to any trademarks, service marks, or trade names of Sun or Sun's licensors is granted hereunder.

(E) Aircraft Product and Nuclear Applications Restriction

SOFTWARE IS NOT DESIGNED OR INTENDED FOR USE IN ON-LINE CONTROL OF AIRCRAFT, AIR TRAFFIC, AIRCRAFT NAVIGATION OR AIRCRAFT COMMUNICATIONS; OR IN THE DESIGN, CONSTRUCTION, OPERATION OR MAINTENANCE OF ANY NUCLEAR FACILITY. SUN DISCLAIMS ANY EXPRESS OR IMPLIED WARRANTY OF FITNESS FOR SUCH USES. LICENSEE REPRESENTS AND WARRANTS THAT IT WILL NOT USE THE SOFTWARE FOR SUCH PURPOSES.

2. CONFIDENTIALITY

The Software is the confidential and proprietary information of Sun and/or its licensors. The Software is protected by United States copyright law and international treaty. Unauthorized reproduction or distribution is subject to civil and criminal penalties. Licensee agrees to take adequate steps to protect the Software from unauthorized disclosure or use.

3. TRADEMARKS AND LOGOS

This Agreement does not authorize Licensee to use any Sun name, trademark, or logo. Licensee acknowledges that Sun owns the Java trademark and all Java-related trademarks, logos and icons including the Coffee Cup and Duke ("Java Marks") and agrees to: (i) comply with the Java Trademark Guidelines at http://java.sun.com/trademarks.html; (ii) not do anything harmful to or inconsistent with Sun's rights in the Java Marks; and (iii) assist Sun in protecting those rights, including assigning to Sun any rights acquired by Licensee in any Java Mark.

4. TERM, TERMINATION AND SURVIVAL

(A) The Agreement shall automatically terminate 180 days after production release of the next version of the Software by Sun.

(B) Licensee may terminate this Agreement at any time by destroying all copies of the Software.

(C) This Agreement will immediately terminate without notice if Licensee fails to comply with any obligation of this Agreement.

(D) Upon termination, Licensee must immediately cease use of and destroy the Software or, upon request from Sun, return the Software to Sun.

(E) The provisions set forth in paragraphs 1 (D), 2, 5, 7, 8, 9, and 10 will survive termination or expiration of this Agreement.

5. NO WARRANTY

THE SOFTWARE IS PROVIDED TO LICENSEE "AS IS". ALL EXPRESS OR IMPLIED CONDITIONS, REPRESENTATIONS, AND WARRANTIES, INCLUDING ANY IMPLIED WARRANTY OF MERCHANTABILITY, SATISFACTORY QUALITY, FITNESS FOR A PARTICULAR PURPOSE, OR NON-INFRINGEMENT, ARE DISCLAIMED, EXCEPT TO THE EXTENT THAT SUCH DISCLAIMERS ARE HELD TO BE LEGALLY INVALID.

6. MAINTENANCE AND SUPPORT

Sun has no obligation to provide maintenance or support for the Software under this Agreement.

7. LIMITATION OF DAMAGES

TO THE EXTENT NOT PROHIBITED BY APPLICABLE LAW, SUN'S AGGREGATE LIABILITY TO LICENSEE OR TO ANY THIRD PARTY FOR CLAIMS RELATING TO THIS AGREEMENT, WHETHER FOR BREACH OR IN TORT, WILL BE LIMITED TO THE FEES PAID BY LICENSEE FOR SOFTWARE WHICH IS THE SUBJECT MATTER OF THE CLAIMS. IN NO EVENT WILL SUN BE LIABLE FOR ANY INDIRECT, PUNITIVE, SPECIAL, INCIDENTAL OR CONSEQUENTIAL DAMAGE IN CONNECTION WITH OR ARISING OUT OF THIS AGREEMENT (INCLUDING LOSS OF BUSINESS, REVENUE, PROFITS, USE, DATA OR OTHER ECONOMIC ADVANTAGE), HOWEVER IT ARISES, WHETHER FOR BREACH OR IN TORT, EVEN IF SUN HAS BEEN PREVIOUSLY ADVISED OF THE POSSIBILITY OF SUCH DAMAGE. LIABILITY FOR DAMAGES WILL BE LIMITED AND EXCLUDED, EVEN IF ANY EXCLUSIVE REMEDY PROVIDED FOR IN THIS AGREEMENT FAILS OF ITS ESSENTIAL PURPOSE.

8. GOVERNMENT USER

Rights in Data: If procured by, or provided to, the U.S. Government, use, duplication, or disclosure of technical data is subject to restrictions as set forth in FAR 52.227-14(g)(2), Rights in Data-General (June 1987); and for computer software and computer software documentation, FAR 52-227-19, Commercial Computer Software-Restricted Rights (June 1987). However, if under DOD, use, duplication, or disclosure of technical data is subject to DFARS 252.227-7015(b), Technical Data-Commercial Items (June 1995); and for computer software and computer software documentation, as specified in the license under which the computer software was procured pursuant to DFARS 227.7202- 3(a). Licensee shall not provide Software nor technical data to any third party, including the U.S. Government, unless such third party accepts the same restrictions. Licensee is responsible for ensuring that proper notice is given to all such third parties and that the Software and technical data are properly marked.

9. EXPORT LAW

Licensee acknowledges and agrees that this Software and/or technology is subject to the U.S. Export Administration Laws and Regulations. Diversion of such Software and/or technology contrary to U.S. law is prohibited. Licensee agrees that none of this Software and/or technology, nor any direct product therefrom, is being or will be acquired for, shipped, transferred, or reexported, directly or indirectly, to proscribed or embargoed countries or their nationals, nor be used for nuclear activities, chemical biological weapons, or missile projects unless authorized by the U.S. Government. Proscribed countries are set forth in the U.S. Export Administration Regulations. Countries subject to U.S. embargo are: Cuba, Iran, Iraq, Libya, North Korea, Syria, and the Sudan. This list is subject to change without further notice from Sun, and Licensee must comply with the list as it exists in fact. Licensee certifies that it is not on the U.S. Department of Commerce's Denied Persons List or affiliated lists or on the U.S. Department of Treasury's Specially Designated Nationals List. Licensee agrees to comply strictly with all U.S. export laws and assumes sole responsibility for obtaining licenses to export or reexport as may be required.

Licensee is responsible for complying with any applicable local laws and regulations, including but not limited to, the export and import laws and regulations of other countries.

10. GOVERNING LAW, JURISDICTION AND VENUE

Any action related to this Agreement shall be governed by California law and controlling U.S. federal law, and choice of law rules of any jurisdiction shall not apply. The parties agree that any action shall be brought in the United States District Court for the Northern District of California or the California superior Court for the County of Santa Clara, as applicable, and the parties hereby submit exclusively to the personal jurisdiction and venue of the United States District Court for the Northern District of California and the California Superior Court of the county of Santa Clara.

11. NO ASSIGNMENT

Neither party may assign or otherwise transfer any of its rights or obligations under this Agreement, without the prior written consent of the other party, except that Sun may assign its right to payment and may assign this Agreement to an affiliated company.

12. OFFICIAL LANGUAGE

The official text of this Agreement is in the English language and any interpretation or construction of this Agreement will be based thereon. In the event that this Agreement or any documents or notices related to it are translated into any other language, the English language version will control.

13. ENTIRE AGREEMENT

This Agreement is the parties' entire agreement relating to the Software. It supersedes all prior or contemporaneous oral or written communications, proposals, warranties, and representations with respect to its subject matter, and following Licensee's acceptance of this license by clicking on the "Accept" Button, will prevail over any conflicting or additional terms of any subsequent quote, order, acknowledgment, or any other communications by or between the parties. No modification to this Agreement will be binding, unless in writing and signed by an authorized representative of each party.

FORTE™ FOR JAVA™ RELEASE 2.0, COMMUNITY EDITION LICENSE

This product or document is protected by copyright and distributed under licenses restricting its use, copying, distribution, and decompilation. No part of this product or related documentation may be reporduced in any form by any means without prior written authorization of Sun and its licensors, if any.

Third party software, including font technology, is copyrighted and licensed from Sun suppliers.

This product includes software developed by the Apache Software Foundation (http://www.apache.org/).

Sun, Sun Microsystems, the Sun logo, Java, Forte, NetBeans, Solaris, iPlanet, StarOffice, StarPortal, Jini, Jiro are trademarked or registered trademarks of Sun Microsystems, Inc. in the U.S. and other countries.

Federal Acquisitions: Commercial Software--Government Users Subject to Standard License Terms and Conditions.

The DEITEL & DEITEL Suite of Products...

BOOKS

e-Business & e-Commerce How to Program

BOOK / CD-ROM

©2001, 1254 pp., paper bound w/CD-ROM (0-13-028419-X)

This innovative book explores programming technologies for developing Web-based e-business and e-commerce solutions, and covers e-business and e-commerce models and business issues. Readers learn a full range of options, from "build-your-own" to turnkey solutions. The book examines a number of the top e-businesses (such as Amazon, eBay, Priceline, Travelocity, etc.), explaining the technical details of building successful e-business and e-commerce sites and their underlying business premises. Learn how to implement the dominant e-commerce models — shopping carts, auctions, naming-your-own-price, comparison shopping and bots/ intelligent agents—by using markup languages (HTML, Dynamic HTML and XML), scripting languages (JavaScript, VBScript and Perl), server-side technologies (Active Server Pages and Perl/CGI) and database (SQL and ADO) , security and online payment technologies. Updates are regularly posted to **www.deitel.com** and the book includes a CD-ROM with software tools, source code and live links.

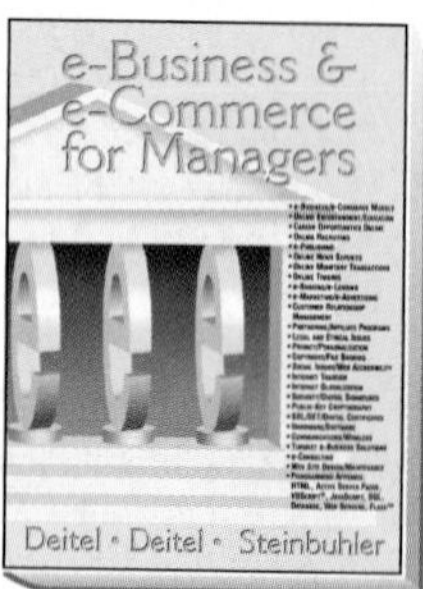

e-Business & e-Commerce for Managers

©2001, 794 pp., paper (0-13-032364-0)

This comprehensive overview of building and managing an e-business explores topics such as the decision to bring a business online, choosing a business model, accepting payments, marketing strategies and security, as well as many other important issues (such as career resources). Features Web resources and online demonstrations that supplement the text and direct readers to additional materials. The book also includes an appendix that develops a complete Web-based shopping cart application using HTML, JavaScript, VBScript, Active Server Pages, ADO, SQL, HTTP, XML and XSL. Plus, company-specific sections provide "real-world" examples of the concepts presented in the book.

Internet & World Wide Web How to Program, Second Edition

BOOK / CD-ROM

©2002, 1300 pp., paper bound w/CD-ROM (0-13-030897-8)

The world's best-selling Internet and Web programming text uses the scripting and markup languages of the Web to present traditional introductory programming concepts. Now you can learn programming fundamentals "wrapped in the metaphor of the Web." Employing the Deitels' signature "live-code™" approach, the book covers markup languages (XHTML, Dynamic HTML), client-side scripting (JavaScript) and server-side scripting (VBScript, ASP, Perl/CGI, Python, PHP, Java servlets, Java Server Pages). The book offers a thorough treatment of programming concepts, with programs that yield visible or audible results in Web pages and Web-based applications. It discusses Internet Explorer, effective Web-based design, multi-tier Web-based applications development, ActiveX® controls and introduces electronic commerce and security. Updated material on **www.deitel.com** and **www.prenhall.com/deitel** provides additional resources for instructors who want to cover Microsoft® or non-Microsoft technologies. The Web site includes an extensive treatment of Netscape® 6 and alternate versions of the code from the Dynamic HTML chapters that will work with non-Microsoft environments as well. The Second Edition also features new and updated material on XHTML, CSS, wireless Internet (WML, WMLScript), Web accessibility, career resources, Python, PHP, XML/XSLT, SVG, SMIL, Web servers, Photoshop Elements, multimedia audio, animation, Macromedia Flash, databases, Perl, CGI, Java servlets, JavaServer Pages, PWS, IIS and Apache.

Python How to Program

BOOK / CD-ROM

©2002, 1000 pp., paper
(0-13-092361-3)

This exciting new book provides a comprehensive introduction to Python — a powerful object-oriented programming language with clear syntax and the ability to bring together various technologies quickly and easily. This book covers introductory programming techniques as well as more advanced topics such as graphical user interfaces, databases, wireless Internet programming, networking and multimedia. Readers will learn principles that are applicable to both systems development and Web programming. The book features the outstanding, consistent and applied pedagogy that the *How to Program* series is known for, including the Deitels' signature Live-Code™ Approach, with thousands of lines of code in hundreds of working programs; hundreds of valuable programming tips identified with icons throughout the text; an extensive set of exercises, projects and case studies; two-color four-way syntax coloring and much more.

XML How to Program

BOOK / CD-ROM

©2001, 934 pp., paper
(0-13-028417-3)

This book is a complete guide to programming in XML. It explains how to use XML to create customized tags and addresses standard custom markup languages for science and technology, multimedia, commerce and other fields. Concise introductions to Java, JavaServer Pages, VBScript, Active Server Pages and Perl/CGI provide readers with the essentials of these programming languages and server-side development technologies to enable them to work effectively with XML. The book also covers cutting-edge topics such as XQL and SMIL, plus a real-world e-commerce case study and a complete chapter on Web accessibility that addresses Voice XML. It also includes tips such as Common Programming Errors, Software Engineering Observations, Portability Tips and Debugging Hints. Other topics covered include XHTML, CSS, DTD, schema, parsers, DOM, SAX, XPath, XLink, namespaces, XBase, XInclude, XPointer, XSL, XSLT, XSL Formatting Objects, JavaServer Pages, XForms, topic maps, X3D, MathML, OpenMath, CML, BML, CDF, RDF, SVG, Cocoon, WML, XBRL, and BizTalk and SOAP Web resources.

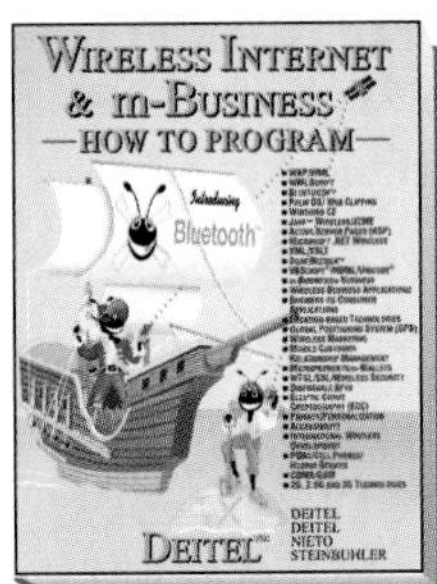

Wireless Internet & Mobile Business How to Program

©2002, 1300 pp., paper
(0-13-062226-5)

While the rapid growth of wireless technologies (such as cell phones, pagers and personal digital assistants) offers many new opportunities for businesses and programmers, it also presents numerous challenges related to issues such as security and standardization. This book offers a thorough treatment of both the management and technical aspects of this expanding area, including current practices and future trends. The first half explores the business issues surrounding wireless technology and mobile business, including an overview of existing and developing communication technologies and the application of business principles to wireless devices. It then turns to programming for the wireless Internet, exploring topics such as WAP (including 2.0), WML, WMLScript, XML, XSL, XSLT, XHTML, Wireless Java Programming, Web Clipping and more. Other topics covered include career resources, location-based services, wireless marketing, wireless payments, security, accessibility, international issues, Palm, PocketPC, Windows CE, i-Mode, Bluetooth, J2ME, MIDP, MIDlets, ASP, Perl and PHP. Also discussed are Microsoft .NET Mobile Framework, BREW, multimedia, Flash, VBScript and legal, ethical and social issues.

Perl How to Program

BOOK / CD-ROM

©2001, 1057 pp., paper
(0-13-028418-1)

This comprehensive guide to Perl programming emphasizes the use of the Common Gateway Interface (CGI) with Perl to create powerful dynamic Web content for e-commerce applications. The book begins with a clear and careful introduction to programming concepts at a level suitable for beginners, and proceeds through advanced topics such as references and complex data structures. Key Perl topics such as regular expressions and string manipulation are covered in detail. The authors address important and topical issues such as object-oriented programming, the Perl database interface (DBI), graphics and security. Also included is a treatment of XML, a bonus chapter introducing the Python programming language, supplemental material on career resources and a complete chapter on Web accessibility. The text also includes tips such as Common Programming Errors, Software Engineering Observations, Portability Tips and Debugging Hints.

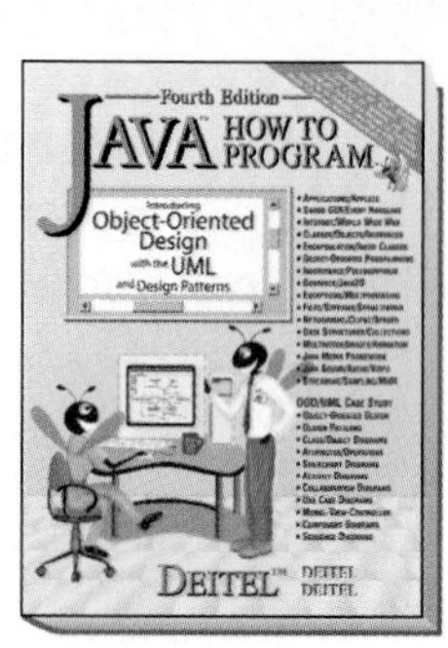

Java How to Program Fourth Edition

BOOK / CD-ROM

©2002, 1100 pp., cloth bound w/CD-ROM (0-13-034151-7)

The world's best-selling Java text is now even better! The Fourth Edition of *Java How to Program* now includes a new focus on object-oriented design with the UML, design patterns, full-color program listings and figures, and the most up-to-date Java coverage available.

Readers will discover key topics in Java programming, such as graphical user interface components, exception handling, multithreading, multimedia, files and streams, networking, data structures, and more. In addition, a new chapter on design patterns explains frequently recurring architectural patterns —information that can help save designers considerable time when building large systems.

The highly detailed optional case study focuses on object-oriented design with the UML and presents fully implemented working Java code.

Updated throughout, the text now includes new and revised discussions on topics such as Swing, graphics, multithreading, multimedia, Java Media Framework, streaming audio, streaming video, socket-and-packet-based networking and career resources. Three introductory chapters heavily emphasize problem solving and programming skills. The chapters on RMI, JDBC, servlets and JavaBeans have been moved to *Advanced Java 2 Platform How to Program*, where they are now covered in much greater depth. (See *Advanced Java 2 Platform How to Program*, at right.)

Advanced Java™ 2 Platform How to Program

BOOK / CD-ROM

©2002, 1000 pp., paper (0-13-089560-1)

Expanding on the world's best-selling Java textbook—*Java How to Program*—*Advanced Java 2 Platform How To Program* presents advanced Java topics for developing sophisticated, user-friendly GUIs; significant, scalable enterprise applications; wireless applications and distributed systems. Focusing on Java 2 Enterprise Edition (J2EE), this textbook integrates technologies such as XML, XSLT, JavaBeans, security, JDBC, JavaServer Pages (JSP), servlets, Remote Method Invocation (RMI), Enterprise JavaBeans (EJB) and design patterns into a significant enterprise case study that leverages J2EE's powerful component model. This textbook also features a case study that integrates Swing, Java2D, drag and drop, XML and design patterns to build a sophisticated drawing application. Additional topics include CORBA, Jini, JavaSpaces, Jiro, Java Management Extensions (JMX) and Peer-to-Peer networking with an introduction to JXTA. This textbook also introduces the Java 2 Micro Edition (J2ME) for building applications for handheld and wireless devices using MIDP and MIDlets. Wireless technologies covered include WAP, WML and i-mode.

C++ How to Program Third Edition

BOOK / CD-ROM

©2001, 1168 pp., paper (0-13-089571-7)

The world's best-selling C++ text teaches programming by emphasizing object-oriented programming, software reuse and component-oriented software construction. This comprehensive book uses the Deitels' signature live-code™ approach, presenting every concept in the context of a complete, working C++ program followed by a screen capture showing the program's output. It also includes a rich collection of exercises and valuable insights in its set of Common Programming Errors, Software Engineering Observations, Portability Tips and Debugging Hints. The Third Edition features an extensive treatment of the Standard Template Library and includes a new case study that focuses on object-oriented design with the UML, illustrating the entire process of object-oriented design from conception to implementation. In addition, it adheres to the latest ANSI/ISO C++ standards. The accompanying CD-ROM contains Microsoft® Visual C++ 6.0 Introductory Edition software, source code for all examples in the text and hyperlinks to C++ demos and Internet resources.

BOOK/MULTIMEDIA PACKAGES

Complete Training Courses

Each complete package includes the corresponding *How to Program Series* book and interactive multimedia CD-ROM. *Complete Training Courses* are perfect for anyone interested in learning Java, C++, Visual Basic, XML, Perl, Internet/World Wide Web and e-commerce programming. They are exceptional and affordable resources for college students and professionals learning programming for the first time or reinforcing their knowledge.

Each *Complete Training Course* is compatible with Windows 95, Windows 98, Windows NT and Windows 2000 and includes the following features:

Intuitive Browser-Based Interface

Whether you choose the Web-based *Complete Training Course* or the CD-ROM, you'll love the new browser-based interface, designed to be easy and accessible to anyone who's ever used a Web browser. Every *Complete Training Course* features the full text, illustrations, and program listings of its corresponding *How to Program* book—all in full color—with full-text searching and hyperlinking.

Further Enhancements to the Deitels' Signature Live-Code™ Approach

Every code sample from the main text can be found in the interactive, multimedia, CD-ROM-based *Cyber Classrooms* included in the *Complete Training Courses*. Syntax coloring of code is included for the *How to Program* books that are published in full color. Even the recent two-color books use effective four-way syntax coloring. The *Cyber Classroom* software is provided in full color for all the Deitel books.

Audio Annotations

Hours of detailed, expert audio descriptions of thousands of lines of code help reinforce concepts.

Easily Executable Code

With one click of the mouse, you can execute the code or save it to your hard drive to manipulate using the programming environment of your choice. With selected *Complete Training Courses*, you can also automatically load all of the code into a development environment such as Microsoft® Visual C++™, enabling you to modify and execute the programs with ease.

Abundant Self-Assessment Material

Practice exams test your understanding with hundreds of text questions and answers in addition to those found in the main text. Hundreds of self-review questions, all with answers, are drawn from the text; as are hundreds of programming exercises, half with answers.

Announcing New Web-Based Versions of the Deitels' *Complete Training Courses!*

The same highly acclaimed material found on the *Cyber Classroom* CD-ROMs is now available at the same price via the World Wide Web! When you order the Web-based version of a *Complete Training Course,* you receive the corresponding *How to Program* book with a URL and password that give you six months of access to the *Cyber Classroom* software via the Web.

To explore a demo of this new option, please visit
http://ptgtraining.com

www.phptr.com/phptrinteractive

The Complete Advanced Java™ 2 Platform Training Course
CD-ROM version (0-13-091277-8)
Web-based version (0-13-065274-1)

The Complete C++ Training Course, Third Edition
CD-ROM version (0-13-089564-4)
Web-based version (0-13-065156-7)

Bonus! You can run the hundreds of C++ programs with the click of a mouse and automatically load them into Microsoft® Visual C++™, allowing you to modify and execute the programs with ease.

The Complete C# Training Course
CD-ROM version (0-13-064584-2)
Web-based version (0-13-065268-7)

The Complete e-Business & e-Commerce Programming Training Course
CD-ROM version (0-13-089549-0)
Web-based version (0-13-065271-7)

The Complete Internet & World Wide Web Programming Training Course, Second Edition
CD-ROM version (0-13-089550-4)
Web-based version (0-13-065256-3)

The Complete Java Training Course, Fourth Edition
CD-ROM version (0-13-064931-7)
Web-based version (0-13-065259-8)

The Complete Perl Training Course
CD-ROM version (0-13-089552-0)
Web-based version (0-13-066108-2)

The Complete Visual Basic 6 Training Course
CD-ROM version (0-13-082929-3)
Web-based version (0-13-065165-6)

Bonus! You can run the hundreds of Visual Basic programs with the click of a mouse and automatically load them into Microsoft®'s Visual Basic® 6 Working Model edition software, allowing you to modify and execute the programs with ease.

The Complete Wireless Internet & Mobile Business Programming Training Course
CD-ROM version (0-13-062335-0)
Web-based version (0-13-065253-9)

The Complete XML Programming Training Course
CD-ROM version (0-13-089557-1)
Web-based version (0-13-065267-9)

Coming Soon:

- ***The Complete Python Training Course***
  CD-ROM version (0-13-067374-9)
  Web-based version (0-13-067378-1)

All of these ISBNs are retail ISBNs. College and university instructors should contact your local Prentice Hall representative or write to cs@prenhall.com for the corresponding student edition ISBNs.

If you would like to purchase the Cyber Classrooms separately...

Prentice Hall offers Multimedia Cyber Classroom CD-ROMs to accompany the *How to Program* series texts for the topics listed at right. If you have already purchased one of these books and would like to purchase a stand-alone copy of the corresponding *Multimedia Cyber Classroom,* you can make your purchase at the following Web site:

www.informit.com/cyberclassrooms

For **Advanced Java Multimedia Cyber Classroom**, ask for product number 0-13-091276-X

For **C# Multimedia Cyber Classroom**, ask for product number 0-13-064587-7

For **C++ Multimedia Cyber Classroom, 3/E**, ask for product number 0-13-089562-8

For **e-Business & e-Commerce Cyber Classroom**, ask for product number 0-13-089540-7

For **Internet & World Wide Web Cyber Classroom, 2/E**, ask for product number 0-13-089559-8

For **Java Multimedia Cyber Classroom, 4/E**, ask for product number 0-13-064935-X

For **Perl Multimedia Cyber Classroom**, ask for product number 0-13-089553-9

For **Visual Basic 6 Multimedia Cyber Classroom**, ask for product number 0-13-083116-6

For **XML Multimedia Cyber Classroom**, ask for product number 0-13-089555-5

For **Wireless Internet & m-Business Programming Multimedia Cyber Classroom**, ask for product number 0-13-062337-7

www.Deitel.InformIT.com

Deitel & Associates, Inc. is partnering with Prentice Hall's parent company, Pearson PLC, and its information technology Web site, InformIT (`www.informit.com`) to launch the Deitel InformIT site at `www.Deitel.InformIT.com`. The Deitel InformIT site is an online resource center that delivers premium IT content, adding new e-Learning offerings to the established Deitel product suite and the ability to purchase Deitel products. The site will contain information on the continuum of Deitel products, including:

- **Free weekly Deitel Buzz e-mail newsletter**
- **Free informational articles**
- **Deitel e-Matter**
- **Books and new e-Books**
- **Instructor-led training**
- **Web-based training**
- **Complete Training Courses/Cyber Classrooms**

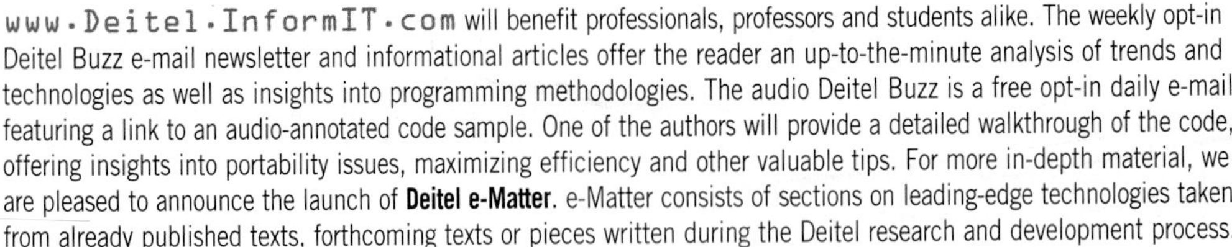

`www.Deitel.InformIT.com` will benefit professionals, professors and students alike. The weekly opt-in Deitel Buzz e-mail newsletter and informational articles offer the reader an up-to-the-minute analysis of trends and technologies as well as insights into programming methodologies. The audio Deitel Buzz is a free opt-in daily e-mail featuring a link to an audio-annotated code sample. One of the authors will provide a detailed walkthrough of the code, offering insights into portability issues, maximizing efficiency and other valuable tips. For more in-depth material, we are pleased to announce the launch of **Deitel e-Matter**. e-Matter consists of sections on leading-edge technologies taken from already published texts, forthcoming texts or pieces written during the Deitel research and development process.

A Sneak Peek at Deitel™ Web-Based Tutorials

Deitel & Associates, Inc. is developing a series of self-paced Web-based tutorials using content from the Cyber Classrooms in their *How to Program Series.* Eventually, it will be possible to access the same cutting-edge content via CD-ROM, the Web, or even wireless devices. New features of these innovative tutorials include:

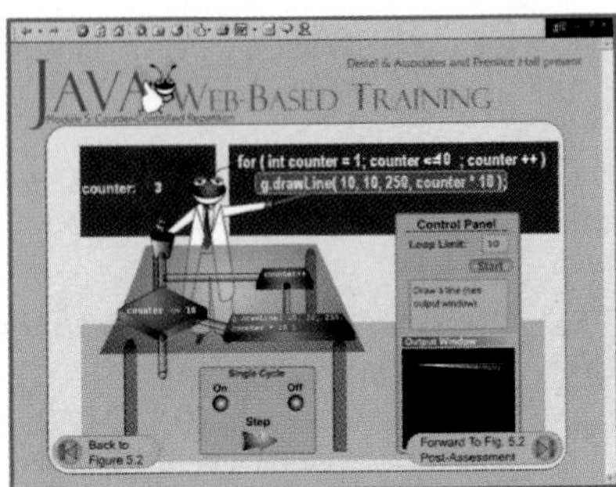

Five-way Flash animation demonstrating looping.

Interactive Questions

Specialized Q icons are attached to particular lines of code. When clicked, the icon provides a question and—upon pressing a button—an answer relating specifically to that line of code.

Dynamic Glossary

Users click on designated keywords, phrases or programming elements, displaying small windows containing definitions.

Interactive Animations

Deitel Web-based tutorial courses take advantage of the small file sizes of vector-based graphics and advancements in the tools used to produce them such as Macromedia™ Flash®, and use cutting-edge compression techniques and streaming media to deliver abundant audio. The Deitel Java Web-based tutorial features an interactive five-way for-loop animation, as pictured above, which includes an animated flowchart, audio and a simulated output window. Future *Cyber Classrooms* will contain animations illustrating important programming concepts such as flow of control and recursion.

Web-based Labs

Gain hands-on knowledge of the concepts you read about in the text. Deitel Web-based tutorial labs present challenging programming assignments and their solutions.

Abundant Audio

The courses deliver hours of streaming audio-based lectures. All code is syntax colored to make it easier to read and comprehend. Future Cyber Classrooms will contain nearly twice the current amount of audio.

Richer Assessment Types

In addition to the true/false questions found in current *Cyber Classrooms*, future versions will contain richer assessment types including fill-in-the-blank and matching questions.

Multiple Content Paths

Future *Cyber Classrooms* will contain multiple paths through the content, optimized for different users. Students will find an abundance of pedagogy designed just for them, while corporate users will find the content arranged in a way that meets their challenging "just-in-time" learning needs.

FORTHCOMING PUBLICATIONS FROM THE DEITELS

For those interested in

Microsoft® Visual Basic .NET

Visual Basic .NET™ How to Program: This book builds on the pedagogy of the first edition, which was developed for Visual Studio 6. It has a much-enhanced treatment of developing Web-based e-business and e-commerce applications. The book includes an extensive treatment of XML and wireless applications, Web Forms and Web Services.

For those interested in

Python

Python How to Program: This book introduces the increasingly popular Python language which makes many application development tasks easier to accomplish than with traditional object-oriented languages. Many people are touting Python as a more effective first language than C++ or Java.

For those interested in

Flash

Flash 6 How to Program: Hundreds of millions of people browse Flash-enabled Web sites daily. This first book in the Deitel Multimedia series introduces the powerful features of Flash 6 and includes a detailed introduction to programming with the Flash 6 scripting language. The key to the book is that it presents a complete treatment of building Flash-centric multi-tier client/server Web-based applications.

For those interested in

Microsoft® Visual C++ .NET

Visual C++ .NET™ How to Program: This book combines the pedagogy and extensive coverage of *C++ How to Program, Third Edition* with a more in-depth treatment of Windows and Internet programming in Visual Studio .NET. We have carefully culled the best material from each of these areas to produce a solid, two-semester, introductory/intermediate level treatment.

For those interested in

C++

Advanced C++ How to Program: This book builds on the pedagogy of *C++ How to Program, Third Edition,* and features more advanced discussions of templates, multiple inheritance and other key topics. We are co-authoring this book with Don Kostuch, one of the world's most experienced C++ educators.

New & Improved Deitel™ Web Site!

Deitel & Associates, Inc. is constantly upgrading `www.deitel.com`. The new site will feature Macromedia™ Flash® enhancements and additional content to create a more valuable resource for students, professors and professionals. Features will include FAQs, Web resources, e-publications and online chat sessions with the authors. We will include streaming audio clips where the authors discuss their publications. Web-based training demos will also be available at the site.

Turn the page to find out more about Deitel & Associates!

License Agreement and Limited Warranty

Using the CD-ROM

The contents of this CD are designed to be accessed through the interface provided in the file **`AUTORUN.EXE`**. If a startup screen does not pop up automatically when you insert the CD into your computer, double click on the icon for **`AUTORUN.EXE`** to launch the program or refer to the file **`README.TXT`** on the CD.

Contents of the CD-ROM

- Java™ 2 SDK, Standard Edition, 1.3.1
- Java Media Framework API 2.1.1
- Forte for Java, Release 2.0, Community Edition
- Java Plug-in HTML Converter 1.3

Software and Hardware System Requirements

- Intel Pentium 166 MHz or faster processor (Forte requires a minimum 350 MHz)
- Microsoft® Windows 95 or later, or
- Microsoft Windows NT 4.0 or later, or
- Red Hat Linux 6.2 or later
- 128 MB of RAM (256 MB recommended)
- CD-ROM drive
- Internet connection and web browser